W9-BDM-462

PowerStudy 4.0

for *Introduction to Psychology*

PowerStudy 4.0

Tom Doyle   Rod Plotnik

With PowerStudy, you can:

- *See and Hear* explanations of the terms and concepts introduced in this text
- *View* animations that demonstrate and clarify challenging concepts
- *Participate* in a variety of interactive quizzes, activities, and critical-thinking questions that refresh and expand your knowledge
- *Identify* areas for improvement and locate the information you need to review concepts
- *Review* the concepts presented in the text

See it, read it, hear it!

For each of the 25 modules in the text (outlined below), **PowerStudy** provides a variety of learning activities including quizzing with immediate feedback, critical-thinking exercises, key terms, a chapter outline, and web links. **Super Modules** (highlighted in bold below) are extensive, fully narrated presentations with animations, videos, and interactive activities that explain and expand the text paragraph by paragraph.

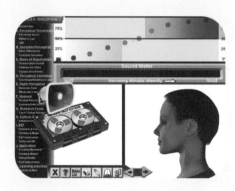

The dynamic, interactive partner to your text that can help you succeed in the course!

PowerStudy's numerous activities help your students focus, think critically, and review

Learning Activities

As the screen shot to the right illustrates, **PowerStudy** offers a variety of animated learning activities. In addition, you can check your mastery of key text concepts by taking a Summary Test, True-False Quiz, or a Multiple-Choice Test. The program's Immediate Feedback feature lets you assess your understanding of important introductory psychology topics.

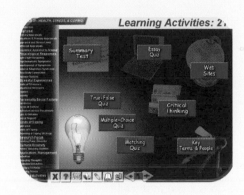

Furthermore, the program includes Internet links that take you to carefully selected websites that help build your knowledge of the topics covered in class. **PowerStudy**'s Critical Thinking Activities encourage you to answer questions about interesting newspaper articles and apply what you've learned as you do so.

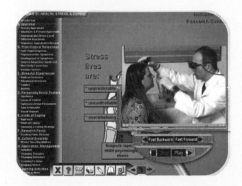

Video Segments

In the program's Video Segments, a clinical setting gives you an overview of a real-world situation. In the example at left, you can explore health and stress.

Interactivity

Learn interactively by doing! With **PowerStudy** you're actively involved in your own learning—building and reinforcing your understanding of key concepts in psychology.

If **PowerStudy** was not ordered with your text, you can purchase the program online at **academic.cengage.com/psychology.**

INTRODUCTION TO

PSYCHOLOGY

8TH EDITION

ROD PLOTNIK
San Diego State University

HAIG KOUYOUMDJIAN
UC Berkeley Extension

WADSWORTH
CENGAGE Learning

Australia • Brazil • Japan • Korea • Mexico • Singapore • Spain • United Kingdom • United States

Introduction to Psychology, Eighth Edition
Rod Plotnik, Haig Kouyoumdjian

Publisher: Michele Sordi

Senior Development Editor: Kate Barnes

Freelance Development Editor: Jim Strandberg

Assistant Editor: Magnolia Molcan

Senior Editorial Assistant: Erin Miskelly

Senior Technology Project Manager: Bessie Weiss

Marketing Manager: Sara Swangard'

Marketing Assistant: Melanie Cregger

Marketing Communications Manager: Linda Yip

Project Manager, Editorial Production: Mary Noel

Creative Director: Rob Hugel

Art Director: Vernon Boes

Print Buyer: Judy Inouye

Permissions Editors: Roberta Broyer, Linda L Rill

Production Service: Nancy Shammas, New Leaf Publishing Services

Text Designers: Rod Plotnik, Andy Norris

Photo Researcher: Linda L Rill

Copy Editor: Carol Reitz

Illustrators: Tim Jacobus, Jacobus Studio Inc., Bill Rieser, Bill Ogden, Phillip Dvorak, Mike Meyer

Cover Designer: Paula Goldstein

Cover Image: Roger Knox

Compositor: LaurelTech Integrated Publishing Solutions

© 2008, 2005 Wadsworth, Cengage Learning

ALL RIGHTS RESERVED. No part of this work covered by the copyright herein may be reproduced, transmitted, stored, or used in any form or by any means graphic, electronic, or mechanical, including but not limited to photocopying, recording, scanning, digitizing, taping, Web distribution, information networks, or information storage and retrieval systems, except as permitted under Section 107 or 108 of the 1976 United States Copyright Act, without the prior written permission of the publisher.

For product information and technology assistance, contact us at **Cengage Learning Customer & Sales Support, 1-800-354-9706**
For permission to use material from this text or product, submit all requests online at **cengage.com/permissions**
Further permissions questions can be emailed to **permissionrequest@cengage.com**

ExamView® and *ExamView Pro*® are registered trademarks of FSCreations, Inc. Windows is a registered trademark of the Microsoft Corporation used herein under license. Macintosh and Power Macintosh are registered trademarks of Apple Computer, Inc. Used herein under license.

COPYRIGHT © 2008 Cengage Learning, Inc. All Rights Reserved. Cengage Learning *WebTutor*™ is a trademark of Cengage Learning, Inc.

Library of Congress Control Number: 2007928073

Student Edition:
ISBN-13: 978-0-495-10318-9
ISBN-10: 0-495-10318-7

Cloth Edition:
ISBN-13: 978-0-495-10317-2
ISBN-10: 0-495-10317-9

Loose-leaf Edition:
ISBN-13: 978-0-495-10319-6
ISBN-10: 0-495-10319-5

Wadsworth
10 Davis Drive
Belmont, CA 94002-3098
USA

Cengage Learning is a leading provider of customized learning solutions with office locations around the globe, including Singapore, the United Kingdom, Australia, Mexico, Brazil, and Japan. Locate your local office at: **international.cengage.com/region**

Cengage Learning products are represented in Canada by Nelson Education, Ltd.

For your course and learning solutions, visit **academic.cengage.com**
Purchase any of our products at your local college store or at our preferred online store **www.ichapters.com**

Printed in Canada
3 4 5 6 7 11 10 09

To all students everywhere

We begin each revision with great enthusiasm, which usually begins to fade at the halfway point. The one sure way we have to revive our motivation is to read the many uplifting students' comments that we have received. To show you what we mean, we've included a sample of their wonderful comments, for which we are eternally grateful. (If you too would like to comment on the text, please fill out and send in the form on the last page of this text.)

The psychology book was amazing. I do not know how and where to begin, because I just loved it so much.
Natosha, Saint Dominic Academy

I really liked how easy the book was to comprehend. The examples help make the definitions easy to memorize.
Natalie, Ononadaga Community College

The diagrams were easy to understand. Good pictures and real-life examples people can *relate* to. Best psychology book I've read.
Sarah, Rochester Community College

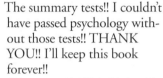

Since I consider myself a visual learner, I benefited a lot from the pictures, drawings, and graphs included throughout the book. Also the "chunking" made the material fun to learn.
Roxanne, Wharton County Junior College

How visual it is. The many pictures helped me to remember the text better. The simple writing style, but still academic, was helpful to make it interesting. I am really glad that we read this book. It made my course!
Julia, Norwalk Community College

I enjoyed so much the photos, the text, the stories, the whole layout of the book—I truly learned just from reading and remembered things because of the way they were used in the book, like next to a picture or highlighted!
Richelle, Western Iowa Tech Community College

This book was marvelous!!! I recommend this textbook to others. This was a "perfect" textbook.
Andrea, Mount San Antonio College

The summary tests!! I couldn't have passed psychology without those tests!! THANK YOU!! I'll keep this book forever!!
Shannon, Griffith University

I truly enjoyed the "little stories." They help me understand what we were studying. Please continue on with the Cultural Diversity sections!
Pharik, Platt College

This is one of the best textbooks I've read and enjoyed; you did a great job organizing and writing material in such a friendly way. I plan on keeping this book as I enjoyed it so much.
Janet, Ivy Tech Community College

The newspaper articles at the end of each chapter were so interesting, I wanted to read every single one. Thank you for putting together such a visual book and making everything seem so much more interesting.
Tracy, Wayne Community College

CONTENTS

MODULE 1:
Discovering Psychology 2

MODULE 2:
Psychology & Science 26

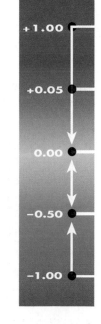

Most Stressful
8. Vomiting
7. Feeling nausea
6. Receiving injection
5. In treatment room
4. Smelling chemicals
3. In waiting room
2. Entering clinic
1. Driving to clinic

MODULE 11: Types of Memory 238

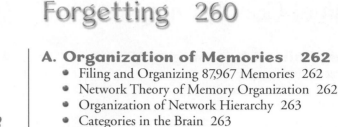

MODULE 12: Remembering & Forgetting 260

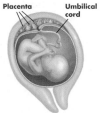

1. Oral
2. Anal
3. Phallic
4. Latency
5. Genital

Should I take one marshmallow now or wait and get two?

I read my horoscope every day, and it's always right on the mark.

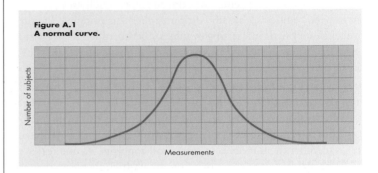
Figure A.1
A normal curve.

Number of subjects

Measurements

TO THE INSTRUCTOR: Changes and Features

What's Different About This Approach?

One of the first things instructors notice about this textbook is that it looks different from more traditional texts. This book looks different because its method of presenting information is based on well-known principles of learning and memory.

One principle is that if information is presented in an interesting way, then students learn and remember the concepts much more readily. Like previous editions, the 8th edition applies this principle by integrating the text with interesting graphics so that students have visual cues to help them learn and remember. As students often say, "I'm a visual learner, so this text is perfect for me."

Another principle is that if information is organized or "chunked" into smaller units, then students learn and remember the material better. As in previous editions, the 8th edition applies this principle by organizing information into smaller and smaller segments to help students remember the hundreds of terms and concepts. As one reviewer said, "The material is broken down into small, friendly pieces that are easy for students to understand."

Thus, this text looks different because it uses "chunking" and visual learning, which help students better learn and remember. One reviewer said, "I was very pleased to find that students were reading the text, discussing the material, and using the study guide. In fact, they sometimes asked questions about parts of the chapters not assigned."

What Are the Major Changes?

During the past decade, new findings in the related areas of biology, genetics, and cognitive neuroscience have had a great impact on the field of psychology. Examples of new and interesting findings include research showing that being rejected activates a part of the brain that responds to physical pain and receiving support from a loved one reduces activity in our brain area that produces stress hormones. Because such findings help psychologists better understand and explain behavior, we have included many new and exciting discoveries not only from the field of psychology but also from the related fields of biology, genetics, and cognitive neuroscience.

New References and Figures. We have used feedback from readers and reviewers in revising and adding new figures and illustrations, which provide effective visual cues for better learning and remembering. Finally, in updating the 8th edition, we have added more than 1,000 new references, all from recent years.

Here are some examples of the major changes in the 8th edition:

MODULE 1: Discovering Psychology. A new discussion is presented on the link between social problems associated with autism and less activity in mirror neurons; Japan has a higher rate of autism than other countries; new statistics show the slowly rising rates of ethnic minority psychologists; students who are confident in their academic abilities and have higher expectations of academic success adjust better to their first year in college and get better grades; psychologists in New Mexico and Louisiana can write prescriptions for drugs; people with autism think visually.

MODULE 2: Psychology & Science. A new discussion tells that the use of cough medication is an example of a placebo effect; advances in stem cell research using animal models give hope of better recovery for people with spinal-cord injuries; PETs show that the brains of individuals given placebos to relieve pain release natural painkillers after the placebo is promised; MRIs show smaller brain areas (prefrontal lobe, corpus callosum, cerebellum) in children with ADHD; Ritalin increases positive classroom behaviors of children with ADHD; the Animal Research Act is discussed.

MODULE 3: Brain's Building Blocks. The incidence of Alzheimer's disease is 2–3 times higher among people with a parent or sibling who has the disease; there are new discussions on the world's first face transplant, on multiple sclerosis and how it affects the central nervous system, on new evidence of a biological link between anxiety and alcohol use, on the use of a mirror box to treat phantom limb pain, and on experimental treatments for Parkinson's disease, including stem cells, fetal tissue transplants, thalamotomy, and deep brain stimulation.

MODULE 4: Incredible Nervous System. New research shows that humans are more intelligent than chimpanzees because humans have an enormous number of basic neurons, not more sophisticated neurons; fMRIs show that the parietal lobe is involved in a variety of cognitive functions (language abilities, visual and auditory attention); new research deals with sex differences in dopamine production and how the amygdala remembers emotionally arousing experiences; women have smaller folds in some parts of their cortex and have faster blood flow to the brain than men; hemispheric specialization can begin as early as 2–3 months of age; the debate about brain death continues.

MODULE 5: Sensation. There is new information that the placebo effect for reducing pain results in increased activity in parts of the brain responsible for pain perception and negative emotions (anxiety); hypnosis changes brain activity and a person's perception of pain; a new discussion tells how dread activates the brain's pain center; powerful beliefs in the effectiveness of acupuncture for reducing pain can change people's perceptions of pain; current advances in artificial vision include having a tiny camera placed inside the eye rather than on eyeglasses; a new article deals with Congenital Insensitivity to Pain with Anhidrosis (CIPA).

MODULE 6: Perception. New research shows that digital mammograms are better at detecting cancerous tumors in women who have a lot of connective breast tissue; people's expectations can unknowingly influence their perceptions; when people genuinely deny racial biases, results reveal racial attitudes beneath their awareness; there are cultural differences not only in how people recall memories of visual scenes, but also in how people physically see images in scenes; virtual reality is now being used to perform surgeries, including one surgeon successfully performing remote robotic surgery.

MODULE 7: Sleep & Dreams. A new discussion focuses on the food-entrainable circadian clock and its role in obesity; morning people tend to be conscientious introverts, while evening people are usually impulsive extroverts; the ventrolateral preoptic nucleus (VPN) in rats is activated by the neurotransmitter adenosine; 42 million sleeping pill prescriptions are filled each year in the United States; cognitive-behavioral therapy is at least as effective as sleeping pills in reducing chronic insomnia; sleep-deprived doctors show impairments in attention, judgment, and reaction times like people who are intoxicated.

MODULE 8: Hypnosis & Drugs. A new discussion focuses on the rapid spread of methamphetamine use; efforts to eliminate cocaine in the United States remain unsuccessful; the U.S. Surgeon General reported that secondhand smoke kills tens of thousands of nonsmokers a year and no level of secondhand smoke is safe; the U.S. government has granted a few researchers permission to investigate the effects of MDMA; eleven states allow marijuana to be prescribed by doctors and used legally for medical reasons; police officers are now using interactive learning exercises in the DARE program, rather than lecturing on the dangers of drugs; a new article discusses how caffeine increases activity in brain areas associated with working memory and attention.

MODULE 9: Classical Conditioning. A new article discusses how visual images and marketing messages about brands of cola influence the brains of cola drinkers in a way that likely alters their taste perception or preference.

MODULE 10: Operant & Cognitive Approaches. New information suggests the best way to address symptoms of autism is to enroll children with autism in intensive behavioral treatment programs (20–40 hours a week) as early as possible; Lovaas's behavior modification program is best suited to help those with less severe symptoms of autism; 61% of parents believe spanking is an acceptable form of discipline for young children, and 95% of 2- and 4-year-olds have been spanked during the past year; a new article describes how operant conditioning techniques are used to train killer whales.

MODULE 11: Types of Memory. New research suggests that the same hormones that help us recall emotional experiences may block memories of what happened moments before the emotional event; the accuracy of recovered memories should be questioned because people usually recall memories in the presence of others; flashbulb memories represent a special kind of automatic encoding that occurs when events are emotionally and personally interesting; flashbulb memories can last 60 years or longer; a new article discusses how phony beliefs can change people's behaviors.

MODULE 12: Remembering & Forgetting. New research using brain scans found that the amygdala plays a critical role in the long-term processing of emotionally intense experiences; people with damage to their hippocampus are able to recall remote personal events; genetically altered mice show improved memory for both pleasant and unpleasant experiences; new research has used the survey method to examine the accuracy of adolescents' memory of their sexual histories; nearly 200 people in the United States have been wrongfully convicted of crimes but have been freed because of DNA evidence, and three-quarters of these people had been convicted on (mistaken) eyewitness testimony; the cognitive interview increases correct recall and avoids making suggestions that might create false memories and errors of source misattribution in children, adults, and senior citizens from varying educational backgrounds.

MODULE 13: Intelligence. New research finds that men's self-reports of IQ are higher than women's estimates, and both men and women report higher IQs for their fathers than for their mothers; two

new kinds of intelligence are added to Gardner's multiple-intelligence theory (naturalistic intelligence and existential intelligence); the Wechsler Intelligence Scale for Children has been revised (WISC-IV); gifted children who have demanding, critical parents are at risk for developing social and emotional problems; the difference in IQs between African Americans and Whites has narrowed by 4–7 points, which suggests environmental factors have a significant influence on IQ; a new discussion deals with how a prodigy's brain develops; long-term follow-up of children who had been in Head Start found that at age 40, these adults were more likely to have earned college degrees and to have owned a home and less likely to have criminal records.

MODULE 14: Thought & Language. New research finds that parents with manic-depression, as well as their children, have higher scores on tests of creativity; a new discussion on how people often base decisions on emotion rather than intellect includes research findings on activation of the amygdala while people make gambling and political decisions; the choice of which language to use in responding to questions may lead to changes in the personalities of people who are bilingual; two genes that contribute to dyslexia have been identified; dolphins communicate with each other in order to perform complex "tandem" movements.

MODULE 15: Motivation. New information links genes to several behaviors that trigger the brain's reward/pleasure center, including obesity, gambling, nicotine addiction, and sexual activity; a commonly found genetic variation increases the risk for obesity; the Czech Republic has the world's highest death rate from heart disease; American males are more satisfied with their weight, are less influenced by mass media, and develop fewer eating problems than American females; the hormone kisspeptin stimulates the production of androgen and estrogen to prepare the human body for reproduction; having older biological brothers increases the likelihood of a man having a homosexual orientation; activation of the brain area associated with sexual responses is determined by sexual orientation and not biological sex; anti-HIV drugs have enabled AIDS patients to have a life expectancy of 24 years; the first once-a-day pill for HIV treatment is now available; new research focuses on how poor and minority students can overcome educational disadvantages through programs that not only teach them academics but also help them build character; obesity may result from an addiction to food.

MODULE 16: Emotion. New research finds that people with damage to their amygdala identify faces as being more trustworthy and approachable than others do; drug and behavioral treatments have been successful in helping people suppress impulsive and violent emotions; men are reported to be better at recognizing angry faces, while women are reported to be better at recognizing facial expressions signaling happiness, sadness, surprise, and disgust; the best method to measure happiness is to track emotions throughout the day; mirror neurons help us perceive emotions in others; compared to nonliars, pathological liars have 22% more prefrontal white matter, which is linked to the ability to deceive others; new lie detector tests measure brain activity, use eye scans, and observe brief, involuntary changes in facial expressions.

MODULE 17: Infancy & Childhood. There is a new discussion on reactive attachment disorder; 1,000 genetic disorders can now be tested for and identified; screening tests can detect Down's syndrome up to 96% of the time; infants born to smoking mothers are at an increased risk for developing ADHD, sudden infant death syndrome (SIDS), and respiratory infections; new research finds prenatal exposure to air pollutants can have a negative impact on children's cognitive development; infants who are outgoing and friendly show increased activity in brain areas associated with positive emotions; sex differences in physical aggression are evident in children as young as 17 months; 9–32% of women and 5–10% of men report having been sexually abused during childhood; 57.8% of child-abuse offenders are women and 42.2% are men.

MODULE 18: Adolescence & Adulthood. New findings show that a hormone called kisspeptin is released by the hypothalamus during menarche, which helps to stimulate the pituitary gland to produce female hormones; only 31% of boys and 21% of girls who are sexually active report using contraceptives each time they have intercourse; alcohol causes more injury to teenage brains than it does to adult brains; siblings have a strong influence on who we become; brains of people in middle and late adulthood are increasingly flexible and adaptable; the area of the brain associated with strong negative emotions becomes less active with age, allowing older adults to have a positivity bias; an increasing number of women are graduating from top business schools, but few women hold top positions in *Fortune* 500 companies; stress results in the aging of DNA; assisted suicide is now legal in the Netherlands, Belgium, and Switzerland; a new article discusses the dangers of teens driving.

MODULE 19: Freudian & Humanistic Theories. New findings on positive regard show that patients in a hospital experience less anxiety and stress when visited by dogs rather than people; positive regard is used in the classroom to help at-risk students succeed; neuroscientists are examining many of Freud's questions about the mind; some recent studies show that the Rorschach test has high reliability and validity; a new article discusses how Freud's personality theory may explain obesity.

MODULE 20: Social Cognitive & Trait Theories. A new example to help explain social cognitive theory is Wangari Maathai, founder of the Green Belt Movement and 2004 Nobel Peace Prize recipient; the new example of actor Michael J. Fox shows how beliefs have a great influence on personality, motivation, and behavior; new information deals with the cultural influences that encourage women to become suicide bombers; updates discuss the use of personality tests in helping employers find applicants who fit.

MODULE 21: Health, Stress & Coping. A new example of a college student diagnosed with panic disorder explains the mind-body connection and appraisal of stress; broken-heart syndrome is a condition that mimics a massive heart attack and is triggered by emotional stress; time spent on vacation enhances people's well-being by decreasing their complaints about health problems and exhaustion; a new example of Shaun White, professional skateboarder, explains hardiness; an internal locus of control may be most important in Western cultures that emphasize autonomy and personal accomplishments; optimists may live longer than pessimists; new discussion focuses on positive psychology and its three components (positive emotions, positive individual traits, and positive institutions) as well as on Type D behavior; married women under extreme stress feel immediate relief upon holding their husband's hand; a new Research Focus section is

on evaluating treatment for panic disorder; Buddhist monks can rid themselves of negative emotions through gamma brain wave activity during meditation; a new article treats coping with cancer.

MODULE 22: Assessment & Anxiety Disorders. New information indicates that 51% of people will develop at least one lifetime disorder and the most common mental disorder is anxiety; psychotherapy is at least as effective as drug therapy in treating generalized anxiety disorder; brain scans show that for people with medically unexplainable paralysis, the emotional areas of their brains are activated inappropriately and may inhibit the functioning of the motor cortex; mass hysteria was reported in a group of 50 teenage girls in Vietnam; the article on why women marry killers in prison is updated.

MODULE 23: Mood Disorders & Schizophrenia. New research using brain scans found the anterior cingulate cortex is overactive in very depressed people, which allows negative emotions to overwhelm thoughts and moods; between 50% and 67% of depressed patients benefit from trying more than one antidepressant medication; the use of antidepressant medication following ECT reduces relapse rates; between 50% and 80% of prisoners meet the criteria for a diagnosis of antisocial personality disorder; antisocial personality disorder is three times more common in men than in women; schizophrenia depends on a combination of genes, and no one gene alone has a strong genetic influence; a slight excess of a protein in the prefrontal cortex of patients with schizophrenia may explain commons symptoms of the disorder; compared to older typical neuroleptics, newer atypical neuroleptics are at least as effective in reducing positive symptoms, more effective in reducing negative symptoms, and better at preventing relapse; a new example of Jeffrey Ingram, a 40-year-old man found in Denver, is used to explain dissociative fugue; a new article discusses psychopaths.

MODULE 24: Therapies. New information indicates that psychologists in New Mexico and Louisiana can now prescribe medications; Freud's influence is popular in today's culture, with 43% of adults believing that dreams reflect unconscious desires and 30% believing that an adult's psychological problems can be traced back to childhood; in vivo exposure is a very effective treatment for about 85% of people with obsessive-compulsive disorder.

MODULE 25: Social Psychology. A new discussion of social neuroscience includes research on human empathy and rejection; a new example of Carol Bartz, successful businesswoman, illustrates the glass ceiling; another new example is Floyd Cochran, White supremacist turned anti-hate leader; fMRIs used during an Asch-type study show that information provided by others may actually change what we see and that going against the group can be an unpleasant experience; a modified replication of Milgram's obedience study found that 70% of subjects pressed the most dangerous button for 150 volts; teens are more willing to disclose sexual information when their anonymity is guaranteed on the Internet; a specific gene variant influences brain development to make someone more likely to engage in impulsive violence, but only when combined with environmental stress; rape prevention programs are increasingly popular on college campuses; brain death has been legalized in Japan, and many Japanese have changed their attitudes about death and are increasingly accepting organ transplants; a new article presents the debate over teens receiving the cervical cancer vaccine.

Now that you've read about some of the changes in the 8th edition, we'll discuss the major features of the text.

MODULE 6
Perception

 PowerStudy 4.0™ Complete Module

120

Modules. One of the features best liked by both instructors and students is that the text is organized into smaller units called *modules*, which are shorter (20–30 pages) and more manageable than traditional chapters (45–50 pages). The 8th edition has 25 *modules,* which can easily be organized, omitted, or rearranged into any order. Because individual modules all have the same structure, each one can stand on its own.

Advantage. Instructors said that, compared to longer and more traditional chapters, they preferred the shorter *modules,* which allow greater flexibility in planning and personalizing one's course.

Example. The sample page on your left, which is the opening page of Module 6, Perception, shows that each *module* begins with a complete outline. In this outline, the major heads are designated by letter (A. Perceptual Thresholds) and provide students with an overview of the entire module.

Under each major head are a number of subheads, which provide a more detailed outline of the major concepts covered in the module.

Outline. Students can use the *module's* outline to organize their lecture notes as well as to find and review selected material.

Visual learning. Many students who have used this text have commented that they are visual learners and that the visual layout of the text greatly helped them better understand and remember difficult concepts. The visual layout of this text involves two approaches: integrating text and graphics and using "chunking."

Text/graphic integration. Each of the 609 pages of this text has been individually formatted so that text and graphics are always integrated. An example of text/graphic integration is shown in the sample page on the right (Module 4). Students never have to search for a distant figure or graph because the text is always integrated with its related graphic.

Chunking. The second method used to help students better understand and remember the material is to break down difficult or complex concepts into smaller, more manageable "chunks." For example, in this sample page, the relatively complex structure and function of the major parts of the brain are broken down into a series of easily grasped smaller chunks or a series of steps.

Definitions. Finally, the sample page shows that students need never search for definitions because they are always **boldface and printed in blue.** Students need only look for **blue** words to easily find and review definitions.

Major Parts of the Brain

Can someone be shot in the head but not die?

A human brain (right figure), which can easily be held in one hand, weighs about 1,350 grams, or 3 pounds, and has the consistency of firm Jell-O. The brain is protected by a thick skull and covered with thin, tough, plasticlike membranes. If shot in the head, a person may or may not die depending on which area was damaged. For example, damage to an area in the forebrain would result in paralysis, damage to an area in the midbrain would result in coma, but damage to an area in the hindbrain would certainly result in death.

We'll begin our exploration of the brain by looking at its three major parts—forebrain, midbrain, and hindbrain—beginning with the forebrain.

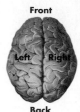

Front
Left Right
Back

1 Forebrain

When you look at the brain, what you are actually seeing is almost all forebrain (figure above). The *forebrain*, which is the largest part of the brain, has right and left sides that are called hemispheres. The hemispheres, connected by a wide band of fibers, are responsible for an incredible number of functions, including learning and memory, speaking and language, having emotional responses, experiencing sensations, initiating voluntary movements, planning, and making decisions.

The large structure outlined in orange to the left shows only the right hemisphere of the forebrain. The forebrain's right and left hemispheres are both shown in the figure at the top right. The forebrain is very well developed in humans.

2 Midbrain

If a boxer is knocked unconscious, part of the reason lies in the midbrain.

The *midbrain* has a reward or pleasure center, which is stimulated by food, sex, money, music, attractive faces, and some drugs (cocaine); has areas for visual and auditory reflexes, such as automatically turning your head toward a noise; and contains the reticular formation, which arouses the forebrain so that it is ready to process information from the senses (Holroyd & Coles, 2002).

If the reticular formation were seriously damaged—by a blow to the head, for example—a person would be unconscious and might go into a coma because the forebrain could not be aroused (E. Goldberg et al., 1989; Parvizi & Damasio, 2003).

Side view of the brain's right hemisphere

3 Hindbrain

The structures and functions of the hindbrain, which are found in very primitive brains, such as the alligator's, have remained constant through millions of years of evolution. The *hindbrain* has three distinct structures: the pons, medulla, and cerebellum.

3a Pons

If someone has a serious sleep disorder, it may involve the pons. In Latin, *pons* means "bridge," which suggests its function.

The *pons* functions as a bridge to transmit messages between the spinal cord and brain. The pons also makes the chemicals involved in sleep (Purves et al., 2004).

3b Medulla

If someone dies of a drug overdose, the cause of death probably involved the medulla.

The *medulla*, which is located at the top of the spinal cord, includes a group of cells that control vital reflexes, such as respiration, heart rate, and blood pressure.

Large amounts of alcohol, heroin, or other depressant drugs suppress the functions of cells in the medulla and cause death by stopping breathing.

3c Cerebellum

A person suspected of drunken driving may fail the test of rapidly touching a finger to the nose because of alcohol's effects on the cerebellum.

The *cerebellum*, which is located at the very back and underneath the brain, is involved in coordinating motor movements but not in initiating voluntary movements.

The cerebellum is also involved in performing timed motor responses, such as those needed in playing games or sports, and in automatic or reflexive learning, such as blinking the eye to a signal, which is called classical conditioning (discussed in Module 9) (Hazeltine & Ivry, 2002; Spencer et al., 2003).

Because alcohol is a depressant drug and interferes with the functions of the cerebellum, an intoxicated person would experience decreased coordination and have difficulty rapidly touching a finger to the nose, which is one of the tests for being drunk.

Of the brain's three parts, the forebrain is the largest, most evolved, and most responsible for an enormous range of personal, social, emotional, and cognitive behaviors. For those reasons, we'll examine the forebrain in more detail.

C. ORGANIZATION OF THE BRAIN **73**

✔ Concept Review

1. An emotion is defined in terms of four components: You interpret or (a)_____ some stimulus, thought, or event in terms of your well-being; you have a subjective (b)_____, such as being happy or fearful; you experience bodily responses, such as increased heart rate and breathing, which are called (c)_____ responses; and you often show (d)_____ behaviors, such as crying or smiling.

2. A peripheral theory says that emotions result from specific physiological changes in our bodies and that each emotion has a different physiological pattern. This theory, which says that we feel fear because we run, is called the _____ theory.

3. Another peripheral theory says that feedback from the movement of facial muscles and skin is interpreted by your brain as an emotion; this theory is called the (a)_____ theory. Although emotions can occur without feedback from facial muscles, facial feedback can influence your mood and contribute to the (b)_____ of an emotion.

4. A theory of emotions that grew out of the work of Schachter and Singer says that your interpretation, appraisal, thought, or memory of a situation, object, or event can contribute to, or result in, your experiencing different emotional states. This is called the _____ theory.

5. The most recent approach to understanding emotions studies the neural bases of mood and emotion by focusing on the brain's neural circuits that evaluate stimuli and produce or contribute to our experiencing and expressing different emotional states. This is called the _____ approach.

6. Emotions have four qualities: They are expressed in stereotypic (a)_____ expressions and have distinctive (b)_____ responses; they are less controllable and may not respond to (c)_____; they influence many (d)_____ functions; and some emotions, such as smiling, are (e)_____ in the brain. The brain area that functions to detect and evaluate stimuli, especially threatening ones, and to store memories with emotional content is called the (f)_____. Because this brain structure receives sensory information so quickly, it triggers a fearful reaction without (g)_____. The brain structure involved in producing emotions from thoughts alone and in analyzing the emotional consequences of actions is called the (h)_____.

7. Specific inherited facial patterns or expressions that signal specific feelings or emotional states across cultures, such as a smile signaling a happy state, are called (a)_____. These emotional expressions, which include anger, happiness, fear, surprise, disgust, sadness, and contempt, are thought to have evolved because they had important (b)_____ and _____ functions for our ancestors.

8. According to one theory, we inherit the neural structure and physiology to express and experience emotions, and we evolved basic emotional patterns to adapt to and solve problems important for our survival; this is called the (a)_____ theory. Facial expressions that accompany emotions send signals about how one (b)_____ and what one intends to do. Emotions focus one's (c)_____ so one can better respond to emotional situations and also increases (d)_____ of situations that may be either beneficial or dangerous to one's well-being.

Difficult tasks
Most tasks

9. Your performance on a task depends on the amount of physiological arousal and the difficulty of the task. For many tasks, moderate arousal helps performance; for new or difficult tasks, low arousal is better; and for easy or well-learned tasks, high arousal may facilitate performance. This relationship between arousal and performance is known as the _____.

10. According to one theory, you soon become accustomed to big happy events, such as getting a car; this theory is called the (a)_____. Long-term happiness is less dependent on wealth and more dependent on pursuing your own personal (b)_____ and developing meaningful (c)_____. Some people are just generally happier and some are generally less happy because of their happiness (d)_____.

11. Specific cultural norms that regulate when, where, and how much emotion we should or should not express in different situations are called _____. These rules explain why emotional expressions and intensity of emotions differ across cultures.

Answers: *1. (a) appraise, (b) feeling, (c) physiological, (d) observable; 2. James-Lange; 3. (a) facial feedback, (b) intensity; 4. cognitive appraisal; 5. affective neuroscience; 6. (a) facial, (b) physiological, (c) reason, (d) cognitive, (e) hard-wired, (f) amygdala, (g) awareness or conscious thought, (h) prefrontal cortex; 7. (a) universal facial expressions, (b) adaptive, survival; 8. (a) evolutionary, (b) feels, (c) attention, (d) memory, recall; 9. Yerkes-Dodson law; 10. (a) adaptation level theory, (b) goals, (c) relationships, (d) set point; 11. display rules*

368

Often-asked question. How many times have students asked, "What should I study for the test?" One way to answer this question is to tell students to complete the two built-in quizzes that appear in each module. One quiz is the *Concept Review* (shown here), and the second is the *Summary Test* (shown on page xxix).

Integrated approach. The sample page on the left shows a *Concept Review* (Module 16), which has the unique feature of repeating the graphics that were first linked to the major concepts discussed in the text. This repeated use of visual cues has been shown to increase the learning or encoding of information as well as to promote visual learning.

Reading versus knowing. One reason for including quizzes within the text is that students may think that they know the material because they have read it. However, studies show that students cannot judge how well they actually know the material unless they test their knowledge of specific information. The *Concept Review* gives students a chance to test their knowledge of major terms discussed in the text.

Student feedback on the *Concept Review* has been very positive. Students like the visual learning approach of having the graphics integrated with the concepts, and they find that the *Concept Review* is a great way to test their knowledge.

Cultural Diversity: Opens Students' Minds

Different viewpoints. One goal of an Introductory Psychology course is to challenge and broaden students' viewpoints by providing information about other cultures. Because of their limited experience of other cultures, students may be unaware that similar behaviors are viewed very differently in other cultures. For this reason, each of the 25 modules includes a *Cultural Diversity* feature.

Example. In the sample page on the right, the *Cultural Diversity* feature (Module 20) describes the cultural and personal reasons people become suicide bombers.

Topics. Other *Cultural Diversity* topics include:

Module 1: Early Discrimination

Module 2: Use of Placebos

Module 4: Brain Size & Racial Myths

Module 7: Incidence of SAD

Module 8: Alcoholism Rates

Module 9: Conditioning Dental Fears

Module 12: Aborigines Versus White Australians

Module 16: Emotions Across Cultures

Module 17: Gender Roles

Module 19: Unexpected High Achievement

Module 21: Tibetan Monks

Module 22: An Asian Disorder

Module 24: Different Healer

The *Cultural Diversity* feature gives students a chance to see the world through very different eyes.

F. Cultural Diversity: Suicide Bombers

Why was Arien the exception?

One of the most difficult and tragic issues for Westerners to understand is the reasons behind suicide bombers. Recently, a young woman agreed to tell her story of how she became a suicide bomber (Bennet, 2002).

Arien Ahmed (right photo) was a 20-year-old Palestinian student of business administration at Bethlehem University. Five days after she had volunteered to become a suicide bomber, she was pulled out of a marketing lecture and shown

> I believe Israeli forces killed my fiancé and I want to avenge his death.

how to trigger a bomb inside a backpack. She got into a old car with another would-be killer and went on her mission dressed as an Israeli woman. As she walked through an Israeli town carrying a heavy backpack containing a bomb surrounded with nails, she began to have second thoughts. She described a kind of awakening and remembered a childhood belief "that nobody has the right to stop anybody's life." At that moment she decided not to go through with the bombing. She was later arrested by Israeli police (Bennet, 2002). Arien was a rare exception, since suicide bombers almost never fail to complete their deadly missions.

Cultural & Personal Reasons

After Arien was arrested, she said that she agreed to tell her story to discourage other Palestinians from becoming suicide bombers and to gain sympathy for herself. The Israeli Security Agency, which allowed Arien to be interviewed by newspaper reporters, appeared eager to show how easily militants manipulate susceptible people and send them to kill and die (Bennet, 2002).

What conditions lead to suicide attacks? In the mid-1990s, there were more than 20 suicide attacks throughout Turkey. The attacks have since stopped because the Turkish government undertook steps to satisfy the rebel forces' demands. Before 1990, there were no suicide attacks in Chechnya. Since then suicide attacks have begun as Chechnyans fight to win their independence from Russia. For example, in 2003, there were at least seven suicide attacks in Chechnya that killed 165 people. All but one of the Chechnyan suicide bombers were women (Zakaria, 2003). From 1993 to 2003, there were almost 200 Palestinian suicide bomb attacks in Israel, which killed and wounded many hundreds of citizens.

What motivates a suicide bomber? Arien appeared to have been motivated by both personal and cultural reasons. As she told Israeli security agents, her strong *personal reason* was that she wanted to avenge the death of her fiancé, whom she believed had been killed by Israeli forces (who said that her fiancé accidentally blew himself up). After his death, she said, "So I lost all my future." Arien's recruiters told her that dying as a suicide attacker would earn her the reward of rejoining her slain fiancé in paradise. Even though Arien now calls her attempt to be a suicide bomber a mistake, she said she understood it. "It's a result of the situation we live in. There are also innocent people killed on both sides" (Bennet, 2002, p. A1).

There are also strong Muslim *cultural influences* that encourage women, such as Arien, to become suicide bombers. For example, during the past several years, women have been increasingly involved in Palestinian terrorism largely because their involvement is unsuspected by others and their actions receive heightened media attention. The use of women as suicide bombers is also thought to convey

There were 200 suicide bombings in Israel.

the seriousness of the threat and to make the men involved act more aggressively (Berko & Erez, 2006; Bloom, 2005). Jyad Sarraj, a Palestinian psychiatrist, states he cannot criticize the suicide bombers because their culture considers them to be martyrs and martyrs are considered prophets, who are revered (Sarraj, 2002). Other experts state the increasing numbers of women who are becoming suicide bombers shows that women are taking a step forward in achieving status equal to men (Bloom, 2005).

Do suicide bombers share certain traits? Almost all of the suicide bombers have been Muslim, relatively young, single (one was the mother of a 3-year-old), varying in education, with some knowledge of political causes and terror tactics (Bennet, 2002; Zakaria, 2003). These traits tend to be general, however, and apply to many Palestinians who do not become suicide bombers. Israel's national security force studied suicide bombers, and their results are puzzling. They didn't find any specific personality profile or traits that differentiated suicide bombers from nonbombers. However, as in Arien's case, some powerful, tragic emotional event, such as the death of her fiancé, may be the final hurt that, combined with cultural forces, led her to become a suicide bomber.

What does the future hold? Because of strong Muslim cultural influences, such as suicide bombers being considered martyrs, some Palestinians hope their own children will be suicide bombers and thus become martyrs. There are others who oppose suicide attacks, such as the group of 55 Palestinian intellectuals who issued a public plea to halt the suicide bombing attacks on innocent Israeli civilians. Government officials believe that suicide attacks will continue until there is a peace settlement in the Middle East. Until then, violent Muslim groups will continue to use suicide bombers because they have widespread cultural approval and are an effective method of killing, instilling fear, and spreading their political message (Bennet, 2002).

Next, we'll briefly review the four major theories of personality to help you understand their major points.

F. *CULTURAL DIVERSITY: SUICIDE BOMBERS* **471**

F. Research Focus:
Treatment for Panic Disorder

How Effective Is Treatment for Panic Disorder?

How is panic disorder best treated?

We have discussed stress and coping in general, and now we return to the case of Luisa, the 23-year-old college student with panic disorder. Remember Luisa had unexpected episodes in which she experienced rapid heart rate, a sense of suffocation, trembling of her arms and legs, dizziness, and chest pain. She felt so frightened by these episodes she worried she might die. Luisa's experience of having panic disorder is not uncommon. Many adults suffer from panic disorder, and fortunately there are treatment options available to them. Psychologists conduct research studies to learn which treatment or combination of treatments is most effective for problems such as panic disorder. Next, we'll discover which research method psychologists use to determine the effectiveness of treatments, as well as discuss research findings on the treatment of panic disorder.

1 Research Methods

In Module 2, we discussed several ways psychologists answer questions, including case studies and experiments, each of which has advantages and disadvantages.

A *case study* is an in-depth analysis of the thoughts, feelings, beliefs, or behaviors of an individual, without much ability to control or manipulate situations or variables.

For example, much of the initial information on how the brain functions came from case studies on individuals who had tumors, gunshot wounds, or accidental damage. Similarly, psychologists can learn about how individuals cope with panic disorder by observing and questioning them as they progress through treatment to identify how they cope and adjust to their condition.

When it is possible to control or manipulate situations or variables, the preferred choice of research method is an experiment.

An *experiment* is a method for identifying cause-and-effect relationships by following a set of guidelines that describe how to control, manipulate, and measure variables, while at the same time minimizing the possibility of error and bias.

Experiments permit great control over manipulating treatments and measuring subjects' responses. Also, they allow research data to be collected on a group of people, rather than on only one person, as in a case study, enabling the results to be more meaningful to a large group of people. Fortunately, psychologists can use experiments to compare the effectiveness of various treatments for panic disorder. We will learn about one such experiment, but before we do, let's learn about the most common treatments available for panic disorder.

2 How Can Panic Disorder Be Treated?

In Luisa's case, her treatment began with medication only, and a few months later she received a combination of medication and psychotherapy. Panic disorder is usually treated with drugs—benzodiazepines (tranquilizers, such as diazepam) or antidepressants (Prozac-like drugs, which are serotonin reuptake inhibitors or SSRIs)—and/or psychotherapy. Many more people with panic disorder receive drugs than psychotherapy, mostly because they seek treatment from their primary care physician rather than a psychologist. One popular type of psychotherapy used to treat panic disorder is cognitive-behavioral therapy or CBT (p. 559), which views the physiological arousal symptoms as a learned fear of certain bodily sensations and views the fear of being in closed or crowded situations as a behavioral response to expecting that the bodily sensations will intensify into a full-blown panic attack (Craske & Barlow, 2001). Given the various treatment options available for panic disorder, how do psychologists know for sure which treatment or combination of treatments is most effective?

Luisa received medication and psychotherapy.

3 Which Treatment Is Most Effective?

A comprehensive experiment including more than 300 people diagnosed with panic disorder used random assignment to place each participant in one of five treatment groups: drug only (a benzodiazepine), CBT only, placebo only, CBT plus drug, and CBT plus placebo (Craske & Barlow, 2001). The results showed that people who received drugs or CBT, as well as the combined treatments, showed more improvement than people in the placebo-only group. In regard to short-term treatment effects (measured after three months of treatment), CBT plus drugs was not better than CBT plus placebo, and people receiving combined treatments showed no more improvements than people receiving individual treatments. In regard to long-term treatment effects (six months after treatment had ended), many people in the drug-only group and CBT-plus-drug group relapsed. Thus, people treated with CBT alone or in combination with placebo did better than those who took medication. Though this study used only a benzodiazepine for drug treatment, similar research studies using an SSRI show comparable results. This suggests that CBT has a better long-term treatment benefit for panic disorder than medication.

4 Conclusions

By using an experiment, researchers found that the use of CBT and drugs, either individually or combined, worked about equally well in the short term. However, the use of CBT without drugs led to the best long-term treatment effects. It is well established that over 80% of people with panic disorder who receive CBT will be panic-free at the end of treatment, and they generally continue to show long-term treatment benefits (Craske & Barlow, 2001). Therefore, treatment for panic disorder should include CBT.

Next, we'll look at how some monks develop mind-over-body control.

500 *Module 21* HEALTH, STRESS & COPING

Feature. In teaching Introductory Psychology, an instructor's important but difficult goal is to explain how psychologists use a variety of research methods and techniques to answer questions. To reach this goal, each of the 25 modules includes a *Research Focus* that explains how psychologists answer questions through experiments, case studies, self-reports, and surveys.

Example. In the sample page on the left, the *Research Focus* (Module 21) explains how psychologists use research methods to examine the effectiveness of treatment for panic disorder.

Topics. Other *Research Focus* topics include:

Module 2: ADHD Controversies

Module 3: What Is a Phantom Limb?

Module 5: Mind over Body?

Module 7: Circadian Preference

Module 8: Drug Prevention

Module 10: Noncompliance

Module 12: Memory Accuracy

Module 16: Emotional Intelligence

Module 17: Temperament

Module 19: Shyness

Module 20: 180-Degree Change

Module 22: School Shootings

Each of the 25 modules includes a *Research Focus,* which discusses the research methods and techniques that psychologists use to answer questions.

Real world. Students are very interested in how psychologists apply research findings and use basic principles to solve or treat real-life problems.

Example. In the sample page on the right, the *Application* (Module 3) describes the various experimental treatments available for Parkinson's disease, which include the use of human stem cells, a stereotaxic procedure to place tissue in the brain, removing part of the thalamus, and deep brain stimulation (pp. 60–61).

Topics. Other *Application* topics include:

Module 1: Study Skills

Module 2: Research Concerns

Module 4: Split Brain

Module 5: Artificial Senses

Module 7: Sleep Problems & Treatments

Module 8: Treatment for Drug Abuse

Module 9: Conditioned Fear & Nausea

Module 10: Behavior Modification

Module 11: Unusual Memories

Module 12: Eyewitness Testimony

Module 16: Lie Detection

Module 17: Child Abuse

Module 18: Suicide

Module 21: Stress Management Programs

Module 22: Treating Phobias

Module 23: Dealing with Mild Depression

Module 25: Controlling Aggression

The *Application* sections show the practical side of psychology—how psychological principles are applied to real-life situations.

I. Application Experimental Treatments

Parkinson's Disease

Why do Michael's arms and legs shake?

Michael J. Fox is a talented actor who has starred in popular TV series, such as "Family Ties" and "Spin City," and numerous movies, including the *Back to the Future* trilogy. He was really good at his job until he noticed a twitch in his left pinkie (Fox, 2002). Within only 6 months, this twitch spread to his whole hand. Michael tried to conceal his symptoms from the public by using medication to calm his tremors, and he was successful doing so for the first seven years (Dudley, 2006). However, it became increasingly difficult to hide his symptoms as he began having tremors that would shake his entire arm. Also, his legs would shake or become really stiff, making it difficult for him to walk. Eventually, these symptoms led Michael to quit his starring role in "Spin City," a popular TV show (Weinraub, 2000).

Michael had all the symptoms of Parkinson's disease.

Parkinson's disease includes symptoms of tremors and shakes in the limbs, a slowing of voluntary movements, muscle stiffness, problems with balance and coordination, and feelings of depression. As the disease progresses, patients develop a peculiar walk and may suddenly freeze in space for minutes or hours at a time.

Michael's Parkinson's symptoms worsened because neurons in his *basal ganglia,* a group of structures located in the center of the brain that are involved in regulating movements, were running out of the neurotransmitter dopamine. Without a sufficient supply of dopamine in the basal ganglia, the brain loses its ability to control movement.

Like most Parkinson's patients, Michael was placed on a medication called L-dopa, which boosts the levels of dopamine in the brain, enabling him to have better control over his movements. Unfortunately, patients must take ever-increasing amounts of L-dopa, until the drug itself causes involuntary jerky movements that may be as bad as those produced by Parkinson's disease. Thus, L-dopa does not cure the symptoms of Parkinson's disease, and after prolonged use (5 to 10 years), L-dopa's beneficial effects may be replaced by unwanted jerky movements (Mercuri & Bernardi, 2005).

In the United States, about 1.5 million adults, usually over the age of 50, have Parkinson's disease. In rare cases, such as Michael's, people are diagnosed with young-onset Parkinson's disease (Michael was only 30). The causes of Parkinson's disease include genetic and possible environmental factors (Schmid, 2002). To date, Parkinson's has no cure but, as you'll see, several experimental treatments are under study.

Issues Involving Transplants

Why not just use drugs?

Human cells. As we learned above, the prolonged use of L-dopa to treat Parkinson's disease produces unwanted side effects. Because of these disappointing long-term results, researchers are investigating alternative treatments, such as fetal brain tissue transplants.

Previously, researchers had shown that when fetal rat brain tissue was transplanted into older rats, the fetal neurons lived, grew, functioned, and allowed brain-damaged older rats to relearn the solutions to mazes (Shetty & Turner, 1996). Following successful fetal transplants in rats and monkeys, researchers have transplanted human fetal brain tissue into patients with Parkinson's disease (Roitberg & Kordower, 2004).

The primary reason for using 6- to 8-week-old fetal tissue for transplants is that this fetal tissue has a unique ability to survive and make connections in a patient's brain or body. Because fetal brain tissue is primed for growth, it has a far greater chance of survival after transplantation than does tissue from mature brains (C. Holden, 2002). More recently, researchers are exploring the use of stem cells to treat Parkinson's disease and spinal cord injuries.

Embryonic stem cells have the ability to form new brain cells.

Stem cells. About four days after a sperm has fertilized an egg, the resulting embryo, which is about the size of the period in this sentence (see p. 379), has divided and formed embryonic stem cells (shown on left).

Stem cells, not discovered until 1998, have the amazing capacity to change into and become any one of the 220 cells that make up a human body, including skin, heart, liver, bones, and neurons.

The discovery of stem cells creates possibilities for treating various body and neurological diseases. For example, when embryonic animal stem cells were transplanted into rats and mice with spinal cord injuries, the stem cells imitated the neighboring neurons and developed into new neurons that, in turn, helped the animals regain their lost functions (N. Wade, 2002b).

The use of human embryonic stem cells is controversial for ethical and political reasons. That's because these embryos, which are fertilized in laboratories and have the potential to develop into humans, are destroyed when the stem cells are removed. On moral grounds, President George W. Bush limited federal funds for stem cell research. Because stem cell research has such potential, however, it has received wide support and funding from private and state sources (Perez-Pena, 2003). Michael J. Fox believes embryonic stem cells are very promising, and he advocates for stem cell research in hopes it may lead to finding a cure for Parkinson's disease (Business Week online, 2004).

Next, we'll take a closer look at how fetal and stem cells are used in treating Parkinson's. We'll also learn about other experimental treatment options, including the procedure used to remove part of Michael's brain.

60 *Module 3* BRAIN'S BUILDING BLOCKS

Summary Test

A. Overview: Human Brain

1. The brain is composed of a trillion cells that can be divided into two groups. One group of cells has specialized extensions for receiving and transmitting information. These cells, which are called (a)_____, are involved in communicating with other neurons, receiving sensory information, and regulating muscles, glands, and organs. The other group of cells provide the scaffolding to guide and support neurons, insulate neurons, and release chemicals that influence neuron functions. These cells are much more numerous than neurons and are called (b)_____.

2. There is a major difference between the growth of neurons in the brains of humans and in the brains of birds. A mature human brain is normally not capable of developing new (a)_____, which are almost totally present at the time of birth. In contrast, a mature (b)_____ brain has the capacity to develop new neurons.

3. The age-old question of how the brain's membranes, fluids, and chemicals are involved in generating complex mental activities, such as thoughts, images, and feelings, is called the _____ question.

B. Neurons: Structure & Function

4. Although neurons come in wondrous shapes and sizes, they all share three structures. The structure that maintains the entire neuron in working order, manufactures chemicals, and provides fuel is called the (a)_____. The structure with many branchlike extensions that receive signals from other neurons, muscles, or organs and conduct these signals to the cell body is called a (b)_____. The single threadlike extension that leaves the cell body and carries signals to other neurons, muscles, or organs is called the (c)_____. At the very end of this structure are individual swellings called (d)_____, which contain tiny vesicles filled with (e)_____.

5. Surrounding most axons is a fatty material called the (a)_____. This material acts like (b)_____ and diminishes interference from electrical signals traveling in neighboring axons.

6. Neurons do not make physical contact with one another or with other organs. Instead, there is an infinitely small space between a neuron's end bulbs and neighboring dendrites, cell bodies, or other organs. This space is called the (a)_____. When an axon's end bulbs secrete a neurotransmitter, it flows across this space and affects the (b)_____ on the neighboring membrane.

C. Neurons Versus Nerves

7. There are major differences between neurons and nerves. Cells with specialized extensions for conducting electrical signals are called (a)_____. These cells, which are located in the brain and spinal cord, make up the (b)_____ nervous system. Stringlike bundles of neurons' axons and dendrites, which are held together by connective tissue, are called (c)_____. These stringlike bundles, which are located throughout the body, make up the (d)_____ nervous system. Nerves carry information back and forth between the body and the spinal cord. If a neuron in the central nervous system is damaged, it normally does not have the capacity to (e)_____. In comparison, a nerve in the (f)_____ nervous system has the capacity to regrow or reattach if cut or damaged. The mature human brain has a limited ability to regrow (g)_____ throughout adulthood.

D. Sending Information

Action Potential

8. The axon membrane has (a)_____ that can be opened or closed. These gates keep some ions inside the membrane and other ions outside. If the axon is ready to conduct but not actually conducting an impulse, the axon is said to be in the (b)_____ state. In this state, most of the positively charged (c)_____ ions are on the outside of the membrane and all the negatively charged (d)_____ ions are trapped inside. In the resting state, the outside of the membrane has a (e)_____ charge compared to the (f)_____ charge on the inside. The process responsible for picking up and transporting sodium ions from the inside to the outside of the axon membrane is called the (g)_____.

9. If a stimulus is strong enough to excite a neuron, two things happen to its axon. First, the stimulus will eventually open the axon's (a)_____. Second, after the gates are opened, the (b)_____ pump is stopped, and all the positive (c)_____ ions rush inside because they are attracted to the negatively charged protein ions. The rush of sodium ions inside generates a tiny electric current that is called the

Problem. How often have you heard students say, "I read the material three times but still did poorly on the test"? The problem is that students may think they know the material because they have a general idea of what they have read. However, researchers found that students are poor judges of how well they really know material unless they test themselves on specific questions.

Remembering. The sample page on the left shows part of the *Summary Test* (Module 3), which gives students a chance to test their knowledge by answering specific questions. The reason the *Summary Test* (and the *Concept Review*) uses fill-in-the-blank questions instead of multiple choice is that fill-in-the-blank questions require recall, while multiple-choice questions require only recognition. Thus, fill-in-the-blank questions are a better test of a student's memory.

Two tests. Each module contains two tests. The first is the *Concept Review* (discussed on page xxv), which occurs toward the end of each module and allows students to test their knowledge of major concepts.

The second is the *Summary Test*, which occurs at the end of each module and allows students to check their knowledge of the entire module. Students' comments indicate that they like the *Summary Test* because it's a great way to review all the material.

Mind challenge. An important goal of an Introductory Psychology course is to give students practice in critical thinking, which includes using concepts that they have learned in the modules to evaluate information from other sources. To accomplish this goal, we ask students to apply what they have learned by reading and evaluating an interesting and current newspaper article.

Research indicates that newspaper articles are a good way to create interest, nurture curiosity, and stimulate critical thinking and writing (Hollander, 2000).

Example. The sample page on the right shows the *Critical Thinking* feature (Module 5), which contains an interesting newspaper article that relates to one of the major topics (pain sensation) discussed in the module. Students are asked to think about and evaluate the article by answering five to six questions that are placed next to it.

Getting started. Because many students need help in thinking about and answering questions, there are brief suggested answers at the bottom of the page to help them get on the right track. The suggested answers show students how they can use information in the module to evaluate statements in the article.

Class discussions. A newspaper article, which appears at the end of each module, is also great for stimulating class discussions.

Critical Thinking

Newspaper Article

What Would It Be Like Never to Feel Pain?

At the young age of 5, Ashlyn Blocker has already experienced many serious physical injuries. She's had a massive abrasion to the cornea of her eye, terrible burns, and hundreds of bite marks from fire ants. She's also severely damaged her tongue, cheek, and lips, knocked out most of her front teeth, and crushed her fingers in a door frame. Other children would scream in pain from experiencing any of these injuries, but Ashlyn never yelled, nor did she shed a tear. "I can't feel my boo-boos," she says (Tresniowski et al., 2005). Ashlyn is unique from most other children because she cannot feel pain.

Ashlyn has a rare and incurable genetic disorder called CIPA (congenital insensitivity to pain with anhidrosis). People with CIPA lack pain and temperature sensation, yet have no other sensory deficits. These individuals cannot feel pain and temperature because they lack nerve fibers responsible for carrying the sensation of pain, heat, and cold to the brain. Anhidrosis, or the inability to sweat, can cause life-threatening problems such as developing dangerously high fevers because people aren't able to lower their body temperature by sweating.

Living life without feeling pain is not as wonderful as one might think. Pain serves an important function by telling our brain that something is wrong and something needs to be done to correct it. Imagine having appendicitis and not feeling pain. Appendicitis is especially dangerous for people with CIPA because they wouldn't know a problem existed until after their appendix burst. Also, while most people shift their body weight when feeling pain in their joints, CIPA prevents people from sensing this pain and often results in joint problems. Lack of pain sensitivity can lead to other problems including bone fractures and infections. For example, Ashlyn recently had tonsillitis that went undetected for six months.

Despite the daily challenges Ashlyn faces, she looks like an ordinary girl who enjoys doing the same things others her age do. She likes to swing on the playground and enjoys being tickled and hugged by her parents. Ashlyn is fortunate to have support from her parents and school officials to ensure her safety while allowing her to enjoy her childhood. "There is no reason to think she won't have a normal life," says Dr. Lawrence Shapiro, an internationally recognized child psychologist. Ashlyn's parents describe her as having the "best laugh in the world" and state "she's going to conquer the world" (Tresniowski et al., 2005). (Adapted from Morton, 2004; Tresniowski et al., 2005)

© 2005 Eric Larson/Light of Day, Inc.

Questions

1. What type of research method would you use to learn about the life of a person who cannot feel pain?

2. What type of neuron is responsible for people experiencing pain, heat, and cold?

3. How helpful would acupuncture be as a treatment for people with CIPA?

4. How might CIPA affect Ashlyn's ability to learn from her mistakes of injuring herself?

5. Why is it that Ashlyn cannot sense pain or heat, but she can feel her parents tickling and hugging her?

Suggested Answers

1. A case study is an in-depth analysis of the thoughts, feelings, beliefs, or behaviors of one person. There are very few people who cannot feel pain, and so a thorough study of one person would be helpful.
2. Afferent neurons carry information in the form of electrical signals to the spinal cord and brain. Signals for sensing pain, heat, and cold are not being carried to the brain in people with CIPA.
3. Acupuncture is a procedure used to reduce various kinds of pain. People with CIPA do not feel pain, and therefore acupuncture would not be an effective treatment.
4. Most children learn to avoid engaging in behaviors that result in pain. For example, children quickly learn not to touch a hot flame after burning their hands by doing so. Learning not to engage in repetitive self-injurious behavior is challenging for Ashlyn because she cannot feel pain.
5. The same nerve ending responds to pain and temperature, but other nerve endings (such as hair receptors) respond to different types of touch stimulation, such as pressure, making it is possible for Ashlyn to feel her parents tickling and hugging her.

118 *Module 5* SENSATION

Links to Learning

Key Terms/Key People

Learning Activities

- **POWERSTUDY FOR INTRODUCTION TO PSYCHOLOGY 4.0**
  by Tom Doyle and Rod Plotnik
  Check out the quizzes and learning activities for "Sensation" on **PowerStudy** and:
  - Test your knowledge using an interactive version of the Summary Test on pages 116 and 117. Also access related quizzing—true/false, multiple choice, and matching.
  - Explore an interactive version of the Critical Thinking exercise "What Would It Be Like Never to Feel Pain?" on page 118.
  - You will also find key terms, a chapter outline including a chapter abstract, and a special extended list of hotlinked websites that correlate to this module.

- **CengageNOW**
  academic.cengage.com/login
  Need help studying? This site is your one-stop study shop. Take a Pre-Test and CengageNOW will generate a Personalized Study Plan based on your test results. The Study Plan will identify the topics you need to review and direct you to online resources to help you master those topics. You can then take a Post Test to determine the concepts you have mastered and what you still need to work on.

- **INTRODUCTION TO PSYCHOLOGY BOOK COMPANION WEBSITE**
  academic.cengage.com/psychology/plotnik
  Visit your book companion website where you will find more resources to help you study. At this site, you will find Learning Objectives, Internet Exercises, quizzing, flash cards, and a pronunciation glossary.

- **STUDY GUIDE and WEBTUTOR**
  Check the corresponding module in your Study Guide for effective student tips and help learning the material presented. Also go to **academic.cengage.com/webtutor** for an interactive version of the Study Guide features.

Study Questions

*A. **Eye: Vision**—What kinds of problems in the visual system could result in some form of blindness? (**Suggested answer page 621**)

B. **Ear: Audition**—What kinds of problems in the auditory system *could result in some form of deafness? (**Suggested answer page 622**)

C. **Vestibular System: Balance**—How do placebos help about 40–60% of people who suffer from motion sickness?

D. **Chemical Senses**—How might a master chef's chemical senses differ from yours? (**Suggested answer page 622**)

*E. **Touch**—What would happen if touch receptors did not show adaptation?

F. **Cultural Diversity: Disgust**—Why do people often show disgust when offered a new but edible food?

G. **Research Focus: Mind over Body?**—Why are some drugs initially reported to be effective but later proven to be worthless?

H. **Pain**—Why can some individuals stand more pain than others?

I. **Application: Artificial Senses**—Why is it so difficult to build an artificial eye or ear that duplicates the real one?

*These questions are answered in Appendix B.

Links to Learning offers students the following opportunities:

Key Terms/Key People allows students to check and review all the important concepts in the module.

Self-Study Assessment gives students Pre- and Post-Tests so they can easily test their knowledge.

PowerStudy 4.0 consists of cross-platform CDs that contain 40- to 50-minute multimedia presentations with over 40 videos. Each presentation is fully narrated and includes animations, interactive activities, and many quizzes.

PowerStudy 4.0 has complete content and coverage for Modules 2, 3, 4, 6, 7, 8, 9, 10, 11, 12, 17, 21, 22, and 23 and includes interactive tests, quizzes, and Critical Thinking activities for all the remaining modules. A more detailed description of ***PowerStudy 4.0*** appears on pages xxxv–xxxviii.

CengageNOW has a Pre-Test to help students study and a Post-Test to show what they have learned and have yet to master.

WebTutor offers students online tutorials and quizzes.

Study Guide, by Matthew Enos, offers study aids and quizzes.

Study Questions ask students to apply what they have learned in each module. Questions with an asterisk mean that suggested answers and possible strategies for answering study questions are given in Appendix B, beginning on page 618.

SUPPLEMENTS

PowerStudy for Introduction to Psychology 4.0 0-495-50335-5
Cross-platform CD-ROMs, created by Tom Doyle and Rod Plotnik. *PowerStudy* includes nine 40–50-minute interactive multimedia presentations called SuperModules. These SuperModules accompany the following modules in *Introduction to Psychology,* 8th edition: Module 2: Psychology & Science; Module 3: Brain's Building Blocks; Module 4: Incredible Nervous System; Module 6: Perception; Module 7: Sleep & Dreams; Module 8: Hypnosis & Drugs; Module 9: Classical Conditioning; Module 10: Operant & Cognitive Approaches; Module 11: Types of Memory; Module 12: Remembering & Forgetting; Module 17: Infancy & Childhood; Module 21: Health, Stress & Coping; Module 22: Assessment & Anxiety Disorders; and Module 23: Mood Disorders & Schizophrenia. The CD-ROM modules for all other chapters include interactive tests and quizzing, a Critical Thinking exercise, key terms, module outlines, and hotlinked websites.

Instructor's Resource Manual 0-495-10417-5
Written by Gail Knapp of Mott Community College. The manual includes teaching tips for new instructors, module outlines, the Resource Integration Guide, websites, student projects, suggested videos, and films—as well as complete "Active Learning Exercises" and handout masters that simplify course preparation.

Test Bank 0-495-10422-1
Written by Gregory Cutler of Bay de Noc Community College. This test bank includes over 150 multiple-choice, 25 true/false, and 10 short-answer essay questions per module. Thirty test items per module will be available to students in the form of online quizzes and are clearly identified as such. Fifteen questions per module are pulled from the Study Guide and the *PowerStudy* CD-ROM. (These are also clearly identified as such.) This edition also includes questions based on the Critical Thinking feature. Each test item will be referenced to the text by page number and topic, will be labeled with question type (applied, conceptual, or factual), and will have an indicated level of difficulty. Also available in ExamView electronic format.

ExamView Computerized Testing 0-495-10420-5
Create, deliver, and customize tests and study guides (both print and online) in minutes with this easy-to-use assessment and tutorial system. ExamView offers both a Quick Test Wizard and an Online Test Wizard that guide you step by step through the process of creating tests, while its "what you see is what you get" interface allows you to see the test you are creating on the screen exactly as it will print or display online. You can build tests of up to 250 questions using up to 12 question types. Using ExamView's complete word-processing capabilities, you can enter an unlimited number of new questions or edit existing questions.

Multimedia Manager Instructor's Resource CD-ROM
0-495-10421-3
The Multimedia Manager helps you to enhance your Microsoft® PowerPoint® lecture with art from this textbook, videos, animations, and your own materials! This one-stop lecture and course-preparation tool makes it easy for you to assemble, edit, publish, and present custom lectures for your course, using PowerPoint. The Multimedia Manager provides text-specific lecture outlines written by John Phelan of Western Oklahoma State College, art from Plotnik's text, videos, and animations that you can combine with your own material. The result is a powerful, personalized, media-enhanced presentation. The CD-ROM also contains a full Instructor's Resource Manual, Test Bank, and other instructor resources.

Study Guide 0-495-10416-7
Written by Matthew Enos of Harold Washington College, the Study Guide includes module outlines, effective student tips, key terms, learning objectives, language development tools, The Big Picture questions, *PowerStudy 4.0* integration, and true/false, matching, essay, and multiple-choice questions. It also includes a "How English Works" section, by John Thissen of Harold Washington College. Answers to all testing items are found on the last page of the Study Guide module.

CengageNOW IAC: 0-495-50057-7
CengageNOW for *Introduction to Psychology* includes a personalized study system that provides a pretest and a posttest for each chapter, written by Paul Kochmanski of Erie Community College. CengageNOW Personalized Study is a diagnostic tool consisting of a chapter-specific Pre-Test, Study Plan, and Post-Test that utilize valuable text-specific assets to empower students to master concepts, prepare for exams, and be more involved in class. CengageNOW features a variety of valuable assets including an integrated eBook, videos, simulations, and animations that help students gain a deeper understanding of important concepts.

WebTutor Advantage on WebCT IAC: 0-495-41074-8
With WebTutor's text-specific, preformatted content and total flexibility, you can easily create and manage your own personal website! WebTutor's course management tool gives you the ability to provide virtual office hours, post syllabi, set up threaded discussions, track student progress with the quizzing material, and much more. For students, WebTutor includes all content from the Book Companion Website, plus many additional study items, such learning objectives; Self-Assessment including a Pre-Test, a Personalized Study Plan, and a Post-Test; vocabulary mastery items include Glossary flashcards (with audio) and crossword puzzles; multiple practice quizzes; simulations; and additional Web resources. WebTutor also provides robust communication tools, such as a course calendar, asynchronous discussion, real-time chat, a whiteboard, and an integrated e-mail system. Available at a discounted package price with the text; contact your Cengage Learning representative for more information.

WebTutor Advantage on Blackboard IAC: 0-495-10468-X
With WebTutor's text-specific, preformatted content and total flexibility, you can easily create and manage your own personal website! WebTutor's course management tool gives you the ability to provide virtual office hours, post syllabi, set up threaded discussions, track student progress with the quizzing material, and much more. For students, WebTutor includes all content from the Book Companion Website, plus many additional study items, such as learning objectives;

Self-Assessment including a Pre-Test, a Personalized Study Plan, and a Post-Test; vocabulary mastery items including Glossary flashcards (with audio) and crossword puzzles; multiple practice quizzes; simulations; and additional Web resources. WebTutor also provides robust communication tools, such as a course calendar, asynchronous discussion, real-time chat, a whiteboard, and an integrated e-mail system. Available at a discounted package price with the text; contact your Cengage Learning representative for more information.

JoinIn on Turning Point   0-495-10423-X

JoinIn™ on TurningPoint® is the easiest way to turn your lecture hall into a personal, fully interactive experience for your students. JoinIn turns your ordinary PowerPoint application into powerful audience response software allowing you to take attendance, poll students on key issues to spark discussion, check student comprehension of difficult concepts, collect student demographics to better assess student needs, and even administer quizzes without collecting paper or grading. In addition, we provide interactive slide sets that you can modify and merge with any existing PowerPoint lecture slides for a seamless classroom presentation. Please consult your local Cengage Learning representative for details or visit academic.cengage.com/join in for FAQs and a demonstration.

Companion Website   0-495-41047-0

When you adopt *Introduction to Psychology,* you and your students will have access to a rich array of teaching and learning resources that you won't find anywhere else. This outstanding site features learning objectives, multiple-choice and true/false quizzes, essay questions, glossary, weblinks, flashcards, crossword puzzles, and more!

Videos for Introductory Psychology

ABC® Videos for Introductory Psychology. These one- to four-minute video clips, aWadsworth exclusive, allow you to integrate the news-gathering and programming power of ABC into the classroom to show students the relevance of psychology to daily life. Organized by course topics, these compelling clips are ideal for launching lectures and encouraging discussion. Adopters receive one new, updated video each year. A Wadsworth Exclusive from Cengage Learning!

Psychology Digital Video Library 3.0   0-495-09063-8

Psychology Digital Video Library Version 3.0 CD-ROM. This CD-ROM contains a diverse selection of more than 100 classic and contemporary clips, including "Little Albert," the "Action Potential of a Neuron," "Parts of the Brain," and many more! The digital library offers a convenient way to access an appropriate clip for every lecture. An accompanying Digital Video Handbook offers a detailed description, approximate running time, and references to related media clips. It also offers objective quizzes and Critical Thinking questions for each clip, as well as instructions on how to embed clips into your PowerPoint presentations. Available exclusively to instructors who adopt Cengage Learning psychology texts.

The Psychology Major's Handbook, Second Edition
ISBN-10: 0-534-53387-6; ISBN-13: 9-780-534533-878

By Tara L. Kuther, Western Connecticut State University. This book offers undergraduate students the information they need to make informed decisions about whether to pursue psychology as a major and career and how to succeed in psychology. The author encourages the student to become an active learner and take control of his or her education and future.

Cross-Cultural Perspectives in Introductory Psychology, 4th Edition
0-534-54653-6

By William F. Price, North Country Community College, and Richley H. Crapo, Utah State University. This book contains 27 articles on cultural groups around the globe and is an ideal companion volume to any introductory psychology text. Each cross-cultural reading or vignette enriches the traditional material of the course. These articles were specifically chosen to increase student understanding of the similarities and differences among the peoples of the world as they relate to psychological principles, concepts, and issues. Available at a discounted package price with the text. Contact your Cengage Learning representative for more information.

Challenging Your Preconceptions: Thinking Critically About Psychology, 2nd Edition   0-534-26739-4

By Randolph A. Smith, Ouachita Baptist University. This is an ideal supplement for any introductory psychology text. The book covers critical thinking within the context of research methods and statistics; biological bases of behavior; sensation and perception; altered states of consciousness; learning; memory; testing; motivation; therapy; and abnormal and social psychology.

Writing with Style—APA Style Made Easy, 3rd Edition
0-534-63432-X

Author Lenore T. Szuchman, Florida International University, succinctly provides the basics of style as presented by the Fifth Edition of the APA's *Publication Manual.* This accessible and invaluable workbook-style reference guide will help students smoothly make the transition from writing for composition classes to writing for psychology classes.

Critical Thinking in Psychology: Separating Sense from Nonsense, 2nd Edition
ISBN-10: 0-534-63459-1 | ISBN-13: 9-780-534-63459-9

John Ruscio Elizabethtown College. Do your students have the tools to distinguish the true science of human thought and behavior from pop psychology? John Ruscio's book provides a tangible and compelling framework for making that distinction. Because we are inundated with "scientific" claims, the author does not merely differentiate science and pseudoscience, but goes further to teach the fundamentals of scientific reasoning on which students can base their evaluation of information.

TO THE STUDENT: A Different Kind of Textbook

Looks different. This textbook looks different because it uses visual learning techniques, such as breaking material into smaller units and integrating text and graphics. Every definition is boldface and printed in blue so that you can identify it easily.

Concept Review. This is a test of how well you remember some of the key concepts. As you fill in the blanks of the Concept Review, you'll be learning important terms and concepts.

Summary Test. This lets you check how well you remember the material from the entire module. Taking the Summary Test is also an excellent way to review all the major terms discussed in the module.

Critical Thinking. At the end of each module are several Critical Thinking activities, including study questions and questions about an interesting newspaper article.

Key Terms/Key People. There's a list of key terms/people (with page numbers) at the end of each module.

Study Guide. To give you additional help in mastering a module, the *Study Guide* contains outlines of each module plus a variety of questions (multiple-choice, true/false, matching) that give you many chances to test your mastery of the material.

PowerStudy 4.0. These CDs contain narrated lectures, interactive tests, and over 40 videos—an exciting new way to learn.

B. Neurons: Structure & Function

Parts of the Neuron

Why could Ina think, move, and talk?

Before Ina developed Alzheimer's disease, she was able to engage in an incredible variety of cognitive and physical behaviors. She was able to think, remember, walk, smile, and speak—all because of the activity of millions of microscopic brain cells called neurons. We'll examine the neuron, which comes in many wondrous shapes and sizes and has only three basic structures—cell body, dendrites, and axon.

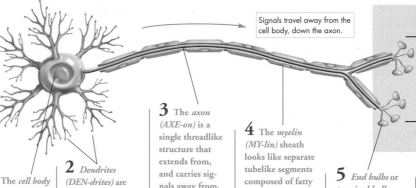

Signals travel away from the cell body, down the axon.

1 The *cell body* (or *soma*) is a relatively large, egg-shaped structure that provides fuel, manufactures chemicals, and maintains the entire neuron in working order.

In the center of the cell body is a small oval shape representing the nucleus, which contains genetic instructions (in the form of DNA) for both the manufacture of chemicals and the regulation of the neuron.

2 *Dendrites (DEN-drites)* are branchlike extensions that arise from the cell body; they receive signals from other neurons, muscles, or sense organs and pass these signals to the cell body.

At the time of birth, a neuron has few dendrites. After birth, dendrites undergo dramatic growth that accounts for much of the increase in brain size. As dendrites grow, they make connections and form communication networks between neurons and other cells or organs.

3 The *axon (AXE-on)* is a single threadlike structure that extends from, and carries signals away from, the cell body to neighboring neurons, organs, or muscles.

Here the axon is indicated by an orange line inside the tube composed of separate gray segments. Axons vary in length from less than a hair's breadth to as long as 3 feet (from your spinal cord to your toes). An axon conducts electrical signals to a neighboring organ (heart), a muscle, or another neuron.

4 The *myelin (MY-lin)* sheath looks like separate tubelike segments composed of fatty material that wraps around and insulates an axon. The myelin sheath prevents interference from electrical signals generated in adjacent axons.

The axons of most large neurons, including motor neurons, have myelin sheaths. You may have heard the brain described as consisting of gray and white matter. Gray is the color of cell bodies, while white is the color of myelin sheaths.

5 *End bulbs* or *terminal bulbs* look like tiny bubbles that are located at the extreme ends of the axon's branches. Each end bulb is like a miniature container that stores chemicals called neurotransmitters, which are used to communicate with neighboring cells.

End bulbs reach right up to, but do not physically touch, the surface of a neighboring organ (heart), muscle (head), or another cell body.

6 The *synapse (SIN-apse)* is an infinitely small space (20–30 billionths of a meter) that exists between an end bulb and its adjacent body organ (heart), muscles (head), or cell body.

When stimulated by electrical signals from the axon, the end bulbs eject neurotransmitters into the synapse. The neurotransmitters cross the synapse and act like switches to turn adjacent cells on or off. We'll explain this switching process a little later.

Alzheimer's Disease and Neurons

Alzheimer's brain is smaller because it has lost many neurons.

Size of normal brain with all of its neurons intact.

In Alzheimer's disease there is an excessive buildup of gluelike substances, which gradually destroy neurons (Cowley, 2002). In Ina's case, these gluelike substances will destroy more and more of her neurons, causing her brain to actually shrink, as shown by the very deep creases in the Alzheimer's brain (left photo). Researchers recently discovered an experimental vaccine that may help stop the buildup of these gluelike killer substances, and they continue to search for other interventions (Check, 2003).

We have discussed the structure and function of neurons, but it is important not to confuse neurons (in your brain and spinal cord) with nerves (in your body).

50 *Module 3* BRAIN'S BUILDING BLOCKS

New Version!

PowerStudy 4.0™ for Introduction to Psychology

What It Is and How to Use It

PowerStudy 4.0 for Introduction to Psychology is your study *partner*—helping you to do your best in this course! **PowerStudy 4.0** consists of cross-platform CDs that are organized to work with every module in this textbook. **PowerStudy 4.0**'s instructive, colorful multimedia presentations actively involve you in your own learning in ways that lead to greater understanding of the material, better retention, *and* better grades on exams!

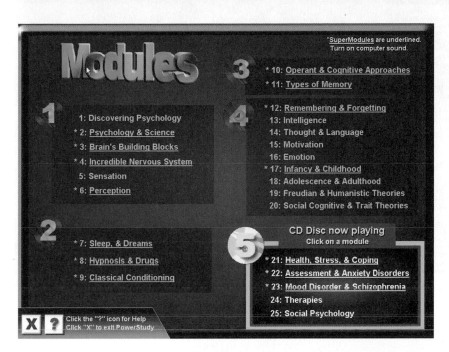

From this screen, click on any module to begin. This easy-to-use opening screen lists all the modules available on **PowerStudy 4.0**'s CD set. You'll notice that **PowerStudy 4.0** highlights the CD you are currently playing.

Choose from PowerStudy 4.0's 11 modules and 14 Super Modules!

PowerStudy 4.0 contains a CD module for each of this book's 25 modules. Fourteen **PowerStudy** modules are **Super Modules**. Each **Super Module** is a 40- to 50-minute multimedia presentation that interactively covers all key topics in the corresponding book module with fascinating animations, activities, self-quizzes, and Critical Thinking questions. The remaining 11 CD-ROM modules contain helpful study information—an interactive version of the book's Summary Test, quizzes, interactive Critical Thinking exercises, key terms, chapter outlines, and a list of websites.

Topic access is so simple and easy!

The opening screen for each module displays the module outline (as shown here on Module 21's opening screen). Because **PowerStudy 4.0** uses the same organization and covers the same topics as this textbook, you can easily locate interactive help on **PowerStudy 4.0** for every important topic you read about in the book.

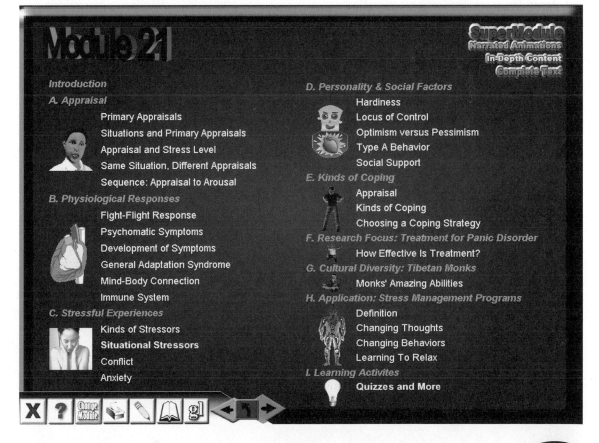

PowerStudy 4.0™ for Introduction to Psychology

On-screen menus, icons, and arrows—for easy *click-and-go* navigation!

With *PowerStudy 4.0*'s on-screen menus, navigation is a snap. As shown here, the menu appears on the left side of the screen and lists the same topics and subtopics as those discussed in this textbook's corresponding module. So, if you need further explanation of any of the topics in this book's Modules 2, 3, 4, 6, 7, 8, 9, 10, 11, 12, 17, 21, 22, or 23, you can visit the CD's corresponding **Super Modules** to hear and see a multimedia presentation on those particular topics. The remaining 11 CD-ROM modules contain helpful study information—an interactive version of the book's Summary Test, quizzing, interactive Critical Thinking exercises, key terms, chapter outlines, and a list of hot-linked websites. You'll also discover how easy it is to move from topic to topic and module to module—thanks to the handy icons and navigation arrows at the bottom of the screen!

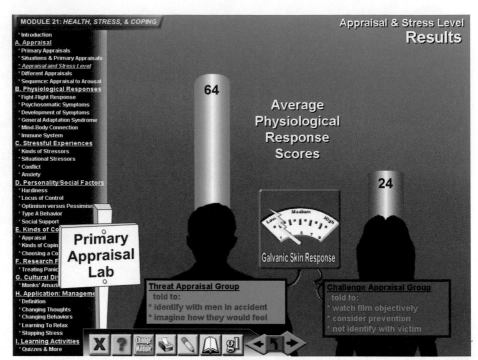

You'll learn interactively by *doing*!

With *PowerStudy 4.0*, you are actively involved in your own learning—building and reinforcing your understanding of psychology's important concepts

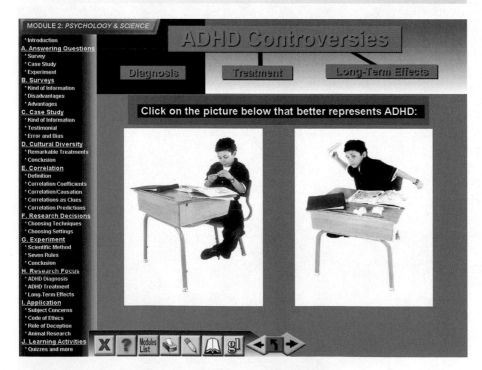

interactively. For example, in the screen shown here from **Super Module 2**, you role-play as a therapist who must diagnose attention-deficit/hyperactivity disorder in children. Throughout *PowerStudy 4.0*, you'll have plenty of opportunities to learn by doing—especially in the program's 14 **Super Modules**:

Super Module 2: Psychology & Science
Super Module 3: Brain's Building Blocks
Super Module 4: Incredible Nervous System
Super Module 6: Perception
Super Module 7: Sleep & Dreams
Super Module 8: Hypnosis & Drugs
Super Module 9: Classical Conditioning
Super Module 10: Operant & Cognitive
   Approaches
Super Module 11: Types of Memory
Super Module 12: Remembering & Forgetting
Super Module 17: Infancy & Childhood—
   NEW Super Module!
Super Module 21: Health, Stress &
   Coping—**NEW Super Module!**
Super Module 22: Assessment & Anxiety
   Disorders
Super Module 23: Mood Disorders &
   Schizophrenia

Animations help you understand complex concepts!

A real advantage of *PowerStudy 4.0*'s multimedia format is its ability to use animations to help explain psychology's complex concepts and topics. For instance, in **Super Module 9**, you'll find animations designed to help you understand classical and operant conditioning. For example, the animation shown in the screen to the left illustrates how through operant conditioning a cat learns to open a cage to get food.

Video segments show you what psychologists do!

Video segments are included within all *PowerStudy 4.0* **Super Modules**. Many video segments show psychologists discussing their work and in clinical settings, so you get a real-world understanding of the *science* of psychology and its vital work in actual practice. For example, the video you see in the screen to the right how stress impacts the immune system.

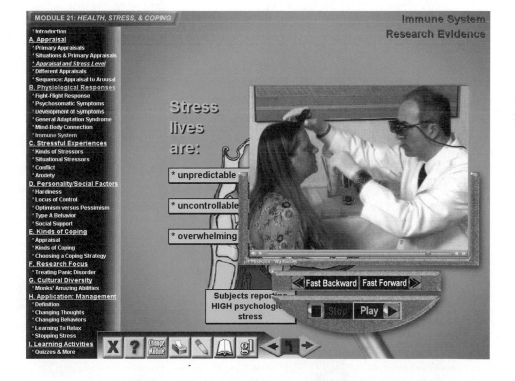

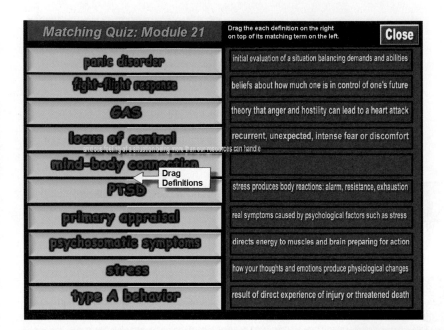

Matching Quiz: Module 21 — Drag the each definition on the right on top of its matching term on the left. **Close**

Terms	Definitions
panic disorder	initial evaluation of a situation balancing demands and abilities
fight-flight response	beliefs about how much one is in control of one's future
GAS	theory that anger and hostility can lead to a heart attack
locus of control	recurrent, unexpected, intense fear or discomfort
mind-body connection	
PTSD	stress produces body reactions: alarm, resistance, exhaustion
primary appraisal	real symptoms caused by psychological factors such as stress
psychosomatic symptoms	directs energy to muscles and brain preparing for action
stress	how your thoughts and emotions produce physiological changes
type A behavior	result of direct experience of injury or threatened death

anxious feeling of a situation being more than our resources can handle — Drag Definitions

Interactive quizzes reinforce learning!
PowerStudy 4.0 is loaded with a wide variety of quizzing. The format is interactive so you can immediately check your answers. For example, in this matching quiz from Module 21, you can click on a function and drag it to its appropriate match. In this case, the "anxious feeling of a situation being more than our resources can handle," matches with "Stress." If you drag it to an incorrect match, the program will let you know.

Many activities help you focus, think critically, and review!

As this screen shows, *PowerStudy 4.0* offers a variety of learning activities. You can check your knowledge by taking a **Summary Test**, **True-False Quiz**, or **Multiple-Choice Quiz**—and get immediate feedback on your answers. You can also click on **Websites** that link you to *PowerStudy*'s carefully selected Internet sites—enriching your knowledge of topics being discussed in class. And you can also engage in *PowerStudy 4.0*'s **Critical Thinking** activities by answering questions about interesting newspaper articles or applying your knowledge as you answer study questions.

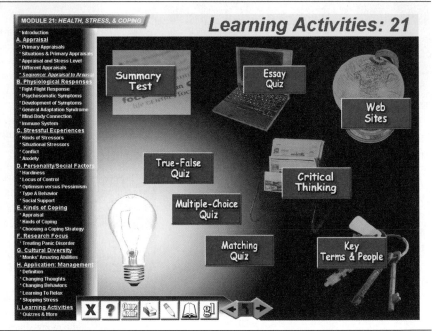

MODULE 21: HEALTH, STRESS, & COPING

Learning Activities: 21

- Introduction
- **A. Appraisal**
  - Primary Appraisals
  - Situations & Primary Appraisals
  - Appraisal and Stress Level
  - Different Appraisals
  - *Sequence: Appraisal to Arousal*
- **B. Physiological Responses**
  - Fight-Flight Response
  - Psychosomatic Symptoms
  - Development of Symptoms
  - General Adaptation Syndrome
  - Mind-Body Connection
  - Immune System
- **C. Stressful Experiences**
  - Kinds of Stressors
  - Situational Stressors
  - Conflict
  - Anxiety
- **D. Personality/Social Factors**
  - Hardiness
  - Locus of Control
  - Optimism versus Pessimism
  - Type A Behavior
  - Social Support
- **E. Kinds of Coping**
  - Appraisal
  - Kinds of Coping
  - Choosing a Coping Strategy
- **F. Research Focus**
  - Treating Panic Disorder
- **G. Cultural Diversity**
  - Monks' Amazing Abilities
- **H. Application: Management**
  - Definition
  - Changing Thoughts
  - Changing Behaviors
  - Learning To Relax
  - Stopping Stress
- **I. Learning Activities**
  - Quizzes & More

Summary Test · Essay Quiz · Web Sites · True-False Quiz · Critical Thinking · Multiple-Choice Quiz · Matching Quiz · Key Terms & People

Watch for the PowerStudy icon as you read this book.

PowerStudy icons located throughout the textbook are your cues to visit the CD-ROM for interactive ways to reinforce your reading!

PowerStudy 4.0™

Early Formation

At the beginning of this module, we described how 14-month-old Jeff had already learned a number of concepts, such as juice, cookie, car, ball, apple, cat, dog, and bunny. Many children 10 to 16 months old

BLOCKS

By 10 to 16 months, infants learn

Categories in the Brain

A child's ability to form and develop concepts is helped not only by having a stimulating environment but also by how the brain is organized. Brain scans and brain stimulation of normal subjects and tests on brain-damaged individuals showed that different visual concepts, such as animals, faces, vegetables/fruits, and nonliving things, as well as auditory concepts, such as animal, human, and tool sounds, are processed and stored in different parts of the brain (Ilmberger et al., 2002; Lewis et al.,

Module 4
B. Studying the Living Brain
Module 11
D. Long-Term Memory: Storing

Functions of Concepts

If you woke up one day to find that you had lost all your concepts, you would indeed have a very bad day. That's because concepts perform two important functions: They organize information and help us

ACKNOWLEDGEMENTS AND MANY THANKS

After more than 20 years of working on my own, I have decided that it was time to cut back on my workload and take on a coauthor for the 8th edition. The coauthor I chose has such unique qualifications that if I had told you about them, you might have thought I made them up. For that reason, I will let my new coauthor, Haig Kouyoumdjian, tell you his own story and, after reading it, you will understand why he is so ideally and perfectly suited for this project (even though I still have trouble pronouncing his name). **Rod Plotnik**

When I took my first college psychology class at Diablo Valley College, I had the opportunity to use *Introduction to Psychology* (3rd ed.) by Rod Plotnik. I can still recall the many conversations I had with peers and family members sharing the fascinating stories I read about and my overall enthusiasm for the textbook. For the first time ever, I did the unimaginable; that is, I began reading ahead because I was impatient to read the next great story and learn the next interesting concept. Plotnik's text sparked my interest in psychology, and I went on to pursue a Bachelor of Science degree at Saint Mary's College of California, a liberal arts college in the San Francisco Bay Area.

My interest in psychology continued to deepen while in college, and I went on to receive a Master of Arts degree in psychology at San Diego State University, where I had the unique experience of working closely with Rod Plotnik, who at that time was a professor in the department and supervisor of the graduate teaching associates training program. Under Plotnik's close supervision, I began teaching undergraduate Introduction to Psychology courses at the university using his 4th and 5th editions.

Following my education and training at San Diego State University, I attended University of Nebraska–Lincoln, where I received a Ph.D. in Clinical Psychology. While there, I continued to teach Introduction to Psychology courses and used Plotnik's 6th edition. My primary areas of research focused on child maltreatment and Latino mental health, which resulted in several publications. I was also actively engaged in teaching-related research, which resulted in a publication and several presentations.

After receiving my Ph.D, I worked as a psychologist in an outpatient medical center, providing mental health services to youths, adults, and families. Currently, I am teaching Introduction to Psychology using Plotnik's 7th edition at University of California, Berkeley, Extension and Diablo Valley College, where I was first introduced to Plotnik's text.

My various teaching experiences have strengthened my interest in the practice and study of teaching. I especially enjoy stimulating students by using visual learning approaches, such as breaking educational content into small, meaningful chunks of information and presenting visual cues to help students better process, retrieve, and remember information. As such, it is with great pleasure and appreciation that I join Rod Plotnik in coauthoring *Introduction to Psychology* (8th ed.). **Haig Kouyoumdjian**

In revising the 8th edition, we worked with a remarkable group of creative people, each of whom deserves special thanks.

Publisher. The 8th edition benefited from the wonderful addition of Michele Sordi, who brings much enthusiasm, new ideas, and commitment to making this textbook better and better. This textbook would not be where it is now without the many years of past support from Vicki Knight.

Developmental Editors. Jim Strandberg's suggestions certainly improved the quality of this revision and his encouragement was always much appreciated. Kate Barnes wrote the materials for the Learning Activities section of each module and was the very best in coordinating many important facets of this revision.

Cover Designers. As always, Vernon Boes does excellent work as our art director. Roger Knox is the creative person who did the wonderful cover image, and Paula Goldstein did a fantastic cover design.

Concept Illustrators. Bill Riesser continued to create wonderful new illustrations and figures. New to this edition is Tim Jacobus, whose incredible illustrative talent helped make this book visually amazing.

Photo Researcher. Once again, Linda Rill was in charge of photo research and permissions, and there is no one as committed and talented at this as Linda.

Manuscript Editor. We had the best manuscript editor ever in Carol Reitz, whose editorial skills really did improve the book.

Production: Part 1. The job of Nancy Shammas at New Leaf Publishing Services was to make sure that every page was perfect and ready for print. Keeping track of everything at Wadsworth Publishing was Mary Noel, who made sure that everything was where it should be.

Production: Part 2. Shelly Bonham and Ed Scanlon of LaurelTech made sure the individual pages were turned into a complete book. They kept track of over 2,000 photos and pieces of artwork and kept the book on schedule. They also had the tough job of checking and correcting all of the QuarkXpress files.

Marketing Communication. The great advertising copy was done by Jean Thomson. Thank you to Linda Yip, our marketing communications manager.

Sales. Sara Swangard makes sure that all sales representatives know what the book is about and how to describe it to potential adopters. Her energy and commitment to make this book a success are unstoppable and much appreciated!

Study Guide. Matthew Enos uses his friendly and helpful teaching skills to write the *Study Guide,* whose previous editions are highly praised by students. John Thissen did a great job on the *Study Guide*'s language workout section.

Supplements. Magnolia Molcan, assistant editor, was responsible for organizing and keeping track of all the many supplements. Once again, Gail Knapp used her creative talents to revise the *Instructor's Resource Manual* and make it one of the best ever. Greg Cutler continued to use his critical thinking skills to write the *Test Bank,* which has always recieved high marks. John Phelan was the multimedia manager who developed the Instructor's Resource CD-ROM, which is full of helpful teaching tools. Paul Kochmanski wrote self-assessment questions that help students determine what they know and what they should learn.

PowerStudy 4.0. Professor Tom Doyle is one of the brightest and most creative people we know. No one is as talented as Tom when it comes to developing *PowerStudy,* an interactive multimedia presentation for students. Bessie Weiss, technology project manager, assisted Tom in the development of *PowerStudy.*

Thomson Higher Education. We thank our CEO Susan Badger, who supported the nontraditional look of the 8th edition and also the development of the revolutionary learning tool, *PowerStudy.*

And finally... While working on revisions, I alternated between "It's wonderful," and "I quit." Through it all, my friend and colleague Sandy Mollenauer provided emotional support, encouragement, and understanding. **Rod Plotnik**

During this revision, there were too many times I responded to invites with "I'd love to, but I have another deadline to meet." Now, *I* can do the inviting! Thank you to my family for their love and many years of support and sacrifices. And thank you to my wife, Zepure, for her unwavering confidence, endless patience, and graceful support—all while going through her own challenging medical career. **Haig Kouyoumdjian**

REVIEWERS AND MANY THANKS

We especially want to thank the many reviewers who put in an amazing amount of time and energy to consider and comment on various aspects of this textbook.

We would like to explain why we were not able to include all your valuable suggestions.

Sometimes your suggestions were great but required inserting material for which there simply was no room.

Other times, one reviewer might suggest changing something that another reviewer really liked, so we tried to work out the best compromise.

Still other times, reviewers forcefully argued for entirely different points so that we felt like the proverbial starving donkey trying to decide which way to turn between two stacks of hay.

For all these reasons, we could not make all your suggested changes but we did give them a great deal of thought and used as many as we possibly could.

We do want each reviewer to know that his or her efforts were invaluable in the process of revising and developing a textbook. If it were within our power, we would triple your honorariums and give you each a year-long sabbatical.

Glen Adams, Harding University
Nelson Adams, Winston-Salem State University
Marlene Adelman, Norwalk Community Technical College
Edward Aronow, Montclair State University
Irwin Badin, Montclair State University
George Bagwell, Colorado Mountain College-Alpine Campus
Roger Bailey, Southwestern College
Susan Barnett, Northwestern State University
Beth Barton, Coastal Carolina Community College
Beth Benoit, University of Massachusetts-Lowell
John B. Benson, Texarcana College
Joan Bihun, University of Colorado at Denver
Kristen Biondolillo, Arkansas State University
Angela Blankenship, Halifax Community College
Pamela Braverman Schmidt, Salem State College
Linda Brunton, Columbia State Community College
Lawrence Burns, Grand Valley State University
Ronald Caldwell, Blue Mountain Community College
James Calhoun, University of Georgia
Peter Caprioglio, Middlesex Community Technical College
Donna M. Casperson, Harrisburg Area Community College
Hank Cetola, Adrian College
Larry Christensen, Salt Lake Community College
Saundra K. Ciccarelli, Gulf Coast Community College
Gerald S. Clack, Loyola University
J. Craig Clarke, Salisbury State University
Randy Cole, Piedmont Technical College
Jay Coleman, University of South Carolina, Columbia
Richard T. Colgan, Bridgewater State College
Lorry J. Cology, Owens Community College
Laurie Corey, Westchester Community College
Shaunna Crossen, Penn State University, Berk-Lehigh Valley College
Sandy Deabler, North Harris College
Paul H. Del Nero, Towson State University
Bradley Donohue, University of Nevada, Las Vegas
Michael Durnam, Adams State College
Jean Edwards, Jones County Junior College
Tami Eggleston, McKendree College
Nolen U. Embry, Lexington Community College
Charles H. Evans, LaGrange College

Melissa Faber, Lima Technical College
Mike Fass, Miami-Dade Community College, North Campus
Diane Feibel, Raymond Walters College
Bob Ferguson, Buena Vista University
Michael Firmin, Cedarville University
Rita Flattley, Pima Community College
Mary Beth Foster, Purdue University
Jan Francis, Santa Rosa Junior College
Grace Galliano, Kennesaw State College
John T. Garrett, Texas State Technical College
Robert Gates, Cisco Junior College
Andrew Getzfeld, New Jersey City University
Marjan Ghahramanlou, The Community College of Baltimore, Catonsville
Kendra Gilds, Lane Community College
Philip Gray, D'Youville College
Charles M. Greene, Florida Community College at Jacksonville
Lynn Haller, Morehead State University
Verneda Hamm Baugh, Kean University
Bill Hardgrave, Aims Community College
Sheryl Hartman, Miami-Dade Community College
Roger Hock, Mendocino College
Quentin Hollis, Bowling Green Community College
Debra Lee Hollister, Valencia Community College
Donna Holmes, Becker College
Lucinda Hutman, Elgin Community College
Terry Isbell, Northwestern State University
Wendy Jefferson-Jackson, Montgomery College
Charles Jeffreys, Seattle Central Community College
Eleanor Jones, Tidewater Community College
Linda V. Jones, Ph.D., Blinn College
Joanne Karpinen, Hope College
Stan Kary, St. Louis Community College at Florissant Valley
Paul Kasenow, Henderson Community College
Don Kates, College of DuPage
Mark Kelland, Lansing Community College
Arthur D. Kemp, Ph.D., Central Missouri State University
Richard Kirk, Texas State Technical College
Dan Klaus, Community College of Beaver City
Gail Knapp, Mott Community College

John C. Koeppel, University of Southern Mississippi
Jan Kottke, California State University-San Bernardino
Haig Kouyoumdjian, University of Nebraska, Lincoln
Joan Krueger, Harold Washington College
Matthew Krug, Wisconsin Lutheran College
Doug Krull, Northern Kentucky University
Diane J. Krumm, College of Lake County
Raymond Launier, Santa Barbara City College
Kristen Lavallee, Penn State University
Eamonn J. Lester, St. Philips College
John Lindsay, Georgia College & State University
Alan Lipman, Georgetown University
Karsten Look, Columbus State Community College
Jerry Lundgren, Flathead Valley Community College
Linda V. Jones, Ph.D., Blinn College
Frank MacHovec, Rappahannock Community College
Sandra Madison, Delgado Community College
Laura Madson, New Mexico State University
Ernest Marquez, Elgin Community College
Peter Matsos, Riverside Community College
Grant McLaren, Edinboro University
Mary Lee Meiners, San Diego Miramar College
Diane Mello-Goldner, Pine Manor College
Laurence Miller, Western Washington University
Lesley Annette Miller, Triton College
Malcolm Miller, Fanshawe College
Gloria Mitchell, De Anza College
Alinde Moore, Ashland University
John T. Nixon, SUNY-Canton
Peggy Norwood, Community College of Aurora
Art Olguin, Santa Barbara City College
Carol Pandey, Pierce College
Christine Panyard, University of Detroit-Mercy
Jeff Parsons, Rockefeller University
Ron Payne, San Joaquin Delta College
Bob Pellegrini, San Jose State University
Julie Penley, El Paso Community College
Judith Phillips, Palomar College
James Previte, Victor Valley College
Joan Rafter, Hudson Community College
Robert R. Rainey, Jr., Florida Community College at Jacksonville
Lillian Range, University of Southern Mississippi
S. Peter Resta, Prince George's Community College
Melissa Riley, University of Mississippi
Vicki Ritts, St. Louis Community College, Meramac
Bret Roark, Oklahoma Baptist University
Ann E. Garrett Robinson, Gateway Community Technical College
Harvey Schiffman, Rutgers University Piscataway Campus
Michael Schuller, Fresno City College
Alan Schultz, Prince George's Community College

Robert Schultz, Fulton Montgomery Community College
Debra Schwiesow, Creighton University
Harold Siegel, Rutger's University Newark Campus
N. Clayton Silver, University of Nevada, Las Vegas
Kimberly Eretzian Smirles, Emmanuel College
James Spencer, West Virginia State College
Deborah Steinberg, Jefferson Community College
Mark Stewart, American River College
Kimberly Stoker, Holmes Community College
Julie Stokes, California State University-Fullerton
Ted Sturman, University of Southern Maine
Clayton N. Tatro, Garden City Community College
Annette Taylor, University of San Diego
Clayton Teem, Gainesville College
Andy Thomas, Tennessee Technical University
Larry Till, Cerritos College
Susan Troy, Northeast Iowa Community College
Jane Vecchio, Holyoke Community College
Randy Vinzant, Hinds Community College
Jeff Wachsmuth, Napa Valley College
Benjamin Wallace, Cleveland State University
James Ward, Western New England College
Janice Weaver, Ferris State University
Mary Scott West, Virginia Intermont College
Fred W. Whitford, Montana State University
John Whittle, Northern Essex Community College
Ellen Williams, Mesa Community College
Matthew J. Zagumny, Tennessee Technological University
Gene Zingarelli, Santa Rosa Community College

Special help on the 8th edition

Aneeq Ahmad, Henderson State University
William T. Brown, Norwalk Community College
Ili Castillo, Houston Community College
Julile P. Dilday, Halifax Community College
Nolen Embry-Bailey, Bluegrass Community and Technical College
Troianne Grayson, Florida Community College at Jacksonville, South Campus
Mike Grevlos, Southeast Technical Institute
Tonya Honeycutt, Johnson County Community College
Mark Kavanaugh, Kennebec Community College
Irv Lichtman, Houston Community College
Chitra Ranganathan, Framingham State College
John Roop, North Georgia College and State University
Matt Rossano, Southeastern Louisiana University
John Santelli, Fairleigh Dickinson University
Daniel J. Tomasulo, New Jersey City University
Stephen P. Weinert, Cuyamaca College
Melissa Wright, The Victoria College
Gene Zingarelli, Santa Rosa Junior College

MODULE 1
Discovering Psychology

Introduction

Growing Up in a Strange World

Why does Donna flap her hands?

When Donna was about 3 years old, she ate lettuce because she liked rabbits and they ate lettuce. She ate jelly because it looked like colored glass and she liked to look at colored glass.

She was told to make friends, but Donna had her own friends. She had a pair of green eyes named Willie, which hid under her bed, and wisps, which were tiny, transparent spots that hung in the air around her.

When people spoke, their words were strange sounds with no meaning, like mumble jumble. Donna did learn the sounds of letters and how they fit together to make words. Although she didn't learn the meanings of words, she loved their sounds when she said them out loud. As a child, she was tested for deafness because she did not use language like other children. She did not learn that words had meaning until she was a teenager.

Some autistic children show rapid hand flapping.

When people talked to Donna, especially people with loud or excited voices, she heard only "blah, blah, blah." Too much excited talk or overstimulation caused Donna to stare straight ahead and appear to be frozen. Donna later called this state "involuntarily anesthetized."

Donna was in and out of many schools because she failed her exams, refused to take part in class activities, walked out of classes she didn't like, and sometimes threw things.

When Donna did make a friend, she tried to avoid getting a friendly hug, which made her feel as if she were burning up inside and going to faint. Eventually she learned to tolerate being hugged but never liked it (D. Williams, 1992). Donna Williams had all the symptoms of autism.

Although relatively rare, autism affects 3 to 4 times as many boys as girls, occurs in all parts of the world, and is thought to be 10 times more prevalent now than it was 20 years ago (Fombonne, 2005; NICHD, 2005). Some parents blamed the increase in autism on childhood vaccinations, but researchers have shown this is not true (Goin-Kochel & Myers, 2005). Researchers believe the increase in autism is due, in part, to better diagnosis in recent years and to environmental factors that may trigger autism in people whose genes make them vulnerable to it (Yeargin-Allsop et al., 2003). Although no specific genetic link to autism has been found, researchers believe they are getting closer to finding a link (Bacchelli & Maestrini, 2006; Segurado et al., 2005).

Some autistic children avoid social interactions.

***Autism* is marked by especially abnormal or impaired development in social interactions, such as hiding to avoid people, not making eye contact, not wanting to be touched. Autism is marked by difficulties in communicating, such as grave problems in developing spoken language or in initiating conversations. Autistics are characterized by having very few activities and interests, spending long periods repeating the same behaviors (hand flapping), or following the same rituals. Signs of autism usually appear when a child is 2 or 3 years old (American Psychiatric Association, 2000).**

A very small percentage of autistics are called *savants* because they have incredible artistic or memory skills. For example, one savant has memorized 7,600 books; another can speak only 100 words but can play over 7,000 songs, most heard only once; another can solve calendar puzzles, such as figuring out the day of the week for a date ten years ago (Treffert & Wallace, 2002).

Donna Williams (1992) is an example of a savant who developed exceptional language skills. At age 25, in four almost-nonstop weeks, she wrote a 500-page book that described what it was like to be autistic. In this and her second book (D. Williams, 1994), Donna describes how common sights, sounds, and images become strangely distorted, which makes getting through an ordinary day like finding one's way out of a terribly complex maze.

As we describe Donna's experiences, you'll see how psychologists try to answer questions about complex behaviors, such as autism, as well as countless other behaviors that are discussed in the 25 modules of this text. For example, one question that psychologists have studied involves a problem that you may be interested in—test anxiety.

Test Anxiety

Why are your hands sweating?

If you're like many other students, you probably experience some degree of test anxiety.

***Test anxiety* refers to a combination of physiological, emotional, and cognitive components that are caused by the stress of taking exams and that may interfere with one's ability to think, reason, and plan (Oostdam & Meijer, 2003).**

For some students, test anxiety is an unpleasant experience but doesn't necessarily interfere with exam performance. For other students, test anxiety not only is an unpleasant experience but also seriously interferes with doing well on exams. We'll discuss what psychologists have discovered about test anxiety, such as its different components, why students differ in how much test anxiety they feel, and, perhaps most important, how to decrease test anxiety.

There are several ways to decrease test anxiety.

What's Coming

In this module, we'll explore the goals of psychology, the major approaches that psychologists use to understand behavior and answer questions, the historical roots of psychology, current research areas, and possible careers in the broad field of psychology. Let's begin with how psychologists study complex problems, such as Donna's autistic behaviors.

A. Definition & Goals

Definition of Psychology

What do psychologists study?

When you think of psychology, you may think of helping people with mental problems. However, psychologists study a broad range of behaviors, including Donna's autistic behaviors and students' test anxiety, as well as hundreds of other behaviors. For this reason, we need a very broad definition of psychology.

Psychology is the systematic, scientific study of behaviors and mental processes.

What's important about this definition is that each of its terms has a broad meaning. For example, *behaviors* refers to observable actions or responses in both humans and animals. Behaviors might include eating, speaking, laughing, running, reading, and sleeping. *Mental processes,* which are not directly observable, refer to a wide range of complex mental processes, such as thinking, imagining, studying, and dreaming. The current broad definition of psychology grew out of discussions and heated arguments among early psychologists, who defined psychology much more specifically, as we'll discuss later in this module.

Although the current definition of psychology is very broad, psychologists usually have four specific goals in mind when they study some behavior or mental process, such as Donna's autistic experiences.

Goals of Psychology

What are some of Donna's unusual behaviors?

Donna (photo below) knows that she has some unusual behaviors. For example, she says that she doesn't like to be touched, held, or hugged, doesn't like to make eye contact when speaking to people, hates to talk to someone who has a loud voice, and really dislikes meeting strangers. If you were a psychologist studying Donna's unusual behaviors, you would have the following four goals in mind: to describe, explain, predict, and control her behavior.

1 Describe Donna says that when she was a child, she wondered what people were saying to her because words were just lists of meaningless sounds. When people or things bothered her, she would endlessly tap or twirl her fingers to create movements that completely held her attention and helped her escape from a world that often made no sense.

The first goal of psychology is to describe the different ways that organisms behave.

As psychologists begin to describe the behaviors and mental processes of autistic children, such as difficulties in learning language, they begin to understand how autistic children behave. After describing behavior, psychologists try to explain behavior, the second goal.

2 Explain Donna's mother believed that autism was caused by evil spirits. Donna thinks her autism may result from metabolic imbalance.

The second goal of psychology is to explain the causes of behavior.

The explanation of autism has changed as psychologists learn more about this complex problem. In the 1950s, psychologists explained that children became autistic if they were reared by parents who were cold and rejecting (Blakeslee, 2000). In the 1990s, researchers discovered that autism is caused by genetic and biological factors that result in a maldeveloped brain (Courchesne et al., 2003). Being able to describe and explain behavior helps psychologists reach the third goal, which is to predict behavior.

Psychology's goals are to describe, explain, predict, and control Donna's autistic behaviors.

3 Predict Donna says that one of her biggest problems is being so overloaded by visual sensations that she literally freezes in place. She tries to predict when she will freeze up by estimating how many new stimuli she must adjust to.

The third goal of psychology is to predict how organisms will behave in certain situations.

However, psychologists may have difficulty predicting how autistic children will behave in certain situations unless they have already described and explained their behaviors. For example, from the first two goals, psychologists know that autistic children are easily overwhelmed by strange stimuli and have difficulty paying attention. Based on this information, psychologists can predict that autistic children will have difficulty learning in a school environment because there are too many activities and stimuli in the classroom (Gresham et al., 1999). However, if psychologists can predict behavior, then they can often control behavior.

4 Control Donna knows one reason she fears meeting people is that social interactions cause a tremendous sensory overload that makes her freeze up. She controls her social fear by making a rule to meet only one person at a time.

For some psychologists, the fourth goal of psychology is to control an organism's behavior. However, the idea of control has both positive and negative sides. The positive side is that psychologists can help people, such as Donna, learn to control undesirable behaviors by teaching better methods of self-control and ways to deal with situations and relationships (Howlin, 1997). The negative side is the concern that psychologists might control people's behaviors without their knowledge or consent. In Module 2, we'll discuss the strict guidelines that psychologists have established to prevent potential abuse of controlling behavior and to protect the rights and privacy of individuals, patients, and participants in experiments.

Because many behaviors, such as autism, are enormously complex, psychologists use a combination of different approaches to reach the four goals of describing, explaining, predicting, and controlling behavior. To reach these goals, psychologists may use one or a combination of the following six approaches.

B. Modern Approaches

How do psychologists answer questions?

Psychologists have many questions about Donna's unusual behaviors. For example, why did Donna believe that objects were alive and made their own sounds? "My bed was my friend; my coat protected me and kept me inside; things that made noise had their own unique voices, which said vroom, ping, or whatever. I told my shoes where they were going so they would take me there" (Blakely, 1994, p. 14).

Why did Donna initially hear words as meaningless sounds that people were constantly saying to her? Why did she develop her own signaling

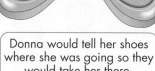

Donna would tell her shoes where she was going so they would take her there.

system, such as raising two fingers or scrunching her toes to signal that no one could reach her? Why did she freeze up when staring at soap bubbles in the sink? In trying to answer questions about Donna's strange and intriguing behaviors, psychologists would use a combination of different approaches.

Approaches to the understanding of behavior include the biological, cognitive, behavioral, psychoanalytic, humanistic, and cross-cultural. Each approach has a different focus or perspective and may use a different research method or technique. We'll summarize these six commonly used approaches and then discuss them in more detail on the following pages.

1 As a child, was Donna unable to learn that words had meaning because of some problem with the development of her brain?

The *biological approach* focuses on how our genes, hormones, and nervous system interact with our environments to influence learning, personality, memory, motivation, emotions, and coping techniques.

2 How was Donna able to develop her own signaling system that involved gestures instead of words?

The *cognitive approach* examines how we process, store, and use information and how this information influences what we attend to, perceive, learn, remember, believe, and feel.

3 Why did Donna make it a rule to avoid leaving soap bubbles in the sink?

The *behavioral approach* studies how organisms learn new behaviors or modify existing ones, depending on whether events in their environments reward or punish these behaviors.

4 Why did Donna develop alternate personalities, such as Willie who had "hateful glaring eyes, a rigid corpselike stance, and clenched fists"?

The *psychoanalytic approach* stresses the influence of unconscious fears, desires, and motivations on thoughts, behaviors, and the development of personality traits and psychological problems later in life.

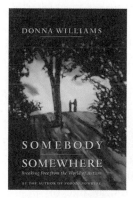

5 How was Donna able to overcome her early language problems and write a book in four weeks?

The *humanistic approach* emphasizes that each individual has great freedom in directing his or her future, a large capacity for personal growth, a considerable amount of intrinsic worth, and enormous potential for self-fulfillment.

6 Why did her mother believe that autism was caused by evil spirits? What do other peoples and cultures believe causes it?

The *cross-cultural approach* examines the influence of cultural and ethnic similarities and differences on psychological and social functioning of a culture's members.

By using one or more of these six different approaches, psychologists can look at autism from different viewpoints and stand a better chance of reaching psychology's four goals: to describe, explain, predict, and control behavior. We'll use the problems of autism and test anxiety to show how each approach examines these problems from a different perspective.

B. Modern Approaches

Biological Approach

Are their brains different?

As Donna explains, autism has a huge effect on all parts of her life. "Autism makes me feel everything at once without knowing what I am feeling. Or it cuts me off from feeling anything at all" (D. Williams, 1994, p. 237). Donna's description of how autism so drastically affects her life raises questions about whether her brain has not developed normally or functions differently. To answer these questions, researchers use the biological approach.

The *biological approach* examines how our genes, hormones, and nervous system interact with our environments to influence learning, personality, memory, motivation, emotions, coping techniques, and other traits and abilities.

Researchers using the biological approach, often called psychobiologists, use different research methods, including taking computerized photos of how the living brain functions (p. 70). For example, the top figure (based on computerized photos of living brains) shows that the normal brain uses one area (blue—fusiform gyrus) to process *faces* of people and a different area (red—inferior temporal gyrus) to process inanimate *objects*, such as a chair. In comparison, the bottom figure shows that the autistic brain uses the area that usually processes inanimate objects (red—inferior temporal gyrus) to also process human faces (Schultz et al., 2000). In addition, researchers reported that, based on brain wave activity, 3-year-old autistic children were unable to distinguish their mother's face from that of strangers but could distinguish between favorite and new toys (Dawson et al., 2002). These studies are examples of using the biological approach to look inside the human brain to explain why autistic individuals show little interest in

Normal brain

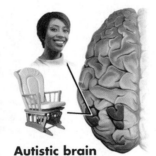

Autistic brain

looking at a person's face during social interactions or in identifying facial emotional expressions.

Psychobiologists have shown that genetic factors influence a wide range of human behaviors, which we'll discuss throughout this text. The genes (p. 68) use a chemical alphabet to write instructions for the development of the brain and body and the manufacture of chemicals that affect mental health, learning, emotions, personality traits, and everything we do (Rutter & Silberg, 2002). For example, it is known that autism runs in families, and this genetic involvement is supported by the finding that if one identical twin has autism, then there is as high as a 90% chance the other twin will have signs of autistic behavior (M. H. Lewis & Lazoritz, 2005). This finding is an example of using the biological approach to answer questions by looking for defects in the genes.

Also using the biological approach, researchers found that social problems associated with autism are linked to less activity in brain cells responsible for human empathy (mirror neurons). These cells allow us to put ourselves in other people's shoes and experience how they feel. Reduced activity in these cells helps explain why children with autism misunderstand verbal and nonverbal cues suggesting a variety of emotions felt by others, including happiness, sadness, and anger (Dapretto et al., 2006).

Essentially, psychobiologists study how the brain affects the mind, and vice versa. They may study an experience that many students are familiar with, called test anxiety.

Biological Approach to Test Anxiety

Why do my hands sweat?

You've probably experienced one component of test anxiety, called the emotional component. This component includes a variety of physiological responses, such as increased heart rate, dry mouth, and sweaty palms. An interesting feature of sweaty palms, called palmar sweating, is that it is caused by stressful feelings and is not related to changes in room temperature (L. A. Goldsmith, 2003). In fact, palmar sweating is one of the measures used in the lie detector test, which we'll discuss in Module 16.

As you take an exam—or even think about taking one—your stressful thoughts trigger the emotional component, which can interfere with processing information and increase your chances of making mistakes (Cassady & Johnson, 2002).

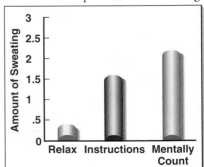

Sweaty hands often indicate stress.

The graph on the right shows how easily your stressful thoughts can trigger palmar sweating, which is one measure of the emotional component of test anxiety. As subjects listened to instructions telling them to do mental arithmetic, which involved them counting backward from 100 in steps of 7, there was a significant increase in palmar sweating. Then, once subjects started to actually do the mental arithmetic, their palmar sweating increased even more (Kobayashi et al., 2003). If simply listening to instructions about having to do a simple task of counting backward increased palmar sweating, a sign of physiological and emotional arousal, imagine the increased arousal that occurs while taking an exam!

(bar graph: Amount of Sweating on the y-axis from 0 to 3; x-axis categories: Relax, Instructions, Mentally Count)

In fact, symptoms of test anxiety may include shaky legs, racing heart, physical illness, or even crying during an exam (V. Strauss, 2004). In Module 21, we'll describe several methods of controlling stress that will be useful in controlling the emotional component of test anxiety.

Cognitive Approach

Was Donna an unusual autistic?

Autistic individuals usually have difficulty developing language skills. For example, Donna writes, "Autism makes me hear other people's words but be unable to know what the words mean. Autism stops me from finding and using my own words when I want to. Or makes me use all the words and silly things I do not want to say" (D. Williams, 1994, p. 237). Although Donna did not understand words until she was an adolescent, she eventually learned to both speak and write, has written two very creative books (D. Williams, 1992, 1994), and has learned French and German. Because of her remarkable language abilities, Donna is said to be a high-functioning autistic, or *savant*. To discover why autistic individuals differ in their development of language and social skills, psychologists use the cognitive approach.

The *cognitive approach* **focuses on how we process, store, and use information and how this information influences what we attend to, perceive, learn, remember, believe, and feel.**

Unlike Donna Williams who speaks fluently and is considered a high-functioning autistic, the photo on the right shows Tito Mukhopadhyay, a severely autistic teenager who often seems overcome by various movements, whose speech is virtually unintelligible, but who has the unusual ability of being able to answer questions or explain what he's thinking or doing by writing or typing on the keyboard he is holding. For example, when Tito was being tested in a laboratory, he repeatedly stopped and started bursts of activity, such as rocking rhythmically, standing and spinning, making loud smacking noises, or flapping his fingers. When asked why he does this, Tito didn't answer verbally but wrote, "I am calming myself. My senses are so disconnected I lose my body,

Tito is severely autistic but can type answers to questions.

so I flap. If I don't do this, I feel scattered and anxious" (Blakeslee, 2002, p. D1). When asked why he doesn't look at people when he talks, he wrote that he can concentrate on only one sense at a time and most of the time he chooses hearing. Thus, there is a major cognitive difference between normal individuals who can respond simultaneously to more than one sensory input, such as seeing and hearing, and autistics who are limited to concentrating on one sense at a time.

Some cognitive researchers combine the study of cognitive skills with identifying their corresponding areas in the brain. This exciting new approach is called cognitive neuroscience (Purves et al., 2004).

Cognitive neuroscience **involves taking pictures and identifying the structures and functions of the living brain during performance of a wide variety of mental or cognitive processes, such as thinking, planning, naming, and recognizing objects.**

For example, when listening to a conversation, 95% of right-handers use primarily the left sides of their brains and very little of the right sides to process this verbal information. In contrast, researchers found that autistic individuals used primarily the right sides of their brains and very little of the left sides when listening to a conversation (Flagg et al., 2005). This reversing of brain sides as well as difficulties in processing verbal information may help explain why autistic individuals have problems acquiring cognitive, language, and communication skills.

In recent years, the cognitive approach along with its newer relative, cognitive neuroscience, have become very popular because they have proved useful in answering questions about many aspects of cognitive skills, emotions, personality traits, and social behaviors (Cacioppo, 2002; Cacioppo et al., 2003).

For example, the cognitive approach has much to say about test anxiety, especially about worrying too much.

Cognitive Approach to Test Anxiety

Can you worry too much?

Students who experience test anxiety must deal with two components. The first component, which we already described, is increased physiological arousal, which is the emotional component. Cognitive psychologists have identified a second component, the cognitive component, which is excessive worrying, usually about doing poorly on exams.

Excessive worrying about your performance can interfere with your ability to read accurately, understand what you are reading, and identify important concepts (Cassady & Johnson, 2002). Thus, it is easy to see how excessive anxiety and worrying can impair academic performance (Chapell et al., 2005). Research measuring students' worry and anxiety about school performance in both 4th- to 6th-

What happens if I worry too much about exams?

graders and college freshmen showed that females report significantly greater worry and anxiety about their school performance than males (Everson et al., 1994; Pomerantz et al., 2002). The reasons females report greater worry and anxiety than males may be that they are more sensitive to negative feedback, such as grades and exam scores, and more concerned with pleasing others, such as teachers (Altermatt & Pomerantz, 2003; Zeidner, 1998).

In related studies, researchers found that the cognitive component could either help or hinder performance. Students who channeled their worry into complaining rather than studying performed poorly because their worry interfered with their reading the exam material and caused them to make more reading errors (Calvo & Carreiras, 1993). In contrast, students who channeled their worry into studying performed better and achieved higher grades because they were better prepared (Endler et al., 1994).

These studies indicate that the cognitive component of test anxiety—excessive worrying—may either help or hinder cognitive performance, depending on how students channel their worries.

B. Modern Approaches

No leaving soap suds in the sink!

Why have a "no soap suds" rule?

If Donna happened to leave soap suds in the sink, she might see a rainbow of colors reflected in the bubbles. She would become so completely absorbed in looking at the brilliant colors that she could not move; she would be in a state of temporary paralysis. Donna made her "no soap suds" rule to prevent the environment from triggering an autistic behavior—temporary paralysis. Donna and her husband, who is also autistic, have developed many rules to control some of their unwanted behaviors. Here are some of their rules: *No lining feet up with furniture; No making the fruit in the bowl symmetrical; No reading newspaper headlines in gas stations or at newsstands* (Blakely, 1994, p. 43). These rules, which help Donna and her husband avoid performing repetitive and stereotyped behaviors, illustrate the behavioral approach.

The *behavioral approach* analyzes how organisms learn new behaviors or modify existing ones, depending on whether events in their environments reward or punish these behaviors.

Donna and her husband's rules are examples of a basic behavioral principle: Rewards or punishments can modify, change, or control behavior. Psychologists use behavioral principles to teach people to be more assertive or less depressed, to toilet train young children, and to change many other behaviors. Psychologists use behavioral principles to train animals to press levers, to use symbols to communicate, and to perform behaviors on cue in movies and television shows.

Seeing a dazzling rainbow in soap suds stopped Donna in her tracks.

Largely through the creative work and original ideas of B. F. Skinner (1989), the behavioral approach has grown into a major force in psychology. Skinner's ideas stress the study of observable behaviors, the importance of environmental reinforcers (reward and punishment), and the exclusion of mental processes. His ideas, often referred to as strict behaviorism, continue to have an impact on psychology. In Module 10, we'll explain how Skinner's ideas were integrated into a program that taught autistic children new social behaviors that enabled them to enter and do well in public grade schools.

However, some behaviorists, such as Albert Bandura (2001a), disagree with strict behaviorism and have formulated a theory that includes mental or cognitive processes in addition to observable behaviors. According to Bandura's *social cognitive approach,* our behaviors are influenced not only by environmental events and reinforcers but also by observation, imitation, and thought processes. In Module 10, we'll discuss how Bandura's ideas explain why some children develop a fear of bugs.

Behaviorists have developed a number of techniques for changing behaviors that can be applied to both animals and humans. Next, you will see how they have used self-management skills to reduce the cognitive component of test anxiety.

Behavioral Approach to Test Anxiety

Can I redirect my worrying?

We discussed how excessive worrying, which is the cognitive component of test anxiety, can improve test performance if you can channel your worry into studying for exams. One method to redirect worry into studying more is to use a system of *self-management* based on a number of behavioral principles (D. V. Kennedy & Doepke, 1999).

Researchers found that the following self-management practices are related to increasing studying time and achieving better grades: (1) select a place that you use exclusively for study; (2) reward yourself for studying; (3) keep a record of your study time; (4) establish priorities among projects; (5) specify a time for each task; (6) complete one task before going on to another. Notice that each of these self-management practices derives from our basic behavioral principle: Events in your environment can modify your behaviors through rewards and punishments. As the graph on the right shows, 53% of freshmen who learned and used self-management practices survived into their sophomore year compared to the survival rate of only 7% of freshmen who did not learn self-management practices (Long et al., 1994).

In later modules, we'll give many examples of how behavioral principles can be used to modify a wide range of behaviors and thought patterns.

 I heard that self-management can help me stay in college.

1. Researchers identified freshmen who had poor study skills and divided them into two groups. One group was given a self-management course to improve their study skills, while a second group was not.

53%

7%

2. 7% of freshmen who **did not take** the self-management course survived into the second semester of their sophomore year.

3. 53% of freshmen who **did take** the self-management course survived into the second semester of their sophomore year.

How was Donna's childhood?

When she was about 3 years old, Donna faced a number of personal problems: having an alcoholic mother who hit and verbally abused her, having a father who was often gone, and being sent to a "special needs" school. Apparently in trying to deal with these problems, Donna developed other personalities. One personality was Willie, a child with "hateful glaring eyes, a pinched-up mouth, rigid corpselike stance, and clenched fists," who stamped and spit but also did well in school. The other was Carol, a charming, cooperative little girl who could act normal and make friends (S. Reed & Cook, 1993). Why Donna developed other personalities to deal with difficult childhood experiences would be carefully looked at in the psychoanalytic approach (Lanyado & Horne, 1999).

The *psychoanalytic approach* is based on the belief that childhood experiences greatly influence the development of later personality traits and psychological problems. It also stresses the influence of unconscious fears, desires, and motivations on thoughts and behaviors.

In the late 1800s, Sigmund Freud, a physician, treated a number of patients with psychological problems. On the basis of insights from therapy sessions, Freud proposed some revolutionary ideas about the human mind and personality development. For example,

Donna had an alcoholic and verbally abusive mother and a mostly absent father.

one hallmark of Sigmund Freud's psychoanalytic approach is the idea that the first five years have a profound effect on later personality development. According to the psychoanalytic approach, Donna's first five years with a verbally abusive mother and mostly absent father would profoundly affect her later personality development.

In addition, Freud reasoned that thoughts or feelings that make us feel fearful or guilty, that threaten our self-esteem, or that come from unresolved sexual conflicts are automatically placed deep into our unconscious. In turn, these unconscious, threatening thoughts and feelings give rise to anxiety, fear, or psychological problems. Because Freud's patients could not uncover their unconscious fears, he developed several techniques, such as dream interpretation, to bring hidden fears to the surface. Freud's belief in an unconscious force that influenced human thought and behavior was another of his revolutionary ideas (Fayek, 2005).

Many of Freud's beliefs, such as the existence of unconscious feelings and fears, have survived, while other ideas, such as the all-importance of a person's first five years, have received less support. Many of Freud's terms, such as id, ego, superego, and libido, have become part of our everyday language. We'll discuss Freud's theory of personality in Module 19.

Unlike the biological, cognitive, and behavioral approaches, the psychoanalytic approach would search for hidden or unconscious forces underlying test anxiety.

Psychoanalytic Approach to Test Anxiety

Is test anxiety related to procrastination?

We discussed two components of test anxiety—excessive worrying and increased physiological responses—that can impair a student's performance on exams. Researchers also found that students with high test anxiety are much more likely to procrastinate than students with low test anxiety (N. A. Milgram et al., 1992).

Procrastination refers to the tendency to always put off completing a task to the point of feeling anxious or uncomfortable about one's delay.

Researchers estimate that about 20% of adults are chronic procrastinators and from 30 to 70% of students procrastinate or deliberately delay completing assignments or studying for exams (Ferrari & Tice, 2000). Some of the more obvious reasons students give for procrastinating include being lazy or undisciplined, lacking motivation, and not knowing how to organize their time or set deadlines (Ariely & Wertenbroch, 2002).

However, the psychoanalytic approach would look beneath these obvious reasons and try to identify unconscious personality problems that may underlie procrastination. Because unconscious reasons for procrastination are difficult to uncover, psychologists studied the personality of procrastinators by giving them standard paper-and-pencil personality tests.

Based on personality tests, researchers concluded that students who are regular procrastinators may have low self-esteem, are too dependent on others, or have such a strong fear of failure that they do not start the task (Blunt & Pychyl,

The best thing for you to do is to put off doing anything for a few more days.

2000). Thus, the psychoanalytic approach would point to underlying personality problems as the probable cause of procrastination.

The psychoanalytic approach would also study how childhood experiences may have led to procrastination. For instance, researchers found that procrastinators tend to be raised by authoritarian parents who stress overachievement, set unrealistic goals for their children, or link achievement to giving parental love and approval. A child who is raised by parents like these may feel very anxious when he or she fails at some task and will be tempted to put off such tasks in the future (Pychyl et al., 2002).

Psychologists know that ingrained personality characteristics, such as procrastination, remain relatively stable and persist across time unless a person makes a deliberate effort to change them. In Modules 21, 23, and 24, we'll discuss several effective methods that psychologists have developed to change personality characteristics.

B. Modern Approaches

What was Donna's potential?

Donna says that one reason she wrote her books was to escape her prison of autism. Autism has trapped her in a world where she sometimes blinks compulsively, switches lights on and off for long periods of time, rocks back and forth, freezes up, stares off into space without being able to stop herself, hates to be touched, cannot stand to enter public places, and hates to make eye contact with others (D. Williams, 1992).

When Donna and her husband were dating, they confided to each other that they didn't feel sexual attraction or sexual feelings like other couples. Something had been left out of their lives and made them asexual (D. Williams, 1994).

Donna's struggle to free herself from autism, develop close personal relationships, and reach her true potential characterizes the humanistic approach.

The _humanistic approach_ emphasizes that each individual has great freedom in directing his or her future, a large capacity for achieving personal growth, a considerable amount of intrinsic worth, and enormous potential for self-fulfillment.

Donna echoes the humanistic approach when she writes, "Autism tried to rob me of life, of friendship, of caring, of sharing, of showing interest, of using my intelligence . . . it tries to bury me alive. . . ." The last words in her book are "I CAN

DONNA WILLIAMS

SOMEBODY
SOMEWHERE

Breaking Free from the World of Autism

BY THE AUTHOR OF _NOBODY NOWHERE_

Although the vast majority of autistics have great difficulty with language, Donna had an amazing ability for written and spoken language.

FIGHT AUTISM. . . . I WILL CONTROL IT. . . . IT WILL NOT CONTROL ME" (D. Williams, 1994, p. 238).

Humanists believe that, like Donna, we may have to struggle to reach our potential, but we have control of our fate and are free to become whatever we are capable of being. The humanistic approach emphasizes the positive side of human nature, its creative tendencies, and its inclination to build caring relationships. This concept of human nature—freedom, potential, creativity—is the most distinctive feature of the humanistic approach and sets it far apart from the behavioral and psychoanalytic approaches (Giorgi, 2005).

The humanistic approach officially began in the early 1960s with the publication of the _Journal of Humanistic Psychology_. One of the major figures behind establishing the journal and the humanistic approach was Abraham Maslow, who had become dissatisfied with the behavioral and psychoanalytic approaches. To paraphrase Maslow (1968), the humanistic approach was to be a new way of perceiving and thinking about the individual's capacity, freedom, and potential for growth. Many of humanism's ideas have been incorporated into approaches for counseling and psychotherapy.

Because of its free-will concept of human nature and its lack of rigorous experimental methods, many behaviorists regard the humanistic approach as more of a philosophy of life than a science of human behavior.

The humanistic approach also applies to dealing with a student's problems, such as test anxiety and procrastination.

Humanistic Approach to Test Anxiety

How can students reach their potentials?

The first year of college can be a difficult adjustment for many students, since it is more demanding and stressful than high school. Researchers wanted to learn which specific factors lead to high academic performance and successful adjustment among first-year college students. They found that students who were confident in their academic abilities performed significantly better than students who were less confident, and they adjusted better to college. Also, students who had higher expectations for academic success, such as performing well in courses, received better grades (Chemers et al., 2001). Based on these findings, it is evident that believing in one's abilities and potential is an important factor in being a successful student. These results may be useful for educators in helping students who do poorly in school to not give up but rather try to develop their academic potential.

What are the ways that I can improve?

Psychologists have also studied students whose academic performance ranged from poor to very good in order to develop a profile of a successful student. Studies showed that successful students share a number of similar characteristics: they feel competent about meeting the demands of their classes; they believe they can handle test situations; they are very good at organizing their study time and leisure time; they prepare themselves for tests and do not procrastinate (Kleijn et al., 1994).

Based on studies of students' performances, the humanistic approach would say that just as successful students found ways to reach their academic potential, all students should search for ways to reach their own potentials. The humanistic approach emphasizes that students have the capacity to choose, that each is unique or special, and that students should have faith in their personal or subjective feelings (Hansen, 2000).

Cross-Cultural Approach

How is autism diagnosed in other cultures?

Let's look at differences in how countries diagnose autism.

United States. A psychologist in the United States first described the symptoms of autism 60 years ago (L. Kanner, 1943). Then autism was thought to be caused by environmental factors, such as having "cold" parents. In the 1960s, the focus changed to searching for biological causes (Rimland, 1964). In the United States, the diagnosis of autism usually occurs early, between ages 2 and 3, making it possible to begin treatment at a young age.

China. Autism was not recognized in China until 1987, and there are three reasons for this delay (Tao, 1987). First, most Chinese could not imagine that any disorder, such as autism, could occur in infancy. Second, many Chinese parents were unaware of an infant's developmental stages, such as when an infant first develops social and verbal skills. Third, Chinese parents generally believed that infants would grow out of any early difficulties. Efforts are under way to alert parents and medical professionals about the importance of making an early diagnosis and beginning early treatment (Tao & Yang, 1997).

Germany. The recognition of autism in Germany began in the late 1940s. Unlike the U.S. policy to diagnose autism early, clinicians in Germany rarely diagnose autism in children younger than 5 years. Efforts are under way to change this policy and diagnose and begin treatment of autism at an earlier age (Schmidt, 1997).

Japan. Autism was first diagnosed in Japan in 1945. It is interesting that Japan has higher rates of autism than other countries, and the rates are rising. Some believed that the rising rates were due to a childhood vaccine, but research has disproved this (Honda et al., 2005). Instead, the higher occurrence of autism in Japan may be due to Japanese clinicians' special efforts to detect signs of autism in children as well as in infants (Brasic, 2005; Yasuda & Matsuishi, 2002).

These differences in diagnosing autism show the influence of cultural factors and the use of the cross-cultural approach in psychology (Kagitcibasi & Poortinga, 2000; Triandis & Suh, 2002).

The *cross-cultural approach* studies the influence of cultural and ethnic similarities and differences on psychological and social functioning.

As you'll see next, there are also cross-cultural differences in how students respond to test anxiety.

Cross-Cultural Approach to Test Anxiety

How do other cultures deal with test anxiety?

Culture plays an important role in determining the intensity and expression of anxiety. For example, the highest test anxiety scores were reported by students in Egypt, Jordan, and Hungary. The lowest test anxiety scores were reported by students in China, Italy, Japan, and the Netherlands. Test anxiety scores of students in the United States were somewhere in the middle (Zeidner, 1998).

Some cultural factors that play a role in determining levels of text anxiety include importance of academic success, career opportunities, parental expectations, perceptions of

Students' level of test anxiety depends on their cultural values.

being evaluated, and students' expectations. Researchers suggest that higher test anxiety may also result from special environmental and educational problems or increased competition because of fewer educational opportunities (Zeidner, 1998).

Researchers also discovered that how students evaluate success depends on their cultural values. For example, students in Chile admired successful students, whether or not they thought the success resulted from expending great effort or having natural ability. In contrast, American students admired successful students much more if they thought the success resulted from expending great effort rather than having natural ability (Betancourt & Lopez, 1993). This study shows how the cross-cultural approach provides different and interesting answers to the same question (Keller & Greenfield, 2000).

Many Approaches, Many Answers

Of the six approaches that we have discussed, the cross-cultural approach is the most recent. This approach began in the early 1970s with the publication of the *Journal of Cross-Cultural Psychology* and has since grown in popularity (Triandis & Suh, 2002). In each module, we will highlight a cross-cultural study, which will be indicated by the symbol of multicultural people shown on the right.

The reason modern psychology uses many different approaches to study the same behavior is that the different viewpoint of each approach serves to provide additional information. By combining information from the biological,

cognitive, behavioral, psychoanalytic, humanistic, and cross-cultural approaches, psychologists stand a better chance of reaching their four goals of describing, explaining, predicting, and controlling behavior.

We have discussed the approaches used by modern psychologists so that you can compare them with the different approaches used by early psychologists. As you compare early and modern approaches, you can appreciate how much psychology has changed in the past 100 years.

This symbol indicates a cultural diversity topic.

C. Historical Approaches

How did psychology begin?

Imagine living in the late 1800s and early 1900s, when the electric light, radio, and airplane were being invented and the average human life span was about 30 years. This was the time when psychology broke away from philosophy and became a separate field of study. As they developed this new area, early psychologists hotly debated its definition, approach, and goals (Benjamin, 2000). We'll highlight those early psychologists whose ideas and criticisms shaped the field. We'll begin with the person considered to be the father of psychology, Wilhelm Wundt.

Structuralism: Elements of the Mind

Who established the first lab?

WILHELM WUNDT 1832–1920

There were no bands or celebrations when Wilhelm Wundt established the first psychology laboratory in 1879, in Leipzig, Germany. In fact, his laboratory was housed in several rooms in a shabby building that contained rather simple equipment, such as platforms, various balls, telegraph keys, and metronomes. The heavily bearded Wundt, now considered the father of psychology, would ask subjects to drop balls from a platform or listen to a metronome (figure below) and report their own sensations. Wundt and his followers were analyzing their sensations, which they thought was the key to analyzing the structure of the mind (Hergenhahn, 2004). For this reason they were called structuralists and their approach was called structuralism.

Structuralism **was the study of the most basic elements, primarily sensations and perceptions, that make up our conscious mental experiences.**

Just as you might assemble hundreds of pieces of a jigsaw puzzle into a completed picture, structuralists tried to combine hundreds of sensations into a complete conscious experience. Perhaps Wundt's greatest contribution was his method of introspection.

Introspection **was a method of exploring conscious mental processes by asking subjects to look inward and report their sensations and perceptions.**

For example, after listening to a beating metronome, the subjects would be asked to report whether their sensations were pleasant, unpleasant, exciting, or relaxing. However, introspection was heavily criticized for being an unscientific method because it was solely dependent on subjects' self-reports, which could be biased, rather than on objective measurements. Although Wundt's approach was the first, it had little impact on modern psychology. The modern-day cognitive approach also studies mental processes, but with different scientific methods and much broader interests than those of Wundt.

Can you describe each sensation you hear?

It wasn't long before Wundt's approach was criticized for being too narrow and subjective in primarily studying sensations. These criticisms resulted in another new approach, called functionalism.

Functionalism: Functions of the Mind

Who wrote the first textbook?

WILLIAM JAMES 1842–1910

For twelve years, William James labored over a book called *The Principles of Psychology*, which was published in 1890 and included almost every topic that is now part of psychology textbooks: learning, sensation, memory, reasoning, attention, feelings, consciousness, and a revolutionary theory of emotions.

For example, why do you feel fear when running from a raging wolf? You might answer that an angry wolf (figure below) is a terrifying creature that causes fear and makes you run—fear makes you run. Not so, according to James, who reasoned that the act of running causes a specific set of physiological responses that your brain interprets as fear—running makes you afraid. According to James, emotions were caused by physiological changes; thus, running produced fear. You'll find out if James's theory of emotions was correct in Module 16.

Unlike Wundt, who saw mental activities as composed of basic elements, James viewed mental activities as having developed through ages of evolution because of their adaptive functions, such as helping humans survive. James was interested in the goals, purposes, and functions of the mind, an approach called functionalism.

Functionalism, **which was the study of the function rather than the structure of consciousness, was interested in how our minds adapt to our changing environment.**

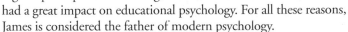

Functionalism did not last as a unique approach, but many of James's ideas grew into current areas of study, such as emotions, attention, and memory (Hergenhahn, 2004). In addition, James suggested ways to apply psychological principles to teaching, which

Does running from an angry wolf cause fear?

had a great impact on educational psychology. For all these reasons, James is considered the father of modern psychology.

Notice that James disagreed with Wundt's structural approach and pushed psychology toward looking at how the mind functions and adapts to our ever-changing world. About the same time that James was criticizing Wundt's structuralism, another group also found reasons to disagree with Wundt; this group was the Gestalt psychologists.

Gestalt Approach: Sensations Versus Perceptions

Who said, "Wundt is wrong"?

When you see a road hazard sign like the one in the photo below, you think the lights forming the arrow are actually moving in one direction. This motion, however, is only an illusion; the lights are stationary and are only flashing on and off.

The illusion that flashing lights appear to move was first studied in 1912 by three psychologists: Max Wertheimer, Wolfgang Köhler, and Kurt Koffka. They reported that they had created the perception of movement by briefly flashing one light and then, a short time later, a second light. Although the two bulbs were fixed, the light actually appeared to move from one to the other. They called this the *phi phenomenon;* today it is known as *apparent motion.*

**MAX WERTHEIMER
1883–1943**

Wertheimer and his colleagues believed that the perception of apparent motion could not be explained by the structuralists, who said that the movement resulted from simply adding together the sensations from two fixed lights. Instead, Wertheimer argued that perceptual experiences, such as perceiving moving lights, resulted from analyzing a "whole pattern," or, in German, a *Gestalt.*

The *Gestalt approach* emphasized that perception is more than the sum of its parts and studied how sensations are assembled into meaningful perceptual experiences.

In our example, Gestalt psychologists would explain that your experience of perceiving moving traffic lights is much more than and very different from what is actually happening—fixed lights flashing in sequence. These kinds of findings could not be explained by the structuralists and pointed out the limitations of their approach (D. J. Murray et al., 2000).

After all these years, many principles of the Gestalt approach are still used to explain how we perceive objects. We'll discuss many of the Gestalt principles of perception in Module 6.

Why do blinking lights seem to move?

Behaviorism: Observable Behaviors

Who offered a guarantee?

"Give me a dozen healthy infants, well-formed, and my own special world to bring them up in and I'll guarantee to take any one at random and train him to become any type of specialist I might select—doctor, lawyer, artist . . ." (Watson, 1924).

**JOHN B. WATSON
1878–1958**

These words come from John B. Watson, who published a landmark paper in 1913 titled "Psychology as a Behaviorist Views It." In it, he rejected Wundt's structuralism and its study of mental elements and conscious processes. He rejected introspection as a psychological technique because its results could not be scientifically verified by other psychologists. Instead, John Watson boldly stated that psychology should be considered an objective, experimental science, whose goal should be the analysis of observable behaviors and the prediction and control of those behaviors (Harzem, 2004). It is a small step from these ideas to Watson's boast, "Give me a dozen healthy infants . . . ," which illustrates the behavioral approach.

The *behavioral approach* emphasized the objective, scientific analysis of observable behaviors.

Can anyone guarantee what I will become?

From the 1920s to the 1960s, behaviorism was the dominant force in American psychology. Part of this dominance was due to the work of B. F. Skinner and other behaviorists, who expanded and developed Watson's ideas into the modern-day behavioral approach, which is fully discussed in Module 10. However, beginning in the 1970s and continuing into the present, behaviorism's dominance was challenged by the cognitive approach, whose popularity throughout the 1990s surpassed behaviorism (R. B. Evans, 1999).

Survival of Approaches

Which approaches survived?

The survival of each approach—structuralism, functionalism, Gestalt, and behaviorism—depended on its ability to survive its criticisms. Criticisms of Wundt's structural approach gave rise to the functional approach of James and the Gestalt approach of Wertheimer, Köhler, and Koffka. Criticisms of all three approaches—structural, functional, and Gestalt—gave rise to Watson's behavioral approach. Another approach, Sigmund Freud's psychoanalytic approach (see p. 9), which emphasized the influence of unconscious processes, disagreed with Watson's strict behavioral approach and developed largely in parallel with these other approaches. These disagreements in approaches resulted in heated debates among early psychologists, but they helped psychology develop into the scientific field it is today (R. B. Evans, 1999).

Although early American psychologists differed in their approaches, they shared one underlying theme that was a sign of their times. They discriminated against women and minorities in both academic and career settings. Such discriminatory practices were widespread in early times, and we'll examine that issue next.

D. Cultural Diversity: Early Discrimination

Because psychologists focus on studying and understanding human behavior, you would expect them to be among the first to recognize the mistreatment of and discrimination against other groups. However, psychologists are human and, being human, they knowingly or unknowingly adopted and carried out the discriminatory practices that were operating at the time. This means that, for the first 75 of its more than 100 years of existence, the academic policies and career opportunities of American psychology were determined by White males, who both intentionally and unintentionally discriminated against women and people of color. Here are just a few examples.

Women in Psychology

Why couldn't she enter graduate school?

The reason Mary Calkins (on right) could not enter graduate school was that she was a woman, and many universities (Johns Hopkins, Harvard, Columbia) would not admit women. Since Calkins was a faculty member and had established a laboratory in psychology at Wellesley College in 1891, she petitioned and was allowed to take seminars at Harvard. There, she completed all requirements for a Ph.D. and was recommended for a doctorate by her professors, but the Harvard administration declined to grant it because she was a woman (Furumoto, 1989). It was not until 1908 that a woman, Margaret Washburn, was awarded a Ph.D. in psychology.

Mary Calkins was not given a Ph.D. because she was a woman.

Even after women began obtaining doctorates, the only positions open to them were teaching jobs at women's colleges or normal schools, which trained high school teachers (Furumoto & Scarborough, 1986). During the past 25 years, women have made great progress in the field. However, even though women currently earn more Ph.D.s in psychology than men, in 1991 there were more full-time male psychologists (39,180) than women (20,100). In addition, female psychologists earn less than male psychologists, and fewer women are editors of psychology journals (Rabasca, 2000b). Not only did women face discrimination in psychology, but so did people of color.

Minorities in Psychology

Why so few minority students?

In psychology's early days, only a few northern White universities accepted Black students, while all southern White universities denied admission to Black students.

The first African American woman to receive a Ph.D. in psychology was Ruth Howard (photo below), who graduated from the University of Minnesota in 1934. She had a successful career as a clinical psychologist and school consultant.

Between 1920 and 1966, only 8 Ph.D.s in psychology were awarded to Black students, compared to 3,767 doctorates to Whites (R. V. Guthrie, 1976). In 1996, 168 Ph.D.s were awarded to African Americans, 183 to Hispanics, 23 to Native Americans, 131 to Asians, and 2,939 to Whites (Rabasca, 2000b).

During the early 1900s, few degrees were awarded to Hispanics. One early exception was

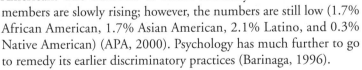

Ruth Howard was the first Black woman to get a Ph.D. in 1934.

George Sanchez (photo below), who conducted pioneering work on the cultural bias of intelligence tests given to minority students. Sanchez criticized the claim that Mexican Americans were mentally inferior, saying the claim was based solely on intelligence tests. He showed that intelligence tests contained many questions that were biased against minorities and thus resulted in their lower scores (R. V. Guthrie, 1976).

From the founding of the American Psychological Association in 1892 to 1990, its cumulative membership was 128,000. Of those members, only 700 were African American, 700 were Latino, and 70 were Native American. The numbers of ethnic minority members are slowly rising; however, the numbers are still low (1.7% African American, 1.7% Asian American, 2.1% Latino, and 0.3% Native American) (APA, 2000). Psychology has much further to go to remedy its earlier discriminatory practices (Barinaga, 1996).

George Sanchez found intelligence tests were culturally biased.

Righting the Wrongs

How much success?

Today, people of color are still underrepresented in academic departments and in graduate programs in psychology, although their numbers and influence are increasing (APA, 2004b).

The American Psychological Association (APA) recognized the need to recruit more ethnic minorities and formed a special group to reach this goal. The group established numerous journals to promote the causes of women and ethnic minorities (DeAngelis, 1966) and sponsored a program to visit high schools and teach minority students about careers in psychology (Dittman, 2005). The APA has an official policy supporting equal opportunities "for persons regardless of race, gender, age, religion, disability, sexual orientation and national origin" (Tomes, 2000).

In the late 1990s, several states banned affirmative action programs, which had helped minority students enter college. As a result, university enrollments of minority students in these states have dropped (J. Steinberg, 2003). Colleges are now searching for other ways to recruit minority students (Marklein, 2002).

✔ Concept Review

1. The systematic, scientific study of behaviors and mental processes is called _____.

2. The four goals of psychology are to (a)_____ what organisms do, to (b)_____ the causes of behavior, to (c)_____ behavior in new situations, and to (d)_____ behavior, which has both positive and negative aspects.

3. The approach that focuses on how one's nervous system, hormones, and genes interact with the environment is called the _____ approach.

4. The approach that studies how people think, solve problems, and process information is called the _____ approach.

5. The approach that analyzes how environmental rewards and punishments shape, change, or motivate behavior is called the _____ approach.

6. The approach that stresses the influence of unconscious feelings, fears, or desires on the development of behavior, personality, and psychological problems is called the (a)_____ approach. This approach also emphasizes the importance of early (b)_____ experiences.

7. The approach that emphasizes freedom of choice, self-fulfillment, and attaining one's potential is called the (a)_____ approach. Many of this approach's concepts have been taken up and used in (b)_____.

8. The newest approach, which focuses on cultural and ethnic influences on behavior, is called the _____ approach.

9. Wundt studied the elements that made up the conscious mind and called this approach (a)_____. Subjects were asked to observe the workings of their minds, a technique that Wundt called (b)_____. Modern-day psychologists who study mental activities with more objective and scientific methods are said to use the (c)_____ approach.

10. William James disagreed with Wundt's structuralism and instead emphasized the functions, goals, and purposes of the mind and its adaptation to the environment; he called this approach (a)_____. James also applied the principles of psychology to teaching, so his approach had a great effect on the field of (b)_____ psychology.

11. Some psychologists disagreed with Wundt's approach of structuralism and instead believed that perceptions are more than the sum of many individual (a)_____. These psychologists called their approach the (b)_____ approach, which studied how sensations were assembled into meaningful (c)_____.

12. John Watson disagreed with Wundt's approach, which was called (a)_____, and disagreed with Wundt's technique of studying the mind, which was called (b)_____. Instead, Watson emphasized the objective, scientific analysis of observable behaviors, which was known as the (c)_____ approach. Later, this approach became a dominant force in psychology through the work of behaviorist (d)_____.

Answers: 1. psychology; 2. (a) describe, (b) explain, (c) predict, (d) control; 3. biological; 4. cognitive; 5. behavioral; 6. (a) psychoanalytic, (b) childhood; 7. (a) humanistic, (b) counseling or psychotherapy; 8. cross-cultural; 9. (a) structuralism, (b) introspection, (c) cognitive; 10. (a) functionalism, (b) educational; 11. (a) sensations, (b) Gestalt, (c) perceptions; 12. (a) structuralism, (b) introspection, (c) behavioral, (d) B. F. Skinner

E. Research Focus: Taking Class Notes

*How good
are your
class notes?*

As you listen to lectures in class, you'll probably be taking notes. But how do you know if you're using the best system or strategy? To research some particular behavior, such as note-taking, psychologists first ask a very specific research question: Which system or strategy for taking notes results in the best performance on tests? One researcher answered this question by using a combination of behavioral and cognitive approaches (A. King, 1992). As we describe this interesting study, notice how it involves the four goals of psychology, beginning with the first goal, describing behavior.

How can I make my notes better?

1st Goal: Describe Behavior

The researcher divided college students into three different groups. Each group was given a different method or strategy for taking notes. As described below, students practiced three different strategies for taking notes: review notes, summarize notes, and answer questions about notes.

A. Review Notes

The strategy that most students use is to try to write down as much as possible of what the professor says. Then, before exams, students review their notes, hoping they took good class notes.

B. Summarize Notes

Students took notes as usual but, after the lecture, used their notes to write a summary of the lecture in their own words.

Students were shown how to identify a main topic and, in their own words, write a sentence about it. Then they identified a subtopic and wrote a sentence that related it to the main topic. When linked together, these sentences created a summary of the lecture, written in the students' own words.

C. Answer Questions about Notes

Students took notes as usual but, after the lecture, used their notes to ask and answer questions about the lecture material. Students were given a set of 13 general questions, such as: **What is the main idea of . . . ? How would you use . . . to . . . ? What is a new example of . . . ? What is the difference between . . . and . . . ?** Students answered each of these questions using their class notes.

After practicing one of these three note-taking strategies, students watched a videotaped lecture and used their particular strategy for taking notes.

2nd Goal: Explain Behavior

A week after each group had watched a videotaped lecture, they were given an exam. The graph on the right shows that the group who used the strategy of taking notes plus answering questions scored significantly higher than the other two groups. The researcher explained that students who took notes and then answered questions about their notes retained more information than students who employed the other two strategies (A. King, 1992).

Average Score on Exam

34	Review notes
45	Summarize notes
51	Answer questions

3rd Goal: Predict Behavior

On the basis of these results, the researcher predicts that students who use the strategy that combines note-taking with answering questions are likely to retain more information and perform better on exams than students who use traditional note-taking methods, such as writing as much as they can and then reviewing their notes before exams.

4th Goal: Control Behavior

Students can increase their chances of getting better grades by taking the time to learn a better note-taking strategy. This new strategy involves taking notes and then answering, in their own word, a series of general questions about the lecture material. Although this new note-taking strategy takes a little time to learn, the payoff will be better performance on exams. This and other research show the connection between good note-taking skills and higher test performance (Peverly et al., 2003).

Purpose of the Research Focus

This study shows how psychologists answered a very practical and important question about how best to take lecture notes. We'll use the Research Focus to show how psychologists use different approaches and research techniques to answer a variety of interesting questions about human behavior.

Each time you see this symbol, it will indicate a Research Focus, which occurs in each module.

Although a large percentage of psychologists engage in research, you'll see next how many others work in a variety of career settings that may or may not involve research.

F. Careers in Psychology

What's a psychologist? Many students think that psychologists are primarily counselors and therapists, even though advanced degrees in psychology are awarded in a dozen different areas. Obtaining an advanced degree in psychology requires that one finish college and spend about two to three years in postgraduate study to obtain a master's degree or four to five years in postgraduate study to obtain a Ph.D. Some careers or work settings require a master's degree, while others require a Ph.D. Many students are confused about the difference between a psychologist, a clinical or counseling psychologist, and a psychiatrist.

It usually takes about 4 to 5 years after college to become a psychologist.

A *psychologist* is usually someone who has completed 4 to 5 years of postgraduate education and has obtained a Ph.D., PsyD., or Ed.D. in psychology.

A *clinical psychologist* has a Ph.D., PsyD., or Ed.D., has specialized in a clinical subarea, and has spent an additional year in a supervised therapy setting to gain experience in diagnosing and treating a wide range of abnormal behaviors.

Similar to clinical psychologists are *counseling psychologists,* who provide many of the same services but usually work with different problems, such as those involving marriage, family, or career counseling. Neither clinical nor counseling psychologists assess the neurological causes of mental problems. Until recently no psychologists in the United States have been able to prescribe drugs. Now, psychologists in New Mexico and Louisiana who have completed special medical training can prescribe drugs like psychiatrists (Levin, 2005).

A *psychiatrist* is a medical doctor (M.D.) who has spent several years in clinical training, which includes diagnosing possible physical and neurological causes of abnormal behaviors and treating these behaviors, often with prescription drugs. Psychologists can work in the following career settings.

Are psychologists usually therapists? As you can see in the pie chart below, the majority (49%) of psychologists are therapists, while the rest work in four other settings. In the United States and Canada, most psychologists have a Ph.D., PsyD., or Ed.D., which requires 4 to 5 years of study after college. In many other countries, most psychologists have a college degree, which requires four to five years of study after high school (Helmes & Pachana, 2005). Since the 1950s, there has been an increase in psychologists who provide therapy/health services and a decline in those who work in academic/research settings.

The U.S. Department of Labor predicts that employment opportunities for psychologists will grow much faster than the average for other occupations in the coming years (U.S. Dept. of Labor, 2006). Here's a breakdown of where psychologists in the United States currently work (D. Smith, 2002).

49% The largest percentage (49%) of psychologists work as clinical or counseling psychologists in either a *private practice* or *therapy setting,* such as a psychological or psychiatric clinic; a mental health center; a psychiatric, drug, or rehabilitation ward of a hospital; or a private office. The duties of clinical or counseling psychologists might involve doing individual or group therapy; helping patients with problems involving drugs, stress, weight, marriage, family, or career; designing programs for healthier living; or testing patients for psychological problems that developed from some neurological problem.

28% The second largest percentage (28%) of psychologists work in the *academic settings* of universities and colleges. Academic psychologists often engage in some combination of classroom teaching, mentoring or helping students, and doing research in their areas of interest.

13% The third largest percentage (13%) of psychologists work in a variety of other kinds of jobs and *career settings.*

6% The fourth largest percentage (6%) of psychologists work in *industrial settings,* such as businesses, corporations, and consulting firms. These psychologists, often called industrial/organizational psychologists, may work at selecting personnel, increasing production, or improving job satisfaction and employer–employee relations.

4% The smallest percentage (4%) work in *secondary schools and other settings.* For example, school psychologists conduct academic and career testing and provide counseling for a variety of psychological problems (learning disabilities, attention-deficit/hyperactivity disorder).

If you are thinking of entering the field of psychology today, you have a wide and exciting range of career choices. For those who decide to engage in research, we'll next discuss seven of the more popular research areas that psychologists choose.

G. Research Areas

Which area should I choose?

As you proceed through your introductory psychology course, you'll find that the world of psychology has been divided into at least seven general areas. And, if you go on and enter graduate school in psychology, you'll be expected to specialize in one of these seven areas. Students often find it difficult to choose only one special area of psychology, since they may be interested in two or three. For example, I switched areas three times before deciding upon one of the seven. The reason graduate students are asked to choose one area is that there is such an enormous amount of information that it takes great effort to master even one area. As you read about each research area, think about which one you might prefer. (Percentages given below do not add up to 100% because some miscellaneous areas are not included.)

Social and Personality

How does being in a group affect one's behavior?

How does one develop certain personality traits?

How important is physical attractiveness in making first impressions?

These questions come from the two different and sometimes overlapping areas of social psychology and personality psychology.

Social psychology involves the study of social interactions, stereotypes, prejudices, attitudes, conformity, group behaviors, and aggression.

Personality psychology involves the study of personality development, personality change, assessment, and abnormal behaviors.

Many social/personality psychologists work in academic settings, but some work as consultants and personnel managers in business. About 22% of psychologists choose social psychology and 5% choose personality.

Developmental

Why do some babies cry more than others?

What impact does abuse have on children?

What happens to teenagers during puberty?

What happens to our sex drive as we age?

You would be asking these kinds of questions if you were a developmental psychologist.

Developmental psychology examines moral, social, emotional, and cognitive development throughout a person's entire life.

Some developmental psychologists focus on changes in infancy and childhood, while others trace changes through adolescence, adulthood, and old age. They work in academic settings and may consult on day care or programs for the aging. About 25% of psychologists choose this specialty.

Experimental

Why does an animal press a bar to obtain food?

Can learning principles be used to treat a phobia?

Why do we feel fear when we see a snake?

What is taste aversion?

These kinds of questions interest experimental psychologists.

Experimental psychology includes areas of sensation, perception, learning, human performance, motivation, and emotion.

Experimental psychologists conduct much of their research under carefully controlled laboratory conditions, with both animal and human subjects. About 16% of psychologists specialize in experimental psychology. Most work in academic settings, but some also work in business, industry, and government.

Biological

How do psychiatric medications change brain chemistry?

How do brain cells change during Alzheimer's disease?

What happens to the brain during a dream?

Do genes affect your intelligence?

Physiological psychologists or psychobiologists study the biological basis of learning and memory; the effects of brain damage; the causes of sleep and wakefulness; the basis of hunger, thirst, and sex; the effects of stress on the body; and the ways in which drugs influence behavior.

Biological psychology or *psychobiology* **involves research on the physical and chemical changes that occur during stress, learning, and emotions, as well as how our genetic makeup, brain, and nervous system interact with our environments and influence our behaviors.**

Psychobiologists work in academic settings, hospitals, and private research laboratories. About 8% of psychologists choose this area.

Cognitive

What was unique about Einstein's thought processes?

What's the best way to learn new information?

Does memory get worse with age?

Do men and women think differently?

If these questions interest you, think about being a cognitive psychologist.

Cognitive psychology **involves how we process, store, and retrieve information and how cognitive processes influence our behaviors.**

Cognitive research includes memory, thinking, language, creativity, and decision making. Newer areas, such as artificial intelligence, combine knowledge of the brain's functions with computer programming in an attempt to duplicate human thinking and intelligence.

Earlier we discussed a relatively new area that combines cognitive and biological approaches and is called cognitive neuroscience. About 5% of psychologists select this area.

Psychometrics

What do college entrance tests show?

What career best fits my abilities?

How do tests assess abnormal behaviors?

These questions introduce an area called psychometrics, which involves the construction, administration, and interpretation of psychological tests.

Psychometrics **focuses on the measurement of people's abilities, skills, intelligence, personality, and abnormal behaviors.**

To accomplish their goals, psychologists in this area focus on developing a wide range of psychological tests, which must be continually updated and checked for usefulness and cultural biases. Some of these tests are used to assess people's skills and abilities, as well as to predict their performance in certain careers and situations, such as college or business. About 5% of psychologists select this area.

Making Decisions

What should I do?

If you decide to become a psychologist, you will need to make a series of decisions. The first is whether to obtain a master's degree or a Ph.D. The next decision involves which setting to work in: choosing among private practice, clinic or hospital setting, academic research and/or teaching, industry/business, or counseling and testing in a school setting. You'll also need to specialize in one of the seven areas: social, personality, developmental, experimental, biological, cognitive, or psychometrics. After making all these decisions, you are on your way to having a very interesting and exciting career.

Next, we're going to use research findings from several research areas, including personality, experimental, and cognitive, and give you tips on how to improve your study skills.

H. Application — Study Skills

Improving Study Habits

What problems do over 50% of freshmen report?

In a survey of college freshmen, 57% reported they had poor study habits, and 54% said they had problems managing their time (Thombs, 1995). We'll discuss ways to deal with both of these problems, beginning with ways to improve study habits.

Common complaint. The most common student complaint we hear after exams is, "I read the book and went over my notes three times and still got a C." This complaint points to the most common mistake students make in studying for exams. Because students read the material and go over their notes several times, they may have a general feeling they know the material. For example, you have just read about the six modern approaches, the historical approaches, and the differences between a psychologist, clinical psychologist, and psychiatrist. Having read this material, you may generally feel that you know it. However, researchers have discovered a startling fact: There is almost no relationship between how well students think they know material and how well they perform on an exam (Cull & Zechmeister, 1994; Mazzoni & Cornoldi, 1993).

Poor judges. The reason students tend to be poor judges of what they know is they base their judgments more on what they *generally* know rather than on what they *specifically* remember (Glenberg et al., 1987). For example, you might generally remember the six approaches. However, on an exam you will be asked for specific information, such as names and definitions. One of the best ways to judge how prepared you are for an exam is to test yourself and get feedback from answering specific questions. For instance, can you list the six approaches and define each one? Because answering specific questions is one way to judge your learning, we built specific questions and answers into this text. You can test yourself by answering questions in the Concept Review in each module and by answering questions in the Summary Test at the end of each module.

How do I know when I've studied enough to take a test?

Reducing distractions. When we ask students about their study habits, we often learn they listen to music, watch TV, answer phone calls, or use the Internet while studying. These study habits can lead to lower exam scores (Gurung, 2005). One way students can improve their study habits is by eliminating all distractions.

Time management. A common problem students have is managing their time—specifically, underestimating how long it will take to study all the material. For example, researchers found that about 50% of college students repeatedly anticipated finishing a task earlier than they actually did (Buehler et al., 1994). Part of the problem is that students do not allow enough time for studying more difficult items. Researchers found that students who plan to set aside extra time for studying more difficult items increase their chances of remembering the material (Allgood et al., 2000). One way to achieve better time management involves setting the right kinds of goals.

Remember:
To judge how well prepared you are for an exam, ask yourself specific questions about the material. You can do that by taking the tests built into each module—Concept Review and Summary Test.

Setting Goals

What's the best kind of goal to set?

Another way to better manage your study time is to set the right goals, which can vary from studying for a certain period of time to studying until you feel you are well prepared (Flippo & Caverly, 2000). Which of the following goals do you think would make your study time more efficient and improve your test performance?

1 Set a **time goal**, such as studying 10 hours a week or more, and then keep track of your study time during the semester.

Should my goal be to study 10 hours a week?

2 Set a **general goal**, such as trying to study hard and stay on schedule; then, try to reach this goal during the semester.

3 Set a **specific performance goal,** such as answering at least 80% of the Summary Test questions correctly for each module.

To determine which of these three goals leads to more effective studying, researchers told three different groups of students to set time goals, general goals, or specific performance goals when they studied on their own. The researchers found that students who set specific performance goals did significantly better on the final exam than students who set time or general goals (M. Morgan, 1985). Thus, if you want to improve your study skills, you should think less about the total time you study and concentrate more on reaching a specific performance goal every week. For example, the first week your goal might be to correctly answer 80% of the Summary Test questions. Once you have reached this goal, you could aim to answer 90% of the questions correctly. Following a study plan based on specific performance goals is the key to better time management (Wolters, 2003).

As you'll see next, one way to motivate yourself to reach your performance goals is to reward yourself at the right times.

Remember:
One way to make your study time more efficient is to set a specific performance goal and keep track of your progress.

What if you reach a goal?

One problem many students have is getting and staying motivated. One reliable solution is to give yourself a reward when you reach a specific goal, such as answering 80% of the questions correctly. The reward may be a special treat (such as a CD, meal, movie, or time with friends) or a positive statement (such as "I'm doing really well" or "I'm going to get a good grade on the test"). Giving yourself a reward (self-reinforcement) is an effective way to improve performance (Allgood et al., 2000).

Motivate yourself with rewards.

Remember:
Immediately after you reach a specific goal, give yourself a reward, which will both maintain and improve your motivation.

Another way to improve your performance is to take great notes. Students generally make two kinds of mistakes in taking notes. One is to try to write down everything the instructor says, which is impossible and leads to confusing notes. The other is to mechanically copy down terms or concepts that they do not understand but hope to learn by sheer memorization, which is difficult. Researchers have four suggestions for taking good notes (Armbruster, 2000):

1 Write down the information in your own words. This approach will ensure that you understand the material and will increase your chances of remembering it.

2 Use headings or an outline format. This method will help you better organize and remember the material.

3 Try to associate new lecture or text material with material that you already know. It's easier to remember new information if you can relate it to your existing knowledge. That is the reason we have paired terms in the Concept Review section with illustrations, drawings, and photos that you are familiar with from earlier in the text.

4 As we discussed in the Research Focus (p. 16), you can improve your note-taking by asking yourself questions, such as: What is the main idea of . . . ? What is an example of . . . ? How is . . . related to what we studied earlier? Writing the answers in your own words will give you a better chance of remembering the material (A. King, 1992).

Even though you may take great notes and set performance goals, if you procrastinate and put off getting started, as 30 to 70% of students report doing, your best-laid plans will come to nothing (Senécal et al., 1995). We already discussed some of the reasons behind procrastination (p. 9), and here we'll look at ways to overcome it.

Remember:
Go through your lecture notes, ask questions, and write down answers in your own words.

How do you get started?

Some students find the task of reading assignments, studying for exams, or writing papers so difficult that they cannot bring themselves to start. If you have problems with procrastinating, here are three things you should do to get started (Ariely & Wertenbroch, 2002; Blunt & Pychyl, 2000).

1 *Stop thinking about the final goal*—reading 30 pages or taking two midterm exams—which may seem too overwhelming.

2 Break the final assignment down into a number of *smaller goals* that are less overwhelming and easier to accomplish. Work on the first small goal, and when you finish it, go on to the next small goal. Continue until you have completed all the small goals.

3 Write down a *realistic schedule* for reaching each of your smaller goals. This schedule should indicate the time and place for study and what you will accomplish that day. Use a variety of self-reinforcements to stay on your daily schedule and accomplish your specific goals.

Everyone procrastinates a little, but it becomes a problem if you continually put off starting important projects that have deadlines, such as exams and papers. Take the advice of professionals on stopping procrastination: get organized, set specific goals, and reward yourself (Ariely & Wertenbroch, 2002).

Use three steps to overcome procrastination.

If you adopt these tested methods for improving your study skills, you'll greatly increase your chances of being a successful student (Flippo et al., 2000).

Remember:
One of the most effective ways to start a large assignment is to break it down into a series of smaller goals and work on each goal separately.

Unusual Excuses for Missing Exams

✔ I missed the exam because of my uncle's funeral, and I can't take the make-up tomorrow because I just found out my aunt has a brain tumor.

✔ I can't be at the exam because my cat is having kittens and I'm her coach.

✔ I want to reschedule the final because my grandmother is a nun.

✔ I can't take the exam on Monday because my mom is getting married on Sunday and I'll be too drunk to drive back to school.

✔ I couldn't be at the exam because I had to attend the funeral of my girlfriend's dog.

✔ I can't take the the test Friday because my mother is having a vasectomy. (D. A. Bernstein, 1993, p. 4)

✔ Summary Test

A. Definition & Goals

1. The broad definition of psychology is the systematic, scientific study of (a)_____ and (b)_____. The term in (a) refers to observable responses of animals and humans, and the term in (b) refers to processes that are not directly observable, such as thoughts, ideas, and dreams.

2. All psychologists agree that the first three goals of psychology are to (a)_____ what organisms do, to (b)_____ how organisms behave as they do, and to (c)_____ how they will respond in the future and in different situations. Some psychologists add a fourth goal, which is to (d)_____ behavior and thus curb or eliminate psychological and social problems.

B. Modern Approaches

3. Because behavior is often so complex, psychologists study it using six different approaches. The approach that focuses on how a person's genetic makeup, hormones, and nervous system interact with the environment to influence a wide range of behaviors is called the _____ approach.

4. The approach that studies how organisms learn new behaviors or change or modify existing ones in response to influences from the environment is called the (a)_____ approach. There are two versions of this approach. One that primarily studies observable behaviors and excludes mental events is called (b)_____ and is best expressed by the ideas of B. F. Skinner; the other, which includes observable behaviors plus cognitive processes, is called the (c)_____ approach and is expressed by the ideas of Albert Bandura and his colleagues.

5. An approach that examines how our unconscious fears, desires, and motivations influence behaviors, thoughts, and personality and cause psychological problems is called the _____ approach. Sigmund Freud developed this approach, as well as the technique of dream interpretation, to bring unconscious ideas to the surface.

6. The approach that investigates how people attend to, store, and process information and how this information affects learning, remembering, feeling, and believing is called the _____ approach.

7. An approach that emphasizes people's capacity for personal growth, freedom in choosing their future, and potential for self-fulfillment is called the _____ approach. One of the founders of this approach was Abraham Maslow.

8. The approach that studies how cultural and ethnic similarities and differences influence psychological and social functioning is called the _____ approach.

C. Historical Approaches

9. Considered the father of psychology, Wilhelm Wundt developed an approach called (a)_____. This approach studied the elements of the conscious mind by using a self-report technique called (b)_____. Wundt's approach was the beginning of today's cognitive approach.

10. Disagreeing with Wundt's approach, William James said that it was important to study functions rather than elements of the mind. Accordingly, James studied the functions of consciousness as well as how mental processes continuously flow and adapt to input from the environment. This approach is called _____. James's ideas contributed to the modern area of psychology and have also influenced educational psychology.

11. Also disagreeing with Wundt's approach was a group of psychologists, led by Wertheimer, Köhler, and Koffka, who stated that perceptions cannot be explained by breaking them down into individual elements or sensations. Instead, they believed that perceptions are more than the sum of individual sensations, an idea called the _____ approach.

12. Another psychologist who disagreed with Wundt's approach was John B. Watson. He stated that psychology should use scientific principles to study only observable behaviors and not mental events, an approach called _____. Watson's approach gave rise to the modern behavioral approach.

D. Cultural Diversity: Early Discrimination

13. During the first 75 of its more than 100 years of existence, the field of psychology discriminated against (a)_____ and (b)_____, as indicated by the very limited number of these individuals who were granted Ph.D.s or offered positions in major universities. During the past 25 years, the American Psychological Association, minority organizations, and most universities and colleges have been actively recruiting minorities and helping them enter the field of psychology.

E. Research Focus: Taking Class Notes

14. Three different strategies for note-taking were studied: note-taking plus review, which means writing down almost everything the instructor says; note-taking plus questions, which means asking and answering questions about the lecture material; and note-taking plus summary, which means writing a summary of the lecture in your own words. The note-taking strategy that resulted in the highest exam grades involved (a)_____, and the note-taking strategy that resulted in the lowest exam grades involved (b)_____.

F. Careers in Psychology

15. There are five major settings in which psychologists work and

establish careers. The largest percentage of psychologists work in private practice or (a)_____ settings, where they diagnose and help clients with psychological problems. The second largest group work in (b)_____ settings, doing a combination of teaching and research. The third largest group work in a (c)_____ of settings. The fourth largest group work in (d)_____ settings, where they are involved in selecting personnel, increasing job satisfaction, and improving worker–management relations. The fifth largest group work in other settings, such as (e)_____, where they do academic testing and counseling.

G. Research Areas

16. There are six common subareas in which psychologists specialize. Those who are interested in prejudice, attitudes, and group behaviors or in personality development and change specialize in (a)_____ psychology. Those interested in social, emotional, and cognitive changes across the life span specialize in (b)_____ psychology. Those interested in studying sensation, perceptions, learning, and motivation, often under laboratory conditions, specialize in

(c)_____ psychology. Those interested in the interaction among genes, the nervous system, and the environment choose (d)_____. Those interested in how people process, store, and retrieve information choose (e)_____ psychology, and those who are interested in the measurement and testing of skills, abilities, personality, and mental problems specialize in (f)_____.

H. Application: Study Skills

17. A common mistake that many students make is that, when they plan their study schedules, they often _____ the time it will take to complete a task.

18. Another common mistake that students make is that they think they know the material after reading the text and reviewing their notes. A better way to judge how prepared you are for an exam is to ask yourself specific (a)_____ rather than to trust your judgment about what you think you know. A good way to make your study time more efficient is to set specific (b)_____ and

keep track of your progress. Immediately after you reach a specific performance goal, give yourself a (c)_____, which will both maintain and improve your motivation. To improve your lecture notes, try to associate new lecture material with what you already know, and use your notes to ask and answer (d)_____ in your own words. One of the most effective ways to overcome a strong tendency to delay starting a task, known as (e)_____, is to stop thinking about the final goal. Instead, break down a large assignment into a series of smaller goals and work on each goal separately. Finally, it's best to set a realistic (f)_____ in order to accomplish each of the smaller goals.

Answers: *1. (a) behaviors, (b) mental processes; 2. (a) describe, (b) explain, (c) predict, (d) control; 3. biological; 4. (a) behavioral, (b) strict behaviorism, (c) social learning; 5. psychoanalytic; 6. cognitive; 7. humanistic; 8. cross-cultural; 9. (a) structuralism, (b) introspection; 10. functionalism; 11. Gestalt; 12. behaviorism; 13. (a) women, (b) minorities; 14. (a) answering questions, (b) reviewing notes; 15. (a) therapy or clinical, (b) academic, (c) variety, (d) industrial, (e) schools; 16. (a) social and personality, (b) developmental, (c) experimental, (d) biological or physiological psychology, (e) cognitive, (f) psychometrics; 17. underestimate; 18. (a) questions, (b) performance goals, (c) reward, (d) questions, (e) procrastination, (f) schedule*

Critical Thinking

How Do Autistic People Think?

Questions

Test your thinking power by answering the following questions. If you need help, check the suggested answers at the bottom.

1. What three childhood symptoms of autism do Donna (introduced on p. 3) and Temple share in common?

2. Which area of specialization in psychology would be best able to understand how Temple thinks in pictures?

3. Of the six modern approaches to psychology, which should you use to study someone with autism?

As a young child, Temple Grandin had a few peculiarities. She had great difficulty learning to speak and understanding language, but had an incredible eye for color and great artistic talent. Temple didn't know how to relate with other children and preferred to be alone, often rocking herself back and forth for hours. She was so sensitive to touch that she refused to allow anyone to touch her. Temple was unusually sensitive to sounds. She compared hearing the school bell to a "dentist's drill" (J. P. Shapiro, 1996) sounding in her ear. She described going through each day feeling anxious as if she was constantly "being mugged on the New York subway" (J. P. Shapiro, 1996).

Temple was diagnosed with autism at the age of 3, and doctors were certain she wouldn't ever be successful. What they didn't know is how much Temple would prove them wrong. Her childhood art projects provided a glimpse into Temple's unique way of thinking. While most of us think in words, Temple, like many others with autism, thinks in pictures. She compares her memory to a full-length movie in her head that she can replay over and over again. She can even view the movies from different points of view, which help her notice small details that other-

wise would have been overlooked.

Temple has made remarkable accomplishments by applying her visual way of thinking to her love of animals (see photo). For example, she placed herself "inside a cow's head" to see the world through its eyes. By doing so she realized how frightening it is for cattle to approach the dip vat, a deep swimming pool filled with pesticide that cattle enter to rid them of ticks and other parasites. Cattle would panic while going down a steep and slippery slope and then become even more frightened as they unexpectedly dropped into water. To reduce the fear cattle had of the dip vat, Temple used her visual way of thinking to design equipment with a less steep and slippery walkway, as well as a more comfortable way for cattle to enter the water.

Using her unique way of thinking in pictures, Temple has become the most accomplished and well-known autistic adult in the world. She has taken the lead in designing and advocating for the use of more humane equipment with animals. Temple Grandin earned a doctorate degree in animal science and is currently a university professor, prominent author and speaker, and a consultant for the care and handling of livestock. (Adapted from Fenly, 2006; Grandin, 1992, 2002; J. P. Shapiro, 1996)

4. What social skill does Temple have (unlike many with autism) that allows her to put herself "inside a cow's head"?

5. How would a humanistic psychologist understand Temple's accomplishments?

Suggested Answers

1. Three symptoms of autism Donna and Temple share in common are poor social relationships, sensitivity to touch and sound, and difficulty learning to speak and understand language.

2. Cognitive psychology studies how we process, store, and retrieve information. One of its primary goals is to better understand how people think.

3. None of the approaches is necessarily better than the others. Rather, each approach adds a different kind of information. By using several or all six of the approaches, we can more thoroughly understand someone with autism.

4. As we learned on page 6, empathy is an important social skill allowing us to put ourselves in other people's shoes and experience how they feel. People with autism generally have difficulty expressing empathy; however, Temple conveys much empathy toward cattle.

5. Unlike the doctors who were certain Temple would not be successful, humanistic psychologists believe that all people have free will, creativity, the ability to achieve personal growth, and an enormous potential for self-fulfillment. Humanistic psychologists would say that by working hard and believing in her abilities, Temple was able to reach her potential.

Links to Learning

Learning Activities

- ***POWERSTUDY FOR INTRODUCTION TO PSYCHOLOGY 4.0***

by Tom Doyle and Rod Plotnik
Check out the quizzes and learning activities for "Discovering Psychology" on **PowerStudy** and:
  - Test your knowledge using an interactive version of the Summary Test on pages 22 and 23. Also access related quizzing—true/false, multiple choice, and matching.
  - Explore an interactive version of the Critical Thinking exercise "How Do Autistic People Think?" on page 24.
  - You will also find key terms, a chapter outline including a chapter abstract, and a special extended list of hotlinked websites that correlate to this module.

- *CengageNOW*

academic.cengage.com/login
Need help studying? This site is your one-stop study shop.
Take a Pre-Test and CengageNOW will generate a Personalized Study Plan based on your test results. The Study Plan will identify the topics you need to review and direct you to online resources to help you master those topics. You can then take a Post-Test to determine the concepts you have mastered and what you still need to work on.

- ***INTRODUCTION TO PSYCHOLOGY BOOK COMPANION WEBSITE***

academic.cengage.com/psychology/plotnik
Visit your book companion website where you will find more resources to help you study. At this site, you will find Learning Objectives, Internet Exercises, quizzing, flash cards, and a pronunciation glossary.

- ***STUDY GUIDE and WEBTUTOR***
Check the corresponding module in your Study Guide for effective student tips and for help learning the material presented. Also go to **academic.cengage.com/webtutor** for an interactive version of the Study Guide features.

Study Questions

*A. **Definition & Goals**—How would you rank the four goals of psychology in terms of importance? (**Suggested answer page 619**)

B. **Modern Approaches**—How would psychologists use the six modern approaches to study whether alcoholism runs in families?

C. **Historical Approaches**—Do any of these historical approaches match your stereotype of what psychology is all about?

*D. **Cultural Diversity: Early Discrimination**—Why would discriminatory practices exist in psychology, an area devoted to studying human behavior? (**Suggested answer page 619**)

E. **Research Focus: Taking Class Notes**—What could you do to improve your note-taking skills?

F. **Careers in Psychology**—If you're thinking about a career in psychology, what setting would you choose?

G. **Research Areas**—Which of the six subareas of psychology would you study to help people manage stress?

*H. **Application: Study Skills**—What changes would you make to study most efficiently? (**Suggested answer page 619**)

*These questions are answered in Appendix B.

MODULE 2
Psychology & Science

The Origin Of
MAN

 PowerStudy 4.0™ Complete Module

Introduction

Dusty's Problem

What's wrong with Dusty's behavior?

It was 5:00 in the morning when Dusty began throwing a fit. As if driven by an inner motor, all 50 pounds of him was flying around the room, wailing and kicking. This raging activity went on for about 30 minutes; then he headed downstairs for breakfast. While his mother was busy in the kitchen, Dusty grabbed a box of cereal and kicked it around the room, spreading cereal everywhere. When his mother told him to clean up the mess, he got the dustpan but began picking it apart, piece by piece. Next he grabbed three rolls of toilet paper and unraveled them around the house. By then, it was only 7:30. Dusty had not been given his pill because he was seeing his doctor at 4:00 that day (adapted from *Time*, July 18, 1994).

Seven-year-old Dusty has a behavioral problem that has been surrounded with controversy. Dusty was diagnosed as being hyperactive, a problem that is officially called attention-deficit/hyperactivity disorder, or ADHD (American Psychiatric Association, 2000).

Attention-deficit/hyperactivity disorder, or *ADHD*, is not diagnosed by any medical tests but on the basis of the occurrence of certain behavioral problems. A child must have six or more symptoms of inattention, such as making careless mistakes in schoolwork, not following instructions, and being easily distracted, and six or more symptoms of hyperactivity, such as fidgeting, leaving classroom seat, running about when should not, and talking excessively. These symptoms should have been present from an early age, persisted for at least six months, and contributed to maladaptive development.

One controversy surrounding ADHD involves diagnosis. Since ADHD is based not on medical tests but rather on the occurrence of certain behavioral problems, how can children with ADHD be distinguished from those who are naturally outgoing and rambunctious (Sciutto et al., 2000)? Because of this difficulty, the American Academy of Pediatrics issued guidelines for diagnosing ADHD (Tanner, 2000). These guidelines stressed that, before the diagnosis of ADHD is made, a number of the symptoms described above should be present for at least six months. The guidelines focused on children aged 6 to 12 because there isn't sufficient evidence for making the diagnosis of ADHD at earlier ages. The goal of these guidelines is to prevent merely rambunctious youngsters from being overmedicated while ensuring that children with ADHD get the help they need (Root & Resnick, 2003).

Another controversy is how to treat children with ADHD. To help control Dusty's ADHD, he is given a popular drug that is a relatively powerful stimulant, called Ritalin *(WRIT-ah-lin)*. Ritalin's effects are similar to those of another stimulant, amphetamine. Researchers do not understand why stimulant drugs, such as Ritalin and amphetamine (Adderall), decrease activity in children. Spending on drugs to treat ADHD is about $1 billion a year, and drug manufacturers spend about $2.5 billion on marketing (Novak, 2001).

Seven-year-old Dusty has been diagnosed with ADHD.

Perhaps the major questions surrounding the use of Ritalin concern whether it is being overprescribed, whether it is the most effective treatment, and how long a child with ADHD should remain on the drug (Root & Resnick, 2003). In addition, Ritalin, especially in larger doses, does have side effects that may include loss of appetite and problems with sleeping. A related question is whether children with ADHD should be kept on a diet free of artificial dyes, sweeteners, and sugar, which some parents claim worsen the symptoms. We'll answer these questions in this module.

We're going to use Dusty's problem with ADHD to show how researchers pursue the four goals of psychology that we discussed in Module 1. In Dusty's case, the four goals are (1) to describe Dusty's symptoms, (2) to explain their causes, (3) to predict their occurrence, and (4) to control Dusty's behavior through some behavioral therapy or drug treatment.

Rhino Horn and Cough Medicine

Can beliefs cure like real medicine?

One interesting aspect of trying to control unwanted symptoms with a drug treatment is that sometimes the drug is not really a drug because it has no proven medical effects. For example, in many parts of Asia, people take powdered rhino horn because they believe that it is a medicine for treating hundreds of physical and mental problems. Similarly, in the United States, people are spending billions of dollars a year on over-the-counter cough medicines, including cough syrups and cough drops, even though there is no reliable scientific evidence that cough medications work (J. W. Payne, 2006). The use of rhino horn and cough medicine, both questionable medical treatments, raises the interesting question of how much one's mind or one's beliefs contribute to the development or treatment of physical symptoms. We'll discuss methods that researchers use to decide whether the effectiveness of a treatment is due to a drug's medical effect or the person's beliefs.

Can rhino horn cure all kinds of problems?

What's Coming

Our main focus in this module is to explore the methods that researchers use to answer questions, such as how to treat ADHD and why placebos work. Specifically, we'll discuss the advantages and disadvantages of three major research methods—surveys, case studies, and experiments. We'll explain which research procedures can identify cause-and-effect relationships and which cannot. We begin with an overview of the three major research methods that psychologists use to answer questions.

A. Answering Questions

How do researchers study ADHD?

As you look at the photo of Dusty on the right, you see a young boy ready to explode into an uncontrolled burst of activity, a major symptom of ADHD. Twenty-five years ago, ADHD was a relatively small problem in the United States, while today it is the most commonly diagnosed behavioral problem in children. ADHD is surrounded with controversy. For example, its name has been changed from hyperactivity to minimal brain damage to attention-deficit disorder and most recently to attention-deficit/hyperactivity disorder (ADHD). The diagnosis of ADHD is not straightforward, since it is based on behavioral symptoms rather than medical tests. The proposed causes of ADHD

Researchers use three different research methods to study ADHD.

are many, including various genetic, neurological, cultural, and dietary factors (Root & Resnick, 2003). Finally, the most popular treatment of ADHD involves giving children a stimulant drug.

In the middle of these controversies are parents like Dusty's mother, who, after dealing with a hyperactive and impulsive child from an early age, have little doubt that ADHD exists and that Ritalin decreases hyperactivity and impulsivity. At the same time, critics warn that ADHD may be misdiagnosed or overdiagnosed and that, while Ritalin may reduce activity, it may fail to improve academic performance in grade-school children (Jensen, 1999).

As researchers work to resolve all the controversies surrounding ADHD, they are using three major research methods—survey, case study, and experiment.

Survey

Suppose you wish to know how many children have ADHD, whether it occurs more in boys or girls, which treatment is the most popular, and how many children continue to have problems when they become adults. Researchers obtain this information with surveys.

A *survey* is a way to obtain information by asking many individuals—either person to person, by telephone, or by mail—to answer a fixed set of questions about particular subjects.

The disadvantage of a survey is that such information can contain errors or be biased because people may not remember accurately or answer truthfully. The advantage of a survey is that it is an efficient way to obtain much information from a large number of people.

But if researchers wanted to know more about a particular person, they would use a case study.

Case Study

Suppose you wish to know in greater detail about how a single child, such as Dusty, developed ADHD, performs in school, makes friends, plays team sports, and deals with everyday problems. Or suppose you wish to know about how a family copes with a child who has ADHD. For example, one mother said, "Ritalin doesn't take away the problems at all. It just helps him focus on what he's doing. You can talk to him; he can get his school work done. It still takes him a long time to get things done. He's still behind, emotionally and socially" (*San Diego Tribune,* November 27, 1989). When another mother was told that sugar doesn't increase activity, she replied, "I say, they're nuts! Where were they last Christmas when my sons ate candy canes and green frosting for days and never slept!" (*Los Angeles Times,* February 9, 1994). Researchers gather in-depth data about a particular individual with a case study.

A *case study* is an in-depth analysis of the thoughts, feelings, beliefs, experiences, behaviors, or problems of a single individual.

One disadvantage of a case study is that its detailed information about a particular person, such as Dusty, may not apply to other children with ADHD.

One advantage of a case study is that its detailed information allows greater understanding of a particular person's life.

But if researchers wanted to establish whether sugar really increases activity in children with ADHD, they would use an experiment.

Experiment

Suppose you thought that sugar or artificial dyes caused hyperactivity in your child and you wondered if this were true. For example, based on case studies and parents' reports, one researcher thought that certain artificial dyes, chemicals, and sweeteners increased the activity and impulsive behavior of children diagnosed with ADHD (Feingold, 1975). When researchers want to identify a cause-and-effect relationship, such as whether sugar increases activity, they use an experiment.

An *experiment* is a method for identifying cause-and-effect relationships by following a set of rules and guidelines that minimize the possibility of error, bias, and chance occurrences.

A disadvantage of an experiment is that information obtained in one experimental situation or laboratory setting may not apply to other situations. An experiment's primary advantage is that it has the greatest potential for identifying cause-and-effect relationships with less error and bias than either surveys or case studies.

Which method is best?

Very often, researchers use all three research methods—survey, case study, and experiment—because each provides a different kind of information. Surveys provide information about fixed questions from a large number of people. Case studies give in-depth information about a single person. Experiments point to cause-and-effect relationships. We'll discuss the advantages and disadvantages of each of the three methods, beginning with surveys.

Kind of Information

What do surveys tell us?

Almost every day the media report some new survey. Although surveys tell us what others believe or how they behave, survey questions can be written to bias the answers; moreover, people may not always answer truthfully (N. Schwartz, 1999). For example, how many people do you think always wash their hands after going to the bathroom? We'll sample some surveys and then discuss their problems.

Do you wash your hands?

Although 91% of the people surveyed by telephone said that they always washed their hands after using a public bathroom, direct observation of 6,336 people in six major cities found that only 82% really do and that women (90%) washed their hands more often than men (75%) (Bakalar, 2005).

What's your biggest worry?

A survey of 251,323 college freshmen (class of 2000) reported that 66% are worried about not having the money to finish college (Weiss, 1997). In a telephone survey of 2,012 adults, 55% said they are dissatisfied with the quality of health care in the United States ("Survey Finds," 2005).

How many children are diagnosed with ADHD?

Recent surveys report that 6% of U.S. school-age children are diagnosed with ADHD and that there may be cultural and ethnic differences in the diagnosis of ADHD. The lowest incidence of ADHD is reported in Asian Americans and the highest in African American boys, even though their symptoms appear very similar to those of White boys (Popper et al., 2003; Root & Resnick, 2003).

These examples show that surveys provide a great deal of useful information. However, surveys have potential problems with accuracy (as in the hand-washing survey) and, as you'll see next, with how questions are worded and who asks the questions.

Disadvantages

How questions are worded

You may be surprised to learn that surveys may get very different results depending on how questions are worded. Here are two examples:

QUESTION: "Would you say that **industry** contributes more or less to air pollution than **traffic**?"
Traffic contributes more: **24%**
Industry contributes more: 57%

QUESTION: "Would you say that **traffic** contributes more or less to air pollution than **industry**?"
Traffic contributes more: **45%**
Industry contributes more: 32%

These two examples indicate that the way questions are phrased and the way the possible answers are ordered can greatly influence people's responses and, in this case, produce opposite results (reported in *U.S. News & World Report,* Dec. 4, 1995, p. 55).

Who asks the questions

You may also be surprised to learn that the sex or race of the questioner can also affect how people answer the questions.

QUESTION: "The problems faced by Blacks were brought on by Blacks themselves."
When the interviewer was **White, 62%** of Whites who were interviewed agreed.
When the interviewer was **Black, 46%** of Whites who were interviewed agreed.

These two examples indicate that when asked about sensitive or emotional issues, people take into account the race of the interviewer and tend to give socially acceptable rather than honest answers (*U.S. News & World Report,* Dec. 4, 1995, p. 55).

We can conclude that surveys can be biased because people may not answer questions truthfully, may give socially acceptable answers, or may feel pressured to answer in certain ways. Also, surveys can be biased by how questions are worded and by interviewing a group of people who do not represent the general population (Mazor et al., 2002; N. Schwartz, 1999). Despite these potential problems, surveys have advantages.

Advantages

While guarding against error and bias, surveys can be a useful research tool to quickly and efficiently collect information on behaviors, beliefs, experiences, and attitudes from a large sample of people and can compare answers from various ethnic, age, socioeconomic, and cultural groups.

For example, surveys suggest that ADHD interferes with performance in school settings, decreases the chances of graduating from high school, and may lead to conduct disorder problems in adolescence as well as continued problems in adulthood (Root & Resnick, 2003).

Because surveys indicate that children with ADHD have major problems in school settings, psychologists are developing methods for improving performance. These methods include: teaching ADHD children how to organize their work, giving them constant feedback on reaching their goals, and starting programs that train teachers and families to work together to help ADHD children control their disruptive behaviors (Hechtman et al., 2004). Thus, another advantage of surveys is their ability to identify problems and evaluate treatment programs.

However, if researchers wish to focus on a particular individual rather than a group, they use a case study.

C. Case Study

What's a case study?

Sometimes researchers answer questions by studying a single individual in great detail, which is called a case study.

A *case study* is an in-depth analysis of the thoughts, feelings, beliefs, or behaviors of a single person.

We'll use a different case study, this time focusing on Nick, who is now 11 years old and diagnosed as having ADHD. From the age of 3, Nick has had problems paying attention and completing tasks. Because he was so easily distracted, Nick needed to be called as many as 19 times before he answered,

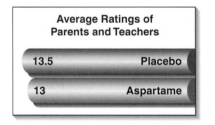

couldn't seem to finish tying his shoes, couldn't pay attention in school, and alternated between bouts of frustration and being an angel. In the first grade, Nick was put on Ritalin, and it made an immediate difference. He called it a "concentrating medicine," and although he still has academic problems, he can better focus on and complete a project (Leavy, 1996). This case study tells us that Ritalin helped Nick concentrate but only partially solved his academic problems. Sometimes case studies help answer questions, but as you'll see next, case studies can also result in wrong or biased answers.

Personal Case Study: Testimonial

Why did parents make a mistake?

Observations from case studies may be misinterpreted if the observer has preconceived notions of what to look for. For example, beginning in the mid-1970s, parents were told that food with artificial additives, dyes, and preservatives could cause hyperactivity in children (Feingold, 1975). Shortly after, parents reported that, yes indeed, artificial additives caused a sudden increase in restlessness and irritability in their hyperactive children (Feingold, 1975). The parents' reports and beliefs that additives cause hyperactivity are examples of another kind of case study, called a testimonial.

A *testimonial* is a statement in support of a particular viewpoint based on detailed observations of a person's own personal experience.

However, contrary to the parents' testimonials, researchers have generally found that amounts of artificial additives within a normal

Average Ratings of Parents and Teachers

13.5	Placebo
13	Aspartame

range did not affect hyperactivity (Kinsbourne, 1994). More recently, there are testimonials from parents that children with attention-deficit disorder who ate foods with an artificial sweetener, aspartame (Nutrasweet), showed noticeable increases in symptoms.

To test the accuracy of these recent testimonials, researchers asked teachers and parents to evaluate the behaviors and cognitive functions of children who were given a capsule containing either ten times their normal daily intake of aspartame or a placebo. Neither parent, child, nor teacher knew if the capsule contained aspartame or the placebo. As the graph on the left shows, there was little or no difference between the effect of aspartame (Nutrasweet) and that of the placebo on the behaviors or cognitive functions of children with attention-deficit disorder (B. A. Shaywitz et al., 1994). Although testimonials from parents, friends, or peers can be very convincing, we'll point out two problems that make testimonials especially susceptible to error.

Error and Bias

What's the problem with testimonials?

One of the major problems with testimonials is that they are based on our personal observations, which have great potential for error and bias. For example, if parents reported that sweeteners increased their son's activity, we would have to rule out personal beliefs and self-fulfilling prophecies.

Personal beliefs. If parents hear that artificial sweeteners may cause physical or psychological problems, they may interpret their child's problems as caused by artificial sweeteners. Because of biased perceptions, parents may overlook other potential causes, such as frustration, anger, or changes in the child's environment, and make the error of focusing only on artificial sweeteners. If we believe strongly in something, it may bias our perception and cause us to credit an unrelated treatment or event as the reason for some change.

Parents mistakenly believed that artificial sweeteners caused ADHD.

Self-fulfilling prophecy. If parents believe that artificial sweeteners cause problems, they may behave in ways—being more strict or less sympathetic—that cause the problems to occur. This phenomenon is called a self-fulfilling prophecy.

A *self-fulfilling prophecy* involves having a strong belief or making a statement (prophecy) about a future behavior and then acting, usually unknowingly, to fulfill or carry out the behavior.

If we strongly believe that something is going to happen, we may unknowingly behave in such a way as to make it happen (R. Rosenthal, 2003). Self-fulfilling prophecies reinforce testimonials and thus keep our biased beliefs alive.

The main disadvantage of testimonials is their high potential for error and bias. But they have the advantage of providing detailed information that may point to potential answers or lead to future studies. We'll discuss how case studies are used in developmental research in Module 18 and clinical research in Module 21.

Next, we'll discuss how testimonials are a popular source of information, especially when we are talking about placebos.

D. Cultural Diversity: Use of Placebos

Examples of Mind over Body

Have you taken a placebo?

Psychologists are interested in how the mind influences the body, such as happens when someone takes a pill that happens to be a placebo.

A *placebo* **is some intervention, such as taking a pill, receiving an injection, or undergoing an operation, that resembles medical therapy but that, in fact, has no medical effects.**

A *placebo effect* **is a change in the patient's illness that is attributable to an imagined treatment rather than to a medical treatment.**

> ## Placebo
> Placebos are sugar pills.

For example, the results of a study involving children who were depressed showed that an antidepressant medication (Zoloft) decreased depression in 69% of children. However, 59% of the children reported equally good results from taking another pill that proved to be a placebo (in this case a sugar pill) (Saxbe, 2004). Researchers estimate that between 35 and 75% of patients benefit from placebos for a variety of problems (pain, depression, headaches, warts) (Christensen, 2001).

Researchers believe that placebos work by reducing tension and distress and by creating powerful self-fulfilling prophecies so that individuals think and behave as if the drug, actually a placebo, is effective (Christensen, 2001). In a recent study, subjects were injected in the jaw with a pain-inducing solution and then researchers falsely told subjects they had been injected with pain-relieving medication. Pictures of subjects' brains were then taken (PET, p. 71), and results showed that for those people who said they felt less pain, their brain released natural painkillers after the placebo was injected (Haslinger, 2005). Thus, placebos may work because individuals' beliefs and thoughts are powerful enough to produce the same relief that is provided by real drugs.

As you'll see, testimonials from around the world claim that different kinds of placebos can cure a wide variety of symptoms.

Rhino Horn	*Bear Gallbladders*	*Tiger Bones*	*Cough Medication*

Millions of people in China, Thailand, South Korea, and Taiwan claim that rhino horn is an aphrodisiac, will increase their sexual desire and stamina, and is a cure for everything from headaches and nosebleeds to high fevers and typhoid. However, the basic ingredient of rhino horn is compacted hair (keratin), which has no proven medicinal powers (*Sierra*, November/December 1989). A single rhino horn weighing about 4 to 5 pounds will bring from $25,000 to $50,000 on the black market. In the early 1900s, there were about 1 million rhinos. By 1994, poachers had reduced the total number of rhinos to about 10,000, as the desire for rhino horns continued to grow (Berger & Cunningham, 1994).

In parts of Asia, a very popular "medicine" to treat many kinds of physical problems is a tablet made from bear gallbladders. Some traders are substituting pig gallbladders for 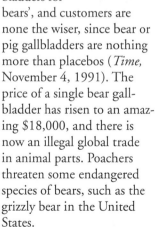 bears', and customers are none the wiser, since bear or pig gallbladders are nothing more than placebos (*Time*, November 4, 1991). The price of a single bear gallbladder has risen to an amazing $18,000, and there is now an illegal global trade in animal parts. Poachers threaten some endangered species of bears, such as the grizzly bear in the United States.

In the early 1900s, there were 100,000 tigers in Asia, but by 1994 there were fewer than 5,000. The chief reason for this precipitous decline is the use of tiger bones to treat ulcers, typhoid, malaria, dysentery, and burns, to increase longevity, to guard newborn babies from infection, and to cure devil possession (Friend, 1997). In addition, wealthy Taiwanese pay $320 for a bowl of tiger penis soup that is thought to increase flagging libidos (Nagarahole, 1994). Tiger bones and tiger penises function as powerful placebos in traditional Asian medicine.

When we have a cold with a relentless cough, many of us purchase cough syrup. In the United States, billions of dollars are spent every year on cough medications (cough syrups and lozenges), yet there is no scientific evidence that these over-the-counter medications work (Ignelzi, 2006a; J. W. Payne, 2006). In one study with children who had coughs, results showed that children who were given a commonly used cough syrup did no better than those given a nonmedicated syrup (placebo) (Querna, 2004).

Conclusion: Testimonials and Placebos

Why are placebos so popular?

The main reason placebos are used worldwide, even to the point of destroying certain wild animals, is that the placebo's beneficial "medical" effects are supported by countless testimonials. For example, compared to the results of surveys, testimonials are much more convincing because they are based on real-life experiences of friends, peers, and parents, who are honest and believable. However, it is common for people, honest and trustworthy, to unknowingly make a mistake and conclude a rhino horn, bear gallbladder, tiger bone, or cough medication is producing a beneficial "medical" effect when the beneficial effect is actually being caused by the individual's mental thoughts influencing the brain or body's functioning (Christensen, 2001).

As you'll see next, people often make mistakes about the effect of placebos because there is often no way to figure out what causes what.

E. Correlation

Research suggests that ADHD has a genetic basis.

What's a correlation?

The photo on the left shows Dusty running wild in a supermarket. Researchers would like to know if Dusty's hyperactivity has a genetic basis. One way to identify genetic factors is to study genetic twins because they share 100% of their genes in common. Suppose you were studying the occurrence of ADHD in identical male twins and found that about 70% of the time, if one identical twin had ADHD so did the second twin (Root & Resnick, 2003). This strong relationship between behaviors in identical twins suggests a genetic basis for ADHD. Such a relationship is called a correlation.

A *correlation* is an association or relationship between the occurrence of two or more events.

For example, if one twin has hyperactivity, a correlation will tell us the likelihood that the other twin also has hyperactivity. The likelihood or strength of a relationship between two events is called a correlation coefficient.

A *correlation coefficient* is a number that indicates the strength of a relationship between two or more events: the closer the number is to −1.00 or +1.00, the greater is the strength of the relationship.

We'll explain correlation coefficients in more detail because they can be confusing.

Correlation Coefficients

What are these numbers?

There are two major points to understand about correlations:

First, a correlation means there is an association between two or more events. For example, there is an association, or correlation, between the sex of a child and the occurrence of ADHD; 4 to 5 times more boys are diagnosed with ADHD than girls.

A second point to understand about correlations is that the strength of the relationship or association is measured by a number called a correlation coefficient. Because the correlation coefficient ranges from +1.00 to −1.00, its meaning can be confusing. In the boxes on the right, we'll describe what correlation coefficients mean, beginning at the top of the scale with a +1.00.

+1.00

+0.50

0.00

−0.50

−1.00

If each of 20 identical pairs showed equal levels of hyperactivity, the correlation coefficient would be positive and perfect and would be indicated by a +1.00 correlation coefficient.

A **perfect positive correlation coefficient** of +1.00 means that an increase in one event is always matched by an equal increase in a second event. For example, if one identical twin has hyperactivity, then the other twin always has hyperactivity. A correlation of +1.00 is virtually never found in applied psychological research (Hemphill, 2003).

If some identical pairs but not all 20 pairs were similar in hyperactivity, the result would be a positive correlation coefficient, which can range from +0.01 to +0.99.

A **positive correlation coefficient** indicates that as one event tends to increase, the second event tends to, but does not always, increase.

As the coefficient increases from +0.01 to +0.99, it indicates a strengthening of the relationship between the occurrence of two events.

If one twin of 20 pairs showed hyperactivity while the other twin sometimes did and sometimes did not show hyperactivity, the result would be no association, or zero correlation (0.00).

A **zero correlation** indicates that there is no relationship between the occurrence of one event and the occurrence of a second event.

If, in some identical pairs, one twin showed an increase while the other showed an equivalent decrease in activity, the result would be a negative correlation coefficient, which can range from −0.01 to −0.99.

A **negative correlation coefficient** indicates that as one event tends to increase, the second event tends to, but does not always, decrease.

As the coefficient increases in absolute magnitude from −0.01 to −0.99, it indicates a strengthening in the relationship of one event increasing and the other decreasing.

If one twin of 20 identical pairs showed hyperactivity and the second twin always showed decreased activity, the correlation coefficient would be negative and perfect and would be indicated by a −1.00 correlation coefficient.

A **perfect negative correlation coefficient** of −1.00 means that an increase in one event is always matched by an equal decrease in a second event. For example, if one identical twin has hyperactivity, then the other twin always has decreased activity. A correlation of −1.00 is virtually never found in applied psychological research (Hemphill, 2003).

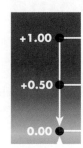

Can you recognize a correlation?

The media often headline interesting findings: Thin people live longer than heavier ones; overweight people earn less money than their peers; wearing school uniforms decreases violence. Before you assume that one event causes the other, such as thinness causing one to live longer, you must check to see what researchers did. If researchers measured only the relationship between two events, such as thinness and length of life, then it's a correlation. In fact, all three findings reported here are correlations. The reason you should check whether some finding is a correlation is that correlations have one very important limitation: They do not identify what causes what. For example, let's look closely at findings about breast feeding and intelligence test scores.

Correlation Versus Causation

The biggest mistake people make in discussing correlations is assuming that they show cause and effect. For instance, many parents have been told that breast feeding their infant leads to greater intelligence. The graph on the right shows that duration of breast feeding was correlated with an increase in intelligence test scores during adulthood. Since an increase in the duration of breast feeding was associated with an increase in intelligence test scores, this is a positive correlation (Mortensen, 2002).

Does breast feeding increase intelligence?

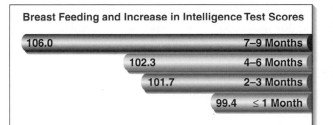

Breast Feeding and Increase in Intelligence Test Scores

106.0	7–9 Months
102.3	4–6 Months
101.7	2–3 Months
99.4	≤ 1 Month

Although the correlation between breast-feeding duration and intelligence test scores was impressive, you must keep in mind that even though breast feeding may have caused the increase in test scores, correlations themselves cannot demonstrate cause and effect between variables. For example, over the past 32 years, there is a +0.88 correlation between which professional football team (American or National League) wins the Super Bowl and whether the stock market rises or falls. Although +0.88 is a very high positive correlation, it only shows a relationship between two variables because winning a Super Bowl could not possibly cause a rise or fall in the stock market.

Although correlations cannot indicate cause-and-effect relationships, they do serve two very useful purposes: Correlations help predict behavior and also point to where to look for possible causes, as has happened in the case of lung cancer.

Correlation as Clues

Although cigarette smoke was positively correlated with lung cancer (right graph), it was unknown whether smoking was the *cause* of cancer. Acting on the clue that some ingredient of cigarette smoke might trigger the development of lung cancer, researchers rubbed tar, an ingredient of cigarette smoke, on the skin of animals. After repeated applications over a period of time, the animals developed cancerous growths. This research proved that tar could cause cancer. More recently, researchers discovered that one particular ingredient of cigarette smoke (benzo[a]pyrene) turns off a gene that normally suppresses tumors. When that particular gene is turned off by cigarette smoke, lung cancer develops (Liu et al., 2005). In this case, correlations told researchers where to look for causes of lung cancer. In other cases, correlations help predict behavior.

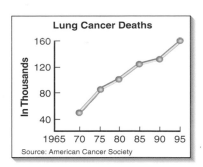

Lung Cancer Deaths

In Thousands

Source: American Cancer Society

Correlation and Predictions

One way to predict how well students will do in academic settings is by looking at their IQ scores. For example, there is a reasonably high correlation, from +0.60 to +0.70, between IQ scores and performance in academic settings (Anastasi & Urbina, 1997). Thus, we would predict that individuals who score high on IQ tests have the skills to do well in college. However, IQ scores are only relatively good predictors for any single individual because doing well in college involves not only academic skills but also many other motivational, emotional, and personality factors that we'll discuss in Module 13.

So far, we have discussed the advantages and disadvantages of two major research methods—surveys and case studies—that psychologists use to answer questions. We have also explained a statistical procedure—correlation—that shows the strength of relationships and points to possible causes of behaviors. Next, we'll describe the other kinds of research decisions that psychologists make as they try to understand and explain behavior.

Do IQ scores predict academic success?

F. Decisions about Doing Research

Choosing Research Techniques

What's the best technique for answering a question?
You are constantly asking questions about human behavior, such as "Why did she say that?" or "Why did he behave that way?" Similarly, psychologists are continually asking questions, such as "What percentage of the population is gay?" or "Of what use are SAT scores?" or "How do we diagnose ADHD?"or "Can human stem cell transplants cure paralysis?" After asking one of these questions, psychologists must decide which research technique or procedure best answers it. We'll describe four different techniques for finding answers.

Questionnaires and Interviews

What percentage of the population is gay? This question is often answered by doing a survey using interviews or questionnaires.

An *interview* **is a technique for obtaining information by asking questions, ranging from open-ended to highly structured, about a subject's behaviors and attitudes, usually in a one-on-one situation.**

A *questionnaire* **is a technique for obtaining information by asking subjects to read a list of written questions and check off specific answers.**

You might think this question about what percentage of the population is gay would be relatively easy to answer. But three different surveys have reported three different answers: 2.3%, 10%, and 22% (Billy et al., 1993; Janus & Janus, 1993; Kinsey et al., 1948). These different answers resulted from surveys using differently worded questions, different groups of people, and different kinds of interview techniques. As we discussed earlier, when it comes to surveys on personal issues—such as Did you vote? Do you wear seat belts? Do you go to church? or What is your sexual preference?—people may give a desirable rather than a honest answer.

Laboratory Experiments

How do we diagnose ADHD? As of this writing, the diagnosis of ADHD is based primarily on behavioral symptoms, which are less reliable than medical tests. For this reason, researchers are currently searching for more reliable tests to diagnose ADHD. To identify such tests, researchers are using laboratory experiments.

A *laboratory experiment* **is a technique to gather information about the brain, genes, or behavior with the least error and bias by using a controlled environment that allows careful observation and measurement.**

For example, in the photo on the right, a boy is taking a laboratory test that is believed to be an accurate way of diagnosing ADHD. In this test, children wear special goggles to monitor their eye

> Can a laboratory or psychological test be used to diagnose ADHD?

movements and are asked to follow spots of light moving across the screen. Children with ADHD are expected to be able to follow the light for only 3 to 5 seconds, whereas children without ADHD may be able to follow the light for as long as 5 minutes (Vince, 2005).

Standardized Tests

Of what use are SAT scores? The standardized test that you may be most familiar with is the SAT, which is given to many high-school seniors to help predict how they will perform in college. Each year only 0.05% of students who take the SAT score a perfect 1600, a feat accomplished for the first time in 1997 by twins, Courtney and Chris (photo on left).

A *standardized test* **is a technique to obtain information by administering a psychological test that has been standardized, which means that the test has been given to hundreds of people and shown to reliably measure thought patterns, personality traits, emotions, or behaviors.**

One disadvantage of standardized tests, such as the SAT, is that they may be biased toward a certain group of people. One advantage of standardized tests is that they allow

> Courtney and Chris scored perfect 1600s on the SAT.

comparisons to be made across schools, states, and groups of people (Anastasi & Urbina, 1997). Another well-known standardized test is the IQ test, which we'll discuss in Module 13.

Animal Models

Can human stem cell transplants cure paralysis? Over 250,000 people in the United States are living with a spinal-cord injury resulting in some paralysis (Szabo, 2004). Scientists have been trying to find a cure for paralysis for many years, and recently they have made some exciting advances with the use of animal models.

An *animal model* **involves examining or manipulating some behavioral, genetic, or physiological factor that closely approximates some human problem, disease, or condition.**

For example, mice that received human stem cell (p. 60) transplants following a spinal-cord injury showed long-term improvements in walking, compared to mice that didn't receive the transplants (Cummings et al., 2005). Advances in stem cell research using animal models give hope for a better recovery for people with spinal-cord injuries. One advantage of the animal model is that it answers questions about physiological factors that cannot be investigated in humans.

> Mice are used to study human stem cell transplants.

Deciding which one or combination of these four research techniques to use depends on the kind of question being asked. As you'll see next, the kind of question also influences which research setting to use.

Choosing Research Settings

Which problems do children with ADHD have?

In trying to understand the kinds of problems faced by children with ADHD, psychologists study these children in different research settings, which may include observing them in the home, in the classroom, on the playground, or at their individual work. In addition, researchers may try to find the causes of ADHD by using different research settings, which may include studying children in the laboratory, hospital, or clinic. All these research settings can be grouped under either laboratory or naturalistic environments. We'll explain each setting and compare their advantages and disadvantages, beginning with more naturalistic environments.

Naturalistic Setting

Parents and teachers want to know if ADHD children have different problems at home (photo below) than in school. Researchers answer this question by studying ADHD children in different naturalistic settings (home versus school) (J. E. Allen, 2000).

Does this ADHD child have different problems in school than at home?

A *naturalistic setting* is a relatively normal environment in which researchers gather information by observing individuals' behaviors without attempting to change or control the situation.

For example, observations of children with ADHD in school settings indicate that they have difficulty remaining in their seats, don't pay attention to the teacher, don't complete their projects, can't sit still, get into trouble, are rude to other students, and get angry when they don't get their way. Parents report that, at home, ADHD children do not respond when called, throw tantrums when frustrated, and have periods of great activity (Hancock, 1996; Henker & Whalen, 1989). Based on these naturalistic observations, researchers and pediatricians developed a list of primary symptoms of ADHD (Tanner, 2000). Similarly, psychologists study how normal people behave in different naturalistic settings, including schools, workplaces, college dormitories, bars, sports arenas, and homeless shelters. One problem with naturalistic observations is that the psychologists' own beliefs or values may bias their observations and cause them to misperceive or misinterpret behaviors. One advantage of naturalistic observations is the opportunity to study behaviors in real-life situations and environments, which cannot or would not be duplicated in the laboratory.

Case studies. As we discussed earlier, a single individual may be studied in his or her natural environment, and this is called a case study. The case study approach is often used in clinical psychology to understand the development of a personality or psychological problem or in developmental psychology to examine a person's behavior across his or her life span.

One *disadvantage* of a case study is that the information obtained is unique to an individual and may not apply to, or help us understand, the behaviors of others. One *advantage* of a case study is that psychologists can obtain detailed descriptions and insights into aspects of an individual's complex life and behaviors that cannot be obtained in other ways.

As you can see, naturalistic settings are very useful for observing how individuals behave in relatively normal environments. However, since naturalistic settings are uncontrolled and many things happen, researchers find it difficult to identify what causes what. For this reason, researchers may have to answer some questions in a more controlled setting, such as a laboratory or clinic.

Laboratory Setting

Is there something different about the brains of children with ADHD? Questions about the brain are usually answered under very controlled conditions, such as in a laboratory setting.

A *laboratory setting* involves studying individuals under systematic and controlled conditions, with many of the real-world influences eliminated.

For example, researchers used special techniques (MRI brain scans, p. 70) that actually took pictures of the living brains of children with and without ADHD. Researchers focused on specific areas of the brain involved in paying attention and controlling impulses, which are difficult for ADHD children. Findings showed that ADHD children had smaller total brain size and smaller sizes of specific brain areas involved in paying attention and controlling impulses (prefrontal lobes, corpus callosum, cerebellum) (D. E. Hill et al., 2003). Researchers continue to investigate what specific areas of the brain are involved in ADHD.

Researchers use laboratory settings to study and identify a wide range of psychological and biological factors involved in motivation, emotion, learning, memory, drug use, sleep, intelligence, and mental disorders.

One disadvantage of laboratory settings is that they may be so controlled or artificial that their results are not always transferable to, or meaningful for, real-life situations. However, one advantage of the laboratory setting is that psychologists can carefully control and manipulate one or more treatments while reducing error or bias from other situational or environmental factors.

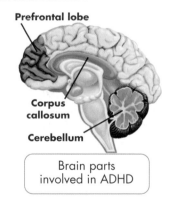

Prefrontal lobe

Corpus callosum

Cerebellum

Brain parts involved in ADHD

Psychologists may use both naturalistic and laboratory settings to obtain a broader understanding of some behavior or problem, such as ADHD (Root & Resnick, 2003).

Researchers may combine the advantages of naturalistic and laboratory settings to identify cause-and-effect relationships. That's what happened when psychologists answered the difficult question: Does Ritalin help children with ADHD?

G. Scientific Method: Experiment

Advantages of the Scientific Method

How do researchers reduce error and bias?

There have been many different treatments, including diets, vitamins, drugs, and behavior therapy, that claimed to help children with ADHD, such as Dusty (right photo). To discover which of these claims were valid, researchers followed a general approach called the scientific method.

The *scientific method* **is an approach of gathering information and answering questions so that errors and biases are minimized.**

Remember that information from surveys, case studies, and testimonials has considerable potential for error and bias. Remember too that information from correlations can suggest, but not pinpoint, cause-and-effect relationships. One way to both reduce error

It takes 7 rules to do an experiment on ADHD.

and bias and identify cause-and-effect relationships is to do an experiment.

An *experiment* **is a method of identifying cause-and-effect relationships by following a set of rules and guidelines that minimize the possibility of error, bias, and chance occurrences.**

An experiment, which is an example of using the scientific method, is the most powerful method for finding what causes what. We will divide an experiment into seven rules that are intended to reduce error and bias and identify the cause of an effect.

Conducting an Experiment: Seven Rules

Why seven rules?

Some researchers and parents claimed that diets without sugar, artificial colors, and additives reduced ADHD symptoms, but most of these claims proved false because the rules to reduce error had not been followed (Kinsbourne, 1994). Here are seven rules that reduce error and bias and that researchers follow when conducting an experiment.

Rule 1: Ask

Every experiment begins with one or more specific questions that are changed into specific hypotheses.

A *hypothesis* **is an educated guess about some phenomenon and is stated in precise, concrete language to rule out any confusion or error in the meaning of its terms.**

Hypothesis:

Ritalin will increase positive classroom behaviors of children diagnosed with ADHD.

Researchers develop different hypotheses based on their own observations or previous research findings. Following this first rule, researchers change the general question—Does Ritalin help children with ADHD?—into a very concrete hypothesis: Ritalin will increase the positive classroom behaviors of children with ADHD.

Rule 2: Identify

After researchers have made their hypothesis, they identify a treatment that will be administered to the subjects. This treatment is called the independent variable.

The *independent variable* **is a treatment or something that the researcher controls or manipulates.**

The independent variable may be a single treatment, such as a single drug dose, or various levels of the same treatment, such as different doses of the same drug.

Independent Variable:

Drug treatment

In our experiment, the independent variable is administering three different doses of Ritalin and a placebo.

After researchers choose the treatment, they next identify the behavior(s) of the subjects, called the dependent variable, that will be used to measure the effects of the treatment.

Dependent Variable:

Child's negative classroom behaviors

The *dependent variable* **is one or more of the subjects' behaviors that are used to measure the potential effects of the treatment or independent variable.**

The dependent variable, so called because it is dependent on the treatment, can include a wide range of behaviors, such as observable responses, self-reports of cognitive processes, or recordings of physiological responses from the body or brain. In the present experiment, the dependent variable is the teacher's rating of the child's positive classroom behaviors.

Rule 3: Choose

After researchers identify the independent and dependent variables, they next choose the subjects for the experiment. Researchers want to choose participants who are representative of the entire group or population, and they do this through a process called random selection.

Random selection **means that each participant in a sample population has an equal chance of being selected for the experiment.**

Random Selection

Examples of random selection include the way lottery numbers are drawn and selecting people using a random number table.

The reason researchers randomly select participants is to avoid any potential error or bias that may come from their knowingly or unknowingly wanting to choose the "best" subjects for their experiment.

Rule 4: Assign

After randomly choosing the subjects, researchers then randomly assign participants to different groups, either an experimental group or a control group.

The *experimental group* is composed of those who receive the treatment.

The *control group* is composed of participants who undergo all the same procedures as the experimental participants except that the control participants do not receive the treatment.

In this study, some of the children are assigned to the experimental group and receive Ritalin; the other children are assigned to the control group and receive a similar-looking pill that is a placebo.

The reason participants are randomly assigned to either the experimental or control group is to take into account or control for other factors or traits, such as intelligence, social class, economic level, age, personality variables, sex, and genetic differences. Randomly assigning participants reduces the chances that these factors will bias the results.

Rule 5: Manipulate

After assigning participants to experimental and control groups, researchers manipulate the independent variable by administering the treatment (or one level of the treatment) to the experimental group. Researchers give the same conditions to the control group but give them a different level of the treatment, no treatment, or a placebo.

For example, in this study, researchers give the experimental group a pill containing Ritalin, while the control group receives a placebo. Drugs and placebos are given with special care in a double-blind procedure.

A *double-blind procedure* means that neither participants nor researchers know which group is receiving which treatment.

Double-blind procedure is an important research tool.

A double-blind procedure is essential in drug research to control for self-fulfilling prophecies, placebo effects (see p. 31), and possible influences or biases of the experimenters.

Rule 6: Measure

By manipulating the treatment so that the experimental group receives a different treatment than the control group, researchers are able to measure how the independent variable (treatment) affects those behaviors that have been selected as the dependent variables.

For example, the hypothesis in this study is: Ritalin will increase the positive classroom behaviors of children with ADHD. Researchers observe whether treatment (Ritalin or placebo) changes positive behaviors of ADHD children in the classroom. Positive behaviors, whose frequencies are counted for 30-minute periods, include following a variety of classroom rules, such as remaining in seat, not disturbing others, not swearing or teasing, and following instructions. As the graph at the right indicates, ADHD children given placebos follow classroom rules 69% of the time, compared with 87% for the children given Ritalin (Pelham et al., 2005). Thus, compared to placebos, Ritalin increases positive behaviors in the classroom. However, to

Positive Behaviors in the Classroom

87%	Ritalin
69%	Placebo

be absolutely sure, researchers must analyze the results more carefully by using statistical procedures.

Rule 7: Analyze

Although there appears to be a large increase in positive behaviors, from 69% for the placebo control group to 87% for the Ritalin experimental group, researchers must analyze the size of these differences with statistical procedures.

Statistical procedures are used to determine whether differences observed in dependent variables (behaviors) are due to independent variables (treatment) or to error or chance occurrence.

Statistical analysis shows if the result occurred by chance.

Using statistical procedures, which are described in Appendix A, researchers compared the effect of the placebo with that of Ritalin on positive behaviors. They concluded that, compared with the placebo, Ritalin significantly increased positive behaviors. In this case, significantly means there was a 95% likelihood that it was Ritalin and not some error or chance occurrence that increased positive behaviors (Pelham et al., 2005).

These significant findings support the hypothesis that Ritalin increases positive classroom behaviors of children with ADHD.

Conclusion

What does an experiment tell you?

By following these seven rules for conducting an experiment, researchers reduced the chances that error or bias would distort the major finding, which was that Ritalin increased the positive behaviors of children in the classroom. This example shows that when an experiment is run according to these seven rules, it is a much more powerful method for identifying cause-and-effect relationships than are surveys, testimonials, correlations, or case studies. Even so, researchers usually repeat experiments many times before being confident that the answers they found were correct. That's why a newly reported finding, no matter how significant, is usually regarded as questionable until other researchers have been able to repeat the experiment and replicate the finding.

After the Concept Review, we'll discuss why, after 20 years of research, there are still controversies surrounding ADHD.

✔ Concept Review

1. If psychologists obtain information through an in-depth analysis of the thoughts, beliefs, or behaviors of a single person, this method is called a (a)_____. If a method is used that minimizes error and identifies cause-and-effect relationships, it is called an (b)_____. If individuals are asked a fixed set of questions, it is called a (c)_____. If individuals make statements in support of a particular viewpoint on the basis of personal experience, it is called a (d)_____.

2. Some intervention that is designed to look like a medical treatment but that has no actual medical effect is called a (a)_____. A change in a patient's illness that is due to a supposed treatment and not to any medical therapy is called a (b)_____.

3. Psychologists describe the association, relationship, or linkage among two or more events as a (a)_____. They describe the strength of such a relationship by a number called the (b)_____, which may vary from −1.00 to +1.00. If an increase in one event is associated with an increase in a second event, this relationship is called a (c)_____ correlation. If an increase in one event is associated with a decrease in a second event, this relationship is called a (d)_____ correlation. Finding that two or more events are linked together does not prove that one event (e)_____ the other.

4. Psychologists use at least five common research techniques. They can ask subjects oral or written questions by using (a)_____ and (b)_____. They might ask subjects to answer questions on established tests, which are called (c)_____ tests. They might observe and measure behaviors, brains, or genes with the least error and bias by using a controlled environment, called a (d)_____. They could study some question or problem in animals by developing an (e)_____ that closely approximates the human condition.

5. If psychologists study individuals in their real-life environments, without trying to control the situation, they are using a (a)_____ setting. A variation of this approach is to study a single individual in great depth in his or her own environment, which is called a (b)_____. If psychologists study individuals under carefully controlled conditions, they are using a (c)_____ setting.

Prefrontal lobe
Corpus callosum
Cerebellum

6. One example of searching for cause-and-effect relationships by following the rules and guidelines of the scientific method is to answer questions by conducting an _____, which has seven rules.

7. If you are conducting an experiment, you should follow 7 rules.

Rule 1 is to *ask* specific questions in very concrete terms: these statements are called (a)_____.

Ritalin

Rule 2 is to *identify* the treatment, which is called the (b)_____, and to choose the behaviors or responses that will be observed to judge the effectiveness of the treatment. These behaviors or responses are called the (c)_____.

Rule 3 is to *choose* subjects through a process called (d)_____, which gives everyone in a sample population an equal chance of being selected.

Rule 4 is to *assign* subjects to different groups by random selection. The group that will receive the treatment is called the (e)_____, and the group that undergoes everything but the treatment is called the (f)_____.

Rule 5 is to *manipulate* the (g)_____ by administering it to the experimental group but not the control group.

Placebo

Rule 6 is to *measure* the effects of the independent variable on behaviors that have been selected as the (h)_____.

Rule 7 is to *analyze* the difference between the experimental and control groups by using (i)_____.

8. Researchers usually repeat experiments many times to make sure that their _____ are correct.

Answers: *1. (a) case study, (b) experiment, (c) survey, (d) testimonial; 2. (a) placebo, (b) placebo effect; 3. (a) correlation, (b) correlation coefficient, (c) positive, (d) negative, (e) causes; 4. (a) questionnaires, (b) interviews, (c) standardized, (d) laboratory experiment, (e) animal model; 5. (a) naturalistic, (b) case study, (c) laboratory; 6. experiment; 7. (a) hypotheses, (b) independent variable, (c) dependent variable, (d) random selection, (e) experimental group, (f) control group, (g) independent variable, (h) dependent variables, (i) statistical procedures; 8. answers or results*

H. Research Focus: ADHD Controversies

Why do controversies still remain?

You might ask why, after 35 years of research, there are still controversies over how best to diagnose and treat ADHD. Although researchers have reached the first goal of psychology, which is to describe ADHD, they have not reached the second goal, which is to explain the causes of ADHD, which will lead to better treatment. Explaining the causes of ADHD means combining biological, psychological, behavioral, and cultural factors, which is a slow process. We'll review the current controversies involving ADHD to show how far researchers have come and how far they have to go.

Controversy: Diagnosis

The first controversy involves the accuracy and reliability of how ADHD is diagnosed. In the United States, about 3 to 5 million school-age children are diagnosed with ADHD, with 4 to 5 times as many boys having ADHD as girls (Root & Resnick, 2003).

The controversy arises from the fact that the current diagnosis of ADHD is based solely on reported and observed behavioral symptoms rather than on medical or laboratory tests. Because the behavioral symptoms vary in severity (more or less), setting (home versus school), and culture (fewer Asian American children than African American), there is the potential for misdiagnosis (Root & Resnick, 2003). For example, parents or teachers may label a child as having ADHD if the child is overwhelmed by the demands of school and

There are three big controversies surrounding ADHD.

acts outgoing, rambunctious, or difficult to discipline (Sinha, 2001). Because of diagnostic difficulties, pediatricians and family doctors were recently given the following guidelines for diagnosing ADHD: Children should be 6–12 years old, show six or more symptoms of inattention and hyperactivity, have symptoms for at least six months, and symptoms should occur in both home and school (J. E. Allen, 2000). The purpose of the guidelines is to prevent the merely rambunctious child from being diagnosed with ADHD and given unnecessary drugs.

The controversy regarding the diagnosis of ADHD will continue until the development of medical tests that confirm the behavioral symptoms, which are not always clear-cut (Root & Resnick, 2003).

Controversy: Treatment

The second controversy involves how best to treat ADHD. As we discussed earlier (p. 30), researchers found that using certain diets that avoid artificial flavors and colors, preservatives, artificial sweeteners, and sugars did little to reduce or stop hyperactive behaviors (Kinsbourne, 1994). More recently, a group of experts in the treatment of ADHD have compared nondrug and drug treatments for ADHD and made the following recommendations.

NONDRUG, BEHAVIORAL TREATMENT

There is a nondrug, behavioral treatment program that involves changing or modifying undesirable behaviors by using learning principles (p. 232). Such a behavioral treatment program, which requires considerable efforts by the parents, has been effective in reducing ADHD symptoms (Root & Resnick, 2003).

Use of Ritalin 600% increase since 1993

Experts in the treatment of ADHD recommend a behavioral treatment program be used for preschool-age children with ADHD, for milder forms of ADHD, for children who also have deficits in social skills, and when the family prefers the nondrug, behavioral treatment.

COMBINED DRUG AND BEHAVIORAL TREATMENT

A combination of Ritalin (methylphenidate) and behavioral treatment is recommended when children have severe ADHD, when children also have significant aggression or serious problems in school, when ADHD symptoms cause a major disruption in home or school, or when there is need for a rapid response to severe ADHD symptoms (Conners et al., 2001). The use of Ritalin has risen 600% since 1993, and total ADHD medication sales more than quadrupled between 2000 and 2004 (Alonso-Zaldivar, 2006; Haislip, 2003). Currently, there are nearly 3.3 million Americans age 19 or younger who are using ADHD medications (Bridges, 2006).

ADHD medications help to decrease children's hyperactivity and increase their ability to pay attention; however, they may cause side effects, including sleeping and eating problems, headaches, and abdominal pain (Martins et al., 2004). Because of the risk for serious side effects and the alarming increase in Ritalin use, the Food and Drug Administration recommended that Ritalin and other similar drugs include a warning (*N.Y. Times,* 2006). The use of drug and/or behavioral treatment for ADHD depends on an accurate diagnosis, the severity of symptoms, and concerns of teachers and parents.

Controversy: Long-Term Effects

The third controversy involves the long-term effects of ADHD. It used to be thought that children outgrew ADHD, but researchers have found that even when ADHD children are treated with Ritalin, 65% continue to have problems as adults. In fact, 1.5 million adults in the United States take ADHD medication (Alonso-Zaldivar, 2006). Adults with ADHD are less likely to graduate from high school and college, and more likely to get fired from jobs and have relationship problems (Elias, 2005a; *Medical News Today,* 2005). Because ADHD

is a continuing problem, the use of medication and/or behavioral programs that focus on setting goals, establishing rules, and rewarding performance should be encouraged to help those with ADHD deal with adolescence and adulthood (Jensen, 1999).

The controversies surrounding ADHD point out the difficulties in understanding, explaining, and treating complex human problems, such as ADHD. Using Ritalin to treat children also raises questions about the rights of subjects, both humans and animals, in research.

I. Application Research Concerns

Concerns about Being a Subject

What's it like to be a subject?

When you hear about a new research finding—such as a drug to control weight or treat depression, or the discovery of a gene related to happiness, or ways to improve memory—you rarely think about the treatment of subjects, humans and animals, used in these experiments.

For example, if you were asked to volunteer to be a participant, you would certainly be concerned about whether someone has checked to ensure that the experiment is safe, that there are safeguards to protect you from potential psychological or physical harm, and that you won't be unfairly deceived or made to feel foolish. These are all real concerns, and we'll discuss each one in turn.

Additionally, a separate and controversial question concerns the use of animals in research. We'll answer this question in some detail, since there are many misconceptions about the use and misuse of animals in research.

We'll begin by considering the concerns of human subjects.

Code of Ethics

If you are a college student, there is a good possibility that you will be asked to participate in a psychology experiment. If you are considering becoming a subject, you may wonder what kinds of safeguards are used to protect subjects' rights and privacy.

The American Psychological Association has published a code of ethics and conduct for psychologists to follow when doing research, counseling, teaching, and related activities (American Psychological Association, 2002). This code of ethics spells out the responsibilities of psychologists and the rights of participants.

Besides having to follow a code of ethics, psychologists must submit the details of their research programs, especially those with the potential for causing psychological or physical harm, to university and/or federal research committees (institutional review boards). The job of these research committees is to protect the participants (human or animal) by carefully checking the proposed experiments for any harmful procedures (Breckler, 2006).

Are my rights protected?

Experiments are not approved unless any potentially damaging effects can be eliminated or counteracted. Counteracting potentially harmful effects is usually done by thoroughly describing the experiment, a process called debriefing.

Debriefing includes explaining the purpose and method of the experiment, asking the participants their feelings about being participants in the experiment, and helping the participants deal with possible doubts or guilt that arise from their behaviors in the experiment.

During the debriefing sessions, researchers will answer any questions or discuss any problems that participants may have. The purpose of debriefing is to make sure that participants have been treated fairly and have no lingering psychological or physical concerns or worries that come from participating in an experiment (Aronson et al., 2004).

Role of Deception

When recruiting participants for their experiments, psychologists usually give the experiments titles, such as "Study of eyewitness testimony" or "Effects of alcohol on memory." The reason for using such general titles is that researchers do not want to create specific expectations that may bias how potential participants will behave. It is well known that an experiment's results may be biased by a number of factors: by participants' expectations of how they should behave, by their unknowingly behaving according to self-fulfilling prophecies, or by their efforts to make themselves look good or to please the experimenter.

One way that researchers control for participants' expectations is to use bogus procedures or instructions that prevent participants from learning the experiment's true purpose. However, before researchers can use bogus or deceptive methodology, they must

Will they try to trick or deceive me?

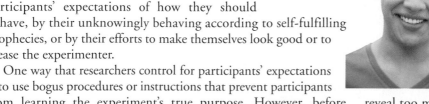

satisfy the American Psychological Association's (2002) code of ethics. For example, researchers must justify the deceptive techniques by the scientific, educational, or applied value of the study and can only use deception if no other reasonable way to test the hypothesis is available (APA, 2002).

Another way to avoid bias from participants' expectations is to keep both the researcher and participants in the dark about the experiment's true purpose by using a double-blind procedure. As discussed earlier (p. 37), a double-blind procedure means that neither participants nor researchers are aware of the experiment's treatment or purpose.

Thus, researchers must be careful not to reveal too many details about their experiments lest they bias how potential subjects may behave.

How many animals are used in research?

It is estimated that over 25 million animals are used each year in biomedical research, which includes the fields of psychology, biology, medicine, and pharmaceuticals (Humane Society, 2006). Although these numbers seem large, they are small in comparison to the 5 billion chickens eaten annually by people in the United States. However, it is the use of animals in research that has generated the most concern and debate (Rowan, 1997).

In the field of psychology, about 95% of the nonhuman animals used by researchers are rats, mice, and birds, while the remaining 5% consist of various other animals such as cats, dogs, and monkeys (S. Carpenter, 2001). We'll examine the justification for using animals in research and how their rights are protected.

Are research animals mistreated?

You may have seen a disturbing photo or heard about a laboratory animal being mistreated (Barnard & Kaufman, 1997). The fact is that, of the millions of animals used in research, only a few cases of animal mistreatment have been confirmed. That is because scientists know that proper care and treatment of their laboratory animals are vital to the success of their research. To abolish the use of all laboratory animals because of one or two isolated cases of mistreatment would be like abolishing all medical practice because of isolated cases of malpractice. Instead, researchers support the Animal Research Act, which balances the rights of animals to be treated with care with the needs for advancing the medical, physiological, and psychological health of humans (Albright et al., 2005).

Is the use of animals justified?

Adrian Morrison, director of the National Institute of Mental Health's Program for Animal Research Issues, offers this view, "Because I do experimental surgery, I go through a soul-searching every couple of months, asking myself whether I really want to continue working on cats. The answer is always yes because I know that there is no other way for medicine to progress but through animal experimentation and that basic research ultimately leads to unforeseen benefits" (Morrison, 1993).

According to Frederick King, the former chair of the American Psychological Association's Committee on Animal Research and Experimentation, animal research has resulted in major medical advances, new treatments for human diseases, and a better understanding of human disorders (F. A. King et al., 1988).

In the field of psychology, animal research and animal models have led to a better understanding of how stress affects one's psychological and physical health, mechanisms underlying learning and memory, the development of anxiety and fears, and the effects of sensory deprivation on development, to mention but a few (Dingfelder, 2006; Mukerjee, 1997).

Researchers are currently using animals to study epilepsy, Alzheimer's disease, fetal alcohol syndrome, schizophrenia, AIDS, and transplantation of brain tissue, none of which is possible with human subjects.

Who checks on the use of animals in research?

Numerous government and university regulations ensure the proper care and humane treatment of laboratory animals. For example, the U.S. Department of Agriculture conducts periodic inspections of all animal research facilities to ensure proper housing and to oversee experimental procedures that might cause pain or distress. Universities hire veterinarians to regularly monitor the care and treatment of laboratory animals. Finally, universities have animal subject committees with authority to decide whether sufficient justification exists for using animals in specific research projects (Kalat, 2004).

How do we strike a balance?

One of the basic issues in animal research is how to strike the right balance between animal rights and research needs (Albright et al., 2005). Based on past, present, and potential future benefits of animal research, many experts in the scientific, medical, and mental health communities believe that the conscientious and responsible use of animals in research is justified and should continue. This is especially true in light of recent rules that regulate the safe and humane treatment of animals kept in laboratories or used in research (Botting & Morrison, 1997; Kalat, 2004).

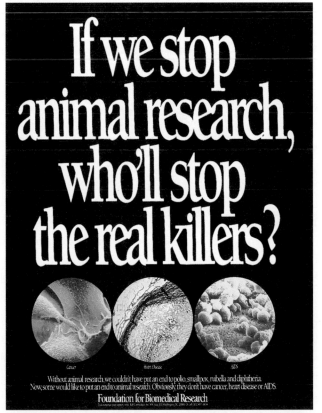

The small print in the poster reads, "Without animal research, we couldn't have put an end to polio, smallpox, rubella and diphtheria. Now, some would like to put an end to animal research. Obviously, they don't have cancer, heart disease or AIDS."

✔ Summary Test

A. Answering Questions

1. Psychologists use at least three methods to answer questions or obtain information. An in-depth analysis of a single person's thoughts and behaviors is called a (a)_____. One advantage of this method is that researchers obtain detailed information about a person, but one disadvantage is that such information may not apply to others. Asking a large number of individuals a fixed set of questions is called a (b)_____. Gathering information in a controlled laboratory setting is called an (c)_____.

B. Surveys

2. Measuring the attitudes, beliefs, and behaviors of a large sample of individuals by asking a set of questions is called a _____. One advantage of this method is that psychologists can quickly and efficiently collect information about a large number of people. One disadvantage is that people may answer in a way that they think is more socially acceptable.

C. Case Study

3. A statement that supports a particular viewpoint and is based on a person's own experience is called a (a)_____, which has two potential sources of error and bias. First, strongly held personal beliefs may bias an individual's (b)_____ of events. Second, believing strongly that something will happen and then unknowingly acting in such a way as to make that something occur is a source of error called (c)_____. This source of error is one of the major reasons that people believe that their (d)_____ are true.

D. Cultural Diversity: Use of Placebos

4. Some intervention that resembles a medical therapy but that, in fact, has no medical effects is called a (a)_____. If a person reports an improvement in some medical condition that is due to a supposed treatment rather than some medical therapy, that is called a (b)_____. One reason people around the world believe in placebos is that people give (c)_____ to their effectiveness.

E. Correlation

5. If two or more events are associated or linked to-gether, they are said to be (a)_____. The strength of this association is indicated by a number called the (b)_____, which has a range from −1.00 to +1.00.

6. If there were a perfect association between two events—for example, when one increased, the other did also—this would be called a (a)_____. If an increase in one event is usually, but not always, accompanied by an increase in a second event, this would be called a (b)_____. If an increase in one event is always accompanied by a decrease in a second event, this is called a (c)_____. If an increase in one event is usually, but not always, accompanied by a decrease in a second event, this is called a (d)_____.

7. Although a correlation indicates that two or more events are occurring in some pattern, a correlation does not identify which event may (a)_____ the other(s). Although correlations do not identify cause-and-effect relationships, they do provide (b)_____ as to where to look for causes and they help to (c)_____ behavior.

+1.00
+0.50
0.00
−0.50
−1.00

F. Decisions about Doing Research

8. Psychologists may answer some question by using one or more of five commonly used research techniques. Asking questions about people's attitudes and behaviors, usually in a one-on-one situation, is using an (a)_____. Asking subjects to read a list of questions and indicate a specific answer is using a (b)_____. Asking subjects to complete established tests that measure personality, intelligence, or other behaviors is using (c)_____. If psychologists study subjects' behaviors under carefully controlled conditions that allow manipulation of the treatment, they are conducting a (d)_____. Psychologists can study a problem using animals by developing an (e)_____, which closely approximates the human disease or condition.

Prefrontal lobe

Corpus callosum

Cerebellum

9. Psychologists conduct research in two common settings. If psychologists obtain information by observing an individual's behaviors in his or her environment, without attempts to control or manipulate the situation, they would be using a _____. The *advantage* of this method is that it gives information that would be difficult to obtain or duplicate in a laboratory. The *disadvantage* of this method is that the psychologists' own beliefs or values may bias their observations and cause them to misinterpret the behaviors under observation.

10. If psychologists study a single individual in considerable depth in his or her own environment, they are using a _____. The *advantage* of this method is that it results in detailed descriptions and insights into many aspects of an individual's life. The *disadvantage* is that the information obtained may be unique and not applicable to others.

11. If psychologists want to study individuals under controlled and systematic conditions, with many of the real-life factors removed, they do the study in a _____. The *advantage* of this setting is that it permits greater control and manipulation of many conditions while ruling out possible contaminating factors. The *disadvantage* of this setting is that it may be too artificial or controlled, so that the results may not necessarily apply to real-life situations.

G. Scientific Method: Experiment

12. The scientific method offers a set of rules or guidelines on how to conduct research with a minimum of error or bias. We have divided these guidelines into seven rules. **Rule 1** is to make a

statement in precise, concrete terms. Such a statement is called a (a)_____, which researchers often develop based on previous observations or studies. **Rule 2** is to identify the treatment or something the experimenter manipulates, which is called the (b)_____. In addition, the experimenter selects behaviors that are to be used to measure the potential effects of the treatment. These selected behaviors are called the (c)_____, and they may include a wide range of behaviors, such as cognitive processes, observable behaviors, or measurable physiological responses. **Rule 3** is to choose subjects so that each one in a sample has an equal chance of being selected. One procedure for doing so is called (d)_____. **Rule 4** is to assign subjects randomly to one of two groups. The group that will receive the treatment is called the (e)_____, and the group that will undergo everything but the treatment is called the (f)_____. **Rule 5** is to manipulate the (g)_____ by administering it (or one level of it) to the experimental group but not to the control group. The procedure for preventing researchers or subjects from knowing who is getting the

treatment is called the (h)_____. **Rule 6** is to measure the effects of the independent variable on behaviors that have been selected as the (i)_____. **Rule 7** is to analyze differences between behaviors of subjects in the experimental group and those in the control group by using various (j)_____, which determine whether differences were due to the treatment or to chance occurrences. By following these seven rules, researchers reduce the chances that (k)_____ caused their results.

H. Research Focus: ADHD Controversies

13. One controversy over ADHD is that, as of this writing, the diagnosis of ADHD is based on (a)_____ observations, which are not always clear-cut, rather than on more reliable (b)_____ tests. Another controversy involves how best to treat ADHD. For more severe ADHD, researchers recommend a combination of (c)_____ and (d)_____ treatment. However, even though Ritalin can decrease hyperactivity in children and increase their ability to pay (e)_____, Ritalin does not necessarily improve reading or social skills and does not necessarily reduce problems occurring during adolescence and adulthood.

I. Application: Research Concerns

14. One method of counteracting potential harmful effects on experimental subjects is by thoroughly _____ them. This includes explaining the purpose and method of the experiment, asking subjects about their feelings, and helping subjects deal with possible doubts or problems arising from the experiment.

15. The justification for using _____ in research is that it has resulted in major medical advances, treatments for diseases, and understanding of human disorders.

Answers: *1. (a) case study, (b) survey, (c) experiment; 2. survey; 3. (a) testimonial, (b) perceptions, (c) self-fulfilling prophecy, (d) testimonials; 4. (a) placebo, (b) placebo effect, (c) testimonials; 5. (a) correlated, (b) correlation coefficient; 6. (a) perfect positive correlation, (b) positive correlation, (c) perfect negative correlation, (d) negative correlation; 7. (a) cause, (b) clues, (c) predict; 8. (a) interview, (b) questionnaire, (c) standardized tests, (d) laboratory study or experiment, (e) animal model; 9. naturalistic setting; 10. case study; 11. laboratory setting; 12. (a) hypothesis, (b) independent variable, (c) dependent variables, (d) random selection, (e) experimental group, (f) control group, (g) independent variable, (h) double-blind procedure, (i) dependent variables, (j) statistical procedures, (k) error or bias; 13. (a) behavioral, (b) medical or laboratory, (c) Ritalin, (d) behavioral, (e) attention; 14. debriefing; 15. animals*

Critical Thinking

Does Binge Drinking Cause Later Health Problems?

Questions

1. What are the three major methods for answering questions in psychology, and which method was used in this study?

2. Do the results of this study show a cause-and-effect relationship between teenage binge drinking and poorer health for young adults? Why or why not?

It is well known that adolescent drinking causes plenty of immediate health problems such as sleeplessness, fatigue, headaches, and lower cognitive functioning. But does adolescent binge drinking (having at least 5 alcoholic drinks on one occasion) have any long-term effects on health? According to a recent study, the answer is yes. Binge drinking during adolescence was found to have a variety of long-term, negative health consequences, and the risks remained even for people who stopped drinking during their teenage years.

Researchers at the University of Washington followed 808 people (about equal numbers of males and females) from ages 10 to 24, interviewing them numerous times asking about their drinking and other drug use, exercise habits, and health. They identified four types of teenage drinkers: nonbinge drinkers (including nondrinkers), who never or rarely engaged in binge drinking; chronic heavy drinkers, who drank throughout adolescence; escalators, who started drinking in mid-adolescence and quickly increased their alcohol use; and late onsetters, who began drinking late in their teenage years.

Findings showed that nonbinge drinkers were in the best health at age 24, based on weight, physical activity, blood pressure, and number of times they got sick. Chronic heavy drinkers were in the worst physical health. For example, compared to nonbinge drinkers, they were almost 4 times as likely to be overweight and to have high blood pressure. Also, late onsetters were more likely to get sick than nonbinge drinkers, but surprisingly escalators were not found to have poorer health than teens who did not binge drink.

The researchers adjusted the study's statistical analyses to account for factors that might explain the findings, such as income level, gender, ethnicity, and level of drinking at age 24. Even so, they still found teenage binge drinking to be associated with later health problems. These results support the role of alcohol in long-term health risk.

Although these findings are impressive, the researchers cannot conclude that adolescent binge drinking causes later health problems. Instead, they state that those who binge drink may choose certain lifestyles and engage in certain behaviors that more directly contribute to poorer health. When these factors are better understood, interventions can be more effective in reducing the occurrence of teenage binge drinking. (Adapted from Oesterle et al., 2004; Querna, 2004)

3. Why were "escalators" found not to have poorer health than "nonbinge drinkers"?

4. What should alcohol prevention programs emphasize to help reduce teenage binge drinking?

5. What are the advantage and disadvantage of this study?

Suggested Answers

1. The three major methods for answering questions are survey, case study, and experiment. In this study, researchers asked people questions about their drinking and physical health, so this study used the survey method.

2. Surveys cannot show cause-and-effect relationships but only correlations between events: teenagers who engaged in binge drinking more often had poorer physical health as young adults than those who engaged in binge drinking less often. To show a cause-and-effect relationship, this study would have to be designed as an experiment in which an experimental group got one treatment (alcohol) while a control group got no or different treatment (no alcohol/placebo).

3. This is difficult to know for certain. It may be helpful to examine additional aspects of physical health (cholesterol, family history) and health behaviors (diet, routine medical care).

4. Alcohol prevention programs should emphasize the immediate and long-term negative consequences resulting from adolescent binge drinking.

5. The advantage of this survey study is that it suggests an unexpected cause or explanation for why some young adults have poorer health (adolescent binge drinking). One disadvantage of this survey study is that it cannot identify cause-and-effect relationships.

Links to Learning

Learning Activities

- ***POWERSTUDY FOR INTRODUCTION TO PSYCHOLOGY 4.0***

by Tom Doyle and Rod Plotnik

    SuperModule: Check out "Psychology & Science" on **PowerStudy**. This module is self-paced, fully narrated, and includes:

    - Videos—Imbedded videos discuss the definition, treatment, behaviors, and possible overdiagnosis of ADHD.
    - Interactive surveys, an entire section on cultural diversity, an explanation of correlation, and an ADHD diagnosis section where you can become the therapist. You will also find numerous drag and drop exercises to help you remember the difference between methods of research and decide which is best for different circumstances.
    - An interactive version of the Summary Test on pages 42 and 43. Also access related quizzing—true/false, multiple choice and matching.
    - An interactive version of the Critical Thinking exercise "Does Binge Drinking Cause Later Health Problems?" on page 44.
    - Key terms, a chapter outline including chapter abstract, and a special extended list of hotlinked websites that correlate to this module.

- ***CengageNOW***

academic.cengage.com/login

    Need help studying? This site is your one-stop study shop. Take a Pre-Test and CengageNOW will generate a Personalized Study Plan based on your test results. The Study Plan will identify the topics you need to review and direct you to online resources to help you master those topics. You can then take a Post-Test to determine the concepts you have mastered and what you still need to work on.

- ***INTRODUCTION TO PSYCHOLOGY BOOK COMPANION WEBSITE***
academic.cengage.com/psychology/plotnik

    Visit your book companion website where you will find more resources to help you study. At this site, you will find Learning Objectives, Internet Exercises, quizzing, flash cards, and a pronunciation glossary.

- ***STUDY GUIDE and WEBTUTOR***

    Check the corresponding module in your Study Guide for effective student tips and help learning the material presented. Also go to **academic.cengage.com/webtutor** for an interactive version of the Study Guide features.

Study Questions

*A. Answering Questions—Which method would you use to find out if caffeine improves memory? (**Suggested answer page 619**)

B. Surveys—How believable is a recent survey that reported that people never lie to their best friends?

C. Case Study—Why do some people put more faith in testimonials than in proven research?

*D. Cultural Diversity: Use of Placebos—Why do Americans think it strange that Asians use rhino horn as medicine? (**Suggested answer page 620**)

E. Correlation—How would you explain the positive correlation (0.60) researchers found between drinking coffee and being sexually active after age 60?

*F. Decisions about Doing Research—Which research techniques and settings would you use to study mental problems in the homeless? (**Suggested answer page 620**)

G. Scientific Method: Experiment—How would you determine whether taking vitamin B reduces stress?

H. Research Focus: ADHD Controversies—If you had a child who might have ADHD, what would you do?

I. Application: Research Concerns—What concerns might a student have about volunteering to be a subject in an experiment?

*These questions are answered in Appendix B.

MODULE 3
Brain's Building Blocks

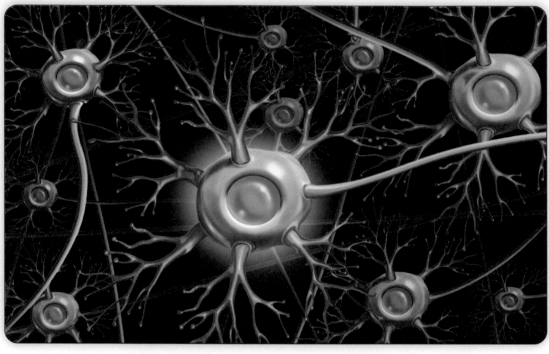

 PowerStudy 4.0™ Complete Module

Introduction

Losing One's Mind

Why does 71-year-old Ina think the baby is hers?

Her children had always called their mother, Ina, "the Rock of Gibraltar." Ina could fix the plumbing, hang wallpaper, and prepare a full dinner from scratch every night, while keeping her six children out of trouble. She could swim faster than anyone, she wanted to be a basketball player, and her late husband called her the most beautiful woman he had ever seen.

But that was before she started to forget things and repeat herself, which could just be part of getting old. What could explain her mopping the kitchen floor at 2:00 in the morning and refusing to go to bed? Or wearing the same dirty clothes day after day, something she had never done in her entire life? Or being confused at housework? Or thinking that her granddaughter (right photo) is her own child?

Because Ina had always been so healthy, her six grown children thought that she must have suffered a stroke or that she was depressed. When they took Ina in for a checkup, a neurologist confirmed their worst fears. Ina had Alzheimer's *(ALTS-hi-mers)* disease.

In 10% of the cases, *Alzheimer's disease* begins after age 50, but in 90% of the cases, it begins after age 65. Its initial symptoms are problems with memory, such as forgetting and repeating things, getting lost, and being mildly confused. There are also cognitive deficits, such as problems with language, difficulties in recognizing objects, and inability to plan and organize tasks. Over a period of five to ten years, these symptoms worsen and result in profound memory loss, lack of recognition of family and friends, deterioration in personality, and emotional outbursts. There is widespread damage to the brain, especially the hippocampus, which is involved in memory. At present, there is no cure for Alzheimer's, which is always fatal (NIH, 2005).

In the United States, Alzheimer's is one of the leading causes of death among adults. Currently, there are more than 4 million people in the United States and 16 million people worldwide who have Alzheimer's disease. The number of patients is projected to rise dramatically in the coming decades (right graph) as people are expected to live longer. It is estimated that nearly half of those over 85 have Alzheimer's (P. R. Solomon & Murphy, 2005).

Ina's condition worsened through the coming months. She had trouble completing even the simplest tasks, and the day after having a big Thanksgiving celebration with her family, she asked where she had spent the holiday. At times, she recognized her grown children; at other times, she thought they were her cousins. Ina must now be watched almost every minute so she does not hurt herself or wander off and get lost (adapted from *Newsweek,* December 18, 1989).

She was the family's "Rock of Gibraltar" until she developed Alzheimer's.

For Ina, the worst is yet to come. Her memory will totally disintegrate, she will be completely bedridden, and she will not know who she is or recognize the family she has lovingly raised. When she dies—for Alzheimer's has, at present, no cure—Ina will have lost her memory, her wonderful personality, and all signs of humanity.

Diagnosis and Causes

In Ina's case as well as all cases of individuals with memory and cognitive difficulties, Alzheimer's is diagnosed by identifying a combination of behavioral, neurological, physical, and psychological symptoms. Recently, researchers were successful in diagnosing Alzheimer's by injecting chemical markers and identifying brain damage from pictures of living brains (PET scans, p. 71) (Zhang et al., 2005).

Researchers now believe they are close to figuring out the causes of Alzheimer's disease, which involve genetic, neurological, and possible environmental factors (S. A. Small & Mayeux, 2005). For example, Alzheimer's incidence is two to three times higher among individuals who have a parent or sibling with Alzheimer's, and the rate of developing the disease increases when additional family members also have the illness (Alzheimer's Association, 2005). Researchers also identified several chemicals (proteins and peptides) that occur naturally in all brains but, for some reason, begin to multiply and are believed to cause Alzheimer's. These chemicals act like glue that eventually destroys brain cells (Brendza et al., 2005). With these new leads, researchers are optimistic about finding the causes of and developing treatments for Alzheimer's. New treatments are needed because current drugs are only moderately effective in treating early symptoms of Alzheimer's disease (NIH, 2005).

What's Coming

The reason Alzheimer's disease eventually destroyed Ina's memory, personality, and humanity is this disease gradually destroys the building blocks that form the brain's informational network. We'll explain the two groups of brain cells—glial cells and neurons—that make up this network. We'll discuss how the cells in one group—neurons—have a remarkable ability to receive and send information. You'll discover how brain cells communicate with chemicals that have the ability to start or stop the flow of information. Finally, we'll explain an experimental treatment of implanting neurons to treat brain diseases. We'll use the story of Ina and Alzheimer's disease to illustrate the brain's building blocks.

Dementia on the rise
Alzheimer's patients in the U.S.

[Graph: Millions (y-axis from 0 to 18) vs. years 1990, 2010, 2030, 2050 (projection). Line rises from 3.7 to 16.]

A. Overview: Human Brain

As Alzheimer's disease slowly destroys Ina's brain, she is also slowly losing her mind. In Ina's case, Alzheimer's disease has progressed to the point that she can no longer recognize her own children or remember her family gathering on Thanksgiving day.

We'll use Ina's brain and her current problems with Alzheimer's disease to answer four related questions: Why isn't the brain a nose? What's in the brain? Can a brain grow new neurons? Can you take a picture of the mind?

Development of the Brain

Why isn't the brain a nose?

The fact that your brain does not develop into a nose is because of instructions contained in your genes.

Genes are chains of chemicals arranged like rungs on a twisting ladder (right figure). There are about 20,000–25,000 genes that contain chemical instructions equal to about 300,000 pages of typed instructions (IHGSC, 2004). The chemical instructions in the genes program the development of millions of individual parts into a complex body and brain.

An amazing feature of the 20,000–25,000 genes is they are contained in a fertilized egg, which is a single cell about the size of a grain of sand. We'll explain more about the genes and their chemical instructions in the next module (see p. 68).

In the brain's early stages of development, it looks nothing like the final product. For example, the figure below looks more like some strange animal than what it really is, a six-week-old human embryo with a developing brain.

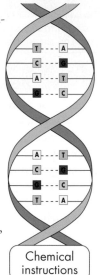

| T --- A |
| C --- G |
| A --- T |
| G --- C |

| A --- T |
| C --- G |
| G --- C |
| T --- A |

Chemical instructions

SIX-WEEK-OLD BRAIN. This drawing represents a greatly enlarged six-week-old human embryo. The 3 labeled areas (in 3 colors) will eventually develop into the 3 major divisions of the mature human brain that is shown below.

3 major divisions of 6-week-old brain

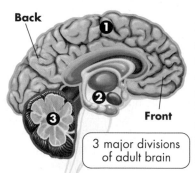

Back

Front

3 major divisions of adult brain

MATURE BRAIN. The 3 labeled areas represent the 3 major divisions of the mature brain that we'll discuss in the next module. The mature human brain (side view) weighs almost 3 pounds and contains about 1 trillion cells (Ropper & Brown, 2005).

In the case of Ina, who developed Alzheimer's disease, researchers think that some of her genetic instructions were faulty. The faulty instructions resulted in an abnormal buildup in the brain of a gluelike substance that gradually destroys brain cells (Cowley, 2000b). Next, we'll explain the two different kinds of brain cells and which ones are destroyed by Alzheimer's disease.

Structure of the Brain

What's in your brain?

On the left is a top view of a human brain. It is shaped like a small wrinkled melon, weighs about 1,350 grams (less than 3 pounds), has a pinkish-white color, and has the consistency of firm Jell-O.

Top view of human brain

Your brain is fueled by sugar (glucose) and has about 1 trillion cells that can be divided into two groups—glial cells and neurons.

GLIAL CELLS. The most numerous brain cells, about 900 billion, are called glial *(GLEE-all)* cells.

Glial cells have at least three functions: providing scaffolding to guide the growth of developing neurons and support mature neurons; wrapping around neurons to form a kind of insulation to prevent interference from other electrical signals; and releasing chemicals that influence a neuron's growth and function (Fields & Stevens-Graham, 2002).

Glial cell

A star-shaped glial cell (astrocyte) is shown above. Glial cells grow throughout one's lifetime. If something causes the uncontrolled growth of glial cells, the result is brain cancer. Alzheimer's disease does not usually destroy glial cells, but it does destroy the second kind of brain cells, which are called neurons.

NEURONS. The second group of brain cells, which number about 100 billion, are called neurons *(NER-ons);* one is shown on the right.

A *neuron* is a brain cell with two specialized extensions. One extension is for receiving electrical signals, and a second, longer extension is for transmitting electrical signals.

Depending upon their size, neurons receive and transmit electrical signals at speeds of up to 200 miles per hour over distances from a fraction of an inch to over 3 feet, such as from your toe to your spinal cord.

Neurons form a vast, miniaturized informational network that allows us to receive sensory information, control muscle movement, regulate digestion, secrete hormones, and engage in complex mental processes such as thinking, imagining, dreaming, and remembering.

Neuron

Ina's brain was constructed from two kinds of building blocks—glial cells and neurons. However, it is the neurons that Alzheimer's disease gradually destroys; the result is that Ina's brain is losing its ability to transmit information, causing memory and cognitive difficulties. Why neurons do not usually repair or replace themselves is our next topic.

Growth of New Neurons

Can a brain grow new neurons?

If you had a bird's brain, you could grow new neurons every spring. A male canary learns to sing a breeding song in the spring, but when breeding season is over, the ability to sing the song disappears. However, come next spring, an adult canary's brain begins growing about 20,000 new neurons a day, and, during this short period, the bird relearns the breeding song. These new neurons result in a 50% or more increase in neurons in two areas of the canary's brain (left figure) that control singing (G. Miller, 2003). Without a doubt, an adult canary's brain can regularly grow new neurons (Barinaga, 2003).

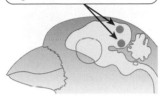

The two red dots show two areas of the mature canary's brain that increase by 50% with the growth of new neurons.

PRIMATE BRAINS. Does the fact that adult canaries as well as adult mice, rats, and other animals can grow new neurons also hold true for adult human brains (Barinaga, 2003a)? Researchers believe that, with few exceptions, the brains of adult primates, such as humans and chimpanzees, develop almost all their neurons at birth and adult brains do not grow new neurons (Kornack & Rakic, 2001).

The few exceptions to the finding that new neurons do not grow in adult brains were found in two areas of the brain—hippocampus (p. 80) and olfactory bulb (p. 107). Researchers concluded that adult monkey and human brains are capable of growing a relatively limited number of new neurons throughout adulthood and that some of these new neurons play an important role in our continuing ability to learn and remember new things (van Praag et al., 2002).

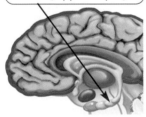

Growth of new neurons is found in this area of mature human brain (hippocampus).

REPAIRING THE BRAIN. Besides having a limited capacity to grow new neurons throughout adulthood, mature human brains also have a limited capacity to replace, rewire, or repair damaged neurons, such as after a stroke, gunshot wound, or blow to the head (Silver & Miller, 2004). One reason neurons have only a limited capacity to be repaired or rewired after damage is that there is a genetic program that turns off regrowth when neurons become fully grown (McKerracher & Ellezam, 2002). This limited capacity of the adult brain to rewire itself by forming new connections helps explain why people may recover some, but rarely all, of the functions initially lost after brain damage (Gage, 2003). Recent advances in stem cell research suggest the human brain may be able to grow more neurons. If this were possible, the brain could repair damage caused by an accident or disease, such as Alzheimer's (Wong et al., 2005).

The reason Alzheimer's disease is so destructive and eventually leads to death is that this disease destroys neurons many times faster than the brain's limited capacity for regrowth, repair, or rewiring. As Alzheimer's destroys Ina's brain, what is happening to her mind?

Brain Versus Mind

Can you take a picture of the mind?

As Alzheimer's disease destroys Ina's brain, she is also losing her mind, which brings us to the mind-body question.

The *mind-body question* asks how complex mental activities, such as feeling, thinking, and learning, can be explained by the physical, chemical, and electrical activities of the brain.

Through the centuries, philosophers and scientists have given different answers to the mind-body question, some believing the mind and brain are separate things and others saying the mind and brain are one and the same (Gelder, 2005).

For example, Nobel Prize winner and geneticist Francis Crick (2002) believes the mind *is* the brain: "You, your joys and your sorrows, your memories and your ambition, your sense of personal identity and free will, are in fact no more than the behavior of a vast assembly of nerve cells and their associated molecules." Although some agree with Crick's answer—that the mind and brain are the same—others reply that mental activities cannot be reduced to the physical activities of the brain (Mahoney, 2005).

Another answer comes from Nobel Prize winner and neurophysiologist Roger Sperry (1993), who said that the brain is like a coin with two sides. One side consists of physical reactions, such as making chemicals that neurons use for communicating. The other side consists of all of our mental functions, such as thinking, imagining, and deciding. According to Sperry, the brain's chemicals (physical side) influence consciousness and mental activities, which, in turn, influence the production of more or different brain chemicals. There is considerable support for Sperry's idea of continuous interaction between the physical and mental sides (Wakefeld, 2001).

ALZHEIMER'S. In Ina's case, as Alzheimer's disease destroys her brain, she also loses more and more of her mental activities, such as knowing, thinking, and deciding. Researchers can now study a person's mental activities by taking pictures or brain scans of the neural activities going on inside the living brain (brain scans are discussed on pp. 70–71). For example, the top right brain scan shows a great amount of neural activity occurring inside a normal brain (red/yellow indicate most neural activity, blue/green indicate least activity). In comparison, the bottom right brain scan shows relatively little neural activity and thus relatively little mental activity occurring inside an Alzheimer's brain. These kinds of brain scans show that neural activities and mental activities are closely linked, and researchers are studying how these links occur (Mosconi et al., 2005).

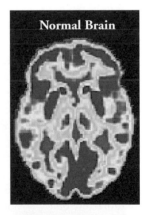

Normal Brain

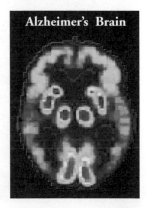

Alzheimer's Brain

Knowing now how important neurons are to your mental and physical functions, we next examine them in more detail.

B. Neurons: Structure & Function

Why could Ina think, move, and talk?

Before Ina developed Alzheimer's disease, she was able to engage in an incredible variety of cognitive and physical behaviors. She was able to think, remember, walk, smile, and speak—all because of the activity of millions of microscopic brain cells called neurons. We'll examine the neuron, which comes in many wondrous shapes and sizes and has only three basic structures—cell body, dendrites, and axon.

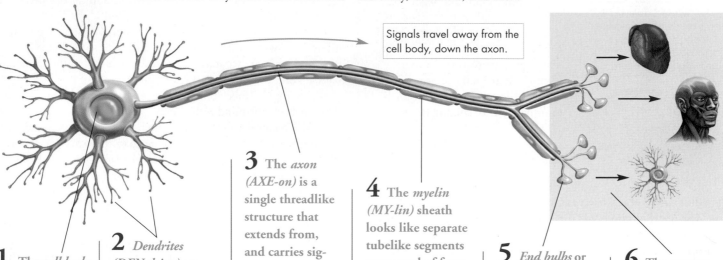

Signals travel away from the cell body, down the axon.

1 The *cell body* (or soma) is a relatively large, egg-shaped structure that provides fuel, manufactures chemicals, and maintains the entire neuron in working order.

In the center of the cell body is a small oval shape representing the nucleus, which contains genetic instructions (in the form of DNA) for both the manufacture of chemicals and the regulation of the neuron.

2 *Dendrites (DEN-drites)* are branchlike extensions that arise from the cell body; they receive signals from other neurons, muscles, or sense organs and pass these signals to the cell body.

At the time of birth, a neuron has few dendrites. After birth, dendrites undergo dramatic growth that accounts for much of the increase in brain size. As dendrites grow, they make connections and form communication networks between neurons and other cells or organs.

3 The *axon (AXE-on)* is a single threadlike structure that extends from, and carries signals away from, the cell body to neighboring neurons, organs, or muscles.

Here the axon is indicated by an orange line inside the tube composed of separate gray segments. Axons vary in length from less than a hair's breadth to as long as 3 feet (from your spinal cord to your toes). An axon conducts electrical signals to a neighboring organ (heart), a muscle, or another neuron.

4 The *myelin (MY-lin)* sheath looks like separate tubelike segments composed of fatty material that wraps around and insulates an axon. The myelin sheath prevents interference from electrical signals generated in adjacent axons.

The axons of most large neurons, including motor neurons, have myelin sheaths. You may have heard the brain described as consisting of gray and white matter. Gray is the color of cell bodies, while white is the color of myelin sheaths.

5 *End bulbs* or *terminal bulbs* look like tiny bubbles that are located at the extreme ends of the axon's branches. Each end bulb is like a miniature container that stores chemicals called neurotransmitters, which are used to communicate with neighboring cells.

End bulbs reach right up to, but do not physically touch, the surface of a neighboring organ (heart), muscle (head), or another cell body.

6 The *synapse (SIN-apse)* is an infinitely small space (20–30 billionths of a meter) that exists between an end bulb and its adjacent body organ (heart), muscles (head), or cell body.

When stimulated by electrical signals from the axon, the end bulbs eject neurotransmitters into the synapse. The neurotransmitters cross the synapse and act like switches to turn adjacent cells on or off. We'll explain this switching process a little later.

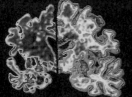

Alzheimer's brain is smaller because it has lost many neurons.

Size of normal brain with all of its neurons intact.

In Alzheimer's disease there is an excessive buildup of gluelike substances, which gradually destroy neurons (Cowley, 2002). In Ina's case, these gluelike substances will destroy more and more of her neurons, causing her brain to actually shrink, as shown by the very deep creases in the Alzheimer's brain (left photo). Researchers recently discovered an experimental vaccine that may help stop the buildup of these gluelike killer substances, and they continue to search for other interventions (Check, 2003).

We have discussed the structure and function of neurons, but it is important not to confuse neurons (in your brain and spinal cord) with nerves (in your body).

C. Neurons Versus Nerves

Reattaching Limbs

What's unusual about John's arms?

John Thomas was 18 when a farm machine ripped off both of his arms just below his shoulders. Since he was home alone, he had to walk to the farmhouse, kick open the front door, and with a pencil clenched in his teeth, dial the phone for help. When paramedics arrived, he reminded them to get his two arms, which were still stuck in the farm equipment. John was taken to the hospital, where doctors reattached both arms (indicated by red arrows in left photo).

Three months later, John could raise his arms up in the air but could not move them below his elbows. After three years of physical therapy and 15 operations, John could raise his reattached arms over his head, make fists, and grip with his hands. Surgeons believe that John will continue to improve with years of physical therapy (*USA Today*, January 12, 1995). In another case, a donor hand was attached to the arm of a person whose own hand was severed (P. Smith, 2003).

Both his arms were torn off and then reattached.

Transplanting a Face

Can parts of your face be transplanted onto someone else's?

More recently, French doctors performed the world's first-ever face transplant, a very risky and complex procedure. Doctors removed facial tissue from a dead woman's face and transplanted it onto Isabelle, a 38-year-old woman whose face had been severely disfigured by a dog. She received a new nose, lips, and chin during the surgery (right) (C. Gorman, 2005b). A few months after the surgery, Isabelle said, "I can open my mouth and eat. I feel my lips, my nose and my mouth" (A. Doland, 2006). There is still risk of her body rejecting the donor's facial tissue in the future, but so far the surgery appears to have been a success.

The fact that severed nerves in arms, hands, or faces can be reattached but neurons in a severed spinal cord are difficult to reattach illustrates a major difference between the peripheral and central nervous systems.

Doctors gave Isabelle a new mouth, nose, and chin.

Peripheral Nervous System

Why can limbs be reattached?

Severed limbs can be reattached and regain movement and sensation because their nerves are part of the peripheral nervous system.

The *peripheral nervous system* is made up of nerves, which are located throughout the body except in the brain and spinal cord.

Nerves are stringlike bundles of axons and dendrites that come from the spinal cord and are held together by connective tissue (shown in red in right figure). Nerves carry information from the senses, skin, muscles, and the body's organs to and from the spinal cord. Nerves in the peripheral nervous system have the ability to regrow or reattach if severed or damaged.

Peripheral nerves can be reattached.

The fact that nerves can regrow means that severed limbs can be reattached and limb transplants are possible. However, limb transplants are risky because a person must take drugs long-term to suppress his or her own immune system, whose normal job is to destroy "foreign" things, such as a donor's transplanted limb. When his or her own immune system is suppressed, a person is at risk for getting serious infectious diseases (Lake et al., 2004).

The remarkable ability of nerves to regrow and be reattached distinguishes them from neurons.

Central Nervous System

Why do Montel's feet hurt?

People may have numbness or paralysis after damage to their brain or spinal cord because of what neurons cannot easily do.

The *central nervous system* is made up of neurons located in the brain and spinal cord (shown in blue in left figure).

The adult human brain has a limited capacity to grow new neurons and a limited ability to make new connections. Once damaged, neurons usually die and are not replaced.

Because neurons have such a limited capacity for repair or regrowth, people who have an injured or damaged brain or spinal cord experience some loss of sensation and motor movement, depending upon the severity of the damage. For example, Montel Williams (right photo) has suffered from intense pain in his feet and legs for many years as a result of *multiple sclerosis*, a disease that attacks the myelin sheaths that wrap around and insulate cells in the central nervous system.

Montel was diagnosed with multiple sclerosis.

As a result of this damage, messages between the brain and other parts of the body are disrupted, often causing problems in motor coordination, strength, and sensation (Falcon, 2002).

Currently, one of the most exciting areas of research involves techniques that stimulate the regrowth or repair of damaged neurons. For example, axons, which carry information up and down the spinal cord, normally wither and die after injury. Two methods to promote the regrowth of axons are providing tubes that guide their growth and injecting growth-producing chemicals (M. E. Schwab, 2002). The newest approach for treating brain damage is to replace damaged neurons by transplanting fetal tissue or stem cells (taken from embyros) into the damaged area. This method has great potential for treating brain and spinal cord diseases, such as Alzheimer's and multiple sclerosis (Capello et al., 2005; Wong et al., 2005). We'll discuss fetal tissue transplants in the Application section.

Now that you know the structure of the neuron, we'll explain one of its amazing functions: sending information at speeds approaching 200 miles per hour.

D. Sending Information

1 Feeling a Sharp Object

When you step on a sharp object, you seem to feel the pain almost immediately because neurons send signals at speeds approaching 200 mph. To feel the pain involves the following series of electrochemical events:

A. Some stimulus, such as a tack, causes a change in physical energy. The tack produces mechanical pressure on the bottom of your foot.

B. Your skin has sensors that pick up the mechanical pressure and transform it into electrical signals. (We'll discuss various kinds of sensors in Module 5.)

C. The sensors' electrical signals are sent by the neuron's axon to various areas in the spinal cord and brain.

D. Finally, your brain interprets these electrical signals as "pain."

We're going to focus on step C and explain how axons send electrical signals by using the analogy of a battery. We'll begin by enlarging the inside of an axon.

2 Axon Membrane: Chemical Gates

Just as a battery has a protective covering, so too does the axon. Think of an axon as a long tube that is not only filled with fluid but also surrounded with fluid. The axon's tube is formed by a thin membrane, similar to a battery's outside covering, which keeps the fluid separate and also has special gates.

The *axon membrane* **has chemical gates (shown in red) that can open to allow electrically charged particles** to enter or can close to keep out electrically charged particles.

Just as a battery's power comes from its electrically charged chemicals, so does the axon's power to send information. In fact, the axon's electrically charged particles are the key to making it a living battery.

3 Ions: Charged Particles

The fluid inside and outside the axon contains ions.

Ions **are chemical particles that have electrical charges. Ions follow two rules: Opposite charges attract (figure below), and like charges repel.**

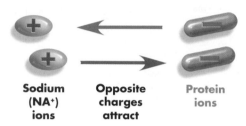

Sodium (NA⁺) ions   Opposite charges attract   Protein ions

The fluid contains several different ions, such as sodium, potassium, chloride, and protein. The axon's function is often explained by discussing sodium and potassium ions. However, it is simpler and easier to focus on just sodium ions, which have positive charges and are abbreviated Na^+, and large protein ions, which have negative charges and are labeled protein⁻. Because they have opposite charges, Na^+ ions will be attracted to protein⁻ ions (figure above).

Because the axon's membrane separates the positive sodium ions from the negative protein ions, we have the makings of a living battery, as shown in section 4 on the next page.

6 Sending Information

One mistake students make is to think that the axon has ONE action potential, similar to the bang of a gunshot. However, unlike a gunshot, the axon has numerous individual action potentials that move down the axon, segment by segment; this movement is called the nerve impulse.

The *nerve impulse* **refers to the series of separate action potentials that take place segment by segment as they move down the length of an axon.**

Thus, instead of a single bang, a nerve impulse goes down the length of the axon very much like a lit fuse. Once lit, a fuse doesn't go off in a single bang but rather burns continuously until it reaches the end. This movement of a nerve impulse all the way down to the end of an axon is actually a natural law.

7 All-or-None Law

Why does a nerve impulse travel down the axon's entire length? The answer is the all-or-none law.

The *all-or-none law* **says that, if an action potential starts at the beginning of an axon, the action potential will continue at the same speed, segment by segment, to the very end of the axon.**

You'll see how the all-or-none law works in the next figure.

8 Nerve Impulse

Notice in this drawing, which continues on the next page, that the nerve impulse is made up of a sequence of six action potentials, with the first action potential occurring at the beginning of the axon.

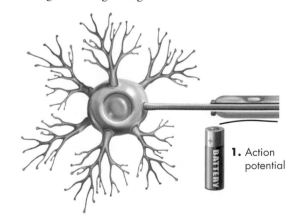

1. Action potential

4 Resting State: Charged Battery

The axon membrane separates positively charged sodium ions on the outside from negatively charged protein ions on the inside. This separation produces a miniature chemical battery that is not yet discharging and, thus, is said to be in its resting state.

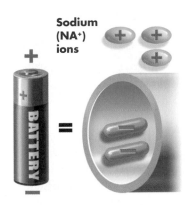

Sodium (NA⁺) ions

The *resting state* means that the axon has a charge, or potential; it resembles a battery. The charge, or potential, results from the axon membrane separating positive ions on the outside from negative ions on the inside (left figure).

The axon membrane has a charge across it during the resting state because of several factors, the primary one being the sodium pump. (To simplify our explanation of the resting state, we won't discuss other pump or transport systems.)

The *sodium pump* is a transport process that picks up any sodium ions that enter the axon's chemical gates and returns them back outside. Thus, the sodium pump is responsible for keeping the axon charged by returning and keeping sodium ions outside the axon membrane.

In the resting state, the axon is similar to a fully charged battery. Let's see what happens when the resting state is disrupted and the battery discharges.

5 Action Potential: Sending Information

If a stimulus, such as stepping on a tack, is large enough to excite a neuron, two things will happen to its axon. First, the stimulus will eventually open the axon's chemical gates by stopping the sodium pump. Second, when the stoppage of the sodium pump causes the gates to open, thousands of positive sodium ions will rush inside because of their attraction to the negative protein ions. The rush of sodium ions inside the axon is called the action potential.

The *action potential* is a tiny electric current that is generated when the positive sodium ions rush inside the axon. The enormous increase of sodium ions inside the axon causes the inside of the axon to reverse its charge. The inside becomes positive, while the outside becomes negative.

Action Potential

Inside = positive

Outside = negative

5a Just as a current flows when you connect the poles of a battery, current also flows when sodium ions rush through the opened gates of the axon membrane.

5b During an action potential, the inside of the axon changes to positive and the outside changes to negative. Immediately after the action potential, the sodium pump starts up and returns the axon to the resting state.

At this point, imagine that an action potential has started at the beginning of an axon. How action potentials whiz at race-car speeds down the entire length of an axon is what we'll examine next in the section below, Sequence: Nerve Impulse.

8a According to the all-or-none law, once a nerve impulse begins, it goes to the end of the axon. This means that when action potential 1 occurs, it will be followed in order by potentials 2, 3, 4, 5, and 6. After the occurrence of each action potential, the axon membrane at that point quickly returns to its resting state.

8b Notice that the *myelin sheath* has regular breaks where the axon is bare and uninsulated. It is at these bare points that the axon's gates open and the action potential takes place.

9 End Bulbs and Neurotransmitters

Once the nerve impulse reaches the end of the axon, the very last action potential, 6, affects the end bulbs, which are located at the very end of the axon. This last action potential triggers the end bulbs to release their neurotransmitters. Once released, neurotransmitters cross the synapse and, depending upon the kind, they will either excite or inhibit the function of neighboring organs (heart), muscles (head), or cell bodies.

As you can now see, neurotransmitters are critical for communicating with neighboring organs, muscles, and other neurons. We'll examine transmitters in more detail and show you how they excite or inhibit.

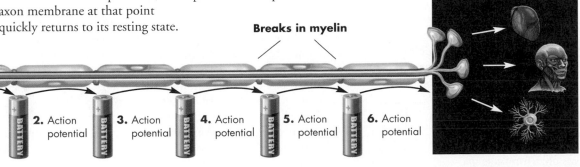

Breaks in myelin

2. Action potential   **3.** Action potential   **4.** Action potential   **5.** Action potential   **6.** Action potential

E. Transmitters

What makes your heart pound?

There's no doubt that you have felt your heart pounding when you are afraid, stressed, or angry. One reason for your pounding heart has to do with transmitters.

A *transmitter* is a chemical messenger that carries information between nerves and body organs, such as muscles and heart.

Everything you do, including thinking, deciding, talking, and getting angry, involves transmitters. For example, imagine seeing someone back into your brand new car and then just drive away. You would certainly become angry and your heart would pound. Let's see why getting angry can increase your heart rate from a normal 60 to 70 beats per minute to over 180.

> Why does my heart rate increase when I get angry?

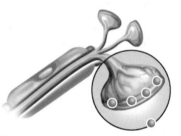

1 In the figure on the left, you see the end of an axon with 3 branches. At the end of the bottom branch is a greatly enlarged *end bulb.* Inside the bulb are 4 colored circles that represent transmitters.

2 When the action potential hits the *end bulb,* it causes a miniature explosion, and the transmitters are ejected outside. Once ejected, transmitters cross a tiny space, or synapse, and, in this case, reach the nearby heart muscle. Think of transmitters as chemical keys that fit into chemical locks on the surface of the heart muscle. End bulbs usually hold either excitatory or inhibitory transmitters, which have opposite effects.

Transmitters

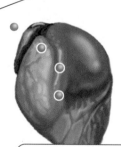

> Transmitters can increase or decrease heart rate.

3 Strong emotions cause the release of *excitatory transmitters,* which open chemical locks in the heart muscle and cause it to beat faster (left figure). When you get very angry, excitatory transmitters may cause your heart rate to double or even triple its rate. When you start to calm down, there is a release of *inhibitory transmitters,* which block chemical locks in the heart muscle and decrease its rate (right figure). Think of transmitters acting like chemical messengers that either excite or inhibit nearby body organs (heart), neurons, or muscle fibers. One special class of transmitters that are made in the brain are called neurotransmitters.

Excitatory

Inhibitory

What makes your brain work?

Writing a paper on a computer requires your brain to use millions of neurons that communicate with one another by using chemicals called neurotransmitters. *Neurotransmitters* are about a dozen different chemicals that are made by neurons and then used for communication between neurons during the performance of mental or physical activities.

Since billions of neurons that are packed tightly together use different neurotransmitters for eating, sleeping, talking, thinking, and dreaming, why don't neurotransmitters get all mixed up? The answer is that neurotransmitters are similar to chemical keys that fit into only specific chemical locks.

> What happens in my brain when I use my computer?

1 The figure on the left again shows the end of an axon with 3 branches. We have again enlarged one *end bulb* to show that it contains neurotransmitters (4 colored circles).

2 The action potential causes the end bulbs to eject their neurotransmitters (yellow circles), which, in turn, cross the synapse and, in this case, land on the surface of nearby dendrites. The surface of one dendrite is enlarged (right figure) to show its *receptors* (white notches), which are special areas that function like chemical locks.

Neurotransmitters

Receptors

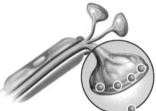

> Receptors on dendrites are like chemical locks.

3 Although there are many different neurotransmitters, each one has a unique chemical key that fits and opens only certain chemical locks, or receptors. Thus, billions of neurons use this system of chemical keys that open or close matching locks to communicate and to participate in so many different activities. Also, remember that some neurotransmitters are *excitatory*—they open receptor locks and turn on neurons—while others are *inhibitory*—they close locks and turn off neurons.

Since neurons use neurotransmitters to communicate, any drug that acts like or interferes with neurotransmitters has the potential to change how the brain functions and how we feel, think, and behave. For example, here's what alcohol does.

What does alcohol do? Drinking alcoholic beverages usually raises the level of alcohol in the blood, which is measured in terms of blood alcohol content (BAC). For example, at low to medium doses (0.01–0.06 BAC), alcohol causes friendliness, loss of inhibitions, decreased self-control, and impaired social judgment; after 3 or 4 drinks, the average person's BAC will range from 0.08 to 0.1, which meets the legal definition of drunkenness in most states. (Alcohol is discussed more fully in Module 8.)

Why do I feel different after drinking?

Alcohol (ethyl alcohol) is a psychoactive drug that is classified as a depressant, which means that it depresses the activity of the central nervous system.

Alcohol has been around for 3,000 years, but researchers have only recently determined its many effects on the brain. We'll discuss one of its major effects on the brain.

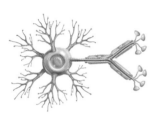

GABA neurons. Alcohol affects the nervous system in a number of ways, blocking some neural receptors and stimulating others. For example, some neurons are excited by a neurotransmitter called GABA *(GAH-bah)*, which the brain normally manufactures. This means that GABA neurons (figure above) have chemical locks that can be opened by chemical keys in the form of the neurotransmitter GABA (Koolman, 2005).

GABA keys. Now here's the interesting part. Alcohol molecules so closely resemble those of the GABA neurotransmitter that alcohol can function like GABA keys and open GABA receptors (figure right). Opening GABA receptors excites GABA neurons. Although it seems backward, when GABA neurons are *excited,* they *decrease* neural activity and produce inhibitory effects, such as a loss of inhibitions and self-control, as well as reduced anxiety. In fact, one reason alcohol has become so popular is that many people drink alcohol to feel less anxious and more relaxed. It is interesting that there appears to be a biological link between alcohol and anxiety. Researchers found that a deficiency in a specific brain protein is associated with high anxiety and excessive alcohol use (Wand, 2005).

Alcohol mimics neurotransmitter.

GABA receptor

We learned that alcohol affects the brain by imitating a naturally occurring neurotransmitter, GABA. Let's now look at the effects other drugs have on the brain's neurotransmitters.

What are the latest discoveries? There are a number of well-known neurotransmitters, such as acetylcholine, GABA, norepinephrine, epinephrine, dopamine, and serotonin. And researchers continue to discover new ones to add to the list of neurotransmitters.

Endorphins. In the 1970s, researchers discovered that the brain makes its own painkiller, very similar to morphine. They called this neurotransmitter endorphin, which is secreted to decrease the effects of pain during great bodily stress, such as an accident (Drolet et al., 2001). We'll discuss the effects of endorphins on page 113.

Anandamide. In the early 1990s, researchers discovered a somewhat surprising neurotransmitter, called anandamide, which is similar in chemical makeup to THC, the active ingredient in marijuana (discussed on p. 186) (Fackelmann, 1993). The figure on the right shows a horizontal section of a rat brain treated with a radioactive version of anandamide. The yellow areas, which were most affected by anandamide, are involved in memory, motor coordination, and emotions (Herkenham, 1996). Anandamide may help people regulate emotions, which would help them to better deal with anxiety and stress (Gaetani et al., 2003).

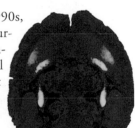

Yellow areas show where marijuana-like anandamide acts.

Nitric oxide. In the mid-1990s, researchers discovered that a gas, nitric oxide, functions like a neurotransmitter and may be involved in regulating emotions. For example, mice genetically altered to lack nitric oxide were six times more likely to pick a fight (right figure) compared to normal mice (R. J. Nelson et al., 1995). Researchers now believe nitric oxide may be involved in regulating aggressive and impulsive behaviors not only in mice but also in humans (Chiavegatto & Nelson, 2003).

Other chemicals. Currently, researchers have identified over a dozen chemicals that

Changing neurotransmitter levels in rats causes increased aggression.

have all the characteristics of neurotransmitters and up to 100 chemicals that influence communication between neurons but do not have all the characteristics of more traditional neurotransmitters (S. Snyder, 2002). The important point to remember about neurotransmitters is that their system of chemical keys and locks permits very effective communication among billions of neurons, which allow us to move, sense, think, feel, and perform hundreds of other functions.

Now that you are familiar with neurons and neurotransmitters, we'll explain a response that many of you have experienced—what happened when you touched a hot object.

F. Reflex Responses

Definition and Sequence

Can you move without thinking?

If you accidentally touched a hot light bulb, your hand would instantly jerk away, without any conscious thought or effort on your part. This is an example of a reflex.

A *reflex* is an unlearned, involuntary reaction to some stimulus. The neural connections or network underlying a reflex is prewired by genetic instructions.

In some cases, such as when a doctor taps your knee, the knee-jerk reflex is controlled by the spinal cord. In other cases, such as when someone shines a bright light into your eye, the pupillary reflex causes the pupil to constrict. We are all born with a number of programmed reflexes, and all reflexes share the same two or three steps, depending upon how they are wired in the nervous system.

One reason reflexes occur so quickly is that they are genetically programmed and involve relatively few neural connections, which saves time. Here's the sequence for how a reflex occurs:

1 **Sensors.** The skin of your fingers has specialized sensors, or receptors, that are sensitive to heat. When you touch a hot light bulb, these skin sensors trigger neurons that start the withdrawal reflex.

2 **Afferent neuron.** From the receptors in your skin, long dendrites carry "pain information" in the form of electrical signals to the spinal cord. These dendrites are part of sensory, or afferent, neurons (red arrows).

Afferent (AFF-er-ent), or *sensory, neuron*s carry information from the senses to the spinal cord.

Sensory neurons may have dendrites 2 to 3 feet long, to reach from the tips of your fingers to the spinal cord. When the pain information enters the spinal cord, it is transmitted to a second neuron.

3 **Interneuron.** Once the afferent neuron reaches the spinal cord, it transmits the pain information to a second neuron, called an interneuron.

An *interneuron* is a relatively short neuron whose primary task is making connections between other neurons.

In this example, an interneuron transmits the pain information to a third neuron, called the efferent, or motor, neuron.

4 **Efferent neuron.** Inside the spinal cord, an interneuron transfers information to a third neuron, called an efferent, or motor, neuron (blue arrows).

Efferent (EFF-er-ent), or *motor, neurons* carry information away from the spinal cord to produce responses in various muscles and organs throughout the body.

From the spinal cord, an efferent (motor) neuron sends electrical signals on its 2- to 3-foot-long axon to the muscles in the hand. These electrical signals contain "movement information" and cause the hand to withdraw quickly and without any thought on your part.

In addition, an interneuron will send the pain information to other neurons that speed this information to different parts of the brain. These different parts interpret the electrical signals coming from your hand as being hot and painful. At this point your brain may direct motor neurons to move your facial and vocal muscles so that you look pained and yell "Ouch!" or something much more intense.

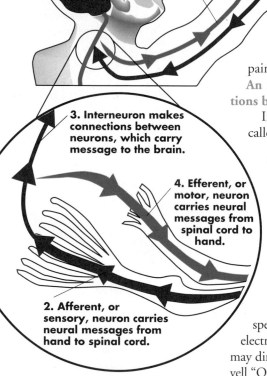

Afferent, or sensory, neuron

Efferent, or motor, neuron

3. Interneuron makes connections between neurons, which carry message to the brain.

4. Efferent, or motor, neuron carries neural messages from spinal cord to hand.

2. Afferent, or sensory, neuron carries neural messages from hand to spinal cord.

Functions of a Reflex

The primary reason you automatically withdraw your hand when touching a hot object, turn your head in the direction of a loud noise, or vomit after eating tainted food has to do with survival. Reflexes, which have evolved through millions of years, protect body parts from injury and harm and automatically regulate physiological responses, such as heart rate, respiration, and blood pressure. One primitive reflex that is no longer useful in our modern times is called piloerection, which causes the hair to stand up on your arms when you are cold. Piloerection helped keep heat in by fluffing hair for better insulation, but clothes now do a better job.

After the Concept Review, we'll discuss a very strange neural phenomenon that you may have heard of—phantom limb.

✔ Concept Review

1. The structure that nourishes and maintains the entire neuron is the (a)_____. Branchlike extensions that receive signals from senses and the environment are called (b)_____. A single threadlike extension that speeds signals away from the cell body toward a neighboring cell is the (c)_____. A tubelike structure that insulates the axon from interference by neighboring signals is the (d)_____. Tiny swellings at the very end of the axon are called (e)_____, which store neurotransmitters.

2. Chemicals that have electrical charges are called (a)_____. They obey the rule that opposite charges attract and like charges repel. Although the fluid of the axon contains a number of ions, we have focused on only two, a positively charged (b)_____ ion whose symbol is Na⁺ and a negatively charged (c)_____ ion.

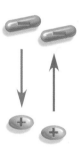

3. If an axon membrane has a potential similar to a charged battery, the axon is in the (a)_____. During this state, the ions outside the membrane are positively charged (b)_____ ions; the ions inside the membrane are negatively charged (c)_____ ions.

4. If an axon membrane is in a state similar to a discharging battery, the axon is generating an (a)_____. During this potential, the chemical gates open and positively charged (b)_____ rush inside, changing the inside of the membrane to a (c)_____ charge, while the outside of the membrane has a (d)_____ charge. As the action potential moves down the axon, it is called an (e)_____. Once it is generated, the impulse travels from the beginning to the end of the axon; this phenomenon is referred to as the (f)_____.

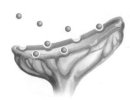

5. The end bulbs of one neuron are separated from the dendrites of a neighboring neuron by an extremely small space called the (a)_____. Into this space, end bulbs release chemicals, called (b)_____, which open/excite or block/inhibit neighboring receptors.

6. From end bulbs, chemical keys or (a)_____ are secreted into the synapse. These chemical keys open matching locks called (b)_____, which are located on the surface of neighboring dendrites, muscles, or organs. Neurotransmitters that open a receptor's lock are called (c)_____; neurotransmitters that block a receptor's lock are called (d)_____.

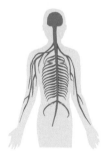

7. Neurons in the brain and spinal cord make up the (a)_____. If neurons are damaged, they have little ability to (b)_____ and usually die. The mature human brain has a limited ability to regrow (c)_____ throughout adulthood. Information from the body's senses, skin, organs, and muscles is carried to and from the spinal cord by nerves that make up the (d)_____. If this nervous system is damaged, (e)_____ in this system have a remarkable ability to regrow and make new connections. If your finger were accidentally cut off, it could be (f)_____ and there is a good chance that your finger would regain most of its sensory and motor functions.

8. If you touch a sharp object, your hand automatically withdraws because of a prewired reflex response. Neurons that carry "pain information" to the spinal cord are called (a)_____ neurons. Inside the spinal cord, there are short neurons, called (b)_____, that make connections between other neurons that carry information to the brain. Neurons that carry information away from the spinal cord to muscles or organs are called (c)_____ neurons.

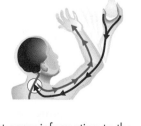

Answers: 1. (a) cell body or soma, (b) dendrites, (c) axon, (d) myelin sheath, (e) end bulbs; 2. (a) ions, (b) sodium, (c) protein; 3. (a) resting state, (b) sodium, (c) protein; 4. (a) action potential, (b) sodium ions, (c) positive, (d) negative, (e) impulse, or nerve impulse, (f) all-or-none law; 5. (a) synapse, (b) neurotransmitters; 6. (a) neurotransmitters, (b) receptors, (c) excitatory, (d) inhibitory; 7. (a) central nervous system, (b) regrow, repair, or reconnect, (c) neurons, (d) peripheral nervous system, (e) nerves, (f) reattached; 8. (a) sensory, or afferent, (b) interneurons, (c) motor, or efferent

G. Research Focus: What Is a Phantom Limb?

Case Study

Why did Donald cut off his leg?

An interesting and puzzling question for researchers to answer is: How can someone feel a phantom limb?

This question especially applies to Donald Wyman, who was a bulldozer driver working alone on trees in a remote forest. A giant oak tree accidentally fell and pinned him to the ground. With no one close enough to hear his shouts for help, Donald realized his only hope to get out from under the tree and survive was to cut off his leg, which he did with a 3-inch pocket knife. Although bleeding badly, he dragged himself to his truck and

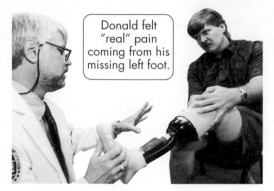

Donald felt "real" pain coming from his missing left foot.

drove a mile and a half to get help. Even though his leg was recovered, it was too damaged to be reattached. Donald is now learning to walk with an artificial leg (left photo) that is fitted to the stump.

Donald is recovering but he says, "The toughest part since the accident is dealing with phantom pain. It feels like somebody's holding an electrical shock to your foot that's not there. It makes you jump around" (*USA Today*, August 31, 1993, p. 2A). Donald's case introduces you to the strange phenomenon of phantom limb.

Definition and Data

What is phantom limb?

Very few symptoms have so surprised doctors as when patients reported feeling strange sensations or movements in arms or legs that had been amputated, a phenomenon called phantom limb.

Phantom limb **refers to feeling sensations or movements coming from a limb that has been amputated. The sensations and movements are extremely vivid, as if the limb were still present.**

As the graph on the right shows, the vast majority of individuals felt sensations ("pins and needles") or intense pain coming from their removed limbs. Patients insist that the phantom limb pain is real pain and not merely memories of earlier pain (A. Hill et al., 1996). In

other cases, amputees felt that their removed limbs were not only still present but stuck in certain positions, such as straight out from their bodies, so they felt they had to be very careful not to hit their phantom limbs when going through doorways (Katz, 1992).

Scientists have been struggling for many years to better understand what causes the feelings of sensations and movements coming from phantom limbs.

Patients' Reports after Removal of Limbs

80–100%	Report sensations
70–80%	Report pain

Answers and Treatment

Answers. Early researchers thought that the phantom limb sensations came from cut nerves remaining in the stump or from the spinal cord. Researchers now believe the origin of phantom limb sensations must be the brain itself (Melzack, 1997). But, researchers are puzzled about how the brain generates these sensations.

The newest and most supported answer about the origin of phantom limb sensations comes from researcher Ronald Melzack, who has been studying this problem for over 40 years (Melzack, 1989, 1997). He states that each of us has a genetically programmed system of sensations that results in our knowing where our body parts are and in our developing an image of our body. Based on sensations from body parts, Melzack believes the brain pieces together a complete body image. Thus, having a body image, the brain can generate sensations as coming from any body part, even if that part is a phantom limb. Although Melzack's theory must still be tested, many researchers agree that it is the best available answer to the long-standing question involving phantom limbs (Flor et al., 1995).

Because traditional medical treatment has had limited success in treating phantom limb pain, researchers are looking for more creative and effective treatments (R. A. Sherman, 1997).

Treatment. One interesting treatment method has been to create an illusion that the phantom limb exists. This has been done by having people with amputations of the arm and phantom limb pain place their arm inside a mirror box. Looking into the box, they see the reverse image of their remaining arm on the mirror, rather than a missing limb (right photo). By helping patients recreate a complete body image, the use of mirrors has had some success in reducing phantom pain in lower and upper limb amputations (MacLachlan et al., 2003, 2004). Researchers are also investigating the effectiveness of virtual reality in reducing phantom limb pain (Battles, 2004).

The phantom limb phenomenon points out that the brain sometimes functions in mysterious ways. Less mysterious is how certain drugs affect the functioning of the brain and the body.

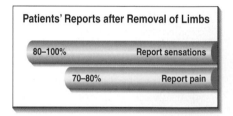

This mirror box can help to reduce phantom limb pain.

H. Cultural Diversity: Plants & Drugs

Where did the first drugs come from?

The very first drugs that affected neurotransmitters came from various plants, which people used long before researchers knew what those plants contained. We'll discuss three such drugs—cocaine, curare, and mescaline—which come from plants found in different parts of the world. We'll explain what these plants contain and their actions on the nervous systems.

Cocaine: Blocking Reuptake

For almost 3,500 years, South American Indians have chewed leaves of the coca plant. Following this ancient custom, adult Indians habitually carry bags of toasted coca leaves, which contain cocaine. Throughout the day, they chew small amounts of coca leaves to relieve fatigue and feelings of hunger. Here's how cocaine affects neurotransmitters.

The drawing on the right shows a neuron's end bulb containing the neurotransmitter dopamine *(DOPE-ah-mean)*. Once released, dopamine (colored blue circles) reaches the dendrite's receptors, opens their chemical locks, and activates the neuron. However, after a short period of time, the neurotransmitter is normally removed by being transported back into the end bulb through a process called reuptake.

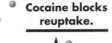

Cocaine blocks reuptake.

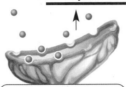

Cocaine works by blocking reuptake.

Reuptake **is a process through which some neurotransmitters, such as dopamine, are removed from the synapse by being transported back into the end bulbs.**

If reuptake does not occur, the released neurotransmitter would continually affect the neuron by remaining longer in the synapse. What cocaine does is block reuptake so that dopamine remains longer in the synapse (Sadock & Sadock, 2005). Because cocaine blocks reuptake, neurons are stimulated longer, resulting in the physiological arousal and feelings of euphoria that are associated with cocaine usage. Researchers now understand why South American Indians chewed coca leaves. The cocaine released from chewing coca leaves blocked the reuptake of dopamine, which in turn caused physiological arousal that relieved fatigue and feelings of hunger.

Curare: Blocking Receptors

When hunting animals, the Indians of Peru and Ecuador coat the ends of blowdarts with the juice of a tropical vine that contains the paralyzing drug curare.

Curare (cure-RAH-ree) **is a drug that enters the bloodstream, reaches the muscles, and blocks receptors on muscles. As a result, the neurotransmitter that normally activates muscles, which is called acetylcholine, is blocked, and muscles are paralyzed (M. R. Lee, 2005).**

Once hit by a curare-tipped blowdart, an animal's limb muscles become paralyzed, followed by paralysis of chest muscles used to breathe.

Why did Indians coat blowdarts with curare?

Curare is an example of a drug that stops neural transmission by blocking the muscles' receptors. Today, the purified active ingredient in curare (tubocurarine chloride) is used to induce muscle paralysis in humans, such as when doctors insert a breathing tube down a patient's throat. Curare doesn't easily enter the brain because the body's blood must go through a filtering system before it can enter the brain. This filtering system, called the *blood-brain barrier,* prevents some, but not all, potentially harmful substances in the body's blood supply from reaching the brain.

Mescaline: Mimicking a Neurotransmitter

A golf-ball-sized, gray-green plant (right photo) called peyote cactus grows in Mexico and the southwestern United States. Peyote contains mescaline (Stahl, 2000).

Mescaline (MESS-ka-lin) **is a drug that causes physiological arousal as well as visual hallucinations. Mescaline's chemical keys are similar to those of the neurotransmitter norepinephrine** *(nor-epee-NEFF-rin).*

Because mescaline's chemical keys open the same chemical locks (receptors) as norepinephrine, mescaline produces its effects by mimicking the actions of norepinephrine.

In 1965, an estimated 250,000 members of the Native American Church in the United States and Canada won a Supreme Court case that permits them to be the only group legally authorized to use peyote in their religious services. To enhance meditation, members may

Mescaline comes from peyote cactus.

eat from 4 to 12 peyote buttons, which results in visual sensations, euphoria, and sometimes nausea and vomiting.

Conclusion. These three plants—cocaine, curare, and mescaline—contain potent drugs that illustrate three different ways of affecting the nervous system. Researchers have discovered numerous plants, including the opium poppy, marijuana, and "magic" mushrooms, that contain drugs that in turn affect neurotransmitters (discussed in Module 8).

Neurotransmitters are the keys that turn the brain's functions on or off. For example, Alzheimer's disease interferes with neurons and neurotransmitters and turns off the brain's functions. Such is the case with another terrible disease, called Parkinson's, which we'll discuss next.

I. Application Experimental Treatments

Parkinson's Disease

Why do Michael's arms and legs shake?

Michael J. Fox is a talented actor who has starred in popular TV series, such as "Family Ties" and "Spin City," and numerous movies, including the *Back to the Future* trilogy. He was really good at his job until he noticed a twitch in his left pinkie (Fox, 2002). Within only 6 months, this twitch spread to his whole hand. Michael tried to conceal his symptoms from the public by using medication to calm his tremors, and he was successful doing so for the first seven years (Dudley, 2006). However, it became increasingly difficult to hide his symptoms as he began having tremors that would shake his entire arm. Also, his legs would shake or become really stiff, making it difficult for him to walk. Eventually, these symptoms led Michael to quit his starring role in "Spin City," a popular TV show (Weinraub, 2000).

Michael had all the symptoms of Parkinson's disease.

Parkinson's disease includes symptoms of tremors and shakes in the limbs, a slowing of voluntary movements, muscle stiffness, problems with balance and coordination, and feelings of depression. As the disease progresses, patients develop a peculiar walk and may suddenly freeze in space for minutes or hours at a time.

Michael's Parkinson's symptoms worsened because neurons in his *basal ganglia,* a group of structures located in the center of the brain that are involved in regulating movements, were running out of the neurotransmitter dopamine. Without a sufficient supply of dopamine in the basal ganglia, the brain loses its ability to control movement.

Like most Parkinson's patients, Michael was placed on a medication called L-dopa, which boosts the levels of dopamine in the brain, enabling him to have better control over his movements. Unfortunately, patients must take ever-increasing amounts of L-dopa, until the drug itself causes involuntary jerky movements that may be as bad as those produced by Parkinson's disease. Thus, L-dopa does not cure the symptoms of Parkinson's disease, and after prolonged use (5 to 10 years), L-dopa's beneficial effects may be replaced by unwanted jerky movements (Mercuri & Bernardi, 2005).

In the United States, about 1.5 million adults, usually over the age of 50, have Parkinson's disease. In rare cases, such as Michael's, people are diagnosed with young-onset Parkinson's disease (Michael was only 30). The causes of Parkinson's disease include genetic and possible environmental factors (Schmid, 2002). To date, Parkinson's has no cure but, as you'll see, several experimental treatments are under study.

Issues Involving Transplants

Why not just use drugs?

Human cells. As we learned above, the prolonged use of L-dopa to treat Parkinson's disease produces unwanted side effects. Because of these disappointing long-term results, researchers are investigating alternative treatments, such as fetal brain tissue transplants.

Previously, researchers had shown that when fetal rat brain tissue was transplanted into older rats, the fetal neurons lived, grew, functioned, and allowed brain-damaged older rats to relearn the solutions to mazes (Shetty & Turner, 1996). Following successful fetal transplants in rats and monkeys, researchers have transplanted human fetal brain tissue into patients with Parkinson's disease (Roitberg & Kordower, 2004).

The primary reason for using 6- to 8-week-old fetal tissue for transplants is that this fetal tissue has a unique ability to survive and make connections in a patient's brain or body. Because fetal brain tissue is primed for growth, it has a far greater chance of survival after transplantation than does tissue from mature brains (C. Holden, 2002). More recently, researchers are exploring the use of stem cells to treat Parkinson's disease and spinal cord injuries.

Embryonic stem cells have the ability to form new brain cells.

Stem cells. About four days after a sperm has fertilized an egg, the resulting embryo, which is about the size of the period in this sentence (see p. 379), has divided and formed embryonic stem cells (shown on left).

Stem cells, not discovered until 1998, have the amazing capacity to change into and become any one of the 220 cells that make up a human body, including skin, heart, liver, bones, and neurons.

The discovery of stem cells creates possibilities for treating various body and neurological diseases. For example, when embryonic animal stem cells were transplanted into rats and mice with spinal cord injuries, the stem cells imitated the neighboring neurons and developed into new neurons that, in turn, helped the animals regain their lost functions (N. Wade, 2002b).

The use of human embryonic stem cells is controversial for ethical and political reasons. That's because these embryos, which are fertilized in laboratories and have the potential to develop into humans, are destroyed when the stem cells are removed. On moral grounds, President George W. Bush limited federal funds for stem cell research. Because stem cell research has such potential, however, it has received wide support and funding from private and state sources (Perez-Pena, 2003). Michael J. Fox believes embryonic stem cells are very promising, and he advocates for stem cell research in hopes it may lead to finding a cure for Parkinson's disease (Business Week online, 2004).

Next, we'll take a closer look at how fetal and stem cells are used in treating Parkinson's. We'll also learn about other experimental treatment options, including the procedure used to remove part of Michael's brain.

Placing tissue in the brain. A neurosurgeon can transplant fetal cells or stem cells into a precise location in either animal or human brains by using the stereotaxic procedure.

The *stereotaxic procedure* (right figure) involves fixing a patient's head in a holder and drilling a small hole through the skull. The holder has a syringe that can be precisely guided to inject cells into a predetermined location in the brain.

In the figure, a large part of the skull has been removed to show the brain, but in actual surgery, only a small, pencil-sized hole is drilled in the patient's skull. A long needle from the syringe (lower left in the figure) extends from the holder into the patient's brain area that is involved with regulating movement, the basal ganglia. The surgeon will inject fetal or stem cells into the designated brain area.

The advantages of the stereotaxic procedure are that a thin syringe can be placed in precise locations in the brain and that it causes relatively little damage to the brain. The stereotaxic procedure can be used to either inject solutions or, as we'll later learn, destroy diseased brain tissue.

In this illustration, a large portion of the top of the left side of the skull has been cut away. In addition, the top part of the brain has been removed to show the position of the left basal ganglia, which lie deep inside the brain.

The patient's head is held firmly in place by a device called the stereotaxic instrument, which also holds a precisely guided syringe (shown in bottom left). The syringe's needle injects donor fetal brain tissue exactly into the basal ganglia.

This yellow oval represents millions of fetal cells that have been inserted into the basal ganglia by using a long, thin needle. With modern techniques, only a small area of the skull need be opened (about the size of a pencil), and fetal tissue can be injected with relatively little damage to the brain.

Based on a number of experimental treatments, researchers learned that when injected into a human adult brain, fetal tissue does survive and function. Fetal tissue transplants have benefited some people, but others have reported serious side effects. Therefore, critics suggest that researchers identify the best location for injecting the tissue into the brain and aim to prevent the unwanted motor side effects by determining the optimum number of fetal cells to inject (Kolata, 2001).

Stem cell research is still in its infancy, but already remarkable success has been reported in using stem cells to treat animals with spinal cord or brain injury (Isacson et al., 2003). Researchers are currently studying how to use stem cells to treat human spinal cord injury and diseases such as Parkinson's. Researchers are hopeful that the use of stem cells will help replace cells damaged during the progression of Parkinson's disease, and consequently restore lost function (such as motor control) (Sonntag et al., 2005).

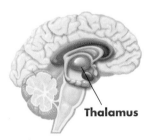

Thalamus

Michael J. Fox chose to have part of his thalamus removed.

Removing part of the brain. People with Parkinson's disease have regained control over their limbs after having part of their thalamus (p. 80) removed. The thalamus is an oval-shaped structure (see right) of the brain that closely interacts with the basal ganglia. One of its functions is to help make voluntary motor movements, such as when a person wants to move a leg to walk (Murat et al., 2005).

Michael J. Fox chose to have a thalamotomy, a surgery that removed part of his thalamus. During the procedure, a stereotaxic procedure was used to drill a hole in his skull and apply heat to destroy very precise sections of his thalamus. Michael's surgeon warned him that the procedure would not cure his Parkinson's, but if successful, it would stop the severe tremors in his arm. The surgery was a success in Michael's case, as most of his severe tremors went away. He now takes medication to control his milder tremors (Fox, 2002).

Thalamotomy has proven to have a high success rate, but there are serious risks, including paralysis, coma, and death. Therefore, this procedure is used only in severe cases of Parkinson's, such as Michael's. Doctors treated Michael with medication for several years before suggesting he undergo a dangerous surgery (Fox, 2002).

Brain stimulation. About 30,000 people in the United States have received deep brain stimulation, a relatively new surgical procedure that involves implanting electrodes into the thalamus and placing a battery-powered stimulator under the collarbone. The electrodes are wired to the stimulator, which provides electrical stimulation to the thalamus. The patient controls the stimulation by using a remote control to turn it on and off. This procedure helps the thalamus function better and, as a result, reduces or eliminates tremors (Fischman, 2006; Pahwa & Lyons, 2003).

The advantages of deep brain stimulation include being able to undo the surgery and to modify the level of stimulation. The limitation of this procedure, however, is the need for close, long-term medical follow-up to ensure that everything is working properly. For example, the batteries need to be surgically replaced every one to three years (Pahwa & Lyons, 2003).

Given its effectiveness and relatively minimal risk, some researchers believe deep brain stimulation will replace procedures that remove part of the brain, such as the thalamotomy performed on Michael J. Fox (Murat et al., 2005).

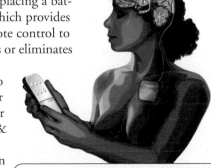

Electrodes implanted into the thalamus provide stimulation to help reduce tremors.

✔ Summary Test

A. Overview: Human Brain

1. The brain is composed of a trillion cells that can be divided into two groups. One group of cells has specialized extensions for receiving and transmitting information. These cells, which are called (a)_____, are involved in communicating with other neurons, receiving sensory information, and regulating muscles, glands, and organs. The other group of cells provide the scaffolding to guide and support neurons, insulate neurons, and release chemicals that influence neuron functions. These cells are much more numerous than neurons and are called (b)_____.

2. There is a major difference between the growth of neurons in the brains of humans and in the brains of birds. A mature human brain is normally not capable of developing new (a)_____, which are almost totally present at the time of birth. In contrast, a mature (b)_____ brain has the capacity to develop new neurons.

3. The age-old question of how the brain's membranes, fluids, and chemicals are involved in generating complex mental activities, such as thoughts, images, and feelings, is called the _____ question.

B. Neurons: Structure & Function

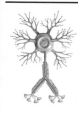

4. Although neurons come in wondrous shapes and sizes, they all share three structures. The structure that maintains the entire neuron in working order, manufactures chemicals, and provides fuel is called the (a)_____. The structure with many branchlike extensions that receive signals from other neurons, muscles, or organs and conduct these signals to the cell body is called a (b)_____. The single threadlike extension that leaves the cell body and carries signals to other neurons, muscles, or organs is called the (c)_____. At the very end of this structure are individual swellings called (d)_____, which contain tiny vesicles filled with (e)_____.

5. Surrounding most axons is a fatty material called the (a)_____. This material acts like (b)_____ and diminishes interference from electrical signals traveling in neighboring axons.

6. Neurons do not make physical contact with one another or with other organs. Instead, there is an infinitely small space between a neuron's end bulbs and neighboring dendrites, cell bodies, or other organs. This space is called the (a)_____. When an axon's end bulbs secrete a neurotransmitter, it flows across this space and affects the (b)_____ on the neighboring membrane.

C. Neurons Versus Nerves

7. There are major differences between neurons and nerves. Cells with specialized extensions for conducting electrical signals are called (a)_____. These cells, which are located in the brain and spinal cord, make up the (b)_____ nervous system. Stringlike bundles of neurons' axons and dendrites, which are held together by connective tissue, are called (c)_____. These stringlike bundles, which are located throughout the body, make up the (d)_____ nervous system. Nerves carry information back and forth between the body and the spinal cord. If a neuron in the central nervous system is damaged, it normally does not have the capacity to (e)_____. In comparison, a nerve in the (f)_____ nervous system has the capacity to regrow or reattach if cut or damaged. The mature human brain has a limited ability to regrow (g)_____ throughout adulthood.

D. Sending Information

Action Potential

8. The axon membrane has (a)_____ that can be opened or closed. These gates keep some ions inside the membrane and other ions outside. If the axon is ready to conduct but not actually conducting an impulse, the axon is said to be in the (b)_____ state. In this state, most of the positively charged (c)_____ ions are on the outside of the membrane and all the negatively charged (d)_____ ions are trapped inside. In the resting state, the outside of the membrane has a (e)_____ charge compared to the (f)_____ charge on the inside. The process responsible for picking up and transporting sodium ions from the inside to the outside of the axon membrane is called the (g)_____.

9. If a stimulus is strong enough to excite a neuron, two things happen to its axon. First, the stimulus will eventually open the axon's (a)_____. Second, after the gates are opened, the (b)_____ pump is stopped, and all the positive (c)_____ ions rush inside because they are attracted to the negatively charged protein ions. The rush of sodium ions inside generates a tiny electric current that is called the (d)_____. When this current is generated, the inside of the axon membrane changes to a (e)_____ charge and the outside changes to a (f)_____ charge.

10. Once an action potential starts in the axon, it continues, segment by segment, down the entire length of the axon, creating the (a)_____. Once an action potential is triggered in the segment at the beginning of the axon, other action potentials will be triggered in sequence down the entire length of the axon; this phenomenon is called the (b)_____.

E. Transmitters

11. Once started, the action potential will reach the end bulbs at the end of the axon. The action potential excites the end bulbs and causes them to secrete (a)_____ that were stored in the end bulbs. Neurotransmitters function like chemical keys that unlock chemical locks or (b)_____, which are located on neighboring neurons, muscles, or other organs. If neurotransmitters open the receptors' locks on neighboring cells, they are said to be (c)_____. If neurotransmitters block the receptors' locks, they are said to be (d)_____. Because of these different actions, neurotransmitters can cause different and even opposite responses in neurons, muscles, or organs. There are about a dozen well-known neurotransmitters. One of the newly discovered neurotransmitters that has a chemical makeup similar to THC in marijuana is called (e)_____ and is involved in emotions and motor coordination.

F. Reflex Responses

12. The movement of automatically withdrawing your hand after touching a hot object is called a (a)_____, which involves several or more neurons. Information is carried to the spinal cord by the (b)_____ neuron. Information is carried from the spinal cord to the muscle by the (c)_____ neuron. Connections between efferent (motor) and afferent (sensory) neurons are made by relatively short (d)_____, which also send signals to the brain. The functions of reflexes include protecting body parts from (e)_____ and automatically regulating the (f)_____ responses of the body.

G. Research Focus: What Is a Phantom Limb?

13. The experience of sensations from a limb that has been amputated is called the (a)_____ phenomenon. About 70–80% of patients report sensations of intense pain coming from limbs that have been amputated. A recent explanation of phantom limb sensations is that they arise from the brain's genetically programmed system of sensations that allows the brain to know the locations of all the body's (b)_____.

H. Cultural Diversity: Plants & Drugs

14. One of cocaine's effects on the nervous system is to block the process of (a)_____ so that the neurotransmitter remains longer in the synapse, which causes physiological arousal. A drug that blocks receptors on muscles and causes muscle paralysis is (b)_____. A drug that mimics the naturally occurring neurotransmitter norepinephrine and can produce visual hallucinations is (c)_____.

I. Application: Experimental Treatments

15. The tremors and rigidity of Parkinson's disease result when a group of structures that regulate movement, called the (a)_____, lose their supply of dopamine. In experimental treatment, fetal brain cells or stem cells can be transplanted into a precise location of a patient's brain by a technique called the (b)_____ procedure. Cells that have the amazing capacity to develop into any of the 220 cells that make up the human body are called (c)_____. These cells can be used to treat spinal cord injuries and diseases like Alzheimer's and Parkinson's because stem cells can develop into (d)_____.

Answers: *1. (a) neurons, (b) glial cells; 2. (a) neurons, (b) bird; 3. mind-body; 4. (a) cell body, or soma, (b) dendrite, (c) axon, (d) end bulbs, (e) neurotransmitters; 5. (a) myelin sheath, (b) insulation; 6. (a) synapse, (b) receptors; 7. (a) neurons, (b) central, (c) nerves, (d) peripheral, (e) regrow, (f) peripheral, (g) neurons; 8. (a) chemical gates, (b) resting, (c) sodium, (d) protein, (e) positive, (f) negative, (g) sodium pump; 9. (a) chemical gates, (b) sodium, (c) sodium, (d) action potential, (e) positive, (f) negative; 10. (a) nerve impulse, (b) all-or-none law; 11. (a) neurotransmitters, (b) receptors, (c) excitatory, (d) inhibitory, (e) anandamide; 12. (a) reflex, or reflex response, (b) sensory, or afferent, (c) motor, or efferent, (d) interneurons, (e) injury or harm, (f) physiological; 13. (a) phantom limb, (b) parts; 14. (a) reuptake, (b) curare, (c) mescaline; 15. (a) basal ganglia, (b) stereotaxic, (c) stem cells, (d) neurons*

Critical Thinking

Would You Want a Head Transplant?

Questions

1. From what you know about the central nervous system, what's the major problem in transplanting a head?

2. Why do researchers first develop new medical procedures in animals before trying them on humans?

3. Why do damaged neurons usually wither and die instead of regrowing?

Everyone knows the story of Dr. Frankenstein, who transplanted a brain into a dead body and brought this creature to life with a jolt from a lightning bolt. As a serious and respected researcher, Dr. Robert J. White, Harvard Medical School graduate and professor of neurosurgery at Case Western Reserve University, believes that a complete head (including brain) transplant is becoming increasingly possible.

Dr. White has been working for the past 40 years on the possibility of transplanting a head. In the 1960s, he succeeded in removing brains from monkeys and keeping the brains alive in special solutions for up to 22 hours. In the 1970s, he successfully removed the complete head from one rhesus monkey and transplanted it onto the body of another monkey. He reports that this "new" monkey with the transplanted head regained consciousness, tried to bite the researchers, moved its eyes, and lived for eight days—dying of lung failure. Although transplanting a head has a number of practical applications, it also raises ethical, religious, and moral questions.

As to practical applications, a head transplant would mean that if quadriplegics' bodies developed life-threatening problems, they could have their healthy heads (and brains) transplanted onto healthy donor bodies and thus keep on living. (Quadriplegics have damaged spinal cords that prevent all movement

and sensations from the neck down and often develop life-threatening lung problems.) Because researchers have not yet solved the problem of how to reconnect spinal cords, the quadriplegic's head could not send or receive information from the donor's body. But if you were a quadriplegic with a diseased and dying body, would you want the choice and chance of living a little longer by having your healthy head transplanted onto a donor's healthy body?

Among the ethical and moral questions are whether someone with a healthy head should be allowed to live on top of a stranger's body. Or, how would a family react to knowing that their dead son's or daughter's body is still alive? Among the religious questions are, What happens to a person's mind or soul when the person's head is now transplanted onto a different body? Or, is it right to separate the head from the body for any reason?

Dr. White answers these questions by saying that defining death is a medical and not a religious issue. He believes the body is essentially an "energy pack" and concludes by saying, "If a procedure can help somebody live longer, I think most doctors and patients are willing to do what they can, particularly if the alternative is death." (Adapted from S. LaFee, At hand and ahead, *San Diego Union Tribune,* March 8, 2000, p. E-1)

4. What advances have been made in getting damaged neurons to regrow and in developing new neurons?

5. How do many neuroscientists view the mind-brain distinction?

6. How does Dr. White answer questions about the mind and soul?

Suggested Answers

1. Surgeons can transplant many body organs (hearts, lungs, kidneys, even hands) because peripheral nerves regrow. However, the major problem in transplanting a complete head involves reconnecting the head's spinal cord to the spinal cord in the donor's body. That's because damaged or severed neurons that are in the central nervous system do not usually reconnect or regrow.

2. This raises the ethical question of whether animals should be used in research. The major reason researchers first use animals to develop complicated medical procedures, such as heart or future head transplants, is to work out problems and avoid life-threatening risks to humans (see p. 41).

3. Damaged neurons (central nervous system) usually wither and die because of a built-in genetic program that turns off future

regrowth or repair once a neuron is fully grown (see p. 49).

4. Researchers are stimulating damaged neurons to regrow by providing tubes to guide regrowth and by injecting growth-producing chemicals. Experimental treatments include injecting stem cells or fetal tissue into the brain (see pp. 51, 60, and 61).

5. As discussed on page 49, the age-old mind-body (brain) question has several answers. Some philosophers believe that the mind (spirit or soul) and brain are separate things. In contrast, many researchers believe that the mind and the brain are either the same thing or like two sides of a coin.

6. Dr. White seems to believe that the mind (soul, spirit) and brain are one and the same, since he defines death as being a medical rather than a spiritual problem.

Links to Learning

action potential, 53

afferent neurons, 56

alcohol, 55

all-or-none law, 52

Alzheimer's disease, 47

anandamide, 55

axon, 50

axon membrane, 52

basal ganglia, 60

birds' brains, 49

cell body, 50

central nervous system, 51

cocaine, 59

curare, 59

dendrites, 50

efferent neurons, 56

end bulbs, 50

endorphins, 55

excitatory neurotransmitters, 54

fetal tissue transplants, 60

GABA neurons, 55

gene, 48

glial cell, 48

growth of new neurons, 49

inhibitory neurotransmitters, 54

interneuron, 56

ions, 52

mature brain, 48

mescaline, 59

mind-body question, 49

multiple sclerosis, 51

myelin sheath, 50

nerve, 51

nerve impulse, 52

neuron, 48

neurotransmitter, 54

nitric oxide, 55

Parkinson's disease, 60

peripheral nervous system, 51

phantom limb, 58

primate brains, 49

reattaching limbs, 51

reflex, 56

reflex functions, 56

reflex sequence, 56

repair of neurons, 51

repairing the brain, 49

resting state, 53

reuptake, 59

six-week-old brain, 48

sodium pump, 53

stem cells, 60

stereotaxic procedure, 61

synapse, 50

transmitter, 54

Learning Activities

- ● **POWERSTUDY FOR INTRODUCTION TO PSYCHOLOGY 4.0**
  by Tom Doyle and Rod Plotnik

  SuperModule: Check out "Brain's Building Blocks" on **PowerStudy**. It includes complete paragraph-by-paragraph explanations of all content using fully-narrated animations and graphics. An onscreen toolbar allows immediate access to text, text outline, and module glossary with notetaking and printing capabilities. This module also includes:

  - • Videos—Ina's daughter discusses the impact of Alzheimer's on her mother and the family.
  - • A multitude of animations designed to help you understand each section of your text—for example, an overview of the brain and coverage of difficult concepts like the action potential.
  - • A test of your knowledge using an interactive version of the Summary Test on pages 62 and 63. Also access related quizzing—true/false, multiple choice, and matching.
  - • An interactive version of the Critical Thinking exercise "Would You Want a Head Transplant?" on page 64.
  - • Key terms, a chapter outline including chapter abstract, and a special extended list of hotlinked websites that correlate to this module.

- ● *CengageNOW*
  academic.cengage.com/login

  Need help studying? This site is your one-stop study shop.
  Take a Pre-Test and CengageNOW will generate a Personalized Study Plan based on your test results. The Study Plan will identify the topics you need to review and direct you to online resources to help you master those topics. You can then take a Post-Test to determine the concepts you have mastered and what you still need to work on.

- ● **INTRODUCTION TO PSYCHOLOGY BOOK COMPANION WEBSITE**
  academic.cengage.com/psychology/plotnik

  Visit your book companion website where you will find more resources to help you study. At this site, you will find Learning Objectives, Internet Exercises, quizzing, flash cards, and a pronunciation glossary.

- ● *STUDY GUIDE and WEBTUTOR*

  Check the corresponding module in your Study Guide for effective student tips and help learning the material presented. Also go to **academic.cengage.com/webtutor** for an interactive version of the Study Guide features.

Study Questions

*A. **Overview: Human Brain**—Why is it really smart to drive a car only if it is equipped with driver- and passenger-side airbags? (**Suggested answer page 620**)

B. **Neurons: Structure & Function**—How would you decide if a piece of tissue came from the brain or from a muscle?

C. **Neurons Versus Nerves**—Headline—"Chimp Brain Transplanted into Human Skull." Is this possible?

*D. **Sending Information**—How are the structure and function of the axon like those of a battery? (**Suggested answer page 620**)

E. **Transmitters**—What are some of the ways that nerve gas could cause death?

F. **Reflex Responses**—How might the reflexes of professional tennis players differ from those of amateurs?

G. **Research Focus: What Is a Phantom Limb?**—What problems might you have after your hand was amputated?

*H. **Cultural Diversity: Plants & Drugs**—What are the different ways that drugs can affect neurotransmitters? (**Suggested answer page 620**)

I. **Application: Experimental Treatments**—Would you recommend that a family member with Parkinson's be treated with a fetal transplant?

*These questions are answered in Appendix B.

MODULE 4
Incredible Nervous System

 PowerStudy 4.0™ Complete Module

Lucy's Brain: Earliest Ancestor

Although Lucy was fully grown, she was short and slightly built, standing a little under 4 feet tall and weighing about 55 pounds. She had an apelike head, and her face (left drawing) had a large brow above her eyes and a protruding jaw that held big, uneven front teeth. Lucy had a lot of hair, was very muscular, walked upright on slightly bent legs, and had powerful arms for climbing trees to search for fruits and nuts.

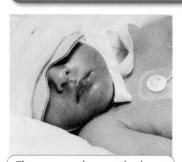

Anthropologists think that Lucy did not make tools, knew nothing of fire, and conversed with hand gestures, waves, and grunts. Lucy's small skull held a brain that was only about the size of a chimpanzee's, which is about one-third the size of ours. The males of her species were about a foot taller than Lucy and at least two-thirds heavier.

A possible human ancestor lived 3–4 million years ago.

Anthropologists believe that Lucy's species, formally named *Australopithecus afarensis*, lived about 3 to 4 million years ago and may be the earliest ancestor of modern humans (A. Gibbons, 2002).

We'll use Lucy's brain to illustrate how the human brain is thought to have evolved and increased in size over 3 million years.

Baby Theresa's Brain: Fatal Flaw

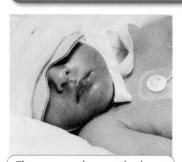

Theresa was born with almost all of her brain missing.

The press called her Baby Theresa. She was one of about 1,000 babies born each year in the United States with a disorder called anencephaly *(an-in-CEPH-ah-lee)*, which is always fatal in the first few years (Cunningham et al., 2005).

Baby Theresa (left photo) was born with almost no brain and therefore would never develop the functions we associate with being human, such as thinking, talking, reasoning, and planning. She survived for 9 days because a very primitive part of her brain was functioning to keep her alive. This small, primitive brain area lies directly above the spinal cord and regulates vital reflexes, such as breathing, blood pressure, and heart rate. These vital reflexes kept her alive for a short time.

We'll use Baby Theresa's tragic case to illustrate some of the different structures and functions of the brain.

Steve's Brain: Cruel Fate

When Steve walked into the hotel, he felt an incredible pain in his head. He was 28 years old, a successful journalist, and in excellent health, but something terrible was happening.

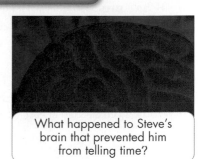

What happened to Steve's brain that prevented him from telling time?

He could barely talk to the hotel clerk, who said that Steve's room wasn't ready. Steve slowly walked to a chair and sat down to wait. He glanced at the clock on the wall to check the time. He could clearly see the hands of the clock, but he could not figure out the time. Like a small child, he said out loud, "The big hand is on twelve and the little hand is on eight." When he heard the words, he knew it was 8 o'clock and wondered why he could tell time by sound but not by sight (Fishman, 1988).

We'll use Steve's unsettling experience to show some of the symptoms of brain damage and how neurologists can examine the living brain.

Scott's Brain: Wrong Instructions

"As a very young baby, Scott seemed okay," said his mother, Cindy. "He cooed and smiled at the right times. He babbled at the right times. He seemed normal" (LaFee, 1996, p. E-1). But it was his constant crying that scared her. Scott would walk outside and burst into tears, and no one could comfort him.

As Scott (right photo) got older, other problems developed. He couldn't sit up, he refused to play with other children, and often he was off in a world of his own. An examination of Scott's genetic makeup revealed that he had inherited fragile X syndrome, which is the most common cause of an inherited developmental disorder (Van Esch, 2006).

Scott has a genetic defect that affects his functioning.

We'll use Scott's problem to explain how genetic instructions are written and what happens when the instructions have errors.

What's Coming

The brains of Lucy, Baby Theresa, Steve, and Scott raise a number of questions. Lucy's brain brings up the question of evolution, which says that modern brains have been evolving for 3 million years. Baby Theresa's brain raises the question of what it means to be human. Steve's brain brings up the questions of what happens when brains are damaged and how doctors can look inside living brains. Finally, Scott's brain raises the questions of how brains develop and why things go wrong. We'll answer these questions as well as discuss all the major structures and functions of the human brain.

Let's begin with how genetic instructions are written.

A. Genes & Evolution

What makes brains different? Your brain and body developed according to complex chemical instructions that were written in a human cell no larger than a grain of sand. The reason brains and bodies have different shapes, colors, and abilities is that they develop from different instructions, which are written at the moment of fertilization.

1 Fertilization. Human life has its beginnings when a father's sperm, which contains 23 chromosomes, penetrates a mother's egg, which contains 23 chromosomes. The result is a fertilized cell called a zygote (shown below).

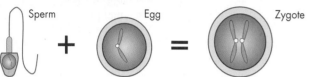

Sperm   Egg   Zygote

2 Zygote. A zygote (figure above), which is about the size of a grain of sand, is the largest human cell.

A *zygote* is a cell that results when an egg is fertilized. A zygote contains 46 chromosomes arranged in 23 pairs.

A zygote contains the equivalent of 300,000 pages of type-written instructions. For simplicity, the zygote shown above has only 1 pair of chromosomes instead of the usual 23 pairs.

3 Chromosomes. Inside the very tiny zygote are 23 pairs of chromosomes, which contain chemical instructions for development of the brain and body.

A *chromosome* is a short, rodlike, microscopic structure that contains tightly coiled strands of the chemical DNA, which is an abbreviation for deoxyribonucleic *(dee-ox-ee-RYE-bow-new-CLEE-ick)* acid. Each cell of the human body (except for the sperm and egg) contains 46 chromosomes arranged in 23 pairs.

For the sake of simplicity, the cell above contains only 4 pairs of chromosomes instead of the usual 23 pairs.

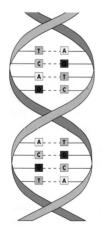

4 Chemical alphabet. Each chromosome contains a long, coiled strand of DNA, which resembles a ladder (left figure) that has been twisted over and over upon itself.

Each rung of the DNA ladder is made up of four chemicals. The order in which the four different chemicals combine to form rungs creates a microscopic chemical alphabet. This chemical alphabet is used to write instructions for the development and assembly of the 100 trillion highly specialized cells that make up the brain and body (R. J. Sternberg, 2001).

5 Genes and proteins. On each chromosome are specific segments that contain particular instructions. In the chromosome on the right, each segment is represented by a green band, which represents the location of a gene.

A *gene* is a specific segment on the long strand of DNA that contains instructions for making proteins. Proteins are chemical building blocks from which all the parts of the brain and body are constructed.

For example, genes determine physical traits (eye color, shape of ear lobes) as well as contribute to the development of emotional, cognitive, and behavioral traits (Angier, 2003). When researchers discover a new gene, it means they have identified the exact location of the gene on its chromosome.

6 Genome. The Human Genome Project, which began in 1995 and cost over $2.7 billion, reached its first goal in 2003 of mapping all the human genes (Mestel, 2003a). Unlike earlier estimates of 100,000 human genes, researchers found only about 20,000–25,000 human genes (about the same number as in a mouse) on the 23 pairs of chromosomes (IHGSC, 2004). Researchers are now working on the project's other goals: to understand how humans develop physical and psychological traits, to identify sources of genetic diseases, to develop new drugs, and to use gene therapy to treat genetic problems (Kolata, 2003).

7 Scott's brain: An error in instructions. Earlier, we told you about Scott's unusual physical and behavioral problems. Scott has an inherited genetic disorder called fragile X syndrome.

***Fragile X syndrome,* an inherited developmental disability, is due to a defect in the X chromosome (shown here as the pinched end of the X chromosome). It can result in physical changes, such as a relatively large head with protruding ears, as well as mild to profound mental retardation.**

Fragile X syndrome, which can include changes in both physical features and brain development, illustrates what happens when there is an error in genetic instructions (Van Esch, 2006). We'll discuss other problems caused by errors in genetic instructions, such as Down syndrome, on page 380.

Scott has fragile X syndrome.

Genetic factors. The Human Genome Project and related genetic research are having a tremendous influence on psychology. Researchers are discovering how genetic factors interact with the environment to result in the development of mental retardation, emotional and personality traits, mental disorders, and various cognitive abilities (N. Wade, 2003a).

Next, we'll discuss how genetic changes are thought to have affected brain development over millions of years.

What is evolution?

In 1859, Charles Darwin stunned much of the Western world by publishing *Origin of Species*, a revolutionary theory of how species originate, which was the basis for his now-famous theory of evolution.

The *theory of evolution* says that different species arose from a common ancestor and that those species that survived were best adapted to meet the demands of their environments.

Although Darwin's theory of evolution is just that—a theory—it has received broad scientific support from both fossil records and more recent examination of genetic similarities and differences among species (Mayr, 2000). The fact that many scientists hold to the theory of evolution clashes with deeply held religious beliefs that place humans on a family tree of their own. According to the theory of evolution, present-day humans descended from a creature that split off from apes millions of years ago. Supporting the theory of evolution is the finding that humans and chimpanzees share at least 98% of their DNA or genetic instructions. Humans are more intelligent than chimpanzees not because they have more sophisticated neurons; rather, an enormous number of basic neurons and countless more interactions between neurons are responsible for making humans so brainy (Sapolsky, 2006).

We will discuss three supposed human ancestors that represent three major milestones in how the human brain is thought to have evolved and developed.

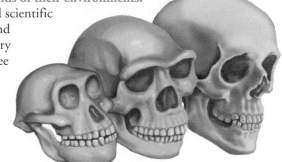

Australopithecus afarensis *Homo erectus* *Homo sapiens*

Increasing skull and brain size of proposed ancestors

Perhaps the First Human Brain

Of the three skulls shown above, the smallest one (far left) is thought to have belonged to one of our earliest ancestors, who lived about 3 to 4 million years ago. This proposed ancestor has been given a common name, Lucy, and a scientific name, *Australopithecus afarensis*. Lucy's brain weighed about 500 grams, which is about the size of a chimpanzee's brain and about one-third the size of our brains. Lucy's brain size and skeleton suggest a closer resemblance to apes than to humans. She had long powerful arms and short legs and is thought to have lived mainly on leaves and fruit.

Anthropologists conclude, on the basis of Lucy's rather limited brain size, that her species did not make tools, did not have language, knew nothing of fire, and thus represents the most primitive kind of human (A. Gibbons, 2002; Lemonick & Dorfman, 1999). Lucy's line died out about a million years ago. Anthropologists believe that another line branched out from Lucy's and gave rise to our genus, which is called *Homo;* this process was accompanied eventually by a threefold increase in brain size.

Brain Doubles in Size

The skull in the middle, which is almost twice as large as Lucy's, belongs to a species named *Homo erectus*. (*Homo* means "man" and *erectus* means "upright.") *Homo erectus,*  who lived about one and a half million years ago, is thought to be part of the genus from which modern humans eventually evolved. *Homo erectus* developed a thick-boned skeleton designed for walking upright and was about as tall as modern humans. They are thought to have added meat to their diets.

With a brain size of about 1,000 grams, which was twice as large as Lucy's, *Homo erectus* had increased abilities and made a wide variety of stone tools. The finest was a tear-shaped hand ax, whose production required much more extensive work than any previous tools. There is considerable debate about whether tool-making or the development of language was the main pressure for the doubling in brain size in *Homo erectus* (Gore, 1997; Leonard, 2002). Descendants of *Homo erectus* evolved a still larger brain; these individuals were called *Homo sapiens*.

Brain Triples in Size

The largest skull, on the far right, comes from a modern human, who is called *Homo sapiens* (*sapiens* means "wise"). Our species began about 400,000 years ago and continues to the present day. *Homo sapiens* evolved a brain that weighs about 1,350 grams, or about 3 pounds, which is the average size of our brains today and almost three times the size of Lucy's. With such a significant increase in brain size came four dramatic changes: *Homo sapiens* began growing crops instead of relying on hunting; started to live in social communities instead of roaming the country; developed language, which was a far better way to communicate than grunts and gestures; and painted beautiful and colorful representations of animals and humans.

Two forces are thought to be responsible for the evolution of the human brain and its tripling in size: genetic changes or mutations, which are accidental changes in genetic instructions, and natural selection, which means that only those best fitted to their environments will survive (Balter, 2002; Toner, 2006).

Anthropologists believe that it took millions of years for our brains to evolve to their current size. Next, we'll describe how researchers study our modern brains.

B. Studying the Living Brain

Brain Scans

Can we look inside the human skull?

We have explained how genetic instructions guide the development and assembly of billions of parts that make up the human brain. We have discussed the anthropologists' belief that the human brain tripled in size through 3 million years of evolution. Now we begin exploring the structure and function of your own brain.

Looking at the skull on the right raises an interesting question: How can researchers look inside the half-inch-thick skull and study the living brain without causing any

New techniques can take pictures through the skull.

damage? The answer is that during the past 10 years, researchers have developed several brain-scanning techniques that can look through the thick skull and picture the brain with astonishing clarity yet cause no damage to the extremely delicate brain cells. By using these almost science-fiction techniques, researchers are mapping a variety of cognitive functions (attention, language, memory, motor skills) as well as sites of emotional feelings and appetite (Geliebter et al., 2006; N. Kitayama et al., 2006; Penn, 2006). We'll discuss several brain-scanning techniques that take pictures through the skull.

Brain Scans: MRI & fMRI

Why would Steve have an MRI?

At the beginning of this module, we told you about Steve, who was a successful journalist in excellent health. As he walked into his hotel, he felt a sudden searing pain in his head. As he waited for his room, he looked up at the clock and suddenly felt fear because he could clearly see the numbers and the hands but could not figure out the time.

Later, the neurologist told Steve that a blood vessel had burst and blood had flowed into the surrounding area of the brain. The neurologist could identify the exact location and extent of the damaged area by using one of the new brain-scanning techniques, called an MRI (photo below).

MRI, or magnetic resonance imaging, **involves passing nonharmful radio frequencies through the brain. A computer measures how these signals interact with brain cells and transforms this interaction into an incredibly detailed image of the brain (or body). MRIs are used to study the structure of the brain.**

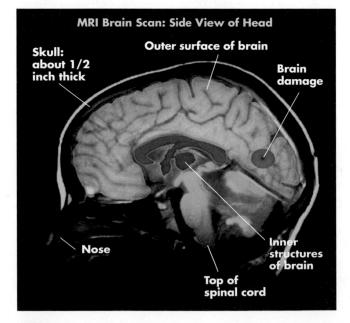

MRI Brain Scan: Side View of Head

Skull: about 1/2 inch thick

Outer surface of brain

Brain damage

Nose

Inner structures of brain

Top of spinal cord

During an MRI procedure, Steve would lie with his head in the center of a giant, donut-shaped machine. Reflections from the radio waves are computer analyzed and developed into very detailed pictures of the living brain, as shown in the photo (below left).

There is also a newer and different version of the MRI, called the fMRI.

The "f" in *fMRI* **(functional magnetic resonance imaging) stands for** *functional* **and measures the activity of specific neurons that are functioning during cognitive tasks, such as thinking, listening, or reading.**

For example, the fMRI on the right shows that while children were watching violence on TV, an increase in activity occurred in an area of the brain called the amygdala (p. 80), which researchers believe is involved in evaluating emotional situations, especially fear or threat (J. P. Murray et al., 2006). Notice that *fMRI* scans can map activities of neurons that are involved in various cognitive *functions.* In comparison, *MRI* scans show the location of *structures* inside the brain as well as identify tumors and sites of brain damage, as shown in the left photo.

Amygdala responds to watching televised violence.

Brain damage. During Steve's MRI scan, images of his brain—slice by slice—appeared on a television screen. Suddenly, standing out from the normal grayish image of a brain slice was an unusual area that indicated dead brain cells (small red area on right of MRI scan). Because the damaged neurons were located in a brain area involved with processing visual information, Steve had experienced visual problems, such as being unable to tell the time by looking at a clock, even though he could see the hands of the clock. However, since only a small part of his visual area was affected, most other functions, such as walking, feeling, speaking, and hearing, were normal. The reason Steve could figure out the time by saying aloud where the big and little hands of the clock were located was that his hearing areas were undamaged.

Advantage. The advantage of the two kinds of MRI scans is they use nonharmful radio frequencies and give very detailed views of structures and functions inside the living brain (Ropper & Brown, 2005). The use of these two kinds of MRI scans has greatly increased our understanding of the brain.

We'll discuss one other brain-scanning technique, called the PET scan, which, similar to the fMRI, is also used to identify cognitive functions.

Are there pictures of thinking?

Currently, one of the most exciting approaches in biological psychology is the area of cognitive neuroscience (p. 7), which involves using imaging techniques to literally light up your thoughts and feelings.

PET scan, or positron emission tomography, involves injecting a slightly radioactive solution into the blood and then measuring the amount of radiation absorbed by brain cells called neurons. Very active neurons absorb more radioactive solution than less active ones. Different levels of absorption are represented by colors   red and

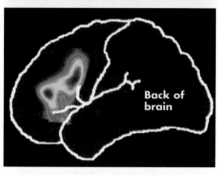

PET scan indicates that when you LOOK at a word, maximum neural activity—areas of red and yellow—occurs in the BACK of your brain.

PET scan indicates that when you SPEAK a word, maximum neural activity—areas of red and yellow—occurs in the FRONT of your brain.

yellow indicate maximum activity of neurons, while blue and green indicate minimal activity.

Pictures of thinking and speaking. The PET scan at the top left shows that when the subject was "looking at words" but not speaking them, most neural activity occurred near the back of the brain, which is involved in processing visual information. The PET scan at the bottom left shows that when the subject was "speaking words" instead of just thinking about them, most neural activity occurred near the front part of the brain, which is involved in speaking (Raichle, 1994).

Neuroimaging. Both PET and fMRI scans are used to identify and map the living brain's neural activity as a person performs complex behavioral and cognitive tasks, such as seeing, moving, thinking, speaking, empathizing, trusting, and even reacting to TV violence (McCarthy, 2005). Currently, PET scans are being replaced by the newer fMRI scans because fMRI scans do not require the injection of slightly radioactive solutions (Ropper & Brown, 2005).

Next, we'll discuss how brain scans were used to study an interesting puzzle in cognitive neuroscience.

How do you know if it's a camel or pliers?

An interesting cognitive puzzle is how you can so easily identify thousands of objects. This is a job for PET scans.

Naming animals. As shown at the top right, the thoughts of subjects as they *silently* named animals (camel) activated an area in the back of the brain that is involved in processing visual information. Researchers think this visual area helps us distinguish sizes, shapes, and colors, such as distinguishing a camel from a horse.

Naming tools. As shown at the bottom right, the thoughts of subjects as they *silently* named tools (pliers) activated an area in the front of the brain. Researchers think this frontal area helps us think about how we use tools (A. Martin et al., 1996).

Researchers concluded that you are able to identify thousands of objects, in large part, because the brain has two separate built-in systems: one for thoughts about naming animals, which involves distinguishing between sizes, shapes, and colors, and another for thoughts about naming tools, which involves thinking about how tools are used (A. Martin et al., 1996). Other researchers agree that when you see an object, the brain is genetically wired to place different objects, such as tools, animals, faces, and vegetables, into different categories, which are located in different areas of the brain. With this system, you can quickly and easily perceive and make sense of all the objects in your world (J. W. Lewis et al., 2005).

As we discussed in Module 1 (p. 7), this study is an example of a relatively new area called *cognitive neuroscience,* which identifies and maps differences in neural activity to understand the bases for cognitive functions (Gazzaniga, 2004).

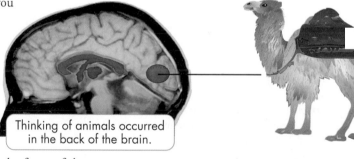

Thinking of animals occurred in the back of the brain.

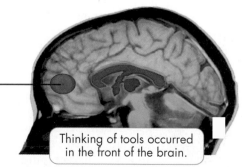

Thinking of tools occurred in the front of the brain.

Later on, we'll discuss a wide range of cognitive processes being studied using brain scans.

Now that you are familiar with ways to study the living brain, we can begin to examine the brain's specific structures and interesting functions.

C. Organization of the Brain

Divisions of the Nervous System

How many nervous systems?

Because you have one brain, you may think that means you have one nervous system. In fact, your brain is much more complex: It has two major nervous systems, one of which has four subdivisions. We'll explain the overall organization of the brain's several nervous systems, beginning with its two major divisions, the central and peripheral nervous systems.

A. Major Divisions of the Nervous System

CENTRAL NERVOUS SYSTEM—CNS

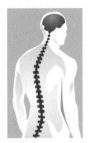

You are capable of many complex cognitive functions—such as thinking, speaking, and reading, as well as moving, feeling, seeing, and hearing—because of your central nervous system.

The *central nervous system* is made up of the brain and spinal cord. From the bottom of the brain emerges the spinal cord, which is made up of neurons and bundles of axons and dendrites that carry information back and forth between the brain and the body.

We'll discuss the major parts of the brain throughout this module.

PERIPHERAL NERVOUS SYSTEM—PNS

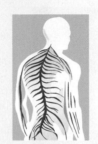

You are able to move your muscles, receive sensations from your body, and perform many other bodily responses because of the peripheral nervous system.

The *peripheral nervous system* includes all the nerves that extend from the spinal cord and carry messages to and from various muscles, glands, and sense organs located throughout the body.

The peripheral nervous system has two subdivisions, the somatic and autonomic nervous systems.

B. Subdivisions of the PNS

SOMATIC NERVOUS SYSTEM

The *somatic nervous system* consists of a network of nerves that connect either to sensory receptors or to muscles that you can move voluntarily, such as muscles in your limbs, back, neck, and chest. Nerves in the somatic nervous system usually contain two kinds of fibers. Afferent, or sensory, fibers carry information from sensory receptors in the skin, muscles, and other organs to the spinal cord and brain. Efferent, or motor, fibers carry information from the brain and spinal cord to the muscles.

For example, this gymnast controls her muscles, knows where her arms and legs are located in space, and maintains her coordination and balance because the somatic nervous system sends electrical signals back and forth to her brain.

ANS—AUTONOMIC NERVOUS SYSTEM

The *autonomic nervous system* regulates heart rate, breathing, blood pressure, digestion, hormone secretion, and other functions. The autonomic nervous system usually functions without conscious effort, which means that only a few of its responses, such as breathing, can also be controlled voluntarily.

The autonomic nervous system also has two subdivisions, the sympathetic and parasympathetic divisions.

C. Subdivisions of the ANS

SYMPATHETIC DIVISION

The *sympathetic division,* which is triggered by threatening or challenging physical or psychological stimuli, increases physiological arousal and prepares the body for action.

For example, the sight of a frightening snake would trigger the sympathetic division, which, in turn, would arouse the body for action, such as fighting or fleeing.

PARASYMPATHETIC DIVISION

The *parasympathetic division* returns the body to a calmer, relaxed state and is involved in digestion.

For example, when you are feeling calm and relaxed or digesting food, your parasympathetic system is activated.

Now that you know the overall organization of the nervous system, we'll focus on major parts of the brain.

Front

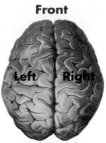

Left **Right**

Back

A human brain (right figure), which can easily be held in one hand, weighs about 1,350 grams, or 3 pounds, and has the consistency of firm Jell-O. The brain is protected by a thick skull and covered with thin, tough, plasticlike membranes. If shot in the head, a person may or may not die depending on which area was damaged. For example, damage to an area in the forebrain would result in paralysis, damage to an area in the midbrain would result in coma, but damage to an area in the hindbrain would certainly result in death.

Can someone be shot in the head but not die?

We'll begin our exploration of the brain by looking at its three major parts—forebrain, midbrain, and hindbrain—beginning with the forebrain.

2 Midbrain

If a boxer is knocked unconscious, part of the reason lies in the midbrain.

The *midbrain* has a reward or pleasure center, which is stimulated by food, sex, money, music, attractive faces, and some drugs (cocaine); has areas for visual and auditory reflexes, such as automatically turning your head toward a noise; and contains the reticular formation, which arouses the forebrain so that it is ready to process information from the senses (Holroyd & Coles, 2002).

If the reticular formation were seriously damaged—by a blow to the head, for example—a person would be unconscious and might go into a coma because the forebrain could not be aroused (E. Goldberg et al., 1989; Parvizi & Damasio, 2003).

1 Forebrain

When you look at the brain, what you are actually seeing is almost all forebrain (figure above). The *forebrain,* which is the largest part of the brain, has right and left sides that are called hemispheres. The hemispheres, connected by a wide band of fibers, are responsible for an incredible number of functions, including learning and memory, speaking and language, having emotional responses, experiencing sensations, initiating voluntary movements, planning, and making decisions.

The large structure outlined in orange to the left shows only the right hemisphere of the forebrain. The forebrain's right and left hemispheres are both shown in the figure at the top right. The forebrain is very well developed in humans.

Side view of the brain's right hemisphere

3 Hindbrain

The structures and functions of the hindbrain, which are found in very primitive brains, such as the alligator's, have remained constant through millions of years of evolution. The *hindbrain* has three distinct structures: the pons, medulla, and cerebellum.

3a Pons

If someone has a serious sleep disorder, it may involve the pons. In Latin, *pons* means "bridge," which suggests its function.

The *pons* functions as a bridge to transmit messages between the spinal cord and brain. The pons also makes the chemicals involved in sleep (Purves et al., 2004).

3b Medulla

If someone dies of a drug overdose, the cause of death probably involved the medulla.

The *medulla,* which is located at the top of the spinal cord, includes a group of cells that control vital reflexes, such as respiration, heart rate, and blood pressure.

Large amounts of alcohol, heroin, or other depressant drugs suppress the functions of cells in the medulla and cause death by stopping breathing.

3c Cerebellum

A person suspected of drunken driving may fail the test of rapidly touching a finger to the nose because of alcohol's effects on the cerebellum.

The *cerebellum,* which is located at the very back and underneath the brain, is involved in coordinating motor movements but not in initiating voluntary movements.

The cerebellum is also involved in performing timed motor responses, such as those needed in playing games or sports, and in automatic or reflexive learning, such as blinking the eye to a signal, which is called classical conditioning (discussed in Module 9) (Hazeltine & Ivry, 2002; Spencer et al., 2003).

Because alcohol is a depressant drug and interferes with the functions of the cerebellum, an intoxicated person would experience decreased coordination and have difficulty rapidly touching a finger to the nose, which is one of the tests for being drunk.

Of the brain's three parts, the forebrain is the largest, most evolved, and most responsible for an enormous range of personal, social, emotional, and cognitive behaviors. For those reasons, we'll examine the forebrain in more detail.

D. Control Centers: Four Lobes

How do you package 1 trillion cells?

How would you design a brain to hold 1 trillion cells (100 billion neurons and 900 billion glial cells) and be no bigger than a small melon and weigh no more than 3 pounds? You would need to make the cells microscopic in size, which they are, and to organize the billions of cells into different but interconnected areas, which they are. But would you have thought to make the brain's surface very wrinkled? Here's why.

WRINKLED CORTEX

In the photo below, you see a computer-enhanced picture of the outside of an adult human brain, which has a very wrinkled surface that is called the cortex (in Latin, *cortex* means "cover").

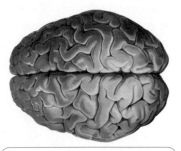

Brain's surface shows its wrinkled cortex.

The *cortex* **is a thin layer of cells that essentially covers the entire surface of the forebrain. The vast majority of our neurons are located in the cortex, which folds over on itself so that it forms a large surface area.**

To understand the advantage of having a wrinkled cortex, just imagine having to put a large sheet of paper about 18 inches square into a small match box that is 3 inches square. One solution is to crumple (wrinkle) the sheet of paper until it easily fits into the tiny match box. Similarly, imagine many billions of neurons laid on a sheet of paper about 18 inches square. When this large sheet of neurons is wrinkled, the cortex can fit snugly into our much smaller, rounded skulls.

Early researchers divided the wrinkled cortex into four different areas, or lobes, each of which has different functions.

FOUR LOBES

As you look at the brain's cortex, you see a wrinkled surface of peaks and valleys with very few distinguishing features. However, the cortex's appearance is deceiving because its hundreds of different functions are organized into four separate areas called lobes.

The cortex is divided into four separate areas, or *lobes,* each with different functions: the *frontal lobe* is involved with personality, emotions, and motor behaviors; the *parietal (puh-RYE-it-all) lobe* is involved with perception and sensory experiences; the *occipital (ock-SIP-pih-tull) lobe* is involved with processing visual information; and the *temporal (TEM-purr-all) lobe* is involved with hearing and speaking.

The one brain structure that most clearly distinguishes you from other animals is your well-developed cortex, which allows you to read, understand, talk about, and remember the concepts in this text. To understand what life would be like without a cortex, we'll return to the case of Baby Theresa, who was born without any lobes and thus no cortex.

Cortex is divided into four different areas, or lobes.

BABY THERESA'S BRAIN: A FATAL DEFECT

At the beginning of this module, we told you about Baby Theresa, who was one of the 1,000 babies born each year in the United States with almost no brain. This rare condition, caused by errors in genetic instructions, is called anencephaly (Greer, 2005).

Anencephaly (an-in-CEPH-ah-lee) **refers to the condition of being born with little or no brain. If some brain or nervous tissue is present, it is totally exposed and often damaged because the top of the skull is missing. Survival is usually limited to days; the longest has been two months.**

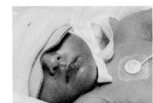

Theresa has anencephaly, meaning little or no brain.

Anencephaly is always fatal because it also includes other serious physical defects, such as damage to the skull (Goetz, 2003). Baby Theresa (photo above), who survived only nine days, had almost no brain tissue and almost no skull (bandaged area above eyes). Lacking most of a brain means that she would be incapable of perceiving, thinking, speaking, planning, or making decisions.

The figure below shows that a baby born with anencephaly has no forebrain. One reason babies with anencephaly may survive for days or weeks is that they may have parts of their hindbrain. As discussed earlier, the hindbrain contains the pons and medulla. The medulla controls vital reflexes, such as breathing, heart rate, and blood pressure, which together can maintain life for a period of time.

This example of anencephaly shows that without the forebrain, a baby may be physiologically alive but show no signs of having a mind or possessing cognitive abilities associated with being human. In a real sense, it is the functions of the forebrain's four lobes that define us as human and distinguish us from all other creatures.

No forebrain
Medulla

Medulla kept Theresa alive.

Because the four lobes are vital to our existence as humans, we'll discuss each lobe in turn. We'll begin with the frontal lobe and a tragic accident.

What does the biggest lobe do?

The frontal lobe (right figure) is the largest of the brain's four lobes and has a number of important functions (E. Goldberg, 2001; Sylvester et al., 2003).

The *frontal lobe*, which is located in the front part of the brain, includes a huge area of cortex. The frontal lobe is involved in many functions: performing voluntary motor movements, interpreting and performing emotional behaviors, behaving normally in social situations, maintaining a healthy personality, paying attention to things in the environment, making decisions, and executing plans. Because the frontal lobe is involved in making decisions, planning, reasoning, and carrying out behaviors, it is said to have executive functions, much like the duties of a company's executive officer.

Our first clue about the functions of the frontal lobe came from an unusual accident in 1848; our more recent knowledge comes from research using brain scans (fMRI and PET scans). Let's first go back in time and meet Phineas Gage, whose accident led to the discovery of one of the frontal lobe's important functions.

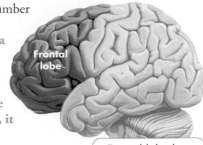

Frontal lobe

Frontal lobe has executive functions.

A TERRIBLE ACCIDENT

The accident occurred at about half past four on the afternoon of September 13, 1848, near the small town of Cavendish, Vermont. Railroad crewmen were about to blast a rock that blocked their way. Foreman Phineas Gage filled a deep, narrow hole in the rock with powder and rammed in a long iron rod to tamp down the charge before covering it with sand. But the tamping iron rubbed against the side of the shaft, and a spark ignited the powder. The massive rod—$3\frac{1}{2}$ feet long, $1\frac{1}{4}$ inches in diameter, and weighing 13 pounds—shot from the hole under the force of the explosion. It struck Phineas just beneath his left eye and tore through his skull. It shot out the top of his head and landed some 50 yards away.

Phineas survived, but, following the accident, his personality changed: He went from being a popular, friendly foreman to acting impatient, cursing his workers, and refusing to honor his promises.

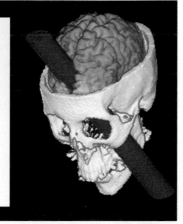

A massive rod (right image) weighing 13 pounds was accidentally driven through the front part of Phineas Gage's frontal lobe. The result, which was similar to having a frontal lobotomy, caused Phineas to have emotional outbursts and problems in making decisions, something he did not experience before this accident.

Researchers recently used Phineas's preserved skull to reconstruct the site and extent of his brain damage. As the figure above shows, the iron rod had passed through and extensively damaged Phineas's frontal lobe. Researchers concluded that Phineas had suffered a crude form of frontal lobotomy, which caused deficits in processing of emotion and decision making that result after damage to the frontal lobe (H. Damasio et al., 1994).

Beginning in the 1930s, doctors performed thousands of lobotomies to treat various mental and behavioral problems.

FRONTAL LOBOTOMY

In 1936, Egas Moniz, a Portuguese neurologist, used an untested surgical treatment, called frontal lobotomy, to treat individuals with severe emotional problems (Tierney, 2000).

A *frontal lobotomy* was a surgical procedure in which about one-third of the front part of the frontal lobe (figure below) was cut away from the rest of the brain.

Moniz first reported that frontal lobotomies did reduce emotional problems in about 35% of severely agitated human patients, although he did no controlled or follow-up studies to check long-term effects (Weinberger et al., 1995). Based on Moniz's reports of success, about 18,000 frontal lobotomies were performed in the 1940s and 1950s on emotionally disturbed patients who were primarily confined to state mental hospitals that had no other treatments.

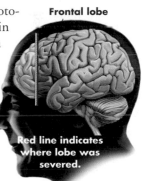

Frontal lobe

Red line indicates where lobe was severed.

RESULTS OF LOBOTOMIES

Initially, neurologists reported good short-term effects, but better controlled, long-term studies on frontal lobotomies found mixed results: Some patients did become less violent, but others showed no improvement and some became worse. Even those whose social-emotional behaviors improved were often left with serious problems in other areas, such as having difficulty in making and carrying out plans, adjusting to new social demands, or behaving with appropriate emotional responses in social situations (Mashour et al., 2005).

Two things happened in the early 1950s that ended the use of frontal lobotomies to treat social-emotional problems. First, follow-up research indicated that lobotomies were no more successful in relieving social-emotional problems than doing nothing. Second, antipsychotic drugs were discovered and showed greater success in treating serious social-emotional problems (Mashour et al., 2005).

From using frontal lobotomies as treatment, researchers learned two things: (1) careful follow-up work is essential before declaring a treatment successful and (2) the frontal lobe has many different, important functions, which we'll look at next.

D. Control Centers: Four Lobes

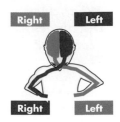

How do you move your right hand?

The organization of the frontal lobe is somewhat confusing because it has such a wide range of functions, from motor movements to cognitive processes. We'll first focus on motor movements, which have a very unusual feature.

In the figure on the right, notice that nerves from the right hemisphere (blue) cross over and control the movements of the left hand and left side of the body; nerves from the left hemisphere (red) cross over and control the movements of the right hand and right side of the body. The ability to move your hand or any other part of your body depends on the motor cortex in the right and left frontal lobes.

1 Location of Motor Cortex

To move your right hand, you will use the motor cortex in your left frontal lobe.

The *motor cortex* is a narrow strip of cortex that is located on the back edge of the frontal lobe and extends down its side. The motor cortex is involved in the initiation of all voluntary movements. The right motor cortex controls muscles on the left side of the body and vice versa.

You can move any individual part of your body at will because of how the motor cortex is organized.

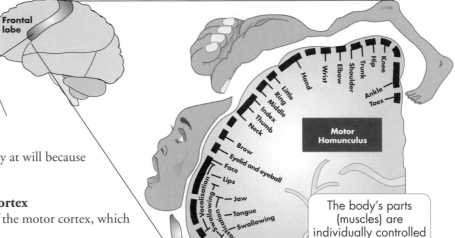

The body's parts (muscles) are individually controlled by the motor cortex.

2 Organization and Function of Motor Cortex

The figure on the right shows an enlarged part of the motor cortex, which is organized in two interesting ways.

First, a larger body part (notice huge hand area) indicates relatively more area on the motor cortex and thus more ability to perform complex movements. A smaller body part (notice small knee area) indicates relatively less area on the motor cortex and thus less ability to perform complex movements. This unusual drawing, which uses sizes of body parts to show the ability to perform complex movements, is called the ***motor homunculus (ho-MONK-you-luss).*** **Second,** each body part has its own area on the motor cortex. This means that damage to one part of the motor cortex could result in paralysis of that part yet spare most other parts. However, recent studies indicate that motor cortex is not as discretely organized as once believed. Instead of each body part having a different, discrete area, there is considerable overlap between body parts in the motor cortex (Helmuth, 2002). Finally, notice that the motor cortex makes up only a relatively small part of the entire frontal lobe.

In a surprising finding, there was vigorous activity in the motor cortex when people did nothing more than silently read action words. For example, when people read the word *lick*, activity occurred in parts of the motor cortex associated with the tongue and mouth (Hauk et al., 2004). This means that besides triggering voluntary movements, the motor cortex responds to simply hearing action words, such as *kick, hit,* or *run.* Next, we'll explain the frontal lobe's other functions.

3 Other Functions of Frontal Lobe

Brain damage. Much of our knowledge of other frontal lobe functions comes from individuals who had damage to that area. By studying patients like Phineas Gage, researchers found that damage to frontal lobes may result in disruption of personality as well as emotional swings. From studying patients with damage to frontal lobes, researchers found that frontal lobes are involved in paying attention, remembering things, making good decisions, and planning and organizing events (Stuss & Levine, 2002).

Brain scans. Researchers have also identified frontal lobe functions by taking brain scans while subjects performed various tasks. For example, after subjects were shown a series of word pairs, such as *ordeal* and *roach*, they were shown one word from each pair *(ordeal)* and were asked to either think about or avoid thinking about the associated word *(roach).* fMRI scans, such as the one shown below indicated that people who best avoided thinking about the associated word had maximum activity in the frontal lobe. This means the frontal lobe is involved in memory, specifically intentional forgetting (M. C. Anderson et al., 2004). Other studies indicate the frontal lobe is involved in paying attention and learning rules of social behavior (A. Damasio, 1999).

Executive function. Because the frontal lobes are involved in paying attention, organizing, planning, deciding, and carrying out various cognitive tasks and social-emotional behaviors, they are said to have an executive function—that is, act similar to a smart, successful executive of a large organization (Plumet et al., 2005).

Immediately behind the frontal lobe is the parietal lobe, which, among other things, keeps track of your body's limbs.

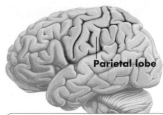

Parietal lobe

Parietal lobe processes information from body parts.

How do you know where your feet are? Every second of every minute of every day, your brain must keep track of what's touching your skin, where your feet and hands are, and whether you're walking or running. All this is automatically and efficiently done by your parietal lobe (right figure).

The *parietal lobe* **is located directly behind the frontal lobe. The parietal lobe's functions include processing sensory information from body parts, which includes touching, locating positions of limbs, and feeling temperature and pain, and carrying out several cognitive functions, such as attending to and perceiving objects.**

For example, the ability to know what you're touching involves the parietal lobe's somatosensory cortex.

1 Location of Somatosensory Cortex

Knowing what you're touching or how hot to make the water for your shower involves the somatosensory cortex.

The *somatosensory cortex* **is a narrow strip of cortex that is located on the front edge of the parietal lobe and extends down its side. The somatosensory cortex processes sensory information about touch, location of limbs, pain, and temperature. The right somatosensory cortex receives information from the left side of the body and vice versa.**

Your lips are much more sensitive than your elbows because of the way the somatosensory cortex is organized.

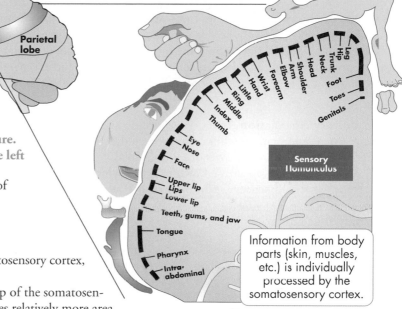

Parietal lobe

Sensory Homunculus

Information from body parts (skin, muscles, etc.) is individually processed by the somatosensory cortex.

2 Organization of Somatosensory Cortex

The large figure on the right shows an enlarged part of the somatosensory cortex, which is also cleverly organized.

First, notice the different sizes of the body parts drawn on top of the somatosensory cortex. A larger body part (notice large area for lips) indicates relatively more area on the somatosensory cortex and thus more sensitivity to external stimulation. A smaller body part (notice small nose area) indicates relatively less area on the somatosensory cortex and thus less sensitivity to external stimulation. This unusual drawing, which uses sizes of body parts to indicate amount of sensitivity to external stimulation, is called the ***sensory homunculus*** *(ho-MONK-you-luss).* In Latin, *homunculus* means "little man." Notice that the somatosensory cortex makes up only a small part of the parietal lobe.

Second, notice that each body part has its own area on the somatosensory cortex. This means that damage to one part of the somatosensory cortex could result in loss of feeling to one part of the body yet completely spare all others. Next, we'll explain the parietal lobe's other functions.

3 Other Functions of Parietal Lobe

Brain damage. When you put your hand in your pocket, you can easily distinguish a key from a stick of chewing gum because your parietal lobe digests information about texture, shape, and size and "tells you" what the object is. However, patients with damage to the back of their parietal lobes cannot recognize common objects by touch or feel (Bear et al., 1996). Evidence that the parietal lobes are involved in other cognitive processes comes from studies using brain scans, such as the fMRI.

fMRI scans. Subjects were asked to participate in a writing exercise while researchers investigated changes in their brain activity. fMRI scans, such as the one shown here, indicated that maximum activity

Parietal lobe

Maximum activity

Back of brain

during this task occurred in the parietal lobe (Menon & Desmond, 2001). Another fMRI study on people who fluently speak a second language indicated the parietal lobe was more developed (or larger) than in those who spoke only one language (Mechelli et al., 2004).

Researchers concluded that the parietal lobe is involved in language abilities, such as writing and speaking a second language. Other fMRI studies indicate the parietal lobe is involved in additional cognitive functions, such as visual and auditory attention (Hao et al., 2005; Shomstein & Yantis, 2006).

Immediately below the parietal lobe is the temporal lobe, which we'll examine next.

D. Control Centers: Four Lobes

Did you hear your name?

You recognize your name when you hear it spoken; because of the way sound is processed in the temporal lobe, you know it's not just some meaningless noise.

The temporal lobe is located directly below the parietal lobe and is involved in hearing, speaking coherently, and understanding verbal and written material.

As you'll see, the process of hearing and recognizing your name involves two steps and two different brain areas.

1a Primary Auditory Cortex

The first step in hearing your name occurs when sounds reach specific areas in the temporal lobe called the primary auditory (hearing) cortex—there is one in each lobe.

The primary auditory cortex (shown in red), which is located on the top edge of each temporal lobe, receives electrical signals from receptors in the ears and transforms these signals into meaningless sound sensations, such as vowels and consonants.

At this point, you would not be able to recognize your name because the primary auditory cortex only changes electrical signals from the ears into basic sensations, such as individual sounds, clicks, or noises. For these meaningless sound sensations to become recognizable words, they must be sent to another area in the temporal lobe, called the auditory association area (Whalen et al., 2006).

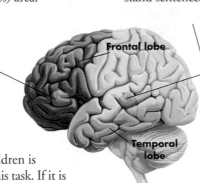

Temporal lobe processes auditory (hearing) information.

1b Auditory Association Area

The second step in recognizing your name is when the primary auditory cortex sends its electrical signals to the auditory association area; there is one in each lobe.

The auditory association area (shown in blue), which is located directly below the primary auditory cortex, transforms basic sensory information, such as noises or sounds, into recognizable auditory information, such as words or music.

It is only after auditory information is sent by the primary auditory cortex to the auditory association area that you would recognize sounds as your name, or words, or music (Whalen et al., 2006). So, it is safe to say that you hear with your brain rather than your ears.

Besides being involved in hearing, the temporal lobe has other areas that are critical for speaking and understanding words and sentences.

2 Broca's Area—Frontal Lobe

Just as hearing your name is a two-step process, so is speaking a sentence. The first step is putting words together, which involves an area in the frontal lobe called Broca's *(BROKE-ahs)* area.

Broca's area, which is usually located in the left frontal lobe, is necessary for combining sounds into words and arranging words into meaningful sentences. Damage to this area results in Broca's aphasia (ah-PHASE-zz-ah), which means a person cannot speak in fluent sentences but can understand written and spoken words.

The reason that saying words and putting words into sentences come naturally to small children is that Broca's area is genetically programmed to do this task. If it is damaged, people with Broca's aphasia have difficulty putting words into sentences. For example, a patient was asked, "What have you been doing in the hospital?" The patient answered, "Yes, sure. Me go, er, uh, P.T. non o'cot, speech . . . two times . . . read . . . wr . . . ripe, er, rike, er, write . . . practice . . . get-ting better" (H. Gardner, 1976, p. 61). The patient was trying to say, "I go to P.T. (physical therapy) at one o'clock to practice speaking, reading, and writing, and I'm getting better."

A patient with Broca's aphasia cannot speak fluently but can still understand words and sentences because of a second area in the temporal lobe—Wernicke's area (Dronkers et al., 2004).

3 Wernicke's Area—Temporal Lobe

The first step in speaking is using Broca's area to combine sounds into words and arrange words into sentences. The second step is to understand sentences, which involves Wernicke's *(VERN-ick-ees)* area.

Wernicke's area, which is usually located in the left temporal lobe, is necessary for speaking in coherent sentences and for understanding speech. Damage to this area results in Wernicke's aphasia, which is a difficulty in understanding spoken or written words and a difficulty in putting words into meaningful sentences.

For example, a patient with Wernicke's aphasia said, "You know, once in awhile I get caught up, I mention the tarripoi, a month ago, quite a little, I've done a lot well" (H. Gardner, 1976, p. 68). As this meaningless sentence shows, Wernicke's area is critical for combining words into meaningful sentences and being able to speak coherently (Mesulam, 2005).

Due to genetic factors, most right-handers (96%) and a majority of left-handers (70–80%) have Broca's and Wernicke's areas in the left hemisphere. In about 20% of left-handers, the language areas are in either the right hemisphere or both hemispheres (B. Bower, 2002b).

Compared to many other animals, humans rely more heavily on visual information, which is processed in the occipital lobe, our next topic.

Can you see better than dogs?

Dogs have poor color vision and rely more on their sense of smell. In comparison, all primates, which include monkeys, apes, and humans, have a relatively poor sense of smell and rely more on vision for gathering information about their environments.

If you have ever been hit on the back of the head and saw "stars," you already know that vision is located in the occipital lobe.

The *occipital lobe* is located at the very back of the brain and is involved in processing visual information, which includes seeing colors and perceiving and recognizing objects, animals, and people.

Although you see and recognize things with great ease, it is actually a complicated two-step process. Here, we'll give only an overview of that process; we'll go into more detail in Module 5.

1 Vision

When you look in the mirror and see your face, you don't realize that seeing your face involves two steps and two different areas in the occipital lobe (Maldonado et al., 1997). The first step in seeing your face involves the primary visual cortex.

The *primary visual cortex,* which is located at the very back of the occipital lobe, receives electrical signals from receptors in the eyes and transforms these signals into meaningless basic visual sensations, such as lights, lines, shadows, colors, and textures.

Since the primary visual cortex produces only meaningless visual sensations (lights, lines, shadows), you do not yet see your face. Transforming meaningless visual sensations into a meaningful visual object occurs in the visual association area (B. Bower, 2002b).

The *visual association area,* which is located next to the primary visual cortex, transforms basic sensations, such as lights, lines, colors, and textures, into complete, meaningful visual perceptions, such as persons, objects, or animals.

Occipital lobe

Occipital lobe processes visual (seeing) information.

When the second step works properly, there is an increase in activity in the visual association area and a decrease in activity in the primary visual cortex as basic sensations are turned into meaningful perceptions (S. O. Murray et al., 2002). If there are problems in the second step, the person can still see parts of objects but has difficulty combining the parts and seeing or recognizing the whole object (B. Bower, 1996).

We'll discuss two unusual visual problems that result from damage to association areas.

2 Visual Agnosia

Since the visual association area is critical for recognizing faces, shapes, and objects, damage to this area results in difficulties of recognition, a condition called visual agnosia *(ag-NO-zee-ah).*

In *visual agnosia,* the individual fails to recognize some object, person, or color, yet has the ability to see and even describe pieces or parts of some visual stimulus.

Here's what happened when a patient with damage to the visual association area was asked to simply copy an object.

A patient who has visual agnosia was asked to make a copy of this horse, something most everyone can do.

The patient drew each part of the horse separately and could not combine individual parts into a meaningful image.

Patients with visual agnosia can see individual parts of an object, such as a horse's leg, but, because of damage to visual association areas, have great difficulty combining parts to perceive or draw a complete and recognizable image, such as a complete horse (Maratsos & Matheny, 1994). Damage to association areas can also result in seeing only half of one's world.

3 Neglect Syndrome

Individuals who have damage to association areas, usually in occipital and parietal lobes, and usually in the right hemisphere, experience a very strange problem called the neglect syndrome.

The *neglect syndrome* refers to the failure of a patient to see objects or parts of the body on the side opposite the brain damage. Patients may dress only one side of their body and deny that opposite body parts are theirs ("that's not my leg").

Here's how a patient with neglect syndrome drew an object.

 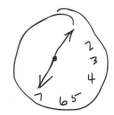

A patient with neglect syndrome caused by right-sided brain damage was asked to copy this clock.

The patient drew only the right side of the clock because he did not see or recognize things on his left side.

After a stroke or other damage, usually to the occipital and parietal association areas in the right hemisphere, patients may behave as if the left sides of objects or their own bodies no longer exist: they may not shave or dress the left sides of their bodies, which they do not recognize. Neglect syndrome shows the important function of association areas in recognizing things (Purves et al., 2004).

Now we'll journey beneath the cortex and explore a group of structures that existed in evolutionarily very old, primitive brains.

E. Limbic System: Old Brain

How are you like an alligator? Your cortex is involved in numerous cognitive functions, such as thinking, deciding, planning, and speaking, as well as other sensory and motor behaviors. But what triggers your wide range of emotional experiences, such as feeling happy, sad, or angry? The answer lies deeper inside the brain, where you'll find a number of interconnected structures that are involved in emotions and are called the limbic system (R. J. Dolan, 2002).

The *limbic system* refers to a group of about half a dozen interconnected structures that make up the core of the forebrain. The limbic system's structures are involved with regulating many motivational behaviors such as obtaining food, drink, and sex; with organizing emotional behaviors such as fear, anger, and aggression; and with storing memories.

The limbic system is often referred to as our primitive, or animal, brain because its same structures are found in the brains of animals that are evolutionarily very old, such as alligators. The alligator's limbic system, which essentially makes up its entire forebrain, is involved in smelling out prey, defending territory, hunting, fighting, reproducing, eating, and remembering. The human limbic system, which makes up only a small part of our forebrain, is involved in similar behaviors.

Alligators and humans have limbic systems.

We'll discuss some of the major structures and functions of the limbic system. The drawing below shows the right hemisphere (the left hemisphere is cut away). Notice that the limbic structures are surrounded by the forebrain, whose executive functions regulate the limbic system's emotional and motivational behaviors.

Important Parts of the Limbic System

1 One limbic structure that is a master control for many emotional responses is the hypothalamus *(high-po-THAL-ah-mus)*.

The *hypothalamus* regulates many motivational behaviors, including eating, drinking, and sexual responses; emotional behaviors, such as arousing the body when fighting or fleeing; and the secretion of hormones, such as occurs at puberty.

In addition, the hypothalamus controls the two divisions of the autonomic nervous system discussed on the next page.

The next limbic structure, the amygdala, is also involved in emotions but more in forming and remembering them.

2 The *amygdala (ah-MIG-duh-la),* located in the tip of the temporal lobe, receives input from all the senses. It plays a major role in evaluating the emotional significance of stimuli and facial expressions, especially those involving fear, distress, or threat.

When the amygdala is damaged, patients had difficulty recognizing emotional facial expressions and animals did not learn to fear or avoid dangerous situations. Brain scans indicate that the amygdala is involved in identifying emotional facial expressions (Hamann et al., 2002). Researchers report that the amygdala is critical in recognizing emotional facial expressions, including happy faces but especially faces indicating fear, distress, or threat; evaluating emotional situations, especially involving threat or danger; and adding emotional feelings to happy or sad events (going to a funeral, remembering a joke) (R. J. Dolan, 2002).

3 This limbic structure, which is like a miniature computer that gathers and processes information from your senses, is called the thalamus *(THAL-ah-mus)*.

The *thalamus* is involved in receiving sensory information, doing some initial processing, and then relaying the sensory information to areas of the cortex, including the somatosensory cortex, primary auditory cortex, and primary visual cortex.

For example, if the thalamus malfunctions, you might have difficulty processing sensory information (hearing or seeing).

Our last limbic structure, the hippocampus, is involved in saving your memories.

4 The *hippocampus,* which is a curved structure inside the temporal lobe, is involved in saving many kinds of fleeting memories by putting them into permanent storage in various parts of the brain.

For example, humans with damage to the hippocampus have difficulty remembering new facts, places, faces, or conversations because these new events cannot be placed into permanent storage (Bayley et al., 2003). Think of the hippocampus, which is involved in saving things in long-term storage (see p. 268), as functioning like the "Save" command on your computer.

Limbic system versus frontal lobe. Some of the basic emotional feelings triggered by the limbic system (anger, rage, fear, panic) carry the potential for self-injury or injury to others. Researchers found that our larger and evolutionarily newer frontal lobe, which is involved in thinking, deciding, and planning, plays a critical role in controlling the limbic system's powerful urges (R. J. Dolan, 2002).

One particular structure in the limbic system, the hypothalamus, also has an important role in regulating the autonomic nervous system, which we'll examine next.

Why don't you worry about breathing?

You are unaware of what regulates your breathing, heart rate, hormone secretions, or body temperature. You're not concerned about these vital functions because they are usually controlled by a separate nervous system, called the autonomic nervous system, which, in turn, is regulated by a master control center, the hypothalamus (discussed on the preceding page).

The autonomic nervous system, which regulates numerous physiological responses, has two divisions, the sympathetic and parasympathetic nervous systems. The sympathetic division is activated when you suddenly see a snake; then the parasympathetic division helps you relax (Faller et al., 2004). We'll explain some of the specific and automatic functions of the sympathetic and parasympathetic divisions.

Sympathetic Nervous System

If you were on a nature hike and suddenly saw a snake, your cortex would activate the hypothalamus, which in turn triggers the sympathetic division of the autonomic nervous system (S. Johnson, 2003).

The *sympathetic division*, **which is one part of the autonomic nervous system, is triggered by threatening or challenging physical stimuli, such as a snake, or by psychological stimuli, such as the thought of having to give a public speech. Once triggered, the sympathetic division increases the body's physiological arousal.**

All of the physiological responses listed in the left-hand column under *Sympathetic,* such as increased heart rate, inhibited digestion, and dilated pupils, put your body into a state of heightened physiological arousal, which is called the fight-flight response.

The *fight-flight response*, **which is a state of increased physiological arousal caused by activation of the sympathetic division, helps the body cope with and survive threatening situations.**

You have no doubt experienced the fight-flight response many times, such as when you felt your heart pound and your mouth go dry. Later, we'll discuss the role of the fight-flight response in stressful situations and its role in psychosomatic diseases (pp. 484–489).

Parasympathetic Nervous System

After you have been physiologically aroused by seeing a snake, it is usually some time before your body returns to a calmer state. The process of decreasing physiological arousal and calming down your body is triggered by the hypothalamus, which activates the parasympathetic division.

The *parasympathetic division*, **which is the other part of the autonomic nervous system, decreases physiological arousal and helps return the body to a calmer, more relaxed state. It also stimulates digestion during eating.**

As shown in the right column under the heading *Parasympathetic,* the parasympathetic division, once activated, decreases physiological arousal by decreasing heart rate, stimulating digestion, and constricting pupils. These responses result in the body returning to a more relaxed state.

In dealing with stress, we'll discuss many relaxation techniques (pp. 502–503), such as the relaxation response, various forms of meditation, and biofeedback, which help increase parasympathetic activity, decrease body arousal, and thus help you calm down after stressful experiences.

Sympathetic		Parasympathetic
Pupils dilated, dry; far vision	*Eyes*	Pupils constricted, moist; near vision
Dry	*Mouth*	Salivation
Goose bumps	*Skin*	No goose bumps
Sweaty	*Palms*	Dry
Passages dilated	*Lungs*	Passages constricted
Increased rate	*Heart*	Decreased rate
Supply maximum to muscles	*Blood*	Supply maximum to internal organs
Increased activity	*Adrenal glands*	Decreased activity
Inhibited	*Digestion*	Stimulated
Climax	*Sexual functions*	Arousal

Homeostasis

One problem that some students face is becoming too stressed or upset by life's events. Because it is potentially harmful to your body to stay stressed or aroused, the autonomic nervous system tries to keep the body's arousal at an optimum level, a state called homeostasis.

Homeostasis (ho-me-oh-STAY-sis) **means that the sympathetic and parasympathetic systems work together to keep the body's level of arousal in balance for optimum functioning.**

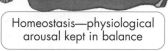

Homeostasis—physiological arousal kept in balance

For instance, your body's balance, or homeostasis, may be upset by the continuous stress of final exams or a difficult relationship. Such stress usually results in continuous physiological arousal and any number of physical problems, including headaches, stomachaches, tight muscles, or fatigue. These physical symptoms, which are called psychosomatic problems, may result in real pain. We'll discuss these problems in Module 21: Health, Stress & Coping (pp. 480–507).

Besides triggering your autonomic nervous system, the hypothalamus is also involved in regulating a complex hormonal system, which we'll examine next.

F. Endocrine System

What is your chemical system?

You have two major systems for sending signals to the body's muscles, glands, and organs. We have already discussed the nervous system, which uses neurons, nerves, and neurotransmitters to send information throughout the body. The second major system for sending information is called the endocrine system.

The *endocrine system* is made up of numerous glands that are located throughout the body. These glands secrete various chemicals, called *hormones,* which affect organs, muscles, and other glands in the body.

The location and function of some of the endocrine system's glands are shown in the figure below.

Control Center

In many ways, the *hypothalamus,* which is located in the lower middle part of the brain, controls much of the endocrine system by regulating the pituitary gland, which is located directly below and outside the brain. The hypothalamus is often called the control center of the endocrine system.

Hypo-thalamus

Posterior pituitary

Anterior pituitary

The drawing on the left shows that the hypothalamus is connected to the pituitary gland.

Other Glands

We'll describe some of the endocrine system's major glands as well as their dysfunctions.

The *pituitary gland,* a key component of the endocrine system, hangs directly below the hypothalamus, to which it is connected by a narrow stalk. The pituitary gland is divided into anterior (front) and posterior (back) sections.

Posterior pituitary. The rear portion of the pituitary regulates water and salt balance.

Dysfunction: Lack of hormones causes a less common form of diabetes.

Anterior pituitary. The front part of the pituitary regulates growth through secretion of growth hormone and produces hormones that control the adrenal cortex, pancreas, thyroid, and gonads.

Dysfunction: Too little growth hormone produces dwarfism; too much causes gigantism. Other problems in the pituitary cause problems in the glands it regulates.

Pancreas. This organ regulates the level of sugar in the bloodstream by secreting insulin.

Dysfunction: Lack of insulin results in the more common form of diabetes, while too much causes hypoglycemia (low blood sugar).

The endocrine system controls glands located throughout the body.

Thyroid. This gland, which is located in the neck, regulates metabolism through secretion of hormones.

Dysfunction: Hormone deficiency during development leads to stunted growth and mental retardation. Undersecretion during adulthood leads to reduction in motivation. Oversecretion results in high metabolism, weight loss, and nervousness.

Adrenal glands. The adrenal cortex (outside part) secretes hormones that regulate sugar and salt balances and help the body resist stress; they are also responsible for growth of pubic hair, a secondary sexual characteristic. The adrenal medulla (inside part) secretes two hormones that arouse the body to deal with stress and emergencies: epinephrine (adrenaline) and norepinephrine (noradrenaline).

Dysfunction: With a lack of cortical hormones, the body's responses are unable to cope with stress.

Gonads. In females, the ovaries produce hormones that regulate sexual development, ovulation, and growth of sex organs. In males, the testes produce hormones that regulate sexual development, production of sperm, and growth of sex organs.

Dysfunction: Lack of sex hormones during puberty results in lack of secondary sexual characteristics (facial and body hair, muscles in males, breasts in females).

Up to this point, we have examined many of the structures and functions that make up the incredible nervous and endocrine systems. After the Concept Review, we'll discuss a question that students often ask: Do the brains of males differ from those of females?

Concept Review

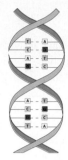

1. A hairlike structure that contains tightly coiled strands of the chemical DNA (deoxyribonucleic acid) is called a (a)_____. A specific segment on the strand of DNA that contains instructions for making proteins is called a (b)_____. A theory that different species arose from a common ancestor and that those species survived that were best adapted to meet the demands of their environments is called the theory of (c)_____.

2. There are several techniques for studying the living brain. One method for identifying structures in the brain involves measuring nonharmful radio frequencies as they pass through the brain; this is called an (a)_____ scan. Another method that is used to study functions of the brain involves measuring the amounts of low-level radioactive substances absorbed by brain cells; this is called a (b)_____ scan.

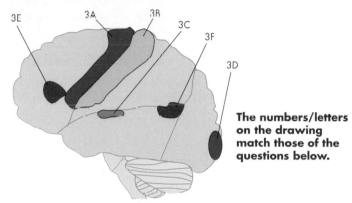

The numbers/letters on the drawing match those of the questions below.

3A. The cortical area that controls voluntary movements is called the (a)_____ and is located in the (b)_____ lobe.

3B. The cortical area that receives input from sensory receptors in the skin, muscles, and joints is called the (a)_____ and is located in the (b)_____ lobe.

3C. The cortical area that receives input from sensory receptors in the ears is called the (a)_____ and is located in the (b)_____ lobe.

3D. The cortical area that receives input from sensory receptors in the eyes is called the (a)_____ and is located in the (b)_____ lobe.

3E. The cortical area that is necessary to produce words and arrange them into sentences is called (a)_____ and is located in the (b)_____ lobe.

3F. The cortical area that is necessary for understanding spoken and written words and putting words into meaningful sentences is called (a)_____ and is located in the (b)_____ lobe.

4. The two major divisions of the nervous system are the (a)_____ and the (b)_____. In turn, the peripheral nervous system has two parts: one part is a network of nerves that are connected either to sensory receptors or to muscles that you can move voluntarily and is called the (c)_____; another part regulates heart rate, breathing, blood pressure, digestion, secretion of hormones, and other functions and is called the (d)_____. The brain itself is divided into three major parts: (e)_____, _____, and _____.

5. The old brain that is involved with many motivational and emotional behaviors is called the (a)_____. One structure of the limbic system, the hypothalamus, controls the autonomic nervous system, which has two divisions. The division that responds by increasing the body's physiological arousal is called the (b)_____. This division triggers an increased state of physiological arousal so that the body can cope with threatening situations; this state is called the (c)_____. The other division of the autonomic nervous system that is primarily responsible for returning the body to a calm or relaxed state and is involved in digestion is called the (d)_____. These two divisions work together to keep the body in physiological balance so that it remains or returns to a state of optimal functioning; this state is called (e)_____.

6. A system made up of numerous glands that are located throughout the body and that secrete various hormones is called the (a)_____. The brain area that can be considered the master control for this system is the (b)_____. This brain area is connected to and controls one of the endocrine system's major glands that has an anterior and posterior part and is collectively called the (c)_____.

Answers: *1. (a) chromosome, (b) gene, (c) evolution; 2. (a) MRI, (b) PET; 3A. (a) motor cortex, (b) frontal; 3B. (a) somatosensory cortex, (b) parietal; 3C. (a) primary auditory cortex, (b) temporal; 3D. (a) primary visual cortex, (b) occipital; 3E. (a) Broca's area, (b) frontal; 3F. (a) Wernicke's area, (b) temporal; 4. (a) central nervous system, (b) peripheral nervous system, (c) somatic nervous system, (d) autonomic nervous system, (e) forebrain, midbrain, hindbrain; 5. (a) limbic system, (b) sympathetic nervous system, (c) fight-flight response, (d) parasympathetic nervous system, (e) homeostasis; 6. (a) endocrine system, (b) hypothalamus, (c) pituitary gland*

G. Research Focus:
Sex Differences in the Brain?

Is this kind of research sexist?

Throughout history, politicians have criticized or misused research depending on what was "politically correct" (Lilienfeld, 2003). For example, in the 1920s, U.S. politicians misused research on IQ scores to justify passing discriminatory immigration quotas (p. 296) (S. J. Gould, 1981). In the 1980s, many politicians were critical of homosexuality and denied federal money for AIDS research until the virus became a threat to the heterosexual population (Shilts, 1988). In the 1980s and 1990s, research on sex differences was criticized as "sexist" because it went against the "politically correct" belief that male and female brains are essentially the same (Azar, 1997).

However, using brain scans, researchers have recently reported interesting differences in the structure and function of male and female brains, which are called sex differences (Cahill, 2005; Carne et al., 2006).

Sex, **or** *gender,* *differences* **refer to structural or functional differences in cognitive, behavioral, or brain processes that arise from being a male or a female.**

Sex differences are not good, bad, or sexist but simply ways in which males and females differ. Here are some interesting sex differences.

Differences in Solving Problems

The rotating figure problem is a rather difficult spatial problem, as follows. First, study the target figure on the left. Then, from the three choices at the right, identify the same figure, even though it has been rotated.

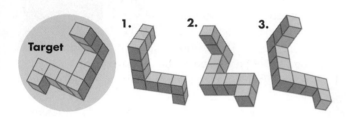

The key to solving this problem is the ability to rotate the target figure in your mind until it matches the rotation of one of the three choices. Researchers consistently report faster or more accurate performance by males than by females in solving rotating figure problems (Kimura, 1992). (Correct answer is 1.)

There are other tasks at which women perform better than men.

For example, look at the house outlined in black (figure above) and find its twin among the three choices. Women are generally faster on these kinds of tests, which measure perceptual speed. In addition, women usually score higher on tests of verbal fluency, in which you must list as many words as you can that begin with the same letter, as in the figure below (Halpern, 2000).

One explanation for these sex differences in skills is that they result from differences in

Limp, Livery, Love, Laser, Liquid, Low, Like, Lag, Live, Lug, Light, Lift, Liver, Lime, Leg, Load, Lap, Lucid, . . .

socialization and learning. Another explanation is that these sex differences have evolved from different skills needed by early humans. Males with good spatial skills had an advantage in hunting, and females with good communication skills had an advantage in child-rearing (Springer & Deutsch, 1997).

Researchers have now begun to look for sex differences in how the brain itself functions.

Differences between Female and Male Brains

To check for sex differences between male and female brains, researchers took brain scans while subjects were solving rotating figure problems.

Problem solving. As seen in the right figure, brain scans taken during problem solving showed that maximum neural activity in *males* occurred in the right frontal area. In contrast, maximum neural activity in *females* occurred in the right parietal-temporal area. Researchers concluded that solv-

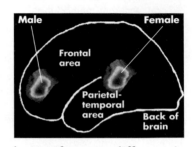

ing rotating figure problems showed a significant sex difference in terms of which brain areas were activated, which in turn may be the basis for sex differences in performance on this task (Alivisatos & Petrides, 1997).

Another interesting PET study found that while escaping from a three-dimensional virtual-reality maze, men were significantly faster (average: 2 min., 22 sec) than women (average: 3 min., 16 sec). Also, men used both sides of their hippocampus, which saves data into permanent storage, while women used only the right hippocampus. Researchers concluded that these brain differences may explain why men are better at finding a specific place in a strange city (Gron et al., 2000).

Emotional memories. How do men and women remember intense emotional experiences? Brain scans (fMRI) were taken while men and women viewed images they rated as ranging from emotionally neutral to highly arousing. Two weeks later, subjects were asked to pick out images they had seen earlier. Men with better memories for emotionally arousing images had greater activity in the right hemisphere amygdala, whereas women with better memories for emotionally arousing images had greater activity in the left hemisphere amygdala. Researchers concluded that there are sex differences in how the amygdala remembers emotionally arousing experiences (Cahill et al., 2004).

Movement and coordination. Researchers recently found a difference in how male and female brains make a major neurotransmitter (dopamine), which is responsible for controlling movement and coordination. This may help explain why men are more likely than women to develop Parkinson's disease (p. 60) (Gramling, 2006).

In finding sex differences in the brain, researchers warn against using such differences as the basis for promoting discriminatory practices or furthering a particular political agenda (L. Rogers, 2001).

H. Cultural Diversity: Brain Size & Racial Myths

Skull Size and Intelligence

Which race had the biggest brain?

When he died in 1851, the *New York Times* proudly said that Samuel George Morton, scientist and physician, had one of the best reputations among scholars throughout the world. Morton had spent his lifetime collecting skulls of different races to determine which race had the biggest brain. During Morton's time, it was generally accepted that a bigger brain meant greater intelligence and innate mental ability.

Results in 1839. Morton estimated the size of a brain by pouring tiny lead pellets (the size of present-day BBs) into each skull and then measuring the number of pellets. Using this procedure, he arrived at the following ranking of brain

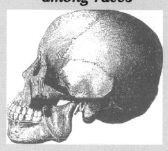

No significant differences in brain size among races

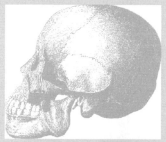

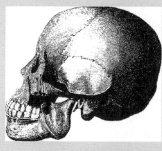

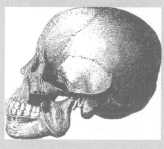

size in different races, from biggest to smallest (see skulls on left): 1, White (Caucasian); 2, yellow (Mongolian); 3, brown (American Indian); and 4, Black (Negro). Along with his racial ranking of decreasing brain size, Morton also believed there was a corresponding decrease in behavioral and cognitive skills (Morton, 1839, cited in S. J. Gould, 1981).

Reanalyzed in 1980. Stephen Jay Gould, a renowned evolutionary biologist, reanalyzed Morton's data on brain size and, unlike Morton's findings, found *no significant difference* in brain size among the four races. Furthermore, Gould concluded that Morton's strong biases that Caucasians should have the biggest brains had unknowingly swayed his scientific judgment to fit his racial prejudices of the 1800s (S. J. Gould, 1981).

Major error. Morton's major error was that he included skulls that matched his personal biased expectations and omitted skulls that did not support his racial beliefs. That is, Morton chose bigger skulls to match his bias of Whites being more intelligent and smaller skulls for other races, whom he considered to be less intelligent (S. J. Gould, 1994).

Although Morton had the reputation for being a respected scholar and although he had asked a legitimate research question—Are there differences in brain size?—he was unable to prevent his strong personal beliefs from biasing his research and finding what he strongly but mistakenly believed.

One way current researchers guard against the problem of biasing their results is by having scientists in other laboratories repeat their studies. If the original findings are repeated in other laboratories, then scientists can be reasonably confident that their original results are valid.

Brain Size and Intelligence

What do brain scans show?

Researchers have studied the relationship between brain size and IQ scores by using brain scans (p. 70), which precisely measure the size of the human brain. For example, researchers found a moderate correlation (+0.45) between the number of neurons in the frontal lobe, which has an executive function (p. 76), and IQ scores (P. M. Thompson et al., 2001). This positive correlation means that, generally, the more neurons in the frontal lobe, the higher the IQ scores.

Female brains. If there is a positive correlation between number of neurons in the frontal lobe and IQ scores, we might expect women generally to have lower IQ scores than men, since their brains, as well as their heads, are about 9–12% smaller than men's (Witelson et al., 2006). Because there is no evidence that women do have lower IQ scores than men,

Women's heads and brains are about 10% smaller than men's.

how do we explain this contradiction?

Although women's brains are smaller, they have 15–20% more neurons than in men's larger brains, and the brain cells of women are more tightly packed together (L. M. Williams et al., 2005). Women even have more folds in some parts of the cortex than men do, which may compensate for their smaller brain size (Luders et al., 2004). Last, blood flow to the brain is faster in women than in men, which may reduce the loss of cognitive abilities due to aging (L. M. Williams et al., 2005).

Correlations. Since studies report a positive correlation between brain size and IQ scores, we'll briefly review what *correlation* means. A correlation indicates only the existence of a relationship between two events; it does not identify the cause and effect. For example, being in a stimulating environment may promote brain growth and result in higher IQ scores, or being born with a larger brain may allow one to absorb more from one's environment and score higher on IQ tests. Thus, a positive correlation between brain size and intelligence may be scientifically interesting but has little practical application.

Before we complete our journey through the brain, we'll take you on one last trip, perhaps the most interesting of all. We'll see what happens when the brain is literally cut in two.

Definition and Testing

Why did Victoria choose a split brain?

Since about the age of 6, Victoria had seizures (also called epileptic seizures). During the seizures, she would lose consciousness and fall to the floor. Although her muscles would jerk uncontrollably, she felt no pain and would remember nothing of the experience. She was given anticonvulsant medicine, which prevented any further seizures until she was 18.

Split-brain operation. When Victoria was 18, for some unknown reason, her seizures returned with greater intensity. And to her dismay, anticonvulsant medication no longer had any effect. The seizures continued for ten years. Finally, when she was 27, she decided that her best chance of reducing her frightening, uncontrollable seizures was to have an operation that had a high probability of producing serious side effects. In this operation, a neurosurgeon would sever the major connection between her right and left hemispheres, leaving her with what is called a split brain (figure below).

Having to choose between a future of uncontrollable seizures and the potential problems of having a split brain, Victoria chose the operation (Sidtis et al., 1981).

In addition to Victoria (identified as V.P. in published reports), dozens of other individuals have also chosen to have a split-brain operation when they found that medicine no longer prevented their severe, uncontrollable seizures.

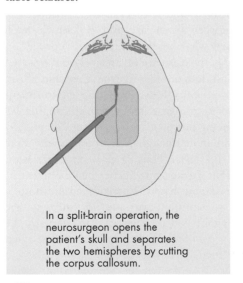

In a split-brain operation, the neurosurgeon opens the patient's skull and separates the two hemispheres by cutting the corpus callosum.

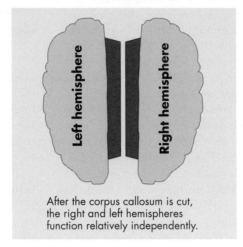

After the corpus callosum is cut, the right and left hemispheres function relatively independently.

A *split-brain operation* involves cutting the wide band of fibers, called the corpus callosum, that connects the right and left hemispheres (figure above). The corpus callosum has 200 million nerve fibers that allow information to pass back and forth between the hemispheres.

A split-brain operation not only disrupts the major pathway between the hemispheres but, to a large extent, leaves each hemisphere functioning independently. In many split-brain patients, severing the corpus callosum prevented the spread of seizures from one hemisphere to the other and thus reduced their frequency and occurrence (Holt, 2005).

Major breakthrough. It was 1961 when researcher Michael S. Gazzaniga and his colleagues tested the first split-brain patient, known as W.J. in the literature. Researchers first flashed on a screen a number of colors, letters, and pictures of objects. These stimuli were flashed so that they went only to W.J.'s left hemisphere, and he had no difficulty naming them. Then researchers flashed the same stimuli so that they went only to W.J.'s right hemisphere, and W.J. seemed to see nothing, to be blind (Gazzaniga et al., 1962). Gazzaniga calls the discovery that W.J.'s right hemisphere was saying nothing "one of those unforgettable moments in life." Was it true that W.J.'s left hemisphere could talk but not his right?

Testing a patient. To determine what each hemisphere can and cannot do, we can watch as Gazzaniga tests Victoria after her split-brain operation.

Victoria is asked to stare at the black dot between *HE* and *ART* as the word *HEART* is displayed on a screen. Because Victoria's hemispheres are split, information from each side of the black dot will go only to the opposite hemisphere (figure below). This means that Victoria's left hemisphere will see only the word *ART* and her right hemisphere will see only the word *HE*.

When asked, "What did you see?" Victoria says that she saw the word *ART* because it was projected to the left hemisphere, which has the ability to speak.

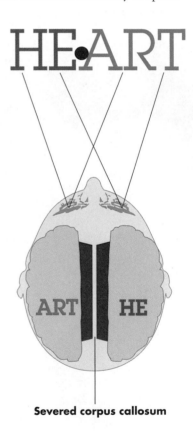

Severed corpus callosum

Although Victoria's right hemisphere saw the word *HE,* the right hemisphere turns out to be mute, meaning that it cannot say what it saw. However, Victoria can point with her left hand to a photo of a man (HE), indicating that the right hemisphere understood the question and saw the word *HE*. (Victoria points with her left hand because her right hemisphere controls the left side of the body.) Although the effects of having a split brain are obvious under special testing, the effects are not so apparent in everyday life.

How does a split brain affect behavior?

Initially after her operation, Victoria reported that when she would choose clothes from her closet, her right hand would grab a blouse but then her left hand would put it back. However, these obvious conflicts between hemispheres are rare and disappear with time.

Four months after her operation, Victoria was alert and talked easily about past and present events. She could read, write, reason, and perform everyday functions such as eating, dressing, and walking, as well as carry on normal conversations. For Victoria with her split brain, as well as for most of us with normal brains, only the left hemisphere can express itself through the spoken word (Gazzaniga, 2000). If the speech area is in the left hemisphere, the right hemisphere is usually mute. (For a small percentage of left-handers, the speech area is in the right hemisphere and the left hemisphere is usually mute.) After testing split-brain patients, researchers discovered that each hemisphere is specialized for performing certain tasks (Gazzaniga, 2005).

Different Functions of Hemispheres

Before observing split-brain patients, researchers knew very little about how each hemisphere functioned. But after studying the behaviors of split-brain patients, researchers gained a whole new understanding of what task each hemisphere does best.

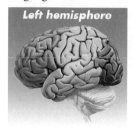

Verbal. Left hemisphere is very good at all language-related abilities: speaking, understanding language, carrying on a conversation, reading, writing, spelling.

Mathematical. Left hemisphere is very good at mathematical skills: adding, subtracting, multiplying, dividing, solving complex problems in calculus and physics, and so on. Generally, the right hemisphere can perform simple addition and subtraction but not more complex mathematics (Sperry, 1974).

Analytic. Left hemisphere appears to process information by analyzing each separate piece that makes up a whole. For example, the left hemisphere would recognize a face by analyzing piece by piece its many separate parts: nose, eyes, lips, cheeks, and so on—a relatively slow process (J. Levy & Trevarthen, 1976).

Recognizing self. Left hemisphere is primarily involved in identifying one's own face, distinguishing one's face from others, as well as in memories and knowledge of oneself. Thus, the left brain contributes to the conscious understanding of oneself (Turk, 2002).

Nonverbal. Although usually mute, the right hemisphere has a childlike ability to read, write, spell, and understand speech (Gazzaniga, 1998). For example, when spoken to, the right hemisphere can understand simple sentences and read simple words.

Spatial. Right hemisphere is very good at solving spatial problems, such as arranging blocks to match a geometric design. Because hemispheres control opposite sides of the body, the left hand (right hemisphere) is best at arranging blocks, a spatial task.

Holistic. Right hemisphere appears to process information by combining parts into a meaningful whole. For this reason, the right hemisphere is better at recognizing and identifying whole faces (J. Levy et al., 1972). The right hemisphere is also good at making and recognizing emotional facial expressions (Springer & Deutsch, 1997).

Recognizing others. Right hemisphere is involved in recognizing familiar faces but not in recognizing one's own face, which primarily involves the left hemisphere (Turk, 2002).

After comparing the left and right hemispheres' functions, you can see that each hemisphere has specialized skills and is better at performing particular tasks. Some hemisphere specializations begin very early in life. For example, left-brain specialization for language appears as early as 2 to 3 months of age (B. Bower, 2003a). These differences raise a popular question: Am I right-brained or left-brained?

The popular press has exaggerated the idea that you are either "right-brained"—creative, intuitive—or "left-brained"—reasonable, logical, and rational.

According to Jerre Levy (1985), who has devoted her career to studying how the brain's hemispheres interact, these distinctions are much too simple. She believes that we are constantly using both hemispheres, since each hemisphere is specialized for processing certain kinds of information. For example, when you read a novel, you are probably using programs in the left hemisphere that allow you to understand language in written form. But at the same time, you are using programs in the right hemisphere to keep track of the overall story, appreciate its humor and emotional content, and interpret any illustrations. Although hemispheres may sometimes work alone, they share much of their information by passing it quickly back and forth through the corpus callosum.

How is my brain organized? Michael Gazzaniga (1998), a cognitive neuroscientist who has studied split-brain patients for over 45 years, believes that each hemisphere of the brain has many different mental programs, such as sensing, thinking, learning, feeling, and speaking, all of which can function simultaneously. For example, when you see someone smile, your brain uses dozens of mental programs from each hemisphere to receive, interpret, and respond to this relatively simple emotional facial expression.

According to Gazzaniga, the brain and mind are built from separate units or modules that are interconnected and work together to carry out specific functions, much as your computer uses many separate programs to perform many different tasks.

✔ Summary Test

A. Genes & Evolution

1. A fertilized egg, which is called a (a)_____, contains 46 chromosomes arranged in 23 pairs. A hairlike structure that contains tightly coiled strands of the chemical DNA (deoxyribonucleic acid) is called a (b)_____. A specific segment on the strand of DNA that contains instructions for making proteins is called a (c)_____.

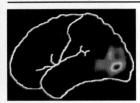

2. In 1859, Charles Darwin published a revolutionary theory of (a)_____, which said that different species arose from a common (b)_____ and that those species survived that were best adapted to meet the demands of their (c)_____.

B. Studying the Living Brain

3. There are several recently developed techniques for studying the living brain. One technique, which measures nonharmful radio frequencies as they pass through the brain, is called an (a)_____ and is used to identify structures in the living brain. Another technique measures how much of a radioactive substance is taken up by brain cells and is called a (b)_____. This kind of scan is used to study brain function and identify the most and least active parts.

C. Organization of the Brain

4. The human nervous system is divided into two major parts. The brain and spinal cord make up the (a)_____. The network of nerves outside the brain and spinal cord makes up the (b)_____.

5. The peripheral nervous system is further divided into two parts. One part is made up of a network of nerves that either carry messages to muscles and organs throughout the body or carry input from sensory receptors to the spinal cord; this is called the (a)_____. The second part of the peripheral nervous system, which regulates heart rate, breathing, digestion, secretion of hormones, and related responses, is called the (b)_____.

6. The human brain is divided into three major parts. The largest part is involved in cognitive responses that we characterize as most human. This part is called the (a)_____, which is divided into right and left hemispheres. The part that is involved in controlling vital reflexes, sleeping, and coordinating body movements is called the (b)_____. The part that is involved in visual

and auditory reflexes, as well as alerting the brain to incoming sensations, is called the (c)_____.

7. Beginning in the midbrain and extending downward is a long column of cells called the _____ that alerts the forebrain to incoming sensory information.

8. The hindbrain consists of three structures. The structure that serves as a bridge to connect the brain and body and also manufactures chemicals involved in sleep is called the (a)_____. The structure that controls vital reflexes, such as heart rate, blood pressure, and respiration, is called the (b)_____. The structure that was assumed to be involved primarily in coordinating body movements but has recently been found to have a role in cognitive functions, such as short-term memory, following rules, and carrying out plans, is called the (c)_____.

D. Control Centers: Four Lobes

9. The thin outside layer of cells that has a wrinkled look and covers almost the entire forebrain is called the (a)_____. This layer of cells is divided into four separate areas or lobes: (b)_____, _____, _____, and _____.

10. The lobe that is involved in controlling social-emotional behaviors, maintaining a healthy personality, and making and carrying out plans is called the _____ lobe.

11. At the back edge of the frontal lobe is a continuous strip called the _____, which controls the movement of voluntary muscles. Body parts that have greater capacity for complicated muscle movement have more area on the motor cortex devoted to them.

12. Along the front edge of the parietal lobe is a continuous strip that receives sensations from the body and is called the _____. Body parts with greater sensitivity have more area on the somatosensory cortex devoted to them.

13. An area on the upper edge of the temporal lobe that receives signals from receptors in the ears and changes them into basic auditory sensations is called the (a)_____. For most individuals, an area in the left temporal lobe is involved in understanding and speaking coherently; it is called (b)_____ area. Damage to this area results in inability to understand spoken and written speech or to speak coherently, a problem called (c)_____. An area in the frontal lobe, called (d)_____, is necessary for producing words and arranging them into fluent sentences. If this area is damaged, the result is a speech problem called (e)_____.

14. An area at the very back of the occipital lobe that receives signals from receptors in the eyes and changes them into basic visual sensations is called the _____.

15. The vast majority of the cortex making up the four lobes is involved in adding meaning, interpretations, and associations to sensory stimuli, as well as in many cognitive functions. Together, these areas are called _____ areas.

E. Limbic System: Old Brain

16. Inside the forebrain is a central core of interconnected structures known as the primitive, or "animal," brain or, more technically, the (a)_____. Four of the areas that make up the limbic system are the (b)_____, _____, _____, and _____, which are all involved in motivational and emotional behaviors.

17. One structure of the limbic system, the hypothalamus, controls the autonomic nervous system, which has two divisions. The one that arouses the body, increases physiological responses (such as heart rate and blood pressure), and prepares the body for the fight-flight response is called the (a)_____. The division that calms down the body and aids digestion is called the (b)_____. These two divisions work together to keep the body's internal organs in a balanced physiological state, which is called (c)_____.

F. Endocrine System

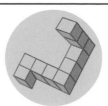

18. Besides the nervous system, a network of glands regulates organs through the secretion of hormones. This chemical system is called the (a)_____. A major gland that controls other glands in this system is the (b)_____ gland, which has an anterior and posterior parts.

G. Research Focus: Sex Differences in the Brain?

19. Structural or functional differences in the brain that arise from being male or female are called _____. One example of sex differences in the brain is that males primarily use the frontal area to solve spatial problems, while females use the parietal-temporal area.

H. Cultural Diversity: Brain Size & Racial Myths

20. In the 1800s, one scientist measured skull size and concluded that a larger brain indicated more intelligence and that the races could be ranked by brain size. However, further analysis of this researcher's data indicated that there was no basis for ranking races by (a)_____. More recent experiments that precisely measured brain size with MRI scans found a modest correlation between brain size and (b)_____. However, we do not know if a stimulating environment causes the brain to grow more or if a larger brain is able to absorb more from the environment.

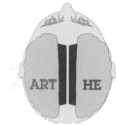

I. Application: Split Brain

21. The two hemispheres are connected by a major bundle of fibers that is called the _____. Severing this structure produces a condition called a split brain.

22. For most individuals, mental programs for language, speech, and mathematics, as well as for distinguishing one's face from others and for memories and knowledge of oneself, are located in the (a)_____; mental programs for solving spatial problems, processing emotional responses, and recognizing familiar faces are located in the (b)_____. In addition, the hemispheres process information in different ways. The left hemisphere processes information in a more piece-by-piece fashion or (c)_____ way. In comparison, the right hemisphere processes information as a meaningful whole; that is, it uses a more (d)_____ approach.

23. One theory of brain organization says that your brain has many separate but interconnected _____ programs that function and work together so that you can perform many cognitive skills.

Answers: *1. (a) zygote, (b) chromosome, (c) gene; 2. (a) evolution, (b) ancestor, (c) environment; 3. (a) MRI scan, (b) PET scan; 4. (a) central nervous system, (b) peripheral nervous system; 5. (a) somatic nervous system, (b) autonomic nervous system; 6. (a) forebrain, (b) hindbrain, (c) midbrain; 7. reticular formation; 8. (a) pons, (b) medulla, (c) cerebellum; 9. (a) cortex, (b) frontal, parietal, temporal, occipital; 10. frontal; 11. motor cortex; 12. somatosensory cortex; 13. (a) primary auditory cortex, (b) Wernicke's, (c) Wernicke's aphasia, (d) Broca's area, (e) Broca's aphasia; 14. primary visual cortex; 15. association; 16. (a) limbic system, (b) hippocampus, hypothalamus, thalamus, amygdala; 17. (a) sympathetic division, (b) parasympathetic division, (c) homeostasis; 18. (a) endocrine system, (b) pituitary; 19. sex differences; 20. (a) brain size, (b) intelligence; 21. corpus callosum; 22. (a) left hemisphere, (b) right hemisphere, (c) analytic, (d) holistic; 23. mental*

Critical Thinking

When Is a Person Brain Dead?

Questions

1. What part of the brain allows Terri to breathe?

2. How would Terri respond to being poked with a needle?

3. Do Terri's abilities to function fit with severe damage to the cortex?

Terri Schiavo, a 27-year-old woman, suffers a heart attack that results in her losing consciousness. During the next 15 years, she never regains consciousness and lives in nursing homes under constant care. Terri is fed and hydrated through tubes, and has her diapers changed regularly. She can still breathe without a respirator and can even open her eyes. Terri will at times turn toward her mother's voice and smile, make sounds similar to laughter, and has seemingly followed a balloon with her eyes. Despite these abilities and movements, Terri remains completely unaware of her surroundings.

Doctors describe Terri's condition as a persistent vegetative state, meaning she has severe brain damage to the cortex resulting in long-term loss of cognitive function and awareness, but retains basic physiological functions, such as breathing and the sleep-wake cycle. Doctors say that her responses, including following an object with her eyes, are reflexive, not intentional, and commonly occur spontaneously with people in a vegetative state.

As a result of being in a vegetative state for over a decade, Terri's brain severely deteriorated. Brain scans (see top photo) show that much of her cortex is gone and is replaced with spinal fluid, a condition that is incurable. All that remains is enough of a brain stem (includes midbrain, pons, and medulla,

p. 73) to keep certain basic life functions working (e.g., heart rate, breathing, arousal, visual and auditory reflexes). Many doctors conclude Terri will forever remain unconscious and be completely dependent on others, as she has been for the past 15 years.

Given the doctors' serious doubt that Terri's condition will ever improve, how long should she remain on a feeding tube? This question stirred tremendous debate between her husband who wanted the feeding tube to be removed and her parents who wanted it to remain. The decision over Terri's future even received attention by the courts, the President, religious leaders, and many protestors arguing both sides of the debate. Some referred to removing the feeding tube as euthanasia, while others believed she died years ago following her heart attack.

Finally, after years of controversy, the court ordered the removal of the feeding tube. Terri died 13 days following its removal, and her autopsy showed she had massive and irreversible brain damage that shrunk her brain to about half of its expected size and she was blind. The medical examiner commented on Terri's potential for recovery by stating: "No amount of therapy or treatment would have regenerated the massive loss of neurons" (Associated Press, 2005b). (Adapted from Associated Press, 2005a, 2005b; Eisenberg, 2005; Russell, 2005)

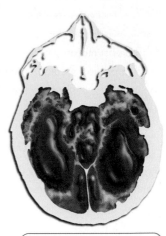

Brain scan shows dark blue areas that are filled with fluid, which has replaced brain tissue.

4. What defines brain death?

5. What type of treatment(s) can be used to help regenerate neurons?

Suggested Answers

1. The medulla is located at the top of the spinal cord and controls vital reflexes, such as breathing, heart rate, and blood pressure.
2. Terri's body may flinch even though she is unaware of being poked, and she would not feel any pain because her cortex, responsible for experiencing pain, is severely damaged.
3. Yes. The cortex is responsible for hundreds of "higher-order" functions, such as planning, deciding, reasoning, seeing, speaking, and hearing, none of which Terri is able to do.
4. Brain death can be defined as whole-brain or higher-brain death. Whole-brain death means the cortex and brain stem have shut

down, leaving the person unable to move or breathe independently, and there is no brain activity. Higher-brain death means the brain stem still functions, keeping the vital organs working, but the cortex is shut off. Terri's brain stem is functioning, so she is brain dead only according to the higher-brain death definition.

5. Still experimental treatments, fetal brain tissue transplants (p. 60) show promise in surviving and making new connections in the brain, and stem cell transplants (p. 60) are being used to form new neurons.

Links to Learning

Learning Activities

- **POWERSTUDY FOR INTRODUCTION TO PSYCHOLOGY 4.0**
  by Tom Doyle and Rod Plotnik

  SuperModule: Check out "Incredible Nervous System" on **PowerStudy**. It includes complete paragraph-by-paragraph explanations of all content using fully-narrated animations and graphics. An onscreen toolbar allows immediate access to text, text outline, and module glossary with notetaking and printing capabilities. This module also includes:

  - Videos—Imbedded videos cover scans of the nervous system, an exploration of temporal lobe damage, and a demonstration of split brain research.
  - A multitude of animations—for example, a breakdown of the chromosomal genetic instructions and a virtual discussion of the different types of brain imaging techniques.
  - A test of your knowledge using an interactive version of the Summary Test on pages 88 and 89. Also access related quizzing—true/false, multiple choice, and matching.
  - An interactive version of the Critical Thinking exercise "When Is a Person Brain Dead??" on page 90.
  - Key terms, a chapter outline including chapter abstract, and a special extended list of hotlinked websites that correlate to this module.

- *CengageNOW*
  academic.cengage.com/login

  Need help studying? This site is your one-stop study shop.
  Take a Pre-Test and CengageNOW will generate a Personalized Study Plan based on your test results. The Study Plan will identify the topics you need to review and direct you to online resources to help you master those topics. You can then take a Post-Test to determine the concepts you have mastered and what you still need to work on.

- **INTRODUCTION TO PSYCHOLOGY BOOK COMPANION WEBSITE**
  academic.cengage.com/psychology/plotnik

  Visit your book companion website where you will find more resources to help you study. At this site, you will find Learning Objectives, Internet Exercises, quizzing, flash cards, and a pronunciation glossary.

- *STUDY GUIDE and WEBTUTOR*
  Check the corresponding module in your Study Guide for effective student tips and help learning the material presented. Also go to **academic.cengage.com/webtutor** for an interactive version of the Study Guide features.

Study Questions

*A. **Genes & Evolution**—If a species of humans with 5-pound brains were discovered, would their behavior differ from ours? (**Suggested answer page 621**)

*B. **Studying the Living Brain**—How would you know if a professional boxer had brain damage? (**Suggested answer page 621**)

C. **Organization of the Brain**—If you had to give up one part of your brain, which one would you sacrifice?

D. **Control Centers: Four Lobes**—Which brain functions would computers be the best and worst at imitating?

E. **Limbic System: Old Brain**—What would happen if your limbic system were replaced with one from an alligator?

F. **Endocrine System**—What is one reason for the different bodies of football players, soccer players, and jockeys?

G. **Research Focus: Sex Differences in the Brain?**—What's the danger of identifying sex differences in the brain?

*H. **Cultural Diversity: Brain Size & Racial Myths**—Why is there a continuing interest in whether a bigger brain is more intelligent? (**Suggested answer page 621**)

I. **Application: Split Brain**—If you were supposed to act like a person with a split brain, what would you do differently?

*These questions are answered in Appendix B.

MODULE 5
Sensation

Electric Billboard in the Brain

Can Katie see without her eyes?

Katie was looking at an electric billboard made up of 36 dots of blue, purple, red, and yellow light. The billboard wasn't on the front of a store or sports stadium; it was in her own head.

When Katie was 22, she lost her eyesight to glaucoma and lived in total darkness for the next 20 years. At the age of 42, she volunteered to have experimental surgery in which 36 tiny gold wires were implanted into the occipital lobe in the back of her brain, which is the area that processes visual information. When researchers pushed a switch, a low-level, non-harmful electrical current passed through these gold wires and activated brain cells. When the brain cells in Katie's visual area were activated, she reported seeing flashes of colored light. By adjusting the electrical current, researchers could vary the brightness and size of the flashes from a tiny dot to the size of a nickel.

Because the implanted gold wires formed a rectangular grid of 36 dots (see figure above), researchers could apply current to particular wires in the grid to form patterns of flashing dots. For example, when the flashing dots formed the pattern shown in the

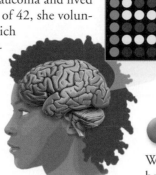

figure, Katie reported seeing the letter "S" (adapted from *Los Angeles Times,* October 30, 1992).

She can "see" the letter "S" when her brain is stimulated.

Although Katie is officially blind because her eyes are not functioning, she can still "see" flashes of colored lights when the visual area of her brain is electrically stimulated. This fact raises an interesting question: How is it possible to see without using one's eyes? As we answer this question, you'll discover that the eye, ear, nose, tongue, and skin are smaller, more complicated, and better recorders than any of the newest, miniaturized, high-tech video cameras, recorders, or digital disks on the market.

What's Coming

We'll discuss six of the major human senses—vision, hearing, balance (vestibular system), taste, olfaction (smell), and touch. We'll also explain how you see color, why some long-playing rock-and-roll musicians have become partially deaf, why you get motion sickness, and why your sense of taste decreases when you have a cold. Although your sense organs—eye, ear, tongue, nose, and skin—look so very different, they all share the three characteristics defined next.

Three Definitions

Your eyes, ears, nose, skin, and tongue are complex, miniaturized, living sense organs that automatically gather information about your environment. We begin with three definitions that will help you understand sensation.

1 Transduction. The first thing each sense organ must do is to change or transform some physical energy, such as molecules of skunk spray, into electrical signals, a process called transduction.

Electrical signal

Transduction refers to the process in which a sense organ changes, or transforms, physical energy into electrical signals that become neural impulses, which may be sent to the brain for processing.

For example, transduction occurs when a skunk's molecules enter your nose, which transforms the molecules into electrical signals, or impulses, that are interpreted by your brain as the very unpleasant odor of a skunk.

2 Adaptation. A short period of time after putting on glasses, jewelry, or clothes, you no longer "feel" them, a process called adaptation.

Adaptation refers to the decreasing response of the sense organs, the more they are exposed to a continuous level of stimulation.

For example, the continuous stimulation of glasses, jewelry, or clothes on your skin results in adaptation so that soon you no longer feel them. Some sense organs adapt very quickly, and some very slowly. However, sense organs do not adapt to intense forms of stimulation, because such stimulation may cause physical damage. Instead, intense stimulation, such as from a very hot shower, may cause pain, which warns us of possible injury.

3 Sensations versus perceptions. Gathering information about the world involves two steps. In the first step, electrical signals reach the brain and are changed into sensations.

Sensations are relatively meaningless bits of information (left figure) that result when the brain processes electrical signals that come from the sense organs.

In the second step, the brain quickly changes sensations, which you're not aware of, into perceptions.

Perceptions are meaningful sensory experiences (right figure) that result after the brain combines hundreds of sensations.

For example, visual sensations would resemble the top figure, showing meaningless lines, colors, and shapes. Visual perceptions would be like the bottom figure, showing a complete "sad-happy" face.

While all sensations begin with step 1, transduction, sense organs use different mechanisms to do it. We'll start with how the visual system works.

A. Eye: Vision

Why can't you see radio waves?

Each sense organ has a different shape and structure; it can receive only a certain kind of stimulus, or physical energy. For instance, the reason you cannot see radio waves is that their waves are not the right length. Although radio waves, along with light waves from the sun, are all forms of electromagnetic energy, they vary in wavelength. For example, the figure below shows that X rays are very short and AM radio waves are very long. Notice that only a small, specific range of wavelengths that come from a light source, called the visible spectrum, is able to excite receptors in your eyes.

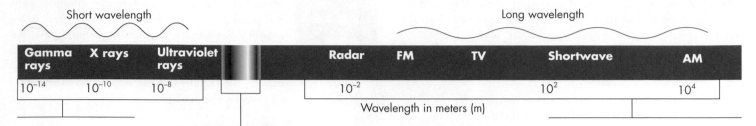

Short wavelength · Long wavelength

| Gamma rays | X rays | Ultraviolet rays | | Radar | FM | TV | Shortwave | AM |

10^{-14} 10^{-10} 10^{-8} 10^{-2} 10^{2} 10^{4}

Wavelength in meters (m)

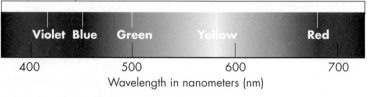

Violet Blue   Green   Yellow   Red

400   500   600   700

Wavelength in nanometers (nm)

Invisible—too short. On this side of the electromagnetic energy spectrum are shorter wavelengths, including gamma rays, X rays, and ultraviolet rays. These waves are invisible to the human eye because their lengths are too short to stimulate our receptors. However, some birds (such as hummingbirds) and insects can see ultraviolet rays to help them find food.

Visible—just right. Near the middle of the electromagnetic spectrum is a small range of waves that make up the visible spectrum.

The *visible spectrum* is one particular segment of electromagnetic energy that we can see because these waves are the right length to stimulate receptors in the eye.

The reason you can see a giraffe is that its body reflects light waves from the visible spectrum back to your eyes. One function of the eyes is to absorb light waves that are reflected back from all the objects in your environment.

Invisible—too long. On this side of the electromagnetic spectrum are longer wavelengths, such as radio and television waves. These waves are invisible to the human eye because their lengths are too long to stimulate the receptors in the eye. Imagine the awful distraction of seeing radio and television waves all day long!

Stimulus. Thus, the most effective stimulus for vision is energy (light waves) from the visible spectrum. However, for you to see anything, reflected light waves must be gathered and changed into electrical signals, and for that process—transduction—we must look inside the eye itself.

Structure and Function

How can you see a giraffe?

For you to see a 16-foot-tall giraffe, your eyes perform two separate processes. First, the eyes gather and focus light waves into a precise area at the back of your eyes. Second, this area absorbs and transforms light waves into impulses, a process known as transduction. We'll follow the path of light waves from the giraffe to the back of your eyes in a series of 7 steps.

1 Image reversed. Notice that, at the back of the eye, the giraffe appears upside down. Even though the giraffe is focused upside down in the eye, somehow the brain turns the giraffe—and all other objects we see—right side up so that we see the world as it really is.

2 Light waves. The problem with light waves is that after they strike an object, such as a giraffe, they are reflected back in a broad beam. You cannot see the giraffe unless your eyes change this broad beam of light waves into a narrow, focused one. Your eye has two structures, the cornea and the lens, that bring an image into focus, much as a camera does.

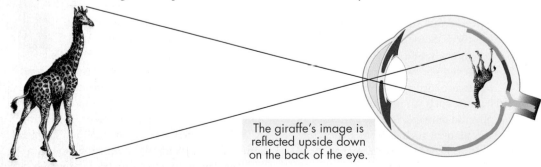

The giraffe's image is reflected upside down on the back of the eye.

3 Cornea. The broad beam of light reflected from the giraffe passes first through the cornea.

The *cornea* is the rounded, transparent covering over the front of your eye. As the light waves pass through the cornea, its curved surface bends, or focuses, the waves into a narrower beam.

4 Pupil. After passing through the cornea, light waves next go through the pupil.

The *pupil* is a round opening at the front of your eye that allows light waves to pass into the eye's interior.

Your pupil grows larger or smaller because of a muscle called the iris.

5 Iris. The opening of the pupil is surrounded by the iris.

The *iris* is a circular muscle that surrounds the pupil and controls the amount of light entering the eye. In dim light, the iris relaxes, allowing more light to enter—the pupil dilates; in bright light, the iris constricts, allowing less light to enter—the pupil constricts. The iris muscle contains the pigment that gives your eye its characteristic color.

If you look in a mirror in bright light, you will see that the iris is constricted and that your pupil—the black dot in the center of your eye—is very small.

6 Lens. After passing through the cornea and pupil, light waves reach the lens.

The *lens* is a transparent, oval structure whose curved surface bends and focuses light waves into an even narrower beam. The lens is attached to muscles that adjust the curve of the lens, which, in turn, adjusts the focusing.

For the eye to see distant objects, light waves need less bending (focusing), so muscles automatically stretch the lens so that its surface is less curved. To see near objects, light waves need more focusing, so muscles relax and allow the surface of the lens to become very curved. Making the lens more or less curved causes light waves to be focused into a very narrow beam that must be projected precisely onto an area at the very back of the eye, called the retina.

7 Retina. Although light waves have been bent and focused, transduction hasn't yet occurred. That is about to change as light waves reach the retina.

The *retina*, located at the very back of the eyeball, is a thin film that contains cells that are extremely sensitive to light. These light-sensitive cells, called photoreceptors, begin the process of transduction by absorbing light waves.

On the following page, we'll describe the two kinds of photoreceptors, how they absorb light waves, and how they carry out the process of transduction. For some people, light waves cannot be focused precisely on the retina because of a problem with the shape of their eyeballs.

Eyeball's Shape and Laser Eye Surgery

Eyeball. Some of us are born with perfectly shaped eyeballs, which contributes to having almost perfect vision. Others, however, are born with eyeballs that are a little too long or too short, resulting in two common visual problems: nearsightedness and farsightedness.

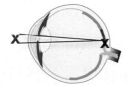 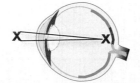  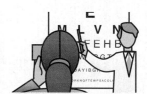

Normal vision. The shape of your eyeball is primarily determined by genetic instructions. If your eyeball is shaped so that objects are perfectly focused on the back of your retina (**black X**), then both the near and distant objects will appear clear and sharp and you will have very good vision (20/20).

Nearsighted. If you inherit an eyeball that is too long, you are likely nearsighted.

Nearsightedness (myopia) results when the eyeball is too long so that objects are focused at a point in front of the retina (**black X**). In this case, near objects are clear, but distant objects appear blurry.

Common treatments involve corrective lenses or eye surgery.

Farsighted. If you inherit an eyeball that is too short, you are likely farsighted.

Farsightedness (hyperopia) occurs when the eyeball is too short so that objects are focused at a point slightly behind the retina (**black X**). In this case, distant objects are clear, but near objects appear blurry.

Common treatments involve corrective lenses or eye surgery.

Eye surgery. Currently, a popular and successful treatment to correct nearsighted vision is called LASIK. In this procedure, the surface of the eye is folded back and a laser is used to reshape the exposed cornea so that light waves are correctly bent and focused on the retina (Koch & Harvey, 2006).

Next, we'll examine the retina more closely and see exactly how transduction occurs.

A. Eye: Vision

What happens to light waves? Some miniaturized electronic cameras can record amazingly detailed video pictures. But they are primitive compared to the retina, whose microscopic cells can transform light waves into impulses that carry detailed information to the brain about all kinds of shapes, shadows, sizes, textures, and colors. Think of the retina as a combination of a video camera and a computer whose batteries never run out as it transforms light waves into impulses—the process of transduction. And here's how transduction occurs.

You already know that an object, such as a giraffe, reflects light waves that enter the eye and are bent, focused, and projected precisely on the retina, at the very back of the eyeball.

The *retina* has three layers of cells. The back layer contains two kinds of photoreceptors that begin the process of transduction, changing light waves into electrical signals. One kind of photoreceptor with a rodlike shape is called a rod and is located primarily in the periphery of the retina. The other photoreceptor with a conelike shape is called a cone and is located primarily in the center of the retina in an area called the *fovea (FOH-vee-ah)*.

We have enlarged a section of retina to show that it has three layers. We'll explain the function of each layer. Start with #1, located below the figure on the far right, and move left to #3.

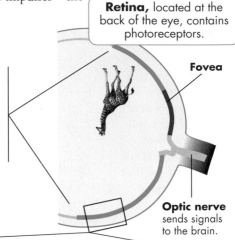

Retina, located at the back of the eye, contains photoreceptors.

Fovea

Optic nerve sends signals to the brain.

Retina blown up to show its 3 layers.

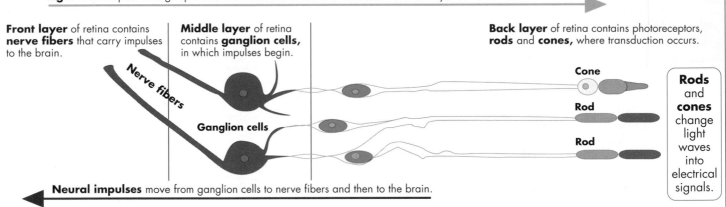

Light waves pass through spaces between cells to reach rods and cones in back layer of the retina.

Front layer of retina contains **nerve fibers** that carry impulses to the brain.

Middle layer of retina contains **ganglion cells,** in which impulses begin.

Back layer of retina contains photoreceptors, **rods** and **cones,** where transduction occurs.

Nerve fibers

Ganglion cells

Cone

Rod

Rod

Rods and **cones** change light waves into electrical signals.

Neural impulses move from ganglion cells to nerve fibers and then to the brain.

3 *Nerve impulses* generated in ganglion cells exit the back of the eye through the *optic nerve*, which carries impulses toward the brain. The point where the optic nerve exits the eye has no receptors and is called the **blind spot**. You don't notice the blind spot because your eyes are continually moving.

What's surprising about the eye is that it does not "see" but rather is a sophisticated computer for transduction, for changing light waves into impulses. For you to "see something," impulses must reach the visual areas in the brain, our next stop.

2 The process of *transduction* begins when chemicals in the rods and cones break down after absorbing light waves. This chemical breakdown generates a tiny electrical force that, if large enough, triggers *nerve impulses* in neighboring *ganglion* cells; now, transduction is complete.

1 Each eye has about 120 million rods, most located in the retina's periphery.

Rods are photoreceptors that contain a single chemical, called rhodopsin *(row-DOP-sin)*, which is activated by small amounts of light. Because rods are extremely light sensitive, they allow us to see in dim light, but to see only black, white, and shades of gray.

To see color, we need the cones. Each eye has about 6 million cones, most located in the retina's fovea (Goldstein, 2007).

Cones are photoreceptors that contain three chemicals called opsins *(OP-sins)*, which are activated in bright light and allow us to see color. Unlike rods, cones are wired individually to neighboring cells; this one-on-one system of relaying information allows us to see fine details.

Next, we finally get to transduction, which begins in the rods and cones.

How do you see rock stars?

There is a lot of truth to the old saying, "Seeing is believing," but most people don't realize that the "seeing" takes place in the brain, not in the eye. So far, we have traced the paths along which light waves enter the eye, are focused on the retina, are changed into impulses, and leave the eye on the optic nerve. Now we will follow the optic nerve as it reaches its final destination in the occipital lobe, at the back of the brain. There, the occipital lobe changes light waves into colorful rock stars.

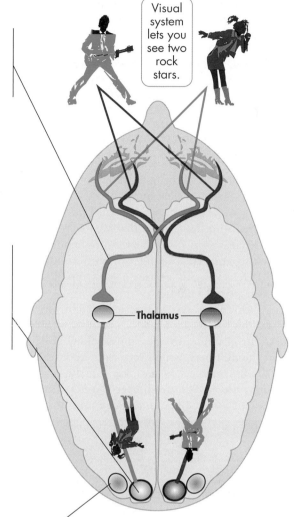

Visual system lets you see two rock stars.

Thalamus

1 Optic nerve. Nerve impulses flow through the optic nerve as it exits from the back of the eye. This exit point creates a blind spot that we do not normally see because our eyes are constantly moving and cover any areas that might be in the blind spot.

The optic nerves partially cross over and make a major stop in the *thalamus*, which does some initial processing. The thalamus relays the impulses to the back of the occipital lobe in the right and left hemispheres.

2 Primary visual cortex. At the very back of each occipital lobe lies a primary visual cortex, which transforms nerve impulses into simple visual sensations, such as texture, lines, and colors. At this point, you would report seeing only these basic sensations (left figure), not the complete figure of a rock star.

Researchers estimate that about 25% of the entire cortex is devoted to processing visual information, more area than to any other sensory input (Goldstein, 2007). The visual cortex contains many different cells that respond to many different kinds of visual stimulation.

Meaningless stimuli

Specialized cells. From the Nobel Prize–winning research of David Hubel and Torsten Wiesel (1979), we know that different cells in the *primary visual cortex* respond to specific kinds of visual stimuli. For example, some cortical cells respond to lines of a particular width, others to lines at a particular angle, and still others to lines moving in a particular direction. These specialized cortical cells transform different stimuli into simple visual sensations, such as shadows, lines, textures, or angles.

Stimulation or blindness. At the beginning of this module, we told you about Katie, who had 36 tiny wires implanted into her primary visual cortex. When electricity was passed through these wires to stimulate neurons, Katie reported seeing flashes of colored light. She did not see meaningful images, such as a singer, because neurons in the primary visual cortex produce only simple visual sensations.

If part of your primary visual cortex were damaged, you would have a blind spot in the visual field, similar to looking through glasses with tiny black spots painted on the lens. Damage to the entire primary visual cortex in both hemispheres would result in almost total blindness; the ability to tell night from day might remain.

However, to make sense of what you see, such as a rock star, nerve impulses must be sent from the primary visual cortex to neighboring visual association areas.

3 Visual association areas. The primary visual cortex sends simple visual sensations (actually, impulses) to neighboring association areas, which add meaning or *associations* (Tong, 2003). In our example, the association area receives sensations of texture, line, movement, orientation, and color and assembles them into a meaningful image of a complete rock star (left figure). There are visual association areas in each hemisphere. If part of your visual association area were damaged, you would experience *visual agnosia*, which is difficulty in assembling simple visual sensations into more complex, meaningful images (Ropper & Brown, 2005). For instance, a person with visual agnosia could see pieces of things but would have difficulty combining pieces and recognizing them as whole, meaningful objects (see p. 79).

Meaningful rock star

Researchers can use brain scans to show actual neural activity that is occurring in the visual association areas.

4 This slightly modified brain scan (p. 70) shows that when a subject is silently looking at and reading words, maximum neural activity occurs in the primary visual cortex and nearby visual association areas (red and yellow indicate maximum neural activity; blue and green indicate least). These visual areas are located in the occipital lobe (back of the brain). The visual association areas are involved in many visual activities, such as reading, writing, and perceiving objects, animals, people, and colors (Gaillard et al., 2006; Storbeck et al., 2006).

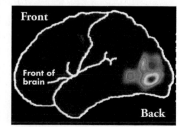

Front

Front of brain

Back

Next, we'll explain how the visual system transforms light waves into all the colors of the rainbow.

A. Eye: Vision

What is red? Debra was born with opaque films over her lenses (cataracts) that made her almost totally blind. For her first 28 years, she could tell night from day but see little else. When a newly developed operation restored much of her vision, she cried with delight as she looked around her hospital room and saw things she had only imagined. "Colors were a real surprise to me," Debra said. "They were so bright. You can't conceive what colors are until you've seen them. I couldn't imagine what a red apple looked like and now I can hold one and actually see red" (*San Diego Tribune,* April 3, 1984).

Red is actually long light waves.

Like Debra, you might assume that a red apple is really red, but you are about to discover otherwise. Objects, such as a red apple, do not have colors. Instead, objects reflect light waves whose different wavelengths are transformed by your visual system into the experience of seeing colors. So, what is red? The answer is that the color red is actually produced by a certain kind of wavelength.

How light waves are turned into millions of colors is a wondrous and interesting process, which begins with a ray of sunlight.

Making Colors from Wavelengths

1. A ray of sunlight is called white light because it contains all the light waves in the visible spectrum, which is what humans can see.

2. As white light passes through a prism, it is separated into light waves that vary in length. Nature creates prisms in the form of raindrops, which separate the passing sunlight into waves of different lengths, creating a spectrum of colors that we call a rainbow.

3. Our visual system transforms light waves of various lengths into millions of different colors. For example, in the figure below, notice that the numbers, which vary from about 400 to 700 (nanometers, or nm), indicate the length of light waves. We see shorter wavelengths as shades of violet, blue, and green, and longer

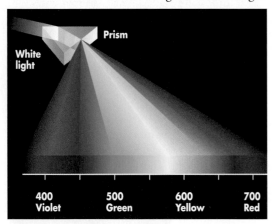

wavelengths as shades of yellow, orange, and red (Despopoulous & Silbernagl, 2003).

You see an apple as red because the apple reflects longer light waves, which your brain interprets as red.

Actually, how our visual system transforms light waves into color is explained by two different theories—the trichromatic and opponent-process theories—which we'll examine next.

Trichromatic Theory

The explanation of how you see the many colors in the native face (left photo) began over 200 years ago with the early work of a British physicist, Thomas Young. It was his research that laid the basis for a theory of how you see colors, called the trichromatic *(TRI-crow-MAH-tic)* theory of color.

All colors are made from mixing 3 primary colors: red, green, and blue.

The *trichromatic theory* says that there are three different kinds of cones in the retina, and each cone contains one of three different light-sensitive chemicals, called opsins. Each of the three opsins is most responsive to wavelengths that correspond to each of the three primary colors: blue, green, and red. All other colors can be mixed from these three primary colors.

According to the recent version of the trichromatic theory, you see the red around the man's eyes because this area reflects light waves of a longer wavelength. You see the green in the feathers because they reflect light waves of medium length. You see the blue in the headband because it reflects light waves of shorter length. The different lengths of light waves are absorbed by three different cones whose chemicals (opsins) are most sensitive to one of the three primary colors—red, green, blue (right figure). Thus, wavelengths of different lengths are changed into one of the three primary colors, which are mixed to produce all colors (Goldstein, 2007).

Until recently, color vision was believed to involve only three genes, one each to code the three primary colors of red, green, and blue. Researchers discovered that we had as many as two to nine genes (thus two to nine cones) that code the longer wavelengths involved in seeing red (Neitz & Neitz, 1995). This means that seeing a particular color, such as red, depends on how many color genes you have inherited.

For example, which bar on the TV (below) you label as "red" depends on which of the genes (two to nine) you've inherited. One person may label deep scarlet as "red" while another sees a pale red. This means that different people may see and label the "same" color, red, very differently (scarlet to pale red), and this difference explains why people may not agree about adjusting the color (red) on their television sets (Lipkin, 1995; Yanoff et al., 2003). Thus, your perception of the color "red" may differ from someone who has different "color genes."

People do NOT all see the same color of red.

To understand how color coding occurs in the brain, we need to examine the second theory of color vision, the opponent-process theory.

Opponent-Process Theory

If you stare at a red square for about 20 seconds and then immediately look at a white piece of paper, you'll see a green square, which is called an afterimage.

An *afterimage* is a visual sensation that continues after the original stimulus is removed.

And if you stare at a blue square, you'll see a yellow afterimage. On the basis of his work with afterimages, physiologist Ewald Hering suggested that the visual system codes color by using two complementary pairs—red-green and blue-yellow. Hering's idea became known as the opponent-process theory.

The *opponent-process theory* says that ganglion cells in the retina and cells in the thalamus of the brain respond to two pairs of colors—red-green and blue-yellow. When these cells are excited, they respond to one color of the pair; when inhibited, they respond to the complementary pair.

For example, some ganglion and thalamic cells use a *red-green* paired combination: they signal red when excited and green when inhibited.

Other ganglion and thalamic cells use a *yellow-blue* paired combination: they signal blue when excited and yellow when inhibited.

Thus, different parts of the visual system use different methods to code different colors.

Theories Combined

Because we see colors so automatically and naturally, we don't realize it involves both the opponent-process and trichromatic theories. Here's what happens when we combine the two theories to explain color vision.

First, the trichromatic theory says that there are usually three different kinds of cones (there may be as many as nine) in the retina. Each cone absorbs light waves of different lengths, which correspond to the three primary colors of blue, green, and red. Second, when electrical signals (color information) reach the ganglion cells in the retina and neurons in the thalamus, they use the opponent-process theory, which involves a pair of colors: Activation results in one color of a pair, and inhibition results in the other color. Third, nerve

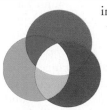
impulses carry this color information to the visual cortex, where other neurons respond and give us the experience of seeing thousands of colors, which can be made by combining the three primary colors of red, green, and blue.

Although most of us have good color vision, some individuals have varying degrees of color blindness.

Color Blindness

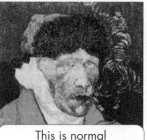
This is normal color vision.

The vast majority of us have normal color vision. We see the man on the left with a pinkish face, pale yellow scarf, purple hat, blue coat with orange trim, and brown pipe giving off yellow smoke, all against a two-toned orange background. However, about 1 out of 20 men in the United States see this same man in different shades of greens (photo below right) because they have inherited the most common form of color blindness.

Color blindness is the inability to distinguish two or more shades in the color spectrum. There are several kinds of color blindness.

Monochromats (MOHN-oh-crow-mats) have total color blindness; their worlds look like black-and-white movies. This kind of color blindness is rare and results from individuals having only rods or only one kind of functioning cone (instead of three).

This is red-green color blindness.

Dichromats (DIE-crow-mats) usually have trouble distinguishing red from green because they have just two kinds of cones. This is an inherited genetic defect, found mostly in males, that results in seeing mostly shades of green (right photo) but differs in severity (Neitz et al., 1996).

People don't always realize they have color blindness. For example, a little boy came home complaining about being chased by a green dog. The dog really looked green to the little boy; he did not know he had a form of color blindness.

People in some occupations, such as electrical technicians, are screened for color blindness because they must identify differently colored wires.

Below, you see two circles filled with colored dots that are part of a test for color blindness. An individual taking this test is asked to look at each circle and identify what, if any, number is formed by the colored dots.

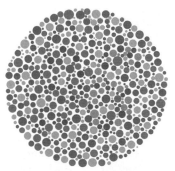

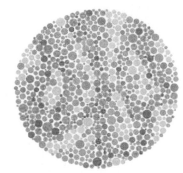

Individuals with normal vision see the number 96, while people with red-green color deficits find this number difficult or impossible to see.

Those with normal color vision and total color blindness should not be able to read any number. The majority of those with red-green deficiencies should read the number 5.

From our discussion of the eye's structure and function, you can see that the eye is an engineering marvel that makes even the most sophisticated video camera seem like an expensive toy.

Next, we'll examine an equally astonishing sense organ, the ear.

B. Ear: Audition

What happens when someone yells?

When a cheerleader gives a big yell, she is actually producing the yell by letting out air so that it is alternately compressed and expanded into traveling waves, called sound waves.

Sound waves, **which are the stimuli for hearing (audition), resemble ripples of different sizes. Similar to ripples on a pond, sound waves travel through space with varying heights and frequency. Height, which is the distance from the bottom to the top of a sound wave, is called amplitude. Frequency refers to the number of sound waves that occur within 1 second.**

We'll demonstrate the concept of amplitude by comparing sound waves of a cheerleader's yell with a child's whisper.

Amplitude and Loudness

Yell. As a cheerleader yells, she lets out an enormous amount of air that is compressed and expanded into very large traveling waves (shown below). Large sound waves are described as having high amplitude, which the brain interprets as loud sounds.

High amplitude means big sound waves and loud sounds.

Whisper. As a child whispers a secret to his friend, he lets out a small amount of air that is compressed and expanded into very small traveling waves. Small sound waves are described as having low amplitude, which the brain interprets as soft sounds.

 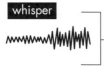

Low amplitude means small sound waves and soft sounds.

Relationship: amplitude and loudness. You have no difficulty distinguishing between a cheerleader's yell and a child's whisper because your auditory system automatically uses the amplitude of the sound waves to calculate loudness (Ganong, 2005).

Loudness **is your subjective experience of a sound's intensity. The brain calculates loudness from specific physical energy, in this case the amplitude of sound waves.**

A whisper, which results in low-amplitude sound waves, is just above our threshold of hearing. The loudest yell on record, which resulted in high-amplitude sound waves, was about as loud as sound heard near speakers at a rock concert.

If the brain uses amplitude to calculate loudness, what does it use to calculate a sound's low or high pitch?

Frequency and Pitch

Screech or boom. As you listen to someone playing a keyboard, you can tell the difference between high and low notes because your brain is continually discriminating between high and low sounds, which is called pitch.

High frequency means sound waves are close together, resulting in high sounds or pitch.

Low frequency means sound waves are apart, resulting in low sounds or pitch.

High note. Striking the top key on a keyboard produces sound waves that travel rapidly and are described as having high frequency. The brain interprets high frequency as high notes or high pitch.

Low note. Striking the bottom key on a keyboard produces sound waves that travel slowly and are described as having low frequency. The brain interprets slow frequency as low notes or low pitch.

Relationship: frequency and pitch. When you hear a sound, your auditory system automatically uses frequency to calculate pitch (Ganong, 2005).

Pitch **is our subjective experience of a sound being high or low, which the brain calculates from specific physical stimuli, in this case the speed or frequency of sound waves. The frequency of sound waves is measured in cycles, which refers to how many sound waves occur within 1 second.**

For example, playing the keyboard's highest key produces sound waves with a fast frequency (4,000 cycles per second), which results in high sounds or high pitch; the keyboard's lowest key produces sound waves of slower frequency (27 cycles per second), which results in low sounds or low pitch.

Hearing range. Humans hear sounds only within a certain range of frequencies, and this range decreases with age. For example, infants have the widest range of hearing, from frequencies of 20 to 20,000 cycles per second. For college students, it is perhaps 30 to 18,000 cycles per second. With further aging, the hearing range decreases even more so that by age 70, many people have trouble hearing sounds above 6,000 cycles per second.

Next, we'll see how loud a jet plane is compared to a whisper.

How loud is the library?

MEASURING SOUND WAVES

If the sign on the right were posted in the library, you might not know that it refers to loudness, which is measured in decibels (dB).

A *decibel* is a unit to measure loudness, just as an inch is a measure of length. Our threshold for hearing ranges from 0 decibels, which is absolutely no sound, to 140 decibels, which can produce pain and permanent hearing loss.

The following table contains common sounds with their decibel levels. Notice especially those sound levels that can cause permanent hearing loss.

Please Do Not Talk Above 30 Decibels

Decibel (dB) level	Sounds and their decibel levels	Exposure time and permanent hearing loss
140	Jet engine, gun muzzle blast	Any exposure to sounds this loud is painful and dangerous. That's why aircraft ground personnel must wear ear protectors.
120	Rock concert near speakers, thunderclap, record-setting human yell (115 dB)	Exposure for 15 minutes or less can produce hearing loss. Rock musicians and fans who do not use ear plugs risk hearing loss.
100	Chain saw, jackhammer, baby screaming, inside of racing car, firecracker	Exposure for 2 hours or more can cause hearing loss. Workers using loud power tools who do not use ear protectors risk hearing loss.
80	Heavy city traffic, alarm clock at 2 feet, subway, MP3 player, personal CD player	Constant exposure for 8 hours can produce hearing loss. Music lovers should know that stereo headphones can produce sounds from 80 to 115 dB.
60	Conversation, air conditioner at 20 feet, typewriter	Aging decreases hearing sensitivity, and that's why older adults may ask, "What did you say?" indicating that they may not easily hear normal conversations.
30	Whisper, quiet library, car idling in neutral (45 dB)	Today's cars are engineered for quietness. At idle, many cars are almost as quiet as a library; and at 65 mph (70 dB), they are not much louder than a conversation.
0	Threshold of hearing	If you were boating in the middle of a calm lake, you might say, "Now, this is really quiet." In comparison, most of us are accustomed to relatively noisy city environments.

DECIBELS AND DEAFNESS

It is now well established that continuous exposure to sounds with higher decibel levels for certain periods of time can produce permanent hearing loss. For example, rock musicians, rock fans, hunters, drivers of heavy machinery, airplane workers, and stereo headphone listeners who take no precautions against high decibel levels may suffer significant, permanent hearing losses later (Lalwani & Snow, 2006).

At the end of this module (p. 115) we'll discuss different causes of deafness and treatment. Now, we'll take you inside the ear and explain how it turns sound waves into wonderful sounds.

B. Ear: Audition

Outer, Middle, and Inner Ear

Is that the Rolling Stones or a barking dog?

Most of us think that we hear with our ears and that's how we tell the difference between, for example, the music of the Rolling Stones and the barking of a dog. But nothing is further from the truth. What really happens is that both music and a dog's barks produce only sound waves, which are just the stimulus for hearing (audition). Your ears receive sound waves, but it is your brain that actually does the hearing, distinguishing the difference between the Stones' song, "(I Can't Get No) Satisfaction," and a dog's barks. It's a complicated journey; the first step begins in the outer ear.

1 Outer Ear

The only reason your ear has that peculiar shape and sticks out from the side of your head is to gather in sound waves. Thus, sound waves produced by the Rolling Stones are gathered by your outer ear.

The *outer* ear consists of three structures: external ear, auditory canal, and tympanic membrane.

The *external ear* is an oval-shaped structure that protrudes from the side of the head. The function of the external ear is to pick up sound waves and send them down a long, narrow tunnel called the auditory canal.

1a The *auditory canal* is a long tube that funnels sound waves down its length so that the waves strike a thin, taut membrane—the eardrum, or tympanic membrane.

In some cases, the auditory canal may become clogged with ear wax, which interferes with sound waves on their way to the eardrum. Ear wax should be removed by a professional so as not to damage the fragile eardrum.

1b The *tympanic (tim-PAN-ick) membrane* is a taut, thin structure commonly called the eardrum. Sound waves strike the tympanic membrane and cause it to vibrate. The tympanic membrane passes the vibrations on to the first of three small bones to which it is attached.

The tympanic membrane marks the boundary between the outer ear and the middle ear, described below left in #2.

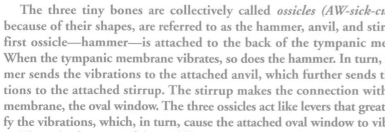

Sound waves

2 Middle Ear

The middle ear functions like a radio's amplifier; it picks up and increases, or amplifies, vibrations.

The *middle ear* is a bony cavity that is sealed at each end by membranes. The two membranes are connected by three small bones.

The three tiny bones are collectively called *ossicles (AW-sick-culls)* and, because of their shapes, are referred to as the hammer, anvil, and stirrup. The first ossicle—hammer—is attached to the back of the tympanic membrane. When the tympanic membrane vibrates, so does the hammer. In turn, the hammer sends the vibrations to the attached anvil, which further sends the vibrations to the attached stirrup. The stirrup makes the connection with the end membrane, the oval window. The three ossicles act like levers that greatly amplify the vibrations, which, in turn, cause the attached oval window to vibrate.

Thus, the function of the middle ear is to pick up vibrations produced by the tympanic membrane, amplify these vibrations, and pass them on to the oval window, which marks the end of middle ear and beginning of the inner ear.

3 Inner Ear

The inner ear contains two main structures that are sealed in bony cavities: the cochlea, which is involved in hearing, and the vestibular system, which is involved in balance. We'll discuss the vestibular system on page 105; now, we'll focus on the cochlea.

The *cochlea (KOCK-lee-ah)*, located in the inner ear, has a bony coiled exterior that resembles a snail's shell. The cochlea contains the receptors for hearing, and its function is transduction—transforming vibrations into nerve impulses that are sent to the brain for processing into auditory information.

Researchers liken the cochlea to an exquisite miniature box that is made of bone and contains precious jewels, which in this case are miniature cells that are the receptors for hearing.

On the next page, we have enlarged and opened the cochlea so you can see the auditory receptors.

3 Inner Ear (continued)

3a If you were to take two drinking straws, hold them side by side, and then wind them around your finger, you would have a huge model of a cochlea. The cochlea consists of two long narrow tubes (straws) separated by membranes (basilar and tectorial) but joined together and rolled up, or coiled. The beginning of the coiled compartments is sealed by a membrane, the oval window. So when the ossicles vibrate the oval window, the oval window vibrates the fluid in the cochlea's tubes, where the auditory receptors are located.

3b The auditory receptors, called *hair cells,* are miniature hair-shaped cells that stick up from the cochlea's bottom membrane, called the *basilar (BAZ-ih-lahr) membrane.* Vibration of fluid in the cochlear tubes causes movement of the basilar membrane, which literally bends the hair cells. The mechanical bending of the hair cells generates miniature electrical forces that, if large enough, trigger nerve impulses (transduction). Nerve impulses leave the cochlea as explained at right in #3c.

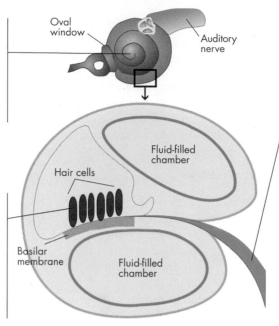

Cochlea changes vibrations into electrical signals.

Cross Section of Cochlea

3c The *auditory nerve* is a band of fibers that carry nerve impulses (electrical signals) to the auditory cortex of the brain for processing.

Now the cochlea has completed its role of transduction—transforming vibrations into nerve impulses. However, you won't report hearing anything until the impulses reach your brain.

Auditory Brain Areas

How do we tell noise from music?

Just as your eye does not see, your ear does not hear. Rather, sense organs, such as the ear, perform only transduction—transform physical energy into nerve impulses. You don't hear or recognize sound as noise, music, or words until nerve impulses are processed by various auditory areas in the temporal lobes of your brain.

4 Sensations and Perceptions

After nerve impulses reach the brain, a two-step process occurs in which nerve impulses are transformed first into meaningless bits of sounds and then into meaningful sounds. The first step occurs in the primary auditory area, explained in #4a.

4a The *primary auditory cortex,* which is located at the top edge of the temporal lobe, transforms nerve impulses (electrical signals) into basic auditory sensations, such as meaningless sounds and tones of various pitches and loudness.

Next, the primary auditory cortex sends impulses (sensations) to the auditory association area, explained in #4b.

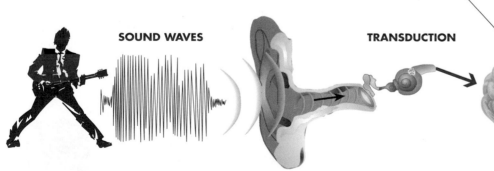

SOUND WAVES **TRANSDUCTION** **HEARING**

Temporal lobe

4b The *auditory association area* receives meaningless auditory sensations in the form of neural impulses from the neighboring primary auditory cortex. The auditory association area combines meaningless auditory sensations into perceptions, which are meaningful melodies, songs, words, or sentences.

It takes only a moment from the time sound waves enter your ear until you say, "That's the Stones' song, '(I Can't Get No) Satisfaction.'" But during that amazing moment, sound waves were changed into impulses, impulses into sensations, and finally, sensations into perceptions (Goldstein, 2007).

Now we'll explain how the brain uses nerve impulses to calculate where a sound is coming from, whether it is a high or low sound, and whether it is a loud or soft sound.

B. Ear: Audition

Where's the sound coming from?

If someone yelled "Watch out!" you would immediately turn your head toward the source of the sound because your brain automatically calculates the source's location. The brain calculates not only the source of the voice but also whether the voice calling your name is high or low or loud or soft. Thus, sound waves contain an amazing amount of information. We'll begin with how your brain calculates the direction of where a sound is coming from.

Calculating Direction

You automatically turn toward the source of the yell "Watch out!" because your brain instantly calculates the direction or source.

The brain determines the *direction of a sound* by calculating the slight difference in time (see #1 in right figure) that it takes sound waves to reach the two ears, which are about six inches apart (see #2 in right figure) (Goldstein, 2007).

If you have difficulty telling where a sound is coming from, the sound is probably arriving at both ears simultaneously. To locate the direction, you can turn your head from side to side, causing the sound to reach one ear before the other.

The brain uses other cues to calculate a sound's high or low pitch.

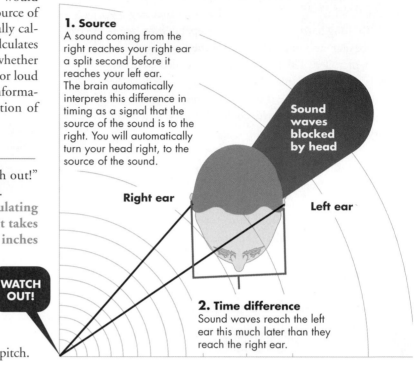

1. Source
A sound coming from the right reaches your right ear a split second before it reaches your left ear. The brain automatically interprets this difference in timing as a signal that the source of the sound is to the right. You will automatically turn your head right, to the source of the sound.

Sound waves blocked by head

Right ear

Left ear

WATCH OUT!

2. Time difference
Sound waves reach the left ear this much later than they reach the right ear.

Calculating Pitch

Imagine the low, menacing growl of a lion and then the high screech of fingernails on the chalkboard. Your subjective experience of a sound being high or low is referred to as pitch. Exactly how the cochlea codes pitch and the brain interprets the code is rather complicated. We'll focus on two better-known theories of pitch, the frequency and place theories.

The frequency and place theories explain how we perceive pitch.

The *frequency theory,* which applies only to low-pitched sounds, says that the rate at which nerve impulses reach the brain determines how low the pitch of a sound is.

For example, the brain interprets a frequency rate of 50 impulses per second as a lower sound than one with a frequency rate of 200 impulses per second. Hearing the low-pitched roar of a lion involves the frequency theory. Hearing higher-pitched sounds, however, such as the screech of fingernails on a chalkboard, involves another theory, the place theory.

The *place theory* says that the brain determines medium- to higher-pitched sounds on the basis of the place on the basilar membrane where maximum vibration occurs.

For example, lower-pitched sounds cause maximum vibrations near the beginning of the cochlea's basilar membrane, while higher-pitched sounds cause maximum vibrations near the end of the membrane. Our auditory system combines the frequency and place theories to transform sound waves into perceptions of low- to high-pitched sounds (Goldstein, 2007).

The brain does one more thing: It calculates how loud a sound is.

Calculating Loudness

You can easily tell the difference between a yell and a whisper because your auditory system transforms the intensity of sound waves into the subjective experiences of a soft whisper or a loud yell. This transformation occurs inside the cochlea.

Compared to a yell, a whisper produces low-amplitude sound waves that set off the following chain of events: fewer vibrations of the tympanic membrane, less movement of fluid in the cochlea, less movement of the basilar membrane, fewer bent hair cells, less electrical force, and finally, fewer nerve impulses sent to the brain, which interprets these signals as a soft sound.

The brain calculates *loudness* primarily from the frequency or rate of how fast or how slowly nerve impulses arrive from the auditory nerve.

For example, the brain interprets a slower rate of impulses as a softer tone (whisper) and a faster rate as a louder tone (yell) (Goldstein, 2007).

Earlier, we said that there are two structures in the inner ear, the cochlea and the vestibular system. If you have ever stood on your head, you have firsthand experience with the vestibular system, our next topic.

The brain calculates loudness from frequency of nerve impulses.

C. Vestibular System: Balance

Position and Balance

What else is in the inner ear?

Vestibular system says you're upside down.

I guarantee that one question you never ask is "Where is my head?" Even though your head is in a hundred different positions throughout the day, you rarely forget to duck it as you enter a car or forget whether you're standing on your feet or your hands. That's because the position of your head is automatically tracked by another sense, called your vestibular system.

The *vestibular system,* which is located above the cochlea in the inner ear, includes three *semicircular canals,* resembling bony arches, which are set at different angles (right figure). Each of the semicircular canals is filled with fluid that moves in response to movements of your head. In the canals are sensors (hair cells) that respond to the movement of the fluid. The functions of the vestibular system include sensing the position of the head, keeping the head upright, and maintaining balance.

The vestibular system uses information on the position of your head to indicate whether you're standing on your hands or your feet. A gymnast (left figure) relies heavily on his or her vestibular system to keep balance. Sometimes an inner ear infection affects the vestibular system and results in dizziness, nausea, and the inability to balance. And as you'll see next, the vestibular system is also involved in motion sickness.

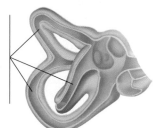

Semicircular canals

Motion Sickness

Why am I getting sick?

One of my (R.P.) terrible childhood memories is sitting in the back seat of a moving car and after 30 minutes of curving roads feeling a cold sweat followed by nausea, dizziness, and an extreme desire to lie down anywhere—stationary. Along with about 25% of the U.S. population, I experienced moderate to severe signs of motion sickness. About 55% of people experience only mild symptoms, while the remaining 20% are lucky and rarely experience any. Researchers think that motion sickness results when information provided by the vestibular system doesn't match information coming from other senses (Ignelzi, 2006).

Motion sickness results from mismatch between vestibular and visual systems.

Motion sickness, which consists of feelings of discomfort, nausea, and dizziness in a moving vehicle, is believed to develop when there is a sensory mismatch between the information from the vestibular system—that your head is physically bouncing around—and the information reported by your eyes—that objects in the distance look fairly steady.

Infants below age 2 rarely have motion sickness, but susceptibility increases from 2 to about 12. After 12, susceptibility decreases in both men and women. Researchers suspect that genetic and not personality factors determine susceptibility to motion sickness (Ignelzi, 2006b).

A number of drugs reduce the symptoms of motion sickness. As an alternative to drugs, military pilots reported a significant reduction in motion sickness after completing a training program that taught them how to regulate several physiological responses to decrease their symptoms (Cowings et al., 2005). Other research found that people who used special breathing techniques reported significantly less nausea during an activity designed to induce motion sickness than people who did not learn the breathing techniques (Sang et al., 2003, 2005). Also, the use of ginger or a relief band (a bracelet that emits electronic pulses) may help to reduce motion sickness (Ignelzi, 2006).

Malfunctioning of the vestibular system can cause terrible symptoms.

Meniere's Disease and Vertigo

Why is the room spinning?

Imagine suddenly having ringing in your ears like Niagara Falls, walking into the bathroom to find the toilet spinning out of range, or vomiting more than 30 times a day. These are all symptoms of the dreaded Meniere's disease.

Meniere's (main-YERS) disease **results from a malfunction of the semicircular canals of the vestibular system. The symptoms include sudden attacks of dizziness, nausea, vomiting, spinning, and head-splitting buzzing sounds.**

About 615,000 Americans are diagnosed with Meniere's disease, but it is estimated that over 6 million Americans suffer from the disease, which is thought to be caused by a viral infection of the inner ear (Pray & Pray, 2005). The vestibular system is also involved in another problem, called vertigo.

Vertigo, **whose symptoms are dizziness and nausea, results from malfunction of the semicircular canals of the vestibular system.**

Sophie, 57 years old, was sitting at the dining table. Suddenly she felt dizzy, fell out of her chair, crawled to the bathroom, and vomited. She had to lie in bed to keep from spinning. Sophie was diagnosed as having vertigo and sought help from a "dizzy" clinic (Jauhar, 2001).

Meniere's disease and vertigo share some symptoms and have no known cures. There are "dizzy" clinics that use drug and nondrug methods to decrease symptoms that involve malfunctions of the vestibular system.

If you happen to be reading this book in a car or on a plane and feel a little queasy, relax before reading the next section, which is about tasting and smelling food.

D. Chemical Senses

How does your tongue taste?

You rarely think about the thousands of chemicals you put into your mouth every day, but you do know when something tastes very good or very bad. You also know that if you burn your tongue on hot foods or liquids, your sense of taste can be markedly decreased.

Taste is called a chemical sense because the stimuli are various chemicals. On the surface of the tongue are receptors, called taste buds, for five basic tastes: sweet, salty, sour, bitter, and umami. The function of taste buds is to perform transduction, which means transforming chemical reactions into nerve impulses.

As you imagine biting into and chewing a very bitter slice of lemon, we'll explain how your tongue tastes.

1 Tongue: Five Basic Tastes

You're probably familiar with four basic tastes—*sweet, salty, sour,* and *bitter.* There now appears to be a fifth, called *umami,* a meaty-cheesy taste found in cheese, meat, pizza, and MSG (Svitil, 2006). The right figure shows the areas on the tongue that have the most sensors or taste buds.

The reason many of us have a sweet tooth is that, as newborns, we inherited an innate preference for sweet and salty (Netting, 2001). Like most animals, humans avoid bitter-tasting substances, presumably because many poisonous substances taste bitter (Barinaga, 2000). If you are one of those who like sour lemonade, you know that people can learn to like bitter substances. Tasting begins with what happens in the trenches on the surface of your tongue.

2 Surface of the Tongue

As you chew the lemon, its chemicals, which are the *stimuli* for taste, break down into molecules. In turn, these molecules mix with saliva and run down into narrow trenches on the surface of the tongue. Once inside the trenches, the molecules stimulate the taste buds.

3 Taste Buds

Buried in the trenches on the surface of the tongue are many hundreds of bulblike taste buds.

Taste buds, which are shaped like miniature onions, are the receptors for taste. Chemicals dissolved in the saliva activate the taste buds, which produce nerve impulses that eventually reach areas in the brain's parietal lobe. The brain transforms these nerve impulses into sensations of taste.

Taste buds live in a relatively toxic environment and are continuously exposed to heat, cold, spices, bacteria, and saliva. As a result, taste buds wear out and are replaced about every ten days. The human tongue can have as many as 10,000 taste buds and as few as 500; the number remains constant throughout life (Goldstein, 2007).

Tongue contains sensors (taste buds) for five tastes.

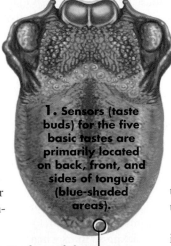

1. Sensors (taste buds) for the five basic tastes are primarily located on back, front, and sides of tongue (blue-shaded areas).

2. Surface of the tongue

Trench contains buried taste buds.

3. Taste buds

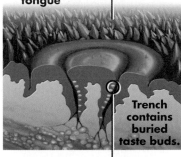

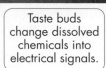

Taste buds change dissolved chemicals into electrical signals.

4 All Tongues Are Not the Same

In rare cases, individuals are born without any taste buds and cannot taste anything because they have a genetically determined disorder (Mass et al., 2005). In contrast, about 25% of the population are supertasters, which means they may have two to three times more taste buds than normal, which results in increased sensitivity to sweet, bitter, sour, and salty. For example, supertasters taste sugar to be twice as sweet as most people and get more intense oral burning sensations from the chemical (capsaicin) in chili peppers. Supertasters find grapefruit juice too bitter and don't like broccoli because it also contains a bitter chemical (Bhattacharya, 2003).

Researchers found that being a supertaster is an inherited trait and speculate that it may have had some evolutionary advantage. For example, supertasters would be better able to judge whether fruits or berries were poisonous (Bartoshuk, 1997). Today, supertasters may work for food manufacturers and rate the taste of new food products.

But for all of us, our ability to taste is greatly affected by our ability to smell.

5 Flavor: Taste and Smell

If taste receptors are sensitive to only five basic tastes, how can you tell the difference between two sweet tastes, such as a brownie and vanilla ice cream, or between two sour tastes, such as lemon juice and vinegar? The truth is that a considerable percentage of the sensations we attribute to taste are actually contributed by our sense of smell (Kalat, 2007).

We experience *flavor* when we combine the sensations of taste and smell.

You have no doubt experienced the limitations of your taste buds' abilities when you had a cold, which blocks the nasal passages and cuts out the sense of smell. Without smell, foods we usually love now taste very bland.

Since our taste of foods is greatly enhanced by the sense of smell, we'll examine smell, or olfaction, next.

How does your nose smell?

Every year people in the United States spend about $3 billion on perfumes to make themselves smell better (Banay, 2006). You may have been impressed that your tongue has up to 10,000 taste buds, but that number pales in comparison to the nose's 6 million receptor cells (Doty, 2001). That's why the sense of smell, more properly called olfaction, is 10,000 times more sensitive than taste (Lindstrom, 2005).

Olfaction is called a chemical sense because its stimuli are various chemicals that are carried by the air. The upper part of the nose has a small area that contains receptor cells for olfaction. The function of the olfactory receptors is transduction, to transform chemical reactions into nerve impulses.

We'll explain the steps for olfaction by having you imagine crossing paths with an angry skunk.

1 Stimulus

An angry skunk protects itself by spraying thousands of molecules, which are carried by the air and drawn into your nose as you breathe. The reason you can smell substances such as skunk spray is that these substances are volatile. A volatile substance is one that can release molecules into the air at room temperature. For example, volatile substances include skunk spray, perfumes, and warm brownies, but not glass or steel. We can smell only volatile substances, but first they must reach the olfactory cells in the nose.

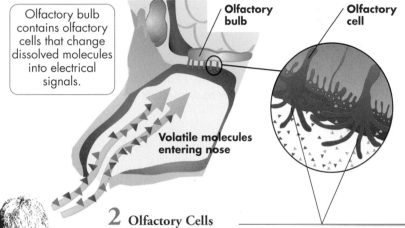

Olfactory bulb contains olfactory cells that change dissolved molecules into electrical signals.

Olfactory bulb

Olfactory cell

Volatile molecules entering nose

2 Olfactory Cells

Olfactory cells are the receptors for smell and are located in two 1-inch-square patches of tissue in the uppermost part of the nasal passages. Olfactory cells are covered with mucus, a gluey film into which volatile molecules dissolve and stimulate the underlying olfactory cells. The olfactory cells trigger nerve impulses that travel to the brain, which interprets the impulses as different smells.

As you breathe, a small percentage of the air entering your nose reaches the upper surface of your nasal passages, where the olfactory receptors are located. People can lose their sense of smell if a virus or inflammation destroys the olfactory receptors, or if a blow to the head damages the neural network that carries impulses to the brain (Lalwani & Snow, 2006; Ropper & Brown, 2005). About 6%, 17%, and 29% of people in their 50s, 60s, and 70s, lose the ability to detect common odors (C. Murphy et al., 2002). You don't actually smell anything until neural impulses reach your brain.

3 Sensations and Memories

Nerve impulses from the olfactory cells travel first to the olfactory bulb, which is a tiny, grape-shaped area (green structure in diagram of nose) that lies directly above the olfactory cells at the bottom of the brain. From here, impulses are relayed to the primary olfactory cortex (also called the piriform cortex) located underneath the brain. This cortex transforms nerve impulses into the olfactory sensations of a skunk's spray or a sweet perfume (Doty, 2001).

Although we can identify as many as 10,000 different odors, we soon stop smelling scents we are repeatedly exposed to (deodorants, perfumes) because of decreased responding called adaptation, in the olfactory cells (Jacob et al., 2006).

Smell, in terms of evolution, is a very primitive sense and has important functions.

A nose worth $100,000?

Sophia Grojsman is one of only a dozen master perfumers in the United States who are responsible for creating some of the best-known perfumes (Calvin Klein, Estée Lauder). Known in the trade as a "nose," she earns over $100,000 a year because there is no scientific/computer substitute for her nose and brain's ability to identify, remember, and mix fragrances that elicit pleasant memories and moods. One reason a computerized nose has not yet replaced a human nose is that scientists are only now beginning to understand which combinations of molecular qualities (weight, shape) and olfactory receptors determine which of 10,000 different odors humans can smell (Buck, 1999).

4 Functions of Olfaction

One function of smell is to intensify the taste of food. For example, you could not tell a licorice from an orange jelly bean with your nose held closed. A second function is to warn of potentially dangerous foods; the repulsive odor of spoiled or rotten food does this very effectively. A third and more recently discovered function is to elicit strong memories, often associated with emotional feelings; for example, the smell of pumpkin pie may remind you of a festive family gathering (Ropper & Brown, 2005). For many animals, such as cats and dogs, smell also functions to locate food, mates, and territory.

Next, we examine the sense of touch and explain what happens when you pet a cat.

E. Touch

Definition

What happens when fingers feel fur?

If you were to draw your hand across the surface of a cat, you would have the sensations of touching something soft and furry. These sensations are part of the sense of touch.

The sense of *touch* includes pressure, temperature, and pain. Beneath the outer layer of skin are a half-dozen miniature sensors that are receptors for the sense of touch. The function of the touch sensors is to change mechanical pressure or temperature variations into nerve impulses that are sent to the brain for processing.

We'll examine several miniature mechanical sensors and explain how they function.

Receptors in the Skin

If you were to closely examine the surface of your skin, you would see a relatively smooth membrane covered in some places with hair. Some "touch" sensors are wound around hair follicles (the backs of your arms) and are slightly different from sensors in skin without hair (your palms). However, before we discuss several major touch receptors, we need to examine the different layers of the skin.

1 Skin. The skin, which is the body's largest organ, has three layers. The *outermost layer* of skin is a thin film of dead cells containing no receptors. Immediately below the dead layer are the first receptors, which look like groups of threadlike extensions. In the *middle and fatty layers* of skin are a variety of receptors with different shapes and functions. Some of the major sensors in the middle layer of skin are hair receptors.

2 Hair receptors. In the middle layer are free nerve endings that are wrapped around the base of each hair follicle; these are called *hair receptors.* Hair receptors respond or fire with a burst of activity when hairs are first bent. However, if hairs remain bent for a period of time, the receptors cease firing, an example of *sensory adaptation.* When you first put on a watch, it bends hairs, causing hair receptors to fire; your brain interprets this firing as pressure on your wrist. If you keep the watch on and it remains in place, keeping the hairs bent, the hair receptors adapt or cease firing, and you no longer feel pressure from your watch, even though it is still there. Your skin contains some receptors that adapt rapidly (hair receptors) and others that adapt slowly. Adaptation prevents your sense of touch from being overloaded.

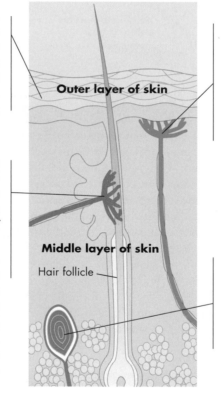

Outer layer of skin

Middle layer of skin

Hair follicle

3 Free nerve endings. Near the bottom of the outer layer of skin is a group of threadlike extensions; these are called *free nerve endings* because they have nothing protecting or surrounding them. One question about free nerve endings is how the same receptor can transmit information about both temperature and pain. Researchers think that different patterns of neural activity may signal different sensations—for example, slow bursts of firing for temperature and fast bursts for pain (Ferster & Spruston, 1995).

4 Pacinian corpuscle. In the fatty layer of skin is the largest touch sensor, called the *Pacinian corpuscle (pa-SIN-ee-in CORE-pus-sole).* This receptor, which has distinctive layers like a slice of onion, is highly sensitive to touch, is the only receptor that responds to vibration, and adapts very quickly.

All these receptors send their electrical signals to the brain.

Brain Areas

Did I touch my nose or my toe?

When pressure (touch), temperature, or pain stimulates the skin's receptors, they perform transduction and change these forms of energy into nerve impulses. The impulses go up the spinal cord and eventually reach the brain's somatosensory cortex.

The *somatosensory cortex,* which is located in the parietal lobe, transforms nerve impulses into sensations of touch, temperature, and pain. You know which part is being stimulated because, as we explained earlier (p. 77), different parts of the body are represented on different areas of the somatosensory cortex.

Somatosensory cortex

Parietal lobe

Compared with touch and temperature, the sense of pain is different because it has no specific stimulus and can be suppressed by psychological factors. We'll discuss these interesting aspects of pain, along with acupuncture, later in this module. We'll also discuss later how psychological factors can make foods that we think are truly disgusting become delicacies in other parts of the world. But first, try out your memory on the Concept Review.

✔ Concept Review

EYE: Numbers on the eye match the numbers of the questions.

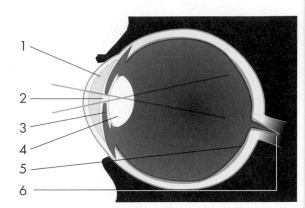

1. A transparent, curved structure at the front of the eye, called the _____, focuses or bends light waves into a more narrow beam.

2. A round opening at the front of the eye that allows varying amounts of light to enter the eye is called the _____.

3. A circular, pigmented muscle that dilates or constricts, thus increasing or decreasing the size of the pupil, is called the _____.

4. The function of the transparent, oval structure called the _____ is to bend light waves into a narrower beam of light and focus the beam precisely on a layer of cells in the very back of the eye.

5. Lining the back of the eye is a filmlike layer called the (a)_____, which contains several layers of cells. The back layer of cells has two kinds of photoreceptors, called (b)_____ and (c)_____.

6. This band of nerve fibers, called the (a)_____, exits from the back of the eye and carries impulses to the brain. The point at which this nerve exits is called the (b)_____ because it contains no rods or cones.

EAR: Numbers on the ear match the numbers of the questions.

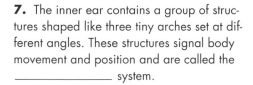 

1. The funnel-like structure called the _____ gathers in sound waves from the environment.

2. The short tunnel called the _____ carries sound waves that strike a membrane.

3. The thin, taut membrane at the end of the auditory canal, called the _____, transforms sound waves into vibrations.

4. The three small bones (hammer, anvil, and stirrup) called the (a)_____ are part of the middle ear. They transform vibrations of the tympanic membrane into mechanical movements, which in turn vibrate a second membrane, called the (b)_____.

5. The coiled, fluid-filled structure called the (a)_____ is one part of the inner ear. It contains auditory receptors called (b)_____ that are attached to the basilar membrane.

6. The band of fibers called the _____ carries nerve impulses from the cochlea to the brain.

7. The inner ear contains a group of structures shaped like three tiny arches set at different angles. These structures signal body movement and position and are called the _____ system.

9. Substances give off volatile molecules that are drawn into the nose, dissolve in mucus, and activate the (a)_____. The function of these cells is to produce (b)_____ that are sent to the olfactory bulb and brain for processing.

8. Sensors that are located on the surfaces of the tongue respond to five basic tastes, which are (a)_____, _____, _____, _____, and the newly found taste called _____. The sensors or receptors for taste are called (b)_____.

10. There are several kinds of touch receptors: the (a)_____ is fast adapting; the (b)_____ is also fast adapting; the (c)_____ responds to both touch and vibration.

Hair follicle

Answers: EYE: 1. cornea; 2. pupil; 3. iris; 4. lens; 5. (a) retina, (b) rods, (c) cones; 6. (a) optic nerve, (b) blind spot; EAR: 1. external ear; 2. auditory canal; 3. tympanic membrane (eardrum); 4. (a) ossicles, (b) oval window; 5. (a) cochlea, (b) hair cells; 6. auditory nerve; 7. vestibular; 8. (a) sweet, salty, sour, bitter, umami, (b) taste buds; 9. (a) olfactory cells, (b) nerve impulses; 10. (a) free nerve ending, (b) hair receptor, (c) Pacinian corpuscle

Psychological Factors

Would you eat a worm?

We have discussed how senses transform physical energy into impulses, which eventually become sensations and then perceptions. However, your perceptions are usually influenced by psychological factors, such as learning, emotion, and motivation, so that you never perceive the world exactly like someone else. For example, when offered a fish eye to eat, many of us would react with great disgust. The facial expression to express disgust (right photo) is similar across cultures.

Disgust is triggered by the presence of a variety of contaminated or offensive things, including certain foods, body products, and gore. We show disgust, which is a universally recognized facial

expression, by closing the eyes, narrowing the nostrils, curling the lips downward, and sometimes sticking out the tongue (left photo).

Disgust is considered a basic emotion and is specifically related to a particular motivational system (hunger). People around the world express disgust in the same way. Children begin to show the facial expression for disgust between the ages of 2 and 4, a time when they are learning which foods in their culture are judged edible and which are considered repugnant (Rozin et al., 2000).

Cultural influence. Your particular culture has a strong influence on which foods you learn to perceive as disgusting and which you think are delicious. We'll describe some foods that are considered delicious in some cultures and disgusting in others.

Plump Grubs

For most U.S. citizens, eating a round, soft, white worm would be totally unthinkable. For the Asmat of New Guinea, however, a favorite delicacy is a plump, white, 2-inch larva—the beetle grub. The natives harvest dozens of the grubs, put them on bamboo slivers, and roast them. A photographer from the United States who did a story on the Asmat tried to eat a roasted grub, but his American tastes would not let him swallow it (Kirk, 1972).

Fish Eyes and Whale Fat

Although some Americans have developed a taste for raw fish (sushi), a common dish in Japan, most would certainly gag at the thought of eating raw fish eyes. Yet for some Inuit (Eskimo) children, raw fish eyes are like candy. Here you see a young girl using the Inuits' all-purpose knife to gouge out the eye of an already-filleted Arctic fish.

Eskimos also hunt a type of whale (the narwhal) that provides much of their protein. They consider the layer of fat under the skin *(mukluk)* a delicacy, and they eat it raw or dried.

Milk and Blood

Several tribes in East Africa supplement their diet with fresh blood that is sometimes mixed with milk. They obtain the blood by puncturing a cow's jugular vein with a sharp arrow. A cow can be bled many times and suffer no ill effects. The blood-milk drink is a rich source of protein and iron.

CULTURAL INFLUENCES ON DISGUST

The reaction of U.S. college students to eating white, plump grubs (on right, actual size) or cold, glassy fish eyes or having a warm drink of blood mixed with milk is almost always disgust. Researchers believe that showing disgust originally evolved to signal rejection of potentially contaminated or dangerous foods. Today, however, because of cultural and psychological influences, we may show disgust for eating a variety of noncontaminated foods (cat, dog, or horse meat) or situations (touching a dead person) (Rozin et al., 2000). The fact that the same things are viewed as all right in one culture but as disgusting in another graphically shows how much cultural values can influence and bias perceptions.

Just as psychological factors are involved in perceiving taste, they are also involved in experiencing pain.

G. Research Focus: Mind over Body?

Definitions and Research Methods

Can sugar pills reduce pain?

One of the truly amazing research findings is how sugar pills or placebos can somehow "trick" us into feeling or getting better. For example, because many of us believe that we will be helped by taking pills, about one-third of the population report feeling much better or having less pain after taking a pill, not knowing that it was only a sugar pill—a placebo.

A *placebo* is some intervention, such as taking a pill, receiving an injection, or undergoing an operation, that resembles medical therapy but that, in fact, has no medical effects.

A *placebo effect* is a change in the patient's illness (for better or worse) that is due to the patient's beliefs or expectations rather than the medical treatment.

One of the strongest and most studied placebo effects is the ability for placebos to relieve pain (G. A. Hoffman et al., 2005). For example, if people take a pill for headache pain and *believe* or *expect* that the pill will decrease their pain, about 30 to 60% of people will actually feel less pain after taking a placebo (Talbot, 2000).

Because the placebo effect can occur after taking any pill (injection or medical procedure), researchers needed to find a method that could separate a person's expectations and beliefs from the actual effects of a new drug or medical treatment. The method researchers use to separate the effects of a person's expectations (placebo effect) from a pill or medical treatment is called the double-blind design.

In a *double-blind procedure*, neither the researchers ("blind") nor the subjects ("blind") know who is receiving what treatment. Because neither researchers nor subjects know who is receiving which treatment, the researchers' or subjects' expectations have a chance to equally affect both treatments (drug and placebo).

For example, in a double-blind design, headache sufferers would be told that they will be given one of two different kinds of pills to decrease pain. Unknown to the subjects ("blind") and the researchers ("blind"), one of the pills is a drug and one is a placebo. If subjects taking the drug report the same decrease in pain as those taking the placebo, researchers conclude the drug is no better than a placebo. If subjects taking the drug report less pain than those taking the placebo, researchers conclude the drug is medically useful because it is better than a placebo.

> Only a double-blind procedure can tell if a treatment is real or a placebo.

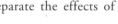

REAL MEDICINE? **SUGAR PILL?**

Over the past 25 years, hundreds of double-blind experiments have found that 30 to 98% of people have reported beneficial effects after taking placebos (Talbot, 2000). More recently, researchers found that the placebo effect for decreasing pain results in increased activity in parts of the brain responsible for pain perception and negative emotions such as anxiety (Kong et al., 2006). What follows are samples of research study findings that demonstrate how people's expectations and beliefs can change placebos into powerful medicine.

Placebo Results

Here are four convincing examples of pain reduction that involved placebos and double-blind procedures (J. A. Turner et al., 1994).

98% of patients originally reported marked or complete relief of pain from ulcers after medical treatment (gastric freezing). However, in a later double-blind procedure, this treatment was shown to be ineffective.

85% of patients originally reported a reduction in pain from *Herpes simplex* (cold sores and genital sores) after a drug treatment. However, in a later double-blind procedure, this drug was proved to be ineffective.

56% of patients reported a decrease in heart pain (angina pectoris) after being given a medical procedure that, unknown to the patient, involved only a skin incision.

35% of patients who had arthroscopic knee surgery reported decreased pain. About 250,000 patients a year get this surgery ($5,000 each). In a double-blind study, the placebo group (sham surgery) reported a similar decrease (Moseley et al., 2002).

Conclusion: Mind over Body!

Based on findings like those given above, researchers have reached three conclusions (W. A. Brown, 1997; Talbot, 2000).

First, potentially very powerful placebo effects, such as reducing pain, getting over colds, or speeding recovery from medical procedures, have been greatly underestimated.

Second, both medication (pills, injections) and fake surgeries can produce significant placebo effects, such as reducing pain, in 30 to 98% of patients.

Third, and of great interest to psychologists, placebos indicate a powerful mind-over-body interaction. This mind-over-body interaction explains why people may really experience and report surprising health benefits from taking a wide variety of placebos on the market, such as unproven herbal remedies.

Researchers suggest that placebos may work by creating positive expectations and beliefs that reduce anxiety and stress. In turn, the reduction of anxiety results in perceiving less pain. And the reduction in stress improves functioning of the immune system so that the body can better fight off toxins and make a quicker recovery from some problem (W. A. Brown, 1997). Thus, there is no question that our minds have powerful effects on our bodies.

Next, we'll examine pain in more detail and see how mental factors can affect the perception of pain.

H. Pain

What causes pain?

All of us can relate to pain because at one time or another we have all felt various degrees of pain.

Pain **is an unpleasant sensory and emotional experience that may result from tissue damage, one's thoughts or beliefs, or environmental stressors (job, traffic). Pain receptors in the body send nerve impulses to the somatosensory and limbic areas of the brain, where impulses are changed into pain sensations. Pain is essential for survival: it warns us to avoid or escape dangerous situations or stimuli and makes us take time to recover from injury.**

This definition of pain differs from the other senses in three ways. First, pain results from many different stimuli (physical injury, loud noises, bright lights, psychological and social stressors), while each of the other senses responds primarily to a single stimulus. Second, the pain's intensity depends not only on the physical stimulus but also on a number of social and psychological factors, including attentional or emotional states. Third, the treatment of pain depends not only on treating any physical injury but also on reducing psychological and

emotional distress that may have caused or contributed to the painful sensations (Keefe et al., 2002).

Researchers recognize that pain is a complex process that may or may not include tissue damage and usually involves social, psychological, and emotional factors, which can cause, increase, or decrease painful sensations (Keefe et al., 2002). For example, after men had hot metal plates placed on the backs of their hands, they were given an injection of either a painkiller or a placebo (they did not know which—double-blind procedure). Brain scans showed that the placebo injections that had reduced pain had activated pain-reducing brain circuits that were similar to the circuits activated by real painkillers (Petrovic et al., 2002; Ploghaus et al., 2003). In another study, researchers showed that hypnosis could change brain activity along with a person's perception of pain (Basbaum & Julius, 2006). These studies demonstrate how one's beliefs (in placebos) can activate circuits in the brain that, in turn, may result in significant changes in perception (decrease in pain).

Other psychological factors, such as changes in attention, can also alter perception of pain and answer an interesting question: Why do headaches come and go, depending on what you are doing?

How does the mind stop pain?

Although a headache is painful, the pain may come and go as you shift your attention or become absorbed in some project. This phenomenon is explained by the gate control theory of pain (Melzack & Wall, 1983).

The *gate control theory* **of pain says that nonpainful nerve impulses (shifting attention) compete with pain impulses (headache) in trying to reach the brain. This competition creates a bottleneck, or neural gate, that limits the number of impulses that can be transmitted. Thus, shifting one's attention or rubbing an injured area may increase the passage of nonpainful impulses and thereby decrease the passage of painful impulses; as a result, the sensation of pain is dulled. The neural gate isn't a physical structure but rather refers to the competition between nonpainful and painful impulses as they try to reach the brain.**

The gate control theory explains that you may not notice pain from a headache or injury while thoroughly involved in some other activity because impulses from that activity close the neural gate and block the passage of painful impulses (right figure above: NO PAIN). However, when you become less involved, there are fewer nonpainful impulses, the neural gate opens (left figure above: PAIN), and you again notice the pain as painful impulses reach the brain (Kugelmann, 1998).

The gate control theory explains how a professional football quarterback was able to play the last six minutes

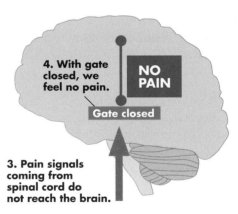

of an important football game with a broken ankle (Associated Press, 2002). The gate control theory says that a football player's intense attentional and emotional involvement in the game caused his brain to send nonpainful impulses that closed neural gates in the spinal cord. The closed neural gates blocked impulses from a painful ankle from reaching his brain and thus prevented feelings of pain. Later, when the game was over, the quarterback's attentional and emotional states calmed down, the neural gates opened, impulses from his broken ankle reached his brain, and he felt considerable pain.

PAIN: PHYSICAL AND PSYCHOLOGICAL

According to the gate control theory, your perception of pain depends not only on a stressful mental state or physical injury but also on a variety of psychological, emotional, and social factors, which can either decrease or increase your perception of pain (Pincus & Morley, 2001).

Your perception of pain from a serious injury can also be reduced by your brain's ability to secrete its own pain-reducing chemicals, called endorphins.

Does the brain make its own painkillers?

Someone who has experienced a serious injury—in football, for example—will usually report that initially the pain was bearable but with time the pain became much worse. One reason pain seems less intense immediately after injury is that the brain produces endorphins.

Endorphins (en-DOOR-fins) are chemicals produced by the brain and secreted in response to injury or severe physical or psychological stress. The pain-reducing properties of endorphins are similar to those of morphine, a powerful painkilling drug.

Brain releases endorphins in times of great pain, stress, or fear.

The brain produces endorphins in situations that evoke great fear, anxiety, stress, or bodily injury, as well as after intense aerobic activity (Tripathi et al., 1993). For example, subjects with severe jaw pain produced increased levels of endorphins after they received a placebo injection, and subjects who reported the greatest pain relief showed the greatest endorphin release (Zubieta et al., 2005). In other research, patients showed increased levels of endorphins after their teeth nerves were touched or the bandages were removed from badly burned areas of their bodies (Szyfelbein et al., 1985). These studies indicate that the brain produces endorphins to reduce pain during times of intense physical stress. Endorphins and other painkillers (heroin, morphine, codeine) act mostly to stop receptors from signaling severe, persistent pain, but they do not stop receptors from signaling quick, sharp pain, as from a pinprick (Taddese et al., 1995).

Next, we'll look at the connection between dread and your brain's pain center.

How is dread related to pain?

Recent studies found evidence for dread being connected to the pain centers of the brain. One such study placed participants into a brain scanner (fMRI) and offered them the choice of receiving a stronger shock now or a weaker shock in the future. Some participants dreaded the shock so much that they chose to receive the stronger shock instead of waiting to receive a weaker one. Brain imaging of these "extreme-dreaders" showed heightened activity in the brain's pain center. Thus, dread is not simply an emotional response to fear or anxiety; rather, a significant component of dread involves devoting attention to the expected and unpleasant physical threat (in this case shock) (Berns et al., 2006). These results suggest that when it comes to getting root canal surgery or receiving a painful shot, it is not the actual procedure people dread most, but rather the waiting time (Blakeslee, 2006).

I want my root canal now!

Next, we'll learn how having thin needles inserted into your body can help reduce pain.

Can an ancient technique reduce pain?

Initially, scientists trained in the rigorous methods of the West (in particular, the United States) expressed great doubt about an ancient Chinese pain-reducing procedure, traced back to 2500 B.C., called acupuncture.

Acupuncture is a procedure in which a trained practitioner inserts thin needles into various points on the body's surface and then manually twirls or electrically stimulates the needles. After 10–20 minutes of needle stimulation, patients often report a reduction in various kinds of pain.

The mysterious part of this procedure is that the points of insertion—such as those shown in the photograph on the right—were mapped thousands of years ago and, as researchers now know, are often far removed from the sites of painful injury.

Today, modern scientists have explained some of the mystery surrounding acupuncture. First, the points of needle insertion, which seem unrelated to the points of injury, are often close to known pathways that conduct pain. Second, there is some evidence that stimulation of these points causes secretion of endorphins, which we know can reduce pain. For example, if patients are first given a drug (naloxone) that blocks secretion of endorphins, acupuncture does not reduce pain. Third, fMRI brain scans showed that acupuncture decreases neural activity in brain areas involved in pain sensations (Hui et al., 2000; Ulett, 2003).

Studies on the effectiveness of acupuncture in reducing pain of headaches and back pain indicate that 50 to 80% of patients reported short-term improvement, but after six months, about 50% of the patients reported a return of their painful symptoms (Ceniceros & Brown, 1998). The National Institutes of Health concluded that acupuncture is effective for nausea (from chemotherapy or morning sickness) and some kinds of pain (after dental treatment) (C. Holden, 1997). A recent study investigating the impact of a placebo treatment (fake acupuncture treatment) applied equal amounts of heat to people's right and left arms. Researchers then told participants they were being given acupuncture treatment on their right arm, but what the participants didn't know is that the treatment was a sham. Results showed that people reported feeling significantly less pain in their right arms than in their left arms even though equally intense heat was applied to both arms (Kong et al., 2006). This study suggests that the power of people's belief that acupuncture can reduce pain is strong enough to change their perception of pain.

Next, we turn to a very practical question: Can a sense be replaced if it is damaged? Of the five major senses—vision, audition, taste, olfaction, and touch—damage to vision and audition is especially disastrous to the quality of life. For that reason, researchers are trying to develop artificial eyes and ears.

Acupuncture is effective for nausea, headaches, and some kinds of pain.

I. Application Artificial Senses

Artificial Visual System

Is an artificial eye possible?

The cause and degree of blindness depend on which part of the visual system is affected. For example, a person would be totally blind if the photoreceptors (rods and cones) in the retina were destroyed (retinitis pigmentosa, an inherited disease) or if the entire retina or optic nerve were damaged. First, we'll look at a microchip that could be implanted into the retina to replace photoreceptors damaged by disease.

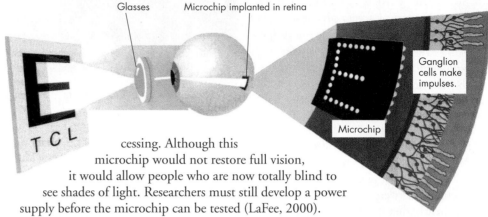

Glasses | Microchip implanted in retina

Ganglion cells make impulses.

Microchip

1 Artificial photoreceptors. Some individuals are blind because the front part of the eye is functioning but the photoreceptors (rods and cones) in the retina are damaged by accident or disease. For these individuals, researchers are developing a microchip the size of a match head (black square with white "E") that would be implanted in the back of the retina. This microchip would change light waves into electrical signals that would activate the middle layer of ganglion cells, which are undamaged. The ganglion cells would then make impulses that travel on to the brain for pro- cessing. Although this microchip would not restore full vision, it would allow people who are now totally blind to see shades of light. Researchers must still develop a power supply before the microchip can be tested (LaFee, 2000).

For individuals who are blind because their entire eye or optic nerve is damaged, researchers are developing a complete artificial eye that would send impulses directly to the brain.

2 Artificial eye and brain implant. At the beginning of this module, we told you about Katie, who was completely blind because both her eyes were damaged. In Katie's case, 36 tiny wires or electrodes were implanted directly into her visual cortex. When these electrodes were stimulated, Katie saw 36 dots of light, which is far fewer than needed for something as simple as avoiding objects while walking.

In another attempt to restore some vision (figure below), a blind patient was fitted with a miniature camera that sent electrical signals to 100 electrodes that were implanted directly into the visual cortex, located in the occipital lobe. When activated, the electrodes stimulated neurons in the visual cortex and produced 100 tiny spots of light. This patient could see the letter S when some of the 100 electrodes were stimulated (LaFee, 2000). Although the 100 electrodes in this patient's visual cortex provided more visual information than did Katie's 36, neither patient was able to see the outlines of objects or walk around without using canes.

However, recently, researchers made a significant step forward in developing an artificial visual system.

Camera sent electrical signals directly to brain.

3 Functional vision. The major goal in developing an artificial visual system is to provide enough visual information so a blind person can function, such as reading letters and distinguishing between and avoiding objects while walking around a room. Researchers are getting closer to reaching this goal.

Jerry, a 62-year-old man who has been blind since the age of 36, volunteered for having electrodes implanted into his brain's visual cortex (right photo). Jerry also wears a pair of glasses that, on one side, hold a tiny camera and, on the other side, an ultrasonic range finder. The range finder analyzes echoes from high-frequency sounds (beyond our range of hearing) that provide information on location, size, and distance of objects. The tiny camera provides visual information that is like

Artificial visual system lets Jerry "see" a 2-inch-high letter.

looking through a tunnel opening about 2 inches wide and 8 inches high. Both devices send electrical signals to a small computer that Jerry wears on his hip. In turn, the computer analyzes and relays electrical information to a panel of electrodes that were implanted into and stimulate the visual area in Jerry's occipital lobe (white cords going into skull) (Dobelle, 2000).

Using this device, Jerry can recognize a 2-inch letter from 5 feet away and avoid large objects as he moves around a room. As a result of receiving several upgrades to his device over the years, Jerry can now navigate the subway system on his own. This is one of the first examples of using a camera and brain implant to create useful vision (J. Anderson, 2005). The development of devices to help provide blind people with useful and functional visual information is advancing. Currently, researchers are trying to put a tiny camera inside the eye rather than on eyeglasses, which would allow people to scan their environment by simply moving their eyes, rather than moving their heads (Keats, 2006).

Researchers are also developing an artificial cochlea for the inner ear.

What causes deafness?

There are two major kinds of deafness that have different effects, causes, and treatments. The most severe kind of deafness is caused by damage to the inner ear and is called neural deafness. A less severe kind of deafness is caused by problems in the middle ear and is called conduction deafness.

Conduction Deafness

About 28 million Americans, almost 10% of the population, have hearing loss called conduction deafness (Rutherford, 2001).

Conduction deafness **can be caused by wax in the auditory canal, injury to the tympanic membrane, or malfunction of the ossicles. All of these conditions interfere with the transmission of vibrations from the tympanic membrane to the fluid of the cochlea, resulting in degrees of hearing loss.**

Conduction deafness, occurring in 40% of adults over 70, can often be treated with a hearing aid, which replaces the function of the middle ear. Hearing aids pick up sound waves, change them to vibrations, and send them through the skull to the inner ear.

Neural Deafness

Hellen Keller, who was born deaf and blind, said, "To be deaf is a greater affliction than to be blind." Hellen Keller had neural deafness, which, unlike conduction deafness, is not helped by hearing aids.

Neural deafness **can be caused by damage to the auditory receptors (hair cells), which prevents the production of impulses, or by damage to the auditory nerve, which prevents nerve impulses from reaching the brain. Since neither hair cells nor auditory nerve fibers regenerate, neural deafness was generally untreatable until the development of the cochlear implant.**

Currently, the only approved treatment for certain kinds of neural deafness is the cochlear implant described below.

Cochlear Implants

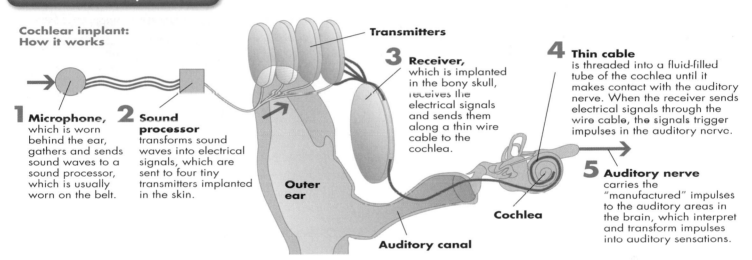

Cochlear implant: How it works

1 Microphone, which is worn behind the ear, gathers and sends sound waves to a sound processor, which is usually worn on the belt.

2 Sound processor transforms sound waves into electrical signals, which are sent to four tiny transmitters implanted in the skin.

Outer ear

Transmitters

3 Receiver, which is implanted in the bony skull, receives the electrical signals and sends them along a thin wire cable to the cochlea.

4 Thin cable is threaded into a fluid-filled tube of the cochlea until it makes contact with the auditory nerve. When the receiver sends electrical signals through the wire cable, the signals trigger impulses in the auditory nerve.

5 Auditory nerve carries the "manufactured" impulses to the auditory areas in the brain, which interpret and transform impulses into auditory sensations.

Cochlea

Auditory canal

Can deaf people hear?

If the auditory nerve is intact, a cochlear implant (figure above) can be used to treat neural deafness that is caused by damaged hair cells, which affects about 90% of those with hearing impairment (Rauschecker & Shannon, 2002).

The *cochlear implant* **is a miniature electronic device that is surgically implanted into the cochlea. The cochlear implant changes sound waves into electrical signals that are fed into the auditory nerve, which carries them to the brain for processing.**

As you proceed step by step through the figure above, notice that the cochlear implant first changes sound waves into electrical signals (1, 2, and 3) and then sends the electrical signals into the auditory nerve (4), which sends impulses to the brain (5).

Worldwide, about 100,000 adults and children with severe neural deafness have received cochlear implants (up from 5,000 in 1990) (Denworth, 2006). The child in the photo at right, deaf from birth, is reacting to hearing his first sounds after receiving a cochlear implant.

Using the newest cochlear implants (cost up to $50,000), adults who had learned to speak before they became deaf were able to understand about 80% of sen-

This child, deaf from birth, reacts after hearing with cochlear implant.

tences without any facial cues and from 90 to 100% of sentences when watching the speaker's face and lips (speech reading). Many could converse on the telephone (B. Stone, 2002; Svirsky et al., 2000).

The results are more complicated for children who did not learn to speak before becoming deaf. Researchers reported that when cochlear implants were put in before age $3\frac{1}{2}$, deaf children had the best neurological development, while implants after age 7 resulted in the poorest auditory development (Seppa, 2005). That's because brains of younger children are more flexible or plastic, which means younger brains are better able to develop neurological responses to auditory information and learn to hear and speak (Rauschecker & Shannon, 2002). For example, Julia received an implant when she was $2\frac{1}{2}$, and at age 9 she speaks and reads above her age level (Reisler, 2002). Very young children need intensive speech rehabilitation after cochlear implants (Sharp, 2000). Thus, cochlear implants have proven effective in many adults, adolescents, and children who experienced profound deafness (Dorman, 2003).

As we end this module, notice that we primarily discussed how senses transform energy into electrical impulses. Next, in Module 6, we'll focus on how "meaningless" sensations turn into meaningful perceptions.

✔ Summary Test

A. Eye: Vision

1. Waves in about the middle of the electromagnetic spectrum are visible because they can be absorbed by the human eye. These waves make up the _____ and can be absorbed by receptors at the back of the eye.

2. Upon entering the eye, light waves pass first through a curved, thin, transparent structure called the (a)_____, whose function is to bend or focus light waves into a narrower beam. Next, light waves pass through an opening in the eye called the (b)_____. Around this opening is a circular, pigmented muscle called the (c)_____; its function is to dilate or constrict, thus increasing or decreasing the amount of entering light. Finally, light waves pass through a transparent, oval structure called the (d)_____, whose function is to further focus light waves precisely on the photosensitive back surface of the eye, which is called the (e)_____.

3. The retina has several layers of cells, but only the very back layer contains photoreceptors. The photoreceptors that are used to see in dim light and transmit only black, white, and shades of gray are called (a)_____. Photoreceptors that are used to see in bright light and transmit colors are called (b)_____.

4. When rods absorb light waves, a chemical called (a)_____ breaks down and in turn generates tiny electrical forces that trigger (b)_____ in neighboring cells. Similarly, when cones absorb light waves, chemicals called (c)_____ break down and generate tiny electrical forces.

5. Nerve impulses generated in the eye travel along fibers that combine to form the (a)_____ nerve. This nerve carries nerve impulses to an area in the back of each occipital lobe called the (b)_____, which transforms impulses into simple visual (c)_____, such as lines, shadows, colors, and textures. If the primary visual cortex were totally damaged, the person would be essentially blind. Simple, meaningless sensations are transformed into complete, meaningful images when nerve impulses reach an area of the brain known as (d)_____.

6. We see color because our eyes absorb light waves of different (a)_____, which are transformed by the visual system into our experience of seeing colors. One theory of color applies to how the cones function; this is the (b)_____ theory. A second theory of color applies to how the ganglion and thalamic cells function; this is called the (c)_____ theory of color.

B. Ear: Audition

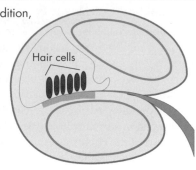

Hair cells

7. The stimuli for hearing, or audition, are sound waves, which have several physical characteristics. The physical characteristic of amplitude or height of sound waves is transformed into the subjective experience of (a)_____, which is measured in units called (b)_____. The frequency of sound waves (cycles per second) is transformed into the subjective experience of (c)_____, which for humans ranges from about 20 to 20,000 cycles per second.

8. The outer ear is composed of a funnel-like shape, called the external ear, whose function is to gather (a)_____. These waves travel down a short tunnel called the (b)_____ and strike a thin, taut membrane called the (c)_____, whose function is to transform sound waves into (d)_____.

9. The middle ear has three tiny bones (hammer, anvil, and stirrup), which together are called (a)_____. Vibrations in the tympanic membrane produce mechanical movements in the ossicles, the third of which is attached to another thin membrane, called the (b)_____, which is made to vibrate.

10. Of several structures in the inner ear, one is a coiled, fluid-filled, tubelike apparatus called the (a)_____, which contains the auditory receptors, called (b)_____. Movement of the fluid in the tube causes movement of the basilar membrane, which in turn causes bending of the hair cells, generating a tiny (c)_____. If this is large enough, it will trigger nerve impulses, which leave the cochlea via the (d)_____ and travel to the brain.

11. Nerve impulses are transformed into rather simple, meaningless auditory sensations when they reach the (a)_____, which is located in the temporal lobe. These sensations are transformed into meaningful and complete melodies, songs, words, or sentences by the auditory (b)_____.

12. To tell the direction of a sound, the brain analyzes the differences in time and intensity between (a)_____ arriving at the left and right ears. The brain determines degrees of loudness by using the (b)_____ of the arriving impulses. The discrimination of different tones or pitches is explained by the (c)_____ and _____ theories.

C. Vestibular System: Balance

13. Besides the cochlea, the inner ear contains three arch-shaped, fluid-filled structures called _____. The movement of fluid in these organs provides signals that the brain interprets in terms of the movement and position of the head and body. The vestibular system is also involved in motion sickness, Meniere's disease, and vertigo.

D. Chemical Senses

14. Sensors on the tongue respond to five basic tastes: (a)_____, _____, _____, _____, and _____. The receptors for taste, which are called (b)_____, trigger nerve impulses that travel to the brain, which then transforms them into the sensations of taste.

15. Volatile airborne substances are drawn into the upper part of the nose, where they dissolve in a thin film of mucus. Underneath the mucus are layers of receptors for olfaction (smell), which are called (a)_____. These receptors trigger impulses that travel to an area underneath the brain called the (b)_____. This area transforms impulses into hundreds of different odors.

E. Touch

16. The sense of touch actually provides information on three different kinds of stimuli: (a)_____, _____, and _____. The various layers of skin contain different kinds of touch receptors that have different speeds of adaptation. Receptors for the sense of touch trigger nerve impulses that travel to an area in the brain's parietal lobe, called the (b)_____. This area transforms impulses into sensations of pressure, temperature, and pain. The more sensitive the area of the body is to touch, the larger is its area on the cortex.

Hair follicle

F. Cultural Diversity: Disgust

17. A universal facial expression that indicates rejection of food is called (a)_____. Besides our innate preferences for sweet and salty foods and avoidance of bitter substances, most of our tastes are (b)_____ and particular to our culture. The fact that foods considered fine in one culture may seem disgusting to people in another culture indicates how much psychological factors influence taste.

G. Research Focus: Mind over Body?

18. In order to control for the placebo effect, researchers use an experimental design in which neither the researchers nor subjects know who is receiving what treatment. This is the _____ design, which controls for the expectations of both researchers and subjects.

H. Pain

19. After an injury, you feel two different kinds of pain sensations: at first, there is sharp, localized pain, which is followed by a duller, more generalized pain. The receptors for pain are (a)_____, which send impulses to two areas of the brain, specifically the (b)_____ and _____. If you rub an injured area or become totally absorbed in another activity, you may experience a reduction of pain, which is explained by the (c)_____. Immediately following a serious injury or great physical stress, the brain produces pain-reducing chemicals called (d)_____.

I. Application: Artificial Senses

20. There are two basic causes of deafness. If the cause is wax in the auditory canal, injury to the tympanic membrane, or malfunction of the ossicles, it is called (a)_____ deafness. If the cause is damage to hair cells in the cochlea or to the auditory nerve, it is called (b)_____ deafness. One treatment for neural deafness is to use a (c)_____, which is more effective if individuals have learned to speak before becoming deaf.

Answers: 1. visible spectrum; 2. (a) cornea, (b) pupil, (c) iris, (d) lens, (e) retina; 3. (a) rods, (b) cones; 4. (a) rhodopsin, (b) impulses, (c) opsins; 5. (a) optic, (b) primary visual cortex, (c) sensations, (d) association areas; 6. (a) lengths, (b) trichromatic, (c) opponent-process; 7. (a) loudness, (b) decibels, (c) pitch; 8. (a) sound waves, (b) auditory canal, (c) eardrum or tympanic membrane, (d) vibrations; 9. (a) ossicles, (b) oval window; 10. (a) cochlea, (b) hair cells, (c) electrical force, (d) auditory nerve; 11. (a) primary auditory cortex, (b) association areas; 12. (a) sound waves, (b) rate, (c) frequency, place; 13. vestibular organs; 14. (a) bitter, sour, salty, sweet, umami, (b) taste buds; 15. (a) olfactory cells, (b) primary olfactory cortex; 16. (a) pressure, temperature, pain, (b) somatosensory cortex; 17. (a) disgust, (b) learned; 18. double-blind; 19. (a) free nerve endings, (b) somatosensory area, limbic system, (c) gate control theory, (d) endorphins; 20. (a) conduction, (b) neural, (c) cochlear implant

Critical Thinking

What Would It Be Like Never to Feel Pain?

© 2005 Eric Larson/Light of Day, Inc.

Questions

1. What type of research method would you use to learn about the life of a person who cannot feel pain?

2. What type of neuron is responsible for people experiencing pain, heat, and cold?

3. How helpful would acupuncture be as a treatment for people with CIPA?

4. How might CIPA affect Ashlyn's ability to learn from her mistakes of injuring herself?

5. Why is it that Ashlyn cannot sense pain or heat, but she can feel her parents tickling and hugging her?

At the young age of 5, Ashlyn Blocker has already experienced many serious physical injuries. She's had a massive abrasion to the cornea of her eye, terrible burns, and hundreds of bite marks from fire ants. She's also severely damaged her tongue, cheek, and lips, knocked out most of her front teeth, and crushed her fingers in a door frame. Other children would scream in pain from experiencing any of these injuries, but Ashlyn never yelled, nor did she shed a tear. "I can't feel my boo-boos," she says (Tresniowski et al., 2005). Ashlyn is unique from most other children because she cannot feel pain.

Ashlyn has a rare and incurable genetic disorder called CIPA (congenital insensitivity to pain with anhidrosis). People with CIPA lack pain and temperature sensation, yet have no other sensory deficits. These individuals cannot feel pain and temperature because they lack nerve fibers responsible for carrying the sensation of pain, heat, and cold to the brain. Anhidrosis, or the inability to sweat, can cause life-threatening problems such as developing dangerously high fevers because people aren't able to lower their body temperature by sweating.

Living life without feeling pain is not as wonderful as one might think. Pain serves an important function by telling our brain that something is wrong and something needs to be done to correct it. Imagine having appendicitis and not feeling pain. Appendicitis is especially dangerous for people with CIPA because they wouldn't know a problem existed until after their appendix burst. Also, while most people shift their body weight when feeling pain in their joints, CIPA prevents people from sensing this pain and often results in joint problems. Lack of pain sensitivity can lead to other problems including bone fractures and infections. For example, Ashlyn recently had tonsillitis that went undetected for six months.

Despite the daily challenges Ashlyn faces, she looks like an ordinary girl who enjoys doing the same things others her age do. She likes to swing on the playground and enjoys being tickled and hugged by her parents. Ashlyn is fortunate to have support from her parents and school officials to ensure her safety while allowing her to enjoy her childhood. "There is no reason to think she won't have a normal life," says Dr. Lawrence Shapiro, an internationally recognized child psychologist. Ashlyn's parents describe her as having the "best laugh in the world" and state "she's going to conquer the world" (Tresniowski et al., 2005). (Adapted from Morton, 2004; Tresniowski et al., 2005)

1. A case study is an in-depth analysis of the thoughts, feelings, beliefs, or behaviors of one person. There are very few people who cannot feel pain, and so a thorough study of one person would be helpful.
2. Afferent neurons carry information in the form of electrical signals to the spinal cord and brain. Signals for sensing pain, heat, and cold are not being carried to the brain in people with CIPA.
3. Acupuncture is a procedure used to reduce various kinds of pain. People with CIPA do not feel pain, and therefore acupuncture would not be an effective treatment.
4. Most children learn to avoid engaging in behaviors that result in pain. For example, children quickly learn not to touch a hot flame after burning their hands by doing so. Learning not to engage in repetitive self-injurious behavior is challenging for Ashlyn because she cannot feel pain.
5. The same nerve ending responds to pain and temperature, but other nerve endings (such as hair receptors) respond to different types of touch stimulation, such as pressure, making it is possible for Ashlyn to feel her parents tickling and hugging her.

Links to Learning

Key Terms/Key People

acupuncture, 113	motion sickness, 105
adaptation, 93	nearsightedness, 95
afterimage, 99	neural deafness, 115
amplitude, 100	olfaction, 107
auditory association area, 103	olfactory cells, 107
auditory canal, 102	opponent-process theory, 99
auditory nerve, 103	optic nerve, 97
basilar membrane, 103	ossicles, 102
cochlea, 102	outer ear, 102
cochlear implant, 115	pain, 112
color blindness, 99	perceptions, 93
conduction deafness, 115	pitch, 100
cones, 96	place theory, 104
cornea, 95	placebo, 111
decibel, 101	placebo effect, 111
dichromats, 99	primary auditory cortex, 103
direction of sound, 104	primary visual cortex, 97
disgust, 110	pupil, 95
double-blind study, 111	retina, 95, 96
dread, 113	rods, 96
endorphins, 113	sensations, 93
external ear, 102	somatosensory cortex, 108
farsightedness, 95	sound waves, 100
flavor, 106	taste, 106
frequency theory, 104	taste buds, 106
gate control theory, 112	touch, 108
hair cells, 103	transduction, 93
inner ear, 102	trichromatic theory, 98
iris, 95	tympanic membrane, 102
lens, 95	vertigo, 105
loudness, 100, 104	vestibular system, 105
Meniere's disease, 105	visible spectrum, 94
middle ear, 102	visual agnosia, 97
monochromats, 99	visual association areas, 97

Learning Activities

- **POWERSTUDY FOR INTRODUCTION TO PSYCHOLOGY 4.0**
  by Tom Doyle and Rod Plotnik
  Check out the quizzes and learning activities for "Sensation" on **PowerStudy** and:
  - Test your knowledge using an interactive version of the Summary Test on pages 116 and 117. Also access related quizzing—true/false, multiple choice, and matching.
  - Explore an interactive version of the Critical Thinking exercise "What Would It Be Like Never to Feel Pain?" on page 118.
  - You will also find key terms, a chapter outline including a chapter abstract, and a special extended list of hotlinked websites that correlate to this module.

- **CengageNOW**
  academic.cengage.com/login

  Need help studying? This site is your one-stop study shop. Take a Pre-Test and CengageNOW will generate a Personalized Study Plan based on your test results. The Study Plan will identify the topics you need to review and direct you to online resources to help you master those topics. You can then take a Post-Test to determine the concepts you have mastered and what you still need to work on.

- **INTRODUCTION TO PSYCHOLOGY BOOK COMPANION WEBSITE**
  academic.cengage.com/psychology/plotnik

  Visit your book companion website where you will find more resources to help you study. At this site, you will find Learning Objectives, Internet Exercises, quizzing, flash cards, and a pronunciation glossary.

- **STUDY GUIDE and WEBTUTOR**
  Check the corresponding module in your Study Guide for effective student tips and help learning the material presented. Also go to **academic.cengage.com/webtutor** for an interactive version of the Study Guide features.

Study Questions

*A. **Eye: Vision**—What kinds of problems in the visual system could result in some form of blindness? (**Suggested answer page 621**)

B. **Ear: Audition**—What kinds of problems in the auditory system *could result in some form of deafness? (**Suggested answer page 622**)

C. **Vestibular System: Balance**—How do placebos help about 40–60% of people who suffer from motion sickness?

D. **Chemical Senses**—How might a master chef's chemical senses differ from yours? (**Suggested answer page 622**)

*E. **Touch**—What would happen if touch receptors did not show adaptation?

F. **Cultural Diversity: Disgust**—Why do people often show disgust when offered a new but edible food?

G. **Research Focus: Mind over Body?**—Why are some drugs initially reported to be effective but later proven to be worthless?

H. **Pain**—Why can some individuals stand more pain than others?

I. **Application: Artificial Senses**—Why is it so difficult to build an artificial eye or ear that duplicates the real one?

*These questions are answered in Appendix B.

MODULE 6
Perception

 PowerStudy 4.0™ Complete Module

Silent Messages

How can I be more confident?

Although it seemed like an ordinary week, Maria and her 7-year-old daughter, Gabrielle, would be involved in three relatively normal events that could change their lives forever.

On Tuesday, Maria's new boss unfairly criticized her work and made her feel insecure and unsure of herself. During her lunch hour, she browsed through a bookstore to find something on building confidence. She was intrigued by an audiotape titled "Improve Self-Esteem." The instructions read, "The listener hears only relaxing music, but the unconscious hears and automatically processes subliminal messages that boost self-esteem. In a few short weeks, the listener is guaranteed to have more confidence and self-

Can subliminal tapes change a person's behaviors?

esteem. If you're not completely satisfied, return the tape for a full refund." Maria had heard about tapes with subliminal persuasion from a friend who claimed that she used a weight-reduction tape that helped her lose 20 pounds. When Maria asked about the effectiveness of subliminal tapes, the salesperson said that he had a friend who increased his motivation to study by listening to one of these tapes. Maria smiled and said, "Well, it's guaranteed, so what have I got to lose?" She bought the tape, put it in her purse, and as she walked out the door, she was already feeling a little more confident.

Nice Dog, Mean Dog

What's a mean dog?

On Saturday afternoon, Maria took her daughter, Gabrielle, to play at the local park, which had slides, swings, ropes, and even a small trampoline. As Gabrielle was walking toward the trampoline, she saw a beautiful brown dog sitting by its owner. Gabrielle loved animals, and she ran toward the dog. The dog's owner was deep in conversation and did not notice the cute little girl running toward the beautiful Doberman. As Gabrielle came closer, she thrust out her hands to pet the dog's smooth black nose. The movement of Gabrielle's hands startled the dog, who reflexively snarled and then snapped at the hands coming at its nose. Gabrielle felt the pain as the dog's teeth nipped two of her fingers, which immediately started to bleed. The owner turned to see what had happened and quickly pulled the dog away as Maria came running. Maria took Gabrielle in her arms, soothed her, and then examined the small cuts on her fingers. Gabrielle looked at her bleeding fingers and then at the big, ugly, brown dog that had bit her and said in a tearful voice, "I hate that dog. Bad dog." Seeing her daughter's reaction, Maria began to have doubts about her plans to surprise Gabrielle with a cute little puppy for her birthday.

How does a bad experience create a bad perception?

White Spot

Can the doctor be sure?

On Friday, Maria had to take time from work for her annual physical exam, which included a mammogram. In the past, the doctor had simply said that the results of her mammogram were negative. This time, the doctor brought in her mammogram, which looked like an X ray. He pointed to a small white spot and said in a concerned voice, "I'm afraid that this tiny white dot may be a cancerous tumor." The doctor's words took her breath away. Finally, Maria asked in a terrified whisper, "Are you absolutely sure that spot is cancer?" The doctor paused for a minute, looked again at the mammogram, and said, "I can't be absolutely sure the spot is cancerous until we do a biopsy. All I can say is that there is a good possibility that it is." As Maria scheduled her biopsy, she would never forget seeing that white spot on the mammogram.

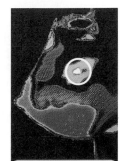

Why should two doctors read each mammogram?

Perceiving Things

What are the three questions?

At first glance, these three events—buying a subliminal tape, being bitten by a dog, and seeing a spot on a mammogram—seem to have nothing in common. In fact, these events raise three basic questions about how we perceive things.

Maria's subliminal tape raises the first question: Are there things that we perceive but are not aware of, and can these things influence our behaviors (R. L. Abrams & Greenwald, 2000)?

Maria's mammogram raises the second question: How large or unusual must things be before our senses can detect them? This is a very important question, since the answer may have serious health consequences (Pisano et al., 2005).

Finally, Gabrielle's painful experience with a dog raises the third question: How much are the things we perceive influenced or biased by our cultural, learning, emotional, and personal experiences (Goldstein, 2007)? These three questions are the key to understanding how we perceive our world.

What's Coming

We'll discuss what perceptual thresholds are, how sensations differ from perceptions, how sensations are combined to form perceptions, how objects can undergo great changes yet appear the same to us, how our senses are fooled by illusions, how cultural experiences change perceptions, whether there is good evidence for ESP (extrasensory perception), and whether the newest kind of perceiving, called virtual reality, can fool our senses into believing we're in a three-dimensional world.

Let's start with the first and most basic perceptual question: At what point do you become aware of seeing, hearing, smelling, tasting, or feeling some stimulus, object, or event?

A. Perceptual Thresholds

When do you know something is happening?

Imagine suddenly becoming deaf or blind, unable to hear what people are saying or to see where you are going. Only then would you realize that your senses provide a continuous stream of information about your world. Your senses tell you that something is out there, and your perceptions tell you what that something is. However, there are some sounds and objects you may not be aware of because the level of stimulation is too low and does not exceed the threshold of a particular sense.

Threshold **refers to a point above which a stimulus is perceived and below which it is not perceived. The threshold determines when we first become aware of a stimulus.**

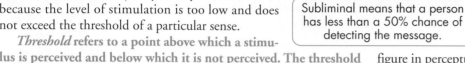

IMPROVE SELF-ESTEEM

Subliminal means that a person has less than a 50% chance of detecting the message.

For example, Maria is not aware of, or does not hear, subliminal messages recorded on tape because these messages are below her absolute threshold for hearing. To understand how the absolute threshold is determined, imagine that Maria is presented with a series of auditory messages that slowly increase in intensity. Maria is asked to press a button when she first hears a message. You may think that there will be a certain level or absolute value of intensity (loudness) at which Maria will first report hearing a tone. The idea that there is an absolute threshold was proposed by Gustav Fechner (1860), an important historical figure in perceptual research. However, as you'll see, Fechner had difficulty identifying the absolute threshold as he defined it.

1 At first, *Gustav Fechner (FECK-ner)* defined the absolute threshold as the smallest amount of stimulus energy (such as sound or light) that can be observed or experienced.

According to Fechner's definition, if Maria's hearing could always be measured under exactly the same conditions, her absolute threshold would always remain the same. Although Fechner tried various methods to identify absolute thresholds, he found that an individual's threshold was not absolute and, in fact, differed depending on the subject's alertness and the test situation. Because of this variability in measurement, researchers had to redefine absolute threshold.

2 The graph below shows how the absolute threshold was redefined.

Absolute threshold **is the intensity level of a stimulus such that a person will have a 50% chance of detecting it.**

According to this updated definition, Maria's absolute threshold is the point on the graph where she has a 50% chance of hearing the message.

Once we have determined Maria's absolute threshold for hearing messages, we can define a subliminal stimulus.

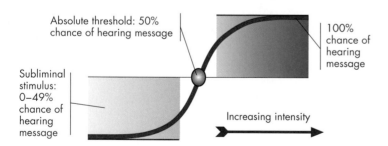

Absolute threshold: 50% chance of hearing message

100% chance of hearing message

Subliminal stimulus: 0–49% chance of hearing message

Increasing intensity

3 The graph above shows that a subliminal stimulus can occur at any point below the absolute threshold (50% chance of hearing).

A *subliminal stimulus* **has an intensity that gives a person less than a 50% chance of detecting the stimulus.**

Because subliminal messages can occur in a wide range (0–49%), Maria may or may not report hearing them on the tape. For example, Maria would never report hearing messages of very low intensity (0% level) but may sometimes report hearing messages of higher intensity (49%).

We'll discuss whether subliminal messages can change behaviors or attitudes, such as increasing self-esteem, in the Research Focus (p. 135).

4 Although the concept of an absolute threshold may seem abstract, it has very real consequences in detecting breast cancer.

Each year, over 200,000 women are diagnosed with breast cancer and over 40,000 women die of the disease, making it the most frequently occurring cancer in American women and,

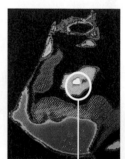

Possible cancerous breast tumor stands out as a white spot.

after lung cancer, the second-leading cancer killer (R. Stein, 2006). Doctors read about 25 million mammograms (X rays of breasts) each year to look for white spots that usually stand out on a black background; these white spots indicate tumors (photo above). However, about 40% of women have so much connective breast tissue, which also appears white, that tiny white tumors may go undetected. This problem, combined with doctors' lack of expertise, results in missing up to 30% of tumors on mammograms (DiIulio, 2004; Pisano et al., 2005).

Accuracy problems. Researchers are constantly looking for ways to lower the threshold for detecting cancerous tumors and thus save patients' lives. One study found that when mammograms were read independently by two doctors, the accuracy of identifying cancerous tumors increased by 20% (M. Healy, 2000). Recently, digital mammograms, which allow for images to be enhanced or magnified on a computer screen, have been found to be better at detecting cancerous tumors in women who have a lot of connective breast tissue (Pisano et al., 2005).

The problem of determining thresholds also applies to the question of how we know a stimulus has decreased or increased in intensity. We'll discuss this next.

Why is that music still too loud?

Suppose people are playing music too loud and you ask them to turn down the volume. Even after they turn it down, it may still seem just as loud as before. The explanation for this phenomenon can be found in the work of another historical figure in perception, E. H. Weber (VEY-ber).

Weber worked on the problem of how we judge whether a stimulus, such as loud music, has increased or decreased in intensity. This problem involves measuring the difference in thresholds between two stimuli, such as very loud music and not-quite-so-loud music. To solve this problem, Weber (1834) developed the concept of a just noticeable difference.

Smallest detectable increase or decrease in sound is a JND.

A *just noticeable difference*, or *JND*, refers to the smallest increase or decrease in the intensity of a stimulus that a person is able to detect.

For example, to measure a just noticeable difference in weight, Weber asked people to compare stimuli of varying intensities and indicate when they could detect a difference between them. He discovered that if he presented two stimuli with very low intensities, such as a 2-ounce weight versus a 3-ounce weight, people could easily detect the difference between them. However, if he presented stimuli with high intensities, such as a 40-pound weight versus a 41-pound weight, people could no longer detect the difference. For higher-intensity stimuli, such as heavy weights, a much larger difference in intensity was required for the difference to be noticed (Kantowitz et al., 2005).

Weber's observations on what it takes to detect just noticeable differences were the basis for what became known as Weber's law.

Weber's law states that the increase in intensity of a stimulus needed to produce a just noticeable difference grows in proportion to the intensity of the initial stimulus.

We'll use Weber's law (please read right figure) to explain how if someone is playing the stereo very loud, it must be turned down a great deal, usually more than the person prefers to turn it down, for you to detect a just noticeable decrease in volume.

Weber's Law Explained

Weber's law explains that, at lower intensities, small changes between two stimuli can be detected as just noticeable differences (JNDs); however, at higher intensities, only larger changes between two stimuli can be detected as JNDs.

Stimulus: Lower ⟶ Higher

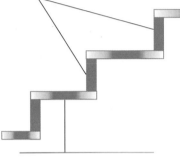

1 JND. The same height of each step illustrates your ability to detect "one sensory unit" of a *just noticeable difference* between the loudness of two sounds.

2 Lower intensities. The small width of this step indicates that, at lower intensities, you need only a *small difference* in order to detect a just noticeable difference between the loudness of two sounds. This statement follows from Weber's law, which says that only a small difference in intensity is required for you to detect a just noticeable difference when judging stimuli of lower intensity.

3 Higher intensities. The considerable width of this step indicates that, at higher sound intensities, you need a *larger difference* to detect a just noticeable difference between the loudness of two sounds. This statement follows from Weber's law, which says that a larger difference in intensity is required for you to detect a just noticeable difference when judging stimuli of higher intensity.

Besides explaining the problem with loud stereos, Weber's law has many practical applications, such as how to detect a difference in the softness of towels.

Just Noticeable Difference (JND) and Soft Towels

Which towel is softer?

Every year, industry and business spend billions of dollars to make sure that consumers can detect just noticeable differences between this year's and last year's cars, shampoos, cereals, and fashions. For example, consumers spend millions of dollars each year on fabric softeners, which are added during washing and are claimed to make clothes feel softer. To test such claims, researchers asked subjects to feel towels washed with and without a fabric softener and rate the softness of the towels on a scale from 1 (hard) to 30 (very soft). Subjects gave an average softness rating of 5 to towels washed repeatedly without softener and an average rating of 18 to towels washed with softener. Researchers concluded that fabric softeners worked, since subjects could easily detect a just noticeable difference in softness (S. I. Ali & Begum, 1994). This is but one practical application of Weber's law and just noticeable difference (JND) in industry.

Judging the softness of towels involves noting JND.

So far, we've focused on how you become aware of and detect stimuli and distinguish between their intensities. Next, we'll discuss one of the most interesting questions in perception: How do you change meaningless bits of sensations into meaningful and complete perceptions?

B. Sensation Versus Perception

How can I be successful and adapt and happy?

Much of your success in being happy and successful depends on your ability to respond intelligently and adapt appropriately to changes in your environment (NAMHC, 1996). The first step in responding and adapting involves gathering millions of meaningless sensations and changing them into useful perceptions. Because your brain changes sensations into perceptions so quickly, automatically, and with very little awareness, you might assume that what you see (sense) is what you perceive. However, the process of changing sensations into perceptions is influenced by whether you are alert, sleepy, worried, emotional, motivated, or affected by the use of a legal or illegal drug. For example, drinking alcohol causes perceptions in social situations to be less rational and more uninhibited, causing people under its influence to act aggressively, make terrible decisions, create problems, or say really dumb things (R. Goldberg, 2006; Maisto et al., 2004). As you are about to discover, sensing and perceiving are as different as night and day.

For example, quickly glance at the black-and-white figure below on the left and then look away and describe what you saw.

Sensations

Initially, the left figure appears to be a bunch of meaningless lines, spaces, and blobs, which, for the sake of simplicity, we'll take the liberty of calling visual sensations. In real life, we rarely if ever experience sensations because, as we'll explain on the next page, they are immediately turned into perceptions.

A *sensation* is our first awareness of some outside stimulus. An outside stimulus activates sensory receptors, which in turn produce electrical signals that are transformed by the brain into meaningless bits of information.

Sensations are MEANINGLESS bits of information.

You can approximate how visual sensations may look by placing half of a ping-pong ball over your eye. As you look through this nearly opaque ping-pong ball, you'll see shadows, textures, and dark shapes but nothing meaningful; these are similar to sensations.

Another example that illustrates the difference between sensations and perceptions is the photo below. Your first impression consists of meaningless shapes, textures, and blotches of color, which we'll again take the liberty of calling visual sensations. However, you can turn these meaningless sensations into a meaningful image—a perception—by using the following clues. This photo is an ultrasound image of a fetus in the womb. The fetus is lying on his back with his rounded tummy on the left and his large head on the right. Above his head is the right arm and hand, and you can even count the five tiny fingers. You can also see that the fetus is sucking on his thumb. Once you know what to look for, you automatically change the random blotches of colors and shapes into the perception of a fetus.

Obviously, it would be impossible to respond, adapt, and survive if you had to rely only on sensations. You can now appreciate the importance of changing sensations into perceptions.

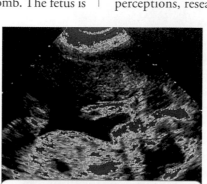

You can turn this sensation into a perception by reading the text (left).

Perceptions

As you look at the right stimulus, your brain is processing many thousands of visual sensations involving lines, curves, textures, shadows, and colors. Then, instantaneously, automatically, and without awareness, your brain combines these thousands of sensations into a perception—an orange tiger's face against a green background.

Perceptions are MEANINGFUL patterns, images, or sounds.

A *perception* is the experience we have after our brain assembles and combines thousands of individual, meaningless sensations into a meaningful pattern or image. However, our perceptions are rarely exact replicas of the original stimuli. Rather, our perceptions are usually changed, biased, colored, or distorted by our unique set of experiences. Thus, perceptions are our personal interpretations of the real world.

If you now look at the black-and-white drawing on the upper left, your brain will automatically combine the formerly meaningless shapes and blobs into a tiger's face. This is an approximate example of how meaningless sensations are automatically combined to form meaningful perceptions.

One important feature of perceptions is that they are rarely exact copies of the real world. For example, people who listen to the same song or music can react very differently (happy, relaxed, agitated, bored). To study how personal preferences for music can bias our perceptions, researchers assigned students who preferred listening to classical music over other types of music to groups that were instructed to sit and relax while listening to either 20 minutes of classical music or 20 minutes of rock music. Researchers used physiological measures to record anxiety levels both before and after subjects listened to music. Findings showed that only those subjects who listened to their favorite kind of music (classical music) had a decrease in anxiety levels (Salamon et al., 2003).

To show that no two individuals perceive the world in exactly the same way, we'll explain how your personal experiences change, bias, and even distort your perceptions.

How does a "nice" doggie become a "bad" doggie?

It is most unlikely that you have ever experienced a "pure" sensation because your brain automatically and instantaneously changes sensations into perceptions. Despite what you may think, perceptions do not exactly mirror events, people, situations, and objects in your environment. Rather, perceptions are interpretations, which means that your perceptions are changed or biased by your personal experiences, memories, emotions, and motivations. For

example, at the beginning of this module we told you how 7-year-old Gabrielle's perception of a dog was changed from "nice" to "bad" by her personal experience of being bitten. The next time Gabrielle sees a dog, she won't see just a four-legged creature with ears, nose, and tail; she will see a "bad" four-legged creature. To understand how sensations become perceptions, we have divided the perceptual process into a series of discrete steps that, in real life, are much more complex and interactive.

There are five steps in forming perceptions.

1 Stimulus. Since normally we experience only perceptions, we are not aware of many preceding steps. The first step begins with some stimulus, which is any change of energy in the environment, such as light waves, sound waves, mechanical pressure, or chemicals. The stimulus activates sense receptors in the eyes, ears, skin, nose, or mouth. In Gabrielle's case, the stimuli are light waves reflecting off the body of a large, brown dog.

A stimulus (dog) activates receptors in the senses.

2 Transduction. After entering Gabrielle's eyes, light waves are focused on the retina, which contains photoreceptors that are sensitive to light. The light waves are absorbed by photoreceptors, which change physical energy into electrical signals, called transduction. The electrical signals are changed into impulses that travel to the brain. Sense organs do not produce sensations but simply transform energy into electrical signals.

Senses change stimulus into electrical signals.

3 Brain: primary areas. Impulses from sense organs first go to different primary areas of the brain. For example, impulses from the ear go to the temporal lobe, from touch to the parietal lobe, and from the eye to areas in the occipital lobe. When impulses reach primary areas in the occipital lobe, they are first changed into sensations. However, Gabrielle would not report seeing sensations.

Occipital lobe

Primary areas of brain change electrical signals into sensations.

4 Brain: association areas. Each sense sends its particular impulses to a different primary area of the brain where impulses are changed into sensations, which are meaningless bits of information, such as shapes, colors, and textures (top right). The "sensation" impulses are then sent to the appropriate association area in the brain. The association areas change meaningless bits into meaningful images, called perceptions, such as a dog (bottom right).

In Gabrielle's case, impulses from her eyes would be changed into visual sensations by the primary visual area and into perceptions by the visual association areas. However, Gabrielle's perception of a dog would be changed, biased, and even distorted by many psychological, emotional, and cultural factors.

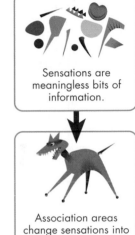

Sensations are meaningless bits of information.

Association areas change sensations into perceptions—dog.

5 Personalized perceptions. Each of us has a unique set of personal experiences, emotions, and memories that are automatically added to our perceptions by other areas of the brain. As a result, our perceptions are not a mirror but a changed, biased, or even distorted copy of the real world (Goldstein, 2007). For example, the visual areas of Gabrielle's brain automatically assemble many thousands of sensations into a meaningful pattern, which in this case is a dog. Now, however, Gabrielle doesn't see just an ordinary brown dog because other brain areas add her emotional experience of being bitten. Thus, Gabrielle perceives this brown, four-legged creature to be a "bad dog." For this same reason, two people can look at the same dog and have very different perceptions, such as cute dog, great dog, bad dog, smelly dog, or friendly dog. Thus, your perceptions are personalized interpretations rather than true copies of objects, animals, people, and situations in the real world.

The process of assembling and organizing sensations into perceptions was of great interest to early psychologists, who disagreed on how perceptions were formed. As you'll see next, their debate resulted in a very interesting perceptual controversy.

Perceptions do not mirror reality but rather include our biases, emotions, and memories to reflect reality.

C. Rules of Organization

What was the great debate?
In the early 1900s, two groups of psychologists engaged in a heated debate over how perceptions are formed. One group, called the structuralists, strongly believed that we added together thousands of sensations to form a perception. Another group, called the Gestalt psychologists, just as strongly believed that sensations were not added but rather combined according to a set of innate rules to form a perception (D. J. Murray et al., 2000). One group won the debate and you might guess which one before you read further.

Structuralists	*Gestalt Psychologists*

As you look at the scene in the middle of this page, you perceive a fountain at the bottom with shrubs and palm trees on the sides, all topped by a large dome of glass windows. Is it possible that your brain combined many thousands of individual sensations to produce this complex perception? If you answer yes, you agree with the structuralists.

The *structuralists* believed that you add together hundreds of basic elements to form complex perceptions. They also believed that you can work backward to break down perceptions into smaller and smaller units, or elements.

Structuralists spent hundreds of hours analyzing how perceptions, such as a falling ball, might be broken down into basic units or elements. They believed that once they understood the process of breaking down perceptions, they would know how basic units are recombined to form perceptions. Thus, structuralists believed that you add together basic units to form perceptions, much as you would add a column of numbers to get a total.

Do you add together basic elements to form perceptions or does your brain have rules for forming perceptions?

For example, structuralists would say that you add together hundreds of basic units, such as colors, bricks, leaves, branches, tiles, pieces of glass, and bits of steel, to form the perception of the scene above. However, the structuralists' explanation of adding bits to form a perception was hotly denied by Gestalt psychologists.

The Gestalt psychologists said that perceptions were much too complex to be formed by simply adding sensations together; instead, they believed that perceptions were formed according to a set of rules.

Gestalt psychologists **believed that our brains follow a set of rules that specify how individual elements are to be organized into a meaningful pattern, or perception.**

Unlike the structuralists, the Gestalt psychologists said that perceptions do not result from adding sensations. Rather, perceptions result from our brain's ability to organize sensations according to a set of rules, much as our brain follows a set of rules for organizing words into meaningful sentences (Donderi, 2006).

So how would Gestalt psychologists explain your perception of the scene on the left? They would say that your perception was not formed by simply adding bits of tile, steel, and foliage into a whole image. Rather, your brain automatically used a set of rules to combine these elements to form a unified whole. To emphasize their point, Gestalt psychologists came up with a catchy phrase, "The whole is more than the sum of its parts," to mean that perceptions are not merely combined sensations. The Gestalt psychologists went one step further; they came up with a list of organizational rules.

Who won the debate?
Gestalt psychologists won their debate with the structuralists for two reasons. The first reason comes from our own personal perceptual experiences. For example, as you look again at the beautiful scene above, we must reveal that it is entirely fake. The scene, which looks so realistic and three-dimensional, is actually painted on a flat wall. It seems impossible that we could have such a complex, three-dimensional perceptual experience from simply combining bits and pieces of bricks, branches, leaves, and steel. This fake but truly realistic scene makes the Gestalt motto come to life: "The whole is more than the sum of its parts."

Equally convincing evidence that the whole is greater than the sum of its parts came from a remarkably detailed series of studies in which Gestalt psychologists presented stimuli to subjects and then asked them to describe what they perceived (Rock & Palmer, 1990). On the basis of subjects' reports, researchers discovered that forming perceptions involved more than simply adding and combining individual elements. Modern research has generally supported the early Gestalt conclusion that our brains actually do follow a set of rules for organizing and forming perceptions (Palmer et al., 2003). We'll explain these rules for organizing perceptions next.

How many rules are there?

It is very hard to believe that the scene on the preceding page (repeated here on the right) was actually painted on a flat wall. One reason you perceive this scene as complex and 3-dimensional is that the painter followed many of the Gestalt rules of organization (Han & Humphreys, 1999).

Rules of organization, which were identified by Gestalt psychologists, specify how our brains combine and organize individual pieces or elements into a meaningful perception.

As you look at the scene, your brain automatically organizes many hundreds of visual stimuli, including colors, textures, shadows, bricks, steel, glass, leaves, and branches, according to one or more of the six perceptual rules of organization described below. We'll use a relatively simple figure to illustrate each rule.

Figure-Ground

One of the most basic rules in organizing perceptions is picking out the object from its background. As you look at the figure on the left, you will automatically see a white object standing out against a red background, which illustrates the figure-ground principle.

The *figure-ground rule* states that, in organizing stimuli, we tend to **automatically distinguish between a figure and a ground: The figure, with more detail, stands out against the background, which has less detail.**

There is some evidence that our ability to separate figure from ground is an innate response. For example, individuals who were blind from an early age and had their sight restored as adults were able to distinguish between figure and ground with little or no training (Senden, 1960). The figure-ground rule is one of the first rules that our brain uses to organize stimuli into a perception (Vecera, 2002). This particular image is interesting because, as you continue to stare at it, the figure and ground will suddenly reverse and you'll see profiles of two faces. However, in the real world, the images and objects we usually perceive are not reversible because they have more distinct shapes (Humphreys & Muller, 2000).

Similarity

As you look at this figure filled with light and dark blue dots, you see a dark blue numeral 2. The *similarity rule* states that, in organizing stimuli, we group together elements that appear similar.

The similarity rule causes us to group the dark blue dots together and prevents us from seeing the figure as a random arrangement of light and dark blue dots.

Closure

Although the lines are incomplete, you can easily perceive this drawing as a cat or dog.

The *closure rule* states that, in organizing stimuli, we tend to fill in any missing parts of a figure and see the figure as complete.

For example, the closure rule explains why you can fill in letters missing on a sign or pieces missing in a jigsaw puzzle.

Proximity

Notice that although there are exactly eight circles in each horizontal line, you perceive each line as formed by a different number of groups of circles.

The *proximity rule* states that, in organizing stimuli, we group together objects that are physically close to one another.

You automatically group circles that are close together and thus perceive the first line as composed of three groups (Kubovy & Wagemans, 1995).

Simplicity

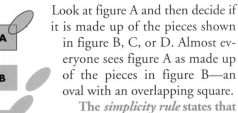

Look at figure A and then decide if it is made up of the pieces shown in figure B, C, or D. Almost everyone sees figure A as made up of the pieces in figure B—an oval with an overlapping square.

The *simplicity rule* states that stimuli are organized in the simplest way possible.

For example, almost no one sees figure A as having been formed from the complicated pieces shown in figure C or figure D. This rule says that we tend to perceive complex figures as divided into several simpler figures (Shimaya, 1997).

Continuity

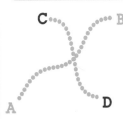

As you scan this figure, keep track of the path that your eyes follow. If you are like most people, your eyes will move from left to right in a continuous line, following the path from A to B or from C to D.

The *continuity rule* states that, in organizing stimuli, we tend to favor smooth or continuous paths when interpreting a series of points or lines.

For example, the rule of continuity predicts that you do not see a line that begins at A and then turns abruptly to C or to D.

Conclusion. These figures demonstrate the Gestalt rules of organizing stimuli into perceptions. Young children slowly learn these perceptual rules and begin to use them as early as 7 months (Quinn et al., 2002). As adults we often use these rules to organize thousands of stimuli into perceptions, especially stimuli in print and advertisements.

Next, we turn to another interesting perceptual question: How can objects change yet appear to remain the same?

D. Perceptual Constancy

Size, Shape, Brightness & Color Constancy

Why don't speeding cars shrink? Perception is full of interesting puzzles, such as how cars, people, and pets can constantly change their shapes as they move about yet we perceive them as remaining the same size and shape. For example, a car doesn't grow smaller as it speeds away, even though its shape on your retina grows smaller and smaller. A door doesn't become a trapezoid as you walk through it, even though that's what happens to its shape on your retina. These are examples of how perceptions remain constant, a phenomenon called perceptual constancy.

Perceptual constancy refers to our tendency to perceive **sizes, shapes, brightness, and colors as remaining the same even though their physical characteristics are constantly changing.**

We'll discuss four kinds of perceptual constancy—size, shape, brightness, and color.

Size Constancy

Imagine a world in which you perceived that every car, person, or animal became smaller as it moved away. Fortunately, we are spared from coping with so much stimulus change by perceptual constancy, one type of which is size constancy.

Size constancy refers to our tendency to perceive objects as remaining the same size even when their images on the retina are continually growing or shrinking.

As a car drives away, it projects a smaller and smaller image on your retina (left figure). Although the retinal image grows smaller, you do not perceive the car as shrinking because of size constancy. A similar process happens as a car drives toward you.

As the same car drives closer, notice in the figure below how it projects a larger image on your retina. However, because of size constancy, you do not perceive the car as becoming larger.

Size constancy is something you have learned from experience with moving objects. You have learned that objects do not increase or decrease in size as they move about. For example, an individual who was blind since birth and had his vision restored as an adult looked out a fourth-story window and reported seeing tiny creatures moving on the sidewalk. Because he had not learned size constancy, he did not know the tiny creatures were full-size people (Gregory, 1974).

We also perceive shapes as remaining the same.

Shape Constancy

Each time you move a book, its image on your retina changes from a rectangle to a trapezoid. But you see the book's shape as remaining the same because of shape constancy.

Shape constancy refers to your tendency to perceive an object as retaining its same shape even though when you view it from different angles, its shape is continually changing its image on the retina.

The figure below shows that when you look down at a rectangular book, it projects a rectangular shape on your retina.

However, if you move the book farther away, it projects trapezoidal shapes on your retina (figure below), but you still perceive the book as rectangular because of shape constancy.

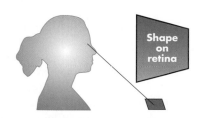

Besides size and shape constancy, there is also brightness and color constancy.

Brightness and Color Constancy

If you look into your dimly lit closet, all the brightly colored clothes will appear dull and grayish. However, because of brightness and color constancy, you still perceive brightness and colors and have no trouble selecting a red shirt.

Brightness constancy refers to the tendency to perceive brightness as remaining the same in changing illumination.

Color constancy refers to the tendency to perceive colors as remaining stable despite differences in lighting.

For example, if you looked at this young girl's sweater in bright sunlight, it would be a bright yellow.

If you looked at her same yellow sweater in dim light, you would still perceive the color as a shade of yellow, although it is duller. Because of color constancy, colors seem about the same even when lighting conditions change.

However, if the light is very dim, objects will appear mostly gray because you lose color vision in very dim light.

Perceptual constancy is important because it transforms a potentially ever-changing, chaotic world into one with stability and comforting sameness.

Our next perceptual puzzle is how our eyes can see only two-dimensional images but our brain can transform them into a three-dimensional world.

Binocular (Two Eyes) Depth Cues

How can you see in three dimensions?

Normally, movies are shown in only two dimensions, height and width. But if you have ever seen a movie in 3-D (using special glasses to see three dimensions: height, width, and depth), you know the thrill of watching objects or animals leap off the screen so realistically that you duck or turn your head. You may not have realized that your eyes automatically give you a free, no-glasses, 3-D view of the world. And the amazing part of seeing in 3-D is that everything projected on the retina is in only two dimensions, height and width, which means that your brain combines a number of different cues to add a third dimension—depth (J. M. Harris & Dean, 2003).

Seeing in 3-D means seeing length, width, and DEPTH.

Depth perception refers to the ability of your eye and brain to add a third dimension, depth, to all visual perceptions, even though images projected on the retina are in only two dimensions, height and width.

The object on the left has been given a three-dimensional look by making it seem to have depth. It is impossible for most sighted people to imagine a world without depth, since they rely on depth perception to move and locate objects in space. The cues for depth perception are divided into two major classes: binocular and monocular.

Binocular depth cues depend on the movement of both eyes (*bi* means "two"; *ocular* means "eye").

We'll start with two binocular cues, convergence and retinal disparity.

Convergence

When you have an eye exam, the doctor usually asks you to follow the end of her finger as she holds it a few feet away and then slowly moves it closer until it touches your nose. This is a test for convergence.

Convergence refers to a binocular cue for depth perception based on signals sent from muscles that turn the eyes. To focus on near or approaching objects, these muscles turn the eyes inward, toward the nose. The brain uses the signals sent by these muscles to determine the distance of the object.

The woman in the photo at the right is demonstrating the ultimate in convergence as she looks at

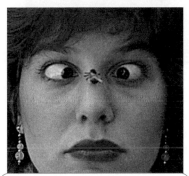

During convergence the eyes turn inward to see objects up close.

the fly on her nose. You can experience convergence by holding a finger in front of your nose and slowly bringing it closer to your nose. Your finger appears to move closer to your nose because the muscles that are turning the eyes inward produce signals corresponding to convergence. The more your eyes turn inward or converge, the nearer the object appears in space. The woman in the photo knows the fly is on her nose because of convergent clues from her turned-in eyes.

The second binocular cue comes from having an eye on each side of your face.

Retinal Disparity

One reason it's an advantage to have an eye on each side of your face is that each eye has a slightly different view of the world, which provides another binocular cue for depth perception called retinal disparity.

Retinal disparity refers to a binocular depth cue that depends on the distance between the eyes. Because of their different positions, each eye receives a slightly different image. The difference between the right and left eyes' images is the retinal disparity. The brain interprets a large retinal disparity to mean a close object and a small retinal disparity to mean a distant object.

The figure at the left shows how retinal disparity occurs: The difference between the image seen by the left eye (1) and the one seen by the right eye (2) results in retinal disparity (3).

1. Left eye sees a slightly different image of the fly.

3. Brain combines the two slightly different images from left and right eyes and gives us a perception of depth.

2. Right eye sees a slightly different image of the fly.

Another example of retinal disparity occurs when viewers wear special glasses to watch a 3-D movie, which has width, height, and depth. Standard 3-D glasses use a red and a green lens, which is a technique to allow the right and left eyes to perceive slightly different views of the same scene. As a result, the brain receives two slightly different images. As the brain automatically combines the slightly different images, we get the feeling of depth—for example, seeing a mad dog jump out of the movie screen into the audience (followed by much screaming).

Individuals who have only one eye still have depth perception because there are a number of one-eyed, or monocular, cues for depth perception, which we'll explain next.

E. Depth Perception

Could a Cyclops land an airplane?

A mythical creature called the Cyclops had only one eye in the middle of his forehead. Although a Cyclops would lack depth perception cues associated with retinal disparity, he would have depth perception cues associated with having one eye, or being monocular (*mon* means "one").

I could land an airplane with one eye!

This means that a Cyclops or an individual with one good eye could land an airplane because of monocular depth cues.

Monocular depth cues **are produced by signals from a single eye. Monocular cues most commonly arise from the way objects are arranged in the environment.**

We'll show you seven of the most common monocular cues for perceiving depth.

Linear perspective makes you see the road as going on forever.

Interposition makes you see the fish in front as closer and those in back as farther away.

1 Linear Perspective

As you look down a long stretch of highway, the parallel lines formed by the sides of the road appear to come together, or converge, at a distant point. This convergence is a monocular cue for distance and is called linear perspective.

Linear perspective **is a monocular depth cue that results as parallel lines come together, or converge, in the distance.**

Relative size makes you see the larger man as closer and the smaller men as farther away.

2 Relative Size

You expect the runners in the photo above to be the same size. However, since the runner on the right appears larger, you perceive him as closer, while the runner on the left appears smaller and, thus, farther away. The relative size of objects is a monocular cue for distance.

Relative size **is a monocular cue for depth that results when we expect two objects to be the same size and they are not. In that case, the larger of the two objects will appear closer and the smaller will appear farther away.**

3 Interposition

As you look at the school of fish in the photo above, you can easily perceive which fish are in front and which are in back, even though all the fish are about the same size. You can identify and point out which fish are closest to you and which are farthest away by using the monocular depth cue of overlap, which is called interposition.

Interposition **is a monocular cue for depth perception that comes into play when objects overlap. The overlapping object appears closer and the object that is overlapped appears farther away.**

Light makes the outlines of the footprints appear closer, while shadow makes the imprints seem farther away.

4 *Light and Shadow*

Notice how the brightly lit edges of the footprints appear closer, while the shadowy imprint in the sand appears to recede. Also, the sunny side of the sand dune seems closer, while the back side in shadows appears farther away. The monocular depth cues shown here involve the interplay of light and shadows.

Light and shadow **make up monocular cues for depth perception: Brightly lit objects appear closer, while objects in shadows appear farther away.**

Texture gradient makes you see the sharply detailed, cracked mud as being closer.

5 *Texture Gradient*

You can't help but notice how the wide, detailed surface cracks in the mud seem closer, while the less detailed and narrower cracks appear farther away. These sharp changes in surface details are monocular depth cues created by texture gradients.

Texture gradient **is a monocular depth cue in which areas with sharp, detailed texture are interpreted as being closer and those with less sharpness and poorer detail are perceived as more distant.**

6 *Atmospheric Perspective*

One of the depth cues you may have overlooked is created by changes in the atmosphere. For example, both the man sitting on the chair and the edge of the cliff appear much closer than the fog-shrouded hills and landscape in the background. These monocular depth cues are created by changes in the atmosphere.

Atmospheric perspective **is a monocular depth cue that is created by the presence of dust, smog, clouds, or water vapor. We perceive clearer objects as being nearer, and we perceive hazy or cloudy objects as being farther away.**

Atmospheric perspective makes clear objects seem nearer and hazy objects as being farther away.

7 *Motion Parallax*

In this photo, you can easily tell which riders seem closer to you and which appear farther away. That's because you perceive fast-moving or blurry objects (horsemen on the right) as being closer to you and slower-

Motion parallax makes blurry objects appear closer and clear objects as being farther away.

moving or clearer objects (horsemen on the left) as being farther away. These monocular depth cues come from the way you perceive motion.

Motion parallax **is a monocular depth cue based on the speed of moving objects. We perceive objects that appear to be moving at high speed as closer to us than those moving more slowly or appearing stationary.**

We have just discussed seven monocular cues involved in perceiving depth and distance accurately. Because they are monocular cues—needing only one eye—it means that people with only one eye have depth perception good enough to land a plane, drive a car, or play various sports such as baseball and tennis. If you wish to try some of these monocular cues, just hold your hand over one eye and see if you can avoid objects as you walk around a room.

We turn next to occasions where our perceptual system is fooled, and we see things that are not there. Welcome to the world of illusions.

F. Illusions

What is an illusion?

There are two reasons that much of the time your perceptions of cars, people, food, trees, animals, furniture, and professors are reasonably accurate reflections but, because of emotional, motivational, and cultural influences, never exact copies of reality.

First, we inherit similar sensory systems whose information is processed and interpreted by similar areas of the brain (Franz et al., 2000). However, damage to sensory areas of the brain can result in very distorted perceptions, such as the neglect syndrome (p. 79), in which people do not perceive one side of their body or one side of their environment. The second reason our perceptions are reasonably accurate is that we learn from common experience about the sizes, shapes, and colors of objects. But we've already discussed how perceptions can be biased or distorted by previous emotional and learning experiences, such as perceiving dogs differently after being bitten by one. Now we come to another way that perceptions can be distorted: by changing the actual perceptual cues so you perceive something unlikely, which is called an illusion.

An *illusion* is a perceptual experience in which you perceive an image as being so strangely distorted that, in reality, it cannot and does not exist. An illusion is created by manipulating the perceptual cues so that your brain can no longer correctly interpret space, size, and depth cues.

This impossible figure seems to have two or three prongs!

For example, if you look at the right end of this tuning fork, it appears to have two prongs. But if you look at the left end, it appears to have three prongs. You're looking at a figure that most of us cannot draw because it seems impossible.

An *impossible figure* is a perceptual experience in which a drawing seems to defy basic geometric laws.

One reason the tuning fork appears impossible to figure out and is almost impossible for you to draw has to do with your previous experience with line drawings in books. Because you have seen many three-dimensional objects drawn in books, you tend to perceive the left side of the tuning fork as being three-dimensional (three forks) but you tend to perceive the right side as being two-dimensional (two forks). Later on in the Cultural Diversity feature (p. 137), you'll learn why Africans can easily draw this impossible figure while most college professors cannot (Coren & Ward, 1993).

In this example, we perceive an illusion because the tuning fork is drawn to confuse our previous experiences with two- and three-dimensional objects. One of the oldest illusions that you have often experienced is the moon illusion, which has proven very difficult to explain (H. E. Ross & Plug, 2002).

Moon Illusion

Moon appears to be huge when it's near the horizon.

Moon appears 50% smaller when it's high in the sky.

The moon illusion has intrigued people for centuries because it is so impressive. The left photo shows that when a full moon is near the horizon, it appears (or gives the illusion of being) as much as 50% larger than when it is high in the sky (right photo). Here's the interesting part: You perceive this 50% increase in size even though the size of both moons on your retinas is exactly the same.

For over 50 years, researchers have proposed different theories for the moon illusion. Currently, no single theory can explain the moon illusion completely and it is believed that several factors contribute to it. The most important factor has to do with how the view of the landscape surrounding the moon influences our depth perception (H. E. Ross & Plug, 2002).

When we view the moon on the horizon, we see it in relation to the landscape (trees, mountains, buildings), which consists of depth information. In contrast, because we view the elevated moon through empty space, there are no cues to indicate distance. Thus, our brains perceive the moon on the horizon to be farther away than the elevated moon. Consequently, since the size of both moons on our retinas is exactly the same and the moon on the horizon is perceived as being farther away, our brain compensates to correct this inconsistency by inflating our perception of the size of the moon on the horizon. Consistent with this theory, researchers found that subjects estimated the horizon moon to be much farther away and interpreted its size as being larger. Likewise, subjects estimated the elevated moon to be closer and perceived it as being smaller (L. Kaufman, 2000).

Besides naturally occurring illusions, there are others that humans have created. One of the most interesting illusions comes from looking inside the Ames room.

Ames Room

Adult woman appears smaller than young boy.

In the Ames room (left photo), you perceive the boy on the right to be twice as tall as the woman on the left. In fact, the boy is smaller than the woman but appears larger because of the design of the Ames room.

The Ames room, named after its designer, shows that our perception of size can be distorted by changing depth cues.

The reason the boy appears to be twice as tall as the woman is that the room has a peculiar shape and you are looking in from a fixed peephole. To see how the Ames room changes your depth cues, look at the diagram of the Ames room in the drawing below right.

If you view the Ames room from the fixed peephole, the room appears rectangular and matches your previous

experience with rooms, which are usually rectangular. However, as the right figure shows, the Ames room is actually shaped in an odd way: The left corner is twice as far away from the peephole as the right corner. This means that the woman is actually twice as far away from you as the boy. However, the Ames room's odd shape makes you think that you are seeing the two people from the same distance, and this (illusion) makes the farther woman appear to be shorter than the boy (Goldstein, 2007).

The next two illusions either change your perceptual cues or rely too much on your previous perceptual experiences.

Ponzo Illusion

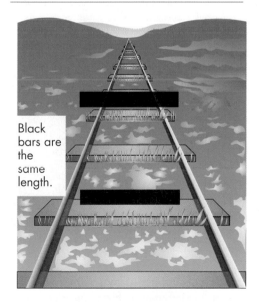

Black bars are the same length.

In the figure above, the top black bar appears to be much longer than the bottom black bar. However, if you measure these two bars, you will discover that they are exactly the same size. This is the **Ponzo illusion.** I clearly remember measuring the first time I saw this picture because I couldn't believe the bars were the same size. You perceive the top bar as being farther away, and you have learned from experience that if two objects appear to be the same size but one is farther away, the more distant object must be larger; thus, the top bar appears longer.

Müller-Lyer Illusion

The figures at the left and right illustrate the **Müller-Lyer illusion.** Notice that the left arrow appears noticeably shorter than the right arrow. However, if you measure them, you'll prove that the arrows are of equal length.

Left and right arrows are the same length.

One explanation for this illusion is that you are relying on size cues learned from your previous experience with corners of rooms. You have learned that if a corner of a room extends outward, it is closer; this experience distorts your perception so that the left arrow appears to be shorter. In contrast, you have learned that if a corner of a room recedes inward, it is farther away, and this experience makes you perceive the right arrow as longer (Goldstein, 2007). Illusions are fun, but what have we learned?

Learning from Illusions

Most of the time, you perceive the world with reasonable accuracy by using a set of proven perceptual cues for size, shape, and depth. However, illusions teach us that when proven perceptual cues are changed or manipulated, our reliable perceptual processes can be deceived, and we see something unreal or an illusion. Illusions also teach us that perception is a very active process, in which we continually rely on and apply previous experiences with objects when we perceive new situations. For example, you'll discover later (p. 140) how the entertainment industry changes the perceptual rule of closure to create movies, whose motion is a brilliant illusion. After the Concept Review, we'll discuss a form of perception that the U.S. Congress almost outlawed.

Concept Review

 **1.** This figure illustrates the concept of the _____, which is defined as the intensity level of a stimulus such that a person will have a 50% chance of detecting it.

2. The smallest increase or decrease in the intensity of a stimulus that a person can detect is called a (a)_____. The increase in intensity of a stimulus needed to produce a just noticeable difference grows in proportion to the intensity of the initial stimulus; this is called (b)_____ law.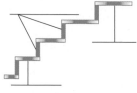

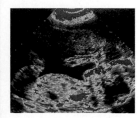 **3.** Our first awareness of sensory information, in the form of meaningless bits of information, is called a (a)_____. When many bits of sensory information have been assembled into a meaningful image, it is called a (b)_____, which can be biased or distorted by our unique set of experiences.

4. Early psychologists discovered a set of rules or principles that our brains use to automatically group or arrange stimuli into perceptual experiences. These early researchers, who were called _____ psychologists, disagreed with other early psychologists, who were called structuralists.

 5. You automatically separate an image into a more dominant, detailed figure and a less detailed background according to the _____ rule.

6. You fill in missing parts to form a complete image as a result of the _____ rule.

7. You see this image as formed by an oval and an overlying square because of the _____ rule.

 8. You divide each line of this figure into separate groups of objects according to the _____ rule.

9. In this figure, you see a blue numeral 2 instead of light and dark blue circles because of the _____ rule.

10. In this figure, you see a continuous line from A to B, rather than a line from A to C, following the _____ rule.

11. Although physical qualities of stimuli may change, you may perceive them as remaining the same because of (a)_____. For example, as a car drives away from you, its image on your retina becomes smaller but you know that the car does not shrink in size because of (b)_____ constancy. When you close a door, its shape on your retina changes from a rectangle to a trapezoid, but you perceive the door as remaining the same because of (c)_____ constancy. If you had a bright red car, it would appear red in bright light and still appear to be red in dimmer light because of (d)_____ constancy.

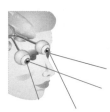 **12.** Cues for depth perception that depend on both eyes are called (a)_____ cues. Cues for depth perception that depend on a single eye are called (b)_____ cues. The bin-ocular cue that occurs when your eyes move inward to track a fly landing on your nose is called (c)_____. The binocular cue that occurs when each eye receives a slightly different image is called (d)_____.

13. Monocular cues for depth perception include: cues from overlapping objects, called (a)_____; cues from two parallel lines converging, called (b)_____; cues from larger and smaller images, called (c)_____; cues from the presence of dust and smog, called (d)_____; and cues from nearer and farther objects moving at different speeds, called (e)_____.

14. If perceptual cues are so changed that our brains can no longer interpret them correctly, we perceive a distorted image of reality, called an (a)_____. Such a distorted perception illustrates that perception is an active process and that we rely on previous (b)_____ when perceiving new situations.

Answers: *1. absolute threshold; 2. (a) just noticeable difference, (b) Weber's; 3. (a) sensation, (b) perception; 4. Gestalt; 5. figure-ground; 6. closure; 7. simplicity; 8. proximity; 9. similarity; 10. continuity; 11. (a) perceptual constancy, (b) size, (c) shape, (d) color; 12. (a) binocular, (b) monocular, (c) convergence, (d) retinal disparity; 13. (a) interposition, (b) linear perspective, (c) relative size, (d) atmospheric perspective, (e) motion parallax; 14. (a) illusion, (b) experiences*

G. Research Focus: Influencing Perception

Can "Unsensed Messages" Change Behavior?

Why did people buy more popcorn? Sometimes research questions come from unusual places—in this case, a movie theater. In the late 1950s, moviegoers were reported to have bought 50% more popcorn and 18% more Coca-Cola when the words "Eat popcorn" and "Drink Coca-Cola" were projected subliminally (1/3,000 of a second) during the regular movie (J. V. McConnell et al., 1958). The concern that advertisers might change consumers' buying habits without their knowledge prompted the U.S. Congress to consider banning any form of subliminal advertising. Congress did not take legislative action because subliminal advertising proved to be ineffective (Pratkanis, 1992). However, history seems to be repeating itself as advertisers now claim that subliminal tapes can change specific behaviors (Epley et al., 1999).

Eat popcorn!

Changing Specific Behaviors

At the beginning of this module, we told you about Maria, who, like millions of other Americans, purchased an audiotape because it claimed to contain subliminal persuasion that would effortlessly change her behavior.

A *subliminal message* is a brief auditory or visual message that is presented below the absolute threshold, which means that there is less than a 50% chance that the message will be perceived.

To answer the research question, Can subliminal messages change specific behaviors?, researchers conducted a well-designed experiment that used a double-blind procedure.

Labels did not match subliminal messages.

Method. For several weeks, subjects listened to two different tapes titled either "Improve Self-Esteem" or "Improve Memory." Then they rated any improvement in these behaviors.

Double-blind procedure. Researchers had to control for any possible placebo effects, such as subjects' showing improvement because they believed they were hearing powerful subliminal messages. Therefore, subjects were not told which subliminal messages the tapes contained. For example, some tapes labeled "Improve Memory" contained subliminal messages for improving memory, while others contained subliminal messages for improving self-esteem. Thus, because of the double-blind procedure, subjects were unaware of the fact that some tapes' subliminal messages did not match the tapes' labels.

But, subjects believed what the labels said.

Results. About 50% of the subjects reported improvements in either self-esteem or memory. However, subjects reported improvements in behavior based on what the **tapes' labels promised** rather than on what the subliminal messages were. For example, a subject who listened to a tape labeled "Improve Self-Esteem" reported improvements in self-esteem even though the tape contained subliminal messages for improving memory. These results suggest a self-fulfilling prophecy at work.

Self-fulfilling prophecies involve having strong beliefs about changing some behavior and then acting, unknowingly, to change that behavior.

Researchers concluded that subliminal messages in self-help tapes did not affect the behavior they were designed to change. Instead, any changes in behavior resulted from listeners' beliefs that the tapes would be effective (Epley et al., 1999).

Although subliminal messages are ineffective in changing specific behaviors, there is evidence that unconscious attitudes can unknowingly or subliminally influence perception.

Influencing Perceptions

Is it possible to have biased attitudes and be unaware of having them? If so, can these unknown or unconscious attitudes influence our perceptions? These questions are similar to those Mahzarin Banaji, a researcher at Harvard, has been asking for many years now. In one very interesting study, she wanted to determine whether people's expectations could unknowingly influence their perceptions (Vedantam, 2005).

Method. Fifty business executives viewed a black-and-white video clip of a basketball game in which the players were making quick passes and rapidly changing positions. The executives were asked to count the number of passes made during the video clip. When the video clip ended, executives excitedly shouted out answers. However, Banaji was not interested in their answers and instead asked whether anyone had seen anything unusual. The video watched by the executives did in fact show something unusual; about halfway through the video clip, a woman with an open white umbrella slowly walked through the screen from one end to the other. How many of the executives do you think noticed something so obvious?

Results. It turns out that none of the fifty executives noticed the woman with the white umbrella. Banaji played the video clip for the executives again and this time told them not to pay attention to the basketball passes. When the woman appeared, the executives could not believe they had not noticed something so obvious and worried that hidden biases could influence them in other ways.

These results indicate that people's expectations can unknowingly or subliminally influence their perceptions. Other research has also shown that subtle cues often influence people without their awareness. Several studies focused on racial biases found that even when people genuinely deny having racial biases, results reveal that they hold biased racial attitudes without their awareness. Thus, people's unconscious attitudes can unknowingly influence their behaviors and potentially influence the way people make important decisions, such as those made in the hiring process or in court trials (Lehrman, 2006; Vedantam, 2005).

Next, you'll see how cultural values and experiences can also unknowingly change what you perceive.

H. Cultural Diversity: Influence on Perceptions

What Do Cultural Influences Do?

If you visit ethnic sections of large U.S. cities, such as Chinatown or Little Italy, or visit foreign countries, you become aware of cultural differences and influences. For example, this photo shows two Japanese women in traditional robes and setting, which symbolize the different cultural influences of Japan compared to Western countries.

Cultural influences are persuasive pressures that encourage members of a particular society or ethnic group to conform to shared behaviors, values, and beliefs.

What if you were raised in a different culture?

No one doubts that cultural influences affect the way people eat, dress, talk, and socialize. But you are less likely to notice how cultural influences also affect how you perceive things in your own environment.

For example, cultural anthropologists, who study behaviors in natural settings in other cultures, have reported intriguing examples of how cultural experiences influence perceptual processes. We'll begin with a remarkable finding of why natives were unable to perceive common objects in photos.

Perception of Photos

Could not recognize a dog in a black/white photo

A cultural anthropologist showed African natives black-and-white photos of a cow and a dog, two animals the natives were very familiar with. But when the natives looked at the black-and-white photos, they seemed very puzzled because they did not see any animals. Their expressions suggested that the anthropologist was lying about the black-and-white photos showing a cow and a dog. Next, the anthropologist showed the natives color photos of the same two animals. The natives looked at the color photos and smiled and nodded as they now recognized and pointed to the color photos of the cow and dog (Deregowski, 1980).

Because the people of this tribe had never seen black-and-white photos, they had no experience in recognizing

The thing without color is nothing.

The thing with color is a dog.

animals in this format. But when they were shown color photographs, which showed a world more similar to the one they experienced, they immediately recognized the cow and dog. Most likely, the natives drew on their everyday experiences with objects in full color and could recognize what they saw in the photo from what they saw in the real world. This is an example of how cultural experiences can influence perceptual skills, such as the ability to recognize familiar images presented in different photo formats.

How we describe images is another example of how culture influences what we perceive.

Could recognize a dog in a color photo

Perception of Images

Please look at the photo below for a few seconds and then close your eyes and describe what you saw. Richard Nisbett (2000) and colleagues found that what you see or think about depends, to a large extent, on your culture.

For example, after looking at the underwater scene, Americans tended to begin their descriptions by focusing on the largest fish and making statements like "There was what looked like a trout swimming to the left." Americans are much more likely to zero in on the biggest fish, the brightest object, the fish moving the fastest.

Compared to Americans, Japanese subjects were much more likely to begin by setting the scene, saying, for example, "The bottom was rocky." On average, Japanese subjects made 70% more statements about how the background looked than Americans did and twice as many statements about the relationships between the fish and the backgrounds. For instance, Japanese subjects were more likely to say, "The big fish swam past the gray seaweed."

Generally, Americans analyze objects separately, which is called analytical thinking—see-

Look at the photo briefly and then close your eyes and describe it.

ing a forest and focusing more on separate trees. In comparison, Easterners (Japanese, Chinese, and Koreans) tend to think more about the relationship between objects and backgrounds, which is called holistic thinking—seeing a forest and thinking about how trees combine to make up a forest (Chua et al., 2005).

These differences in thinking and perceiving (analytical versus holistic) have been thought to primarily come from differences in social and religious practices, languages, and even geography (S. Kitayama et al., 2003; Nisbett & Miyamoto, 2005). A recent study found that differences in how Americans and the Chinese recall and report their memories may result from culturally different viewing patterns (Chua et al., 2005). For instance, when presented with naturalistic scenes, Americans looked at the focal object more quickly and spent more time looking at it; the Chinese moved their eyes more, especially between the object and the background. Thus, cultural differences in people's perceptions are based not only on how people recall and report their memories, but also on how people physically see images.

Cultures also influence how we see cartoons.

For just a moment, look at the cartoon drawing of the dog (below) and notice what its tail is doing. Then look at the female figure (right) and describe what the figure is doing.

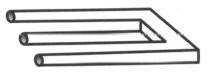

Most people in Western cultures immediately perceive what is happening: the dog is wagging its tail and the figure is spinning. Because of our Western cultural experience with cartoon drawings, we have learned to recognize that certain kinds of repeated images (the dog's tail) and certain lines and circles (the dancing figure) indicate movement. We have learned and become so accustomed to seeing these kinds of cartoon drawings indicate motion that the tail and the dancer really do seem to be in motion.

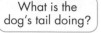

What is the dog's tail doing?

What is this dancer doing?

However, people from non-Western cultures, who have no experience with these cartoon drawings, do not perceive the dog's tail or the figure as moving. Non-Westerners see only an unusual dog that has three tails and a strange figure that is surrounded by circles; they do not perceive any indication of movement in these drawings (S. Friedman & Stevenson, 1980). This is a perfect example of how Western cultural influences shape our perceptions, often without our realizing.

If part of your cultural experience involves seeing 3-dimensional objects in books, you won't be able to draw the next figure.

Perception of 3 Dimensions

Can you draw this impossible figure?

This is the same impossible figure that you saw earlier. As you look at it, it changes almost magically back and forth between a two-pronged and a three-pronged tuning fork. The illusion is that the middle fork is unreal because it seems to come out of nowhere.

When people from industrialized nations try to draw this figure from memory, they almost surely fail. What is interesting is that Africans who have no formal education do not see any illusion but perceive only a two-dimensional pattern of flat lines, which they find easy to draw from memory. In contrast, people with formal education, who have spent years looking at three-dimensional representations in books, perceive this object as having three dimensions, a pattern that is almost impossible to draw (Coren & Ward, 1993).

I can draw that strange thing.

Perception of Beauty

Do you think this woman is attractive?

In the past, when Burmese girls were about 5 years old, they put a brass coil one-third-inch wide around their necks. As they grew older, girls added more brass coils until they had from 19 to 25 wrapped around their necks, sometimes weighing over 10 pounds. The appearance of long necks, caused by the brass coils was perceived as being very attractive by Burmese people, who live in southeast Asia. This custom eventually declined as neck coils were no longer considered beautiful, just cruel and uncomfortable. Recently, however, the custom has been revived because now tourists come and pay about $6 to see and take photos of women with brass neck coils (Moe & Son, 2005).

This example illustrates how cultural values influence our perceptions of personal beauty.

Perceptual Sets

Do you think this muscular body is beautiful?

From our previous cultural experiences with images and objects, we develop certain expectations about how things should be; these expectations are called perceptual sets.

Perceptual sets are learned expectations that are based on our personal, social, or cultural experiences. These expectations automatically add information, meaning, or feelings to our perceptions and thus change or bias our perceptions.

For example, as you look at this bodybuilder, you automatically add personal feelings, such as like/dislike and approve/disapprove, as well as impressions of physical characteristics: height, about 6 feet, and weight, about 225 pounds. Because of your perceptual set for bodybuilders, you expect them to be large, and so you will be surprised to learn that this bodybuilder is only 5 feet 2 inches tall and weighs 182 pounds. One function of perceptual sets is to automatically fill in information or add feelings that can greatly modify our perceptions.

These examples show that we rarely perceive the world exactly as it is. Rather, our perceptions can be changed, biased, or distorted by experiences, such as cultural influences and perceptual sets.

Next, we'll discuss a controversial kind of perception that goes by the initials ESP.

I. ESP: Extrasensory Perception

Definition and Controversy

What are psychic powers?

No one doubts your ability to receive information through one or more of your major senses—seeing, hearing, tasting, smelling, and touching—because this ability has been repeatedly demonstrated and reliably measured. In comparison, most research psychologists do not believe that you can receive information outside normal sensory channels, which is called extrasensory perception, because this phenomenon has been neither repeatedly demonstrated nor reliably measured (D. J. Bem & Honorton, 1994).

Extrasensory perception (ESP) **is a group of psychic experiences that involve perceiving or sending information (images) outside normal sensory processes or channels. ESP includes four general abilities—telepathy, precognition, clairvoyance, and psychokinesis.** *Telepathy* **is the ability to transfer one's thoughts to another or to read the thoughts of others.** *Precognition* **is the ability to foretell events.** *Clairvoyance* **is the ability to perceive events or objects that are out of sight.** *Psychokinesis* **is the ability to exert mind over matter—for example, by moving objects without touching them. Together, these psychic powers or extrasensory perceptions are called psi phenomena.**

The term *psi* **refers to the processing of information or transfer of energy by methods that have no known physical or biological mechanisms and that seem to stretch the laws of physics.**

Psi refers to getting information by methods that defy the laws of physics.

Believing in ESP. According to the most recent Gallup polls, 41% of adult Americans believe in ESP, 31% believe in communication between minds without the use of regular senses, 21% believe they can communicate mentally with someone who has died, and as many as 55% believe in psychics (D. W. Moore, 2005). The reason so many Americans but so few research psychologists believe in ESP is that researchers demand hard, scientific evidence rather than evidence from testimonials, which are based on personal beliefs or experiences and have a high potential for error and bias.

Testimonials as evidence. In discussing testimonials (p. 30), we pointed out that they seem convincing because they are based on personal experiences. However, there are many examples of testimonials that, when evaluated with scientifically designed experiments, were found to be unproven. For example, researchers found that 35 to 98% of individuals who gave testimonials about becoming ill or getting well after taking a pill, dietary supplement, or herb had unknowingly taken a placebo, a medically useless treatment (Cowley, 2000a). Because many people are so convinced and so willing to provide testimonials that some treatment works (actually a placebo), scientists must seriously question any evidence arising from testimonials. Questioning testimonial evidence applies especially to ESP, which is outside normal senses, defies physical and biological explanations, and stretches the laws of physics (P. Kurtz, 1995; Nisbet, 1998).

Another reason researchers demand reliable and repeatable evidence to prove the existence of ESP is that some demonstrations of psi phenomena have involved trickery or questionable methodology. For example, at least one well-known researcher has used trickery and magic to duplicate many of the better-known demonstrations of ESP, such as mentally bending spoons, starting broken watches, moving objects, and reading messages in sealed envelopes. This researcher's name is the Amazing Randi.

Trickery and Magic

Could you spot a trick?

According to James Randi, known as the Amazing Randi (on the left in the photo), and others acquainted with magic, much of what passes for extrasensory perception is actually done through trickery (Steiner, 1989; Ybarra, 1991). For example, to show how easily people may be fooled, Randi sent two young magicians (also in the photo) to a lab that studied psychic phenomena. Instead of admitting they were magicians, the pair claimed to have psychic powers and to perform psychic feats, such as mentally bending keys and making images on film. After 120 hours of testing, the lab's researchers, who had carefully conducted and supervised the ESP demonstrations, concluded that the two did indeed have genuine psychic abilities. The lab's researchers were not expecting trickery, had not taken steps to prevent it, and were thus totally fooled into believing they were witnessing ESP.

The Amazing Randi (left), professional magician, sent two young magicians to fool researchers into believing they had psychic powers.

Several years ago, a television show under the supervision of James Randi offered $100,000 to anyone who could demonstrate psychic powers. Twelve people claimed to have psychic powers, such as identifying through interviews the astrological signs under which people were born, seeing the auras of people standing behind screens, and correctly reading Zener cards (showing five symbols: square, circle, wavy lines, plus sign, and star). Of the 12 people who claimed psychic powers, none scored above chance on any of these tasks (Steiner, 1989). Although people may claim psychic powers, most cannot demonstrate such powers under controlled conditions, which eliminate trickery, magic, and educated guessing. On the next page, we'll learn how one popular TV psychic responded to being asked to take James Randi's test to prove she had psychic powers.

James Randi has repeatedly shown that people untrained in recognizing trickery cannot distinguish between psychic feats and skillful tricks. To eliminate any trickery, claims of psychic abilities must withstand the scrutiny of scientific investigation. Let's see how a controlled ESP experiment is designed and conducted.

How do researchers study psychic abilities?

One of the more common demonstrations of psychic ability is to use Zener cards, which show five symbols—circle, waves, square, plus sign, and star (on right). A researcher holds up the back of one card and asks the subject to guess the symbol on the front. If there were 100 trials, the subject could identify 20 symbols correctly simply by guessing (chance level). However, if a subject identifies 25 symbols correctly, which is above chance level, does that mean the subject has psychic powers? This is a simplified example of a very complicated statistical question: How can we determine whether a person has psychic powers or is just guessing correctly? Therefore, to solve one major problem in psi research—how to eliminate guesswork and trickery—researchers use a state-of-the-art method called the Ganzfeld procedure.

The *Ganzfeld procedure* is a controlled method for eliminating trickery, error, and bias while testing telepathic communication between a sender—the person who sends the message—and a receiver—the person who receives the message.

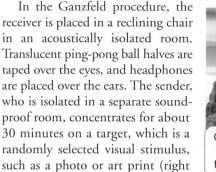

Symbols used to study ESP

In the Ganzfeld procedure, the receiver is placed in a reclining chair in an acoustically isolated room. Translucent ping-pong ball halves are taped over the eyes, and headphones are placed over the ears. The sender, who is isolated in a separate soundproof room, concentrates for about 30 minutes on a target, which is a randomly selected visual stimulus, such as a photo or art print (right figure). At the end of this period, the receiver is shown four different stimuli and asked which one most closely matches what the receiver was imagining. Because there are four stimuli, the receiver will guess the target correctly 25% of the time. Thus, if the receiver correctly identifies the target more than 25% of the time, it is above chance level and indicates something else is occurring, perhaps extrasensory perception (D. J. Bem & Honorton, 1994).

Ganzfeld procedure involves mentally sending this picture to a person in another room.

We have described the Ganzfeld procedure in detail to illustrate the precautions and scientific methodology that researchers must use to rule out the potential for trickery, error, and bias. The next question is perhaps the most interesting of all: What have researchers learned from recent Ganzfeld experiments?

Status of ESP and TV Psychics

What is the scientific status of ESP?

The history of psychic research is filled with controversy, especially about replication, which is the ability of other researchers to do similar experiments and obtain similar results. For example, Daryl Bem and Charles Honorton (1994), two respected researchers, reported that the Ganzfeld procedure (described above) provided evidence for mental telepathy; that is, one person mentally transferred information to a person in another room. The biggest question about Bem and Honorton's controversial mental telepathy results was whether their findings could be repeated or replicated by other researchers.

Importance of replication. Science has a powerful weapon for evaluating research findings, called **replication,** that simply says: If other scientists cannot repeat the results, the results probably occurred by chance. More recently, researchers evaluated the results of 30 Ganzfeld experiments conducted by 7 independent researchers. These researchers reported that the original Ganzfeld finding, which supported some kind of mental telepathy, could not be replicated (Milton & Wiseman, 1999). This failure to replicate the Ganzfeld experiments, which represent the best-controlled studies on ESP to date, means that there is currently little or no reliable scientific

The best-known mental telepathy results could not be replicated.

evidence to support the existence of ESP or psi phenomena (Milton & Wiseman, 2001). One of the biggest problems with ESP is that those who claim to have it are rarely subjected to scientific study. Such is the case with so-called psychic hotlines.

Television psychics. There is no test or training for becoming a psychic, so anyone can claim to be one. Many alleged TV psychics were recruited through want ads and paid $15 to $20 an hour to answer questions from strangers (Nisbet, 1998). TV psychics have been so popular that at one time they took in $100 million a year.

Sylvia Browne is a well-known TV psychic who has become a multimillionaire by writing books, providing psychic readings in person (cost $700) and over the phone (cost $200), and making regular appearances on *The Montel Williams Show*, where she gives advice and claims to connect viewers with their loved ones who have died. Sylvia Browne has been repeatedly asked by the Amazing Randi to take his controlled test to prove she has psychic powers. Despite agreeing on national TV that she would do so, now years later she has yet to take the test (R. Friedman, 2006). There is no scientific evidence that self-proclaimed psychics are better at knowing or predicting the future than would occur by chance (Sheaffer, 1997).

TV psychic, Sylvia Browne, refuses to take a controlled test to prove her psychic powers.

Next, we'll discuss several other forms of perceptions that fool our senses into believing that fixed things are moving.

J. Application Creating Perceptions

Can we create new perceptions?

About 20,000 years ago, early humans *(Homo sapiens)* created some of the earliest images by using earth pigments to paint prancing horses on the sides of their caves (right photo) (S. Fritz, 1995). About 3,000 years ago, Egyptians created some of the most impressive images with their enormous and long-lasting pyramids. Today, computer researchers are using virtual reality techniques to develop new images and perceptions that can put you in the middle of a mind-blowing three-dimensional world. We'll begin our look at how perceptions are created with an old perceptual device that is used in modern billboards.

Painted 20,000 years ago

Creating Movement

The father of the flashing lights used in today's billboards, movie marquees, and traffic arrows was a distinguished Gestalt psychologist named Max Wertheimer. In the early 1900s, Wertheimer spent a considerable amount of time in a darkened room, where he experimented with flashing first one light and then a second light that was positioned some distance away. He discovered that if the time between flashing one light and then the other was adjusted just right, the two flashes were actually perceived as a moving spot of light rather than as two separate flashes. He called this illusion phi movement.

Phi movement refers to the illusion that lights that are actually stationary seem to be moving. This illusory movement, which

Neon billboards use flashing lights to create the illusion of movement.

today is called apparent motion, is created by flashing closely positioned stationary lights at regular intervals.

Each time you pass a traffic arrow composed of flashing lights or perceive a moving string of lights used in an advertising sign, you are seeing a practical application of Wertheimer's phi movement. This phi movement was one of the first examples of how ordinary visual stimuli could be adjusted to create an illusion.

Another example of creating wonderful moving illusions with stationary visual stimuli came from the remarkable genius of Thomas Edison, who invented motion pictures in 1893.

Creating Movies

Movies create the illusion of motion by showing a series of fixed images.

If you attend a track meet and watch a 100-meter race and then, minutes later, watch a videotaped replay of the same race, you perceive motion produced in two very different ways. One kind of motion is real, while the other is an illusion.

Real motion refers to your perception of any stimulus or object that actually moves in space.

As you watch a live 100-meter race, you are perceiving real motion. However, when you watch a replay of that same race, you are seeing apparent motion.

Apparent motion refers to an illusion that a stimulus or object is moving in space when, in fact, the stimulus or object is stationary. The illusion of apparent motion is created by rapidly showing a series of stationary images, each of which has a slightly different position or posture than the one before.

The principle for creating apparent motion is deceptively simple and can be easily discovered by examining the positions of the runner's body in each frame of the time-lapse photo shown above.

Beginning on the left side of the photo, notice that each frame shows only a slight change in the position of the runner's body. However, if these frames were presented rapidly—for example, at the movie standard of 24 frames per second—you would perceive the illusion of an athlete running down the track.

In a series of ingenious experiments, researchers discovered that several complex mechanisms built into our visual system detect cues that produce the illusion of motion (Ramachandran & Anstis, 1986). One such cue is the closure principle, which means that our brains fill in the motion expected to occur between images that vary only slightly in position and are presented in rapid sequence. Without apparent motion, there would be no movies, television, or flip books.

Currently, researchers have developed a procedure that creates a three-dimensional perceptual experience of walking through a house, dissecting a frog, or doing complicated human surgery. This is the brave new world of virtual reality.

Creating Virtual Reality

What is a surgical robot?

The invention of the movie camera was revolutionary because it created a new perceptual experience: the illusion that still pictures moved. Currently, another perceptual revolution is under way, and it's called virtual reality.

Virtual reality **refers to a perceptual experience of being inside an object, moving through an environment, or carrying out some action that is created or simulated by computer.**

Remote and robotic surgery. In a medical application of virtual reality, surgeons can now practice their skills with surgical simulators on virtual cadavers. Research shows that the use of virtual reality significantly improves surgeons' skills and reduces their error rates ("New virtual reality," 2006; Seymour et al., 2002). Virtual reality is also being used on real patients. For example, a surgeon can insert and maneuver a tiny camera and surgical tools in patients through pencil-thin incisions. The surgeon operates by maneuvering robotic arms (photo below), which are steadier and more precise than human arms. Robotic surgery has already been performed more than 10,000 times in many procedures, includ-

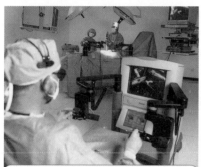

Doctors use virtual reality to guide a robot to perform operations.

ing the removal of prostate cancers and brain tumors, as well as heart bypass surgery, middle-ear surgery, and pediatric surgeries (Berlinger, 2006; Fox, 2005; Mackenzie, 2000; "Medical robot," 2002). Another truly amazing advance in surgical technology is the ability for a surgeon to perform remote surgery using a robot (Berlinger, 2006). For instance, one surgeon in New York robotically removed a gallbladder from a patient in France with no complications!

Psychotherapy. In a psychological application of virtual reality, clients with such fears as spiders, flying, or heights are exposed to the feared stimuli in a three-dimensional environment where everything appears very real.

Therapists use virtual reality to treat phobias (fear of spiders).

In this photo, a client is being treated for fear of spiders. She wears a plastic helmet that contains a computer monitor that puts her inside a virtual reality kitchen in which she sees, touches, and kills spiders. For example, Joanne Cartwright suffered a debilitating fear of spiders. "I washed my truck every night before I went to work in case there were webs," she said. "I put all my clothes in plastic bags and taped duct tape around my doors so spiders couldn't get in. I thought I was going to have a mental breakdown" (Robbins, 2000, p. D6). After receiving 12 virtual reality sessions to decrease her fear, Joanne said, "I'm amazed because I am doing all this stuff I could never do— camping, hunting and hiking" (Carlin, 2000). Psychotherapists report success in using virtual reality therapy to treat a wide variety of phobias, as well as posttraumatic stress disorder (PTSD) (see p. 491) (Bergfield, 2006; H. G. Hoffman, 2004).

The next topic focuses on how much your first impressions of other people depend on your perceptions of their physical appearances.

Creating First Impressions

Can you name these faces?

Social psychologists have discovered that facial features have a significant effect on our first impressions and perceptions of people. For example, researchers found that we perceive an attractive person as being more interesting, sociable, intelligent, outgoing, and kind (Lemley, 2000). Similarly, first impressions are also influenced by racial stereotypes, both positive and negative, based on physical features such as skin color and hair style. Hollywood hair stylists know that the kind, amount, color, and style of actors' hair can radically change their appearance and our impressions of them. In fact, they use different hair styles to match different roles. For instance, look at the three photos on the right and try to correctly identify each of these famous personalities (answers at the end).

Besides hair color and style, skin color has a considerable impact on first perceptions and impressions. To illustrate how skin color can greatly change your perceptions of people, look at the two photos on the far right and try to correctly identify these two famous people.

Who . . .

. . . am . . .

. . . I?

You may have guessed correctly that the two people are the actor-politician Arnold Schwarzenegger of the United States and Queen Elizabeth of England. The editors of *Colors, the Multicultural Magazine* published these computer-colored images to ask their readers: What percentage of your understanding of someone is formed by race? After looking at Queen Elizabeth with the skin color of an Indian and at Arnold Schwarzenegger with the skin color of an African American, you can judge for yourself how much facial coloring influences your impressions and perceptions of others. We'll discuss more on how we perceive people and form impressions in Module 25.

Who are we?

The factors involved in forming first impressions as well as in creating moving lights, movies, and virtual reality illustrate an important, underlying principle of perception: Our perceptions, which may be changed or biased by personal experiences, are interpretations rather than exact copies of reality.

(Correct answers top to bottom: actress Marilyn Monroe, radio personality Howard Stern, actress Julia Roberts)

Summary Test

A. Perceptual Thresholds

1. We discussed three basic questions that psychologists ask about perception. Our first question—At what point are we aware of a stimulus?— can be answered by measuring the threshold of a stimulus, which is a point above which a stimulus is perceived and below which it is not. The intensity level at which a person has a 50% chance of perceiving the stimulus is called the _____.

2. Our second question—At what point do we know a stimulus intensity has increased or decreased?—can be answered by measuring the smallest increase or decrease in the intensity of a stimulus that a person can detect; this is called a (a)_____. It has been found that the increase in stimulus intensity needed to produce a just noticeable difference increases in proportion to the intensity of the initial stimulus; this is called (b)_____ law.

B. Sensation Versus Perception

3. Our third question—How are meaningless sensations combined into meaningful perceptions?—can be answered by analyzing our own perceptual experiences. Our first awareness of some outside stimulus is called a (a)_____. This awareness results when some change in energy activates sensory receptors, which produce signals that, in turn, are transformed by the brain into meaningless sensory experiences. When many individual sensations are assembled into a meaningful experience, image, or pattern, it is called a (b)_____. The latter is not an exact replica of the real world but rather a copy that has been changed, biased, or distorted by our unique set of (c)_____. Our brain transforms sensations into perceptions instantaneously, automatically, and without our awareness.

4. The (a)_____ argued that we can explain how perceptions are formed by dividing perceptions into smaller and smaller elements. They believed that we combine basic elements to form a perception. In contrast, the (b)_____ psychologists replied that the formation of perceptions cannot be understood by simply breaking perceptions down into individual components and then studying how we reassemble them. They argued that "the whole is more than the sum of its parts," by which they meant that perceptions are more than a combination of individual elements. The Gestalt psychologists believed that the brain has rules for assembling perceptions, which they called principles of (c)_____.

C. Rules of Organization

5. Many of the rules of perceptual organization involve ways of grouping or arranging stimuli. According to one of these rules, the first thing we do is automatically separate an image into two parts: the more detailed feature of an image becomes the (a)_____ and the less detailed aspects become the (b)_____. According to the (c)_____ rule, stimuli tend to be organized in the most basic, elementary way. According to the (d)_____ rule, stimuli that appear the same tend to be grouped together. According to the (e)_____ rule, stimuli that are near one another tend to be grouped together. According to the (f)_____ rule, stimuli that are arranged in a smooth line or curve tend to be perceived as forming a continuous path. According to the (g)_____ rule, we tend to fill in the missing parts of a figure and perceive it as complete.

D. Perceptual Constancy

6. Although the size, shape, brightness, and color of objects are constantly changing, we tend to see them as remaining the same, a phenomenon that is called (a)_____. A person walking away does not appear to grow smaller, even though the image on the retina is decreasing in size, because of (b)_____ constancy. Even though the image of a door that is opened and closed changes on the retina from a rectangle to a trapezoid, we see it as retaining its rectangular outline because of (c)_____ constancy. Even though the color and brightness inside a car are altered when we drive from bright into dim light, we tend to see little change because of (d)_____ and _____ constancy.

E. Depth Perception

7. The visual system transforms the two-dimensional image (height and width) of stimuli projected onto the retina into a three-dimensional experience by adding depth. Cues for depth that are dependent on both eyes are called (a)_____; cues for depth that are dependent on only a single eye are called (b)_____. The binocular cue for depth that arises when muscles turn your eyes inward is called (c)_____. The binocular cue for depth that arises because the two eyes send slightly different images to the brain is called (d)_____.

8. There are a number of monocular cues for depth. When an object appears closer because it overlaps another, the cue is called (a)_____. When parallel lines seem to stretch to a point at the horizon and create a sense of distance, the cue is called (b)_____. When two figures are expected to be the same size but one is larger and thus appears closer, the cue is called (c)_____. If dust or smog makes objects appear hazy and thus farther away, the cue is called (d)_____. As texture changes from sharp and detailed to dull and monotonous, it creates the impression of distance; this cue is called (e)_____. The play of light and shadow gives objects a three-dimensional look, a cue that is called (f)_____. As you ride in a car, the impression that near objects are speeding by and far objects are barely moving is called (g)_____.

F. Illusions

9. For much of the time, our perceptions are relatively accurate reflections of the world (except for anything added by our attentional, motivational, or emotional filters). However, if perceptual cues that we have learned to use and rely on are greatly changed, the result is a distorted image, called an _____. Although illusions are extreme examples, they illustrate that perception is an active, ongoing process in which we use past experiences to interpret current sensory experiences.

G. Research Focus: Influencing Perception

10. Brief auditory or visual messages that are presented below the  absolute threshold, which means that their chance of being heard or seen is less than 50%, are called (a)_____. Researchers have concluded that any behavioral changes attributed to subliminal messages actually result because listeners' strong belief that a behavior will change leads them to act, unknowingly, to change that behavior; this is called a (b)_____.

H. Cultural Diversity: Influence on Perceptions

11. Experiences that are typical of a society and shared by its members are called _____ influences. These influences have significant effects on the perception of images, constancy, depth, and motion.

12. Because of cultural influences, Americans tend to engage more in (a)_____ thinking, while Easterners (Japanese) engage more in (b)_____ thinking.

I. ESP: Extrasensory Perception

13. The perception and transmission of thoughts or images by other than normal sensory channels are referred to as psychic experiences or (a)_____ phenomena. ESP, which stands for (b)_____, includes four psychic abilities. The ability to transfer one's thoughts to another or read another's thoughts is called (c)_____. The ability to foretell events is called (d)_____. The ability to perceive events or objects that are out of sight is called (e)_____. The ability to move objects without touching them is called (f)_____. Two reasons many researchers are skeptical of psychic abilities are that some supposedly psychic phenomena were actually accomplished with (g)_____ and some previous studies that supported ESP had questionable (h)_____. Although some studies supported the occurrence of psi phenomena, recent studies showed that the experiments that supported psi phenomena could not be (i)_____

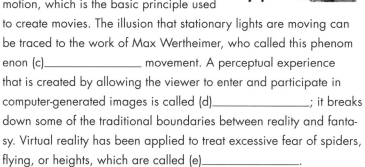

J. Application: Creating Perceptions

14. When you view objects moving in space, it is called (a)_____ motion. When you view images of stationary objects that are presented in a rapid sequence, it is called (b)_____ motion, which is the basic principle used to create movies. The illusion that stationary lights are moving can be traced to the work of Max Wertheimer, who called this phenomenon (c)_____ movement. A perceptual experience that is created by allowing the viewer to enter and participate in computer-generated images is called (d)_____; it breaks down some of the traditional boundaries between reality and fantasy. Virtual reality has been applied to treat excessive fear of spiders, flying, or heights, which are called (e)_____.

Answers: 1. absolute threshold; 2. (a) just noticeable difference, (b) Weber's; 3. (a) sensation, (b) perception, (c) experiences; 4. (a) structuralists, (b) Gestalt, (c) perceptual organization; 5. (a) figure, (b) ground, (c) simplicity, (d) similarity, (e) proximity, (f) continuity, (g) closure; 6. (a) perceptual constancy, (b) size, (c) shape, (d) color, brightness; 7. (a) binocular, (b) monocular, (c) convergence, (d) retinal disparity; 8. (a) interposition, (b) linear perspective, (c) relative size, (d) atmospheric perspective, (e) texture gradient, (f) light and shadow, (g) motion parallax; 9. illusion; 10. (a) subliminal messages, (b) self-fulfilling prophecy; 11. cultural; 12. (a) analytical, (b) holistic; 13. (a) psi, (b) extrasensory perception, (c) telepathy, (d) precognition, (e) clairvoyance, (f) psychokinesis, (g) trickery, (h) methodology, (i) replicated; 14. (a) real, (b) apparent, (c) phi, (d) virtual reality, (e) phobias

Critical Thinking

Can See but Not Recognize His Wife's Face

Questions

1. Why did extensive scarring of the cornea cause total blindness in Mike's right eye?

2. Why did Mike have to wait until 1999 to have the stem cell procedure, and why is there controversy over using these amazing stem cells?

3. Although Mike could see through his right eye, why was his vision so poor?

4. What happened to Mike's brain that prevents him from combining his wife's facial features into a recognizable face?

5. What does Mike's normal ability to track moving objects tell us about his brain?

When Mike May was 3 years old, a jar of fuel for a lantern exploded, completely destroying his left eye and so badly scarring the right eye's cornea that his right eye became totally blind. Being totally blind did not stop Mike from playing flag football in elementary school, playing soccer in college, and earning a master's degree.

In 1999, 43 years after Mike was blinded, a surgeon tried to repair Mike's eye by placing stem cells on his right cornea. The stem cells replaced the scarred tissue and literally remade the front of his eye. Next, Mike received a corneal transplant, which allowed light waves to pass into his eye and continue on through a perfectly good lens, retina, optic nerve, and finally the brain's area for processing visual stimuli.

The surgeon believed that Mike would be able to see out of his right eye since everything from the cornea to his brain was in perfect working order. However, when the bandage was removed and Mike looked at the eye chart, instead of recognizing the big **E** from 20 feet away (20/20 vision), he needed to get within 2 feet (20/500 vision). Mike's vision was very poor.

In the first months after surgery, he could see that there were objects on a table, but he could not distinguish between two different objects, such as a ball from a cube, which is a very easy task, even for young sighted children.

Although Mike can see his wife's face and has seen it hundreds of times since surgery, he cannot recognize it. Distinguishing faces and emotional expressions is impossible for Mike and will likely remain so. The reason sighted people can recognize complex objects, such as faces, is that, from birth on, all kinds of visual stimuli were projected to the brain, which had to learn how to combine these stimuli into meaningful perceptions, such as faces, ball, cubes, or animals. Brain scans show that when Mike is looking at faces and objects, that part of his brain that would normally be activated when recognizing objects is silent.

Although Mike has trouble distinguishing between and recognizing objects, he is able to track a moving object and is pretty good at catching a ball thrown to him. Brain scans show that when he is looking at a moving ball, the motion-detection part of his brain is active, similar to a normal brain.

When Mike goes walking, he still depends on his dog or taps his cane on the sidewalk. Even though he can "see," he describes himself as "a blind man with vision." (Adapted from M. Abrams, 2002)

Suggested Answers

1. As discussed in Module 5 (pp. 94–95), the cornea is the rounded, transparent covering over the front of the eye. The cornea allows light waves to pass into the eye, and its rounded surface bends or focuses light waves onto the lens. Because Mike's cornea was so badly scarred, no light waves could pass into his eye, resulting in total blindness, even though the rest of his optical system (lens, retina, optic nerve, brain's visual areas) was intact.

2. As discussed in Module 3 (p. 60), stem cells, which were not discovered until 1998, have the amazing capacity to change into and become hundreds of other kinds of cells. The use of human embryonic stem cells involves moral and ethical objections because human embryos are destroyed in the process.

3. There is a difference between seeing and perceiving. Mike can see that something is there, but he cannot easily distinguish or perceive what that "something" is.

4. Because Mike was totally blinded at age 3, his brain was prevented from receiving normal visual stimulation during its development, so his brain was never programmed for perceiving and recognizing visual stimuli, such as a face. Visual stimulation during early childhood is critical and explains why it is now too late for Mike to develop complex visual perceptual skills.

5. When Mike was successfully tracking a moving ball, brain scans showed activity in the motion-detection area of his brain. This means that, unlike developing the ability to distinguish between objects, detecting motion is hard-wired into the brain and does not require years of visual stimulation for normal development.

Links to Learning

Learning Activities

- ***POWERSTUDY FOR INTRODUCTION TO PSYCHOLOGY 4.0***
  by Tom Doyle and Rod Plotnik

  SuperModule: Check out "Perception" on **PowerStudy.** It includes complete paragraph-by-paragraph explanations of all content using fully narrated animations and graphics. An onscreen toolbar allows immediate access to text, text outline, and module glossary with notetaking and printing capabilities. This module also includes:
  - Video—Imbedded videos cover motion parallax, the Ames room, and virtual reality therapy.
  - A multitude of animations designed to help you understand each section of your text.
  - A test of your knowledge using an interactive version of the Summary Test on pages 142 and 143. Also access related quizzing—true/false, multiple choice, and matching.
  - An interactive version of the Critical Thinking exercise "Can See But Not Recognize His Wife's Face" on page 144.
  - Key terms, a chapter outline including chapter abstract, and a special extended list of hotlinked websites that correlate to this module.

- *CengageNOW*
  academic.cengage.com/login

  Need help studying? This site is your one-stop study shop. Take a Pre-Test and CengageNOW will generate a Personalized Study Plan based on your test results. The Study Plan will identify the topics you need to review and direct you to online resources to help you master those topics. You can then take a Post-Test to determine the concepts you have mastered and what you still need to work on.

- ***INTRODUCTION TO PSYCHOLOGY BOOK COMPANION WEBSITE***
  academic.cengage.com/psychology/plotnik

  Visit your book companion website where you will find more resources to help you study. At this site, you will find Learning Objectives, Internet Exercises, quizzing, flash cards, and a pronunciation glossary.

- ***STUDY GUIDE and WEBTUTOR***
  Check the corresponding module in your Study Guide for effective student tips and help learning the material presented. Also go to **academic.cengage.com/webtutor** for an interactive version of the Study Guide features.

Study Questions

*****A. Perceptual Thresholds**—How does Weber's law apply to how old you perceive someone to be? (**Suggested answer page 622**)

*****B. Sensation Versus Perception**—What would your life be like if your brain could receive sensations but could not assemble them into perceptions? (**Suggested answer page 622**)

C. Rules of Organization—Why can you still read the message on a faded and torn billboard sign?

D. Perceptual Constancy—If you suddenly lost all perceptual constancy, what specific problems would you have?

E. Depth Perception—Would a one-eyed pitcher have any particular problems playing baseball?

F. Illusions—What has to happen to our perceptual processes before we see an illusion?

G. Research Focus: Influencing Perception—Could advertisers make any honest claims for subliminal tapes?

*****H. Cultural Diversity: Influence on Perceptions**—When foreigners visit the United States, what do you think they perceive differently? (**Suggested answer page 622**)

I. ESP: Extrasensory Perception—How could you test your friend's claim of having had a psychic experience?

J. Application: Creating Perceptions—What do illusions add to our perceptions of the world?

*These questions are answered in Appendix B.

MODULE 7
Sleep & Dreams

 PowerStudy 4.0™ Complete Module

Living in a Cave

Would you answer this ad?

The advertisement read: "We are looking for a hardy subject to live alone in an underground cave for four months. We'll provide board, room, and a monthly allowance. It will be necessary to take daily physiological measurements, measure brain waves, and collect blood samples."

Twenty people answered this ad, but researchers selected Stefania because she seemed to have the inner strength, motivation, and stamina to complete the entire four months. On the chosen day, Stefania crawled 30 feet underground with her favorite books into a 20-by-12-foot Plexiglas module, which had been sealed off from sunlight, radio, television, and other time cues.

During her first month underground, Stefania's concentration seemed to come and go. She appeared depressed, and she snapped at researchers when they asked her to do routine measurements. She had strange dreams—for example, that her computer monitor had turned into a TV that was talking to her. After several months, however, she became more comfortable with her underground isolation. She followed a regular routine of taking her body temperature, heart rate, and blood pressure and typing the results into a computer monitor, her only link with the outside world.

Without clocks, radio, television, or the sun, Stefania found it difficult to keep track of time, which seemed to have slowed down. When told she could leave her underground cave (photo below) because her 130 days were up, she felt certain she had been underground only about 60 days. Her time underground, which was a women's record (the men's record is 210 days), allowed researchers to closely monitor her sleeping and waking behaviors in the absence of all light and time cues (adapted from *Newsweek*, June 5, 1989).

Stefania leaves an underground cave in which she had lived for 130 days without any time cues (clocks, sunshine, radio, TV).

Asking Stefania to live in a cave for many months was not a publicity stunt but a way to answer questions about how long a day is and how much one sleeps when there are no light cues. To answer these questions, researchers used a **case study** approach, which meant studying Stefania's behaviors and physiological responses in great detail and depth and doing so in a reasonably naturalistic setting. Researchers discovered that the preferred length of a day is not 24 hours and that during a particular kind of sleep Stefania's eyes moved back and forth as if she were watching a ping-pong game. The significance of these eye movements emphasizes the fact that some major discoveries in science occur quite by accident.

Chance Discovery

Why are your eyes moving?

In the early days of sleep research, psychologists were observing changes in sleeping subjects and noticed that during a certain stage of sleep a person's eyes suddenly began to move rapidly back and forth. This back-and-forth eye movement can actually be seen under the eyelids in the photos below. Even more interesting, when subjects were awakened during

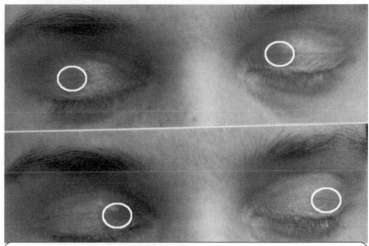

During one kind of sleep (REM—rapid eye movement sleep), the eyes dart back and forth beneath the eye lids.

rapid eye movement, they usually reported that they had been dreaming. This chance observation of rapid eye movement and its high association, or correlation, with dreaming gave researchers a reliable method to identify and study dreaming in the laboratory (Dement & Kleitman, 1957).

These examples show how researchers study waking, sleeping, and dreaming in different settings, including underground caves and sleep laboratories, and also how they were helped along by a chance discovery.

What's Coming

We'll discuss the preferred length of a day, how you know when to sleep and wake up, what happens to your body and brain during sleep, how much sleep you need, why you sleep, and common sleep problems and their treatments. We'll also discuss the one question students always ask: What do dreams mean? All these areas fit neatly under a much broader phenomenon that we call awareness, or consciousness, and that is where we'll begin.

A. Continuum of Consiousness

Are you conscious now?

One curious and amazing feature of consciousness is that, at some point, the person is actually observing himself or herself (Rochat, 2003). For example, how do you know that at this very moment you are conscious?

Consciousness refers to different levels of awareness of one's thoughts and feelings. It may include creating images in one's mind, following one's thought processes, or having unique emotional experiences.

One way you know that you are conscious is that you are aware of your own thoughts and existence (Pinker, 2000). You may think that when awake you are conscious and when asleep you are unconscious, but there is actually a continuum of consciousness.

The *continuum of consciousness* refers to a wide range of experiences, from being acutely aware and alert to being totally unaware and unresponsive.

We'll summarize some of the experiences that make up the continuum of consciousness.

Controlled Processes

A big problem with car phones is that we have the ability to focus all of our attention on only one thing, which is an example of controlled processes.

Controlled processes are activities that require full awareness, alertness, and concentration to reach some goal. The focused attention required in carrying out controlled processes usually interferes with the execution of other ongoing activities.

Talking on a car phone while driving is a controlled process.

A controlled process, such as talking on a car phone, involves focusing most of your attention on talking and little on driving. There's less problem if the driving is easy, but if you need to take quick action, your driving will likely suffer because your attention is primarily focused on your phone conversation (P. J. Cooper et al., 2003). For example, people who use car phones have four times the risk of having an accident. For that reason, hand-held car phones have been banned in New York, New Jersey, Connecticut, the District of Columbia, and many countries around the world (Associated Press, 2005; Repanshek, 2006).

Automatic Processes

Eating while reading is an automatic process.

Since this woman's attention is focused primarily on reading an important report, she is almost automatically eating the donut; this is an example of an automatic process.

Automatic processes are activities that require little awareness, take minimal attention, and do not interfere with other ongoing activities.

Examples of automatic processes include eating while reading or watching television and driving a car along a familiar route while listening to the radio or thinking of something else.

Although we seem to concentrate less during automatic processes, at some level we are conscious of what is occurring. For instance, as we drive on automatic pilot, we avoid neighboring cars and can usually take quick evasive action during emergencies.

Daydreaming

Many of us engage in a pleasurable form of consciousness that is called daydreaming.

Daydreaming is an activity that requires a low level of awareness, often occurs during automatic processes, and involves fantasizing or dreaming while awake.

We may begin daydreaming in a relatively conscious state and then drift into a state between sleep and wakefulness. Usually we daydream in situations that require little attention or during repetitive or boring activities.

Most daydreams are rather ordinary, such as thinking about getting one's hair cut, planning where to eat, pondering some problem, or fantasizing a date. These

Men's and women's daydreams are similar.

kinds of daydreams serve to remind us of important things in our future. Although you might guess otherwise, men's and women's daydreams are remarkably similar in frequency, vividness, and realism (Klinger, 1987).

Altered States

Over 3,000 years ago, Egyptians brewed alcohol to reach altered states of consciousness (Samuel, 1996).

Altered states of consciousness result from using any number of procedures—such as meditation, psychoactive drugs, hypnosis, or sleep deprivation—to produce an awareness that differs from normal consciousness.

For example, this woman is using a form of meditation to focus all her attention on a single image or thought, free her mind from all external restraints, and enter an altered state of consciousness.

Meditation is an altered state.

In an interesting series of studies on himself, neuropsychologist John Lilly (1972) repeatedly took LSD (when it was legal) and reported that it caused unusual, bizarre, and sometimes frightening altered states of consciousness. For example, he described leaving his body, seeing it from above, and being afraid that he would not be able to return safely to it.

The chief characteristic of altered states, whichever way they are produced, is that we perceive our internal and external environments or worlds in ways very different from normal perception.

Sleep and Dreams

We enter an altered state of consciousness every night when we go to sleep.

Sleep **consists of five different stages that involve different levels of awareness, consciousness, and responsiveness, as well as different levels of physiological arousal. The deepest state of sleep borders on unconsciousness.**

Because of our decreased awareness, 8 hours of sleep may seem like one continuous state. However, it is actually composed of different states of body arousal and consciousness (Czeisler et al., 2006). One interesting sleep state involves dreaming.

Dreaming **is a unique state of consciousness in which we are asleep but experience a variety of astonishing visual, auditory, and tactile images, often connected in strange ways and often in color. People blind from birth have only auditory or tactile dreams.**

Newborns sleep about 17 hours a day.

During the initial stage of sleep, we are often aware of stimuli in our environment. However, as we pass into the deepest stage of sleep, we may sleeptalk or sleepwalk and children may experience frightening night terrors but have no awareness or memory of them.

Most of this module focuses on waking, sleeping, and dreaming.

Unconscious and Implicit Memory

We told you that one of Sigmund Freud's revolutionary ideas was his concept of the unconscious (see pp. 9, 434–437).

According to Freud's theory, when we are faced with very threatening wishes or desires, especially if they are sexual or aggressive, we automatically defend our self-esteem by placing these psychologically threatening thoughts into a mental place of which we are not aware, called the *unconscious.* **We cannot voluntarily recall unconscious thoughts or images.**

Freud believed that we can become aware of our unconscious thoughts only through a process of free association or dream interpretation, both of which are explained on page 435.

Freud's idea of the unconscious is different from implicit memory.

Somewhat related to Freud's theory of the unconscious is a new concept developed by cognitive neuroscientists called implicit or nondeclarative memory (Frensch & Runger, 2003).

Implicit **or** *nondeclarative memory* **means learning without awareness, such as occurs in emotional situations or in acquiring habits. We are unaware of such learning, which can influence our conscious feelings, thoughts, and behaviors.**

For example, you cannot describe the complex motor movements your feet make as they walk down stairs because such motor memories are stored in implicit memory, which you are unaware of and cannot voluntarily recall. Implicit memory explains why people cannot recall and are unaware of why or how they learned to fear a tiny spider, fell in love, fainted at the sight of blood, or learned (classically conditioned) to make a happy or sad facial expression (Poldrack & Packard, 2003). Implicit memory emphasizes the learning and influence of many different kinds of motor and emotional memories and is different from Freud's unconscious, which focuses on the influence of threatening memories (Kihlstrom, 1993).

Unconsciousness

If you have ever fainted, gotten general anesthesia, or been knocked out from a blow to the head, you have experienced being unconscious or unconsciousness.

Unconsciousness, **which can result from disease, trauma, a blow to the head, or general medical anesthesia, results in total lack of sensory awareness and complete loss of responsiveness to one's environment.**

Unconsciousness results from a head knock, disease, or general anesthesia.

For example, a boxer's goal is to knock out the opponent with a quick blow to the head that produces a temporary state of unconsciousness. Being in an accident can damage the brain and cause different levels of unconsciousness and result in different kinds of comas. In some comas, a person appears to be asleep and has absolutely no awareness or responsiveness; this is called a vegetative state. People in vegetative comas are unconscious and in some cases brain-dead, which means they will never again regain consciousness.

Several Kinds

Why is it so mysterious?

Consciousness is so mysterious because it is a continuum of states, which range from the tragic unconsciousness of being in a vegetative coma to the keen alertness of controlled processes during a final exam. Although it is difficult to define consciousness, you know what it feels like to be conscious and aware of your thoughts and surroundings. Neuroscientists find there is no single seat of consciousness; rather it results from interactions among many different areas of the brain, depending upon the kinds of thoughts, images, or stimuli to which you are attending (Edelman, 2003).

Although you have experienced having conscious beliefs and desires, Freud believed that there was also an active, unconscious psychological process that defended you against threatening sexual and aggressive thoughts, of which you are totally unaware. In partial support of Freud's theory, cognitive neuroscientists use the concept of implicit or nondeclarative memory to explain how you can be unaware of perceiving various stimuli, such as words, objects, faces, and emotional events, and even learn simple responses (classical conditioning). Although you are not aware of this unconscious learning, you can be unknowingly influenced by the thoughts, memories, feelings, and behaviors stored in your implicit memory (Guterl, 2002; Petty et al., 2006).

One obvious sign of consciousness is being awake, which is regulated by a clock in the brain, our next topic.

B. Rhythms of Sleeping & Waking

Biological Clocks

How long is a day?

Sleep researchers studied Stefania (left photo), who is shown coming out of her modernized cave after 130 days. Stefania was asked to live in a cave so researchers could study her biological clocks.

Biological clocks are internal timing devices that are genetically set to regulate various physiological responses for different periods of time.

Stefania's sleep-wake cycle in the cave was regulated by a biological clock.

Biological clocks can be set for hours (secretion of urine), for a single day (rise and fall in internal body temperature), or for many days (women's 28-day menstrual cycle). We are interested in a biological clock that is set for a single day and produces what is called a circadian (*sir-KAY-dee-un*) rhythm (*circa* means "about"; *diem* means "day").

A *circadian rhythm* refers to a biological clock that is genetically programmed to regulate physiological responses within a time period of 24 hours (about one day).

Length of day. You are most familiar with the circadian rhythm that regulates your sleep-wake cycle. In previous studies, when researchers removed all time cues (light, clock, radio, television) from cave dwellers like Stefania, the circadian clock day was believed to lengthen from 24 hours to about 25 hours (Young, 2000). However, in a better controlled study, researchers reported that for both young (mean age 24) and older (mean age 67) adults, the sleep-wake circadian clock is genetically set for a day lasting an average of 24 hours and 18 minutes (Czeisler et al., 1999).

Resetting the circadian clock. Because your circadian clock is genetically set for about 24 hours, 18 minutes, it must be reset each day to match our agreed upon 24-hour-long day. The resetting stimulus is morning sunlight, which stimulates newly discovered light-detecting cells in the eye's retina (see p. 96) (Berson, 2003). These *retinal cells*, which are involved in sensing the amount of light and are not involved in seeing, send electrical signals to the brain's circadian clock (described below) and reset it by about 18 minutes each day (Menaker, 2003).

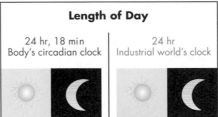

Length of Day

| 24 hr, 18 min | 24 hr |
| Body's circadian clock | Industrial world's clock |

Problems. If your circadian clock is not properly reset each day, it may result in problems getting to sleep, getting over jet lag, and adjusting to working the night shift (see next page). Although the circadian clock was long known to exist, only recently have researchers identified its exact location in the brain.

Location of Biological Clocks

Where is the circadian clock?

It may seem strange to think of having clocks in your brain. Actually you have several clocks, including the biological circadian sleep-wake clock located in a group of cells in the brain's suprachiasmatic (*SUE-pra-kye-as-MAT-ick*) nucleus (R. Y. Moore, 2006).

The *suprachiasmatic nucleus* is one of many groups of cells that make up the hypothalamus, which lies in the lower middle of the brain. The suprachiasmatic nucleus is a sophisticated biological clock that regulates a number of circadian rhythms, including the sleep-wake cycle. Because this nucleus receives direct input from the eyes, the suprachiasmatic cells are highly responsive to changes in light.

SUPRACHIASMATIC NUCLEUS

OPTIC NERVE

The sleep-wake circadian clock is located in the suprachiasmatic nucleus.

Since light regulates sleep-wake circadian rhythms, the absence of light should disrupt circadian rhythms in blind people and cause sleep problems. Researchers found that many blind people do report sleep problems (Lamberg, 2006). However, a small percentage of completely blind people reported no sleep problems because the pathway for transmitting light from their eyes directly to the suprachiasmatic nucleus, which is not involved in seeing, was intact (Barinaga, 2002; R. Y. Moore, 1997).

Besides the 24-hour sleep-wake circadian clock, you also have other clocks in your brain, including one that measures shorter periods of time, called an interval timing clock (Rao, 2002).

The *interval timing clock,* which can be started and stopped like a stopwatch, gauges the passage of seconds, minutes, or hours and helps people and animals time their movements, such as knowing when to start or stop doing some activity (taking a one-hour nap and actually waking up about an hour later). The interval timing clock is located in a part of the brain known as the basal ganglia (see p. 60).

Another clock in your brain is regulated by food.

The *food-entrainable circadian clock* (also referred to as the *midnight-snack clock*) regulates eating patterns in people and animals and might be responsible for late-night eating in people. Thus, obese people, many of whom eat more than half their calories at night, may have an abnormality in their clock, which is located in the hypothalamus (see p. 80) (C. Brownlee, 2006; Mieda et al., 2006).

Walking around with several fine-tuned biological clocks in your head is great for timing activities. However, if your circadian sleep-wake clock is interfered with or not properly reset, you may have various sleep-wake problems.

Circadian Problems and Treatments

What if circadian clock is upset?

Here's the basic problem: For most of the industrial world, a day is agreed to be exactly 24 hours long, but for your genetically set sleep-wake circadian clock, a day is an average of 24 hours and 18 minutes. This difference means that your sleep-wake clock must be reset about 18 minutes each day. The resetting stimulus is bright morning sunlight, which our eyes send directly to the suprachiasmatic nucleus. This daily resetting of our sleep-wake clocks about 18 minutes usually occurs automatically. However, if our circadian clocks are not properly reset, we may experience decreased cognitive performance, work-related and traffic accidents, jet lag, and various sleep disorders (K. Wright, 2002).

Accidents

Staying awake when your sleep-wake clock calls for sleep results in decreased performance in cognitive and motor skills (Drummond, 2000).

Highway Accidents

Saturday 2–3 A.M.	509
Sunday 1–2 A.M.	475
Other hours	203

Source: Data from National Highway Traffic Administration, 1992

For example, the graph above shows that highway accidents occur most often in the early morning. Although drug usage plays a significant role in traffic accidents, another factor is that the early morning hours are a time when our bodies and brains are in a sleep rhythm. Similarly, employees who work the graveyard shift (about 1–8 A.M.) also experience the highest number of accidents, reaching their lowest point, or "dead zone," at about 5 A.M., when it is very difficult to stay alert (Stutts et al., 2002).

The reason shift workers and late-night drivers have more accidents is that their sleep-wake clocks have prepared their bodies for sleep, which means they feel sleepy, are less attentive and alert, and are often in a lousy mood (Ohayon et al., 2002).

Circadian rhythms can also create problems for long-distance travelers.

Jet Lag

If you flew from west coast to east coast, you would cross three time zones, experience a 3-hour difference in time, and most likely have jet lag the next day.

Jet lag is the experience of fatigue, lack of concentration, and reduced cognitive skills that occurs when travelers' biological circadian clocks are out of step or synchrony with the external clock times at their new locations.

Generally, it takes about one day to reset your circadian clock for each hour of time change.

Jet lag occurs when a body's circadian clock gets out of synchrony.

After 3 months in space, astronauts experience "space lag" or sleeplessness because their circadian clocks are not being properly reset (Monk et al., 2001).

Next, you'll see how researchers are studying ways to more effectively reset our biological clocks.

Resetting Clock

Researcher Charles Czeisler (1994) spent ten years trying to convince his colleagues that light could reset circadian clocks. After he finally succeeded, other researchers used his and their own research to obtain patents for something called light therapy (Nowak, 1994).

Light therapy is the use of bright artificial light to reset circadian clocks and so combat the insomnia and drowsiness that plague shift workers and jet-lag sufferers. It also helps people with sleeping disorders in which the body fails to stay in time with the external environment.

For example, researchers report that workers who had been exposed to bright light and then shifted to night work showed improvement in alertness, performance, and job satisfaction (Czeisler et al., 1995). Exposure to bright light (about 20 times brighter) at certain times reset the workers' suprachiasmatic nucleus and resulted in a closer match between their internal circadian clocks and their external shifted clock times.

Light therapy is still a relatively new treatment but has enormous potential for resetting our sleep-wake clocks, and more recently it has been used to treat depression (B. Bower, 2005; Tompkins, 2003a, 2003b).

Another factor involved in setting the sleep-wake clock is a hormone from a gland that was once thought useless.

Melatonin

One of the big scientific surprises of the mid-1990s was the discovery of a use for melatonin, which was first identified in the 1950s (Brzezinski, 1997).

Melatonin is a hormone that is secreted by the pineal gland, an oval-shaped group of cells that is located in the center of the human brain. Melatonin secretion increases with darkness and decreases with light. The suprachiasmatic nucleus regulates the secretion of melatonin, which plays a role in the regulation of circadian rhythms and in promoting sleep.

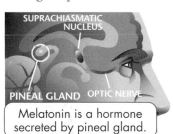

Melatonin is a hormone secreted by pineal gland.

Although early testimonials and some studies claimed that melatonin reduced jet lag, a later double-blind study reported that melatonin was no better than a placebo (sugar pill) in reducing jet lag (Spitzer et al., 1999). Previous reports of melatonin reducing jet lag were probably due to users' expectations (Rose & Kahan, 2001). However, melatonin helped individuals with medical problems resulting from chronically disrupted circadian clocks sleep better and experience less fatigue (Nagtegaal et al., 2000).

Next, we'll examine what happens inside the brain and body during sleep.

C. World of Sleep

Stages of Sleep

Does my brain sleep?

The first thing to know about sleep is that your brain never totally sleeps but is active throughout the night. To track your brain's activity during sleep, researchers would attach dozens of tiny wires or electrodes to your scalp and body and record electrical brain activity as you passed through the stages of sleep.

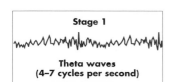

Going to sleep involves going through several different stages.

The *stages of sleep* refer to distinctive changes in the electrical activity of the brain and accompanying physiological responses of the body that occur as you pass through different phases of sleep.

As shown in the graph at the top, brain waves are described in terms of frequency

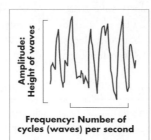

Amplitude: Height of waves

Frequency: Number of cycles (waves) per second

(speed) and amplitude (height). They are recorded by a complex machine called an EEG, or electroencephalogram. Each stage of sleep can be recognized by its distinctive pattern of EEGs, which we'll explain here.

ALPHA STAGE

Before actually going into the first stage of sleep, you briefly pass through a relaxed and drowsy state, marked by characteristic alpha waves.

The *alpha stage* is marked by feelings of being relaxed and drowsy, usually with the eyes closed. Alpha waves have low amplitude and high frequency (8–12 cycles per second).

After spending a brief time relaxing in the alpha stage, you enter stage 1 of non-REM sleep.

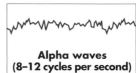

Alpha waves (8–12 cycles per second)

Non-REM Sleep

What happens during sleep?

The second thing to know about sleep is that it is divided into two major categories, called non-REM and REM. We'll discuss non-REM first.

Non-REM sleep is where you spend approximately 80% of your sleep time. Non-REM is divided into sleep stages 1, 2, 3, and 4; each stage is identified by a particular pattern of brain waves and physiological responses. (REM stands for rapid eye movement.)

You begin in sleep stage 1 and gradually enter stages 2, 3, and 4 (Hirshkowitz et al., 1997).

Stage 1

This is the lightest stage of sleep.

Stage 1 sleep is a transition from wakefulness to sleep and lasts 1–7 minutes. In it, you gradually lose responsiveness to stimuli and experience drifting thoughts and images. Stage 1 is marked by the presence of theta waves, which are lower in amplitude and lower in frequency (4–7 cycles per second) than alpha waves.

Stage 1

Theta waves (4–7 cycles per second)

Although stage 1 is usually labeled a sleep stage, some individuals who are aroused from it feel as if they have been awake.

Next, you enter stage 2 sleep.

Stage 2

This is the first stage of what researchers call real sleep.

Stage 2 sleep marks the beginning of what we know as sleep, since subjects who are awakened in stage 2 report having been asleep. EEG tracings show high-frequency bursts of brain activity called sleep spindles.

Stage 2

Sleep spindles

As you pass through stage 2, your muscle tension, heart rate, respiration, and body temperature gradually decrease, and it becomes more difficult for you to be awakened.

Stages 3 and 4

About 30–45 minutes after drifting off into sleep, you pass through stage 3 and then enter into stage 4 sleep.

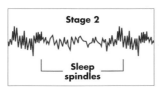

Stage 4 sleep, which is also called slow-wave or delta sleep, is characterized by waves of very high amplitude and very low frequency (less than 4 cycles per second) called delta waves. Stage 4 is often considered the deepest stage of sleep because it is the most difficult from which to be awakened. During stage 4, heart rate, respiration, temperature, and blood flow to the brain are reduced, and there is a marked secretion of GH (growth hormone), which controls levels of metabolism, physical growth, and brain development.

As you pass through stages 3 and 4, your muscle tension, heart rate, respiration, and temperature decrease still further, and it becomes very difficult for you to be awakened.

After spending a few minutes to an hour in stage 4, you will backtrack through stages 3 and 2 and then pass into a new stage, called REM sleep, which is associated with dreaming.

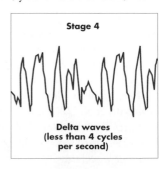

Stage 4

Delta waves (less than 4 cycles per second)

When do you dream?

We have discussed one major category of sleep, non-REM, and now move on to the second major category of sleep, which goes by the initials REM.

REM sleep makes up the remaining 20% of your sleep time. It is pronounced "rem" and stands for rapid eye movement sleep because your eyes move rapidly back and forth behind closed lids. REM brain waves have high frequency and low amplitude and look very similar to beta waves, which occur when you are wide awake and alert. During REM sleep, your body is physiologically very aroused, but all your voluntary muscles are paralyzed. REM sleep is highly associated with dreaming.

REM Sleep

(14–25 cycles per second)

You pass into REM sleep about five or six times throughout the night with about 30 to 90 minutes between periods. You remain in each period of REM sleep for 15 to 45 minutes and then pass back into non-REM sleep.

Characteristics of REM Sleep

When REM sleep was first discovered in the early 1950s, researchers found it difficult to believe their unusual findings: Although you are asleep during REM, your body and brain are in a general state of physiological arousal (Aserinsky & Kleitman, 1953). For example, during REM sleep, your heart rate and blood pressure may be twice as high as during non-REM sleep (Dement, 1999). Because of this strange combination of being asleep yet physiologically aroused, REM sleep is often called *paradoxical sleep.* (A *paradox* is something with contradictory qualities.)

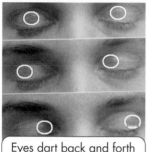

Eyes dart back and forth as a sign of REM sleep.

Another unusual feature of REM sleep is that its brain waves are very similar to those recorded when a person is wide awake and alert. By looking at brain wave recordings alone, researchers cannot tell whether a person is in REM sleep or wide awake. Only the additional recording of rapid eye movements indicates the occurrence of REM sleep.

Although many physiological responses are greatly increased, you completely lose the muscle tension (tonus) in your neck and limbs so that you are essentially paralyzed. However, involuntary muscles that regulate heart, lungs, and other body organs continue to function. Researchers think that humans evolved muscle paralysis of their limbs during REM sleep so that they would not act out violent dreams by running, fighting, or jumping about and injuring themselves (Schenck, 2003). In fact, this actually happens in REM behavior disorder.

In *REM behavior disorder,* which usually occurs in older people, voluntary muscles are not paralyzed, and sleepers can and do act out their dreams, such as fighting off attackers in dreams. In some cases, REM behavior disorder is caused by known neurological damage, but in other cases, the causes are unknown (Mahowlad, 2003).

So not only is REM a paradoxical sleep but it also signals dreaming.

REM—Dreaming and Remembering

Dreaming. One of the biggest breakthroughs in dream research was the finding that about 80–90% of the times when subjects are awakened from a REM period, they report having vivid, complex, and relatively long dreams, such as flying like a bird (right figure) (Dement, 1999). In contrast, only about 10% of subjects awakened from non-REM sleep report similar kinds of dreams.

One of the first questions asked was what happens when people are deprived of REM sleep and dreaming by being awakened whenever their physiological signs show they are starting a REM period. Many subjects

Dreaming usually occurs during REM sleep.

have been deprived of REM sleep and dreaming without showing any major behavioral or physiological effects (Bonnet, 2005). However, suppressing REM sleep does produce a curious phenomenon called REM rebound.

REM rebound refers to individuals spending an increased percentage of time in REM sleep if they were deprived of REM sleep on the previous nights.

Remembering. The occurrence of REM rebound suggests a need for REM sleep, and one such need involves memory. In one study, subjects learned to press a button when they spotted a moving target on a screen. Subjects tested on the same day as training showed a modest improvement. However, when subjects were tested the next day, those subjects allowed to get the most REM sleep (slept 8 hours) showed the greatest improvement compared to subjects who got the least REM (slept 6 hours). Researchers concluded that REM sleep helps us store or encode information in memory and advise students to get a good night's sleep so that what they studied the previous day has a chance to be stored in the brain's memory (Stickgold, 2000, 2005).

A short time after awakening from sleep, you enter a state of being awake and alert. This state has distinctive brain activity called beta waves (right figure), which are characterized by high frequency and low amplitude and are very similar to those waves observed during REM sleep.

Awake and Alert

Beta waves
(14–25 cycles per second)

How alert you feel in the morning partly depends on whether you are a morning or an evening person, which we'll discuss in the Research Focus on page 155.

Although you now have an overview of the different sleep stages, you may be surprised to discover that how you go through the different stages is somewhat like riding a roller coaster.

C. World of Sleep

Why is sleep like a roller-coaster ride? When you go to sleep at night, you may think that you simply sleep for 8 hours, perhaps toss and turn a little, and even do some dreaming. But sleep is not one unbroken state; rather, it is a series of recurring stages, similar to the ups and downs of a roller-coaster ride. We'll describe a typical night's pattern for George, a college sophomore, who goes to bed about 11 P.M. and gets up about 7 A.M. As we take you through the figure below, notice that non-REM sleep is indicated by the wide blue

A night's sleep is like a roller-coaster ride through different stages of sleep.

line and REM sleep is indicated by red inserts. The numbers 1 to 4 refer to sleep stages 1, 2, 3, and 4 of non-REM sleep, which we discussed earlier.

Researchers have studied and plotted changes in brain waves, physiological arousal, and dreaming as subjects progressed through the stages of sleep (L. Rosenthal, 2006). Here's what George will experience on a typical roller-coaster-like ride through the different stages of a night's sleep.

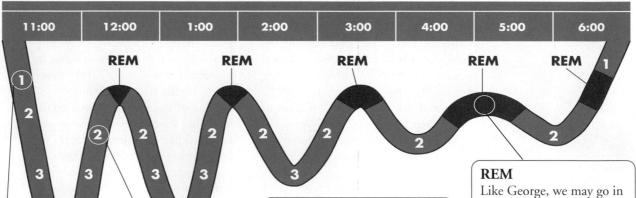

Here's what happens during a normal night's sleep.

STAGE 1

As George becomes drowsy, he will enter non-REM stage 1, which is the transition between being awake and asleep.

As sleep progresses, he will continue to the next stage, non-REM stage 2, which is the first stage of real sleep. During stage 2, he may experience short, fragmented thoughts, so that if he is awakened, he may think he was dreaming.

He will continue through non-REM stage 3 and finally reach non-REM stage 4. When George enters non-REM stage 4, which is slow-wave, or delta, sleep, he will be very difficult to waken. After staying in stage 4 for some minutes to an hour, he will backtrack to stages 3 and then 2.

STAGE 2

After George reaches non-REM stage 2, he does not awaken but rather enters REM sleep. He will remain in REM for 15–45 minutes and, if awakened, will likely report dreaming. When in REM, his body is in a high state of physiological arousal, but his voluntary limb muscles are essentially paralyzed. If George experiences nightmares during REM, he will not act them out or injure himself because he cannot move.

After the REM period, he goes back down through non-REM stages 2, 3, and 4.

STAGE 4

It is during stage 4 that George may sleepwalk, sleeptalk, or perform other activities, such as partially awakening to turn off the alarm, pull up the covers, or get up and go to the bathroom. However, George will remember nothing of what happens in non-REM stage 4, such as sleeptalking with his roommate or walking to the kitchen and getting a snack. He will remain in stage 4 for a period of time before again backtracking to non-REM stages 3 and 2, and then to his second REM period of the night.

Children sometimes wake up terrified during non-REM stage 4. These experiences are called night terrors (see p. 163), but the children will have no memory of them the next day. Also, bedwetting, a condition in which children are unable to control urination while asleep, occurs during non-REM stage 4.

REM

Like George, we may go in and out of REM sleep five or six times, with REM periods becoming longer toward morning. If George wants to remember his dreams, he should try when he first wakes up, since his last REM period may have occurred only minutes before.

Recent findings indicate that getting as many REM periods as possible is important in helping the brain store material learned the previous day (Stickgold, 2000).

If George has a difficult time awakening from sleep, it may be because he was in stage 4, the hardest stage to awaken from.

Like George, we all go through the sleep stages in about the same sequence. However, there's a reason that some of us hate mornings more than others.

D. Research Focus: Circadian Preference

Are You a Morning or Evening Person?

Are you an early bird or a night owl?

Some students are early birds and seem to like morning classes, while night owls hate them. Researchers studied differences between early birds and night owls by developing and using a questionnaire.

A *questionnaire* is a method for obtaining information by asking subjects to read a list of written questions and check off or rate their preferences for specific answers.

The morning/evening questionnaire asked subjects to rate their preferred times for going to bed, getting up, and engaging in physical and mental activities, as well as their feelings of alertness in the morning and evening. The graph here shows the results from this questionnaire.

Morning person

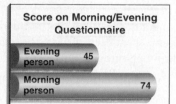

Score on Morning/Evening Questionnaire

Evening person — 45

Morning person — 74

Morning persons (score above 74) prefer to get up earlier, go to bed earlier, and engage in morning activities. *Evening persons* (score below 45) prefer to get up later, go to bed later, and engage in afternoon-evening activities. Those individuals who scored between 45 and 74 did not express a strong morning or evening preference (J. P. Guthrie et al., 1995).

Researchers found that there was a morning/evening continuum with strong preferences on either end and mixed or no preferences in the middle (Andershed, 2005). One reason a person may have a strong morning or evening preference is that an inherited genetic circadian rhythm regulates body temperature, which, in turn, affects going to sleep at night and getting up in the morning.

Evening person

Body Temperature

Your body has several circadian rhythms, and one of them is the sleep-wake cycle, which is regulated by the suprachiasmatic nucleus in the hypothalamus. Another circadian rhythm, also thought to be regulated by the suprachiasmatic nucleus, involves body temperature, which falls as we go to sleep and rises after we get up (Ropper & Brown, 2005). The graph on the right shows how changes in body temperature over a 24-hour period influence sleep preferences.

Getting up. Our body temperature is low in the morning and rises throughout the day, when we are most active. The temperature of a morning person rises more quickly, so this person gets up earlier than an evening person. In fact, body temperature in a morning person may rise

1–3 hours earlier than the temperature in an evening person (Duffy, 2002; Tankova et al., 1994).

Body temperature (°F)

94 96 8 100 2 4 6

Morning person's temperature rises more quickly and person gets up earlier.

Morning person's temperature peaks earlier and person goes to bed earlier.

98.6°

Evening person's temperature rises 1 to 3 hours later and person gets up later.

Evening person's temperature peaks 1 to 3 hours later and person goes to bed later.

6 A.M.   12 noon   6 P.M.   12 midnight

Changes in body temperature influence sleep preferences.

Going to bed. The body temperature of a morning person peaks earlier in the evening, so this person goes to bed earlier than an evening person. An evening person's body temperature peaks 1–3 hours later, so this person goes to bed later. Researchers think that the suprachiasmatic nucleus regulates the rise and fall of body temperature, which in turn determines whether you are a confirmed morning or evening person.

In addition, there are some interesting behavioral differences between morning and evening people.

Behavioral Differences

Researchers found that students who were morning people reported being more alert at 8 A.M., took more morning classes, performed better in morning classes, and studied more in the morning than did students who were evening people (Duffy, 2002; J. P. Guthrie et al., 1995). Students who were evening people but began classes in the morning had more attention problems and poorer performance and complained of daytime sleepiness (Giannotti et al., 2002).

Researchers found that people who worked night shifts or who had to rotate through afternoon and late evening times tended to be evening persons (Adan, 1992).

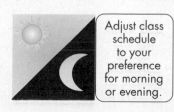

Adjust class schedule to your preference for morning or evening.

When looking at personality differences, researchers found that morning people tend to be conscientious introverts while evening people tend to be impulsive extroverts (K. Gilbert, 2006).

Finally, researchers found no differences between sexes in their preferences for being a morning or evening person. But, they did find that in the course of normal aging, people tend to become physiologically and behaviorally more like morning persons after age 50, which explains why grandparents are usually early to bed and early to rise (Duffy, 2002).

Although people differ in being morning or evening persons, they do share similar brain structures involved in putting them to sleep and waking them up, our next topic.

E. Questions about Sleep

Most adults need 7–8 hours of sleep.

By the time you are 25 years old, you have fallen asleep over 9,000 times and have spent about 72,000 hours asleep. There are usually four questions that students ask about sleep: How much sleep do I need? Why do I sleep? What happens if I go without sleep? What causes sleep? We'll discuss each of these questions in turn.

How Much Sleep Do I Need?

What's the best amount for me?

According to a national survey, 16% of adults sleep less than 6 hours a night, 24% sleep 6–6.9 hours, 31% sleep 7–7.9 hours, and 26% sleep 8 or more hours. Overall, adults in America sleep an average of 6.9 hours a night (NSF, 2005). If we took a survey of babies, the time spent sleeping would be dramatically different, as shown in the pie charts below.

Beginning at birth and continuing through old age, there is a gradual change in the total time we spend sleeping, the percentage of time we spend in REM sleep, and the kinds of sleep problems we experience.

INFANCY AND CHILDHOOD
From infancy to adolescence, the total amount of time spent in sleep and the percentage spent in REM gradually decline. For example, a newborn sleeps about 17 hours a day, and 50% of that time is spent in REM; a 4-year-old sleeps about 10 hours a day, and 25–30% of that time is spent in REM.

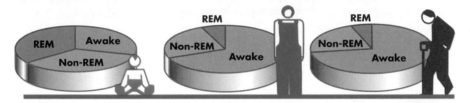

ADOLESCENCE AND ADULTHOOD Researchers recently found that, compared to adults, adolescents need more sleep (about 9 hours) and their circadian clocks favor going to bed later and getting up later (Hathaway, 2006; MFMER, 2005). Researchers concluded that adolescents who must get up early (6 or 7 A.M.) for classes are often sleep deprived, which may interfere with their performance (Millman et al., 2005). One solution is for high-school classes to start an hour later so adolescents can get sufficient sleep. At about age 20, adolescents adopt the sleep pattern of adults, which is to get approximately 7–8 hours of sleep a night, with about 20% or less being REM sleep.

OLD AGE
Upon reaching our sixties, total sleep time drops to about 6.5 hours a day, but the percentage of REM sleep remains about the same (20%) (Ropper & Brown, 2005). In people over 55, 66% experience symptoms of a sleep problem (trouble getting to sleep or staying asleep, interrupted breathing), and they compensate by taking a nap during the day (NSF, 2003, 2004).

Why Do I Sleep?

Is my brain being repaired?

One reason we know sleep is important comes from studies of animals who are deprived of sleep. Rats can live about 16 days without food (water provided) and about 17 days without sleep (Rechtschaffen, 1997). So far, the longest a human has voluntarily gone without sleep is 11 days (discussed on next page). We'll explain two currently popular theories—the repair and adaptive theories—of why we spend about one-third of each day asleep.

Repair theory says sleep restores brain and body.

The *repair theory* suggests that activities during the day deplete key factors in our brain or body that are replenished or repaired by sleep. The repair theory says that sleep is primarily a restorative process.

The repair theory is supported by three findings. First, during stage 4 sleep there is a marked secretion of growth hormone, which controls aspects of metabolism, physical growth, and brain development (C. M. Shapiro, 1981). Second, during sleep there is increased production of immune cells to fight off infection (Born et al., 1997). Third, during wakefulness there is a decline in the brain's energy stores (glycogen), which are restored during sleep and are needed for normal functioning and survival (Geiger, 2002). The brain needs sleep to grow, repair its immune system, and restore its energy and chemicals (J. M. Siegel, 2003).

The *adaptive theory* suggests that sleep evolved because it prevented early humans and animals from wasting energy and exposing themselves to the dangers of nocturnal predators (Webb, 1992).

Support for the adaptive theory comes from observations that large predatory animals, such as lions,

Adaptive theory says sleep helps us avoid dangers.

sleep a lot and wherever they wish, while prey animals, such as antelope, sleep far less and in protected areas. Many birds sleep with one hemisphere at a time, to guard against predators (Sillery, 2002). Animals (humans) that rely primarily on visual cues and have little night vision have evolved a circadian clock for sleeping at night and thus avoid becoming prey (Hirshkowitz et al., 1997).

The adaptive and repair theories are not really at odds. Both have support but just focus on different reasons for sleep.

What If I Miss Sleep?

Can you go without sleep?

One method of investigating why sleep is important is to study people or animals who are sleep deprived. The record for sleep deprivation was set by a young adult who went without sleep for 11 days, or 264 hours (L. C. Johnson et al., 1965). On his 11th day without sleep, this young man beat the researcher in a pinball game, which indicates he was still awake and alert. Here's what happens when people are sleep deprived.

EFFECTS ON THE BODY

Sleep deprivation, even for 264 hours, has minimal effect on physiological functions controlled by the autonomic nervous system, such as a person's heart rate or blood pressure (Kato et al., 2000). However, sleep deprivation can lead to serious health problems. For instance, sleep deprivation may compromise our immune system, which means that for most people, sleep deprivation could increase their vulnerability to some viral or bacterial infections (Dement, 1999). Also, sleep deprivation puts the body in high alert, increasing production of stress hormones and elevating blood pressure, which are major risk factors for health conditions such as heart disease, stroke, and cancer (R. Stein, 2005). In other research, sleep deprivation was linked to changes in appetite-related hormones and elevated amounts of the hormone insulin. Researchers concluded that sleep deprivation increased the risk for obesity and diabetes (Spiegal, 2006).

EFFECTS ON THE BRAIN

Sleep deprivation can cause irritability and unhappiness and interfere with tasks that require vigilance and concentration, such as recalling and recognizing words and doing math tests (Ropper & Brown, 2005). People who are greatly sleep deprived, such as sled-dog racers who averaged 2 hours of sleep a night during the 12-day Iditarod race, reported vivid hallucinations, such as seeing blazing fireplaces, only to awake lying in the cold snow (Balzar, 1997). Researchers found that sleep deprivation depleted vital energy stores (gylcogen) in the brain (Geiger, 2002). Various degrees of sleep deprivation cause moodiness and hallucinations, interfere with cognitive performance, and deplete the brain's vital energy stores.

What Causes Sleep?

How do you go to sleep?

After getting into bed, most of us fall asleep within 5–30 minutes and sleep an average of 7 8 hours (range about 6 to 10). Going to sleep involves a very complicated process during which different areas of the brain are activated or deactivated. The whole sleep process begins with something flipping the master switch for sleep.

MASTER SLEEP SWITCH

VPN is sleep switch.

The master switch for sleep is in a nucleus of the brain called the VPN (Garcia-Rill et al., 2006).

The *VPN— ventrolateral preoptic nucleus*—is a group of cells in the hypothalamus that act like a master switch for sleep. When turned on, the VPN secretes a neurotransmitter (GABA) that turns off areas that keep the brain awake. When the VPN is turned off, certain brain areas become active and you wake up.

Researchers don't know how the VPN in humans is turned on and off, but they recently found that the VPN in rats is activated by the neurotransmitter adenosine (Gallopin et al., 2005). Next, we'll look at one brain area the VPN turns off.

RETICULAR FORMATION

In order for the forebrain to receive and process information from the senses, it must be aroused and alerted by the reticular formation.

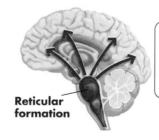

Reticular formation is turned off to go to sleep.

Reticular formation

The *reticular formation,* a column of cells that stretches the length of the brain stem, arouses and alerts the forebrain and prepares it to receive information from all the senses.

The reticular formation is important in keeping the forebrain alert and in producing a state of wakefulness (Ropper, 2006). If the reticular formation is stimulated in sleeping animals, they awaken; if it is seriously damaged in animals or humans, they lapse into permanent unconsciousness or coma.

GOING TO SLEEP

The master sleep switch and the reticular formation are but two of the factors regulating sleep. Here is the probable sequence for going to sleep.

First, the time of day you go to sleep is regulated by the circadian clock, which is influenced by the suprachiasmatic nucleus of the hypothalamus (R. Y. Moore, 2006).

Second, something turns on your master sleep switch, which is located in the VPN (ventrolateral preoptic nucleus). In turn, the VPN turns off areas that arouse your brain, such as the reticular formation (Garcia-Rill et al., 2006).

Third, a number of different chemicals and neurotransmitters, some of which are manufactured in the pons, regulate when you go into and out of non-REM and REM sleep and when you awaken (Czeisler et al., 2006).

Fourth, the circadian rhythm that regulates your body temperature is tied in with sleep, since  Four factors for sleep you go to sleep when your temperature falls and wake up when your temperature rises (Ropper & Brown, 2005).

Thus, the reasons you go to sleep and wake up involve a complex interaction among the circadian clock, brain areas, sleep-inducing chemicals, and body temperature.

After the Concept Review, we'll describe a psychological problem whose cause seems related to decreased sunlight.

Concept Review

1. The various levels of awareness of one's thoughts and feelings, as well as of other internal and external stimuli, are referred to as (a)_____. This experience varies on a continuum from very aware and alert to totally unaware and unresponsive. Activities that require full awareness and alertness and may interfere with other ongoing endeavors are called (b)_____. In comparison, activities that require little awareness and minimal attention and that do not interfere with other ongoing endeavors are called (c)_____.

2. The biological clock that is set for a day of about 24 hours is called a (a)_____. This rhythm regulates our sleep-wake cycle, which is set to an average day of 24 hours and 18 minutes. Our circadian clock is reset by 18 minutes each day to match our agreed upon 24-hour day. The circadian clock is located in the brain's hypothalamus, in a small part called the (b)_____.

3. If your circadian rhythm is out of step with local time, you may feel fatigued and disoriented, a traveler's complaint called (a)_____. Workers and drivers have more accidents during the early-morning hours because their sleep-wake clock is telling them it's time to (b)_____. Researchers have reset circadian rhythms by exposing subjects and night workers to periods of bright light; this is called (c)_____ therapy.

4. Near the center of the human brain is an oval group of cells, collectively called the pineal gland, that secrete a hormone called (a)_____. The gland secretes the hormone during dark periods and stops when it gets light. In many animals, this hormone plays a major role in the regulation of (b)_____ rhythms.

SUPRACHIASMATIC NUCLEUS

PINEAL GLAND   OPTIC NERVE

5. During a night's sleep, we gradually pass through five stages. Stage 1, which is a transition between waking and sleeping, has brain waves known as (a)_____. Stage 2 has brain waves with bursts of activity that are called (b)_____. Stage 3 and especially stage 4 are marked by high-amplitude, low-frequency (c)_____. Stage 4 is often considered the deepest stage of sleep because it is the most difficult from which to be awakened. During stage 4, heart rate, respiration, temperature, and blood flow to the brain are (d)_____. Together, stages 1, 2, 3, and 4 are referred to as (e)_____, in which we spend about 80% of our sleep time. About five or six times throughout the night, we enter a paradoxical state called (f)_____, which accounts for the remaining 20% of our sleep time. This stage is characterized by increased physiological arousal, "alert and awake" brain waves, and vivid dreaming.

6. From birth through old age, there is a decrease in total sleep time, from about 17 hours in newborns to 6.5 hours after age 60. In addition, one stage of sleep, called _____, decreases from 50% of sleep time in infancy to 20% in adulthood.

7. There are two different but not incompatible theories of why we sleep. The theory that says the purpose of sleep is to restore factors depleted throughout the day is the (a)_____. The theory that says sleep is based on an evolutionary need to conserve energy and escape nocturnal harm is the (b)_____.

8. Going to sleep is regulated by the following factors. An area in the hypothalamus that is the master sleep switch is called the (a)_____. An area in the hypothalamus that regulates circadian rhythms is called the (b)_____ nucleus. A brain area that contributes to our staying awake by sending neural signals that alert and arouse the forebrain is called the (c)_____. Several different sleep chemicals and (d)_____, some of which are made in the pons, regulate going into and out of the stages of sleep. In addition, we go to sleep several hours after a fall in body (e)_____ and get up when it starts to rise.

Answers: *1. (a) consciousness, (b) controlled processes, (c) automatic processes; 2. (a) circadian rhythm, (b) suprachiasmatic nucleus; 3. (a) jet lag, (b) sleep, (c) light; 4. (a) melatonin, (b) circadian; 5. (a) theta waves, (b) sleep spindles, (c) delta waves, (d) reduced, (e) non-REM sleep, (f) REM sleep; 6. REM sleep; 7. (a) repair theory, (b) adaptive theory; 8. (a) VPN, or ventrolateral preoptic nucleus, (b) suprachiasmatic, (c) reticular formation, (d) neurotransmitters, (e) temperature*

F. Cultural Diversity: Incidence of SAD

Problem and Treatment

Does light affect your mood?

Problem. For many animals, including humans, sunlight has a direct influence on resetting the circadian clock and affecting circadian rhythms. However, it was only recently that researchers found a direct nerve connection from receptors in the retina, which is located in the back of the eye, to a nucleus in the brain (suprachiasmatic nucleus in the hypothalamus—p. 150). This particular nerve pathway is not involved with seeing things but only with sensing the presence and amount of light, either sunlight or artificial light (Young, 2000). This means that humans have a neural pathway that is very responsive to the presence of light and may be involved in a mental health problem called seasonal affective disorder, or SAD.

Seasonal affective disorder, or *SAD,* is a pattern of depressive symptoms, such as loss of interest or pleasure in nearly all activities. Depressed feelings cycle with the seasons, typically beginning in fall or winter and going away in spring, when days are longer and sunnier. Along with depression are

Seasonal affective disorder (SAD) occurs in fall/winter.

lethargy, excessive sleepiness, overeating, weight gain, and craving for carbohydrates. Recently, SAD has become a subtype (Seasonal Pattern Specifier) of major depression (American Psychiatric Association, 2000).

Cause and Treatment. What might trigger SAD is the amount of a brain neurotransmitter, serotonin, and the amount of a hormone made mostly at night, melatonin. Researchers suggest that the decreased sunlight in fall and winter causes a decrease in the amount of serotonin and an increase in melatonin, which may both act to trigger SAD (Anstett, 2006; G. W. Lambert et al., 2002).

A nondrug treatment for SAD involves exposing a person to bright light in the morning for about 30 minutes. This treatment helps as many as 70% of individuals diagnosed with SAD (Anstett, 2006).

Because decreased sunlight appears to trigger SAD, you would expect the fewest cases of SAD in southern Florida, more cases in northern New Hampshire with its gloomy winters, and even more cases in northern Iceland, which has harsh winters with little or no sunlight.

Occurrence of SAD

Where is the highest rate of SAD?

As predicted, the graph shows that the incidence of SAD is very low (1.4%) among people who live in sunny Florida but about five times higher (7.3%) among people who live under the gray winter skies of northern New Hampshire (Magnusson, 2000). However, far north of New Hampshire is Iceland (see map), which has far less sunlight in fall and winter than New Hampshire. In spite of having less sunlight, Icelanders have only about half the incidence of SAD (3.6%) compared to residents of New Hampshire (Axelsson et al., 2002).

1.4 % SAD in Florida

3.6 % SAD in Iceland

7.3 % SAD in New Hampshire

When researchers try to explain any unusual or unpredicted findings, they first check the methods and procedures used to measure the dependent variable, which in this case is the occurrence of SAD. However, researchers in Iceland used the same methods (questionnaires) and procedures that were used by researchers in the United States (Magnusson, 2000). If research methods and procedures were similar, what else would explain why the highest incidence of SAD was reported in New Hampshire and not in Iceland?

Cultural Differences

What's different about Icelanders?

Why did Icelanders report less than half the incidence of SAD, even though they have far less sunlight in fall and winter than residents of New Hampshire (see map)?

Researchers concluded that differences in methods, questionnaires, and residents' lifestyles or occupations could not explain this discrepancy. Rather, there may be two other explanations that involve cultural and genetic differences.

For 1,000 years, Icelanders have lived rather isolated in a very demanding, low-sunlight environment. Because of very harsh and unyielding environmental demands, Icelanders may have developed an emotional hardiness to deal with especially gloomy winters that trigger almost twice as many cases of SAD among residents of the northeastern United States.

Cultural differences explain why Iceland (far north) has less SAD than New Hampshire.

Another explanation for Icelanders' low incidence of SAD may involve genetic factors. For example, researchers studied a population of immigrants in Canada who were wholly of Icelandic descent. The incidence of SAD in the Icelandic immigrants was unexpectedly much lower than found in other residents of the same general area. Researchers concluded that the lower frequency of SAD in Icelanders is puzzling and may reflect both genetic and cultural differences, such as learning how to deal with isolation and living in harsh environments (Axelsson et al., 2002; Magnusson & Partonen, 2005).

Next, we'll discuss four explanations for something most of us experience every night—dreaming.

G. World of Dreams

What do dreams mean?

Although some people insist that they never dream, research suggests that everyone dreams during the night, even though many have forgotten their dreams by morning. In sleep laboratories, people awakened from REM periods report 80–100% of the time that they were having dreams with vivid, colorful, even bizarre images. Less frequently, people awakened from non-REM sleep or right after going to sleep may report dreaming of dull, repetitive thoughts or of colorful images as reported after REM sleep (Domhoff, 2003). However, what you think of as dreaming usually occurs during REM sleep (B. Bower, 2001). For example, how might the following dream be interpreted?

I am in an elevator sitting by myself against the wall. A girl comes in, and I say, "Come sit by me," and she sits by me. (I don't even know her.) I lean over and try to kiss her, and she says, "No, don't do that." I say, "How come?" and she says something

There are several different interpretations of dreams.

about her acne, and I say it doesn't matter and she laughs, and we end up kissing and stuff on the elevator. Then these parents get on, and the elevator is real shaky, and I think that the elevator will crash or get stuck (adapted from D. B. Cohen, 1979).

Figuring out what dreams mean is a popular and scholarly activity for the more than 400 psychologists, physiologists, anthropologists, artists, "dream workers," and swamis who attend the annual meeting of the Association for the Study of Dreams. The focus of this group is to discover meaning in dreams—no easy task, since there are numerous theories. We'll discuss three currently popular psychological theories of dream interpretation as well as one thousand-year-old theory of dreams from the Inuit or Eskimo people.

We'll begin our discussion of dreams with the most famous and still controversial theory, Freud's theory of dream interpretation.

1 Freud's Theory of Dream Interpretation

In the preface to his famous book, *The Interpretation of Dreams*, Freud (1900) wrote, "This book contains, even according to my present-day judgment, the most valuable of all the discoveries it has been my good fortune to make. Insight such as this falls to one's lot but once in a lifetime." Before 1900, psychologists believed that dreams were meaningless and bizarre images. However, Freud's theory changed all that when he said that dreams were a way ("the royal road") to reach our unconscious thoughts and desires.

Freud's theory of dreams says that we have a "censor" that protects us from realizing threatening and unconscious desires or wishes, especially those involving sex or aggression. To protect us from having threatening thoughts, the "censor" transforms our secret, guilt-ridden, and anxiety-provoking desires into harmless symbols that appear in our dreams and do not disturb our sleep or conscious thoughts.

Freud believed dreams reveal repressed desires.

Freud made two main points that no one had made before: Dreams contained symbols that had meaning, and dreams could be interpreted. For example, Freud (1900) said that male sex symbols are long objects, such as sticks, umbrellas, and pencils; female sex symbols are hollow things, such as caves, jars, and keyholes. Freud believed a psychoanalyst's (Freudian therapist) task was to interpret or decode dream symbols, which were "the royal road" or way to uncover a client's threatening but unconscious desires, needs, defenses, fears, and emotions (B. Bower, 2001).

Current psychoanalysts agree with Freud that dreams have meaning and can represent past, present, or future concerns, fears, or worries (R. Greenberg & Perlman, 1999). However, as you'll see next, many non-Freudian therapists disagree with Freud's idea that a dream's contents are necessarily symbols or disguised thoughts for threatening, unconscious wishes and desires (Domhoff, 2003).

2 Extensions of Waking Life

Many therapists and some current psychoanalysts believe that dreams are extensions of waking life (Kramer, 2006).

The theory that *dreams are extensions of waking life* means that our dreams reflect the same thoughts, fears, concerns, problems, and emotions that we have when awake.

Therapist and researcher Rosalind Cartwright (1988), director of Rush Sleep Disorder Service, says, "People simply don't remember their dreams very well. The therapist's task is often like trying to reconstruct a 500-page novel from just the last page. But dreams collected from a single night in the sleep lab read like chapters in a book. They illuminate current concerns and the feelings attached to them" (p. 36). Cartwright believes that patients suffering from depression or marital problems cope with their problems by repeating their fears and concerns in their dreams. She advises that as soon as you awaken from a reoccurring bad dream, you should figure out why the dream is upsetting and then visualize how you would like the dream to end the next time it occurs. With practice, people can gain control over reoccurring bad dreams. Cartwright concludes that there

Therapists believe dreams reflect waking concerns.

is probably little reason to pay attention to dreams unless they keep you from sleeping or cause you to wake up in a panic (Cartwright, 2002). In these cases, therapists find dream interpretation a useful tool in helping clients better understand the personal and emotional problems that are contributing to their bad dreams.

Other researchers believe that dreams have a variety of uses, ranging from dealing with threatening situations, resolving personal and emotional problems, sparking artistic creativity, to even solving scientific, mathematical, or other kinds of puzzles (B. Bower, 2001).

The next theory looks at dreams as reflecting neural activity.

3 Activation-Synthesis Theory

In the late 1970s, psychiatrist and neurophysiologist J. Allan Hobson published a new theory of dreams that totally disagreed with many therapists' as well as Freud's theory of dreams. Recently, Hobson (2002) published a revised version of this 1970s theory.

The activation-synthesis theory says that dreaming occurs because brain areas that provide reasoned cognitive control during the waking state are shut down. As a result, the sleeping brain is stimulated by different chemical and neural influences that result in hallucinations, delusions, high emotions, and bizarre thought patterns that we call dreams.

Unlike Freud, Hobson believes that dream interpretation is questionable, since there is no way to know whether dreams are just bizarre events or contain useful or valid information about a person's problems.

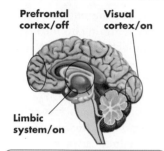

Prefrontal cortex/off **Visual cortex/on**

Limbic system/on

During REM, prefrontal cortex turned off; visual cortex and limbic system turned on.

Brain scans. The bases for Hobson's revised theory come from brain scans of neural activity taken while subjects were in REM sleep. Researchers reported that during REM sleep, the area responsible for executive functions (prefrontal cortex), such as thinking, planning, and reasoning, had reduced activity, while areas involved in emotions (limbic system) and visual experiences (visual cortex) had increased activity (A. R. Braun et al., 1998). Hobson believes that this pattern of brain activity explains why dreams are emotional (limbic system/on) and full of visual images (visual cortex/on) but are often strange, bizarre, and poorly planned or thought out (prefrontal cortex/off) (Domhoff, 2003). Similar to the other dream theories, the activation-synthesis theory also has critics. They believe the content of dreams can contain useful and meaningful information about a person's life (Domhoff, 2005a, 2005b).

How do dream theories from European-Western cultures compare with those from native cultures, such as the Inuit (formerly called Eskimo)?

4 Entering the Spiritual World

The Inuit or Eskimo people have lived for thousands of years in isolation along the arctic coasts of North America. The Inuit, along with other native people, believe that dreams are ways to enter the spiritual world (E. G. Foulks, 1992).

The Inuit believes that in dreaming, one enters the spiritual world, where the souls of animals, supernaturals, and departed relatives are made known. Through dreams, forces in the spiritual world help a living person reflect on some present or future event.

Inuits believe you enter the spiritual world through dreams.

Although the Inuit live in a far different time, place, and culture than did Sigmund Freud or Western therapists, there are numerous parallels between their theories of dreams. For example, the Inuit, Freud, and Western therapists all believed that past forces, wishes, or concerns could be revealed to the dreamer and that these wishes, concerns, or desires could take symbolic forms. Inuit shamans, who were thought to possess spiritual powers, function like Freudian trained psychoanalysts or Western trained therapists, who are sometimes needed to interpret dream symbols or unravel the meaning of dreams. Notice, however, that each dream theory has a unique focus: Freud says that dreams are ways to reach the unconscious; modern therapists hold that dreams represent waking problems; and the Inuit believe that dreams are ways to enter the spiritual world.

Next, we'll examine what people dream about.

Typical Dreams

What do people dream about?

Although many animals, including bats, whales, monkeys, moles, dogs, and cats (but not snakes), have REM sleep, we do not know if they dream. We know that humans dream because they tell us. Thousands of descriptions of dreams have been obtained from people who had just been aroused from REM sleep and others who were asked to record their dreams at home. One researcher (Van de Castle, 1994) has catalogued these descriptions and found that typical dreams have the following characteristics:

- dreams have several characters;
- they involve motion such as running or walking;
- they are more likely to take place indoors than outside;
- they are filled with visual sensations but rarely include sensations of taste, smell, or pain;
- they seem bizarre because we disregard physical laws by flying or falling without injury;
- they may be recurrent—for example, dreams of being threatened, being pursued, or trying to hide;
- they more frequently involve emotions of anxiety or fear than joy or happiness;
- they rarely involve sexual encounters and are almost never about sexual intercourse;
- rarely can we control or dream about something we intend to;

Many people dream about flying, running, falling, or hiding.

- dreams usually have visual imagery and are in color in sighted people, but in people blind from birth, dreams are never visual but only tactile, olfactory (smell), or gustatory (taste).

Researchers conclude that although individual dreams represent unique experiences, the format in which we dream, such as flying, falling, running, or hiding, is shared by others (Domhoff, 2003). One common question is: Why do some better remember their dreams? One researcher found that the ability to remember dreams was positively related or correlated with how well one can create mental images during waking and was not related to verbal ability, which might influence dream recall (D. Foulkes, 2003).

Sometimes dreams can turn into nightmares, which we'll discuss next in considering sleep problems and treatments.

Occurrence

How big is the problem? In the United States, about 50–70 million people experience some kind of sleep problem (Gupta, 2006). For example, some adults stop breathing in their sleep (sleep apnea); some have trouble going to or staying asleep (insomnia); a small percentage go from being wide awake to a very deep sleep quickly and without warning (narcolepsy); and 69% of all children experience some type of sleep disturbance at least a few nights a week (Carskadon, 2006). We'll discuss a number of these sleep problems as well as possible treatments, beginning with one of the more common problems, insomnia.

Insomnia

In the United States, about 33% of adults report some type of insomnia (Ohayon & Guilleminault, 2006).

Insomnia refers to difficulties in either going to sleep or staying asleep through the night. Insomnia is associated with a number of daytime complaints, including fatigue, impairment of concentration, memory difficulty, and lack of well-being.

Psychological causes. Common psychological causes of insomnia include experiencing an overload of stressful events, worrying about personal or job-related dif-

ficulties, grieving over a loss or death, and coping with mental health problems. For many middle-aged working people, job stress is a major cause of insomnia and other sleep problems (Kalimo et al., 2000). For students, common causes of insomnia are worry about exams, personal problems, and changes in sleep schedule, such as staying up late Saturday night and sleeping late on Sunday morning. Then Sunday night students are not tired at the usual time and may experience insomnia.

Physiological causes. Common physiological causes of insomnia include changing to night-shift work, which upsets circadian rhythms, having medical problems or chronic pain, and abusing alcohol or other substances (sedatives). All can disrupt going to and staying asleep.

There are effective nondrug (psychological) and drug treatments for bouts of insomnia.

Nondrug Treatment

Nondrug treatments for insomnia may differ in method, but all have the same goal: to stop the person from excessive worrying and reduce tension, which are major psychological causes of insomnia. One proven cognitive-behavioral method of reducing insomnia is to establish an optimal sleep pattern (Bootzin & Rider, 1997).

Establishing an Optimal Sleep Pattern

Follow these eight steps so that sleeping becomes more regular and efficient.

1. Go to bed only when you are sleepy, not by convention or habit.

2. Put the light out immediately when you get into bed.

3. Do not read or watch television in bed, since these are activities that you do when awake.

4. If you are not asleep within 20 minutes, get out of bed and sit and relax in another room until you are tired again. Relaxation can include tensing and relaxing your muscles or using visual imagery, which involves closing your eyes and concentrating on some calm scene or image for several minutes.

5. Repeat step 4 as often as required, and also if you wake up for any long periods of time.

6. Set the alarm to the same time each morning, so that your time of waking is always the same. This step is very important because oversleeping or sleeping in is one of the primary causes of insomnia the next night.

7. Do not nap during the day because it will throw off your sleep schedule that night.

8. Follow this program rigidly for several weeks to establish an efficient and regular pattern of sleep.

Results. In one study, participants who had chronic insomnia reduced their time awake (after going to sleep) by 54% using cognitive-behavioral therapy, compared to 16% using relaxation exercises and 12% using a placebo treatment (Edinger et al., 2001).

Serious problems with chronic insomnia may be treated, in the short term, with drugs.

Drug Treatment

Many stressful situations, such as losing a loved one, going through a divorce, or dealing with a physical injury, may result in chronic insomnia, which is defined as lasting longer than three weeks. In these cases, doctors may prescribe one of the following sleep-inducing drugs.

Benzodiazepines (ben-zo-die-AS-ah-peens) (Dalmane, Xanax, Restoril) reduce anxiety, worry, and stress and are effective and relatively safe when taken in moderate doses in the short-term (2–4 weeks) treatment of insomnia (Czeisler et al., 2006).

However, prolonged use of benzodiazepines, especially at higher doses, may lead to dependence on the drug

and serious side effects, such as memory loss and excessive sleepiness. Reduced side effects are one advantage of the next drugs.

Nonbenzodiazepines (Ambien, Sonata, Lunesta) are rapidly becoming popular sleeping pills because they are fast acting, reduce daytime drowsiness, have fewer cognitive side effects, and are less likely to lead to dependence (Lee-Chiong & Sateia, 2006).

In the United States alone, about 42 million sleeping pill prescriptions were filled in 2005 and sales of sleeping pills reached $2.8 billion (Saul, 2006; Szabo, 2006). However, studies have found that cognitive-behavioral therapy is either as effective as or superior to sleeping pills in treating and reducing chronic insomnia (Perlis et al., 2003; Sivertsen et al., 2006).

Sleep Apnea

In the United States, about 20 million adults have insomnia because they stop breathing, a problem called sleep apnea.

Sleep apnea refers to repeated periods during sleep when a person stops breathing for 10 seconds or longer. The person may repeatedly stop breathing, momentarily wake up, resume breathing, and return to sleep. Repeated awakenings during the night result in insomnia and leave the person exhausted during the day but not knowing the cause of the tiredness.

The chances of developing sleep apnea increase if a person is an intense and frequent snorer, is overweight, uses alcohol, or takes sedatives (benzodiazepines) (Chokroverty, 2000). Some people with sleep apnea may wake up an astonishing 200–400 times a night, which also results in insomnia (Czeisler et al., 2006).

The simplest treatment for sleep apnea is to sew tennis balls into the back of a pajama top so the person cannot lie on his or her back, which increases the chances of sleep apnea. For more severe cases, the most effective therapy is a device that blows air into a mask worn over the nose that helps keep air passages open (see photo below). An alternative treatment is for people to wear a mouth device that helps to move the lower jaw forward and thus open the airway (H. Fields, 2006). In severe cases, people may undergo surgery to remove tonsils or alter the position of the jaw (J. E. Brody, 2002).

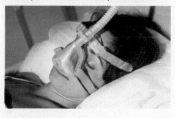

Narcolepsy

"I have lived with narcolepsy for 45 years. . . . I was directly responsible for several near-fatal automobile accidents. The simple joys everyone takes for granted are, for the most part, denied me. I would literally sleep the rest of my life away" (NCSDR, 1993, p. 16).

Narcolepsy (NAR-ko-lep-see) is a chronic disorder that is marked by excessive sleepiness, usually in the form of sleep attacks or short periods of sleep throughout the day. The sleep attacks are accompanied by brief periods of REM sleep and loss of muscle control (cataplexy), which may be triggered by big emotional changes.

Narcoleptics describe their sleep attacks as irresistible. They report falling asleep in very inappropriate places, such as while carrying on a conversation or driving a car. In many cases, these sleep attacks make it difficult for narcoleptics to lead normal lives.

Like humans, some dogs get narcolepsy, such as the one held below by famous sleep researcher William Dement. Researchers have recently discovered that narcolepsy occurred in dogs and mice when certain brain cells, called hypocretin neurons, either were absent or did not respond normally (Mignot, 2000). Researchers also found very little hypocretin in the spinal fluid of narcoleptics (Mignot, 2002). When "narcoleptic" dogs were given the missing hypocretin, their narcoleptic symptoms were reversed. Researchers believe that, in five years, a hypocretin-based medicine could be on the market and provide a new and effective way to treat narcolepsy, which affects about 135,000 Americans.

Sleep Disturbances

NIGHT TERRORS

A 4-year-old boy sits up in the night and begins screaming. This is an example of a night terror.

Night terrors, which occur during stage 3 or 4 (delta sleep), are frightening experiences that often start with a piercing scream, followed by sudden waking in a fearful state with rapid breathing and increased heart rate. However, the next morning the child has no memory of the frightening experience. About 3–7% of children have night terrors.

A child in the grip of night terrors is difficult to calm and, even if severely shaken, may need several minutes to regain full awareness. Night terrors are most common in children aged 5–7 and disappear by adolescence (Heussler, 2005). Caregivers should take enough time to comfort and soothe the frightened child, who usually will go back to sleep.

NIGHTMARES

Besides night terrors, about 25–70% of all children aged 3–6 have nightmares, and about 47% of college students report having them once a month (Picchioni et al., 2002).

Nightmares, which occur during REM sleep, are very frightening and anxiety-producing images that occur during dreaming. Nightmares usually involve great danger— being attacked, injured, or pursued. Upon awakening, the person can usually describe the nightmare in great detail.

Nightmares usually stop when the person wakes, but feelings of anxiety or fear may persist for some time; it may be difficult to go back to sleep. One effective treatment for nightmares involves regular use of anxiety-reduction techniques (described in Module 21).

SLEEPWALKING

One of the more unusual sleep disturbances is sleepwalking.

Sleepwalking usually occurs in stage 3 or 4 (delta sleep) and consists of getting up and walking while literally sound asleep. Sleepwalkers generally have poor coordination, are clumsy but can avoid objects, can engage in very limited conversation, and have no memory of sleepwalking.

Occasional sleepwalking is considered normal in children; frequent sleepwalking in adults may be caused by increased stress, sleep deprivation, or mental problems (Dement, 1999). Sleepwalking can be a serious problem because of the potential for injury and harm to oneself and others (imagine sleepwalking out of the house onto the highway).

Sleep researchers estimate that as many as 70 million Americans have one or more of the sleep problems discussed above. Sleep disorders clinics have been set up to treat the more serious problems (R. S. Rosenberg, 2006).

Summary Test

A. Continuum of Consciousness

1. The awareness of our own thoughts and feelings, as well as of other internal and external stimuli, is called (a)_____, which occurs on a continuum from being very alert to being very unresponsive.  Those activities that require our full awareness and concentration to reach some goal are called (b)_____. Those activities that require little awareness and minimal attention and that do not interfere with other ongoing activities are called (c)_____.

2. Fantasizing or dreaming while awake, which often occurs during automatic processes, is called (a)_____. If, under the influence of drugs, meditation, or hypnosis, we perceive our internal and external environments in ways that differ from normal, we may be said to have entered (b)_____ of consciousness. Sigmund Freud suggested that we push unacceptable wishes or desires into our (c)_____. A blow to the head or general anesthesia can produce complete loss of awareness, which is called (d)_____. Mental and emotional processes that, although we are unaware of them, influence our conscious thoughts and behaviors form a kind of memory called (e)_____.

B. Rhythms of Sleeping & Waking

3. A biological clock that is set to run on a time cycle of 24–25 hours is called a (a)_____. In animals (and probably humans) the biological clock for the sleep-wake cycle is located in a part of the hypothalamus called the (b)_____.

4. If we travel across time zones and our circadian rhythm gets out of phase with the local clock time, we experience difficulty in going to sleep and getting up at normal times, a condition known as (a)_____. Researchers have been able to reset circadian rhythms in workers by exposing them to bright light during certain times; this is called (b)_____ therapy.

5. In the center of the animal and human brain is the pineal gland, a small group of cells that secrete the hormone _____. This hormone has a major role in regulating the sleep-wake cycle in animals; its role in humans is less clear.

C. World of Sleep

6. Researchers study sleep and wakefulness by recording the activity of brain cells and muscles. Electrical brain activity is recorded in tracings called an (a)_____. The height of a wave is called its (b)_____, and the number of wave cycles that occur in one second is called the (c)_____.

7. If you are awake and alert, your brain waves have a very high frequency and low amplitude and are called (a)_____ waves. If you close your eyes and become relaxed and drowsy, your brain waves remain low in amplitude but decrease slightly in frequency; these are called (b)_____ waves.

8. Researchers divide sleep into five stages. Stage 1, the transition from wakefulness to sleep, is marked by (a)_____ waves and a feeling of gradually losing responsiveness to the outside world. Stage 2 represents the first real phase of sleep and is marked by high-frequency bursts of brain activity called (b)_____. In stage 3 and especially stage 4, there are high-amplitude, low-frequency brain waves called (c)_____. Stage 4 may be considered the deepest stage of sleep, since it is the most difficult from which to wake someone. Together, stages 1, 2, 3, and 4 are referred to as (d)_____ sleep, which makes up about 80% of sleep time.

9. About every 30–90 minutes throughout sleep, you leave stage 4 (delta sleep) and progress backward to stage 2. From stage 2, you enter a new stage of sleep marked by high-frequency, low-amplitude brain waves that look identical to (a)_____ waves. This stage is called (b)_____ sleep because your eyes move rapidly back and forth underneath closed eyelids. During this stage, you are asleep and lose muscle tension in the neck and limbs. However, your brain waves are like those when you are awake and alert, and there is increased arousal of many physiological responses. When awakened from this stage, people usually (80–100% of the time) report that they have been (c)_____.

D. Research Focus: Circadian Preference

10. People who prefer to get up earlier, go to bed earlier, and engage in morning activities and whose body temperature rises more quickly in the morning and peaks earlier at night are called (a)_____. People who prefer to get up later, go to bed later, and engage in afternoon-evening activities and whose body temperature rises more slowly in the morning and peaks later at night are called (b)_____.

E. Questions about Sleep

11. Going to sleep is regulated by the following factors. An area in the hypothalamus that is the master sleep switch is called the (a)_____. An area in the hypothalamus that regulates circadian rhythms is called the (b)_____. A brain area that contributes to our staying awake by sending neural signals that alert and arouse the forebrain is called the (c)_____. Several different sleep chemicals and (d)_____, some of which are made in the pons, regulate going into and out of the stages of sleep. In addition, we go to sleep several hours after a fall in body (e)_____ and get up when it starts to rise.

REM

Non-REM

Awake

12. From infancy through old age, there is a gradual reduction in total (a)_____ time, from about 17 to 6.5 hours, and a reduction in the percentage of (b)_____ sleep, from about 50% to 20%.

13. The theory that says we sleep because we use up vital factors during the day that must be replaced at night is called the (a)_____ theory. The theory that says we sleep to conserve energy and avoid potential harm and injury from nocturnal predators is called the (b)_____ theory.

14. When we are sleep deprived, the next day we have difficulty performing tasks that require (a)_____. Sleep deprivation also affects the body, as measured by a decrease in killer cells, which are important in the functioning of our (b)_____ system, which fights off infections and toxic agents.

F. Cultural Diversity: Incidence of SAD

15. The occurrence of a pattern of depressive symptoms that generally begin in the fall and winter and disappear in the spring is called (a)_____. Although the incidence of this disorder is lower in Florida and higher in the northeastern United States, it is not higher in Iceland, which is much farther north than New Hampshire. One reason Icelanders report a lower incidence of SAD is because of their (b)_____ values.

Iceland

G. World of Dreams

16. According to Freud's theory, we have a "censor" that protects us from (a)_____. This involves transforming threatening, unconscious desires into harmless symbols. According to Hobson's revised theory, called the (b)_____, the sleeping brain produces hallucinations, delusions, high emotions, and bizarre thoughts that we call dreams. During REM sleep, some parts of the brain are turned on, (c)_____, and some are turned off, (d)_____. According to many therapists and sleep-dream researchers, such as Cartwright, dreams are (e)_____ of waking thoughts and concerns, especially emotional ones, and provide clues to a person's problems. According to the Inuit culture, dreams are a way to enter the (f)_____ world.

H. Application: Sleep Problems & Treatments

17. A common sleep problem that includes difficulty in going to sleep or remaining asleep throughout the night is called (a)_____. A nondrug treatment is to use a proven (b)_____ method. Drug treatment for insomnia usually involves prescribing (c)_____. Insomnia caused when the sleeper stops breathing and wakes up is called (d)_____.

18. If children wake up screaming and in a great fright, they have experienced (a)_____ but will remember nothing the next morning. When adults experience emotionally charged, frightening images during their dreams, they are having (b)_____. If a person walks or carries out other behaviors during sleep, it is called (c)_____, which may be caused by increased stress. A relatively rare condition that involves irresistible attacks of sleepiness, brief periods of REM, and often loss of muscle control is called (d)_____.

Answers: *1. (a) consciousness, (b) controlled processes, (c) automatic processes; 2. (a) daydreaming, (b) altered states, (c) unconscious, (d) unconsciousness, (e) implicit or nondeclarative memory; 3. (a) circadian rhythm, (b) suprachiasmatic nucleus; 4. (a) jet lag, (b) light; 5. melatonin; 6. (a) electroencephalogram, or EEG, (b) amplitude, (c) frequency; 7. (a) beta, (b) alpha; 8. (a) theta, (b) sleep spindles, (c) delta waves, (d) non-REM; 9. (a) beta, (b) REM, (c) dreaming; 10. (a) morning people, (b) evening people; 11. (a) ventrolateral preoptic nucleus, (b) suprachiasmatic nucleus, (c) reticular formation, (d) neurotransmitters, (e) temperature; 12. (a) sleep, (b) REM; 13. (a) repair, (b) adaptive; 14. (a) concentration, (b) immune; 15. (a) SAD, or seasonal affective disorder, (b) cultural; 16. (a) threatening desires/wishes, (b) activation-synthesis theory, (c) limbic system and visual cortex, (d) prefrontal cortex, (e) extensions, (f) spiritual; 17. (a) insomnia, (b) cognitive-behavioral, (c) benzodiazepines or nonbenzodiazepines, (d) sleep apnea; 18. (a) night terrors, (b) nightmares, (c) sleepwalking, (d) narcolepsy*

Critical Thinking

How Good Is a Sleep-Deprived Doctor?

It may come as a surprise to learn that some of the worst work conditions occur in some of the major hospitals in the United States. For example, interns and residents, who are doctors in training, often work 36-hour shifts and 100-hour weeks. As a result, doctors in training may spend practically all of their waking hours in the hospital, with little time to be concerned about their own physical and mental health.

The primary reason that doctors in training are usually required to work long hours is that teaching hospitals keep costs down by relying on young doctors to provide low-cost labor. But for the first time, doctors in training are allowed to join a labor union called the Committee of Interns and Residents, which aims to reduce the excessive required work hours for doctors in training.

A 32-year-old Stanford University doctor remembers her years in training at a major teaching hospital: "I was chronically fatigued, so tired I felt as if I was operating in a daze sometimes. You go into medicine for idealistic reasons, but by the end of a grueling internship, you see each patient you admit to the hospital as a barrier to getting sleep" (Pear, p. 2D).

William Dement, a well-known sleep researcher, strongly believes that "sleep deprivation contributes to medical errors" and that "with more hours of sleep, doctors make fewer errors" (Pear, p. 2D). In fact, recent research found that longer shifts resulted in interns making 36% more medical errors.

One interesting study used a simulator to test the driving abilities of residents both after working intensely for a month and when they were relatively rested but had 3–4 alcoholic drinks. In each circumstance, residents had trouble driving at a constant speed and they went off the road at least once. Fatigued residents and people who are intoxicated show comparable impairments in attention, judgment, and reaction time.

In 2002, the American Medical Association endorsed an 80-hour work week with no more than 24 hours at a time. Still, after their long shifts, many interns and residents continue to do paperwork, study, or attend class before going home. These long training hours not only may compromise the physical and mental health of trainees, but also places their safety at risk. For instance, compared to interns who work 12 or fewer hours, interns working at least 24 hours were found to be twice as likely to have a car accident on the way home.

There are controls on how many hours pilots can fly and truck drivers can drive, so why aren't there stricter limits on hours that doctors in training can work? (Adapted from Abelson, 2002; Arnedt et al., 2005; Associated Press, 2004; S. L. Cohen, 2000; Fackelmann, 2005; Gupta, 2002; Pear, 2000)

Questions

1. Why do you think the medical establishment opposed the formation of a labor union for doctors in training?

2. How does sleep deprivation affect the body and the brain?

3. Despite Dement's observations and research, why don't teaching hospitals put a stop to overworking doctors in training?

4. Why do most work and traffic accidents occur early in the morning?

5. Why are there controls on pilots and truck drivers but not on doctors in training?

1. Because medical treatment and costs keep rising, training hospitals try to hold costs down by giving doctors in training long, hard hours, a potentially dangerous work practice that is permitted in no other workplace where people's lives are at stake.

2. Researchers report that sleep deprivation has little effect on heart rate or blood pressure but decreases the immune system's ability to fight off infections. However, researchers found that sleep deprivation does interfere with concentration and performing cognitive tasks, such as would be required when doctors prescribe or perform medical treatment for patients.

3. Although Dement concluded that sleep deprivation contributes to medical errors, many teaching hospitals continue to overwork doctors in training primarily for economic reasons—to have a source of low-cost labor and help keep costs down.

4. Most highway and work accidents occur in the early morning because that is when our genetically set circadian rhythms say that our bodies should be asleep. For this reason, it's difficult to stay awake and alert in the early morning hours.

5. Teaching hospitals are able to maintain working conditions that would be considered unsafe in most other professions partly because it is a very big business with considerable political clout.

Links to Learning

Learning Activities

- ***POWERSTUDY FOR INTRODUCTION TO PSYCHOLOGY 4.0***

by Tom Doyle and Rod Plotnik

  SuperModule: Check out "Sleep & Dreams" on **PowerStudy.** It includes complete paragraph-by-paragraph explanations of all content using fully-narrated animations and graphics. An onscreen toolbar allows immediate access to text, text outline, and module glossary with notetaking and printing capabilities. This module also includes:
  - Video—Imbedded videos and animations walk you through the exciting world of sleep and dreams.
  - A test of your knowledge using an interactive version of the Summary Test on pages 164 and 165. Also access related quizzing—true/false, multiple choice, and matching.
  - An interactive version of the Critical Thinking exercise "How Good Is a Sleep-Deprived Doctor?" on page 166.
  - Key terms, a chapter outline including chapter abstract, and a special extended list of hotlinked websites that correlate to this module.

- *CengageNOW*
  academic.cengage.com/login
  Need help studying? This site is your one-stop study shop.
  Take a Pre-Test and CengageNOW will generate a Personalized Study Plan based on your test results. The Study Plan will identify the topics you need to review and direct you to online resources to help you master those topics. You can then take a Post-Test to determine the concepts you have mastered and what you still need to work on.

- ***INTRODUCTION TO PSYCHOLOGY BOOK COMPANION WEBSITE***

  academic.cengage.com/psychology/plotnik
  Visit your book companion website where you will find more resources to help you study. At this site, you will find Learning Objectives, Internet Exercises, quizzing, flash cards, and a pronunciation glossary.

- ***STUDY GUIDE and WEBTUTOR***
  Check the corresponding module in your Study Guide for effective student tips and help learning the material presented. Also go to **academic.cengage.com/webtutor** for an interactive version of the Study Guide features.

Study Questions

*A. **Continuum of Consciousness**—How many different states of consciousness have you been in today? (**Suggested answer page 622**)

B. **Rhythms of Sleeping & Waking**—If an ad promised a device to cure jet lag, what would the device do?

C. **World of Sleep**—How would we know whether astronauts in space were awake, asleep, or dreaming?

*D. **Research Focus: Circadian Preference**—What kind of problems might arise if a morning person married an evening person? (**Suggested answer page 623**)

E. **Questions about Sleep**—If researchers discovered the perfect sleeping pill, how might it work?

*F. **Cultural Diversity: Incidence of SAD**—What cultural values might New Hampshire residents have that contribute to their incidence of SAD? (**Suggested answer page 623**)

G. **World of Dreams**—Which of the four theories most closely matches your personal beliefs about what dreams mean?

H. **Application: Sleep Problems & Treatments**—If you worked in a clinic that treated sleep problems, what kinds of symptoms would your patients have?

*These questions are answered in Appendix B.

MODULE 8
Hypnosis & Drugs

 PowerStudy 4.0™ Complete Module

Introduction

Hypnosis

Why do people do stupid things?

Consider the experience of one of us (R.P.) some years ago. One night a friend and I were sitting in the front row of one of the longest-running nightclub acts in San Diego. We were going to watch a psychologist-turned-performer who entertained locals and tourists by hypnotizing volunteers from the audience and asking them to perform funny, strange, and somewhat embarrassing acts on a stage. Before the hypnotist appeared, my friend Paul repeated for the tenth time that nothing would get him up on that stage.

Finally the lights dimmed, and the hypnotist appeared. He was a very good performer and soon had the audience laughing at his jokes and believing that he was a wonderful, trustworthy human being.

"Now we come to the interesting part," the hypnotist said in a low, soothing voice. "Just sit back and relax and, if you wish, follow my suggestions." The hypnotist slowly repeated a list of suggestions: "You cannot bend your right arm . . . you cannot close your eyes . . . your left arm will become rigid and slowly rise above your head." As I looked around the dimly lit room, a number of rigid left arms were slowly rising. To my surprise, one of those arms was Paul's. (I could not or would not raise my arm, for fear that some of my students were in the audience and would never let me forget whatever foolish behavior I might have performed.)

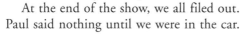

After being hypnotized, shy Paul imitated Elvis.

At the end of the show, we all filed out. Paul said nothing until we were in the car. Then he turned and asked, "Why did you let me get on stage and be hypnotized? You better not tell anyone."

I smiled and replied, "You were terrific. That was the best imitation of Elvis Presley ever done by a reluctant friend." Then I added, "I might have been tempted to try Mick Jagger."

Although I have changed Paul's name and minor details to protect his pride and reputation, his story is essentially true and illustrates some of the strange behaviors that occur under hypnosis.

For over 200 years, psychologists have puzzled over what hypnosis really is. Some believe hypnosis is a special state during which individuals experience hallucinations (seeing an imaginary fly), carry out suggestions (swatting an imaginary fly), or report decreased pain after receiving a painful stimulus (M. R. Nash, 2001). Recently, researchers have questioned whether hypnosis is a special state, since they found that nonhypnotized individuals responded to imaginative suggestions (see an imaginary fly) just as if they were hypnotized (Kirsch & Braffman, 2001). We'll discuss the debate over what hypnosis really is.

Local newspapers often carry ads claiming that hypnosis can help you stop smoking, lose weight, get rid of phobias, induce immediate relaxation, reduce pain, or increase motivation to tackle difficult projects. We'll discuss whether these claims for hypnosis are true as well as current medical uses of hypnosis.

Drugs

What was the first bicycle trip?

Although only some psychologists believe that hypnosis may change a person's state of consciousness, most agree that there are a number of drugs, legal and illegal, that can alter consciousness. One example of how a drug greatly altered consciousness happened quite by chance and began with a bike ride.

On April 19, 1943, Albert Hofmann left his laboratory, got on his bike, and began pedaling his regular route home. As Albert pedaled, the world around him began to change into threatening, wavering forms that appeared distorted, as if he was looking into a curved mirror.

Once he reached home and entered his house, the familiar objects and pieces of furniture assumed grotesque and threatening forms that were in continual motion. After a while, the threatening forms disappeared, and he began to enjoy an incredible display of visual sensations and illusions. Albert saw fantastic images that opened and closed in circles and spirals that seemed to explode into colored fountains. Even stranger, sounds such as the passing of a car or opening of a door were transformed into visual images with changing forms and colors (adapted from Hofmann, 1983).

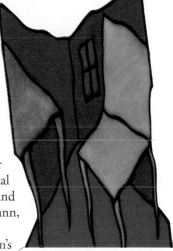

Albert Hofmann tried out his newly discovered drug (LSD) and watched his furniture change into strange shapes.

The cause of Albert Hofmann's startling visual experiences was a drug that Hofmann had previously discovered in his laboratory and had taken before his bike ride. The drug was LSD (d-lysergic acid diethylamide) and is now well known to cause strange and bizarre visual experiences, called hallucinations. Because Hofmann had not known about LSD's great potency (compared to other drugs, a very small dose of LSD has a very large effect), he had actually taken a dose that was four times the usual amount. We will discuss LSD as well as other illegal and legal drugs that can alter consciousness.

What's Coming

We'll discuss what hypnosis is, how a person is hypnotized, what a person does and does not do under hypnosis, and the uses of hypnosis. We'll examine the use and abuse of both legal and illegal drugs, such as stimulants, hallucinogens, opiates, marijuana, and alcohol. We'll discuss how drugs affect the nervous system, their dangers, and the treatments for drug abuse.

Let's begin with an interesting and supposedly mind-altering force called animal magnetism.

A. Hypnosis

What is hypnosis?

In the late 1700s, Anton Mesmer was the hit of Paris, France, as he claimed to cure a variety of symptoms by passing a force into a patient's body; he called this force animal magnetism. So many patients testified to the success of animal magnetism as a treatment that a committee of the French Academy of Science was appointed to investigate. The committee concluded that many of Mesmer's patients were indeed cured of various psychosomatic problems. However, the committee thought it safer to ban the future use of animal magnetism because they could neither identify what it was nor verify Mesmer's claims that such a force existed (Shermer, 2002). Mesmer's name lives on in our vocabulary: We use the term *mesmerized* to describe someone who is acting strangely because he or she has been spellbound or hypnotized.

Today we know that Mesmer was not creating animal magnetism but rather was inducing hypnosis. Here's the definition agreed to by the American Psychological Association's Division of Psychological Hypnosis (1993):

Hypnosis **is a procedure in which a researcher, clinician, or hypnotist suggests that a person will experience changes in sensations, perceptions, thoughts, feelings, or behaviors.**

We'll begin by answering three questions that are often asked about hypnosis.

Who Can Be Hypnotized?

Despite what you may have seen on television or at a stage show, not everyone can be easily hypnotized.

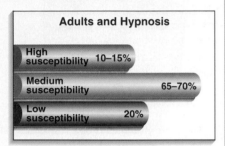

Adults and Hypnosis

High susceptibility 10–15%
Medium susceptibility 65–70%
Low susceptibility 20%

As shown in the graph above, there is considerable variation in susceptibility to being hypnotized: About 20% of adults have low susceptibility to hypnosis, which means that they cannot be easily hypnotized. About 65–70% of adults have medium susceptibility, and the remaining 10–15% have high susceptibility to being hypnotized (Spiegal, 2005).

Hypnotic susceptibility is not correlated with introversion, extraversion, social position, intelligence, willpower, sex, compliance, gullibility, being highly motivated, or being a placebo responder (Kirsch & Lynn, 1995; M. R. Nash, 2001).

The one trait that was highly correlated with susceptibility to hypnosis was a truly remarkable ability to respond to imaginative suggestions. Individuals who had this trait were highly susceptible to being hypnotized (Kirsch & Braffman, 2001).

Who Is Susceptible?

The standard test for susceptibility is to hypnotize a person and then give a fixed set of suggestions (Weitzenhoffer, 2002). The best-known test is the Stanford Hypnotic Susceptibility Scale, which asks the individual to carry out a series of both simple suggestions—for example, "Your arm is moving up"—and complex suggestions—for example, "Your body is heavy and you cannot stand up."

For instance, the person in the photo below is carrying out the hypnotic suggestion, "Your right arm is weightless and moving up." One such scale has a series of 12 activities.

This man is being tested for susceptibility to being hypnotized.

Individuals who score high on the Stanford scale are usually easily hypnotized and tend to remain so across their lifetimes (M. R. Nash, 2001).

The process used to hypnotize a person is called hypnotic induction.

How Is Someone Hypnotized?

Although different procedures are used, most use some of the following suggestions for hypnotic induction.

Hypnotic induction **refers to inducing hypnosis by first asking a person to either stare at an object or close his or her eyes and then suggesting that the person is becoming very relaxed.**

For example, here is a commonly used method for hypnotic induction:

1. The hypnotist creates a sense of trust, so that the individual feels comfortable.
2. The hypnotist suggests that the subject concentrate on something, such as the sound of the hypnotist's voice, an object, or an image.
3. The hypnotist suggests what the subject will experience during hypnosis—for example, becoming relaxed, feeling sleepy, or having a floating feeling. The hypnotist may say, "I am going to count from one to ten, and with each count you will drift more and more deeply into hypnosis" (B. L. Bates, 1994).

Inducing hypnosis may involve 3 steps.

This procedure works on both individuals and groups, provided the individuals are all susceptible to hypnosis.

During hypnosis, subjects are not asleep, keep their ability to control their behaviors, are aware of their surroundings, adhere to their usual moral standards, and are capable of saying no or of stopping hypnosis. For these reasons, hypnosis is not a dangerous procedure when used by an experienced researcher or clinician, and hypnosis has useful medical and therapeutic benefits (M. R. Nash, 2001).

Perhaps the biggest debates surrounding hypnosis are what actually happens when a person is hypnotized and whether hypnotic induction is even needed. These are our next questions.

What happens during hypnosis? The explanation of why Paul got on the stage and imitated Elvis has changed significantly over the past 40 years. Early on, being hypnotized was believed to put a person into a trancelike state. In the late 1990s, the trancelike state was dropped for lack of evidence and some believed that being hypnotized put individuals into an altered state of consciousness. More recently, researchers believe that some individuals, hypnotized or not, have the amazing personal ability to respond to imaginative suggestions (Kirsch & Braffman, 2001). We'll discuss these two different views of hypnosis.

Altered State Theory of Hypnosis

Perhaps Paul got on stage and imitated Elvis because hypnosis put him into an altered or disconnected state.

The *altered state theory of hypnosis* holds that hypnosis puts a person into an altered state of consciousness, during which the person is disconnected from reality, and so is able to experience and respond to various suggestions (M. R. Nash, 2001).

For example, individuals were hypnotized and given suggestions that their raised hands were getting heavy or that they would feel no pain. When no longer hypnotized, these individuals said, "My hand became heavy and moved down by itself" or "Suddenly I found myself feeling no pain" (M. R. Nash, 2001, p. 49). Researcher Michael Nash (2001), editor-in-chief of *The International Journal of Clinical and Experimental Hypnosis,* believes hypnosis disconnects an individual from reality so that the individual does things without conscious intent. Nash explains that with hypnosis, scientists can temporarily create hallucinations, compulsions, certain types of memory loss, false memories, and delusions (bee buzzing around your head).

Explanation: Altered or disconnected state. Here's how the altered or disconnected state theory of hypnosis explains why shy Paul got on stage and imitated Elvis Presley.

> **1. Hypnotic induction.** The hypnotist uses hypnotic induction: "Just sit back, relax, and follow my suggestions." The hypnotist slowly repeats a list of suggestions: "You cannot bend your right arm . . . you cannot close your eyes . . . your left arm will become rigid and slowly rise above your head . . . ," etc.

> **2. Susceptibility.** Paul easily responds to the hypnotist's suggestion and, without conscious intent, raises his left arm. This means that he is one of the 10–15% or more who is easily hypnotized and would score high on a hypnotic susceptibility scale.

> **3. Hypnosis.** According to the altered state theory, hypnosis disconnects Paul from reality. In this state, he may automatically and without conscious intent follow a wide range of suggestions, such as getting up on stage and imitating Elvis.

Conclusion. Hypnosis is one method of inducing an individual to follow, without conscious intent, certain suggestions that range from having hallucinations to reducing pain.

Sociocognitive Theory of Hypnosis

Perhaps Paul got up on stage and imitated Elvis because of personal abilities and social pressures—the sociocognitive theory.

The *sociocognitive theory of hypnosis* says that behaviors observed during hypnosis result not from being hypnotized, but rather from having the special ability of responding to imaginative suggestions and social pressures (Kirsch & Braffman, 2001).

Psychologist Irving Kirsch, who has published more than 85 articles on hypnosis, found that all the phenomena produced during hypnosis have also occurred in subjects who were not hypnotized.

Explanation: Special abilities and social pressures. Here's how the sociocognitive theory of hypnosis explains why shy Paul got on stage and imitated Elvis Presley.

> **NO hypnotic induction.** According to the sociocognitive theory of hypnosis, individuals do not have to be hypnotized because about 30% or more already have a special and amazing ability called imaginative suggestibility (Kirsch & Braffman, 2001).

> **1. Imaginative suggestibility.** The reason Paul does NOT need to be hypnotized is that he is one of those 30% or more who have imaginative suggestibility. This a special ability to alter one's experiences and produce hallucinations, experience partial paralysis, have selective amnesia, and reduce pain. Individuals who have imaginative suggestibility can perform these unusual behaviors from suggestion alone, without having to go through formal hypnotic induction (being hypnotized) (Kirsch & Braffman, 2001).

> **2. Imaginative suggestions without hypnosis.** According to the sociocognitive theory, Paul is one of those individuals who has the special ability to respond in a totally focused way to imaginative suggestions, such as getting up on stage and imitating Elvis.

Conclusion. Some people have a trait called imaginative suggestibility, which is the amazing ability to experience and perform a wide variety of unusual behaviors when given the suggestion, with or without being hypnotized (Kirsch & Braffman, 2001).

Next, we'll discuss some of the unusual behaviors that can be experienced and performed by individuals who, according to one theory, have been hypnotized or, according to another theory, have the trait of imaginative suggestibility.

A. Hypnosis

What are some of the unusual behaviors?

Stage hypnotists can get volunteers to perform a variety of unusual behaviors, such as pretending they are chickens, falling asleep after counting to 5, or singing like Elvis. However, keep in mind that individuals responsive to hypnosis most likely have the trait of imaginative suggestibility, which means that they can perform these behaviors with or without being hypnotized (Kirsch & Braffman, 2001).

Hypnotic Analgesia

Hypnosis has long been known to reduce pain; this is called hypnotic analgesia.

Hypnotic analgesia (an-nall-GEEZ-ee-ah) **refers to a reduction in pain reported by clients after they had undergone hypnosis and received suggestions that reduced their anxiety and promoted relaxation.**

Researchers used PET scans to show that hypnosis reduced the subjects' unpleasant feelings of pain though not the sensations of pain (Rainville et al., 1997). This means that when subjects put their hands into hot water they felt pain as usual but, depending on the hypnotic suggestions, reported it as either more or less unpleasant. Hypnotic analgesia proved useful in helping patients cope with painful medical or dental treatments (Montgomery et al., 2000).

Posthypnotic Suggestion

If subjects perform some behavior on cue after hypnosis, it's called a posthypnotic suggestion.

A *posthypnotic suggestion* **is given to the subject during hypnosis about performing a particular behavior to a specific cue when the subject comes out of hypnosis.**

Some believe that subjects who follow posthypnotic suggestions are acting automatically in response to a predetermined cue, such as smiling when they hear the word *student*. However, researchers have shown that subjects perform posthypnotic suggestions if they believe it is expected of them but stop performing if they believe the experiment is over or they are no longer being observed (Spanos, 1996).

Posthypnotic Amnesia

"When you wake up, you will not remember what happened." This suggestion is used to produce posthypnotic amnesia.

Posthypnotic amnesia **is not remembering what happened during hypnosis if the hypnotist suggested that, upon awakening, the person would forget what took place during hypnosis.**

One explanation is that the person forgets because the experiences have been repressed and made unavailable to normal consciousness. However, there is good evidence that, after they come out of hypnosis, what people remember or forget depends on what they think or believe the hypnotist wants them to remember or forget (Spanos, 1996). For instance, people who are instructed to not remember anything usually report not remembering, but when pressed, many of these same people admit they do in fact remember the information (Kirsch & Lynn, 1998).

Age Regression

Could the 31-year-old woman shown at the left be hypnotized and sent back to being the 3-year-old child shown below? This phenomenon is called age regression.

Age regression **refers to subjects under hypnosis being asked to regress, or return in time, to an earlier age, such as early childhood.**

Researchers have found that during age regression, hypnotized subjects do not relive their earlier experiences as some believe but rather play the role of being a child. After an exhaustive review of more than 100 years of hypnosis research on age regression, one researcher concluded that there was no evidence that adults actually went back or regressed in time (Kirsch et al., 1993). Thus, researchers believe that, during age regression, hypnotized adults are not reliving childhood experiences but merely acting as they expect children to behave (M. R. Nash, 2001).

Imagined Perception

When a hypnotized subject responds to a suggestion such as "Try to swat that fly," it is called an imagined perception.

An *imagined perception* **refers to experiencing sensations, perceiving stimuli, or performing behaviors that come from one's imagination.**

Hypnotherapists use many forms of imagined perceptions in treating clients' problems. For example, one client imagined he was an armored knight on a great horse. After several therapy sessions, the therapist asked the client to remove the armor and discover his true self, which turned out to be a person afraid of his flaws (Eisen, 1994).

Conclusions

Researchers agree that hypnotized subjects are not faking or acting out their responses but seem to be actually experiencing such behaviors as hypnotic analgesia, imagined perception, age regression, and posthypnotic suggestion and amnesia. What researchers disagree about is why these behaviors occur. Some researchers believe that these behaviors occur because hypnosis puts individuals into an altered or disconnected state (M. R. Nash, 2001). Other researchers believe that individuals who are highly susceptible to hypnosis have a trait called imaginative suggestibility, which allows these individuals to totally focus and carry out suggestions, whether or not they are hypnotized (Kirsch & Braffman, 2001).

Next, we'll examine some of the uses of hypnosis.

How is hypnosis used?

You have probably seen hypnosis used in entertainment, such as when people in the audience volunteer to come up on stage and be hypnotized and then perform unusual and often funny behaviors, such as Paul's wild imitation of Elvis. However, there are also serious and legitimate uses of hypnosis in medical, dental, therapeutic, and behavioral settings.

Medical and Dental Uses

In both medical and dental settings, hypnosis can be used to reduce pain through hypnotic analgesia, to reduce fear and anxiety by helping individuals relax, or to help patients deal with health problems by motivating them to make the best of a difficult situation (Patterson & Jensen, 2003). However, clients who are highly susceptible to hypnosis are better able to respond to suggestions for pain reduction and body relaxation than are low-susceptibility clients (B. L. Bates, 1994). As the graph below shows, highly susceptible people reported feeling the lowest level of pain during a procedure in which pain was produced by binding their arm, which cuts off the blood supply and results in considerable pain (H. J. Crawford et al., 1993).

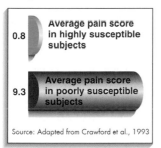

0.8	Average pain score in highly susceptible subjects
9.3	Average pain score in poorly susceptible subjects

Source: Adapted from Crawford et al., 1993

Hypnosis can be helpful in preparing people for anxiety-provoking procedures. For instance, the woman above seeks hypnosis to help cope with her fear about having painful dental work performed. As part of her hypnosis, she hears, "Your jaw, mouth, gums, and throat become so relaxed that the muscles get soft ... and as your jaw is opened gently and your gums are examined, your entire body will feel more and more relaxed."

Next, we'll look at what happens in the brain during hypnotic analgesia.

Brain scans. Researchers used PET scans (p. 71) to measure activity in different parts of the brain after subjects were hypnotized and told to place their hands in lukewarm (95°F) or "painfully hot" (115°F) water. Hypnotic suggestions to think of pain as *more unpleasant* (more painful) resulted in *decreased* brain activity in the frontal lobe (anterior cingulate cortex), while hypnotic suggestions to think of pain as *less unpleasant* (less painful) resulted in *increased* brain activity in the same area. In comparison, hypnotic instructions that pain was more or less unpleasant did not increase or decrease brain activity in the parietal lobe (somatosensory cortex), which indicates the reception of pain sensations (Rainville et al., 1997). Researchers concluded that hypnotic suggestions can change a person's *perception* of pain as more or less unpleasant, but hypnotic suggestions do not affect *receiving* pain sensations. This means that during hypnotic analgesia, subjects feel pain, but how much it bothers them depends on whether hypnotic suggestions are to think of pain as being more or less unpleasant. That is, the hypnotized subjects' thoughts or expectations actually change their perceptions of pain (Ploghaus et al., 2003).

Therapeutic and Behavioral Uses

Hypnosis has been used in therapy for the past 100 years. In the early 1900s, Sigmund Freud (1905) used hypnosis with his patients. More recently, Milton Erickson (1980/1941), who is generally acknowledged to be the world's leading practitioner of therapeutic hypnosis, said that hypnosis made clients more open and receptive to alternative ways of problem solving. However, hypnosis is not for all clients; some people find hypnosis frightening because they fear losing control or because they believe it indicates a lack of willpower (Kirsch, 1994).

Therapists who often use hypnosis along with other techniques generally report that it is very useful in helping clients reveal their personalities, gain insights into their lives, and arrive at solutions to their problems. Research on hypnotherapy indicates that hypnosis can be a powerful tool that leads to successful outcomes when used in therapeutic settings (M. B. Nash, 2001).

Clients who are highly susceptible to hypnosis generally respond better to suggestions aimed at treating a wide range of psychosomatic problems, which involve mind-body interactions. For example, hypnosis has been successfully used to reduce pain, decrease asthma attacks, remove warts, and relieve tension. But hypnosis is not as successful with problems of self-control, such as helping clients quit smoking, stop overeating, stop excessive drinking, or overcome other habits that interfere with optimal functioning (B. L. Bates, 1994; J. P. Green & Lynn, 2000).

The graph below shows the percentage of subjects who continued to smoke after receiving three different treatment programs. Notice that after three weeks of treatment, hypnosis was not statistically more suc-

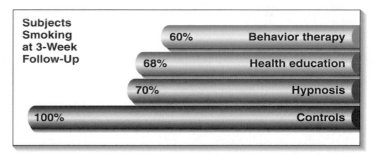

Subjects Smoking at 3-Week Follow-Up		
60%	Behavior therapy
68%	Health education
70%	Hypnosis
100%	Controls

cessful in motivating people to stop smoking than was health education or behavior modification. From these results, we can conclude that all three programs were about equally effective and significantly better than controls (no treatment program) (J. P. Green & Lynn, 2000; Rabkin et al., 1984). Clinicians generally conclude that hypnosis by itself is not a miracle treatment but can be a useful technique when combined with other procedures (Lynn et al., 2000).

Although helpful in a therapeutic setting, evidence obtained under hypnosis is not allowed in most U.S. courts. That's because an examiner's questions or suggestions may bias or mislead a hypnotized witness into agreeing to something that was suggested but did not happen. Generally, hypnotized witnesses give unreliable testimony (Perry, 1997).

Next, we'll discuss the use, abuse, and effects of drugs.

B. Drugs: Overview

Why do people use drugs?

For the past 6,000 years, humans have used legal and illegal drugs, and current usage continues to increase as do drug-related problems (Glantz & Hartel, 1999). For example, Americans spend over $150 billion a year on legal and illegal drugs, and the resulting problems—personal, medical, legal, and job related—cost society a whopping $484 billion a year (Volkow, 2004).

The reasons people use drugs include obtaining pleasure, joy, and euphoria; meeting social expectations; giving in to peer pressure; dealing with or escaping stress, anxiety, and tension; avoiding pain; and achieving altered states of consciousness (R. Goldberg, 2006).

One researcher, reviewing 200 years of drug use in the United States, concluded that we have gone through regular cycles of tolerant and intolerant attitudes toward drug usage. Because history

Americans spend $150 billion annually on drugs.

tends to repeat itself, the researcher warns that our society will continue to face various physical and psychological problems related to drugs (Musto, 1999).

In the sections that follow, we'll discuss stimulants, opiates, hallucinogens, alcohol, marijuana, and other commonly used psychoactive drugs.

Psychoactive drugs **are chemicals that affect our nervous systems and, as a result, may alter consciousness and awareness, influence how we sense and perceive things, and modify our moods, feelings, emotions, and thoughts. Psychoactive drugs are both licit (legal)—coffee, alcohol, and tobacco—and illicit (illegal)—marijuana, heroin, cocaine, and LSD.**

Although all psychoactive drugs affect our nervous systems, how they affect our behaviors depends on our psychological state and other social factors, such as peer pressure and society's values. To illustrate how drug usage involves both pharmacological and psychological factors, we describe a famous person who had a serious drug problem.

What famous therapist had a drug problem?

When this famous person was 38, his doctor told him to stop smoking because it was causing irregular heart beats. Although he tried to cut down, he was soon back to smoking his usual 20 cigars a day. When his heart problems grew worse, he stopped again. However, he experienced such terrible depression and mood swings that he started smoking to escape the psychological torture. When he was 67, small sores were discovered in his mouth and diagnosed as cancer. During the next 16 years, he had 33 operations on his mouth and jaw for cancer but continued smoking. By age 79, most of his jaw had been removed and replaced by an

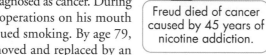

Freud died of cancer caused by 45 years of nicotine addiction.

artificial one. He was in continual pain and was barely able to swallow or talk. However, he continued to smoke an endless series of cigars. In 1939, at age 83, he died of cancer caused by 45 years of heavy smoking (Brecher, 1972; E. Jones, 1953).

Our famous person is none other than Sigmund Freud, the father of psychoanalysis. Freud had a serious drug problem most of his professional life—he was addicted to tobacco (nicotine). In spite of his great insights into the problems of others, he tried but could not treat his own drug addiction. Freud's struggle with smoking illustrates four important terms related to drug use and abuse—addicton, tolerance, dependency, and withdrawal symptoms (American Psychiatric Association, 2000).

Addiction

One reason Freud continued to smoke despite a heart condition was that he had an addiction.

Addiction **means a person has developed a behavioral pattern of drug abuse that is marked by an overwhelming and compulsive desire to obtain and use the drug; even after stopping, the person has a strong tendency to relapse and begin using the drug again.**

The reason Freud relapsed each time he tried to give up smoking was that he was addicted to nicotine.

Tolerance

One reason Freud smoked as many as 20 cigars daily was that he had developed a tolerance to nicotine.

Tolerance **means that after a person uses a drug repeatedly over a period of time, the original dose of the drug no longer produces the desired effect so that a person must take increasingly larger doses of the drug to achieve the same behavioral effect.**

Becoming tolerant was a sign that Freud had become dependent on nicotine.

Dependency

Another reason Freud found it difficult to quit smoking was that he had developed a dependency on nicotine.

Dependency **refers to a change in the nervous system so that a person now needs to take the drug to prevent the occurrence of painful withdrawal symptoms.**

Addiction and dependency combine to make stopping doubly difficult.

Withdrawal Symptoms

Being dependent on nicotine, Freud had withdrawal symptoms when he stopped smoking.

Withdrawal symptoms **are painful physical and psychological symptoms that occur after a drug-dependent person stops using the drug.**

Freud described his withdrawal symptoms as being depressed, having images of dying, and feeling so tortured that it was beyond his human power to bear (E. Jones, 1953).

Next, we'll examine a number of specific drugs that people use.

Which drugs do people use?

The graph on the right shows current users of legal and illegal drugs in the United States. (A current user is defined as someone who reported using a drug in the past month.)

The most recent national statistics show that almost 20 million Americans spend over $62 billion on illegal drugs each year (ONDCP, 2000; SAMHSA, 2006).

Because drug treatment programs are more cost-effective than imprisonment, many health professionals recommend reducing illegal drug use by spending more on drug education, counseling, and treatment (Egan, 1999; Vastag, 2003).

Because of the cost and relative ineffectiveness of the current "drug

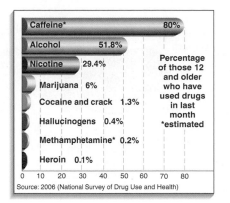

Caffeine*		80%
Alcohol	51.8%	
Nicotine	29.4%	
Marijuana	6%	
Cocaine and crack	1.3%	
Hallucinogens	0.4%	
Methamphetamine*	0.2%	
Heroin	0.1%	

Percentage of those 12 and older who have used drugs in last month *estimated

0 10 20 30 40 50 60 70 80

Source: 2006 (National Survey of Drug Use and Health)

war," doctors, federal judges, and political writers have proposed controlling illegal drugs either by legalization, which means illegal drugs can be used but with age restrictions, or by decriminalization, which means drugs remain illegal but criminal penalties are replaced with fines. No one knows the effect drug legalization or decriminalization might have on drug use or related personal and social problems in a country as large as the United States (Huggins, 2005).

Whether legal or illegal, psychoactive drugs alter one's consciousness, emotions, and thoughts by affecting the brain's communication network.

How do drugs work?

You may remember from Module 3 that the nervous system communicates by using chemical messengers called neurotransmitters. You can think of neurotransmitters as acting like chemical keys that open or close chemical locks on neighboring neurons (right figure). Many drugs act by opening or closing chemical locks, which in turn results in increased or decreased neural activity. However, how drugs affect each person's nervous system partly involves genetic factors. For example, researchers found that identical twins, who share 100% of their

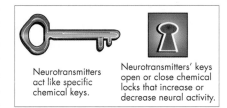

Neurotransmitters act like specific chemical keys.

Neurotransmitters' keys open or close chemical locks that increase or decrease neural activity.

genes, were much more similar in their use and abuse of drugs than fraternal twins, who share only 50% of their genes. These findings apply in countries where there are high rates of drug problems (United States) and in those with low rates (Norway) (Kendler et al., 2000a, 2006). This means that genetic factors influence the development and functioning of the nervous system, which in turn can increase or decrease the risk of a person using and abusing drugs. We'll discuss ways that drugs affect the nervous system and activate the brain's reward/pleasure center to cause addiction and dependency.

1 Drugs Affect Neurotransmitters

Your nervous system makes several dozen neurotransmitters as well as many other chemicals (neuromodulators) that act like chemical messengers. After neurons release neurotransmitters, they act like chemical keys that search for and then either open or close chemical locks to either excite or inhibit neighboring neurons, organs, or muscles. For example, morphine's chemical structure closely resembles that of the neurotransmitter endorphin (see p. 113). As a result of this similarity, morphine acts like, or mimics, endorphin by affecting the same chemical locks, which decreases pain. Thus, some drugs produce their effects by *mimicking* the way neurotransmitters work (Ropper & Brown, 2005).

After being excited, neurons secrete neurotransmitters, which move across a tiny space (synapse) and affect neighboring neurons' receptors (see p. 54). However, after a brief period, the neurotransmitters are reabsorbed back into the neuron. The action by which neurotransmitters are removed from the synapse through reabsorption is called *reuptake.* If reuptake did not occur, neurotransmitters would remain in the synapse, and neurons would be continuously stimulated. Thus, some drugs, such as cocaine, block reuptake, which leads to increased neural stimulation that causes increased physiological and psychological arousal (Mendelson et al., 2006).

Some drugs have a powerful affect on the brain's reward/pleasure center.

Morphine and heroin are similar to brain's neurotransmitters.

2 Drugs Affect Brain's Reward/Pleasure Center

Some drugs, especially cocaine and methamphetamine, activate the brain's *reward/pleasure center.* This center includes the nucleus accumbens and ventral tegmental area (right figure) and involves the neurotransmitter dopamine (S. L. Hauser & Beal, 2006). These drugs produce their effects by directly activating the brain's reward/pleasure center. The reward/pleasure center is also activated when one eats a favorite food, has sex, and does other pleasurable activities (Nestler & Malenka, 2004).

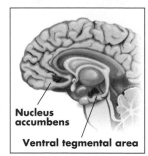

Nucleus accumbens

Ventral tegmental area

Addiction/dependency. Some drugs, such as cocaine and methamphetamine, activate the reward/pleasure center by increasing dopamine levels. However, repeated drug usage depletes dopamine levels, so the user must continue to use more drugs to activate the reward/pleasure center and avoid feeling depressed. When the reward/pleasure center becomes dependent on outside drugs, the user is addicted and dependent. Thus, drug addiction and dependency involve real changes in the brain's chemistry (Nestler & Malenka, 2004).

Next, we'll examine the more frequently used drugs.

C. Stimulants

Definition

What are stimulants?

"Two pills beat a month's vacation." This marketing slogan was used to sell amphetamines in Sweden in the 1940s. It resulted in epidemic usage that peaked in the mid-1960s.

In the 1940s, American doctors prescribed amphetamines as safe energizers, mood enhancers, and appetite suppressors. By the 1960s, billions of doses of amphetamines were being used in the United States and their usage had become a serious problem.

In the 1940s, Japanese workers used amphetamines to keep factory production high during World War II. After the war, many students, night workers, and people displaced by the war began to use "wake-amines." Amphetamine use spread until, in 1954, 2 million Japanese had become abusers and addicts (Brecher, 1972).

Amphetamine slogan in the 1940s: "Two pills beat a month's vacation."

By the early 1970s, most countries had brought amphetamine usage under control by regulating prescriptions, decreasing supply, and placing stiffer penalties. However, at present, amphetamine-like stimulants, such as methamphetamine (crystal) and cocaine, are widely available on the black market.

All *stimulants,* **including cocaine, amphetamines, caffeine, and nicotine, increase activity of the central nervous system and result in heightened alertness, arousal, euphoria, and decreased appetite. Dose for dose, cocaine and amphetamines are considered powerful stimulants because they produce a strong effect with a small dose; caffeine and nicotine are considered mild stimulants.**

We'll discuss the more widely used stimulants—amphetamines, cocaine, caffeine, and nicotine.

Amphetamines

Is it still a problem?

During the 1960s, amphetamine pills were heavily prescribed to treat a wide range of problems, including fatigue, depression, and being overweight. This was also the time that young adults, called "flower children," took large doses of amphetamines that resulted in their having true paranoid psychotic symptoms, which resulted in their being called "speed freaks." Amphetamine usage peaked in the mid-1960s, when over 31 million prescriptions were written for dieting and about 25 tons of legitimately manufactured amphetamines were diverted to illegal sales (Hanson & Venturelli, 1998). Finally, in 1971, the Food and Drug Administration (FDA) outlawed the prescription of amphetamines for everything except attention-deficit/hyperactivity disorder (ADHD) (p. 39) and narcolepsy (p. 163).

Following a "drug war" on cocaine in the late 1980s, there was a dramatic increase in using a form of amphetamine called methamphetamine, which is manufactured in illegal home laboratories. In many countries, the possession or use of methamphetamine is illegal and yet the use of methamphetamine is quickly spreading in the United States and worldwide. Karen Tandy, a U.S. drug enforcement official, commented on the nation's use of methamphetamine: "Meth has spread like wildfire across the Unites States. It has burned out communities, scorched childhoods, and charred once happy and productive lives beyond recognition" (Eggen, 2005). In Japan, methamphetamine has become the most popular illegal drug (Magnier, 2000).

Drug

In 2001, authorities raided about 8,000 illegal crystal methamphetamine laboratories in the United States. Methamphetamine labs are becoming increasingly common in the West, Southwest, and Midwest (Crea, 2003; Sanchez, 2001).

Methamphetamine **(D-methamphetamine) is close to amphetamine in both its chemical makeup and its physical and psychological effects. Unlike amphetamine, which is taken in pill form, methamphetamine (meth, speed, crank, crystal, ice) can be smoked or snorted and produces an almost instantaneous high. Both amphetamine and methamphetamine cause marked increases in blood pressure and heart rate and produce feelings of enhanced mood, alertness, and energy. However, both have a high risk for addiction and dependency.**

"It's the ultimate high. . . . It makes you feel so powerful. You have tons of energy. . . . I loved it. I craved it" (Witkin, 1995, p. 50). So said 23-year-old Tara, who became addicted to and dependent on meth and whose euphoria eventually turned into a terrible nightmare.

Nervous System

The primary effect of amphetamines and related drugs (methamphetamine) is to increase the release of the neurotransmitter dopamine and also to block its reuptake (Mendelson et al., 2006). Researchers are learning that the release of dopamine occurs during a wide range of pleasurable activities, such as sex (Esch & Stefano, 2005). Thus, drugs like methamphetamine are both desirable and dangerous because they increase the release of dopamine, which causes very pleasurable feelings.

Dangers

"I couldn't get high. No matter how much I did . . . nothing made me happy," said 23-year-old Tara, who was a methamphetamine user (Witkin, 1995, p. 50).

At first, users of methamphetamine have periods of restless activity and perform repetitive behaviors. Later, the initial euphoria is replaced with depression, agitation, insomnia, and true paranoid feelings. Recently, methamphetamine users were found to have 15% fewer dopamine receptors, which are involved in the reward/pleasure center (Riddle et al., 2006; Volkow et al., 2003). Fewer dopamine receptors decrease one's ability to experience normal pleasures and contribute to further drug usage. Long-term risks include stroke, liver damage, memory loss, and extreme weight loss (Jefferson, 2005).

Another powerful stimulant is cocaine, which we'll discuss next.

Why has it been used for 3,000 years?

For 3,000 years, the ancient Incas and their descendants, the indigenous Andean people of Peru, have chewed coca leaves as they made demanding journeys through the high mountains. Some minutes after chewing the leaves, which contain cocaine, they reported feeling more vigor and strength and less fatigue, hunger, thirst, and cold. Coca leaves contain very little cocaine and produce stimulation equivalent to that experienced by coffee (caffeine) drinkers (McCarry, 1996). Few psychological or physical problems are observed in those who chew coca leaves, partly because they consume very little cocaine and because this activity is part of their culture. However, natives who have switched from chewing coca leaves to using the more concentrated cocaine powder have reported many more problems (R. K. Siegel, 1989).

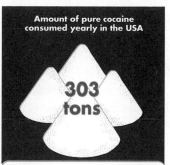

Amount of pure cocaine consumed yearly in the USA

303 tons

Americans spend about $35 BILLION annually on cocaine.

In the United States, an increase in usage of one illegal drug is partly due to which other drug is being targeted for enforcement. For example, the U.S. government's crackdown on amphetamine usage in the 1970s was largely responsible for the increased popularity of cocaine, whose usage reached epidemic proportions in the 1980s. In turn, the 1980s were marked by the government's "war" on cocaine, which was partly responsible for an upsurge in methamphetamine usage in the 1990s.

Since the cocaine epidemic of the late 1980s, usage of cocaine in the United States is reportedly down by 10–35%. For more than 25 years, law enforcement has been working to eliminate cocaine and other drugs. The United States has spent nearly $5 billion in the past six years to eliminate Columbia's coca crops, but the availability of cocaine in the United States is unchanged (Forero, 2006). The figure at left shows that cocaine is now a $35-billion-a-year illegal industry with about 2.4 million users (Brodzinsky, 2006; SAMHSA, 2006).

Drug

Cocaine can be sniffed or snorted, since it is absorbed by many of the body's membranes. If cocaine is changed into a highly concentrated form, which is called *crack,* it can be smoked or injected and produces an instantaneous but short-lived high.

Cocaine, **which comes from the leaves of the coca plant, has physiological and behavioral effects very similar to amphetamine. Like amphetamine, cocaine produces increased heart rate and blood pressure, enhanced mood, alertness, increased activity, decreased appetite, and diminished fatigue. With higher doses, cocaine can produce anxiety, emotional instability, and suspiciousness.**

When humans or monkeys have unlimited access to pure cocaine, they will use it continually, to the point of starvation and death. Only extreme shock will reduce an addicted monkey's use of cocaine, and only extreme problems involving health, legal, or personal difficulties will reduce an addicted human's intake.

Nervous System

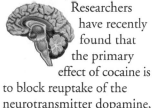

Researchers have recently found that the primary effect of cocaine is to block reuptake of the neurotransmitter dopamine, which means that dopamine stays around longer to excite neighboring neurons (Mendelson et al., 2006).

Researchers also found that cocaine excites one kind of neural receptor (dopamine) to produce pleasure/euphoria and another kind of receptor (glutamate) to produce a craving for more of the drug (Dackis & O'Brien, 2003). Like amphetamine, cocaine results in increased physiological and psychological arousal.

When applied to an external area of the body, cocaine can block the conduction of nerve impulses. For this reason, cocaine is classified as a local anesthetic and that is its only legal usage.

Dangers

In *moderate doses,* cocaine produces a short-acting high (10–30 minutes) that includes bursts of energy, arousal, and alertness. Users tend to believe that they are thinking more clearly and performing better, but, in fact, they overestimate the quality of their work. In *large doses,* cocaine can result in serious physical and psychological problems, which may include hallucinations and feelings of bugs crawling under the skin as well as addiction.

Many physical problems result from cocaine abuse, including lack of appetite, headaches, insomnia, irritability, heart attacks, strokes, seizures, damage to cartilage of the nose (if snorted), and increased risk of HIV (if injected). Also, respiratory failure, which may lead to sudden death, can result from relatively low doses (NIDA, 2006a).

Recently, heavy cocaine usage was found to significantly reduce the levels of dopamine receptors in the brain's reward/pleasure center. This reduction results in two disastrous consequences: First, the user must take larger doses of cocaine to experience the same pleasure and this continues the addiction; second, the user will find decreased pleasure in previously normal experiences (a good meal or companionship) and seek pleasure in continued use of drugs. This motivates the user to continue to gain pleasure by using cocaine and to avoid seeking treatment (Begley, 2001a).

Cocaine users often go through the vicious circle of feeling depressed as the effect wears off, wanting and using more cocaine to relieve the depression, and so on (Ropper & Brown, 2005). Thus, heavy users often require professional help to break out of their addictive vicious circles (Lamberg, 2004).

Next, we turn to two legal drugs that are the most widely used stimulants—caffeine and nicotine.

C. Stimulants

What's the most widely used drug in the world?

Caffeine, which has been used for the past 2,000 years, is the most widely used psychoactive drug in the world (A. Smith, 2005). In the United States, more than 172 million adults drink coffee daily (Associated Press, 2006; R. Goldberg, 2004). One 8-ounce cup of regular coffee, two cups of regular tea, two diet colas, or four regular-sized chocolate bars all contain about 100 milligrams of caffeine. The average amount of caffeine consumed in the United States is 238 milligrams per person per day, compared to 400 milligrams in Sweden and England and a worldwide average of 76 milligrams (Bowman, 2005).

Drug

Many users do not consider caffeine an addicting drug. *Caffeine,* a mild stimulant, produces physiological and psychological arousal, including decreased fatigue and drowsiness, feelings of alertness, and improved reaction times.

Moderate doses of caffeine improved performance in sleep-deprived drivers but had little effect on reducing motor impairment from alcohol (Fillmore et al., 2002; Reyner & Horne, 2000).

Nervous System

Caffeine belongs to a group of chemicals called xanthines *(ZAN-thenes),* which have a number of effects. One effect is to block certain receptors (adenosine receptors) in the brain, which results in stimulation and mild arousal (Keisler & Armsey, 2006).

Dangers

Researchers found that mild to heavy doses of caffeine (125–800 milligrams; two cups of coffee = 200 mg) can result in addiction and dependency similar to those produced by alcohol, nicotine, and cocaine (Strain et al., 1994). Higher doses of caffeine (300–1,000 milligrams) can result in depression, tension, and anxiety (DeAngelis, 1994).

Abruptly stopping the consumption of caffeine, especially medium to heavy doses, usually results in a number of uncomfortable withdrawal symptoms, such as increased headaches, irritability, fatigue, difficulty concentrating, and intense craving for caffeine (Condor, 2004). These symptoms usually disappear within 5–7 days. Obviously, caffeine is a real drug, as is the nicotine in tobacco products.

What causes the most deaths?

After caffeine, nicotine is the world's most widely used psychoactive drug. In the United States, over 70 million people use tobacco products, and over 2 million teens begin using cigarettes each year (SAMHSA, 2006).

The graph at the right shows that, in the United States, the highest number of deaths (435,000) results from using tobacco (Mokdad et al., 2004). For this reason, the U.S. Surgeon General concluded that cigarette smoking is the single largest avoidable cause of death in our society and the most important public health issue of our time (USDHHS, 2006).

Causes of Death in the United States
435,000 Tobacco
365,000 Diet and activity patterns
85,000 Alcohol
29,000 Guns

Drug

Nicotine has long been classified a stimulant drug, but not until 1997 was it officially classified an addictive drug (Koch, 2000).

Nicotine is a stimulant because it triggers the brain's reward/pleasure center to produce good feelings. In low doses, nicotine improves attention, concentration, and short-term memory. Regular use of nicotine causes addiction and dependency, and stopping leads to withdrawal symptoms.

Researchers now think they know why about 30 million American smokers try to quit each year and fail.

Nervous System

Nicotine stimulates the production of dopamine, which is used by the brain's reward/pleasure center to produce good feelings. Nicotine also stops other controlling cells from turning off the pleasure areas, so the overall result is that smoking produces a relative long-lasting good feeling (Mansvelder et al., 2003). Thus, smokers find it so difficult to quit because they are addicted to nicotine and really crave the good feeling.

Dangers

Nicotine is a very addicting drug, and it has serious health consequences. Over 400,000 American smokers die each year from lung and heart problems, and for thousands more, smoking causes sexual problems, including impotency (CDC, 2000; McKay, 2005). In 2006, the U.S. Surgeon General concluded that secondhand smoke kills tens of thousands of nonsmokers a year and reported there is no safe level of secondhand smoke exposure (O'Neil, 2006).

Because nicotine is addictive, a habitual smoker will experience withdrawal symptoms when trying to quit. Withdrawal symptoms range in severity and include nervousness, irritability, difficulty in concentrating, sleep disturbances, and a strong craving to light up again. Stop-smoking programs, including counseling and some combination of nicotine patch, pill, or gum, are all about equally effective—10 to 25% remained smoke free one year later (Vergano, 2001). This means that about 75% of smokers who tried to quit failed to do so, despite receiving nicotine.

Unlike stimulants, the next group of drugs, called opiates, produce the opposite effect.

Opium, Morphine, Heroin

How popular is heroin?

Beginning in 6000 B.C., opiates have been used around the world. Opiates were legal in the early 1800s, when the active ingredient in the juice of the opium poppy was found to be morphine. In the late 1800s, morphine was chemically altered to make heroin, which like opium is addictive. Law enforcement agencies usually refer to opiates as *narcotics*.

In the early 1900s, the sale and use of narcotics (opium, morphine, and heroin) were made illegal and a wildly lucrative worldwide opium black market began. In spite of restrictive laws and billions spent on enforcement, opiates are still readily available in most major U.S. cities (Schuckit, 2000).

In 1980, heroin was about 7% pure, but current heroin is about 50% pure, which means that instead of being injected, it can be smoked. Smoking appeals to and is more popular with new users; the beginning age has dropped to 18 years (Leinwand, 2000).

The number of Americans who use heroin regularly is estimated to be 136,000 (SAMHSA, 2006). The graph at left shows that compared to 85,000 drug-related deaths a year from alcohol, there were about 4,800 heroin-related deaths (SAMHSA, 2000, 2005a). The possession or use of opium, morphine, and heroin is illegal.

85,000 Alcohol

4,800 Heroin

Drug-Related Deaths per Year

Drug

Opiates produce similar effects, but users generally prefer to inject heroin because then it reaches the brain more quickly and produces the biggest "rush."

Opiates, such as opium, morphine, and heroin, produce three primary effects: analgesia (pain reduction); opiate euphoria, which is often described as a pleasurable state between waking and sleeping; and constipation. Continued use of opiates results in tolerance, addiction, and dependency.

One rock star (Anthony Kiedis of "Red Hot Chili Peppers") described using heroin for the first time as "a great feeling. . . . It's like you're opening a door that leads you into a different world. You discover a brand new universe" (NY Rock, 2002). However, with constant usage, his brain developed a tolerance to heroin, which means he had to take larger and larger doses to achieve a high and ended up developing many life problems (Kiedis, 2004).

Nervous System

In the 1970s, researchers discovered that the brain has naturally occurring receptors for opiates (Pert et al., 1974). When morphine reaches the brain's receptors, it produces feelings of euphoria and analgesia. In addition, the gastrointestinal tract has opiate receptors, whose stimulation results in constipation.

Researchers discovered that the brain not only has its own opiate receptors but also produces its own morphinelike chemicals. These chemicals, which function as neurotransmitters, are called *endorphins* and are found to have the same analgesic properties as morphine (Pleuvry, 2005).

Dangers

Anthony Kiedis, who injected heroin, said, "If you haven't ever put a needle in your arm, don't ever do it . . . it's horrible, and I don't want anyone to ever have to feel like I'm feeling right now. Let me do the suffering for you" (Kiedis, 2004, p. 179).

After several weeks of regular use, a person's brain produces less of its own endorphins and relies more on the outside supply of opiates. As a result, a person becomes addicted to taking opiates and must administer one or more doses daily to prevent withdrawal symptoms.

Withdrawal symptoms, which include hot and cold flashes, sweating, muscle tremors, nausea, and stomach cramps, are not life threatening and last 5–8 days. An overdose of opiates depresses the neural control of breathing, and a person dies from respiratory failure (Mendelson et al., 2006).

Treatment

In Great Britain, where heroin addiction is considered a health problem, heroin addicts who chose methadone injections instead of heroin use showed significant reductions in drug use and crime during a 12-month period (Metrebian et al., 2001). In contrast, in the United States, heroin addiction is considered a criminal problem, and addicts have limited or no access to regular medical treatment. In a 33-year follow-up study of heroin addicts in the United States, researchers reported that only 6% were in a medical treatment program, 40% had used heroin in the past year, and many had severe health problems or spent time in prison (Hser et al., 2001). Researchers concluded that, if heroin users do not quit by age 30, they are unlikely ever to stop. The most common treatment for heroin addiction is to maintain addicts on methadone, which is an addictive, synthetic drug similar to opium. Methadone treatment programs, which are not widely available, can be relatively effective in preventing heroin use, reducing criminal activities, and preventing loss of employment (Vocci et al., 2005).

The biggest change in treating heroin addiction in the United States is a new federally approved drug (buprenorphine) that blocks the craving for heroin (Rubin, 2006). Because this drug is given in a doctor's office, it signals that heroin addiction is more of a medical problem, similar to the treatment of heroin addiction in Great Britain (Amass, 2003).

Next, we'll consider the hallucinogens, which alter the brain chemistry to produce strange experiences and perceptions.

Opium poppy contains morphine.

E. Hallucinogens

What is a hallucinogen?

In many parts of the world and in many different cultures, plants and fungi (mushrooms) have long been used to produce visions or hallucinations as part of cultural or religious experiences. However, Caucasians in the United States rarely used hallucinogens until the 1950s and 1960s, when these drugs gained popularity as part of the hippie subculture. Researchers have once again begun to study the potential therapeutic uses of hallucinogens, which have also gained back

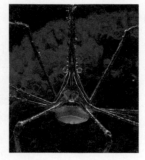

some of their former popularity (Golub et al., 2001).

Hallucinogens **are psychoactive drugs that can produce strange and unusual perceptual, sensory, and cognitive experiences, which the person sees or hears but knows that they are not occurring in reality. Such nonreality-based experiences are called** *hallucinations.*

We'll focus on four of the more commonly used hallucinogens: LSD, psilocybin, mescaline, and a designer drug called ecstasy.

LSD

What does LSD do?

At the beginning of this module, we told you of the strange bike ride of Albert Hofmann, who in 1943 discovered LSD (*d*-lysergic acid diethylamide). However, LSD did not become popular in America until the mid-1960s. Since then, LSD has gradually fallen in popularity, but there were reports of a slight increase in usage in the 1990s (Schuckit, 2000). In 2005, there were about 243,000 new LSD users (age 12 and older), compared to the 872,000 who began using cocaine (SAMHSA, 2006). Possession or use of LSD is illegal.

Drug

LSD is a very potent drug because it produces hallucinogenic experiences at very low doses.

LSD **produces strange experiences, which include visual hallucinations, perceptual distortions, increased sensory awareness, and intense psychological feelings.**

An LSD experience, or "trip," may last 8–10 hours.

Nervous System

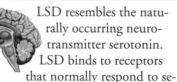

LSD resembles the naturally occurring neurotransmitter serotonin. LSD binds to receptors that normally respond to serotonin, and the net effect is increased stimulation of these neurons (D. L. Nelson, 2004). The majority of serotonin receptors are located on neurons in the brain's outermost layer, the cerebral cortex, which is involved in receiving sensations, creating perceptions, thinking, and imagining.

Dangers

LSD's psychological effects partially depend on the setting and the person's state of mind. If a person is tense or anxious or in an unfamiliar setting, he or she may experience a bad trip. If severe, a bad trip may lead to psychotic reactions (especially paranoid feelings) that require hospitalization. Sometime after the hallucinogenic experience, users may experience frightening flashbacks that occur for no apparent reason. There have been no reports of physical addiction to LSD or death from overdose, but users do quickly develop a tolerance to LSD (R. Goldberg, 2006).

Psilocybin

What are "magic mushrooms"?

The existence of "magic mushrooms" was suggested by carvings of the ancient Aztec Indians, who lived around 500 B.C. In 1957, archaeologists sent samples of the supposedly magic mushrooms *(Psilocybe mexicana)* to none

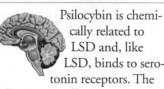

other than Albert Hofmann, who identified the active ingredient as psilocybin. Hofmann also tried magic mushrooms (left photo) and reported that they produced an "awake dream" that included a whirlpool of pictures rapidly changing shape and color (Hofmann, 1983). Possession or use of psilocybin is illegal.

Drug

The active ingredient in magic mushrooms is psilocybin.

Psilocybin **in low doses produces pleasant and relaxed feelings; medium doses produce perceptual distortions in time and space; high doses produce distortions in perceptions and body image and sometimes hallucinations.**

Nervous System

Psilocybin is chemically related to LSD and, like LSD, binds to serotonin receptors. The hallucinatory effects produced by psilocybin are comparable to those from LSD but last half as long (Carter et al., 2005).

Dangers

The dangers of psilocybin come not from physical harm to the brain or body but rather from its potential for inducing psychotic states that may persist long after the experience is expected to end (Espiard et al., 2005). In addition, accidental poisonings are common among those who eat poisonous mushrooms, mistaking them for magic mushrooms.

What is peyote?

In the 1500s, Spanish soldiers noted that the Aztec Indians of South America ate peyote cactus as part of their religious ceremonies. Peyote cactus contains about 30 psychoactive chemicals; one of the more potent is the drug mescaline.

In 1965, the Native American Church of North America won a battle in the U.S. Supreme Court for the legal right to use peyote as a sacrament in their Christian ritual. Participants in this ritual usually sit around a fire and eat peyote buttons. This is followed by meditation, during which the participants feel removed from earthly

cares and experience unusual visual perceptions, such as seeing a vast field of golden jewels that move and change (Liska, 1994). Beginning about ten years ago, Native American Indians in the U.S. armed forces were allowed to use peyote in religious rituals (A. Gardner, 2005).

The possession or use of mescaline is illegal for all except those who belong to the Native American Church.

Drug

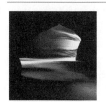

Mescaline is about 2,500–4,000 times less potent than LSD.

Mescaline is the active ingredient in the peyote cactus. At high doses, mescaline produces very clear and vivid visual hallucinations, such as latticework, cobweb figures, tunnels, and spirals, which appear in various colors and intense brightness. Mescaline does not impair the intellect or cloud consciousness.

As with most hallucinogens, the setting and user's psychological state influence the experience.

Nervous System

Mescaline reaches maximum concentration in the brain about 2–4 hours after someone eats buttons of peyote cactus. Mescaline primarily increases the activity of the neurotransmitters norepinephrine and dopamine (Stahl, 2000). In addition, mescaline activates the sympathetic nervous system to produce physiological arousal, such as increased heart rate and temperature and sometimes vomiting.

Dangers

During a mescaline experience, which can last 6–8 hours, users may experience headaches and vomiting. When street samples of mescaline were analyzed in a number of cities, researchers found that the chemical was rarely mescaline. Instead "street mescaline" was usually other hallucinogens, such as LSD or PCP (Hanson et al., 2006).

Can hallucinogens be made?

The mid-1980s saw the appearance of so-called designer drugs.

Designer drugs refer to manufactured or synthetic drugs that are designed to resemble already existing illegal psychoactive drugs and to produce or mimic their psychoactive effects.

For example, a drug designer can start with an amphetamine molecule and alter it in hundreds of ways. Because designer drugs are manufactured in home laboratories, users have no guarantees

that these drugs are safe to use. Of the dozen or so designer drugs available, we'll focus on one, MDMA, which was first used in the 1970s and whose street name is "ecstasy." In the late 1990s, ecstasy increased in popularity across the United States, and in 2005, there were about 500,000 current users (age 12 and older) (SAMHSA, 2006). Ecstasy has become the drug of choice at rave parties (left photo), which feature all-night music and dancing. The U.S. government banned research on MDMA in 1985, and only recently have a few researchers received permission to study its effects (Kohn, 2004). Possession or use of MDMA is illegal.

Drug

After alcohol and marijuana, ecstasy is the drug of choice among teens (Leinwand, 2002).

MDMA, or *ecstasy,* resembles both mescaline (hallucinogen) and amphetamine (stimulant). MDMA heightens sensations, gives a euphoric rush, raises body temperature, and creates feelings of warmth and empathy.

For these reasons, some suggest that ecstasy may be useful in some kinds of therapy (Adam, 2005).

Nervous System

MDMA causes neurons to release large amounts of two neurotransmitters, serotonin and dopamine, which stimulate the brain's reward/pleasure center. Afterward, users may feel depressed and have attention and memory deficits. The worry is that MDMA may cause brain damage (Kohn, 2004).

Dangers

In recreational doses, MDMA trips can last 6 hours and include euphoria, high energy, jaw clenching, teeth grinding, increased body temperature, and insomnia. At higher doses, trips include panic, rapid heart beat, high body temperature, paranoia, and psychotic-like symptoms (Baylen & Rosenberg, 2006). MDMA depletes some of the brain's transmitters (serotonin and dopamine) (Montoya et al., 2002). However, a sobering report that a single dose of MDMA caused neurological problems in monkeys and might do the same in humans has since been retracted because the researchers could not replicate their own findings (Ricaurte, 2003; Ricaurte et al., 2002).

The psychoactive drug we'll examine next is widely used, potentially very dangerous, and legal.

F. Alcohol

What if alcohol was banned?

The first brewery appeared in Egypt in about 3700 B.C., making alcohol the oldest drug to be made by humans (Samuel, 1996). Alcohol has grown in popularity worldwide, and its usage has been associated with a wide range of problems, such as motor coordination (right figure). If alcohol causes so many problems, why not just ban it?

In 1919, the U.S. Congress passed the Eighteenth Amendment, which prohibited the sale and manufacture of alcohol. However, Americans did not want to give up alcohol, so a lucrative black market developed and supplied illegal alcohol. After 14 years of black-market alcohol and failed prohibition, the U.S. Congress repealed prohibition in 1933. The lesson learned from prohibition was that it is impossible to pass a law to ban a drug that is

Party begins.

2 drinks later.

4 drinks later.

5 drinks later.

7 drinks in all.

126 million Americans drink alcohol and 19 million have problems.

so popular and widely used (Musto, 1996).

In 2005, about 126 million Americans age 12 and older drank alcohol. Of these, about 28% were underage (12–20 years old), 23% were binge drinkers (consumed 5 drinks in a row at same occasion), and about 7% were heavy drinkers (5 drinks in a row on 5 different days in the past month). The heavy drinkers are most likely to be alcoholics, who develop a variety of serious behavioral, neurological, social, legal, or medical problems (SAMHSA, 2006).

We'll discuss heavy drinkers and alcoholism in the Cultural Diversity section (p. 185), but first we'll explain alcohol's effects on the user's brain, body, and behaviors.

Although we'll use the term *alcohol,* we actually mean *ethyl alcohol,* which is safe to drink. The level of alcohol is measured in percentage in the blood, which is called blood alcohol content, or BAC. For example, after 3–4 drinks in an hour, the average person's BAC will range from 0.08 to 0.1. The national legal definition of being drunk is now 0.08. A drink is defined as one cocktail, one 5-ounce glass of wine, or one 12-ounce bottle of beer. It makes no difference whether you drink hard liquor, wine, or beer, since they all contain ethyl alcohol, which affects the nervous system and results in behavioral and emotional changes.

Drug

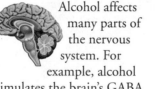

Alcohol is not a stimulant but a depressant.

Alcohol (ethyl alcohol) **is a psychoactive drug that is classified as a depressant, which means that it depresses activity of the central nervous system. Initially, alcohol seems like a stimulant because it reduces inhibitions, but later it depresses many physiological and psychological responses.**

The effects of alcohol depend greatly on how much a person drinks. After a few drinks (0.01–0.05 BAC), alcohol causes friendliness and loss of inhibitions. After four or five drinks (0.06–0.10 BAC), alcohol seriously impairs motor coordination (driving), cognitive abilities, decision making, and speech. After very many drinks (0.4 BAC and higher), alcohol may cause coma and death. For example, a 19-year-old college student died after an 11-hour drinking binge that led to a BAC of 0.44—about 30–40 drinks (ABC News, 2004).

Nervous System

Alcohol affects many parts of the nervous system. For example, alcohol stimulates the brain's GABA *(GAH-bah)* neural receptors, which leads to feeling less anxious and less inhibited (Schuckit, 2006). Alcohol also impairs the anterior cingulate cortex, which monitors the control of motor actions. When this area is impaired, drinkers will fail to recognize their impaired motor performance (driving a car) and continue to drive (Ridderinkhof et al., 2002). In very high doses (0.5 BAC), alcohol depresses vital breathing reflexes in the brain stem (medulla), and this may totally stop breathing and result in death.

Dangers

The morning after a bout of heavy drinking (3–7 drinks), a person usually experiences a *hangover,* which may include upset stomach, dizziness, fatigue, headache, and depression. There is presently no cure for hangovers, which are troublesome and painful but not life threatening.

Repeated and heavy drinking can result in tolerance, addiction, and dependency. *Tolerance* means that a person must drink more to experience the same behavioral effects. *Addiction* means an intense craving for alcohol, and *dependency* means if the person stops drinking, he or she will experience serious *withdrawal symptoms,* which may include shaking, nausea, anxiety, diarrhea, hallucinations, and disorientation.

Another serious problem is *blackouts,* which occur after heavy and repeated drinking. During a blackout, a person seems to behave normally but when sober cannot recall what happened. If the blackout lasts for hours or days, it is probable that the person is an alcoholic.

Repeated and heavy drinking can also result in liver damage, alcoholism, and brain damage.

Who's at risk for becoming an alcoholic?

Of the 126 million Americans who drink alcohol, almost 19 million will develop alcoholism. Researchers believe that a number of psychological and genetic risk factors increase the chances that a person will drink alcohol AND become an alcoholic. For example, one's risk of becoming an alcoholic is 3–4 times higher if one comes

19 million alcoholics

from a family whose parents are alcoholic. However, it's important to remember that risk factors increase the chances but do not guarantee that someone who drinks will become an alcoholic.

We'll discuss both genetic and psychological risk factors that may lead to a person abusing alcohol.

Psychological Risk Factors

Researchers found that children whose parents (either or both) are alcoholics develop a number of unusual, abnormal, or maladaptive psychological and emotional traits that are called *psychological risk factors* (Schuckit, 2000). For example, these childhood risk factors include being easily bored, engaging in risk-taking or sensation-seeking behaviors, and acting impulsively or overemotionally when faced with stressful situations (Legrand et al., 2005; Song, 2006).

When children with these psychological risk factors become adults, they may have a tendency to imitate the behavior of their alcoholic parent and abuse alcohol when faced with personal, social, stressful, or work-related difficulties. However, besides psychological risk factors for abusing alcohol, there are also genetic risk factors (Edenberg & Foroud, 2006).

Genetic Risk Factors

Besides psychological risk factors, there are also *genetic risk factors,* which refer to inherited biases or predispositions that increase the potential for alcoholism. For example, if one identical twin was an alcoholic, there was a 39% chance that the other twin was also. In comparison, if one fraternal twin was an alcoholic, there was a 16% chance that the other twin was also. Based on genetic studies, researchers estimate that genetic factors contribute about 60% to the reasons a person becomes an alcoholic (Schuckit, 2006).

One way genetic factors work is by making a person less sensitive to alcohol, meaning that a person has to drink more to feel its effects, and drinking more is a risk factor for becoming an alcoholic (Schuckit, 2006). Researchers find that genes set a person's sensitivity by affecting a number of different neurotransmitter systems (GABA, NMDA, dopamine, and serotonin) (DePetrillo, 2003; Li, 2000). For example, monkeys who have inherited low levels of serotonin are the ones with little impulse control and the urge to drink until drunk (Higley, 2002). Researchers caution that there is not one "alcoholic" gene that puts one at risk for alcoholism but perhaps as many as eight genes, which in turn interact with the environment to increase the risk for alcoholism (Edenberg & Foroud, 2006).

Because neither every child of an alcoholic parent nor both members of a pair of identical twins become an alcoholic, genetic risk factors alone do not lead to alcoholism. Rather, researchers believe that alcoholism results from the interaction between genetic and psychological risk factors (Lesch, 2005).

The use and abuse of alcohol are associated with a wide range of problems.

Problems with Alcohol

Why is alcohol so dangerous?

The reason alcohol is considered such a dangerous drug is that its use and abuse are linked to many problems in the United States:

✔ 80–90% of all campus rapes involve drinking on the part of the assailant, victim, or both;

✔ 68% of manslaughter convictions and 63% of assaults involve alcohol;

✔ 63% of episodes in which husbands batter their wives involve alcohol;

✔ 41% of traffic deaths involve alcohol;

✔ 44% of college students and 75% of fraternity/sorority students said they had binged—women drank 4 or men drank 5 successive drinks at least once in the last two weeks;

✔ 37% of pedestrians killed by an automobile were under the influence of alcohol at the time;

✔ 11% of workplace accidents involve alcohol;

✔ 8–21% of suicides involve alcohol;

✔ 7% of college freshmen who drop out do so because of alcohol;

44% of college students and 75% of fraternity/sorority students report having binged.

✔ alcoholism is a factor in 25% of all hospital admissions;

✔ alcohol is the leading cause of mental retardation due to fetal alcohol syndrome (FAS);

✔ alcohol is the most serious problem facing U.S. high schools, surpassing apathy and poor discipline by a wide margins;

✔ alcoholism and alcohol abuse cost an estimated $150 billion per year to lost production, health and welfare services, property damage, and medical expenses (Hingson & Winter, 2003; Morse, 2002; NHTA, 2003; Norungolo, 2005; Schuckit, 2000).

Because alcohol is significantly involved in so many medical, social, emotional, legal, job-related, and personal problems, many consider it to be one of the most dangerous of all the legal and illegal drugs (Naimi et al., 2003).

After you have had a chance to test your knowledge with the Concept Review, we'll discuss the worldwide problem of alcoholism.

✔ Concept Review

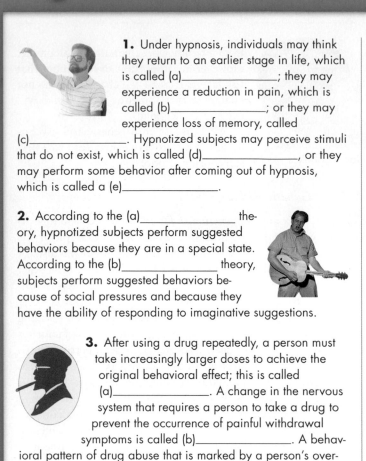

1. Under hypnosis, individuals may think they return to an earlier stage in life, which is called (a)_____; they may experience a reduction in pain, which is called (b)_____; or they may experience loss of memory, called (c)_____. Hypnotized subjects may perceive stimuli that do not exist, which is called (d)_____, or they may perform some behavior after coming out of hypnosis, which is called a (e)_____.

2. According to the (a)_____ theory, hypnotized subjects perform suggested behaviors because they are in a special state. According to the (b)_____ theory, subjects perform suggested behaviors because of social pressures and because they have the ability of responding to imaginative suggestions.

3. After using a drug repeatedly, a person must take increasingly larger doses to achieve the original behavioral effect; this is called (a)_____. A change in the nervous system that requires a person to take a drug to prevent the occurrence of painful withdrawal symptoms is called (b)_____. A behavioral pattern of drug abuse that is marked by a person's overwhelming and compulsive desire to obtain and use the drug is called an (c)_____. Painful physical and psychological symptoms that occur after a drug-dependent person stops using the drug are called (d)_____.

4. Drugs that affect the nervous system and result in altered awareness and consciousness, as well as changes in mood, cognition, and perception, are called _____.

5. Some drugs act like (a)_____ keys that are so similar to neurotransmitters that these drugs open the chemical (b)_____ of nearby neurons by acting like or (c)_____ the action of regularly occurring neurotransmitters. Some drugs prevent the neuron's reabsorption of neurotransmitters by slowing down a process called (d)_____. Some drugs act on the nucleus accumbens and ventral tegmental area, which are parts of the brain's (e)_____ center.

6. Those drugs that result in increased arousal, alertness, and euphoria are called (a)_____. The potent stimulant that comes from a plant, can be sniffed or smoked, and produces short-acting alertness and euphoria is (b)_____. The potent stimulant that is a form of amphetamine, is smoked, and produces longer-lasting alertness and euphoria is known on the street as (c)_____. The world's most widely used stimulant, which produces mild arousal and alertness, is (d)_____. The drug that is the single greatest avoidable cause of death in the United States is (e)_____. This drug triggers dopamine, which stimulates the brain's reward/pleasure center.

7. Drugs that produce unusual or distorted perceptual, sensory, and cognitive experiences that do not correspond to external reality are called (a)_____. One of the most powerful of these drugs, which can cause trips that last 8–10 hours, is (b)_____. A drug that is found in certain mushrooms is (c)_____; one that is found in peyote cactus is (d)_____.

8. Synthetic drugs that are variations of known psychoactive drugs and are manufactured in illegal laboratories are called (a)_____. One designer drug that is part stimulant and part hallucinogen is (b)_____.

9. Drugs that have three primary effects—analgesia, a state of waking sleep, and constipation—are called (a)_____. Continued use of these drugs causes the user to become (b)_____; if the user stops using the drug, he or she will experience painful (c)_____.

10. The psychoactive drug that depresses the functions of the central nervous system is (a)_____. At low doses, it causes friendliness and loss of (b)_____; at medium doses, it impairs social (c)_____; and, at higher doses, it seriously impairs (d)_____ coordination.

11. Certain individuals may develop or inherit different factors that make them at risk for becoming alcoholics. For example, a child raised by alcoholic parents may develop unusual, abnormal, or maladaptive psychological and emotional traits; these are called (a)_____ risk factors. In addition, a child may inherit predispositions for abusing alcohol, such as being less sensitive to alcohol; these are called (b)_____ risk factors.

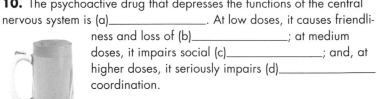

Answers: 1. (a) age regression, (b) hypnotic analgesia, (c) posthypnotic amnesia, (d) imagined perception, (e) posthypnotic suggestion; 2. (a) altered state, (b) sociocognitive; 3. (a) tolerance, (b) dependence, (c) addiction, (d) withdrawal symptoms; 4. psychoactive drugs; 5. (a) chemical, (b) locks, (c) mimicking, (d) reuptake, (e) reward/pleasure; 6. (a) stimulants, (b) cocaine, (c) methamphetamine (crack, crystal, or ice), (d) caffeine, (e) nicotine; 7. (a) hallucinogens, (b) LSD, (c) psilocybin, (d) mescaline; 8. (a) designer drugs, (b) MDMA or ecstasy; 9. (a) opiates, (b) addicted, (c) withdrawal symptoms; 10. (a) alcohol (ethyl alcohol), (b) inhibitions, (c) judgment, (d) motor; 11. (a) psychological, (b) genetic

G. Cultural Diversity: Alcoholism Rates

What is alcoholism?

One of the interesting questions that applies to all drugs is why some people can use a drug usually in moderation and rarely abuse it, while others use the same drug but often abuse it and usually develop serious problems. For example, of the approximately 110 million U.S. citizens who drink alcohol, about 10 to 14 million abuse it, drink to excess, and develop alcoholism.

Alcoholism involves heavy drinking (sometimes a quart a day) for a long period of time, usually many years. Alcoholics are addicted (have intense craving) and are dependent on

First signs of alcoholism appear in the early 20s.

alcohol (must drink to avoid withdrawal symptoms). They continue to use alcohol despite developing major substance-related life problems, such as neglecting family, work, or school duties, having repeated legal or criminal incidents, and experiencing difficulties in personal or social relationships (American Psychiatric Association, 2000).

One answer to why only certain drinkers abuse the drug and become alcoholics comes from studying various risk factors, such as psychological and genetic influences, which we discussed earlier. Now, we'll examine another risk factor—cultural influences.

Genetic Risk Factors

After the very first drink of alcohol, some individuals respond with a sudden reddening of the face. This reaction is called *facial flushing* and is caused by the absence of a liver enzyme involved in metabolizing alcohol.

Facial flushing from alcohol is a genetic trait and rarely occurs in Caucasians (Whites) but does occur in about 30–50% of Asians (photo below) (Schuckit, 2000). Asians with significant facial flushing, such as Taiwanese, Chinese, and Japanese, tend to drink less and have lower rates of alcoholism than Asians who show less facial

Asians with most facial flushing have lower rates of drinking and alcoholism.

flushing, such as Koreans (Assanangkornchai et al., 2003). These findings show that facial flushing, which occurs in some cultures more than others, is linked to a *genetic risk factor* that influences the chances of becoming an alcoholic.

Cultural Risk Factors

Different cultures have different values and pressures that may encourage or discourage alcohol abuse. For instance, researchers studied 48,000 adults (age 18 and older) in six different cultures to answer two questions: Do rates of alcoholism differ across cultures? What cultural values influence the rate of alcoholism?

The answer to the first question is shown in the graph below. Rates of alcoholism did differ across cultures, from a low of 0.5% among Taiwanese to a high of 22% among Koreans (Helzer & Canino, 1992).

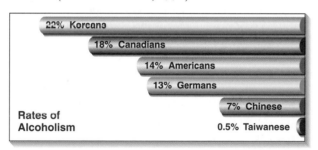

Rates of Alcoholism

- 22% Koreans
- 18% Canadians
- 14% Americans
- 13% Germans
- 7% Chinese
- 0.5% Taiwanese

The answer to the second question—What cultural values influence the rate of alcoholism?—was also partly answered. For example, the high rate of alcoholism in Korea is almost entirely in men, who are encouraged by cultural pressures to drink heavily in certain social situations, such as at the end of the workday, when co-workers are encouraged to have drinking contests. The medium rate of alcoholism found in Germany, the United States, and Canada was related to the stresses of living in heavily industrialized societies. The below-average rate of alcoholism found in China and especially Taiwan was influenced by the Confucian moral code, which has strong cultural-religious taboos against drinking or showing drunken behavior in public. These findings indicate that *cultural risk factors* can either encourage or discourage the development of alcoholism.

However, despite the different rates of alcoholism across cultures, there are some striking similarities.

Across Cultures

Although rates of alcoholism differed widely across cultures, from 0.5% to 22%, researchers found many similarities in how people developed alcoholism and the problems they had (Helzer & Canino, 1992; Peele, 1997). Here are some similarities that occurred across cultures:

■ the average age when the first symptoms of alcoholism appear was in the early twenties or mid-twenties;

■ the average number of major life problems among alcoholics was 4–6;

■ the average duration of alcoholism was 8–10 years;

■ the average pattern of drinking involved daily heavy drinking, often a quart a day;

■ men were five times more likely to develop alcoholism than were women;

■ depression was about twice as likely to be diagnosed in alcoholics as in nonalcoholics;

■ the overall mortality rate from alcoholism did not differ among cultures.

Researchers concluded that although cultural—genetic and psychological—risk factors had a significant influence on the *rate* of alcoholism, cultural factors had little effect on the *development*, symptoms, sex differences, and mental disorders associated with alcoholism.

Next, we'll focus on the most widely used illegal drug in the United States.

H. Marijuana

What's the most widely used illegal drug?

The most widely used illegal drug in the United States is marijuana, with 14.6 million current users (SAMHSA, 2005b). The graph on the right shows that, compared to other illegal drugs, no deaths have been reported from marijuana usage, which can still cause health problems (Cloud, 2002).

Marijuana is believed to be the leading U.S. cash crop; growers make an estimated $25 billion yearly (D. Campbell, 2003). In comparison, corn growers make $19 billion.

Medical marijuana. Research shows that marijuana can be effective in treating nausea and vomiting associated with chemotherapy, appetite loss in AIDS patients, eye disease (glaucoma), muscle spasticity in patients with multiple sclerosis, and some forms of pain (Cole, 2005). For these reasons, 11 states have passed laws and others are considering laws that allow marijuana to be prescribed by doctors and used legally for medical problems (Associated Press, 2006; N. Johnson, 2006). However, these state laws are in conflict with federal laws, which outlaw all uses of marijuana, including medical. This federal/state conflict will continue to receive increasing attention as drug manufacturers release promising medications based on extracts of high-grade marijuana plants. Already, one such drug (Sativex) has proven effective in treating chronic pain symptoms of patients with multiple sclerosis and arthritis, but it is now available only in Canada (J. Davis, 2005).

4,000	Heroin
3,618	Cocaine
	Marijuana 0

Drug-Related Deaths per Year

Gateway effect. There are 600,000 marijuana arrests a year. One reason for enforcing tough penalties against marijuana usage is the *gateway effect,* which says that using marijuana leads young people to try harder drugs (cocaine, heroin). However, the gateway effect has been challenged by researchers who found that genetic and environmental predispositions explain equally well why some marijuana users go on to try harder drugs (Morral et al., 2002). In any case, marijuana is illegal and can cause problems.

Drug

As is true of many psychoactive drugs, some of marijuana's effects depend on the user's initial mood and state of mental health. For example, older patients who used marijuana to treat glaucoma or nausea complained about its "strange side effect," which was feeling high or euphoric, which is the very effect that young users seek in smoking marijuana (Tramer et al., 2001).

Marijuana **is a psychoactive drug whose primary active ingredient is THC (tetrahydrocannabinol), which is found in the leaves of the cannabis plant. The average marijuana cigarette ("joint") contains 2.5–11.0 mg of THC, which is a tenfold increase over the amount of THC found in marijuana in the 1970s. THC is rapidly absorbed by the lungs and in 5–10 minutes produces a high that lasts for several hours. The type of high is closely related to the dose: Low doses produce mild euphoria; moderate doses produce perceptual and time distortions; and high doses may produce hallucinations, delusions, and distortions of body image (Hanson et al., 2002).**

Depending on the user's state of mind, marijuana can either heighten or distort pleasant or unpleasant experiences, moods, or feelings.

Nervous System

In 1964, researchers identified and synthesized THC, the main mind-altering substance in marijuana.

In 1990, researchers discovered a specific receptor for THC in the brains of rats and humans (Matsuda et al., 1990). These THC receptors are located throughout the brain, including the hippocampus, which is involved in short-term memory; the cerebral cortex, which is involved in higher cognitive functions; the limbic system, which is involved in emotions; and the cerebellum and basal ganglia, which are involved in motor control, timing, and coordination (Iversen, 2000). Mammalian brains (such as humans) contain extremely high levels of THC receptors, which suggests they may be involved in important brain functions (Iversen, 2000).

In 1993, researchers found that the brain itself makes a chemical, called anandamide, that stimulates THC receptors. Anandamide, a naturally occurring brain chemical, has been shown to be one of the brain's neurotransmitters, whose actions are currently under study (Piomelli, 1999).

Thus, the brain not only has receptors for THC but also makes a THC-like chemical, called anandamide.

Dangers

Marijuana can cause temporary changes in cognitive functioning, such as interfering with short-term memory and ability to drive a car, boat, or plane, because it impairs reaction time, judgment, and peripheral vision (Schuckit, 2000). At high doses, marijuana may cause toxic psychoses, including delusions, paranoia, and feelings of terror (Fergusson et al., 2005). However, there is no conclusive evidence that prolonged marijuana use causes permanent damage to brain or nervous system makeup (Cloud, 2002). Marijuana can also temporarily decrease secretion of various hormones and effectiveness of the immune system.

Marijuana causes many of the same kinds of respiratory problems as smoking tobacco, including bronchitis and asthma attacks. Because marijuana smoke contains 50% more cancer-causing substances and users hold smoke in their lungs longer, the effects of smoking 1 joint of marijuana are similar to those of 4 cigarettes (Biello, 2006).

Some, but not all, regular, heavy users of marijuana develop addiction and dependency. And when heavy users stop, some, but not all, experience withdrawal symptoms, usually described as feeling irritable, restless, and nervous (N. T. Smith, 2002).

Now we'll examine a popular program to prevent drug usage in teenagers.

I. Research Focus: Drug Prevention

For over 30 years, schools have tried dozens of drug prevention programs, such as providing knowledge about drugs and their risks, helping students make the right decisions, and recently, developing skills to resist social and peer pressures to use drugs. We want to focus on a popular and well-financed school-based drug prevention program called DARE.

DARE (Drug Abuse Resistance Education) is based on the idea of using social influence and role-playing to discourage adolescents from starting drug use and to encourage them to refuse drugs in the future. This program is taught in grade-school classrooms by trained, uniformed police officers.

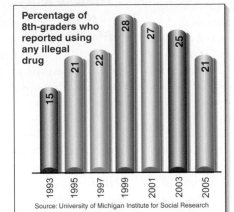

Percentage of 8th-graders who reported using any illegal drug

1993	1995	1997	1999	2001	2003	2005
15	21	22	28	27	25	21

Source: University of Michigan Institute for Social Research

Begun in 1983, DARE has become the most popular drug education school program, with an annual budget of about $700 million. Currently, thousands of DARE police officers speak to 26 million grade-school children in over 75% of the school districts in the United States and in 53 other countries (DARE, 2006a, 2006b).

The question you might ask is: Why has DARE remained so popular even though the left graph shows that teenage use of illegal drugs almost doubled from 1993 to 1999 and dropped only slightly in recent years (NIDA, 2006b)? This question brings us to one of the major uses of research: to evaluate the effectiveness of intervention programs that claim to change behavior. Here's how and what researchers discovered when they evaluated the effectiveness of the DARE program.

Method and Procedure

Researchers selected 36 elementary schools in urban, suburban, and rural areas in Illinois. Schools were paired to control for ethnic differences and income levels of parents. Students in one school of a pair were the experimental group and received DARE training, while students in the other school of the pair were the control group and did not receive DARE training. A total of 1,803 students took part in the study.

Before DARE began, students were pretested to determine their attitudes toward drugs and their use of drugs. Then students in the experimental schools began the DARE program, which consisted of educational sessions lasting 45–60 minutes that are taught in the classroom by uniformed police officers.

Immediately after the DARE program and also one, two, and three years later, students were re-tested on their attitudes toward drugs and their actual use of drugs.

Although the DARE program was very popular with police and school officials, researchers found that it was mostly ineffective.

Results and Discussion

Researchers found that going through project DARE had no statistically significant effect on whether students did or did not start smoking, drinking alcohol, or drinking to get drunk. These disappointing results were found immediately after the DARE program ended, as well as 1, 2, and 3 years later. There was a significant increase in self-esteem, but this gain was short-lived and was apparently not strong enough to help students resist using drugs in the future.

Researchers concluded that, although the police officers were well trained and popular among students, there was little evidence that being in project DARE had any direct influence on adolescents' use of drugs or on attitudes and skills related to preventing drug use (Ennett et al., 1994).

Other researchers who analyzed dozens of similar studies involving thousands of teenagers also concluded that DARE had "a limited to essentially nonexistent effect" on drug use in teenagers (S. Glass, 1998; Research Triangle Institute, 1994). A recent 10-year follow-up of the DARE program also found what other studies had reported: DARE had no effect on preventing the future use of illegal drugs (Janofsky, 2000; Lynam et al., 1999).

Conclusion

Despite DARE's large federal financial support and widespread popularity among police, politicians, school administrators, and parents, researchers have repeatedly found that the DARE program was ineffective in preventing future drug use in teenagers. In fact, researchers have found that almost all school-based prevention programs have failed to reduce teen drug usage in the long term (more than one year) (Cuijpers, 2003).

The DARE program became so popular and well financed because it received such glowing testimonials from its police officers, school officials, and politicians. However, as discussed in Module 2, evidence from testimonials is questionable because they are based on personal experiences, which have great potential for error and bias. The best way to evaluate the effectiveness of any program designed to change behavior, such as DARE, is to use the scientific method, which limits error and bias. This Research Focus shows the importance of basing evaluations on hard scientific evidence rather than on glowing testimonials, which may be distorted by error and bias.

Because of the program's proven ineffectiveness, police officers are no longer lecturing on the dangers of drugs. Instead, the new DARE program uses interactive learning, such as mock courtroom exercises, to help students stay away from drugs (E. S. McConnell, 2006).

If a teenager or adult does develop a drug habit, what kind of help does he or she receive in a drug treatment program?

Application Treatment for Drug Abuse

Developing a Problem

What are the risks for drug abuse?

Here's a case study that shows how psychological risks helped push Martin into abusing alcohol and becoming an alcoholic.

In high school, Martin got good grades but still felt insecure, especially about his sexual abilities. His solution was to act like a "rugged, hard-drinking person." But, instead of helping, hard drinking made him feel more insecure in relationships and made it more difficult for him to perform sexually.

When Martin entered college, he continued to have low self-esteem and feared that someone would discover that his sexual performance did not match his bragging. As he had done in high school, he buried his fears in having 5–10 drinks on weekends.

Despite his drinking bouts, Martin's knack for learning helped him finish college with good grades and even get into medical school. However, between college and medical school, he took a job driving a beer truck and drank half a dozen beers after work.

In medical school, Martin drank regularly because alcohol reduced his feelings of "self-loathing" and gave him an "instant" sense of self-worth. Despite heavy drinking, Martin's talents for mastering academic subjects helped him finish medical school.

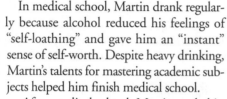

Many start out believing that alcohol is the solution.

After medical school, Martin settled in the Midwest, developed a successful medical clinic, got married, and had a family. However, throughout this period, he continued to drink heavily and began having blackouts. His wife could stand his drinking no longer, and one day she took the children and left. Martin began using painkillers, writing his own prescriptions.

Finally, one cold afternoon as Martin sat home with his booze and painkillers, the police arrested him for writing illegal prescriptions. Martin was forced to enter a psychiatric hospital for drug treatment (adapted from Khantzian & Mack, 1994).

Some of the psychological risks that pushed Martin to become a drug abuser are clear: For most of his life, he suffered from feelings of low self-esteem, worthlessness, and fears of not performing sexually. Hoping to solve his problems with drugs, Martin instead made them worse with substance abuse, the most common mental health problem among men (Kessler et al., 1994).

The former director of the National Institute on Drug Abuse, Alan Leshner, believes that the process of a voluntary drug user turning into an addict, as happened to Martin, results from a combination of psychological risks and actual changes inside the brain. Based on considerable research, Leshner makes the case that changes in the brain's structure and function from heavy drug use result in the equivalent of a brain disease, which in turn keeps the addiction going. For this reason, he cautions against blaming addicts for their drug addiction. Instead he recommends programs that treat both the brain disease by reducing drug usage and the psychological problems by actively involving the user in returning to normal functioning without drugs (Leshner, 2001).

Substance Abuse and Treatment

What is a drug problem?

Like Martin, about 5–15% of those who use legal or illegal drugs develop a serious drug problem called substance abuse.

Substance abuse refers to a maladaptive behavioral pattern of using a drug or medicine so frequently that significant problems develop: failing to meet major obligations and having multiple legal, social, family, health, work, or interpersonal problems. These problems must occur repeatedly during the same 12-month period (American Psychiatric Association, 2000).

Individuals with substance abuse usually need professional help.

Most substance abusers need professional help and treatment to get straightened out. Martin entered a treatment program that is based on the Minnesota model, which is used in about 95% of inpatient drug treatment centers in the United States. The *Minnesota model* recognizes that the drug user has lost control when it comes to drugs, may be vulnerable to using other mood-altering substances, cannot solve the drug problem alone, must rebuild his or her life without drugs, and must strive for total abstinence (McElrath, 1997; Owen, 2003).

We'll follow Martin's progress as he goes through a typical drug treatment program based on the Minnesota model.

Step 1. Admit the Problem

Why don't people seek treatment?

The fact that Martin did not seek help for his drug problem until he was arrested points out an important difference between most individuals treated for drug problems and those treated for mental health problems.

Generally, individuals with mental health problems seek help voluntarily because they want to stop their suffering or unhappiness. In contrast, many individuals with drug problems do not recognize that they have a problem and do not seek help voluntarily. Thus, the first step in getting treatment is admitting that one has a drug problem. Although this step appears obvious, in reality it represents a hurdle that many drug abusers have a difficult time getting over. What happens is that drug users believe that drugs are the solution to their problems, fears, insecurities, and worries.

Alcoholics deny that they have a problem.

For almost 10 years, Martin believed that alcohol was the solution to his sexual and social fears. In fact, the opposite was true. Heavy drug use became the problem, even though Martin and most users refuse to admit it. Convincing heavy drug users to seek treatment often requires the efforts of their family, loved ones, and employer, as well as a judge or doctor (Schuckit, 2000).

Step 2. Enter a Program

Every day in the United States, about 2.8 million people receive treatment for alcoholism in either an inpatient (hospital) or outpatient (clinic) setting (SAMHSA, 2006). In Martin's case, he was required to enter an inpatient (hospital) drug treatment program because he was both addicted and depressed, would not admit to having a problem, and would not seek help on his own. In comparison, most alcoholics (85%) are treated in clinics as outpatients.

Most in- or outpatient drug treatment programs involve the following steps and goals: Martin receives a complete medical checkup and a two-week period of detoxification (getting drug free), and then a team consisting of a physician, psychologist, counselor, and nurse discusses the treatment's four goals with Martin (Winters et al., 2000).

First goal. Help Martin face up to his drinking problem. It is not uncommon for a drug abuser to deny that he or she has a problem with drugs, even though it is obvious to everyone else.

Second goal. Have Martin begin a program of stress management, so that he can reduce his anxiety and tension without drinking. Stress management involves the substitution of relaxation exercises and other enjoyable activities (sports, hobbies) for the escape and enjoyment that alcohol has provided.

Third goal. Give Martin an opportunity to share his experiences in group therapy. Group sessions helped Martin realize that he was not suffering alone, that it was important for him to make plans for the future, and that he might have to make new, nondrinking friends once he left the program.

Fourth goal. Perhaps the most important goal is to help Martin face and overcome his psychological risk factors, which include personal and social problems that had contributed to his drug abuse.

> Three different therapies, including AA, were equally effective.

Step 3. Get Therapy

Regarding the fourth goal, you may wonder which kind of therapy is most effective in helping drug abusers. One answer comes from a 8-year study on over 1,700 individuals, all diagnosed as alcohol-dependent. This study compared the effectiveness of three different programs.

Three therapies. After volunteering for this study, individuals were randomly assigned to a 12-week treatment program that involved one of the following three therapies. *Cognitive-behavioral therapy* focuses on helping patients develop skills to control their thoughts about alcohol and learn to control their urges to drink. *Motivational therapy* helps clients recognize and utilize their personal resources and encourages them to take personal responsibility to abstain from drinking. The *12-step approach* is used in traditional Alcoholics Anonymous (AA) programs. The AA therapy or program promotes spiritual awakening, and its 12 steps serve as a guide for recovery and abstinence. AA believes that drug abuse is a disease, that a person must surrender to and ask God for help, and that total abstinence is the only solution.

Because these three therapies represent three different philosophies or approaches, many professionals believed that one therapy might be more effective than another.

Effectiveness. Researchers found that, before therapy, all individuals drank heavily on about 25 out of 30 days per month. In comparison, a year after finishing therapy, 35% reported not drinking at all, while 65% had slipped, or relapsed, into drinking again. Of the 65% who had relapsed, 40% reported periods of at least 3 consecutive days of heavy drinking.

There was little difference in the effectiveness of the three programs, which was somewhat surprising in view of their different approaches to drug treatment (Project Match Research Group, 1997).

Rate of success. The effectiveness of a drug treatment program is measured by how many clients remain abstinent (do not use drugs) for a period of one year. Success rates range from 30 to 45%, which means that 55 to 70% relapse or return to drinking during the year following treatment (Fuller & Hiller-Sturmhofel, 1999). For most drug treatment programs, the goal is total abstinence. However, there is an ongoing debate over whether alcoholics can learn to use drugs in moderate amounts. So far, there is very little research to show that long-term alcoholics can learn to drink moderately and responsibly (Rivera, 2000).

In 2002, a new drug (acamprosate) was approved for treating alcoholism. It's no wonder drug, but alcoholics who took the drug were able to stay sober 16% longer than those without it (Roan, 2002). However, this new drug is much less effective if not combined with cognitive behavioral therapy, which helps alcoholics rebuild their lives (Schuckit, 2002).

Following drug treatment program, patients are encouraged to join a support group in their community.

Step 4. Stay Sober

After treatment, recovering alcoholics as well as other drug addicts are encouraged to join a community support group to help fight relapse, or returning to drugs. The most popular and successful aftercare program for alcoholics is Alcoholics Anonymous (AA); a similar program for other drug users is Narcotics Anonymous (NA). After drug treatment, AA and NA provide programs to help prevent relapse, which occurs in 55 to 70% of former drug users.

Relapse can be triggered by a single exposure to the drug, by being with people or in places associated with using the drug, or by acute and chronic stressors.

To help patients deal with relapse, therapists have developed a program called relapse prevention therapy, which includes helping patients recognize high-risk situations that might trigger relapse, rehearsing strategies for dealing with high-risk situations, such as avoiding old drinking buddies, and learning how to deal with drug cravings. Because the majority of drug users relapse, this therapy also helps patients recover from a relapse (Foxhall, 2001).

> About 55–70% of recovering alcoholics suffer relapse.

Thus, a person with a drug problem initially needs help to get off a drug, then treatment to recover, then a support group, and finally relapse therapy to deal with relapse and try to remain drug free.

✔ Summary Test

A. Hypnosis

1. Hypnosis is defined as an altered state of awareness, attention, and alertness, during which a person is usually much more open to the (a)_____ of a hypnotist or therapist. About 10–15% of adults are easily hypnotized, while 20% are difficult to hypnotize. The procedure used to hypnotize someone is called (b)_____.

2. Under hypnosis, subjects will experience or perform the following _____: age regression, imagined perception, posthypnotic amnesia, posthypnotic suggestions, and hypnotic analgesia.

3. According to the (a)_____ theory, hypnotized subjects perform suggested behaviors because they are in a special state. According to the (b)_____ theory, subjects perform suggested behaviors, not because they are hypnotized, but because these individuals have the amazing ability of responding to imaginative suggestions and because of social pressures.

4. In dental and medical settings, hypnosis is used to help patients deal with painful procedures by producing (a)_____. In therapeutic settings, hypnosis is used in combination with other behavioral and cognitive treatments to help clients reveal their personalities and gain insights. However, hypnosis is not very successful in dealing with problems that involve (b)_____.

B. Drugs: Overview

5. Regular use of a drug usually results in one or more of the following. A behavioral pattern of drug abuse that is marked by an overwhelming and compulsive desire to obtain and use the drug is called an (a)_____. If the nervous system becomes accustomed to having the drug and needs the drug for normal functioning, the user is said to have developed a (b)_____. If a habitual user suddenly stops taking the drug, he or she will experience unpleasant or painful (c)_____. After using a drug over a period of time, a person must take a larger dose to achieve the original behavioral effect because this person has developed a (d)_____ for the drug.

6. Drugs that affect the nervous system by altering consciousness, awareness, sensations, perceptions, mood, and cognitive processes are called _____ drugs.

7. Some drugs act like (a)_____ keys that open neurons' chemical (b)_____, and some prevent the neuron's reabsorption of neurotransmitters, called (c)_____. Some drugs act on the brain's powerful (d)_____ center.

C. Stimulants

8. Drugs that increase activity of the nervous system and result in heightened alertness, arousal, and euphoria and decreased appetite and fatigue are called _____.

9. In moderate doses, cocaine produces short-lived enhancement of _____. In heavy doses, it can produce addiction; serious psychological effects, such as frightening hallucinations; and serious physical problems, such as heart irregularity, convulsions, and death.

10. A form of amphetamine called _____ produces a quick high, is very addictive, and has become a major drug problem.

11. The most widely used legal psychoactive drug in the world is _____, which affects brain receptors and, depending on the dose, produces physiological arousal, a mild feeling of alertness, increased reaction time, and decreased fatigue and drowsiness.

12. The legal drug that is second to caffeine in worldwide usage is _____, which triggers the production of dopamine.

D. Opiates

13. All opiates produce three primary effects: a reduction in pain, which is called (a)_____; a twilight state between waking and sleeping, which is called (b)_____; and (c)_____, which permits their use as a treatment for diarrhea. With continued use of opiates, users develop tolerance, addiction, and an intense craving for the drug. The brain also produces its own morphinelike chemicals, called (d)_____.

E. Hallucinogens

14. Drugs that act on the brain (and body) to produce perceptual, sensory, and cognitive experiences that do not match the external reality are called (a)_____. Sometime after using LSD, a user may suddenly have a frightening, drug-related experience called a (b)_____. Examples of hallucinogenic drugs are LSD, psilocybin, and mescaline. Drugs that are manufactured or altered to produce psychoactive effects are called (c)_____; an example is (d)_____.

F. Alcohol

15. Alcohol is classified as a (a)_____ because it decreases the activity of the central nervous system by stimulating neural receptors called (b)_____ receptors. Heavy and repeated drinking can result in periods of seemingly normal behavior that the drinker, when sober, cannot recall at all; these periods are called (c)_____. Alcohol abuse is a major contributor to personal problems, fatal traffic accidents, birth defects, homicides, assaults, date rape, and suicide.

16. A drinker's risk of becoming an alcoholic increases 3–4 times if members of his or her family are alcoholics. The risk of developing alcoholism is increased by having difficulties in showing trust and being overdependent in relationships, which are called (a)_____ factors, and also by the inheritance of predispositions for alcoholism, which are called (b)_____ factors.

G. Cultural Diversity: Alcoholism Rates

17. About 10–14% of American drinkers become _____, defined as people who have drunk heavily for a long period of time, are addicted to and have an intense craving for alcohol, and have developed major life problems because of drinking.

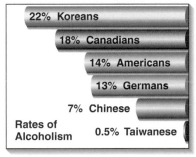

Rates of Alcoholism	
22%	Koreans
18%	Canadians
14%	Americans
13%	Germans
7%	Chinese
0.5%	Taiwanese

18. One reason the Chinese and Taiwanese have low rates of alcoholism is that these societies are heavily influenced by the Confucian moral code, which discourages _____ in public.

H. Marijuana

19. The most widely used illegal drug in the United States is (a)_____. In low doses it produces mild euphoria, in moderate doses it produces distortions in perception and time, and in high doses it may produce hallucinations and delusions. Researchers discovered that the brain has neural locks, or THC (b)_____, that are highly concentrated in the brain and respond to the THC in marijuana. The brain makes its own chemical, called (c)_____, which is one of the brain's own (d)_____ and closely resembles THC. Throughout the brain are many THC receptors that are involved in a number of behaviors, including (e)_____.

I. Research Focus: Drug Prevention

20. The most popular program to prevent drug use in teenagers is called (a)_____, which involves police officers lecturing to students about the dangers of drugs. However, researchers found that this popular and well-financed program was not effective in preventing future drug use. One reason DARE grew in popularity was because school officials and police officers gave DARE glowing (b)_____. Compared to scientific evidence, testimonials are much less reliable because they have a relatively high potential for (c)_____.

J. Application: Treatment for Drug Abuse

21. A maladaptive pattern of continued usage of a substance—drug or medicine—that results in significant legal, personal, or other problems over a 12-month period is called _____.

22. Programs that treat drug abusers have four steps: The first step is admitting that one has a (a)_____. The second step is entering a (b)_____, which has four goals. The third step is to get (c)_____ to help overcome drug abuse. The fourth step is to remain (d)_____.

23. Researchers found that three different kinds of therapy—cognitive-behavioral, motivational, and AA's 12-step approach—were about (a)_____ in helping alcoholics stop drinking. Although 35% of individuals stopped drinking, 65% started drinking again, which is called (b)_____. Part of recovery is learning how to deal with relapse, called (c)_____ therapy. In addition, recovering addicts are encouraged to join a community (d)_____ group, which helps them remain drug free.

Answers: 1. (a) suggestions, (b) hypnotic induction; 2. behaviors; 3. (a) altered state, (b) sociocognitive; 4. (a) analgesia, (b) self-control; 5. (a) addiction, (b) dependence, (c) withdrawal symptoms, (d) tolerance; 6. psychoactive; 7. (a) chemical, (b) locks, (c) reuptake, (d) reward/pleasure; 8. stimulants; 9. activity, mood, or energy; 10. methamphetamine; 11. caffeine; 12. nicotine; 13. (a) analgesia, (b) opiate euphoria, (c) constipation, (d) endorphins; 14. (a) hallucinogens, (b) flashback, (c) designer drugs, (d) MDMA, or ecstasy; 15. (a) depressant, (b) GABA, (c) blackouts; 16. (a) psychological risk, (b) genetic risk; 17. alcoholics; 18. drunkenness; 19. (a) marijuana, (b) receptors, (c) anandamide, (d) neurotransmitters, (e) memory, emotions, motor control, higher cognitive functions; 20. (a) DARE, (b) testimonials, (c) error and bias; 21. substance abuse; 22. (a) drug problem, (b) treatment program, (c) therapy, (d) drug free; 23. (a) equally effective, (b) relapse, (c) relapse, (d) support

Critical Thinking

Does Caffeine Make You Smarter?

Questions

1. How does caffeine make us more upbeat, alert, and focused?

2. Why did researchers use fMRI brain scans instead of MRI scans?

3. Why were the two beverages made to look and taste the same?

4. Can the researchers conclude that caffeine, and not something else, was the cause of subjects' improved memory?

5. Can drinking more than two cups of coffee improve memory even more?

Almost all of us drink caffeinated beverages to feel better—more upbeat, alert, and focused. Many college students drink caffeinated beverages to stay awake studying for an exam or completing a term paper. Is it possible that in addition to keeping us from nodding off, caffeine can make us more intellegent?

A recent study explored the effect of caffeine on one intellectual function—memory. Researchers conducted a laboratory experiment (see p. 34) in which they gave subjects a caffeinated drink or a caffeine-free drink (placebo) through a straw while they were in a fMRI machine (see p. 70). Subjects were not told which drink they were being given, and both drinks looked and tasted the same as researchers simply dissolved caffeine (the equivalent of two cups of coffee) in water to create the caffeinated beverage.

Twenty minutes after drinking and while lying in the brain scan machine, subjects were given a memory test that involved being presented with a random sequence of letters and having to decide whether the current letter was the same or different from the letter presented two letters ago. Subjects were told to respond as quickly as possible by tapping response pads with their fingers. Also, during different testing sessions, each subject went through a caffeine and placebo scan.

Results showed that after taking caffeine, subjects had faster reaction times and increased activity in the areas of the brain responsible for working memory

and attention. Working memory, or short-term memory, stores information for about 30 seconds (see p. 240). Subjects used working memory to store information about the letters they saw to help remember the letter presented two letters ago. When subjects drank the placebo (caffeine free), there were no changes in the brain areas responsible for working memory. Researchers concluded that caffeine affects brain activity, which makes us more alert and better able to remember information.

Drinking two cups of coffee may improve your memory, but it will not make you more intelligent. As a research psychologist, Harris Lieberman, says, "I use the word intelligence as an inherent trait, something permanently part of your makeup" (Lemonick, 2006, p. 95). He explains that caffeine cannot change intelligence, but what it can do is improve your attention, mood, and energy level. For instance, when you're feeling drowsy and you take caffeine, many intellectual functions, such as attention, logical reasoning, and reaction time, improve. Thus, though caffeine cannot make you more intelligent, it can help you to better use the intellectual abilities you already have. (Adapted from Billingsley, 2005; Koppelstaetter et al., 2005; Lemonick, 2006; RSNA, 2005)

Suggested Answers

1. Researchers are still trying to answer this question. What they know is that caffeine blocks receptors in the brain that accept the neurotransmitter adenosine, which acts to lower brain activity. The result is stimulation and mild physiological and psychological arousal.

2. Researchers used the fMRI brain scan because they were interested in how the brain functions during a cognitive task, such as memory. The MRI brain scan examines the structure of the brain and is most useful in determining where and to what extent the brain has been damaged.

3. It is important for subjects not to know when they are receiving caffeine or a placebo to control for self-fulfilling prophecies (p. 30)

and placebo effects (p. 31). If subjects were to know when they were drinking caffeine or a placebo, their expectations (e.g., "caffeine will make me more alert") might bias their performance.

4. Yes. The research design used in the study was a placebo-controlled experiment, which eliminates chances of error and determines cause and effect.

5. There is no research to support that drinking more than two cups of coffee will lead to further memory improvement. On the contrary, high caffeine consumption can make a person feel jittery and anxious and may interfere with sleep.

Links to Learning

Key Terms/Key People

Learning Activities

- **POWERSTUDY FOR INTRODUCTION TO PSYCHOLOGY 4.0**

  PowerStudy 4.0™

  by Tom Doyle and Rod Plotnik

  SuperModule: Check out "Hypnosis & Drugs" on **PowerStudy.**
  It includes complete paragraph-by-paragraph explanations of all content using fully-narrated animations and graphics. An onscreen toolbar allows immediate access to text, text outline, and module glossary with notetaking and printing capabilities. This module also includes:

  - Video—Imbedded videos cover topics like why nicotine is so addicitve, hypnosis, and alcoholism.
  - A test of your knowledge using an interactive version of the Summary Test on pages 190 and 191. Also access related quizzing—true/false, multiple choice, and matching.
  - An interactive version of the Critical Thinking exercise "Does Caffeine Make You Smarter?" on page 192.
  - Key terms, a chapter outline including chapter abstract, and a special extended list of hotlinked websites that correlate to this module.

- *CengageNOW*

  CENGAGENOW™

  academic.cengage.com/login

  Need help studying? This site is your one-stop study shop.
  Take a Pre-Test and CengageNOW will generate a Personalized Study Plan based on your test results. The Study Plan will identify the topics you need to review and direct you to online resources to help you master those topics. You can then take a Post-Test to determine the concepts you have mastered and what you still need to work on.

- **INTRODUCTION TO PSYCHOLOGY BOOK COMPANION WEBSITE**

  www

  academic.cengage.com/psychology/plotnik

  Visit your book companion website where you will find more resources to help you study. At this site, you will find Learning Objectives, Internet Exercises, quizzing, flash cards, and a pronunciation glossary.

- *STUDY GUIDE and WEBTUTOR*

  WebTUTOR

  Check the corresponding module in your Study Guide for effective student tips and help learning the material presented. Also go to **academic.cengage.com/webtutor** for an interactive version of the Study Guide features.

Study Questions

*A. Hypnosis—A student has great test anxiety, which is interfering with his success in college. Would hypnosis help? (**Suggested answer page 623**)

B. Drugs: Overview—Keeping in mind that Americans spend over $62 billion annually on illegal drugs, what is your position on their legalization?

C. Stimulants—Why don't most Americans think that caffeine and nicotine are drugs that can be addictive?

D. Opiates—Why do you think that our brains manufacture their own morphinelike chemicals, called endorphins?

E. Hallucinogens—Why is there a long history of people's use of hallucinogens in religious ceremonies?

*F. Alcohol—If researchers know who has an increased risk for alcoholism, at what age should such a person be told? (**Suggested answer page 623**)

G. Cultural Diversity: Alcoholism Rates—Why are there such striking similarities in the development of alcoholism across different cultures?

*H. Marijuana—A regular user of marijuana says that he can drive just fine after smoking. Would you ride with him? (**Suggested answer page 624**)

I. Research Focus: Drug Prevention—Can you think of reasons a 17-week course in drug abuse prevention might not be effective for adolescents?

J. Application: Treatment for Drug Abuse—Why are individuals who have been successfully treated for drug abuse so often tempted to relapse and use drugs again?

*These questions are answered in Appendix B.

MODULE 9
Classical Conditioning

 PowerStudy 4.0™ Complete Module

Introduction

It's Only Aftershave

What happened to Carla?

"I've got an unusual problem and I thought you might be able to explain what happened." Carla, one of my (R.P.) students, looked troubled.

"I'll help if I can," I replied, and asked her to sit down.

"It all started when my dentist told me that I needed a lot of work on my teeth and gums. I spent many mornings in the dentist's chair, and even though he gave me Novocain, it was painful and very uncomfortable. But here's the strange part that I wish you would explain. I had recently bought my boyfriend a new aftershave, and as the dentist worked on my teeth, I noticed that he was using the same one. You'll think this is silly, but now when I smell my boyfriend's aftershave, I start to feel tense and anxious."

Carla stopped and waited to see if I would tell her that she was just being silly. I didn't, and she continued.

"Finally, I told my boyfriend that he would have to stop using the aftershave I had bought him because it was the same as my dentist's and the smell made me anxious. Well, we got into a big argument because he said that he was nothing like my dentist and I was just being silly. So now my teeth are great, but I feel myself getting anxious each time we get close and I smell his aftershave."

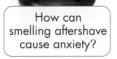

How can smelling aftershave cause anxiety?

I assured Carla that she was not being silly and that many people get conditioned in the dentist's chair. In fact, patients have reported feeling anxious when they enter the dentist's office, smell the antiseptic odor, or hear the sound of the drill (Settineri et al., 2005; Taani et al., 2005). I explained that, without her knowing, she had been conditioned to feel fear each time she smelled her dentist's aftershave and how that conditioning had transferred to her boyfriend's aftershave. Before I explained how to get "unconditioned," I told her how after only one terrifying experience, I too had been conditioned.

It's Only a Needle

What happened to Rod?

I was about 8 years old when I had to get an injection from my local doctor, whom I really liked. He warned me in a kindly way that the injection might hurt a little. I was feeling OK until I saw the long needle on the syringe. I tried to be brave and think of my fuzzy dog, but as soon as I felt that long needle enter my little butt, everything started to spin. I remember sinking slowly to the floor, and then everything went dark. When I came to, the doctor told me that I had fainted.

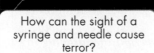

How can the sight of a syringe and needle cause terror?

Even after all these years, the sight of a needle can still strike terror into me. To prevent fainting, I always lie down when getting an injection or giving blood. But I'm not alone in my fear of needles and injections; about 10 to 20% of the general population report a similar fear and many others have some aversion to needles (Page et al., 1997; Sibbitt, 2006).

Besides learning to fear needles and blood, people can unknowingly learn to feel sick and nauseated, just as Michelle did.

It's Only Dish Soap

What happened to Michelle?

Michelle was nervous and afraid as the nurse put a needle into the vein in her left arm and then opened a valve that allowed chemicals to drip into her bloodstream. Michelle was in the process of receiving chemotherapy to treat her cancer. One serious side effect of chemotherapy is severe nausea, which Michelle experienced after each treatment.

What Michelle wasn't prepared for was how other things could trigger her nausea. In one case, the odor of her dishwashing liquid, which smelled similar to the chemotherapy room, made her feel nauseated. She had to change her brand of detergent because its odor made her salivate, which was the first sign of oncoming nausea (Wittman, 1994). Without her awareness, Michelle had been conditioned to feel nauseated by numerous stimuli involved in her chemotherapy (McRonald & Fleisher, 2005).

The cases of Michelle, Carla, and myself show how we had been conditioned to fear relatively ordinary things, such as aftershave lotion, needles, and the smell of detergent. This conditioning illustrates one kind of learning.

How can smelling dish soap cause nausea?

Learning **is a relatively enduring or permanent change in behavior that results from previous experience with certain stimuli and responses. The term** *behavior* **includes both unobservable mental events (thoughts, images) and observable responses (fainting, salivating, vomiting).**

In all three cases, conditioning resulted in a relatively enduring change in behavior. In fact, mine has lasted almost 50 years. What happened to each of us involved a particular kind of learning, called classical conditioning, which we'll discuss in this module.

What's Coming

We'll first discuss three different kinds of learning and then focus on one, classical conditioning. We'll examine how classical conditioning is established and tested, how we respond after being classically conditioned, what we learn during classical conditioning, and how classical conditioning is used in therapy. Let's begin with a look at three different kinds of learning.

A. Three Kinds of Learning

Why is some learning easier? Some things are difficult to learn, such as all the terms in this module. Other things are easy to learn, such as fear of an injection. To understand why some learning is easy and some hard, we'll visit three different laboratories. You'll see how psychologists identified three different principles that underlie three different kinds of learning: classical conditioning, operant conditioning, and cognitive learning.

Classical Conditioning

Why does the dog salivate? It is the early 1900s, and you are working as a technician in Russia in the laboratory of Ivan Pavlov. He has already won a Nobel Prize for his studies on the reflexes involved in digestion. For example, he found that when food is placed in a dog's mouth, the food triggers the reflex of salivation (R. B. Evans, 1999).

As a lab technician, your task is to place various kinds of food in a dog's mouth and measure the amount of salivation. But soon you encounter a problem. After you have placed food in a dog's mouth on a number of occasions, the dog begins to salivate merely at the sight of the food.

At first, Pavlov considered this sort of anticipatory salivation to be a bothersome problem. Later, he reasoned that the dog's salivation at the sight of food was also a reflex, but one that the dog had somehow *learned.*

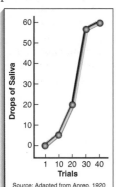
Source: Adapted from Anrep, 1920

In a well-known experiment, Pavlov rang a bell before putting food in the dog's mouth.

As shown in this graph, after a number of trials of hearing a bell paired with food, the dog salivated at the sound of the bell alone, a phenomenon that Pavlov called a *conditioned reflex* and today is called classical conditioning. Classical conditioning was an important discovery because it allowed researchers to study learning in an observable, or objective, way (Honey, 2000).

Classical conditioning is a kind of learning in which a neutral stimulus acquires the ability to produce a response that was originally produced by a different stimulus.

Next, we'll visit a lab in the United States and observe a different kind of learning.

Operant Conditioning

Why does the cat escape? It is the late 1800s, and you are now working in the laboratory of the American psychologist E. L. Thorndike. Your task is to place a cat in a box with a door that can be opened from the inside by hitting a simple latch. Outside the box is a fish on a dish. You are to record the length of time it takes the cat to hit the latch, open the door, and get the fish.

Thorndike studied how a cat learned to open a cage to get food nearby.

On the first trial, the cat sniffs around the box, sticks its paw in various places, accidentally hits the latch, opens the door, and gets the fish. You place the cat back into the box for another trial. Again the cat moves around, accidentally strikes the latch, and gets the fish. After many such trials, the cat learns to spend its time around the latch and eventually to hit the latch and get the fish in a very short time.

To explain the cat's goal-directed behavior, Thorndike formulated the law of effect.

The *law of effect* says that if some random actions are followed by a pleasurable consequence or reward, such actions are strengthened and will likely occur in the future.

Thorndike's law of effect was important because it identified a learning process different from Pavlov's conditioned reflex. Today, the law of effect has become part of operant conditioning (R. B. Evans, 1999).

Operant conditioning refers to a kind of learning in which the consequences that follow some behavior increase or decrease the likelihood of that behavior's occurrence in the future.

We will discuss operant conditioning in *Module 10.* Our next lab has a big plastic doll and a bunch of kids.

Cognitive Learning

Why do they punch the doll? It is the 1960s, and you are in Albert Bandura's laboratory, where children are watching a film of an adult who is repeatedly hitting and kicking a big plastic doll. Following this film, the children are observed during play.

Bandura found that children who had watched the film of an adult modeling aggressive behavior played more aggressively than children who had not seen the film (Bandura et al., 1963). The children's change in behavior, which was increased aggressive responses, did not seem to be based on Pavlov's conditioned reflexes or Thorndike's law of effect. Instead, the entire learning process appeared to take place in the children's minds, without their performing any observable responses or receiving any noticeable rewards. These mental learning processes are part of cognitive learning, which is a relatively new approach that began in the 1960s (Chance, 2006).

Cognitive learning is a kind of learning that involves mental processes, such as attention and memory; may be learned through observation or imitation; and may not involve any external rewards or require the person to perform any observable behaviors.

Bandura's study demonstrated a third principle of learning, which essentially says that we can learn through observation or imitation. ***We will discuss cognitive learning in Modules 10, 11, and 12.***

Now, let's return to Pavlov's laboratory and examine his famous discovery in greater detail.

B. Procedure: Classical Conditioning

What's the procedure? Imagine that you are an assistant in Pavlov's laboratory and your subject is a dog named Sam. You are using a procedure that will result in Sam's salivating when he hears a bell, a response that Pavlov called a ***conditioned reflex***. Today, we call Pavlov's procedure ***classical conditioning***, which involves the following three steps.

Step 1. *Choosing Stimulus and Response*

Terms. Before you begin the procedure to establish classical conditioning in Sam, you need to identify three critical terms: *neutral stimulus, unconditioned stimulus,* and *unconditioned response.*

Neutral stimulus. You need to choose a neutral stimulus.

A *neutral stimulus* is some stimulus that causes a sensory response, such as being seen, heard, or smelled, but does not produce the reflex being tested.

Your neutral stimulus will be a tone (bell), which Sam the dog hears but which does not normally produce the reflex of salivation.

Unconditioned stimulus. You need to choose an unconditioned stimulus, or UCS.

An *unconditioned stimulus,* or *UCS,* is some stimulus that triggers or elicits a physiological reflex, such as salivation or eye blink.

Your unconditioned stimulus will be food, which when presented to Sam will elicit the salivation reflex, that is, will make Sam salivate.

Unconditioned response. Finally, you need to select and measure an unconditioned response, or UCR.

The *unconditioned response,* or *UCR,* is an unlearned, innate, involuntary physiological reflex that is elicited by the unconditioned stimulus.

For instance, salivation is an unconditioned response that is elicited by food. In this case, the sight of food, which is the unconditioned stimulus, will elicit salivation in Sam, which is the unconditioned response.

Step 2. *Establishing Classical Conditioning*

Trial. A common procedure to establish classical conditioning is for you first to present the neutral stimulus and then, a short time later, to present the unconditioned stimulus. The presentation of both stimuli is called a *trial.*

Neutral stimulus. In a typical trial, you will pair the neutral stimulus, the tone, with the unconditioned stimulus, the food. Generally, you will first present the neutral stimulus (tone) and then, a short time later, present the unconditioned stimulus (food).

 +

Unconditioned stimulus (UCS). Some seconds (but less than a minute) after the tone begins, you present the unconditioned stimulus, a piece of food, which elicits salivation. This trial procedure is the one most frequently used in classical conditioning.

→

Unconditioned response (UCR). The unconditioned stimulus, food, elicits the unconditioned response, salivation, in Sam. Food and salivation are said to be unconditioned because the effect on Sam is inborn and not dependent on some prior training or learning.

Step 3. *Testing for Conditioning*

Only CS. After you have given Sam 10 to 100 trials, you will test for the occurrence of classical conditioning. You test by presenting the tone (conditioned stimulus) without showing Sam the food (unconditioned stimulus).

Conditioned stimulus. If Sam salivates when you present the tone alone, it means that the tone has become a conditioned stimulus.

A *conditioned stimulus,* or *CS,* is a formerly neutral stimulus that has acquired the ability to elicit a response that was previously elicited by the unconditioned stimulus.

In this example, the tone, an originally neutral stimulus, became the CS.

 →

Conditioned response. When Sam salivates to the tone alone, this response is called the conditioned response.

The *conditioned response,* or *CR,* which is elicited by the conditioned stimulus, is similar to, but not identical in size or amount to, the unconditioned response.

One thing to remember is that the conditioned response is usually similar in appearance but smaller in amount or magnitude than the unconditioned response. This means that Sam's conditioned response will involve less salivation to the tone (conditioned stimulus) than to the food (unconditioned stimulus).

Predict. One question you may ask about classical conditioning is: What exactly did Sam learn during this procedure? One thing Sam learned was that the sound of a bell predicted the very likely occurrence of food (Rescorla, 1988). Classical conditioning helps animals and humans predict what's going to happen and thus provides information that may be useful for their survival (D. A. Lieberman, 2004).

Next, we'll use the concepts of classical conditioning to explain how Carla was conditioned to her dentist's aftershave.

B. Procedure: Classical Conditioning

Terms in Classical Conditioning

What happened to Carla?

After many trips to her dentist, Carla unknowingly experienced classical conditioning, which explains why she now feels anxious and tense when she smells a certain aftershave lotion. As we review the steps involved in classical conditioning, you will see how they apply to Carla's situation.

Step 1. Selecting Stimulus and Response

Terms. To explain how classical conditioning occurs, it's best to start by identifying three terms: *neutral stimulus, unconditioned stimulus,* and *unconditioned response.*

The *neutral stimulus* in Carla's situation was the odor of the dentist's aftershave lotion, which she smelled while experiencing pain in the dentist's chair. The aftershave is a neutral stimulus because although it affected Carla (she smelled it), it did not initially produce feelings of anxiety. In fact, initially Carla liked the smell.

The *unconditioned stimulus* for Carla was one or more of several dental procedures, including injections, drillings, and fillings. These dental procedures are unconditioned stimuli (UCS) because they elicited the unconditioned response (UCR), which was feeling anxious and tense.

The *unconditioned response* was Carla's feeling of anxiety, which is a combination of physiological reflexes, such as increased heart rate and blood pressure and rapid breathing, as well as negative emotional reactions. Carla's unconditioned response (anxiety) was elicited by the unconditioned stimulus (painful dental procedure).

Step 2. Establishing Classical Conditioning

Trial. One procedure to establish classical conditioning is for the neutral stimulus to occur first and be followed by the unconditioned stimulus. Each presentation of both stimuli is called a *trial.*

In Carla's case, the *neutral stimulus* was smelling the dentist's aftershave while she was experiencing a number of painful dental procedures.

+

Carla's many trips to the dentist resulted in her having repeated trials that involved occurrence of the *neutral stimulus,* smelling the dentist's aftershave, and occurrence of the *unconditioned stimulus,* having painful dental procedures.

→

The painful dental procedures elicited the *unconditioned response* (feelings of anxiety) as well as other physiological responses, such as increases in heart rate, blood pressure, and breathing rate.

Step 3. Testing for Conditioning

Only CS. A test for classical conditioning is to observe whether the neutral stimulus, when presented alone, elicits the conditioned response.

Conditioned stimulus. When Carla smelled her boyfriend's aftershave, which was the same as the dentist's, she felt anxious. The aftershave's smell, formerly a neutral stimulus, had become a *conditioned stimulus* because it elicited anxiety, the conditioned response.

Conditioned response. Whenever Carla smelled the aftershave (conditioned stimulus) used by both her dentist and her boyfriend, it elicited the *conditioned response,* feeling anxious. However, remember that the conditioned response is similar to, but of lesser intensity than, the unconditioned response. Thus, the anxiety elicited by smelling the aftershave was similar to, but not as great as, the anxiety Carla felt during painful dental procedures.

Dental fears. Through classical conditioning, Carla learned that the smell of a certain aftershave predicted the likely occurrence of pain and made her feel anxious. Researchers suggest that people who developed an extreme fear or phobia of dental procedures learned such fears through classical conditioning (Skaret & Soevdsnes, 2005; Townsend et al., 2000). However, just as classical conditioning can elicit fears, it can also be used to treat them through an "unconditioning" procedure that we'll discuss in the Application section on page 206.

Next, we'll describe several other behaviors that are associated with classical conditioning.

C. Other Conditioning Concepts

What else happened to Carla?

Carla's experience in the dentist's office of being classically conditioned to feel anxious when she smelled a particular aftershave has some other interesting features. Carla found that similar odors also elicited anxious feelings but that other odors did not; her anxiety when smelling her boyfriend's aftershave gradually decreased, but accidentally meeting the dentist and smelling his aftershave triggered some anxiety. Pavlov found that these phenomena were associated with classical conditioning, and he named them generalization, discrimination, extinction, and spontaneous recovery.

1. Generalization

Why her shampoo?

During Carla's conditioning trials, the neutral stimulus, which was the odor of the dentist's aftershave, became the conditioned stimulus that elicited the conditioned response, anxiety. However, Carla may also feel anxiety when smelling other similar odors, such as her own hair shampoo; this phenomenon is called generalization.

Generalization is the tendency for a stimulus that is similar to the original conditioned stimulus to elicit a response that is similar to the conditioned response. Usually, the more similar the new stimulus is to the original conditioned stimulus, the larger will be the conditioned response.

Pavlov suggested that generalization had an adaptive value because it allowed us to make an appropriate response to stimuli that are similar to the original one. For example, although you may never see your friend's smiling face in exactly the same situation, generalization ensures that the smiling face will usually elicit positive feelings.

Reacting to similar odors is generalization.

2. Discrimination

Why not her nail polish?

Carla discovered that smells very different from that of the aftershave did not elicit anxiety; this phenomenon is called discrimination.

Discrimination occurs during classical conditioning when an organism learns to make a particular response to some stimuli but not to others.

For example, Carla had learned that a particular aftershave's smell predicted the likelihood of a painful dental procedure. In contrast, the smell of her nail polish, which was very different from that of the aftershave, predicted not painful dental procedures but nice-looking fingernails.

Discrimination also has an adaptive value because there are times when it is important to respond differently to related stimuli. For example, you would respond differently to the auditory stimulus of a police siren than to the auditory stimulus of a baby's cries.

Not reacting to a new odor is discrimination.

3. Extinction

What about her boyfriend?

If Carla's boyfriend did not change his aftershave and she repeatedly smelled it, she would learn that it was never followed by painful dental procedures, and its smell would gradually stop making her feel anxious; this phenomenon is called extinction.

Extinction refers to a procedure in which a conditioned stimulus is repeatedly presented without the unconditioned stimulus and, as a result, the conditioned stimulus tends to no longer elicit the conditioned response.

The procedure for extinguishing a conditioned response is used in therapeutic settings to reduce fears or phobias. For example, clients who had a conditioned fear of needles and receiving injections were repeatedly shown needles and given injections by qualified nurses. After exposure to the conditioned stimuli during a 3-hour period, 81% of the clients reported a significant reduction in fear of needles and receiving injections (Ost et al., 1992). This kind of exposure therapy is a practical application of Pavlov's work and will be discussed more fully in Module 22.

Not reacting to a previously powerful stimulus is extinction.

4. Spontaneous Recovery

Would the anxiety come back?

Suppose Carla's conditioned anxiety to the smell of the aftershave had been extinguished by having her repeatedly smell her boyfriend's lotion without experiencing any painful consequences. Some time later, when Carla happened to accidentally meet her dentist in the local supermarket, she might spontaneously show the conditioned response and feel anxiety when smelling his aftershave; this is called spontaneous recovery (D. C. Brooks, 2000).

Spontaneous recovery is the tendency for the conditioned response to reappear after being extinguished even though there have been no further conditioning trials.

Spontaneous recovery of the conditioned response will not persist for long and will be of lesser magnitude than the original conditioned response. If the conditioned stimulus (smell of aftershave) is not presented again with the unconditioned stimulus (painful dental procedure), the spontaneously recovered conditioned response will again undergo extinction and cease to occur. Thus, once Carla had been classically conditioned, she would have experienced one or more of these four phenomena.

Having a reaction come back is spontaneous recovery.

Now that you are familiar with the procedure and concepts of classical conditioning, we'll explore its widespread occurrence in the real world.

D. Adaptive Value & Uses

How useful is classical conditioning?

Pavlov believed that animals and people evolved the capacity for classical conditioning because it had an adaptive value (Lieberman, 2004).

Adaptive value refers to the usefulness of certain abilities or traits that have evolved in animals and humans and tend to increase their chances of survival, such as finding food, acquiring mates, and avoiding pain and injury.

We'll discuss several examples, such as learning to avoid certain tastes, salivating at the sight of food, and avoiding pain, which support Pavlov's view that classical conditioning is useful because it has an adaptive value.

Taste-Aversion Learning

What do you learn from getting sick?

Rat exterminators have firsthand knowledge of classical conditioning's adaptive value. Exterminators find that while some rats eat enough bait poison to die, others eat only enough to get sick. Once rats get sick on a particular bait poison, they quickly learn to avoid its smell or taste, called *bait shyness,* and never again eat that bait poison. This kind of learning is a form of classical conditioning called taste-aversion learning (Koh & Bernstein, 2005).

Taste-aversion learning is how rats avoid poison.

Taste-aversion learning refers to associating a particular sensory cue (smell, taste, sound, or sight) with getting sick and thereafter avoiding that particular sensory cue in the future.

The adaptive value of taste-aversion learning for rats is obvious: By quickly learning to avoid the smells or taste associated with getting sick, such as eating poison bait, they are more likely to survive.

Humans. It is likely that in your lifetime, you too will experience taste-aversion learning. For example, if you have eaten something and gotten sick after taking a thrill ride, you may avoid the smell or taste of that particular food (D. A. Lieberman, 2004). Similarly, people who get sick from drinking too much of a particular alcoholic drink (often a sweet or distinctive-tasting drink) avoid that drink for a long period of time (Lieberman, 2000).

I'm starting to get a sick feeling!!!

Taste-aversion learning may also warn us away from eating poisonous plants that cause illness or even death, such as eating certain varieties of mushrooms. All these examples of taste-aversion learning show the adaptive value of classical conditioning, which is to keep us away from potentially unpleasant or dangerous situations, such as taking thrill rides, overdrinking, or eating poisonous plants.

As many people have learned, taste-aversion learning can develop after a single experience and may last weeks, months, or even as long as 4 to 5 years (Logue et al., 1981; Rozin, 1986).

The study of taste-aversion learning changed two long-held beliefs about classical conditioning.

Explanation

Is only one trial enough?

For a long time, psychologists believed that bait shyness was not due to classical conditioning. They were sure that classical conditioning required many trials (not a single trial of getting sick) and that the neutral stimulus (smell or taste) must be followed within seconds by the unconditioned response (nausea), and certainly not hours later (getting sick). Psychologist John Garcia thought otherwise.

One-trial learning. Garcia showed that taste-aversion learning did occur in one trial and, more surprisingly, did occur even though there was an hour or more delay between the neutral stimulus (smell or taste) and the unconditioned response (sickness or vomiting). Garcia's findings proved that taste-aversion learning is a form of classical conditioning (Koh & Bernstein, 2005).

Taste-aversion learning occurs in one trial.

Preparedness. An interesting finding was that animals acquired taste aversion differently. For example, rats, which have poor vision but great senses of taste and olfaction (smell), acquired taste aversion easily to smell and taste cues but were rarely conditioned to light cues (Garcia et al., 1966). Similarly, quails, which have poor olfaction but great vision, acquired taste aversion more easily to visual cues (Wilcoxon et al., 1971). Garcia concluded that, depending on the animal, different stimuli or cues have different potentials for becoming conditioned stimuli. These findings challenged the long-standing belief in classical conditioning that all stimuli (smell, taste, visual, auditory) have an equal chance of becoming conditioned stimuli. Garcia's finding that some stimuli were more easily conditioned than others was called preparedness (Seligman, 1970).

Preparedness refers to the phenomenon that animals and humans are biologically prepared to associate some combinations of conditioned and unconditioned stimuli more easily than others.

The idea of preparedness means that different animals are genetically prepared to use different senses to detect stimuli that are important to their survival and adaptation. For example, John Garcia and his colleagues (1974) applied their knowledge of preparedness and taste aversion to the problem of sheep-killing by coyotes. They baited grazing areas with pieces of sheep flesh

Taste-aversion learning is used to stop coyotes from eating sheep.

laced with a chemical that caused coyotes to become nauseated and ill. As a result, coyotes that had acquired a taste aversion showed an estimated 30–60% reduction in sheep-killing (B. Bower, 1997; Gustavson et al., 1976). Taste-aversion learning has applications for sheep ranchers and for people who get sick from overdrinking or eating before going on thrill rides (Loy & Hall, 2002).

Classical Conditioning and Adaptive Value

Why do blue jays avoid monarchs?

Taste-aversion learning helps rats survive by alerting them to the smell and taste of poison, and it also warns blue jays, who feast on butterflies, not to eat monarch butterflies. Monarch butterflies, which have a distinctive coloring pattern, contain a chemical that, when eaten, will make birds sick. Through taste aversion, blue jays learn that the distinctive color pattern of monarch butterflies predicts getting sick, and so blue jays avoid eating monarch butterflies.

Like monarch butterflies, many animals have evolved with distinctive markings or colors that, through taste-aversion learning, have become conditioned stimuli that serve as warnings to predators. Thus, classically conditioned taste aversion has survival value for animals. In contrast, things that taste good can produce a classically conditioned response in humans that is also adaptive.

Through taste-aversion learning blue jays learn to avoid monarchs.

Hot fudge sundaes. The next time you enter a restaurant, read the menu, think about food, and see people eating, notice that you are salivating even though you have no food in your own mouth. Just as Pavlov's dog was conditioned to salivate at the sound of a bell, we have also become conditioned to salivate when only thinking about, imagining, smelling, or seeing food. This is a clear example of how many different kinds of neutral stimuli, such as reading a menu, seeing people eat, or imagining food, can become conditioned stimuli that elicit a conditioned response—salivation.

Salivation serves a very useful purpose: It is a reflex response that normally occurs when you place food in your mouth. One purpose of salivation is to lubricate your mouth and throat to make chewing and swallowing food easier. Thus, being classically conditioned to salivate when reading a menu prepares your mouth for the soon-to-arrive food.

Conditioned salivation and taste-aversion learning are examples of how classical conditioning can have an adaptive value (D. A. Lieberman, 2004).

Next, we'll examine how emotional responses can be classically conditioned.

Does thinking about food make you salivate?

Classical Conditioning and Emotions

Why do people fear needles?

At the beginning of this module, I told a sad but true childhood story of getting an injection that elicited such pain and fear that I fainted. Even 50 years later, I still fear injections and needles and always lie down to avoid fainting. In my case, you can easily identify each element of classical conditioning: The neutral stimulus is the sight of the needle; the unconditioned stimulus is the injection; and the unconditioned response is pain and fear. After a painful injection, the formerly neutral stimulus, the needle, becomes a conditioned stimulus and elicits the conditioned response, which is fear and even fainting. Because this situation involved the

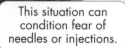

This situation can condition fear of needles or injections.

conditioning of an emotional response, my fear of injections and needles is called a conditioned emotional response (Rachman, 2002).

A conditioned emotional response refers to feeling some positive or negative emotion, such as happiness, fear, or anxiety, when experiencing a stimulus that initially accompanied a pleasant or painful event.

Conditioned emotional responses can have survival value, such as learning to fear and avoid stimuli that signal dangerous situations, like the sound of a rattlesnake or wail of a siren (McNally & Westbrook, 2006). Conditioned emotional responses can also signal pleasant situations. For example, many couples have a special song that becomes emotionally associated with their relationship. When this song is heard by one in the absence of the other, it can elicit strong emotional and romantic feelings. Thus, different kinds of stimuli can be classically conditioned to elicit strong conditioned emotional responses.

Classical Conditioning in the Brain

Where does it happen?

The young man in the photo is wearing head gear that delivers a tone (conditioned stimulus) followed by a puff of air (unconditioned stimulus) that elicits his eye blink reflex (unconditioned response). With this classical conditioning procedure, individuals learn to blink about 90% of the time to the tone alone (conditioned response), before the air puff occurs. For both humans and animals, classical conditioning of the eye blink requires the cerebellum (right figure). Lacking the cerebellum, neither humans nor animals can acquire the conditioned eye blink response, which is a highly specific motor response (Gerwig et al., 2003).

Conditioning eye blink reflex

In contrast to the classically conditioned eye blink reflex, which is a motor response, the young boy on the right is acquiring a classically conditioned emotional response—fear of needles and injections. In both humans and animals, acquiring a conditioned emotional response, especially involving fear, involves a different brain structure called the amygdala (p. 80) (Dityatev & Bolshakov, 2005). Thus, classically conditioning responses in humans or animals involve different areas of the brain, depending on whether the responses are motor or emotional.

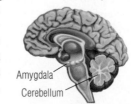

Conditioning emotional response

Next, we'll go to the heart of classical conditioning and examine how and why classical conditioning works.

Amygdala
Cerebellum

E. Three Explanations

Do you salivate when thinking of pizza?

Although most of us have had the experience of salivating when thinking about or seeing a favorite food, such as a pizza, researchers have given different explanations of what happens or what is learned during conditioning. We'll discuss three theories—stimulus substitution, contiguity theory, and cognitive perspective—that offer different explanations of why nearly all of us salivate when only thinking about or seeing a delicious pizza.

Stimulus Substitution & Contiguity Theory

Does the bell substitute for food?

The first explanation of classical conditioning came from Pavlov, who said the reason a dog salivated to a tone was that the tone became a substitute for the food, a theory he called stimulus substitution.

Stimulus substitution means that a neural bond or association forms in the brain between the neutral stimulus (tone) and unconditioned stimulus (food). After repeated trials, the neutral stimulus becomes the conditioned stimulus (tone) and acts like a substitute for the unconditioned stimulus (food). Thereafter, the conditioned stimulus (tone) elicits a conditioned response (salivation) that is similar to that of the unconditioned stimulus.

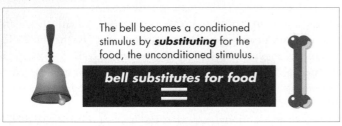

The bell becomes a conditioned stimulus by **substituting** for the food, the unconditioned stimulus.

bell substitutes for food
=

According to stimulus substitution theory, you salivate when you see a pizza because the act of seeing a pizza (conditioned stimulus) becomes bonded in your nervous system to the pizza itself (unconditioned stimulus). Because of this neural bond or association, the sight of pizza substitutes for the pizza, so that just the sight of a pizza can elicit salivation (conditioned response).

However, researchers discovered that the responses elicited by the unconditioned stimulus were often slightly different from those elicited by the conditioned stimulus. For example, following the unconditioned stimulus, a dog salivated and always chewed, but, following the conditioned stimulus, it salivated but rarely chewed (Zener, 1937). As a result of this and other criticisms of Pavlov's stimulus substitution theory, researchers suggested a different explanation, the contiguity theory.

The *contiguity theory* says that classical conditioning occurs because two stimuli (neutral stimulus and unconditioned stimulus) are paired close together in time (are contiguous). As a result of this contiguous pairing, the neutral stimulus becomes the conditioned stimulus, which elicits the conditioned response.

The contiguity theory says that because seeing a pizza is paired closely in time with eating it, the sight alone begins to elicit salivation. Contiguity theory was the most popular explanation of classical conditioning until the 1960s, when it was challenged by the clever research of psychologist Robert Rescorla (1966).

Cognitive Perspective

Does the bell predict food is coming?

To the surprise of many researchers, Robert Rescorla (1966, 1987, 1988) showed that an association between neutral and unconditioned stimuli did not necessarily occur when the two stimuli were closely paired in time. Instead, he found that classical conditioning occurred when a neutral stimulus contained information about what was coming next; this explanation is called the cognitive perspective.

The *cognitive perspective* says that an organism learns a predictable relationship between two stimuli such that the occurrence of one stimulus (neutral stimulus) predicts the occurrence of another (unconditioned stimulus). In other words, classical conditioning occurs because the organism learns what to expect.

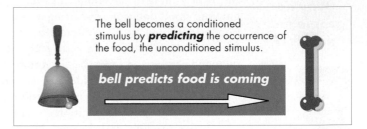

The bell becomes a conditioned stimulus by **predicting** the occurrence of the food, the unconditioned stimulus.

bell predicts food is coming

For example, the cognitive perspective theory would explain that you salivate to the sight of pizza because you have learned a predictable relationship: Seeing a pizza (conditioned stimulus) often leads to eating one (unconditioned stimulus), and your expectation causes salivation (conditioned response).

Support for the cognitive perspective comes from a number of findings. For example, classical conditioning works best if the neutral stimulus (tone) occurs slightly before the unconditioned stimulus (food). In this sequence, the organism learns a relationship between two stimuli: Tone predicts food. However, if the sequence is reversed and the unconditioned stimulus appears before the neutral stimulus, this is called *backward conditioning* and does not usually result in classical conditioning.

The cognitive perspective would explain that backward conditioning makes it impossible to predict a relationship between the neutral and unconditioned stimuli and thus does not usually result in classical conditioning. Currently, there is widespread support for the cognitive perspective, which says that classical conditioning involves learning about predictable relationships, or learning about cause and effect (Pearce & Bouton, 2003).

After the Concept Review, we'll discuss a well-known study of classical conditioning that involves the famous "Little Albert."

✓ Concept Review

1. In classical conditioning, one of the stimuli that is chosen has two characteristics: The stimulus, such as a tone, must cause some reaction, such as being heard, seen, tasted, or smelled, but it must not elicit the unconditioned response. A stimulus with these two characteristics is called a _____.

2. In classical conditioning, a second stimulus is chosen that can elicit an unlearned, involuntary physiological reflex, such as salivation. This stimulus is called an _____.

3. In classical conditioning, the unconditioned stimulus elicits an unlearned, involuntary physiological reflex, such as salivation, which is called the _____.

4. A typical trial in classical conditioning involves first presenting the (a)_____ and then, a short time later, presenting the (b)_____.

5. On the very first conditioning trial, the neutral stimulus (tone) did not itself elicit the unconditioned response (salivation). However, on the first trial, the presentation of food, which is called the (a)_____, did elicit salivation, called the (b)_____.

6. After a dozen trials that paired the tone with the food, you noticed that as soon as the tone was presented, the dog salivated. Because the tone itself elicited a response similar to that elicited by the unconditioned stimulus (food), the tone is called the (a)_____. The salivation elicited by the tone itself is called the (b)_____.

7. During classical conditioning, there is a tendency for a stimulus similar to the original conditioned stimulus to elicit a response similar to the conditioned response. This tendency is called _____.

8. During classical conditioning, an organism learns to make a particular response to some stimuli but not to others; this phenomenon is called _____.

9. If a conditioned stimulus is repeatedly presented *without* the unconditioned stimulus, there is a tendency for the conditioned stimulus to no longer elicit the conditioned response. This phenomenon is called _____.

10. The tendency for the conditioned response to reappear some time later, even though there are no further conditioning trials, is called _____.

11. The kind of learning in which the cues (smell, taste, auditory, or visual) of a particular stimulus are associated with an unpleasant response, such as nausea or vomiting, is called (a)_____. This kind of learning can even occur after only a single (b)_____.

12. According to Pavlov's original explanation, classical conditioning occurs because of (a)_____, which means that the conditioned stimulus (tone) bonds to the unconditioned stimulus (food). Through this bond, or association, the conditioned stimulus (tone) elicits the conditioned response (salivation) by substituting for the (b)_____ (food). Pavlov's explanation of classical conditioning was criticized, and researchers suggested instead that conditioning occurs because two stimuli are paired close together in time. This explanation, which is called (c)_____ theory, has been challenged, in turn, by more recent explanations.

13. The current and widely accepted explanation of classical conditioning, which is called the (a)_____ perspective, states that animals and humans learn a predictable relationship between stimuli. According to this explanation, a dog learns predictable relationships, such as a tone predicting the occurrence of (b)_____.

Answers: *1. neutral stimulus; 2. unconditioned stimulus (UCS); 3. unconditioned response (UCR); 4. (a) neutral stimulus, (b) unconditioned stimulus (UCS); 5. (a) unconditioned stimulus (UCS), (b) unconditioned response (UCR); 6. (a) conditioned stimulus (CS), (b) conditioned response (CR); 7. generalization; 8. discrimination; 9. extinction; 10. spontaneous recovery; 11. (a) taste-aversion learning, (b) trial; 12. (a) stimulus substitution, (b) unconditioned stimulus, (c) contiguity; 13. (a) cognitive, (b) food*

F. Research Focus: Conditioning Little Albert

Can Emotional Responses Be Conditioned?

Why did Little Albert fear white animals?

One of the first attempts to study the development of emotional responses, such as becoming fearful, occurred in the 1920s. At this time, psychologists did not yet know if emotional responses could be conditioned. John Watson realized that he could use Pavlov's conditioning procedure to study the development of emotional behaviors in an objective way. As you may remember from Module 1, John Watson (p. 13) was a strong supporter of behaviorism, which emphasized the study of observable behaviors and the rejection of unobservable mental or cognitive events.

What follows is a first in psychology: an important classic experiment on conditioning emotions that John Watson and his student assistant, Rosalie Rayner, published in 1920.

Method: Identify Terms

Watson questioned the role that conditioning played in the development of emotional responses in children. To answer his question, Watson (photo) tried to classically condition an emotional response in a child.

Subject: Nine-month-old infant.
The subject, known later as Little Albert, was described as healthy, stolid, and unemotional, since "no one had ever seen him in a state of rage and fear. The infant practically never cried" (Watson & Rayner, 1920, p. 3).

Neutral stimulus: White rat.
Watson briefly confronted 9-month-old Albert with a succession of objects, including a white rat, a rabbit, and a dog. "At no time did this infant ever show fear in any situation" (Watson & Rayner, 1920, p. 2).

Rat is neutral stimulus.

Unconditioned stimulus: Noise.
Standing behind Albert, the researchers hit a hammer on a metal bar, which made a loud noise and elicited startle and crying. "This is the first time an emotional situation in the laboratory has produced any fear or crying in Albert" (Watson & Rayner, 1920, p. 3).

BANG !

Bang is UCS.

Unconditioned response: Startle/cry.
Startle and crying were observable and measurable emotional responses that indicated the baby was feeling and expressing fear.

After Watson identified the three elements of classical conditioning, he and his assistant, Rayner, began the procedure for classical conditioning.

Fear is UCR.

Procedure: Establish and Test for Classical Conditioning

Establish. At the age of 11 months, Albert was given repeated trials consisting of a neutral stimulus, a white rat, followed by an unconditioned stimulus, a loud noise. During early trials, he startled at the sight of the rat and on later trials he also cried.

Rat (neutral stimulus) plus loud bang (UCS) elicits fear response (UCR).

Test. When first presented with the rat alone (no noise), Albert only startled. Then he was given additional conditioning trials and retested with the rat alone (no noise). "The instant the rat was shown the baby began to cry" (Watson & Rayner, 1920, p. 5). Thus, Watson had succeeded in classically conditioning Albert's emotional response (fear).

Classical conditioning: rat (CS) alone elicits fear response (CR).

Results and Conclusions

Watson and Rayner had shown that Albert developed a conditioned emotional response of startle and crying to the sight of a rat, which lasted about a week and then diminished, or underwent *extinction.*

After Albert was conditioned to fear a white rat, he was shown other objects to test for *generalization.* For example, he crawled away and cried at the sight of a rabbit, and he turned away and cried at the sight of a fur coat. But he showed no fear of blocks, paper, or Watson's hairy head, which indicates *discrimination.*

Watson's conditioning of Albert was more of a demonstration than a rigorously controlled experiment. For example, Watson and Rayner did not use a standardized procedure for presenting stimuli, and they sometimes removed Albert's thumb from his mouth, which may have made him cry. Watson was also criticized for not unconditioning Albert's fears before he left the hospital.

Rabbit elicits fear (CR) is an example of generalization.

Although other researchers failed to replicate Watson and Rayner's results, this was the first demonstration that emotional responses could be classically conditioned in humans (Samelson, 1980). Watson's demonstration laid the groundwork for explaining how people can acquire conditioned emotional responses, such as developing a fear of needles or injections.

We've discussed how emotional responses can be conditioned; next, we'll show how conditioned emotional responses can influence a person's behavior.

In the Dentist's Chair

What goes on at the dentist's?

As you sit in the dentist's chair, two interesting psychological factors are at work: the possibility of being classically conditioned and the possibility of perceiving more or less pain (Johnsen et al., 2003).

Earlier, we discussed the likely possibility of being classically conditioned during dental treatment. For example, in the dentist's chair you'll receive unconditioned stimuli (injection, drilling), which elicit unconditioned responses (pain, fear, and anxiety), which, in turn, can be conditioned to a variety of neutral stimuli

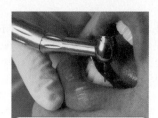

Classical conditioning: smell (CS) plus drilling (UCS) elicits pain (UCR).

(smells, sights, sounds, or images). At the beginning of this module we discussed how Carla's anxiety was conditioned to the smell of the dentist's aftershave lotion (see p. 198).

As we also discussed earlier, pain is somewhat unlike other senses in that the intensity of pain can be increased or decreased by a number of psychological factors, such as your ability to relax or refocus your attention on something else (see p. 112). Now we'll discuss how cultural factors can influence the conditioning of dental fears, which in turn can increase or decrease the visits to dentists in different countries (Milgrom et al., 1994).

Cultural Practices

Which citizens have most dental fears?

As the graph below indicates, the percentage of children reporting high levels of dental fear is considerably greater in the United States and Asia (Singapore and Japan) than in Scandinavia (Norway and Sweden) (Chellappah et al., 1990; Klingberg & Hwang, 1994; Milgrom et al., 1994; Neverlien & Johnsen, 1991).

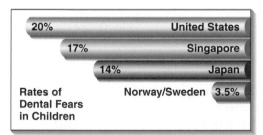

Rates of Dental Fears in Children

United States	20%
Singapore	17%
Japan	14%
Norway/Sweden	3.5%

One reason for cultural differences in rates of dental fear is that the countries have different systems of dental care. In Scandinavian countries, dental care is part of a free, universal health care program available to all citizens. Because it is free and easily available, Scandinavian children tend to receive regular dental care rather than be treated only for dental emergencies. These children view dental treatment as unpleasant but necessary.

In contrast, neither America nor Japan provides free, universal dental coverage. Consequently, some children receive treatment only when there is a serious and painful dental problem. As a result, a child's first dental experience is more painful and something to be avoided. This is an example of how cultural practices influence the "painfulness" of dental treatments.

Origins

When did dental fears develop?

American and Asian adults who reported high rates of dental fears were asked when their fears began. About 66% replied that they acquired their dental fears in childhood or adolescence, often after a painful treatment that was necessitated by a dental emergency (Milgrom et al., 1995; Poulton et al., 1997). These fearful adults reported that the more painful their childhood dental experiences had been, the greater was their fear (Milgrom et al., 1992).

Researchers concluded that the majority of dental fears are acquired in childhood or adolescence, often through classical conditioning. In addition, these fears can keep individuals from asking for or receiving dental treatment for future but necessary dental problems (Abrahamsson et al., 2002).

Effects of Fear

Which citizens most avoid dentists?

Once dental fears are established, about 20–40% of these individuals report avoiding regular checkups or routine dental treatment (graph below). Usually, these individuals seek dental treatment only when they have emergency problems,

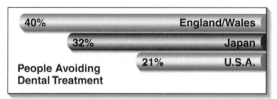

People Avoiding Dental Treatment

England/Wales	40%
Japan	32%
U.S.A.	21%

which tend to involve very painful procedures. As a result, painful emergency dental procedures strengthen their already high level of fears and start a new vicious circle of avoiding dental treatment until the next emergency. From our knowledge of classical conditioning, we know that one way to reduce high levels of dental fear is to receive regular, nonpainful dental checkups and treatment, which will extinguish some of the conditioned emotional responses (Litt et al., 1999).

Based on these data, researchers concluded that cultural differences, such as the kind and frequency of dental treatment in childhood and adolescence, affect both a child's perception of pain and the occurrence of conditioned emotional responses—in this case, fear of dentists (Milgrom et al., 1994).

Next, we'll examine another kind of treatment—chemotherapy for cancer—that also involves classical conditioning and results in a terrible problem—conditioned nausea.

H. **Application** Conditioned Fear & Nausea

Examples of Classical Conditioning

Why do people faint from fear? At the beginning of this module, I related my childhood experience of receiving an injection and then fainting. This one trial of classical conditioning resulted in my fear of needles, which remains with me to this present day.

Conditioned emotional response

My experience illustrates the powerful effect that conditioned emotional responses can have on our behavior. If you still doubt that relatively nonthreatening stimuli (needle, blood) can be conditioned to elicit such a powerful physiological response as fainting, you'll be convinced by the next study (Page, 2003).

Conditioned Emotional Response

About 5–20% of adults report a fear of needles, injections, or seeing blood that often began before the age of 10 (Vogele et al., 2003). Wondering why some people feel faint at the sight of blood, researchers asked 30 such subjects to watch a movie on open-heart surgery as their heart rates were monitored. During the movie, 4 of the 30 subjects unexpectedly fainted.

For example, the graph shows that after 4 minutes of watching the open-heart surgery movie, one subject

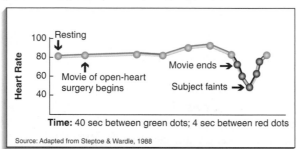

Time: 40 sec between green dots; 4 sec between red dots

Source: Adapted from Steptoe & Wardle, 1988

became so fearful and anxious that his body went into mild shock and he fainted. The reason this subject fainted from simply watching a movie on open-heart surgery was that he had developed a conditioned emotional response, intense fear, to the sight of blood (Steptoe & Wardle, 1988). Intense fear triggers tremendous changes in heart rate and blood pressure that can cause many physiological changes, including fainting.

Classical conditioning can also trigger nausea to a particular odor.

Anticipatory Nausea

At the beginning of this module, we told you about Michelle, who was receiving chemotherapy treatment for breast cancer. One side effect of the powerful anticancer drugs used in chemotherapy is nausea, which may be accompanied by severe vomiting that lasts 6–12 hours.

As Michelle received additional chemotherapy injections, she experienced nausea when she smelled the treatment room or smelled her dish soap, which smelled like the treatment room. Michelle's problem is called anticipatory nausea.

Anticipatory nausea refers to feelings of nausea that are elicited by stimuli associated with nausea-inducing chemotherapy treat-

Anticipatory nausea is an example of classical conditioning.

ments. Patients experience nausea after treatment but also before or in anticipation of their treatment. Researchers believe that conditioned nausea occurs through classical conditioning.

For example, by their fourth injection, 60–70% of the patients who receive chemotherapy experience anticipatory nausea when they encounter smells, sounds, sights, or images related to treatment (Montgomery & Bovbjerg, 1997). Even 1–2 years after treatment ends, patients may continue to experience anticipatory nausea if they encounter cues associated with chemotherapy (Fredrickson et al., 1993). What makes conditioned nausea especially troublesome is that current medication does not always control it (ACS, 2005).

First we'll discuss how conditioned nausea occurs and then how it can be controlled with a nonmedical treatment.

Conditioning Anticipatory Nausea

A few weeks after beginning her chemotherapy, Michelle began to experience anticipatory nausea that was triggered by a number of different stimuli, including the smell of her dish detergent, which smelled similar to the treatment room. Now that you know her situation, perhaps you can identify the terms and explain how classical conditioning occurred.

- **Neutral stimulus** is the smell of the treatment room and her dish detergent, which initially did not cause any nausea.
- **Unconditioned stimulus** is the chemotherapy, which elicits nausea and vomiting.
- **Unconditioned responses** are the nausea and vomiting, which were elicited by chemotherapy, the unconditioned stimulus.

- **Conditioning trials** involve presenting the neutral stimulus, smell of the treatment room (same as her detergent), with the unconditioned stimulus, the chemotherapy.
- **Conditioned stimulus** (smell of the treatment room or detergent), when presented by itself, now elicits the conditioned response (nausea).

Once established, anticipatory nausea can be very difficult to treat and control with drugs (Montgomery & Bovbjerg, 1997). Even after chemotherapy ends, anticipatory nausea may reappear for a while, which is an example of spontaneous recovery.

Dish soap is CS.

However, there is a nonmedical treatment for anticipatory nausea, which is also based on classical conditioning. This treatment is called systematic desensitization, which we'll discuss next.

Can you "uncondition" fearful things?

Because of repeated chemotherapy sessions, Michelle developed anticipatory nausea (right photo), which was not relieved by medication.

She is now going to try a nonmedical treatment called systematic desensitization.

Systematic desensitization **is a procedure based on classical conditioning, in which a person imagines or visualizes fearful or anxiety-evoking stimuli and then immediately uses deep relaxation to overcome the anxiety. Systematic desensitization is a form of counterconditioning because it replaces, or counters, fear and anxiety with relaxation.**

Learning to decrease anxiety through systematic desensitization

Essentially, systematic desensitization is a procedure to "uncondition," or overcome, fearful stimuli by pairing anxiety-provoking thoughts or images with feelings of relaxation. Systematic desensitization was developed by Joseph Wolpe in the early 1950s and has become one of the most frequently used nonmedical therapies for relief of anxiety and fears in both children and adults (M. A. Williams & Gross, 1994). Just as anticipatory nausea is based on Pavlov's classical conditioning, so too is systematic desensitization (Lieberman, 2004).

In Michelle's case, she will try to "uncondition," or override, the anxiety-producing cues of chemotherapy, such as smells and sights, with feelings of relaxation. The procedure for systematic desensitization involves the three steps described below (Wolpe & Lazarus, 1966).

Systematic Desensitization Procedure: Three Steps

Step 1. Learning to relax

Michelle is taught to relax by tensing and relaxing sets of muscles, beginning with the muscles in her toes and continuing up

1st step is learning to relax on cue.

to the muscles in her calves, thighs, back, arms, shoulders, neck, and finally face and forehead. She practices doing this intentional relaxation for about 15 to 20 minutes every day for several weeks.

After learning how to relax her body at will, she goes on to Step 2.

Step 2. Making an anxiety hierarchy

Most Stressful
8. Vomiting
7. Feeling nausea
6. Receiving injection
5. In treatment room
4. Smelling chemicals
3. In waiting room
2. Entering clinic
1. Driving to clinic

2nd step is making a list of items that elicit anxiety.

Michelle makes up a list of 7–12 stressful situations associated with chemotherapy treatment. As shown above, she arranges her list of situations in a hierarchy that goes from least to most stressful. For example, the least stressful situations are driving to and entering the clinic, and the most stressful are nausea and vomiting. Now she's ready for Step 3.

Step 3. Imagining and relaxing

Michelle *first* puts herself into a deeply relaxed state and then vividly imagines the least stressful situation, driving to the clinic. She is told to remain in a relaxed state while imagining this situation. If she becomes anxious or stressed, she is told to stop imagining this situation and return instead to a relaxed state. Once she is sufficiently relaxed, she again imagines driving to the clinic. If she can imagine driving to the clinic while remaining in a relaxed state, she goes to the next stressful situation.

Most Stressful
8. Vomiting
7. Feeling nausea
6. Receiving injection
5. In treatment room
4. Smelling chemicals
3. In waiting room
2. Entering clinic
1. Driving to clinic

3rd step is combining relaxation with items in anxiety hierarchy.

She then imagines entering the clinic, while remaining in a relaxed state. She continues up the anxiety hierarchy, imagining in turn each of the eight stressful stimuli while keeping herself in a relaxed state. At the first sign of feeling anxious, she stops and returns to a relaxed state. After returning to a relaxed state, she continues with this procedure until she reaches the most stressful situation in her anxiety hierarchy.

Effectiveness of Systematic Desensitization

As Michelle associates relaxation with each stressful situation in the hierarchy, she overcomes, or counterconditions, each stimulus. In other words, systematic desensitization can be thought of as using relaxation to get rid of the stressful and anxious feelings that have become associated with the stimuli that are listed in the hierarchy.

Systematic desensitization has been found to be very effective in treating a variety of fearful and anxiety-producing behaviors, including conditioned nausea and fear of blood, injections, snakes, and

speaking in public (Chambless & Ollendick, 2001; Spiegler & Guevremont, 2003).

We have discussed the many sides of classical conditioning, from salivation to fainting, from taste aversion to little Albert's conditioned emotional responses, from bait shyness in rats to dental fears in humans, from anticipatory nausea to systematic desensitization. It's evident that classical conditioning has a considerable influence on many of our thoughts, emotions, and behaviors.

Summary Test

A. Three Kinds of Learning

1. A relatively permanent change in behavior that involves specific stimuli and/or responses that change as a result of experience is a definition of _____. The change in behavior includes both unobservable mental events and observable behavioral responses.

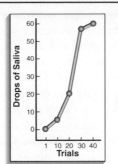

2. Psychologists have identified three different principles that are the basis for three different kinds of learning. One kind of learning can be traced to Pavlov's well-known experiment in which a bell was sounded and then food was placed in a dog's mouth. After a number of trials in which the bell and food were presented, the dog began to salivate to the bell alone. Pavlov called this kind of learning a conditioned reflex, which today is called _____.

3. A second kind of learning grew out of Thorndike's observations of cats learning to escape from a box. To explain a cat's goal-directed behavior of hitting a latch to get food, Thorndike formulated a principle of learning called the (a)_____. This law states that if certain random actions are followed by a pleasurable consequence or reward, such actions are strengthened and will likely occur in the future. Today, the law of effect has become part of the second kind of learning that is called (b)_____.

4. A third kind of learning involves mental processes, such as attention and memory; may be learned through observation or imitation; and may not involve any external rewards or require the person to perform any observable behaviors. This kind of learning is called _____.

B. Procedure: Classical Conditioning

5. Suppose you wanted to classically condition your roommate to salivate at the sight of a psychology textbook. One procedure for establishing classical conditioning would be to present two stimuli close together in time. The presentation of the two stimuli is called a trial. In our example, a typical trial would involve first presenting a psychology textbook, initially called the (a)_____, which does not elicit salivation. A short time later, you would present a piece of brownie, called the (b)_____ stimulus, which elicits salivation. Salivation, an innate, automatic, and involuntary physiological reflex, is called the (c)_____.

6. After giving your roommate about a dozen trials, you observe that, as soon as you show him the psychology text, he begins to salivate. Because the sight of the psychology textbook itself elicits salivation, the psychology text has become a (a)_____. The roommate's salivation at the sight of the psychology book, presented alone, is called the (b)_____. You know that classical conditioning is established when the neutral stimulus becomes the (c)_____ and elicits the (d)_____. Compared to the unconditioned response, the conditioned response is usually similar in appearance but smaller in amount or magnitude.

C. Other Conditioning Concepts

7. The more similar the new stimulus is to the original conditioned stimulus, the stronger or larger the conditioned response will usually be. During classical conditioning, there is a tendency for a stimulus similar to the original conditioned stimulus to elicit a response similar to the conditioned response. This tendency is called _____.

8. During classical conditioning, an organism learns to make a particular response to some stimuli but not to others; this phenomenon is called _____.

9. If a conditioned stimulus is repeatedly presented without the unconditioned stimulus, there is a tendency for the conditioned stimulus to no longer elicit the conditioned response; this phenomenon is called (a)_____. However, if some time later you again presented the psychology text to your roommate without giving him a brownie, he would show salivation, the conditioned response. This recurrence of the conditioned response after it has been extinguished is called (b)_____.

D. Adaptive Value & Uses

10. After receiving an injection, people may develop fear or anxiety in the presence of stimuli associated with the treatment. If we feel fear or anxiety in the presence of some stimulus that precedes a painful or aversive event, we are experiencing a _____.

11. A powerful form of classical conditioning occurs in real life when a neutral stimulus is paired with an unpleasant response, such as nausea or vomiting. The result of this conditioning is called _____. This form of classical conditioning is unusual in two ways: It may be acquired in a single trial and may last a relatively long period of time; and there may be a considerable lapse of time between the presentations of the two stimuli.

12. We now know that animals and humans are biologically prepared to associate certain combinations of conditioned and unconditioned stimuli more easily than others. This phenomenon is called

_____.

13. Classical conditioning of the eye blink reflex, which is a motor response, requires a brain structure called the (a)_____. Acquiring a classically conditioned emotional response, especially involving fear, involves a different brain structure called the (b)_____.

14. The occurrence of salivation in response to the thought, sight, or smell of food is helpful to digestion and shows that classical conditioning has an _____ role or value.

E. Three Explanations

15. According to Pavlov's explanation, classical conditioning occurs because a neural bond or association forms between the conditioned stimulus and unconditioned stimulus so that the conditioned stimulus eventually substitutes for the unconditioned stimulus. Pavlov's explanation is called _____.

16. The explanation that says that classical conditioning occurs because two stimuli (the neutral and unconditioned stimuli) are paired close together in time is called the _____ theory. However, researchers have shown that contiguity or simply pairing stimuli close together does not necessarily produce classical conditioning.

17. The explanation of classical conditioning that says that an organism learns a relationship between two stimuli such that the occurrence of one stimulus predicts the occurrence of the other is called the (a)_____. This theory is supported by the idea that classical conditioning is not usually learned if the unconditioned stimulus appears before the neutral stimulus, a procedure that is called (b)_____.

F. Research Focus: Conditioning Little Albert

18. An emotional response, fear, was classically conditioned in Little Albert by presenting a white rat, which was the 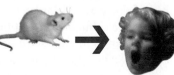 (a)_____, and then making a loud noise, which was the (b)_____; in turn, the loud noise elicited crying, which was the (c)_____. Albert's conditioned emotional response, crying, also occurred in the presence of stimuli

similar to the white rat, such as a rabbit; this phenomenon is called (d)_____. Albert did not cry at the sight of blocks or papers; this phenomenon is called (e)_____. Watson and Rayner were the first to demonstrate that (f)_____ responses could be classically conditioned in humans.

G. Cultural Diversity: Conditioning Dental Fears

19. In the United States and Asia, the percentage of children reporting (a)_____ is considerably greater than in Scandinavia. A likely reason for this difference in dental fears is different (b)_____ practices. The majority of people with high levels of dental fears report that these fears originated in childhood, probably through the occurrence of (c)_____.

H. Application: Conditioned Fear & Nausea

20. During chemotherapy, 60–70% of the patients develop nausea in anticipation of, or when encountering stimuli associated with, the actual treatment. This type of nausea, which is called _____, cannot always be treated with drugs and may persist long after the chemotherapy ends. Researchers believe that conditioned nausea is learned through classical conditioning.

Most Stressful
8. Vomiting
7. Feeling nausea
6. Receiving injection
5. In treatment room
4. Smelling chemicals
3. In waiting room
2. Entering clinic
1. Driving to clinic

21. A nondrug treatment for conditioned nausea involves a procedure based on classical conditioning in which a person imagines or visualizes fearful or anxiety-evoking stimuli and then immediately uses deep (a)_____ to decrease the anxiety associated with these stimuli. This procedure, which is called (b)_____, is a form of counterconditioning because it uses deep relaxation to replace or decrease the fear or anxiety with particular (c)_____ that are arranged in a hierarchy.

Answers: 1. learning; 2. classical conditioning; 3. (a) law of effect, (b) operant conditioning; 4. cognitive learning; 5. (a) neutral stimulus, (b) unconditioned stimulus, (c) unconditioned response; 6. (a) conditioned stimulus, (b) conditioned response, (c) conditioned stimulus, (d) unconditioned response; 7. generalization; 8. discrimination; 9. (a) extinction, (b) spontaneous recovery; 10. conditioned emotional response; 11. taste-aversion learning; 12. preparedness; 13. (a) cerebellum, (b) amygdala; 14. adaptive, or survival; 15. stimulus substitution; 16. contiguity; 17. (a) cognitive perspective, (b) backward conditioning; 18. (a) neutral stimulus, (b) unconditioned stimulus, (c) unconditioned response, (d) generalization, (e) discrimination, (f) conditioned emotional; 19. (a) dental fears, (b) cultural, (c) classical conditioning; 20. anticipatory nausea; 21. (a) relaxation, (b) systematic desensitization, (c) stimuli or situations

Critical Thinking

Can Beliefs Change Your Brain?

Coke® and Pepsi® are almost identical chemically and physically (they are carbonated, brown in color, and have similar ingredients), yet people usually have a strong preference for one over the other. Can this preference be explained simply as a matter of difference in taste, or is there something else occurring in the brain that makes us choose Coke over Pepsi, or vice versa?

Samuel McClure and his colleagues examined how cultural messages may be more influential than taste in people's preferences for cola. In this study, subjects were placed into a fMRI machine with a tube in their mouth that delivered small amounts of cola while their brain activity was measured. In one condition, the drinks were "anonymous"; that is, one drink had Coke and the other Pepsi, but subjects were not told which they were drinking. In the second condition, the drinks were "semianonymous," which means one of the two drinks was labeled either Coke or Pepsi, but the second drink was unlabeled and was secretly the same cola as the labeled drink. In both conditions, either flashes of light or pictures of a Coke or Pepsi can (which informed subjects of the cola they were drinking) preceded the tastes of cola. In addition to subjects being unaware of the contents of the unlabeled drinks, researchers who analyzed the data did not know which drink was given to subjects.

Researchers first examined cola preference and brain response when colas were presented anonymously. Results showed that when subjects did not know which brand of cola they were drinking, they were equally as likely to choose Coke or Pepsi as their favorite. Also, the part of the brain that responds to rewards or pleasure was activated as they drank either cola.

Cola preference and brain response were also examined when subjects had knowledge about which cola they were drinking. When one cup was labeled Coke and the other was unlabeled, subjects preferred Coke, even though the unlabeled drink was also Coke. The same was not true for Pepsi. Also, when subjects knew they were drinking Coke, not only was there increased activity in the part of the brain that responds to rewards, but also memory-related brain regions involved in recalling cultural influences were activated.

Researchers concluded that when subjects knew they were drinking Coke, their brain responded not only to flavor but also to other things it knows about the product. These results suggest that the visual images and marketing messages about brands of cola have influenced the brains of cola drinkers in a way that likely alters taste perception or preference. (Adapted from McClure et al., 2004a, 2004b)

Questions

1. How does an fMRI measure brain activity?

2. What is the name of this research approach in which neither the subjects nor the researchers knew who received which kind of cola?

3. Why was the part of the brain that responds to rewards activated?

4. Why were the memory-related brain regions activated when subjects knew they were drinking Coke, but not when subjects knew they were drinking Pepsi?

5. How might these results be useful to companies interested in developing a cola to compete with Coke or other products similar to those that have strong brand images?

1. In this brain scan, nonharmful radio frequencies are used to measure the activity of specific neurons that are functioning during various tasks, such as tasting and making decisions.
2. In studying effects of chemicals or drugs, researchers use a double-blind procedure (pp. 37 and 111), in which neither the subjects nor researchers know who got which treatment. The double-blind procedure greatly reduces error and bias that can come from beliefs or expectations of either subjects or researchers.
3. The reward/pleasure center of the brain is activated when a person eats a favorite food, has sex, and does other pleasurable activities, such as drinking a highly sugared beverage like Coke or Pepsi.
4. One explanation for why memory-related brain regions involved in recalling cultural influences were activated only when subjects knew they were drinking Coke is the brand image of Coke may be more culturally familiar than that of Pepsi.
5. Companies should be cautious about developing a cola similar to Coke or other products similar to favored brands because it will take a lot of effort and expense to have people buy a new product that competes with an existing one with a strong brand.

Links to Learning

Key Terms/Key People

adaptive value, 200

anticipatory nausea, 206

anxiety hierarchy, 207

classical conditioning, 196

cognitive learning, 196

cognitive perspective, 202

conditioned emotional response, 201

conditioned response, 197

conditioned stimulus, 197

conditioning anticipatory nausea, 206

conditioning Little Albert, 204

contiguity theory, 202

cultural effects on dental fear, 205

dental fear, 205

discrimination, 199

establishing classical conditioning, 197–198

extinction, 199

fear of injections, 206

fear of needles, 206

generalization, 199

law of effect, 196

learning, 195

learning to relax, 207

neutral stimulus, 197

one-trial learning, 200

operant conditioning, 196

Pavlov's experiment, 197

preparedness, 200

selecting stimulus and response, 197–198

spontaneous recovery, 199

stimulus substitution, 202

survival value, 201

systematic desensitization, 207

systematic desensitization procedure, 207

taste-aversion learning, 200

taste-aversion learning in coyotes, 200

taste-aversion learning in humans, 200

testing for conditioning, 197–198

unconditioned response (UCR), 197

unconditioned stimulus (UCS), 197

Learning Activities

- **POWERSTUDY FOR INTRODUCTION TO PSYCHOLOGY 4.0**
  by Tom Doyle and Rod Plotnik

  SuperModule: Check out "Classical Conditioning" on **PowerStudy.** It includes complete paragraph-by-paragraph explanations of all content using fully-narrated animations and graphics. An onscreen toolbar allows immediate access to text, text outline, and module glossary with notetaking and printing capabilities. This module also includes:
  - Videos—Imbedded videos discuss taste aversion in wolves and present a historic 1920 video of Watson's Little Albert.
  - A multitude of animations designed to help you understand classical and operant conditioning and cognitive learning. Get help with concepts like the difference between conditioned and unconditioned responses and stimuli.
  - A test of your knowledge using an interactive version of the Summary Test on pages 208 and 209. Also access related quizzing—true/false, multiple choice, and matching.
  - An interactive version of the Critical Thinking exercise "Can Beliefs Change Your Brain?" on page 210.
  - Key terms, a chapter outline, and hotlinked websites.

- **CengageNOW**
  academic.cengage.com/login

  Need help studying? This site is your one-stop study shop.
  Take a Pre-Test and CengageNOW will generate a Personalized Study Plan based on your test results. The Study Plan will identify the topics you need to review and direct you to online resources to help you master those topics. You can then take a Post-Test to determine the concepts you have mastered and what you still need to work on.

- **INTRODUCTION TO PSYCHOLOGY BOOK COMPANION WEBSITE**
  academic.cengage.com/psychology/plotnik

  Visit your book companion website where you will find more resources to help you study. At this site, you will find Learning Objectives, Internet Exercises, quizzing, flash cards, and a pronunciation glossary.

- **STUDY GUIDE and WEBTUTOR**

  Check the corresponding module in your Study Guide for effective student tips and help learning the material presented. Also go to **academic.cengage.com/webtutor** for an interactive version of the Study Guide features.

Study Questions

*A. **Three Kinds of Learning**—Can you recall situations in which you have experienced each of the three kinds of learning? (**Suggested answer page 624**)

*B. **Procedure: Classical Conditioning**—How do you explain why your heart pounds when you hear the words "There will be a test next class"? (**Suggested answer page 624**)

C. **Other Conditioning Concepts**—If a child were bitten by a small brown dog, can you predict what other animals the child would fear?

D. **Adaptive Value & Uses**—Using the terms and procedures of classical conditioning, can you explain how a person might develop a fear of flying?

E. **Three Explanations**—How would you explain why your cat runs into the kitchen and salivates each time you open the refrigerator door?

F. **Research Focus: Conditioning Little Albert**—What happens when you look into your rear-view mirror and see a police car's flashing lights?

G. **Cultural Diversity: Conditioning Dental Fears**—As a parent, how can you decrease the chances that your child will become fearful of dental treatment?

*H. **Application: Conditioned Fear & Nausea**—How would systematic desensitization be used to help reduce a student's test anxiety? (**Suggested answer page 624**)

*These questions are answered in Appendix B.

MODULE 10
Operant & Cognitive Approaches

 PowerStudy 4.0™ Complete Module

Learning 45 Commands

How did Bart become a movie star? It was an unusual movie for two reasons. First, there was almost no dialogue: Human actors spoke only 657 words. Second, the star of the movie was a nonspeaking, nonhuman, 12-year-old, 10-foot-tall, 1,800-pound, enormous brown Kodiak bear named Bart (shown on the left). Bart is one of the world's largest land-dwelling carnivores and can, with one swipe of his massive 12-inch paw, demolish anything in his path. Yet, in the movie, there was big bad Bart, sitting peacefully on his haunches, cradling a small bear cub in his arms. "So what?" you might say, but what you don't know is that, in the wild, a Kodiak bear normally kills and eats any cub it encounters.

Because Bart was found as a cub and raised by a human trainer, Bart grew to act more like an overgrown teddy bear than a natural-born killer. For his role in the movie *The Bear,* Bart learned to perform 45 behaviors on cue, such as sitting, running, standing up, roaring, and, most difficult of all, cradling a teddy bear, which is not what an adult bear does in the wild.

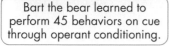

Bart the bear learned to perform 45 behaviors on cue through operant conditioning.

The training procedure seems deceptively simple: Each time Bart performed a behavior on cue, the trainer, Doug Seus, gave Bart an affectionate back scratch, an ear rub, or a juicy apple or pear. For example, when the trainer raised his arms high in the air, it was the signal for Bart to sit and hold the teddy bear. After Bart correctly performed this behavior, Doug would give him a reward. After Bart learned to perform all these behaviors with a stuffed teddy bear, a live bear cub was substituted and the scene was filmed for the movie (Cerone, 1989).

Bart learned to perform 45 behaviors on cue through a kind of learning called operant conditioning.

Operant conditioning, **also called instrumental conditioning, is a kind of learning in which an animal or human performs some behavior, and the following consequence (reward or punishment) increases or decreases the chance that an animal or human will again perform that same behavior.**

For example, if Bart performed a particular behavior, such as picking up a teddy bear, the consequence that followed—getting a rewarding apple—increased the chance that Bart would again pick up the teddy bear. Because of what Bart learned through operant conditioning, he starred in 20 movies and became the highest paid animal actor, making about $10,000 a day (Brennan, 1997). That's a salary that most of us would be very happy to bear!

Operant conditioning seems rather straightforward. You perform an action or operate on your environment, such as studying hard. The consequence of your studying, such as how well you do on exams, increases or decreases the likelihood that you will perform the same behavior—studying hard—in the future.

Besides learning by having your behaviors rewarded or punished, you can also learn in a very different way.

Learning to Skateboard

What did Tony Hawk learn from just watching? In operant conditioning, the learning process is out in the open: Bart performs an observable behavior (holds a teddy bear), which is followed by an observable consequence (gets an apple). But there is another kind of learning that involves unobservable mental processes and unobservable rewards that you may give yourself. This kind of learning, called cognitive learning, is partly how Tony Hawk learned to skate.

Tony Hawk is recognized as the greatest skateboarder of all time. But Tony did not always have a talent for skating. When Tony was 9 years old, his brother gave him his old skateboard. Tony had seen his brother skate before, and he tried to skate just like him. Tony then visited a skate park, where he was awed by how quickly skaters went up, down, and around walls. He was also amazed at how they daringly spun while high up in the air. Tony wanted to be as talented as the skaters at the park, and he went on to practice every chance he had. When Tony was asked why he enjoyed skating as a child, he replied, "I liked that no one was telling me how to do it" (CBS News, 2004). Instead, Tony learned by observing how his friends and professionals skated at the park: "I would watch them and try to learn from them. I'd imitate them" (Hawk, 2002, p. 30). On his own initiative and without any special guidance, Tony learned to skate by imitating others.

The process Tony used to learn skateboarding is very different from the operant conditioning procedure used to teach Bart new behaviors. During operant conditioning, Bart performed observable behaviors that were influenced by observable consequences. In comparison, Tony learned how to skateboard through observation

Tony Hawk learned to skateboard partly from watching others.

and imitation, which involved unobservable mental processes and is called cognitive learning. We'll discuss cognitive learning later in this module.

What's Coming

In the first half of this module, we'll discuss the history and procedure of operant conditioning, how operant conditioning differs from classical conditioning, how consequences or reinforcers work, and other examples of operant conditioning. In the second half of this module, we'll explain the history of cognitive learning, the theory behind observational learning, and the role of insight learning.

We'll begin with an important study that involved a cat, a puzzle box, and a smelly fish.

A. Operant Conditioning

How did Bart become a movie star?

We told you how a trainer used operant conditioning to teach Bart to perform 45 different behaviors on cue. Operant conditioning has now been applied to many different settings, such as training animals to perform, training children to use the potty, stopping retarded children from injuring themselves, and helping autistic children learn social behaviors. However, the discovery of operant behavior involved two different researchers who worked in two different laboratories on two different kinds of problems. So that you can appreciate the thinking that led to operant conditioning, we'll visit the laboratories of the two important researchers—E. L. Thorndike and B. F. Skinner.

Thorndike's Law of Effect

E. L. THORNDIKE (1874–1949)

It's the late 1800s, and we're in the laboratory of E. L. Thorndike, who is interested in animal intelligence—specifically, in measuring their capacity for reasoning.

Unlike pet owners who assume from anecdotal observations that their animals are intelligent, Thorndike devised a simple but clever way to measure reasoning in a more objective way. He built a series of puzzle boxes from which a cat could escape by learning to make a specific response, such as pulling a string or pressing a bar. Outside the puzzle box was a reward for escaping— a piece of fish.

We watch Thorndike place a cat in the puzzle box and record its escape time. After Thorndike graphs the data (graph below), we see a gradual lessening in the time needed to escape. Notice that on the first trial the cat needed over 240 seconds to hit the escape latch, but by the last trial, the cat hits the escape latch in less than 60 seconds.

Thorndike explains that, with repeated trials, the cat spends more time around the latch, which increases the chances of finding and

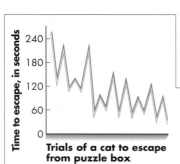

Trials of a cat to escape from puzzle box

Law of effect: In escaping puzzle box, cat's successful responses are strengthened and this results in quicker escape times.

hitting the latch and more quickly escaping to get the fish. To explain why a cat's random trial-and-error behaviors gradually turned into efficient, goal-directed behaviors, Thorndike formulated the law of effect.

The *law of effect* states that behaviors followed by positive consequences are strengthened, while behaviors followed by negative consequences are weakened.

Thorndike's (1898) findings were significant because they suggested that the law of effect was a basic law of learning and provided an objective procedure to study it. Thorndike's emphasis on studying the consequences of goal-directed behavior was further developed and expanded by B. F. Skinner.

Skinner's Operant Conditioning

B. F. SKINNER (1904–1990)

It's the 1930s, and we're in the laboratory of B. F. Skinner, who is interested in analyzing ongoing behaviors of animals. Skinner explains that Thorndike's law of effect is useful, since it describes how animals are rewarded for making particular responses. However, in order to analyze ongoing behaviors, you must have an objective way to measure them. Skinner's clever solution is a unit of behavior he calls an operant response (Skinner, 1938).

An *operant response* is a response that can be modified by its consequences and is a meaningful unit of ongoing behavior that can be easily measured.

For example, suppose that out of curiosity Bart picks up a teddy bear. His picking up the teddy bear is an example of an operant response because Bart is acting or operating on the environment. The consequence of his picking up the teddy bear is that he receives an apple, which is a desirable effect. This desirable effect modifies his response by increasing the chances that Bart will repeat the same response.

By measuring or recording operant responses, Skinner can analyze animals' ongoing behaviors during learning. He calls this kind of learning *operant conditioning,* which focuses on how consequences (rewards or punishments) affect behaviors.

A simple example of operant conditioning occurs when a rat in an experimental box accidentally presses a bar. If the bar press is followed by food, this consequence increases the chance that the rat will press the bar again. As the rat presses the bar more times, more food follows, which in turn increases the chances that the rat will continue to press the bar (indicated by the rise of the blue line in the figure below).

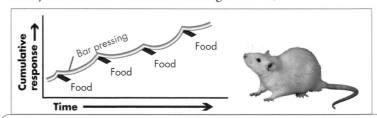

Rat learns to press a bar, which increases the chances of getting food.

Using his newly developed procedure of operant conditioning, B. F. Skinner spent the next 50 years exploring and analyzing learning in rats, pigeons, schoolchildren, and adults.

The 1920s and 1930s gave learning a mighty jolt with the discovery of two general principles—Pavlov's classical conditioning and Skinner's operant conditioning. For the first time, psychologists had two methods to analyze learning processes in an objective way.

Now we'll examine Skinner's ingenious procedure for operant conditioning in more detail.

Why does a rat press a bar?

A rat may initially press a bar out of curiosity, and whether it presses the bar again depends on the consequences. To show how consequences can affect behavior, imagine that you are looking over Skinner's shoulder as he places a rat into a box.

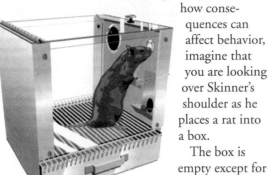

Skinner box contains bar and food cup.

The box is empty except for a bar jutting out from one side and an empty food cup below and to the side of the bar (above figure). This box, called a *Skinner box,* is automated to record the animal's bar presses and deliver food pellets. The Skinner box is an efficient way to study how an animal's ongoing behaviors may be modified by changing the consequences of what happens after a bar press.

As you watch, Skinner explains that the rat is a good subject for operant conditioning because it can use its front paws to manipulate objects, such as a bar, and it has a tendency to explore its environment, which means that it will eventually find the bar, touch it, or even press it.

Skinner goes on to explain the following three factors that are involved in operantly conditioning a rat to press a bar in the Skinner box.

1 The rat has not been fed for some hours so that it will be active and more likely to eat the food reward. A hungry rat tends to roam restlessly about, sniffing at whatever it finds.

2 The goal is to condition the rat to press the bar. By pressing the bar, the rat operates on its environment; thus, this response is called an *operant response.*

3 Skinner explains that a naive rat does not usually waltz over and press the bar. In conditioning a rat to press a bar, Skinner will use a procedure called shaping.

Shaping **is a procedure in which an experimenter successively reinforces behaviors that lead up to or approximate the desired behavior.**

For example, if the desired behavior is pressing the bar, here's how shaping works.

Shaping: Facing the Bar

Skinner places a white rat into the (Skinner) box, closes the door, and watches the rat through a one-way mirror. At first, the rat wanders around the back of the box, but when it turns and faces the bar, Skinner releases a food pellet that makes a noise as it drops into the food cup. The rat hears the pellet drop, approaches the food cup, then sees, sniffs, and eats the pellet. After eating, the rat moves away to explore the box. But, as soon as the rat turns and faces the bar, Skinner releases another pellet. The rat hears the noise, goes to the food cup, sniffs, and eats the pellet. Shaping is going well.

Shaping: Touching the Bar

As shaping continues, Skinner decides to reinforce the rat only when it actually moves toward the bar. Skinner waits and as soon as the rat faces and then moves toward the bar, Skinner releases another pellet. After eating the pellet, the rat wanders a bit but soon returns to the bar and actually sniffs it. A fourth pellet immediately drops into the cup, and the rat eats it. When the rat places one paw on the bar, a fifth pellet drops into the cup. Notice how Skinner has shaped the rat to spend all its time near the bar.

Shaping: Pressing the Bar

As soon as the rat actually puts its paws on the bar, Skinner releases a pellet. After eating, the rat puts its paws back on the bar and gets a pellet. Now Skinner waits until the rat puts its paws on the bar and actually happens to press down, which releases another pellet. Soon, the rat is pressing the bar over and over to get pellets. Notice how Skinner reinforced the rat's behaviors that led up to or approximated the desired behavior of bar pressing.

Immediate Reinforcement

Depending on the rat and the trainer's experience, it may take from minutes to an hour to shape a rat to press a bar. Skinner explains that in shaping behavior, the food pellet, or *reinforcer,* should follow *immediately* after the desired behavior. By following immediately, the reinforcer is associated with the desired behavior and not with some other behavior that just happens to occur. If the reinforcer is delayed, the animal may be reinforced for some undesired or superstitious behavior.

Superstitious behavior **is a behavior that increases in frequency because its occurrence is accidentally paired with the delivery of a reinforcer.**

When I (R.P.) was a graduate student, I conditioned my share of superstitious rat behaviors, such as making them turn in circles or stand up instead of pressing the bar. That's because I accidentally but immediately reinforced a rat after it performed the wrong behavior.

Humans, especially professional baseball players, report a variety of superstitious behaviors that were accidentally reinforced by getting a hit. For example, a five-time batting champion (Wade Boggs) ate chicken every day he played, allowed no one else to touch his bats, and believed each bat had a certain number of hits. Once a batter's superstitious behaviors are reinforced, especially by getting a big hit or home run, superstitious behaviors tend to persist and can be very difficult to eliminate. You probably have some of your own!

Next, we'll discuss some interesting examples of operant conditioning in very young humans.

A. Operant Conditioning

Have you been operantly conditioned?

Without realizing it, you may be performing a wide range of behaviors learned through operant conditioning. For example, operant conditioning was involved if you learned to put money into a jukebox to hear music, drive through a yellow traffic light to avoid stopping, study for hours to get good grades, or give flowers to your honey to see him or her smile. And you may continually perform

these behaviors because they are followed by reinforcers that increase the chances that you will perform these same behaviors again. To help you better understand how operant conditioning works, we'll discuss how its procedures and principles have been used by parents to solve two relatively common problems: getting young children to use the toilet and to stop refusing to eat a wide variety of healthy foods.

Toilet Training

Imagine that you are a parent of 3-year-old Sheryl, who is physically mature enough to begin toilet training. Here's how operant conditioning techniques can be applied to teach toilet training.

1. Target behavior. The target behavior or goal is for Sheryl to urinate in the toilet.

4 steps in toilet training

2. Preparation. Before training begins, put all of Sheryl's toys away so that she will not be distracted. Then give her a large glass of apple juice, so that she will have to urinate soon.

3. Reinforcers. Select reinforcers, which can be candy, verbal praise, or a hug. Each time Sheryl performs or emits a desired behavior, you immediately reinforce it. The reinforcer increases the likelihood that the behavior will be repeated.

4. Shaping. Just as Skinner used the shaping procedure in conditioning a rat to press a bar, you can use a similar shaping procedure in conditioning Sheryl to use the toilet. Each time Sheryl performs a behavior that leads to the target behavior (using the toilet), give her a treat, verbal praise, or a hug. For instance, when Sheryl says that she has to go potty, say, "That's great." When Sheryl enters the bathroom, say, "What a good girl." When she lowers her pants by herself, say, "You're doing really well." After Sheryl urinates into the toilet, give her a big hug and perhaps a treat.

Mothers who were supervised as they used this training procedure needed 4–18 hours to toilet train their 2- to 3-year-olds (Berk & Patrick, 1990; Matson & Ollendick, 1977). However, children vary in when they are ready to begin toilet training and operant conditioning. Researchers advise that "in most cases there's no clear benefit to starting training before 24 to 27 months and in fact kids who start early often take longer to finish" (N. Blum, 2003).

Another difficulty parents face is when children eat only one or two favorite foods and refuse all others.

Food Refusal

Some young children with no medical problems may develop a habit of eating only certain foods and refusing all others, which may result in having an unhealthy diet or low weight (Patel et al., 2002). Researchers taught parents how to use the principles of operant conditioning to overcome food refusal in their young children.

1. Target behavior. The target behavior or goal was for the child to taste, chew, and eat a food (usually fruits or vegetables) that she or he has persistently refused to eat.

2. Preparation. Researchers first showed mothers how to shape and reinforce target behaviors. Next, each mother shaped the target behavior in her child in the home setting.

3. Reinforcers. Each time the child performed or emitted a target behavior, the mother immediately reinforced the child with a positive reinforcer, such as praise, attention, or a smile.

4. Shaping. The shaping procedure consisted of having the child notice the food and let it be placed in his or her mouth, letting the child taste the food, and, finally, having the child chew and swallow the food.

The graph below explains and shows the success of using operant conditioning to overcome food refusal in young children (Werle et al., 1993).

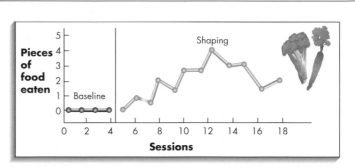

Baseline: During these four sessions, the mother offered nonpreferred food to her child, who refused the food each time.

Shaping: During these sessions, the mother shaped the child to accept nonpreferred food by giving praise, attention, and smiles each time her child made a response that was similar to or approximated the target behavior (chewing and swallowing food). Shaping proved effective in overcoming the child's habit of food refusal. Compare the child's food refusal during baseline to that during shaping sessions.

Notice that the same principles of operant conditioning apply whether the goal is to condition a child to use the potty, to overcome food refusal, or to train Bart the bear to pick up and hold a teddy bear.

Next, we'll compare the principles of operant and classical conditioning.

Operant Versus Classical Conditioning

How are they different?

Earlier in this module, we discussed how Bart the bear was operantly conditioned to hold a teddy bear—something he would never do in the wild. As you may remember from Module 9, we discussed how Sam the dog was classically conditioned to salivate to the sound of a bell—something he would not

Bart—classically or operantly conditioned?

usually do. Although both operant and classical conditioning lead to learning, they have very different procedures and principles, which may be a little confusing. We'll try to clear up any confusion by doing a side-by-side comparison of the principles and procedures of operant and classical conditioning by using the same subject, Bart, one of the world's largest subjects.

Operant Conditioning

1 Goal. The goal of operant conditioning is to *increase or decrease the rate* of some response, which usually involves shaping. In Bart's case, the goal was to increase his rate of holding a teddy bear.

2 Voluntary response. Bart's behavior of holding a teddy bear is a voluntary response because he can perform it at will. Bart must first perform a voluntary response before getting a reward.

3 Emitted response. Bart voluntarily performs or emits some response, which Skinner called the operant response (holding teddy bear). Skinner used the term *emit* to indicate that the organism acts or operates on the environment. In most cases, animals and humans are shaped to emit the desired responses.

4 Contingent on behavior. Bart's performance of the desired response depends on, or is *contingent* on, the consequences, or what happens next. For example, each time Bart holds the teddy bear, the consequence is that he receives an apple. The apple, which is a reward (reinforcer), increases the chances that Bart will perform the desired response in the future.

The reinforcer must occur *immediately after* the desired response. In Bart's case, the reinforcer (apple) would be given immediately after Bart holds the teddy bear. If the reinforcer occurs too late, the result may be the conditioning of unwanted or superstitious responses.

5 Consequences. An animal or human's performance of some behavior is dependent or contingent on its *consequences*—that is, on what happens next. For example, the consequence of Bart's picking up and holding a teddy bear was to get an apple.

Thus, in operant conditioning, an animal or human learns that performing or *emitting* some behavior is followed by a *consequence* (reward or punishment), which, in turn, increases or decreases the chances of performing that behavior again.

Classical Conditioning

1 Goal. The goal of classical conditioning is to create a new response to a *neutral stimulus*. In Bart's case, he will make a new response, salivation, to the sound of a horn, which is the neutral stimulus because it does not usually cause Bart to salivate.

2 Involuntary response. Salivation is an example of a *physiological reflex*. Physiological reflexes (salivation, eye blink) are triggered or elicited by some stimulus and therefore called involuntary responses.

3 Elicited response. As Bart eats an apple, it will trigger the involuntary physiological reflex of salivation. Thus, eating the apple, which is called the *unconditioned stimulus*, triggers or elicits an involuntary reflex response, salivation, which is called the *unconditioned response*.

4 Conditioned response. Bart was given repeated trials during which the neutral stimulus (horn's sound) was presented and followed by the unconditioned stimulus (apple). After repeated trials, Bart learned a relationship between the two stimuli: The horn's sound is followed by an apple. The horn's sound, or neutral stimulus, becomes the *conditioned stimulus* when its sound alone, before the occurrence of the apple, elicits salivation, which is the *conditioned response*.

For best results, the neutral stimulus is presented slightly before the unconditioned stimulus. If the unconditioned stimulus is presented before the neutral stimulus, this is called *backward conditioning* and produces little if any conditioning.

5 Expectancy. According to the *cognitive perspective* of classical conditioning, an animal or human learns a predictable relationship between, or develops an expectancy about, the neutral and unconditioned stimuli. This means Bart learned to *expect* that the neutral stimulus (horn's sound) is always followed by the unconditioned stimulus (apple). Thus, in classical conditioning, the animal or human learns a *predictable relationship* between stimuli.

One major difference between operant and classical conditioning is that in operant conditioning, the performance of some response depends on its consequence (rewards or punishment). We'll discuss the effects of different kinds of consequences next.

B. Reinforcers

Why are consequences important?

Notice where the man is sitting as he saws off a tree limb. His behavior illustrates a key principle of operant conditioning, which is that *consequences are contingent on behavior.* In this case, the man will fall on his head (consequence) if he cuts off the tree limb (behavior). Furthermore, this consequence will make the tree trimmer think twice before repeating this stupid behavior. Thus, consequences affect behavior, and in operant conditioning, there are two kinds of consequences—reinforcement and punishment.

There are serious consequences to this man's behavior!

Reinforcement is a consequence that occurs after a behavior and increases the chance that the behavior will occur again.

For example, one of the main reasons you study hard for exams is to get good grades (reinforcement). The consequence of getting a good grade increases the chances that you'll study hard for future exams.

Punishment is a consequence that occurs after a behavior and decreases the chance that the behavior will occur again.

For example, one high school used punishment to reduce students' absentee rates. Students who got more than eight unexcused absences lost very desirable privileges (no football games, no prom). In this case, punishing consequences decreased from 15% to 4% the chance of students playing hookey from school (Chavez, 1994).

Sometimes reinforcement and punishment are used together to control some behavior, as was done in treating a serious behavioral disorder called pica.

Pica is a behavioral disorder, often seen in individuals with mental retardation, that involves eating inedible objects or unhealthy substances. This can result in serious physical problems, including lead poisoning, intestinal blockage, and parasites.

Here's an example of how both reinforcement and punishment were used to treat an adolescent who suffered from pica.

CHANGING THE CONSEQUENCES

Walt was 15 years old and suffered from profound retardation. One of Walt's problems was pica, which included eating bits of paper and clothing, metal and plastic objects, and especially paint chips, from which he had gotten lead poisoning.

To control his pica, Walt was given a tray containing nonfood items (fake paint chips made from flour) and food items (crackers). Each time Walt chose a food item, he received a reinforcement—verbal praise. When Walt chose a paint chip, he received a mild punishment—having his face washed for 20 seconds. The graph below shows how the consequences (reinforcement or punishment) greatly modified Walt's pica behavior (C. R. Johnson et al., 1994).

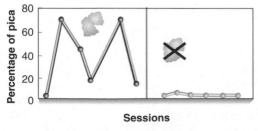

Baseline: During these sessions, Walt chose the nonfood items 10–80% of the time. Compare the baseline with training sessions.

Training: During these sessions, Walt was reinforced with praise for choosing food items and punished with face washing for choosing nonfood items. These consequences greatly modified his behaviors so that he chose primarily food items.

In this study, reinforcement and punishment proved an effective combination to treat a potentially dangerous problem. Next, we'll discuss two kinds of reinforcements.

How are an apple and an "F" alike?

Although getting an apple and getting a grade of "F" seem very different, they are both consequences that can increase the occurrence of certain behaviors. There are two kinds of reinforcements, or consequences—positive and negative—that increase the occurrence of behaviors.

POSITIVE REINFORCEMENT

Immediately after Bart the bear emitted or performed a behavior (holding a teddy bear), the trainer gave him an apple to increase the likelihood of his repeating that behavior. This situation is an example of positive reinforcement.

Positive reinforcement refers to the presentation of a stimulus that increases the probability that a behavior will occur again.

A *positive reinforcer* is a stimulus that increases the likelihood that a response will occur again.

For example, if you ask a friend for money and get it, the money is a positive reinforcer that will increase the chances of your asking again. There's a second kind of reinforcement, called negative reinforcement.

NEGATIVE REINFORCEMENT

If you have a headache and take an aspirin to get rid of it, your response of taking an aspirin is an example of negative reinforcement.

Negative reinforcement refers to an aversive (unpleasant) stimulus whose removal increases the likelihood that the preceding response will occur again.

If taking an aspirin removes your headache (aversive or unpleasant stimulus), then your response of taking an aspirin is negatively reinforced because it removes the headache and thus increases the chances of your taking an aspirin in the future. Don't be confused by the fact that both positive and negative reinforcers *increase* the frequency of the responses they follow.

Besides positive and negative reinforcers, there are also primary reinforcers, such as food, and secondary reinforcers, such as money and coupons.

How are chocolate and a coupon alike?

A student might repeat a behavior, such as study, because the consequence is food, a primary reinforcer, or be quiet on the school bus because the consequence is a coupon, a secondary reinforcer.

PRIMARY REINFORCERS

If you made yourself study for 2 hours before rewarding yourself with chocolate, you would be using a primary reinforcer.

Food: primary reinforcer

A *primary reinforcer* is a stimulus, such as food, water, or sex, that is innately satisfying and requires no learning on the part of the subject to become pleasurable.

Primary reinforcers, such as eating, drinking, or having sex, are unlearned and innately pleasurable. Brain scans (p. 70) showed that these activities, including eating chocolate, activate the brain's built-in or inherited reward/pleasure center (Begley, 2001; D. Small, 2001). Although brain scans were discovered after Skinner, they have proven him right: Primary reinforcers are innately satisfying and require no training because they automatically activate the brain's built-in reward/pleasure center. In our example, chocolate is a primary reinforcer for studying. However, many behaviors are aided or maintained by secondary reinforcers.

SECONDARY REINFORCERS

A school bus driver used a secondary reinforcer when he gave each child a coupon good for a pizza if he or she was quiet on the bus. A coupon is an example of a secondary reinforcer.

A *secondary reinforcer* is any stimulus that has acquired its reinforcing power through experience; secondary reinforcers are learned, such as by being paired with primary reinforcers or other secondary reinforcers.

Coupons, money, grades, and praise are examples of secondary reinforcers because their value is learned or acquired through experience (LeBlanc et al., 2000). For example, children learned that coupons were valuable because they could be redeemed for pizza. The coupons became secondary reinforcers that encouraged children to choose a seat quickly and sit quietly so that the driver could get rolling in 5 minutes (George, 1995). Many of our behaviors are increased or maintained by secondary reinforcers.

Coupons, or secondary reinforcers, encourage children's good behaviors.

Unlike primary and secondary reinforcers, which are consequences that increase behaviors, punishment has a very different effect.

Are there different kinds of punishment?

It is helpful to distinguish between positive and negative punishment.

Positive punishment refers to presenting an aversive (unpleasant) stimulus (such as spanking) after a response. The aversive stimulus decreases the chances that the response will recur.

Negative punishment refers to removing a reinforcing stimulus (a child's allowance) after a response. This removal decreases the chances that the response will recur.

Both positive and negative punishment function as "stop signs"; they stop or decrease the occurrence of a behavior. We'll discuss negative punishment in the Application section. Here, we'll explain how positive punishment was used to treat a serious disorder called self-injurious behavior.

Self-injurious behavior refers to serious and sometimes life-threatening physical damage that a person inflicts on his or her own body; this may include body or head banging, biting, kicking, poking ears or eyes, pulling hair, or intense scratching.

About 8–14% of mentally retarded individuals who live in large residential treatment facilities engage in self-injurious behavior (D. E. Williams et al., 1993). Here's an example of a treatment program that used positive punishment.

POSITIVE PUNISHMENT

Since all other treatments had failed, the State Committee for Behavior Therapy approved a program of using positive punishment to treat

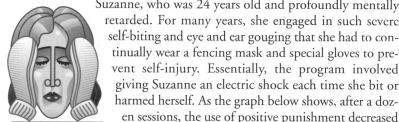

She had to wear special gloves so she wouldn't injure herself.

Suzanne, who was 24 years old and profoundly mentally retarded. For many years, she engaged in such severe self-biting and eye and ear gouging that she had to continually wear a fencing mask and special gloves to prevent self-injury. Essentially, the program involved giving Suzanne an electric shock each time she bit or harmed herself. As the graph below shows, after a dozen sessions, the use of positive punishment decreased Suzanne's self-injurious behaviors by 99%, to almost zero. After 69 treatment sessions, Suzanne's protective face mask and gloves were removed, and for the first time in 15 years, Suzanne began to feed herself, perform personal care, and refrain from self-injury (D. E. Williams et al., 1993). We'll discuss the pros and cons of using punishment in the Application section on page 233.

Self-Injurious Behaviors per Minute	
Before treatment	9.3
After punishment	0.07

Before punishment is used, other nonpunishment treatments based on operant conditioning are always tried. For example, some self-injurious behaviors decreased if the therapist gave attention (reinforcement) only when the patient stopped engaging in injurious behaviors or if the therapist reinforced the patient for performing particular noninjurious behaviors, such as playing games or eating candy (Olson & Houlihan, 2000).

Although somewhat confusing, remember that positive and negative punishment *decrease* the likelihood of a behavior occurring again, while positive and negative reinforcement *increase* the likelihood of a behavior occurring again.

C. Schedules of Reinforcement

Skinner's Contributions

Why are consequences important?

On September 20, 1971, *Time* magazine recognized B. F. Skinner's influence and accomplishments in psychology and education by putting him on its cover (right photo). Just a year earlier, the *American Psychologist* rated B. F. Skinner second, after Freud, in influence on 20th-century psychology.

Skinner is perhaps best known for his discovery of operant conditioning, which is a powerful method for analyzing the individual behaviors of animals and humans. Part of his method was to study how different kinds of consequences or reinforcements affected behavior, and this led to his study of different schedules of reinforcement.

B. F. Skinner (1904–1990)

A *schedule of reinforcement* refers to a program or rule that determines how and when the occurrence of a response will be followed by a reinforcer.

Skinner pointed out many examples of how schedules of reinforcement both maintained and controlled behaviors. For example, slot machine players don't realize that they are paid off according to a schedule of reinforcement that encourages rapid responding.

Skinner was able to study how different schedules of reinforcement affected behavior because he developed a clever method to record ongoing, individual behaviors. His method included the use of the now-famous "Skinner box" and something called the cumulative record.

Measuring Ongoing Behavior

Skinner showed how different schedules of reinforcement affected an animal's or a human's ongoing behavior with something called a cumulative record.

A *cumulative record* is a continuous written record that shows an animal's or a human's individual responses and reinforcements.

A rat in a Skinner box is shown on the left and a cumulative record is shown below. When the rat is not pressing the bar, a pen draws a straight line on a long roll of paper that unwinds slowly and continuously to the left. When the rat presses the bar, the pen moves up a notch. When the rat makes numerous responses, the pen moves up many notches to draw a line that resembles a stairway going up. If the rat presses the bar slowly, the pen notches up gradually, resulting in a gentler slope. If the rat responds

Rat in a Skinner box

Pen

Sloped line: series of rapid responses

Blip: reinforcement

Upward notch: one response

Blip: reinforcement

Flat line: no responses

quickly, the pen notches up more quickly, resulting in a steeper slope. A downward blip indicates that the rat received a food pellet, or reinforcement (only two are shown). The cumulative record shows you an animal's ongoing responses and reinforcements across time.

We'll first look at how two general schedules of reinforcement—continuous and partial reinforcement—can greatly affect ongoing behavior.

Schedules of Reinforcement

When I (H.K.) first began training my dog to "shake hands," I gave her a treat each time she responded to my command by shaking my hand. Later on, when she had mostly learned to shake hands, I gave her a treat only some of the time. These situations illustrate two general schedules of reinforcement—continuous and partial.

CONTINUOUS REINFORCEMENT

Giving my dog a treat each time she responded to my command by shaking my hand illustrates the schedule of continuous reinforcement.

Continuous reinforcement means that every occurrence of the operant response results in delivery of the reinforcer.

In the real world, relatively few of our behaviors are on a continuous reinforcement schedule because very few things or people are as reliable as my dog. Continuous reinforcement is often used in the initial stages of operant conditioning because it results in rapid learning of some behavior.

Every response is reinforced.

PARTIAL REINFORCEMENT

After my dog had mostly learned to shake hands on command, I gave her a treat about every fifth time, which illustrates the schedule of partial reinforcement.

Partial reinforcement refers to a situation in which responding is reinforced only some of the time.

In the real world, many of our behaviors are on a partial reinforcement schedule, which is very effective in maintaining behavior over the long run. My dog keeps shaking my hand on command because some of the time she gets a treat.

We'll discuss the four common schedules of partial reinforcement and show how differently they affect behavior.

Only some responses are reinforced.

Which schedule are you on?

We'll discuss four different schedules of partial reinforcement, each of which has a different effect on controlling and maintaining animal and human behaviors.

Fixed-Ratio Schedule

If factory workers are paid after packing six boxes, they are on a fixed-ratio schedule.

Fixed-ratio schedule **means that a reinforcer occurs only after a fixed number of responses are made by the subject.**

A fixed-ratio schedule is often used to pay assembly-line workers because it results in fast rates of work.

Fixed-Interval Schedule

If a surfer gets a big wave to ride (the reinforcer) every 30 seconds (waves come in regular sets of big and small), he is on a fixed-interval schedule.

Fixed-interval schedule **means that a reinforcer occurs following the first response that occurs after a fixed interval of time.**

A fixed-interval schedule has slow responding at first, but as the time for the reinforcer nears, responses increase.

Variable-Ratio Schedule

If a slot machine pays off after an average of 25 pulls, the gambler is on a variable-ratio schedule.

Variable-ratio schedule **means that a reinforcer is delivered after an average number of correct responses has occurred.**

The variable-ratio schedule produces a high rate of responding because the person (gambler) doesn't know which response will finally produce the payoff.

Variable-Interval Schedule

If a bus arrives (the reinforcer) at your stop an average of 7 minutes late but at variable intervals, the bus rider is on a variable-interval schedule. This reinforces your arriving just a few minutes late for your bus.

Variable-interval schedule **means that a reinforcer occurs following the first correct response after an average amount of time has passed.**

A variable-interval schedule results in a more regular rate of responding than does a fixed-interval schedule.

In the real world, many of our behaviors are maintained on one or more of these four schedules of partial reinforcement.

Next, we'll describe an interesting and unusual application of Skinner's principles of operant conditioning.

How smart are dolphins?

After the Gulf War, ships carrying food and medicine had to wait outside the ports until the many underwater mines were located. Because the water was dark and murky, human divers could not easily detect the mines, but dolphins had no difficulty, since they can "see" by using sound waves or echolocation to find objects. Dolphins are trained to detect mines similar to how dogs are trained to detect explosives: Their trainers applied Skinner's principles of operant conditioning.

Trainer and dolphin

1. A dolphin has been trained to wait and circle around an inflatable boat. On the trainer's signal (discriminative stimulus), the dolphin dives and uses echolocation to find the mine in the murky water. Echolocation involves emitting sound waves (too high for humans to hear) and analyzing the waves that are reflected back from objects. The dolphin's echolocation is so sensitive that it can detect a quarter-sized metal disk 100 feet away, no matter how murky the water is.

2. After locating the mine, the dolphin returns to the surface and is trained to touch a rubber disk at the front of the boat. The trainer rewards the dolphin with a fish for this and many other behaviors.

3. The trainer places on the dolphin's nose a hollow cone attached to a plastic cylinder that rides on the dolphin's back. Again, the dolphin dives and echolocates the mine, but it has been trained not to touch the mine. When close to the mine, the dolphin is trained to release the nose cone, and the cylinder break opens and releases an anchor.

4. The anchor (sound transmitter) falls to the bottom while the cylinder rises to the surface to mark the location of the mine. Human divers use the cylinder to locate and then detonate the mine. The dolphin is always removed from the area before the mine is detonated. A Navy spokesperson says that the dolphins are well cared for and, for that reason, live in captivity as long as or longer than in the wild (Friend, 2003).

Through operant conditioning, dolphins learned to perform this complex series of behaviors. During operant conditioning, a number of other things are also happening.

D. Other Conditioning Concepts

What else did Bart learn?

During the time that Bart was being operantly conditioned to pick up and hold a teddy bear to a hand signal, he simultaneously learned a number of other things, such as to also hold a bear cub, not to obey commands from a stranger, and to stop picking up the teddy bear if he was no longer given apples (reinforcers). You may remember these phenomena—generalization, discrimination, extinction, and spontaneous recovery—from our discussion of classical conditioning in Module 9 (see p. 199). We'll explain how the same terms also apply to operant conditioning.

Generalization

In the movie, Bart was supposed to pick up and hold a bear cub on command. However, in the wild, adult male Kodiak bears don't pick up and hold cubs; instead, they usually kill them.

Generalization: Bart transfers his response from teddy bear to live cub.

Although Bart was relatively tame, his trainer took no chances of Bart's wilder nature coming out and killing the bear cub. For this reason, the trainer started by conducting the initial conditioning with a stuffed teddy bear. Only after Bart had learned to pick up and hold the teddy bear on cue did the trainer substitute a live bear cub. As the trainer had predicted, Bart transferred his holding the teddy bear to holding the live bear cub, a phenomenon called generalization.

In operant conditioning, *generalization* means that an animal or person emits the same response to similar stimuli.

In classical conditioning, *generalization* is the tendency for a stimulus similar to the original conditioned stimulus to elicit a response similar to the conditioned response.

A common and sometimes embarrassing example of generalization occurs when a young child generalizes the word "Daddy" to other males who appear similar to the child's real father. As quickly as possible, embarrassed parents teach their child to discriminate between the real father and other adult males.

Discrimination

Since Bart had been raised and trained by a particular adult male, he had learned to obey and take cues only from his trainer and not from other males. This is an example of discrimination.

In operant conditioning, *discrimination* means that a response is emitted in the presence of a stimulus that is reinforced and not in the presence of unreinforced stimuli.

In classical conditioning, *discrimination* is the tendency for some stimuli but not others to elicit a conditioned response.

One problem with Bart was that he would repeatedly pick up and hold the teddy bear to receive an apple. To control this problem, the trainer used a cue—raising his arms in the air—to signal that only then would Bart receive an apple for his behavior. This is an example of a discriminative stimulus.

A *discriminative stimulus* is a cue that a behavior will be reinforced.

Discrimination: Bart obeys signals from his trainer but not from a stranger.

If you pay close attention to an animal trainer, you'll notice that discriminative stimuli, such as a hand signal or whistle, are used to signal the animal that the next behavior will be reinforced.

Young children learn to discriminate between stimuli when their parents reinforce their saying "Daddy" in the presence of their real fathers but do not reinforce their children when they call strangers "Daddy."

Extinction and Spontaneous Recovery

Even after filming ended, Bart continued to perform his trained behaviors for a while. However, after a period of time when these behaviors were no longer reinforced, they gradually diminished and ceased. This is an example of extinction.

In operant conditioning, *extinction* refers to the reduction in an operant response when it is no longer followed by the reinforcer.

In classical conditioning, *extinction* refers to the reduction in a response when the conditioned stimulus is no longer followed by the unconditioned stimulus.

Extinction: Bart stops behaviors if reinforcers stop. Spontaneous recovery: After extinction, Bart's behavior returns.

After undergoing extinction, Bart may show spontaneous recovery.

In operant conditioning, *spontaneous recovery* refers to a temporary recovery in the rate of responding.

In classical conditioning, *spontaneous recovery* refers to the temporary occurrence of the conditioned response to the presence of the conditioned stimulus.

Remember that all four phenomena—generalization, discrimination, extinction, and spontaneous recovery—occur in both operant and classical conditioning.

One distinctive characteristic of operant conditioning is that it usually has an observable response and an observable reinforcer. Next, we turn to cognitive learning, which may have neither observable response nor observable reinforcer.

E. Cognitive Learning

How did Tony Hawk learn?

At the beginning of this module, we told you about Tony Hawk, who as a child loved to watch skateboarders at the park. He began to practice skateboarding every chance he had so that he could imitate what he saw. Tony learned how to skateboard not from classical or operant conditioning but from another kind of learning process called cognitive learning.

Cognitive learning, **which involves mental processes such as attention and memory, says that learning can occur through observation or imitation and such**

He learned by observing.

learning may not involve any external rewards or require a person to perform any observable behaviors.

The roots of cognitive learning extend back to the work of Wilhelm Wundt in the late 1800s (p. 12) and Edward Tolman in the 1930s. It died in the 1950s, was reborn in the 1960s, and became popular in the 1990s. Currently, cognitive learning is extremely useful in explaining both animal and human behavior and was vital to the development of a new area called cognitive neuroscience (p. 71) (Bandura, 2001a). We'll begin by discussing what three famous psychologists had to say about cognitive learning.

Against: B. F. Skinner

Eight days before his death, B. F. Skinner was honored by the American Psychological Association (APA) with the first APA Citation for Outstanding Lifetime Contribution to Psychology. In his acceptance speech to over 1,000 friends and colleagues, Skinner spoke of how psychology was splitting between those who were studying feelings and cognitive processes and those who were studying observable

behaviors, such as animals under controlled conditions (figure at right). In a sharp criticism of cognitive learning, Skinner said, "As far as I'm concerned, cognitive science is the creationism [downfall] of psychology" (Vargas, 1991, p. 1).

Skinner's severe criticism of studying cognitive processes caused many in the audience to gasp and only a few to applaud (Vargas, 1991).

In the 1950s and 1960s, Skinner had advocated that psychology's goal should be to study primarily observable behaviors rather than cognitive processes.

However, psychologists gradually discovered that cognitive processes played a major role in human and animal activities and that such activities could not be understood or explained from observable behaviors alone. Today, the study of cognitive processes is a major goal of psychology (Bandura, 2001a).

In Favor: Edward Tolman

In the 1930s, about the same time that Skinner was emphasizing observable behaviors, Tolman was exploring hidden mental processes. For example, he would place rats individually in a maze, such as the one shown below, and allow each rat time to explore the maze with no food present. Then, with food present in the maze's food box, he would test the rat to see which path it took. The rat learned very quickly to take the shortest path. Next, Tolman blocked the shortest path to the food box. The first time the rat encountered the blocked shortest path, it selected the next shortest path to the food box. According to Tolman (1948), the rat selected the next shortest path because it had developed a cognitive map of the maze.

A *cognitive map* is a mental representation in the brain of the layout of an environment and its features.

Tolman showed that rats, in addition to forming a cognitive map, learned the layout of a maze without being reinforced, a position very different from Skinner's. Tolman's position is making a comeback as psychologists currently study a variety of cognitive processes in animals (D. A. Lieberman, 2000). Tolman's study of cognitive processes in animals laid the groundwork for the study of cognitive processes in humans, which is best shown by the current theory of Albert Bandura (2001a).

In Favor: Albert Bandura

Bandura began as a behaviorist in the Skinnerian tradition, which means focusing on observable behaviors and avoiding study of mental events. Since then he has almost entirely shifted to a cognitive approach. In many of his studies, Bandura (1986) has focused on how humans learn through observing things. For example, Bandura says that a child can learn to hate spiders simply by observing the behaviors of someone who shows a great fear of spiders. This is an example of social cognitive learning.

Social cognitive learning **results from watching, imitating, and modeling and does not require the observer to perform any observable behavior or receive any observable reward.**

Just as Tolman found that learning occurred while rats were exploring, Bandura found that humans learned while observing and that much (most) of human learning takes place through observation. Observational learning, which involves numerous cognitive processes, is a 180-degree change from Skinner's position, which had emphasized observable, noncognitive behaviors.

Following the death of Skinner in 1990, the study of cognitive processes has ballooned in popularity and usefulness. We'll introduce you to cognitive learning by describing one of Bandura's best-known studies, which involved a doll and a considerable amount of kicking and screaming.

E. Cognitive Learning

Do children learn by watching?

Perhaps a dozen experiments in psychology have become classics because they were the first to demonstrate some very important principles. One such classic experiment demonstrated the conditioning of emotional responses in "Little Albert" (p. 204). Another classic is Albert Bandura (1965) and his colleagues' demonstration that children learned aggressive behaviors by watching an adult's aggressive behaviors. Learning through watching is called observational learning, which is a form of cognitive learning.

Bobo Doll Experiment

Why did children kick the Bobo doll?

One reason this Bobo doll study is a classic experiment is that it challenged the earlier idea that learning occurred through either classical or operant conditioning. You'll see that children learned to perform aggressive responses simply from watching.

Procedure. In one part of the room, preschool children were involved in their own art projects. In another part of the room, an adult got up and, for the next 10 minutes, kicked, hit, and yelled ("Hit him! Kick him!") at a large, inflated Bobo doll. Some children watched the model's aggressive behaviors, while other children did not.

After watching, children imitated adults kicking doll.

Sometime later, each child was subjected to a mildly frustrating situation and then placed in a room with toys, including the Bobo doll. Without the child's knowledge, researchers observed the child's behaviors.

Results. Children who had observed the model's aggressive attacks on the Bobo doll also kicked, hit, and yelled ("Hit him! Kick him!") at the doll. Through observational learning alone, these children had learned the model's aggressive behaviors and were now performing them. In comparison, the children who had not observed the model's behaviors did not hit or kick the Bobo doll after they had been mildly frustrated.

Conclusion. Bandura's point is that these children learned to perform specific aggressive behaviors not by practicing or being reinforced but simply by watching a live model perform these behaviors. Observational learning is sometimes called modeling because it involves watching a model and later imitating the behavior.

Another interesting finding of the Bobo doll studies was that children may learn by observing but then not perform the observed behavior. This is an example of the learning-performance distinction.

Learning Versus Performance

Do you learn but not show it?

Is it possible that people can learn by observing but not necessarily perform what they have learned? To answer this question, Bandura and colleagues asked a group of children to watch a movie in which someone hit and kicked a Bobo doll. However, after hitting and kicking the doll, the person in the film was punished by being soundly criticized and spanked. Next, each child was left alone in a room filled with toys, including a Bobo doll.

As the experimenters watched each child through a one-way mirror, they found that more boys than girls imitated the model and performed aggressive behaviors on Bobo. But not all the children imitated the model's aggressive behaviors. Next, each child who had not imitated the model's aggressive behaviors on Bobo was offered a reward (a sticker or some fruit juice) to imitate the model's behavior. With the promise of a reward, all of the children imitated the model's aggressive behaviors. We'll examine in more detail the girls' imitated aggressive behaviors, which were similar to the boys' but more dramatic.

As the graph below shows, girls imitated an average of 0.5 aggressive behaviors after watching a film of a model who performed aggressive behaviors on Bobo and then was punished for being aggressive.

In other words, after observing a model being punished for aggressive behaviors, girls imitated almost none of the model's aggressive behaviors. However, when the same girls were promised a reward for imitating the model's aggressive behaviors, these girls imitated an average of 3.0 aggressive behaviors (Bandura, 1965).

Average Number of Aggressive Responses		
0.5	Watched punished model	
3.0	Rewarded for imitating	

So what does this experiment show? It shows that the girls had actually *learned* the model's aggressive behaviors through observation but that some did not *perform* these behaviors until they were rewarded for doing so (Bandura, 1965). This is an example of the learning-performance distinction.

The *learning-performance distinction* means that learning may occur but may not always be measured by, or immediately evident in, performance.

The learning-performance distinction may be demonstrated by young children, often to the embarrassment of their parents. For instance, a young child may overhear a "dirty" word but not repeat the word until out in public. Repeating a "dirty" word shows that the child had learned the word through observation but waited until later to imitate the parent and actually say (perform) the "dirty" word.

Child imitates adult's speech.

Based on the Bobo doll study and others, Bandura developed a theory of cognitive learning that we'll examine next.

Would you hold this spider?

The idea that humans gather information about their environments and the behaviors of others through observation is a key part of Bandura's (2001a) social cognitive theory of learning.

Social *cognitive theory* emphasizes the importance of observation, imitation, and self-reward in the development and learning of social skills, personal interactions, and many other behaviors. Unlike operant and classical conditioning, this theory says that it is not necessary to perform any observable behaviors or receive any external rewards to learn.

Bandura believes that four processes—attention, memory, imitation, and motivation—operate during social cognitive learning. We'll explain how these processes operate in decreasing fear of spiders and snakes.

Social Cognitive Learning: Four Processes

1 Attention

The observer must pay attention to what the model says or does. In the photo at right, a nonfrightened woman (model) holds a huge spider while another woman (observer) looks on in amazement.

2 Memory

The observer must store or remember the information so that it can be retrieved and used later. The observer in the photo will store the image of seeing a nonfrightened woman (model) holding a spider.

3 Imitation

The observer must be able to use the remembered information to guide his or her own actions and thus imitate the model's behavior.

After observing fearless woman, woman in back may learn not to fear spiders.

The observer in the photo will later try to imitate the model's nonfrightened facial expression and manner when holding a spider.

4 Motivation

The observer must have some reason or incentive to imitate the model's behavior. The observer in the photo is motivated to overcome her fear of spiders because she wants to go on camping trips.

If this observer can successfully imitate the model's calm behavior, then she will overcome her fear of spiders and be able to go camping with her friends. This example shows how Bandura's four mental processes operate during social cognitive learning.

The next study by Bandura shows how social cognitive learning, which usually takes some time and effort, decreased fear of snakes.

Social Cognitive Learning Applied to Fear of Snakes

Background. Although most people are wary of snakes, some develop an intense fear of them. Bandura and colleagues recruited subjects who had developed such an intense fear of snakes that they avoided many normal outdoor activities, such as hiking or gardening (Bandura et al., 1969). The subjects' fear of snakes was objectively measured by noting how many of 29 steps of increasingly frightening actions they would perform. For example, step 1 was approaching a glass cage containing a snake; step 29 was putting the snake in their laps and letting it crawl around while holding their hands at their sides.

Social cognitive learning helped this woman overcome her fear of snakes.

Treatment. One group of subjects watched as a model handled a live, 4-foot, harmless king snake. After watching for 15 minutes, subjects were invited to gradually move closer to the snake. Then the model demonstrated touching the snake and asked the subjects to imitate her actions. As the model held the snake, subjects were encouraged to touch the snake with a gloved hand. Another group of subjects, who also reported an intense fear of snakes, received no treatment (control group).

Results and conclusion. As the graph below shows, subjects who watched a live model handle a snake and who imitated some of the model's behaviors scored an average of 27 on the 29-step approach scale.

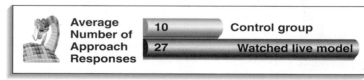

Average Number of Approach Responses

| 10 | Control group |
| 27 | Watched live model |

In contrast, control subjects scored an average of only 10 approach behaviors on the 29-step scale. This study clearly showed that behavior can be greatly changed through social cognitive learning, which emphasized observation and imitation.

Bandura believes that humans acquire a great amount of information about fears, social roles, discrimination, and personal interactions through social cognitive learning. We'll discuss other aspects of cognitive learning and memory in Modules 11 and 12.

Next, we'll describe another kind of cognitive learning that involves what is often described as the "ah-ha!" feeling.

E. Cognitive Learning

What's the "ah-ha!" feeling?

Earlier we told you that Thorndike studied how cats learned to escape from a puzzle box to get a piece of fish. Thorndike concluded that learning occurred through a process of trial and error as cats gradually formed associations between moving the latch and opening the door. None of the cats showed any evidence of suddenly discovering the solution of how to escape the box.

About the same time that Thorndike in America was studying the trial-and-error learning of cats escaping from a puzzle box, Wolfgang Köhler in Germany was studying how

AH-HA!

Flash of insight

chimpanzees learned to obtain bananas that were out of reach. Köhler challenged Thorndike's conclusion that animals learned only through trial and error. Köhler suggested instead that cats and other animals that were observed under the proper circumstances could solve a problem in a sudden flash, known as insight or "ah-ha!" (Cook, 2002).

Insight **is a mental process marked by the sudden and unexpected solution to a problem: a phenomenon often called the "ah-ha!" experience.**

Here's an example of Köhler's chimp, Sultan, who showed insight in getting a banana that was hanging out of reach.

Insight in Animals

How did the chimp get the banana?

This classic experiment in psychology suggested a new kind of learning.

What Köhler (1925) did was to hang a banana from the ceiling in a room that had a box placed off to one side. The banana was too high for Sultan the chimp to grab by reaching or jumping. When Sultan first entered the room, he paced restlessly for about 5 minutes. Then he got the box, moved it toward the banana, climbed onto the box, jumped up, and seized the banana. On his second try, Sultan quickly moved the box directly beneath the banana and jumped up to get it.

What intrigued Köhler about Sultan's problem-solving behavior was that it seemed to differ greatly from the random trial-and-error behavior of Thorndike's cats. Before Sultan arrived at a solution, he might pace about, sit quietly, or vainly grasp at the out-of-reach banana. Then, all of a sudden, he seemed to hit on the solution and immediately executed a complicated set of behaviors, such as standing on a box, to get the banana. Köhler believed that Sultan's sudden solution to a problem was an example of *insight,* a mental process quite different from what Thorndike had observed in the random trial-and-error learning of cats.

However, critics of Köhler's insight studies pointed out that he did not explain how chimps solved problems; rather, he simply described the process. Critics also noted that chimpanzees that were best at solving Köhler's problems were those that had had the most experience getting or retrieving objects. Thus, the development of insight seems to depend, to a large extent, on previous experience.

Köhler replied that his studies on insight were more a way to study problem solving than an explanation of what was happening in the chimp's head. The significance of Köhler's work was that it represented a method for studying learning that was different from either classical conditioning or random trial-and-error learning (Pierce, 1999). Since the early 1990s, there has been a renewed interest in studying the workings of the animal mind, which is currently called animal cognition (D. A. Lieberman, 2000).

Let's look at an example of insight learning in humans.

Chimp stood on a box to be able to reach the banana.

Insight in Humans

Can you solve this puzzle?

Just as Sultan the chimp seemed to suddenly arrive at a solution to a problem, humans also report the experience of suddenly and unexpectedly solving a challenging or difficult problem. We call this phenomenon the "ah-ha!" experience or a flash of insight (Cook, 2002). You may have an "ah-ha!" experience if you can figure out what critical piece of information is needed to make the following story make sense.

A man walks into a bar and asks for a glass of water. The bartender points a gun at the man. The man says "Thank you" and walks out.

If you solved this puzzle, you had an insight!

Obviously, something critical happened between two events: ". . . asks for a glass of water" and "The bartender points a gun at the man." Some subjects solved this problem in a relatively short time, while others could not solve this problem in the 2-hour time limit.

Neither one of us could solve the problem until we read the hint: The man has hiccups. Think about cures for hiccups and you may have an "ah-ha!" experience (answer at bottom of page). There was a difference between nonsolvers and solvers in the cognitive strategy that they used. The nonsolvers focused on the obvious elements, such as man, bartender, gun, and glass of water, and not on new concepts (hiccups, cure) that would lead to a solution. In comparison, the solvers spent more time on bringing in new information, and when they finally found the missing piece of information (cure for hiccups), the solution arrived suddenly, like the "ah-ha!" experience that Köhler defined as insight (Durso et al., 1994).

We have discussed three examples of cognitive learning: Tolman's idea of cognitive maps, Bandura's theory of social cognitive learning, and Köhler's study of insightful problem solving. In addition, we'll discuss cognitive learning in Modules 11 and 12.

After the Concept Review, we'll explain why biological factors make some things easier and some things harder to learn.

Answer: The man drank the water, but it didn't cure his hiccups. The bartender thought a surprise or fright might do the trick. He points a gun at the man, who is frightened, and so his hiccups stop. The man says "Thank you" and walks out.

✔ Concept Review

1. The kind of learning in which the consequences that follow some behavior increase or decrease the likelihood that the behavior will occur in the future is called _____.

2. In operant conditioning, the organism voluntarily performs or (a)_____ a behavior. Immediately following an emitted behavior, the occurrence of a (b)_____ increases the likelihood that the behavior will occur again.

3. Because an organism may not immediately emit the desired behavior, a procedure is used to reinforce behaviors that lead to or approximate the final target behavior. This procedure is called _____.

4. In operant conditioning, the term *consequences* refers to either (a)_____, which increases the likelihood that a behavior will occur again, or (b)_____, which decreases the likelihood that a behavior will occur again.

5. If the occurrence of some response is increased because it is followed by a pleasant stimulus, the stimulus is called a (a)_____. An increase in the occurrence of some response because it is followed either by the removal of an unpleasant stimulus or by avoiding the stimulus is called (b)_____.

6. A stimulus, such as food, water, or sex, that is innately satisfying and requires no learning to become pleasurable is a (a)_____. A stimulus, such as grades or praise, that has acquired its reinforcing power through experience and learning is a (b)_____.

7. The various ways that reinforcers occur after a behavior has been emitted are referred to as (a)_____ of reinforcement. For example, if each and every target behavior is reinforced, it is called a (b)_____ schedule of reinforcement. If behaviors are not reinforced each time they occur, it is called a (c)_____ schedule of reinforcement.

8. When an organism emits the same response to similar stimuli, it is called (a)_____. When a response is emitted in the presence of a stimulus that is reinforced and not in the presence of unreinforced stimuli, it is called (b)_____. A decrease in emitting a behavior because it is no longer reinforced is called (c)_____. If an organism performs a behavior without its being reinforced, it is called (d)_____.

9. A kind of learning that involves mental processes, that may be learned through observation and imitation, and that may not require any external rewards or the performance of any observable behaviors is referred to as _____.

10. Tolman studied the behavior of rats that were allowed to explore a maze without any reward given. When food was present, rats quickly learned to select the next shortest path if a previously taken path was blocked. Tolman said that rats had developed a mental representation of the layout, which he called a _____.

11. Although an organism may learn a behavior through observation or exploration, the organism may not immediately demonstrate or perform the newly learned behavior. This phenomenon is known as the _____ distinction.

12. According to Bandura, one form of learning that develops through watching and imitation and that does not require the observer to perform any observable behavior or receive a reinforcer is called (a)_____ learning. Bandura believes that humans gather much information from their (b)_____ through social cognitive learning.

13. Bandura's theory of social cognitive learning involves four mental processes. The observer must pay (a)_____ to what the model says or does. The observer must then code the information and be able to retrieve it from (b)_____ for use at a later time. The observer must be able to use the coded information to guide his or her (c)_____ in performing and imitating the model's behavior. Finally, the observer must be (d)_____ to perform the behavior, which involves some reason, reinforcement, or incentive.

14. In Köhler's study of problem solving in chimps, he identified a mental process marked by the sudden occurrence of a solution, which he termed (a)_____. This phenomenon is another example of (b)_____ learning.

Answers: *1. operant conditioning; 2. (a) emits, (b) reinforcement or reinforcer; 3. shaping; 4. (a) reinforcement, (b) punishment; 5. (a) positive reinforcer, (b) negative reinforcement; 6. (a) primary reinforcer, (b) secondary reinforcer; 7. (a) schedules, (b) continuous, (c) partial; 8. (a) generalization, (b) discrimination, (c) extinction, (d) spontaneous recovery; 9. cognitive learning; 10. cognitive map; 11. learning-performance; 12. (a) social cognitive, (b) environments; 13. (a) attention, (b) memory, (c) motor control, (d) motivated; 14. (a) insight, (b) cognitive*

F. Biological Factors

Definition

Why would a monkey make a snowball?

You may remember having difficulty learning to read, write, ride a bike, drive a car, put on makeup, or shave. But do you remember having problems learning to play? For a young child, playing just seems to come naturally. Just as children engage in play behavior with little or no encouragement, reward, or learning, so too do monkeys. For example, young monkeys learn to roll snowballs and carry them around for apparently no other reason than for play (right photo). In fact, most young mammals engage in various play behaviors, which are not easily explained by the three traditional learning procedures—classical conditioning, operant conditioning, and cognitive learning (S. Brownlee, 1997). Observations of animals and humans indicate that

Animals have innate tendencies, such as playing with objects.

some behaviors, such as play, are easily and effortlessly learned partly because of innate biological factors.

Biological factors **refer to innate tendencies or predispositions that may either facilitate or inhibit certain kinds of learning.**

Researchers suggest that animals and humans may have evolved biological predispositions to learn play behaviors because they have adaptive functions—for example, developing social relationships among peers and learning behaviors useful for adult roles (Bekoff, 2001; Dugatkin & Bekoff, 2003). This means that animals and humans have innate biological factors or predispositions that make certain kinds of learning, such as play behavior, very easy and effortless.

Besides play behavior, we'll discuss two other examples of learning—imprinting and preparedness—that are learned early and easily because of biological factors.

Imprinting

Why do young chicks follow their mother?

Soon after they hatch and without any apparent learning, baby chicks follow their mother hen. This following behavior was not explained by any of the principles of learning identified by Pavlov (classical conditioning), Thorndike (trial-and-error learning), or Skinner (operant conditioning). The baby chick's seemingly unlearned behavior of following its mother was a different kind of learning that was first identified by ethologists.

Ethologists **are behavioral biologists who observe and study animal behavior in the animal's natural environment or under relatively naturalistic conditions.**

For example, an Austrian ethologist, Konrad Lorenz (1952), studied chicks, goslings, and ducks, which can all move around minutes after hatching. He discovered that these baby animals followed the first moving object they saw, which was usually their mother. This following behavior is an example of imprinting.

Baby ducks automatically follow first moving object.

Imprinting **refers to inherited tendencies or responses that are displayed by newborn animals when they encounter certain stimuli in their environment.**

Imprinting is an unlearned behavior that is based on biological factors and that has great survival value: It increases the chances that newly hatched birds will remain with and follow their parent instead of wandering off into the waiting jaws of predators. Besides being unlearned, Lorenz noted two other major differences between imprinting and other kinds of learning.

Sensitive period. Unlike classical conditioning, operant conditioning, and cognitive learning, which occur throughout an animal's life, imprinting occurs best during the first few hours after hatching. This brief time period is called the critical, or sensitive, period.

The *critical,* **or** *sensitive, period* **refers to a relatively brief time during which learning is most likely to occur.**

Normally, the first object that newly hatched ducks see is their parent, upon whom they imprint. Thus, imprinting is a way for newly hatched animals to establish social attachments to members of their species. Although newly hatched birds will imprint on almost any moving object that they first see, including a human, a colored ball, or a glove, they imprint more strongly on moving objects that look or sound like their parent. Only birds that can walk immediately after hatching show imprinting, which promotes their survival (Bateson, 1991).

Irreversible. Unlike classical conditioning, operant conditioning, and cognitive learning, whose effects are usually reversible, imprinting is essentially irreversible. Most likely, imprinting evolved to be irreversible so that a young duck would not imprint on its mother one week and then imprint on a sly fox the next week.

In a program to prevent the California condor from becoming extinct, condor chicks are hatched at the San Diego Zoo and raised by humans. Because imprinting occurs very early and is irreversible, special precautions are taken so that the condor will not imprint on humans.

For example, the young condor chick shown on the right is being fed by a puppet that resembles an adult condor's head rather than a human's hand. The "puppet mother" helps the young condor imprint on real condor characteristics. When this condor grows up and is introduced into the wild, it will establish social relationships with, and attempt to mate with, its own species.

"Puppet mother" feeds baby condor.

Another example of how biological factors increase the ease and speed of learning is evident in something called prepared learning.

Why was learning to talk so easy?

You easily learned to talk but probably had trouble learning to read because of how your brain is organized, which illustrates the importance of biological factors. We'll discuss how biological factors help humans learn to speak different languages and birds learn to remember thousands of places where they hid food.

Incredible Memory

How do birds remember?

There are small birds, called Clark's nutcrackers, that live in an area where almost no food is available in the winter. During autumn, nutcrackers hide stores of food in underground places in perhaps as many as 2,500 to 6,000 different locations. During winter, nutcrackers survive by finding and digging up their hidden stores of food. How do nutcrackers locate their thousands of hidden stores? One explanation is preparedness, which we discussed earlier (p. 200).

Remembers thousands of hidden food places

Preparedness, or prepared learning, refers to the innate or biological tendency of animals to recognize, attend to, and store certain cues over others, as well as to associate some combinations of conditioned and unconditioned stimuli more easily than others.

Under seminatural conditions, researchers observed the amazing ability of nutcrackers to hide and find hundreds of hidden stores of food. Researchers found that nutcrackers use natural landmarks (trees, stones, bushes) to form cognitive maps that help them remember the locations of their hidden stores (B. M. Gibson & Kamil, 2001; Kamil & Cheng, 2001).

One reason nutcrackers have such phenomenal memories is that the areas of their brains involved in memory are larger than the same areas in birds that do not store food. Specifically, the hippocampus, which is involved in transferring short-term memories into long-term memories, is larger in nutcrackers than in nonstoring birds (S. D. Healy et al., 2005). Thus, the nutcracker is biologically prepared for surviving winters by having a larger hippocampus (right figure), which helps it better remember the locations of thousands of food stores.

Hippocampus

Just as some birds are biologically prepared to remember the locations of critical hidden stores, humans are biologically prepared to make sounds and speak at least one of 6,800 different languages.

Incredible Sounds

How do infants make "word" sounds?

In the late 1940s, two psychologists raised a chimp in their home, along with their own child, because they wanted to know if this "speaking" environment would help a chimp learn to speak. However, after 6 years of trying, the chimp had learned to say a grand total of three words: "mama," "papa," and "cup" (Hayes & Hayes, 1951). At that time, these two psychologists did not know that the chimp's vocal apparatus and brain were not biologically prepared to produce sounds and words necessary for human speech (see the discussion of animal language on pp. 322–323).

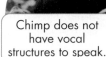

Chimp does not have vocal structures to speak.

The reason humans but not chimps or other animals learn to speak so easily is that humans' vocal apparatus and brains are biologically prepared, or innately wired, for speaking (Pinker, 1994).

For example, the brain of a newborn infant is biologically prepared to recognize the difference between human speech sounds. Researchers discovered this ability by playing speech sounds to infants whose rate of sucking on a nipple was being recorded. After newborns heard the sound "ba" over and over, their rate of sucking slowed, indicating that they were paying little attention to the sound. But, as soon as researchers played the sound "pa," the infants' rate of sucking increased, indicating that they had noticed the relatively small change between the sounds "ba" and "pa." This study showed that infants' brains are prewired or biologically prepared (below figure) to recognize and discriminate among sounds that are essential for learning speech (Buonomano & Merzenich, 1995). In fact, infants all around the world make similar babbling sounds, which indicates the influence and importance of biological factors in learning to speak.

Infant's brain is prewired for speaking.

Conclusion. The learning principles of Pavlov, Thorndike, and Skinner do not, by themselves, explain how rats form cognitive maps, how infants easily produce and discriminate among human speech sounds, how nutcrackers remember thousands of hiding places for stored food, why monkeys spend time making and rolling snowballs, and why newborn chicks follow the first moving object. All these examples indicate how innate biological factors, such as differences in size or organization of brain structures, play a major role in preparing and helping animals and humans learn certain kinds of behaviors that are useful for maintenance and survival.

Broca's area is prewired to combine sounds into words.

Wernicke's area is prewired to combine words into sentences.

Two brain areas are prewired for speaking.

Next, we'll return to operant conditioning and discuss how its learning principles helped parents manage childhood problems.

G. Research Focus: Noncompliance

Why study a single subject? When researchers study a group of subjects, information on any single subject may be lost in the group's combined scores. One advantage of operant conditioning is that a researcher can observe, study, and modify the ongoing behavior of a single subject. The ability to focus on a single subject's behavior makes operant conditioning a powerful procedure for changing undesirable behaviors. One kind of undesirable behavior in young children can be the persistent refusal of parental requests. We'll look at 4-year-old Morgan, who is becoming unmanageable because of a problem called noncompliance.

Noncompliance refers to a child refusing to follow directions, carry out a request, or obey a command given by a parent or caregiver.

NO!

Child constantly refusing or saying "NO" is a common complaint of many parents.

Noncompliance is a common complaint of parents in general and the most frequent problem of parents who bring their children to clinics for treatment of behavioral problems (Kalb & Loeber, 2003; Wierson & Forehand, 1994).

When saying "NO!" becomes a big problem, parents can be trained to use operant conditioning to decrease their child's persistent refusal. Parental training may involve different kinds of operant conditioning procedures, such as using verbal praise or giving attention to increase the occurrence of positive behaviors or using negative punishment to decrease undesirable behaviors. We'll focus on one form of negative punishment—time-out.

Time-out is a form of negative punishment in which reinforcing stimuli are removed after an undesirable response. This removal decreases the chances that the undesired response will recur.

Because Morgan persistently said "NO!" to her mother's requests, researchers showed Morgan's mother how to use time-out periods.

Study: Using Time-Out to Reduce Noncompliance

NO!

Researchers began by explaining to parents how to use the principles of operant conditioning to overcome a child's persistent "NO!"

Subjects. They were 4-year-old girls who were normal in every way but had a long history of saying "NO!" to parental requests. Their mothers had volunteered for this study because they wanted help with this problem.

Procedure. Researchers first observed mothers making typical requests and noted the children's rate of refusal, which is called the baseline. Then, mothers were shown how to use several procedures, but we'll focus on the most successful, time-outs.

If Morgan's mother made a request and Morgan complied, her mother reinforced Morgan's response with praise. However, if Morgan refused, her mother used the time-out procedure. Morgan was led to the corner of another room and told to do nothing (no TV, books, or toys) but to sit silently in a chair facing the wall for 1 minute. After 1 minute, Morgan was allowed to leave the corner and rejoin her mother. At that point, the mother made another request of Morgan. If Morgan complied, praise was given; if she showed noncompliance ("NO!"), the time-out procedure was used. All procedures were conducted in Morgan's home by her mother.

Results. The changes in Morgan's behavior after her mother began using time-out periods are shown in the graph below (Rortvedt & Miltenberger, 1994).

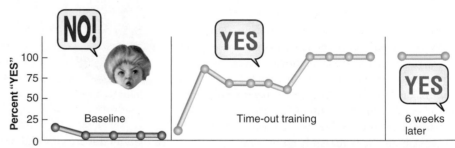

Baseline: Remember that during baseline, the researcher observed only the number of times that Morgan refused or agreed with her mother's request. During baseline, Morgan's mother made 5–8 requests during each session. Notice that during the last five sessions, Morgan showed mostly 0% compliance, despite her mother's scolding, pleading, or reprimanding.

Time-out: During time-out training, each time Morgan refused her mother's request, she was given a time-out period. Notice that Morgan's percentage of compliance started out at 12%, reached 60% on sessions 8–11, and then reached 100%.

Six weeks later, in a follow-up session using time-out, Morgan again showed 100% compliance with her mother's requests.

Conclusion. Studies like this show that the time-out procedure is effective in reducing undesirable behaviors, including noncompliance, temper tantrums, and disruptive activities (J. Taylor & Miller, 1997). The time-out procedure is an example of negative punishment, in which removing some stimulus, freedom to play, decreases the undesirable response, noncompliance. Negative punishment (time-out) is generally preferable to positive punishment (spanking) because positive punishment may cause negative emotional reactions as well as negative feelings toward the punisher (parents). The time-out procedure is an example of how operant conditioning principles may be applied to modify human behavior. We'll discuss the pros and cons of punishment more fully in the Application section on page 233.

Dealing with noncompliance is one example of how learning principles can be applied to human behavior. Another example involves learning how to play the violin.

Suzuki's method of teaching young children to play musical instruments has many similarities with Bandura's principles of social cognitive learning.

What's the Suzuki method?

In the 1940s, a violin player and teacher from Japan, Shinichi Suzuki, developed a remarkably successful method for teaching violin playing to very young children (Suzuki, 1998). His method, called the *Suzuki method,* was brought to the United States in the mid-1960s and has generated incredible enthusiasm among children, parents, and music teachers ever since (Lamb, 1990).

It's interesting to learn that the basic principles of the Suzuki method for teaching young children to play the violin are very similar to Bandura's four mental processes for social cognitive learning. What's different is that Suzuki developed his learning principles after years of actually teaching young children to play the violin, while Bandura developed his four mental processes of observational learning after years of research with young children. We'll discuss how even though Suzuki the teacher and Bandura the researcher lived in very different cultures thousands of miles apart, their experiences led them to very similar conclusions about how children learn.

Different Cultures but Similar Learning Principles

1 Attention

Bandura states that the observer must pay attention to what the model says and does.

Similarly, Suzuki advises parents to teach violin information only when the child is actually looking at and watching the parent. Parents are told to stop teaching and wait if the child rolls on the floor, jumps up and down, walks backward, or talks about unrelated things.

The recommended age for starting a child with the Suzuki method is 3 for girls and 4 for boys. Parents are cautioned, however, that the attention span of the 3- to 4-year-old child is extremely limited, usually from 30 seconds to at most several minutes at a time.

2 Memory

Bandura says that the observer must code the information in such a way that it can be retrieved and used later.

Similarly, Suzuki tells parents that they should present information in ways that a young child can understand (Bandura would say code). Because a 3- to 4-year-old child does not have fully developed verbal skills or memory, little time is spent giving verbal instructions. Instead, the young child is given violin information through games and exercises. For example, children are taught how to hold the violin, use the bow, and press the strings by first playing games with their hands. Children are taught how to read music (notes) only when they are older and have gained some technical skill at playing the violin.

3 Imitation

Bandura says the observer must be able to use the information to guide his or her own actions and thus imitate the model's behavior.

Similarly, Suzuki suggests that children start at about 3 or 4 years old, the earliest age when they can physically perform the required movements and imitate their parents and teachers. Girls can start earlier than boys because girls physically mature earlier. For other instruments, the starting times are different—piano, 4–5 years; cello, 5 years; flute, 9 years—because these instruments require more physical dexterity. As you have probably guessed, 3- and 4-year-olds start with miniature violins and move up to bigger ones as they develop.

4 Motivation

Bandura says that the observer must have some reason, reinforcement, or incentive to perform the model's behaviors.

Similarly, Suzuki emphasizes that the most important role of the parent is to constantly reward and reinforce the child for observing and "doing what Mommy or Daddy is doing." Suzuki recommends several ways to keep motivation high in young children: Be an active and interested model for the child, play violin games that are fun for the child, avoid games or lessons that involve competition, and *never* push the child beyond the level that he or she is capable of reaching (Slone, 1985).

Social cognitive learning involves attention, memory, imitation, and motivation.

Conclusion. Parents and teachers who have used the Suzuki method report great success (Lamb, 1990). As you can judge, the basic principles of the Suzuki method for teaching violin are quite similar to Bandura's four mental processes for social cognitive learning. Both Suzuki and Bandura recognized the importance of observational learning and how much information children can learn from watching and imitating models. Suzuki's successful method of teaching violin to young children provides support for Bandura's four mental processes that he believes are involved in social cognitive learning.

Next, we'll discuss how operant learning principles were used to develop a method for teaching autistic children.

I. Application: Behavior Modification

Definitions

What is behavior mod?

In this module, we discussed using operant conditioning principles to decrease food refusal in young children, to toilet train children (p. 216), to prevent eating paint chips (p. 218), to stop a severe form of self-injury (p. 219), and to decrease noncompliance (refusal) in children (p. 230). These are all examples of behavior modification (Miltenberger, 2004).

Behavior modification is a treatment or therapy that changes or modifies problems or undesirable behaviors by using principles of learning based on operant conditioning, classical conditioning, and social cognitive learning.

For over 35 years, psychologist and researcher Ivar Lovaas of the University of California at Los Angeles has used behavior modification or, more colloquially, behavior mod to treat autism.

Autism is marked by poor development in social relationships, such as not wanting to be touched, not making eye contact, and hiding to avoid people (see drawing); great difficulty developing language and communicating; very few activities and interests;

Behavior mod is used to treat autism.

and long periods of time spent repeating the same behaviors or motor patterns, or following rituals that interfere with more normal functioning. Symptoms range from mild to severe and usually appear when a child is about 2 to 3 years old (American Psychiatric Association, 2000). (We discussed the symptoms and causes of autism more thoroughly in Module 1.)

Parents, doctors, and policy makers all agree that the best method to address the above symptoms, especially deficits in forming relationships and communicating, in autistic children is to enroll them in intensive behavioral treatment (between 20 and 40 hours a week) as early as possible. There is no evidence that any treatment leads to a complete recovery, but without treatment, many autistics will remain socially unresponsive (Carey, 2004; Kabot et al., 2003). We'll discuss the behavior mod treatment developed by Ivar Lovaas, who combined principles of operant conditioning and social cognitive learning (Lovaas & Buch, 1997).

Behavior Modification and Autism

What kind of training?

Lovaas's program at UCLA, which is called the Young Autism Project, treats 2- to 3-year-old autistic children with a 40-hour-per-week program that runs for 2 to 3 years. Here's part of the program.

Program. Lovaas's training program actually consists of hundreds of separate teaching programs, many of them using principles of operant conditioning: Select a specific *target behavior*, *shape the behavior*, and use *positive reinforcers* of praise and food that are given immediately after the child emits the desired behavior. For example, here's a program to increase making eye contact.

Target behavior is getting the child to make eye contact following the command "Look at me."

Shaping the behavior involves two steps.

Step 1. Have the child sit in a chair facing you. Give the command "Look at me" every 5–10 seconds. When the child makes a correct response of looking at you, say "Good looking" and simultaneously reward the child with food.

Step 2. Continue until the child repeatedly obeys the command "Look at me." Then gradually increase the duration of the child's eye contact from 1 second to periods of 2 to 3 seconds.

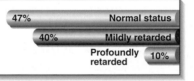

47% improved.

Using this behavior mod program, therapists and parents have had success in teaching autistic children to make eye contact, to stop constant rocking, to respond to verbal requests such as "Wash your hands," to interact with peers, to speak, and to engage in school tasks such as reading and writing (Lovaas, 1993).

Results. Lovaas and his colleagues did a long-term study of 19 children diagnosed as autistic. Behavior modification training went on for at least 40 hours per week for 2 years or more. The graph above shows that, at the end of training, 47% (9/19) of the autistic children reached normal status (Lovaas, 1987). These children acquired sufficient

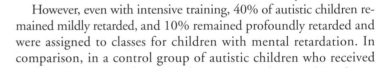

47%	Normal status
40%	Mildly retarded
Profoundly retarded	10%

language, social, play, and self-help behaviors to enter preschool and go on to successfully complete first grade in public school. Many of the children did so well that the teachers did not know they were autistic.

However, even with intensive training, 40% of autistic children remained mildly retarded, and 10% remained profoundly retarded and were assigned to classes for children with mental retardation. In comparison, in a control group of autistic children who received only minimal treatment, only 2% achieved normal intellectual and educational functioning, while 45% remained mildly retarded and 53% remained severely retarded (Eikeseth, 2001; Lovaas & Buch, 1997; McEachin et al., 1993). Lovaas and colleagues concluded that without intensive behavior modification treatment, autistic children will continue to show severe behavioral deficits.

Follow-up. A six-year follow-up study of the nine children who had reached normal status found that they had kept their gains and were still functioning normally (Lovaas, 1999). A later follow-up study of the same nine children, then 20 to 30 years old, showed that eight appeared normal—that is, did not score differently from other normal adults on a variety of tests—while one had personality problems but would not be classified as autistic (Lovaas, 1999).

However, critics questioned whether the results from these nine individuals can be applied to all autistic children (Gresham et al., 1999). Recent research indicates that Lovaas's behavior mod is best suited to help those with less severe symptoms and it may not lead to improvement in those with more severe symptoms (Carey, 2004).

Health care specialists concluded that autism therapy can be effective provided it begins early (child 2–3 years old) and includes one-on-one training for a minimum of 25 hours a week, 12 months a year for several years (Tarkan, 2002). However, such therapy is so costly ($72,000 a year) that fewer than 10% of autistic children are receiving the recommended level of treatment (Lord, 2002; Wallis, 2006).

Biofeedback

How can we reduce tension?

Many people develop a variety of psychosomatic problems, which result from stressful or disturbing thoughts that lead to real aches and pains in the body. For example, psychosomatic problems include back pain, muscle tension, high blood pressure, stomach distress, and headaches. One procedure to reduce psychosomatic problems is based on operant conditioning and is called biofeedback.

Biofeedback **is a training procedure through which a person is made aware of his or her physiological responses, such as muscle activity, heart rate, blood pressure, or temperature. After becoming aware of these physiological responses, a person tries to control them to decrease psychosomatic problems.**

Stress may cause a buildup of muscle tension.

For example, headaches may be caused or worsened by muscle tension, of which the sufferer may be totally unaware. The left figure shows that the forehead and neck have wide bands of muscles where tension can lead to pain and discomfort. Through video or audio (bio)feedback, a person can be made aware of muscle tension and learn how to reduce it.

As shown in the photo below, small sensors attached to the client's forehead detect activity in the large muscle that stretches across the top front part of the head. The woman is trying to relax her forehead muscle by imagining relaxing scenes, thinking relaxing thoughts, or actually tensing and relaxing the muscle itself. The target behavior is a decrease in the forehead's muscle tension. To reach this target behavior, the client practices thinking about or imagining relaxing scenes that result in a decrease in muscle tension. A decrease in muscle tension is signaled by a decrease in an audio signal, which acts as a reinforcer. After a number of these sessions, the client learns to decrease muscle tension with the goal of staying relaxed the next time she gets upset.

Biofeedback helps in learning to control physiological responses.

Biofeedback is often used in conjunction with other forms of medical treatment or psychotherapy and can help a person reduce blood pressure, decrease headaches, and reduce anxiety (deCharms et al., 2005; Stetter & Kupper, 2002). We'll discuss other methods of reducing stress and associated psychosomatic problems in Module 21.

Our last example deals with concerns about using punishment to decrease undesirable behaviors.

Pros and Cons of Punishment

Should it be used?

About 61% of parents believe spanking is an acceptable form of discipline for young children, and 94% of 3- and 4-year-olds have been spanked during the past year (O'Callahgan, 2006). Since spanking may immediately stop undesirable behaviors, it has been and remains a popular form of discipline. But spanking is surrounded with controversy because it is associated with numerous negative side effects and may be a less desirable form of punishment (discipline) than the time-out procedure (Benjet & Kazdin, 2003). We'll discuss the pros and cons of each.

SPANKING: POSITIVE PUNISHMENT

Since spanking involves the presentation of an aversive stimulus (pain), it is an example of positive punishment. Researchers disagree on the use of spanking. Some argue that all spanking is bad because it is associated with numerous short- and long-term negative side effects, such as the child imitating and modeling aggressive behavior and developing other conduct problems (Gershoff, 2002). Others agree that severe spanking administered by harsh parents is always bad but mild to moderate spanking used as one form of discipline by loving parents does not necessarily have undesirable or negative side effects (Baumrind et al., 2002).

Effects of punishment depend on its usage.

Some of the undesirable effects of positive punishment can be reduced if it is given immediately after the behavior, if it is just severe enough to be effective, if it is delivered consistently, if the child is told the reason for the punishment, and, perhaps most important, if punishment is used in combination with positively reinforcing a desirable behavior (Benjet & Kazdin, 2003). One disadvantage of positive punishment is that it points out only what the child should not do, while positive reinforcers have the advantage of encouraging the child to engage in desirable behaviors.

TIME-OUT: NEGATIVE PUNISHMENT

Another form of discipline is time-out, which was discussed earlier (p. 230). Time-out is an example of negative punishment because it involves the removal of a reinforcing stimulus (desirable reward) so that some undesirable response will not recur. For example, after misbehaving, a child is given a time-out period (stays in a corner without games, books, or toys). Time-out is most effective when used consistently and combined with teaching the child alternative desired behaviors using positive reinforcers (J. Taylor & Miller, 1997).

Time-out has fewer undesirable side effects than spanking.

Compared to spanking, time-out has fewer undesirable side effects; it does not provide a model of aggression and does not elicit severe negative emotional reactions. Thus, when it is necessary to discipline a child, care should be taken in choosing between positive punishment (spanking) and negative punishment (time-out). Although both kinds of punishment stop or suppress undesirable behaviors, spanking has more negative side effects than time-out, and time-out has been shown to be effective in eliminating undesirable behaviors. Both kinds of punishment are best used in combination with positive reinforcers so the child also learns to perform desirable behaviors (Nichols, 2004).

Summary Test

A. Operant Conditioning

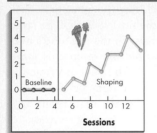

1. A kind of learning in which the consequences that follow some behavior increase or decrease the likelihood that the behavior will occur again is called _____.

2. To explain how random trial-and-error behaviors of cats became goal-directed behaviors, Thorndike formulated the _____, which says that behaviors are strengthened by positive consequences and weakened by negative consequences.

3. Skinner used the term *operant* (a)_____ to describe something that can be modified by its consequences. Operant responses provide one way to separate ongoing behaviors into units that can be observed and measured. Skinner believed that Pavlov's conditioning, which involves physiological (b)_____, was not very useful in understanding other forms of ongoing behaviors.

4. Suppose you wished to operantly condition your dog, Bingo, to sit up. The procedure would be as follows. You would give Bingo a treat, which is called a (a)_____, after he emits a desired behavior. Because it is unlikely that Bingo will initially sit up, you will use a procedure called (b)_____, which is a process of reinforcing those behaviors that lead up to or approximate the final desired behavior—sitting up. Immediately after Bingo emitted a desired behavior, you would give him a (c)_____.

5. Any behavior that increases in frequency because of an accidental pairing of a reinforcer and that behavior is called a _____ behavior.

6. The essence of operant conditioning can be summed up as follows: Consequences or reinforcers are contingent on _____.

7. If you compare classical and operant conditioning, you will find the following differences. In classical conditioning, the response is an involuntary (a)_____ that is elicited by the (b)_____. In operant conditioning, the response is a voluntary (c)_____ that is performed or (d)_____ by the organism. In classical conditioning, the unconditioned stimulus is presented at the beginning of a trial and elicits the (e)_____. In operant conditioning, the organism emits a behavior that is immediately followed by a (f)_____.

B. Reinforcers

8. In operant conditioning, the term *consequences* refers to what happens after the occurrence of a behavior. If a consequence increases the likelihood that a behavior will occur again, it is called a (a)_____. If a consequence decreases the likelihood that a behavior will occur again, it is called a (b)_____.

9. If a stimulus increases the chances that a response will occur again, that stimulus is called a (a)_____. If the removal of an aversive stimulus increases the chances that a response will occur again, that aversive stimulus is called a (b)_____. Both positive and negative reinforcements (c)_____ the frequency of the response they follow. In contrast, punishment is a consequence that (d)_____ the likelihood that a behavior will occur again.

10. The stimuli of food, water, and sex, which are innately satisfying and require no learning to become pleasurable, are called (a)_____. The stimuli of praise, money, and good grades have acquired their reinforcing properties through experience; these stimuli are called (b)_____.

C. Schedules of Reinforcement

11. A program or rule that determines how and when the occurrence of a response will be followed by a reinforcer is called a _____.

12. If you received reinforcement every time you performed a good deed, you would be on a (a)_____ schedule. This schedule is often used at the beginning of operant conditioning because it results in a rapid rate of learning. If your good deeds were not reinforced every time, you would be on a (b)_____ schedule. This schedule is more effective in maintaining the target behavior in the long run. There are four kinds of partial reinforcement schedules.

D. Other Conditioning Concepts

13. The phenomenon in which an organism emits the same response to similar stimuli is called (a)_____. If a response is emitted in the presence of a reinforced stimulus but not in the presence of unreinforced stimuli, the organism is exhibiting (b)_____. If an organism's response is no longer reinforced, it will stop emitting this behavior, which is an example of (c)_____. However, even without reinforcement, an organism may perform the behavior, which is an example of (d)_____.

E. Cognitive Learning

14. The kind of learning that involves mental processes such as attention and memory, that may be learned through observation and imitation, and that may not involve any external rewards or require the person to perform any observable behaviors is called (a) _____. According to Tolman, rats developed a mental representation of the layout of their environment, which he called a (b)_____.

15. If an observer learns a behavior through observation but does not immediately perform the behavior, this is an example of the _____ distinction.

16. During his studies of problem solving in chimpanzees, Köhler used the term _____ to describe a mental process marked by the sudden occurrence of a solution.

17. Köhler's study of insightful problem solving, Bandura's theory of observational learning, and Tolman's idea of cognitive maps represent three kinds of _____ learning.

F. Biological Factors

18. Innate tendencies or predispositions that may either facilitate or inhibit learning are referred to as _____.

19. The innate tendency of newborn birds to follow the first moving object that they encounter soon after birth is called (a)_____. This kind of learning occurs best during a critical or sensitive period and is essentially (b)_____. One function of imprinting is to form social attachments between members of a species.

20. The innate tendency of animals to recognize, attend to, and store certain cues over others and associate some combinations of conditioned and unconditioned stimuli is referred to as _____. An example of this tendency is observed in Clark's nutcrackers, which are preprogrammed to bury and remember thousands of hidden stores of food.

G. Research Focus: Noncompliance

21. One of the most common problems faced by parents is dealing with a child who refuses to follow directions or carry out a request or command. This refusal behavior is called _____.

22. An effective way to deal with a child's noncompliance is to use a procedure that involves placing a child in a situation where there is no chance of reinforcers. This mild form of nonphysical punishment is called _____.

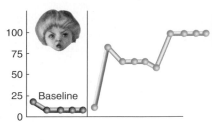

Baseline

100
75
50
25
0

H. Cultural Diversity: East Meets West

23. Suzuki's method and Bandura's theory both emphasize observation, modeling, and imitation. Specifically, both Suzuki and Bandura focus on four concepts: paying (a)_____ to the model, placing the information in (b)_____, using the information to (c)_____ the model's actions, and having (d)_____ to perform the behavior.

I. Application: Behavior Modification

24. Using principles of operant conditioning to change human behavior is referred to as (a)_____. Using these same principles to help individuals learn to control (increase or decrease) some physiological response, such as muscle activity or temperature, is called (b)_____.

25. If an aversive stimulus is presented immediately after a particular response, the response will be suppressed; this procedure is called (a)_____. If a reinforcing stimulus is removed immediately after a particular response, the response will be suppressed; this procedure is called (b)_____. A poorly chosen form of punishment, such as spanking, may have undesirable side effects, such as developing (c)_____ problems and serving as a model for future (d)_____ behaviors.

Answers: *1. operant conditioning; 2. law of effect; 3. (a) response, (b) reflexes; 4. (a) reinforcer, (b) shaping, (c) reinforcer; 5. superstitious; 6. behavior; 7. (a) reflex, (b) unconditioned stimulus, (c) behavior, (d) emitted, (e) unconditioned response, (f) reinforcer; 8. (a) reinforcer, (b) punishment; 9. (a) positive reinforcer, (b) negative reinforcer, (c) increase, (d) decreases; 10. (a) primary reinforcers, (b) secondary reinforcers; 11. schedule of reinforcement; 12. (a) continuous reinforcement, (b) partial reinforcement; 13. (a) generalization, (b) discrimination, (c) extinction, (d) spontaneous recovery; 14. (a) social cognitive learning, (b) cognitive map; 15. learning-performance; 16. insight; 17. cognitive; 18. biological factors; 19. (a) imprinting, (b) irreversible; 20. preparedness, or prepared learning; 21. noncompliance; 22. time-out; 23. (a) attention, (b) memory, (c) imitate, (d) motivation; 24. (a) behavior modification, (b) biofeedback; 25. (a) positive punishment, (b) negative punishment, (c) conduct, (d) aggressive*

Critical Thinking

How Do You Train a Killer Whale?

If you have ever been to a marine park, then you most certainly have been entertained by watching the marvelous marine animal performances. In just one show an enormous killer whale jumps through a ring suspended in air, waves to audience members with its fins, swims backward while standing up on its tail, and gently kisses a brave volunteer. Whales are taught to perform these impressive behaviors with the use of operant and classical conditioning techniques.

Operant conditioning is used to train whales because when the consequences of performing a specific behavior are reinforcing, the whale will likely repeat the behavior. Positive reinforcers for whales may include food, toys, back scratches, being sprayed with a hose, or another favorite activity. Giving the whale positive reinforcers immediately after it performs a specific behavior makes it likely that the behavior will increase in frequency, duration, and intensity in a similar situation.

The use of classical conditioning is also necessary to teach a whale to perform complex behaviors. Because it is not always possible to reinforce the whale immediately after it performs a specific behavior, trainers must use a signal (whistle) to provide the whale with immediate feedback that it has correctly performed the desired behavior. A whale learns the meaning of the whistle by the trainer whistling before giving the whale food. Over the course of several trials, the whale comes to associate the whistle with receiving food and the whale performs the behavior to get the reinforcement.

Once the association between the whistle and the reinforcer is established, whales can be taught to perform complex behaviors. First, the whale is taught to follow a target, such as a long stick with a ball at the end. The target guides the whale in a direction and when the target touches the whale, the trainer blows the whistle and reinforces the whale. After this is done several times, the target is moved farther away and the trainer waits for the whale to touch it before providing reinforcement. The whale learns that making contact with the target results in being reinforced. Now, when the whale performs a behavior that is close to the desired behavior, the trainer whistles and the whale approaches the trainer to receive a positive reinforce.

Teaching whales to perform behaviors may appear like a relatively easy task while watching the trainers and whales interact on stage, but the truth is training whales to perform is very challenging work. Trainers need to be committed, patient, and friendly to earn the whale's trust, and even then it can take months or even years to teach a whale a complex set of behaviors. (Adapted from Animal training at SeaWorld, 2002; Aqua facts: Training marine mammals, 2006)

Questions

1. How do we know what a reinforcer is for a whale?

2. Why isn't punishment used to train a whale to perform behaviors?

3. Why is it important to reinforce the whale *immediately* after it performs a desired behavior?

4. What should a trainer do if a whale performs a behavior incorrectly?

5. Can whales learn to do tricks by just watching other whales perform?

Suggested Answers

1. Whales cannot tell us what they like and don't like, and not all whales have the same preferences. Thus, trainers examine the frequency of the behavior after providing a reinforcer. If the frequency increases, the trainer knows the consequence was a reinforcer. If the frequency decreases, the trainer will try using other consequences until one increases the frequency of the desired behavior.
2. Punishment only points out what the whale should not do, while reinforcers point out what the whale should do. Also, punishment can increase aggressive behaviors in some whales.
3. When a reinforcer immediately follows a desired behavior, the whale associates the reinforcer with the desired behavior and not some other behavior that just happens to occur. If the reinforcer is delayed even for a few seconds, the whale may be reinforced for an undesired or superstitious behavior.
4. If a whale performs a behavior incorrectly, the trainer must be sure to avoid giving any reinforcement. In such a case, the trainer should remain motionless and silent for a few seconds, making sure there is no possibility the whale will think its behavior earned approval.
5. Yes. Whales can learn to imitate some behaviors just by watching other whales, a process known as observational learning. Also, whales that are trained with experienced whales may learn to perform behaviors at a faster rate.

Links to Learning

Learning Activities

- **POWERSTUDY FOR INTRODUCTION TO PSYCHOLOGY 4.0**

  by Tom Doyle and Rod Plotnik

  SuperModule: Check out the "Operant & Cognitive Approaches" on **PowerStudy.** It includes complete paragraph-by-paragraph explanations of all content using fully-narrated animations and graphics. An onscreen toolbar allows immediate access to text, text outline, and module glossary with notetaking and printing capabilities. This module also includes:

  - Videos—Imbedded videos present important discussions like operant conditioning and the Skinner box, treatment of snake phobia, and predisposition to play behavior.
  - A multitude of animations designed to help you understand the components of operant and cognitive learning. A virtual test helps you identify the differences between operant and cognitive learning, and a vitual rat in a Skinner box helps illustrate schedules of reinforcement.
  - A test of your knowledge using an interactive version of the Summary Test on pages 234 and 235. Also access related quizzing—true/false, multiple choice, and matching.
  - An interactive version of the Critical Thinking exercise "How Do You Train a Killer Whale?" on page 236.
  - Key terms, a chapter outline, and hotlinked websites.

- **CengageNOW**
  academic.cengage.com/login

  Need help studying? This site is your one-stop study shop. Take a Pre-Test and CengageNOW will generate a Personalized Study Plan based on your test results. The Study Plan will identify the topics you need to review and direct you to online resources to help you master those topics. You can then take a Post-Test to determine the concepts you have mastered and what you still need to work on.

- **INTRODUCTION TO PSYCHOLOGY BOOK COMPANION WEBSITE**
  academic.cengage.com/psychology/plotnik

  Visit your book companion website where you will find more resources to help you study. At this site, you will find Learning Objectives, Internet Exercises, quizzing, flash cards, and a pronunciation glossary.

- **STUDY GUIDE and WEBTUTOR**

  Check the corresponding module in your Study Guide for effective student tips and help learning the material presented. Also go to **academic.cengage.com/webtutor** for an interactive version of the Study Guide features.

Study Questions

*A. Operant Conditioning—How do you explain why your significant other sulks every time something is wrong even though you've told him or her that it bugs you? (**Suggested answer page 625**)

*B. Reinforcers—How would you use operant conditioning to change a rude friend into a more likable and friendly person? (**Suggested answer page 625**)

C. Schedules of Reinforcement—Which schedules of partial reinforcement best apply to the following behaviors: eating, studying, going to the movies, dating?

D. Other Conditioning Concepts—The first time you visit your 2-year-old niece, she takes one look at you and starts to cry. What happened?

E. Cognitive Learning—Why should parents be especially concerned about what they say and do in the presence of their children?

F. Biological Factors—A 14-year-old boy graduated from college with outstanding grades. How could he learn so much so early?

G. Research Focus: Noncompliance—Why might parents yell, threaten, or spank rather than use a time-out to deal with a child's constant refusals?

*H. Cultural Diversity: East Meets West—Why do the same principles of learning work in very different cultures? (**Suggested answer page 625**)

I. Application: Behavior Modification—How could techniques of behavior modification be used in a computer program to teach children how to do math problems?

*These questions are answered in Appendix B.

MODULE 11
Types of Memory

 PowerStudy 4.0™ Complete Module

Introduction

Incredible Memory

What's a super memory?

Rajan Mahadevan stood before the packed house of the International Congress on Yoga and Meditation. He recited, from memory, the first 31,811 digits of pi, which is often rounded off to two decimal places, or 3.14. He did not err until the 31,812th digit. This feat took 3 hours and 44 minutes and earned him a place in *The Guinness Book of World Records*.

Rajan memorized 31,811 digits of pi in exact order.

Researcher Charles Thompson discovered that Rajan can quickly recall the digit at any location within the first 10,000 digits of pi. This would be equivalent to memorizing the names of 10,000 people seated in numbered seats and then recalling the name of any single person, such as the one sitting in seat 2,141. Rajan can repeat a string of 60 numbers after a single hearing, while most of us can repeat about 7–10 random numbers. Rajan is one of a half-dozen people worldwide with such gargantuan memory powers.

Despite Rajan's unbelievable ability to memorize numbers, he seems to be worse than average at recalling faces, and he constantly forgets where he put his keys (C. Thompson et al., 1993). Rajan's pi record has since been broken a few times. Most recently, Akira Haraguchi correctly repeated the first 100,000 digits of pi in about 16 hours (Associated Press, 2006).

Few people have such incredible memories and, unfortunately, many others have memory problems. Next, we'll learn about a man who has very serious problems with his memory.

Memory Problem

How important is memory?

Imagine what life would be like without memory. For Clive Wearing, that's a grim reality.

At age 40, Clive Wearing, a musician, got a disease that caused brain damage resulting in severe memory impairment. For instance, despite having written a book on a classical composer, he cannot remember any information about the composer. Clive can no longer enjoy reading books or watching movies because he is unable to follow the plot. Each time Clive sees his wife, he excitedly greets her as if he has not seen her in years, even though she may have left the room for only a moment. He cannot recall his wedding day or the names of his children.

Clive has very serious memory problems caused by a disease that damaged his brain.

The disease did spare Clive some of his memory. Even though Clive cannot remember being educated in music, he remembers how to play the piano, conduct an orchestra, and sing.

When Clive tells others about his life, he says it is "precisely like death. I'd like to be alive" (J. Goodwin, 2006, p. 125). He does not feel alive because for the past 20 years, his memory problems have robbed him of a past and future. Clive lives in a never-ending present. His wife describes his memory by explaining, "It's as if Clive's every conscious moment is like waking up for the first time" (J. Goodwin, 2006, p. 126). Clive's problems with memory significantly affect his quality of life and clearly demonstrate the importance of memory.

Definitions

What are the three processes?

Rajan's amazing ability to recall thousands of digits and Clive's very serious memory problems involve three different memory processes.

Memory **is the ability to retain information over time through three processes: encoding (forming), storing, and retrieving. Memories are not copies but representations of the world that vary in accuracy and are subject to error and bias.**

We'll briefly define each of the three memory processes because they are the keys to understanding the interesting and complex process of how we remember and thus create the world we live in.

1 *Encoding*

Rajan developed a method or code to form memories for digits, a process called encoding.

Encoding **refers to making mental representations of information so that it can be placed into our memories.**

For example, Rajan encoded the number 111 by associating it with Admiral Nelson, who happened to have one eye, one arm, and one leg.

2 *Storing*

Rajan used associations to encode information because associations are also useful for storing information.

Storing **is the process of placing encoded information into relatively permanent mental storage for later recall.**

New information that is stored by making associations with old or familiar information is much easier to remember, or retrieve.

3 *Retrieving*

Rajan was able to recall, or retrieve, 31,811 digits in order.

Retrieving **is the process of getting or recalling information that has been placed into short-term or long-term storage.**

Only a half-dozen people in the entire world can match Rajan's feat of encoding, storing, and retrieving thousands of digits in order. Most people vary in their accuracy to recall information. For example, adolescents were questioned about dating, their families, and general activities. When asked the same questions 30 years later, they made many errors in recalling the same information (Offer et al., 2000).

We'll discuss three kinds of memory, how memories are encoded, why emotional memories are long-lasting, the issue of repressed memories, and some unusual memory abilities. We'll start with an overview of the three kinds of memory.

239

A. Three Types of Memory

What are the three types?

We often talk about memory as though it were a single process. In fact, a popular model of memory divides it into three different processes: sensory, short-term, and long-term memory (Baddeley, 2006). To illustrate each of these processes, we'll examine what happens as you walk through a big-city mall.

Sensory Memory

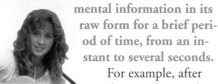

As you walk through a busy mall, you are bombarded by hundreds of sights, smells, and sounds, including the music of a lone guitarist playing for spare change. Many of these stimuli reach your sensory memory.

Sensory memory **refers to an initial process that receives and holds environmental information in its raw form for a brief period of time, from an instant to several seconds.**

For example, after reaching your ears, the guitarist's sounds are held in sensory memory for a second or two. What you do next will determine what happens to the guitarist's sounds that are in your sensory memory.

If you pay no more attention to these sounds in sensory memory, they automatically *disappear* without a trace.

However, if you pay attention to the guitarist's music, the auditory information in sensory memory is transferred into another memory process called short-term memory (Baddeley, 2004).

Short-Term Memory

Because a few notes of the guitarist's song sounded interesting, you shifted your attention to that particular information in sensory memory. Paying attention to information in sensory memory causes it to be automatically transferred into short-term memory.

Short-term memory, **also called** *working memory,* **refers to another process that can hold only a limited amount of information—an average of seven items—for only a short period of time—2 to 30 seconds.**

Once a limited amount of information is transferred into short-term, or working, memory, it will remain there for up to 30 seconds. If during this time you become more involved in the information, such as humming to the music, the information will remain in short-term memory for a longer period of time.

However, the music will *disappear* after a short time unless it is transferred into permanent storage, called long-term memory (Baddeley, 2004).

Long-Term Memory

If you become mentally engaged in humming along or wondering why the guitarist's music sounds familiar, there is a good chance that this mental activity will transfer the music from short-term into long-term memory.

Long-term memory **refers to the process of storing almost unlimited amounts of information over long periods of time.**

For example, you have stored hundreds of songs, terms, faces, and conversations in your long-term memory—information that is potentially available for retrieval. However, from personal experience, you know that you cannot always retrieve things you learned and know you know. In Module 12, we'll discuss reasons for forgetting information stored in long-term memory.

Now that you know what the three memory processes are, we'll explain how they work together.

Memory Processes

1 **Sensory memory.** We'll explain how the three types of memory described above work and how paying or not paying attention to something determines what is remembered and what is forgotten.

Imagine listening to a lecture. All the information that enters your sensory memory remains for seconds or less. If you *do not pay attention* to information in sensory memory, it is forgotten. If you *do pay attention* to particular information, such as the instructor's words, this information is automatically transferred into short-term memory.

2 **Short-term memory.** If you *do not pay attention* to information in short-term memory, it is not encoded and is forgotten. If you *do pay attention* by rehearsing the information, such as taking notes, the information will be encoded for storage in long-term memory. That's why it helps to take lecture notes.

3 **Long-term memory.** Information that is encoded for storage in long-term memory will remain there on a *relatively permanent basis.* Whether or not you can recall the instructor's words from long-term memory depends partly on how they are encoded, which we'll discuss later. This means that poor class notes may result in poor encoding and poor recall on exams. The secret to great encoding and great recall is to associate new information with old, which we'll also discuss later.

Now that we have given you an overview of memory, we'll discuss each of the three types of memory in more detail.

Incoming information → Sensory memory → Selective attention → Short-term memory → *REHEARSING* → Encoded for storage → Long-term memory

Three types of memory, each with a different function

NO attention → Forgotten

NOT encoded → Forgotten

Do you have a mental video recorder? Your brain has a mental video-audio recorder that automatically receives and holds incoming sensory information for only seconds or less. This brief period provides just enough time for you to decide whether some particular incoming sensory information is important or interesting and therefore demands your further attention. We'll examine two different kinds of sensory memory: visual sensory memory, called iconic memory, and auditory sensory memory, called echoic memory.

Iconic Memory

What happens when you blink? About 14,000 times a waking day, your eyes blink and you are totally blind during the blinks (Casselman, 2006; Garbarini, 2005). However, the world doesn't disappear during the eye blinks because of a special sensory memory, which is called iconic *(eye-CON-ick)* memory.

Iconic memory **is a form of sensory memory that automatically holds visual information for about a quarter of a second or more; as soon as you shift your attention, the information disappears.** (The word *icon* means "image.")

You don't "go blind" when both eyes close completely during a blink (about one-third of a second) because the visual scene is briefly held in iconic memory (O'Regan et al., 2000). When your eyes reopen, you don't realize that your eyes were completely closed during the blink because "you kept seeing" the visual information that was briefly stored in iconic memory. Without iconic memory, your world would disappear into darkness during each eye blink.

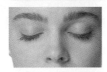

Iconic memory briefly holds visual information during eye blink.

IDENTIFYING ICONIC MEMORY

Here's the first study that showed the existence and length of iconic memory.

Procedure. Individual subjects sat in front of a screen upon which 12 letters (three rows of four letters) appeared for a very brief period of time (50 milliseconds, or 50/1,000 of a second). After each presentation, subjects were asked to recall a particular row of letters.

Results and conclusion. As shown in the left graph, if subjects responded immediately (0.0-second delay) after seeing the letters, they remembered an average of nine letters. However, a delay of merely 0.5 second reduced memory to an average of six letters, and a delay of 1.0 second reduced memory to an average of only four letters (Sperling, 1960).

Number of Letters Remembered

Delay in Seconds	
0.0	9 letters
0.5	6 letters
1.0	4 letters

Notice that an increased delay in responding resulted in subjects' remembering fewer letters, which indicated the brief duration of iconic memory—seconds or less.

This study demonstrated a sensory memory for visual information, which was called iconic memory. The sensory memory for auditory information is called echoic memory.

Echoic Memory

What did you hear? Without realizing, you have already experienced auditory sensory memory, which is called echoic (eh-KO-ick) memory.

Echoic memory **is a form of sensory memory that holds auditory information for 1 or 2 seconds.**

For instance, suppose you are absorbed in reading a novel and a friend asks you a question. You stop reading and ask, "What did you say?" As soon as those words are out of your mouth, you realize that you can recall, or play back, your friend's exact words. You can play back these words because they are still in echoic memory, which may last as

What did you say?

Oh, yes. Now I remember.

Echoic memory briefly holds sounds.

long as 2 seconds. In addition to letting you play back things you thought you did not hear, echoic memory also lets you hold speech sounds long enough to know that sequences of certain sounds form words (Norman, 1982). Researchers discovered that the length of echoic memory increases as children grow into adults (Gomes et al., 1999).

Here's a quick review of the functions of iconic and echoic memories.

Functions of Sensory Memory

1 **Prevents being overwhelmed.** Sensory memory keeps you from being overwhelmed by too many incoming stimuli because any sensory information you do not attend to will vanish in seconds.

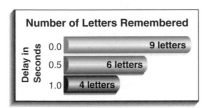

Incoming information → Sensory memory → NO attention → Forgotten

2 **Gives decision time.** Sensory memory gives you a few seconds to decide whether some incoming sensory information is interesting or important. Information you pay attention to will automatically be transferred to short-term memory.

3 **Provides stability, playback, and recognition.** Iconic memory makes things in your visual world appear smooth and continuous, such as "seeing" even during blinking. Echoic memory lets you play back auditory information, such as holding separate sounds so that you can recognize them as words.

If you attend to information in sensory memory, it goes into short-term memory, the next topic.

C. Short-Term Memory: Working

What was that phone number?

You have just looked up a phone number, which you keep repeating as you dial to order a pizza. After giving your order and hanging up, you can't remember the number. This example shows two characteristics of short-term memory.

Short-term memory, more recently called *working memory,* refers to a process that can hold a limited amount of information—an average of seven items—for a limited period of time—2 to 30 seconds. However, the relatively short duration can be lengthened by repeating or rehearsing the information.

For good reason, telephone numbers and postal ZIP codes are seven numbers or fewer because that is about the limit of short-term memory.

Clive Wearing's prefrontal cortex is damaged.

Prefrontal cortex

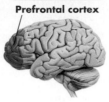

Recent studies found that when you are paying attention and using working memory to perform a variety of cognitive tasks, such as looking for a face in a crowd, maximum neural activity occurs in various areas of the prefrontal cortex (Pessoa & Ungerleider, 2004). The prefrontal cortex of Clive Wearing, discussed in the beginning of this module, is damaged and he can remember certain types of information for only 7 seconds. Thus, his working memory is impaired and he cannot remember a phone number for longer than a few seconds.

Although extremely useful, working or short-term memory has the two characteristics of limited duration and limited capacity.

Two Features

LIMITED DURATION

The new telephone number that you looked up will remain in short-term memory for a brief time, usually from 2 to 30 seconds, and then disappear. However, you can keep information longer in short-term memory by using maintenance rehearsal.

Short-term memory holds items for 2-30 seconds.

Maintenance rehearsal refers to the practice of intentionally repeating or rehearsing information so that it remains longer in short-term memory.

Researchers studied how long information is remembered without practice or rehearsal by asking participants to remember a series of consonants composed of three meaningless letters, such as CHJ. Participants were prevented from rehearsing, or repeating, these consonants by having them count backward immediately after seeing the groups of three letters. As the graph below shows, 80% of the participants recalled the groups of three letters after 3 seconds. However, only 10% of the participants recalled the groups of three letters after 15 seconds (L. R. Peterson & Peterson, 1950). Since almost all the participants had forgotten the groups of three letters after 15 seconds (if they were prevented from rehearsing), this study clearly showed that information disappears from your short-term memory within seconds unless you continually repeat or rehearse the information.

You can increase the time that information remains in short-term memory by using maintenance rehearsal. However, during maintenance rehearsal, which involves repeating the same thing over and over, new information cannot enter short-term memory.

Not only does short-term or working memory have a limited duration, it also has a limited capacity.

(Graph: Percent of Items Correctly Recalled vs. Interval in Seconds; y-axis 20, 40, 60, 80, 100; x-axis 3, 6, 9, 12, 15. Legend: CHJ BDK MXF RTQ)

LIMITED CAPACITY

In previous modules, we pointed out several studies that are considered classic because they challenged old concepts or identified significant new information. One such classic study is that of George Miller (1956), who was the first to discover that short-term memory can hold only about seven items or bits, plus or minus two. Although this seems like too small a number, researchers have repeatedly confirmed Miller's original finding (Baddeley, 2004). Thus, one reason telephone numbers worldwide are generally limited to seven digits is that seven matches the capacity of short-term memory.

It is easy to confirm Miller's finding with a *memory span test,* which measures the total number of digits that we can repeat back in the correct order after a single hearing. For example, students make few errors when they are asked to repeat seven or eight digits,

Short-term memory holds about 7 items.

make some errors with a list of eight or nine digits, and make many errors when they repeat a list that is longer than nine digits. One of the main reasons information disappears from short-term memory is interference (Lieberman, 2004).

Interference results when new information enters short-term memory and overwrites or pushes out information that is already there.

For example, if you are trying to remember a phone number and someone asks you a question, the question interferes with or wipes away the phone number. One way to prevent interference is through rehearsal. However, once we stop rehearsing, the information in short-term memory may disappear.

Although short-term memory has limited capacity and duration, it is possible to increase both. For example, we use a classroom demonstration in which we guarantee that any student can learn to memorize a list of 23 digits, in exact order, in just 25 seconds. This impressive memory demonstration, which always works, is accomplished by knowing how to use something called chunking.

Chunking

How does Rajan remember 1113121735 1802?

Although short-term memory briefly holds an average of about seven items, it is possible to increase the length of each item by using a process called chunking (Kimball & Holyoak, 2005).

Chunking **is combining separate items of information into a larger unit, or chunk, and then remembering chunks of information rather than individual items.**

One of the interesting things about Rajan's prodigious memory for numbers is his ability to chunk. For instance, in about 2 minutes Rajan (right photo) memorized 36 random numbers (in a block of 6 × 6) written on a blackboard. He was able to repeat the numbers forward and backward and to state the numbers in any individual row, column, or diagonal.

When asked about his method for memorizing numbers, he replied that he automatically arranged the numbers into chunks and gave the chunks a name.

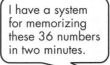

I have a system for memorizing these 36 numbers in two minutes.

111312
173518
028537
873625
419803
291728

For example, here's how he chunked the first 14 numbers: 11131217351802. He chunked 111 and named it "Nelson" because Admiral Nelson had one eye, one arm, and one leg; he chunked 312 and named it the "area code of Chicago"; he chunked 1735 and named it "29" because Ben Franklin was 29 in 1735; and he chunked 1802 as "plus 2" because John Adams occupied the White House in 1800. When Rajan wants to recall the numbers, he does so by remembering a string of associations: Nelson, area code of Chicago, Ben Franklin, and John Adams. As Rajan explains, he doesn't know why he makes particular associations; they just come to him.

Sometimes we use chunking without thinking about it. For example, to remember the 11-digit phone number 16228759211, we break it into four chunks: 1-622-875-9211.

As first suggested by George Miller (1956), chunking is a powerful memory tool that greatly increases the amount of information that you can hold in short-term memory. Rajan's ability to chunk numbers helped him develop an incredible memory, and the use of chunking can improve your memory, too.

Next, we'll review three important functions of short-term memory.

Functions of Short-Term Memory

Why is it also called working memory?

Short-term memory is like having a mental computer screen that stores a limited amount of information that is automatically erased after a brief period of time and replaced by new information, and so the cycle continues. *Short-term memory* is also called *working memory* to indicate that it's an active process. Using brain scans, researchers found that short-term memory involves the front part of the brain, especially the prefrontal area (Pessoa & Ungerleider, 2004).

There are three important points to remember about short-term memory: 1st—paying attention transfers information into short-term memory; 2nd—after a short time, information disappears unless it is rehearsed; and 3rd—some information is eventually transferred from short-term memory into permanent storage.

1 *Attending*

Imagine driving along with your radio on while a friend in the passenger seat is talking about the weekend. A tremendous amount of information is entering your sensory memory, but you avoid stimulus overload because incoming information automatically vanishes in seconds unless you pay attention to it.

The moment you pay attention to information in sensory memory, that information enters short-term memory for further processing. For example, while your friend is talking, you don't pay attention to the radio until your favorite song comes on and enters sensory memory. As you pay attention, you hear the radio, even though it has been playing the whole time. One function of short-term memory is that it allows us *to selectively attend to information that is relevant and disregard everything else.*

Once information enters short-term, or working, memory, several things may happen.

2 *Rehearsing*

Once information enters short-term memory, it usually remains for only seconds unless you rehearse it. For example, the announcer on the car radio gives a phone number to call for free movie tickets. But unless

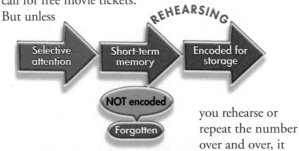

you rehearse or repeat the number over and over, it will probably disappear from your short-term memory because of interference from newly arriving information. Another function of short-term memory is that it allows you *to hold information for a short period of time until you decide what to do with it.*

If you rehearse the information in short-term memory, you increase the chances of storing it.

3 *Storing*

Rehearsing information not only holds that information in short-term memory but also helps *to store or encode information in long-term memory.* Later, we'll discuss two different kinds of rehearsing (p. 249) and explain why one kind of rehearsing is better than the other for storing or encoding information in long-term memory.

Next, we'll describe the steps in the memory process and why some things are stored in long-term memory.

D. Long-Term Memory: Storing

Putting Information into Long-Term Memory

Is it a thing or a process? Don't think of sensory memory, short-term memory, and long-term memory as *things* or *places* but rather as ongoing and interacting *processes*. To show how these different memory processes interact, we'll describe what happens as you hear a new song on the car radio or iPod and try to remember the song's title.

1 Sensory memory. As you drive down the highway, you're half listening to the car radio. Among the incoming information, which is held for seconds or less in sensory memory, are the words, "Remember this song, 'Love Is Like Chocolate,' and win two movie tickets."

2 Attention. If you do NOT pay attention to information about winning tickets, it will disappear from sensory memory. If the chance to win tickets gets your attention, information about the song title, "Love Is Like Chocolate," is automatically transferred into short-term memory.

3 Short-term memory. Once the song title is in short-term memory, you have a short time (2–30 seconds) for further processing. If you lose interest in the title or are distracted by traffic, the title will most likely disappear and be forgotten. However, if you rehearse the title or, better yet, form a new association, the title will likely be transferred into and encoded in your long-term memory.

4 Encoding. You place information in long-term memory through a process called encoding. *Encoding* **is the process of transferring information from short-term to long-term memory by paying attention to it, repeating or rehearsing it, or forming new associations.**

For example, if you simply repeat the title or don't make any new associations, the title may not be encoded at all or may be poorly encoded and thus difficult to recall from long-term memory. However, if you find the title, "Love Is Like Chocolate," to be catchy or unusual, or you form a new association, such as thinking of a chocolate-shaped heart, you will be successful in encoding this title into long-term memory.

We'll discuss ways to improve encoding information and thus improve recalling information later in this module.

5 Long-term memory. Once the song title is encoded in long-term memory, it has the potential to remain there for your lifetime.

Long-term memory **refers to the process of storing almost unlimited amounts of information over long periods of time with the potential of retrieving, or remembering, such information in the future.**

For example, later you may try to recall the song title from long-term memory by placing it back into short-term memory. How easily and accurately you can recall or retrieve information depends on many factors (S. C. Brown & Craik, 2005).

6 Retrieving. When people talk about remembering something, they usually mean retrieving or recalling information from long-term memory.

Retrieving **is the process of selecting information from long-term memory and transferring it back into short-term memory.**

There are several reasons you can't remember or retrieve the song's title. You may not have effectively encoded the title into long-term memory because you got distracted or neglected to form a new association (chocolate heart). The key to successfully retrieving information from long-term memory is to effectively encode information, usually by making associations between new and old information, which we'll soon discuss.

Features of Long-Term Memory

How big and how accurate? **Capacity and permanency.** Researchers estimate that long-term memory has an almost unlimited capacity to store information. Anything stored has the potential to last a lifetime, provided drugs or disease do not damage the brain's memory circuits (Bahrick, 2000).

Chances of retrieval. Although all information in long-term memory has the potential to be retrieved, how much you can actually retrieve depends on a number of factors, including how it was encoded and the amount of interference from related information. The next question is: How accurate are your long-term memories?

Accuracy of long-term memory. Researchers found that the content and accuracy of long-term memories may undergo change and distortion across time and not always be as accurate as people think. For example, college freshmen were asked to recall grades from all four years of high school. As the graph below shows, students accurately recalled 89% of grades of A but

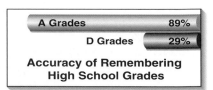

Accuracy of Remembering High School Grades

only 29% of grades of D. Thus, students were much more accurate recalling positive events, grades of A, than they were recalling negative events, grades of D (Bahrick et al., 1996).

This and other studies show that we do not recall all events with the same accuracy, sometimes inflating positive events and eliminating negative ones (Koriat et al., 2000). The reasons we may change, distort, or forget information will be discussed in Module 12.

Next, we'll explain how psychologists demonstrated the existence of two separate memory processes: a short-term and a long-term memory process.

What is the evidence?

Most researchers agree that there are two memory systems (Neath & Surprenant, 2003). One system involves short-term memory, which stores limited information for a brief period of time and then the information disappears. For example, a stranger tells you his or her name, but a few minutes later you have totally forgotten the name because it disappeared from short-term memory. A second system involves long-term memory, which stores large amounts of information for very long periods of time. For example,

you can recall in great detail many childhood memories that years ago were stored in long-term memory. Other evidence for two memory systems comes from findings that brain damage can wipe out long-term memory while completely sparing short-term memory. Still other evidence for two memory systems comes from research on how you remember items in a relatively long list. We'll give you a chance to memorize a list of items, which will show that you have two separate memory systems—short- and long-term memory.

Primacy Versus Recency

Can you remember this list?

Please read the following list only once and try to remember the animals' names:

bear, giraffe, wolf, fly, deer,
elk, gorilla, elephant, frog, snail,
turtle, shark, ant, owl

Immediately after reading this list, write down (in any order) as many of the animals' names as you can remember.

If you examine the list of names that you wrote down, you'll discover a definite pattern to the order of the names that you remembered. For example, here's the order in which names in the above list would most likely be remembered.

First items: Primacy effect. In studies using similar lists, subjects more easily recalled the *first* four or five items (bear, giraffe, wolf, fly) because subjects had more time to rehearse the first words presented. As a result of rehearsing, these first names were transferred to and stored in long-term memory, from which they were recalled. This phenomenon is called the primacy effect.

The *primacy effect* refers to better recall, or improvement in retention, of information presented at the beginning of a task.

Middle items. Subjects did not recall many items from the *middle*  of the list (gorilla, elephant, frog) because they did not have much time to rehearse them. When they tried to remember items from the middle of the list, their attention and time were split between trying to remember the previous terms and trying to rehearse new ones. Less rehearsal meant that fewer middle names were stored in long-term memory; more interference meant that fewer names remained in short-term memory.

Last items: Recency effect. Subjects more easily recalled the *last* four or five items (turtle, shark, ant, owl) because they were still available in short-term memory and could be read off a mental list. This phenomenon is called the recency effect.

The *recency effect* refers to better recall, or improvement in retention, of information presented at the end of a task.

Together, these two effects are called the primacy-recency effect.

The *primacy-recency effect* refers to better recall of information presented at the beginning and end of a task.

As we'll explain next, the primacy-recency effect is evidence that short- and long-term memory are two separate processes.

Short-Term Versus Long-Term Memory

Why didn't you remember "elephant"?

One reason you probably didn't remember the name "elephant" is that it came from the middle of the list. The middle section of a list is usually least remembered because that information may no longer be retained in short-term memory and may not have been encoded in long-term memory. Evidence for the primacy-recency effect is shown in the graph below (Glanzer & Cunitz, 1966).

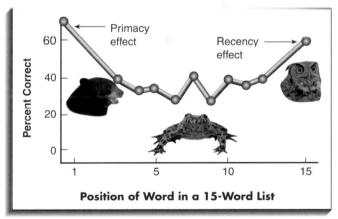

Position of Word in a 15-Word List

For example, subjects showed better recall (70%) for the first items presented, which is the primacy effect. The primacy effect occurs because subjects have more time to rehearse the first items, which increases the chances of transferring these items into long-term memory. Remember that rehearsal has two functions: keeping information longer in short-term memory and promoting encoding—the transfer of information into long-term memory.

In addition, subjects showed better recall (60%) for the last items presented, which is the recency effect. Sometimes subjects say that they can still "hear these words" and usually report these items first. The recency effect occurs because the last items are still in short-term memory, from which they are recalled (Glanzer & Cunitz, 1966).

The occurrence of the primacy-recency effect suggested the existence of two separate kinds of memory processes, which we now call short-term and long-term memory (R. C. Atkinson & Shiffrin, 1968; Neath & Surprenant, 2003).

Next, you'll discover that instead of one, there are several different kinds of long-term memory.

D. Long-Term Memory: Storing

Declarative Versus Procedural or Nondeclarative

Why does Clive play the piano but forget names?

After brain damage, Clive Wearing (photo below) remembered how to play the piano but forgot the names of his children and had no memory of his wedding. Clive retained some memory abilities while losing others because different types of memory are stored differently in the brain. For instance, the ability to play the piano uses one type of long-term memory, and remembering names and personal experiences uses a second type of long-term memory. The discovery that there are two kinds of long-term memory is a relatively new finding, and like many discoveries in science, it was found quite by accident.

Researchers were testing a patient, well known in memory circles as H. M., who suffered severe memory loss because of an earlier brain operation to reduce his seizures. H. M.'s task seemed simple: draw a star by guiding your hand while looking into a mirror. However, this mirror-drawing test is relatively difficult because looking into a mirror reverses all hand movements: up is down and down is up. As H. M. did this task each day, his drawing improved, indicating that he was learning and remembering the necessary motor skills. But here's the strange part. Each and every day, H. M. would insist that he had never seen or done mirror-drawing before (N. J. Cohen, 1984).

How could H. M. have no memory of mirror-drawing, yet show a steady improvement in his performance as he practiced it each day? Based on H. M.'s mirror-drawing as well as data from other patients and numerous animal studies, researchers discovered that there are two different kinds of long-term memory, each involving different areas of the brain (Nyberg & Cabeza, 2005; Squire, 1994).

You'll understand why H. M. could improve at mirror-drawing but not remember doing it after you learn about the two kinds of long-term memory—declarative and procedural.

Declarative Memory

Which bird cannot fly?
What did you eat for breakfast?

You would recall or retrieve answers to these questions from one particular kind of long-term memory called declarative memory.

Declarative memory involves memories for facts or events, such as scenes, stories, words, conversations, faces, or daily events. We are aware of and can recall, or retrieve, these kinds of memories.

There are two kinds of declarative memory—semantic and episodic (Eichenbaum, 2004).

Semantic memory
"Which bird cannot fly?" asks you to remember a fact, which involves semantic *(sah-MANT-ik)* memory.

Semantic memory **is a type of declarative memory and involves knowledge of facts, concepts, words, definitions, and language rules.**

Most of what you *learn* in classes (facts, terms, definitions) goes into semantic memory (Eichenbaum, 2004).

Episodic memory
"What did you eat for breakfast?" asks you to remember an event, which involves episodic *(ep-ih-SAW-dik)* memory.

Episodic memory **is a type of declarative memory and involves knowledge of specific events, personal experiences (episodes), or activities, such as naming or describing favorite restaurants, movies, songs, habits, or hobbies.**

Most of your college activities and experiences go into episodic memory (Tulving, 2002).

Since his brain operation, H. M. cannot remember new facts (semantic memory) or events (episodic memory). Thus, H. M. has lost declarative memory, which explains why he does not remember events, such as doing mirror-drawing (Squire et al., 2004).

However, H. M.'s motor skills improved during mirror-drawing, which indicates another kind of long-term memory.

Procedural or Nondeclarative Memory

How did you learn to play tennis?
Why are you afraid of spiders?

Even though you can play tennis and are afraid of spiders, you can't explain how you control your muscles to play tennis or why you're so terrified of such a tiny (usually harmless) bug. That's because motor skills and emotional feelings are stored in procedural memory.

Procedural memory, **also called** *nondeclarative memory,* **involves memories for motor skills (playing tennis), some cognitive skills (learning to read), and emotional behaviors learned through classical conditioning (fear of spiders). We cannot recall or retrieve procedural memories.**

Even if you have not played tennis for years, you can pick up a racket and still remember how to serve because that information is stored in procedural memory. But you cannot describe the sequence of movements needed to serve a ball because these skills are stored in procedural memory. Similarly, if you learned to fear spiders through classical conditioning, you cannot explain why you're afraid because the reasons are stored in procedural memory. Although procedural memories greatly influence our behavior, we have neither awareness of nor ability to recall these memories (Mayes, 2005).

Now we can explain H. M.'s strange behavior. He was able to improve at mirror-drawing because it involved learning a motor skill that was stored in procedural memory. But he could not talk about the skill because no one is aware of or can recall procedural memories. Although H. M. gradually improved at mirror-drawing, he could not remember the event of sitting down and drawing because that involves declarative (episodic) memories, which were damaged in his brain surgery (Hilts, 1995). The study of H. M. is a classic study because it first demonstrated the existence of two kinds of long-term memory: declarative memory and procedural memory. We'll discuss the brain systems underlying these types of long-term memory in Module 12.

E. Research Focus: Do Emotions Affect Memories?

Hormones and Memories

Do hormones affect memories? Many of us have vivid memories that involve highly charged emotional situations (Goldstein, 2005). For example, imagine the emotional excitement Halle Berry (right photo) felt when she became the first African-American woman to win an Oscar for Best Actress. During her acceptance speech, Halle said, "This moment is so much bigger than me" (Berry, 2002). Halle was so overwhelmed by the experience she could hardly contain her tears of joy. She will remember this event the rest of her life because something happens during strong emotions that increases the chances of remembering the particular situation, person, or event.

Caption (photo): Excitatory hormones can "stamp in" memories.

What actually happens to improve memory during an emotional event was studied in a long-term research program that began in animals. In Module 2 we explained that researchers may use an animal model (p. 34) to answer questions that for safety, moral, or ethical reasons cannot be studied in humans. Because of safety concerns, neuropsychologist James McGaugh (1999) began using an animal model to study how hormones produced during emotional states affect memory. He found that certain drugs or hormones associated with emotional experiences could either increase or decrease the recall of long-term memories. For example, if rats were given an injection of a hormone (epinephrine) that is normally produced by the body during emotional or stressful states, rats remembered better what they had just learned (McGaugh, 1990). This was a new and interesting finding and made him wonder why emotional experiences improve long-term memories for related events.

After McGaugh found that the "emotional" hormones and drugs could be safely used in animals, he began his work with human subjects. His study on animals and humans of why emotional events seemed to "stamp in" memories spanned 40 years of research. Here's one of his interesting studies.

Memories of Emotional Events

Can drugs block emotional memories? After almost 20 years of research using an animal model, McGaugh found a way to safely study this phenomenon in humans.

Subjects. Those in the experimental group received a drug (propranolol) that decreases or blocks the effects of hormones (epinephrine and norepinephrine) that are normally produced during emotional states. After taking this drug, experimental subjects would still feel emotions, but the drug would block the secretion of those emotionally produced hormones that had been shown to increase memory in animals. Subjects in the control group received a placebo, but because of the double-blind procedure, no subjects knew whether they were given a drug or a placebo.

Procedure. So that the drugs would have time to act, subjects were given either a placebo or the drug 1 hour before seeing a series of slides. To prevent their expectations from biasing the results, subjects did not know whether they got a drug or a placebo.

Each subject watched a series of 12 slides and heard an accompanying story. The beginning of the slide story was emotionally neutral and simply described a mother leaving home with her son to visit her husband's workplace. The middle of the slide story was emotionally charged and described the son having a terrible accident in which his feet were severed and his skull was damaged. The end of the slide story was emotionally neutral and described the mother leaving the hospital to pick up her other child from preschool. Subjects were tested for retention of the slide story a week later.

Hypothesis. Based on their results from the animal model, McGaugh and his colleagues guessed that if a drug blocked the effects of memory-enhancing hormones normally produced during emotional situations, subjects who took the drug should show poor retention for emotional events.

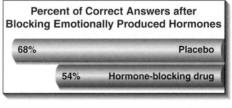

Percent of Correct Answers after Blocking Emotionally Produced Hormones

68%	Placebo
54%	Hormone-blocking drug

Results and conclusion. Researchers found that both drug and placebo subjects remembered about the same number of neutral events. However, the graph below shows that, compared to subjects in the placebo group, subjects given a drug that blocked "emotional" hormones remembered significantly fewer emotionally charged events (Cahill et al., 1994). Other studies on humans found that intense feelings triggered by emotional or stressful situations are encoded, or "carved in stone," by hormones released during emotionally charged situations and that these memories are better remembered (McGaugh, 1999). More recent research suggests that the same "emotional" hormones that help us recall emotional experiences may block memories of what happened moments before the emotional event (Strange et al., 2003). McGaugh's research is a good example of using an animal model to lay the basis for similar studies in humans. But of what use is it to animals or humans for emotional memories to be better remembered?

Based on years of research, McGaugh believes that one reason emotions seem to "stamp in" memories is to help a species survive. For instance, if emotions stamped in memories of dramatic or life-threatening situations, our early ancestors would better pay attention to and remember to avoid these dangers and thus increase their chances of survival (R. J. Dolan, 2002). An important clinical application of McGaugh's research is that it explains why bad emotional memories, such as those formed after witnessing or being in a terrible accident or suffering physical or sexual abuse, are stamped in and thus become so powerful and so difficult to treat and overcome.

While McGaugh's research shows that emotional feelings are easily encoded, you'll see next that nonemotional information, such as learning terms and definitions, can be encoded only with hard work.

F. Encoding: Transferring

How do we store memories?

It's very common for someone to say, "Let me tell you about my day," and then proceed to describe in great detail a long list of mostly bad things, including long, word-for-word conversations. You can easily recall these detailed personal experiences, even though you took no notes. That's because many personal experiences are automatically, and with no effort on your part, encoded in your long-term memory.

Encoding **refers to acquiring information or storing information in memory by changing this information into neural or memory codes.**

> Let me tell you about my awful day. First . . .

Why is it that detailed personal experiences and conversation seem to be encoded effortlessly and automatically and easily recalled? Why is it that much of book learning, such as memorizing terms or definitions, usually requires deliberate effort and considerable time and may still not be easily recalled when taking exams? The answer is that there are to two different kinds of encoding: automatic and effortful encoding.

> Encoded for storage → Long-term memory

Automatic Encoding

Why are some things easy to encode?

Just as most of us can easily and in great detail recall all the annoying things that happened today, the person below is recalling a long list of very detailed personal activities that were automatically encoded into his long-term memory. In fact, many personal events (often unpleasant ones), as well as things we're interested in (movies, music, sports) and a wide range of skills (riding a bike) and habits, are automatically encoded (Murnane et al., 1999).

Automatic encoding **is the transfer of information from short-term into long-term memory without any effort and usually without any awareness.**

> I bought this hat at a second-hand store for a quarter, and then I bought these shoes from a guy who said that he makes them from old tires . . .

Personal events. One reason many of your personal experiences and conversations are automatically encoded is that they hold your interest and attention and easily fit together with hundreds of previous associations. Because personal experiences, which are examples of *episodic information,* are encoded automatically into long-term memory, you can easily recall lengthy conversations, facts about movies and sports figures, television shows, clothes you bought, or food you ate.

Interesting facts. You may know avid sports fans or watchers of popular TV programs who remember an amazing number of facts and details, seemingly without effort. Because these kinds of facts (*semantic information)* are personally interesting and fit with previous associations, they are automatically and easily encoded into declarative long-term memory.

Skills and habits. Learning how to perform various motor skills, such as playing tennis or riding a bike, and developing habits, such as brushing your teeth, are examples of *procedural information,* which is also encoded automatically. For example, H. M. learned and remembered how to mirror-draw because mirror-drawing is a motor skill that is automatically encoded into procedural long-term memory.

On the other hand, factual or technical information from textbooks is usually not encoded automatically but rather requires deliberate, or effortful, encoding, which we'll discuss next.

Effortful Encoding

Why are some things hard to encode?

The person below is pulling his hair because learning unfamiliar or complicated material almost always involves *semantic information,* such as complex terms, which is difficult to encode because such information is often uninteresting, complicated, or requires making new or difficult associations. For all these reasons, semantic information, such as terms, can be encoded only with considerable concentration and effort.

Effortful encoding **involves the transfer of information from short-term into long-term memory either by working hard to repeat or rehearse the information or, especially, by making associations between new and old information.**

> I've been studying these terms for hours and I still can't remember their definitions.

You already know that some information, such as learning a skill, habit, or interesting personal event, is often encoded effortlessly and automatically. In contrast, semantic information, such as learning hundreds of new or difficult terms, facts, concepts, or equations, usually requires effortful encoding because you must form hundreds of new associations. Forming new associations is often just plain hard work and is made even more difficult if you are simultaneously taking two or three difficult classes or have limited time because of other responsibilities, such as a part-time job.

Although there are two methods of effortful encoding—rehearsing and forming associations—the most effective method involves forming associations between the new information that you are trying to learn and the old information that you have already stored in long-term memory. The better the effortful encoding, the better the recall on exams. We'll explain the two methods of effortful encoding, rehearsing and forming associations, and why the second method is more effective and results in better recall.

How much do you remember?

Think of encoding information in your brain as similar to saving information on a gigantic computer hard drive. Unless you have a very good system for labeling and filing the hundreds of computer files, you will have great difficulty finding or retrieving a particular file from the hard drive. Similarly, how easily you can remember or retrieve a particular memory from your brain depends on how much effort you used to encode the information. There are two kinds of effortful encoding: maintenance rehearsal and elaborative rehearsal (S. C. Brown & Craik, 2005).

MAINTENANCE REHEARSAL

The easiest way to remember information for only a short period of time, such as a new phone number, for example, 926-4029, is to simply repeat or rehearse it. This kind of effortful encoding is called maintenance rehearsal.

Maintenance rehearsal **refers to simply repeating or rehearsing the information rather than forming any new associations.**

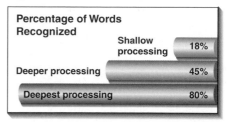

Maintenance rehearsal works best for maintaining or keeping information longer in *short-term memory*, such as remembering a phone number for a few seconds while dialing it. However, if you want to remember the phone number later, maintenance rehearsal is not a good encoding process because it does not include a system for keeping track of how and where that particular phone number will be

Maintenance rehearsal is not a very effective encoding process.

stored. If you need to remember a phone number for a long period of time and avoid having to keep looking it up, you'll need to use another form of effortful encoding called elaborative rehearsal.

ELABORATIVE REHEARSAL

There are some phone numbers and much information from lectures and textbooks that you want to encode so that you remember the information for long periods of time. To have the greatest chance for remembering something, it's best to encode information using elaborative rehearsal.

Elaborative rehearsal **involves using effort to actively make meaningful associations between new information that you wish to remember and old or familiar information that is already stored in long-term memory.**

For example, using elaborative rehearsal, you could associate this phone number, 926-4029, with age: An old person is "926," I'm not "40," but I wish I were "29." To recall this number, you think of the different age associations and those associations lead to the phone number.

To test the usefulness of elaborative rehearsal, students were asked to remember many groups of three words each, such as *dog, bike,* and *street.* Students who encoded the words with maintenance rehearsal (repeating words) did poorly on recall. In comparison, students who encoded the words using elaborative rehearsal, that is, taking the effort to make associations among the three words (dog rides a bike down the street), had significantly better recall (McDaniel & Einstein, 1986).

Elaborative rehearsal is a very effective encoding process.

Effectiveness. Elaborative rehearsal is such an effective system of encoding because by making associations between new and old information, you create cues for locating or retrieving the new information from long-term memory. For example, thinking of the association (dog rides a bike down the street) helps you remember the three words (dog, bike, street).

How important are associations?

The poorest system for encoding information is to simply repeat the information, which is maintenance rehearsal. The best encoding system is to make associations, which is elaborative rehearsal. How much effort and time you put into encoding information is the basis for the levels-of-processing theory (Craik & Lockhart, 1972).

The *levels-of-processing theory* **says that remembering depends on how information is encoded. If you encode by paying attention only to basic features (length of phone number), information is encoded at a shallow level and results in poor recall. If you encode by making new associations, this information will be encoded at a deeper level, which results in better recall.**

For example, students were shown a series of words and asked a question after each one. The questions were of three types, designed to trigger three different levels of processing.

1. Shallow processing question:
"Is the word printed in capital letters?" Asks about one physical feature of the word.

2. Deeper processing question:
"Does the word rhyme with *rain?*" Asks about sound properties of the word.

3. Deepest processing question:
"Does the word fit into the sentence 'She was late for the _____'?" Asks about the meaning of the word.

After students answered these questions, they were tested to see how many of the original words they recognized.

Percentage of Words Recognized

Shallow processing	18%
Deeper processing	45%
Deepest processing	80%

As shown in the graph above, students recognized the smallest percentage of words after shallow processing and the most after the deepest processing (Craik & Tulving, 1975).

This study clearly demonstrates that the system you use to process or encode information has a great effect on how easily you can remember or retrieve the information (Roediger et al., 2002). As we'll discuss in Module 12, a major reason for forgetting is poor encoding (S. C. Brown & Craik, 2005).

Next, we'll discuss a kind of memory that has resulted in great controversy because of the difficulties in determining whether the event ever happened.

G. Repressed Memories

Recovered Memories

Who's to blame? The man in the photo on the right was accused by his daughter, Holly (left photo), of allegedly molesting her beginning when she was 6 years old. Holly's memories of sexual abuse first surfaced during therapy sessions 13 years later, when she was 19. The father sued Holly's therapist for implanting false memories. The jury partly agreed with the father in deciding that Holly's memories were probably false and that the therapist had not implanted the memories but had carelessly reinforced them (K. Butler, 1994). A state appeals court dismissed Holly's case against her father because some of her testimony about sexual abuse was obtained under sodium amytal, the so-called truth serum, which was administered by her therapist. Because testimony taken under

"He abused me."

"I did not."

sodium amytal is often unreliable, it has been barred in California's courts since 1959 (*Los Angeles Times,* August 21, 1997).

Holly's case illustrates one of the more explosive issues in psychology, the problem of repressed and recovered memories.

Psychiatrist Harold Lief, one of the first to question the accuracy of repressed memories, said, "We don't know what percent of these recovered memories are real and what percent are pseudomemories (false). . . . But we do know there are hundreds, maybe thousands of cases of pseudomemories and that many families have been destroyed by them" (J. E. Brody, 2000a, p. D8).

We'll discuss four major issues related to repressed and recovered memories.

Definition of Repressed Memories

What's different about a repressed memory? The idea of repressed memories is based on Sigmund Freud's theory of repression, which underlies much of his psychoanalytic theory of personality (discussed in Module 19).

Repression **is the process by which the mind pushes a memory of some threatening or traumatic event deep into the unconscious. Once in the unconscious, the repressed memory cannot be retrieved at will and may remain there until something releases it and the person remembers it.**

Some therapists believe that children who are sexually abused cope with such traumatic situations and their feelings of guilt by repressing the memories. For example, a client may enter therapy with sexual problems or a mood disorder and later in therapy uncover repressed memories, such as being sexually abused as a child, as the cause of her current problems. Clients usually have total amnesia

Repressed memories are difficult to recover.

(loss of memory) for the traumatic experience, their recovery of repressed memories usually occurs in the first 12 months of therapy, and recovered memories usually involve specific incidents (Andrews et al., 2000).

Based on clients' experiences, many therapists believe that repressed memories of sexual abuse do occur. However, a prominent memory researcher disagrees: "The idea that forgetting in abuse survivors is caused by a special repression mechanism—something more powerful than conscious suppression—is still without a scientific basis" (Schacter, 1996, p. 264). Thus, the controversy over repressed memories continues.

Researcher Elizabeth Loftus (1997b, 2005a) partly blames increased reports of recovered memories on some therapeutic practices.

Therapist's Role in Recovered Memories

How does a therapist know? Some therapists who treat survivors of incest and other traumatic situations maintain that repressed memories are so completely blocked that it may take deliberate suggestion and effort to release them, sometimes using images, hypnosis, or so-called truth serum, sodium amytal.

For example, in one case a client recalls that her therapist insisted that she showed signs of having been sexually abused during childhood and probably had terrible memories buried in her unconscious. The client was dubious at first but, wanting to please her therapist, finally admitted to being raped at the age of 4. However, after leaving the hospital and enlisting help from new therapists, she concluded that the sexual assaults had never happened (B. Bower, 1993a). Whatever the therapists' good intentions, Loftus (1993, 1997b) and others wonder if some therapists

The therapist may have suggested traumatic memories.

are suggesting or implanting traumatic memories in their clients rather than releasing repressed ones (Schooler & Eich, 2005). Loftus suggests that therapists not assume that the cause of psychological problems must be an earlier traumatic experience and cautions against aggressive efforts to recover traumatic memories (Loftus, 2003b).

Fortunately, there are many examples of therapists who have helped clients recover and deal with terrible repressed memories (Gold et al., 1994). Thus, therapists are in the difficult position of distinguishing accurate accounts of repressed memories from those that may have been shaped or reinforced by the suggestions or expectations of the therapist (Baddeley, 2004).

Questions about whether suggestions can influence repressed memories raise the issue of whether false memories can be implanted.

Implanting False Memories

Do people believe "fake" memories?

Because, in some cases, it appears that therapists' suggestions may have contributed to implanting false memories, researchers studied whether fake memories could in fact be implanted and later recalled as being "true."

Researchers gave 24 adults a booklet that contained descriptions of three events that occurred when each adult was 5 years old (Loftus, 1997a). Two of the childhood events had *really happened* because they were obtained from parents or relatives. One childhood event of being lost in a shopping mall, crying, being comforted by an elderly woman, and finally getting reunited with the family had *not happened,* according to parents and relatives. After reading the three events described in the booklet, the adults (aged 18–53) were asked to write what they remembered of the event or, if they did not remember, to write "I do not remember this."

The graph above shows that 68% of subjects remembered some or most of the two *true events* from their childhood. However, about 29% also said that they remembered having experienced the

Percentage of Subjects Who Remembered True and False Memories

| Recalled events after reading booklet | False | 29% |
| | True | 68% |

About 29% of subjects said that they remembered a childhood event that never happened (false) and 68% remembered childhood events that did happen (true).

one *false event of* being lost in the mall at age 5 (Loftus, 1997a).

Researchers concluded that although the memory of being lost in a mall is neither as terrible nor as terrifying as the memory of being abused, this study does show that false memories can be implanted through suggestion alone. Even on a follow-up interview, subjects continued to insist that they remembered the false event.

There are now many similar studies reporting that false memories can be implanted in both children and adults (Loftus, 2003a; S. M. Smith et al., 2003). However, the fact that false memories can be implanted and later recalled as true does in no way disprove the occurrence of repressed memories. Rather, studies on implanting false memories simply show that a false suggestion can grow into a vivid, detailed, and believable personal memory (Ceci, 2000; Loftus, 2000).

The repeated finding that false memories can be implanted in children and adults and later remembered as "true" raises a question about the accuracy of repressed memories that are later recovered and believed to be true.

Accuracy of Recovered Memories

How accurate are repressed memories?

Some individuals may initially enter therapy for help with mood disorders or eating problems, but during the course of therapy, they recovered memories, apparently repressed, of childhood sexual abuse. Since researchers have shown that "false" memories can be implanted through suggestion and believed to be "true" memories, some question the accuracy of a client's recovered memories.

In a few cases, the accuracy of recovered memories can be established. For example, a client who suffered from obesity entered a hospital weight-reduction program that also included psychotherapy. During therapy, she experienced flashbacks of being sexually abused from about age 5 by her older brother, who had since been killed in the war. When she searched through his things, she found a diary in which he had described sexual experiments with his little sister (B. Bower, 1993a). In this case, the woman's repressed memories of sexual abuse were proved accurate by confirming evidence, her brother's diary.

In many cases, the accuracy of recovered memories cannot be clearly established because there is no collaborating evidence of the client's report that the traumatic event really did occur 20–30 years earlier (Roediger & McDermott, 2005). Therapists tend to believe their client's report of recovered memories partly because there is little reason for their client to lie and partly because the recovered memories may explain their client's current problems (Loftus, 1993).

There is reason to question the accuracy of recovered memories because people usually do not recall the memories on their own,

Some question the accuracy of repressed memories.

but often do so with the help of therapists or support groups (Roediger & McDermott, 2005). Additionally, if the memories were obtained under hypnosis or "truth serum" (sodium amytal), they may not be accurate, since people often become more open to suggestion and may later recall events that had been suggested during hypnosis as being true (Lynn et al., 2003).

Another reason to question the accuracy of recovered memories is reports of more than 300 clients who later retracted charges of childhood sexual abuse based on memories that were recovered in therapy (de Rivera, 1997). In about a dozen other cases, clients have successfully sued and won large monetary awards from their therapists for implanting false memories of child abuse (Loftus, 1999). All these examples question the accuracy of some recovered memories.

Conclusions. Memory researcher Elizabeth Loftus (1997a, 2003a) states there are examples of recovered memories that are accurate. However, she questions the accuracy of recovered memories for three reasons: Research has shown that memories that are very detailed but later proven false can be implanted in both children and adults; some clients later retracted their recovered memories; and memories might have been implanted by therapists' suggestions and/or the clients needed and used these memories to explain their current psychological problems. For these reasons, new guidelines caution therapists against using forceful or persuasive suggestions that might elicit memories from their clients (J. E. Brody, 2000a).

The debate over repressed and recovered memories, which reached its peak in the mid-1990s, has recently decreased because some therapists have been sued by their patients over the accuracy of recovered memories and researchers have showed that false memories could be implanted in both children and adults (Lynn et al., 2003).

✔ Concept Review

1. Three processes are involved in memory: the process in which information is placed or stored in memory by making mental representations is called (a)_____; the process of placing encoded information into a permanent mental state is called (b)_____; the process of getting information out of short-term or permanent storage is called (c)_____.

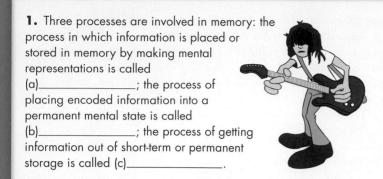

2. The initial step in memory is a process that holds visual and auditory information in its raw form for a very brief period of time, from an instant to several seconds; this process is called _____.

3. Memory that holds raw visual information for up to a quarter of a second is called (a)_____. Memory that holds raw auditory information for up to several seconds is called (b)_____. The process for controlling the transfer of information from sensory memory to the next memory process is (c)_____.

4. The kind of memory that has a limited capacity of about seven items (plus or minus two) and a short duration (2–30 seconds) for unrehearsed information is called either (a)_____ or _____. One way to increase this memory capacity is by combining separate pieces of information into larger units, which is called (b)_____. One way to increase the duration of this memory is by repeating the information, which is called (c)_____.

5. The kind of memory that can store almost unlimited amounts of information over a long period of time is _____, whose accuracy may undergo change and distortion across time.

6. The process for controlling the transfer of information from short-term memory into long-term memory is called _____, which may be automatic or may involve deliberate effort.

7. The process for selecting information from long-term memory and transferring it back into short-term memory is _____.

8. The better recall of items at the beginning of a list is called the (a)_____ effect. The better recall of items at the end of a list is called the (b)_____ effect. Evidence that there are two kinds of memory, short- and long-term, comes from the (c)_____ effect.

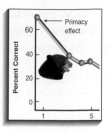

9. There are two kinds of encoding. Simply repeating or rehearsing the information is called (a)_____. Actively making associations between new and old information already stored is called (b)_____.

10. One kind of long-term memory that involves memories for facts or events, such as scenes, stories, words, conversations, faces, or daily events, is called (a)_____ memory. We can retrieve these memories and are conscious of them. One kind of declarative memory that involves events or personal experiences is called (b)_____ memory. A second kind of declarative memory that involves general knowledge, facts, or definitions of words is called (c)_____ memory.

11. A second kind of long-term memory that involves performing motor or perceptual tasks, carrying out habits, and responding to stimuli because of classical conditioning is called _____ memory. We cannot retrieve these memories and are not conscious of them.

12. Something happens that is so threatening, shocking, or traumatic that our mind pushes that memory into the unconscious, from which it cannot be retrieved at will. This phenomenon is called _____.

13. During very emotional or stressful situations, the body secretes chemicals called (a)_____ that act to make encoding very effective, and this results in vivid, long-term memories. Researchers believe that this hormonal encoding system for stressful or emotional events has helped our species (b)_____.

Answers: *1. (a) encoding, (b) storage, (c) retrieval; 2. sensory memory; 3. (a) iconic memory, (b) echoic memory, (c) attention; 4. (a) short-term, or working, memory, (b) chunking, (c) rehearsal, or maintenance rehearsal; 5. long-term memory; 6. encoding; 7. retrieval; 8. (a) primacy, (b) recency, (c) primacy-recency; 9. (a) maintenance rehearsal, (b) elaborative rehearsal; 10. (a) declarative, (b) episodic, (c) semantic; 11. procedural or nondeclarative; 12. repression, or repressed memory; 13. (a) hormones, (b) survive*

H. Cultural Diversity: Oral Versus Written

United States Versus Africa

What do you remember best?

If you went to grade school in the United States, you spent considerable time in your first 8 years learning to read and write. In the U.S. culture, reading and writing skills are viewed as being not only very important for personal growth and development but also necessary for achieving success in one's career. For similar reasons, the schools of many industrialized cultures place heavy emphasis on teaching reading and writing, which allow individuals to encode great amounts of information in long-term memory. In addition, reading and writing skills are necessary for being admitted to and doing well in college.

In contrast, if you went to grade school in the more rural countries of Africa, you would have spent your first 8 or so years learning primarily through the spoken word rather than the written word. In the less industrialized countries of Africa, such as Ghana, there are fewer

In more rural parts of Africa (Ghana), children must rely more on oral than written information.

public or private schools, fewer textbooks and libraries. As a result, these cultures are said to have a strong *oral tradition,* which means that these people have considerable practice in passing on information through speaking and retelling. The Ghana culture emphasizes the oral tradition, which means encoding information after hearing it rather than after reading it.

With Ghana's emphasis on oral tradition, we would expect that African people would better encode and remember information that was spoken. In comparison, with the United States' emphasis on *written tradition*, we would expect that American people would better encode and remember information that was read rather than spoken. Let's see if this hypothesis has been supported.

Remembering Spoken Information

WAR OF THE GHOSTS

One night, two young men from Egulac went down to the river to hunt seals, and while they were there it became foggy and calm. Then they heard war cries, and they thought: "Maybe this is a war party." They escaped to the shore and hid behind a log. Now canoes came up, and they heard the noise of paddles and saw one canoe coming up to them. There were five men in the canoe, and they said:

"What do you think? We wish to take you along. We are going up the river to make war on the people."

One of the young men said: "I have no arrows."

"Arrows are in the canoe," they said.

"I will not go along. I might be killed. My relatives do not know where I have gone. But you," he said, turning to the other, "may go with them."

So one of the young men went, but the other returned home.

And the warriors went up the river to a town on the other side of Kalama. The people came down to the water, and they began to fight, and many were killed (story continues but is too long for full reprint).

Who best remembers what they heard?

On the left is part of a story called "War of the Ghosts," which was read aloud in English to college students at Winneba Training College in Ghana and at New York University. Each group of students heard the story twice and were told to just listen to the story so that they would not take notes on their own. They were not told that they would be tested on its content.

Although English was not the native language of the Ghanaian students, they had learned English in previous schooling, and English was used exclusively in their Training College. Sixteen days after hearing "War of the Ghosts," students were asked to write down as much of the text as they could remember. Researchers scored the amount and accuracy of recalled information by counting the number of ideas or themes and the total number of words (330). The "War of the Ghosts" story has been used frequently in memory research because it can be broken down into 21 themes, or ideas, and easily scored. For example, two of the 21 themes or ideas are (1) two young men went to hunt seals and (2) they heard war cries.

As the graph on the right shows, Ghanaian students remembered a significantly higher percentage of themes and a larger number of words than did American students. The Ghanaian students' superior performance was even more remarkable since they were tested by having to write the themes or ideas in English, which was their second language.

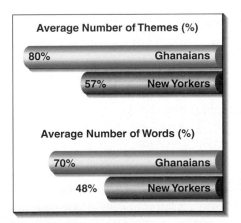

Average Number of Themes (%)

80% — Ghanaians
57% — New Yorkers

Average Number of Words (%)

70% — Ghanaians
48% — New Yorkers

These results support the idea that the Ghanaian students showed superior recall of spoken information because of their long oral tradition, which involves practicing encoding information through hearing rather than reading (B. M. Ross & Millsom, 1970). This study indicates that a culture's emphasis on how information is presented or taught can influence how information or events are encoded and how easily they can be recalled.

Next, we'll examine some unusual cases of encoding and retrieving information.

I. Application Unusual Memories

Photographic Memory

Can you recall everything?

One kind of unusual memory that many of us wish we had is the ability to remember everything with little or no difficulty. Such an amazing memory is commonly called a photographic memory.

Photographic memory, **which occurs in adults, is the ability to form sharp, detailed visual images after examining a picture or page for a short period of time and to recall the entire image at a later date.**

There are no reports of someone developing a photographic memory and only one or two reports of adults who had a truly photographic memory (Stromeyer, 1970). Sometimes people with exceptional memories are mislabeled as having photographic memories (W. L. Adams, 2006; Higbee, 2001). For example, Rajan, who we described earlier as memorizing 31,811 numbers, denies that he has a photographic memory.

She could perfectly visualize her class notes so didn't have to study for exams.

At a recent national memory contest (U.S. Memoriad), Tatiana Cooley (left photo) came in first by doing incredible memory feats, such as pairing 70 names and faces after studying a stack of 100 faces for just 20 minutes. As a child, Tatiana's mother would read to her, and when Tatiana was $2\frac{1}{2}$ years old, she read one of the books back to her mother. In college, Tatiana says, "I remember visualizing the notes that I had taken in class and being able to recall them verbatim for tests so I didn't have to study" (P. Rogers & Morehouse, 1999, p. 90). To keep her memory sharp, she spends 45 minutes each day memorizing the order in which cards appear in a freshly shuffled deck. Wow! Tatiana's ability to visually remember her notes during exams comes close to satisfying the definition for having a photographic memory.

Although there are few examples of adults with photographic memories, a very small percentage of children do have photographic memories.

Eidetic Imagery

Can you memorize this picture?

A small number of children have the ability to look at a picture for a few seconds and then describe it in great detail. This kind of remarkable memory is called eidetic *(eye-DET-ick)* imagery.

Eidetic imagery, **which is a form of photographic memory that occurs in children, is the ability to examine a picture or page for 10–30 seconds and then for several minutes hold in one's mind a detailed visual image of the material.**

For example, an 11-year-old girl was given the following instructions: "Look at this picture from Rudyard Kipling's *The Jungle Book* for a few minutes. Hold the details of this picture in your mind's eye for several minutes. Now, close your eyes and describe what you see."

After the picture (at right) was removed, the young girl closed her eyes and, without hesitation, she described the picture in great detail, as follows: "Ground is dark greenish brown, then there's a mama and a little leopard and there's a native sitting against him. Then there's a pool with a crab coming out . . . with a fish in it, and I think there are turtles walking in front and a porcupine down near the right. There's a tree that separates a cow in half. The cow's brown and white, and there's something up in the tree—I can't see the bottom right-hand corner. There's a sun with a lot of rays on it near the top on the right . . . eight rays . . . the porcupine has a lot of bristles on it . . . the right is disappearing. I can still see that cow that's divided by the tree . . . Oh, there's a crocodile or alligator in the right-hand corner . . . It's very faint . . . It's gone" (Haber, 1980, p. 72).

What is unusual about her description is not only the amount of detail but also the fact that she seems to be examining a vivid visual image of the actual drawing that seems to be held for a time in her mind's eye.

This girl's description is an example of eidetic imagery, which has been shown to be a real phenomenon that occurs in only about 5–8% of preadolescent children. The small percentage of children with eidetic imagery almost always lose the ability around adolescence (Neath & Surprenant, 2003). Why eidetic imagery drops out in adults is not known, but some suggest it may be because adults learn to use and rely more on words than on pictures (Crowder, 1992). The one or two times eidetic imagery did occur in adults it was usually called photographic memory.

Many of us have experienced a very vivid and detailed memory that is called a "flashbulb memory."

Eidetic imagery: The young girl closed her eyes and, without hesitation, she described the picture in great detail, as follows: "Ground is dark greenish brown, there's a little leopard, and there's a native sitting against him. There's a pool with a crab coming out and fish in it, and a turtle walking, and at the top a sun with lots of rays. . . ."

What makes a memory so vivid?

Although it happened about 20 years ago, I (H. K.) have a detailed memory of my cabin in the Santa Cruz Mountains of California shaking and then seesawing on the edge of a mountain during a frightening earthquake. I can play back this terrible scene in great detail and vivid color as if I were actually experiencing an earthquake. Many individuals have had a similar experience, and this kind of memory event is called a flashbulb memory (R. Brown & Kulik, 1977).

Flashbulb memories **are vivid recollections, usually in great detail, of dramatic or emotionally charged incidents that are of interest to the person. This information is encoded effortlessly and may last for long periods of time.**

IMPACT AND ACCURACY

Do you remember precisely what you were doing when you first learned of the 9-11 attacks? Flashbulb memories usually involve events that are extremely surprising, are emotionally arousing, or have very important meaning or consequences for the person. For example, when people were questioned about what they were doing when they heard that President Kennedy or Reagan had been shot, or when the space shuttle *Challenger* exploded, about 80–90% could recall vivid details seven months later (Pillemer, 1984). Researchers concluded that only events that are personally significant and have an emotional impact result in the formation of flashbulb memories (P. S. R. Davidson & Glisky, 2002).

Although flashbulb memories are reported with great confidence and in vivid details, this does not mean the memories are necessarily accurate. That's because people mistake the vividness of flashbulb memories for their accuracy. In fact, researchers report that although flashbulb memories are very vivid, this does not guarantee any special accuracy (Talarico & Rubin, 2003).

MOST-REMEMBERED EVENTS

As you can see in the center table, the top five flashbulb memories of college students involved a car accident, a college roommate, high school graduation and prom, and a romantic experience, all of which are emotionally charged events (D. C. Rubin & Kozin, 1984).

Initially, flashbulb memories were claimed to represent a special kind of memory that was complete, accurate, vivid, and immune to forgetting (R. Brown & Kulik, 1977). Since then, several studies have investigated these claims and reported that flashbulb memories do not seem to be a separate, special kind of memory because flashbulb memories are subject to inaccuracies, change with retelling, and are even forgotten over time (Weaver & Krug, 2004).

Examples of Flashbulb Memories

Cues	Percent*
A car accident you were in or witnessed	85
When you first met your college roommate	82
Night of your high school graduation	81
Night of your senior prom (if you went or not)	78
An early romantic experience	77
A time you had to speak in front of an audience	72
When you got your college admissions letter	65
Your first date—the moment you met him/her	57
Day President Reagan was shot in Washington	52
Night President Nixon resigned	41
First time you flew in an airplane	40
Moment you opened your SAT scores	33
Your 17th birthday	30
Day of the first space shuttle flight	24
The last time you ate a holiday dinner at home	23
Your first college class	21
The first time your parents left you alone for some time	19
Your 13th birthday	12

*Percentage of students in the memory experiment who reported that events on the experimenter's list were of flashbulb quality (D. C. Rubin & Kozin, 1984).

REMOTE HISTORICAL EVENTS

In a study of flashbulb memory, Danes (people from Denmark) who lived through the Nazi occupation and liberation during World War II and Danes born during or after World War II were asked questions about the days of the occupation and liberation, such as what the weather conditions were like and what they were doing when they heard the news. Nearly all the older Danes reported having flashbulb memories, being able to recall detailed personal memories about the two war events. Also, the majority of older Danes but very few younger Danes accurately recalled weather conditions. These researchers concluded that flashbulb memories represent a special kind of automatic encoding that occurs when events are emotionally and personally interesting. The results of this study and other research show that flashbulb memories can last 60 years or even longer (Berntsen & Thomsen, 2005).

BRAINS AND HORMONES

Researchers think the reason flashbulb memories are so detailed and long-lasting is that their emotionally arousing content activates a special brain area and several hormones. For example, researchers believe that flashbulb memories involve a brain structure called the amygdala (p. 80), which plays a key role in processing and encoding strong emotional experiences (Davidson & Glisky, 2002).

Also, in the Research Focus on page 247, we discussed how emotionally triggered hormones are involved in encoding long-term memories as if "in stone" (McGaugh, 1999). The secretion of these "emotional" hormones is thought to play an important role in encoding emotionally charged personal experiences into long-lasting memories (Schooler & Eich, 2005).

PICTURES VERSUS IMPRESSIONS

Each of us has a remarkable memory system that can encode, store, and retrieve unlimited amounts of information over long periods of time. But it's important to remember that memories are not perfect pictures of objects, people, and events but rather our personal impressions of these things. For example, the things that you remember when you're in a good mood and having a "good day" are very different from the things that you remember when you're in a bad mood and having a "bad day." This means that what you remember and recall may be changed, biased, or distorted by a wide range of emotional feelings, personal experiences, stressful situations, or social influences (Roediger & McDermott, 2005).

✔ Summary Test

A. Three Types of Memory

1. The study of memory, which is the ability to retain information over time, includes three separate processes. The first process—placing information in memory—is called (a)_____. The second process, which is filing information in memory, is called (b)_____. The third process—commonly referred to as remembering—is called (c)_____.

2. Although we think of memory as a single event, it is really a complex sequence that may be separated into three different kinds of memory. The initial memory process that holds raw information for up to several seconds is called _____. During this time, you have the chance to identify or pay attention to new information.

3. If you pay attention to information in sensory memory, this information is automatically transferred into a second kind of memory process, called _____ memory.

4. If you rehearse or think about information in short-term memory, that information will usually be transferred or encoded into the third, more permanent kind of memory process called _____.

B. Sensory Memory: Recording

5. Visual sensory memory, known as (a)_____ memory, lasts about a quarter of a second. Auditory memory, known as (b)_____ memory, may last as long as two seconds. Sensory memory has many functions; for example, it prevents you from being overwhelmed by too much incoming information and gives you time to identify the incoming data and pay attention to them.

C. Short–Term Memory: Working

6. If you pay attention to information in sensory memory, it is automatically transferred to short-term memory, which has two main characteristics. The first is that unrehearsed information will disappear after 2–30 seconds, indicating that short-term memory has a limited (a)_____. The second characteristic is that short-term memory can hold only about seven items (plus or minus two), indicating that short-term memory has a limited (b)_____. You can increase the length of time that information remains in short-

term memory by intentionally repeating the information, which is called (c)_____. You can considerably increase the capacity of short-term memory by combining separate items of information into larger units, which is called (d)_____.

D. Long-Term Memory: Storing

7. Let's follow the progress of information from the time it enters sensory memory to its storage in long-term memory. For an instant to several seconds, incoming raw information is held in (a)_____. If you do not pay attention to this information, it disappears forever; if you pay attention, that information is automatically transferred to short-term memory. The transfer of information from sensory memory to short-term memory is controlled by the process of (b)_____.

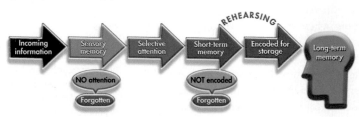

8. If information in short-term memory is not (a)_____, it will disappear in 2–30 seconds. If you rehearse or think about information in short-term memory, it may be transferred into long-term memory. The transfer of information from short-term into long-term memory is controlled by a process called (b)_____. In some cases, information is transferred automatically; in other cases, this transfer process may require deliberate effort.

9. The process of selecting information from long-term memory and transferring it back into short-term memory is called _____. Because information has been encoded into long-term memory does not guarantee that such information can always or easily be remembered or retrieved.

10. One demonstration of the existence of, and difference between, short-term and long-term memory is observed in the order that subjects remember items from a multiple-item list. Subjects tend to have better recall of items at the beginning of a list; this tendency is called the (a)_____ effect and involves long-term memory. Subjects tend to have better recall of items at the end of the list; this tendency is called the (b)_____ effect and involves short-term memory. The order in which subjects recall items from a long list is called the (c)_____ effect.

11. There are two different kinds of long-term memory. One kind involves memories of facts or events, such as scenes, stories, words, conversations, faces, or daily events. We can retrieve these memories and are conscious of them; they constitute (a)_____ memory. There are two kinds of declarative memory. One kind consists of factual knowledge of the world, concepts, word definitions, and language rules; this is called (b)_____ memory. The second kind of declarative memory consists of knowledge about personal experiences (episodes) or activities; this is called (c)_____ memory.

12. A second kind of long-term memory involves memories for performing motor or perceptual tasks, carrying out habits, and responding to stimuli because of classical conditioning; this is called _____ memory. We cannot retrieve these memories and are not conscious of them.

E. Research Focus: Do Emotions Affect Memories?

13. There are times when for safety, moral, or ethical reasons researchers cannot use human subjects but instead use an (a)_____ model. Using this model, researchers found that during emotional or stressful situations, the body secretes chemicals called (b)_____, which make encoding so effective that these situations become very vivid long-term memories. One reason for the evolution of this carved-in-stone memory system is to help the species survive by remembering dangerous situations.

F. Encoding: Transferring

14. The process of storing information in memory by making mental representations is called (a)_____. There are two processes for encoding information. Most procedural and episodic information is transferred from short-term into long-term memory without any effort, and usually without any awareness, through a process called (b)_____ encoding. Much semantic information is transferred from short-term into long-term memory by deliberate attempts to repeat, rehearse, or make associations. Together, these deliberate attempts are referred to as (c)_____ encoding.

15. There are two kinds of effortful encoding, which differ in their effectiveness. Encoding by simply repeating or rehearsing the information is called (a)_____. This method is not very effective because it involves little thinking about the information or making new associations. Encoding that involves thinking about the information and making new associations is called (b)_____.

16. One theory says that memory depends on how information is encoded in the mind. If we pay attention only to basic features of the information, it is encoded at a shallow level, and poor memory results. If we form new associations, the information is encoded at a deeper level, and good memory results. This theory is called _____.

G. Repressed Memories

17. If something happens that is threatening, shocking, or traumatic, our minds may push that information deep into the unconscious, from which it may one day be released and enter consciousness. This phenomenon is called (a)_____ and is the theory behind the formation of (b)_____ memories. Unless there is corroborating evidence, the accuracy of repressed memories is difficult to establish.

H. Cultural Diversity: Oral Versus Written

18. Students from Ghana, Africa, remembered more information when it was read to them than did American students who heard the same information. These results show how Ghana's tradition of passing on information orally, which is an example of _____ influences, improves both encoding and recalling or retrieving information.

I. Application: Unusual Memories

19. The ability of certain children to examine a picture or page for 10–30 seconds and then retain a detailed visual image of the material for several minutes is called (a)_____ imagery. In adults, the ability to form sharp, detailed visual images after a short period and recall the entire image at a later date is called (b)_____ memory. Memories that are vivid recollections, usually in great detail, of dramatic or emotionally charged incidents are called (c) _____. Although very vivid, these memories are not necessarily completely accurate.

Answers: *1. (a) encoding, (b) storing, (c) retrieving; 2. sensory memory; 3. short-term, or working; 4. long-term memory; 5. (a) iconic, (b) echoic; 6. (a) duration, (b) capacity, (c) maintenance rehearsal, (d) chunking; 7. (a) sensory memory, (b) attention; 8. (a) rehearsed, (b) encoding; 9. retrieval, or retrieving; 10. (a) primacy, (b) recency, (c) primacy-recency; 11. (a) declarative, (b) semantic, (c) episodic; 12. procedural or nondeclarative; 13. (a) animal, (b) hormones; 14. (a) encoding, (b) automatic, (c) effortful; 15. (a) maintenance rehearsal, (b) elaborative rehearsal; 16. levels of processing; 17. (a) repression, (b) repressed; 18. cultural; 19. (a) eidetic, (b) photographic, (c) flashbulb memories*

Critical Thinking

Can Phony Beliefs Change Your Behavior?

It's been well established that people can be made to believe "fake" memories, but can "fake" memories change people's behavior? Research psychologist Elizabeth Loftus of the University of California–Irvine and her colleagues studied whether simply suggesting food preferences can change what people decide to eat. To answer this question, these researchers asked college-aged subjects to complete questionnaires on their personalities and food experiences. As part of the questionnaires, subjects were asked about childhood food experiences, such as whether they "ate a piece of banana cream pie."

One week after completing the questionnaires, subjects returned and were told that their responses were used to create a "unique" profile of their early childhood food experiences. Everyone's profile included generic statements such as they disliked spinach, enjoyed eating bananas, and felt happy when a classmate brought sweets to school. In addition, the profiles of a group of subjects included one completely made-up point: "Felt ill after eating strawberry ice cream." The remaining subjects were the control group and their profiles did not include a statement about getting ill as a result of eating strawberry ice cream.

When subjects in the false memory group were told the questionnaire results showed they had a bad childhood experience with strawberry ice cream, researchers asked several follow-up questions about the phony memory, such as where they were when they got sick and who else witnessed the event. About 41% of subjects given the false memory believed they had once gotten sick from eating strawberry ice cream. Some of these subjects even reported details about the experience such as "may have gotten sick after eating seven cups of ice cream."

During this same visit subjects completed a second questionnaire about eating preferences and many of these "believers" (20 of the 47) now reported less preference for and less willingness to eat strawberry ice cream. In contrast, the control group of subjects who did not receive false feedback did not show any change in their preference for strawberry ice cream.

As many people have learned, a strong and long-lasting aversion to a certain food can develop after only one bad childhood experience. Loftus gives an example that a novel food such as béarnaise sauce may make a person sick one time and lead to avoiding the food in the future. The current study suggests it is possible for such an aversion to occur based only on a false memory. Loftus and her colleagues are now examining whether false memories of really liking certain healthy vegetables during childhood can be implanted and make people more likely to eat such foods as adults. (Adapted from D. M. Bernstein et al., 2005a; Loftus, 2005; Park, 2005; Skloot, 2006; M. Smith, 2005)

Questions

1. What type of long-term memory is used to recall a bad childhood experience with food?

2. Why were researchers able to implant false memories in these subjects?

3. Would the results be different if subjects were presented with a bowl of strawberry ice cream instead of being asked to report their preference on a questionnaire?

4. What type of learning occurs when a person has a bad experience with food and then avoids eating it?

5. Should physicians implant false memories to help patients lose weight?

Suggested Answers

1. When you recall a childhood event, such as feeling ill after eating a certain food, you are using a type of declarative memory called episodic memory. Episodic memory is a type of long-term memory that involves knowledge of specific events and personal experiences.

2. It is likely that false memories can be implanted only in people who are unaware of the mental manipulation. Subjects in this study did not know they were being deceived, and this is why they were highly suggestible.

3. The research design of the current study is limited because it involved a laboratory setting rather than a naturalistic setting. If this study was conducted in a naturalistic setting such as at an ice cream shop, the results may be different.

4. Taste-aversion learning refers to associating a particular sensory cue (such as the taste of strawberry ice cream) with getting sick and thereafter avoiding that particular sensory cue in the future.

5. The results of this study may have implications for dieters, but it is unethical to lie to a patient even if the doctor believes it will benefit the patient. Also, false memories may work only for foods that are infrequently eaten. For instance, researchers have not been able to create false memories of people associating commonly eaten unhealthy foods, such as potato chips and chocolate chip cookies, with feeling ill.

Links to Learning

Learning Activities

- ***POWERSTUDY FOR INTRODUCTION TO PSYCHOLOGY 4.0***

  by Tom Doyle and Rod Plotnik

  SuperModule: Check out "Types of Memory" on **PowerStudy.** It includes complete paragraph-by-paragraph explanations of all content using fully-narrated animations and graphics. An onscreen toolbar allows immediate access to text, text outline, and module glossary with notetaking and printing capabilities. This module also includes:

  - Videos—Imbedded videos explore Rajan's phenomenal ability to remember. Other imbedded videos discuss short-term memory, memory and the brain, chunking, and false memories.
  - A multitude of animations—for example, a virtual dolphin teaches you about the training procedure for mine detection, and an animated exercise helps you remember the three main types of memory—sensory, short-term, and long-term.
  - A test of your knowledge using an interactive version of the Summary Test on pages 256 and 257. Also access related quizzes.
  - An interactive version of the Critical Thinking exercise "Can Phony Beliefs Change Your Behavior?" on page 258.
  - Key terms, a chapter outline, and hotlinked websites.

- *CengageNOW*

  academic.cengage.com/login

  Need help studying? This site is your one-stop study shop. Take a Pre-Test and CengageNOW will generate a Personalized Study Plan based on your test results. The Study Plan will identify the topics you need to review and direct you to online resources to help you master those topics. You can then take a Post-Test to determine the concepts you have mastered and what you still need to work on.

- ***INTRODUCTION TO PSYCHOLOGY BOOK COMPANION WEBSITE***

  academic.cengage.com/psychology/plotnik

  Visit your book companion website where you will find more resources to help you study. At this site, you will find Learning Objectives, Internet Exercises, quizzing, flash cards, and a pronunciation glossary.

- *STUDY GUIDE and WEBTUTOR*

  Check the corresponding module in your Study Guide for effective student tips and help learning the material presented. Also go to **academic.cengage.com/webtutor** for an interactive version of the Study Guide features.

Study Questions

*A. Three Types of Memory—Why does seeing an ambulance speed by remind you of your father's heart attack and his trip to the hospital? (**Suggested answer page 625**)

B. Sensory Memory: Recording—Why doesn't the world disappear for the short period of time when your eyes are completely closed during blinking?

C. Short-Term Memory: Working—If you took a drug that blocked short-term memory, what would be different about your life?

D. Long-Term Memory: Storing—What would your life be like if you had declarative memory but no procedural memory?

E. Research Focus: Do Emotions Affect Memories?—Why do people who suffer traumatic situations, such as sexual abuse or job layoffs, have difficulty getting on with their lives?

*F. Encoding: Transferring—Why is it important that teachers make learning interesting and meaningful? (**Suggested answer page 626**)

G. Repressed Memories—What are some of the ways that therapists can guard against clients reporting repressed memories that are false?

*H. Cultural Diversity: Oral Versus Written—How might playing video games affect a child's encoding process? (**Suggested answer page 626**)

I. Application: Unusual Memories—If you could have one unusual memory ability, which would you choose, and how would it make your life different?

*These questions are answered in Appendix B.

MODULE 12
Remembering & Forgetting

 PowerStudy 4.0™ Complete Module

Introduction

Watching a Crime

How much can you remember? It was about nine at night when you entered the campus building, climbed one flight of stairs, and began walking down the long hallway. You had just finished your psychology paper and were going to slip it under the instructor's door. Everything happened very quickly.

From about the middle of the dimly lit hallway, a man with reddish hair and wearing a brown leather jacket jumped out from behind a half-open door and ran at you. Instinctively, you threw out your hands and tried to ward off the oncoming threat. With a quick motion, the man grabbed your blue shoulder bag and pushed you down. At that instant, your eyes met. He pointed at you with a menacing gesture and said, "Don't move or make a sound." Then he checked the hallway, stepped around you, and was gone (adapted from Buckout, 1980).

1,800 people identified the wrong mugger.

A 12-second filmed sequence with a storyline similar to this one was shown on television. In the TV film, the assailant's face was on the screen for several seconds. Next, the viewers were asked to watch a lineup of six men and then to call the TV station and identify which was the assailant. Of the more than 2,000 viewers who called in, only 200 identified the correct man; 1,800 selected the wrong one (Buckout, 1980).

Without looking back, try to answer the following questions (answers at bottom):

A. **B.** **C.**

1. What color was the mugger's jacket? _____
2. What color and type was the student's bag? _____
3. Besides the bag, what else was the student carrying? _____
4. The mugger's exact words were "Don't make a sound." True or false?
5. When thrown down, the student yelled out "Stop!" True or false?
6. Of the 2,000 viewers who called in, 1,800 identified the correct assailant. True or false?

Answers: 1. brown; 2. blue, shoulder bag; 3. psychology paper; 4. false; 5. false; 6. false

Recall Versus Recognition

Which is easier? You probably found the first three questions harder because they involve recall.

Recall **involves retrieving previously learned information without the aid of or with very few external cues.**

For example, in questions 1–3, you were asked to recall colors or objects without having any choices. Students must use recall to answer fill-in-the-blank or essay questions.

You probably thought the last three questions were easier because they involve recognition.

Recognition **involves identifying previously learned information with the help of external cues.**

In questions 4–6, you have only to recognize whether the information provided is correct. Students use recognition to decide which of the choices is correct on multiple-choice tests. Since multiple-choice tests involve recognition, they are generally considered easier than fill-in-the-blank and essay questions, which involve recall. Later in this module, we'll discuss why recall is more difficult than recognition.

Eyewitness Testimony

Which face did you see? Question 6 asks about a very curious result. Although the assailant's face was on the television screen for several seconds, 90% of the viewers identified the *wrong* person in a six-man lineup. (For example, from the six faces below, can you identify the correct mugger? Answer below.) How can you clearly see someone's face and not remember it? The answer to this question comes from studies on how eyewitness memories can be affected by suggestions, misleading questions, and false information. Although we

D. **E.** **F.**

generally assume that eyewitness testimony is the most accurate kind of evidence, you'll see that this is not always true. We'll discuss accuracy and problems of eyewitness testimony at the end of this module. (Mugger had reddish hair.)

What's Coming

We'll discuss how you organize thousands of events, faces, and facts and file this information in long-term memory. We'll explain the most common reasons for forgetting, the biological bases for memory, methods to improve memory, the accuracy of memory, and the accuracy of eyewitness testimony.

We'll begin with a huge problem that you face every day: How do you file away and organize your many, many thousands of memories?

A. Organization of Memories

Filing and Organizing 87,967 Memories

How do you store memories?

One of the great puzzles of memory is how you file and store zillions of things over your lifetime. Suppose this past month you stored 91 faces, 6,340 concepts, 258 songs, 192 names, 97 definitions, 80,987 personal events, 1 dog, and 1 cat. How did you store these 87,967 memories so that you can search and retrieve one particular item from long-term memory?

There are several theories for how we file and organize memories; we'll discuss one of the more popular theories, which is called network theory (J. L. McClelland, 2005).

Network theory says that we store related ideas in separate categories, or files, called nodes. As we make associations among information, we create links among thousands

Network theory says we store memories by filing them into categories.

of nodes, which make up a gigantic interconnected network of files for storing and retrieving information.

Network theory may become clearer if you imagine that the mental files, or nodes, are like thousands of cities on a map and the connections or associations between them are like roads. Just as you follow different roads to go from city to city, you follow different associative pathways to go from idea to idea. Storing new events, faces, and thousands of other things would be similar to erecting new buildings in the cities and also building new roads between the cities (B. Schwartz & Reisberg, 1991). Here's how one cognitive psychologist, Donald Norman, used network theory to explain how he retrieved a particular memory.

Network Theory of Memory Organization

Where do the roads lead?

Just as you might follow a road map (right figure) to reach a particular city, cognitive psychologist Norman followed a cognitive map to remember the name of a particular store in San Diego. Although the mental roads that Norman takes may seem strange, these roads rep-

resent personal associations that he created when he filed, or stored, information in long-term memory. As he follows his associations, or mental roads, he travels the cognitive network from node to node or memory to memory in search of a particular name (Norman, 1982). Please begin reading at node 1 and continue to node 6.

1 Norman's train of thought began with his remembering a party he had attended earlier at a friend's house.

2 The house had associations with smoke detectors on the ceilings of the rooms.

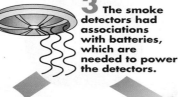

3 The smoke detectors had associations with batteries, which are needed to power the detectors.

4 The batteries had associations with a certain store in San Diego where Norman bought batteries and other items.

5 The department store had associations with many items that he bought, including trays for his slides.

6 As Norman thought of buying slide trays, he remembered the store's name "Nordstrom."

Norman mentally followed a cognitive map, starting with node 1 and following nodes 2, 3, 4, 5, to the name of a store at node 6.

Searching for a Memory

We've all shared Norman's problem of knowing we know something but having difficulty recalling it. This problem relates to how we store memories in long-term memory. According to the network theory of memory, we store memories in nodes that are interconnected after we make new associations. Because the network theory is somewhat complicated, we'll review how it applied to Norman's problem of trying to recall a particular memory.

Nodes. Norman organizes or stores related ideas in separate files, or categories, called nodes. We simplified this process by showing only six nodes, but there may be dozens. Nodes are categories for storing related ideas, such as birds, faces, friends, and store names.

Associations. Norman links the nodes, or categories of ideas, together by making associations or mental roads between new information and old information that was previously stored.

Network. Norman has thousands of interconnected nodes, which form an enormous cognitive network for arranging and storing files. Norman must search through this cognitive network to find a particular node or file, where a specific memory is stored.

Researchers have developed a theory of how we search through thousands of nodes to find a particular one (J. L. McClelland, 2005).

How do you find a specific memory?

How do you find a specific memory to answer these questions: How big is a guppy? Does a rooster have feathers? Does a blue jay have skin? According to network theory, you will search for answers to these questions by using different nodes or memory files.

Nodes are memory files that contain related information organized around a specific topic or category.

According to network theory, the many thousands of nodes or memory files are arranged in a certain kind of order, which is called a network hierarchy (Diesendruck & Shatz, 2001).

A *network hierarchy* refers to the arrangement of nodes or memory files in a certain order or hierarchy. At the bottom of the hierarchy are nodes with very concrete information, which are connected to nodes with somewhat more specific information, which in turn are connected to nodes with general or abstract information.

For example, a partial network hierarchy for nodes or memory files containing information about animals is shown on the right. Depending on whether you're looking for a specific memory (How big is a guppy?) or a more abstract memory (Does a blue jay have skin?), you will search different nodes, as explained next.

1. ANIMAL
2. BIRD
2. FISH
3. BLUE JAY   3. ROOSTER   3. SHARK   3. GUPPY

Network hierarchy: Arranging memory files (nodes) so that general information is in top file (node #1) and specific information is in bottom files (nodes #3)

1. ABSTRACT: ANIMAL

This node, or memory file, contains information that is very abstract and applies to all animals, such as has skin, can move around, eats, and breathes. This category has answers to very general questions about animals—"Does a blue jay have skin?"

2. MORE SPECIFIC: BIRD OR FISH

This node, or memory file, contains information that is somewhat more specific because it applies to many fish or birds, such as has wings, can fly, and has feathers. This category has answers to some-what specific questions about fish or birds—"Does a rooster have feathers?"

3. CONCRETE: BLUE JAY, ROOSTER, SHARK, OR GUPPY

This node, or memory file, contains very concrete information that applies only to a specific animal. This category has answers to very specific questions—"How big is a guppy?" "What color is a shark?"

Conclusion. Because network theory doesn't have all the answers to how you file and store information, researchers are developing more complex models, such as neural networks, that try to imitate how the brain organizes and files millions of bits of information (Ratcliff & McKoon, 2005).

Does the brain come with a built-in filing system?

The network theory's idea that information is filed in interconnected nodes or categories is partly supported by recent findings showing that the brain seems to have its own built-in filing system. For example, researchers found that, depending on which area of the brain is damaged, patients lose the ability to identify or process information dealing with a specific category. In some cases, patients could no longer identify faces but had no problems identifying information in other categories, such as tools, animals, furniture, or plants. In other cases, patients could no longer identify plants but could identify information in different categories (tools, animals, etc.) (Schacter et al., 2005). These findings indicate that the

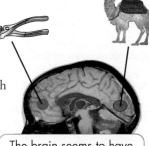

The brain seems to have built-in files or categories.

brain has built-in categories for sorting and filing different kinds of information.

By using another research approach involving brain scans (p. 70), researchers found further evidence that we use different areas of the brain to process different categories. For example, when subjects were asked to think of objects in specific categories, such as faces, tools, or furniture, researchers found that maximum neural activity occurred in different areas of the brain. As shown at the left, when people were thinking of animals, the maximum neural activity occurred in the back of the brain, while thinking of tools produced maximum neural activity in the front of the brain (A. Martin et al., 1996). The finding that the brain comes with prewired categories for processing information helps explain how you can easily sort through a tremendous amount of information and quickly find the answer to a specific question, such as "Does a camel have a hump?" (Low et al., 2003).

B. Forgetting Curves

What's your earliest memory?

The earliest that people in different cultures can recall personal memories averages $3\frac{1}{2}$ years old (Q. Wang, 2003). Researchers did find that children as young as 13 months can recall visual events, such as a sequence of moving toys. However, recalling moving objects is different from recalling personal memories, which is based on having developed a sense of oneself (recognizing the face in mirror as yours), which occurs after age 2 (Howe, 2003). Another reason we rarely remember personal events before age $3\frac{1}{2}$ is that very young children have little or no

Earliest memories at about age $3\frac{1}{2}$

language skills, so they cannot verbally encode early personal memories and cannot recall them even after they do develop language skills (Baddeley, 2004; Simcock & Hayne, 2002). Also, very young children have not yet developed a complete memory circuit in the brain, which is necessary for encoding and retrieving personal memories (Baddeley, 2004; Bauer, 2002). But even though you're now an adult with a completely developed memory brain circuit, why do you still forget things, especially when taking exams?

Unfamiliar and Uninteresting

Could you remember LUD, ZIB?

From your experience studying for exams, you know that just because you verbally encode information by listening, reading, or writing doesn't mean that you'll automatically recall this information on exams. The kinds of events that you are more likely to remember or forget can be demonstrated with forgetting curves.

A *forgetting curve* measures the amount of previously learned information that subjects can recall or recognize across time.

We'll examine how two different kinds of information—unfamiliar and familiar—are remembered by using forgetting curves.

One of the earliest psychologists to study memory and forgetting was Hermann Ebbinghaus, who used himself as his only subject. He got around the fact that people have better memories for more familiar events by memorizing only three-letter nonsense syllables, such as **LUD, ZIB, MUC.**

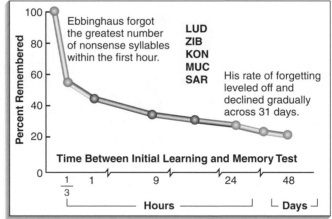

Ebbinghaus forgot the greatest number of nonsense syllables within the first hour.

LUD
ZIB
KON
MUC
SAR

His rate of forgetting leveled off and declined gradually across 31 days.

Time Between Initial Learning and Memory Test

He made up and wrote down hundreds of three-letter nonsense syllables on separate cards and arranged these cards into sets of varying length. To the ticking of a metronome, he turned over each card and read aloud each of the syllables until he had read all the cards in the set. He used only rote memory (made no associations) and needed only one or two readings to memorize a set of seven cards (containing seven nonsense syllables). He needed about 45 readings to memorize a set of 24 cards (Ebbinghaus, 1885/1913).

The forgetting curve on the left shows that Ebbinghaus forgot about half the unfamiliar and uninteresting nonsense syllables within the first hour.

How long do we remember familiar information?

Familiar and Interesting

Can you remember the names of your high school classmates?

Ebbinghaus's nonsense syllables are certainly uninteresting, which helps explain why he forgot half within the first hour. But what about information that is both familiar and interesting, such as the names and faces of your high school graduating class?

The graph below shows that even after 47 years, subjects correctly matched about 80% of their high school classmates' names with faces; they correctly recalled about 25% after 47 years (Bahrick et al., 1975). Subjects did better on recognition tests (matching names to faces) because they were given clues (names). They did poorer on recall tests (seeing

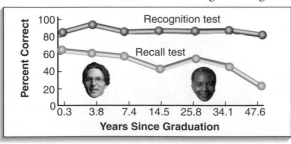

Recognition test

Recall test

Years Since Graduation

faces and asked to recall the names) because they were not given any clues. Similarly, students also show better memory on recognition tests (multiple-choice) than on recall tests (essay or fill-in-the-blank).

Notice that even though names and nonsense syllables were both encoded verbally, subjects correctly recalled about 60% of familiar and interesting information (names and faces) after 7 years, while Ebbinghaus forgot about 80% of the unfamiliar and uninteresting nonsense syllables after about a week. One researcher found that, after 20 years, he best remembered those events that were vivid, rare, and emotionally intense (R. White, 2002).

These studies show that remembering is partly related to how familiar or interesting the information is. However, there are other reasons for forgetting, as you'll see next.

Overview: Forgetting

Why do I forget things?

If asked to describe what happened today, you can accurately recall many personal events, conversations, and countless irritations. However, in spite of hours of study, there are many things you seem to have forgotten when you take an exam.

Forgetting **refers to the inability to retrieve, recall, or recognize information that was stored or is still stored in long-term memory.** We'll summarize a number of reasons people forget things.

Repression

There is a documented case of a man, J.R., who became anxious while watching a movie that featured a main character who struggled with memories of being sexually molested. Later that night, J.R. had a vivid recollection of being sexually abused by a parish priest (Schooler, 1994). J.R.'s case is an example of repression.

Repression, **according to Freud, is a mental process that automatically hides emotionally threatening or anxiety-producing information in the unconscious, from which repressed memories cannot be recalled voluntarily, but something may cause them to enter consciousness at a later time.**

Earlier we discussed the accuracy of recovered repressed memories involving sexual abuse (pp. 250–251). The J.R. example suggests that a traumatic sexual event can be repressed and recovered later. However, prominent memory researchers have questioned the validity of repressed memories, pointing to the possibility that such memories may have been suggested or implanted during the therapeutic process (Lynn et al., 2003).

Poor Retrieval Cues/Poor Encoding

Studying for exams by cramming or using rote memory may lead to forgetting because these techniques result in poor retrieval cues and thus poor encoding or storing.

Retrieval cues **are mental reminders that we create by forming vivid mental images or creating associations between new information and information we already know.**

What if I study for 2 hours?

Many students don't realize that it's not how long but how well they study that matters. Effective studying is not only memorizing but also creating good retrieval cues. The best retrieval cues, which ensure the best encoding, are created by associating new information with information already learned.

For example, instead of just trying to remember that the hippocampus is involved in memory (pp. 80, 84, 229), try to make a new association, such as a hippo remembered its way around campus.

We'll discuss the importance of and how to form good retrieval cues for effective encoding on page 267.

Interference

If you have to study for several exams and take them on the same day, there is a good chance that you may mix up and forget some of the material because of interference.

What if I have two exams?

Interference, **one of the common reasons for forgetting, means that the recall of some particular memory is blocked or prevented by other related memories.**

For example, if you are studying for and taking psychology and sociology tests on the same day, you may find that some of the material on social behavior in psychology is similar to but different from material in sociology, and this mix-up will cause interference and forgetting. Because psychologists believe that interference between material is a common cause of forgetting, we'll focus on two different kinds of interference on the next page.

Amnesia

While showing off her new pair of skates, my sister (R.P.) fell down and cracked her head on the hard Minnesota ice. She was knocked unconscious for a short time, and when she woke up the first thing she said was, "What happened?" She couldn't remember what happened because the blow had caused temporary amnesia.

Amnesia, **which may be temporary or permanent, is loss of memory that may occur after a blow or damage to the brain or after disease (Alzheimer's, p. 47), general anesthesia, certain drugs, or severe psychological trauma.**

Depending on its severity, a blow to the head causes the soft jellylike brain to crash into the hard skull, and this may result in temporary or permanent damage to thousands of neurons (p. 50), which form the communication network of the brain. The reason people who strike their heads during car accidents usually have no memories of the events that occurred immediately before and during the accident is that the brain crashed into the skull, which interferes with the neurons' communication network, disrupts memory, and results in varying degrees of amnesia (Riccio et al., 2003).

Distortion

We may not be aware of the times we misremember something due to memory distortions caused by *bias* or *suggestibility* (G. H. Bower, 2005; Schacter, 2001). For example, bias was operating when college students remembered 89% of their high school A grades but only 29% of D grades or when divorcing couples remembered mostly the bad times, not the good (Bahrick et al., 1996). Suggestibility was operating when victims of crimes wrongly identified persons who were later cleared by DNA evidence (Zernike, 2006). Because of bias and suggestibility, we forget or misremember things, often without being aware of the memory distortion.

Why did I misremember?

Next, we'll more closely examine two important reasons for forgetting—interference and poor retrieval cues.

C. Reasons for Forgetting

What if you study for three exams?

Sooner or later, every student faces the problem of having to take exams in several different courses on the same day. This situation can increase the chances of forgetting material because of something called interference.

The theory of *interference* says that we may forget information not because it is no longer in storage or memory but rather because old or newer related information produces confusion and thus blocks retrieval from memory.

Students who take multiple tests on the same day often complain of studying long and hard but forgetting information that they knew they knew. In this case the culprit may be interference. Similarly, if you take two or more classes in succession, you may find that information from one class interferes with learning or remembering information from the others. We'll explain the two kinds of interference—proactive and retroactive—and how each can lead to forgetting.

Proactive Interference

The first thing to remember about interference is that it can act forward, which is called proactive, or act backward, which is called retroactive. The prefix *pro* means "forward," so *proactive* interference "acts forward" to interfere with recalling newly learned information.

Proactive interference occurs when old information (learned earlier) blocks or disrupts the remembering of related new information (learned later).

Here's how proactive interference can work.

1. Psychology information.
For two hours you study for a test in psychology. The more psychology terms you store in memory, the more potential this psychology information has to "act forward" and disrupt any new and related information you study next.

2. Psychology information acts forward.
For the next two hours you study for a test in sociology. You may experience difficulty in learning and remembering this new sociology information because the previously learned psychology terms can "act forward" and interfere with remembering new and related terms from sociology.

3. Proactive interference.
When you take your sociology exam, you may forget some of the sociology terms you studied because of proactive interference: Previously learned psychology terms "act forward" to interfere with or block the recall of the more recently learned and related sociology terms (Bunting, 2006).

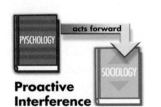

Proactive Interference

Material learned EARLIER (psychology) interferes with learning new information (sociology).

Retroactive Interference

Note that the prefix *retro* means "backward," so *retroactive* interference means "acting backward" to interfere with recalling previously learned information.

Retroactive interference occurs when new information (learned later) blocks or disrupts the retrieval of related old information (learned earlier).

Here's how retroactive interference works.

1. Psychology information.
From 1:00 to 3:00, you study for a test in psychology. Then from 3:00 to 6:00, you study for a test in sociology.

2. Sociology information acts backward.
You may experience difficulty in remembering the psychology terms you learned earlier because the sociology terms recently learned may "act backward" and disrupt earlier learned and related psychology terms.

3. Retroactive interference.
When you take the psychology exam, you may forget some of the psychology terms you studied earlier because of retroactive interference: Recently learned sociology terms "act backward" to interfere with or block the recall of earlier learned and related psychology terms.

Retroactive Interference

Material learned LATER (sociology) disrupts learning new information (psychology).

Interference, both proactive and retroactive, is one of the two most common reasons for forgetting (Roediger & McDermott, 2005). Interference may also cause serious mistakes if eyewitnesses identify the wrong person, as happened in the study we discussed at the beginning of this module.

Why Did Viewers Forget the Mugger's Face?

We began this module by asking why only 200 out of 2,000 viewers correctly identified a mugger's face that was shown for several seconds on television. One reason viewers forgot the mugger's face is that one or both kinds of interference were operating.

If *proactive interference* was operating, it means that previously learned faces acted forward to block or disrupt remembering of the newly observed mugger's face.

If *retroactive interference* was operating, it means that new faces learned since seeing the mugger's face acted backward to block or disrupt remembering of the mugger's face.

Thus, we may forget information that we did indeed store in long-term memory because of one or both kinds of interference.

Besides interference, the other most common reason for forgetting involves inadequate retrieval cues, our next topic.

Where did I park it?

Have you ever parked your car in a mall and later roamed around the huge lot trying to find it? In that case, the reason for your forgetting probably involved poor retrieval cues (S. C. Brown & Craik, 2005).

Retrieval cues **are mental reminders that you create by forming vivid mental images of information or associating new information with information that you already know.**

Poor retrieval cues result in haphazard memory storage.

Retrieval cues are also important in hiding things. Researchers asked students to hide things either in common places, such as drawers or closets, or in unusual places, such as old shoes or cereal boxes. Later, when asked to locate the hidden objects, students remembered objects hidden in common places and forgot those hidden in unusual places (Winograd & Soloway, 1986). Forgetting hiding places (which we have done) and forgetting parking places (which we have done) point to the need for creating good retrieval cues.

Forming Effective Retrieval Cues

One reason we forget things (definitions, names, phone numbers) is that we did not take the time to create effective retrieval cues (discussed on pp. 248–249). You can form effective retrieval cues by creating vivid mental images of the information, making associations between new and old information, or making somewhat bizarre but memorable associations.

For example, researchers wondered which types of sentences students would remember better: common sentences, such as "The sleek new train passes a field of fresh, juicy strawberries," or bizarre sentences, such as "The sleek new train is derailed by the fresh, juicy strawberries." As a computer randomly presented 12 common and 12 bizarre sentences, students were told to form vivid mental images of the scenes. When retested later, subjects recalled significantly more bizarre than common sentences. Researchers concluded that subjects remembered better the bizarre sentences because they formed better mental images or associations, which produced better retrieval cues (Robinson-Riegler & McDaniel, 1994). Poor retrieval cues may also be a problem in eyewitness testimony.

Vivid mental images make great retrieval cues.

Retrieval cues and interference. There have been cases in which eyewitnesses identified assailants who were later proven innocent based on DNA evidence. Even when told that their assailants, who had spent many years in prison, were innocent, the eyewitnesses insisted they had made the correct identifications (Dowling, 2000). One reason eyewitnesses were mistaken is that the emotional and traumatic events prevented them from forming effective *retrieval cues*. Another reason the eyewitnesses made mistakes is *interference;* that is, the faces of the accused assailants somewhat resembled and interfered with their recognizing the real assailants. These examples show that forgetting can result from poor retrieval cues, no associations, or interference (S. C. Brown & Craik, 2005).

Another example of forgetting, which involves retrieval cues and interference, usually begins with someone saying, "It's on the tip of my tongue."

Tip-of-the-Tongue Phenomenon

Most of us have had the frustrating experience of feeling we really do know the name of a movie, person, or song but cannot recall it at this moment. This kind of forgetting is called the tip-of-the-tongue phenomenon.

The *tip-of-the-tongue phenomenon* **refers to having a strong feeling that a particular word can be recalled, but despite making a great effort, we are temporarily unable to recall this particular information. Later, in a different situation, we may recall the information.**

"It's on the tip of my tongue."

Researchers have found that the tip-of-the-tongue phenomenon is nearly universal, occurs about once a week, and most often involves names of people and objects. Its frequency increases with age, and about half of the time the thing is remembered some minutes later (B. L. Schwartz, 1999).

There are two explanations for the tip-of-the-tongue phenomenon. In some cases, information was encoded with inadequate retrieval cues, and so we must think up other associations (first letter of name, where last seen) for recall (Neath & Surprenant, 2003). In other cases, information is being blocked by interference from similar-sounding names or objects. Once we think of something else, the interference stops and the information pops into our memory (Koriat, 2005).

An interesting feature of retrieval cues is that such cues can also come from our states of mind.

What happens when you get angry?

When you yell at someone for doing the same annoying thing again, why is it that a long list of related past annoyances quickly comes to mind? One answer involves state-dependent learning.

State-dependent learning **means that it is easier to recall information when you are in the same physiological or emotional state or setting as when you originally encoded the information.**

For example, getting angry at someone creates an emotional and physiological state that triggers the recall of related past annoyances. Evidence for state-dependent

Being in the same state (emotional) improves recall.

learning comes from a wide range of studies in which subjects (humans, dogs, rats) learned something while they used a certain drug, were in a certain mood, or were in a particular setting and later showed better recall of this information when tested under the original learning conditions (S. C. Brown & Craik, 2005). These state-dependent studies indicate that retrieval cues are created by being in certain physiological or emotional states or in particular settings and that returning to these original states helps recall information that was learned under the same conditions.

Next, we'll look inside the brain to see what happens during remembering and forgetting.

D. Biological Bases of Memory

Where do you put all those memories?

If you learned only 500 new things every day, that adds up to storing 180,000 new memories every year and 3,600,000 memories after twenty years. To figure out how the brain stores and files away 3,600,000 memories (very conservative estimate), researchers have studied formation of memories in sea slugs, which have a relatively simple nervous

system, in brain-damaged individuals, who show deficits in some kinds of memory but not others, and in individuals who are having their brains scanned for neural activity while they are using different kinds of memory (Cabeza & Nyberg, 2003; Zola & Squire, 2005). Based on these studies, researchers have identified the several different areas of the brain that are involved in processing and storing different kinds of thoughts and memories.

1 *Cortex: Short-Term Memories*

When you look up a new phone number, you can hold it in short-term memory long enough to dial the number. Your ability to hold words, facts, and events in short-term memory depends on activity in the *cortex,* which is a thin layer of brain cells that covers the surface of the forebrain (indicated by the thin red line on the outside of the brain).

People may have brain damage that prevents them from storing long-term memories, but if their cortex is intact, they may have short-term memory and be able to carry on relatively normal conversations. However, if they cannot store long-term memories, they would not later remember having those conversations.

2 *Cortex: Long-Term Memories*

If you learn the words to a song, these words are stored in long-term memory. Your ability to remember or recall songs, words, facts, and events for days, months, or years depends on areas widely spread throughout the *cortex.*

People may have brain damage that prevents them from learning or remembering any new songs. However, if they have an intact cortex, they may remember the words from songs they learned before their brain damage because such information would have already been safely stored in their cerebral cortex (indicated by the thin red line on the outside of the brain).

3 *Amygdala: Emotional Memories*

Suppose that each time you hear a particular song associated with a special person, you have a romantic feeling. The romantic feeling associated with this emotional memory is provided by the *amygdala,* which is located in the tip of the temporal lobe and receives input from all the senses. Research using brain scans found that the amygdala plays a critical role in the long-term processing of emotionally intense experiences (Siebert et al., 2003). For example, the amygdala helps us recognize emotional facial expressions, especially fearful or threatening ones, and adds a wide range of emotions (positive and negative) to our memories (R. J. Dolan, 2002; Ohman, 2002). So, humans with damage to the amygdala still have memories but the memories lose their emotional impact, such as no longer finding loud noises unpleasant or no longer recognizing emotional facial expressions (Hamann et al., 2002).

4 *Hippocampus: Transferring Memories*

Just as the "Save" command on your computer transfers a file into permanent storage on your hard drive, the *hippocampus* transfers words, facts, and personal events from short-term memory into permanent long-term memory. The hippocampus is a curved, finger-sized structure that lies beneath the cortex in the temporal lobe.

The hippocampus is vital for storing certain kinds of memories.

Areas of the brain involved in memory

For example, individuals with damage to the hippocampus (and surrounding cortex) cannot save any declarative memories, such as new words, facts, or personal events, because the *hippocampus* is necessary for transferring declarative information from short-term into long-term memory (Zeineh et al., 2003). However, people with hippocampal damage CAN learn and remember *nondeclarative or procedural information,* such as acquiring motor skills or habits (tying one's shoes, walking up the stairs, playing tennis) (R. D. Fields, 2005). But, if asked, people with hippocampal damage CANNOT remember actually performing a motor skill (playing tennis) because performing the skill (I played tennis) is a personal event (declarative memory). Thus, the hippocampus is necessary for transferring declarative information (words, facts, and events) from short-term into long-term memory but not for transferring nondeclarative or procedural information (motor skills and habits) (Zola & Squire, 2005). Until recently, the hippocampus was also believed to be involved in *recalling* remote personal events, such as a childhood birthday, but researchers found that people with damage to their hippocampus are able to recall remote personal events (Bayley et al., 2005).

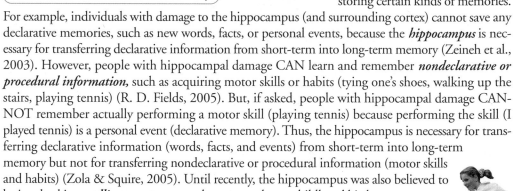

5 *Brain: Memory Model*

Recent findings indicate that your *cortex* stores short-term memories as well as long-term memories; your *hippocampus* transfers or saves declarative information in long-term memory but does not transfer nondeclarative or procedural information into long-term memory; and your *amygdala* adds emotional content to positive and negative memories (Tulving & Craik, 2005). Now that you know the location of memories in the brain, we can examine how individual memories are formed.

How to make a short-term memory?

Suppose you just looked up the phone number 555-9013 and repeat it as you dial. Researchers believe that your brain may store that number in short-term memory by using interconnected groups of neurons that are called neural assemblies.

Neural assemblies **are groups of interconnected neurons whose activation allows information or stimuli to be recognized and held briefly and temporarily in short-term memory.**

The figure on the right shows how a very simplified neural assembly might work. Some information, such as repeating

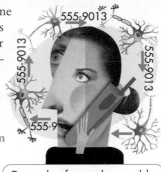

Example of neural assembly

a phone number, activates a neural assembly that holds the phone number in short-term memory. However, if you switch your attention to something else before encoding the number in long-term memory, this neural assembly stops and the phone number is gone and forgotten. Researchers believe that neural assemblies are one mechanism for holding information in short-term memory (E. E. Smith, 2000). However, as you'll see next, permanently storing information in long-term memory involves chemical or structural changes in the neurons themselves.

How to make a long-term memory?

Besides studying memory by genetically altering mice brains, researchers also study memory in sea slugs because their nervous system contains about 20,000 neurons versus billions in the human brain. After the sea slug has learned a simple task, such as tensing its muscular foot in response to a bright light, researchers can dissect the sea slug's nervous system and look for chemical or physical changes associated with learning (Kandel & Abel, 1995). We'll focus on one mechanism—long-term potentiation, or LTP—that researchers believe is involved in forming long-term memories.

LONG-TERM POTENTIATION (LTP)

1 One way to learn the name of the large orange-beaked bird on the left is to repeat its name, "toucan," several times. After you repeat this name (repeated stimulation), some neurons in your brain actually grow and change to form new connections with other neurons (Goldstein, 2005). This neural change, which is involved in forming long-term memories, is part of a complicated process called LTP.

Long-term potentiation, **or** *LTP,* **refers to changes in the structure and function of neurons after they have been repeatedly stimulated.**

For example, by repeating the name "toucan," you are repeatedly stimulating neurons.

2 We'll use only two neurons (perhaps many hundreds are involved) to make the LTP process easier to understand. In the figure below, repeating the name "toucan" stimulates neuron A, which produces LTP and causes neuron A to grow and form new connections with neuron B.

3 LTP changes the structure and function of neuron A so it becomes associated with the name "toucan." To recall the name of this bird, you activate neuron A, which activates its newly formed connections with neuron B, and this combined neural activation forms the basis for your long-

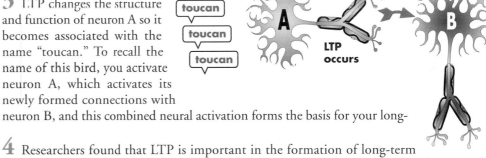

4 Researchers found that LTP is important in the formation of long-term memory because when the occurrence of LTP was chemically or genetically blocked in sea snails or mice, these animals could not learn a classically conditioned response or a water maze (Mayford & Korzus, 2002; Tonegawa & Wilson, 1997). Blocking the occurrence of LTP blocked the formation of long-term memories. Thus, neuroscientists believe the LTP process, which changes the ***structure*** and function of neurons, is the most likely basis for learning and memory in animals and humans (Goldstein, 2005; Tsien, 2000).

How to change memory?

Researchers have changed a mouse's memory by genetically changing its brain. For example, researcher Joe Tsien (2000) inserted a special gene into a fertilized mouse egg that eventually developed into a healthy mouse. The special gene caused changes in a part of the mouse's brain (hippocampus) so that certain brain cells—neurons—could communicate better by making stronger (synaptic) connections with other neurons (see pp. 52–53). The *genetically altered mice,* whose brain cells could better communicate, could also remember which objects they had explored and which objects were new (see right photo) about four

to five times longer than mice with unchanged or normal mice brains. Researchers found that genetically altered mice showed improved memory for both pleasant and unpleasant experiences (Tang et al., 2001). These results demonstrate that certain genes can change the structure of neurons so that they are either better or worse at communicating and better or worse at making memories (Tsien, 2000).

Genes make a mouse smarter.

✔ Concept Review

1. If you retrieve previously learned information without the aid of any external cues, you are using a process of remembering called (a)_____. If you identify or match information that you have previously learned, you are using a process of remembering called (b)_____.

2. Memory files or categories that contain related information organized around a specific topic are called (a)_____. One theory of memory organization says that the separate memory files, or nodes, in which we file related ideas are interconnected in a gigantic system. This idea is called (b)_____.

1. ANIMAL

3. According to network theory, some nodes are arranged so that more concrete information is at the bottom and more abstract information is at the top; this order is called a _____.

4. A diagram of the amount of previously learned information that subjects can recall or recognize across time is called a _____. We tend to remember information that is familiar and interesting and forget information that is unfamiliar and uninteresting.

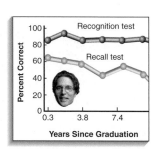

Recognition test

Recall test

Percent Correct

0.3 3.8 7.4
Years Since Graduation

5. According to Sigmund Freud, information that is threatening to our self-concept is automatically driven into our unconscious, from which we cannot retrieve it at will. This process is called _____.

6. One common reason for forgetting is that other related memories already stored in long-term memory may interfere with or block recall of some particular memory; this idea is called _____.

What if I have two exams?

7. Another reason for forgetting comes from a lack of associations between new information and information we already know; this reason has to do with the quality of the _____.

8. Brain damage, a blow to the head, drug use, or severe psychological stress may cause a form of forgetting called (a)_____, which results when the brain's (b)_____ network is temporarily or permanently disrupted.

Why did I misremember?

9. We may not be aware of times when we misremember something because of distortions in memory. Two common causes of memory distortions are _____ and _____.

10. If we forget information not because it is lost from storage but rather because other information gets in the way and blocks its retrieval, this process is called (a)_____. If information learned earlier blocks, interferes with, or disrupts the retrieval of information that was learned later, it is called (b)_____. If information learned later blocks, interferes with, or disrupts the retrieval of information learned earlier, it is called (c)_____.

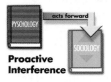

PSYCHOLOGY   acts forward   SOCIOLOGY

Proactive Interference

11. Mental reminders that we create by making images or associating new information with information that we already know are called (a)_____. If you do not form effective retrieval cues when learning new information, you will likely have a difficult time (b)_____ this information from long-term memory.

12. Sometimes, despite making a great effort, you are temporarily unable to recall information that you absolutely know is in your memory. This is called the _____ phenomenon.

13. According to one memory model of the brain, short-term memories are formed and stored in different parts of the (a)_____. Long-term memories are also stored in different parts of the (b)_____, although these kinds of memories are not formed there. Declarative information is transferred by the (c)_____ into long-term memory, which is stored in different parts of the cortex. However, the hippocampus is not involved in transferring motor skills or habits, which are part of (d)_____ information, into long-term memory. Both positive and negative emotional associations are added to memories by an area in the temporal lobe called the (e)_____.

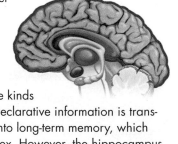

Answers: 1. (a) recall, (b) recognition; 2. (a) nodes, (b) network theory; 3. hierarchy; 4. forgetting curve; 5. repression; 6. interference; 7. retrieval cues; 8. (a) amnesia, (b) communication; 9. bias, suggestibility; 10. (a) interference, (b) proactive interference, (c) retroactive interference; 11. (a) retrieval cues, (b) recalling or retrieving or remembering; 12. tip-of-the-tongue; 13. (a) cortex, (b) cortex, (c) hippocampus, (d) procedural, (e) amygdala

E. Mnemonics: Memorization Methods

Do you complain about forgetting things?

At one time or another, almost everyone complains about forgetting something. Many of our students complain about forgetting information that they really knew but couldn't recall during exams. This kind of forgetting has several causes: There may be *interference (proactive and retroactive)* from information studied for related classes; there may be *poor retrieval* cues that result from trying to learn information by using rote or straight memorization; or students may not use elaborative rehearsal (p. 249), which involves making associations between new and old information.

After about age 40, adults begin to complain about forgetting things that they never forgot before. For example, memory researcher Daniel Schacter, at age 50, complained, "Reading a journal article 15 years ago, I would have it at my fingertips. Now, if I don't deliberately try to relate it to what I already know, or repeat it a few times, I'm less likely to remember it" (Schacter, 1997, p. 56). This kind of forgetting is commonly caused by poor retrieval cues, which result from being busy or distracted and not having or taking the time to create meaningful associations.

How can I improve my memory?

If you hear about memory courses that claim to greatly improve your memory, what these courses usually teach are how to use mnemonic methods.

Mnemonic (ni-MON-ick) methods are ways to improve encoding and create better retrieval cues by forming vivid associations or images, which improve recall.

We'll discuss two common mnemonic methods—method of loci and peg method—that improve memory (Mason & Kohn, 2001).

Method of Loci

If you need to memorize a list of terms, concepts, or names in a particular order, an efficient way is to use the method of loci.

The *method of loci (LOW-sigh)* is an encoding technique that creates visual associations between already memorized places and new items to be memorized.

We'll use the following three steps of the method of loci to memorize names of early psychologists: Wundt, James, and Watson.

Step 1. Memorize a visual sequence of places (*loci* in Latin means "places"), such as places in your apartment where you can store things. Select easily remembered places such as in your kitchen: sink, cabinet, refrigerator, stove, and closet.

Step 2. Create a vivid association for each item to be memorized. For example, picture Wundt hanging from a bridge and saying, "I wundt jump."

Step 3. Once you have created a list of vivid associations, mentally put each psychologist in one of the selected places: Wundt goes in the sink, James in the cabinet, Watson in the refrigerator.

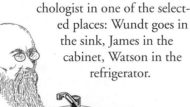

To recall this list of early psychologists, you take an imaginary stroll through your kitchen and mentally note the image stored in each of your memorized places.

Peg Method

Another useful mnemonic device for memorizing a long list, especially in the exact order, is the peg method.

The *peg method* is an encoding technique that creates associations between number-word rhymes and items to be memorized.

The rhymes act like pegs on which you hang items to be memorized. Let's use the two steps of the peg method to memorize our three early psychologists: Wundt, James, Watson.

Step 1. Memorize the list of peg words shown on the left, which consists of a number and its rhyming word.

**one is a bun
two is a shoe
three is a tree
four is a door
five is a hive**

Step 2. Next, associate each of the items you wish to memorize with one of the peg words. For instance, imagine Wundt on a bun, James with two left shoes, and Watson stuck in a tree.

To remember this list of early psychologists, you recall each peg along with its image of an early psychologist that you placed there.

Effectiveness of Methods

A national magazine writer, who was 41 years old and complained about forgetfulness, decided to improve her memory by trying three methods (Yoffe, 1997).

First, she took a 3-hour memory-enhancement class ($49) that focused on the peg method. The magazine writer concluded that the peg method was impressive and if she were back in college, she would use it to memorize all the new facts.

Second, she listened to an audiocassette program ($79) that promised to release the "perfect photographic memory" that everyone already had. The audio program focused on using the peg method without much application to real life. Contrary to the audiocassette's promise, memory researchers report that photographic memories are as rare as duck's teeth (Schacter, 1996).

Third, she read a memory-improvement book ($10) that described the peg method, how to pay attention, and the importance of creating associations and images.

As this writer's experience illustrates, improving one's memory requires making the effort to use good encoding, such as elaborative rehearsal, which means creating good associations that, in turn, produce good retrieval cues and improve memory.

As the percentage of people over 50 increases, so does interest in *memory-enhancing drugs,* such as the popular herbal supplement ginkgo. However, researchers found that ginkgo did NOT improve memory or concentration in healthy adults (P. R. Solomon et al., 2002). Still, the search for effective memory enhancers continues. Researchers have found ways to improve memory in mice, and they are now testing memory-enhancing drugs in humans (Rex et al., 2006).

Next, we'll discuss how cultural influences can affect what you remember.

Retrieval Cues

How do you survive in a desert versus an office meeting?

Suppose you lived in the harsh, endless, barren desert world of western Australia, where many of the native Aborigines live (top photo). For about 30,000 years, the Aborigines have survived by using visual landmarks to remember the exact locations of water, food, and game in vast stretches of unmapped country (R. A. Gould, 1969). Because the Aborigines use few, if any, written records, their survival in this barren desert largely depends on their ability to store, or encode, enormous amounts of visual information, such as landmarks for food, water, and game. Lacking reading and writing skills, Aborigines primarily encode information about the desert by using *visual retrieval cues,* which are later used to recall information.

Survival depends on VISUAL cues.

Survival depends on VERBAL cues.

In contrast, most of us live in an industrial urban culture, in which survival largely depends on the ability to read and write and store an enormous amount of verbal, written, and computer-related information (bottom photo). Successfully surviving in an industrial culture is greatly dependent on the ability to store, or encode, enormous amounts of written and verbal information by using *verbal retrieval cues.*

These two examples show that survival in the aboriginal culture depends on encoding and remembering visual information, while surviving in an industrial culture depends on encoding and remembering verbal (written) information. This cultural difference predicts that people would perform differently on tests, depending on whether the tests emphasized visual or verbal retrieval cues.

Visual Versus Verbal Memory

Psychologist Judith Kearins was not surprised to find that Aborigines scored low on Western-style intelligence tests because these tests emphasize verbal retrieval cues and put Aborigines at a disadvantage. Considering their desert culture, she suspected that Aborigines would perform better on tests that took advantage of their ability to encode with visual retrieval cues.

USING VISUAL CUES

To see if Aborigines were better at visual encoding, Kearins developed a test that emphasized visual retrieval cues. This test consisted of looking at 20 objects that were placed on a board divided into 20 squares. Some objects were natural—stone, feather, leaf; others were manufactured—eraser, thimble, ring. Aborigines and white Australian adolescents were told to study the board for 30 seconds (sample section on right). Then all the objects were heaped into a pile in the center of the board and the children were asked to replace the items in their original locations. The 44 Aborigine adolescents had been reared for the most part in desert tribal ways, had learned a nontraditional form of English as a second language, and were now attending school. The 44 white Australian adolescents lived and attended high school in a relatively large urban area (Perth).

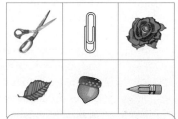

Aborigine students are better at using VISUAL cues than white Australian students.

PERFORMANCE

Kearins tested the adolescents using four different sets of objects—natural, manufactured, and two combinations. The graph below shows that the Aborigine adolescents performed significantly better in placing objects back in their original locations than did the white Australian adolescents (Kearins, 1981). Another group of researchers essentially replicated Kearins's results using a younger population (average age of 9) of Aborigines and white Australians (Klich & Davidson, 1983).

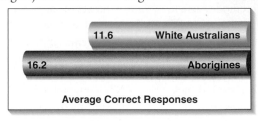

11.6 White Australians

16.2 Aborigines

Average Correct Responses

CULTURE AND RETRIEVAL CUES

Kearins concluded that the Aborigines' survival in the harsh desert landscape encouraged and rewarded their abilities to encode information using visual retrieval cues. In comparison, the urban school setting of the white Australians encouraged and rewarded their ability to encode information using verbal retrieval cues. For example, when questioned about their strategies, many of the Aborigines said that they remembered only the look of the objects on the board. In comparison, white Australians described their strategies in great detail: "I looked at the bottom row and remembered onion, banksia nut, rock, bone, and apple core." These descriptions support the idea that the Aborigines used visual retrieval cues, while the white Australians used verbal retrieval cues. These interesting results suggest that survival needs do shape and reward a particular way of encoding information in memory.

The better performance of Aborigines on visual tasks indicates that culture does influence the encoding and recall of information. Besides culture, other factors, such as the type of information having to be recalled, may also influence memory, as shown next in a study on recalling sexual history in adolescents.

How Accurate Are Students' Memories?

Are students telling the truth?

Many schools across the United States offer sex education in an effort to reduce adolescent sexual activity. Some sex education programs encourage students to take virginity pledges to abstain from sexual intercourse until marriage. These programs are considered to be so important that they are promoted by the U.S. government (Rosenbaum, 2006). But, how do we know whether or not these programs actually reduce adolescent sexual activity? Since sexual activity is not a behavior researchers can observe, research methods used to study sexual activity are limited to the survey method (see p. 28).

Using surveys to question teenagers about intimate behaviors, especially their sexual histories, is very challenging. Adolescents may deliberately report false information because they want to present a desirable self-image or

Surveys are used to question teenagers about their sexual histories.

because they are being influenced by social pressures. If adolescents' behaviors go against their moral or religious beliefs, they may falsify their answers so they are more consistent with their values. Another challenge in obtaining accurate information by using a survey is that when people are asked to report on their past experiences, their survey responses tend to be based on their current beliefs and behaviors more than on past beliefs and behaviors. Thus, if adolescents have recently changed their beliefs or their sexual behaviors, their recollection of the past may be biased (Rosenbaum, 2006).

If adolescents are inaccurately reporting their sexual histories, it becomes impossible to determine whether sex education programs are effective in reducing sexual activity. This serious concern led a researcher to study whether adolescents accurately recall their sexual histories.

Research Method to Evaluate Memory Accuracy

Why do so many students change their answers?

To answer the question of how well adolescents recall their sexual histories, Janet Rosenbaum (2006), a health policy researcher at Harvard University, studied more than 13,000 students in grades 7 to 12 from schools across the United States.

Procedure. The students were questioned two times, a year apart. To respect students' privacy, many personal questions were asked through headphones and students typed their answers into a computer. The questions they were asked included: "Have you ever taken a public or written pledge to remain a virgin until marriage?" Students were also asked if they ever had sexual intercourse.

Results. In the first survey, about 13% of subjects reported having taken a virginity pledge. In the second survey (a year later), only 6% of subjects reported having ever taken a virginity pledge (see left bar graph). Thus, more than half of the subjects who reported having taken a virginity pledge in the first survey later denied having done so. Also, subjects who reported having sexual intercourse for the first time in the second survey were more likely to deny having taken a virginity pledge than those who did not report having sexual intercourse.

First Survey 13%

Second Survey 6%

Report Making Virginity Pledge

When first asked about their sexual histories, about 33% of subjects reported having sexual intercourse, but only 29% of subjects reported having sexual intercourse when questioned during the second survey (see right bar graph). Many subjects who reported having had sexual intercourse during the first survey and who made a virginity pledge for the first time during the second survey denied ever having sexual intercourse. Thus, many subjects changed their minds about their sexual histories, especially if they recently made a virginity pledge.

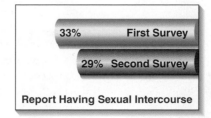

33% First Survey

29% Second Survey

Report Having Sexual Intercourse

Conclusion. Many students changed their responses about their sexual histories and whether or not they had taken a virginity pledge. The results of this study show that adolescents who have sexual intercourse after making a virginity pledge are likely to deny having made a pledge. Also, adolescents who have sexual intercourse before making a virginity pledge are likely to deny their sexual histories.

These results raise concern about the reliability of surveys to collect information about sexual activity among adolescents. One explanation for why students changed their answers is that their beliefs changed during the course of the year between the two surveys and students may recall only memories that are consistent with their current beliefs. Students may even report behaviors that never happened but that are consistent with their new beliefs. These types of reporting errors are not uncommon when using surveys to collect information. Overall, the results show that adolescents' memories for sexual behaviors are often inaccurate.

Just as adolescents may misremember information about their sexual histories, research shows that some adults have difficulty recalling their sexual histories as well (Garry et al., 2002). Adults may also misremember when giving eyewitness testimony, our next topic.

H. Application: Eyewitness Testimony

How Accurate Is an Eyewitness?

The woman on the witness stand was very emotional as she recalled in vivid detail the hour of terror during which two men had forced her into her car, drove away, and later raped her in the front seat. When she was asked if one of the rapists was present in the courtroom, she pointed directly at the defendant sitting at the table and said, "There is no doubt in my mind."

Eyewitness testimony **refers to recalling or recognizing a suspect observed during a potentially very disrupting and distracting emotional situation that may have interfered with accurate remembering.**

For example, the woman's eyewitness testimony was the damning evidence that sent the defendant (an alleged rapist) to prison. After the man spent 10 years in prison, a new defense lawyer asked that the victim's clothes undergo a DNA test, which had not yet been developed at the time of the initial trial. The DNA test proved that the sperm stains on the victim's jeans did not come from the man who was in prison. The man who had been sent to prison because of the victim's eyewitness testimony was found innocent and set free (M. Dolan, 1995). This example points to at least three problems with eyewitness testimony.

I have no doubt that he's the one who raped me!

DNA evidence proved he was not the rapist.

The first problem is that juries assume that eyewitness testimony is the best kind of evidence because it is so accurate and reliable. However, in the United States (as of this writing), nearly 200 people have been wrongfully convicted of crimes and later been freed because of DNA evidence. Of the 200 convictions, about 150 had been based on (mistaken) eyewitness testimony (Zernike, 2006).

Because of apparent problems with eyewitness testimony, the Supreme Court of New York has recently ruled that experts can be called to testify on its reliability and accuracy (McKinley, 2001).

Own-race bias. In the rape case discussed here, the eyewitness was a white female and the accused rapist was a black man. This case brings up another source of eyewitness error: problems in correctly identifying individuals of another race. For example, researchers found that an eyewitness of one race is less accurate when identifying an accused person of another race. The finding that people better recognize faces of their own race than faces of other races is called ***own-race bias,*** which can distort and lessen the accuracy of eyewitness testimony (Ferguson et al., 2001).

A second problem with eyewitness testimony is that the police and juries generally assume that the more confident an eyewitness is, the more accurate is the testimony. For example, the witness in this rape case was very confident when she pointed at the accused man and said, "There is no doubt in my mind." However, there is only a moderate association or correlation (+0.37) between how correct the identification of an eyewitness is and how much confidence the eyewitness feels about his or her identification (Wells & Olson, 2003). This means that an eyewitness's confidence is not a good indication of accuracy.

A third problem with eyewitness testimony is that eyewitnesses may make errors if law enforcement officials ask misleading or biased questions or make suggestions about the perpetrator's identification. In these cases, eyewitnesses may unknowingly accept the misinformation as fact and give unreliable testimony (B. Bower, 2003b). For example, consider the following case of an eyewitness's mistaken identity.

Can an Eyewitness Be Misled?

Some years ago a series of armed robberies occurred in the Wilmington, Delaware, area. The police had few leads in the case until a local citizen said that a Roman Catholic priest, Father Bernard Pagano, looked like the sketch of the robber.

At his trial, seven eyewitnesses positively identified Father Pagano (left photo) as the robber. But at the last minute, another man, Ronald Clouser (right photo), stepped forward and confessed to the robberies and Father Pagano was released (Rodgers, 1982).

As you look at these two photos, you will wonder how this case of mistaken identity could possibly have happened. Ronald Clouser is shorter, 14 years younger, and not nearly as bald as Father Pagano; besides, he has different facial features. Why, then, did seven eyewitnesses say with certainty that Father Pagano was the robber they had seen? One reason involves how the witnesses were questioned. Apparently, before the

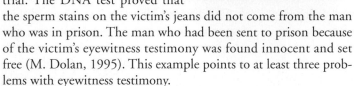

Seven people identified Father Pagano . . .

. . . but Ronald Clouser confessed to being the robber.

witnesses were questioned and shown photos of the suspects, the police had suggested the possibility that the robber was a priest. After being prompted to look for a priest, the witnesses focused on the few similarities Father Pagano had to the real robber. Because Father Pagano was the only suspect wearing a clerical collar, the witnesses concluded that he must be the robber. This example is but one of many that show how eyewitness testimony may be distorted or biased.

Because of potential problems with eyewitness testimony, the U.S. Department of Justice released a guide for collecting and preserving eyewitness evidence (Wells et al., 2000). This guide, based on research findings discussed in this Application section, warns law enforcement agencies about the kinds of errors that eyewitnesses may make. We'll next discuss more of the research findings that show how eyewitness testimony may be changed or biased.

Can Questions Change the Answers?

Because of concern about the reliability of eyewitness testimony, Elizabeth Loftus (1979, 2003) studied whether people can be misled and do misremember, especially if they are given false information. We'll describe some of Loftus's experiments that demonstrate how subjects misremembered what they saw or heard.

DID THE CAR PASS THE BARN?

In one experiment, subjects watched a film of an automobile accident and then were questioned about what they saw. One of the questions contained a false piece of information: "How fast was the red sports car going when it passed the barn while traveling along the country road?" Although there was no barn in the film, 17% of the subjects said they had seen a barn, indicating that people may believe misinformation if it fits the overall scene or pattern (Loftus, 1975).

WAS THERE A STOP SIGN?

In a well-known study by Loftus and colleagues, subjects were first shown slides of a traffic accident involving a stop sign and then asked a series of questions about the accident. Some of the questions were not misleading and asked about the presence of a stop sign. Other questions were deliberately misleading and did not mention the stop sign but asked about the presence of a yield sign. Later, when subjects were asked whether they had seen a stop sign

or a yield sign, those subjects who had been misled by earlier questions about a yield sign were more likely to report seeing a yield sign than subjects who were not misled (Loftus et al., 1978). These results, which show that subjects can be misled by being given false but related information, have been replicated by many other researchers (Neisser & Libby, 2005).

HOW DOES FALSE INFORMATION ALTER MEMORY?

Based on many such studies, Loftus and Hoffman (1989) concluded that if misleading information is introduced during questioning after an event, people may believe this misinformation and report events that they did not see.

According to Loftus, eyewitnesses believed the false information they were told, rather than what they saw, because the false information altered or overwrote their original, true memory (Loftus & Loftus, 1980). This explanation, which has generated much research and debate, says that people misremember because of a memory impairment: the true memory was erased or overwritten (D. G. Payne et al., 1994). However, other researchers argue that the original, true memory is still there but is difficult to retrieve (Zaragoza & Lane, 1994). Whatever the cause, these many studies indicate that people (witnesses) do misremember when given misleading information.

Is What You Say, What You Believe?

The debate over whether false information overwrites the original memory has not been settled. However, what has been settled is that sometimes people do come to believe that they actually remember seeing things that were merely suggested to them; this phenomenon is called source misattribution.

Source misattribution **is a memory error that results when a person has difficulty deciding which of two or more sources a memory came from: Was the source something the person saw or imagined, or was it a suggestion?**

For example, suppose you saw a hit-and-run accident involving a dark red car. During questioning, you are asked the color of the car

Did you see a red or blue car?

that drove off. As you're thinking that the car was dark red, you remember hearing another bystander say, "The car was dark blue." Source misattribution would occur if you said that the car was dark blue (suggestion you heard) rather than dark red (something you saw). Researchers have found that false suggestions, misleading questions, and misinformation can result in source misattribution and create false memories (Roediger & McDermott, 2005). False memories that can result from source misattribution, such as suggestions or misleading questions, are one reason that court officials may question the accuracy of eyewitness testimony.

Which Interview Technique Works Best?

Suppose you had witnessed a robbery but had trouble picking the suspect out of a police lineup. To help you provide reliable information about the suspect, you might be questioned using a procedure called the cognitive interview.

The *cognitive interview* **is a technique for questioning people, such as eyewitnesses, by having them imagine and reconstruct the details of an event, report everything they remember without holding anything back, and narrate the event from different viewpoints.**

The cognitive interview has proved very useful in police interrogation: Detectives trained in cognitive interview techniques obtained 47–60% more information from victims and suspects than detectives using the standard police interrogation method (Gwyer & Clifford, 1997).

A cognitive interview is a more effective method for questioning eyewitnesses.

The cognitive interview is a very effective way to increase correct recall and avoid making suggestions that might create false memories and increase errors of source misattribution in children, adults, and senior citizens from varying educational backgrounds (L. M. Stein & Memon, 2006).

Psychologists have answered many questions about how eyewitnesses can be misled as well as how to improve the reliability of their testimony, which may result in life-or-death decisions. Because most jurors do not know that eyewitness testimonies are unreliable, many courts in the United States allow experts to testify about the reliability of eyewitnesses so juries are made aware of the same studies and findings that you have just read (McVeigh, 2006; Pezdek, 1995). England has gone as far as barring cases when the only evidence is an eyewitness.

✔ Summary Test

A. Organization of Memories

1. If you are asked to retrieve previously learned information without the aid of external cues, you are using a process of remembering called (a)_____, which is generally more difficult. If you are asked to answer multiple-choice questions, you can identify or match information and use a process of remembering called (b)_____, which is generally less difficult.

1. ANIMAL

2. According to one theory of memory organization, we encode or file related ideas in separate categories called _____.

3. We form links between nodes by forming associations. The idea that the interconnected nodes form a gigantic system is called _____ theory.

4. An arrangement in which nodes are organized in a logical manner, with more concrete information at the bottom and more abstract information at the top, is called a _____.

B. Forgetting Curves

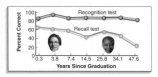

5. If the amount of previously learned information that subjects can recall or recognize across time is plotted, the resulting graph is called a _____. For example, Ebbinghaus demonstrated that the majority of nonsense syllables are forgotten relatively quickly—within hours. However, other studies showed that more relevant and interesting information may be remembered for many years.

C. Reasons for Forgetting

6. If you forget because other memories interfere with or prevent retrieval of some particular memory, it is called (a)_____. If you forget because information that was learned earlier interferes with information learned later, it is called (b)_____ interference. If you forget because information that was learned later interferes with information learned earlier, it is called (c)_____ interference.

7. Forgetting information because it was poorly encoded means that you failed to form new associations or reminders, which results in poor or inadequate _____.

8. Freud said you may forget information that is threatening to your self-concept because it is automatically pushed into your unconscious, from which you cannot retrieve it at will. This idea of Freud's is called _____.

9. If a person experiences a blow to the head, has severe psychological trauma, or takes or is given certain drugs, that person may forget things because of having _____.

10. You may not always be aware of when you misremember something or when your memory is distorted because of the influence of _____ and _____.

11. To increase the chances of remembering items from long-term memory, we can create reminders that associate new information with information that we already know; these reminders are called _____.

12. There are times you are absolutely sure that certain information is stored in memory but you are unable to retrieve it. This experience is called the _____ phenomenon.

13. Besides creating retrieval cues, it may also be easier to recall information when you are in the same physiological or emotional state as when you originally learned it; this phenomenon is called _____.

D. Biological Bases of Memory

14. Different areas of the brain are involved in different memory processes. For example, the ability to hold words, facts, or events (declarative information) in short-term memory depends on activity in the (a)_____. The ability to transfer information about words, facts, and events (declarative information) from short-term into long-term memory depends on activity in the (b)_____. If this structure were damaged, a person could carry on a conversation but would not (c)_____ the conversation the next day.

15. The ability to recall words, facts, and events (declarative information) from the past involves activity in the outer covering of the brain, which is called the (a)_____. For example, if patients have an intact cortex, they can remember past events because these events are already stored in the cortex. However, they may have difficulty remembering any new words, facts, or events (declarative information) because of damage to their (b)_____.

16. The ability to transfer motor skills and habits, which is part of _____ memory, does not involve the hippocampus. Even though a person with damage to the hippocampus can store procedural information, that person would have no memory of having engaged in that event (declarative information).

17. The area of the brain that adds emotional feelings to memories is called the _____. This area is involved in forming a wide range of happy, sad, or fearful memories.

18. Researchers believe that the brain forms and briefly stores short-term memories by using a circuit of interconnected neurons called _____. When these interconnected neurons stop being activated, the short-term memory vanishes unless it has been encoded in long-term memory.

19. Researchers have evidence that the formation and storage of long-term memories involve the repeated stimulation of neurons, which in turn causes neurons to grow and change to form new connections with other neurons; this phenomenon is called (a)_____. When this process was chemically or genetically blocked, animals were unable to form (b)_____, which points to the importance of LTP in forming long-term memories.

E. Mnemonics: Memorization Methods

20. Although we have the capacity to store great amounts of information, we may not be able to recall some of this information because of forgetting. Techniques that use efficient methods of encoding to improve remembering and prevent forgetting are called (a)_____. The major function of these techniques is to create strong (b)_____ that will serve as effective (c)_____.

21. A method that creates visual associations between memorized places and items to be memorized is called the (a)_____. With another method, one creates associations between number-word rhymes and items to be memorized; this method is called the (b)_____.

F. Cultural Diversity: Aborigines Versus White Australians

22. Data from Aborigine and white Australian children suggest that survival needs may shape and reward a particular way of (a)_____ information in memory. For example, in the industrialized world, people (white Australians) are required to store large amounts of (b)_____. However, Aborigines in the wilds of Australia need to be able to store environmental, or (c)_____, to find their way, locate watering places, and thus increase their chances of survival. Researchers found that Aborigines performed better on tests that required (d)_____ retrieval cues and performed less well on tests that required (e)_____ cues.

G. Research Focus: Memory Accuracy

23. Since sexual activity is not a behavior researchers can observe, research methods used to study sexual activity are limited to the (a)_____. Janet Rosenbaum at Harvard University asked more than 13,000 adolescents questions about their sexual histories and whether or not they had ever taken a virginity pledge. Overall, the results of this study show that adolescents' memories for sexual behaviors are often (b)_____.

H. Application: Eyewitness Testimony

24. In 150 out of 200 cases, eyewitnesses identified the wrong suspect, which indicates that such eyewitness testimony is not always (a)_____. Another problem is that the accuracy of an eyewitness is only moderately related to the how much (b)_____ the eyewitness feels. Eyewitnesses have difficulty identifying a suspect of another race; this is called (c)_____. Eyewitness testimony may not be reliable because witnesses may be influenced by officials who ask (d)_____ questions.

25. When a person has difficulty deciding which of two or more sources is responsible for a memory, it is called (a)_____. Researchers found that misleading questions and false information can cause subjects to (b)_____ events.

26. The recall of eyewitnesses may be improved by having them imagine and reconstruct the details of an event, report everything that they remember, and report things from different viewpoints. This method is called the (a)_____. With this method, eyewitnesses remember much more information about the event than they do when asked standard questions. This questioning procedure also helps to eliminate suggestions or source misattributions, which can result in implanting (b)_____ in witnesses.

Answers: *1. (a) recall, (b) recognition; 2. nodes; 3. network; 4. hierarchy; 5. forgetting curve; 6. (a) interference, (b) proactive, (c) retroactive; 7. retrieval cues; 8. repression; 9. amnesia; 10. bias, suggestibility; 11. retrieval cues; 12. tip-of-the-tongue; 13. state-dependent learning; 14. (a) cortex, (b) hippocampus, (c) remember; 15. (a) cortex, (b) hippocampus; 16. procedural; 17. amygdala; 18. neural assemblies; 19. (a) long-term potentiation, or LTP, (b) long-term memories; 20. (a) mnemonics, (b) associations, (c) retrieval cues; 21. (a) method of loci, (b) peg method; 22. (a) encoding, (b) verbal information, (c) visual information, (d) visual, (e) verbal; 23. (a) survey method, (b) inaccurate; 24. (a) accurate or reliable, (b) confidence, (c) own-race bias, (d) misleading; 25. (a) source misattribution, (b) misremember; 26. (a) cognitive interview, (b) false memories*

Critical Thinking

Why Does Wife Forget, Date, and Remarry Husband?

by Michael Haederle

Questions

1. Of the four reasons for forgetting, which one applies to Krickitt?

2. Krickitt's loss of many long-term memories means that which part of her brain was damaged?

3. How was Krickitt able to remember her parents but not her husband, not their apartment, and not their wedding photos?

4. Of the two kinds of long-term memory, which involves Krickitt's having to relearn to drive a car?

5. Which part of Krickitt's brain was undamaged and allowed her to store new long-term memories of Kim?

LAS VEGAS, N.M.—Shortly after their wedding in 1993, Krickitt suffered a severe head injury in a car crash. When she emerged from a month-long coma, she no longer knew Kim (her husband), having lost all memory of the previous 18 months—including meeting and marrying her husband.

Kim stuck by her as she struggled to heal, and against all odds, they courted and fell in love again. . . .

Emerging from her coma around Christmas, Krickitt was as helpless as a newborn. She needed to be fed, diapered, and bathed. The 5-foot-2 former college gymnast, who'd once performed back flips on a balance beam, had to learn to walk again.

"It was sad to see her in this condition," Kim says. But there was worse news. . . .

When quizzed by a nurse, Krickitt knew she was in Phoenix—although she thought it was 1969 (it was really 1993) and Nixon was the president. She also knew who her parents were. . . . Then the nurse asked "Who's your husband?" Krickitt said, "I'm not married." Kim said, "I was devastated—I was crushed, I was hurt so bad. I hit my hand on the wall." . . .

Krickitt visited their Las Vegas home, hoping the familiar surroundings might jog her memory. She wandered through the apartment she'd shared with Kim, gazing at their wedding photos and fingering her china. Nothing clicked.

"I remember asking, 'How did I do the wife thing? Did I cook for you? Did I bring you lunch?'" she says. Krickitt was unable to drive and couldn't remember directions. Kim worried she'd get lost walking the 100 yards to the grocery store. . . . It was the therapist who suggested that Kim and Krickitt start dating as a way of rebuilding their relationship. On their "date nights," they sampled everything their small town had to offer. "We'd go to Pizza Hut," Kim says. "We'd go to Wal-Mart or go bowling." Sometimes he'd bring her roses. . . . With continued therapy and the passage of time, Krickitt has accepted her new life. . . . It was Krickitt who suggested getting married again.

On Valentine's Day he went to her office with a bunch of red roses and proposed on bended knee. . . . They married (above photo) Sept. 18, 1993, and honeymooned in Maui before settling into their new life together in this small northern New Mexico city. (Source: *Los Angeles Times*, May 23, 1996)

Suggested Answers

1. Because of a car accident, Krickitt suffered a severe blow to her head that caused her to go into a coma. In addition, when she came out of her coma, the severe blow to her head caused widespread amnesia, which is forgetting caused by loss of memory.

2. Since long-term memories are stored primarily in the cortex (surface of the brain), this means that areas of Krickitt's cortex were damaged in the accident.

3. Researchers have discovered that different kinds of long-term memories are stored in different parts of the cortex. Krickitt could remember her parents because those memories were stored in a part of her cortex that was undamaged. However, she lost all memory of her husband and being married because those memories were stored in a part of her cortex that was damaged.

4. There are two kinds of long-term memories: declarative and nondeclarative or procedural (p. 246). Learning motor skills and habits involves storing nondeclarative or procedural memories and does not involve the hippocampus.

5. Krickett was able to relearn who Kim was by dating him. Krickett's ability to remember that she was dating and going out with Kim means that she was able to store personal or episodic memories, which are one kind of declarative memories (p. 246). Declarative memories are transferred and stored as long-term memories by the hippocampus, which means that Krickett's hippocampus was undamaged and functioning.

Links to Learning

Learning Activities

- **POWERSTUDY FOR INTRODUCTION TO PSYCHOLOGY 4.0**
  by Tom Doyle and Rod Plotnik
  SuperModule: Check out "Remembering & Forgetting" on **PowerStudy.** It includes complete paragraph-by-paragraph explanations of all content using fully-narrated animations and graphics. An onscreen toolbar allows immediate access to text, text outline, and module glossary with notetaking and printing capabilities. This module also includes:
  - Videos—Imbedded videos explore how we associate names as well as Elizabeth Loftus's research on eyewitness testimony.
  - A test of your knowledge using an interactive version of the Summary Test on pages 276 and 277. Also access related quizzing—true/false, multiple choice, and matching.
  - An interactive version of the Critical Thinking exercise "Why Does Wife Forget, Date, and Remarry Husband?" on page 278.
  - Key terms, a chapter outline including chapter abstract, and a special extended list of hotlinked websites that correlate to this module.

- *CengageNOW*
  academic.cengage.com/login
  Need help studying? This site is your one-stop study shop.
  Take a Pre-Test and CengageNOW will generate a Personalized Study Plan based on your test results. The Study Plan will identify the topics you need to review and direct you to online resources to help you master those topics. You can then take a Post-Test to determine the concepts you have mastered and what you still need to work on.

- **INTRODUCTION TO PSYCHOLOGY BOOK COMPANION WEBSITE**
  academic.cengage.com/psychology/plotnik
  Visit your book companion website where you will find more resources to help you study. At this site, you will find Learning Objectives, Internet Exercises, quizzing, flash cards, and a pronunciation glossary.

- *STUDY GUIDE and WEBTUTOR*
  Check the corresponding module in your Study Guide for effective student tips and help learning the material presented. Also go to **academic.cengage.com/webtutor** for an interactive version of the Study Guide features.

Study Questions

*A. Organization of Memories—How would your memory be affected if you accidentally took a drug that prevented the formation of any new nodes? (**Suggested answer page 626**)

B. Forgetting Curves—Why are you more likely to remember students' names than concepts from high school?

C. Reasons for Forgetting—If you wanted to change your study habits, how would you use information about why we forget?

*D. Biological Bases of Memory—If a virus suddenly destroyed your hippocampus, what effect would it have on your performance in college? (**Suggested answer page 626**)

E. Mnemonics: Memorization Methods—Can you describe a mnemonic method to remember the four reasons for forgetting?

F. Cultural Diversity: Aborigines Versus White Australians—What might be one difference between the ways in which art and English majors encode information?

G. Research Focus: Memory Accuracy—How can you obtain more accurate sexual histories from adolescents?

*H. Application: Eyewitness Testimony—If you were on a jury, what concerns would you have when listening to eyewitness testimony? (**Suggested answer page 626**)

*These questions are answered in Appendix B.

MODULE 13
Intelligence

Mirror, Mirror, on the Wall, Who Is the Most Intelligent of Them All?

Who is the most intelligent?

For the past 200 years, psychologists have been involved in defining and measuring intelligence, which turns out to be a very complicated business. For example, after reading about the five individuals described below, rank them according to your idea of intelligence. After you have read the module, come back to your ranking and see if you would make any changes.

Based on my idea of intelligence, here's how I have ranked the five individuals: #1____, #2____, #3____, #4____, #5____.

| **A. Gregg Cox** | **B. Halle Berry** | **C. Bill Gates** | **D. Steve Lu** | **E. Midori** |

A. Gregg Cox
At age 37, he can speak 64 languages fluently, making him, says *The Guinness Book of World Records,* the planet's greatest linguist. He broke the old record of 58 languages. He began learning languages at age 5, starting with Spanish, Portuguese, Italian, German, and Chinese. Since then, he has been learning about 5 languages a year. He's writing a book—a dictionary.

B. Halle Berry
At age 40, she has already starred in nearly 30 Hollywood movies and become the highest paid African American actress in Hollywood. Not only has she earned an Emmy and a Golden Globe award for her acting, but she also won Best Actress at the Academy Awards in 2002, making her the first African American woman to ever win an Oscar for best actress.

C. Bill Gates
At age 51, he has become the richest man in the United States, worth around $53 billion. He began writing computer programs in eighth grade. As a college sophomore, he dropped out of Harvard and wrote one of the first operating systems to run a computer. In his twenties, he founded Microsoft, whose software operates 90% of the computers in the world.

D. Steve Lu
At age 5, he scored 194 on an IQ test (average is 100). At age 9, he scored 710 on the math part of the SAT (perfect score is 800). He completed 12 years of precollege courses in just 5 years. At age 10, he was a freshman in college. At age 15, he was one of the youngest students ever to be accepted in the graduate computer science program at prestigious Stanford University.

E. Midori
At age 3, she began playing violin. By age 10, she was considered a musical prodigy, another name for a child genius. Also at age 10, she made a big stir in classical music circles by performing professionally with the New York Philharmonic Orchestra. From an early age she was able to memorize and flawlessly perform long and complicated pieces of classical music.

Psychometrics

The problem you faced in trying to rank the intelligence of the above five individuals—Cox, Berry, Gates, Lu, and Midori—is similar to what psychologists faced in having to define and measure intelligence. Since the late 1800s, psychologists have debated the question, What is intelligence? and have developed a number of tests to measure intelligence. Measuring intelligence is part of an area of psychology that is called psychometrics.

Psychometrics, **which is a subarea of psychology, is concerned with developing psychological tests that assess an individual's abilities, skills, beliefs, and personality traits in a wide range of settings—school, industry, or clinic.**

As you'll discover in this module, the measurement of intelligence and the development of intelligence tests are still being debated (Sternberg et al., 2003b).

What's Coming

We'll discuss the different theories of intelligence, how intelligence is measured, the meaning of IQ scores, the problems with intelligence tests, how genetics and environment influence intelligence, and ways to improve environmental opportunities.

We'll begin with a very old but very basic question: How do we define intelligence?

A. Defining Intelligence

What is intelligence?

Gregg Cox: speaks 64 languages

Halle Berry: Oscar-winning actress

Bill Gates: head of Microsoft; $53 billion

Steve Lu: 194 IQ; grad school at age15

Midori: child prodigy; violin genius

When college students were asked to estimate their overall IQs, men's reports of IQ were higher than estimates given by women, and both men and women reported higher IQs for their fathers than for their mothers (Petrides et al., 2004). In fact, over the past 20 years, men have consistently overestimated and women have consistently underestimated their IQs, even though researchers find no sex differences in IQ scores (Colom et al., 2000).

People generally believe IQ scores measure intelligence. But it's not so simple. For example, how did you rank the intelligence of the five individuals in the left photos, each of whom shows a different yet extraordinary skill or talent? Do these examples point to the existence of different kinds of intelligence (H. Gardner, 2006b)?

Many psychologists believe that intelligence is best defined by measuring a variety of cognitive abilities, which is what most intelligence tests measure. For example, Steve Lu received a very high IQ score (194) based on an intelligence test. Others argue that a definition of intelligence based entirely on cognitive abilities is much too narrow. Instead, they believe that there are many kinds of intelligence, such as involving acting skills (Halle Berry), musical abilities (Midori), practical skills (Gregg Cox), or solving problems (Bill Gates) (E. Benson, 2003a; H. Gardner, 2006).

More recently, researchers have pointed to the importance of emotional intelligence, which involves how well people perceive, express, and regulate emotions in themselves and others (Salovey & Pizarro, 2003). Award-winning actors (Halle Berry) certainly have high emotional intelligence. We'll discuss emotional intelligence in Module 16 (p. 369).

Here we'll examine three popular definitions of intelligence, beginning with the oldest and perhaps the most widely accepted definition of intelligence, the two-factor theory.

What is "g"?

In 1904, Charles Spearman reported that he had measured intelligence in an objective way. Spearman was one of the first to use the psychometric approach.

The *psychometric approach* measures or quantifies cognitive abilities or factors that are thought to be involved in intellectual performance.

Spearman (1904) reasoned that by measuring related cognitive factors he would have an objective measure of intelligence. This idea led to his two-factor theory of intelligence.

Spearman's *two-factor theory* says that intelligence has two factors: a general mental ability factor, *g*, which represents what different cognitive tasks have in common, plus many specific factors, *s*, which include specific mental abilities (mathematical, mechanical, or verbal skills).

Spearman believed that factor *g*, or general mental ability, represented a person's mental energy. Today, factor *g* is defined and measured by a person's performance on various and related cognitive abilities. In other words, modern intelligence tests have essentially changed or transformed Spearman's *g* into an objective score, which is commonly known as the IQ score. Today, many psychologists believe that *g*, as represented by IQ scores, is a good measure of a person's general intelligence (Jenson, 2005).

On the basis of Spearman's two-factor theory, which of the five individuals (left photos) is most intelligent?

Many psychologists believe that *g* is the definition of general intelligence, which can be measured by an IQ test and represented by an IQ score. Thus, one way to compare people on intelligence is by using scores from IQ tests. Ranking intelligence by using IQ scores would favor Lu (IQ 194), Gates (one colleague said Gates was "the smartest person he ever knew"), and probably Cox (speaks 64 languages). However, although Berry (Oscar-winning actress) and Midori (violin genius) might score high on IQ tests, they would get little or no credit for having exceptional motor, acting, or music skills.

Steve Lu: 194 IQ; grad school at age 15

ADVANTAGES AND DISADVANTAGES

One advantage of *g* is that it can be objectively defined and measured by an IQ test, which gives a single IQ score that is presumed to reflect a person's general intelligence. Another advantage is that *g* is a good predictor of performance in academic settings and has some success in predicting performance in certain careers (discussed later) (N. Brody, 2000).

One disadvantage of Spearman's *g* is the continuing debate over whether it is the best measure of intelligence. Or as one researcher states, "We know how to measure something called intelligence, but we do not know what has been measured" (N. Brody, 2000, p. 30). A second disadvantage of *g* is that it focuses on cognitive abilities but neglects motor, perceptual, musical, practical, and creative abilities, which some believe indicate other kinds of intelligence (H. Gardner, 2006b). A third disadvantage is that *g* and its focus on cognitive abilities are popular in Western cultures but not in many Asian and African cultures, where being intelligent includes other abilities, such as how one relates to and understands others (E. Benson, 2003b). For these reasons, psychologists critical of *g*'s narrow approach to measuring general intelligence have proposed other definitions and ways to measure intelligence. We'll discuss two other definitions of intelligence.

Multiple-Intelligence Theory

Multiple kinds of intelligence?

Some psychologists reject the idea that intelligence can be reduced to *g* and expressed by a single number, an IQ score. Howard Gardner (1999, 2006b) argues for broadening the definition of intelligence to include different kinds of abilities, an idea he calls the multiple-intelligence theory.

Gardner's multiple-intelligence theory says that instead of one kind of general intelligence, there are at least nine different kinds, which include verbal intelligence, musical intelligence, logical-mathematical intelligence, spatial intelligence, body movement intelligence, intelligence to understand oneself, intelligence to understand others, naturalistic intelligence, and existential intelligence.

Gardner states that standard IQ tests measure primarily verbal and logical-mathematical intelligence and neglect other but equally important kinds of intelligence, such as the ones listed above. Gardner (1999, 2006b) arrived at his theory of multiple kinds of intelligence after studying which abilities remain following brain damage, how savants and prodigies develop their specialized kinds of intelligence, and how people in different environments develop different abilities to adapt and be successful.

Halle Berry: Oscar-winning actress

On the basis of Gardner's multiple-intelligence theory, which of the five individuals (previous page) is most intelligent?

According to Gardner's multiple intelligence theory, there isn't one kind of general intelligence for ranking all individuals. Rather, Gardner views the special abilities of Berry in acting and Midori in music as representing other kinds of intelligence. Gardner argues that none of the five is more intelligent but rather that each of the five individuals shows a different kind of ability or intelligence that was developed and adapted to his or her environment.

Midori: child prodigy; violin genius

ADVANTAGES AND DISADVANTAGES

One advantage of Gardner's multiple-intelligence approach is that it does not reduce intelligence to a single IQ score but rather credits people with having different kinds of intelligence.

Two disadvantages of this approach are not knowing how many kinds of intelligence there are and not having standard measuring techniques to assess different kinds of intelligence (Callahan, 2000).

Agreeing with Gardner that *g* is too narrow a measure of intelligence, Sternberg proposed a triarchic theory.

Triarchic Theory

Three kinds of intelligence?

Criticizing Spearman's *g* as too narrow and current IQ tests as limited to measuring only problem-solving skills and cognitive abilities, psychologist Robert Sternberg defined intelligence by *analyzing* three kinds of reasoning processes that people use in solving problems. Sternberg (2003a) calls his approach the triarchic theory of intelligence.

Sternberg's triarchic theory says that intelligence can be divided into three different kinds of reasoning processes (*triarchic* means "three components"). The first is using analytical or logical thinking skills measured by traditional intelligence tests. The second is using problem-solving skills that require creative thinking and the ability to learn from experience. The third is using practical thinking skills that help a person adjust to, and cope with, his or her sociocultural environment.

Analytical

Problem solving

Practical

Unlike Spearman's *g*, which measures general intelligence by measuring cognitive abilities, Sternberg's theory breaks intelligence down into three reasoning processes: analytical, problem solving, and practical skills.

On the basis of Sternberg's triarchic theory of intelligence, which of the five individuals (previous page) is most intelligent?

According to Sternberg's triarchic theory, there isn't one kind of general intelligence for evaluating these five individuals but rather three different reasoning processes (analytical, problem solving, practical) that contribute to and predict the success of each of the five individuals.

ADVANTAGES AND DISADVANTAGES

One advantage of Sternberg's triarchic theory of intelligence is that it doesn't limit the definition of intelligence to cognitive abilities. Instead, Sternberg's theory evaluates a person's intelligence by measuring three different kinds of reasoning processes and how they contribute to a person's success. For example, a person may be "street smart" or have exceptional practical reasoning skills but may not necessarily score high on traditional intelligence tests.

One disadvantage of the triarchic theory is that Sternberg's research and tests for measuring his proposed three kinds of reasoning processes have so far been criticized as providing little support for his triarchic theory (N. Brody, 2003; Gottfredson, 2003).

Current Status

Western psychologists used the psychometric approach to measure cognitive abilities, which led to the development of intelligence tests and IQ scores and the concept of *g* as the best measure of intelligence (N. Brody, 2000). Standard intelligence tests remain popular because they have proved useful in predicting performance in academic settings, but they are less predictive for career settings. Newer approaches, such as Gardner's multiple-intelligence approach and Sternberg's triarchic approach, which measure additional abilities

and reasoning skills and represent different kinds of intelligence, hope to replace *g* and its IQ score as the best measure of intelligence (H. Gardner, 2006b; Sternberg et al., 2003a). Finally, many Asian and African cultures believe that besides cognitive abilities, intelligence should include the ability to relate to and get along with and understand others.

To see how far intelligence testing has come, we'll go back in time and discuss early attempts to define and measure intelligence.

B. Measuring Intelligence

Earlier Attempts to Measure Intelligence

HEAD SIZE AND INTELLIGENCE

Are bigger brains better?

Efforts to measure intelligence began in earnest in the late 1800s. That's when Francis Galton noticed that intelligent people often had intelligent relatives and concluded that intelligence was, to a large extent, biological or inherited.

In trying to assess inherited intelligence, Galton measured people's heads and recorded the speed of their reactions to various sensory stimuli. However, measures proved to be poorly related to intelligence or academic achievement (S. J. Gould, 1996).

Galton switched gears and tried to correlate head size with students' grade point average. For example, he reported that the average head size of Cambridge students who received A's was about 3.3% larger than that of students who received C's (Galton, 1888). However, a review of later studies showed a very low correlation of 0.15 between head size and intelligence (IQ scores) (Vernon et al., 2000). Such a low correlation has little practical use in measuring or predicting intelligence. For this reason, using head size as a measure of intelligence was abandoned in favor of using skull or brain size.

BRAIN SIZE AND INTELLIGENCE

Efforts to measure intelligence continued with the work of Paul Broca, a famous neurologist in the late 1800s. Broca claimed that there was a relationship between brain size and intelligence, with larger brains indicating more intelligence. However, a later reanalysis of Broca's data indicated that measures of brain size proved to be unreliable and poorly correlated with intelligence (S. J. Gould, 1996).

Recently, the sizes of living brains were measured with brain scans (p. 70), which permit more precise measurement. A review of brain scan studies reported medium-sized positive correlations (+0.33) between brain size and intelligence (IQ scores) (McDaniel, 2005). However, such correlations indicate only that a relationship exists; correlations cannot tell us whether bigger brains lead to increased intelligence or whether more cognitive activity leads to bigger brains. These medium-sized correlations indicate a positive relationship between brain size and intelligence (IQ scores) but are too low to have practical value in actually predicting an individual's intelligence.

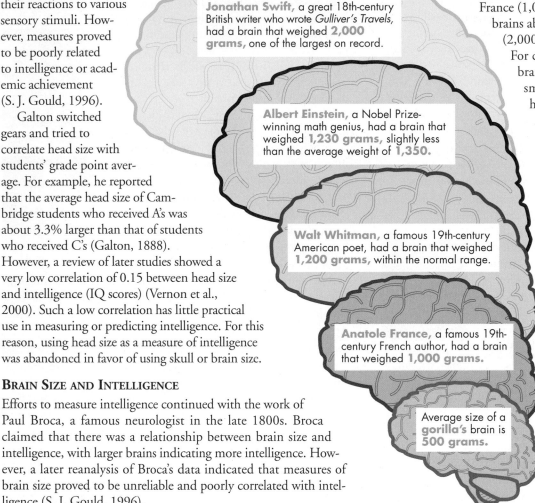

Jonathan Swift, a great 18th-century British writer who wrote *Gulliver's Travels,* had a brain that weighed **2,000 grams,** one of the largest on record.

Albert Einstein, a Nobel Prize-winning math genius, had a brain that weighed **1,230 grams,** slightly less than the average weight of **1,350.**

Walt Whitman, a famous 19th-century American poet, had a brain that weighed **1,200 grams,** within the normal range.

Anatole France, a famous 19th-century French author, had a brain that weighed **1,000 grams.**

Average size of a **gorilla's** brain is **500 grams.**

Brain size doesn't necessarily match performance.

BRAIN SIZE AND ACHIEVEMENT

Early researchers were reluctant to give up the idea that bigger brains were better. They looked for a relationship between brain size and personal achievement, another measure of intelligence. However, as shown in the center illustration, there is enormous variation in brain size and achievement (S. J. Gould, 1996). Notice that Nobel Prize–winner Einstein's brain (1,230 grams) was slightly below average weight and that two famous authors, poet Walt Whitman (1,200 grams) and novelist Anatole France (1,000 grams), achieved literary fame with brains about half the weight of Jonathan Swift's (2,000 grams), one of the heaviest on record. For comparison, we have included a gorilla brain (500 grams), which is actually quite small considering the size of a gorilla head. It is difficult to test a gorilla's intelligence, but at least one is reported to have learned a vocabulary of more than 1,000 hand signs ("Koko's World," 2006).

BRAIN SIZE, SEX DIFFERENCES, AND INTELLIGENCE

Still believing that bigger brains are better, some researchers claimed that women had lower IQ scores than men because women's brains weigh about 10% less than men's (C. Holden, 1995). However, a recent study of over 4,000 women and 6,000 men reported that there was little or no difference in intelligence (IQ scores) between men and women. Researchers concluded that the larger size of men's brains does not result in higher IQs (Colom et al., 2000).

MEASURING INTELLIGENCE

As you have seen, there is a long history of scientists trying to measure intelligence. However, all the early attempts to use head, skull, body, or brain size to measure intelligence failed. In fact, a paper presented in 1904 to a German psychological society concluded that there was little hope of developing psychological tests to measure intelligence in an objective way (Wolf, 1973). What's interesting about this paper is that one of the authors was Alfred Binet, who went on to develop the first intelligence test.

We'll explain how Binet succeeded in developing an intelligence test when so many others had failed.

Why did Binet develop an intelligence test?

In the late 1800s, a gifted French psychologist named Alfred Binet realized that Broca and Galton had failed to assess intelligence by measuring brain size. Binet strongly believed that intelligence was a collection of mental abilities and that the best way to assess intelligence was to measure a person's ability to perform cognitive tasks, such as understanding the meanings of words or being able to follow directions.

Binet was very pessimistic about developing an intelligence test. By a strange twist of fate, he was appointed to a commission that was instructed to develop tests capable of differentiating children of normal intelligence from those who needed special help. Binet accepted this challenge with two goals in mind: The test must be easy to administer without requiring any special laboratory equipment, and the test must clearly distinguish between normal and abnormal mental abilities (N. Brody, 1992). In 1905, Binet and psychiatrist Theodore Simon succeeded in developing the world's first standardized intelligence test, the Binet-Simon Intelligence Scale (Binet & Simon, 1905).

Alfred Binet (1857–1911)

The *Binet-Simon Intelligence Scale* contained items arranged in order of increasing difficulty. The items measured vocabulary, memory, common knowledge, and other cognitive abilities.

The purpose of this first Binet-Simon Intelligence Scale was to distinguish among mentally defective children in the Paris school system. In Binet's time, intellectually deficient children were divided into three groups: idiots (most severely deficient), imbeciles (moderate), and morons (mildest). These terms are no longer used today because they have taken on very negative meanings. The problems with this first test were that it classified children into only three categories (idiots, imbeciles, and morons) and that it did not have a way to express the results in a single score. However, several years later, Binet corrected both of these problems when he introduced the concept of mental level, or mental age.

MENTAL AGE: MEASURE OF INTELLIGENCE

Binet and Simon revised their intelligence scale to solve several problems in their original scale. In this revised test, they arranged the test items in order of increasing difficulty and designed different items to measure different cognitive abilities. For each test item, Binet determined whether an average child of a certain age could answer the question correctly. For example, a child at age level 3 should be able to point to various parts of the face. A child at age level 9 should be able to recite the days of the week. Because the test items were arranged for each age level (age levels 3 to 13), this new test could identify which average age level the child performed at. If a particular child passed all the items that could be answered by an average 3-year-old but none of the items appropriate for older children, that child would be said to have a mental age of 3.

Thus, if a 6-year-old child could answer only questions appropriate for a 3-year-old child, that child would be given a mental age of 3 and would be considered retarded in intellectual development. Binet's intelligence test became popular because a single score represented mental age.

Mental age is a method of estimating a child's intellectual progress by comparing the child's score on an intelligence test to the scores of average children of the same age.

At this point, the Binet-Simon scale gave its results in terms of a mental age but not an IQ score. The idea for computing an IQ score did not occur until some years later, when the scale was revised by L. M. Terman.

Which items could an average 9-year-old answer?

Which items could an average 3-year-old answer?

What was the big change?

The first big change was when Binet and Simon introduced the concept of mental age. The second big change occurred in 1916, when Lewis Terman and his colleagues at Stanford University in California came up with a new and better method to compute the final score. Improving on the concept of expressing the test results in terms of mental age, Terman devised a formula to calculate an intelligence quotient (IQ) score (Terman, 1916).

Intelligence quotient (IQ) is computed by dividing a child's mental age (MA), as measured in an intelligence test, by the child's chronological age (CA) and multiplying the result by 100.

Remember that in Binet's test, mental age was calculated by noting how many items a child answered that were appropriate to a certain age. For example, if a 4-year-old girl passed the test items appropriate for a 5-year-old, she was said to have a mental age of 5. A child's chronological (physical) age is his or her age in months and years. To compute her IQ score, we use Terman's formula, shown below.

$$IQ = \frac{MA}{CA} \times 100$$

IQ (Intelligence quotient) = MA (Mental age) / CA (Chronological age) × 100

Formula for calculating IQ score

Thus, for the child in our example, we substitute 5 for MA, 4 for CA, and multiply by 100. We get: $5/4 = 1.25 \times 100 = 125$. So the child's IQ is 125. An IQ score computed in this traditional way is called a *ratio IQ* because the score represents a ratio of mental to chronological age. Today the ratio IQ has been replaced by the *deviation IQ,* whose computation is too complex to explain here. The reason for the switch from ratio IQ to deviation IQ is that deviation IQ scores more accurately reflect test performance as children get older.

Since the original Binet-Simon scale in 1905, IQ tests have become very popular and have grown into a large business. We'll look more closely at one of the most widely used IQ tests.

B. Measuring Intelligence

Is IQ the same as intelligence?

We are all curious to learn someone's IQ because we believe that this single score reveals a person's real intelligence. For example, try to match these IQ scores— 104, 114, 228—with three famous people—John F. Kennedy, 35th president of the United States; J. D. Salinger, famous novelist *(Catcher in the Rye);* and Marilyn vos Savant, columnist for *Parade* magazine (answers on right). Knowing the IQ scores of these individuals tells us something of their cognitive abilities, but some psychologists believe that cognitive abilities represent only one kind of intelligence. For example, would you expect Salinger, with his average IQ, to be a very creative novelist, or vos Savant, columnist for *Parade* magazine, to have a high IQ twice that of President Kennedy? The achievements of individuals with average or slightly above average IQs suggest that there are other kinds of intelligence, such as practical, emotional, social, and creative, which may be equally important to one's success in life and career (H. Gardner, 2003; Sternberg et al., 2003b). Now, let's see how IQ scores are measured.

John F. Kennedy: 35th U.S. president

Marilyn vos Savant: columnist for *Parade* magazine

J. D. Salinger: author of *Catcher in the Rye*

Answers: *Salinger, 104; Kennedy, 114; and vos Savant, 228, the highest IQ on record (Cowley, 1994)*

Examples of IQ Tests

The most widely used IQ tests are the Wechsler Adult Intelligence Scale (WAIS-III), for ages 16 and older, and the Wechsler Intelligence Scale for Children (WISC-IV), for children of ages 6–16. A trained examiner administers the Wechsler scales on a one-to-one basis.

The *Wechsler Adult Intelligence Scale (WAIS-III)* and *Wechsler Intelligence Scale for Children (WISC-IV)* have items that are organized into various subtests. For example, the verbal section contains a subtest of general information, a subtest of vocabulary, and others. The performance section contains a subtest that involves arranging pictures in a meaningful order, one that requires assembling objects, and one that involves using codes. The verbal and performance scores are combined to give a single IQ score.

Examples of the subtests for WAIS-III are shown on the right. The Verbal Scale (top right) emphasizes language and verbal skills. Because of this emphasis, a person from a deprived environment or for whom English is a second language might have difficulty on this scale because of lack of verbal knowledge rather than lack of cognitive ability.

In an attempt to measure nonverbal skills and rule out other cultural or educational problems, Wechsler added the Performance Scale (lower right). These performance subtests, which measure problem-solving abilities, require considerable concentration and focused effort, which may be difficult for individuals who are very nervous, are poor test takers, or have emotional problems. Although these IQ tests carefully try to measure verbal and nonverbal abilities, you can see that part of one's success on IQ tests depends on nonintellectual factors, such as cultural, educational, or emotional factors (Kaplan & Saccuzzo, 2005). We'll discuss other problems with IQ tests later in this module.

One reason these IQ tests are widely used is that they have two characteristics of good tests: validity and reliability.

WAIS-III Verbal Scale: Subtests

Subtests for the verbal scale include information, comprehension, arithmetic, similarities, digit span, and vocabulary. These examples resemble the WAIS-III items.

Information
On what continent is France?

Comprehension
Why are children required to go to school?

Arithmetic
How many hours will it take to drive 150 miles at 50 miles per hour?

Similarities
How are a calculator and a typewriter alike?

Digit span
Repeat the following numbers backward: 2, 4, 3, 5, 8, 9, 6.

Vocabulary
What does *audacity* mean?

WAIS-III Performance Scale: Subtests

Subtests for the performance scale include digit symbol, block design, picture completion, picture arrangement, and object assembly. These sample items shown on the right resemble those given for each WAIS-III subtest.

Digit symbol

Shown: Fill in:
1 2 3 4 1 4 3 2
○ □ △ ⊙ _ _ _ _

Block design
Assemble blocks to match this design.

Picture completion
Tell me what is missing.

Picture arrangement
Put the pictures in the right order.

Object assembly
Assemble the pieces into a complete object.

Can you analyze handwriting?

How truthful are the claims that intelligence and other personality traits can be identified through analyzing handwriting (Searles, 1998)? For example, which one of the four handwriting samples on the right indicates the highest IQ? (Answer at bottom of page.)

Although handwriting analysis may claim to measure intelligence, research shows that its accuracy is usually no better than a good guess (Tripician, 2000).

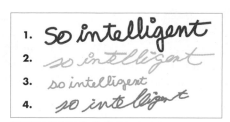

Which handwriting sample, 1, 2, 3, or 4, is from the person with the highest IQ?

The reason handwriting analysis or so-called IQ tests in popular magazines are poor measures of intelligence (IQ) is that they lack at least one of the two important characteristics of a good test. These two characteristics are validity and reliability, which mark the difference between an accurate IQ test (WAIS-III) and an inaccurate test (handwriting analysis).

Validity

Handwriting analysis is fun, but it is a very poor intelligence test because it lacks validity, which is one of the two characteristics of a good test.

Validity **means that the test measures what it is supposed to measure.**

Although the definition of validity seems simple and short, this characteristic makes or breaks a test. For example, numerous studies have shown that handwriting analysis has little or no validity as an intelligence or personality test (Basil, 1989; Tripician, 2000). Because handwriting analysis lacks the characteristic of validity, it means that this test does not accurately measure what it is supposed to measure. Thus, a test with little or no validity produces results that could be produced by guessing or by chance.

The reason handwriting analysis or tests in popular magazines are not checked for validity is that checking validity is a long, expensive, and complicated process. One way to show a test's validity is to give the new test to hundreds of subjects along with other tests whose validity has already been established. Then the subjects' scores on the new test are correlated with their scores on the tests with proven validity. Another way that the validity of intelligence tests, such as the WAIS-III, was established was to show that IQ scores correlated with another measure of intelligence, such as academic performance (A. S. Kaufman, 2000).

However, if IQ scores are valid measures of cognitive abilities and correlate with academic performance, why do some individuals with high IQs do poorly in college? The developer of the Head Start program, Ed Zigler, believes that academic performance depends on three factors: cognitive abilities; achievement, or the amount of knowledge that a person has accumulated; and motivation (Zigler, 1995). This means that a person may have outstanding cognitive abilities but may lack either the achievement or the motivation to succeed in college.

Besides validity, a good intelligence test should also have reliability.

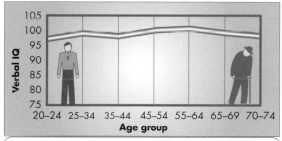

No change in VERBAL IQ scores in seven different age groups indicates that test is reliable.

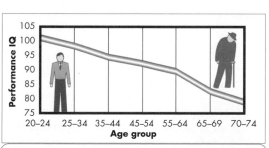

Decrease in OVERALL IQ scores across ages is due to psychological and physiological changes and not reliability problems with IQ test.

Reliability

If your style of handwriting remained constant over time, such as always boldly crossing your *t*'s, then this trait would be reliable.

Reliability **refers to consistency: A person's score on a test at one point in time should be similar to the score obtained by the same person on a similar test at a later point in time.**

For example, if boldly crossed *t*'s indicated that a person is intelligent, then this measure of intelligence would be reliable. However, there is no evidence that boldly crossed *t*'s indicate that a person is intelligent. So, in this case, handwriting analysis would be a reliable test of intelligence, but since it lacks validity (doesn't measure intelligence) it is a worthless test of intelligence.

Now, suppose you took the WAIS-III as a senior in high school and then retook the test as a junior in college. You would find that your IQ scores would be much the same because each time you would be compared with others of your same age. Because your IQ scores remain similar across time, it would mean that the Wechsler scales, like other standardized IQ tests, have reliability (Berg, 2000).

For example, the top graph shows the results of verbal IQ scores when seven different age groups of subjects were given the WAIS-III. Notice that verbal IQ scores are quite stable from ages 20 to 74, indicating that the Wechsler scales score high in reliability (A. S. Kaufman et al., 1989).

But notice that the lower graph shows that there is an overall decrease in performance IQ scores from ages 20 to 74 (A. S. Kaufman et al., 1989). However, this general decrease in performance scores across one's lifetime reflects changes in psychological and physiological functioning rather than a decrease in the test's reliability.

Researchers have shown that current intelligence tests, which measure primarily cognitive abilities, have relatively good validity and reliability (Kaplan & Saccuzzo, 2005). Even though IQ scores can be measured with good reliability and validity, our next question to answer is: What good or use are IQ scores?

(Handwriting answer: I (R.P.) wrote all four samples so that no matter which one you picked, I would come out a winner!)

C. Distribution & Use of IQ Scores

IQ 50–85

The left photo is of Chris Burke, who starred in the television series "Life Goes On." Burke has Down syndrome, a genetic defect that results in varying degrees of mental retardation and physical symptoms (slanting eyes, flattened nose, visual problems). Although Burke has mild or borderline mental retardation, he acted in a TV series and now sings in a band and gives inspirational talks (Horsburgh et al., 2001). Based on his abilities, Burke's IQ is probably between 50 and 85.

In comparison, the photo on the right is of Marilyn vos Savant, who writes a column for *Parade* magazine and has a reported IQ of

228, the highest on record. To compare the IQs of Burke and vos Savant with those of other people, we need to look at the distribution of IQ scores. IQ scores from established intelligence tests, such as the WAIS-III, are said to have a normal distribution.

IQ 228

A *normal distribution* refers to a statistical arrangement of scores so that they resemble the shape of a bell and, thus, is said to be a bell-shaped curve. A bell-shaped curve means the vast majority of scores fall in the middle range, with fewer scores falling near the two extreme ends of the curve.

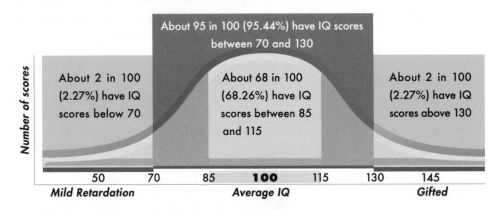

About 95 in 100 (95.44%) have IQ scores between 70 and 130

About 2 in 100 (2.27%) have IQ scores below 70

About 68 in 100 (68.26%) have IQ scores between 85 and 115

About 2 in 100 (2.27%) have IQ scores above 130

Number of scores

50   70   85   100   115   130   145

Mild Retardation   **Average IQ**   **Gifted**

For example, a normal distribution of IQ scores is shown at the left and is bell shaped. The average IQ score is 100, and 95% of IQ scores fall between 70 and 130. An IQ of 70 and below is one sign of mild retardation. An IQ of 130 or higher is one indication of a gifted individual. Thus, one widespread use of IQ tests is to provide general *categories* regarding mental abilities.

Next, we'll examine these guidelines in more detail, beginning with mental retardation.

What is mental retardation?

One use of IQ scores has been to help identify individuals with mental retardation, which was Binet's original goal.

Mental retardation refers to a substantial limitation in present functioning that is characterized by significantly subaverage intellectual functioning, along with related limitations in two of eleven areas, including communication, self-care, home living, social skills, academic skills, leisure, and safety (American Psychiatric Association, 2000).

Psychologists caution against using IQ scores as the sole test for mental retardation. IQ tests are usually used in combination with observations of adaptive skills, which include social, home living, and communication skills. On the basis of IQ scores and adaptive skills, three levels of retardation have been identified.

1 MILD MENTAL RETARDATION

These individuals have IQs that range from 50 to 70. With special training and educational opportunities, they can learn to read and write, gain social competency, master simple occupational skills, and become self-supporting members of society. About 85% of individuals with retardation are in this category.

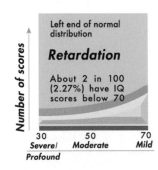

Left end of normal distribution

Retardation

About 2 in 100 (2.27%) have IQ scores below 70

Number of scores

30   50   70
Severe/   Moderate   Mild
Profound

2 MODERATE MENTAL RETARDATION

These individuals have IQs that range from 35 to 55. With special training and educational opportunities, they can learn to become partially independent in their everyday lives, provided they are in a family or self-help setting.

3 SEVERE/PROFOUND MENTAL RETARDATION

These individuals make up 5% of those with mental retardation and have IQs ranging from 20 to 40. With special training and education, they can acquire limited skills in taking care of their personal needs. However, because of impaired motor and verbal abilities, they require considerable supervision their entire lives.

4 CAUSES

There are two general types of mental retardation—organic and cultural-familial.

Organic retardation results from genetic problems or brain damage.

Chris Burke is an example of someone with organic retardation.

Cultural-familial retardation results from a greatly impoverished environment. There is no evidence of genetic or brain damage.

Approximately 5 million Americans have various degrees of mental retardation.

Next, we move to the middle of IQ's normal distribution.

Since the vast majority of people, about 95%, have IQ scores that fall between 70 and 130, it is interesting to see what IQ scores can tell us.

Do IQ Scores Predict Academic Achievement? Because IQ tests measure cognitive abilities that are similar to those used in academic settings, it is no surprise that there is a medium-strength association, or correlation, between IQ scores and grades (0.50) and between IQ scores and total years of education that people complete (0.50) (N. Brody, 1997). However, based on medium-strength correlations alone, it would be difficult to predict a *specific person's academic performance* because performance in academic settings also depends on personal characteristics, such as one's interest in school and willingness to study (Neisser et al., 1996).

IQ scores are useful for predicting academic success.

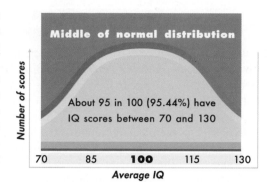

Middle of normal distribution

About 95 in 100 (95.44%) have IQ scores between 70 and 130

Number of scores

70   85   **100**   115   130

Average IQ

Do IQ Scores Predict Job Performance? There is a low- to medium-strength correlation (+0.30 to 0.50) between IQ scores and job performance (Neisser et al., 1996). However, such correlations are not very accurate at predicting a *specific person's job performance* because several noncognitive factors that are not measured by IQ tests, such as personality traits (is a can-do person), emotional traits (can deal with stress and get along with co-workers), and practical know-how (figures out how to get job done), play important roles in predicting job performance (Gottfredson, 2002; Sternberg, 2003b).

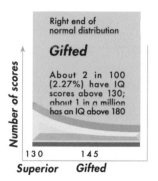

IQ scores are somewhat useful at predicting job performance.

Now, we'll examine the right end of the normal distribution—high IQ scores.

Sho Yano (photo below), whose IQ is 200 plus, entered college at age 9, graduated at age 12, plays classical works on the piano, and is the youngest person ever to start a dual M.D.-Ph.D. program at the University of Chicago. Sho Yano is considered a profoundly gifted child. Although researchers and educators differ in how they define *gifted*, this definition refers to academically gifted children.

A moderately *gifted* child is usually defined by an IQ score between 130 and 150; a profoundly gifted child has an IQ score about 180 or above.

Like Sho Yano, who excels at the piano and medicine, gifted children usually have some superior talent or skill.

When placed in *regular classrooms,* gifted children face a number of problems: They are bored by the lack of stimulation and they may feel lonely or develop social problems because they are labeled nerds or geeks. Researchers recommend that gifted children be placed in special academic programs that challenge and help them develop their potentials (Goode, 2002; Winner, 2000).

How Do Gifted Individuals Turn Out? In the early 1920s, Lewis Terman selected a sample of over 1,500 gifted children with IQs ranging from 135 to 200 (the average was 151) (Hulbert, 2005). Over the next 65 years, researchers repeatedly tested these individuals to determine what they had achieved and how they had adjusted. Although 10–30% more of the gifted men obtained advanced degrees compared with men in the general population, 30% never finished college, and 2% actually flunked out. Although gifted individuals generally showed better health, adjustment, and achievement than people with average IQs, about 9% had serious emotional problems, and 7% committed suicide (Holahan & Sears, 1995; Terman & Oden, 1959). As a group,

IQ of 200+ labels Sho Yano as gifted.

Right end of normal distribution

Gifted

About 2 in 100 (2.27%) have IQ scores above 130; about 1 in a million has an IQ above 180

Number of scores

130   145

Superior   Gifted

these gifted individuals were generally very successful in life but not at the extraordinary level that might have been predicted from their high IQ scores (Colangelo, 1997).

Contrary to Terman's findings, another researcher followed 180 children with IQs over 180 and found that these extremely smart children often developed social problems, such as being more introverted and lonely than their peers (Hollingworth, 2002). Other research found that only gifted children who have demanding and critical parents are more likely to have social and emotional problems than children with normal intelligence (Elias, 2005b).

Researchers have long been interested in brain differences between gifted individuals and those with normal-range intelligence. Recently, researchers found that brain areas responsible for higher cognitive reasoning develop differently in highly intelligent children (we'll discuss this further in the Research Focus section on p. 297) (Shaw et al., 2006). What remains a mystery is why some profoundly gifted children do become brilliant adults while others do not and their brilliance seems to fade (Winner, 2002).

Conclusion. IQ scores, the most popular measure of intelligence, have proven moderately useful in predicting academic performance, in helping to define mental retardation, and in identifying the gifted, but they have low to moderate success in predicting job performance. One reason IQ scores are not more predictive is that they do not measure numerous emotional, motivational, and personality factors that also influence behavior.

While IQ tests have proved useful, we'll next examine potential problems in taking and interpreting IQ tests.

D. Potential Problems of IQ Testing

Binet's Two Warnings

What problems did Binet foresee?

You may remember that Binet's original goal was to develop a test that would distinguish between normal and abnormal mental abilities and thus identify children who were mentally retarded and needed special help and education. Although previous attempts to measure intelligence had failed, Binet and Simon succeeded in developing the first scale that identified children with varying degrees of mental retardation. Binet and Simon's scale was the beginning of the modern-day IQ test. However, even in the early 1900s, Binet realized that intelligence tests could be used in two potentially dangerous ways, so he issued the following two warnings:

> ### BINET'S WARNINGS
>
> **1** Binet warned that ***intelligence tests do not measure innate abilities or natural intelligence;*** rather, they measure an individual's cognitive abilities, which result from both heredity and environment.
>
> **2** Binet warned that ***intelligence tests, by themselves, should not be used to label people*** (for example, "moron," "average," "genius"); rather, intelligence tests should be used to assess an individual's abilities and used in combination with other information to make academic or placement decisions about people.

History shows that neither of Binet's warnings were heeded. In the early 1900s it became common practice to treat IQ scores as measures of innate intelligence and to use IQ scores to label people from "moron" to "genius." The U.S. Congress went so far as to pass laws that restricted immigrants based on assumed levels of innate intelligence (S. J. Gould, 1996), an issue we'll discuss in the Cultural Diversity section (p. 296).

IQ tests have a history of being used to discriminate.

Along with using IQ scores to label individuals came racial and cultural discrimination, some of which continue to the present. For example, a controversial book, *The Bell Curve* (Herrnstein & Murray, 1994), suggests that racial differences in IQ scores are due primarily to genetic factors, something we'll discuss later in this module. For now, we'll examine three issues surrounding IQ tests: cultural bias, other cultures, and nonintellectual factors.

Racial Discrimination

Are IQ tests racially biased?

There have been a number of court cases regarding the appropriate use of IQ tests. Here is one important case and the judge's ruling.

Larry was an African American child who was assigned to special classes for the educa-

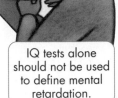

IQ tests alone should not be used to define mental retardation.

ble mentally retarded because he scored below 85 on an IQ test. However, several years later an African American psychologist retested Larry and found that his IQ score was higher than originally thought. Larry was taken out of the special classes, which were considered a dead end, and placed in regular classes that allowed for more advancement. On the basis of Larry's experience, a class action suit was brought against the San Francisco school system on behalf of all African American schoolchildren in the district. The suit was based on the finding that, although African American youngsters made up 27% of all the students enrolled in classes for the mentally retarded, they made up only 4% of the entire school population (Kaplan & Saccuzzo, 2005). African American parents wanted to know why their children were so much more numerous than White children in these special classes. They felt there must be a bias against African American children in the selection process.

Although Larry's case came to trial in the early 1970s, the final decision was given in 1979 by a judge of the federal court of appeals. The judge agreed with the African American parents and found that IQ tests being used in schools (kindergarten through grade 12) to determine mental retardation were biased against people of color. The court ruled that California schools could not place children of color in classes for children with mental retardation on the basis of the IQ test alone. The schools were instructed to come up with an intelligence test that does not favor Whites or else refrain from using a standardized test to identify slow learners.

Definition of mental retardation. In other states, there is disagreement about the role of IQ tests in defining mental retardation and making decisions about placing children in special education classes (BCSSE, 2002). Despite efforts to improve the educational opportunities for African American children in the United States, they continue to be more likely than White children to be placed in classes for children with mental retardation and less

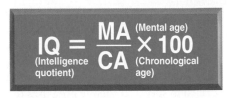

$$IQ = \frac{MA \text{ (Mental age)}}{CA \text{ (Chronological age)}} \times 100$$

(Intelligence quotient)

likely to be placed in classes for gifted children (R. Gardner et al., 2001; Losen & Orfield, 2002). Critics of the special education system argue that African American students are overrepresented not because of their especially high level of disability but because of discriminatory placement procedures, such as the culturally biased IQ tests (Losen & Orfield, 2002; J. P. Shapiro et al., 1993).

Educational decisions. Based on the concerns discussed above, psychologists and educators recommend that IQ tests alone not be used as the primary basis for making decisions about a child's educational future. Instead, they suggest that educational decisions, especially about placing a child in a special education class, be made only after considering a wide range of information, which may include IQ scores but also observations and samples of the child's behavior from other situations (Palomares, 2003).

Cultural Bias

What kind of questions?

One criticism of IQ tests is that they are culturally biased, especially in favor of industrialized communities, such as the White middle class in the United States (Serpell, 2000).

Cultural bias means that the wording of the questions and the experiences on which the questions are based are more familiar to members of some social groups than to others.

For example, consider this question from an older version of the Wechsler Intelligence Scale for Children: "What would you do if you were sent to buy a loaf of bread and the grocer said he did not have any more?"

If you think the answer is "Go to another store," you are correct according to the developers of the Wechsler scale. However, when 200 minority children were asked this same question, 61 said they would go home. Asked to explain their answers, they gave reasonable explanations. Some children answered "Go home" because there were no other stores in their neighborhood. Yet the answer "Go home" would be scored "incorrect," despite it being correct in the child's experience (Hardy et al., 1976). This example shows that different cultural influences and experiences may penalize some children when taking standardized tests of intelligence.

IQ tests are, to some extent, culturally biased.

In today's IQ tests, many of the above kinds of biases have been reduced (A. Kaufman, 2003). However, try as they can, researchers believe that it's virtually impossible to develop an intelligence test completely free of cultural bias because tests will reflect, in some part, the concepts and values of their culture (Greenfield, 2003).

In addition, because IQ tests involve being asked and answering questions, children who have had such experiences in their homes or schools will be better able to take these tests. In some cultures, parents do not engage in question-and-answer sessions with their children as parents do in many Western cultures (Greenfield, 1997). This is another example of how cultural influences can affect a child's performance on standard IQ tests.

Other Cultures

Are there different definitions?

We have discussed how many Western psychologists believe that the best definition of a person's intelligence is something called *g*, which is primarily measured by assessing cognitive abilities and

Other cultures define intelligence to include more than cognitive abilities.

expressed by IQ scores. However, psychologists studying intelligence in non-Western countries, such as in Africa and Asia, find that these cultures have different conceptions and definitions of intelligence.

For example, the Taiwanese conception of intelligence emphasizes how one understands and relates to others, including when and how to show intelligence (Sternberg & Yang, 2003). In Zambia (Africa), parents describe the intelligence of their children as including cognitive abilities as well as showing social responsibility, which is considered equally important (Serpell, 2003). In Micronesia, people demonstrate remarkable navigational skills as they sail long distances using only information from stars and sea currents (Ceci et al., 1997). These navigational abilities certainly indicate a high degree of intelligence that would not be assessed by traditional Western IQ tests.

Thus, the definition of intelligence differs across cultures and challenges the traditional Western concept that intelligence is best measured by something called *g* (Sternberg, 2003b).

Nonintellectual Factors

What if a person is nervous?

Maria is 11 years old and has been in the United States for two years. She had a hard time learning English, is not doing well in school, and is terrified about taking tests. Maria comes to take an IQ test, and the psychologist tries to put her at ease. However, Maria is so afraid of failing the IQ test that she just sits and stares at the floor. The psychologist says, "I'm going to give you a word and you tell me what it means." When Maria hears the word, she is now so anxious that she can't concentrate or think of what to say. Maria will probably do poorly on this IQ test because of nonintellectual factors.

Nonintellectual factors refer to noncognitive factors, such as attitude, experience, and emotional functioning, that may help or hinder performance on tests.

For example, nonintellectual factors such as Maria's shyness, fear of strange situations, and anxiety about failing would certainly hinder her test performance (Oostdam & Meijer, 2003). Thus, students who have test anxiety or who come from an environment with poor educational opportunities would be handicapped in taking IQ tests.

In comparison, a child who is experienced and confident at taking tests has the kind of nonintellectual factors that would aid performance. It is well established that numerous nonintellectual factors can have a great influence on how a person performs on IQ tests (Kaplan & Saccuzzo, 2005).

IQ scores are influenced by emotions and experience.

Next, we'll discuss one of the oldest questions about intelligence, the nature-nurture question.

E. Nature-Nurture Question

Definitions

What is the nature-nurture question?

At the beginning of this module, we told you about Midori (right photo), who began playing violin at age 3 and made her professional debut at age 10. Because Midori was a musical genius at such an early age, her exceptional skill was due to nature or heredity, that is, something she was born with. She played professionally until age 23, when she suddenly withdrew for four months. The official reason for her sudden withdrawal was a "digestive disorder," but some reports said that she was actually suffering from an eating disorder. Midori's problem raises questions about the effects of environment (nurture), specifically how to help a child genius adjust to difficult personal and professional pressures at such a young age (Cariaga, 1995). The difficulty Midori faced in

Midori, child prodigy: "If I went back, I would probably do everything differently."

balancing nature or heredity factors (being a child genius) with nurture or environmental factors (facing difficult personal and professional pressures) brings us to the nature-nurture question.

The *nature-nurture question* asks how nature—hereditary or genetic factors—interacts with nurture—environmental factors—in the development of a person's intellectual, emotional, personal, and social abilities.

In the early 1900s, intelligence was believed to be primarily inherited or due to nature (Terman, 1916). In the 1950s, psychology was heavily influenced by behaviorism, which emphasized nurture or environmental factors in the development of intelligence (B. F. Skinner, 1953). Today, researchers have found that nature and nurture interact and contribute about equally to the development of intelligence (Pinker, 2003).

Twin Studies

What do genes do?

In exploring how nature and nurture contribute to and interact in the development of intelligence, researchers compared IQ scores in siblings (brothers and sisters) and in fraternal and identical twins.

Fraternal twins, like siblings (brothers and sisters), develop from separate eggs and have 50% of their genes in common. *Identical twins* develop from a single egg and thus have identical genes, which means that they have 100% of their genes in common.

Genetic factors. The graph on the right shows that the correlation in IQ scores between identical twins (0.85), who share 100% of their genes, was higher than the correlation between fraternal twins (0.60), who share 50% of their genes, or between siblings (0.45), who also share 50% of their genes (Plomin & Petrill, 1997). These findings, which come from over 100 studies, indicate that genetic factors contribute about 50% to the development of intelligence, which has a rather specific definition (Plomin & Spinath, 2004).

Definition of intelligence. As we have discussed, many researchers define intelligence as relating to Spearman's **g** factor (see p. 282), which is measured by performance on cognitive tests and results in IQ scores. However, some researchers argue that there are other, equally important kinds of intelligence, such as practical (adjusting to one's environment), social (interacting with others), emotional (perceiving and understanding emotions), as well as creative, musical, and insightful intelligence (Sternberg et al., 2003b). As discussed earlier, these kinds of

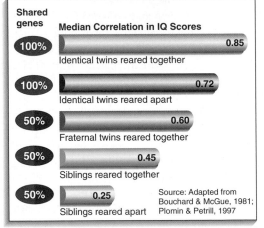

Shared genes	Median Correlation in IQ Scores
100%	0.85 — Identical twins reared together
100%	0.72 — Identical twins reared apart
50%	0.60 — Fraternal twins reared together
50%	0.45 — Siblings reared together
50%	0.25 — Siblings reared apart

Source: Adapted from Bouchard & McGue, 1981; Plomin & Petrill, 1997

intelligence are not measured by standard IQ tests, which primarily focus on measuring cognitive abilities.

Interaction of nature and nurture. When researchers report that genetic factors influence intelligence (IQ scores), they mean that genetic factors influence cognitive abilities to varying degrees, depending on the environment (Bishop et al., 2003). For example, what would happen to cognitive skills if a child were rated as being high or low in interacting with his or her environment?

Interaction. An example of how genetic and environmental factors interact in the development of intelligence comes from a study of 3-year-old children who were identified as being either high or low in exploring their environments, which is a personality trait known as stimulation seeking. These children were later given IQ tests at age 11 to determine if being high or low in stimulation seeking affected their IQs. Researchers reported that children who had been rated high in stimulation seeking at age 3 scored significantly higher on IQ tests compared to children who had been rated low in stimulation seeking at age 3. This significant difference in IQ scores (11 points) was not related to the occupation or education of their parents. Researchers concluded that children high in stimulation seeking were more curious and open to learning from their environments, which in turn enhanced the development of their cognitive abilities and resulted in higher scores on IQ tests (A. Raine et al., 2002).

Thus, genetic factors contribute about 50% to the development of one's intelligence (IQ score), while the other 50% comes from the interaction with environmental factors, which we'll examine next.

How much does environment contribute?

What would happen if children with limited social-educational opportunities and low IQs were adopted by parents who could provide better social-educational opportunities? Researchers reasoned that if environmental factors influence the development of intelligence, then providing more environmental opportunities should increase IQ scores.

A group of French researchers studied children who had been abandoned as babies by their lower-class parents and adopted during the first six months of life into upper-middle-class families. The researchers found that the mean IQ of the adopted children was 14 points higher than the mean IQ of similar children born and raised in lower-class settings by their natural parents. In addition, the adopted children were four times less likely to fail in school. This study suggests that with improved environmental factors—for example, better social-educational opportunities—intellectual development (as measured by IQ scores) and performance in the classroom can be improved (Schiff et al., 1982).

Children adopted into advantaged homes had higher IQ scores.

In a similar study, African American children from impoverished environments were adopted into middle-class families, some White and some African American; all of the families provided many social-educational opportunities for the adopted children. Researchers found that the IQs of the adopted children were as much as 10 points higher than those of African American children who were raised in disadvantaged homes (Scarr & Weinberg, 1976). In a follow-up study, researchers reported that the adopted children, now adolescents, had higher IQ scores than African American children raised in their own communities (Weinberg et al., 1992).

These kinds of studies show that children with poor educational opportunities and low IQ scores can show an increase in IQ scores when they are adopted into families that provide better educational opportunities. Based on data from adoption studies, researchers concluded that nurture or environmental factors contribute to intellectual development (Duyme, 1999).

What is heritability?

In the last 10 years, researchers have made significant progress in answering the nature-nurture question, and one tool they have used is a number called heritability.

Heritability **is a number that indicates the amount or proportion of some ability, characteristic, or trait that can be attributed to genetic factors (nature).**

For example, the figure below shows that heritability (nature) for overall intelligence (measured by IQ tests) was about 50%, which means that 50% of general cognitive ability comes from genetic factors. Researchers were also able to calculate the heritability scores for specific cognitive abilities, such as spatial ability (32%), verbal ability (55%), and memory (55%) (McClearn et al., 1997). These studies on heritability show that genetic factors (nature) contribute about half to intelligence.

The next big step in genetic research is the identification of specific genes or groups of genes that contribute to specific cognitive traits used to measure intelligence (Petrill, 2003).

Notice that the heritability numbers in the graph on the left are in the 50% range, which means that genes do not determine or fix these abilities, because the other 50% is coming from environmental

Estimates of Heritability

Nature — genetic factors	Nurture — environmental factors

Intelligence (general abilities)	
50%	50%

Spatial ability	
32%	68%

Verbal ability	
55%	45%

Memory	
55%	45%

factors. You can think of genetic factors as establishing a range of potential abilities or behaviors, which are shaped and molded through interaction with one's environment. This idea of how genetic factors operate is called the reaction range (Bouchard, 1997).

Reaction range **indicates the extent to which traits, abilities, or IQ scores may increase or decrease as a result of interaction with environmental factors.**

Researchers estimate that the reaction range may vary up or down by as much as 10–15 points in one's IQ score. For example, the figure on the right shows that a person's IQ may vary from 85 to 110, depending on whether he or she has an impoverished or enriched environment (Zigler & Seitz, 1982).

Conclusion. The studies on heritability, twins, and adopted children provide an answer to the nature-nurture question: Nature or heredity contributes about 50% to intelligence (IQ) and environment or nurture contributes about 50%. However, a person's IQ can vary by 10–15 points (IQ reaction range), depending on how heredity interacts with different kinds of environments.

Next, we'll examine the debate over racial differences in IQ scores.

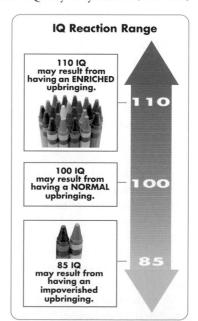

IQ Reaction Range

110 IQ may result from having an ENRICHED upbringing.

110

100 IQ may result from having a NORMAL upbringing.

100

85 IQ may result from having an impoverished upbringing.

85

E. Nature-Nurture Question

Racial Controversy

What is the latest controversy?

In the early 1900s, psychologists believed that intelligence was primarily inherited. This idea reappeared in a relatively recent book, *The Bell Curve,* by psychologist Richard Herrnstein and political scientist Charles Murray (1994). But what brought these authors the greatest publicity was their statement that racial differences in IQ scores were caused primarily by genetic or inherited factors. This and other statements from Herrnstein and Murray's book set off such a heated and often misguided public debate that the American Psychological Association (APA) formed a special task force of prominent researchers. The goal of the APA task force was to summarize what is currently known about intelligence (Neisser et al., 1996). We have already discussed many of the issues raised in the APA report, and we will now focus on the difficult and complex question of racial differences in IQ scores.

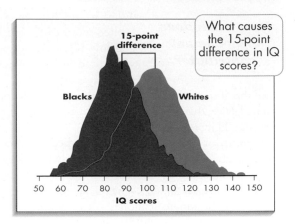

Difference between IQ Scores

Findings. To help you understand the controversy surrounding racial differences in IQ scores, please look at the figure in the upper right. Notice that there are two distributions of IQ scores: The red bell-shaped curve shows the distribution of IQ scores for African Americans (Blacks), and the blue bell-shaped curve shows the distribution of scores for Caucasians (Whites). Although there is much overlap in IQ scores (indicated by overlapping of red and blue areas), researchers generally agree that the average or mean IQ score for African Americans is about 15 points lower than the average IQ score for Caucasians (Bouchard, 1995). This 15-point average difference in IQ scores means that although there are many African Americans with high IQ scores, they are proportionally fewer in number compared to Caucasians.

How...

is...

race...

Two explanations. There are at least two possible explanations for this 15-point difference in average IQ scores. One explanation is that the differences are due to inherited or ***genetic factors:*** African Americans are genetically inferior to Whites. Another explanation is that the difference is due to a number of ***environmental factors:*** African Americans have fewer social, economic, and educational opportunities than Whites do.

Although the authors of *The Bell Curve* emphasized the role of genetic factors, you'll see that the APA task force and many other psychologists disagreed.

decided?

Cause of IQ Differences

Group differences. In a careful review of *The Bell Curve,* one of the leading researchers in the area of intelligence concluded the book offered no convincing evidence that genetic factors were primarily responsible for the 15-point IQ difference between African Americans and Caucasians (Sternberg, 1995). This conclusion is based largely on the distinction between whether genetic factors can influence the development of intelligence in an individual and whether they can influence different development of intelligence among races. The APA task force said that there is good evidence that genetic factors play a significant role in the development of an ***individual's intelligence.*** However, there is no convincing evidence that genetic factors play a primary role in the development of differences in intelligence ***among races.*** Thus, the APA task force challenged Herrnstein and Murray's statement that IQ ***differences among races*** are caused primarily by genetic factors (Neisser et al., 1996).

Although no one knows exactly what causes the differences in IQ scores shown in the above graph, many psychologists suggest a number of environmental factors, such as differences in social-economic classes, educational opportunities, family structures, and career possibilities (Loehlin, 2000). Recent research that shows the difference in IQs between African Americans and Whites is narrowing by 4–7 points also suggests that environmental factors can significantly influence IQ (Dickens & Flynn, 2006). Thus, one of *The Bell Curve*'s major conclusions—that racial differences in IQ scores are based primarily on genetic factors—is not supported by the evidence (Neisser et al., 1996). Two prominent researchers concluded that *The Bell Curve*'s argument for racial inferiority appeared to be based on scientific evidence, but closer examination shows that it was not (S. J. Gould, 1996; Sternberg, 1995).

Differences in skin color. Another problem with *The Bell Curve* is its assumption that skin color is a meaningful way to identify races. For example, based on skin color, to which race would you assign the individuals in the four photos on the left? Researchers report that skin color is not reliable in identifying racial makeup because recent studies on DNA (genetic instructions) indicate that people around the world are much more alike than different (Shriver, 2005). In fact, no matter the color of one's skin, genetic instructions in people around the world vary by only about 3–5% (M. C. King & Motulsky, 2002). Thus, differences in skin color are only skin deep, and skin color is not a reliable measure to assign people to different races when comparing IQ scores (Venter, 2000).

After the Concept Review, we'll discuss how early racial discrimination was based on IQ scores.

Concept Review

1. One approach to measuring intelligence focuses on quantifying cognitive factors or abilities that are involved in intellectual performance; this is called the (a)_____ approach. Charles Spearman used this approach to develop a two-factor theory of intelligence: one factor is **g**, or (b)_____; the second factor is **s**, or (c)_____.

2. In comparison to Spearman's two-factor approach, Howard Gardner's theory says that there are nine kinds of _____, such as verbal skills, math skills, spatial skills, and movement skills.

3. Another approach to measuring intelligence is by analyzing the kinds of (a)_____ processes that people use to solve problems. An example of this approach is Robert Sternberg's (b)_____ theory of intelligence.

4. Alfred Binet developed an intelligence test that estimated intellectual progress by comparing a child's score on an intelligence test to the scores of average children of the same age. Binet called this concept _____.

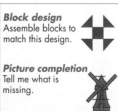

5. Lewis Terman revised Binet's intelligence test, and the most significant change he made was to develop a formula to compute a single score that represents a person's (a)_____. This formula is IQ = (b)_____ age divided by (c)_____ age, times (d)_____.

6. The most widely used series of IQ tests are the (a)_____ Intelligence Scales. These tests organize items into two subtests, which are called (b)_____ and (c)_____ scales. In an attempt to measure nonverbal skills and rule out cultural problems, Wechsler added the (d)_____ scale.

Block design
Assemble blocks to match this design.

Picture completion
Tell me what is missing.

7. A good psychological test has two characteristics. It should give about the same score over time, which is called (a)_____, and it should measure what it is supposed to measure, which is called (b)_____.

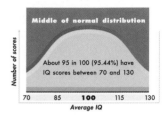

8. If IQ scores can be represented by a bell-shaped curve, the pattern is called a _____. The scores have a symmetrical arrangement, so that the vast majority fall in the middle range and fewer fall near the extreme ends of the range.

Middle of normal distribution

About 95 in 100 (95.44%) have IQ scores between 70 and 130

70   85   **100**   115   130
Average IQ

9. An individual who has a combination of limited mental ability (usually an IQ below 70) and difficulty functioning in everyday life is said to have some degree of (a)_____. If this condition results from genetic problems or brain damage, it is called (b)_____. If this condition results from a greatly impoverished environment, it is called (c)_____. Individuals who have above-average intelligence (usually IQ scores above 130) as well as some superior talent or skill are said to be (d)_____.

Left end of normal distribution
Retardation
About 2 in 100 (2.27%) have IQ scores below 70

30   50   70
Severe/   Moderate   Mild
Profound

Right end of normal distribution
Gifted
About 2 in 100 (2.27%) have IQ scores above 130; about 1 in a million has an IQ above 180

130   145
Superior   Gifted

10. If the wording of test questions and the experiences on which they are based are more familiar to members of some social groups than to others, the test is said to have a (a)_____. Depending on the culture, (b)_____ can be defined in different ways.

11. When we ask how much genetic factors and how much environmental factors contribute to intelligence, we are asking the (a)_____ question. There is good evidence that genetic factors contribute about (b)_____ and environmental factors contribute about (c)_____ to the development of one's intelligence. The extent to which IQ scores may increase or decrease depending on environmental effects is called the (d)_____.

Intelligence (general abilities)
Spatial ability
Verbal ability
Memory

Answers: 1. (a) psychometric, (b) general intelligence, (c) specific abilities; 2. intelligence; 3. (a) reasoning, (b) triarchic; 4. mental age; 5. (a) intelligence quotient or IQ, (b) mental, (c) chronological, (d) 100; 6. (a) Wechsler, (b) verbal, (c) performance, (d) performance; 7. (a) reliability, (b) validity; 8. normal distribution; 9. (a) mental retardation, (b) organic retardation, (c) cultural-familial retardation, (d) gifted; 10. (a) cultural bias, (b) intelligence; 11. (a) nature-nurture, (b) 50%, (c) 50%, (d) reaction range

Misuse of IQ Tests

What were Binet's warnings about using IQ tests?

After Alfred Binet developed the first intelligence tests, he gave two warnings about the potential misuse of IQ tests. He warned that IQ tests do not and should not be used to measure innate intelligence and that IQ tests should not be used to label individuals. However, in the early 1900s the area we know as psychology was just beginning, and American psychologists were very proud of how much they had improved IQ tests. With their improved IQ tests, American psychologists not only used IQ tests to measure what they thought was innate, or inherited, intelligence but also used IQ tests to label people (as morons or imbeciles). As if that weren't bad enough, early psychologists persuaded the U.S. Congress to pass discriminatory immigration laws based on IQ tests. As we look back now, we must conclude that the use and abuse of IQ tests in the early 1900s created one of psychology's sorriest moments. Here's what happened.

In 1924, Congress passed an immigration law to keep out those believed to have low IQs.

Innate Intelligence

One name that we have already mentioned is that of Lewis Terman, who was the guiding force behind revising Binet's intelligence test (which became the Stanford-Binet test) and also developing the formula for computing a single IQ score. Terman, who became head of the Department of Psychology at Stanford University, firmly believed that intelligence was primarily inherited, that intelligence tests measured innate abilities, and that environmental influences were far less important.

One of Terman's goals was to test all children and, on the basis of their IQ scores, to label and sort them into categories of innate abilities. Terman argued that society could use IQ scores (usually of 70 or below) to restrain or eliminate those whose intelligence was too low to lead an effective moral life (Terman, 1916).

Terman hoped to establish minimum intelligence scores necessary for all leading occupations. For example, he believed that people with IQs below 100 should not be given employment that involves prestige or monetary reward. Those with IQs of 75 or below should be unskilled labor, and those with 75–85 IQs should be semiskilled labor. In Terman's world, class boundaries were to be set by innate intelligence, as measured by his Stanford-Binet IQ test (S. J. Gould, 1996; Hunt, 1993).

Terman's belief that IQ tests measured innate intelligence was adopted by another well-known American psychologist, Robert Yerkes.

Classifying Races

Robert Yerkes was a Harvard professor who was asked to develop a test that could be used to classify applicants for the army. Under Yerkes's direction, over 1.75 million World War I army recruits were given IQ tests. From this enormous amount of data, Yerkes (1921) and his colleagues reached three conclusions:

1. They concluded that the average mental age of White American adults was a meager 13 years, slightly above the classification of a moron (a term psychologists used in the early 1900s). The reasons they gave for this low mental age were (using the terminology then current) the unconstrained breeding of the poor and feebleminded and the spread of Negro blood through interracial breeding.

2. They concluded that European immigrants could be ranked on intelligence by their country of origin. The fair peoples of western and northern Europe (Nordics) were most intelligent, while the darker peoples of southern Europe (Mediterraneans) and the Slavs of eastern Europe were less intelligent.

3. They concluded that Negroes were at the bottom of the racial scale in intelligence.

Many of Yerkes's outrageous and discriminatory views resurfaced in the book *The Bell Curve* (Herrnstein & Murray, 1994), which we discussed earlier. Following Yerkes's lead, IQ scores were next used for racial discrimination.

Immigration Laws

The fact that Yerkes ranked European races by intelligence eventually reached members of the U.S. Congress. Outraged by the "fact" that Europeans of "low intelligence" were being allowed into America, members of Congress sought a way to severely limit the immigration of people from southern and eastern Europe. In writing the Immigration Law of 1924, Congress relied, in part, on Yerkes's racial rankings and imposed harsh quotas on those nations they believed to have inferior stock (people from southern and eastern Europe, Alpine and Mediterranean nations).

Stephen Jay Gould (1996), a well-known evolutionary biologist, reviewed Yerkes's data and pointed out a number of problems: poorly administered tests, terrible testing conditions, inconsistent standards for retaking tests, written tests given to illiterate recruits (guaranteeing a low score), and no control for educational level or familiarity with the English language. As a result of these problems, Gould concluded that Yerkes's data were so riddled with errors as to render useless any conclusions about racial differences in intelligence.

Looking back, we see clearly that early psychologists badly misused IQ tests. They forgot that IQ tests are merely one of many tools to assess cognitive abilities, which many consider to be one of many kinds of intelligence (H. Gardner, 1995).

We've discussed how past IQ tests have been misused and how current IQ tests may be biased. Is there a new generation of intelligence tests on the horizon?

G. Research Focus: New Approaches

Can Genius Be Found in the Brain?

There is one question about intelligence that has especially interested researchers: How is the brain of a genius different? For example, how was Albert Einstein able to think of riding through space on a beam of light or create his famous formula ($E = mc^2$), which led to building the atomic bomb?

When Einstein died of heart failure in 1955 at age 76, Dr. Thomas Harvey, who performed the autopsy, removed Einstein's brain and kept it at Princeton University. In 1996, Harvey contacted Dr. Sandra Witelson, a neuroscientist at McMaster University, and asked if she wished to examine Einstein's brain. McMaster University in Ontario, Canada, has a bank of over 100 brains that people have donated for research. Dr. Witelson was able to compare Einstein's 76-year-old brain with brains of similar ages from 35 men and 56 women who were known to have normal intelligence when they died. The results of Dr. Witelson's examination of Einstein's brain are discussed in the figure at the right.

Although the physical differences in Einstein's brain are obvious in the figure,

Normal brain weighs about 1,350 grams. This side view shows the wrinkled cortex, which contains separate areas for different functions (feeling, moving, reading, writing, seeing). Notice the yellow and red areas, which are part of the parietal lobe. The **red area, the inferior parietal lobe,** is especially used for thinking in visual-spatial terms, for mathematical thought, and for imaging how things move in space.

Einstein's brain weighed 1,230 grams, slightly less than normal. Einstein's brain was different in that it lacked the yellow area, which allowed his **red area, the inferior parietal lobe,** to be 15% wider than in normal brains. Researchers believe that Einstein's larger inferior parietal lobe increased his ability to think and imagine such things as space being curved and that time could slow down (Witelson et al., 1999).

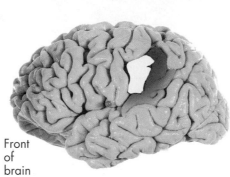

Front of brain

Front of brain

Dr. Witelson cautions that they don't know if every brilliant mathematician has a larger inferior parietal lobe, which is something only further research can answer. Other researchers wonder if genius can ever be measured or located in the brain, since genius involves a mixture of creative insights, culture, and life experiences that may be unique to that person (S. C. Wang, 2000).

How Does a Prodigy's Brain Develop?

What do brain scans show?

With the recent advances in brain scans, researchers are now able to explore brain development like never before. Phillip Shaw and his colleagues (2006) at the National Institute of Mental Health and McGill University in Montreal completed a long-term study examining intelligence and brain development in children.

Method. The team of researchers followed a group of more than 300 children as they aged from 6 to 19. Each child was administered intelligence tests at the start of the study, and MRI brain scans (p. 70) were taken about every two years to measure the size of brain structures.

Results. The thickness of the cortex (p. 74), which is the outer layer of the brain that controls higher cognitive functioning, began thinner in highly intelligent children, but became thicker than the cortexes in children with average intelligence by adolescence. As shown in the brain above, the areas that changed the most were in the front of the brain and in a strip over the top of the brain, which are areas responsible for higher cognitive functioning,

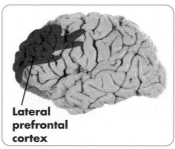

Lateral prefrontal cortex

such as planning and reasoning. By the age of 19, the cortexes of highly intelligent children thinned such that they were equal in thickness to the cortexes of children with average intelligence.

Conclusions. This is the first study to show that the brain develops differently in highly intelligent children. However, it is uncertain what might be causing the changes in cortex thickness. One possible explanation is the thickening may be a result of highly intelligent children developing more neural connections during school years, and the later thinning of the cortex may be due to unused neural connections withering away to make cognitive functioning more efficient.

The role of genes and environment in the changes in the cortex is also unknown. Genes may play an important role as smarter children had different cortex thickness even at a young age. But environmental factors (social activities, schooling, diet) may also have an important role in the thickening of the cortex over the years (Grigorenko, 2006).

Last, this study examined only group differences, and making any predictions based on an individual child is not possible (Giles, 2006).

H. Application — Intervention Programs

Definition of Intervention Programs

Why might a child need a head start?

For a moment, imagine what will happen to Nancy's child. Nancy, who is in her mid-twenties, is a single mother with a 3-year-old child. Nancy lives in a lower-class neighborhood and earns less than $5,000 a year doing part-time work. She has completed only two years of high school, has no family and few friends. What effects do you think Nancy's background, educational level, and current impoverished environment will have on her child? Psychologists would predict that Nancy's 3-year-old child will not likely acquire the social, emotional, and cognitive skills and abilities needed to do well in school or society. Her child may need outside help, which may come from an intervention program (Arnold & Doctoroff, 2003).

Intervention programs create a stimulating environment.

An *intervention program* helps disadvantaged children from low socioeconomic classes to achieve better intellectual, social, and personal-emotional development, as well as physical health.

Intervention programs can give Nancy training in how to be a good parent and provide her child with educational and social opportunities. Perhaps the best-known intervention program in the United States is Head Start, which began in 1965 as a six-to-eight-week program. Researchers later discovered that was too brief to be effective. As a result, Head Start was lengthened to two years, and in 2006, the program enrolled nearly one million 3- to 5-year-olds across the United States (ACF, 2006).

We'll focus on some successful intervention programs for disadvantaged children.

Abecedarian Project

This project's goal was to teach youngsters from disadvantaged environments the cognitive and social skills needed for future success in school. Psychologists identified babies who were at high risk of failing in school because they lived in disadvantaged settings. Most of the mothers had low IQ scores, were African American, young, without a high school education, and single. With the mothers' permission, 2- to 3-month-old infants were assigned either to a control group that did not receive any special treatment or to an experimental group. Children in the experimental group spent 6 or more hours daily, five days a week, in a carefully supervised day-care center that continued for four years until the children entered public school at the age of 5.

After four years of this intense intervention program, children in the Abecedarian Project had IQ scores 12 points higher than control children from disadvantaged environments. Once children left the program, some of their IQ gains decreased. However, when the children were retested at ages 12, 15, and 21, researchers found that the children had shown substantial gains in cognitive and academic abilities as a result of early intervention (F. A. Campbell et al., 2001).

Head Start results in long-term personal and social gains.

Head Start

Head Start, which is a day-care program for disadvantaged children, usually lasts for two years, from ages 3 to 5, and has six goals: preschool education, health screening, mental health services, hot meals, social services for the child and family, and involvement and participation of parents in the program (Zigler & Styfco, 1994). More recently, Head Start has emphasized teaching basic academic skills, such as reading, in order to prepare disadvantaged children to do well in kindergarten (R. T. Cooper, 1999).

Head Start was initially viewed as something of a failure because two to three years after children left Head Start, few if any differences in IQ or other academic scores were found between those children and control groups (Clarke & Clarke, 1989). However, Head Start showed other important long-term beneficial effects (Kirp, 2004; Zigler & Styfco, 1994):

- Adolescents who had been in the Head Start program were more likely to be in classes appropriate for their ages rather than to have had to repeat a class, were less likely to show antisocial or delinquent behavior, and were more likely to hold jobs.
- Mothers whose children had been in the Head Start program reported fewer psychological symptoms, greater feelings of mastery, and greater current life satisfaction.
- Children who had two years of Head Start and an additional two to seven years of educational help were much more successful in graduating from high school (69%) than a control group (49%).
- At the age of 40, adults who had been in Head Start were more likely to have earned college degrees and to have owned a home and a car, and less likely to have criminal records and be drug users.

Another program similar to Head Start, called the Chicago Child Parent Center Program, enrolled children 3–4 years old and lasted for 18 months. Over 1,500 children in this program were tracked from ages 5 to 20 and were found to be more likely to graduate from high school and less likely to be arrested than poor children not in the program (A. J. Reynolds et al., 2001).

From studies like these we can draw two conclusions. First, often early and rather large increases (up to 10 points) in IQ scores do not last after the child leaves the intervention program. Second, programs like Head Start result in a number of long-term benefits, such as better social and personal well-being and increased chances of graduating from high school and avoiding crime (Zigler, 1995; Zigler & Styfco, 2001). These long-term effects indicate that programs like Head Start should not be evaluated solely on IQ scores but also on other personality, motivational, and psychological benefits.

Raising IQ Scores

In the early days of Head Start, psychologists were very encouraged to find that the program initially increased disadvantaged children's IQ scores by about 10 points, a very significant amount. One reason IQ scores can be raised in young children from disadvantaged homes is that these children have not been exposed to and have not acquired the kinds of skills and cultural experiences assessed by IQ tests. However, when disadvantaged children are exposed to the enriched environment of Head Start, these children quickly acquire all kinds of new skills and abilities that help them score higher on IQ tests (Spitz, 1997).

For example, researchers compared two groups of disadvantaged children, all of whom had IQ scores below 80 (100 is considered the average IQ). Some of these children, called the experimental group, were placed in a special educational intervention program from ages 3 to 5. Other children, called the control group, were given no additional training and remained in their home environments.

The figure below shows that, after only one year, children in the experimental group (intervention program) showed a significant increase in IQ scores (about 10 points) compared to the children in the control group who remained in disadvantaged home environments (Schweinhart & Weikart, 1980). However, after the children left the intervention program at the age of 5 and entered public school, their IQ scores began a slow but consistent decline. At the same time, the IQ scores of control children began a gradual increase as they benefited from attending public school. By the age of 11, there was no longer any difference in IQ scores.

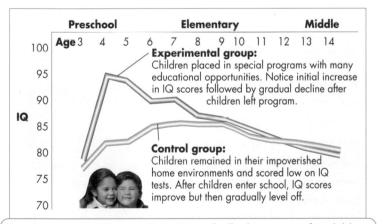

Initial increase in IQ scores (age 4) gradually disappears after children leave Head Start program and return to less stimulating environments.

One reason for this decline in IQ scores is that after children leave an intervention program, they usually return to less stimulating environments, which offer less educational, social, and motivational support. For this reason, researchers make two strong recommendations: First, programs like Head Start should be lengthened from three to at least five or more years so children have more time to learn and practice their newly acquired social, emotional, and academic skills; second, parents must become involved in helping their children develop cognitive skills, such as reading to their children (G. Nelson et al., 2003; Zigler & Styfco, 2001).

Finally, as we discussed earlier, intervention programs should not be evaluated solely on IQ scores but rather on other social, emotional, and psychological gains that are found to be long-lasting.

Need for Intervention Programs

The most successful intervention programs have a strong educational emphasis, well-trained teachers, and a low ratio of children to trained teachers.

Researchers make three important points about the usefulness of intervention programs and the need for day-care centers:

1 Currently, about 14.5 million children in the United States are living in poverty, which is known to have a devastating negative influence on a young child developing important social-emotional skills and cognitive abilities. In addition, living in poverty is known to lower academic achievement and goals, decrease motivation, and contribute to school failure and dropouts (Arnold & Doctoroff, 2003). Intervention programs help reduce the devastating effects that continuing poverty can have on families and give children a much needed head start (Zigler & Styfco, 2001).

2 About 25 to 30% of children live in single-parent families that are below the poverty line (Kassebaum, 1994). In some cases, impoverished family environments lead to neglect or abuse, which has very negative effects on a child's social, emotional, and intellectual development. Intensive intervention programs during the first years of life are effective in reducing and preventing the significant intellectual dysfunction that may result from continuing poverty and lack of environmental support (Zigler & Styfco, 2001).

3 Currently, over 60% of married mothers with infants below the age of 2 are employed outside the home and need to place their young children in day care. A study of 1,300 children in day-care centers in the United States reported that quality day care contributed to a child's well-being and cognitive development. Of the 1,300 children, 83% did just fine in social-emotional adjustment, while 17% experienced some behavior problems, such as being aggressive (NICHD, 2001, 2003). But it is not known if the aggressive behavior was caused by being in day care or by factors in the child's home (Stolberg, 2001).

If day care is needed, researchers emphasize the importance of choosing quality day care, which is one with specially trained teachers and a low ratio of children to teachers.

✔ Summary Test

A. Defining Intelligence

1. A subarea of psychology that is concerned with developing psychological tests to assess an individual's abilities, skills, beliefs, and personality traits in a wide range of settings—school, industry, or clinic—is called _____.

2. Spearman's two-factor theory of intelligence says there is a general factor, called (a)_____, that represents a person's ability to perform complex mental work, such as abstract reasoning and problem solving. The general factor underlies a person's performance across tests. In addition, there is a second factor, called (b)_____, that represents a person's specific mental abilities, such as mathematical or verbal skills. These specific mental abilities may differ across tests.

3. Gardner says that there are at least nine kinds of intelligence: verbal intelligence, musical intelligence, logical-mathematical intelligence, spatial intelligence, body movement intelligence, intelligence to understand oneself, intelligence to understand others, naturalistic intelligence, and existential intelligence. This is called the _____ theory.

4. Sternberg's triarchic theory says that intelligence can be divided into three ways of gathering and processing information (*triarchic* means "three"). The first is using (a)_____ skills, which are measured by traditional intelligence tests. The second is using (b)_____ skills that require creative thinking, the ability to deal with novel situations, and the ability to learn from experience. The third is using (c)_____ skills that help a person adjust to, and cope with, his or her sociocultural environment.

B. Measuring Intelligence

Block design
Assemble blocks to match this design.

Picture completion
Tell me what is missing.

5. In trying to measure intelligence, researchers through the years have learned that neither skull size nor brain weight is an accurate predictor of _____.

6. The first intelligence test, which was developed by (a)_____, measured vocabulary, memory, common knowledge, and other cognitive abilities. By comparing a child's score with the scores of average children at the same age, Binet was able to estimate a child's (b)_____. Thus, the Binet-Simon Intelligence Scale gave its results in terms of mental age, while the IQ score was later developed by

(c)_____, who devised a formula to calculate an individual's intelligence quotient. The formula can be written as IQ = (d)_____.

7. The Wechsler Adult Intelligence Scale (WAIS-III) and Wechsler Intelligence Scale for Children (WISC-IV) have items that are organized into various subtests. Subtests for general information, vocabulary, and verbal comprehension are some of those in the (a)_____ section. Subtests that involve arranging pictures in a meaningful order, assembling objects, and using codes are examples of subtests in the (b)_____ section. An individual receives a separate score for each of the subtests; these scores are then combined to yield overall scores for verbal and performance abilities, which, in turn, are combined into a single score, called an (c)_____ score.

8. A good psychological test must have two qualities. One quality ensures that a person's score on a test at one point in time is similar to a score by the same person on a similar test at a later date; this is called (a)_____. The other quality ensures that a test measures what it is supposed to measure; this is called (b)_____. Although the results from analyzing handwriting may be consistent from time to time, this is a poor test of personality or intelligence because handwriting analysis lacks the quality of (c)_____.

C. Distribution & Use of IQ Scores

9. Suppose IQ scores are in a statistical arrangement that resembles the shape of a bell, with the vast majority of scores falling in the middle range and fewer scores falling near the two extreme ends of the curve. This arrangement is called a _____.

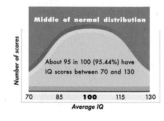

Middle of normal distribution

About 95 in 100 (95.44%) have IQ scores between 70 and 130

Number of scores

70   85   **100**   115   130
Average IQ

10. Substantial limitation in present functioning that is characterized by significantly below average intellectual functioning, along with related limitations in two of eleven areas, including communication, self-care, home living, social skills, and safety, is called _____.

11. There are two general causes of mental retardation: genetic problems or brain damage give rise to (a)_____ retardation, and in the absence of apparent genetic or brain damage, greatly impoverished environments can give rise to (b)_____ retardation. Mental retardation is reflected in IQ scores at one end of the normal distribution. At the other end of the normal distribution of IQ scores are those who are considered (c)_____; such people have above average intelligence (usually IQs above 130) as well as some superior talent or skill.

D. Potential Problems of IQ Testing

12. Binet warned that intelligence tests should not be used to measure (a)_____ mental abilities because intelligence tests measure cognitive abilities, which are influenced by both heredity and environment. Binet also warned that intelligence tests, by themselves, should not be used to (b)_____ people—for example, a moron or a genius. Current IQ tests have been criticized for including wording or experiences that are more familiar to a particular culture, which is called (c)_____. The definition of intelligence differs across (d)_____ and may differ from the Western idea of **g.** One reason individuals may do poorly on IQ tests is noncognitive factors, such as attitude, experience, and emotional functioning, which are called (e)_____.

E. Nature–Nurture Question

13. The (a)_____ question refers to the relative contributions that genetic and environmental factors make to the development of intelligence. On the basis of twin studies, researchers generally conclude that about

Intelligence (general abilities)
Spatial ability
Verbal ability
Memory

(b)_____ of the contribution to intelligence (IQ scores) comes from genetic factors and about (c)_____ comes from environmental factors. Adoption studies support the idea that environmental factors contribute to intellectual development (as measured by IQ scores). The idea that about half of one's intellectual development is dependent on environmental factors has resulted in (d)_____ programs that give impoverished children increased social-educational opportunities. There is little or no cause-and-effect evidence that the average difference in IQ scores between African Americans and Whites is caused primarily by (e)_____ factors.

F. Cultural Diversity: Races, IQs & Immigration

14. Early psychologists ignored Binet's warning about misusing IQ tests. For example, in the early 1900s, Terman believed that IQ tests did measure (a)_____ intelligence, and he wanted to use IQ tests to sort people into categories. Terman's view was adopted by Robert Yerkes, who wanted to use IQ tests to rank the intelligence of

(b)_____ entering the United States. In the 1920s, (c)_____ were written to exclude citizens from certain countries because Yerkes had ranked these individuals low in intelligence.

G. Research Focus: New Approaches

15. In looking for physical differences in Einstein's brain, researchers found that he had a 15% wider (a)_____, which is involved in visual–spatial and mathematical thinking. By using MRI brain scans and intelligence tests, researchers found that the thickness of the brain's cortex began (b)_____ in highly intelligent children, but became (c)_____ than the cortexes in children with average intelligence by adolescence. By the age of 19, the cortex of highly intelligent children was (d)_____ in thickness to that of children with average intelligence.

H. Application: Intervention Programs

16. A program that creates an environment with increased opportunities for intellectual, social, and personality-emotional development is called an (a)_____ program. Although data indicate that IQ increases resulting from intervention programs may be short-lived, there are other long-term positive benefits, such as being more likely to graduate from high school and less likely to be involved in (b)_____ activities. A study of 1,300 children in day-care centers in the United States reported that quality day care contributed to a child's (c)_____ and _____. Researchers emphasize the importance of choosing quality day care, which is one with specially trained (d)_____ and a low ratio of (e)_____ to teachers.

Answers: *1. psychometrics; 2. (a) **g**, (b) **s**; 3. multiple-intelligence; 4. (a) analytical, cognitive, or logical, (b) problem-solving, (c) practical; 5. intelligence; 6. (a) Binet and Simon, (b) mental age, (c) Terman, (d) MA/CA × 100; 7. (a) verbal, (b) performance, (c) IQ; 8. (a) reliability, (b) validity, (c) validity; 9. normal distribution; 10. mental retardation; 11. (a) organic, (b) cultural-familial, (c) gifted; 12. (a) innate, (b) label or classify, (c) cultural bias, (d) cultures, (e) nonintellectual factors; 13. (a) nature–nurture, (b) 50%, (c) 50%, (d) intervention, (e) inherited, or genetic; 14. (a) innate, (b) immigrants, (c) immigration laws, or quotas; 15. (a) inferior parietal lobe, (b) thinner, (c) thicker, (d) equal; 16. (a) intervention, (b) antisocial, delinquent, or criminal, (c) well-being, cognitive development; (d) teachers, (e) children*

Critical Thinking

Can a Successful Bookie Have an IQ of 55?

Questions

1. How smart is Max Weisberg, who as a bookie made $700,000 but didn't hide his illegal activities and kept being arrested by police?

2. What is different about the terms used in the past to describe individuals with IQ scores at the lower end?

3. What are three theories of intelligence, and what would each say about Max's intelligence?

4. Based on the normal distribution, where would Max rank in intelligence, and what would he be capable of doing?

5. Why doesn't Max understand that book-making is illegal and that he must stop or he will keep being arrested?

When Max Weisberg was in his 70s, he continued to be a very successful bookie (person who takes illegal gambling bets). But what's unusual about Max is that even after police repeatedly raided and seized nearly $700,000 in cash from his rundown house, even after he'd been arrested more times than he could remember, he still took no precautions to hide his bookmaking activities. He left gambling slips all over his house, never hid his cash earnings, and openly took bets on the telephone even though the FBI had recorded hours of his conversations. So, how smart is Max, who as a bookie made $700,000 but took no precautions to hide his illegal activities?

Determining how smart Max is is not that easy. In 1939, when Max was 15 years old, he was committed to a state school because of "mental deficiency." Later, he was judged to be "feeble-minded," and still later a probation report on Max read: "mentally deficient: moron, causes undiagnosed." Later on, when Max scored about 55 on an IQ test, he was judged to be in the mentally retarded category.

A psychologist tested Max to find out how someone who was mentally retarded could be a successful bookie. For example, Max had no idea which direction the sun set (west), who wrote "Hamlet" (Shakespeare), who Louis Armstrong was (jazz singer and trumpet player), or

why being a bookie was bad (it's against the law in most states). However, when Max was asked to repeat 8 numbers in correct sequence, his face lit up and he repeated the numbers without an error. When something involves using numbers, Max was as good as a calculator.

Although an IQ of 55 puts Max in the range of mild mental retardation, Max had no trouble remembering and calculating hundreds of complex and difficult numbers related to gambling. For example, if you wanted to make an illegal bet on a professional football team, Max could give you the odds, such as Vikings to win by $10\frac{1}{2}$ points. This means that you win your bet only if the Vikings win by 11 points. If you decided to bet on two or more teams, called "par-leys," or bet "over/under," which uses the total scores of games instead of a single game, Max calculated these very complicated odds without using anything more than the head on his shoulders. A person having this unusual combination of a low IQ score but excelling at some skill, such as numbers, is called a savant, which occurs in about 1 in 2,000 of mentally retarded individuals.

After every arrest, Max told the police that he needed to get out as soon as possible so he could get to a phone and start taking bets. (Adapted from S. Braun, Max the bookie won't stop and that's a sure thing, *Los Angeles Times*, August 7, 1999, p. A1)

1. As a bookie, Max has to be pretty smart to have made $700,000, but he has to be pretty dumb to leave all his gambling slips and cash lying around the house so the police have an easy time finding evidence to arrest him over and over.
2. Notice that the terms used in the past to describe individuals with lower IQs, such as "mentally deficient," "feebleminded," and "moron," were very unfavorable or derogatory and put the individual in a bad light.
3. According to Spearman's *g*, Max would be rated low in intelligence because his IQ is 55 (normal is 100) and Max is given no credit for his practical abilities (being a very successful bookie). According to Gardner's idea of multiple intelligence, Max certainly has exceptional skills in calculating numbers and is intelligent in that sense. According to Sternberg's triarchic theory, Max

certainly shows considerable practical intelligence in his ability to adapt to his environment (being a very successful bookie).
4. Based on the normal distribution of IQ scores, Max's IQ score of 55 falls in the range for borderline mentally retarded (50–75). In this range, Max should be able to read and write, master a simple occupational skill, and be self-supporting. As it turns out, Max is a very successful, self-supporting bookie.
5. Being mentally retarded means that Max has some limited cognitive capacities (not knowing which direction the sun sets). The reason Max believes that being a bookie is OK is that he says that's what he does and has been doing for 40 years. The idea that being a bookie is illegal or immoral is a concept too complex or abstract for Max to understand, no matter how many times it is explained or he is arrested.

Links to Learning

Learning Activities

- **POWERSTUDY FOR INTRODUCTION TO PSYCHOLOGY 4.0**

by Tom Doyle and Rod Plotnik

SuperModule: Check out the quizzes and learning activities for "Intelligence" on **PowerStudy** and:

- Test your knowledge using an interactive version of the Summary Test on pages 300 and 301. Also access related quizzing—true/false, multiple choice, and matching.
- Explore an interactive version of the Critical Thinking exercise "Can a Successful Bookie Have an IQ of 55?" on page 302.
- You will also find key terms, a chapter outline including chapter abstract, and a special extended list of hotlinked websites that correlate to this module.

- *CengageNOW*

academic.cengage.com/login

Need help studying? This site is your one-stop study shop.
Take a Pre-Test and CengageNOW will generate a Personalized Study Plan based on your test results. The Study Plan will identify the topics you need to review and direct you to online resources to help you master those topics. You can then take a Post-Test to determine the concepts you have mastered and what you still need to work on.

- **INTRODUCTION TO PSYCHOLOGY BOOK COMPANION WEBSITE**

academic.cengage.com/psychology/plotnik

Visit your book companion website where you will find more resources to help you study. At this site, you will find Learning Objectives, Internet Exercises, quizzing, flash cards, and a pronunciation glossary.

- **STUDY GUIDE and WEBTUTOR**

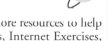

Check the corresponding module in your Study Guide for effective student tips and help learning the material presented. Also go to **academic.cengage.com/webtutor** for an interactive version of the Study Guide features.

Study Questions

*A. **Defining Intelligence**—How intelligent was Ray Kroc, who never finished high school but started the world-famous McDonald's hamburger chain? (**Suggested answer page 627**)

B. **Measuring Intelligence**—Would a new test based on a very accurate count of all the cells in your brain be a good test of intelligence?

C. **Distribution & Use of IQ Scores**—If you were hiring for a large department store, would it help to know the applicants' IQ scores?

*D. **Potential Problems of IQ Testing**—Should we use IQ scores to assign the growing number of students from different cultures to grade levels? (**Suggested answer page 627**)

E. **Nature-Nurture Question**—If parents wanted to adopt a child, how important would it be to know the child's genetic makeup?

F. **Cultural Diversity: Races, IQs & Immigration**—What convinced members of the U.S. Congress to use IQ scores as the basis for immigration laws?

G. **Research Focus: New Approaches**—Would brain scans provide a less biased, more culture-free measure of intelligence than standard IQ tests?

*H. **Application: Intervention Programs**—Since Head Start fails to raise IQ scores over the long run, should its financial support be reduced? (**Suggested answer page 627**)

*These questions are answered in Appendix B.

MODULE 14
Thought & Language

BUTTERFLYALPHABET
KJELL B. SANDVED
www.butterflyalphabet.com

©butterflyalphabet.com

Introduction

Concepts

What is that four-legged thing?

Jeff, who is only 14 months old, walks up to his mother and says, in a somewhat demanding voice, "Juice." Jeff's one-word sentence, "Juice," is shorthand for "Can I please have a glass of orange juice?" Even as a toddler, Jeff already knows a considerable number of words that represent a whole range of objects, such as cookie, car, bottle, bunny, baby, juice, ball, apple, and the most hated words of all for a young child, "wash up." So when Jeff points at an object and says, "Ball," his one-word sentence is short for "That is my ball." Jeff's use of these single-word "sentences" indicates that he is on his way to learning a very complex system of communicating by using language.

Jeff learned that this four-legged animal is a rabbit and not a cat or dog.

Jeff also uses one-word "sentences" to ask questions. For instance, he'll point to a picture in his animal book and ask, "Name?" This means "What is the name of that animal?" Jeff has already learned that a four-legged, fuzzy-tailed, large-eared animal is a bunny; a four-legged, long-nosed animal that barks is a dog; and a four-legged, short-eared animal with a long tail that says "meow" is a cat. Perhaps when Jeff sees an animal, such as a dog, cat, or rabbit, he takes a "mental photo" that he uses for future identifications. But that would mean storing an overwhelming number of "mental photos" of all the animals, objects, and people in his environment. We'll explain a more efficient system that Jeff probably uses to identify animals, objects, and people.

Creativity

How does one become creative?

One of Jeff's favorite things to do is paint the animals in his picture books. Although Jeff makes a terribly wonderful mess, his parents encourage him because they hope that Jeff's early interest in painting may indicate that he has a creative talent for painting or art. How one becomes a creative person is quite a mystery; take the case of Gordon Parks, for example.

No one thought Gordon Parks would amount to much. He was out on the streets at age 15 and never had time to finish high school, where he and his classmates were told, "Don't worry about graduating—it doesn't matter because you're gonna be porters and maids." Parks is African American and grew up in the 1920s, surrounded by segregation, discrimination, and, worst of all, lynchings.

Parks was a teenager when his mother died. He was sent to live with his brother-in-law, but, Parks remembers, "That man didn't like children and didn't want to take me on, and I sensed that the minute I walked into his house." Parks was soon out on the street. He drifted from city to city, lived in flophouses, and worked at odd jobs. What would become of Parks (McKenna, 1994)?

Parks (right photo) lived to his nineties, and with little formal schooling and little professional help, he wrote four volumes of poetry and a best-selling autobiography, *The Learning Tree*. He worked as a professional photographer for *Vogue* and *Life* magazines and directed a few films (*Shaft* and *The Learning Tree*). He wrote 12 books, held an exhibition of his photographs, and published a book of his incredible photos (Grundberg, 2006; Parks, 1997). Parks's early years showed no signs of his creativity. We'll discuss what creativity is and what makes creative people different.

With little formal schooling, Parks became a very creative person.

Cognitive Approach

How does your mind work?

How do toddlers like Jeff learn to speak a complex language and to recognize hundreds of objects? How did Gordon Parks, with little formal schooling, develop the ability to write and express his creativity in so many ways? The answers to these kinds of questions involve figuring out how our minds work. One way to study mental processes is to use the cognitive approach.

The *cognitive approach* is one method of studying how we process, store, and use information and how this information, in turn, influences what we notice, perceive, learn, remember, believe, and feel.

Of all animals, humans have the greatest language ability.

We have already discussed several aspects of the cognitive approach: learning in Modules 9 and 10, and memory and forgetting in Modules 11 and 12. Here we'll explore two other cognitive processes, thinking and language.

Thinking, which is sometimes referred to as reasoning, involves mental processes that are used to form concepts, solve problems, and engage in creative activities.

Language is a special form of communication in which we learn and use complex rules to form and manipulate symbols (words or gestures) that are used to generate an endless number of meaningful sentences.

In fact, thinking and using language are two things we do much better than animals (Hoff, 2005; Woodard, 2005).

What's Coming

We'll discuss how we form concepts, solve problems, think creatively, acquire language, and make decisions. We'll examine why people have difficulty recognizing words (dyslexia) and how language used by animals is different from the language of humans.

We'll begin with the interesting question of how Jeff learned to distinguish a rabbit from a dog, and a dog from a cat.

A. Forming Concepts

#1

Is it a dog, cat, or rabbit?

During your childhood, there was a time when every animal you saw was called a "dog." As a child, you gradually learned to tell the difference between a dog, a cat, and a rabbit by forming a different concept for each animal.

A *concept* is a way to group or classify objects, events, animals, or people based on some features, traits, or characteristics that they all share in common.

How you formed the concept of a dog or cat or rabbit has two different explanations: the exemplar model and the prototype theory (Nosofsky & Zaki, 2002; Olsson et al., 2004).

Exemplar Model

You easily recognize the animals on the left, but the question is How did you know which animal was which? Is it because your mind contains definitions of hundreds of animals?

The *exemplar model* says that you form a concept of an object, event, animal, or person by defining or making a mental list of the essential characteristics of a particular thing.

According to the exemplar model, you formed a concept of a dog, cat, or rabbit by learning its essential characteristics. The essential characteristics of a dog might include that it barks and has a long nose, two ears, two eyes, four legs, some hair, and usually a tail. Similarly, you made mental definitions for all animals. Then, when you looked at the three animals on the left, you automatically sorted through hundreds of animal definitions until you found one that included the essential properties of a dog, cat, or rabbit. Once you found the definition, you knew what the animal was. Although the exemplar model seems like a reasonable method of forming concepts, it has two serious problems.

One way to form concepts is to make definitions.

PROBLEMS WITH THE EXEMPLAR MODEL

Too many features. In real life, it is very difficult to list all the features that define any object (Rey, 1983). For example, if your list of features to define a dog wasn't complete, the list might also apply to wolves, jackals, coyotes, and skunks. If your list of features to define a dog included every possible feature, such a mental list would be complete but take so long to go through that it would be very slow to use. And worse, you would need a long list of defining features for each and every animal, person, and object. Such a great number of mental lists would tax the best of memories.

dog (dog, dag) *n.; pl.* **dogs, dog.**
1. any of a large and varied group of domesticated animals (*Canis familiaris*) that have four legs, a tail, two ears, prominent nose, a hairy coat, and a bark.

Too many exceptions. After making a list of defining features, you would also need to list all the exceptions that do not fit into the dictionary definition of dog. For example, some dogs rarely bark, some are very tiny, some are very large, some are hairless, and some are very fuzzy.

Because of these two problems, you would need to check two mental lists—a long list that contained all the defining features and another that contained all the exceptions—before finding the concept that correctly identified the animal, person, or object.

For these reasons, the exemplar model has generally been replaced by a different theory of how we form concepts: the prototype theory.

Prototype Theory

Please look at the three animals on the right, #1, #2, and #3. Despite the great differences in size, color, and facial features of these animals, prototype theory explains why you can easily and quickly recognize each one as a dog.

Prototype theory says that you form a concept by creating a mental image that is based on the average characteristics of an object. This "average" looking object is called a prototype. To identify a new object, you match it to one of your already formed prototypes of objects, people, or animals.

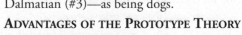
#2

#3

Based on many experiences, you develop prototypes of many different objects, persons, and animals (Rosch, 1978). For example, your prototype of a dog would be a mental image of any particular animal that has *average features* (nose, tail, ears, height, weight). By using your prototype of a dog, you can easily and quickly identify all three animals on the right—the large brown mutt (#1), the tiny Chihuahua (#2), and the colorful Dalmatian (#3)—as being dogs.

ADVANTAGES OF THE PROTOTYPE THEORY

Average features. One advantage of the prototype theory over the exemplar model is that you do not have to make a mental list of all the defining features of an object, which is often impossible. Instead, you form a prototype by creating a mental picture or image of the object, animal, or person that has only average features.

Another way to form concepts is to form prototypes.

Quick recognition. Another advantage of prototype theory is that it can result in quick recognition, as happened when you identified these different-looking animals (#1, #2, and #3) as dogs. The more a new object resembles a prototype, the more quickly you can identify it; the less it matches your prototype, the longer it takes to identify it.

#4

For example, what is the strange animal on the right, #4, and where is its head? Because this animal's features are not close to your dog prototype, it will take you some time to figure out that it has hair like "dreadlocks," its head is on the right, and it's an unusual dog (called a Puli).

Prototype theory, which explains that you form concepts by creating and using prototypes, is widely accepted and has generally replaced the exemplar model (Minda & Smith, 2001).

Next, we'll discuss when children begin forming concepts.

Early Formation

At the beginning of this module, we described how 14-month-old Jeff had already learned a number of concepts, such as juice, cookie, car, ball, apple, cat, dog, and bunny. Many children 10 to 16 months old can form concepts; that is, they can correctly identify

BLOCKS

By 10 to 16 months, infants learn a number of concepts.

different living things (cat, dog, rabbit) as animals and then place each living thing in the correct category (Quinn, 2002; Quinn & Oates, 2004).

Recent studies have reported that children develop many concepts or categories (animal, vegetable, face) by experiencing or interacting with objects and things in their environments, and children show their grasp of concepts even before they have developed much language ability (Mareschal & Quinn, 2001). For example, as 14-month-old Jeff (above photo) plays with different objects in his environment, he will learn that one kind of object is a nonliving thing called a block. Initially, a child's categories may be very broad, such as objects, people, animals, and events.

However, as children gain more experience with objects, animals, people, and things in their environments as well as develop increased language skills, which happens around age 5 (p. 315), they learn to form more complex concepts, such as the qualities of objects—*heavy, shiny, colorful, sweet, bitter*—and the position and placement of objects—*up, down, high, low.* The chances of a child interacting with a wide variety of objects and thus developing many concepts and categories are greatly increased by being raised in a stimulating environment, but chances are hindered in an impoverished one (Quinn, 2002).

Thus, the development and formation of concepts depend, in large part, on the child's opportunity to interact with the environment and, as you'll see next, in part on how the brain is neatly organized to process information into categories.

Categories in the Brain

A child's ability to form and develop concepts is helped not only by having a stimulating environment but also by how the brain is organized. Brain scans and brain stimulation of normal subjects and tests on brain-damaged individuals showed that different visual concepts, such as animals, faces, vegetables/fruits, and nonliving things, as well as auditory concepts, such as animal, human, and tool sounds, are processed and stored in different parts of the brain (Ilmberger et al., 2002; Lewis et al., 2005). Thus, as children interact with and learn to identify different objects, they can easily place different objects into different categories because the brain is already set up to store different categories in different areas (Ilmberger et al., 2002).

This process of placing things into categories occurs very quickly. For example, you quickly and easily recognize the three objects on the right as turtle, apple, and clown, and you easily place them into three different categories: animal, fruit, and person. Researchers explain that you were able to recognize these three things by matching each to your already formed prototypes of a turtle, apple, and clown (Squire & Knowlton, 1995).

One reason you are not aware of forming prototypes or classifying things into categories is that these cognitive processes occur at an unconscious level, which means that you are unaware of and cannot recall what is happening (p. 246). Evidence that forming prototypes and matching things to prototypes occur at an unconscious (implicit) level comes from studies that found that although amnesic patients were able to form prototypes and correctly match things to prototypes, they could not explain how they did it. Researchers concluded that using prototypes involves implicit processes, which we are not aware of and cannot voluntarily recall (Squire & Knowlton, 1995).

As you'll see, not being able to form concepts would make every day a very bad day.

animal

fruit

person

Brain is prewired to make categories.

Functions of Concepts

If you woke up one day to find that you had lost all your concepts, you would indeed have a very bad day. That's because concepts perform two important functions: They organize information and help us avoid relearning (Humphreys & Forde, 2001).

1 Organize information. Concepts allow you to group things into categories and thus better organize and store information in memory. For example, instead of having to store hundreds of mental images of many different kinds of dogs, you can store a single prototype of the average dog.

2 Avoid relearning. By having concepts that can be used to classify and categorize things, you can easily classify new things without having to relearn what each thing is. For example, once you have a concept for a dog, rabbit, cat, or cookie, you do not have to relearn what that thing is on each new encounter.

Without concepts, our cognitive worlds would consist of unconnected pieces of information. In fact, some forms of brain damage destroy a person's ability to form concepts, so that the person is unable to name or categorize what he or she sees (visual agnosia—see p. 79). By using concepts, you can identify, categorize, and store information very efficiently.

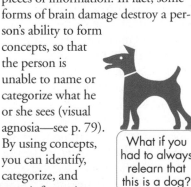

What if you had to always relearn that this is a dog?

There is no doubt that concepts are useful for identifying objects and helping us make sense of our world. Next, you'll see that concepts are valuable for solving problems and thinking creatively.

B. Solving Problems

How do experts solve problems?

In 1997, world chess champion, Garry Kasparov (photo below), lost a chess match for the first time to a powerful computer (McClain, 2005). He played another computer in 2003 and tied (three games each) (Byrne, 2003). This human-versus-computer chess match was all about thinking and problem solving.

Problem solving **involves searching for some rule, plan, or strategy that results in our reaching a certain goal that is currently out of reach.**

In previous matches, Kasparov had always beat the computer because he was the better thinker and problem solver. For Kasparov, as well as for most of us, problem solving involves three states:

> A computer that was unemotional, unconcerned, and uncaring beat me at chess!

(1) the *initial state,* which is thinking about the unsolved problem; (2) the *operations state,* which involves trying various rules or strategies to solve the problem; and (3) the *goal state,* which is reaching the solution. One plan used by expert problem solvers, such as Kasparov, is to think in broad terms of how to solve the problem, while less successful novices become too focused on specifics (Abernethy et al., 1994). For example, when novice players are in a difficult position, they may spend much time calculating possible moves, often planning many moves ahead, yet never find the best solution. An expert player has more knowledge of chess positions and examines fewer, but better, possibilities in much less time (P. E. Ross, 2006). Being a successful problem solver involves using different kinds of thinking, some of which can be progammed into a computer.

Different Ways of Thinking

Can a computer think?

In this man-machine chess match, Kasparov's thinking involved a combination of intuition (clever guesses based on years of experience) and creative mental shortcuts, called heuristics. The computer's "thinking" was more fixed because it has been programmed to use a set of rules that lead to specific outcomes, called algorithms. Solving problems by using algorithms or heuristics illustrates two very different ways of thinking (Lohman, 2000).

Algorithms

If you wanted to win at a variety of games, such as chess, checkers, or bridge, you would follow a fixed set of rules that are called algorithms *(AL-go-rhythms).*

Algorithms **are a fixed set of rules that, if followed correctly, will eventually lead to a solution.**

For example, learning to play chess involves following algorithms that define how pieces move and the results of those moves. The reason relatively few chess players become grand masters like Kasparov is that people vary in their ability to learn and use algorithms.

Initially, the computer was given little chance to beat world chess champion Kasparov because playing chess by using algorithms is a slow process. Instead of using algorithms, chess champion Kasparov was playing with a potentially more powerful set of rules called heuristics.

Heuristics

Kasparov's unique brain, together with his years of experience, allowed him to play chess using heuristics *(hyur-RIS-ticks).*

Heuristics **are rules of thumb, or clever and creative mental shortcuts, that reduce the number of operations and allow one to solve problems more easily and quickly.**

In the late 1990s, Kasparov's clever and creative shortcuts, or heuristics, had given him the advantage over the fixed and not so creative algorithms of computer programs. However, computers now have been programmed with new algorithms that increase their speed of "thinking" from analyzing 100,000 chess moves per second to 2.5 million. As a result of this increased speed, human chess grand masters, whose thinking focuses on using clever heuristics, no longer have a clear advantage over a computer's "thinking" ability (Boyce, 2002).

Besides being used to solve chess problems, heuristics are often used in daily life to make decisions or draw conclusions (Bailenson et al., 2000). A commonly used heuristic is called the availability heuristic.

The *availability heuristic* **says that we rely on information that is more prominent or easily recalled and overlook other information that is available but less prominent or notable.**

For example, the murder rate in the United States actually decreased in the late 1990s. However, during this time, network coverage of homicides increased 473%, which made news of murders more available and, according to the availability heuristic, led people to conclude that murder rates had become epidemic (Comarow, 2001).

Using the availability heuristic to make a decision means taking a mental shortcut. Although heuristics allow us to make quick decisions, they may result in bad decisions, since we make them using shortcuts, which limits the amount of information we use (F. Bower, 1997).

Artificial Intelligence

It took 50 years of effort before scientists learned how to program a computer that could beat Kasparov at chess. One goal of computer science is to develop *artificial intelligence*, which means programming machines (computers, robots) to imitate human thinking and problem-solving abilities.

For example, scientists recently developed a "thinking" program modeled on how the brain thinks (neural network). Scientists programmed a computer with this "thinking" program and the basic rules of checkers. In no time, the computer taught itself to play checkers at the expert level (Fogel, 2000). Can you imagine a computer teaching itself to play expert checkers? This represents a major breakthrough in artificial intelligence—teaching machines to think like humans.

What if you get stuck?

Most of us have had the experience of getting stuck while trying to solve a problem and wondering what to do next. By studying people who are good at problem solving, such as chess players, engineers, and computer programmers, psychologists have identified a number of useful strategies for solving problems. We'll discuss three problem-solving strategies—changing a mental set, using analogies, and forming subgoals. (Solutions to the first two problems appear on page 317.)

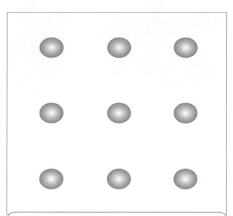

It takes new thinking to connect all dots with 4 straight lines without lifting pencil.

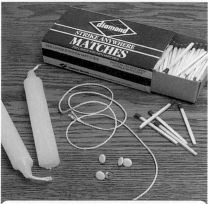

How would you mount a candle on the wall using what you see here?

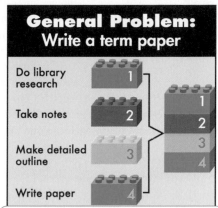

The best strategy for writing a term paper is to break the task into subgoals.

Changing One's Mental Set

Problem. Connect all nine dots shown above by drawing four straight lines without lifting your pencil from the paper or retracing any lines. If, like most people, you have difficulty solving this problem, it may be because of functional fixedness.

Functional fixedness **refers to a mental set that is characterized by the inability to see an object as having a function different from its usual one.**

For instance, you probably have a mental set that a straight line must begin and end on a dot. To solve the nine-dot problem, you need to break out of functional fixedness, which involves thinking of a line as continuing past a dot (Kershaw & Ohlsson, 2004).

The nine-dot puzzle is a good example of the kind of problem that is often solved in a sudden flash, known as insight, which we discussed earlier (p. 226).

Insight **is the sudden grasp of a solution after many incorrect attempts.**

You can increase your chances of solving a problem by insight if you consider the problem from many different viewpoints and unusual angles and if you decrease your anxiety and concern, which will in turn help you to overcome functional fixedness.

Using Analogies

Problem. Imagine that you have a box of matches, two candles, a piece of string, and several tacks, as shown in the photo above. How would you mount a candle on the wall so that it could be used as a light?

You may solve the candle problem in a flash of insight. However, most of us have to develop a strategy to solve the problem, and a good strategy may involve using an analogy.

An *analogy* **is a strategy for finding a similarity between the new situation and an old, familiar situation.**

If you adopt an analogy to solve the candle problem, here's how your thinking might proceed: "I'm familiar with using a shelf to hold a candle on the wall. Which of the objects—candle, string, or box—could serve as a shelf? If I remove the matches, I can tack the box to the wall."

As you gain more experience and knowledge, you become better at using analogies to solve problems. This is one reason that businesses prefer employees with experience: These employees are more likely to use analogies to solve problems.

What about the problem every student must face—writing a paper?

Forming Subgoals

Problem. Suppose your assignment is to write a term paper titled "Creativity and Madness." A useful strategy for writing this paper is to divide the assignment or general problem into a number of subgoals.

Using *subgoals* **is a strategy that involves breaking down the overall problem into separate parts that, when completed in order, will result in a solution.**

As shown in the figure above, the first subgoal is doing library research and finding a number of articles on creativity and madness. The second subgoal is reading the articles and taking notes. The third subgoal is making a detailed outline of the whole paper. A fourth subgoal is using your outline to write the paper. The strategy of working on and completing each specific subgoal makes the overall project more manageable and reduces unproductive worrying and complaining that can interfere with starting and completing your paper.

The strategy of setting specific goals to solve a problem has some advantages: Goals direct and focus your attention, help get you energized and motivated, and increase your persistence and lessen procrastination (Locke & Latham, 2002).

Another problem-solving strategy is to use creative thinking, our next topic.

C. Thinking Creatively

At the beginning of this module, we told you about Gordon Parks (left photo). Parks grew up in the 1920s, a time of segregation, discrimination, and lynchings. As a result of the way Blacks were treated in the 1920s, Parks received little formal schooling or professional help and was told that he should be happy just to look forward to a job as a porter. Despite overwhelming odds, Parks succeeded in writing two novels, four autobiographies, and four volumes of poetry, as well as directing three movies and composing several orchestral scores (Grundberg, 2006). Park was also an excellent photographer who had several exhibitions and also published a book of his incredible photographs (right photo) (Grundberg, 2006; Parks, 1997).

This intriguing story of Gordon Parks raises four interesting questions about creativity: How is creativity defined? Is IQ related to creativity? How do creative people think and behave? Is creativity related to psychological problems? Although there are more than 60 definitions of creativity, we'll begin with the one most commonly used (Boden, 1994).

Gordon Parks was a very creative person even in his 90s.

© The Gordon Parks, Courtesy Howard Greenburg Gallery, NYC

With little formal schooling, Gordon Parks became a very creative movie director, writer, composer, and photographer.

How Is Creativity Defined?

The definition of creative thinking is somewhat different from the definition of a creative individual.

Creative thinking **is a combination of flexibility in thinking and reorganization of understanding to produce innovative ideas and new or novel solutions (Sternberg, 2001).**

A *creative individual* **is someone who regularly solves problems, fashions products, or defines new questions that make an impact on his or her society (H. Gardner, 1993, 2006a).**

People can show evidence of creative thinking in many different ways. For example, recognized creative individuals include Albert Einstein, who formulated the theory of relativity; Michelangelo, who painted the Sistine Chapel; Sigmund Freud, who developed psychoanalysis; Dr. Seuss, who wrote rhyming books for children (and adults); the Rolling Stones, a well-known, 40-year-old rock-and-roll band; Ray Kroc, who founded McDonald's worldwide hamburger chain; and Gordon Parks, who is a writer, director, and photographer.

Because there are so many different examples (and kinds) of creativity, psychologists have used three different approaches to measure creativity: the psychometric, case study, and cognitive approaches (Sternberg & O'Hara, 2000).

Psychometric Approach

This approach, which uses objective problem-solving tasks to measure creativity, focuses on the distinction between two kinds of thinking—convergent and divergent (Guilford, 1967; Runco, 2004).

Convergent thinking **means beginning with a problem and coming up with a single correct solution.**

Examples of convergent thinking include answering multiple-choice questions and solving math problems. The opposite of convergent thinking is divergent thinking.

Divergent thinking **means beginning with a problem and coming up with many different solutions.**

For example, the two problem-solving tasks on page 309 (nine-dot and candle-match puzzles) are used to assess divergent thinking, which is a popular psychometric measure for creativity (Amabile, 1985; Camp, 1994).

Tests of divergent thinking have good reliability, which means that people achieve the same scores across time (Domino, 1994). However, tests of divergent thinking have low validity, which means that creative persons, such as Gordon Parks, may not necessarily score high on psychometric tests of creativity (H. Gardner, 1993).

Case Study Approach

Because the psychometric approach is limited to using objective tests, it provides little insight into creative minds. In comparison, the case study approach analyzes creative persons in great depth and thus provides insight into their development, personality, motivation, and problems.

For example, Howard Gardner (1993) used the case study approach to analyze seven creative people, including Sigmund Freud. Gardner found that creative people are creative in certain areas but poor in others: Freud was very creative in linguistic and personal areas but very poor in spatial and musical areas. Although case studies provide rich insight into creative minds, their findings may be difficult to generalize: Freud's kind of creativity may or may not apply to Gordon Parks's remarkable achievements (Freyd, 1994).

Cognitive Approach

Although case studies provide detailed portraits of creative people, the findings are very personal or subjective and not easily applied to others. In comparison, the cognitive approach tries to build a bridge between the objective measures of the psychometric approach and the subjective descriptions provided by case studies. The cognitive approach, which is also the newest, identifies and measures cognitive mechanisms that are used during creative thinking (Freyd, 1994).

For example, many individuals have reported that one cognitive mechanism vital to creative thinking is the use of mental imagery, which involves thinking in images, without words or mathematical symbols (Finke, 1993). Thus, the cognitive approach involves analyzing the workings of mental imagery and its relationship to creative thinking.

Now, let's see what these three approaches say about creativity.

Is IQ Related to Creativity?

In some cases, such as Michelangelo, Sigmund Freud, and Albert Einstein, creativity seems to be linked to genius. However, creativity is not the same as intelligence, as best illustrated by savants.

Savants refer to about 10% of autistic individuals who show some incredible memory, music, or drawing talent.

Despite their creativity, many savants score below 70 on IQ tests (the average score is 100). For instance, the detailed drawing of a famous Russian church (right photo) was done by Chris, a 16-year-old savant who has little knowledge or use of language and whose IQ is 52 (Sacks, 1995). Studies show that savants lack verbal intelligence but excel in visual intelligence and that their right hemispheres are more active than their left during creative activities (Treffert & Wallace, 2002).

Drawn by a 16-year-old savant with an IQ of 52

Instead of linking creativity to genius, some psychologists believe that creativity involves relatively ordinary cognitive processes that result in extraordinary products (Weisberg, 1993). These creative products include inventions (Post-its, genetic crops), new drugs (Viagra), and computer software (video games).

Compared with the general population, creative scientists, writers, and artists generally score above average, with IQs of 120 and higher. However, when IQs of creative individuals are compared among themselves, there is little correlation between creativity and IQ. In other words, those who are generally recognized as creative do tend to have above-average IQ scores, but those with the highest IQs are not necessarily those who are the most creative (Sternberg & O'Hara, 2000).

How Do Creative People Think and Behave?

Researchers have studied creative individuals to identify what is unusual about their work habits and psychological traits (Helson, 1996; Simonton, 2000). Here are some of their findings.

Focus. Creative people tend to be superior in one particular area, such as dance, music, art, science, or writing, rather than many areas. For example, Einstein (drawing at right) was superior in the logical-spatial area—the theory of relativity ($E = mc^2$)—but poor in the personal area—developing close relationships.

Cognition. Creative individuals have the ability to change mental directions, consider problems from many angles, and make use of mental images. They are also interested in solving unusual problems.

$$E = mc^2$$

Creative people can consider problems from different viewpoints and are driven by strong internal goals.

Personality. On the positive side, creative people tend to be independent, self-confident, unconventional, risk-taking, hard-working, and obsessively committed to their work. On the negative side, they tend to have large egos that make them insensitive to the needs of others. They may pursue their goals at the expense of others, and they may be so absorbed in their work that they exclude others.

Motivation. They are driven by internal values or personal goals; this is called intrinsic motivation. They are less concerned about external rewards such as money or recognition, which is called extrinsic motivation. They are motivated by the challenge of solving problems; their reward is the satisfaction of accomplishment. On average, creative people work on a project for about ten years before reaching their creative peaks.

One question often asked about creative people is whether their creative fires are fueled by psychological or mental problems, such as mood disorders.

Is Creativity Related to Mental Disorders?

There are numerous historical reports of a link between creativity and madness or insanity, more correctly called mental disorders. For example, Mark Twain (Samuel Clemens), Tennessee Williams, Ernest Hemingway, Cole Porter, Edgar Allan Poe, and Hermann Hesse were all reported to suffer from either depression or manic-depression (swings between euphoria and depression) (Jamison, 1995).

A more formal study of 291 creative writers, artists, composers, thinkers, and scientists indicated that 17–46% suffered from mental disorders, especially mood disorders. As the graph on the right shows, writers had the highest percentage of mental disorders, especially alcoholism and depression (R. Post, 1994).

A number of studies indicate that highly creative people experience major mood disorders more often than other groups in the general population (Jamison, 1995). But does the mood disorder contribute to creativity? One study found that

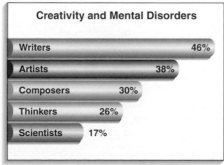

Creativity and Mental Disorders

Writers	46%
Artists	38%
Composers	30%
Thinkers	26%
Scientists	17%

parents with manic-depression (dramatic mood swings), as well as their children, obtained higher scores on tests of creativity than did normal parents and children (Simeonova et al., 2005). This and other research suggests that severe mood change could contribute to creativity by sharpening thoughts and broadening the person's emotional, intellectual, and perceptual views of the world (Jamison, 1995).

Although mental disorders may provide a sense of discomfort that may motivate creative activity, there are many creative individuals (writers) who have achieved creative breakthroughs without having severe emotional problems (J. C. Kaufman & Baer, 2002).

Next, we turn to an important component of creative activities, the development of language.

D. Language: Basic Rules

How many languages are there?

Our ability to use language is one of the most remarkable features of our species (McIntosh & Lobaugh, 2003). Currently, people are believed to speak about 6,900 different languages, but it is estimated that by the next century nearly half of the languages will be extinct (S. Anderson, 2004; Gordon, 2005).

Language is a special form of communication that involves learning complex rules to make and combine symbols (words or gestures) into an endless number of meaningful sentences.

The reason language is such a successful form of communication arises from two amazingly simple principles—words and grammar.

A *word* is an arbitrary pairing between a sound or symbol and a meaning.

For example, the word *parrot* does not look like, sound like, or fly like a parrot, but it refers to a bird we call a parrot because all of us memorized this pairing as children. Young adults are estimated to have about 60,000 such pairings or words in their mental dictionar-

Why is this called a parrot?

ies (Pinker, 1995). However, these 60,000 symbols or words are rather useless unless the users follow similar rules of grammar.

Grammar refers to a set of rules for combining words into phrases and sentences to express an infinite number of thoughts that can be understood by others.

For instance, our mental rules of grammar immediately tell us that the headline "Parrot Bites Man's Nose" means something very different from "Man Bites Parrot's Nose." It may seem surprising, but speakers of all 6,900 languages learned the same four rules.

Four Rules of Language

As children, each of us learned, without much trouble, the four rules of language. Now, as adults, we use these rules without being aware of how or when we use them. To illustrate the four rules of language, we'll use the word *caterpillar*. As a child, you may have watched its strange crawling motion, or perhaps you were even brave enough to pick one up.

1 The first language rule governs phonology.

Phonology (FOE-nawl-uh-gee) specifies how we make the meaningful sounds that are used by a particular language. Any English word can be broken down into phonemes.

Phonemes (FOE-neems) are the basic sounds of consonants and vowels.

For example, the various sounds of *c* and *p* represent different phonemes, which are some of the sounds in the word *caterpillar*. At about 6 months old, babies begin to babble and make basic sounds, or phonemes. We combine phonemes to form words by learning the second rule.

2 The second language rule governs morphology.

Morphology (mor-FAWL-uh-gee) is the system that we use to group phonemes into meaningful combinations of sounds and words.

A *morpheme (MOR-feem)* is the smallest meaningful combination of sounds in a language.

For example, a morpheme may be
a word, such as **cat,**
a letter, such as the **s** in cats,
a prefix, such as the **un-** in **un**breakable,
or a suffix, such as the -**ed** in walk**ed.**

The word **caterpillar** is actually one morpheme, and the word **caterpillars** is two (**caterpillar-s**). After we learn to combine morphemes to form words, we learn to combine words into meaningful sentences by using the third rule.

Learning and using the word *caterpillar* involve four basic rules.

3 The third language rule governs syntax, or grammar.

Syntax, or *grammar,* is a set of rules that specifies how we combine words to form meaningful phrases and sentences.

For example, why doesn't the following sentence make sense?

Caterpillars green long and are.

You instantly realize that this sentence is nonsensical or ungrammatical because it doesn't follow the English grammar rules regarding where we place verbs and conjunctions. If you apply the rules of English grammar, you would rearrange the combination of words to read: "Caterpillars are long and green." Although you may not be able to list all the rules of grammar, you automatically follow them when you speak. One way you know whether the word *bear* is a noun or a verb is by using the fourth rule.

4 The fourth language rule governs semantics.

Semantics (si-MANT-iks) specifies the meanings of words or phrases when they appear in various sentences or contexts.

For instance, as you read "Did Pat pat a caterpillar's back?" how do you know what the word **pat** means, since it appears twice in succession. From your knowledge of semantics, you know that the first **Pat** is a noun and the name of a person, while the second **pat** is a verb, which signals some action.

Somehow you knew that the same word, **pat,** had very different meanings depending on the context. How you know what words mean in different contexts is a very intriguing question.

PowerStudy 4.0™

Module 4
D. Control Centers: Four
   Lobes
Module 10
F. Biological Factors

Understanding Language

One of the great mysteries of using and understanding language can be demonstrated by the following two simple but very different sentences:

You picked up a caterpillar.

A caterpillar was picked up by you.

Despite a different word order, you know that these two sentences mean exactly the same thing. How you know that these different sentences mean exactly the same thing was explained by linguist Noam Chomsky (1957). We'll discuss two of Chomsky's revolutionary principles—mental grammar and innate brain program—that allow us to use and understand spoken language with relative ease (Bever & Montalbetti, 2002).

Mental grammar. Almost every sentence we speak or understand is formed from a brand-new combination of words. Chomsky pointed out that the brain does not have the capacity to contain a list of all the sentences we will ever use. Instead, Chomsky argued that the brain contains a program or *mental grammar* that allows us to combine nouns, verbs, and objects in an endless variety of meaningful sentences. Chomsky's principle of mental grammar answers the question of how we can so easily create so many different sentences. The second question that Chomsky answered was: How do we acquire this mental grammar?

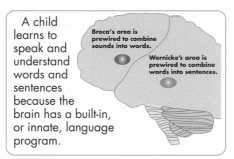

A child learns to speak and understand words and sentences because the brain has a built-in, or innate, language program.

Broca's area is prewired to combine sounds into words.

Wernicke's area is prewired to combine words into sentences.

Innate brain program. How is it possible that 4-year-old children, with no formal schooling and relatively limited instruction from their parents, can speak and understand an endless variety of sentences? For example, the average 4-year-old child can already determine that the sentence "The caterpillar crept slowly across the leaf" is correct but that the sentence "The crept leaf caterpillar slowly the across" is meaningless. Chomsky's answer is that young children can learn these complex and difficult rules of grammar because our brains come with a built-in, or *innate, program* that makes learning the general rules of grammar relatively easy (p. 229). The brain's innate program for learning rules of grammar explains how a child learns most of the complex and difficult rules of grammar by the age of 4 or 5. However, it is the interaction between the gradual development of the brain's innate program and a child's range of environmental experiences that results in learning the complicated rules of grammar (Schlaggar et al., 2002).

But how does an innate grammar program, which could be used by any child in any culture, specify the rules for forming and understanding an endless number of meaningful sentences? Chomsky's answer is perhaps his cleverest contribution.

Different Structure, Same Meaning

One of the most difficult questions that Chomsky had to answer was how an idea can be expressed in several different ways, with different grammatical structures, yet mean the same thing.

He answered this question by making a distinction between two different structures of a sentence: surface structure and deep structure.

Surface structure refers to the actual wording of a sentence, as it is spoken.

Deep structure refers to an underlying meaning that is not spoken but is present in the mind of the listener.

We can illustrate the difference between surface and deep structures with our same two sentences:

You picked up a caterpillar.

A caterpillar was picked up by you.

Notice that these two sentences have different *surface structures,* which means they are worded differently. However, according to Chomsky, you are able to look underneath the different surface structures of the two sentences and recognize that they have the same *deep structure,* which is why you know they have the same meaning.

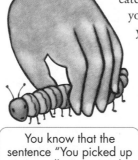

You know that the sentence "You picked up a caterpillar" means the same as "A caterpillar was picked up by you" because you recognize that both have the same deep structure.

Chomsky argues that we learn to shift back and forth between surface and deep structure by applying transformational rules.

Transformational rules are procedures by which we convert our ideas from surface structures into deep structures and from deep structures back into surface ones.

For example, when you hear the two sentences about picking up the caterpillar, you transform the words into their deep structure, which you store in memory. Later, when someone asks what the person did, you use transformational rules to convert the deep structure in your memory back into a surface structure, which can be expressed in differently worded sentences. The distinction between surface and deep structures is part of Chomsky's theory of language.

Chomsky's theory of language says that all languages share a common universal grammar and that children inherit a mental program to learn this universal grammar.

Chomsky's theory of language, which is widely accepted today, was considered a major breakthrough in explaining how we acquire and understand language (Baker, 2002). However, one criticism of Chomsky's theory is that he downplays the importance of different environmental opportunities for hearing and practicing sounds, which have been shown to interact with and influence language development (Schlaggar et al., 2002).

Chomsky's idea of an innate mental grammar would predict that children around the world should go through the same stages of language development. Can this be true for all 6,900 languages?

E. Acquiring Language

What do children's brains do?

If Chomsky is correct that all children inherit the same innate program for learning grammar, then we would expect children from around the world to go through similar stages in developing language and acquiring the rules for using language. And in fact, all children, no matter the culture or the language, do go through the same stages (Pinker, 1994).

Language stages refer to all infants going through four different periods or stages—babbling, single words, two-word combinations, and sentences. All children go through these four stages in the same order, and in each stage, children show new and more complex language skills.

The occurrence of each of the four stages is associated with further development of the brain. At birth, an infant's brain has almost all of its neurons but they have not yet made all their connections (adult brains can grow some new neurons—p. 49).

For example, a 6-month-old infant's brain (left figure) has few neural interconnections, which are associated with performing relatively

6-month-old brain has few connections.

simple behaviors, such as babbling. In comparison, a 24-month-old infant's brain (right figure) has hundreds of neural interconnections, which are associated with more complex behaviors, such as using two-word combinations (Ropper & Brown, 2005).

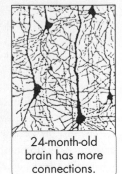
24-month-old brain has more connections.

Here are the four stages that each of us went through in learning to speak and understand the language of our parents or caregivers.

Four Stages in Acquiring Language

1 Babbling

One of the key features in human development is that infants begin to make sounds long before they can say real words. Infants repeat the same sounds over and over, and these sounds are commonly called babbling.

Babbling, which begins at about 6 months, is the first stage in acquiring language. Babbling refers to making one-syllable sounds, such as "deedeedee" or "bababa," which are most common across all languages.

Bababa

A 6-month-old brain has limited capacity for language.

Babbling is an example of an innate "sound" program in the brain that is involved in making and processing sounds that will eventually be used to form words. Researchers have discovered that by 6 months of age, infants have already learned to discriminate between sounds, such as *ba* from *pa,* and to distinguish sounds in their native language from those used in a foreign language (F. Bower, 2000). These findings indicate that, at an early age, infants have already become accustomed to making and hearing sounds that make up their native languages. At about 9 months, babbling sounds begin to resemble more the vowels and consonants that children will actually use in speaking their native languages.

In children who can hear, babbling is oral. In deaf children who have been exposed only to the sign language of their deaf parents, babbling is manual and not oral. That is, these babies babble by repeating the same hand sign over and over (Petitto & Marentette, 1991). This means that the brain has an innate program for acquiring language, whether spoken or sign language.

Through endless babbling, infants learn to control their vocal apparatus so that they can make, change, and repeat sounds and imitate the sounds of their parents or caregivers (Hoff, 2005). After babbling, infants begin to say their first words.

2 Single Word

Shortly before 1 year of age, an infant usually performs a behavior that every parent has been eagerly waiting for: to hear the child's first word. At about 1 year of age, infants begin not only to understand words but also to say single words.

Single words mark the second stage in acquiring language, which occurs at about 1 year of age. Infants say single words that usually refer to what they can see, hear, or feel.

An infant's ability to form sounds into words begins at about 8 months and results from an interaction between the brain's innate language program and the infant's experience with hearing sounds (Jusczyk & Hohne, 1997). About half the infant's single words refer to objects (juice, cookie, doll, dada), and the other half refer to actions, routines, or motions (up, eat, hot, more) (Pinker, 1994). The infant's single words, such as "Milk" or "Go," often stand for longer thoughts such as "I want milk" or "I want to go out."

Milk. Go.

As the infant learns to say words, parents usually respond by speaking in a specific way called parentese (motherese).

Parentese (motherese) is a way of speaking to young children in which the adult speaks in a slower and higher than normal voice, emphasizes and stretches out each word, uses very simple sentences, and repeats words and phrases.

A 1-year-old brain has more connections and more capacity for language.

In a study of mothers in the United States, Russia, and Sweden, researchers found that when talking to their infants, these mothers exaggerated certain sounds (vowel sounds), which they did not do when speaking to their husbands (Kuhl et al., 1997). Another researcher, who spent ten years traveling around the world to record child–parent interactions, concludes that parentese has two functions: getting an infant's attention and stimulating infants to make sounds they will need to speak themselves (Fernald, 1992).

Next, the young child begins to combine words.

3 Two-Word Combinations

Starting around age 2, children begin using single words that they have learned to form two-word combinations.

Two-word combinations, **which represent the third stage in acquiring language, occur at about 2 years of age. Two-word combinations are strings of two words that express various actions ("Me play," "See boy") or relationships ("Hit ball," "Milk gone").**

Hit ball. Me play.

Each of the two words provides a hint about what the child is saying. In addition, the relationship between the two words gives hints about what the child is communicating. For example, "See boy" tells us to look at a specific object; "Daddy shirt" tells us that something belongs to Daddy. The child's new ability to communicate by combining two words and changing their order marks the beginning of learning the rules of grammar. From about 2 years of age through adolescence, a child learns an average of a new word every 2 hours (Pinker, 1994).

A child's language development is partly dependent on how responsive the parent or caretaker is. A responsive parent shows more contact, awareness, and warmth during the child's verbal interactions. For example, infants whose mothers were more responsive to their speech at 13 months had more advanced language abilities, including larger vocabularies at 21 months, compared to children of less responsive mothers (Tamis-LeMonda et al., 2001).

A 2-year-old brain has many connections and more capacity for language.

By the age of 2, a child may have a vocabulary of more than 50 words, many of which will be used in two-word combinations. Although children usually go through a stage of forming single words and then two-word combinations, there is no three-word stage. Instead, at a certain point the child will begin to form sentences, which gradually increase in length through the fourth year.

4 Sentences

Children make a rather large language leap when they progress from relatively simple two-word combinations to using longer and more complex sentences.

Sentences, **which represent the fourth stage of acquiring language, occur at about 4 years of age. Sentences range from three to eight words in length and indicate a growing knowledge of the rules of grammar.**

However, a child's first sentences differ from adult sentences in that the child may omit the "small words" and speak in a pattern that is called telegraphic speech.

Telegraphic speech **is a distinctive pattern of speaking in which the child omits articles** *(the),* **prepositions** *(in, out),* **and parts of verbs.**

For example, an adult may say, "I'm going to the store." A 3- to 4-year-old child may use telegraphic speech (omit article) and say, "I go to store." However, by the time children are 4 or 5 years old, the structure of their sentences improves and indicates that they have learned the basic rules of grammar.

Basic rules of grammar **are the rules for combining nouns, verbs, adjectives, and other parts of speech to form meaningful sentences.**

However, as children learn the rules of grammar, they often make errors of overgeneralization.

I goed to store. I want blue toy.

Overgeneralization **means applying a grammatical rule to cases where it should not be used.**

For example, after a child learns the rule of forming the past tense of many verbs by adding a *d* sound to the end, he or she may overgeneralize this rule and add a *d* to the past tense of irregular verbs (and say, for instance, "I goed to store"). By the time children enter school, they usually have a good grasp of the general rules of their language.

A 4- to 5-year-old brain has significantly more connections so that a child can learn the basic rules of complex grammar.

Going through the Stages

How fast does a child go through the stages?

Parents or caregivers sometimes worry about whether their child is late in developing language. In the real world, normal children pass through the four stages of language at a pace that can vary by a year or more. However, as Chomsky's theory predicts and research has shown, all normal children pass through the four stages, even though some of the stages may begin later or last for shorter or longer periods of time (Pinker, 1994).

As children proceed through the stages, there is a continuous interaction between environmental stimuli and brain development. For example, researchers used brain scans to identify maximum neural activity in 3-month-old infants who were listening to recordings of

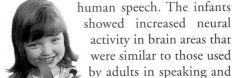

1. Babbling   2. Single word   3. Two words   4. Sentences

human speech. The infants showed increased neural activity in brain areas that were similar to those used by adults in speaking and understanding language (Dehaene-Lambertz et al., 2002). This study shows how environmental stimulation—hearing language sounds—activated the "language areas" of infants' brains long before infants actually begin speaking. This study is a good example of how the brain and environment interact in the development of spoken language and points out the importance of caregivers regularly talking to (verbally stimulating) their infants.

Next, we'll discuss a number of innate (genetic) and environmental interactions that are important in the development of language.

E. Acquiring Language

PowerStudy 4.0™

Module 4
D. Control Centers: Four
Lobes

How does a child learn a particular language? It is quite amazing how children from different countries around the world, such as Bali, China, Nigeria, Sweden, Japan, United States, Mexico, France, Spain, Russia, and Thailand (right photo),

How did he learn to speak Thai?

can acquire the sounds, words, and rules of their particular native language. Each child learns his or her own native language because of an interaction between innate (genetic) and environmental (learning) factors.

What Are Innate Factors?

All children go through the same four language stages because of innate language factors (Albert et al., 2000).

Innate language factors **are genetically programmed physiological and neurological features that facilitate our making speech sounds and acquiring language skills.**

We'll examine three innate language features that work together so that we can learn to speak and use language.

Innate physiological features. We have a specially adapted vocal apparatus (larynx and pharynx) that allows us to make sounds and form words. In comparison, the structures of gorillas' and chimpanzees' vocal apparatus prevent them from making the wide variety of sounds necessary to form words (Lessmoellmann, 2006; Pinker, 1994). Without specialized vocal apparatus, humans would be limited to making "animal" sounds.

Innate neurological features. When people speak or use sign language, certain brain areas are activated. The PET scan above shows a side view of the brain: red and yellow indicate the most neural activity (Petitto, 1997). These findings indicate that the left hemisphere of

The brain is genetically programmed to speak and understand.

the brain is prewired to acquire and use language, whether spoken or signed. In Module 4, we explained how damage to these same language areas (Broca's and Wernicke's areas) disrupts the use and understanding of language (p. 78). Although your brain is prewired for language, there is a best, or critical, time for learning a language.

Innate developmental factors. Researchers have discovered that there is a critical period when acquiring language is the easiest (Stromswold, 1995).

The *critical language period* **is the time from infancy to adolescence when language is easiest to learn. Language is usually more difficult to learn anytime after adolescence.**

For example, immigrant children do very well learning English as a second language, while immigrant adults, who are past the critical period, have more difficulty and do less well (Jackendoff, 1994). The critical period for learning language also explains why learning your native language was easy as a child but, as an adult, learning a foreign language is many times more difficult.

Innate biological factors provide the programming so a child can acquire any one of 6,900 languages. Which particular language the child learns depends on his or her environment (parents).

What Are Environmental Factors?

Social interactions. How each child learns a particular language depends on social interactions, one of the environmental factors.

Environmental language factors **refer to interactions children have with parents, peers, teachers, and others who provide feedback that rewards and encourages language development, as well as provides opportunities for children to observe, imitate, and practice language skills.**

What would happen if a child was deprived of almost all social interactions from ages 1 to 13? Such was the case with Genie, whose mentally disturbed father strapped her to a potty chair in a back room, punished her for making any sounds, and forbid the mother or brother to talk to her. When discovered at age 13 by a social worker, Genie could not speak a single word (Curtiss, 1977). Genie's case illustrates that even though children are prewired by heredity to speak a language, they need certain environmental stimuli, such as listening, speaking, and interacting with others, in order to learn to speak and use language. Genie's case also illustrates the importance of social cognitive learning.

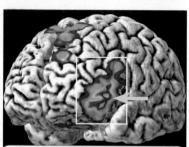

Parentese provides needed stimulation and feedback.

Social cognitive learning **emphasizes the acquisition of language skills through social interactions, which give children a chance to observe, imitate, and practice the sounds, words, and sentences they hear from their parents or caregivers.**

For example, within eight months of training, Genie had acquired a vocabulary of about 200 words. However, Genie's long period of social deprivation left its mark, and even after years of continued social interactions, her language ability did not develop much beyond that of a 2- or 3-year-old child (J. C. Harris, 1995).

Parentese. Researchers found that children who had the biggest vocabularies and performed best on developmental language tests were those whose parents were the most talkative during the child's first two years (Hart & Risley, 1996). These studies show the importance of environmental factors, such as parents stimulating and encouraging language development by speaking in parentese and being responsive to what their child says (Tamis-LeMonda et al., 2001). (We'll discuss parentese further in Critical Thinking on page 326.) These studies indicate that environmental and innate factors interact with and influence a child's ability to acquire language.

When children master language, they have a powerful tool for thinking, as we'll discuss after the Concept Review.

✔ Concept Review

dog (dog, dag) *n.; pl.* **dogs, dog.**
1. any of a large and varied group of domesticated animals (*Canis familiaris*) that have four legs, a tail, two ears, prominent nose, a hairy coat, and a bark.

1. If you form a concept of an object, event, or characteristic by making a list of the properties that define it, you are forming a concept according to the _____ model.

2. If you form a concept by putting together the average characteristics of an object and then seeing whether a new object matches your average object, you are forming a concept according to (a)_____ theory. If you develop an idea of a dog of average age, height, weight, and color, you have formed a (b)_____ of a dog.

3. If you search for some rule, plan, or strategy that results in your reaching a certain goal that is currently out of reach, you are engaging in an activity called (a)_____ During this activity, you go through three states: contemplating the unsolved problem, which is the (b)_____ state; trying out various operations, rules, or strategies to solve the problem, which is the (c)_____ state; and reaching the solution, which is the (d)_____ state.

Answers to problems on page 309

4. Some problems can be solved by following certain rules. If you correctly follow rules that lead to a certain solution, you are using (a)_____. If you follow rules that reduce the number of operations or allow you to take shortcuts in solving problems, you are using (b)_____.

5. When you use a combination of flexibility in thinking and reorganization of understanding to produce innovative ideas and solutions, you are engaging in (a)_____. If you begin with a problem and come up with many different solutions, you are using (b)_____ thinking, which is one definition of creative thinking. The opposite of this type of thinking is beginning with a problem and coming up with the one correct solution; this is called (c)_____ thinking.

6. A system of symbols that we use in thinking, solving problems, and communicating with others is called (a)_____. There are four rules for learning and using language. How we make the meaningful sounds used by a particular language is covered by the rules of (b)_____. Any English word can be broken down into basic sounds of consonants and vowels, which are called (c)_____. How we group phonemes into meaningful combinations of sounds and words is covered by the rules of (d)_____. The smallest meaningful combination of sounds in a language is called a (e)_____. How we combine words to form meaningful phrases and sentences is specified by the rules of (f)_____. How we know the meanings of words in various contexts is covered by the rules of (g)_____.

7. Chomsky explained that a sentence can be stated in different ways and yet have the same meaning. The actual wording of a sentence is called its (a)_____ structure. The underlying meaning of the sentence that is not spoken but is present in the mind of the listener is called the (b)_____ structure. To convert our ideas from surface structures into deep structures and from deep structures back into surface ones, we use (c)_____ rules.

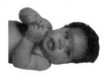

8. In acquiring language, all children go through the same four stages but at different rates. Beginning at about the age of 6 months, a baby begins making one-syllable sounds, such as "bababa," which is called (a)_____. By about 1 year of age, a child forms (b)_____ words, which usually refer to what the child can see, hear, or feel. At about 2 years of age, a child makes (c)_____, which are strings of two words that express various actions ("Me play") or relationships ("Hit ball," "Milk gone"). At about 4 years of age, a child begins forming sentences, which range from three to eight words in length and indicate a growing knowledge of the rules of (d)_____.

9. One reason all children acquire a language in the same order is that there are genetically programmed physiological and neurological features in the brain and vocal apparatus. These are known as (a)_____ factors. Social interactions between the child and others, which offer opportunities for observation, imitation, and practice, are called (b)_____ factors.

Answers: *1. exemplar model; 2. (a) prototype, (b) prototype; 3. (a) problem solving, (b) initial, (c) operations, (d) goal; 4. (a) algorithms, (b) heuristics; 5. (a) creative thinking, (b) divergent, (c) convergent; 6. (a) language, (b) phonology, (c) phonemes, (d) morphology, (e) morpheme, (f) syntax or grammar, (g) semantics; 7. (a) surface, (b) deep, (c) transformational; 8. (a) babbling, (b) single, (c) two-word combinations, (d) grammar or syntax; 9. (a) innate, (b) environmental*

F. Decisions, Thought & Language

How do we make decisions?

We make many decisions each day. Some decisions have very important consequences in our lives, such as choosing a college, career, or spouse. Other decisions have much less importance, such as choosing a flavor of ice cream, the color of a shirt, or a movie to watch. We would like to believe that we make decisions, especially important ones, based on thoughtful reasoning. But how do we actually make decisions?

Imagine that you are in the hospital and a doctor tells you about your treatment options. One of the treatments involves surgery, and you must decide

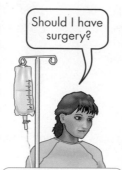

Should I have surgery?

Emotions influence treatment decisions.

whether you want to undergo surgery. Would your decision be influenced differently if a doctor tells you that the survival rate of surgery is 80% *or* that there is a 20% chance of dying from surgery? Even though both statements express the same risk, the 80% chance of survival sounds more appealing than the 20% chance of dying. Thinking about the success of surgery is comforting, but thinking about the failure of surgery makes us uncomfortable (De Martino, 2006a).

Research does show that we often base our decisions on emotion rather than intellect (Vergano, 2006). As we discuss next, recent research on gambling shows what happens in our brains as we make decisions.

Gambling Decisions

Benedetto De Martino (2006b) and his team of researchers (2006) at the University College of London took brain scans of men and women while they were being asked to make a decision about whether or not to gamble. At the start of the study each subject was given about $100. They were then told they could either *"keep"* 40% of their money or *"lose"* 60% of their money if they did not gamble. When subjects were told they could *"keep"* 40% of their money if they chose to not gamble, subjects gambled only 43% of the time. When told they could *"lose"* 60% of their money if they did not gamble, subjects gambled 62% of the time. Even when the chances of winning and losing were identical, the wording of the instructions made a difference in the subjects' decisions.

Gambling decisions are ruled by emotions, not rational thinking.

The results of brain scans showed that the part of the brain responsible for strong negative emotions (amygdala) was very active while subjects were making their decisions, regardless of the choice they made. Researchers concluded that emotions had a strong influence on how subjects made gambling decisions. Further support for the significant role of emotions in decision making comes from research studies showing that people who lack emotions due to brain trauma or injury often have serious difficulties making even simple decisions (A. Damasio, 2006).

Emotions have the power to rule our choices about gambling as well as many other choices we make in life, including how we make political decisions.

Political Decisions

Hillary Clinton and Barack Obama (see right photos) are both Democratic senators who declared their candidacy for president of the United States. How would you decide which candidate to vote for? Would you be able to base your vote only on an objective evaluation of their political positions, or would you be influenced by your feelings about having the first woman or the first African American man be president of the United States?

During presidential elections, people make difficult decisions about which candidate to vote for, and although people may try to make their decisions objectively, a recent research study shows that our political decisions are significantly influenced by our emotions. During the 2004 presidential election, a group of "strong" Republicans and a group of "strong" Democrats were asked to evaluate statements made by George W. Bush (Republican) and

Which would guide your decision to choose between Hillary Clinton (left) and Barack Obama (right) for president—objective thinking or biased emotions?

John Kerry (Democrat) in which both candidates contradicted themselves. Results showed that subjects were not critical of their own candidate, but those who were Republicans were as critical of Kerry as Democrats were of Bush. Brain scans showed that during the task, the part of the brain where reasoning takes place was inactive and subjects made completely biased conclusions by ignoring information that could not be disputed. The most active part of subjects' brains during the task was where emotions are processed, and after subjects made a decision, the part of the brain related to experiencing pleasure and reward was activated (Westen, 2006a, 2006b).

We know emotions can influence or bias our decisions. Because words are so much a part of our reasoning process, we need to know if and how much words can influence or bias our thinking.

Does language influence thinking?

Almost everyone has heard it said that the Inuit (Eskimos) are supposed to have dozens of words for snow because their survival depends on knowing how to travel and hunt in different kinds of snow. This particular observation was first made by amateur linguist Benjamin Whorf (1956), who noticed that languages differed in their vocabularies depending on how much emphasis they gave to different objects and events in their environment. For example, Whorf reasoned that because the Inuit (Eskimos) have many names for snow, they must be able to perceive many more kinds of snow than Americans, for whom snow conditions are less important. On the basis of these kinds of observations, Whorf formulated the theory of linguistic relativity.

The *theory of linguistic relativity* states that the differences among languages result in similar differences in how people think and perceive the world.

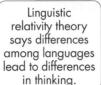

Linguistic relativity theory says differences among languages lead to differences in thinking.

For example, according to the theory of linguistic relativity, people whose language divides colors into only two categories (dark or black and bright or white) should perceive fewer colors. In comparison, people whose language divides colors into eleven categories (black, white, red, yellow, green, blue, brown, purple, pink, orange, gray) should perceive many more colors in their environment. However, researchers discovered that although languages differ in their number of color categories, all languages divide colors into the same basic categories. According to Whorf's theory of linguistic relativity, we would have expected people to perceive colors differently, depending on whether their culture has two or eleven names, but this is not what researchers found (Davies & Corbett, 1997). Thus, people in different cultures seem to perceive colors in similar ways even if they do not have names for different colors (Pinker, 1994).

Now, let's examine Whorf's famous claim that Inuits have more words for snow than do Americans.

Inuit Versus American Words for Snow

In his original article, Whorf (1940) estimated that Inuit (Eskimos) have about seven words for snow: *falling snow, snow on the ground, snow packed hard like ice, slushy snow, drifting snow, snow drift,* and *wind-driven flying snow,* while most Americans use a single word, *snow.* Whorf reasoned that the Inuit's larger vocabulary of snow-related words should make them think and perceive snow very differently than most Americans. Since Whorf's time, the number of snow words attributed to Inuit has ranged from two dozen to about 400 (Pullum, 1991).

We have about the same number of words for snow as you do!

Another linguist did a closer examination and found that Inuit and Americans both have about eight words for snow (English words for snow include *blizzard, sleet, hail, hardpack, powder, avalanche, flurry,* and *dusting*) (L. Martin, 1986). So, as it turns out, Whorf was wrong about how many words Inuit and Americans have for snow. One reason Whorf's story about differences in snow words lives on is that it's a great (but untrue) story (Pullum, 1991).

Although Whorf's story about snow words was untrue, the basic question still remains: Do differences in language mean that people think and perceive the world in different ways? One way to answer this question is to examine how individuals who are bilingual—that is, fluent in two languages—think about and perceive their world.

Thinking in Two Languages

Suppose your native language is Chinese but you are also fluent in English. You are asked to read descriptions of two different people in either Chinese or English and then to write impressions of these individuals. You read a Chinese and an English description of a type of person easily labeled in Chinese—*shi gu,* a person with strong family ties and much worldly experience—but not easily labeled in English. You read an English and a Chinese description of a type of person easily labeled in English—an *artistic* character, a person with artistic abilities who is very temperamental—but not easily labeled in Chinese. Researchers found that when subjects were reading and thinking in Chinese, they formed a clearer impression of the *shi gu* person; when reading and thinking in English, they formed a clearer impression of the artistic character (C. Hoffman et al., 1986). This is one of the few studies that supports the linguistic relativity theory and the idea that language influences thinking (Hardin & Banaji, 1993).

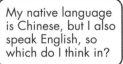

My native language is Chinese, but I also speak English, so which do I think in?

Recent research shows not only that language may influence thinking, but also that it can lead to changes in our personalities. One study including 225 Spanish/English bilingual subjects examined personality characteristics as subjects answered questions in each language. Researchers found that when using English, the bilingual subjects were noticeably more extraverted, agreeable, and conscientious than when speaking in Spanish (Ramirez-Esparza et al., 2006).

We know that words are important tools for thinking, so what happens to an individual's thinking if he or she has great difficulty recognizing printed words? Our next topic is dyslexia.

G. Research Focus: Dyslexia

What Kind of Problem Is Dyslexia?

Was that word "bark" or "dark"?

This Research Focus deals with a real-world problem called dyslexia. *Dyslexia* refers to an unexpected difficulty learning to read despite intelligence, motivation, and education. Causes of dyslexia include genetic factors (defects in neural circuitry) and environmental factors (disadvantaged schooling) (S. E. Shaywitz et al., 2003).

An example of a dyslexic is 16-year-old Steve Goldberg (right photo), who is motivated and intelligent and has won numerous medals for science projects. However, he cannot read or spell

> Why can't I spell the name of my high school?

the name of his high school, read phone numbers, or tell the difference between the words *dark* and *bark*. Dyslexia, which affects boys and girls equally, accounts for 80% of students identified as having learning disabilities.

Although people with dyslexia struggle with a wide range of reading difficulties, many have normal or above-average IQ scores and some have very successful and creative careers: Tom Cruise, movie actor; Jay Leno, TV talk-show host; Agatha Christie, author of 100 mystery books; and Walt Disney, creator of animations (Charkalis, 2005).

In studying dyslexia, researchers combined the cognitive approach—what happens when we read (not what you think)—with the physiological approach—what happens inside the brain.

What's Involved in Reading?

Earlier, we explained that children usually have no difficulty learning to speak because their brains come with innate or prewired areas for speaking (p. 316). Learning to read is entirely different from learning to speak because our brains have no innate areas dedicated specifically to reading. Instead, we must spend many years practicing how to read by learning to use three different brain areas that were originally designed to do something else. That's why reading is so difficult to learn (Eden, 2003).

Reading: 3 steps. Learning to read involves using 3 brain areas, each with a different function (Gorman, 2003; S. E. Shaywitz et al., 2003).

1 **Phoneme (sound) producer.** The first step in reading is to vocalize the word, either silently or out loud. Vocalizing involves changing the letters of each word into their basic sounds, called phonemes. For example, reading the word CAT involves vocalizing or changing the letters C-A-T into the sounds KUH-A-TUH. The phoneme producer is located in brain area #1 (left inferior frontal gyrus) (figure below).

2 **Word analyzer.** After we vocalize or change a word's letters into sounds, the next step is to make a more complete analysis of a written word, such as pulling the word apart into syllables and linking syllables to their appropriate sounds. The word analyzer is located in brain area #2 (left parieto-temporal area). When first learning how to read, children rely heavily on using the phoneme producer and word analyzer.

CAT

3 **Automatic detector.** With practice, brain area #3 (left occipito-temporal area), called the automatic detector, becomes more active. The automatic detector takes on a bigger role by developing a permanent file of words so the reader can recognize words on sight, which makes reading a quick, automatic, and effortless process. Normally, these three processes work together almost simultaneously, like members of a team.

Why Can't Dyslexics Read?

One problem dyslexics have is that their phoneme producer is faulty so they cannot easily or quickly distinguish between phonemes *(ba, pa, la)*, and this results in problems distinguishing between like-sounding words *(bark, park, lark)*, which makes reading difficult (Tallal, 1995). Another problem is that dyslexics have defective neural wiring between the phoneme producer (#1) and the word analyzer (#2) and automatic detector (#3). As a result, they cannot easily or quickly recognize words or their meanings, which makes reading a slow and difficult process (Gorman, 2003; S. E. Shaywitz et al., 2003).

ba
pa
la

Can Training Help?

Because dyslexic children have deficits in the phoneme analyzer, researchers developed computer games to increase phoneme or sound processing, which is the first step in learning to read. After the dyslexic children played computer reading games, brain scans showed that they actually had increased neural activity in brain area #1, phoneme producer, and brain area #2, word analyzer. They also developed better reading skills (Temple et al., 2003).

Parents are advised to encourage their dyslexic children to play rhyming games as well as to have their children read aloud while gently correcting their children's mistakes. Rhyming and reading activities help dyslexic children develop correct associations between sounds and words (Gorman, 2003). According to Dr. Sally Shaywitz (2003), the most successful programs to help dyslexic children use the same core elements: practice with distinguishing between phonemes (playing computer games), building vocabularies, and increasing comprehension.

Reading problems should be identified early, ideally between the ages of 5 and 7, when brain circuitry and reading skills are being developed and can be most easily influenced (Lyon, 1999). Recent research identified two genes that contribute to dyslexia, which means that genetic testing for susceptibility to dyslexia may be possible in the near future (Gruen, 2005).

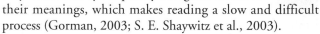

H. Cultural Diversity: Influences on Thinking

Differences in Thinking

How does your culture influence your thinking?

If you spend most of your time in one culture, you probably don't realize how much your culture influences your thinking (Hong et al., 2000). For example, look at the underwater scene at the right and then look away and describe what you saw.

Differences. When American students looked at this underwater scene and then thought about what they saw, they usually began by describing the biggest, brightest, or most outstanding feature—in this case, focusing on the large fish and what it was doing (swimming to the right). In contrast, when Japanese students looked at the same underwater scene and then thought about what they saw, they usually began by describing the background and saying that the bottom was rocky (Had you noticed?) and the water was green (Had you noticed?). They usually discussed how the fish interact with the background, such as the big fish was swimming toward the seaweed. On average, Japanese subjects made 70% more statements about how the background looked than Americans and 100% more statements about the way the objects (fish) interact with the background.

Based on these kinds of findings, researchers concluded that

American students' descriptions of these drawings differed from Japanese students'.

Americans usually analyze each object separately, which is called analytical thinking, such as seeing a forest and focusing on the biggest or strangest trees. In comparison, Asian people (Japanese, Chinese, and Koreans) think more about the relationship between objects and backgrounds, which is called holistic thinking, such as seeing a forest and thinking about how the many different trees make up a beautiful forest (Norenzayan & Nisbett, 2000). Researchers suggest that differences in thinking between Americans and Asians—analytical versus holistic—come from differences in social and religious practices and languages (Nisbett, 2000; Nisbett & Miyamoto, 2005).

Other cultural differences in thinking were revealed when American and Asian (Japanese, Chinese, and Korean) students were asked to watch an animated film that showed one fish swimming in front of other fish (figure below). As you look at this figure, what do you think is happening? American students more often thought that the fish in front was a leader for the other fish. In comparison, Asian students more often thought that the fish in front was being chased by the other fish (Hong et al., 2000). Researchers concluded that cultural factors influence how you think much more than you realize.

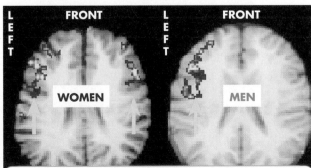

Male–Female Differences

Do men and women think differently?

Just as culture influences how we think, so do gender differences. For about 20 years, linguist Deborah Tannen (1990, 1994) has been recording and analyzing the conversations of men and women. She found that men and women think and use language differently.

MEN AND WOMEN USE LANGUAGE DIFFERENTLY

■ Men more frequently use language to express ideas and solve problems. Women more frequently use language to share concerns, daily experiences, and ordinary thoughts.

■ Men use language to maintain their independence and position in their group. Women use language to create connections and develop feelings of intimacy.

■ Men prefer to attack problems, while women prefer to listen, give support, or be sympathetic.

Tannen concluded that neither the female nor the male use of language, which strongly reflects how they think, is necessarily better; the two styles are just different. She added, however, that men and women need to be aware of basic differences in thinking and using language so they can reduce hurt feelings, avoid misunderstandings, and work to improve communication between the sexes.

fMRI scans showed that women use right and left hemispheres to process language; men use only left.

BRAINS PROCESS WORDS DIFFERENTLY

Not only do men and women use language differently, but their brains may process language differently. Researchers used fMRI brain scans (p. 70) to identify which areas of the brain were most active while men and women performed different language tasks. The fMRI scan below left shows that, in women, activity during certain word-processing tasks occurred almost equally in both the right and left hemispheres (red and yellow areas indicate maximum activity). In contrast, the right fMRI scan shows that, in men, activity during the same word-processing tasks occurred only in the left hemisphere (B. A. Shaywitz et al., 1995). Other research did not find the same hemisphere differences between men and women, but found that they use different parts of the left hemisphere when processing language (Sommer et al., 2004). Generally, researchers believe that brain processes for language are different between men and women but the differences remain unclear. However, differences in brain functioning between men and women do not indicate that one brain is better than another; only that they function differently (Halpern, 2003).

Next, we'll discuss the interesting question of whether animals have language and if my dog really understands what I say.

I. Application Do Animals Have Language?

Criteria for Language

What does my dog understand?

Like most pet owners, I (R.P.) talk to my dog and he usually behaves as if he understands what I say. For example, my dog Bear (photo below) behaves as if he understands "get your toy," "go for walk," "time to eat," and "watch television." The obvious question is: Has Bear learned a language? The answer to this question hinges on the difference between communication and language. Like many animals, Bear has the ability to communicate.

Communication is the ability to use sounds, smells, or gestures to exchange information.

But language is much more than just communication.

Language is a special form of communication in which an individual learns complex rules for using words or gestures to generate and understand an endless number of meaningful sentences.

Although Bear can communicate—that is, understand my commands and act accordingly—he, like most animals, shows no evidence of meeting the four criteria for having real language.

Dogs communicate but don't have a language.

1 Language, which is a special form of communication, involves *learning a set of abstract symbols* (whether words for spoken language or hand signs for sign language).

2 Language involves *using abstract symbols* (words or signs) to express thoughts or indicate objects and events that may or may not be present.

3 Language involves *learning complex rules of grammar* for forming words into meaningful phrases and sentences.

4 Language involves using the rules of grammar to *generate an endless number of meaningful sentences*.

Because some animals, such as dolphins and pygmy chimps, show an amazing ability to communicate, researchers are debating whether animals can satisfy all four criteria for language (Begley, 1998a; Savage-Rumbaugh & Lewin, 1994). We'll examine how close several animals come to satisfying the four criteria.

Dolphins

Do dolphins use language?

Dolphins are considered very intelligent, not only because of their ability to learn but also because in proportion to the size of their bodies, dolphins' brains are the largest of nonhuman mammals (smaller than human brains but larger than brains of great apes) (Tyack, 2000). Because dolphins have relatively large brains, researchers are interested in how well they communicate.

In the wild, dolphins use two kinds of sounds for communication: clicks, which they use to probe the sea and "see" their environment, and whistles, which they use in dolphin-to-dolphin communication, probably to express emotional states and identify the animal to the group (L. Herman, 1999).

In testing the ability of dolphins to communicate, psychologist Louis Herman (1999) has been training dolphins to respond to hand signals or whistles. He has taught two dolphins to respond to approximately 50 such signals (see right photos for an example).

Herman found that dolphins can understand a variety of hand signals and perform behaviors in sequence. For example, the hand signal combination "basket, right, Frisbee, fetch" means "Go to the Frisbee on the right and take it to the basket."

More recently, Herman combined "words" by using gestures or whistles in basic "sentences," such as "ball fetch surface hoop." The two dolphins responded correctly to both familiar and novel "sentences" about 85% of the time. Herman concluded that the ability of

these two dolphins to pass tests of language comprehension (understanding "sentences"), which indicates an understanding of grammar or syntax, means that dolphins have a relatively sophisticated ability to use language (L. Herman, 1999).

Other evidence for dolphins having impressive communication abilities comes from watching a pair of dolphins carry out a complex sequence of movements in synchrony (referred to as "tandem" movements). Herman described these movements by saying that dolphins "may swim in a circle, leap out of water in a spinning motion, and spit water out of their mouths together" (L. Herman, 2006, p. 150). Researchers have yet to determine how dolphins actually communicate information to each other, such as what movements they will make.

Hand signals in top photo tell dolphin to "jump over person," which it does in bottom photo.

Despite Herman's impressive findings, some scientists remain skeptical. For example, David Kastak, a researcher of animal cognition, said, "What dolphins do may turn out to be a lot more complex than what we thought originally, but do they have what we would call language? No. They are not animals using nouns and verbs" (Mastro, 1999, p. E4).

Although dolphins understand a variety of signals, perform behaviors in sequence, form concepts, and even understand "sentences," they show little evidence of using abstract symbols and applying rules of grammar to generate meaningful sentences to communicate information to other dolphins. It is these criteria that distinguish the ability to use language from the ability to communicate with signs, sounds, or gestures.

Next, let's turn to the apes, which in terms of evolution are the animals closest to humans.

Gorilla and Chimpanzee

What does a gorilla know?

Gorillas and chimpanzees have relatively large and well-developed brains. A gorilla's brain weighs about 500 grams, a chimpanzee's about 400 grams, and a human's about 1,350 grams. However, because gorillas and chimpanzees lack the vocal apparatus necessary for making speech sounds, researchers have taught them other forms of language, such as American Sign Language (P. E. Ross, 1991).

Shown on the right is researcher Francine Patterson using sign language to communicate with Koko the gorilla, who has a vocabulary of about 800 signs. Similarly, Beatrice and Allen Gardner (1975) taught sign language to a chimpanzee named Washoe, who after four years of training had learned about 160 signs. The finding that gorillas and chimps can learn sign language raised the question of whether they use language in the same way as humans.

Francine Patterson taught Koko the gorilla a vocabulary of about 800 hand signs.

Psychologist Herbert Terrace (1981) analyzed videotapes of chimps using sign language with their trainers. He was particularly interested in the videotapes of a chimp named Nim, who has learned more than 125 signs, such as "give orange me." After observing over 20,000 of Nim's signs on videotape, Terrace concluded that Nim was using signs more as tools to obtain things than as abstract symbols or words and that Nim never learned to form combinations of more than a few words. Perhaps the most devastating criticism was that Nim had primarily learned to imitate or respond to cues from human teachers rather than learning and using rules of grammar to initiate or produce new sentences.

As a result of criticisms by Terrace and others, research monies to study language in animals mostly disappeared in the 1980s (Savage-Rumbaugh & Lewin, 1994). However, in the late 1980s, new findings on bonobos again raised the question of language in animals.

Bonobo Chimp: Star Pupil

Is this the first real sign of language?

The best evidence for language in animals comes from the work of psychologist Sue Savage-Rumbaugh. She reported that Kanzi, a bonobo (commonly called a pygmy chimp), has remarkable language skills that surpass previous accomplishments of common chimps (Savage-Rumbaugh & Lewin, 1994; Shanker et al., 1999).

Instead of using sign language, Kanzi "speaks" by touching one of 256 symbols on a board (top right photo), each of which stands for a word. For example, Kanzi (bottom right photo) might signal "Want a drink" by touching the symbol for "drink" or signal "Want to play" by touching in sequence two symbols for "hiding" and "play biting."

By the time Kanzi was 6 years old, he had a vocabulary of 90 symbols; at age 12, he knew about 190 symbols but used about 128 regularly. Even more surprising, Kanzi understands about 200 spoken English words, something that common chimps have failed to master.

Perhaps Kanzi's greatest accomplishment is his knowledge of word order. Psychologists tested the ability of Kanzi to respond to 600 spoken English commands that he had not previously encountered, such as "Put the melon in the potty." Savage-Rumbaugh suggests that 17-year-old Kanzi has an ability to use abstract symbols (keyboard) and a kind of primitive grammar (word order)

| BLACKBERRIES | BUTTER | VELVET PLANT |
| SHOT | STRING | PINE CONE |

Examples of symbols and their meanings

Kanzi has an amazing ability to use and respond to either symbols or English words.

for combining symbols that equals the language ability of a 2-year-old child (Savage-Rumbaugh, 1998). Although chimps can learn more than 400 symbols and even string several symbols together, their language ability is nowhere near that of a high-school student, who has a vocabulary of 60,000 words and can string these words together into an endless number of meaningful sentences, often about abstract concepts (love, patriotism, courage, honor) (M. Hauser, 2003).

Why did humans develop a complex language while chimps did not? Researchers now believe that the development of human language was triggered by a major genetic change (R. Klein, 2002). This conclusion is based on a new finding: the discovery of the first human gene (FOXP2) involved specifically in language. Individuals without this "language" gene are normal in other ways but not in communication; they have specific difficulties pronouncing words and speaking grammatically (N. Wade, 2003b). Although ancient humans shared this gene with other animals, researchers discovered that there was an important change in this gene's structure at about the same time that humans and chimps parted evolutionary company.

Some researchers point to a change in the structure of this "language" gene (FOXP2) as the reason that early humans were able to gradually develop their primitive sounds and clicks into the complex, fluent language that we speak today (Paabo, 2003).

Summary Test

A. Forming Concepts

1. There are two theories of how you have formed your concept of a dog and how you form concepts generally. If you form a concept of an object, event, or characteristic by making a list of the properties that define it, you are using the (a)_____ model. If you form a concept by constructing an idea of the ideal object and then seeing whether a new object matches that idea, you are using (b)_____ theory.

2. A concept is a way to group objects, events, or characteristics on the basis of some common property they all share. Concepts perform two important functions: They allow us to (a)_____ objects, and thus better organize and store information in memory, and to identify things without (b) _____.

B. Solving Problems

3. The process of searching for some rule, plan, or strategy that results in reaching a certain goal that is currently out of reach is called (a)_____. We usually go through three states in solving problems: (b)_____, _____, and _____.

4. We win at games by following rules. If we correctly follow a set of rules that lead to a solution, these rules are called (a)_____. As you gain experience with solving problems, you may use rules of thumb that reduce the number of operations or allow you to take shortcuts in solving problems; these shortcuts are called (b)_____. In making everyday decisions, you rely on information that is more prominent or easily recalled and overlook other information that is available but less prominent or notable; this is an example of using the (c)_____ heuristic.

5. By studying how people eventually solve problems, psychologists have discovered a number of useful strategies, including changing our (a)_____. This often involves breaking out of a pattern called (b)_____, in which we cannot see an object as having a function different from its usual one.

6. The sudden grasp of a solution after many incorrect attempts is called (a)_____. Another kind of thinking that is useful in solving problems is to find (b)_____, which are similarities between new situations and familiar situations. Still another useful strategy for solving problems is to break the problem down into a number of (c)_____, which, when completed in order, will result in a solution.

C. Thinking Creatively

7. A combination of flexibility in thinking and reorganization of understanding to produce innovative ideas and solutions is referred to as (a)_____. Psychologists distinguish between two different kinds of thinking. If you begin with a problem and come up with the one correct solution, it is called (b)_____. If you begin with a problem and come up with many different solutions, it is called (c)_____, which is another definition of creative thinking.

D. Language: Basic Rules

8. Our most impressive skill is thought to be a special form of communication in which an individual learns complex rules to manipulate symbols (words or gestures) and so generates an endless number of meaningful sentences; this form of communication is called _____.

9. All of the 6,900 known languages share four basic language rules, which are normally learned during childhood. The first language rule governs (a)_____, which specifies how we make meaningful sounds that are used by a particular language. The second language rule governs (b)_____, which specifies how we group phonemes into meaningful combinations of sounds and words. The third language rule governs (c)_____, which specifies how we combine words to form meaningful phrases and sentences. The fourth language rule governs (d)_____, which specifies the meanings of words in various contexts.

10. The linguist Noam Chomsky distinguished between how a sentence is worded, which he called the (a)_____ structure, and the meaning of the sentence, which he called the (b)_____ structure. Procedures for converting our ideas from surface structures into deep structures and from deep structures back into surface ones are called (c)_____.

E. Acquiring Language

11. Children around the world acquire language in the same four stages that are associated with growth and development of the (a)_____. In the first stage, generally at about the age of 6 months, the infant makes one-syllable sounds; this is called (b)_____. By about 1 year of age, a child forms (c)_____, which usually refer to what the child can see,

hear, or feel. At about 2 years of age, a child makes (d)_____ to express various actions or relationships. At about 4 years of age, a child is forming sentences, which range from three to eight words in length and indicate a growing knowledge of the (e)_____.

12. A child's beginning sentences differ from adult sentences. A child's speech is called (a)_____ because it omits articles, prepositions, and parts of verbs. In learning the rules for combining nouns, verbs, and adjectives into meaningful sentences, children often apply a grammatical rule to cases where it should not be used. This type of error is called (b)_____. Although all children pass through these stages in the same order, they may go through them at different ages and speeds.

13. Children are able to acquire a language with so little formal training because of genetically programmed physiological and neurological features in the brain and vocal apparatus; these features are called (a)_____ factors. One innate factor is the period of time from infancy to adolescence when language is easier to learn, called the (b)_____. Children acquire the sounds and rules of a particular language because of their interactions with their surroundings; these interactions are called (c)_____ factors. The approach that emphasizes observation, exploration, and imitation in language acquisition is (d)_____.

F. Decisions, Thought & Language

14. A study on gambling found that even when people knew that their chances of winning and losing were identical, the wording of what they were told made a difference in their (a)_____. Another study on how the brain responds when people are making political decisions found that the part of the brain where (b)_____ takes place is inactive and the most active part of the brain is where (c)_____ are processed.

15. Whorf has suggested that language determines or influences the way people think and that people with different languages think and perceive their world differently. This is called the theory of _____. There is only weak support for Whorf's theory.

G. Research Focus: Dyslexia

16. About 80% of learning disabilities are accounted for by (a)_____, which is an unexpected difficulty in reading despite intelligence, motivation, and education. The three steps in

reading involve three different brain areas, each with a different function: Brain area #1 is called the (b)_____, brain area #2 is called the (c)_____, and brain area #3 is called the (d)_____. Individuals with dyslexia have a problem with changing letters into sounds or (e)_____ and have faulty (f)_____ connections between brain area #1 and brain areas #2 and #3.

H. Cultural Diversity: Influences on Thinking

17. Men tend to use language to express ideas, maintain their position in the group, and solve (a)_____, while women use language more to share concerns and daily experiences and develop feelings of (b)_____.

18. fMRI scans of the brain have shown that women process some words equally in both (a)_____, while men process words only in the (b)_____ hemisphere.

I. Application: Do Animals Have Language?

19. Many animals have the ability to use sounds, smells, or gestures to exchange information; this is the ability to (a)_____. Another question is whether animals can communicate with abstract symbols; this is called (b)_____. To decide that an animal truly uses language, researchers must show that the animal has learned complex rules of (c)_____ to manipulate symbols (words or gestures) and so generate an endless number of meaningful sentences. The best evidence for language in animals is the (d)_____, who has matched the language ability of a 2-year-old child.

Answers: 1. (a) exemplar, (b) prototype; 2. (a) categorize, (b) relearning; 3. (a) problem solving, (b) initial state, operations state, goal state; 4. (a) algorithms, (b) heuristics, (c) availability; 5. (a) mental set, (b) functional fixedness; 6. (a) insight, (b) analogies, (c) subgoals; 7. (a) creative thinking, (b) convergent thinking, (c) divergent thinking; 8. language; 9. (a) phonology, (b) morphology, (c) syntax or grammar, (d) semantics; 10. (a) surface, (b) deep, (c) transformational rules; 11. (a) brain, (b) babbling, (c) single words, (d) two-word combinations, (e) rules of grammar; 12. (a) telegraphic, (b) overgeneralization; 13. (a) innate, (b) critical language period, (c) environmental, (d) social cognitive learning; 14. (a) decisions, (b) reasoning, (c) emotions; 15. linguistic relativity; 16. (a) dyslexia, (b) phoneme producer, (c) word analyzer, (d) automatic detector, (e) phonemes, (f) neural or brain; 17. (a) problems, (b) intimacy; 18. (a) hemispheres, (b) left; 19. (a) communicate, (b) language, (c) grammar, (d) bonobo (pygmy chimp)

Critical Thinking

Why Do Parents Speak Loudly and Slowly?

by Robert Lee Hotz

Questions

1. What is the term for and what is the purpose of the "baby talk" that parents or caregivers use with their infants?

2. What would happen if parents or caregivers never spoke to their children?

3. Why did the researchers study English, Russian, and Swedish?

4. Why did researchers compare how mothers talked to infants and to other adults?

5. What might happen if mothers or caregivers spoke to infants the same way they spoke to adults?

6. How does the mothers speaking parentese fit in with the critical period for language?

The singsong crooning that every adult instinctively adopts for conversation with a newborn baby is more than patronizing gibberish passing between the generations. It is a universal teaching mechanism rooted in the biology of language and the developing human brain, say neuroscientists Patricia Kuhl and her colleagues at the University of Washington in Seattle, who studied how native speakers of English, Swedish, and Russian talk to infants.

Linguists call the special tone adults reserve for speech with infants "parentese," and the new research indicates it is the same in every culture around the world.

To examine the role of parentese, Kuhl and her colleagues in Russia and Sweden investigated differences in how American, Swedish, and Russian mothers speak to their infants and to other adults. The three languages were chosen because each has a significantly different number of vowel sounds. Russian has five vowel sounds, English nine, and Swedish 16.

The researchers recorded 10 women from each of the three countries talking for 20 minutes to their babies, who ranged in age from 2 to 5 months. Then they recorded the same women talking to other adults. The mothers were told to talk naturally, but were given a list of words containing three common vowel sounds and instructed to work them into their conversations.

For those speaking English, the target words were "bead" for its "ee" vowel sound, "pot" for its "ah" sound, and "boot" for its "oo" sound. Similar words were chosen from Russian and Swedish.

The researchers then used a spectrograph to analyze more than 2,300 instances of how the target words were used in the conversations and discovered that, in all three language groups, the speech directed at infants was stretched out to emphasize the vowel sounds, in contrast to the more normal tone used with adults.

The researchers concluded that the exaggerated speech allowed the mothers to expand the sounds of the vowels so they would be more distinct from each other. It also appears to allow the mothers to produce a greater variety of vowel pronunciations without overlapping other vowel sounds. (Source: *Los Angeles Times,* September 18, 1997)

Suggested Answers

1. "Baby talk" is called parentese (motherese). The purpose of parentese is to teach infants the particular sounds or phonetic building blocks that will be used to form and speak words.
2. For her first 13 years, Genie was punished for making sounds and was never spoken to by her parents. As a result, Genie could not speak a single word and, even with training, developed language skills of only a 2- to 3-year-old child. (Discussion is on page 316.)
3. Researchers chose three different languages because each of these languages had a different number of vowel sounds and researchers wanted to know if mothers would exaggerate the vowel sounds particular to their different languages.
4. Researchers compared how mothers spoke to infants versus adults to see if they used parentese only with infants. It turned out that mothers exaggerated vowel sounds when speaking to their babies but did not when speaking to other adults.
5. If mothers spoke the same to infants and adults, then infants would not hear the slow, exaggerated vowel sounds (parentese) and would have difficulty learning the particular sounds that make up the particular language of their parents.
6. The critical period says that language is easiest to learn between infancy and adolescence. The use of parentese at the beginning of the critical period gives the infant a great start in developing language and successfully going through the four stages of language (babbling, one word, two-word combinations, sentences).

Links to Learning

Learning Activities

- ***POWERSTUDY FOR INTRODUCTION TO PSYCHOLOGY 4.0***
  by Tom Doyle and Rod Plotnik
  Check out the quizzes and learning activities for "Thought & Language" on **PowerStudy** and:
  - Test your knowledge using an interactive version of the Summary Test on pages 324 and 325. Also access related quizzing—true/false, multiple choice, and matching.
  - Explore an interactive version of the Critical Thinking exercise "Why Do Parents Speak Loudly and Slowly?" on page 326.
  - You will also find key terms, a chapter outline including a chapter abstract, and a special extended list of hotlinked websites that correlate to this module.

- ***CengageNOW***
  academic.cengage.com/login
  Need help studying? This site is your one-stop study shop.
  Take a Pre-Test and CengageNOW will generate a Personalized Study Plan based on your test results. The Study Plan will identify the topics you need to review and direct you to online resources to help you master those topics. You can then take a Post-Test to determine the concepts you have mastered and what you still need to work on.

- ***INTRODUCTION TO PSYCHOLOGY BOOK COMPANION WEBSITE***
  academic.cengage.com/psychology/plotnik
  Visit your book companion website where you will find more resources to help you study. At this site, you will find Learning Objectives, Internet Exercises, quizzing, flash cards, and a pronunciation glossary.

- ***STUDY GUIDE and WEBTUTOR***
  Check the corresponding module in your Study Guide for effective student tips and help learning the material presented. Also go to **academic.cengage.com/webtutor** for an interactive version of the Study Guide features.

Study Questions

*A. **Forming Concepts**—Why is it difficult to explain to your younger sister or brother that a whale is a mammal and not a fish? (**Suggested answer page 628**)

B. **Solving Problems**—Why is it easier to win at checkers the longer you have been playing?

C. **Thinking Creatively**—How would you teach people to think more creatively?

D. **Language: Basic Rules**—To develop a secret code for sending computer messages across a network, which language rule should you break?

E. **Acquiring Language**—Why might students in college have more difficulty learning a foreign language than students in grade school?

*F. **Decisions, Thought & Language**—What problems might result when heads of government speak through translators? (**Suggested answer page 628**)

G. **Research Focus: Dyslexia**—Why does dyslexia cause difficulties with reading but not with engineering and inventive abilities?

*H. **Cultural Diversity: Influences on Thinking**—What kinds of social problems can arise from finding differences between male and female brains? (**Suggested answer page 628**)

I. **Application: Do Animals Have Language?**—When a parrot speaks perfect English and understands dozens of commands, can we conclude it is using language?

*These questions are answered in Appendix B.

MODULE 15
Motivation

Introduction

Motivation

Why would a paraplegic climb a mountain?

On a cool September morning, two men began to climb a nearly vertical slope rising over 2,200 feet from the floor of Yosemite National Park. Because of the slope's crumbly granite, fewer than 30 people had completed this particular route up Half Dome, Yosemite's well-known landmark. What made this particular climb very difficult and dangerous was that one of the men, Mark Wellman, is a paraplegic.

Some years before, on a different climb, Mark fell 50 feet into a crevice, hurt his back, and was paralyzed from the waist down. Mark now climbs with his friend Mike Corbett, who takes the lead and sets the supports. Because Mark's legs are paralyzed, he climbs by using the supports to pull himself up inch by inch.

Mark figured that by doing the equivalent of 5,000 pull-ups, each of which would raise him about 6 inches, he could climb the 2,200 feet in seven days. By the end of day seven, however, Mark and Mike were only a little more than halfway up the slope and had to sleep by hanging in sleeping bags anchored to the sheer granite wall.

By day ten, Mark was becoming exhausted as his arms strained to raise his body's weight up the vertical face (left photo). By day 12, the men were almost out of food and water. Finally, on day 13, six days later than planned, Mark pulled himself up the last 6 inches and over the top of Half Dome. When Mark was asked later why he still climbed and risked further injury, he said, "Everyone has their own goals. . . . Never underestimate a person with a disability" (adapted from the *Los Angeles Times*, September 19, 1991, p. A-3).

Reporters who questioned Mark about why he risked his life to climb were really asking about his motivation.

Motivation refers to the various physiological and psychological factors that cause us to act in a specific way at a particular time.

Mark Wellman, a paraplegic, did the equivalent of 5,000 pull-ups to climb the face of Half Dome.

When you are motivated, you usually show three characteristics:

1. You are *energized* to do or engage in some activity.
2. You *direct* your energies toward reaching a specific goal.
3. You have differing *intensities* of feelings about reaching that goal.

We can observe these three characteristics in Mark's behavior:

1. He was energized to perform the equivalent of 5,000 pull-ups during his 13-day climb.
2. He directed his energy toward climbing a particular slope that fewer than 30 other climbers had completed.
3. He felt so intensely about reaching that goal that even when totally exhausted, he still persisted in reaching his goal, the top of Half Dome.

We'll discuss several kinds of motivating forces, including those involved in eating and drinking, sexual behavior, achievement, underachievement, failure, and, of course, climbing mountains.

Achievement

Why did friends call him a "White boy"?

Victor remembers being in the seventh grade when some of his Black buddies called him a "White boy" because they thought he was studying too hard. "You can't be cool if you're smart," says Victor, who was Mission Bay High's student body president, had a 3.7 (A–) grade point average, and planned to attend the University of Southern California in the fall (adapted from the *San Diego Union-Tribune*, June 17, 1994).

Victor (photo below) grew up with an obstacle that goes largely unnoticed and is rarely discussed in public: pressure from students in the same racial or ethnic group not to succeed in the classroom. Faced with this negative peer pressure, some minority students (principally Latino, African American, and Native American teenage boys) stop studying, don't do homework, avoid answering questions in class, join gangs, and even drop out of school.

Similar to Victor's own experience, students who are doing well in school are often accused of "acting white" by peers in their same racial or

Victor was proud of his A– average, but some of his peers believed that being smart wasn't cool.

ethnic group. Educators believe that such a cultural bias against appearing too smart prevents students from achieving their full potential (Fryer, 2005). How Victor overcame this negative peer pressure and did succeed will be discussed later in this module.

What's Coming

We'll look at four general theories that psychologists use to explain motivation, discuss the differences between social and biological needs, and then focus on specific examples, such as hunger, sexual behavior, and achievement. We'll examine why some people are achievers and others are underachievers. We'll discuss why people become overweight and why dieting is so difficult. We'll look at two serious eating disorders that result more from psychological than from biological factors.

We'll begin with four general theories that psychologists use to explain motivation.

A. Theories of Motivation

Why does Mark climb?

For 13 days, sightseers on the Yosemite valley floor watched Mark pull himself up the granite face of Half Dome. Many asked, "Why is he doing that?" The same can be asked of you: Why are you willing to work hard for four to six years to get a college degree? These are questions about motivation. We'll discuss four general theories of motivation—the instinct, incentive, and cognitive theories, and the newest, the brain's reward/pleasure center theory.

Instinct

Is he driven by instincts?

In the early 1900s, William McDougall (1908) claimed that humans were motivated by a variety of instincts.

Instincts are innate tendencies or biological forces that determine behavior.

McDougall listed about half a dozen instincts, such as combat, curiosity, sympathy, and self-assertion. He might have explained Mark's motivation to climb as arising from instincts involving curiosity and self-assertion. But attributing mountain climbing to an instinct is more like labeling than explaining the underlying motivation. At one point, psychologists had proposed over 6,000 instincts to explain every kind of human motivation. Although instincts proved useless in explaining human motivation, they proved useful in explaining animal behaviors because animal researchers redefined instincts as fixed action patterns (FitzGerald, 1993).

A *fixed action pattern* is an innate biological force that predisposes an organism to behave in a fixed way in the presence of a specific environmental condition.

Animals have innate biological tendencies called instincts.

For example, the above photo shows how a baboon is innately predisposed to behave in a fixed aggressive pattern—opens mouth, stares, rises on hind feet—in the face of a specific stimulus, a threatening cheetah. Ethologists, researchers who study animal behaviors, reported that fixed action patterns help animals adapt to their natural environments. For example, in Module 10 (p. 228) we explained how birds that can walk immediately after birth become attached to, or imprinted on, the first moving object (animal, human, or basketball) that the baby bird encounters. Once imprinted, the baby bird continues to interact with that bird or object as if it were its parent. Imprinting is an example of a fixed action pattern that is extremely useful in helping young animals survive (Lorenz, 1952).

Instincts represented an early but failed attempt to explain human motivation. We'll jump from the early 1900s to the early 2000s and examine current research that sheds a new light on human motivation.

Brain: Reward/Pleasure Center

What's his reward for climbing?

During his 13 days climbing Half Dome, Mark was motivated to satisfy various biological needs, such as eating and drinking. The human body is set up genetically to send biological signals to the brain, which is genetically wired to interpret the body's biological signals and thus motivate the person to eat or drink by causing feelings of hunger or thirst (Kalat, 2007). Later we'll describe the body's biological signals and how the brain interprets these signals to produce feelings of hunger or fullness.

One reason you are motivated to eat is that chewing on a favorite food can be so pleasurable. Only recently have researchers discovered that this "eating" pleasure comes from the brain's reward/pleasure center (Dackis & O'Brien, 2001; Dallman et al., 2005).

Food triggers reward center.

The *reward/pleasure center* includes several areas of the brain, such as the nucleus accumbens and the ventral tegmental area, and involves several neurotransmitters, especially dopamine. These components make up a neural circuitry that produces rewarding and pleasurable feelings.

Researchers discovered the brain's reward/pleasure center (figure below) by using newly developed brain scans (fMRI—p. 70) that can identify neural activity in the living brain. For example, researchers found that cocaine produced its pleasurable feelings by activating two brain areas, nucleus accumbens and ventral tegmental area, that are involved in the brain's reward/pleasure center (Dackis & O'Brien, 2001). Using this same technique, researchers found that a number of other activities also triggered the brain's reward/pleasure center. Thus, animals are motivated to continually press a lever to obtain brain stimulation and people are motivated to eat, engage in sex, gamble, use recreational drugs, and listen to "spine-chilling" music because, as brain scans (fMRIs) have shown, all these behaviors activate the brain's reward/pleasure center (Aharon et al., 2001; Bartels, 2002; Begley, 2001a; Blood & Zatorre, 2001; Breiter et al., 2001; Shizgal & Arvanitogiannis, 2003). More recently, genes have been linked to several behaviors that trigger the brain's reward/pleasure center, including obesity, risk-taking behaviors (gambling), nicotine addiction, and sexual activity (Harmon, 2006). This means that having specific variations of genes makes people more likely to engage in these pleasurable activities.

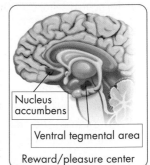

Nucleus accumbens

Ventral tegmental area

Reward/pleasure center

Why does Mark climb? Mark may climb because this behavior activates the brain's reward/pleasure center. He may also be motivated to climb by a variety of psychological factors, such as gaining various incentives or fulfilling his expectations, which we'll examine next.

Incentives

Why do you study? The issue of motivation becomes very personal when we ask you to explain why you sacrificed so much and worked so hard to get into college. Now that you're in college, what is motivating you to study for all those exams and write all those papers? One answer is that you are motivated to get a college degree because it is a very big incentive (Petri & Govern, 2004).

The degree was worth the hard work!

Incentives **are goals that can be either objects or thoughts that we learn to value and that we are motivated to obtain.**

Incentives have two common features. First, they can be either thoughts ("I want to get a degree") or objects (money, clothes) that we LEARN to value. For example, when you were 5 years old, you had not yet learned the value of a good education. Second, the value of incentives can change over time. A pizza is not an incentive at 7 a.m., but it may be an important incentive at 7 p.m. Many of our behaviors are motivated by a variety of incentives, including grades, praise, money, clothes, or academic degrees. You can think of incentives as *pulling* us or motivating us to obtain them.

Would you like a dessert? Incentives explain why there's always room for dessert when we say we are full or why we continue to buy more clothes even when our closets are full. Even though our immediate needs seem to be met ("I'm full" or "I have enough clothes"), highly valued incentives, such as desired foods or great clothes, have the power to motivate or pull us toward obtaining them. Incentives also explain why people often buy things on impulse.

Why does Mark climb? Another reason Mark is motivated to climb probably involves obtaining incentives, such as recognition by national media, speaking invitations, and money ($100,000) from corporate sponsors, which Mark donates to help others with disabilities. However, other equally powerful reasons for Mark's climbing probably involve cognitive factors (Eccles, 2005).

Cognitive Factors

Why do people run marathons? Thousands of people train for months to run grueling 26-mile-long marathons, in which only the top two or three receive any prize money and the rest receive only T-shirts. What motivates people to endure such agony? The answer can be traced to the early 1960s, when psychologists began applying cognitive concepts to explain human motivation (Bandura, 1986; deCharms, 1980; Deci & Ryan, 1985; Weiner, 1991). These cognitive researchers said that one reason people run marathons, usually for no reward other than a T-shirt, has to do with the difference between extrinsic and intrinsic motivation.

Extrinsic motivation **involves engaging in certain activities or behaviors that either reduce biological needs or help us obtain incentives or external rewards.**

Intrinsic motivation **involves engaging in certain activities or behaviors because the behaviors themselves are personally rewarding or because engaging in these activities fulfills our beliefs or expectations.**

Intrinsic motivation explains that people volunteer their services, spend hours on hobbies, run marathons, or work on personal projects because these activities are personally rewarding, fulfilling, or challenging. Intrinsic motivation emphasizes that we are motivated to engage in many behaviors because of our own personal beliefs, expectations, or goals, rather than external incentives (Petri & Govern, 2004).

Why does Mark climb? According to cognitive theory's concept of intrinsic motivation, another reason Mark is motivated to engage in a dangerous and almost impossible climb is that climbing itself is very rewarding to Mark. Mark was an avid climber before he lost the use of his legs, so he continues to climb because it helps him meet his own personal goals and expectations, which are powerful motivators. As Mark said, "Everyone has their own goals."

I need to prove to myself that I can do it!

Explaining Human Motivation

Why did they do that? Why did you pay $65 for a concert ticket? Why did you run a marathon? Why did you study so much for that test? How could you eat a whole pizza? Why did you drink so much last night? The answers to these questions about human behaviors involve three different factors. You may be motivated because certain behaviors trigger the brain's reward/pleasure center. You may be motivated to obtain incentives, which you have learned to value. You may be motivated by cognitive or intrinsic factors, such as wanting to satisfy your personal beliefs, reach certain goals, or fulfill your expectations. Human motivation is so difficult to explain because it may involve all three of these factors. In addition, you can be motivated by emotional factors (anger, fear, happiness) or personality factors (outgoing, shy, uninhibited), which we'll discuss in Modules 16, 19, and 20.

One of the main functions of emotions is to satisfy a number of biological and social needs, which we'll examine next.

B. Biological & Social Needs

How many needs do you have? The most popular daytime television programs are the soap operas, which dramatize a whole range of human needs—the good, the bad, the ugly, and the dumb. As the soap opera characters try to satisfy their needs, they get into endless difficulties. We'll discuss some of the more common biological and social needs.

Biological Needs

What are they doing? It's pretty obvious that the man and his pet pig are about to satisfy their hunger, a basic biological need. *Biological needs are physiological requirements that are critical to our survival and physical well-being.*

Satisfying biological needs

Researchers have identified about a dozen biological needs, such as the needs for food, water, sex, oxygen, sleep, and pain avoidance, all of which help to keep our bodies functioning at their best and thus help us survive (Petri & Govern, 2004).

When genes are defective. Perhaps because biological drives are critical for survival, their automatic regulation is built into a newborn's brain. In rare cases, individuals are born with defective genes that cause biological needs to run amok. For example, some children are born with defective "eating" genes that result in never feeling full but being constantly hungry and obsessed with food and eating (Webb et al., 2006). Children with this genetic problem (the Prader-Willi syndrome affects the hypothalamus) can never be left alone with food because they will eat everything in sight.

Another kind of rare genetic problem affecting only 40 families worldwide destroys the ability to sleep. As individuals with this genetic defect (fatal familial insomnia) reach their 50s, they find that one day they cannot sleep through the night and from then on they never sleep again. Over a period of several months, these individuals lose the ability to walk, speak, and think. Finally, within 15 months, their sleepless body shuts down its functions, resulting in coma and death (Grimes, 2006; Max, 2001). These two examples show that the proper regulation of biological needs is critical for healthy physiological functioning and survival.

When psychological factors interfere. Besides genetic defects, psychological factors can interfere with the regulation of biological needs. For example, some individuals develop the rare eating disorder anorexia nervosa, which involves self-starvation. Without professional help, these individuals may starve themselves to death. Eating disorders show how psychological factors can override basic biological needs. We'll discuss eating disorders in the Application section.

Although there are a relatively limited number of biological needs, there are many more social needs.

Social Needs

Why did they get married? One reason that about 90% of adults in the United States get married is that being married satisfies a number of social needs. *Social needs are needs that are acquired through learning and experience.*

Depending on your learning and experiences, you may acquire dozens of social needs, such as the needs for achievement, affiliation (forming social bonds), fun (play), relaxation, helpfulness, independence, and nurturance (Petri & Govern, 2004).

Getting married satisfies social needs.

One reason marriage is so popular is that it satisfies a number of social needs, including affiliation, nurturance, and achievement. The need for affiliation, or forming lasting, positive attachments, is one of our stronger social needs and is important to maintaining physical health and psychological well-being (Simpson & Tran, 2006).

In some cases, the distinction between biological and social needs is blurred. For example, we may eat or drink not only to satisfy biological needs but also to make social contact or deal with stress. Similarly, we may engage in sex for reproduction, which is a biological need, or to express love and affection, which are social needs. Because we have only so much time and energy to satisfy a relatively large number of biological and social needs, how do we decide which needs to satisfy first? The answer may be found in Maslow's hierarchy.

Satisfying Needs

Which need gets satisfied? You may remember from Module 1 that one of the founders of the humanistic approach in psychology was Abraham Maslow. Maslow was particularly interested in human motivation, especially in how we choose which biological or social need to satisfy. For example, should you study late for an exam and satisfy your social need to achieve, or go to bed at your regular time and satisfy your biological need for sleep? Maslow (1970) proposed that we satisfy our needs in a certain order or according to a set hierarchy (figure on opposite page). *Maslow's hierarchy of needs is an ascending order, or hierarchy, in which biological needs are placed at the bottom and social needs at the top. According to Maslow's hierarchy, we satisfy our biological needs (bottom of hierarchy) before we satisfy our social needs (top of hierarchy).*

Maslow hypothesized that, after we satisfy needs at the bottom level of the hierarchy, we advance up the hierarchy to satisfy the needs at the next level. However, if we are at a higher level and our basic needs are not satisfied, we may come back down the hierarchy.

Do you satisfy biological needs first?

We'll examine Maslow's hierarchy of needs in more detail.

Maslow's Hierarchy of Needs

Which needs do you satisfy first?

If you were very hungry and very lonely at the same time, which need would you satisfy first, your biological need (hunger) or your social need (affiliation)? One answer to this question can be found in Maslow's hierarchy of needs, which says that you satisfy your biological needs before you can turn your attention and energy to fulfilling your personal and social needs. According to Maslow, when it comes to satisfying your needs, you begin at the bottom of the needs hierarchy, with physiological needs, and then work your way toward the top. After you meet the

needs at one level, you advance to the next level. For example, if your physiological needs at Level 1 are satisfied, you advance to Level 2 and work on satisfying your safety needs. Once your safety needs are satisfied, you advance to Level 3, and so forth, up the needs hierarchy.

Maslow's hierarchy of needs is represented by a pyramid and shows the order in which you satisfy your biological and social needs. The first needs you satisfy are physiological or biological ones, so please go to the bottom of the pyramid and begin reading Level 1. Then continue reading Levels 2, 3, 4, and 5, which takes you up the pyramid.

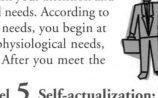

Level 5 **Self-actualization: Fulfillment of one's unique potential.** If we face roadblocks in reaching our true potential, we will feel frustrated. For example, if you are majoring in business and your real interest and talent is music, your need for self-actualization may be unsatisfied. According to Maslow, the highest need is self-actualization, which involves developing and reaching our full potential as unique human beings. However, Maslow cautioned that very few individuals reach the level of self-actualization because it is so difficult and challenging. Examples of individuals who might be said to have reached the level of self-actualization are Abraham Lincoln, Albert Einstein, Eleanor Roosevelt, and Martin Luther King, Jr.

Level 4 **Esteem needs: Achievement, competency, gaining approval and recognition.** During early and middle adulthood, people are especially concerned with achieving their goals and establishing their careers. As we develop skills to gain personal achievement and social recognition, we turn our energies to Level 5.

Level 3 **Love and belonging needs: Affiliation with others and acceptance by others.** Adolescents and young adults, who are beginning to form serious relationships, would be especially interested in fulfilling their needs for love and belonging. After we find love and affection, we advance to Level 4.

Level 2 **Safety needs: Protection from harm.** People who live in high-crime or dangerous areas of the city would be very concerned about satisfying their safety needs. After we find a way to live in a safe and secure environment, we advance to Level 3.

Level 1 **Physiological needs: Food, water, sex, and sleep.** People who are homeless or jobless would be especially concerned with satisfying their physiological needs above all other needs. We must satisfy these basic needs before we advance to Level 2.

Maslow's hierarchy of needs suggests the order in which we satisfy our needs.

Conclusion. One advantage of Maslow's hierarchy is that it integrates biological and social needs into a single framework and proposes a list of priorities for the order in which we satisfy various biological and social needs (Frick, 2000).

One problem with Maslow's hierarchy is that researchers have found it difficult to verify whether his particular order of needs is accurate or to know how to assess some of his needs, especially self-actualization, which very few individuals are able to reach (Geller, 1982). Another problem is that people give different priorities to needs: Some may value love over self-esteem,

or vice versa (Neher, 1991). We'll discuss Maslow's hierarchy of needs later on when we explain humanistic theories of personality (see p. 443). Despite criticisms of Maslow's hierarchy, it remains a useful reminder of the number and complexity of human needs.

To give you a sample of how psychologists study human motivation, we have selected two biological needs—hunger and sex—from Maslow's Level 1 and one social need—achievement—from Maslow's Level 4. We consider these needs in the following sections.

C. Hunger

Optimal Weight

Why don't you see fat wolves? The reason you never see fat wolves is that they, like all animals, have an inherited biological system that carefully regulates their eating so that they maintain their optimal, or ideal, weights (Kolata, 2000b).

Optimal or *ideal weight* **results from an almost perfect balance between how much food an organism eats and how much it needs to meet its body's energy needs.**

In the wild, animals usually eat only to replace fuel used by their bodies, and thus they rarely get fat. In addition, most wild animals use up a tremendous amount of energy in finding food. In comparison, home pets may become fat because their owners,

Animals rely on a biological system to regulate weight.

having the best of intentions, give the pets too much food or food so tasty that their pets eat too much. And unlike wild animals, home-bound pets may have few opportunities to run around and burn off the extra food or surplus calories.

A *calorie* is simply a measure of how much energy food contains. For example, food high in fats (pizza, cheeseburger, french fries, donuts) usually have twice the calories of foods high in protein (fish, chicken, eggs) or high in carbohydrates (vegetables, fruits, grains). The same factors that make pets overweight also make humans overweight.

Overweight

Why the huge increase? Like animals, we humans have an inherited biological system that regulates hunger to keep us at our ideal weights. However, there is currently a worldwide problem of overweight and obesity.

Overweight **means that a person is 20% over the ideal body weight.**

Obesity **means that a person is 30% or more above the ideal body weight.**

The numbers on the right show that, over the years, the percentage of adult Americans who are overweight or obese has increased dramatically, from 26% in 1976 to 64% in 2006 (CDC, 2006b; J. O. Hill et al., 2003). Also, the percentage of American youth who are overweight or obese has increased at alarming rates. About 34% of American youth are overweight and nearly 20% are obese (CDC, 2006a).

1976	26%
2000	55%
2006	64%

Percent of adult Americans who are overweight or obese

Overweight and obesity are primarily caused by two factors: eating more than is required to fuel the body's current energy needs and not getting enough exercise to burn off any extra food (surplus calories) (CDC, 2006c). For example, it is well known that during their freshman year, some students gain 7 to 15 pounds, primarily because of all-you-can eat dining halls and late-night junk food snacks (Hellmich, 2006b; Levitsky, 2003).

Being overweight or obese, which has become a worldwide health problem, significantly shortens people's lifespan and increases their risk for heart disease, stroke, high blood pressure, clogged arteries, kidney failure, and adult-onset diabetes (B. Healy, 2006; J. O. Hill et al., 2003; Hsu, 2006; S. J. Olshansky, 2006). Also, 14% of cancer deaths in men and 20% in women have been attributed to obesity (Calle et al., 2003). In the United States, weight-related costs are estimated to add about $12 billion to the expenses paid by employers (Freudenheim, 2003).

However, solving the problem of being overweight or obese is complicated because eating is influenced by three hunger factors.

Three Hunger Factors

What controls your eating? Hunger is considered a biological drive because eating is essential to our survival. However, the way in which you satisfy your hunger drive—when, where, and how much you eat—is influenced by three different factors: biological, psychosocial, and genetic (J. O. Hill et al., 2003).

Biological hunger factors **come from physiological changes in blood chemistry and signals from digestive organs that provide feedback to the brain, which, in turn, triggers us to eat or stop eating.**

If your eating was regulated primarily by biological factors, as in most animals, you would keep your weight at optimal levels. The fact that 64% of adults are overweight or obese and that some individuals suffer from serious eating problems indicates the influence of both psychosocial and genetic factors.

Psychosocial hunger factors **come from learned associations between food and other stimuli, such as snacking**

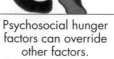

Psychosocial hunger factors can override other factors.

while watching television; sociocultural influences, such as pressures to be thin; and various personality problems, such as depression, dislike of body image, or low self-esteem.

Genetic hunger factors **come from inherited instructions found in our genes. These instructions determine the number of fat cells or metabolic rates of burning off the body's fuel, which push us toward being normal, overweight, or underweight.**

These three hunger factors interact to influence your weight. For example, because of psychosocial factors, some of us eat when we should not, such as during stress. Because of biological factors, some of us may respond too much or too little to feedback from our digestive organs. Because of genetic factors, some of us can eat more calories and still maintain optimal weight.

We'll discuss these three hunger factors, beginning with biological factors.

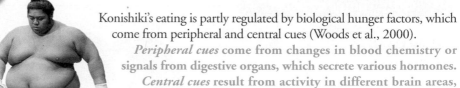
Biological Hunger Factors

Why do you start eating?

The Japanese sumo wrestler on the right is Konishiki, nicknamed Meat Bomb. He is 6 feet 1 inch tall and weighs 580 pounds, which is considered normal by sumo standards but obese by Western medical charts. He maintains his huge body by consuming about 10,000 calories daily, which is 3–5 times the amount required by an average-sized man.

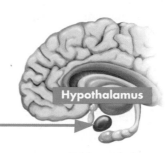

Konishiki's eating is partly regulated by biological hunger factors, which come from peripheral and central cues (Woods et al., 2000). *Peripheral cues* come from changes in blood chemistry or signals from digestive organs, which secrete various hormones. *Central cues* result from activity in different brain areas, which in turn results in increasing or decreasing appetite.

Peripheral and central cues make up a complex biological system that evolved over millions of years to help humans and animals maintain their best weights for survival.

Peripheral Cues

Signals for feeling hungry or full come from a number of body organs that are involved in digestion and regulation of blood sugar (glucose) levels, which is the primary source of fuel for the body and brain.

1 When empty, the *stomach* secretes a newly discovered hormone, ghrelin, which carries "hunger signals" to the brain's hypothalamus, the master control for hunger regulation (Raloff, 2005). When the stomach is full, stretch receptors in its walls send "full signals" to the brain's hypothalamus, which decreases appetite (Chaudri et al., 2006).

2 The *liver* monitors the level of glucose (sugar) in the blood. When the level of glucose (blood sugar) falls, the liver sends "hunger signals" to the brain's hypothalamus; when the level of glucose rises, the liver sends "full signals" to the hypothalamus (Woods et al., 2000).

3 The *intestines* also secrete ghrelin, which carries "hunger signals" to the hypothalamus, increasing appetite. The intestines also secrete another hormone called PYY, which carries "full signals" to the hypothalamus, decreasing appetite (Raloff, 2005). Finally, the intestines secrete a hormone called CCK (cholecystokinin), which signals the hypothalamus to inhibit eating (Chaudri et al., 2006).

4 *Fat cells* secrete a hormone, called leptin, which acts on the brain's hypothalamus. If levels of leptin are falling, the hypothalamus increases appetite; if levels are rising, the hypothalamus decreases appetite. The secretion of leptin helps maintain a constant level of body fat and defend against starving the body to death (Rui, 2005).

Summary. The stomach and intestines secrete a number of "hunger" or "full" hormone signals that act on the hypothalamus, which is the master control for regulating eating and produces central cues for increasing or decreasing appetite.

Central Cues

1 The brain has an area with different groups of cells that are collectively called the *hypothalamus* (left figure). Each group of cells is involved in a different kind of motivation, including regulation of thirst, sexual behavior, sleep, intensity of emotional reactions, and hunger. We'll focus on two particular groups of cells, the lateral and ventromedial hypothalamus, that affect hunger in opposite ways, either increasing or decreasing your appetite.

Hypothalamus

2 The *lateral hypothalamus* refers to a group of brain cells that receives "hunger signals" from digestive organs—increase in ghrelin, fall in level of blood glucose, and fall in levels of leptin. The lateral hypothalamus interprets these "hunger signals" and increases your appetite (Woods et al., 2000).

For example, electrical stimulation of the lateral hypothalamus causes rats to start eating, while destruction of the lateral hypothalamus causes rats to stop eating and even starve without special feeding.

3 The *ventromedial hypothalamus* refers to a group of brain cells that receives "full signals" from digestive organs—a full stomach activates stretch receptors, rise in level of blood glucose, rise in levels of leptin, and increase in the hormones PYY and CCK. The ventromedial hypothalamus interprets these "full signals" and decreases appetite.

For example, electrical stimulation of the ventromedial hypothalamus causes rats to stop eating, while destruction of the ventromedial hypothalamus causes rats to overeat and become obese. In addition, various chemicals affect other cells of the hypothalamus and regulate our appetites for specific foods (B. M. King, 2006).

Summary. The hypothalamus is involved in regulating many different kinds of motivated behaviors; in this case, we focused on hunger. The hypothalamus has one group of cells, called the lateral hypothalamus, that responds to "hunger signals" by increasing your appetite so you start eating. The hypothalamus has another group of cells, called the ventromedial hypothalamus, that responds to "full signals" by decreasing your appetite so you stop eating. This wonderfully complex biological system for regulating hunger is hard-wired and present in a newborn's brain. Although this system is designed to keep us at our ideal weights, we'll discuss a number of genetic and psychological factors that can interfere with this system and cause overeating and even starvation.

C. Hunger

Are identical twins always the same weight?

Researchers generally find that identical twins (photo on right), even when separated soon after birth and reared in adopted families, are much more alike in weight than fraternal twins reared apart (Bouchard et al., 1990). This similarity in weight is due to genetic hunger factors.

Genetic hunger factors come from inherited instructions found in our genes. These instructions determine the number of fat cells or metabolic rates of burning off the body's fuel, which push us toward being normal, overweight, or underweight.

Identical twins share the same genes and thus are similar in weight.

On the basis of twin studies, researchers concluded that inherited factors contribute 70–80% to the maintenance of a particular body size and weight, while environmental factors contribute the other 20–30% (Bulik et al., 2003). The finding that genetic hunger factors contribute 70–80% to having a certain body size and weight explains why identical twins have similar body types. The finding that environmental factors contribute 20–30% to body size explains why one twin may weigh a little more or less than the other.

Recent research shows that people who have a commonly found variation of a gene are at an increased risk of becoming obese. This genetic finding gives hope to the possibility of discovering other common genes involved in obesity (Christman, 2006; Harmon, 2006).

So far, psychologists have identified four genetic hunger factors.

1 We inherit different numbers of fat cells.

Fat cells, **whose number is primarily determined by heredity, do not normally multiply except when people become obese. Fat cells shrink if we are giving up fat and losing weight (left) and greatly enlarge if we are storing fat and gaining weight (right)** (N. R. Carlson, 1998).

People who inherit a larger number of fat cells have the ability to store more fat and are more likely to be fatter than average.

2 We inherit different rates of metabolism.

Metabolic rate **refers to how efficiently our bodies break food down into energy and how quickly our bodies burn off that fuel.**

For example, if you had a low metabolic rate, you would burn less fuel, be more likely to store excess fuel as fat, and thus may have a fatter body. In comparison, if you had a high metabolic rate, you would burn off more fuel, be less likely to store fat, and thus may have a thinner body (left figure). This means that people can consume the same number of calories but, because of different metabolic rates, may maintain, lose, or gain weight. There are only two known activities that can raise metabolic rate: exercise and smoking cigarettes. Researchers found that exercise raises metabolic rate 10–20% and that nicotine raises it 4–10%. That's the reason exercise helps dieters lose weight and smokers generally gain weight when they stop smoking (Audrain et al., 1995).

3 We inherit a set point to maintain a certain amount of body fat.

The *set point* **refers to a certain level of body fat (adipose tissue) that our bodies strive to maintain constant throughout our lives.**

For example, a person whose body has a higher set point will try to maintain a higher level of fat stores and thus have a fatter body (right figure). In comparison, a person whose body has a lower set point will maintain a lower level of fat stores and thus have a thinner body (Woods et al., 2000). If a person diets to reduce the level of fat stores, the body compensates to maintain and build back fat stores by automatically lowering the metabolic rate and thus consuming less fuel. That's the reason dieters may lose weight for the first two or three weeks and then stop losing; the body has lowered its metabolic rate. Researchers concluded that because the body protects its fat stores, long-term dieting will be unsuccessful in treating overweight people unless they also exercise (Leibel et al., 1995).

4 We also inherit weight-regulating genes.

Weight-regulating genes **play a role in influencing appetite, body metabolism, and secretion of hormones (leptin) that regulate fat stores.**

For example, the mouse on the left has a gene that increases a brain chemical (neuropeptide Y) that increased eating so that it weighs three times as much as the normal-weight mouse on the right (Gura, 1997). Researchers have also found a gene that can jack up metabolism so that calories are burned off as heat rather than stored as fat (Warden, 1997). This latter finding may explain why about 10% of the population can stay trim on a diet that would make others fat.

You have seen how genetic hunger factors are involved in the regulation of body fat and weight.

Next, we'll explore several psychological factors involved in the regulation of eating and weight.

Always room for dessert? Many of us have a weakness for certain foods, and mine (R. P.) is for desserts. Even though my biological and genetic hunger factors may tell me (my brain) when to start and stop eating, I can use my large forebrain to override my innately programmed biological and genetic factors. My forebrain allows me to rationalize that one dessert can do no harm. This kind of rationalizing comes under the heading of psychosocial factors.

Psychosocial hunger factors come from learned associations between food and other stimuli, such as snacking while watching television; sociocultural influences, such as pressures to be thin; and various personality traits, such as depression, dislike of body image, or low self-esteem.

Psychosocial hunger factors can have an enormous effect on our eating habits and weight and contribute to many problems associated with eating, such as becoming overweight, eating when stressed or depressed, and bingeing (Ward et al., 2000). We'll discuss three psychosocial hunger factors—learned associations, social-cultural influences, and personality traits.

Learned Associations

The best examples of how *learned associations* influence eating are when we eat not because we're hungry but because it's "lunchtime," because foods smell good, because our friends are eating, or because we can't resist large portions

Extra large box of popcorn has same calories as a meal!

(Hellmich, 2005). For example, an extra large box of popcorn is equivalent in calories (900) to a major meal. Health professionals warn that many Americans prefer large portions and tasty junk foods high in calories, and this has resulted in an increasing rate of overweight and obesity in both children and adults (Hellmich, 2005; Rozin et al., 2003).

Researchers are especially concerned about the continued rise in obesity in children, from 7% in 1980 to 17% in 2004 (Horovitz, 2003; Ogden et al., 2006). Childhood obesity is very difficult to treat, and an obese child has a high probability of becoming an obese adult with the associated health risks we discussed earlier (Hellmich, 2006a).

Health professionals advise us to unlearn many of our learned food associations. We should eat only when hungry and eat smaller portions and healthier foods (Pi-Sunyer, 2003).

Social-Cultural Influences

Examples of how *social-cultural influences* affect food preferences and body weight may be cited from around the world.

Czech Republic. In the 1970s, the Czech Republic government subsidized cheap fatty sausage and dairy products. The result was that 45% of Czech women and a smaller percentage of men are obese. Also, the Czech Republic has the world's highest death rates from heart disease. The government instituted programs to encourage healthier eating habits, which were effective until fast-food restaurants opened all over the country (Elliott, 1995; Jarrett, 2006).

China. In parts of China, fatty fast foods have become very popular along with a more sedentary lifestyle. This has resulted in an increase in obesity and associated diseases of the heart and blood circulation that were previously uncommon in China. In addition, there has been an alarming increase in obesity among children, who are pampered by a culture that prizes well-nourished children as indicating affluence and well-being (Mydans, 2003).

In Chinese "xiao pangzi" means "little fatties."

United States. In the United States, there are many cultural pressures on females to be thin. For example, the mass media advertise that the ideal female is one with a slender body. As a result, many American females report being dissatisfied with their weight and see themselves as overweight even when they are not. An additional problem for females is that their desire to have the ideal slim advertised body may lead to eating disorders (Mayo Clinic, 2006a). In comparison, American males are more satisfied with their weight, less influenced by mass media, and develop fewer eating problems (Hargreaves & Tiggemann, 2006).

Personality Traits

If a person has certain *personality traits,* he or she may be at greater risk for overeating as well as developing serious eating disorders, such as overeating when stressed or depressed, going on food binges (bulimia nervosa), or starving oneself (anorexia nervosa). We'll discuss serious eating problems in the Application section.

The particular personality traits that have been associated with eating problems include depression, anxiety, markedly low self-esteem, heightened sensitivity to rejection, excessive concern with approval from others, high personal standards for achievement, a history of physical or sexual abuse, and the need to have control (over oneself or one's body) (Polivy & Herman, 2002). Someone with these kinds of personality traits, which are often accompanied by stress, anxiety, and emotional upset, may find it very difficult and sometimes almost impossible to control his or her eating (J. E. Brody, 2003). As we'll discuss in the Application section, individuals with serious eating problems may need to seek professional help and counseling.

Although hunger is considered a biological need, you have seen how numerous psychosocial hunger factors can greatly influence where, when, and how the hunger drive is satisfied. And, as we'll discuss in the Application section, there are extreme cases in which psychosocial factors can completely override the hunger drive.

Next, we'll discuss another very important biological need, sexual behavior.

I look too fat!

Personality traits influence eating habits.

D. Sexual Behavior

Why do lions know how to do it?

Although we don't look, sound, or behave the same as lions do, we share similar biological and genetic factors that regulate sexual behavior. The sexual behavior of lions and most animals is controlled chiefly by genetic and biological factors, which means that most animals engage in sex primarily for reproduction.

Genetic sex factors include inherited instructions for the development of sexual organs, the secretion of sex hormones, and the wiring of the neural circuits that control sexual reflexes.

Biological sex factors include the action of sex hormones, which are involved in secondary sexual characteristics (facial hair, breasts), sexual motivation (more so in animals than in humans), and the development of ova and sperm.

Lions, like most animals, generally avoid sexual interactions

In most animals, sexual behavior is regulated by genetic and biological factors.

unless the female is in heat, which means she is ovulating and can be impregnated. In comparison, humans engage in sexual behavior for many reasons, which point to psychological sex factors.

Psychological sex factors play a role in developing a sexual or gender identity, gender role, and sexual orientation. In addition, psychological factors can result in difficulties in the performance or enjoyment of sexual activities.

For example, otherwise healthy men and women may report difficulties in sexual activities arising from stress, anxiety, or guilt, which can interfere with the functioning of genetic and biological sex factors. One reason psychological factors play such an important role in human sexual behavior is that our large forebrains have the capacity to think, reason, and change our minds and thus increase, interfere with, or completely block sexual motivation, performance, or enjoyment.

As we did for the hunger drive, we'll discuss, in order, the influences of genetic, biological, and psychological factors on sexual behavior.

Genetic Influences on Sexual Behavior

Which sex organ?

How we develop a particular sex organ, male or female, is determined primarily by a genetic program that is contained in a single human cell about the size of a grain of sand (Faller et al., 2004).

SEX CHROMOSOME

Unlike the other cells of our body, which contain 46 chromosomes (23 pairs), the sperm and egg each contain half that number and are called sex chromosomes (figure below).

The *sex chromosome,* which is in the sperm or the egg, contains 23 chromosomes, which in turn have genes that contain instructions for determining the sex of the child.

As we discussed earlier (p. 68), each chromosome is made up of a long strand of DNA (deoxyribonucleic acid). On this long strand of DNA are hundreds of genes, which contain the chemically coded instructions for the development and maintenance of our bodies. In the figure above, notice that some sperm have an **X** chromosome and some have a **Y,** which contain different genetic instructions and, as you'll see, result in the development of different sex organs (penis or vagina).

Sperm

or

Egg

1 The human egg contains one of the sex chromosomes, which is always an **X** chromosome. Thus, each human egg has a single **X** chromosome.

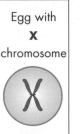
Egg with **X** chromosome

2 A human sperm also contains one of the sex chromosomes. However, the sperm's chromosome can be either an **X** chromosome, which has instructions for development of *female sex organs* and body, or a **Y** chromosome, which has instructions for *male sex organs* and body. Thus, the sperm (**X** or **Y**) determines the sex of the infant.

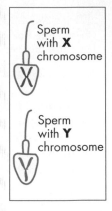
Sperm with **X** chromosome

Sperm with **Y** chromosome

3 During fertilization, a single sperm penetrates an egg and results in a fertilized egg with 23 pairs of chromosomes. If the last pair has the combination **XY,** it means the egg contains the genetic instructions for developing a male's sex organs (top right figure). If the last pair has the combination **XX,** it means the egg contains the genetic instructions for developing a female's sex organs (bottom right figure).

Male instructions
XY

Female instructions
XX

Following fertilization, the human cell, which is called a *zygote,* will divide over and over many thousands of times during the following weeks and months and eventually develop into a female body with female sex organs or a male body with male sex organs.

How an unborn infant actually develops male or female sex organs is an interesting story, especially since everyone begins as a female.

Genetic Influences (continued)

DIFFERENTIATION

Although it would seem that at fertilization you are destined to be either a male or a female, there is actually no physical difference between a male and a female embryo for the first four weeks of development in the womb. During this time period, the embryos are identical and have the potential to develop into either a male or a female. At about the fifth week, the embryo begins to differentiate into either a male or a female because of the presence or absence of certain sex hormones (Bendsen et al., 2006).

MALE SEX ORGAN AND MALE BRAIN

XY =
Testosterone

In an embryo that began from an **XY** fertilized egg, the **Y** sex chromosome has instructions for the development of male testes. At about the fifth week, the testes begin to grow and produce tiny amounts of male hormones or *androgens*, one of which most people know as *testosterone*.

The presence of testosterone does two things: It triggers the development of the male sexual organ (penis), and it programs a particular area of the brain, called the hypothalamus, so that at puberty it triggers the pituitary gland to secrete hormones on a continuous basis, which results in the continuous production of sperm.

Presence
of testosterone
results in a
male brain.

FEMALE SEX ORGANS AND FEMALE BRAIN

XX = No
Testosterone

In an embryo that began from an **XX** fertilized egg, the second **X** sex chromosome contains instructions for the development of ovaries, which do not secrete testosterone.

The absence of testosterone in the developing embryo means two things: It leads to the automatic development of female sexual organs (clitoris and vagina), and the hypothalamus, which is normally programmed for female hormonal functions, keeps its female program. Thus, at puberty, this female-programmed hypothalamus triggers the pituitary gland to secrete hormones on a cyclic basis, which results in the menstrual cycle.

Absence of
testosterone
results in a
female brain.

IMPORTANCE OF TESTOSTERONE

The *presence* of testosterone, which is secreted by fetal testes, results in male sexual organs and a male hypothalamus; the *absence* of testosterone results in female sexual organs and a female hypothalamus (Kalat, 2007).

When the infant is born, the doctor identifies the infant's sex organs and says those famous words, "It's a boy" or "It's a girl." At that point a hormonal clock begins ticking and its alarm will set off biological factors at puberty.

Biological Influences

You have seen how genetic sex factors influence the development of the body's sex organs. The next big event to affect a person's sex organs and sexual motivation occurs at puberty as a result of biological sex factors.

Sex hormones secreted during puberty both directly and indirectly affect our bodies, brains, minds, personalities, self-concepts, and mental health. We'll focus on how sex hormones affect our bodies.

Sex hormones. Before and shortly after birth sex hormones are released in our bodies.

Sex hormones, **which are chemicals secreted by glands, circulate in the bloodstream to influence the brain, body organs, and behaviors. The major male sex hormones secreted by the testes are** *androgens,* **such as testosterone; the major female sex hormones secreted by the ovaries are** *estrogens.*

Testosterone

Sex hormones remain inactive until puberty, when a recently discovered hormone called kisspeptin stimulates the production of androgens and estrogens to prepare the body for reproduction (Kotulak, 2006).

Male–female differences. The presence or absence of testosterone in the womb causes different neural programming so that the male hypothalamus functions differently from the female hypothalamus.

Male
hypothalamus
triggers
release of **testosterone.**

The *male hypothalamus* **triggers a continuous release of androgens, such as testosterone, from the testes. The increased level of androgens causes the development of male secondary sexual characteristics, such as facial and pubic hair, muscle growth, and lowered voice.**

The *female hypothalamus* **triggers a cyclical release of estrogens from the ovaries. The increased level of estrogens causes the development of female secondary sexual characteristics, such as pubic hair, breast development, and widening of the hips. The cyclical release of hormones (estrogen and progesterone) also regulates the menstrual cycle.**

Estrogen

Female
hypothalamus
triggers
release of
estrogen.

SEXUAL MOTIVATION

In humans, normal sexual development and motivation depend upon levels of sex hormones being within the normal range. In rare cases, males are born with an extra X chromosome, XXY or Klinefelter's syndrome, which results in undersized testes and penis, decreased secretion of testosterone, infertility, no development of secondary sexual characteristics at puberty, and little or no interest in sexual activity. However, when given testosterone replacement at puberty, males regain sexual interest and drive (Lanfranco et al., 2004). Thus, the absence of sex hormones interferes with normal sexual development and motivation. But, if a person has a normal level of sex hormones, any increase or decrease in sexual interest and motivation is more dependent on psychological factors, such as feelings, desires, and expectations (Crooks & Baur, 2002). For example, some men and women with normal levels of sex hormones report low sex drives. In these cases, giving additional sex hormones causes little or no increase in the sexual drive, presumably because the causes are psychological (Bancroft, 2002).

As genetic and biological factors guide our bodies toward physical sexual maturity, numerous psychological factors are preparing our minds for psychological sexual maturity. Next, we'll examine these psychological sex factors.

D. Sexual Behavior

Psychological Influences on Sexual Behavior

How do boys and girls become men and women?

As boys and girls go through puberty, various genetic and biological factors prepare their bodies for sexual maturity (Ojeda et al., 2006). At the same time their bodies are developing, boys and girls are observing, imitating, and learning behaviors of their mothers, fathers, older siblings, and other adults in their environments. At this point, psychological sex factors come into play.

Psychological sex factors play a role in developing a sexual or gender identity, gender role, and sexual

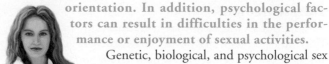

Sex hormones activate many physical and psychological changes.

XY = Testosterone

XX = Estrogen

orientation. In addition, psychological factors can result in difficulties in the performance or enjoyment of sexual activities.

Genetic, biological, and psychological sex factors combine and interact to result in boys and girls developing into sexually mature men and women.

Three psychological sex factors are especially important—gender identity, gender role, and sexual orientation. We'll discuss each in turn, beginning with gender identity.

1st Step: Gender Identity

Between the ages of 2 and 3, a child can correctly answer the question "Are you a boy or a girl?" The correct answer indicates that the child has already acquired the beginnings of a gender identity (Blakemore, 2003).

Gender identity, which was formerly called sexual identity, refers to the individual's subjective experience and feelings of being either a male or a female.

The doctor's words, "It's a girl" or "It's a boy," set in motion the process for acquiring a gender identity. From that point on, parents, siblings, grandparents, and others behave toward male and female infants differently, so that they learn and acquire their proper gender identity (C. L. Martin et al., 2002). For example, the little girl in the right photo is checking out a pretty dress in the mirror, a behavior that she has observed her mother doing and that she is now imitating.

By age 3, children know if they **are** boys or girls.

Gender identity is a psychological sex factor that exerts a powerful influence on future sexual thoughts and behavior, as clearly illustrated in the case of someone with a gender identity disorder, who is commonly referred to as a transsexual.

Gender identity disorder is commonly referred to as transsexualism. A transsexual is a person who has a strong and persistent desire to be the other sex, is uncomfortable about being one's assigned sex, and may wish to live as a member of the other sex (American Psychiatric Association, 2000).

Transsexuals usually have normal genetic and biological (hormonal) factors, but for some reason, they feel and insist that they are trapped in the body of the wrong sex and may adopt the behaviors, dress, and mannerisms of the other sex. There is no clear understanding of why transsexuals reject their biological sex. Current data indicate that the incidence of transsexualism is about the same for males and females (Bartlett et al., 2000). Infrequently, adults with gender identity disorder may seek surgery to change the sex organs that they were born with to the other sex. Because transsexuals acquire gender identities that do not match their external sex organs, they experience problems in thinking and acting and may not easily fit into or be accepted by society (Bartlett et al., 2000). However, the vast majority of people do acquire gender identities that match their external sex organs.

As you acquire a male or female gender identity, you are also acquiring a matching gender role.

2nd Step: Gender Roles

After the first step in becoming psychologically sexually mature, which is acquiring a male or female gender identity—"I'm a boy" or "I'm a girl"—comes the second step, which is acquiring a gender role.

Gender roles, which were formerly called sex roles, refer to the traditional or stereotypic behaviors, attitudes, and personality traits that society designates as masculine or feminine. Gender roles greatly influence how we think and behave.

Between the ages of 3 and 4, American children learn the stereotypic or traditional expectations regarding the kinds of toys, clothes, and occupations for men and women. By the age of 5, children have acquired many of the complex thoughts, expectations, and behaviors that accompany their particular gender role of male or female (Best & Thomas, 2004).

By age 5, a child knows how a boy or girl **behaves.**

For example, young boys learn stereotypic male behaviors, such as playing sports, competing in games, engaging in rough-and-tumble play, and acquiring status in his group. In comparison, girls learn stereotypic female behaviors, such as providing and seeking emotional support, emphasizing physical appearance and clothes, and learning to cooperate and share personal experiences (Eagly et al., 2000; Ruble et al., 2006).

As children, we all learned early on to adopt a male or female gender role, often without being aware of how subtly we were rewarded for imitating and performing appropriate sex-typed behaviors. Learning and adopting a gender role continue through adolescence and into adulthood and result in very different gender roles. For instance, adult American women tend to show stereotypic gender roles that can be described as socially sensitive, nurturing, and concerned with others' welfare. In comparison, adult American men tend to show gender roles that can be described as dominant, controlling, and independent (Eagly et al., 2004).

Dominant Controlling Independent

Sensitive Nurturing Concerned

Function. A major function of gender roles is to influence how we think and behave. Notice that male gender roles—dominant, controlling, and independent—can lead to different kinds of sexual thoughts and behaviors than female gender roles—socially sensitive, nurturing, and concerned. Thus, some of the confusion, conflict, and misunderstanding over sexual behavior come from underlying differences in gender roles. A major task a couple will have in establishing a healthy, loving relationship is to work out the many differences in thoughts, beliefs, and expectations that come from combining two different gender roles.

After we acquire a gender role, the next step involves knowing one's sexual orientation.

3rd Step: Sexual Orientation

In answering the question "Do you find males or females sexually arousing?" you are expressing your sexual orientation, which is the third step in reaching psychological sexual maturity.

Sexual orientation, **also called sexual preference, refers to whether a person is sexually aroused primarily by members of his or her own sex, the opposite sex, or both sexes.**

Homosexual orientation **refers to a pattern of sexual arousal by persons of the same sex.**

Heterosexual orientation **refers to a pattern of sexual arousal by persons of the opposite sex.**

Bisexual orientation **refers to a pattern of sexual arousal by persons of both sexes.**

A recent national survey of sexual orientation found that the vast majority (90%) of the American population reported having a heterosexual orientation, 2% a homosexual orientation, 2% a bisexual orientation, and the remaining 6% declined to identify their sexual orientation (Mosher et al., 2005).

Of several models that explain how we develop a particular sexual orientation, the interactive model is perhaps the most popular (Money, 1987; Zucker, 1990).

The *interactive model of sexual orientation* **says that genetic and biological factors, such as genetic instructions and prenatal hormones, interact with psychological factors, such as the individual's attitudes, personality traits, and behaviors, to influence the development of sexual orientation.**

Genetic and biological factors. There is debate over how much genetic and biological factors influence sexual orientation. Some researchers prefer the term *sexual preference* because it suggests that we have considerable freedom in choosing a sexual orientation and that genetic and biological factors do not play a major role (Baumrind, 1995; Byne, 1997). Other researchers prefer the term *sexual orientation* because they believe genetic and biological factors play a major role (Diamond & Sigmundson, 1997). A case that involved changing a person's gender identity intensified this heated debate.

Changing gender identity. In the 1960s, genetic and biological factors were thought to play minor roles in developing gender identity. That's because some babies who were born with inconclusive sex organs (tiny penis, no testicles) were said to be girls and were raised as girls; others were said to be boys and were raised as boys. Later, when

1st Step: Gender identity

2nd Step: Gender role

3rd Step: Sexual orientation

these children reached puberty, doctors discovered that some of these "girls" actually had the chromosomes of males and some of the "boys" had the chromosomes of females. However, some of those raised as "girls" decided to remain female and received corrective surgery (a vagina) and hormones (developed breasts). Others raised as "boys" decided to remain male and also received corrective surgery and hormones. In these cases, children chose the gender identity and orientation that matched their upbringing, not their genetic makeup. Based on such cases, researchers believed that gender identity and gender orientation could be changed if, before the age of 2, infants were assigned a gender identity and raised accordingly (Money, 1987). However, another case has questioned this belief.

Tragic case. While doctors were doing a routine medical procedure to repair an 8-month-old male's foreskin, they accidentally destroyed the infant's penis. As a result, doctors advised the parents to raise the boy (John) as a girl (Joan). However, since about the age of 8, Joan had been unhappy being and acting like a female and began to suspect that she was really a boy. By the time Joan was 14, she had received corrective surgery (a vagina) and hormonal treatment to physically look like a girl (developed breasts) but was so unhappy she threatened suicide and told doctors she thought she was a boy. After much discussion, doctors agreed to help Joan change back to John. In his 30s, John got married and reported he never liked being a female and was very happy being a male. Based on Joan-John's experience, researchers believe that individuals are genetically and biologically predisposed for having a male or female gender identity, which is not easily changed by being raised a certain way (boy or girl) (Diamond & Sigmundson, 1997). This case suggests that, unlike previously believed, humans may have a genetic predisposition to develop a male or female gender identity and gender orientation.

D. Sexual Behavior

How are men different from women?

After we have acquired a gender identity, gender role, and sexual orientation, there remain the sometimes difficult and complex decisions about when, where, and with whom sexual behavior is appropriate. Virtually every sex survey during the past 30 years reports that men think about sex more, have more sexual partners, reach orgasm more, and masturbate more than women (right graph). Why men consistently report more sexual activity and are allowed more sexual freedom than women has come to be known as the double standard (M. Crawford & Popp, 2003).

The *double standard for sexual behavior* refers to a set of beliefs, values, and expectations that subtly encourages sexual activity in men but discourages the same behavior in women.

The existence of a double standard allowing more freedom in sexual behavior for men than for women is well established (Peplau, 2003). How these male–female differences in sexual behavior came about is explained by two different theories—the biosocial theory and the evolutionary theory.

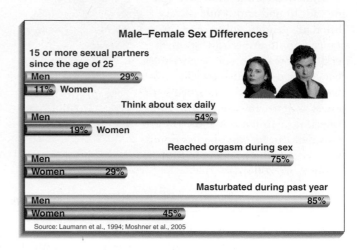

Male–Female Sex Differences

15 or more sexual partners since the age of 25
Men 29%
Women 11%

Think about sex daily
Men 54%
Women 19%

Reached orgasm during sex
Men 75%
Women 29%

Masturbated during past year
Men 85%
Women 45%

Source: Laumann et al., 1994; Moshner et al., 2005

Because of their importance, we'll discuss how each theory explains the male–female differences in sexual behaviors.

Biosocial Theory

There are two major questions about male–female sexual behavior that need answering. First, why do men consistently report greater interest in sex as shown by increased frequency of sexual activities, greater percentage of extramarital affairs, and desire for more sex partners (about 18 partners) than women (about 4 or 5 partners) (Buss & Schmitt, 1993)? Second, in an international study of 37 cultures, 10,000 individuals were asked to state their top priorities in choosing a mate. Across all cultures and all racial, political, and religious groups, why do men generally value physical attractiveness more than women, while women value the financial resources of prospective mates twice as much as men do (Buss et al., 1990)? One answer to these questions comes from the biosocial theory of sexual differences.

Biosocial theory, which emphasizes social and cultural forces, says that differences in sexual activities and in values for selecting mates developed from traditional cultural divisions of labor: Women were primarily childbearers and homemakers, while men were primarily providers and protectors.

According to the biosocial theory, the double standard arose from men's roles as protectors and providers, which allowed them greater control of and access to women and in turn allowed and encouraged greater sexual freedom. In comparison, women's roles restricted and discouraged sexual activities and protected against potential problems with jealousy, which could disrupt or interfere with being successful childbearers and homemakers (right photo) (W. Wood & Eagly, 2002).

Biosocial theory focuses on the importance of different social and cultural pressures that resulted in men and women developing different social roles, which in turn led to men and women developing differences in sexual behavior, which today we call the double standard.

Evolutionary Theory

A different explanation for the differences in sexual behavior between men and women comes from evolutionary theory.

Evolutionary theory, which emphasizes genetic and biological forces, says that our current male–female differences in sexual behavior, which we call the double standard, arise from genetic and biological forces, which in turn grew out of an ancient set of successful mating patterns that helped the species survive.

According to evolutionary theory, men developed a greater interest in sex and desire for many attractive sex partners because it maximized their chances for reproduction. In comparison, women would not benefit from indiscriminate and frequent mating because it would place them at risk for having offspring of low quality and create an unstable environment for raising their children. Instead, women placed a high priority on finding a man who was a good protector and provider, so she and her children would have a better chance for survival, especially during her childbearing years (Gangestad & Simpson, 2000). This evolutionary theory is a relatively new approach to explain the occurrence and development of current male–female differences in sexual behavior (de Waal, 2002).

Although there is considerable debate between supporters of the evolutionary and biosocial theories, some researchers suggest that the best and most complete explanation of male–female sex differences may come from combining the biosocial theory, which emphasizes social-cultural forces, with the evolutionary theory, which emphasizes genetic and biological forces (Baldwin & Baldwin, 1997).

Next, we'll return to a controversial question in sexual behavior: Why does an individual develop a homosexual orientation?

Provider & protector

Childbearer & homemaker

Were the brothers born gay?

According to national surveys, about 3% of the American male population are homosexual (gay) and about 1.5% of the female population are homosexual (lesbian). The question of whether sexual orientation is determined by choice or biological factors results in varied public opinion. A recent survey found that half of American adults believe sexual orientation is a result of *only* biological factors, one-third believe it is a result of choice *and* biological factors, and a smaller percentage believe it is a result of *only* choice (Epstein, 2006).

Both brothers are gay and share similar genetic factors.

National surveys usually find that only a slight majority (56%) of adult Americans approve of homosexuality (C. Goldberg, 1998). Many people say they would be more accepting of homosexuality if it were shown to be a genetic predisposition, since it would be similar to inheriting other preferences, such as being left-handed (Leland, 1994). We'll discuss recent genetic/biological and psychological factors that bear on the question of whether brothers Rick and Randy (left photo) were genetically predisposed to be gay or chose to be gay.

Genetic/Biological Factors

During the past 15 years, there has been a growing search for genetic and hormonal influences that contribute to the development of homosexuality (Rahman & Wilson, 2003). Some evidence comes from the study of sexual orientation in twins. For example, a number of studies on identical male and female twins found that, if one male or female twin of an identical pair was gay, about 31–65% of the time so was the second twin; this compared to 8–30% for fraternal twins and 6–11% for adopted brothers or sisters (Bailey & Zucker, 1995; Kendler et al., 2000b). However, these and other twin studies are criticized because some of the twins were not reared separately, so it is impossible to determine the effects of similar environments on sexual orientation. Still, these results suggest that genes do contribute to the development of homosexual orientation. Another kind of evidence comes from studies on genetic similarities among brothers.

Researchers studied over 900 men who had at least one sibling and examined numerous factors including their sexual orientation, the number of biological and nonbiological siblings they had, and whether or not they lived with their siblings. Results found that the only factor that increases the likelihood of a man having a homosexual orientation is having several older biological brothers. While the national rate of men having a homosexual orientation is about 3%, the rate increases to about 5% for men who have several older biological brothers (Bogaert, 2006a, 2006b). These results further support the role of genes in determining sexual orientation.

To examine biological factors involved in the development of sexual orientation, one study scanned people's brains as they smelled male and female odors associated with sexual attraction. Results showed that in heterosexual men, the hypothalamus (involved in sexual responses—pp. 80, 339) became activated only when smelling the female odor, but in homosexual men, activation occurred only when smelling the male odor. Thus, activation in the part of the brain involved in sexual responses is determined by sexual orientation and not biological sex. However, researchers cannot conclude whether changes in brain activity are the cause or the result of men's sexual orientation (Savic, 2005; Savic et al., 2005).

If there were a genetic/biological predisposition to homosexuality, we might expect that a person would become aware of his or her homosexual orientation before learning about or actually engaging in homosexual behavior and despite pressure from parents, siblings, or peers to develop a heterosexual orientation. Research shows that most people who have a homosexual orientation report becoming aware of their orientation by puberty, usually before knowing much about or engaging in homosexual behavior (Pillard & Bailey, 1995). The average age when homosexual males report beginning to have same-sex attraction is 10, and for homosexual females it is 12 (Savin-Williams, 2005).

All the above findings suggest that, to a certain extent, Rick and Randy were born with genetic or biological tendencies that played a role in the development of a homosexual orientation (Bailey et al., 2000). However, if genetic predisposition were decisive, then we would expect 100% of the pairs of identical twins to have exactly the same sexual orientation, but only about 50% do (Wade, 2005). This means that besides genetic/biological factors influencing the development of a homosexual orientation, there may also be psychological factors.

Psychological Factors

In studying psychological factors, researchers observe the behaviors of young children and consistently find that young boys who prefer girl playmates and girls' toys, avoid rough-and-tumble play, and wear girls' clothing have a tendency to develop a homosexual orientation (Dawood et al., 2000). In addition, adult gay men and lesbian women recall engaging in more behaviors of the opposite sex as children than do heterosexual adults (Bailey & Zucker, 1995). Although these studies are correlational and cannot show cause and effect, they do suggest that certain psychological factors (kinds of play behaviors and preferences) are associated with developing a homosexual orientation (Dawood et al., 2000).

> I knew I was gay before I did anything.

One psychological factor that influenced attitudes on homosexuality was that, until the 1970s, virtually all professional health organizations considered homosexuality to be an abnormal condition that often required psychotherapy to change. However, over the past 30 years, countless studies found that homosexuals scored about the same as heterosexuals on a wide variety of mental health tests, meaning that homosexuals are as mentally healthy as heterosexuals (K. P. Rosenberg, 1994). For these reasons, most professional health organizations now consider homosexuality a normal form or expression of sexual behavior and discourage all discriminatory practices toward homosexuals.

Next, we'll discuss several of the more common sexual problems and their treatments.

D. Sexual Behavior

Sexual Response, Problems, and Treatments

What are some of the problems?

Various surveys report that 10–52% of men and 25–63% of women aged 18 to 59, married and unmarried, experience a variety of sexual problems (Heiman, 2002). Some seek help for their problem, while others are ashamed or embarrassed and suffer in silence. There are two categories of sexual problems—paraphilias and sexual dysfunctions.

Paraphilias, **commonly called sexual deviations, are characterized by repetitive or preferred sexual fantasies involving nonhuman objects, such as sexual attractions to particular articles of clothing (shoes, underclothes).**

Sexual dysfunctions **refer to problems of sexual arousal or orgasm that interfere with adequate functioning during sexual behavior.**

When a person seeks help for a sexual problem, the clinician will check whether the causes are organic or psychological.

Organic factors **refer to medical conditions or drug or medication problems that lead to sexual difficulties.**

For example, certain medical conditions (such as diabetes mellitus), medications (such as antidepressants), and drugs (such as alcohol abuse) can interfere with sexual functioning.

Psychological factors **refer to performance anxiety, sexual trauma, guilt, or failure to communicate, all of which may lead to sexual problems.**

Four-stage model. To understand how psychological factors cause sexual problems, it helps to know Masters and Johnson's (1966) four-stage model of the sexual response.

Masters and Johnson proposed four stages of the human sexual response.

1st stage: Excitement. The body becomes physiologically and sexually aroused, resulting in erection in the male and vaginal lubrication in the female.

2nd stage: Plateau. Sexual and physiological arousal continues in males and females.

3rd stage: Orgasm. Men have rhythmic muscle contractions that cause ejaculation of sperm. Women experience similar rhythmic muscle contractions of the pelvic area. During orgasm, women and men report very pleasurable feelings.

4th stage: Resolution. Physiological responses return to normal.

Problems. Sexual problems can occur at different stages. For example, some individuals cannot reach stage 1, excitement, while others can reach stages 1 and 2 but not stage 3, orgasm.

There were few successful treatments for sexual problems until Masters and Johnson (1970) published their treatment program, which has several stages. First, the therapist provides basic information about the sexual response and helps the couple communicate their feelings. Then the therapist gives the couple "homework," which is designed to reduce performance anxiety. Homework involves learning to pleasure one's partner without genital touching or making sexual demands. This nongenital pleasuring is called *sensate focus.* After using sensate focus, the couple moves on to genital touching and intercourse. Sex therapists have expanded and modified Masters and Johnson's program and report considerable success with treating many sexual problems (Wincze & Carey, 1991).

We'll discuss two common sexual problems and their treatments.

Premature or Rapid Ejaculation

John and Susan had been married for three years and were both 28 years old. When the clinician asked about their problem, Susan said that sex was over in about 30 seconds because that's how long it took for John to have an orgasm. John replied that he had always reached orgasm very quickly and didn't realize it was a problem. Susan said that it was a problem for her (Althof, 1995). John's problem is called premature ejaculation.

Premature or *rapid ejaculation* **refers to persistent or recurrent absence of voluntary control over ejaculation, in which the male ejaculates with minimal sexual stimulation before, upon, or shortly after penetration and before he wishes to.**

Premature or rapid ejaculation is the most common male sexual problem and is reported by 21–33% of adult men (Pryor, 2006). A common treatment for it is called the squeeze technique. First, the partner stimulates the man's penis to nearly full erection. Then, the partner squeezes the head of the penis, which reduces arousal and erection. This squeeze procedure is repeated until the male develops a sense of control over arousal and ejaculation (Heiman, 2002). This procedure has proved successful in treating premature ejaculation.

Inhibited Female Orgasm

Greta and Bill had been married for five years and were in their late twenties. When asked about their problem, Greta said that she didn't think she had ever had an orgasm. She added that she loved Bill very much but that she was becoming less interested in sex (Durand & Barlow, 2006). Greta's problem has a name; it is called inhibited female orgasm.

Inhibited female orgasm **refers to a persistent delay or absence of orgasm after becoming aroused and excited.**

About 8–10% of women never reach orgasm and another 10% reach orgasm only by fantasizing (Haessler & Rosenthal, 2003). Difficulty in reaching orgasm is the most common complaint of women seeking help for sexual problems (Laumann et al., 2005).

Psychological treatment begins with sensate focus, during which the couple learns to pleasure each other and the woman learns to relax and enjoy her body's sensations. The man is told how to help a woman reach orgasm—for example, by using his hand or, in Greta's case, using a vibrator (Durand & Barlow, 2006). This program has proved successful in treating inhibited female orgasm.

Next, we'll discuss a sexual problem that involves a potentially deadly transmitted disease—AIDS.

✔ Concept Review

1. Physiological or psychological factors that cause us to act in a specific way at a particular time are included in the definition of _____.

2. Innate biological forces predispose an animal to behave in a particular way in the presence of a specific environmental condition. These ways of behaving are called _____.

3. There are several areas in the brain, including the nucleus accumbens and ventral tegmental area, that make up a neural circuit called the (a)_____ center. This center especially uses the neurotransmitter (b)_____. Many behaviors (eating, engaging in sex, gambling) that activate this center are (c)_____ with pleasurable feelings.

4. External stimuli, reinforcers, goals, or rewards that may be positive or negative and that motivate one's behavior are called _____.

5. When we perform behaviors to reduce biological needs or obtain various incentives, we are acting under the influence of (a)_____ motivation. When we perform behaviors because they are personally rewarding or because we are following our personal goals, beliefs, or expectations, we are acting under the influence of (b)_____ motivation.

6. Needs that are not critical to your survival but that are acquired through learning and socialization, such as the needs for achievement and affiliation, are called (a)_____ needs. Needs that are critical to your survival and physical well-being, such as food, water, and sex, are called (b)_____ needs.

7. The ascending order or hierarchy with biological needs at the bottom and social needs at the top is _____. This idea assumes that we satisfy our biological needs before we satisfy our social needs.

8. There are three major factors that influence eating. Cues that come from physiological changes are called (a)_____ factors. Cues that come from inherited instructions are called (b)_____ factors. Cues that come from learning and personality traits are called (c)_____ factors.

9. Biological cues for hunger that come from the stomach, liver, intestines, and fat cells are called (a)_____ cues. Biological cues that come from the brain are called (b)_____ cues.

10. The part of the hypothalamus that is involved in feelings of being hungry is called the (a)_____; the part that is involved in feelings of being full is called the (b)_____.

11. We inherit the following genetic factors involved in weight regulation: a certain number of (a)_____ cells that store fat; a certain (b)_____ rate that regulates how fast we burn off fuel; a certain (c)_____ point that maintains a stable amount of body fat; and weight-regulating (d)_____ that influence appetite, metabolism, and hormone secretion.

12. Psychological factors that influence eating include (a)_____ associations, (b)_____ influences, and (c)_____ variables.

13. Genetic sex factors involve the 23rd chromosome, called the (a)_____, which determines the sex of the child. Biological sex factors include sex hormones, which for the male are called (b)_____ and for the female are called (c)_____. Psychological sex factors include the subjective feeling of being male or female, which is called (d)_____; adopting behaviors and traits that society identifies as male or female, which is called (e)_____; and being more sexually aroused by members of the same or opposite sex, which is called (f)_____.

14. Evidence from the sexual orientation of identical twins and the shared genetic material from gay brothers are examples of (a)_____ factors in the development of a homosexual orientation. Young boys who prefer girls' toys and girl playmates and engage in opposite-sex behaviors show a tendency to develop a homosexual orientation, which shows the effects of (b)_____ factors on sexual orientation.

15. A person who has been infected by the human immuno-deficiency virus but has not yet developed any illnesses is said to be (a)_____. A person whose level of T-cells has dropped to 200 per cubic milliliter of blood but who may or may not have developed an illness is defined as having (b)_____.

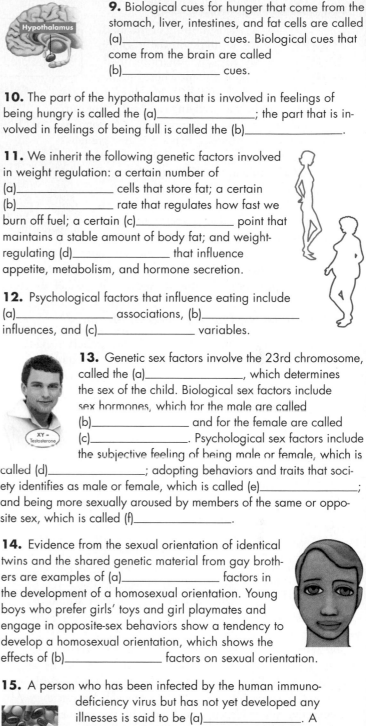

Answers: *1. motivation; 2. fixed action patterns; 3. (a) reward/pleasure, (b) dopamine, (c) rewarded or encouraged; 4. incentives; 5. (a) extrinsic, (b) intrinsic; 6. (a) social, (b) biological; 7. Maslow's hierarchy of needs; 8. (a) biological, (b) genetic, (c) psychosocial; 9. (a) peripheral, (b) central; 10. (a) lateral hypothalamus, (b) ventromedial hypothalamus; 11. (a) fat, (b) metabolic, (c) set, (d) genes; 12. (a) learned, (b) social-cultural, (c) personality; 13. (a) sex chromosome, (b) androgens, (c) estrogens, (d) gender identity, (e) gender role, (f) sexual orientation; 14. (a) genetic, (b) psychological; 15. (a) HIV positive, (b) AIDS*

F. Achievement

Why did Victor succeed?

At the beginning of the module, we told you about Victor, an African American high-school student whose buddies called him a "White boy" because they thought he was studying too hard. "You can't be cool if you're smart," says Victor, who was Mission Bay High's student body president, had a 3.7 (A–) grade point average, and planned to attend the University of Southern California in the fall (adapted from the *San Diego Union-Tribune,* June 17, 1994).

> It doesn't look cool if you work hard for grades.

Victor (right photo) grew up with an obstacle that goes largely unnoticed and is rarely discussed in public: pressure from students in the same racial or ethnic group not to succeed in the classroom (Fryer, 2005). Educators believe that the high dropout rates for minorities result, in part, from peer pressure not to succeed in school or show academic achievement (McWhorter, 2000). For Victor, academic achievement was one of his many social needs.

Social needs, **such as the desire for affiliation or close social bonds, nurturance or need to help and protect others, dominance or need to influence or control others, and achievement or need to excel, are acquired through learning and experience.**

If you are working hard to achieve academic success, you are demonstrating your social need for achievement.

The *achievement need* **refers to the desire to set challenging goals and to persist in pursuing those goals in the face of obstacles, frustrations, and setbacks.**

The achievement need not only is a major concern of college students but also ranks high (Level 4 out of 5) in Maslow's hierarchy of needs. We'll discuss four questions related to the achievement need: How is the need for achievement measured? What is high need for achievement? What is fear of failure? What is underachievement?

How Is the Need for Achievement Measured?

Do you have a strong need to achieve? Researchers David McClelland and John Atkinson tried to answer this question with a test called the Thematic Apperception Test, or TAT.

The *Thematic Apperception Test,* **commonly called the** *TAT,* **is a personality test in which subjects are asked to look at pictures of people in ambiguous situations and to make up stories about what the characters are thinking and feeling and what the outcome will be.**

What do you think is going on in this TAT card?

For example, the sample TAT card on the left shows a young man with a sad expression and a bright sun and fruit tree in the background. If you were taking the TAT, you would be asked to describe what is happening in this card. To measure the level of achievement, your stories would be scored in terms of achievement themes, such as setting goals, competing, or overcoming obstacles (J. W. Atkinson, 1958; D. C. McClelland et al., 1953). The TAT assumes that the strength of your need to achieve will be reflected in the kinds of thoughts and feelings you use to describe the TAT cards. However, TAT stories are difficult to score reliably because there is no objective way to identify which thoughts and feelings indicate level of achievement (Keiser & Prather, 1990). More recently, objective **paper-and-pencil tests** have been developed to measure achievement motivation because these tests are easier to administer and score and have somewhat better reliability and validity than does the TAT (Kaplan & Saccuzzo, 2005).

However, measuring the need for achievement has proved difficult because it relates to intrinsic motivational factors that include beliefs and expectations, which have proved difficult to quantify (Petri & Govern, 2004).

What Is High Need for Achievement?

There is perhaps no better example of individuals with high need for achievement than Olympic athletes. One example is Natalie Coughlin, who is two-time NCAA swimmer of the year, has set two world records and 22 American records, is on track to become the first woman to go under one minute in the 100-meter backstroke, and is one of five finalists for best amateur athlete. She trains four to five hours a day, six days a week, to compete in the Olympics while maintaining a 3.5 grade point average at the University of California, Berkeley (Lieber, 2002). Natalie has all the marks of someone with a high need for achievement (J. W. Atkinson & Raynor, 1974; D. C. McClelland, 1985).

Natalie Coughlin trains 4–5 hours a day, 6 days a week.

High need for achievement **is shown by those who persist longer at tasks; perform better on tasks, activities, or exams; set challenging but realistic goals; compete with others to win; and are attracted to careers that require initiative.**

Although the vast majority of us will not make the Olympics or achieve an A average in college, most of us will show varying degrees of the need to achieve by doing our best, striving for social recognition, and working to achieve material rewards (Hareli & Weiner, 2002).

The idea that there is a need for achievement and that it motivates many of our behaviors has generated a great deal of research. However, measuring a person's need for achievement and making predictions about an individual's level of achievement have proved difficult for two reasons: The TAT and paper-and-pencil tests have limited reliability and validity (p. 287), and achievement motivation is difficult to quantify because it involves intrinsic motivation (p. 331), which includes one's personal beliefs and expectations (Petri & Govern, 2004).

If we consider one side of a coin to be a need for achievement, then the other side is fear of failure and making excuses for failing.

Fear of Failure

Why do some fail? Just as some individuals may be motivated by a need for achievement, others may be motivated by a fear of failure. J. W. Atkinson (1964) believed that, in order to understand why a person succeeds or fails in reaching a goal, we must examine not only a person's need for achievement but also the fear of failure.

Fear of failure **is shown by people who are motivated to avoid failure by choosing easy, nonchallenging tasks where failure is more unlikely to occur.**

For example, fear of failure may motivate a student to study just enough to avoid failing an exam but not enough to get a good grade or set higher academic goals. In fact, the fear of failure is a good predictor of poor grades: The greater a student's fear of failure, the poorer his or her grades (W. E. Herman, 1990). Atkinson said that individuals who are motivated primarily by a fear of failure will never do as well, work as hard, or set goals as high as those who are motivated by a need for achievement. Also, the greater one's fear of failure, the greater the chances of trying to look good by engaging in self-handicapping (Zeidner & Matthews, 2005).

Self-handicapping. If a person is motivated primarily by the fear of failure, how does this individual explain his or her poor performances yet keep a good self-image? One solution is to use self-handicapping (E. Jones & Berglas, 1978).

Self-handicapping **refers to doing things that contribute to failure and then using these very things, knowingly or unknowingly, as excuses for failing to achieve some goal.**

For example, instead of studying for an exam, a student goes to a movie and then does poorly on the test. He excuses his bad grade by saying he didn't study, which is an example of self-handicapping. Researchers found that individuals with low self-esteem are most likely to engage in self-handicapping because it is one way to look good to their peers and thus protect their already low self-esteem (Elliot & Church, 2003). Self-handicapping excuses may involve health (missed sleep, have a cold), drug use (have a hangover), unrealistically high goals (how could I possibly do that), or procrastination (I didn't have enough time). In the short term, self-handicapping helps preserve our positive self-image and self-esteem, but in the long term, it interferes with taking personal responsibility to achieve our goals (Rhodewalt & Vohs, 2005).

One example of how fear of failure affects motivation is seen in individuals who are underachievers.

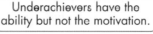

Underachievers have the ability but not the motivation.

Underachievement

Why do some underachieve? One of our friends described his 14-year-old son, Rich, as having all the brains in the world but doing nothing with them. Although Rich is a computer wizard, he gets terrible grades in school, never does his homework, and doesn't seem to have any ambition. Rich might be called an underachiever.

Underachievers **are individuals who score relatively high on tests of ability or intelligence but perform more poorly than their scores would predict.**

The most common examples of underachievers are students who score relatively high on ability or intelligence tests but perform poorly in school or academic settings (Lupart & Pyryt, 1996). Researchers found that underachievement is not related to socioeconomic class, that there are two or three male underachievers for every female, and that about 15% of students are underachievers (McCall, 1994).

Characteristics. The psychological characteristics of underachievers include having a poor self-concept, low self-esteem, and poor peer relationships and being shy or depressed. The cognitive characteristics of underachievers include fear of failure, poor perceptions of their abilities, and lack of persistence. This means that underachievers are less likely to persist in getting their college degrees, holding on to jobs, or maintaining their marriages (McCall, 1994). Thus, underachievement reduces performance in academic, job, and marital settings, and its effects may last through adulthood.

The paradox of underachievement is that underachievers have the abilities but are not motivated to use them. Clinicians, counselors, and researchers are developing treatment programs to help underachievers change their beliefs and expectations so they will develop the motivation to use their considerable abilities (McCall, 1994).

Three Components of Success

Why is a person successful? Explaining why some students are more successful than others involves the interaction of three components that we have just discussed: need for achievement, fear of failure, and psychological factors (self-concept, self-esteem, and confidence in one's abilities). For example, researchers wondered why some minority children from low-income homes were successful in school while others were not. Those minority students who succeeded had higher self-esteem, had more confidence in their abilities, and received more support and encouragement from a parent or caregiver (Finn & Rock, 1997). Researchers also found that students who were more successful in school had come from more stimulating home environments (parents spoke more to children, children had more books and watched less television) (Cleveland et al., 2000). Thus, having a stimulating home environment leads to a higher need for achievement, which in turn leads to more success in life.

Finally, successful students not only worked harder but also liked what they were doing. This "enjoyment of work" is an important cognitive factor that greatly influences motivation and is our next topic.

Need for Achievement + Fear of Failure + Psychological Factors → BEING SUCCESSFUL

F. Achievement

Do you work for love or money?

Each year, over 1,600 seniors compete in the Siemens Westinghouse Science Talent Search to win the most prestigious high-school science award in the United States. One winner was Anne Lee (photo below), a high-school senior from Arizona who has always enjoyed science. Lee's project involved developing software that could help identify the genes responsible for some diseases, such as Alzheimer's and autism (R. Smith, 2005). Lee's love of science translates into a motivating force that comes from various cognitive factors.

Cognitive factors in motivation refer to how people evaluate or perceive a situation and how these evaluations and perceptions influence their willingness to work.

Anne Lee perceives science projects as interesting and enjoyable and works hard to complete them. She plans to major in biology and become a scientific researcher. Compared to Lee's love of science, other students find science projects hard and boring and take science courses only because they are required. The difference between taking science courses because of a love of science and because of course requirements illustrates the difference between two kinds of motivation—intrinsic motivation and extrinsic motivation.

INTRINSIC MOTIVATION
Competent
Determined
Personally rewarding
Enjoyable

Intrinsic motivation involves engaging in certain activities or behaviors without receiving any external rewards because the behaviors themselves are personally rewarding or because engaging in these activities fulfills our beliefs or expectations.

Lee's dedication to science is in large part fueled by intrinsic motivation, which is related to feeling competent, curious, and interested, having self-determination, and enjoying the task, whether it's a science project, work you like, a hobby, or volunteer work. In comparison, extrinsic motivation involves different factors.

Extrinsic motivation involves engaging in certain activities or behaviors that either reduce biological needs or help us obtain incentives and external rewards.

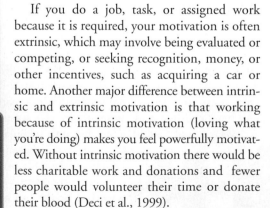

EXTRINSIC MOTIVATION
Competitive
Get recognition
Obtain incentives
Make money

If you do a job, task, or assigned work because it is required, your motivation is often extrinsic, which may involve being evaluated or competing, or seeking recognition, money, or other incentives, such as acquiring a car or home. Another major difference between intrinsic and extrinsic motivation is that working because of intrinsic motivation (loving what you're doing) makes you feel powerfully motivated. Without intrinsic motivation there would be less charitable work and donations and fewer people would volunteer their time or donate their blood (Deci et al., 1999).

So, here's an interesting question: What would happen to intrinsic motivation if you got paid for doing something that you love doing?

What happens if volunteers get paid?

Would receiving money for volunteering to give blood "turn off" or decrease the intrinsic motivation of donors to the point that they might give less blood or none at all?

Researchers generally believed that if people were given external rewards (money, awards, prizes, or tokens) for doing tasks (donating blood) from intrinsic motivation, their performance of and interest in these tasks would decrease (Deci & Moller, 2005). Because of the widely held belief that external rewards decreased intrinsic motivation, many books advised that rewards should not be used in educational settings, hospitals, or volunteer organizations because such rewards would do more harm than good. Recent reviews of this issue indicate that the effects of external rewards on intrinsic motivation are more complex than originally thought.

Researchers have reached three general conclusions about the influence of external rewards on intrinsic motivation (Deci & Moller, 2005; Eisenberger et al., 1999; Lepper et al., 1999). First, giving unexpected external rewards does not decrease intrinsic motivation, but people may come to expect such rewards. Second, giving positive verbal feedback for doing work that was better than others may actually increase intrinsic motivation. Third, giving external rewards for doing minimal work or completing a specific project may decrease intrinsic motivation.

Recent studies indicate that, unlike previously thought, external rewards that are unexpected or involve positive verbal feedback may increase intrinsic motivation. External rewards that are tied to doing minimal work or completing a specific project may decrease intrinsic motivation. For example, when parents or teachers praise children, the praise is likely to increase intrinsic motivation if the praise is sincere and promotes the child's feelings of being competent and independent. In contrast, insincere praise, praise for very small accomplishments, or praise that is controlling rather than rewarding may decrease intrinsic motivation (Deci & Moller, 2005).

People who donate blood are usually intrinsically motivated.

For a long time it was also thought that external rewards automatically decreased creative work and interest. But researchers have found that the effects of giving children a reward for completing a creative task depend on how children perceive the reward. If they perceive the reward as a treat, it will increase their intrinsic interest, but if they see the reward as external pressure to be creative, it will decrease their intrinsic interest (Eisenberger & Armeli, 1997). All these studies show that external rewards influence cognitive factors, which in turn may increase or decrease intrinsic motivation.

Next, we'll examine how poor and minority students can overcome educational disadvantages.

Why Did Poor and Minority Students Do Well?

How should poor and minority students be educated?

There has been a long history of research indicating that poor and minority children do not perform as well as their middle-class and White peers in many schools across the United States. Over many years, it has become increasingly clear that educating poor minority students to the national standards of proficiency is certainly possible, but requires considerable effort.

In order to develop school programs to help poor and minority students overcome their academic disadvantages, education policy makers rely on research findings that identify factors that have an important influence on children's intellectual and academic achievement. For instance, researchers report that parents who are professionals speak more to their children than parents who are on welfare.

Also, children of professionals hear many more words of encouragement than welfare children, and welfare children hear many more words of discouragement than children of professionals. The outcome for young children who hear fewer words spoken by their parents and receive a lot of discouragement is lower IQ scores and poorer academic success than for children who hear many words and receive a lot of encouragement (Hart & Risley, 2006).

Other related research reports that children from middle-class families have parents who are more sensitive, more encouraging, and less detached. Researchers conclude that although wealth influences children's IQs and academic success, parenting style matters even more. Thus, the advantages of middle-class children are due primarily to the language their parents use and their parents' child-rearing approach (Brooks-Gunn, 2006).

Procedure and Results

By using research findings about the disadvantages of poor and minority children to develop education programs, many schools have been able to educate these students to meet and rise above national standards of proficiency. The schools that best educate poor and minority children follow three practices. First, the school day is much longer; the first class often begins before 8 A.M., the last class ends after 4 P.M., and summer vacations are limited to one month. Second, there are clearly stated education goals and principals closely monitor whether or not teachers are achieving the goals. Teachers are very committed to these goals, and some go as far as making themselves available in the evenings to help students with their homework. Third, these schools not only are teaching students academics, but also are teaching them character, such as how to sit in class, make appropriate eye contact, and work cooperatively in a team (Tough, 2006).

Some of the best-recognized schools for their success in educating poor and minority students are operated by KIPP (Knowledge Is Power Program). One of the slogans KIPP schools use to teach students proper classroom behavior is SLANT (Sit up, Listen, Ask questions, Nod, and Track the speaker with their eyes). Children in KIPP schools appreciate the valuable lessons they receive about respectful behavior, saying it even helps them to pay better attention to speakers. KIPP schools use other slogans too, such as the one in the above photo and "All of Us Will Learn." Research findings indicate that the "noncognitive" skills these schools are teaching students, such as patience, respect, self-control, and motivation to work hard, have an important role on children's future academic and career success (Tough, 2006).

Many of the KIPP schools have demonstrated their effectiveness by improving students' performances on state exams. For instance, recent state exam scores for middle-school students at one KIPP school in New York were 12% higher than the state average. When compared to scores from other children in their high-poverty neighborhoods, 86% of KIPP 8th-grade students scored at grade level in math, but only 16% of students attending other schools reached math proficiency. This is especially impressive because when students enter KIPP schools, they are usually at least two grade levels behind (Tough, 2006).

Not only are students taught academics, such as reading and math, but slogans, such as REACH, are used to help them build character.

Conclusions

Children from low-class families who are behind in school need more than the same education provided to middle-class families. These children have a lot of catching up to do and therefore need a better, more intensive education. Results on the effect these special schools have on students' academic performance suggest that schools should not only focus on academics, but also include personality and behavioral curriculum. Programs like KIPP offer promise in reducing the academic achievement and IQ gap between low-class and minority students and middle-class and White students. Yet, these relatively few programs are only a beginning to a large-scale educational issue that requires substantial public school reform (Tough, 2006).

H. Application Eating Problems & Treatments

Dieting: Problems, Concerns, and Benefits

Why is dieting so difficult?

Some of us have learned to eat at certain times (learned associations) or eat when stressed (personality variables), or we come from families that encourage eating to show appreciation (cultural influences). Any of these psychosocial factors—learned associations, personality variables, or cultural influences—can override our genetic and biological factors and result in becoming overweight. The percentage of adult Americans who are overweight or obese has increased dramatically, from 26% in 1976 to 64% in 2006 (CDC, 2006b; J. O. Hill et al., 2003). Losing weight is difficult because the body is genetically designed to store extra calories as fat and because our large forebrains are good at rationalizing why we need to eat another piece of pizza and have a late-night snack.

We'll use the dieting experiences of television talk-show host Oprah Winfrey to illustrate the difficulties of dieting and how best to maintain an optimal weight.

Overweight and Dieting

In the 1970s, when Oprah Winfrey was in her twenties, she weighed about 140 pounds. By the mid-1980s, Oprah weighed about 190 pounds (left photo), which is considered overweight for her height and frame. She described getting home from work and being overwhelmed by a compulsion to eat. When her weight reached 211, she decided it was time for a diet program (B. Greene & Winfrey, 1996).

190 pounds

In the 1980s, Oprah went on a well-publicized diet in which she lost 67 pounds to weigh 142 pounds. She showed off her slim figure on television (right photo) and said she was finally cured of overeating. She was wrong.

In the 1990s, Oprah did not make the necessary changes in her lifestyle and she regained all her lost weight and then some, reaching about 237 pounds (left photo) (*People,* March 14, 2005, p. 148). Like all bodies, Oprah's body has two physiological factors that make it difficult to keep off lost weight.

142 pounds

Physiological factors. One physiological factor is that Oprah's body, which is set up to store a certain amount of fat, automatically adjusts to any decrease in fat stores by lowering its *rate of metabolism* by 25% (J. M. Friedman, 2003). This results in her body more efficiently burning fuel so she must eat even less or exercise more to avoid regaining lost weight. Another physiological factor is that Oprah's body has a *genetically fixed set point,* which maintains her fat stores at a stable level. If the level of fat stores drops below her set point, her body compensates by increasing her appetite so that her fat stores will return to their former level (J. M. Friedman, 2003). This means that the body fights a reduced food intake with two physiological actions: reducing the rate of metabolism and trying to increase fat stores. These factors explain why 90–95% of dieters regain their lost weight within 1 to 2 years and almost certainly after 5 years (Vogel, 1999).

237 pounds

Like most dieters who have regained their lost weight, Oprah admitted, "I didn't do whatever the maintenance program was. I thought I was cured. And that's just not true. You have to find a way to live in the world with food" (*People,* January 14, 1991, p. 84). After dieting, people like Oprah need to develop a *maintenance program* that involves eating less and exercising more.

Psychological factors. Oprah also realized that food had become more than nutrition. "For me, food was comfort, pleasure, love, a friend, everything. Now I consciously work every day at not letting food be a substitute for emotions" (Tresniowski & Bell, 1996, p. 81). Thus, some dieters need a change in lifestyle so that they don't eat when stressed or depressed. In trying to regulate and maintain her weight at a reasonable level (right photo), Oprah has tried a number of diets. Which diet program should one choose?

170 pounds

Diet Program/Lifestyle

In the early 2000s, Oprah's weight climbed again and she went on another diet and lost 33 pounds (Oldenburg, 2002). Oprah's difficulties in controlling her weight confirm the experiences of many dieters who have found it not only difficult to lose weight but even more difficult to keep the weight off. Researchers agree that the best way to keep weight off is by monitoring your weight daily, and when you begin to regain, immediately start eating better and increasing your exercise (Wing, 2005). Researchers found that a program of exercise and diet involves four factors: (1) changing one's attitudes toward food (making it less important); (2) changing one's eating patterns (consuming fewer calories); (3) developing a regular exercise program (a critical part of a weight program); and (4) perhaps the most important, sticking to this weight program over the long term, often for a lifetime (J. E. Brody, 2000b).

Low-fat or low-carbohydrate diet? There has been a big debate over which of these diets is more effective. Dieters report that a low-fat diet works better for some, while a low-carbohydrate diet works better for others. However, researchers report that whichever diet you choose, the ONLY reason you lose weight is that you're consuming fewer calories (Christensen, 2003). And, don't forget the exercise.

Food addiction. Obesity has been suspected to be a result of an addiction to food. But neurological connections between overeating and drug addiction have only recently been found. For instance, overeaters and drug addicts are reported to have deficiencies in dopamine (a chemical that makes us feel good). Also, similar brain activation patterns have been found during food and drug cravings (C. Brownlee, 2005). Thus, obese people may be compulsively driven to eat food just as drug addicts are driven to use drugs.

Next, we'll discuss the causes and treatments of two serious eating disorders.

Must you be thin? On the beautiful tropical island of Fiji, a bulky body had always been viewed as a beautiful body and women complimented each other on gaining weight. But then TV arrived in 1995 and began showing programs like "Melrose Place"

TV programs changed their body image.

(full of young, slender females) and commercials with slim models. After watching these programs, young girls began to develop a different body image, that of being slim. By 1998, the incidence of an eating disorder (bulimia nervosa) had almost doubled to 29% of young girls. Girls said that they wanted to be thin because everyone on TV who has everything is slim (Becker et al., 2002). This is an example of how cultural factors can encourage eating disorders. We'll discuss two serious eating disorders, anorexia nervosa and bulimia nervosa, their causes and treatments.

Anorexia Nervosa

Bonnie (center photo) had developed anorexia nervosa at age 19, when she was in college. She went from 120 to 70 pounds in six months and was hospitalized for treatment (Sohn, 2002). Bonnie, now 35, has the brittle bones of a very old woman because of her eating disorder, anorexia nervosa *(an-uh-REX-see-ah ner-VOH-sah)*.

Anorexia nervosa **is a serious eating disorder characterized by refusing to eat and not maintaining weight at 85% of what is expected, having an intense fear of gaining weight or becoming fat, and missing at least three consecutive menstrual cycles. Anorexics also have a disturbed body image: They see themselves as fat even though they are very thin (American Psychiatric Association, 2000).**

Anorexia nervosa, as defined by these symptoms, is a relatively rare disorder that affects about 1.0% of young women and a much smaller number of men aged 12 to 25.

Risk factors. One risk factor for anorexia nervosa is a dysfunctional family. In Bonnie's case, it was her mom who constantly told her that she was fat and even put padlocks on the kitchen cabinets so she could not have access to food (Sohn, 2002). Another risk involves personality factors, such as being very anxious, compulsive, rigid, and a perfectionist (Bulik, 2006). Recent studies on anorexic identical twins and genetic mapping point to genes on chromosome 1 as being factors in developing a severe form of anorexia nervosa (Kaye, 2002; Tyre, 2005). Thus, there may be multiple risk factors for developing anorexia nervosa.

Anorexics do not see themselves as skinny.

Treatment. Previous psychological treatments for anorexics had limited success, and drugs have not been useful (Walsh et al., 2006). A relatively new treatment program has reported success by using a form of family therapy. Parents are asked to become involved in helping their anorexic daughter to start eating and then gradually letting her control her eating (Tyre, 2005). Parents are coached in how to help their daughter overcome personality problems (discussed above) that may be worsened by adolescent difficulties (LeGrange, 2002). Generally, recovery is difficult: About 10% of anorexics die prematurely; 40% have chronic, recurrent symptoms; and 50% recover enough to maintain a healthy weight and positive self-image (Tyre, 2005).

Bulimia Nervosa

Carol's life seemed perfect when she was growing up, but all the time something was terribly wrong. "It was like I had to live in this fantasy world where everything was sweet and good and I got straight A's," Carol explains. "I started work when I was really young and I would do anything for anyone there and everyone thought I was so nice and so sweet. And I was just dying inside, literally." Carol, who began binge eating at the age of 15, was not overweight to begin with. She would eat a huge amount of food in one brief period and then force herself to vomit as a way of avoiding any weight gain (adapted from the *Daily Aztec,* March 22, 1984). Carol's disorder, which is called bulimia nervosa *(boo-LEE-me-ah ner-VOH-sah),* affects about 2% of the general population and about 8% of people who are overweight or obese (DeAngelis, 2002).

Bulimia nervosa **is characterized by a minimum of two binge-eating episodes per week for at least three months; fear of not being able to stop eating; regularly engaging in vomiting, use of laxatives, or rigorous dieting and fasting; and excessive concern about body shape and weight (APA, 2000).**

Risk factors. One risk factor involves cultural pressures to develop a slim body, as seen in the increase in bulimia nervosa among Fijian girls. Another risk factor involves personality characteristics, such as being excessively concerned about appearance, being too sensitive, and having low self-esteem and high personal standards for achievement. For some, bouts of depression, anxiety, mood swings, and problems with social relationships may trigger episodes of bulimia nervosa, which may lead to obesity (Stice, 2002).

Treatment. The psychological treatment for bulimia nervosa may involve ways to control weight as well as one of two kinds of psychotherapy: cognitive-behavioral therapy, which focuses on substituting positive thoughts for negative ones, or interpersonal therapy, which focuses on improving a person's social functioning (M. J. Cooper, 2005; G. T. Wilson et al., 2002). The drug treatment for bulimia nervosa, which involves the use of antidepressant drugs and possible unwanted side effects, was shown to be less effective than psychotherapy and offered no advantage when combined with psychotherapy (Jacobi et al., 2002). Follow-up studies report that about 50% of bulimics recover fully, 30–39% have some symptoms, and 9–20% have serious symptoms (Clausen, 2004; Collings & King, 1994; DeAngelis, 2002; Keel & Mitchell, 1997).

The eating disorders of anorexia and bulimia nervosa clearly illustrate how various personality and psychosocial factors can not only influence but even override the normal functioning of one of our basic biological needs, hunger.

Summary Test

A. Theories of Motivation

1. The combined physiological and psychological factors that cause you to act in specific ways at particular times are referred to as (a)_____. When motivated, you usually exhibit three characteristics: you are (b)_____ to do something; you (c)_____ your energies toward a specific goal; and you have different (d)_____ of feelings about reaching that goal.

2. There are four general theories that together help explain human motivation. The theory that applies primarily to animal motivation involves innate biological forces that determine behavior. This is called the (a)_____ theory. The reward/pleasure center theory says there are several areas in the brain, including the (b)_____ and _____, that especially use the neurotransmitter (c)_____. Many behaviors (eating, engaging in sex, gambling) that activate this center are (d)_____ with pleasurable feelings. The theory that says we are motivated by external rewards is called the (e)_____ theory. The theory that distinguishes between extrinsic and intrinsic motivations is called the (f)_____ theory. If we are motivated because we find the activities personally rewarding or because they fulfill our beliefs or expectations, our motivation is said to be due to (g)_____ motivation.

B. Biological & Social Needs

3. Food, water, and sleep are examples of (a)_____ needs. In comparison, needs that are acquired through learning and socialization are called (b)_____ needs. The theory that we satisfy our needs in ascending order, with physiological needs first and social needs later, is called (c)_____. According to this theory, needs are divided into five levels: biological, safety, love and belongingness, esteem, and self-actualization.

C. Hunger

4. If there is an almost perfect balance between how much food an organism needs to maintain the body's energy needs and how much the organism actually eats, the organism's weight is said to be (a)_____. Three different factors influence the hunger drive. Factors that come from physiological changes in blood chemistry and signals from digestive organs that provide feedback to the brain, which, in turn, triggers us to eat or stop eating, are called (b)_____ factors. Factors that come from learned associations between food and other stimuli, sociocultural influences, and various personality problems are called (c)_____ factors. Factors that come from inherited instructions contained in our genes are called (d)_____ factors.

5. Biological factors that influence eating come from two different sources. Cues arising from physiological changes in your blood chemistry and signals from your body organs are called (a)_____; cues from your brain are called (b)_____.

6. Genetic factors that influence hunger come from four different sources: the number of cells that store fat, which are called (a)_____; your rate of burning the body's fuel, which is called your (b)_____; the body's tendency to keep a stable amount of fat deposits, which is called the (c)_____; and a number of (d)_____ genes that influence appetite, metabolism, and secretion of hormones regulating fat stores.

D. Sexual Behavior

7. Human sexual behavior is influenced by three different factors. Inherited instructions for the development of sexual organs, hormonal changes at puberty, and neural circuits that control sexual reflexes are called (a)_____ factors. The fact that humans engage in sexual behavior for many reasons besides reproduction and the fact that humans experience sexual difficulties that have no physical or medical basis indicate the influence of (b)_____ factors on sexual behavior. Factors that regulate the secretion of sex hormones, which play a role in the development of secondary sexual characteristics, influence sexual motivation (more so in animals than in humans), regulate the development of ova and sperm, and control the female menstrual cycle, are called (c)_____ factors.

XY = Testosterone

8. Biological sex factors include the secretion of sex hormones, which is controlled by an area of the brain called the (a)_____. The major male sex hormones secreted by the testes are called (b)_____, and the major female sex hormones secreted by the ovaries are (c)_____. When hormone levels are within the normal range, there is little (d)_____ between levels of sex hormones and sexual motivation in humans.

9. Three psychological sex factors include the individual's subjective experience and feelings of being a male or a female, which is called (a)_____; traditional or stereotypic behaviors, attitudes, and personality traits that society designates as masculine or feminine, which are called (b)_____; and whether a person is sexually aroused primarily by members of his or her own sex, the opposite sex, or both sexes, which is called (c)_____.

10. The findings that identical twins are often alike in their sexual orientation and that homosexual brothers shared similar inherited material indicate the influence of (a)_____ factors on homosexual orientation. The finding that genetic factors do not necessarily determine sexual orientation indicates the influence of (b)_____ factors on sexual orientation.

11. There are two kinds of sexual problems. Problems that are characterized by repetitive or preferred sexual fantasies involving nonhuman objects (articles of clothing) are called (a)_____. Problems of sexual arousal or orgasm that interfere with adequate functioning during sexual behavior are called (b)_____. When a person seeks help for a sexual problem, the clinician will check whether the causes are (c)_____ or _____.

12. If a person has been infected by the human immunodeficiency virus (HIV) but has not yet developed one or more of 26 illnesses, that person is said to be (a)_____. A person whose level of T-cells (CD4 immune cells) has dropped to below 200 per cubic milliliter of blood (one-fifth the level of a healthy person) and who may or may not have any other symptoms is said to have (b)_____.

E. Cultural Diversity: Genital Cutting

13. In some cultures the female's external genitalia, usually including her clitoris and surrounding skin (labia minora), are cut away; this practice is called _____. Girls often submit to the fear, pain, and trauma of this procedure so as to gain social status, please their parents, and comply with peer pressure. A number of feminists in Africa have formed a society to fight the sexual mutilation of females.

F. Achievement

14. High in Maslow's needs hierarchy is a desire to set challenging goals and persist in pursuing those goals in the face of obstacles, frustrations, and setbacks. This social need is called the (a)_____. Someone who persists longer at tasks, shows better performance on tasks, activities, or exams, sets challenging but realistic goals, competes with others to win, and is attracted to careers that require initiative is said to have a high (b)_____. Individuals who score relatively high on tests of

ability or intelligence but perform more poorly than their scores would predict are called (c)_____. Individuals who choose either easy, nonchallenging tasks or challenging tasks where failure is probable and expected are said to be motivated by (d)_____.

15. If you engage in behaviors without receiving any external reward but because the behaviors themselves are personally rewarding, you are said to be (a)_____ motivated. If you engage in behaviors to reduce biological needs or obtain external rewards, you are said to be (b)_____ motivated.

G. Research Focus: Overcoming Educational Disadvantages

R E A C H   **16.** Schools that best educate poor and minority students have (a)_____ class days, clearly stated (b)_____, and teach students not only academics but also (c)_____. Research findings indicate that the (d)_____ skills these schools are teaching students, such as patience and respect, have an important effect on children's future academic and career success.

H. Application: Eating Problems & Treatments

17. A healthy weight-maintenance program, which can reduce the risk of serious medical problems of (a)_____ people, involves changing (b)_____ toward food, changing (c)_____ patterns, developing an (d)_____ program, and sticking to a long-term (e)_____ program. Two serious eating disorders are a pattern characterized by bingeing, fear of not being able to stop eating, and regularly purging the body, which is called (f)_____; and another pattern in which a person starves to remain thin, has a fear of being fat, and has a disturbed body image, which is called (g)_____.

Answers: 1. (a) motivation, (b) energized, (c) direct, (d) intensities; 2. (a) instinct, (b) nucleus accumbens, ventral tegmental area, (c) dopamine, (d) rewarded or encouraged, (e) incentive, (f) cognitive, (g) intrinsic; 3. (a) biological, (b) social, (c) Maslow's hierarchy of needs; 4. (a) ideal or optimal, (b) biological, (c) psychosocial, (d) genetic; 5. (a) peripheral cues, (b) central cues; 6. (a) fat cells, (b) metabolic rate, (c) set point, (d) weight-regulating; 7. (a) genetic, (b) psychological, (c) biological; 8. (a) hypothalamus, (b) androgens, (c) estrogens, (d) correlation or association; 9. (a) gender identity, (b) gender roles, (c) sexual orientation; 10. (a) genetic, (b) psychological; 11. (a) paraphilias, (b) sexual dysfunctions, (c) psychological, physiological; 12. (a) HIV positive, (b) AIDS; 13. genital cutting; 14. (a) achievement motive, (b) need for achievement, (c) underachievers, (d) fear of failure; 15. (a) intrinsically, (b) extrinsically; 16. (a) longer, (b) education goals, (c) character, (d) noncognitive; 17. (a) overweight, (b) attitudes, (c) eating, (d) exercise, (e) maintenance, (f) bulimia nervosa, (g) anorexia nervosa

Critical Thinking

How Effective Is Viagra?

Questions

1. What are the two different causes of sexual problems (dysfunctions), and which one applies to Eric?

2. Why do you think that Viagra was discovered by accident?

3. How is the transmitter involved in producing an erection (a gas called nitric oxide) different from most other transmitters discussed earlier (p. 54)?

Eric (not his real name), who was 64 and happily married, was diagnosed with prostate cancer. He chose to have his prostate gland removed, knowing there was a 50–50 chance of becoming impotent, which is the inability to have an erection (also called erectile dysfunction). After surgery, Eric did become impotent and developed a terrible fear that his wife would leave him. Eric volunteered for a study on a brand new drug to treat impotence. For Eric, the new drug worked so well that he called it a "wonder drug" because it gave him back a normal married life. This drug later became known as Viagra (sildenafil).

What's unusual about Viagra is that it was discovered by accident. Scientists were looking for drugs to treat heart disease and found that, while one drug didn't work on heart disease, it did cause erections. Scientists changed goals and began testing the particular drug on men who were impotent.

It was not until the early 1980s that scientists figured out the plumbing behind erections. They discovered that when a man feels aroused, his penis releases a gas, nitric oxide, which activates an enzyme (cyclic GMP), which triggers the blood vessels in the penis to relax, which allows blood to rush in and cause stiffness (erection). Scientists found that Viagra worked by keeping the enzyme around longer so that blood vessels stayed relaxed longer, which allowed blood to flow in and cause an erection.

Estimates are that between 10 and 20 million American men suffer some degree of impotence. For many of these men, the idea of having an erection 20 to 40 minutes after taking Viagra was very appealing. In the first 3 months, sales of Viagra hit $411 million, making it the most successful prescription drug ever. However, after 7 months, sales had fallen 66% to $141 million for a number of reasons.

One reason was that Viagra did not work in 30–40% of men who tried it. Some men experienced unwanted side effects, such as one man who stopped taking Viagra because "your face gets very hot, you feel like your heart is beating faster than it should, there's anxiety" (Leland, 1998, p. 68). Also, although Viagra can cause erections, it may not resolve the underlying sexual difficulties in unhappy relationships. Finally, a few hundred deaths have been associated with Viagra, which resulted in a warning label about not prescribing Viagra for men with certain heart problems.

In women with decreased sexual desire, Viagra has not proved effective, since the percentage of women (21%) who reported improved sexual functioning after Viagra was about the same as for those who took placebos.

For about 70% of men who suffer some degree of impotency, especially after prostate surgery, Viagra appears to be a very good deal. (Adapted from BBC News, 2003; J. S. Cohen, 2001; Horowitz, 1999; Leland, 1998; Mestel, 1999; Roan, 1998)

4. Why might men who were not impotent want to try Viagra?

5. What is one reason that Viagra did not work in 30–40% of those who tried it?

6. What is one reason that Viagra did not improve sexual functioning in women?

Suggested Answers

1. There are two general causes of sexual dysfunctions. One cause involves organic factors, such as medical problems or problems caused by drugs. The other cause involves psychological factors, such as anxiety, sexual trauma, guilt, or communication difficulties, all of which lead to sexual problems. In Eric's case, the cause was organic, since he had no problems with having an erection until his prostate gland was removed.

2. Although finding a pill to treat impotence was a high priority, scientists did not yet understand how erections occurred and so did not know where to look for a drug to treat impotence. It was by accident that scientists, who were initially studying a drug to treat heart disease, found a drug that produced erections.

3. All the transmitters discovered earlier were chemicals (pp. 54–55). That's why finding that the transmitter involved in erections was a gas (nitric oxide) was completely unexpected.

4. Men with no erectile problems may want to try Viagra because they incorrectly believed that Viagra would increase not only erections but also sexual desire and motivation, which it doesn't.

5. The reasons Viagra did not work in 30–40% of men with erectile problems may be serious organic (medical) problems or psychological problems (low sexual motivation, fear or anxiety about performing), which Viagra doesn't necessarily help.

6. One reason Viagra was no more effective than a placebo in improving female sexual functioning was that Viagra essentially deals with the flow of blood into and out of sexual organs and doesn't seem to improve sexual desire. Thus, women's low sexual desire or motivation, which may be a psychological problem, is a difficulty that Viagra doesn't seem to help.

Links to Learning

Learning Activities

- ***POWERSTUDY FOR INTRODUCTION TO PSYCHOLOGY 4.0***

  by Tom Doyle and Rod Plotnik

  Check out the quizzes and learning activities for "Motivation" on **PowerStudy** and:

  - Test your knowledge using an interactive version of the Summary Test on pages 354 and 355. Also access related quizzing—true/false, multiple choice, and matching.
  - Explore an interactive version of the Critical Thinking exercise "How Effective Is Viagra?" on page 356.
  - You will also find key terms, a chapter outline including a chapter abstract, and a special extended list of hotlinked websites that correlate to this module.

- *CengageNOW*

  academic.cengage.com/login

  Need help studying? This site is your one-stop study shop. Take a Pre-Test and CengageNOW will generate a Personalized Study Plan based on your test results. The Study Plan will identify the topics you need to review and direct you to online resources to help you master those topics. You can then take a Post-Test to determine the concepts you have mastered and what you still need to work on.

- ***INTRODUCTION TO PSYCHOLOGY BOOK COMPANION WEBSITE***

  academic.cengage.com/psychology/plotnik

  Visit your book companion website where you will find more resources to help you study. At this site, you will find Learning Objectives, Internet Exercises, quizzing, flash cards, and a pronunciation glossary.

- ***STUDY GUIDE and WEBTUTOR***

  Check the corresponding module in your Study Guide for effective student tips and help learning the material presented. Also go to **academic.cengage.com/webtutor** for an interactive version of the Study Guide features.

Study Questions

*A. Theories of Motivation—Which theory best explains why students work hard to get good grades? (**Suggested answer page 628**)

*B. Biological & Social Needs—How would your needs change if you won a $20-million lottery? (**Suggested answer page 629**)

C. Hunger—As a parent, what would you do to keep you and your children from becoming overweight?

D. Sexual Behavior—What would happen to someone's sexual behavior if, at puberty, no sex hormones were secreted?

E. Cultural Diversity: Genital Cutting—Are there any American cultural traditions that are detrimental to the sexual behavior of men or women?

F. Achievement—Why might some students get the "sophomore blues" and feel less motivated about doing well in college?

G. Research Focus: Overcoming Educational Disadvantages—How can schools better educate poor and minority children while not compromising the education of middle-class and White children?

*H. Application: Eating Problems & Treatments—Would you believe an ad that promised you could "lose weight easily and quickly without dieting or exercise by practicing self-hypnosis"? (**Suggested answer page 629**)

*These questions are answered in Appendix B.

MODULE 16
Emotion

Introduction

Emotional Experience

What did Bethany feel during a shark attack?

What happened to Bethany Hamilton at 7:30 on a Friday morning was something she would never forget. Bethany paddled her surfboard about a quarter mile off the north shore of Kauai, Hawaii, and as she waited to catch the best waves, she noticed the water was clear and calm, like a swimming pool. The waves turned out to be too small to ride so she relaxed by holding the surfboard with her right arm and letting her left arm dangle in the warm water. Suddenly she saw a glimmer of gray in the clear blue water. Almost instantly, Bethany felt tremendous pressure and fierce yanking on her left arm. It was then she realized that the razor-sharp teeth of a 15-foot tiger shark were wrapped tightly around her left arm. When she saw the water around her turn bright red with streaks of her blood, her heart pounded like a hammer and her adrenaline flowed like water from a fire hose. The shark eventually let go of her arm and swam away. With great courage and perseverance, Bethany paddled to the beach as quickly as she could with only her right arm. Her left arm had been violently ripped off almost to the armpit, and the shark even took a big chunk out of her surfboard!

As Bethany approached the beach, people helped her off the surfboard and called for help. She was rushed to the hospital for surgery, and about a week after her stitches were removed, Bethany began surfing again. It was difficult learning to surf with only her right arm, but her extraordinary drive helped her win several surfing competitions after the attack. Although Bethany at times experiences dread and fright that something bad is going to happen again, for the most part, she is as comfortable as other surfers are while in the water (adapted from Hamilton, 2004).

Bethany experienced a variety of emotions during and after her shark attack. During the attack, she felt intense anxiety and fear for her life. When she reached the shore, she felt relieved to be alive but worried about her missing arm. Sometime later, she felt fright about surfing again, but she also felt pride and joy after catching her first big wave after the attack. Although Bethany experienced over a half-dozen emotions, they all shared the same four components (Frijda, 2000).

An *emotion* is defined in terms of four components. First, you interpret or appraise some stimulus (event, object, or thought) in terms of your well-being. Second, you experience a subjective feeling, such as fear or happiness. Third, you have physiological responses, such as changes in heart rate or breathing. Fourth, you may show observable behaviors, such as smiling or crying.

Bethany's experience with the shark illustrates the four components of an emotion:

First, she *interpreted* or *appraised* the stimulus, a shark attack, as a very serious threat to her well-being and survival.

Second, she had the *subjective experience* or *feeling* of fear and terror.

Third, she had a variety of *physiological responses*, such as heart pounding and adrenaline pumping, which cause arousal and prepare the body for action, such as swimming away fast.

Fourth, she showed *overt* or *observable behaviors*, such as fearful facial expressions and rapid paddling to the beach. In some cases, such as playing poker, a person may experience a wide range of emotions but try to hide his or her overt behaviors by showing no facial expression, commonly known as a "poker face." In other cases, cultural factors influence overt behaviors, such as allowing American women but not usually American men to cry in public.

Although there is general agreement that emotions have four components, there is much discussion of the order in which these four components occur (Frijda, 2000). For instance, did Bethany have to think about the shark before she felt fear, or did she feel fear immediately and then think about how terrified she was? We'll discuss this as well as many other questions about emotions, such as why people can identify a fearful face quicker than a happy one.

Bethany was attacked by a shark, which bit off her entire left arm!

Staying Happy

How long do emotions last?

Being attacked by a shark results in a very different emotional experience than winning big bucks in a lottery. Since lotteries began in the late 1970s, about 4,000 people have become instant millionaires. Immediately after winning, the new millionaires reported feeling intense pleasure, being ecstatic, being unbelievably happy, and living in a dream world (Angelo, 1991). But what happens when a winner finally realizes that for the next 20 years he or she will receive a large monthly check? Will the emotional high continue, or will being a millionaire become a taken-for-granted experience?

Ten years after winning a $20-million lottery, would you still be very happy?

Researchers have studied lottery winners to find out what effect such an enormous windfall has had on their lives (CPO, 2006). Later in this module, we'll tell you what the researchers discovered about happiness and how it applies to lottery winners and you.

What's Coming

To realize the importance of emotions, just imagine going through one day without them. We'll discuss how emotions occur; how much our physiological responses, facial expressions, and interpretations contribute to emotions; whether feeling or thinking comes first in experiencing an emotion; whether there is a set of basic or universal facial expressions that occur across all cultures; what the functions of emotions are; how specific emotions work; and how emotions are used in lie detection.

We'll begin our discussion of emotions with how a swimmer's sight of a shark causes him or her to feel fear.

A. Peripheral Theories

Studying Emotions

Why do you feel fear?

Seeing a shark swimming nearby causes instant fear. Explaining how this fear arises has taken three different approaches.

The *peripheral theories of emotions* emphasize how physiological changes in the body give rise to emotional feelings.

The *cognitive appraisal theory of emotions* emphasizes how interpretations or appraisals of situations result in emotional feelings.

The *affective neuroscience approach* studies the underlying neural bases of mood and emotion by focusing on the brain's neural circuits that evaluate stimuli and produce or contribute to experiencing and expressing different emotional states.

We'll begin with one of the peripheral approaches to understanding emotions, the historic James-Lange theory, which says that if you see a bear, you are frightened because you run. Is it true?

James-Lange Theory

This theory, proposed independently in the late 1800s by two psychologists, William James and Carl Lange, emphasizes specific physiological patterns as causing emotional feelings.

The *James-Lange theory says that our brains interpret specific physiological changes as feelings or emotions and that there is a different physiological pattern underlying each emotion.*

James (1884/1969) illustrated his theory with the example of seeing a bear: If you see a bear, "you are frightened because you run" rather than run because you are frightened. According to the James-Lange theory, the order for the occurrence of the four components of an emotion is shown in the right figure.

Criticisms. There are three major criticisms of the James-Lange theory. First, different emotions are not necessarily associated with different patterns of physiological responses. For instance, anger, fear, and sadness share similar physiological patterns of arousal (Cacioppo et al., 2000). Thus, James's bear example was backward: Instead of the act of running making you feel fear, you feel fear and then run.

Second, people whose spinal cords have been severed at the neck are deprived of most of the feedback from their physiological responses (autonomic nervous system), yet they experience emotions with little or no change in

intensity. These data are the opposite of what the James-Lange theory would predict, which is that these people should experience little or no emotion (Chwalisz et al., 1988).

Third, some emotions, such as feeling guilty or jealous, may require a considerable amount of interpretation or appraisal of the situation. The sequence involved in feeling a complex emotion like guilt or jealousy points to the influence of cognitive factors on emotional feelings (Ellsworth & Scherer, 2003).

Intensity. Although researchers showed that physiological changes are not the primary cause of emotions, physiological changes (heart pounding, sweaty palms) may increase the intensity of emotional experiences (Cacioppo et al., 2000).

Next, we turn to the second peripheral theory, the facial feedback theory, which offers a different explanation of how emotions occur.

1. Stimulus (shark) triggers different physiological changes in your body.

2. Your brain interprets different patterns of physiological changes. **Interpret**

3. Different physiological changes produce different emotions (fear).

4. You may or may not show observable responses (scream).

Facial Feedback Theory

The idea that feedback from facial muscles causes emotional feelings originated with Charles Darwin (1872/1965) and evolved into today's facial feedback theory (Keltner & Ekman, 2000).

The *facial feedback theory says that the sensations or feedback from the movement of your facial muscles and skin are interpreted by your brain as different emotions.*

According to facial feedback theory, the four components of emotions occur in the order shown in the figure below.

1. Stimulus (shark) triggers changes in facial muscles and skin.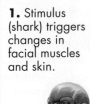

2. Your brain interprets feedback from facial muscles and skin.  **Interpret**

3. Different facial feedback results in feeling different emotions (fear).

4. You may or may not show various observable responses (scream).

Criticisms. While it is true that facial expressions of fear, happiness, sadness, and disgust involve different muscle-skin patterns, there is little evidence that it's the feedback from these different muscle groups that actually causes the emotion. For example, if feedback from facial muscles caused emotions, then individuals whose facial muscles are completely paralyzed should not be able to experience emotions, yet they do report feeling emotions (Heilman, 2000).

Although researchers have not confirmed Darwin's original theory that feedback from facial muscles *alone* is sufficient to produce emotions, they have found that feedback from facial muscles, such as those involved in smiling or crying, may influence your mood and overall emotional feeling and increase the intensity of your subjective emotional experience (Kolb & Taylor, 2000).

The peripheral theories of emotions show that physiological changes in the body and feedback from facial muscles contribute to but do not themselves cause different emotions. What can cause an emotion are the thoughts that go on inside your brain (mind).

B. Cognitive Appraisal Theory

Thoughts and Emotions

Can thoughts cause emotions?

Suppose you won a lottery and felt very happy. Weeks later, the thought of winning still makes you feel very happy. The fact that your thoughts alone can give rise to emotions illustrates the importance of cognitive factors.

Current cognitive theories of emotions can be traced back to the

original research of Stanley Schachter and Jerome Singer (1962), whose classic experiment was the first to show the importance of cognitive interpretation, or appraisal, in contributing to emotional states.

Schachter-Singer Experiment

As shown in the figure below, Schachter and Singer first injected their subjects with a hormone, epinephrine (adrenaline), that caused physiological arousal, such as increased heart rate and blood pressure. However, subjects were told that the injections were vitamins and were not told that they would experience physiological arousal. After the injections, subjects were placed in different situations—a happy one or an angry one. Those subjects in the happy situation often

reported feeling happy, and their observable behaviors were smiles. However, those in the angry situation often reported feeling angry, and their observable behaviors were angry facial expressions. Schachter and Singer explained that subjects did not know that their physiological arousal was caused by hormone injections and they looked around for other causes in their environment. Subjects interpreted environmental cues, such as being in a happy or angry situation, as the cause of their arousal and thus reported feeling happy or angry. The Schachter-Singer cognitive theory was the first to show that cognitive factors, such as your interpretation of events, could influence emotional feelings.

The Schachter-Singer finding that your cognitive processes, such as thoughts, interpretations, and appraisals of situations, can trigger emotions became the basis for today's cognitive appraisal theory of emotions.

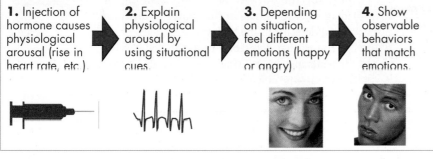

1. Injection of hormone causes physiological arousal (rise in heart rate, etc.)

2. Explain physiological arousal by using situational cues.

3. Depending on situation, feel different emotions (happy or angry).

4. Show observable behaviors that match emotions.

Cognitive Appraisal Theory

The cognitive appraisal theory began with the experiment of Schachter and Singer and developed into its present form because of many researchers (Ellsworth & Scherer, 2003; Lazarus, 2006).

The *cognitive appraisal theory* says that your interpretation or appraisal or thought or memory of a situation, object, or event can contribute to, or result in, your experiencing different emotional states.

Suppose you're thinking about having won the lottery last week and planning what to do with all that money. According to the cognitive appraisal theory, the sequence for how thinking results in feeling happy is shown in the figure on the right.

Thought then emotion. Thinking of your first serious kiss can make you feel happy, while thinking of times you were jealous can make you sad or angry. In these cases, as well as in feeling pride, envy, or compassion, the thinking or appraisal occurs before the emotion (Lazarus, 2006).

Emotion without conscious thought. Imagine being on a nature walk, turning a corner, and seeing a huge snake on the path. In this case, the feeling of fear is instant, without conscious thought or appraisal; you don't have to think "that's a dangerous snake and I better be careful." On the next page, we'll discuss how seeing a snake can elicit fear instantaneously,

before awareness or conscious thoughts can occur (Helmuth, 2003b; Zajonc, 1984). Thus, in some situations, such as those that involve personal relationships, problems at work, fond family memories, or terrible tragedies, thoughts precede and result in emotional feelings. In other situations, such as those involving attack or threat to one's personal survival, emotions can occur instantly, without conscious thought or awareness.

1. The stimulus could be an event, object, or thought: "I won $55 million last week."

2. You appraise or think of what you can do: "I can go on a trip around the world."

3. Appraising or thinking about what you can do brings feelings of happiness and joy.

4. You also have physiological responses and observable behaviors (smiling).

The relatively new finding that certain emotions, especially fear, can occur without conscious thought or awareness brings us to the most recent approach to the study of emotions, called affective neuroscience, which we'll discuss next.

C. Affective Neuroscience Approach

Four Qualities of Emotions

What emotion do you feel?

Seeing this ferocious wolf suddenly appear on your nature walk would cause instant fear. The ability of humans to sense and evaluate stimuli as being more or less desirable to their well-being is an important function of emotions, which have four unique qualities (R. J. Dolan, 2002).

How quickly would you react?

1st. Unlike most psychological states, emotions are felt and *expressed in stereotypic facial expressions,* such as showing a fearful expression (open mouth, raised eyebrows), and accompanied by *distinctive physiological responses* (fear is accompanied by a fast heart rate, quick shallow breathing, and sweaty palms).

2nd. Emotions are *less controllable* than we might like and may *not respond to reason.* For example, advising someone to "calm down" or "control your temper" may have little effect. In fact, some people may need to attend anger management programs to help them gain some rational self-control over their hot tempers.

3rd. Emotions have an enormous *influence on many cognitive processes,* such as making decisions, developing personal relationships, and selecting goals. One reason for this is that you essentially have two brains: an older primitive or animal brain, called the limbic system (p. 80), which regulates emotions, and a newer developed forebrain, which influences but doesn't completely control the limbic system. For example, well-known politicians, who intellectually know better, have gotten into trouble by engaging in illicit sexual activities, and some students, who intellectually know better, admit to doing badly in their freshman year and explain that they were emotionally immature.

4th. Some emotions are *hard-wired in the brain.* That's why babies don't have to learn how to cry to gain attention or express basic needs or learn how to smile to show happiness and form social bonds with their parents or caretakers.

Study of emotions. Recently, the study of emotions has become one of the hottest topics in neuroscience, which studies patients who have discrete brain lesions and psychiatric and neurological disorders. Neuroscientists use brain scanning or imaging techniques to identify structures and neural activities in the living brain. These studies contribute to the new affective neuroscience approach to understand mood and emotions (Heatherton et al., 2004).

The *affective neuroscience approach* studies the underlying neural bases of mood and emotion by focusing on the brain's neural circuits that evaluate stimuli and produce or contribute to experiencing and expressing different emotional states.

The word *affective* suggests affect or emotion. The word *neuroscience* suggests research methods that involve studying patients with neurological disorders and using methods that involve brain scans or imaging to identify neural activity in the living brain.

Emotional Detector and Memorizer

Can you detect a snake quicker than a flower?

Detecting stimuli. If you were shown a number of stimuli, would you detect a snake quicker than a flower? For example, researchers found that, compared to detecting unemotional neutral targets (flowers, mushrooms), we are faster at detecting targets with emotional meaning, such as faces with positive (smiling) or negative (fearful) expressions, and threatening things, such as snakes or spiders. However, we are fastest at identifying emotional stimuli that may pose a threat—fearful faces, snakes (M. A. Williams & Mattingley, 2006). These findings support the idea that our brains have evolved the ability to quickly recognize dangerous things in our environment and thus increase our chances for survival. Further support for this idea comes from scanning or imaging studies (p. 70) that point to an emotional detector in the brain.

Threat to your survival

Emotional detector. Your physical survival depends in part on a brain structure about the size and shape of an almond—the amygdala (Quirk, 2007).

The *amygdala (ah-MIG-duh-la)* is located in the tip of the brain's temporal lobe and receives input from all the senses. Using all this sensory input, the amygdala monitors and evaluates whether stimuli have positive (happy) or negative (fearful) emotional significance for our well-being and survival. It is also involved in storing memories that have emotional content.

One researcher said the amygdala (figure below) is like a guard dog that is constantly sniffing for threats and this gives us an evolutionary advantage in terms of survival (LeDoux, 2003). For example, brain scans indicate the amygdala is especially activated when we view emotional facial expressions indicating fear or distress (Helmuth, 2003b).

When the amygdala is damaged, patients often overlook important emotional cues. For instance, they identify all faces as being more trustworthy and approachable than the rest of us do (Adolphs, 2004; Dobbs, 2006). Similarly, when the amygdala is damaged in animals, they no longer learn to fear and avoid dangerous situations (Hamann et al., 2002).

Amygdala

Amygdala is an emotional detector and memorizer.

Emotional memorizer. Besides being involved in evaluating positive and negative emotional stimuli, the amygdala is also involved in *storing memories with emotional content* (Phelps, 2004). The amygdala is the reason you can remember that a joke is funny or a face is happy or threatening. This means the amygdala is involved in both detecting emotional stimuli and remembering emotional content. How the amygdala detects a snake almost instantaneously is a neat trick.

What happens when you feel fear?

Researchers have used brain scanning or imaging techniques (fMRI—p. 70) to measure neural activity and trace neural pathways or circuits throughout the living brain. We'll focus on the neural activity that occurs when a person is confronted with a fearful stimulus, such as seeing a ferocious wolf. This neural circuit is important for our survival and has received considerable attention (Quirk, 2007; Siegal, 2005).

A. Slower Circuit We'll give a simplified version of the sequence of neural activity in the brain that would occur as you see a ferocious wolf. Visual information about the wolf's shape, size, and color enters the *eyes* (1), which send neural information about the "wolf" to a structure in the brain, called the *thalamus* (2) (THAL-ah-mus). In turn, the thalamus relays the neural information to another part of the brain, called the *visual cortex* (3). The visual cortex transforms the neural signals into the image of a ferocious wolf, and relays the "wolf" information to the *amygdala* (4). The amygdala interprets the neural information and signals the presence of a threat, which results in feelings of fear, an associated fearful facial expression, and probably a lot of yelling and running to escape the threat. And this neural activity happens very fast, in about 0.12 second. However, there is an even faster circuit, that gives a quicker warning.

B. Faster Circuit Researchers have evidence of an even faster circuit for identifying threatening stimuli. As usual, visual information about the wolf enters the *eyes* (1), which send neural information about the "wolf" to the *thalamus* (2). The thalamus sends neural information directly to the *amygdala* (4), saving time by skipping the *visual cortex* (3). This means that the amygdala recognizes the threatening wolf and triggers a fearful response almost instantaneously after seeing the wolf. This is an example of an emotion occurring without any awareness or conscious thought. Researchers believe that this Faster Circuit evolved because its amazingly quick warning of a threatening stimulus greatly improves our chances of avoiding and surviving dangerous stimuli.

C. Prefrontal Cortex The part of your brain that is involved in complex cognitive functions, such as making decisions, planning, and reasoning, is called the *prefrontal cortex* (5). The prefrontal cortex has several functions: It is involved in remembering and experiencing emotions even when the fear object is not present, such as when you tell a friend about your wolf encounter and again feel fear or recall a joke and laugh; it is also involved in anticipating and analyzing the potential rewards, punishments, and emotional consequences of performing or not performing certain behaviors (J. R. Gray et al., 2002). For example, the prefrontal cortex is involved in analyzing the emotional consequences, rewards, and punishments of deciding whether to go to a party instead of studying for an exam. Because reason often has less effect on emotions than you would like, you may decide to go and enjoy the party and live with the potential disappointment and unhappiness of doing poorly on the exam.

In some cases, faulty functioning of the prefrontal cortex, perhaps due to undeveloped neural connections or circuits, may result in less rational control of emotions, which in turn increases the risk for committing impulsive acts of violence or aggression. Researchers warn that this finding points to the need for developing new treatments, both behavioral and drug, to help people suppress impulsive and violent emotions (R. Bradley et al., 2005; Quirk, 2007).

The kinds of studies that we have just discussed illustrate the affective neuroscience approach to understanding emotions as well as emotional disorders.

Why do some have more fears?

Some individuals suffer from social phobias, which means they avoid going out in public because they have an enormous fear of being scrutinized, which would surely result in being humiliated or embarrassed. Researchers wondered if these fears might be reflected in the activity of the amygdala, which evaluates and signals threats from the environment.

Individuals with social phobias and healthy individuals were shown color photos of faces (happy, fearful, angry, and contemptuous) while researchers used brain scans (fMRIs) to record the neural activity of the amygdala. When individuals with social phobias were looking at photos of angry and contemptuous faces, there was increased neural activity in the left amygdala compared to the

activity in healthy individuals. Researchers concluded the amygdala of social phobics is particularly active when processing angry and contemptuous faces (M. B. Stein et al., 2002). This study, which is an example of the affective neuroscience approach, identified neurological factors that may be useful in evaluating and treating emotional disorders.

Phobias and other anxieties are believed to result from there being more neural connections running from the amygdala to the cortex (p. 74) than from the cortex to the amygdala. This explains why our anxieties often control our thoughts and why our thoughts cannot always lower our anxieties (Dobbs, 2006).

Social fears result in an overactive amygdala.

D. Universal Facial Expressions

When did you first smile?

When you were about 4–6 weeks old, you began to smile, which greatly pleased your parents. Smiling is considered one of the universal emotional expressions (Ekman, 2003).

Universal emotional expressions are a number of specific inherited facial patterns or expressions that signal specific feelings or emotional states, such as a smile signaling a happy state.

For example, notice that although the four individuals in the photos come from four different countries, they display similar facial expressions—smiles—which you would interpret as showing happiness.

Why do people from different cultures smile the same way?

Number of expressions. Researchers generally agree that seven facial expressions for emotions are universal, which means they are recognized across cultures: anger, happiness, fear, surprise, disgust, sadness, and contempt (Ekman, 2003; Ekman & Rosenberg, 2005). Other emotions, such as pride, jealousy, and compassion, do not have particular facial expressions.

The existence of universal emotions was scientifically formulated by Charles Darwin (1872/1965), and his ideas have inspired modern-day researchers to study universal emotional expressions (Ekman, 2003). We'll review two kinds of evidence—cross-cultural and genetic—that support the idea of universal emotional expressions.

Cross-Cultural Evidence

How do individuals from relatively isolated cultures in New Guinea, Burma, Thailand, and Borneo (photos top to bottom) know how to smile or what a smile means? One answer is that a smile is one of the unlearned, inherited universal emotional expressions. For example, researchers showed photos of different facial expressions to individuals in 20 different Western cultures and 11 different primitive (illiterate and isolated) cultures. As the graph below indicates, researchers found that individuals in both Western and primitive cultures showed significant agreement on which facial expressions signaled which emotions. Most individuals in Western and primitive cultures agreed that a smile indicated happiness. However, only about one-third of individuals in primitive cultures agreed that an open-mouth and raised-eyebrows expression indicated surprise.

Based on the cross-cultural findings shown in the right graph, researchers concluded that there are innately or biologically determined universal facial expressions for emotions. Universal emotional signals most likely include facial expressions for happiness, surprise, fear, anger, contempt, disgust, and sadness (Ekman, 2003; Ekman & Rosenberg, 2005). Universal emotional expressions are thought to have evolved because they served adaptive and survival functions for our ancestors.

Support for universal emotional expressions also comes from observing the emotional development of infants.

Recognition of Facial Expressions

Expression		Recognition
Happiness	Western	96%
Happiness	Primitive	92%
Surprise	Western	88%
Surprise	Primitive	36%
Anger	Western	81%
Anger	Primitive	46%
Sadness	Western	80%
Sadness	Primitive	52%

Genetic Evidence

How does an infant who is born blind learn to smile? Is it possible that the programming of specific facial expressions, such as smiling, is in the DNA, which is a chemically coded alphabet that contains and writes out genetic instructions for the development of the body and brain? One answer to this question comes from observing the development of emotional expressions in infants.

Researchers found that at 4–6 weeks of age, infants begin to smile, which encourages social bonding with parents. The question is whether an infant's smiling is biologically programmed or whether the infant has learned to smile by observing and imitating the parents' facial expressions. The answer is that even infants born blind, who never observe their parents smiling, begin to smile at 4–6 weeks. This observation supports the idea that some facial expressions, such as smiling, are biologically programmed (Eibl-Eibesfeldt, 1973).

Additional evidence for universal emotions comes from reports that all infants develop facial expressions in a predictable order. For instance, newborns show facial expressions signaling disgust or distress in response to foul tastes or odors, infants 4–6 weeks old begin to smile, infants 3–4 months old show angry and sad facial expressions, and infants 5–7 months old show fear. Because infants in all cultures develop these emotional expressions at about the same age and in the same order, we have further evidence for the existence of universal emotions (Izard, 1993; Kopp & Neufeld, 2003).

Researchers conclude that evidence from cross-cultural studies on facial expressions and on the development of emotional expressions in infants indicates strong biological (genetic) influences on the development of emotional expressions (J. Dunn, 2003). But why should humans have an innate genetic program for the development of facial emotional expressions? There are several interesting answers to this question.

What good are emotions?

To appreciate the value and worth of emotions, try living a single day without feeling or expressing any emotions. It would be one of the worst days of your life because emotions have three important functions. Emotions send powerful *social signals* about how you feel; emotions help you *adapt and survive* in your world; and emotions *arouse and motivate* many of your behaviors. We'll examine each emotional function in turn.

Social Signals

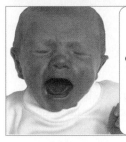

This baby's facial expression is a signal to show others that she is _____.

You would probably fill in the above blank with "distressed, unhappy, in need of something (food, dry diaper)." Thus, one function of emotions is to **send social signals** about one's feelings or needs. Because the baby's facial expression signals distress, she is likely to elicit help, sympathy, or compassion from her parents or caregiver. This is one example of how we may send signals through a variety of facial expressions (Keltner et al., 2003).

Facial expressions that accompany emotions may send social signals about how we feel as well as provide social signals about what we are going to do.

For example, if you smiled at a classmate you did not know, it may signal that you are feeling friendly and perhaps that you wish to talk to and meet this person.

In some cases, there may be gender differences in the ability to recognize facial expressions. For instance, men have been reported to be better than woman at finding angry faces in a crowd, and women have been reported to be better than men in detecting facial expressions signaling happiness, sadness, surprise, and disgust (M. A. Williams & Mattingley, 2006).

A lack of facial expressions may be a symptom of serious emotional disorders, which are discussed in Modules 22 and 23.

Survival, Attention & Memory

If you're walking through a strange neighborhood late at night, you may feel fear. Your sense of fear is a signal that all is not well, so you should be careful. Emotions help us evaluate situations (Rothbart & Sheese, 2007).

The *evolutionary theory of emotions* says that one function of emotions is to help us evaluate objects, people, and situations in terms of how good or bad they are for our well-being and survival (Rozin, 2003).

There are many examples of emotions having survival value: showing anger (below photo) to escape or survive a dangerous or threatening situation, showing disgust to signal the presence of poisonous or rotten food, crying to indicate the need for help or attention, or feeling fear and becoming very watchful when walking home late at night.

This man's facial expression is a signal to show that he is _____, which may help him survive _____ situations.

Besides helping us evaluate situations in terms of our well-being, emotions also affect our attention and memory.

Attention. Feeling very happy when you see your honey means that he or she will get your full attention. Feeling very angry when you are threatened means that you're totally focused on getting out of this situation. These are examples of another function of emotions, which is to **focus one's attention** and thus better detect and respond to emotional situations (Rothbart & Sheese, 2007).

Memory. Earlier we discussed how strong emotions trigger the secretion of hormones that cause memories to be "written in stone" (p. 247). This illustrates that another function of emotions is to **increase memory and recall** of emotionally charged situations (Dobbs, 2006). This results in better remembering situations that are beneficial or dangerous to our well-being.

Arousal and Motivation

Earlier we discussed how Bethany's emotional reaction to seeing a shark included a variety of physiological responses, such as heart pounding and adrenaline pumping, that cause arousal. One major function of emotions is to **produce general arousal**, which prepares the body for some action (Hamm et al., 2003). In Bethany's case, maximum arousal helped her get to shore, but in other cases, such as taking a test, maximum arousal may interfere with performance.

In fact, there is a relationship between emotional arousal and performance on a task. That relationship is called the Yerkes-Dodson law.

The *Yerkes-Dodson law* says that performance on a task is an interaction between the level of physiological arousal and the difficulty of the task. For difficult tasks, low arousal results in better performance; for most tasks, moderate arousal helps performance; and for easy tasks, high arousal may facilitate performance.

If we apply the Yerkes-Dodson law to taking difficult exams, we would predict that a person with high test anxiety (high arousal) would do more poorly than someone with comparable ability but low test anxiety. Researchers confirmed this prediction by finding that students who were highly aroused because of either high test anxiety or much coffee (caffeine) scored more poorly on difficult tests than students who had low test anxiety or were less aroused (less caffeine) (K. J. Anderson, 1994). The graph below shows how the optimum level of arousal for best performance depends on the complexity of the task.

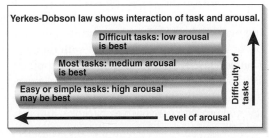

Yerkes-Dobson law shows interaction of task and arousal.

Difficult tasks: low arousal is best

Most tasks: medium arousal is best

Easy or simple tasks: high arousal may be best

Difficulty of tasks

Level of arousal

Besides affecting performance on various tasks, emotions also increase physiological arousal, which forms the basis for lie detector tests, discussed in the Application section (pp. 370–371).

Next, we turn to a positive emotion and the question Why doesn't happiness last longer?

F. Happiness

What makes you happy?

Pam was unmarried, eight months pregnant, and holding down two jobs when she stopped in at Jackson's Food Store for her morning orange juice and one lottery ticket. She remembers praying, "Please, God, let something happen so I can afford a small studio apartment" (S. Reed & Free, 1995, p. 63). The next day she was ecstatic when she discovered that her single lottery ticket was worth $87 million (left photo).

Happiness, usually indicated by smiling and laughing, can result from momentary pleasures, such as a funny commercial; short-term joys, such as a great date; and long-term satisfaction, such as an enjoyable relationship.

Inside the brain, the amygdala is involved in recognizing happy facial expressions and remembering happy occurrences (laughing at jokes) (Berridge, 2003; W. M. Kelley, 2002). In addition, the brain has a special reward/pleasure center that's involved in happiness.

The *reward/pleasure center* includes several areas, such as the nucleus accumbens and ventral tegmental area, and several neurotransmitters, especially dopamine. These and other brain areas make up a neural circuit that produces rewarding and pleasurable feelings, such as happiness.

Researchers found that many behaviors—eating, developing romantic attachments, engaging in sex, gambling, using recreational drugs (cocaine), looking at photos of attractive people, and listening to great music—activate the brain's reward/pleasure center (right figure) and result in happy and pleasurable feelings (Berridge, 2003; Nestler, 2005).

For example, the $87-million check that Pam received activated her brain's reward/pleasure center to trigger much happiness, and this occurrence was stored as a happy memory by her amygdala.

Happiness is about more than measurable physiological processes; it is also about people's unique life experiences. Researchers and therapists often want to measure people's level of happiness. Research shows the best method of measuring happiness is to track emotions through the day by having people write down what they did, when they did it, who they were with, and how they felt (A. Stone, 2004). Beyond day-to-day happiness, what makes people happy in the long term?

I won $87 million dollars!

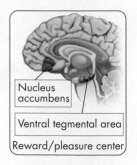

Nucleus accumbens

Ventral tegmental area

Reward/pleasure center

How much happiness can money buy?

When researchers interviewed lottery winners 1 to 24 months after they had won large sums of money, the majority reported positive changes, such as financial security, new possessions, more leisure time, and earlier retirement. However, when asked to rate their happiness one year after winning, lottery winners were no happier than before (Diener & Diener, 1996). Why the happy feeling of winning a lottery doesn't last is explained by the adaptation level theory.

The *adaptation level theory* says that we quickly become accustomed to receiving some good fortune (money, job, car, degree); we take the good fortune for granted within a short period of time; and as a result, the initial impact of our good fortune fades and contributes less to our long-term level of happiness.

According to the adaptation level theory, the immediate emotional high of obtaining good fortune—such as graduating from college, getting married, buying a new car, getting a much-wanted job, or winning a lottery—will fade with time and contributes less and less to our long-term happiness (Brickman et al., 1978; Easterlin, 2003; Seligman, 2002). For example, three weeks after winning $87 million, Pam gave birth to Nicholas, and she said, "Winning the lottery was pretty exciting, but it can't compare to Nicholas. I want him to grow up caring about people and knowing the value of work" (S. Reed & Free, 1995, p. 64).

Long-term happiness. Researchers find that happiness is not a fixed state and does not result from getting more money, cars, clothes, or promotions because these achievements gradually lose their emotional appeal, as predicted by the adaptation level theory. Rather, being happy is a continuous process that is associated with making an effort to enjoy simple, daily pleasurable events, people, or situations. It includes a daily diet of little highs as well as pursuing your own personal goals, developing a sense of meaningfulness, having intimate relationships, and not judging yourself against what others do but by your own yardstick (Lykken, 2003; Seligman, 2002). These findings explain Pam's comment that winning the lottery was great but doesn't compare to the joys and meaningfulness she experiences with her child.

Genetic differences in happiness. One reason that some people are just generally happier than others is one's individual *happiness set point*. Each person has a set point for experiencing a certain level of happiness—some more and some less. Although happiness can go up or down, it generally returns to the person's set point. For example, identical twins showed significantly higher correlations in their happiness ratings (0.44 to 0.52) than did fraternal twins (0.08 to –0.02). Researchers estimate that one's personal level for being happy is set half by inherited or genetic influences, which affect the development of helpful or hurtful cognitive and personality traits, and half by various environmental factors, such as one's career, relationships, and finances (Lykken, 2003).

Although emotional feelings are common to all people, you'll see next that displays of emotional expressions differ across cultures.

Pam said, "Wining the lottery was great, but it can't compare to my baby."

Riches don't guarantee happiness.

Showing Emotions

Do you cover your mouth when you laugh?

When I (R.P.) visited Japan, I noticed that the Japanese covered their mouths when laughing, something we Americans never do. This Japanese-American cultural difference comes from differences in emotional display rules (Ekman, 2003).

Display rules are specific cultural norms or rules that regulate how, when, and where a person expresses emotions and how much emotional expression is appropriate.

Here are examples of how different cultures have developed different display rules for emotional expressions.

Greetings. In some European cultures, the display rule for greeting someone is for the individuals, both men and women, to kiss each other on the cheeks or lips. For Americans, especially straight men, the display rule for greeting is a handshake (maybe a friendly hug), but it is taboo to greet another straight man with a kiss on the cheeks or lips.

Americans don't cover their mouths when they laugh.

Laughing and crying. American display rules generally encourage public displays of emotions, such as open-mouth laughing. In contrast, Japanese display rules for laughing include covering one's open mouth because showing much emotion in public is discouraged (Matsumoto et al., 2002). An Inuit (Eskimo) mother may let a baby cry to send the message that her culture disapproves of the display of negative emotions (Mauss, 2005).

Anger. Among the Inuit (Eskimos), feelings of anger are strongly condemned, but among certain Arab groups, a man's failure to respond with anger is seen as dishonorable (Abu-Lughod, 1986; Briggs, 1970).

These examples show how different cultures have developed different display rules for emotional expressions. One may be unaware of such display rules until visiting another culture (Marsh et al., 2003).

Smiling and interpreting. Display rules can also differ within a culture. For example, American adolescent girls and women smile more than boys and men do, and women are better than men at interpreting nonverbal cues (facial expressions and body gestures) (LaFrance et al., 2003).

Potential problems. Because of different display rules for expressing emotions, people from one culture may run into problems when traveling or conducting business in another culture. For example, Westerners often make direct eye contact and may show emotions during business meetings, while Asians avoid direct eye contact and outward expressions of emotions. Because of increased international travel and business, there are now companies that give advice and training on dealing with the display rules of other cultures (www.communicaid.com).

UK & USA = OK
Japan = MONEY
Brazil = INSULT
France = ZERO

Gestures. Similar to how emotional display rules differ, gestures may also have different emotional meanings in different cultures. For example, the common hand gesture of forming a circle (left figure) has four different meaning—OK, MONEY, INSULT, ZERO—depending on the culture (Bibikova & Koteinikov). These examples show how culture influences the meaning of gestures as well as the expression of emotional display rules.

Depending on your culture, you also rate different emotions as being more or less intense.

Perceiving Emotions

What's the most intense emotion?

Of these five emotions—surprise, anger, happiness, disgust, and sadness—which one do you rate as the most intense? _____

It turns out that your rating depends very much on your culture. For example, because the Japanese have a long history of discouraging any show of emotional intensity in public, researchers guessed that their ratings of emotional intensity would be different from those of Americans, who have a history of showing emotions of all intensities in public (Reitman, 1999).

Researchers asked a group of Japanese and a group of Americans to look at photos of five emotional expressions—anger, surprise, happiness, disgust, and sadness—and rate the intensity of each. Both groups looked at two sets of photos: One depicted a Japanese showing five facial emotional expressions, and the other depicted a Caucasian showing the same five expressions (similar to the photos shown on right).

As predicted, the Japanese gave significantly lower ratings of **emotional intensity** to all five emotional expressions than did the Americans. The Japanese rated disgust as the most intense emotion of the five emotions, while the Americans rated happiness as the most intense (Matsumoto & Ekman, 1989).

This study illustrates how cultures affect the display of emotional expressions and also our perception of an emotion's intensity (Rozin, 2003).

Next, we'll discuss the interesting new area of emotional intelligence.

Japanese rated ***disgust*** as the most intense of five emotions.

Disgust

Americans rated ***happiness*** as the most intense of five emotions.

Happiness

Concept Review

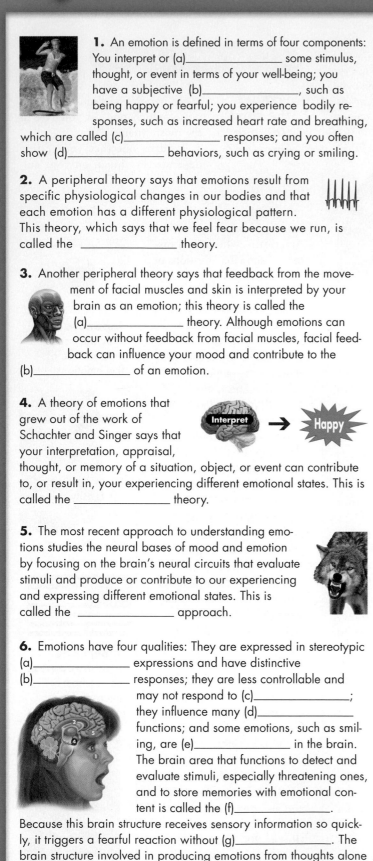

1. An emotion is defined in terms of four components: You interpret or (a)_____ some stimulus, thought, or event in terms of your well-being; you have a subjective (b)_____, such as being happy or fearful; you experience bodily responses, such as increased heart rate and breathing, which are called (c)_____ responses; and you often show (d)_____ behaviors, such as crying or smiling.

2. A peripheral theory says that emotions result from specific physiological changes in our bodies and that each emotion has a different physiological pattern. This theory, which says that we feel fear because we run, is called the _____ theory.

3. Another peripheral theory says that feedback from the movement of facial muscles and skin is interpreted by your brain as an emotion; this theory is called the (a)_____ theory. Although emotions can occur without feedback from facial muscles, facial feedback can influence your mood and contribute to the (b)_____ of an emotion.

4. A theory of emotions that grew out of the work of Schachter and Singer says that your interpretation, appraisal, thought, or memory of a situation, object, or event can contribute to, or result in, your experiencing different emotional states. This is called the _____ theory.

5. The most recent approach to understanding emotions studies the neural bases of mood and emotion by focusing on the brain's neural circuits that evaluate stimuli and produce or contribute to our experiencing and expressing different emotional states. This is called the _____ approach.

6. Emotions have four qualities: They are expressed in stereotypic (a)_____ expressions and have distinctive (b)_____ responses; they are less controllable and may not respond to (c)_____; they influence many (d)_____ functions; and some emotions, such as smiling, are (e)_____ in the brain. The brain area that functions to detect and evaluate stimuli, especially threatening ones, and to store memories with emotional content is called the (f)_____.
Because this brain structure receives sensory information so quickly, it triggers a fearful reaction without (g)_____. The brain structure involved in producing emotions from thoughts alone and in analyzing the emotional consequences of actions is called the (h)_____.

7. Specific inherited facial patterns or expressions that signal specific feelings or emotional states across cultures, such as a smile signaling a happy state, are called (a)_____. These emotional expressions, which include anger, happiness, fear, surprise, disgust, sadness, and contempt, are thought to have evolved because they had important (b)_____ and _____ functions for our ancestors.

8. According to one theory, we inherit the neural structure and physiology to express and experience emotions, and we evolved basic emotional patterns to adapt to and solve problems important for our survival; this is called the (a)_____ theory. Facial expressions that accompany emotions send signals about how one (b)_____ and what one intends to do. Emotions focus one's (c)_____ so one can better respond to emotional situations and also increases (d)_____ of situations that may be either beneficial or dangerous to one's well-being.

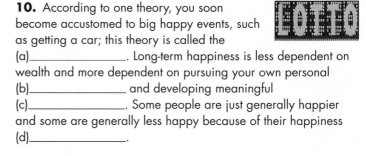

9. Your performance on a task depends on the amount of physiological arousal and the difficulty of the task. For many tasks, moderate arousal helps performance; for new or difficult tasks, low arousal is better; and for easy or well-learned tasks, high arousal may facilitate performance. This relationship between arousal and performance is known as the _____.

10. According to one theory, you soon become accustomed to big happy events, such as getting a car; this theory is called the (a)_____. Long-term happiness is less dependent on wealth and more dependent on pursuing your own personal (b)_____ and developing meaningful (c)_____. Some people are just generally happier and some are generally less happy because of their happiness (d)_____.

11. Specific cultural norms that regulate when, where, and how much emotion we should or should not express in different situations are called _____. These rules explain why emotional expressions and intensity of emotions differ across cultures.

Answers: *1. (a) appraise, (b) feeling, (c) physiological, (d) observable; 2. James-Lange; 3. (a) facial feedback, (b) intensity; 4. cognitive appraisal; 5. affective neuroscience; 6. (a) facial, (b) physiological, (c) reason, (d) cognitive, (e) hard-wired, (f) amygdala, (g) awareness or conscious thought, (h) prefrontal cortex; 7. (a) universal facial expressions, (b) adaptive, survival; 8. (a) evolutionary, (b) feels, (c) attention, (d) memory, recall; 9. Yerkes-Dodson law; 10. (a) adaptation level theory, (b) goals, (c) relationships, (d) set point; 11. display rules*

H. Research Focus: Emotional Intelligence

What Is Emotional Intelligence?

What is it and who has it?

One of the exciting things about being a researcher is the chance to come up with new ideas. This happened in the early 1990s, when researchers came up with the idea of emotional intelligence, which they suggested made people more effective in social situations (Salovey & Mayer, 1990). By the mid-1990s, popular magazines, such as *Time,* declared that emotional intelligence may redefine what it means to be smart and may be the best predictor of success in life (Gibbs, 1995).

Emotional intelligence **is the ability to perceive emotions accurately, to take feelings into account when reasoning, to understand emotions, and to regulate or manage emotions in oneself and others (Salovey & Pizarro, 2003).**

Is emotional intelligence the key to Oprah's success?

Unlike the traditional idea of intelligence involving performance on cognitive tests (IQ scores—p. 282), emotional intelligence involves how well people perceive, express, and regulate emotions in themselves and others. The author of the book *Emotional Intelligence* (Goleman, 1995, 2005) said in an interview, "Oprah Winfrey's ability to read people and identify with them is at the heart of her success" (S. A. Brown, 1996, p. 85). In other words, the reason for Oprah's incredible success as a talk-show host is that she rates very high in emotional intelligence.

For the past decade, researchers have been working to better understand emotional intelligence and just how important it really is.

How Important Is Emotional Intelligence?

All agree that emotions play important roles in our lives.

Here are some common remarks that show how emotions can influence our behaviors.
- "I was so angry, I couldn't think straight."
- "I get worse when people tell me to calm down."
- "When we argue, I often get mad and say the wrong thing."
- "You never try to understand how I feel."
- "Sometimes I act on my feelings, right or wrong."

These kinds of self-reports point to the influence that emotions can have on what we say and do and on our success in life. According to supporters of emotional intelligence, the better our understanding of how emotions work, the more likely we are to find a compromise between our often strong emotional feelings ("I felt like doing that") and our equally strong rational thoughts ("I knew I should not have done that") (Mayer et al., 2000). However, these kinds of self-reports need to be confirmed by a more scientific technique, such as using a valid and reliable emotional intelligence test.

Preliminary findings. Here are some findings reported from recent tests to measure emotional intelligence: Youths who scored higher on emotional intelligence tests were less likely to have smoked cigarettes; school children who scored higher were rated as less aggressive by their peers and as more helpful by their teachers; higher scores on emotional intelligence were related to being more empathetic and satisfied with one's life (Salovey & Pizarro, 2003). These findings are considered preliminary until they are replicated and supported by the findings of other researchers.

However, critics of emotional intelligence point out that in business settings and schools where programs try to teach or improve emotional intelligence, the results have been more hype than substance (G. Matthews et al., 2003). Although there is still considerable debate about the usefulness of emotional intelligence, no one denies that emotions can exert powerful influences on many of our behaviors.

Researchers are only recently beginning to understand how it is that we can perceive, express, and regulate emotions (A. Underwood, 2006). Next, we'll learn about how we perceive emotional expressions.

How Do We Perceive Emotional Expressions?

Scientists have known that we are able to detect emotions, such as fear, anger, and happiness, in people's faces almost instantaneously (M. A. Williams & Mattingley, 2006). Researchers now understand the brain mechanisms that make it possible for us to very easily perceive emotions in others.

Human brains are innately prepared to connect with others in an intimate way, and this enables us to share the emotions of others and be sensitive to their feelings. When we empathize with a friend or family member, the activation pattern in our brains becomes the same as that of the person we are empathizing with (Goleman, 2006a). For instance, by using fMRI scans (p. 70), researchers found that feeling disgust activates similar parts of the brain when people smell a disgusting odor and when they observe a video of someone else feeling disgusted (Rizzolatti et al., 2006). We are able to share the emotions felt by others because of mirror neurons, which track the emotions of the person we are with and replicate the same emotions in us by activating our brains in the same way the other person's brain is activated (Goleman, 2006b).

Mirror neurons help us perceive emotions in others.

Can people from all cultures perceive emotional expressions so easily? This question remains to be explored, but in general, Asian cultures that place greater emphasis on the well-being of a group than of an individual tend to perceive the emotions of others more readily (Goleman, 2006c).

Next, we'll learn about how difficult it is to accurately detect whether someone is lying.

I. Application: Lie Detection

How did a spy pass a lie detector test twice?

For nine years, the Russians paid or promised $4.6 million to Aldrich Ames (photo on right), who was a high-level Central Intelligence Agency official. Later, Ames pleaded guilty to espionage, which involved selling secrets to the Russians. Ames is currently serving a life sentence in prison. The Ames case brings up the issue of lie detection because he reportedly passed at

I lied, but I passed two lie detector tests.

least two lie detector (polygraph) tests during the time that he was selling U.S. secrets to Russia (R. L. Jackson, 1994). The publicity surrounding this case made people ask, "How could Ames be selling secrets and pass two lie detector tests?" The Ames case raises three questions: What is the theory behind lie detection? How is a lie detector test given? How accurate are lie detector tests?

What Is the Theory?

Does the test measure lying?

The lie detector test is based on the four components of an emotion that we discussed earlier. The first component of an emotion is interpreting or appraising a stimulus. In this case, Ames will need to interpret questions such as "Have you ever sold secrets to Russia?" The second component of an emotion is a subjective feeling, such as whether Ames will feel any guilt or fear when he answers "Yes" or "No" to the question "Have you ever sold secrets to Russia?" The third component of an emotion is the occurrence of various physiological responses (figure below). If Mr. Ames feels guilty about selling secrets, then his guilt feeling will be accompanied by physiological arousal, which includes increases in heart rate, blood pressure, breathing, and sweating of the hands. These physiological responses occur automatically and are usually involuntary because they are controlled by the autonomic nervous system (discussed in Module 4). The fourth component of an emotion is the occurrence of some overt behavior, such as a facial expression. Mr. Ames may be able to control his facial expressions and put on a nonemotional poker face. However, neither the presence nor the absence of expressions is critical to the theory behind lie detector tests.

Lie detector (polygraph) tests are based on the theory that, if a person tells a lie, he or she will feel some emotion, such as guilt or fear. Feeling guilty or fearful will be accompanied by involuntary physiological responses, which are difficult to suppress or control and can be measured with a machine called a polygraph.

A polygraph (lie detector) is about the size of a laptop computer (right figure) and measures chest and abdominal muscle movement during respiration, heart rate, blood pressure, and skin conductance or galvanic skin response.

The *galvanic skin response* refers to changes in sweating of the fingers (or palms) that accompany emotional experiences and are independent of perspiration under normal temperatures (Cacioppo et al., 1993).

Chest movement during respiration
Abdominal movement during respiration
Heart rate and blood pressure
Skin conductance

For example, you may remember having sweaty or clammy palms when taking exams, giving a public talk, or meeting someone important, even though the temperature was not unduly hot.

We'll focus on the galvanic skin response because its changes are often the most obvious.

Man hooked up to lie detector (polygraph)

What Is a Lie Detector Test?

Is the suspect lying?

Very few details have been released about how Mr. Ames, who apparently lied, passed two lie detector tests. Instead, we'll use a more detailed report of a man named Floyd, who told the truth but failed two lie detector tests.

Floyd was very surprised when two police officers came to his home. They had a warrant and arrested him for the armed robbery of a liquor store. However, the case against Floyd was weak, since none of the witnesses could positively identify him as the robber. Soon after his arrest, the prosecutor offered to drop all charges if Floyd agreed to take, and pass, a lie detector test. Floyd jumped at the chance to prove his innocence and took the test. He failed the lie detector test but insisted that he had not lied and that he be allowed to take a second one, which he also failed. Eventually Floyd was tried, found guilty, and sent to prison. He served several years behind bars before his lawyer tracked down the real robbers, which proved Floyd's innocence (*Los Angeles Times*, December 22, 1980).

Floyd was given the most commonly used procedure for lie detection in criminal investigations, which is called the Control Question Technique (Bashore & Rapp, 1993; Saxe, 1994).

The *Control Question Technique* refers to a lie detection procedure in which the examiner asks two kinds of questions: neutral questions that elicit little emotional response, and critical questions that are designed to elicit large emotional responses. The person answers only "Yes" or "No" to the questions and, if guilty, is expected to show a greater emotional response to the critical questions than to the neutral questions.

NEUTRAL QUESTIONS

These are general questions, such as "Is your name Floyd?" or "Do you live at a particular place?" These questions are designed to elicit few, if any, emotional responses and are used to establish a baseline for normal physiological responding.

CRITICAL QUESTIONS

These are specific questions about some particular crime or misconduct that only a person who committed the crime would know, such as "Did you rob the liquor store on 5th and Vine?" Critical questions are designed to elicit emotional responses, such as guilt or fear, if the person tells a lie.

As shown in the figure below, Floyd showed very little physiological arousal—as measured by the galvanic skin response—when asked a neutral question, "Is your name Floyd?" However, he showed great physiological arousal when asked a critical question, "Did you rob the liquor store?"

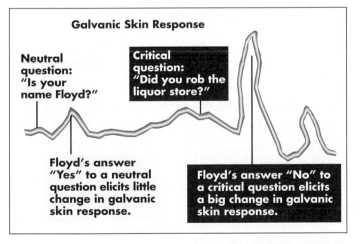

The examiner decides whether the client is lying or telling the truth by looking at the differences in physiological responses between neutral and critical questions. In Floyd's case, he answered "No" to a number of critical questions, such as "Did you rob the liquor store?" But his "No" answers were accompanied by large increases in galvanic skin response (as well as other responses). For those reasons, the examiner decided that Floyd had lied and thus failed the polygraph test. However, when the real robbers were eventually caught, tried, and sentenced, it proved that Floyd had not lied even though he failed the lie detector test twice. Floyd's case, as well as the Ames case, questions the accuracy of lie detector tests.

Why aren't tests allowed in most courts?

If Floyd was innocent, why did he fail two lie detector exams? If Ames was lying, why did he pass two lie detector tests?

The basic problem with lie detector tests is that researchers have been unable to identify a pattern of physiological responses specific to lying. This means that a number of different emotions—such as guilt, fear, nervousness, or worry—can trigger physiological responses that make a person appear to be lying when he or she may be telling the truth (Fiedler et al., 2002). Because of this serious problem, researchers estimate that lie detector tests are wrong about 25–75% of the time (Broad, 2002; Saxe, 1994).

Although low error scores (5–10%) for some lie detector tests have been reported, these data come from less realistic laboratory settings that use simple tasks, such as identifying an object about which the subject—often a college student—has been told to lie (Ben-Shakar & Elaad, 2003). The higher error scores come from field studies that simulate more realistic conditions, in which subjects actually steal objects that they are told will be replaced after the test (Bashore & Rapp, 1993; Honts, 1994).

Innocent or faking. Besides high error scores, lie detector tests have two other problems: In one field study, about 40% of subjects were judged to be lying or maybe lying when they were telling the truth (Honts, 1994); and in another field study, about 50% of guilty people who were told to both press their toes to the ground and bite their tongues during control questions passed lie detector tests (Honts et al., 1994).

Restrictions. Because of the above problems, federal law now prohibits most employers from using polygraph tests to screen employees and most state and federal courts prohibit the use of polygraph evidence (Frazier, 2003). In 1998, the U.S. Supreme Court ruled that polygraph evidence cannot be used in most courts. However, 62% of local law enforcement agencies use lie detectors to screen new employees, and 75% of police believe that polygraph tests are between 86 and 100% effective (K. Johnson, 1999).

New tests. Recent concerns about terrorists and security have increased the need for more reliable methods to detect lies. One of the newest methods involves using brain scans to detect changes in thinking and associated neural activity that occur when lying. Researchers reported distinct patterns of neural activity (prefrontal area) when subjects told lies (Langleben, 2006). Interestingly, researchers studying structural brain abnormalities found that compared to nonliars, pathological liars have 22% more prefrontal white matter, which is linked to the ability to deceive others (Yang et al., 2005a). Although these data are preliminary, they suggest that using brain scans may prove to be a more accurate and reliable way to detect lying (Loviglio, 2003).

Other new tests aiming to improve the accuracy of lie detection include measuring electrical activity of the brain, using eye scans to measure blood flow to the eye, and observing very brief, involuntary facial expression changes (Ekman, 2006; Kluger & Masters, 2006).

One curious and little-known fact about lie detector tests is that they are used primarily in the United States. Lie detector (polygraph) tests are almost unknown and are not used in the rest of the industrialized world (Shenour, 1990).

Summary Test

A. Peripheral Theories

1. We can define an emotion in terms of four components: We interpret or appraise a (a)_____ in terms of our well-being; we have a subjective (b)_____; we experience various (c)_____ responses, such as changes in heart rate and respiration; and we often show (d)_____ behaviors, such as crying or smiling.

2. Several theories explain what causes emotions. Theories that emphasize changes in the body are called (a)_____ theories. One such theory states that emotions result from specific physiological changes in your body and that each emotion has a different physiological basis; this is called the (b)_____ theory. The major criticism of this theory is that different emotions do not always cause different patterns of physiological arousal. However, feedback from physiological changes may increase the (c)_____ of emotional feelings.

3. According to another peripheral theory, sensations or feedback from the movement of facial muscles and skin are interpreted by your brain and result in an emotion; this is called the (a)_____ theory. However, people with paralyzed facial muscles still experience emotions. Facial feedback may influence your (b)_____ as well as increase the (c)_____ of emotional feelings.

B. Cognitive Appraisal Theory

4. A theory of emotions that grew out of the work of Schachter and Singer says that your interpretation, appraisal, thought, or memory of a situation, object, or event can contribute to, or result in, your experiencing different emotional states. This is called the _____ theory.

C. Affective Neuroscience Approach

5. The most recent approach to understanding emotions studies the neural bases of mood and emotion by focusing on the brain's neural circuits that evaluate stimuli and produce or contribute to our experiencing and expressing different emotional states. This is called the _____ approach.

6. Emotions have four qualities: They are expressed in stereotypic (a)_____ expressions and have distinctive (b)_____ responses; they are less controllable and may not respond to (c)_____; they influence many (d)_____ functions; and some emotions, such as smiling, are (e)_____ in the brain. The brain area that functions to detect and evaluate stimuli, especially threatening ones, and to store

memories with emotional content is called the (f)_____. Because this brain structure receives sensory information so quickly, it triggers a fearful reaction without (g)_____. The brain structure involved in producing emotions from thoughts alone and in analyzing the emotional consequences of actions is called the (h)_____.

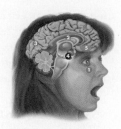

D. Universal Facial Expressions

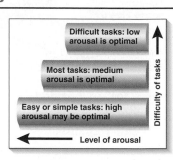

7. Specific inherited facial patterns or expressions that signal specific feelings or emotional states across cultures, such as a smile signaling a happy state, are called (a)_____. These emotional expressions, which are said to include happiness, surprise, fear, anger, contempt, disgust, and sadness, are thought to have evolved because they had important (b)_____ functions for our ancestors. Evidence for universal emotions includes that people in different cultures recognize the same (c)_____ expressions, that infants in different cultures show a predictable (d)_____ in developing facial expressions, and that even blind children, who cannot observe their parents' faces, develop smiling at the same time as sighted children.

E. Functions of Emotions

8. Facial expressions that accompany emotions send signals about how one (a)_____ and what one intends to do. Emotions focus one's (b)_____ so one can better respond to emotional situations and also increases the (c)_____ of situations that may be either beneficial or dangerous to one's well-being.

| Difficult tasks: low arousal is optimal |
| Most tasks: medium arousal is optimal |
| Easy or simple tasks: high arousal may be optimal |

Difficulty of tasks

← Level of arousal

9. According to one theory of emotions, we have inherited the neural structure and physiology to express and experience emotions and we evolved basic emotional patterns to adapt to and solve problems important for our survival; this is called the _____ theory.

10. There is a relationship between emotional arousal and your performance on a task; this relationship is called the (a)_____ law. According to this law, low arousal results in better performance on (b)_____ tasks; for most tasks, (c)_____ arousal helps performance; and for easy tasks, (d)_____ arousal may facilitate performance.

F. Happiness

11. Momentary pleasures, short-term joys, or long-term satisfaction can result in an emotional feeling called (a)_____. This emotion also stimulates the brain's reward/pleasure center, which includes several areas, such as the (b)_____ and _____. The finding that identical twins (share 100% of

genes) are significantly more similar in happiness ratings than fraternal twins (share 50% of genes) shows that (c)_____ factors influence our level of happiness.

12. One theory explains that we quickly become accustomed to receiving some good fortune (money, job, car, degree) and, within a relatively short period of time, take the good fortune for granted. As a result, this good fortune contributes little to our long-term level of happiness; this is called the (a)_____ theory. Research shows that long-term happiness is less dependent upon (b)_____ because we soon adapt to our good fortunes. Instead, long-term happiness is more dependent upon pursuing our own personal (c)_____ and developing meaningful (d)_____. One reason some people are generally more happy and some are generally less happy is that each of us seems to have a happiness (e)_____, which is about half set or influenced by environmental factors and about half set or influenced by inherited or genetic factors.

G. Cultural Diversity: Emotions across Cultures

13. Although many emotional expressions are shared and recognized across cultures, it is also true that cultures have unique rules that regulate how, when, and where we should express emotion and how much emotion is appropriate; these rules are called _____. For example, among the Inuit (Eskimos), feelings of anger are strongly condemned, but among certain Arab groups, a man's failure to respond with anger is seen as dishonorable.

14. Another example of display rules is from a study in which Americans and Japanese rated the intensity of five emotions—surprise, anger, happiness, disgust, and sadness—on a scale from 1 to 10. The emotion rated most intense by the Japanese was (a)_____, while the Americans rated (b)_____ as the most intense of the five emotions. This study illustrates how cultural display rules may differently influence how people perceive the (c)_____ of emotions.

H. Research Focus: Emotional Intelligence

15. The ability to perceive and express emotion, understand and reason with emotion, and regulate emotion in oneself and others is called (a)_____. One reason researchers believe that emotional intelligence is important is that the better we understand how emotions operate, the better are our chances of finding a way to work out compromises between our strong (b)_____ feelings and our equally strong rational (c)_____. We are able to share emotions felt by others because of our (d)_____, which track the emotions of the person we are with and replicate the same emotions in us by activating our brains in the same way the other person's brain is activated.

I. Application: Lie Detection

16. The instrument that is sometimes referred to as a lie detector is correctly called a (a)_____; it measures a person's heart rate, blood pressure, respiration, and emotionally induced hand sweating, which is called the (b)_____ response. To determine whether a person is telling the truth or a lie, the

> Critical question: "Did you rob the liquor store?"
>
> Subject's answer: "No."

examiner compares the person's physiological responses to (c)_____ and _____ questions. The basic problem with lie detector tests is that no pattern of physiological responses has been specifically associated with lying. This means that many emotions can cause increased physiological responses that make the person appear to be lying. Because of the relatively high (d)_____ rate, evidence from lie detector tests is not admitted in most courts of law. The newest method to detect lies involves using brain scans to detect changes in thinking and associated (e)_____ that occur when subjects lie.

Answers: *1. (a) stimulus, (b) feeling, (c) physiological, (d) overt; 2. (a) peripheral, (b) James-Lange, (c) intensity; 3. (a) facial feedback, (b) mood, overall feeling, (c) intensity; 4. cognitive appraisal; 5. affective neuroscience; 6. (a) facial, (b) physiological, (c) reason, (d) cognitive, (e) hardwired, (f) amygdala, (g) awareness or conscious thought, (h) prefrontal cortex; 7. (a) universal emotions, (b) adaptive, survival, (c) facial, (d) order; 8. (a) feels, (b) attention, (c) memory, recall; 9. evolutionary; 10. (a) Yerkes-Dodson, (b) difficult, (c) medium, (d) high; 11. (a) happiness, (b) nucleus accumbens, ventral tegmental area, (c) genetic; 12. (a) adaptation level, (b) wealth or material things, (c) goals, (d) relationships or friends, (e) set point; 13. display rules; 14. (a) disgust, (b) happiness, (c) intensity; 15. (a) emotional intelligence, (b) emotional, (c) thoughts; (d) mirror neurons; 16. (a) polygraph, (b) galvanic skin, (c) neutral, critical, (d) error, (e) neural activity*

Critical Thinking

Why Do They Have to Learn to Smile?

Questions

1. In the United States, why is smiling in social situations considered an acceptable and even desirable way to behave in public?

2. When having to make money is bucking cultural traditions, what do you think will happen?

3. Even though emotional expressions, such as smiling, are considered universal facial expressions, why don't the Japanese smile more?

4. Why is it so difficult for many highly motivated Japanese to learn to smile?

5. Why do you think that smiley, friendly salespeople are more successful and better at building morale?

In the United States it's very common to see people smiling in public because it's a friendly way to interact socially. In fact, many businesses insist that their salespeople smile at customers because smiling makes the customers feel more comfortable and more likely to buy something. But in Japan, people are very reluctant to show emotions in public and that's become a problem.

Japan is currently going through a recession or downturn in business, so there is increased competition to get new customers and keep current customers happy. Said one gas station attendant who is trying to learn to smile more, "In this recession, customers are getting choosy about their gas stations, so you have to think positively. Laughter and a smile are representative of this positive thinking" (Reitman, 1999, p. A1).

But getting salespeople to smile is a radical change in Japan, whose cultural tradition has long emphasized suppressing any public display of emotions, be it happy, sad, or angry. For example, women never smile at their husbands and members of families rarely touch in public and never hug, even when greeting after a long separation. It's still common for women to place a hand over their mouths when they laugh, and men believe that the correct and proper behavior is to show no emotions in public. Unlike American salespeople who often smile and make eye contact with their customers, Japanese salespeople are reserved and greet customers with a simple "welcome"; smiling, up until now, was totally frowned upon.

Because getting salespeople to smile is going against a strong tradition, learning how to smile has grown into a big business in Japan. Employees are now being sent to "smile school," which uses various techniques to teach reluctant and bashful students to smile. For example, one technique in learning how to smile is biting on a chop stick (left photo) and then lifting the edges of the mouth higher than the chopstick. Another technique is to follow "smile" instructions: "Relax the muscle under your nose, loosen up your tongue. Put your hands on your stomach and laugh out loud, feeling the 'poisons' escape" (Reitman, 1999, p. A1).

What is driving all this smiling in Japan is sales and morale. As is well known by American businesses, happy, friendly salespeople are usually the most successful and are great at building company morale. The same is holding true in Japan, where smiley clerks are racking up the most sales and creating a friendly morale.

People in other parts of Asia, such as China, also are not accustomed to smiling in social situations. In fact, volunteers for the 2008 Olympics in Beijing are required to take classes on how to smile to ensure that they portray China as hospitable. (Adapted from Mauss, 2005; Reitman, 1999; UPI, 2006)

1. Smiling is one of the universal facial expressions, which means it occurs and is recognized as a friendly social signal worldwide. However, different countries have different display rules, which regulate how, when, and where its citizens can express emotions. The display rules for the United States encourage the public display of emotional expressions, such as smiling.

2. Cultural display rules have a strong influence on people's behavior (in the United States, women can cry but men should not). It takes a strong motivating force, such as money, to change the cultural display rules, such as making it OK to smile in Japan.

3. Unlike the United States, whose cultural display rules encourage public display of smiling, Japan has had a long tradition of cultural display rules that ban most public display of emotions.

4. Even though many businesses in Japan are now sending their employees to "smile school," employees are finding it difficult to learn to smile because they must first overcome a lifetime habit of being told not to show emotions. Imagine how men in the United States would feel if they were now encouraged to cry in public and were sent to "cry school" to learn how!

5. One reason smiley salespersons are usually more successful is that all their customers come with a built-in or inherited detector for facial expressions, such as smiling. When seeing a salesperson smile (universal facial expression), customers immediately detect that it's a friendly social signal and that the salesperson is acting friendly. As a result, customers feel more friendly and more motivated to agree with the salesperson's suggestions and buy.

Links to Learning

Key Terms/Key People

Learning Activities

- **POWERSTUDY FOR INTRODUCTION TO PSYCHOLOGY 4.0**
by Tom Doyle and Rod Plotnik
Check out the quizzes and learning activities for "Emotion" on **PowerStudy** and:
  - Test your knowledge using an interactive version of the Summary Test on pages 372 and 373. Also access related quizzing—true/false, multiple choice, and matching.
  - Explore an interactive version of the Critical Thinking exercise "Why Do They Have to Learn to Smile?" on page 374.
  - You will also find key terms, a chapter outline including a chapter abstract, and a special extended list of hotlinked websites that correlate to this module.

- **CengageNOW**
academic.cengage.com/login
Need help studying? This site is your one-stop study shop. Take a Pre-Test and CengageNOW will generate a Personalized Study Plan based on your test results. The Study Plan will identify the topics you need to review and direct you to online resources to help you master those topics. You can then take a Post-Test to determine the concepts you have mastered and what you still need to work on.

- **INTRODUCTION TO PSYCHOLOGY BOOK COMPANION WEBSITE**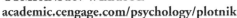
academic.cengage.com/psychology/plotnik
Visit your book companion website where you will find more resources to help you study. At this site, you will find Learning Objectives, Internet Exercises, quizzing, flash cards, and a pronunciation glossary.

- **STUDY GUIDE and WEBTUTOR**
Check the corresponding module in your Study Guide for effective student tips and help learning the material presented. Also go to **academic.cengage.com/webtutor** for an interactive version of the Study Guide features.

Study Questions

*A. **Peripheral Theories**—Does someone with many facial expressions experience more emotions than someone with few facial expressions? (**Suggested answer page 630**)

B. **Cognitive Appraisal Theory**—Why would you get very angry if someone backed into your car but calm down as soon as you discovered your mother had done it?

C. **Affective Neuroscience Approach**—What would happen if you took a drug that decreased the activity of your amygdala?

D. **Universal Facial Expressions**—Do animals express emotions with facial expressions that are similar to humans'?

*E. **Function of Emotions**—Why might people who are madly in love have difficulty making the right decisions? (**Suggested answer page 630**)

F. **Happiness**—How might your level of happiness change after you reach a big goal in your life, such as getting a college degree, new job, or relationship?

G. **Cultural Diversity: Emotions across Cultures**—Is there any truth to the stereotypes that Italians are emotional, British hide their feelings, Germans are serious, and Americans are impulsive?

H. **Research Focus: Emotional Intelligence**—If PET scans could identify emotions, would our criminal justice system benefit from knowing whether violent criminals felt guilt for their crimes?

*I. **Application: Lie Detection**—Would it be fair to use lie detector tests to identify students who are suspected of cheating on exams? (**Suggested answer page 630**)

*These questions are answered in Appendix B.

MODULE 17
Infancy & Childhood

Oliviero Toscani for BENETTON

 PowerStudy 4.0™ Complete Module

Introduction

Nature-Nurture Question

Will Alex ever learn to love a parent?

For the first 3 years of his life, Alex was raised in an orphanage in Romania where the number of infants and children greatly exceeded the number of caregivers. At the orphanage, Alex was given adequate nutrition allowing him to develop well physically, but the affection, stimulation, and comfort he received were far from adequate. Alex, like other children living in Romanian orphanages, spent most of his days alone in a crib with almost no interaction with others. When he cried, no one came to hold or soothe him. He was never given the opportunity to bond with a caregiver.

When Alex was 3 years old, a family living in the United States adopted him. His adoptive mother described him as being friendly and engaging, but also "self-abusive" and having a "dark side." For instance, Alex would make himself go into a seizure by slamming his head on the floor.

He was also aggressive toward others, one time attacking his younger sister, "beating her senseless." When asked if he wanted his adoptive mother to love him, he said to her, "I never want you to love me." When his adoptive mother asked him if he loved her, he replied, "No, I don't love anybody." After years of exhausting every treatment option and still unable to feel loved by Alex, his adoptive parents arranged for Alex to live with another family (Jarriel & Sawyer, 1997).

Until age 3, Alex lived in an orphanage where he didn't receive affection, stimulation, or comfort.

Children like Alex, whose emotional needs (such as forming a stable attachment with a caregiver) go unmet during infancy and early childhood, may develop reactive attachment disorder.

Reactive attachment disorder **is a psychiatric illness characterized by serious problems in emotional attachments to others beginning before age 5. Some symptoms children may show include resisting comfort and affection by parents, being superficially engaging and overly friendly with strangers, having poor peer relationships, and engaging in destructive behavior to themselves and to others (American Psychiatric Association, 2000; Keck & Kupecky, 1995).**

Do all children raised in Romanian orphanages who are later adopted have attachment problems? This question brings up an interesting issue in developmental psychology referred to as the nature-nurture question.

The *nature-nurture question* **asks how much nature (genetic factors) and how much nurture (environmental factors) contributes to a person's biological, emotional, cognitive, personal, and social development.**

Although the nature-nurture question seems like an abstract intellectual issue, it has very practical consequences. For example, in the United States, courts have varied in how they side with biological parents (nature) over adoptive parents (nurture) when awarding custody of an adopted child. Traditionally, courts have favored placement with biological parents, but more recently some courts have begun to favor placement with adoptive parents (M. Dolan, 2002). For example, Dana Wakefield, a juvenile court judge, adamantly states, "In my courtroom, they (children) stay where they've been nurtured. You have to consider who the child feels is the psychological parents. If they have a good bond in that home, I'm not about to break it" (Gibbs, 1993, p. 49).

There are now about 10,000 Romanian children growing up in the United States and nearly all of them initially had serious developmental problems. One researcher studying the adjustment of over 300 Romanian adoptees in the United States found that after the first year, 20% of children reached normal development, 60% showed only mild problems, and the remaining 20% had serious cognitive, behavioral, and emotional problems (Fischer, 1999). The reason some Romanian adoptees have long-term developmental problems while others make significant improvements is complex, involving both biological (nature) and environmental (nurture) factors.

Developmental Psychologists

The questions about why Romanian adoptees vary in how they are affected by being raised in an orphanage and how they later adjust to adoption illustrate the kinds of issues and questions studied by developmental psychologists.

Developmental psychologists **study a person's biological, emotional, cognitive, personal, and social development across the life span, from infancy through late adulthood.**

7-year-old Alex still has serious problems in his emotional attachment to others.

Later in this module, we'll explain how Alex was doing at age 7 and what it means when he is finally able to say "I love you" to a parent. From the work of developmental psychologists, we have learned that the answer to the age-old question of whether nature or nurture is more important is that they are both important and their interaction is the key to understanding how an infant develops into a very complex adult with his or her own personality, behaviors, and goals (Pinker, 2003).

What's Coming

We'll discuss how development is affected by various prenatal factors, such as alcohol, which is the leading known cause of mental retardation. We'll explain the amazing abilities of newborns, the early appearance of a basic emotional makeup, the surprising growth of mental abilities, the different factors that influence social development, and the terrible occurrence of child abuse, which affects more than a million children a year.

We'll begin with a family whose infant son's unusual musical abilities showed how nature and nurture interact.

A. Prenatal Influences

Nature and Nurture

Was he born a violin player?

The reviewer for the *San Francisco Examiner* had listened to an inspired performance and wrote that the violinist "would one day be a master among masters" (Magidoff, 1973, p. 35).

At that point, the "master" was all of 5 years old and had been taking lessons for only six months. His name was Yehudi Menuhin. When Yehudi was 8 years old, he made his first professional appearance. The reviewer wrote, "This is not talent; it is genius!" (Magidoff, 1973, p. 46). Yehudi made his debut in New York at the age of 10, and the reviewer wrote, "What built the world in six days is what contrived the genius of Yehudi. He walks on the waves" (Magidoff, 1973, p. 52).

When only 8 years old, Yehudi made his professional debut.

The amazing musical abilities of young Yehudi certainly classify him as a prodigy.

A *prodigy* is a child who shows a highly unusual talent, ability, or genius at a very early age and does not have mental retardation. A small percentage of autistic children, who have some degree of mental retardation, may also show unusual artistic or mathematical abilities; they are called savants.

Because prodigies demonstrate such unusual abilities so early, they are excellent examples of the interaction between nature (genetic influences) and nurture (learned influences).

Genetic and Environmental Factors

One reason Yehudi Menuhin was a prodigy and could give an inspiring violin performance at the age of 5 was the prenatal (before birth) effects of genetic influences. Prenatal influences, in the form of genetic instructions, regulated the development of Yehudi's brain and body.

Parents. The father contributed half of Yehudi's genetic instructions (23 chromosomes) and the mother contributed half of the genetic instructions (23 chromosomes).

The father and mother were teachers, and both had musical interests. The father had taken six violin lessons when he was a boy, but his grandfather had forbidden him to play any further. The mother had musical ability and took regular cello lessons. Through their chromosomes, the parents passed some of their musical talents on to their three children, Yehudi and his two younger sisters.

Daughters. The two daughters each received half of their genetic instructions from their mother and half from their father. Both daughters, who were younger than Yehudi, showed early musical abilities and began playing piano at the ages of 5 and 7. It is difficult to tell if the daughters had as much natural ability as Yehudi because in the 1930s and 1940s there were few opportunities for women in professional music. As a result, these negative environmental influences actively discouraged the two daughters from developing their potential musical abilities.

Son. Yehudi received half of his genetic instructions from his mother and half from his father. The unique pairing of chromosomes from the mother and father

results in different physical and mental traits for each of the three children. Because Yehudi and his two younger sisters showed great musical ability by age 5, we can assume that their early musical ability was primarily due to genetic or inherited instructions that came from their parents' chromosomes. However, certain environmental factors, such as few opportunities for women musicians, discouraged the sisters from developing their talents. Different environmental factors, such as more opportunities for male musicians, encouraged Yehudi to develop his musical talents.

Interaction. Yehudi Menuhin, who was universally hailed as the greatest child prodigy since Mozart, developed into a legendary violin performer (Magidoff, 1973). The development of Yehudi's musical talents is a perfect example of how nature and nurture interact. You can see that genetic influences (nature) played a major role in wiring his brain so that his incredible musical abilities appeared at a very early age, before he had a chance to learn them. You can also see that environmental influences (nurture), such as being taken to concerts from age 2 on and being encouraged to practice and take lessons, encouraged Yehudi to develop the musical talents that he had inherited from his parents.

Psychologists have long recognized the importance of learning influences, but it is only in about the past ten years that psychologists have also recognized the importance of genetic factors that influence almost every aspect of behavior, including cognitive, social, emotional, and personality development (Baker, 2004). Today, researchers no longer focus on which is more important, nature or nurture, but rather on how nature and nurture interact to influence and regulate our behaviors (Pinker, 2003).

Genetic instructions from our parents can result in our having a wide range of abilities. Next, we'll explain what happens when genetic instructions are damaged—for example, if the mother uses drugs during the prenatal period.

How did you begin? You began as a single cell about the size of a grain of sand. In this tiny cell was the equivalent of about 300,000 pages of instructions for the development of your brain and body. This single cell marks the beginning of the prenatal period.

The *prenatal period* extends from conception to birth and lasts about 266 days (around nine months). It consists of three successive phases: the germinal, embryonic, and fetal stages. During the prenatal period, a single cell will divide and grow to form 200 billion cells.

As we examine the prenatal period, we'll unravel one of the great puzzles of science—how a human being begins, develops, and is born. We'll start with the germinal stage.

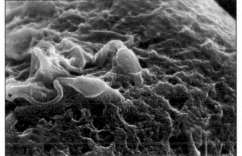

Prenatal Period: Three Stages
1. Germinal Stage
2. Embryonic Stage
3. Fetal Stage

1 Germinal Stage

The germinal stage marks the beginning of our development into a human being.

The *germinal stage* is the first stage of prenatal development and refers to the two-week period following conception.

To understand how conception occurs, we need to back up a little and explain ovulation.

***Ovulation* is the release of an ovum or egg cell from a woman's ovaries.**

In most cases, only a single ovum is released during ovulation, but sometimes two ova are released. If two separate ova are released and fertilized, the result is fraternal twins, who can be two brothers, two sisters, or a brother and sister. Because fraternal twins come from two separate eggs, they are no more genetically alike than any other two children of the same parents. In contrast, if a single ovum splits into two parts after fertilization, the result is identical twins, who share the same genes and thus are genetically alike.

Only one of many sperm will fertilize this egg.

How does conception take place?

If no sperm are present, there can be no fertilization, and the ovum, together with the lining of the uterus, is sloughed off in the process called *menstruation.* If, however, sperm have been deposited in the vagina (100–500 million sperm may be deposited with each act of intercourse), they make their way to the uterus and into the fallopian tubes in search of an ovum to be fertilized.

***Conception,* or *fertilization,* occurs if one of the millions of sperm penetrates the ovum's outer membrane. After the ovum has been penetrated by a single sperm (above photo), its outer membrane changes and becomes impenetrable to the millions of remaining sperm.**

Once the ovum has been fertilized, it is called a ***zygote,*** which is a single cell that is smaller than the dot in the letter *i.* The zygote begins a process of repeated division and, after about a week, consists of about 150 cells. After two weeks, it has become a mass of cells and attaches itself to the wall of the uterus. Once the zygote is implanted, or attached to the wall of the uterus, the embryonic stage begins.

2 Embryonic Stage

During this next stage, the organism begins to develop body organs.

The *embryonic stage* is the second stage of the prenatal period and spans the 2–8 weeks that follow conception; during this stage, cells divide and begin to differentiate into bone, muscle, and body organs.

At about 21 days after conception, the beginnings of the spinal cord and eyes appear; at about 24 days, cells differentiate to form what will become part of the heart; at about 28 days, tiny buds appear that will develop into arms and legs; and at about 42 days, features of the face take shape.

During this stage, the embryo is very fragile, since all of its basic organs are being formed. This is the time when most miscarriages occur and when most major birth defects occur (J. M. Nash, 2002).

Toward the end of the embryonic stage, the organism has developed a number of body organs, such as the heart. The embryo is only about 4 cm long but already has the beginnings of major body organs and limbs and begins to look somewhat human (Cunningham et al., 2005).

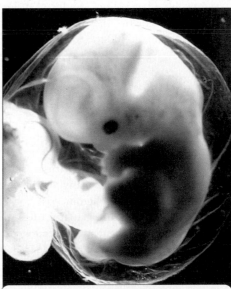

Embryo—about 6 weeks

In the left photo, you can see the head as the large rounded structure at the top, and the black dot on the side of the head is the developing eye. After this second stage of development, which is called the embryonic stage and lasts 2–8 weeks, comes the last stage, which is called the fetal stage.

A. Prenatal Influences

What is the fetal stage?

The embryonic stage is followed by the fetal stage.

The *fetal stage,* which is the third stage in prenatal development, begins two months after conception and lasts until birth.

At the end of the fetal stage, usually 38–42 weeks after conception (or roughly nine months), birth occurs and the fetus becomes a newborn.

During the fetal stage, the fetus develops vital organs, such as lungs, and physical characteristics that are distinctively human. For example, at about six months a fetus has eyes and eyelids that are completely formed (right photo), a fine coating of hair, relatively well-developed external sex organs, and lungs that are beginning to function.

Infants born very prematurely (under six months) will have difficulty surviving because their lungs are not completely formed and they have difficulty breathing. However, a six-month-old fetus usually has lungs well enough developed to begin to show irregular breathing and, for this reason, can survive if born prematurely.

During stage 2, the embryonic stage, and stage 3, the fetal stage, the developing organism is especially vulnerable to toxic agents and chemicals. To help keep out these potentially harmful agents, the developing organism is protected by the placenta.

Placenta and teratogens. Because the fetus experiences rapid body growth and development of the nervous system, it is highly vulnerable to the effects of drugs and other harmful agents. However, the

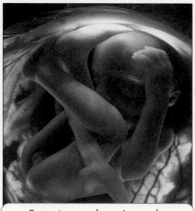

Fetus in womb at 6 months

blood supply of the fetus is partly protected by the placenta (left figure) (Koren, 2004).

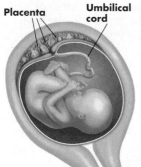

Placenta   Umbilical cord

The *placenta* is an organ that connects the blood supply of the mother to that of the fetus. The placenta acts like a filter, allowing oxygen and nutrients to pass through while keeping out some toxic or harmful substances.

However, certain viruses, such as the HIV virus, and many drugs, including nicotine, caffeine, marijuana, cocaine, and heroin, pass from the placenta into the fetus's blood vessels and thus can affect fetal development. These potentially dangerous agents are called teratogens.

A *teratogen (teh-RAT-oh-gen)* is any agent that can harm a developing fetus (causing deformities or brain damage). It might be a disease (such as genital herpes), a drug (such as alcohol), or another environmental agent (such as chemicals).

Besides harmful chemicals, drugs, or viruses, the developing fetus can also be affected by genetic problems, especially if the parents are carriers of potentially harmful genes (Tay-Sachs) or if the mother is in her forties, which increases the risk for certain fetal genetic problems (Down syndrome). In cases where there is greater potential for fetal genetic problems, the mother may wish to have her fetus tested by a relatively safe process called amniocentesis (Marcus, 2000).

Birth defects and amniocentesis. During the fetal stage, a number of genetic errors can be tested for by amniocentesis *(AM-nee-oh-sen-TEE-sis).*

Amniocentesis, which is a medical test done between weeks 14 and 20 of pregnancy, involves inserting a long needle through the mother's abdominal muscles into the amniotic fluid surrounding the fetus. By withdrawing and analyzing fetal cells in the fluid, doctors can identify a number of genetic problems.

One genetic problem identified by amniocentesis is Down syndrome (p. 288). The risk for it increases in mothers who are in their forties (Cunningham et al., 2005).

Down syndrome results from an extra 21st chromosome and causes abnormal physical traits (a fold of skin at the corner of each eye, a wide tongue, heart defects) and abnormal brain development, resulting in degrees of mental retardation.

Besides Down syndrome, more than 1,000 other genetic disorders can now be tested for and identified (Weil, 2006). A combination of various relatively noninvasive screening tests completed during the first and second trimesters can detect Down syndrome as much as 96% of the time. More invasive fetal DNA testing is even more definitive (Malone et al., 2005). As shown in the graph below, birth defects can occur if something (toxin, drug, genetic malfunction) interferes with developing structures, especially during the embryonic stage (J. M. Nash, 2002).

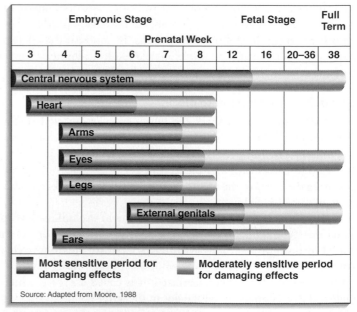

Next, we'll discuss several teratogens (from the Greek word *tera,* meaning "monster") that can pass through the placenta and interfere with fetal growth and development.

How well is the fetus protected? In the womb, the fetus is protected from physical bumps by a wraparound cushion of warm fluid. The fetus is also protected from various teratogens (certain chemicals and drugs) by the filtering system of the placenta (described on p. 380). However, we'll discuss several drugs, both legal and illegal, that can pass through the placenta, reach the fetus, and cause potential neurological, physiological, and psychological problems.

Drug Use and Exposure to Chemicals

Cocaine plus other drugs. Pregnant women who reported using crack cocaine along with other drugs, such as alcohol, tobacco, marijuana, or opiates, had infants with lower birth weights, poor feeding habits, and greater risk for developing other psychological problems, such as lower IQ scores and poor coping skills (Bendersky & Lewis, 1999). Research shows it is not the cocaine alone that is responsible for these physical problems and psychological deficits, but rather the combination of drugs (Frank et al., 2001). This means that children exposed in the womb to cocaine plus other drugs are at risk for developing deficits in cognitive functioning and are more likely to develop behavioral problems than children whose mothers had not used drugs (Chasnoff, 1997; Lester et al., 1998).

Smoking and nicotine. About 13% of pregnant American women smoke, which increases the risk of low birth weight, preterm deliveries, and possible physical problems (Cunningham et al., 2005). In addition, infants born to smoking mothers have 2.5 to 3 times the risk for developing attention-deficit/hyperactivity disorder (p. 27) as well as an increased risk of sudden infant death syndrome (SIDS) and respiratory infections (J. Braun et al., 2006; Dambro, 2006; Linnet et al., 2005). Women who smoke during pregnancy should remember that when they inhale cigarette smoke, so does their fetus.

Lead. It is well known that children exposed to large amounts of lead (paint, gasoline, industry) during pregnancy had lower IQ scores and problems in brain development. More recently, researchers found much lower levels of lead exposure are associated with lower IQ scores in children (Canfield, 2003). Also, there appears to be a link between lead exposure during childhood and the likelihood of later committing antisocial acts, such as assaults and disorderly conduct (Dietrich, 2003). Last, researchers found that children with the highest concentrations of lead in their blood were four times more likely to develop attention-deficit/hyperactivity disorder (p. 27) than children with the lowest concentrations (J. Braun et al., 2006).

Tobacco
Cocaine
Alcohol
Opiates
Marijuana

These drugs can affect the developing fetus.

Air pollutants. New research provides evidence that prenatal exposure to air pollutants, such as gasoline, diesel, and coal, has a negative impact on children's cognitive development. Also, pregnant women exposed to high levels of air pollutants are more likely to have children with low birth weights, fetal growth deficiencies, and delays in physical development. Because it is not possible for pregnant women to completely avoid exposure to air pollutants, environmental changes in vehicles and power plants are important (Harder, 2006).

Alcohol

Heavy drinking—Fetal alcohol syndrome (FAS). In the United States, alcohol is the leading known cause of mental retardation. Alcohol (ethanol) is a teratogen that crosses the placenta, affects the developing fetus, and can result in fetal alcohol syndrome (Mattson et al., 2001).

Fetal alcohol syndrome, or FAS, results from a mother drinking heavily during pregnancy, especially in the first 12 weeks. FAS results in physical changes, such as short stature, flattened nose, and short eye openings (right photo); neurological changes, such as fewer brain connections within the brain structure; and psychological and behavioral problems, such as hyperactivity, impulsive behavior, deficits in information processing and memory, alcohol and drug use, and poor socialization.

Facial features associated with FAS

Children with fetal alcohol syndrome continue to have problems into adolescence and adulthood. For example, follow-up studies up to 21 years after the original diagnosis indicated that FAS individuals tended to remain short, had an average IQ of 68 (normal is 100), were likely to be easily distracted and to misperceive social cues, and were at risk for developing drinking and drug problems (Baer et al., 2003; Streissguth et al., 1999). This means that various physical, neurological, psychological, and behavioral problems associated with fetal alcohol syndrome are long-lasting.

Moderate drinking—Fetal alcohol effects (FAE). Recently, researchers found that moderate drinking (7–14 drinks per week) by pregnant women does not usually result in fetal alcohol syndrome (FAS). However, moderate drinking may result in fetal alcohol exposure (FAE), which is less severe than fetal alcohol syndrome but three times more prevalent (Jacobson & Jacobson, 1999). Researchers report that children with prenatal exposure to alcohol can have growth deficiencies and show deficits in a number of cognitive tasks (learning and memory), academic skills, and fine motor speed and coordination (C. Gorman, 2006; Mattson et al., 2001). Researchers say there is no safe level of alcohol use during pregnancy and therefore it is recommended that women who are pregnant or are planning a pregnancy should not drink any alcohol (C. Gorman, 2006).

We have discussed the three stages of prenatal development, which end with the baby's birth. After the baby gets a pat on the backside and lets out a cry, he or she is ready to take on the world.

B. Newborns' Abilities

Why can't a newborn walk?

Some animals, such as baby elephants (150 pounds), can walk immediately after birth. In comparison, baby humans (7 pounds) cannot walk because neither their leg muscles nor brain areas are well enough developed. However, human infants are born with a surprising number of sensory and motor abilities, such as hearing, grasping, and sucking. How these abilities develop is explained by an inherited genetic program.

Genetic Developmental Program

Conception results in a fertilized egg, which has a genetic program that is equivalent to 300,000 pages of typed instructions for developing the body and brain. The mother and father each contribute 23 chromosomes so each child receives a unique genetic program.

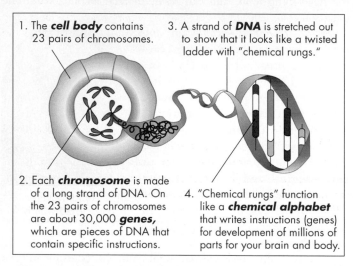

1. The **cell body** contains 23 pairs of chromosomes.

2. Each **chromosome** is made of a long strand of DNA. On the 23 pairs of chromosomes are about 30,000 **genes,** which are pieces of DNA that contain specific instructions.

3. A strand of **DNA** is stretched out to show that it looks like a twisted ladder with "chemical rungs."

4. "Chemical rungs" function like a **chemical alphabet** that writes instructions (genes) for development of millions of parts for your brain and body.

Brain growth. After birth, the genetic program regulates how the brain develops, such as making thousands of connections between neurons. For example, during the first three months of life, the most active areas of the newborn's brain are involved in processing sights, sounds, and touches, preparing the infant for dealing with sensory information from the surrounding environment.

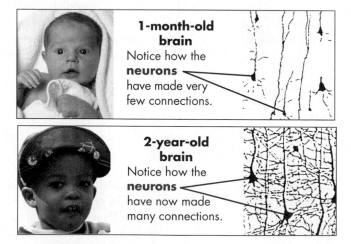

1-month-old brain
Notice how the **neurons** have made very few connections.

2-year-old brain
Notice how the **neurons** have now made many connections.

In the figures above, notice that a 1-month-old brain has very few neural connections, while a 2-year-old brain has many thousands. This enormous increase in neural connections partly explains why the weight of a baby's brain increases from 25% to 75% of its adult weight between birth to 2 years old (Sigelman & Rider, 2006).

Sensory Development

During the nine months of development in the womb, a genetic program is guiding the development of a number of motor and sensory functions that are important for the newborn's survival. Here's a summary of a newborn's sensory abilities.

Faces. Newborns show a preference for their mother's face over strangers' faces in the first few days after birth. Apparently newborns first learn to recognize a person's eyes, a process that occurs through positive stimulation, such as caressing and suckling (E. M. Blass & Camp, 2001). Beginning at 4 months of age, an infant can *visually* distinguish his or her mother's face from a stranger's or an animal's (Wingert & Brant, 2005). By 3 or 4 years of age, an infant's visual abilities are equal to those of an adult.

Hearing. One-month-old infants have very keen hearing and can discriminate small sound variations, such as the difference between *bah* and *pah*. By 6 months, infants have developed the ability to make all the sounds that are necessary to learn the language in which they are raised (Pascalis et al., 2002).

Touch. Newborns also have a well-developed sense of touch and will turn their head when lightly touched on the cheek. Touch will also elicit a number of reflexes, such as grasping and sucking.

Smell and taste. Researchers found that 1-day-old infants could discriminate between a citrus odor and a floral odor (Sullivan et al., 1991). Six-week-old infants can smell the difference between their mother and a stranger (Macfarlane, 1975). Newborns have an inborn preference for both sweet and salt and an inborn dislike of bitter-tasting things.

The senses develop relatively fast.

Depth perception. By the age of 6 months, infants have developed depth perception, which was tested by observing whether they would crawl off a visual "cliff" (E. J. Gibson & Walk, 1960).

A *visual cliff* is a glass tabletop with a checkerboard pattern over part of its surface; the remaining surface consists of clear glass with a checkerboard pattern several feet below, creating the illusion of a clifflike drop to the floor.

An infant is placed on the area with the checkerboard pattern and is encouraged to creep off the cliff. Six-month-old infants hesitate when they reach the clear glass "dropoff," indicating that they have developed depth perception.

Although the genetic program is largely responsible for the early appearance of these sensory abilities, *environmental stimulation,* such as parental touch and play, encourages the infant to further develop these sensory abilities (Collins et al., 2000).

Why do infants crawl before they walk?

"Gloria just took her first step." Parents are proud to note their child's motor accomplishments, which are primarily regulated by a built-in genetic program. As infants learn to crawl and walk, they change from passive observers into very active participants in the family's social life. The first area studied by early developmental psychologists was motor skill development (Thelen, 1995).

Motor development refers to the stages of motor skills that all infants pass through as they acquire the muscular control necessary for making coordinated movements.

Because each child has a unique genetic program, he or she will acquire motor skills at different times (Hadders-Algra, 2002). The development of early motor skills, such as sitting, crawling, and walking, follows two general rules, called the proximodistal and cephalocaudal principles.

1 The *proximodistal principle* states that parts closer to the center of the infant's body (*proximo* in Latin means "near") develop before parts farther away (*distal* in Latin means "far").

For example, activities involving the trunk are mastered before activities involving the arms and legs. For that reason, infants can roll over before they can walk or bring their arms together to grasp a bottle.

2 The *cephalocaudal principle* states that parts of the body closer to the head (*cephalo* in Greek means "head") develop before parts closer to the feet (*caudal* in Greek means "tail").

For example, infants can lift their heads before they can control their trunks enough to sit up, and they can sit up before they can control their legs to crawl. In the figure below, notice the head area (larger) developing before the feet area (smaller).

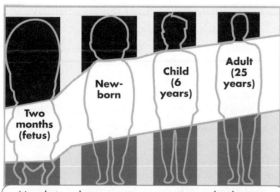

Two months (fetus) | Newborn | Child (6 years) | Adult (25 years)

Head size decreases in proportion to body size.

3 The cephalocaudal and proximodistal principles, which regulate the sequence for developing early motor skills, are part of a process known as maturation.

Maturation refers to developmental changes that are genetically or biologically programmed rather than acquired through learning or life experiences.

In developing motor skills (three right photos), such as sitting up alone, crawling, and walking, all infants in all parts of the world go through the same developmental stages at about the same times. However, if children are given more opportunities to practice their stepping reflex earlier in life, they will begin to walk at an earlier age than children who lack such opportunities (Thelen, 1995). Thus, the development of early motor development is heavily influenced by maturation (genetic program) but the timing can be partly slowed or speeded up by experience/learning (nurture).

4 Parents often note the major milestones in their infants' motor development, such as their first time crawling or walking, because they want to know if their children are within the developmental norms.

Developmental norms refer to the average ages at which children perform various kinds of skills or exhibit abilities or behaviors.

Sitting up alone— average 5.5 months (range 4.5–8.0 months)

Some examples of developmental norms for stages in walking accompany the three photos. Because norms for motor development represent average ages rather than absolute ages, parents should not be disturbed if their infant's motor progress does not match the norms.

By the age of 2, infants have grown into toddlers who can walk up and down stairs and use their hands to hold glasses of juice, operate toys, and, of course, get into a lot of trouble.

5 The reason infants develop skills and abilities at different times is that neural connections develop at different rates. This means that infants cannot perform complex cognitive, sensory, or motor tasks, such as walking, talking, and reading, until appropriate areas of their brains develop neural connections.

Crawling—average 10 months (range 7.0–12.0 months)

Although we have focused on the role of the genetic developmental program (nature), it's important to remember that nature interacts with the environment (nurture) to encourage or discourage the development of various motor, sensory, and cognitive abilities (Hadders-Algra, 2002). For example, infants need appropriate **environmental stimulation** for development of their visual systems (see things), for learning to speak (hear parents speaking), for emotional development (get loving care), and for motor development (explore objects). These examples show how the genetic program needs and interacts with environmental stimulation for the proper development of a child's sensory, motor, and cognitive abilities.

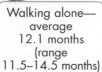

Walking alone— average 12.1 months (range 11.5–14.5 months)

Along with developing motor skills, an infant is also showing emotional changes.

C. Emotional Development

How can sextuplets be so different? Becki is describing the emotional makeup of her sextuplets (photo below). "Brenna, the oldest by 30 seconds, is the affectionate one. Julinan, the second child delivered, is 'Mr. Smiley.' Quinn, the third, is sweet and generous and most adventurous. Claire, fourth oldest, is the boss, as charming as she is tough. Ian, the fifth, is the smallest and loves music, drawing, and sleep. Adrian, the youngest, is the biggest and most gentle" (S. Reed & Breu, 1995, p. 127). Each of these 2-year-old sextuplets has a unique emotional development (J. Bates, 2004).

Each one has a different emotional makeup.

Emotional development **refers to the influence and interaction of genetic factors, brain changes, cognitive factors, coping abilities, and cultural factors in the development of emotional behaviors, expressions, thoughts, and feelings (Goldsmith, 2003).**

Similar to all infants, the sextuplets initially showed a limited number of inherited emotional expressions, including interest, startle, distress, disgust, and a neonatal smile (a half-smile that appears spontaneously for no apparent reason). Also, similar to all infants, during the first two years the sextuplets developed a wide range of emotional expressions and feelings, including *social smiling* (age 4–6 weeks); *anger, surprise,* and *sadness* (age 3–4 months); *fear* (age 5–7 months); *shame* and *shyness* (age 6–8 months); and *contempt* and *guilt* (age 24 months) (Kopp & Neufeld, 2003).

A child's increase in emotional expressions and feelings results from the interaction among genetic, neurological (brain), cognitive, coping, and cultural factors. The interaction of all these factors explains why each of the sextuplets has a unique emotional makeup, ranging from being sweet and gentle to being charming, adventurous, and tough.

We'll focus on one of the genetic factors involved in emotional development, which is called temperament.

Why did the differences show up so early? One reason each of the sextuplets developed such a different emotional makeup so very early in life involves something called temperament.

Temperament **refers to relatively stable and long-lasting individual differences in mood and emotional behavior, which emerge early in childhood because these differences are largely influenced by genetic factors.**

Researchers studied differences in infants' temperaments by interviewing mothers with 2- to 3-month-old infants and then observing these same infants repeatedly over the next seven years. Researchers rated each infant on nine components of temperament, including activity level, attention span, fussiness, and mood. On the basis of these ratings, they divided infants into four categories (Thomas & Chess, 1977).

1 **Easy babies,** who made up 40% of the sample, were happy and cheerful, had regular sleeping and eating habits, and adapted quickly to new situations.

2 **Slow-to-warm-up babies,** who made up 15% of the sample, were more withdrawn, were moody, and tended to take longer to adapt to new situations.

3 **Difficult babies,** who made up 10% of the sample, were fussy, fearful of new situations, and more intense in their reactions. During the course of the seven-year study, difficult babies developed more serious emotional problems than the easy or slow-to-warm-up babies.

4 **No-single-category babies,** who made up 35% of the sample, had a variety of traits and could not be classified into one of the other three categories.

Genetic influence. Infants develop distinct temperaments very early, usually in the first 2–3 months of life, and these temperaments occur largely because of genetic factors rather than learning experiences (J. Bates, 2000). For example, about 10–15% of Caucasian babies inherit an inhibited or fearful temperament (e.g., show physiological arousal in novel situations), while about 40% inherit a fearless temperament (e.g., remain calm in novel situations) (Kagan, 2003a). Differences in temperament are also observed in brain activity. For example, outgoing and friendly 9-month-old babies show increased activity in parts of the brain responsible for positive emotions (Wingert & Brant, 2005).

10% fearful

40% fearless

Environmental influence. About 30% of infants who began with a "fearful" or "fearless" temperament remained that way emotionally into adolescence and adulthood, but 70% showed moderate changes in temperament. One reason for changes in temperament involves environmental factors, such as family influence, poverty level, and educational opportunities, all of which interact with and can change the infant's initial temperament. For example, researcher Jerome Kagan (2003b) explains that an initially "fearful" infant raised in an economically secure home by consistently supportive parents is likely to develop into a popular and accomplished adolescent. In comparison, a "fearful" infant raised in an economically disadvantaged home with parents who are not very supportive and use punishment inconsistently is likely to develop into a delinquent. Thus, whether or not an infant's genetically influenced temperament persists into adolescence and adulthood depends to a considerable extent on the influence and interaction with environmental factors.

Because an infant's temperament influences the development of emotional behavior, it also affects the bond or attachment between parent and child, our next topic.

Attachment

Do infants and parents form a special bond?

For the first 3 years of his life, Alex (right photo) lived in an orphanage where he had no consistent, loving person to take care of him. When he was adopted at age 3, he repeatedly rejected his parents' love and he was never able to express love toward them. Living his first few years of life without close bonding to a parent or caregiver led Alex to have problems in attachment.

Attachment **is a close, fundamental emotional bond that develops between the infant and his or her parents or caregiver.**

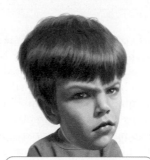

Alex lived in a Romanian orphanage until he was adopted at age 3.

Psychologist John Bowlby (1969) believed that attachment behavior evolved through a process of natural selection. According to his theory, attachment evolved because of its adaptive value, which was to give the infant a better chance of surviving because the parent was close by to provide care and protection. Much of the research on attachment was initiated by Mary Ainsworth (1989), who asked three general questions: How does attachment occur? Are there different kinds of attachment? What are the long-term effects of attachment?

How Does Attachment Occur?

According to attachment theory, babies form an attachment to their parents through a gradual process that begins shortly after birth and continues through early childhood. As newborns, infants have a powerful social signal, crying, which elicits care and sympathy. As 4- to 6-week-old infants, they will begin social smiling (smiling at others), which will elicit joy and pleasure in their parents. At about 6 months, infants begin to give their parents a happy greeting (smiling, holding out their arms) when they reappear after a short absence. These behaviors contribute to children expressing their needs better and understanding their parents' emotional experiences, which ultimately help to build a good parent–child attachment (R. A. Thompson, 1998, 2006).

As the infant develops a closer attachment to her parents, she also shows more distress when her parents leave; this is called separation anxiety.

Separation anxiety **is an infant's distress—as indicated by loud protests, crying, and agitation—whenever the infant's parents temporarily leave.**

According to Ainsworth, separation anxiety is a clear sign the infant has become attached to one or both parents. By the end of the first year, an infant usually shows a close attachment to her parents as well as to one or more other family members.

However, depending on the infant's temperament (easy or difficult) and the mother's attitude (caring or not responsive), different kinds of attachment occur.

Are There Different Kinds of Attachment?

Ainsworth (1979) is best known for developing a method for studying infants' reactions to being separated from, and then reunited with, their mothers. She used these reactions to indicate the kind or quality of the infants' attachment. There are now four different kinds of attachment, but we'll focus on two, which are called secure (65% of infants) and insecure (20% of infants) attachment.

Secure attachment **is characteristic of infants who use their parent as a safe home base from which they can wander off and explore their environments.**

For example, when infants are placed in an unfamiliar room containing many interesting toys, securely attached infants tend to explore freely as long as their parent looks on. If the parent leaves, most of the infants cry. On the parent's return, securely attached infants happily greet the caregiver and are easily soothed. In contrast, some infants show insecure attachment.

Insecure attachment **is characteristic of infants who avoid or show ambivalence or resistance toward their parent or caregiver.**

For example, insecurely attached infants may cling and want to be held one minute but squirm and push away the next minute, displaying a lack of trust in the parent or caregiver.

Researchers found that an infant's sense of trust or attachment was not affected by whether or how long a child was in day care. Instead, what most affected the infant's attachment was a mother's sensitivity, caring, and responsiveness to the infant's needs (NICHD, 1997). Attachments formed in infancy may also affect one's later relationships.

What Are Effects of Attachment?

Because Alex never formed an attachment to a parent during infancy, he will likely have difficulty forming healthy bonds with parents or other adults in the future. As it turned out, despite being adopted by parents who cared tremendously for him and tried everyday to show they loved him, Alex never bonded with them. Even at age 7, he still rejected his parents' affection and did not trust them. Because Alex never developed a secure attachment, when the time came to say good-bye to his parents and meet his new adoptive mother, he left his parents without any hesitation and he immediately called the new woman "mom" and he also told her "I love you."

The kind of attachment formed in infancy is thought to be associated with the success of future relationships. For example, a secure attachment is associated with being more trusting, enjoying relationships more, and dealing better with stress; an insecure attachment is associated with being dependent and having poor social relationships and poor coping skills (Burge et al., 1997; Howard & Medway, 2004). Although the kind of attachment an infant forms—secure or insecure—is thought to have long-term effects on a person's future relationships, there is only moderate research support for this theory (I. Goodwin, 2003).

The kind of attachment an infant forms is partly dependent on temperament. We'll next discuss the kinds and effects of different temperaments.

D. Research Focus: Temperament

How can children be so different? We're going to discuss a series of classic studies by Jerome Kagan (2003a), which changed the way we think about children's temperaments. Kagan wanted to answer a question asked by many parents: Why do children raised by the same parents in the same family grow up with such different emotional makeups? For example, Eric's parents wondered why he (similar to circled child in right photo) was more shy and fearful than his two brothers, would never leave his mother's side to play with other children, was afraid to tell a story to his grade-school class, and feared going into the swimming pool with other children (Elias, 1989). Kagan wondered if Eric was born "fearful" and if he would change as he grew up.

The first problem Kagan faced was to select between two different research methods—longitudinal and cross-sectional methods—to study developmental changes. As we discuss the advantages and disadvantages of each method, you'll understand why Kagan selected the longitudinal method to study temperament.

Why is only one child shy?

Longitudinal Method

One method researchers use to study developmental changes, such as a child's temperament, is the longitudinal method.

A *longitudinal method* means that the same group of individuals is studied repeatedly at many different points in time.

For example, as shown in the figure below, researchers first measure temperaments in a group of 2-year-old children, retest this same group again at age 7, then test them again at age 12, and so on.

Disadvantages. Disadvantages are that researchers must wait many years for their participants to grow older and they must deal with the problem of participants

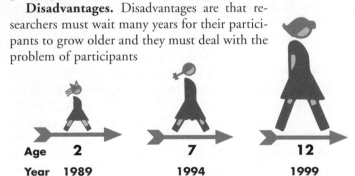

Age	2	7	12
Year	1989	1994	1999

dropping out of the study due to relocation, illness, or death.

Advantage. A major advantage of the longitudinal method is that the same participants are used throughout the study. This means that researchers can track and analyze the development of each participant as he or she ages and confronts new environmental conditions. This ability to track each participant across time is the chief reason researchers prefer to use the longitudinal method to study developmental changes, such as changes in temperament.

Cross-Sectional Method

A *cross-sectional method* means that several groups of different-aged individuals are studied at the same time.

For example, in the figure below, researchers are using the cross-sectional method because they selected a group of 2-year-olds, a group of 7-year-olds, and a group of 12-year-olds and measured their temperaments at the same time.

Advantage. The primary advantage of the cross-sectional method is that researchers can compare any developmental differences, such as in temperaments, across many different age groups, all at

Age	2	7	12
Year		1999	

the same time. This lowers the dropout rate due to relocation, illness, or death and gives immediate results.

Disadvantage. A major disadvantage of the cross-sectional approach is that it does not track the development of the same person across time but rather compares different groups at different ages. This means that both the participants and the environmental conditions are different, which allows for more error and bias in interpreting the results.

Procedure

Choosing the longitudinal method, Jerome Kagan and his colleagues (Kagan, 2003a; Kagan & Snidman, 1991) began by studying the temperaments of 4-month-old infants. These same infants would be retested at different ages, until they reached their early 20s. The initial findings were that some 4-month-olds were fearless while others were fearful, whom he called inhibited children.

Inhibited/fearful children show avoidance,

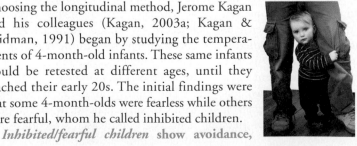

anxiety, or fear (measured by avoiding or crying) when in a strange or novel environment; they also show increased physiological arousal (increased heart rate) and brain activity (increased response of amygdala—threat detector) to novel or strange situations.

Having identified infants with two very different temperaments—inhibited/fearful and fearless—Kagan and his colleagues were able to study how these different temperaments affected emotional development by retesting the same participants across more than 20 years. Here's what they found.

How many were fearful/inhibited? Kagan and his colleagues observed several hundred 4-month-old infants and reported that about one-fourth were classified as inhibited or highly fearful (graph below). An inhibited or highly fearful *infant* showed a high degree of avoidance, fretting, and crying in novel or strange situations. A typical inhibited *child* stayed at the periphery of a large group of peers, reading a book, painting at an easel, or standing in a corner quietly watching another child. One of the best indicators of an inhibited child was that he or she spoke very little and initiated very little spontaneous conversation with unfamiliar peers or adults (Kagan et al., 1988; Kagan & Snidman, 1991).

Temperament at 4 months

23%	Inhibited (fearful)
37%	Uninhibited (fearless)

How many were fearless/uninhibited? About one-third of the *infants* were classified as uninhibited or low-fear individuals (above graph), and the remaining infants were classified in between. A typical fearless/uninhibited *child* was involved in group activities, was very talkative, initiated spontaneous interactions, engaged in conversations, often with smiling and laughter, and showed enthusiasm for social interactions not observed in inhibited children.

Based on these studies, as well as studies that compared identical twins (share 100% of their genes) with fraternal twins (share 50% of their genes), researchers concluded that the influence of genetic factors on emotional development is as high as 60% (Goldsmith, 2003).

How many changed temperaments? About 18% of the very fearful infants remained highly fearful at 14 and 21 months and developed anxious symptoms at about 7 years, but about 80% of infants who were initially classified as very fearful did not develop into very fearful children. However, none of the very fearful children developed into completely fearless ones. This means that having a fearful temperament at infancy puts a person at risk for becoming a fearful child, but the risk for becoming fearful is not completely determined because some do become less fearful (but never fearless) (Kagan, 2003a).

What happens in the brain? Earlier we discussed the brain's emotional detector, called the amygdala (p. 362), which signals threatening or fearful stimuli. Researchers guessed that perhaps fearful infants were born with a more active amygdala. Researchers measured the amygdala's activity (fMRI) in response to novel or familiar faces in 20-year-old adults who had been classified as either fearful or fearless at age 2. Researchers found that adults classified as *fearful* at age 2 had more activity in response to novel faces than did adults initially classified as *fearless*. Researchers suggested that an infant who is born with an overactive amygdala is at risk for having a fearful temperament and later developing into a fearful or shy person (Schwartz et al., 2003).

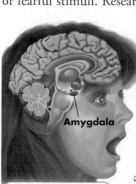

Fearful adults had more activity in the amygdala.

How can parents help a fearful/inhibited child overcome his or her fear and shyness?

This research answers a question asked by many parents: How can children raised by the same parents in the same family have such different temperaments? Part of the answer comes from Kagan's (2003a) series of longitudinal studies, which showed that infants have at least two distinct temperaments—fearful/inhibited or fearless/uninhibited. These two temperaments are relatively stable across time and involve observable behaviors (avoiding and crying), physiological arousal (increased heart rate), and differences in the activity of the brain's emotional detector, the amygdala.

Being fearful is one kind of temperament.

The occurrence of different temperaments in young infants indicates the influence of genetic factors (nature). However, the finding that about 80% of the children's temperaments changed moderately indicates the influence of environmental experiences (nurture) (Pesonen et al., 2003).

Another interesting finding was that although children differed in temperament—inhibited or uninhibited—they did not differ in IQ scores, intellectual abilities, language, memory, or reasoning abilities (Kagan, 1998).

How can parents help fearful children? Researchers advise parents with fearful children to be very caring and supportive and to consistently help their inhibited children deal with minor stressors. With such support, inhibited children learned to control their initial urges to withdraw from strange people or situations. Additionally, researchers suggest that if parents avoid becoming too anxious, overprotective, or angry at their children's extreme fearfulness and timidity, there will be a better chance that the inhibited child will become less anxious in adolescence (Kagan, 1994).

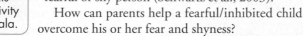

Eric's parents followed this advice. As an infant and child, Eric (similar to left photo) showed signs of being fearful or inhibited. For example, Eric spent two weeks worrying about having to give a book report, which meant standing in front of, and speaking to, the whole class. Eric was sure he couldn't do it. His parents encouraged Eric to role-play giving his book report, so Eric repeated his speech over and over at home until he felt comfortable. When Eric gave his book report to the class, he did very well and felt great afterward (Elias, 1989). With support and understanding, parents can help a fearful child to become more outgoing and less fearful.

At the same time an infant is developing emotional behaviors, he or she is also acquiring numerous cognitive skills and abilities, which we'll discuss next.

E. Cognitive Development

What are blocks for?

We have explained how a newborn's brain and senses develop relatively quickly so that an infant is soon ready to creep and walk and explore and learn about a wondrous world through a process called cognitive development.

Cognitive development **refers to how a person perceives, thinks, and gains an understanding of his or her world through the interaction and influence of genetic and learned factors.**

For example, if you gave blocks to Sam, who is 5 months old (top right photo), he would surely put one into his mouth. If you gave the same blocks to Sam when he was 2 years old, he might stack them (bottom right photo). If you gave the same blocks to Sam when he was an adolescent, he might play a game of throwing them into a can. What Sam does with blocks depends on his experience and level of cognitive development.

Jean Piaget. In the history of developmental psychology, the person who had the greatest impact on the study of cognitive development was Jean Piaget, who was both a biologist and a psychologist. From the 1920s to his death in 1980, Piaget (1929) studied how children solved problems in their natural settings, such as cribs, sandboxes, and playgrounds. Piaget developed one of the most influential theories of cognitive development (Bjorklund, 2005).

Piaget believed that from early on, a child acts like a tiny scientist who is actively involved in making guesses or hypotheses about how the world works. For example, when given blocks, 5-month-old Sam puts them into his mouth, while 2-year-old Sam tries to stack them, and adolescent Sam laughs and plays a game of tossing blocks into a can. Piaget believed that children learned to understand things, such as what to do with blocks, through two active processes that he called assimilation and accommodation.

ASSIMILATION

If you gave 5-month-old Sam a block, he would first try to put it into his mouth because at that age, infants "think" that objects are for sucking on. This mouthing behavior is an example of assimilation.

Blocks are for putting in mouth.

Assimilation **is the process by which a child uses old methods or experiences to deal with new situations.**

At 5 months, Sam will first put a new object into his mouth because his knowledge of objects is that they are for eating or sucking. Thus, Sam will assimilate the new object as something too hard to eat but all right for sucking.

Depending on their age and knowledge, children assimilate blocks in different ways: infants assimilate blocks as something to suck; toddlers assimilate blocks as something to stack or throw; adolescents assimilate blocks as something used to play games; and adults assimilate blocks as something to give to children. The assimilation of new information leads to Piaget's next process—accommodation.

ACCOMMODATION

If you gave 2-year-old Sam the same blocks, he would not try to eat them, but he might try to stack them, which is an example of accommodation.

Accommodation **is the process by which a child changes old methods to deal with or adjust to new situations.**

For example, because of Sam's experience with different kinds of objects, he has learned that square, hard objects are not food but things that can be handled and stacked. Sam's learning to change existing knowledge because of new information (blocks are for stacking, not eating) is an example of accommodation, which is one way that mental growth occurs.

As an infant or child is actively involved in exploring his or her environment, there are many opportunities for assimilation and accommodation, which result in different kinds of cognitive growth and development.

Blocks are for stacking.

According to Piaget, children make big gains in reasoning, thinking, and understanding through active involvement and the processes of assimilation and accommodation. Using these two processes, children go through a series of cognitive stages.

What is Sam thinking?

Piaget is best known for describing the changes or different stages in cognitive development that occur between infancy and adulthood (Bjorklund, 2005).

Piaget's cognitive stages **refer to four different stages—sensorimotor, preoperational, concrete operations, and formal operations—each of which is more advanced than the preceding stage because it involves new reasoning and thinking abilities.**

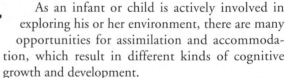

1. Sensorimotor
2. Preoperational
3. Concrete
4. Formal

Although Piaget believed that all people go through the same four cognitive stages, he acknowledged that they may go through the stages at different rates.

Piaget's hypothesis that cognitive development occurs in stages and that each stage involves different kinds of thinking was one of his unique contributions to developmental psychology. We'll explain Piaget's four stages by following Sam through his cognitive development.

Imagine Sam as a newborn infant. His primary way of interacting with the world is through reflexive responses, such as sucking and grasping. By 5 months, Sam has developed enough voluntary muscle control so that he can reach out, grasp things, and put them into his mouth to discover if the things are good to suck on. Sam is in the sensorimotor stage.

The *sensorimotor stage* (from birth to about age 2) is the first of Piaget's cognitive stages. During this stage, infants interact with and learn about their environments by relating their sensory experiences (such as hearing and seeing) to their motor actions (mouthing and grasping).

Hidden objects. At the beginning of the sensorimotor stage, Sam has one thinking problem: remembering that hidden objects still exist. For example, notice in the top left photo that 5-month-old Sam is shown a toy dog. Sam immediately tries to grab it and put part of it in his mouth. This is another example of assimilation; Sam believes that objects are mostly for mouthing.

With doggie in sight, infant tries to touch it.

With doggie hidden, infant acts as if there is no doggie.

However, notice in the bottom left photo that when a screen is placed in front of the dog, Sam looks away. He doesn't push the screen away to get at the toy because, at this point, Sam behaves as if things that are out of sight are out of mind and simply no longer exist. Sam has not learned object permanence.

Object permanence. Beginning at around 9 months, if Sam is shown a toy dog that is then covered by a screen, he will try to push the screen away and look for the dog. Sam has learned that a toy dog that is out of sight still exists behind the screen. This new concept is called object permanence.

Object permanence refers to the understanding that objects or events continue to exist even if they can no longer be heard, touched, or seen.

The concept of object permanence develops slowly over a period of about nine months. By the end of the sensorimotor period (about age 2), an infant will search long and hard for lost or disappeared objects, indicating a fully developed concept of object permanence.

At the end of the sensorimotor stage, 2-year-old Sam can think about things that are not present and can form simple plans for solving problems, such as searching for things.

According to Piaget, after the sensorimotor stage, Sam enters the next stage, called the preoperational stage.

As a 4-year-old, Sam is busy pushing a block around the floor and making noises as he pretends the block is a car. The cognitive ability to pretend is a sign that Sam is going through the preoperational stage.

The ***preoperational stage*** (from about 2 to 7 years old) is the second of Piaget's cognitive stages. During this stage, children learn to use symbols, such as words or mental images, to solve simple problems and to think or talk about things that are not present.

At this stage, Sam is acquiring the cognitive ability to pretend things and to talk about or draw things that are not physically present. Although Sam is learning to use words and images in speech and play, his thinking has a number of interesting limitations that make his thinking different from an adult's. During the preoperational stage, two of his cognitive limitations involve having problems with conservation and engaging in egocentric thinking.

Conservation. As 4-year-old Sam watches you pour milk from a tall, thin glass into a short, wide glass, will he know that the amount of milk remains the same even though its shape changes? This is called the problem of conservation.

Conservation **refers to the fact that even though the shape of some object or substance is changed, the total amount remains the same.**

Here's what happens when 4-year-old Sam is faced with a conservation problem.

In photo #1, 4-year-old Sam watches as his mother fills two short, wide glasses with equal amounts of milk.

In photo #2, Sam sees his mother pour the milk from one short, wide glass into a tall, thin glass. Mother asks, "Does one glass have more milk?"

In photo #3, Sam points to the tall, thin glass as having more milk because the tall glass looks larger. He makes this mistake even though he just saw his mother pour the milk from a short, wide glass.

Sam, like other children at the preoperational stage, will not be able to solve conservation problems until the next stage.

Egocentric thinking. A second problem that Sam has during the preoperational stage is that he makes mistakes or misbehaves because of egocentric thinking.

Egocentric (ee-goh-SEN-trick) thinking **refers to seeing and thinking of the world only from your own viewpoint and having difficulty appreciating someone else's viewpoint.**

Piaget used the term *egocentric thinking* to mean that preoperational children cannot see situations from another person's, such as a parent's, point of view. When they don't get their way, children may get angry or pout because their view of the world is so self-centered.

E. Cognitive Development

<table>
<tr><td>

3. Concrete

Stage 3

Between the ages of 7 and 11, Sam learns that even if things change their shape, they don't lose any quantity or mass, a new concept that occurs during the concrete operations stage.

The *concrete operations stage* (from about 7 to 11 years) is the third of Piaget's cognitive stages. During this stage, children can perform a number of logical mental operations on concrete objects (ones that are physically present).

Conservation. As you may remember, when Sam was 4 years old and in the preoperational stage, he had not mastered the concept of conservation. In the preoperational stage, Sam thought a tall, thin glass held more milk than a short, wide glass. And if 4-year-old Sam watched as a ball of clay (top left photo) was flattened into a long piece (bottom left photo), he would say the long piece was larger.

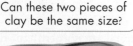

Can these two pieces of clay be the same size?

However, Sam is now 10 years old and has just watched you flatten a ball of clay into a long piece. Sam now says that the long, flattened piece contains the same amount of clay as the ball, even if the shape changed. Similarly, if 10-year-old Sam watched you pour cola from a short glass into a tall glass, he would correctly answer that the amount of cola remained the same. Children gradually master the concept of conservation during the concrete operations stage, and they also get better at classification.

Classification. If you gave a 4-year old, preoperational Sam some red and blue marbles in different sizes (photo below), he would be able to classify the pieces according to a single category, such as size. However, during the concrete operations stage, 10-year-old Sam has acquired the ability to classify the marbles according to two categories, such as color and size, indicating that he has learned a new cognitive skill.

During the concrete stage, children learn to sort objects by both size and color.

New abilities. During the concrete operations stage, children learn to classify or sort objects according to more than one category, and they learn to solve a variety of conservation problems. The reason Piaget called this the *concrete* operations stage is that children can easily classify or figure out relationships between objects provided the objects are actually physically present or "concrete."

However, children at the concrete operations stage still have difficulty figuring out relationships among objects that are not present or situations that are imaginary. Thinking about imaginary or hypothetical situations occurs in Piaget's fourth stage.

</td><td>

4. Formal

Stage 4

Sam is now 17 years old and is surfing the Web for a paper he's writing on what killed the dinosaurs. This kind of abstract thinking indicates that Sam is in the formal operations stage.

The *formal operations stage* (from about 12 years old through adulthood) is Piaget's fourth cognitive stage. During this stage, adolescents and adults develop the ability to think about and solve abstract problems in a logical manner.

Piaget believed that it is during the formal operations stage that adolescents develop thinking and reasoning typical of adults. For example, 17-year-old Sam can compare several theories about why the dinosaurs died, including being destroyed by a giant asteroid, radical temperature change, or some terrible virus. In the formal operations stage, Sam will learn to solve abstract problems in a systematic, logical manner. In comparison, seven years ago when Sam was in the concrete operations stage, he lacked the ability to solve abstract problems. Now that Sam is 17 and in the formal operations stage, Sam is learning to use a computer graphics program as well as solving the latest video game that involves careful planning to outthink seven layers of evil creatures.

How much does the thinking of a 17-year-old differ from that of a 15-year-old?

Once adolescents reach the formal operations stage, they encounter exciting new worlds of abstract ideas and hypothetical concepts. For example, Sam can discuss abstract ideas, such as whether computer hackers should go to jail, if going steady is a good idea, and how strict parents should be. Acquiring the ability to think in a logical, systematic, and abstract way is one of the major characteristics of the formal operations stage and opens up a whole new world of ideas. The cognitive skills associated with the formal operations stage are the very ones that you need to do well in college.

PIAGET'S KEY IDEAS

We have discussed Piaget's cognitive stages in some detail, but there are three ideas that stand out (Larivee et al., 2000):

1 Children gradually and in a step-by-step fashion develop reasoning abilities through the active processes of assimilation and accommodation.

2 Children are naturally curious and intrinsically or self-motivated to explore their worlds and, in the process, develop numerous cognitive skills.

3 Children acquire different kinds of thinking and reasoning abilities as they go through different stages of cognitive development.

Over the past 50 years, researchers have tested Piaget's theories and ideas and made some revisions and modifications.

</td></tr>
</table>

What's happened to Piaget's theory?

Piaget's theory, especially his descriptions of how thinking differs at each of the four cognitive stages, had a tremendous influence on the area of cognitive development (Bjorklund, 2005). However, beginning in the late 1960s and continuing to the present, there have been numerous criticisms of Piaget's theory (Piaget died in 1980). We'll discuss these criticisms along with the current direction of cognitive development.

Impact and Criticisms

Impact of Piaget's theory. For three main reasons, Piaget's theory has had a huge impact on understanding cognitive devel-

Jean Piaget (1896–1980)

opment. First, his theory was far more comprehensive than any other theory at the time. Second, his theory triggered an enormous amount of research and led to the development of other cognitive development theories. Third, many of Piaget's ideas, such as conservation, have proven correct and have been replicated (Sternberg et al., 2003b).

Criticisms. There are three main criticisms. First, Piaget's four stages are not as rigid or orderly as he originally proposed. For example, researchers found that children can solve certain kinds of problems at stages earlier than Piaget proposed (e.g., babies as young as 10 weeks understand object permanence, p. 389) (S. Wang et al., 2005). Because children do show certain thinking skills earlier than would be predicted from Piaget's cognitive stages, his four stages are now seen as not being as rigid or orderly as he initially proposed (Sternberg et al., 2003b).

Second, although Piaget's theory describes the kind of thinking a child can and cannot do at different ages and at different stages, his theory is criticized for not explaining how or why this change occurs (Bruner, 1997). Today, researchers associate changes in thinking with changes in brain development, something unknown to Piaget (Petrill, 2003).

Third, children failed some of the Piagetian tasks not because children lacked the thinking abilities but because they did not understand the instructions. For example, preoperational children can solve some abstract problems, such as who is taller or shorter than someone else, provided the problems are presented simply and are repeated many times. According to Piaget, preoperational children should not be able to solve these simple abstract problems.

Current status. Almost by himself, Piaget began the area of cognitive development. His observational methods to study children and his view that children are active explorers in discovering their worlds are still considered important ideas. However, because of criticisms and new findings on the influence of genetic and neural factors, Piaget's theory is now viewed as having historical importance but is no longer the major force in guiding research in cognitive development (Newcombe, 2002).

New Information

Since Piaget developed his theory, there have been two major changes in understanding and studying cognitive development.

1 Genetic factors. One of the biggest changes has involved identifying genetic factors that influence memory, learning, and many cognitive abilities. For example, research on identical and fraternal twins has shown that genetic factors account for between 20 and 60% of the influence on verbal, spatial, and perceptual abilities as well as on memory (Petrill, 2003). In Piaget's time, the influence of genetic factors on cognitive abilities had not been as clearly established.

Recently, there has been an increasing number of studies showing how genetic factors (nature) interact with a child's environmental and learning experiences (nurture) in the development of cognitive abilities. For example, being outgoing and fearless is related to the kind of temperament an infant inherits (nature) (Kagan, 2003a). Researchers selected 3-year-old children who were rated either high or low in exploring their environments. These same children were given IQ tests at age 11 to determine if being high or low in seeking stimulation affected their IQs. Researchers reported that children who had been rated high in seeking stimulation at age 3 scored significantly higher on IQ tests compared to children who had been rated low in seeking stimulation at age 3. This significant difference in IQ scores (11 points) was not related to the occupation or education of their parents. Researchers concluded that children rated high in seeking stimulation (nature) were more curious and open to learning from their environments (nurture), which in turn enhanced the development of their cognitive abilities and resulted in higher scores on IQ tests (A. Raine et al., 2002). Researchers conclude that genetic factors set a range for many cognitive abilities and these abilities can be either facilitated by a stimulating environment or depressed by an impoverished environment (Bjorklund, 2005).

2 Brain development. Another major change has been our knowledge of how the brain develops. After birth and continuing through adolescence, different areas of the brain develop at different times. For example, the infant on the right doesn't know the doggie is hidden behind the screen because his pre-

Child fails to find the doggie because his prefrontal cortex is not well developed.

frontal cortex is not yet well developed (Kalat, 2007). Similarly, at about age 2, a child learns on average a new word every two hours, in large part because of rapid neural growth in the brain's language areas (Pinker, 1994). These kinds of studies point out that cognitive development results from the interaction among genetic, neural, and environmental factors, much of which was unknown during Piaget's time.

Cognitive development is closely intertwined with and occurs at the same time as social development, which we'll examine next.

F. Social Development

What will happen to Alex?

At the beginning of this module we described how Alex was raised in an orphanage until age 3, at which time he was adopted. Some psychologists wonder how Alex's early emotional difficulties will affect his future social development.

Social development refers to how a person develops a sense of self or a self-identity, develops relationships with others, and develops the kinds of social skills important in personal interactions.

After Alex was adopted, we know that even after a few years with his adoptive parents he never seemed to have made a good adjustment. Some psychologists would not be surprised that Alex never developed close relationships with others or that he never learned social skills important in personal interactions. This is because some psychologists believe the first five years are the most important and that early emotional troubles may lead to later social problems.

Alex's social development is a long and complicated process, which is influenced by many of the emotional and cognitive factors that we have just discussed. We'll describe three different theories of social development, each of which emphasizes a different aspect of behavior.

Freud's Psychosexual Stages

One of the best-known theories is that of Sigmund Freud (1940/1961), who said that each of us goes through five successive psychosexual stages.

The *psychosexual stages* are five different developmental periods—oral, anal, phallic, latency, and genital stages—during which the individual seeks pleasure from different areas of the body that are associated with sexual feelings. Freud emphasized that a child's first five years were most important to social and personality development.

In Freud's theory, there is often conflict between the child and parent. The conflict arises because the child wants immediate satisfaction or gratification of its needs, while the parents often place restrictions on when, where, and how the child's needs should be satisfied. For example, a child may wish

Does an infant's experience during breast feeding have lasting effects?

to be fed immediately, while the parent may want to delay the feeding to a more convenient time. Freud believed that interactions between parent and child in satisfying these psychosexual needs—for example, during breast feeding or toilet training—greatly influence the child's social development and future social interactions. In addition, Freud emphasized the importance of a child's first five years in influencing future social development or future personality problems.

According to Freud, Alex will go through five developmental stages, some of which contain potential conflicts between his desires and his parents' wishes. If his desires are over- or undersatisfied, he may become fixated at one of the first three stages. As you'll see, becoming fixated at one of these stages will hinder his normal social development.

1 Oral Stage	**2 Anal Stage**	**3 Phallic Stage**	**4 Latency Stage**	**5 Genital Stage**
Period: Early infancy—first 18 months of life. **Potential conflict:** The *oral stage* lasts for the first 18 months of life and is a time when the infant's pleasure seeking is centered on the mouth. Pleasure-seeking activities include sucking, chewing, and biting. If Alex were locked into or fixated at this stage because his oral wishes were gratified too much or too little, he would continue to seek oral gratification as an adult.	**Period:** Late infancy—$1\frac{1}{2}$ to 3 years. **Potential conflict:** The *anal stage* lasts from the age of about $1\frac{1}{2}$ to 3 and is a time when the infant's pleasure seeking is centered on the anus and its functions of elimination. If Alex were locked into or fixated at this stage, he would continue to engage in behavioral activities related to retention or elimination. Retention may take the form of being very neat, stingy, or behaviorally rigid. Elimination may take the form of being generous or messy.	**Period:** Early childhood—3 to 6 years. **Potential conflict:** The *phallic (FAL-ik) stage* lasts from about age 3 to 6 and is a time when the infant's pleasure seeking is centered on the genitals. During this stage, Alex will compete with the parent of the same sex (his father) for the affections and pleasures of the parent of the opposite sex (his mother). Problems in resolving this competition (called the Oedipus complex and discussed in Module 19) may result in Alex going through life trying to prove his toughness.	**Period:** Middle and late childhood—from 6 to puberty. The *latency stage*, which lasts from about age 6 to puberty, is a time when the child represses sexual thoughts and engages in nonsexual activities, such as developing social and intellectual skills. At puberty, sexuality reappears and marks the beginning of a new stage.	**Period:** Puberty through adulthood. The *genital stage* lasts from puberty through adulthood and is a time when the individual has renewed sexual desires that he or she seeks to fulfill through relationships with members of the opposite sex. If Alex successfully resolved conflicts in the first three stages, he will have the energy to develop loving relationships and a healthy and mature personality.

According to Freud, Alex's future personality and social development will depend, to a large extent, on what he experiences during the first three psychosexual stages, which occur during his first five years. Freud's psychosexual stages are part of his larger psychoanalytic theory of personality, which we'll discuss more fully in Module 19.

How important is trust?

According to well-known psychologist Erik Erikson, Alex will encounter kinds of problems very different from the psychosexual ones proposed by Freud. Unlike Freud's emphasis on psychosexual issues, Erikson (1963, 1982) focused on psychosocial issues and said that each of us goes through eight psychosocial stages.

The *psychosocial stages* are eight developmental periods during which an individual's primary goal is to satisfy desires associated with social needs. The eight periods are associated, respectively, with issues of trust, autonomy, initiative, industry, identity, intimacy, generativity, and ego integrity.

Erikson hypothesized that from infancy through adulthood we proceed through these stages, each of

Are the effects of psychosocial problems long-lasting?

which is related to a different problem that needs to be resolved. If we successfully deal with the potential problem of each psychosocial stage, we develop positive personality traits and are better able to solve the problem at the next stage. However, if we do not successfully handle the psychosocial problems, we may become anxious, worried, or troubled and develop social or personality problems.

Unlike Freud, Erikson believed that psychosocial needs deserve the greatest emphasis and that social development continues throughout one's lifetime. Thus, Erikson would emphasize Alex's psychosocial needs and downplay the importance of sexuality in the first five years.

We'll explain Erikson's first five stages here and discuss the remaining three stages in Module 18, which deals with social development in adolescents and adults.

Stage 1 Trust versus Mistrust	Stage 2 Autonomy versus Shame and Doubt	Stage 3 Initiative versus Guilt	Stage 4 Industry versus Inferiority	Stage 5 Identity versus Role Confusion
Period: Early infancy—birth through first year. **Potential problem:** Alex comes into the world as a helpless infant who needs much care and attention. If his parents are responsive and sensitive to his needs, Alex will develop what Erikson calls basic trust, which makes it easier for him to trust people later in life. If Alex parents neglect his needs, he may view his world as uncaring, learn to become mistrustful, and have difficulty dealing with the second stage. It appears that Alex did not receive the care and attention he needed during his first year of life.	**Period:** Late infancy—1 to 3 years. **Potential problem:** As Alex begins walking, talking, and exploring, he is bound to get into conflict with the wishes of his parents. Thus, this second stage is a battle of wills between his parents' wishes and Alex's desires to do as he pleases. If his parents encourage Alex to explore, he will develop a sense of independence, or autonomy. If his parents disapprove of or punish Alex's explorations, he may develop a feeling that independence is bad and feel shame and doubt.	**Period:** Early childhood—3 to 5 years. **Potential problem:** As a preschooler, Alex has developed a number of cognitive and social skills that he is expected to use to meet the challenges in his small world. Some of these challenges involve assuming responsibility and making plans. If his parents encourage initiative, Alex will develop the ability to plan and initiate new things. However, if they discourage initiative, he may feel uncomfortable or guilty and may develop a feeling of being unable to plan his future.	**Period:** Middle and late childhood—5 to 12 years. **Potential problem:** Alex's grade school years are an exciting time, filled with participating in school, playing games with other children, and working to complete projects. If Alex can direct his energy into working at and completing tasks, he will develop a feeling of industry. If he has difficulty applying himself and completing homework, he may develop a feeling of inferiority and incompetence.	**Period:** Adolescence. **Potential problem:** Adolescents need to leave behind the carefree, irresponsible, and impulsive behaviors of childhood and develop the more purposeful, responsible, planned behaviors of adults. If Alex is successful in making this change, he will develop a sense of confidence and a positive identity. If he is unsuccessful, he will experience role confusion, which will result in having low self-esteem and becoming socially withdrawn.

According to Erikson, Alex will encounter a particular psychosocial problem at each stage. If he successfully solves the problem, he will develop positive social traits that will help him solve the next problem. If he does not solve the problem, he will develop negative social traits that will hinder his solving a new problem at the next stage.

Evaluation of Erikson's and Freud's theories. Many psychologists agree with Erikson that psychosocial conflicts do contribute to social-emotional development (Bugental & Goodnow, 1998). Erikson said that the first five years were not necessarily the most important and that social development continues throughout one's life. In fact, longitudinal studies show that personality change and development continue well into middle adulthood (Erber, 2005).

Many psychologists also agree with Freud that childhood events are important to social development (Guterl, 2002; Sigelman & Rider, 2006). However, they criticize Freud for emphasizing childhood sexuality while neglecting the influences of social and cognitive factors on social development (Bugental & Goodnow, 1998). In addition, longitudinal studies show that children may overcome a variety of problems during the first five years and still have a well-adjusted personality, contrary to Freud's predictions (E.E. Werner, 1995).

The strength of Erikson's and Freud's theories is they explain the whole of social development, from infancy through adulthood. Their weakness, however, is many of their concepts (trust, autonomy, oral stage, fixation) are more descriptive than explanatory and are very difficult to verify or test experimentally (Austrian, 2002). Next, we'll examine the social cognitive theory of social development.

F. Social Development

Bandura's Social Cognitive Theory

What is the 3-year-old doing?

After watching his daddy bowl, this 3-year-old boy walked up to his daddy, pointed at the ball, and said, "Me too ball." Neither Freud's nor Erikson's theory explains why this boy wanted to learn to bowl, what motivated him to ask his daddy, or why he clapped his hands just like his daddy when the ball hit the pins. Albert Bandura (2001a) says that this little boy, like all of us, develops many of his behaviors and social skills through a variety of social cognitive processes.

The *social cognitive theory* emphasizes the importance of learning through observation, imitation, and self-reward in the development of social skills, interactions, and behaviors. According to this theory, it is not necessary that you perform any observable behaviors or receive any external rewards to learn new social skills because many of your behaviors are self-motivated, or intrinsic.

He watched his daddy bowl and then he wanted to.

Social cognitive theory stresses how you learn by modeling and imitating behaviors you observe in social interactions and situations. For example, after watching his daddy, this boy is intrinsically motivated to imitate many of his daddy's social behaviors. Social cognitive theory emphasizes that children develop social behaviors and skills by watching and imitating the social behaviors of their parents, teachers, and peers.

In comparing Bandura's, Freud's, and Erikson's theories, we notice that although the three theories are very different, they are complementary because each emphasizes a different process. Social cognitive theory emphasizes learning through modeling; Freud's theory focuses on parent–child interactions that occur in satisfying innate biological needs; and Erikson's theory points to the importance of dealing with social needs.

We'll use these theories to explain how some children overcame terrible childhood experiences to develop normal social behaviors.

Resiliency

How do children overcome early problems?

Based on observations of his patients, Freud concluded that social and personality development is essentially completed in the first five years. That is, even though an individual might undergo later social changes, his or her basic social and personality traits are primarily established during the first five years. One way to test Freud's hypothesis is to do a long-term study of children who are faced with major problems. One such child was Delia.

During her first year, Delia's unwed mother was withdrawn and showed little interest in Delia; her father was rarely around. But, during her second year, she was sent to live with her grandparents, who raised Delia in a warm, loving, and caring home environment and later adopted her.

Delia was part of a study of 600 children from a small rural community on the Hawaiian island of Kauai. The children were followed from birth to about 40 (E. E. Werner, 1989; E. E. Werner & Smith, 2001) (right photo of Dr. Werner and children in the study). Like Delia, all the children were exposed to numerous life stresses, including problems during mother's pregnancy, family instability, parents' mental and financial difficulties, and a lower social class environment with limited environmental stimulation. How these life stressors affect children depends on their vulnerability and resiliency.

Vulnerability refers to psychological or environmental difficulties that make children more at risk for developing later personality, behavioral, or social problems.

Resiliency refers to various personality, family, or environmental factors that compensate for increased life stresses so that expected problems do not develop.

Some children were able to overcome terrible childhoods.

In Delia's group of 600 children, about 200 showed increased vulnerability and later developed serious behavioral or learning problems. However, the most remarkable finding is that over 400 of the children showed resiliency and developed into competent and autonomous adults (E. E. Werner & Smith, 2001).

Children like Delia are called resilient, or stress-resistant. These children defy expectations because they develop into well-adapted individuals by learning from their mistakes and despite serious life stressors (C. Gorman, 2005a). For example, despite having an insensitive, unresponsive, young mother and an absent, uncaring father, Delia developed adequate self-esteem, high achievement motivation, a fair degree of insight into her life, and realistic plans for the future.

Researchers identified three factors that contribute to resiliency. One factor was genetic: Children born with *positive temperaments,* meaning they are more smiley and socially responsive, elicited more attention and care. Another factor was related to social cognitive processes: Resilient children had a *substitute caregiver* or teacher whose caring behaviors and social skills could be observed and imitated; as a result, resilient children were socially popular. Another factor involved Erikson's psychosocial stages: Resilient children received *social support, care,* and *trust* from their peers and caregivers and developed well-adjusted social behaviors (Sigelman & Rider, 2006; E. E. Werner & Smith, 2001).

Studies on resilient children show three findings. First, early traumatic emotional events do not necessarily lead to later social-emotional problems, as Freud predicted. Second, a loving, supportive caregiver or teacher can substitute for a disinterested parent. Third, children observe and imitate normal social behaviors modeled by caregivers (R. Brooks & Goldstein, 2002; E. E. Werner & Smith, 2001).

What three words change your life forever?

When you look at the photo of the infant on the right, you can't help asking, Is it a girl or a boy? This question has great importance to social development because it involves gender identity.

Gender identity. By the age of 3, most children learn to label themselves as boys or girls and can classify others as being the same sex or the other sex (Ruble et al., 2006).

Gender identity refers to the individual's subjective experience and feelings of being a female or male.

Once children know their correct sex, they begin to learn and show sex-appropriate behaviors, which are called gender roles.

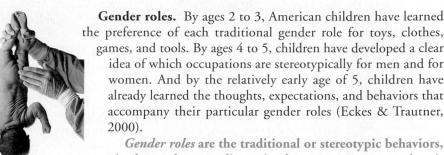

By age 3, this infant will know which sex he or she is.

Gender roles. By ages 2 to 3, American children have learned the preference of each traditional gender role for toys, clothes, games, and tools. By ages 4 to 5, children have developed a clear idea of which occupations are stereotypically for men and for women. And by the relatively early age of 5, children have already learned the thoughts, expectations, and behaviors that accompany their particular gender roles (Eckes & Trautner, 2000).

Gender roles **are the traditional or stereotypic behaviors, attitudes, and personality traits that parents, peers, and society expect us to have because we are male or female.**

Gender roles become part of who we are and have a relatively powerful effect on how we behave, think, and act.

How children acquire gender roles is explained by two somewhat different but related theories: social role theory and cognitive developmental theory (C. L. Martin et al., 2002).

Social Role Theory

In many families, the parents expect a son to behave and act differently than a daughter. How parental expectations influence a child's gender identity is explained by the social role theory (Eagly et al., 2000).

The *social role theory* **emphasizes the influence of social and cognitive processes on how we interpret, organize, and use information. Applied to gender roles, it says that mothers, fathers, teachers, grandparents, friends, and peers expect, respond to, and reward different behaviors in boys than in girls. Under the influence of this differential treatment, boys learn a gender role that is different from girls'.**

For example, the stereotypic gender roles for males include being dominant, controlling, and independent, while gender roles for females include being sensitive, nurturing, and concerned (Eagly & Karau, 2002; W. Wood et al., 1997). According to social role theory, these gender differences originate, to a large extent, because mothers and fathers respond to and reward different behaviors in girls than in boys.

For instance, in playing with boys, fathers were observed to model being assertive and dominant, while in playing with girls, mothers were observed to model being concerned and nurturing (Leaper, 2000). Mothers were found to be more likely to enforce rules when their daughters misbehaved in a way that might be dangerous than when their sons misbehaved in a similar way (Morrongiello & Hogg, 2004). Parents are more likely to encourage dependence in girls, reward boys for conforming to traditional play activities, and reward girls for doing traditional household chores (Keenan & Shaw, 1997). These differences in parents' behaviors support the social role theory idea that parents encourage or discourage behaviors depending on whether these behaviors match traditional boy–girl gender roles.

One criticism of social role theory is that it focuses too much on rewarding and discouraging behaviors and too little on cognitive influences, which are emphasized in the cognitive developmental theory.

Why does she want to be a model?

Cognitive Developmental Theory

When you were a child, you probably learned that there were ways or rules about what boys and girls could and could not do. This childhood experience supports the cognitive developmental theory (C. L. Martin, 2000).

The *cognitive developmental theory* **says that, as children develop mental skills and interact with their environments, they learn one set of rules for male behaviors and another set of rules for female behaviors.**

In this view, children actively process information that results in their learning gender rules regarding which behaviors are correct for girls and wrong for boys and vice versa. On the basis of these rules, children form mental images of how they should act; these images are called gender schemas.

Gender schemas **are sets of information and rules organized around how either a male or a female should think and behave (S. L. Bem, 1985).**

For instance, the traditional gender schema for being a boy includes engaging in rough-and-tumble play and sports, initiating conversations, and exploring; the traditional gender schema for being a girl includes playing with dolls, expressing emotions, listening, and being dependent.

Cognitive developmental theory emphasizes that a child is an active participant in learning a male or female set of rules and schemas, which result in different gender roles (S. L. Bem, 1981).

Both social role theory and cognitive developmental theory predict that the sexes will develop different gender roles.

Why does he want to be a baseball player?

F. Social Development

Girls and boys develop very different gender roles. For example, girls develop traits of being concerned, sensitive, and nurturing (left figure), while boys develop traits of being independent, controlling, and dominant (right figure) (Eckes & Trautner, 2000). These differences in gender traits are explained by two different theories.

CONCERNED SENSITIVE NURTURING

According to **social role theory,** the expectations of parents, peers, and others *reward* or *discourage* different gender roles and behaviors for boys and girls. Social role theory focuses on boys and girls learning different gender roles and behavior because of *outside pressures* from family, peers, and society.

According to **cognitive developmental theory,** children acquire gender schemas or *cognitive rules* that indicate which gender roles and behaviors are right or wrong for boys and girls. Cognitive developmental theory focuses on boys and girls developing different gender roles because of *inside pressures,* which come from their own personal rules.

INDEPENDENT CONTROLLING DOMINANT

These two theories are not mutually exclusive but rather emphasize different factors in the development of gender-role differences and behaviors (C. L. Martin et al., 2002).

We'll discuss how differences in gender traits have important influences on personal, social, and career choices.

Can a woman be elected president?

Career choices. As boys and girls grow into men and women, their different gender roles, which involve different ways for men and women to think, behave, interact socially, and make career choices, are further strengthened by pressures from parents, peers, and society (Eckes & Trautner, 2000). For example, until the early 1990s, gender roles for women did not include careers in law enforcement, armed forces, fire or police departments, or management of large corporations, while gender roles for men did not include careers as nurses, secretaries, or elementary-school teachers. Since then gender roles have changed so that men and especially women have more flexibility and freedom in making job and career choices. However, gender roles still influence career choices, the most obvious being the limited role of women in many Arab societies and the reluctance to elect a woman as president of the United States.

Aggression. Researchers find that, from the age of 2 through college age, males tend to show more rough-and-tumble play, display more aggressive physical and verbal behavior, and commit more violent crimes than females (Kenrick et al., 2004). Sex differences in physical aggression have been found in children as young as 17 months. For example, one study found 17-month-old boys were twice as likely as girls to hit another child frequently (Baillargeon, 2002). Twin and adoption studies indicate the reasons for these sex differences in aggressive behavior include both genetic and environmental factors (Perusse & Gendreau, 2005). Therefore,

Boys and men are more aggressive.

while biological factors help to explain why boys are more aggressive than girls, psychosocial influences also play a key role. For example, researchers found that parents, peers, and society reward boys for acting out, being competitive, and settling their conflicts with fighting. In comparison, "nice girls" don't fight and tend to settle conflicts through talking (Coie & Dodge, 1998). As a result of these biological and psychosocial influences, the gender role for males encourages aggressive behavior and helps explain why the majority of aggressive acts, both social and criminal, are committed by males (DiLalla, 2002; Halpern, 2000).

Different brains. One reason girls and women develop traits of being concerned, sensitive, and nurturing may involve how women's brains process emotional situations. For example, researchers took brain scans (fMRI) while women and men looked at photos, which they graded from neutral (bookcase, landscape) to emotionally intense (crying people, dead body). Weeks later, when the subjects were asked to pick out photos that they had earlier rated as emotionally intense, women correctly remembered 10–15% more than men did. Equally interesting, brain scans taken during viewing of the emotionally intense photos indicated that in women's brains the amygdala and additional areas were more activated than in men's brains. Researchers concluded that, compared to men, women's brains are more effectively wired for processing, coding, and remembering emotional experiences. Researchers suggested that women's greater focus on emotional events may help explain why women report higher rates of clinical depression than men (Canli et al., 2002). These findings also support the evolutionary theory of behavior, which says that in early times women developed particular emotional traits, such as being concerned, sensitive, and nurturing, because these traits were beneficial to women in maintaining a stable family structure and in raising children (Caporael, 2001).

Amygdala

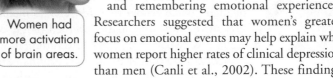

Women had more activation of brain areas.

Another gender difference in brain functions is that women process language by using both sides of their brains, while men use only the left side (Clements et al., 2006). This difference may explain why women are generally better at processing words and performing language tasks (Halpern, 2000).

Conclusion. No amount of brain research will explain all the social differences between males and females. Many other factors, such as temperament, attachment, family background, and environment, may explain why the sexes can be so different (Tyre, 2006). Sex differences in brain function do not mean that one brain is better; any difference found should not be used as the basis for discrimination (Galliano, 2003; L. Rogers, 2001).

What's going on? We have discussed how during infancy and childhood there are amazing increases in sensory abilities and motor skills and wondrous development of emotions, cognitive skills, social interactions, and gender roles. We'll briefly review and summmarize these changes so that you can see the big picture of infant and child development.

| 6 months old | 10 months old | 1 year old | 3 years old |

1 NEWBORNS' ABILITIES

Newborns come with more sensory and perceptual abilities than previously thought. They have a well-developed sense of touch, show an innate preference for sweet and salt, and recognize (smell) their mothers' odors. In a few more months, infants can recognize their mothers' faces, produce speech sounds, and perceive depth. This new and improved version of infants' abilities better explains how they discover the world.

2 MOTOR DEVELOPMENT

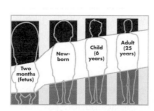

Infants gradually acquire the *coordinated movements* that they need to crawl, sit, stand, and walk. Many motor skills occur in a set sequence called *maturation* that is regulated by genetic programming. Two principles for motor development are that parts closest to the center of the body develop first—the *proximodistal* principle—and parts closer to the head develop first—the *cephalocaudal* principle. With motor development comes the ability to get up and explore.

3 EMOTIONAL DEVELOPMENT

"Good" babies and "difficult" babies show signs of differences in temperament, which is largely influenced by genetic factors. *Temperament* refers to stable differences in attention, arousal, and reaction to new situations; it also affects level of arousal and the development of emotional behaviors. Infants develop many *emotions,* which allow a wide range of wordless communication with the parent and the world. Infants form a close emotional bond with parents (caregiver). This emotional bond, which is called *attachment,* is thought to influence the development of future emotional and social behaviors.

4 COGNITIVE DEVELOPMENT

One theory of cognitive development is *Piaget's theory,* which says that children play an active role in cognitive development by incorporating new information into existing knowledge *(assimilation)* or changing existing knowledge through experience *(accommodation).* Children pass through four different cognitive stages—*(1) sensorimotor, (2) preoperational, (3) concrete operations,* and *(4) formal operations*—in that order but at different rates. With each stage, the child adds a new and qualitatively different kind of thinking or reasoning skill that helps the child make better sense of the world.

5 SOCIAL DEVELOPMENT

At the same time that children are developing emotionally and cognitively, they are also developing socially. *Freud* said that children develop socially by going through five *psychosexual stages* and that during the first three stages, the individual seeks pleasure from different areas of the body associated with sexual feelings. Freud's is the only theory that says the first five years are critical. *Erikson* said that children develop socially by going through eight *psychosocial stages* during which an individual's primary goal is to satisfy desires associated with social needs. According to *Bandura's social cognitive theory,* children develop social skills through imitation, observation, and self-reward. These three theories are not mutually exclusive but rather complement each other by focusing on different factors believed to be important in social development.

6 IMPORTANCE OF CHILDHOOD

How important are events that occur during childhood? In some cases, traumatic events (poverty, parental disinterest) result in later behavioral and social problems, but in other cases, a loving, supportive parent or caregiver compensates for early problems, which results in a resilient child. Although childhood may be an important time for emotional, social, and personality development, both positive and negative personality and social changes continue into middle adulthood.

After the Concept Review we'll examine an interesting and related question: Do children from very different cultures acquire similar or different gender roles and behaviors?

Oliviero Toscani for BENETTON

✔ Concept Review

1. The question that asks how much genetic factors and how much environmental factors contribute to a person's biological, emotional, cognitive, personal, and social development is called the _____ question.

2. The prenatal period, which begins at conception and ends at birth, is composed of three different

stages. The first stage of prenatal development refers to the two-week period following conception; this is called the (a)_____ stage. The second stage of the prenatal period spans the 2–8 weeks that follow conception; this is called the (b)_____ stage. The third stage of the prenatal period begins two months after conception and lasts until birth; this is called the (c)_____ stage.

3. The organ that connects the blood supply of the mother to that of the fetus is called the (a)_____, which acts as a filter. However, some agents, such as drugs, viruses, and chemicals, pass into the fetal blood supply and harm the developing fetus; these agents are called (b)_____. One example of these agents is alcohol, which if drunk heavily by the mother during pregnancy can result in a combination of physical changes and mental retardation in the baby called (c)_____.

Placenta   Umbilical cord

4. Newborns have some visual acuity, respond to touch, and are able to hear, smell, and taste. This indicates that they have relatively well-developed _____.

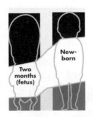

5. The acquisition of the muscular control necessary for coordinated physical activity, which is called (a)_____ development, follows two general principles. The principle that parts of the body closer to the head develop before parts closer to the feet is the (b)_____ principle. The principle that parts closer to the center of the infant's body develop before parts farther away is the (c)_____ principle. Development of motor skills occurs in a sequential and orderly fashion because of a genetic plan; this process is called (d)_____.

Two months (fetus)   Newborn

6. An individual's stable pattern of behavioral and emotional reactions that appear early and are influenced in large part by genetic factors is called his or her _____.

7. The close fundamental emotional bond that develops between the infant and his or her parent or caregiver is called (a)_____. Infants who use their parent as a safe home base from which they can wander off and explore their environments are said to have formed a (b)_____ attachment. Infants who avoid or show ambivalence toward their parents are said to have formed an (c)_____ attachment.

8. Piaget believed that children are actively involved in understanding their world through two basic processes: incorporating new information or experience into existing knowledge is called (a)_____; changing existing knowledge or experience as a result of assimilating some new information is called (b)_____.

9. Piaget's theory of cognitive development includes four stages, each of which is characterized by the development of particular kinds of reasoning. The first stage, during which infants learn about their environments by relating their sensory experiences (such as hearing and seeing) to their motor actions, is called the (a)_____ stage. The second stage, during which infants learn to use symbols to think about things that are not present and to help them solve simple problems, is called the (b)_____ stage. The third stage, during which children learn to perform a number of logical mental operations on objects that are physically present, is called the (c)_____ stage. The fourth stage, during which adolescents and adults develop the ability to think about and solve abstract problems in a logical manner, is called the (d)_____ stage.

10. According to Freud's theory of social development, children go through five developmental periods, which he called _____ stages. During these stages, a child's primary goal is to satisfy desires associated with innate biological needs.

11. According to Albert Bandura's social cognitive theory, we learn social skills through _____, _____, and self–reward.

12. According to Erik Erikson, a person goes through eight developmental periods during which the primary goal is to satisfy desires associated with social needs. Each of these eight periods is called a _____ stage, during which the person works to resolve a potential problem.

Answers: *1. nature-nurture; 2. (a) germinal, (b) embryonic, (c) fetal; 3. (a) placenta, (b) teratogens, (c) fetal alcohol syndrome; 4. senses; 5. (a) motor, (b) cephalocaudal, (c) proximodistal, (d) maturation; 6. temperament; 7. (a) attachment, (b) secure, (c) insecure; 8. (a) assimilation, (b) accommodation; 9. (a) sensorimotor, (b) preoperational, (c) concrete operations, (d) formal operations; 10. psychosexual; 11. observation, imitation; 12. psychosocial*

G. Cultural Diversity: Gender Roles

Identifying Gender Roles

Do cultures have different gender roles?

Although we know that young boys and girls acquire different gender roles, the intriguing question is, Why do little boys generally grow up to be more aggressive and independent, while little girls grow up to be less aggressive and more nurturing? To answer this question, researchers tested hundreds of 5-, 8-, and 11-year-old children in 24 countries to find out if young children from so many different cultures developed similar or different male–female gender roles and behaviors (J. E. Williams & Best, 1990).

> One of these people is a very affectionate person. When they like someone, they hug and kiss them a lot. Which person likes to hug and kiss a lot?

For younger children (5- and 8-year-olds), researchers told 32 brief stories and then asked whether the person in the story was more like a man or a woman; an example is given on the left. For older children (11-year-olds), researchers gave a list of 300 adjectives, such as aggressive, affectionate, calm, bossy, sensitive, loud, and helpful, and asked which adjectives were more likely to be associated with men and which with women. Unlike 5- and 8-year-old children, 11-year-olds were able to understand the meanings of the adjectives and indicate their choices by checking off adjectives that they thought best suited men or women.

Gender Roles across Cultures

Similarities. Researchers found that across the 24 countries, relatively young children showed remarkable similarities in the characteristics that they associated with gender roles.

About 57% of 5-year-old children made stereotyped responses about gender roles by associating people in the stories with a particular sex, either male or female. For example, 5-year-old children associated being strong, aggressive, and dominant with men, while they associated being gentle and affectionate with women. Eight-year-old children had learned even more stereotypic behaviors. They associated being

> Strong, aggressive, dominant, independent, coarse, loud, boastful

weak, emotional, appreciative, excitable, gentle, softhearted, meek, and submissive with women, while they associated being disorderly, cruel, coarse, adventurous, independent, ambitious, loud, and boastful with men (see photos). By the age of 11, the percentage of children who made stereotyped responses about gender roles jumped to 90%.

Differences. Researchers also found that across countries and cultures, interesting differences occurred in children's perceptions of gender roles. For example, in Germany, children associated being adventurous, confident, jolly, and steady with women, while in most other countries, these characteristics were typically associated with men.

In Japan, children associated being dominant and steady with women, while in other countries, these characteristics were typically associated with men.

Conclusions. Researchers concluded that children in 24 different countries and cultures developed knowledge of gender roles relatively early and showed remarkable similarities in choosing different gender roles and behaviors for men and women. Although there were some differences due to cultural values, there were generally more similarities in male–female gender roles across the 24 countries (J. E. Williams & Best, 1990).

> Emotional, appreciative, excitable, gentle, submissive

Two Answers

We began with the question, Why do little boys generally grow up to be more aggressive and independent, while little girls grow up to be less aggressive and more nuturing? To this we add another question, Why do little boys and little girls from 24 different countries and cultures develop such similar male–female gender roles? There are two different but somewhat complementary answers.

The *social role theory* (discussed earlier; p. 395), which emphasizes social and cultural influences, states that gender differences between men and women arise from different divisions of labor.

According to social role theory, male–female gender differences developed from traditional cultural divisions of labor, in which women were childbearers and homemakers, while men were providers and protectors (Eagly et al., 2000). Because men and women performed different duties, men and women were under different social-cultural pressures to develop different gender roles. Another answer comes from a relatively new theory.

The *evolutionary theory,* which emphasizes genetic and biological forces, says that current gender differences are a continuation of the behaviors that evolved from early men and women, who adapted these different behaviors in their attempts to survive the problems of their time.

According to evolutionary theory, men increased their chances for reproduction by being dominant, controlling, and aggressive. In comparison, women increased their chances of raising their children by being concerned, sensitive, and nurturing. According to evolutionary theory, the current male–female gender differences arise from genetic and biological forces that evolved from an ancient set of mating patterns that had initially helped the species to survive (Buss, 1999; Caporael, 2001).

Because social role theory emphasizes cultural influences and evolutionary theory emphasizes genetic and biological forces, researchers suggest that by combining the two theories we can better explain the development of our current male–female gender differences (Baldwin & Baldwin, 1997).

H. Application Child Abuse

What was her terrible secret?

The family had all the trappings of being perfect, including wealth, status, and prestige.

Father. The father was a handsome, intelligent man who served as president of the Denver Area Boy Scout Council and helped establish Denver's Cleo Wallace Village for Handicapped Children. He was a millionaire socialite and a pillar of the Denver community.

Mother. The mother was a good homemaker, who spent all of her time caring for her four children, all girls.

Marilyn. Marilyn was the youngest daughter and described as a golden-haired beauty. In college she was a straight-A student and a swimming champion. At the age of 20, she was crowned Miss America (left photo).

The secret. Marilyn had been sexually abused by her father from the time she was 5 until she was 18, when she moved away to college. However, Marilyn had completely suppressed any knowledge of sexual abuse by her father until she was 24 (suppressed memories are discussed on pages 250–251). She was having a conversation with a former youth minister at her church when she broke down and told her painful secret. She made the minister promise not to tell anyone except her fiancé, who was very sympathetic and understanding, and her oldest sister, who said, "Oh, no! I thought I was the only one" (van Derbur Atler, 1991, p. 91).

At 20, she was crowned Miss America.

Dealing with abuse. Marilyn says that she didn't tell anyone because she didn't want to destroy her family and was afraid her father would go to jail. Thus, she kept her secret and survived by splitting into a day child who seemed normal and happy and a night child who feared her father and suffered his abuse.

Facing the abuser. When Marilyn was 40 years old, the sight of her own 5-year-old daughter triggered terrible memories of her father's abuse and gave her frightening physical symptoms. She knew that her misery would remain until she confronted her father. She met and talked to him for 20 minutes. He did not deny anything and said, "If I had known what this would do to you, I never would have done it" (van Derbur Atler, 1991, p. 94).

Aftermath. At 47, Marilyn van Derbur was named the Outstanding Woman Speaker in America. But she was having terrible bouts of anxiety and couldn't continue her career. Finally, she told her mother about being abused and spent the next seven years in therapy. At 54, Marilyn (right photo) stood before the Adult Incest Survivors Group and publicly revealed her secret: She had been abused for 13 years by her father. Her goal now is to help others who have been abused.

At 54, she admitted being sexually abused by her father.

Marilyn was a victim of one kind of child abuse—sexual abuse. There are several kinds of child abuse.

Kinds of Abuse

How many children are abused?

In the United States, allegations of childhood abuse and neglect are made for 5.5 million children annually (USDHHS, 2006). *Child abuse and neglect (physical and emotional) result from inadequate care or acts of the parent that put the child in danger, cause physical harm or injury, or involve sexual molestation.*

The most common kind of abuse (62%) is neglect, followed in order by physical abuse and sexual abuse (USDHHS, 2006). For example, 2-year-old Brianna was left at home alone for almost three weeks and amazingly survived by drinking water from the toilet and eating any food she could find and unwrap. When the sheriff's department found Brianna, her body was smeared with ketchup and mustard, and the sheriff stated, "Feces and urine were everywhere" (Skipp & Johnson, 2003).

The second most frequently confirmed kind of child abuse (18%) is physical abuse. For example, Karen, who was 10 years old, vividly remembered how much and how often her mother beat her. Her mother would get angry over the tiniest things, grab something handy (shoes, father's belt, potato masher), and start hitting her. One time her mother beat her so hard that Karen's legs turned black and blue. When

Allegations of child abuse are made for 5.5 million children annually.

Karen threatened to tell the police, her mother replied in an angry voice, "Go ahead. They won't believe you and they'll put you in the darkest prison" (*Time,* September 5, 1983).

The third most frequently confirmed kind of child abuse (10%) is sexual abuse. As in Marilyn's case, sexual abuse is most frequently committed by people who know the child, such as an acquaintance or family member, and many children are too fearful of the abuser to report their maltreatment (Douglas & Finkelhor, 2005; Finkelhor, 2002). National surveys of adults indicate that 9–32% of women and 5–10% of men have been sexually abused during their childhood; international surveys suggest similar rates of abuse (7–36% of women, 3–29% of men) (Douglas & Finkelhor, 2005; Emery & Laumann-Billings, 1998). These numbers indicate that sexual abuse, which may result in serious long-term behavioral, social, neural, and personality problems, is an international problem.

The remaining 10% of child abuse cases include emotional neglect and other kinds of abuse that do not easily fit into any category.

We'll focus on three questions related to abuse and neglect: Who abuses children? What problems do abused children suffer? How are abusive parents helped?

Who Abuses Children?

Parents who abuse their children are likely to have low self-esteem and a wide range of personal problems. They are apt to be in distress, unhappy, impulsive, anxious, and aggressive and to have problems with substance abuse (Emery & Laumann-Billings, 1998; Pittman & Buckley, 2006). Recent statistics show 57.8% of people who abused children were women and 42.2% were men. Also, nearly 80% of people who abused children were parents (USDHHS, 2006).

About 30% of abused children become parents who abuse their own children, but a number of *compensatory factors* can prevent this from happening (J. Kaufman & Zigler, 1989). These compensatory factors include having a positive attachment to a caregiver, resolving not to repeat the abuse, having an awareness of one's early abusive experiences, knowing about sex at the time of the abuse, having good self-esteem, experiencing few stressful life events, and having good social support. The path from being abused to becoming an abusive parent is neither direct nor fixed and can be reversed by these compensatory factors (Glasser et al., 2001).

A child who is fussy, irritable, or sickly is more difficult to care for, especially if parents have personal problems of their own (Knutson, 1995). The interaction between a difficult child and troubled parents illustrates the principle of bidirectionality (Maccoby, 1984).

The *principle of bidirectionality* says that a child's behaviors influence how his or her parents respond, and in turn the parents' behaviors influence how the child responds.

According to this principle, child abuse results from an interaction between a child's difficult traits, which tend to elicit maltreatment or abuse from the parents, and the parents' social-emotional and caregiving problems, which make it difficult for them to recognize and meet the needs of their child (J. Miller, 1995). Thus, the combination of a difficult child and parents with their own personal or drug-related problems results in a potentially explosive parent–child interaction that increases the risk for child abuse. Abused children can develop a variety of problems.

> Abuse can leave scars in the brain.

What Problems Do Abused Children Have?

Children who suffer abuse may experience a number of physical, neurological, and psychological problems. The *physical problems* include stomachaches, headaches, bedwetting, and abnormal hormonal changes that indicate their systems are trying to deal with large doses of stress (Yehuda, 2000).

Abused children also suffer a number of *psychological problems,* which include increased anxiety, social withdrawal, delays in social, cognitive, and emotional development, poor school performance, attention problems, and fearful nightmares. They develop stronger reactions to facial expressions of anger, see anger in neutral faces, and have difficulty distinguishing between sad and happy faces (Pollak & Kistler, 2002). As teenagers, abused children experience continuing problems, such as poor self-esteem, depression, loneliness, suicidal impulses, conflicts with friends, and delinquent behaviors (J. L. Davis & Petretic-Jackson, 2000).

Recently, researchers found that childhood abuse can have enduring negative effects on a child's *brain development and neural functioning.* Negative effects include abnormal brain waves that signal abnormal brain functioning, reduction in size of the brain areas that are involved in recognizing and processing emotional cues (hippocampus and amygdala), and reduction in size of the major band of fibers (corpus callosum) responsible for transferring neural information between right and left hemispheres of the brain (Teicher, 2002). These data indicate that maltreatment or abuse at an early age can result in long-lasting deficits and problems in neural development and functioning.

Finally, long-term or longitudinal studies on sexually abused children report that within 12–18 months after sexual abuse stopped, 55–65% of children showed a substantial decrease in symptoms, but 10–24% appeared to get worse. Those children who showed the best recovery were those who received strong support and care from their mothers (Saywitz et al., 2000).

How Are Abusive Parents Helped?

A number of therapy programs that use some combination of cognitive-behavioral therapy (Module 25) and parent-training programs (Module 10) have proven relatively successful in decreasing child abuse. In general, these programs have at least two goals (L. Peterson & Brown, 1994).

1. Overcoming the parent's personal problems. Abusive parents need help in learning about and developing social relationships, which are needed for positive bonding and attachment between parent and child. Abusive parents also need training in basic caregiving skills, which involves learning how to meet the physical, social, and emotional needs of their children. Dealing with abusive parents' personal or drug problems usually requires long-term professional therapy. As parents get their personal or marital problems under control, they can concentrate on improving their interactions with their child.

2. Changing parent–child interactions. Researchers found that abusive parents are less likely to use positive behaviors (smiling, praising, touching) and are more likely to use negative behaviors (threatening, disapproving, showing anger) when dealing with their children (Reid et al., 1981). Therefore, abusive parents need to learn more positive ways of interacting. Parent-training programs, which focus on modifying ways parents interact with their children through behavior modification techniques (discussed in Module 10), are effective in helping parents increase positive interactions with their children (Timmer et al., 2005).

Clinicians and researchers recognize that, in many countries, neglect, physical abuse, and sexual abuse are serious social problems that deserve more community-based prevention methods and treatment programs than are currently available (Coates, 2006; Sanders et al., 2003).

Summary Test

A. Prenatal Influences

1. The time from conception to birth is called the (a)_____ period, which is divided into three parts. The two-week period that immediately follows conception is called the (b)_____ period; it is marked by the zygote dividing into many cells. The period that includes the 2–8 weeks after conception, during which cells continue to divide and begin to differentiate into bone, muscle, and body organs, is called the (c)_____ period. The period of development that begins two months after conception and lasts for about seven months is called the (d)_____ period. At the end of this period, birth occurs and the fetus becomes a newborn.

(Placenta, Umbilical cord)

2. The development of the fetus can be interrupted or damaged by a variety of toxic agents, called (a)_____, which cause malformation of the brain or body and result in birth defects. For example, heavy drinking during pregnancy can cause a combination of physical and psychological deficits called (b)_____, which is the leading known cause of mental retardation in the United States.

B. Newborns' Abilities

(Two months (fetus), New-born)

3. The newborn comes into the world with relatively well-developed sensory and perceptual responses. For example, the newborn can see, but his or her ability to see details, which is called (a)_____, is poor. Six-month-old infants will not crawl off the visual cliff, indicating that they have developed (b)_____ perception. Newborns have good hearing, touch, and smell and an inherited preference for sweet and salt tastes.

4. Motor development, which is the acquisition of the muscle control required for coordinated physical activity, follows two general principles. The principle that parts of the body closer to the head develop before those closer to the feet is called the (a)_____ principle. The principle that parts closer to the center of the body develop before those farther away is called the (b)_____ principle.

5. Development that occurs in a sequential and orderly fashion because of a genetic plan is called (a)_____. The average age at which individuals perform various kinds of motor skills or exhibit abilities or behaviors is reflected in (b)_____.

C. Emotional Development

6. Early and stable individual differences in attention, arousal, and reaction to new things refer to an infant's _____, which is greatly influenced by genetic, or inherited, factors.

7. Newborns have a limited range of emotional expressions that include interest, startle, distress, disgust, and neonatal smile. During the first two years, infants develop a wide range of _____ expressions and feelings that signal the infant's physiological needs and psychological moods.

8. The close emotional bond that develops between infant and parent (caregiver) is called (a)_____. As the infant develops a closer attachment to her parents, she also shows more distress when her parents leave; this distress is called (b)_____.

9. There are two kinds of attachment. Infants who use their caregiver as a safe home base from which they can wander off and explore their environments are said to be (a)_____ attached. This kind of attachment may contribute to better emotional bonds later in life. Infants who avoid or show ambivalence toward their caregivers are said to be (b)_____ attached. For example, these infants may cling and want to be held one minute but squirm and push away the next minute.

D. Research Focus: Temperament

(Age 2, 7)

10. Researchers use two different methods to study developmental processes. Repeatedly studying the same group of individuals at different ages is using the (a)_____ method. Studying different groups of individuals who are of different ages is using the (b)_____ method.

11. Researchers found that about one-fourth of infants show avoidance, anxiety, fear, and increased physiological arousal when in a strange or novel situation. These individuals are called shy or _____, and the majority remain the same into adulthood. This finding supports the idea that temperaments appear early, are stable across time, and are partially under genetic control (nature).

E. Cognitive Development

12. Piaget believed that children participate in their own cognitive development by active involvement through two different processes: incorporating new information or experiences into existing knowledge is called (a)_____; and changing one's knowledge or experiences as a result of assimilating some new information is called (b)_____.

13. Piaget divided cognitive development into four stages. In the first, lasting from birth to about age 2, infants interact with and learn about their environments by relating their sensory experiences to their motor actions; this is called the (a)_____ stage.

A significant development of this stage is the concept that objects or events continue to exist even if they cannot be heard, touched, or seen; this is called (b)_____.

14. In the second stage, lasting from the age of about 2 to 7, children learn to use symbols to think about things that are not present and to help solve simple problems; this is the (a)_____ stage. A limitation in this stage is the tendency to think of the world only from one's own viewpoint, called (b)_____ thinking.

15. The third stage, which lasts from the age of about 7 to 11, is called the (a)_____ stage. During this stage, children can perform a number of logical mental operations on concrete objects (ones that are physically present). The idea that the amount of a substance remains the same even in different shapes, known as (b)_____, is mastered during the third stage.

16. During the fourth and last stage, which lasts from about age 12 through adulthood, the individual develops the ability to think about and solve abstract problems logically; this is called the (a)_____ stage. Each of Piaget's cognitive stages is thought to be qualitatively different from the previous one because each new stage represents the development of some new (b)_____ ability.

F. Social Development

17. How a person develops social relationships, develops a sense of self, and becomes a social being is called (a)_____ development. Three theories of such development each emphasize a different aspect. According to Freud, a person goes through five developmental periods, called (b)_____ stages, during which the primary goal is to satisfy innate biological needs. In contrast, Erikson divided development into eight developmental periods, in which the primary goal is to satisfy social needs; he called these (c)_____ stages. Bandura emphasizes the importance of learning through imitation, observation, and reinforcement; this is called (d)_____ theory.

18. Freud's five psychosexual stages are called the (a)_____, (b)_____, (c)_____, (d)_____, and (e)_____ stages. Freud believed that the first five years leave a lasting impression on the individual's personality and social development.

19. The first five of Erikson's eight stages involve the resolution of a potential social problem between the child and his or her environment. In stage 1, the infant deals with resolving issues surrounding trust versus (a)_____. In stage 2, the toddler must resolve issues

surrounding autonomy versus shame and (b)_____. In stage 3, the younger child deals with issues of initiative versus (c)_____. In stage 4, the older child deals with issues that involve industry versus (d)_____. In stage 5, the adolescent deals with issues that involve identity versus (e)_____.

20. Early psychological difficulties increase a child's (a)_____, which in turn increases the risk for developing later social or personality problems. However, certain emotional traits, family factors, and outside emotional support help a child overcome early problems and are said to help make the child (b)_____ and thus develop normal social behaviors.

21. Expectations of how we should think or behave because we are male or female are called (a)_____. One theory says that these roles develop because parents or caregivers expect, treat, and reward different kinds of behaviors depending on the child's sex; this is the (b)_____ theory. Another theory says that children learn rules for male or female behavior through active involvement with their environments; this is the (c)_____ theory.

G. Cultural Diversity: Gender Roles

22. Although children's perceptions of gender roles show some variation across countries and cultures, it appears that their _____ of gender roles develops in a generally similar way at similar times.

H. Application: Child Abuse

23. Inadequate care, neglect, or acts of the parent that put the child in danger or that cause physical harm or injury or involve sexual molestation compose the definition of (a)_____. According to the principle of (b)_____, the child's behaviors influence how the parents respond and the parents' behaviors influence how the child responds. Two goals of treatment to stop or prevent child abuse are to help parents overcome their (c)_____ problems and to change parent–child interactions from negative to positive.

Answers: 1. (a) prenatal, (b) germinal, (c) embryonic, (d) fetal; 2. (a) teratogens, (b) fetal alcohol syndrome (FAS); 3. (a) visual acuity, (b) depth; 4. (a) cephalocaudal, (b) proximodistal; 5. (a) maturation, (b) developmental norms; 6. temperament; 7. emotional; 8. (a) attachment, (b) separation anxiety; 9. (a) securely, (b) insecurely; 10. (a) longitudinal, (b) cross-sectional; 11. inhibited or fearful; 12. (a) assimilation, (b) accommodation; 13. (a) sensorimotor, (b) object permanence; 14. (a) preoperational, (b) egocentric; 15. (a) concrete operations, (b) conservation; 16. (a) formal operations, (b) reasoning or thinking; 17. (a) social, (b) psychosexual, (c) psychosocial, (d) social cognitive; 18. (a) oral, (b) anal, (c) phallic, (d) latency, (e) genital; 19. (a) mistrust, (b) doubt, (c) guilt, (d) inferiority, (e) role confusion; 20. (a) vulnerability, (b) resilient; 21. (a) gender roles, (b) social role, (c) cognitive developmental; 22. knowledge; 23. (a) child abuse, (b) bidirectionality, (c) personal

Critical Thinking

Can Music Raise a Child's IQ?

Questions

1. The sales clerk supports the Mozart effect by saying that a lot of women are buying the Mozart CD. The sales clerk's statement illustrates what kind of supporting evidence? How good is this kind of evidence?

2. What did the original study say about playing Mozart to children or boosting general intelligence?

3. In what ways did the press and the public change and distort the researchers' original findings?

The young woman, who was 8 months pregnant, asked the sales clerk for the Mozart CD that was supposed to increase a baby's intelligence. The sales clerk said that the Mozart CD was a big seller and that a lot of women were playing Mozart to their unborn children to take full advantage of the Mozart effect.

The "Mozart effect," as it came to be called, was first announced in 1993 with a short study from researchers at the University of Wisconsin–Oshkosh. The researchers played 10 minutes' worth of Mozart's Sonata for Two Pianos in D Major to college students. Then the students took a test that required them to visualize how objects changed over time, such as how a piece of paper that was folded and cut would look when it was unfolded. Subjects who had listened to Mozart showed a slight but temporary rise in scores on this test compared to subjects who sat through 10 minutes of silence. However, the researchers reported that the Mozart effect was not long lasting and had little effect on overall intelligence.

Within no time, the Mozart effect was making headlines around the country: "Mozart Can Boost Intelligence." Advertising for the Mozart CD claimed that listening to Mozart would stimulate young minds, improve intelligence, and raise IQs. Many parents believed the advertising and bought thousands of "Baby Mozart" videotapes and CDs.

One mother said, "I am six months into my pregnancy and almost immediately upon playing the Mozart CD my baby started actively moving. I can really tell he enjoys it even though I can't see him yet." One governor even wanted to pass a law that would give a free Mozart CD to all pregnant women in his state so that their children would have a boost in intelligence.

However, when researchers looked closely at the Mozart effect they reported a different story. A Harvard neuropsychologist analyzed a dozen studies and reported that listening to classical music had no lasting effect on intelligence. Other researchers at Appalachian State University tried repeating the original Mozart study but were unable to find a "Mozart effect" and concluded that listening to classical music did not affect intelligence scores.

However, one nursery had positive proof of one effect. They had been playing classical music to their young children for the past 30 years. Without a doubt, listening to classical music helps kids relax and take their naps. (Adapted from J. Weiss, So-called Mozart effect may be (yawn) just a dream, *San Diego Union-Tribune*, February, 12, 2000, p. E-5; S. M. Jones & Zigler, 2002)

4. In what ways did the new research differ from the original findings?

5. Is it possible that listening to melodic music, such as Mozart, could improve performance on a test?

1. The sales clerk's statement about other mothers buying the Mozart CD is called a testimonial, which has great potential for error and bias and thus is not very reliable evidence.
2. The original study used college students, not children, did not claim that listening to Mozart boosted general intelligence, and said the effect was not long-lasting.
3. Greatly distorting the original findings, the press and general public said that the Mozart effect applied to children, that it boosted IQ scores, and that it would help unborn children.
4. A neuropsychologist reviewed a dozen previous studies and found that listening to classical music had no effect on intelligence. Recent attempts by researchers to repeat or replicate the original study's Mozart effect were not successful; that is, listening to classical music had no effect on test scores.
5. Just as listening to melodic classical music, such as Mozart, relaxed and helped children nap, it may have the same relaxing or calming effect on college students. Thus, feeling more relaxed or less anxious and stressed may improve performance on tests, since we know that stress and anxiety may interfere with and worsen test performance.

Links to Learning

Learning Activities

- **POWERSTUDY FOR INTRODUCTION TO PSYCHOLOGY 4.0** PowerStudy 4.0™
  by Tom Doyle and Rod Plotnik

  SuperModule: Check out "Infancy & Childhood" on PowerStudy. It includes complete paragraph-by-paragraph explanations of all content using fully-narrated animations and graphics. An onscreen toolbar allows immediate access to text, text outline, and module glossary with notetaking and printing capabilities. This module also includes:
  - Video—Imbedded videos discuss many topics including prenatal health issues, development of motor skills, perceiving gender roles, and how early experiences affect brain development.
  - A test of your knowledge using an interactive version of the Summary Test on pages 402 and 403. Also access related quizzing-true/false, multiple choice, and matching.
  - An interactive version of the Critical Thinking exercise "Can Music Raise a Child's IQ?" on page 404.
  - Key terms, a chapter outline including chapter abstract, and a special extended list of hotlinked websites that correlate to this module.

- **CengageNOW**
  academic.cengage.com/login
  Need help studying? This site is your one-stop study shop.
  Take a Pre-Test and CengageNOW will generate a Personalized Study Plan based on your test results. The Study Plan will identify the topics you need to review and direct you to online resources to help you master those topics. You can then take a Post-Test to determine the concepts you have mastered and what you still need to work on.

- **INTRODUCTION TO PSYCHOLOGY BOOK COMPANION WEBSITE**
  academic.cengage.com/psychology/plotnik
  Visit your book companion website where you will find more resources to help you study. At this site, you will find Learning Objectives, Internet Exercises, quizzing, flash cards, and a pronunciation glossary.

- **STUDY GUIDE and WEBTUTOR**
  Check the corresponding module in your Study Guide for effective student tips and help learning the material presented. Also go to **academic.cengage.com/webtutor** for an interactive version of the Study Guide features.

Study Questions

*A. Prenatal Influences—A pregnant woman asks, "Why do I have to worry about ingesting chemicals, since my unborn child has a separate blood supply?" What is your response? (**Suggested answer p. 630**)

B. Newborns' Abilities—A father gives his infant son practice in walking so that the boy will develop early and grow up to be a professional track star. Will this early practice help?

C. Emotional Development—"Parents, stop worrying—emotions depend on genes, not discipline." Is this headline statement correct?

*D. Research Focus: Temperament—Marcie and Jeff love their 6-month-old son but find that he is easily irritated and frightened. What should they do? (**Suggested answer p. 630**)

E. Cognitive Development—Why is it that a 1-year-old child likes to play the game of peek-a-boo but a 7-year-old thinks it is silly?

*F. Social Development—How would Freud's and Erikson's theories apply to a 3-year-old child whose parents are getting divorced? (**Suggested answer p. 631**)

G. Cultural Diversity: Gender Roles—Why do you think that young boys and girls around the world develop relatively similar gender roles?

H. Application: Child Abuse—If one were abused as a child, what kinds of problems might one face as a parent?

*These questions are answered in Appendix B.

MODULE 18
Adolescence & Adulthood

Introduction

Adolescence

Will Branndi become president?

"Do not label me as anything. I'm an individual."

"I will eventually become president. In 2017. I think. I've figured it out. I don't want people to think, 'She's just a kid. She doesn't know what's ahead of her.' I know the presidency will not come easy to me. I'm black, first of all, and I'm a woman. I want to be a lawyer, then work my way up in politics, become like mayor, then senator, then governor . . .

"I know people will look into my past and say, 'Years ago, she did this, she did that, blah, blah, blah.' The worst thing I've ever done is to steal two little five-cent Bazooka gums from a 7-Eleven when I was nine. I don't think they'll count that against me . . .

"Sometimes people just expect me to make trouble because I'm 'one of the black kids.' Do not label me as anything. Label me as individual . . .

"I want everyone to know that some 12-year-olds really do think seriously about the future. I want to be a role model. I'm glad I was born black. I want to tell others, 'Stay in there because you can do just as much good as any other person.'"

Besides talking like a philosopher, Branndi is a fun-loving adolescent who likes rap music, hanging out at the mall with her friends, and "dumb" movies. She is an above-average student, likes to write fairy tales for children, and sings in the youth choir at the neighborhood church (*Los Angeles Times*, December 22, 1991, pp. E-1, E-12).

At age 12, Branndi is just beginning adolescence.

Adolescence is a developmental period, lasting from about ages 12 to 18, during which many biological, cognitive, social, and personality traits change from childlike to adultlike.

While it is true that adolescents, like Branndi, go through dramatic changes, experts now believe that adolescence is not necessarily marked by great psychological turmoil. Psychologists have learned that the majority of teenagers, unlike the terrible adolescents portrayed in the media, do develop a healthy sense of identity, maintain close relationships with their families, and avoid major emotional disorders (Gutgesell & Payne, 2004; Wallace, 2004). After making it through adolescence, most teenagers are ready and eager to enter the adult world.

Adulthood

Did the prom queen live happily ever after?

"I remember standing on stage in front of all the students. I was thinking, 'Can this really happen to me?' It was my junior year of high school, and I had been elected prom queen. It was like being in a fairy tale.

"I cried at my high school graduation, but I was excited about going away to college and being on my own. I considered myself a very sensible, logical, and levelheaded person. So what did I do? I began seriously dating a guy who was my opposite. He was a fun-loving, kidding-around, cocky-type person. I met him in January, got engaged in February, and was married in September. What had love done to my sensible head?

"Only some of the things turned out the way I hoped."

"As I look back over my five years of marriage, I now realize that it was okay but not great. It was great to have two wonderful children. It wasn't great to discover that my husband was having an affair when I was pregnant the second time. We got divorced soon after my daughter was born. It was hard being single again, with two children and no job. Later, my 12-year-old son developed a brain tumor and after two years of suffering, he died. How does one prepare for the death of one's child? Without help from my parents and friends, I would never have survived.

"I'm almost 40 now. My daughter and I are doing pretty well. I think about getting married again. I don't know if I will. You see, I also like my independence. Come back and see me when I'm 70 and I'll tell you what happened" (Wallechinsky, 1986).

Susan had dreamed of finishing college, getting married, and having a family, all of which she did. However, she did not figure on a divorce, having to support herself and her children, and her son's dying of a brain tumor, all before she reached 40. These are some of the joys and pains of adulthood.

MAJOR PERIODS OF CHANGE

Both Susan and Branndi went through periods of great change. Each of us goes through three major developmental periods marked by significant physical, cognitive, personality, and social changes. We discussed childhood in Module 17. Now we'll turn to the other two periods: adolescence and adulthood. Generally, adolescents are more concerned about their physical appearance and finding their identities, while adults are more concerned with establishing a long-term relationship and finding a good job. Thus, the individual's concerns and goals undergo major changes between adolescence and adulthood.

What's Coming

We'll explain the personality, social, cognitive, and physical changes that individuals undergo from adolescence through adulthood and discuss some of the challenges and problems that adolescents and adults face during each of these periods.

We'll begin with perhaps the biggest change in adolescence—puberty.

A. Puberty & Sexual Behavior

Why is puberty such a big deal?

A teenager leaves behind the mind and body of a child and begins to take on the mind and body of an adult. This great change from child to adult is full of challenge, excitement, and anxiety for the adolescent and the parents. Perhaps the biggest event in changing from a child to an adult is the onset of puberty, which is altogether interesting, wondrous, and potentially very stressful.

Puberty refers to a developmental period, between the ages of 9 and 17, when the individual experiences significant biological changes that result in developing secondary sexual characteristics and reaching sexual maturity.

As puberty triggers dramatic changes in the structure and function of our bodies, we simultaneously experience dramatic changes in our thoughts, personalities, and social behaviors. To understand why puberty changed our minds, we must first learn how puberty changed our bodies.

Girls during Puberty

Every girl wants to grow up so she can finally be a woman. Becoming a woman means going through puberty and experiencing three major biological changes that occur between ages 9 and 13. The onset of puberty usually occurs about two years earlier in girls (average of 10.5 years) than in boys (average of 12.5 years).

1 Puberty sets off a surge in *physical growth*, which is marked by an increase in height that starts on average at 9.6 years. This growth spurt begins about 6–12 months before the onset of breast development.

2 Puberty triggers a physiological process that results in a girl's reaching *female sexual maturity*, which primarily involves the onset of menarche.

Menarche is the first menstrual period; it is a signal that ovulation may have occurred and that the girl may have the potential to conceive and bear a child.

In the United States, menarche occurs on average at 12.5 years, about 2.5 years after the beginning of breast development. For reasons of diet, exercise, and genes, age of menarche varies with society and country (S. E. Anderson et al., 2003; Chumlea et al., 2003; Ellison, 2002).

The onset of menarche is triggered by an area of the brain called the *hypothalamus*, which releases a hormone called *kisspeptin* that helps to stimulate the *pituitary gland* to produce hormones. These hormones travel throughout the bloodstream and stimulate the ovaries to greatly increase production of female hormones (Kotulak, 2006; McKie, 2005; Messager, 2006)

Estrogen is one of the major female hormones. At puberty, estrogen levels increase eightfold, which stimulates the development of both primary and secondary sexual characteristics.

3 Puberty marks a major change in the girl's body as she develops female secondary sexual characteristics.

Female secondary sexual characteristics, whose development is triggered by the increased secretion of estrogen, include growth of pubic hair, development of breasts, and widening of hips.

In girls, the onset of secondary sexual characteristics begins at 10.5 years (the range is from age 9 to age 18) and continues for about 4.5 years.

Early versus late maturing. Girls who are early maturing—that is, who go through puberty early—may encounter psychological problems because they have not yet acquired the adult personality traits and social skills that are needed for normal and healthy functioning in their newly developed adult bodies (Dorn et al., 2003).

Boys during Puberty

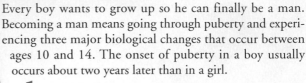

Every boy wants to grow up so he can finally be a man. Becoming a man means going through puberty and experiencing three major biological changes that occur between ages 10 and 14. The onset of puberty in a boy usually occurs about two years later than in a girl.

1 Puberty triggers an increase in *physical growth,* especially height, generally at 13–14 years of age. The increase in height may be dramatic, and a boy may feel strange as he discovers that he is taller than his mother and as tall as or taller than his father.

2 Puberty starts a physiological process that results in a boy's reaching *male sexual maturity,* which includes growth of the genital organs—testes and penis—and production of sperm. The onset of genital growth begins at around 11.5 years (the range is from age 9 to age 16) and continues for approximately three years. The production and release of sperm begin at 12–14 years of age.

The increase in genital growth and the production of sperm are triggered by the *hypothalamus,* which stimulates the male pituitary gland. The pituitary in turn triggers the testes to increase production of testosterone by as much as 18 times more than before puberty.

Testosterone, which is the major male hormone, stimulates the growth of genital organs and the development of secondary sexual characteristics.

3 The increased production of testosterone triggers the development of male secondary sexual characteristics.

Male secondary sexual characteristics, which are triggered by the increased secretion of testosterone, include the growth of pubic and facial hair, development of muscles, and a change (deepening) in voice.

These changes usually occur between 12 and 16 years of age, but there is a wide range in their development.

Early versus late maturing. Generally, boys who are early maturing, which means they go through puberty earlier, are found to be more confident, relaxed, socially responsible, popular, and highly regarded by their peers. In comparison, boys who go through puberty later (are late maturing) are found lacking in self-confidence and self-esteem, more dependent on their parents, and less highly regarded by peers.

However, many of the psychological differences between early- and late-maturing girls and boys decrease and disappear with age (Sigelman & Rider, 2006). One interesting difference between boys and girls during puberty is that generally boys see themselves as being physically attractive, while many girls doubt their attractiveness and are constantly comparing themselves with other girls (Rodriguez-Tome et al., 1993).

During puberty, boys and girls become physically sexually mature, a brand-new body state that raises many difficult questions for adolescents.

Now what do I do?

In the United States, about 30 million youths between the ages of 10 and 17 are looking for answers to a very important and burning question: Now that I am sexually mature, what do I do? For

example, a survey of teenage girls reported that the number one problem they faced revolved around issues of sex and pregnancy (Henry, 1999). Part of the difficulty that adolescents have in making decisions about how to behave sexually is that they receive conflicting answers.

Conflicting Answers

On the one hand, the media (movies, television, magazines), as well as peers, friends, and classmates, often discuss or portray sex in exciting ways that stimulate and encourage adolescents to try sex, often before they are emotionally ready (L. Ali & Scelfo, 2002). For example, in a study of 174 girls, most said that they had been too young (average age was 13) at the time of their first intercourse. The reasons (in order of frequency) that they gave for engaging in sex were that they were physically attracted or curious, were alone with their partner, and knew that all their friends were having sex. Looking back, most of these girls wished they had waited longer before having sexual intercourse because they had not been ready and had not appreciated the risks of pregnancy and disease (S. L. Rosenthal et al., 1997).

Advise. On the other hand, most parents, mental health organizations, and religious groups advise adolescents not to engage in sex too early and to wait until they are more emotionally mature and involved in an intimate relationship (Rabasca, 1999). Researchers advise more parent–teen discussions of sexual behavior because one study found that 50% of mothers whose 14-year-olds were sexually active mistakenly believed their teens were still virgins (R. Blum, 2002). In addition, teens often lack basic information about potential problems, as indicated by 30% of teens who had oral sex but were unaware that this activity could result in sexually transmitted diseases (J. Davis, 2003).

Approach. Trying to explain sexual development in teenagers and the complicated relationship between sex and love has given rise to the BioPsychoSocial model.

The *BioPsychoSocial approach* views adolescent development as a process that occurs simultaneously on many levels and includes hormonal, neural, sexual, cognitive, social, cultural, and personality changes that interact and influence each other (Herdt, 2004; D. L. Tolman et al., 2003).

According to the BioPsychoSocial approach, sexual behavior cannot be discussed independently of hormonal, cognitive, personality, and emotional factors. For example, sex hormones trigger important physical changes but also influence mood and behavioral changes, such as perceiving peers as romantically attractive (J. Schwab et al., 2001). Finding someone romantically attractive naturally leads to seeking a more intimate relationship, which raises the question of becoming sexually active.

Sexual activity of teenage boys and girls is about equal.

Decisions about Becoming Sexually Active

In the late 1980s, 56% of high-school students reported engaging in sexual activity (intercourse), but in the early 2000s, the percentage had dropped to 46% (CDC, 2004). Although the early 2000s marked a decrease in teenage sexual activity, researchers were surprised to find that about 20% of 14-year-olds were sexually active (L. Ali & Scelfo, 2002). In the late 1980s and 1990s, teenage boys reported earlier and more sexual activity than teenage girls, but by the early 2000s, gender differences no longer existed (CDC, 2004; Wells & Twenge, 2005).

Between the late 1980s and early 2000s, the number of teenagers who reported NOT having sexual intercourse rose about 10% (CDC, 2004). The reasons teenagers gave for abstaining from sexual activity included having caring parents, feeling unready, wanting to have some control over their futures, participating in abstinence programs, and having concerns about sexually transmitted diseases. As one teenager said, "Just look at everything—TV, movies. The culture today makes it seem OK to have sex whenever, however or with whoever you want. I just disagree with that"(L. Ali & Scelfo, 2002, p. 63). Besides media influences, many teenagers report that they constantly have to deal with peer pressures to be sexually active or else be considered strange. Teenagers who do become sexually active face a number of potential problems.

Problems. One problem is that the age at which teenagers actually engage in sexual activity is earlier than what they think is the best age. Although the median age for first intercourse was 17.4 years for girls, about half the girls (48%) said that the best age for first intercourse is between 18 and 20 years old. Teenage girls report that sex and pregnancy are the number one issues they face today. However, curiosity, media coverage, and peer pressure play a large role in motivating sexual activity (L. Ali & Scelfo, 2002). Although puberty prepares teenage bodies for engaging in sexual behavior, the majority of teenagers (especially girls) report not being emotionally, psychologically, or mentally prepared to deal with strong sexual desires and feelings.

Another problem is that only 31% of boys and 21% of girls who become sexually active report using contraceptives every time they have intercourse (CDC, 2004). In turn, this can lead to two other major problems: the spread of sexually transmitted diseases, including AIDS, and unwanted pregnancies. Researchers recommend that discussions with trusting and supportive adults can go a long way in helping teenagers make decisions about engaging or not engaging in sexual activity (Kreinin, 2003).

We'll next examine a number of mental and psychological changes that accompany the teenage years.

B. Cognitive & Emotional Changes

Why is Branndi's head spinning?

When most adults and especially current parents of teenagers hear the word *adolescence,* they often get a pained look as they remember a time full of problems. Until the early 1990s, researchers believed that adolescence was primarily a time of storm and stress, of intense feelings, huge mood swings, and irritating parental conflicts. However, current research paints a different picture of adolescence. Yes, storm and stress and intense mood swings and parental conflicts are likely to occur during adolescence, but they come and go and not all adolescents have a terrible time (Arnett, 2000a). Current research also finds that along with the storm and stress, adolescence is a time for tremendous growth in emotional, social, and cognitive development as teenagers go from childhood to adulthood (Lerner & Galambos, 1998).

We have already discussed the dramatic physical changes and sexual feelings that occur during puberty and the problems adolescents have in deciding what to do with their newly developed sexual maturity. Along with sexual maturity, adolescents develop new ways of thinking and reasoning, which represents a major change in cognitive development.

Cognitive development **refers to how a person perceives, thinks, and gains an understanding of his or her world through the interaction and influence of genetic and learned factors.**

"I believe God lets awful things happen to teach us a lesson."

For example, at the beginning of this module we told you that, during adolescence, Branndi (left photo) would undergo major changes in reasoning and thinking. For example, here are some of her thoughts about the condition of the world: "I don't believe in the Pledge of Allegiance. I don't say it, because they're telling a lie—'liberty and justice for all.'. . . My first step into politics will be mayor. I write lots of letters to Tom Bradley [former mayor of Los Angeles] about things like animal rights. But he just sent me, you know, one of those typed things. I don't think it's right . . . I'm very outspoken. I worry about things—sex, rape, and stuff like that . . . I believe in God. I believe God lets awful things happen to teach us a lesson . . ." (*Los Angeles Times,* December 22, 1991, p. E-13).

There's no question that 12-year-old Branndi is full of abstract thinking, is very outspoken, and holds absolute opinions on a variety of concrete and abstract issues. Her views illustrate one of the most significant changes in cognitive development during adolescence, which is the ability to think about abstract issues, such as the meaning of liberty, justice, and God. This kind of abstract thinking indicates that Branndi is entering Piaget's fourth cognitive stage, called formal operations, which marks the beginning of thinking and reasoning like an adult.

Piaget's Cognitive Stages: Continued

What's new about a teenager's thinking?

As you may remember from Module 17, Piaget's theory of cognitive development is that we all go through four distinct **cognitive stage,** (left figure). As we go through each cognitive stage, we acquire a new and distinct kind of reasoning and thinking that is different from and more advanced than the reasoning abilities we possessed at our previous stage. We discussed Piaget's four cognitive stages in Module 17, but we'll review stage 4, the formal operations stage, because it begins in adolescence.

STAGE 4: FORMAL OPERATIONS

The fact that 12-year-old Branndi is using abstract concepts, such as liberty, justice, animal rights, and God, is good evidence that she is entering the formal operations stage.

The *formal operations stage,* the last of Piaget's four cognitive stages, extends from about age 12 through adulthood. During this stage, adolescents and adults develop the

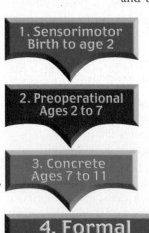

1. Sensorimotor
Birth to age 2

2. Preoperational
Ages 2 to 7

3. Concrete
Ages 7 to 11

4. Formal
Ages 12 thru adulthood

abilities to think about abstract or hypothetical concepts, to consider an issue from another's viewpoint, and to solve cognitive problems in a logical way.

Having the ability to think about and discuss abstract concepts means that adolescents can critically consider their beliefs, attitudes, values, and goals as well as discuss a wide range of topics important to their becoming adults. For instance, when adolescents were asked about their major concerns, tops on their lists were getting married, having friends, getting a good job, and doing well in school. Each of these concerns involves the ability to discuss abstract concepts, which is a cognitive skill that they are learning at the formal operations stage.

"My major concerns are doing well in school and having friends."

One of the interesting questions about adolescents is why some seem so slow to develop thinking and reasoning skills that prepare them to deal with typical problems and stressful situations that occur during adolescence. For example, many adolescents report that they were not prepared to have sex but it just happened, or they fight continually with their parents, or they do stupid things like drink and then drive. Researchers have only recently discovered that the answer involves the developing adolescent's brain.

Brain Development: Reason and Emotion

A difficult problem for parents is dealing with seemingly irresponsible or impulsive bad behaviors or decisions of their teenagers. Parents believe their teens should know better, and until recently, researchers thought that teenagers should know better because they believed that teenage brains were fully developed by puberty. However, new findings indicate that teenage brains are still developing, especially those areas involved in clear thinking and reasoning (Crews, 2006).

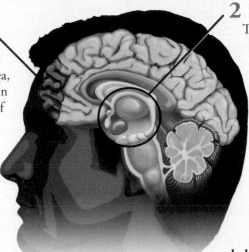

1 Prefrontal cortex: executive functions

Every company has an executive officer who is responsible for making decisions, day-to-day planning, organizing, and thinking about the future. Similarly, our brains have an executive area, called the *prefrontal cortex*, which is involved in similar functions and is located near the front of the brain (p. 75) (right figure).

Researchers used brain scans (p. 70) to take pictures of neural growth and development of teenage brains. Unlike previous beliefs that an adolescent's prefrontal cortex was fully developed, researchers actually found that the adolescent's prefrontal cortex was still in the process of development and thus did not yet have the ability to think, reason, decide, or plan like an adult (Luna, 2006).

Vulnerability. Beginning about age 11 and continuing into young adulthood, the brain undergoes major "rewiring" and reorganization and is especially vulnerable to traumatic adolescent experiences, such as being physically or sexually abused or bullied, feeling depressed, and abusing drugs. Recent research suggests that alcohol causes more injury to teenage brains than it does to adult brains. These kinds of traumatic experiences can interfere with the adolescent's brain developing a healthy and reasonable executive center (Crews, 2001, 2006).

"As executive officer, I'm responsible for thinking, planning, and making decisions."

Risk-taking behavior. The finding that executive functions in the adolescent's brain are not yet fully developed helps explain many of the adolescent's seemingly irresponsible behaviors. For example, adolescents have about twice the rate of adults in transmitting venereal diseases because only 50% think to use condoms; they have 20 times the rate of automobile accidents as adults because adolescents don't worry about drinking, driving, and speeding; and they have the lowest rate for using seat belts (50% do not) of any age group (Irwin et al., 2002). The previous explanation for why adolescents engaged in risk-taking behavior was they felt invulnerable and had no fear of injury. Researchers now report that the underlying explanation for adolescents' tendency to take risks is the executive manager of their behaviors, their prefrontal cortex, is underdeveloped, which means they simply don't have the neural bases to analyze risks and make intelligent decisions (Luna, 2006). We'll discuss how this brain research applies to teen driving in the Critical Thinking section (p. 430).

Another reason adolescents have a tendency to engage in risk-taking behaviors involves a different part of their brain that's involved in emotional behaviors.

2 Limbic system: emotional behaviors

Teenagers are known to act impulsively, such as getting a tongue pierced on a dare, and experience wide mood swings. As one parent said, "It's hot and cold, nasty and nice. One minute loving me, one minute hating me." What parents don't realize is that a teenager's prefrontal cortex, which acts like an executive officer, is not fully developed, so an adolescent has less control over his or her emotional and impulsive behaviors, which involve other brain structures.

Moody, emotional, and impulsive behaviors. As shown in the left figure, in the center of the brain is a circle of structures that make up our emotional brain, called the limbic system (p. 80). The *limbic system* is involved in a wide range of emotional behaviors, such being ecstatic over getting a date, feeling depressed when failing a test, and getting angry when insulted. Research found that sex hormones (testosterone in males and estrogen in females), which are secreted in abundance during puberty, increase the growth of limbic system structures (amygdala, hippocampus). Researchers believe the increased structure and function of the limbic system account for a teenager's irritability as well as the increase in aggressiveness in adolescent males (Giedd, 1999; Yurgelun-Todd, 2004).

"I was dared to get my lip and nose pierced."

Conclusion. Researchers are finding that the adolescent's brain has an underdeveloped prefrontal cortex, or executive officer, but a well-developed limbic system or emotional center (L. Steinberg, 2004). This combination of a weak executive officer and a strong emotional center results in many of the unthinking and irritating behaviors of adolescents, such as taking risks, switching moods, and acting impulsively. As one researcher summarized, "Good judgment is learned but you can't learn it if you don't have the necessary hardware (neural development)" (Yurgelun-Todd, 1999, p. 48).

"One minute I'm laughing and the next I'm crying."

An adolescent's lack of a strong executive officer (prefrontal cortex) will also affect moral judgment, which is our next topic.

B. Cognitive & Emotional Changes

Would you steal to save a friend?

Suppose your best friend is dying of cancer. You hear of a chemist who has just discovered a new wonder drug that could save her life. The chemist is selling the drug for $5,000, many times more than it cost him to make. You try to borrow the full amount but can get only $2,500. You ask the chemist to sell you the drug for $2,500 and he refuses. Later that night, you break into the chemist's laboratory and steal the drug. Should you have done that? Did you decide that it would be all right to steal the drug to save the life of your dying friend? If you did, how did you justify your moral decision? Lawrence Kohlberg (1984) and associates presented similar dilemmas to individuals who were asked to explain their moral decisions. On the basis of such studies, Kohlberg explained the development of moral reasoning in terms of three levels.

Three Levels of Moral Reasoning

Level 1 Self-Interest

The *preconventional level,* which represents Kohlberg's lowest level of moral reasoning, has two stages. At stage 1, moral decisions are based primarily on fear of punishment or the need to be obedient; at stage 2, moral reasoning is guided most by satisfying one's self-interest, which may involve making bargains.

For example, individuals at stage 1 might say that you should not steal the drug because you'll be caught and go to jail. Individuals at stage 2 might say that you can steal the drug and save your best friend, but in return you'll have to give up some freedom by going to jail. Most children are at the preconventional level.

Level 2 Social Approval

The *conventional level,* which represents an intermediate level of moral reasoning, also has two stages. At stage 3, moral decisions are guided most by conforming to the standards of others we value; at stage 4, moral reasoning is determined most by conforming to laws of society.

Individuals at stage 3 might say that you should steal the drug since that is what your family would expect you to do. Individuals at stage 4 might say that you should not steal the drug because of what would happen to society if everybody took what they needed. Many adolescents and adults are at this level.

Level 3 Abstract Ideas

The *postconventional level,* which represents the highest level of moral reasoning, has one stage. At stage 5, moral decisions are made after carefully thinking about all the alternatives and striking a balance between human rights and laws of society.

Individuals at stage 5 might say that one should steal the drug because life is more important than money. (Stage 6, which appeared in earlier versions of Kohlberg's theory, has been omitted in later versions because too few people had reached it.) Some, but not all, adults reach the postconventional level.

Kohlberg's theory has two distinct features. First, he classifies moral reasoning into three distinct levels—preconventional, conventional, and postconventional. Second, he suggests that everyone progresses through the levels in order, from lowest to highest. However, not everyone reaches the higher levels of moral development.

Next, we'll evaluate Kohlberg's theory and its present status.

Evaluating Kohlberg's Theory

Stages. Kohlberg hypothesized that everyone goes through the five stages in sequence, with no skipping of stages. Researchers reviewed 45 Kohlberg-type studies conducted in 27 cultures and concluded that, as Kohlberg assumed, we go through the stages in order but not everyone reaches the higher stages (Damon, 1999; Helwig, 1997).

Thinking versus behaving. One criticism of Kohlberg's moral stages is that they present different kinds of moral thinking that may or may not predict how an individual actually behaves. Thus, Kohlberg focused on development of moral thinking rather than on development of moral behavior in real-life situations (Damon, 1999).

Another criticism, made by Carol Gilligan (1982), is that in making moral decisions, women use more of a *care orientation,* which is based on caring, having concern for others, and avoiding hurt, while men use more of a *justice orientation,* which is based on law, equality, and individual rights. However, there is little support for Gilligan's distinction, and recent reviewers have concluded that both men and women use a mixture of care and justice orientations, depending on the particular moral situation (Jaffee & Hyde, 2000).

Brain or neural factors. Kohlberg constructed his theory before researchers were able to study the structures and functions of the living brain (pp. 70–71). We have explained that the teenage brain has an underdeveloped prefrontal cortex, which results in an underdeveloped executive area and limits a teenager's ability to think, reason, and make intelligent decisions needed for moral reasoning (Luna, 2006). Also supporting the role of the prefrontal cortex in moral reasoning are findings that individuals who had their prefrontal cortex damaged in infancy had difficulty learning the normal social and moral rules in childhood and adolescence. As adults, these individuals showed no guilt or remorse for their extremely bad behaviors and could not get along in social situations (A. Damasio, 1999). More recently, researchers identified different brain areas involved in moral decisions: Making *impersonal moral decisions,* such as keeping the money found in a stranger's wallet, involved areas associated with retrieving information (p. 242); in comparison, making *personal moral decisions,* such as keeping the money found in a fellow worker's wallet, involved areas associated with emotions. Researchers concluded that in making moral decisions, especially those that involve personal concerns (abortion, death penalty, assisted suicide), we use not only reasoning and logic but also our gut feelings or emotions (J. D. Greene et al., 2004).

Moral reasoning and cognitive development are also influenced by the kinds of rules that parents use, which is our next topic.

Were your parents easy or strict?

During adolescence, teenagers experience several major changes in cognitive and emotional development. These changes are influenced by both biological factors, such as brain development, and environmental factors, such as the influence of peers and parents. For instance, if someone asked how your parents raised you, would you answer that they were strict, supportive, easy, or hard? It turns out that parents' rules, standards, and codes of conduct influence how a teenager develops a sense of independence and achievement (Baumrind, 1991). We'll discuss how parental rules can affect the cognitive and emotional development of teenagers.

Personal Experiences

When teenagers were asked how they responded to their parents' rules, here's what Ida and Chris replied (photos below).

Ida, age 17. "I live in a strict Italian home. Sometimes my parents are really, really great, but their rules for me are absolutely ridiculous. So I get around them. My friends will tell you I'm a good kid. I don't drink. I don't do drugs. I don't smoke. But my parents think that, if I've gone out on a Friday night and I ask to go out Saturday, too, I'm asking for the world . . . So I lie a lot . . . A lot of people know I do this, but nobody yells at me for it, because I'm a good kid, and my parents' rules are so ridiculous."

Chris, age 18. "My parents never make their punishments stick. Like, I'll get my Jeep taken away for a week, and I'll get it back within six hours. Why? Because my parents hate to see their kids unhappy, and I know it, so I play right into it. They'll punish me by not letting me go out, so I'll walk around the house, slam the door occasionally, this, that . . . and after awhile this just plays on them, and they feel bad, and they let me out" (*Parade* magazine, July 14, 1991, pp. 6–7. Reprinted with permission from Parade. Copyright © 1991).

Ida says, "I had to get around my parents' strict rules."

Chris says, "I acted unhappy so my parents gave in."

After reading these two descriptions, you can see that Ida's parents are the opposite of Chris's. How do such different styles of parenting affect adolescents' development? To answer this question, psychologist Diana Baumrind (1991, 1993) has been carrying out a series of longitudinal studies on parent–child and parent–adolescent interactions. She has identified a number of parenting styles that are associated with different kinds of adolescent development.

Different Styles of Parenting

We'll focus on three of Baumrind's parenting styles: authoritarian parents, authoritative parents, and permissive parents.

Authoritarian parents **attempt to shape, control, and evaluate the behavior and attitudes of their children in accordance with a set standard of conduct, usually an absolute standard that comes from religious or respected authorities.**

For these parents, obedience is a virtue, and they punish and use harsh discipline to keep the adolescent in line with their rules. This parenting style seems to describe Ida's parents. Boys from authoritarian families are found to be relatively hostile, while girls are found to be relatively dependent and submissive. This description fits Ida, who admits to problems with being independent.

Authoritative parents **attempt to direct their children's activities in a rational and intelligent way. They are supportive, loving, and committed, encourage verbal give-and-take, and discuss their rules and policies with their children.**

Authoritative parents value being expressive and independent but are also demanding. The children of such parents tend to be competent. In addition, girls are achievement-oriented and boys are friendly and cooperative.

Permissive parents **are less controlling and behave with a nonpunishing and accepting attitude toward their children's impulses, desires, and actions; they consult with their children about policy decisions, make few demands, and tend to use reason rather than direct power.**

This parenting style seems to describe Chris's parents. Girls with such parents are less socially assertive, and both boys and girls are less achievement-oriented.

Effects of Parenting Styles

Each of the three parenting styles has different costs and benefits. Authoritarian parents, who are very demanding, benefit by preventing adolescent behavioral problems but at some cost to adolescents, who tend to be more conforming and have lower self-esteem. Authoritative parents, who state their values clearly, benefit by having loving and supportive parent–teenager interactions, which further benefit their teenagers, who tend to be more friendly, cooperative, and achievement-oriented (Hickman et al., 2000; Vazsonyi et al., 2003). Permissive parents benefit by having to make fewer demands and enforcing fewer rules but at some cost to adolescents, who may be less socially assertive and less achievement-oriented than adolescents with authoritative parents (Baumrind, 1991, 1993). Thus, different parenting styles can have significantly different effects on the cognitive, social, and personality development of adolescents.

Which is better, being too easy or too strict?

Even though parenting styles influence adolescent development, new research finds that siblings may have the strongest influence on who we become in the long term. This isn't too surprising as we spend every day of our childhood with our siblings and they remain in our lives long after our parents leave us. Through all of the sibling conflict, we learn how to negotiate, compromise, and maintain lasting relationships, which can help us to have successful adult relationships, such as those with our spouse/partner and colleagues (Kluger, 2006b).

B. Cognitive & Emotional Changes

What are the major changes?

In the United States, there are about 30 million youths (ages 10 to 17) who are currently going through adolescence, a period of considerable physical,

There are 30 million of us.

neurological (brain), cognitive, and emotional change. Although adolescence is a time of some storm and stress, it is also a time for tremendous personal growth. We'll review some of the major changes that occur during adolescence.

1 GIRLS DURING PUBERTY

Puberty sets off a surge in physical growth, which is marked by an increase in height that starts on average at 9.6 years. Puberty triggers a physiological process that results in a girl's reaching *female sexual maturity,* which involves primarily the onset of *menarche,* or the first menstrual period, at an average age of 12.5 years. The onset of menarche is triggered by the *hypothalamus,* which releases a hormone called *kisspeptin* that helps to stimulate the *pituitary gland* to produce hormones (Kotulak, 2006). These hormones stimulate the ovaries to produce female hormones including *estrogen,* which stimulates the development of both primary and secondary sexual characteristics, such as development of pubic hair and breasts.

2 BOYS DURING PUBERTY

Puberty triggers an increase in physical growth, especially height, generally at 13 or 14 years of age. Puberty starts a physiological process that results in a boy's reaching *male sexual maturity,* which includes growth of the genital organs—testes and penis—and production of sperm at 12–14 years of age. The increase in genital growth and the production of sperm are triggered by the *hypothalamus,* which stimulates the male pituitary gland. The pituitary in turn triggers the testes to increase production of *testosterone,* which is the major male hormone and stimulates the growth of genital organs and the development of secondary sexual characteristics, such as growth of pubic and facial hair, development of muscles, and a change (deepening) in voice.

3 SEXUAL MATURITY

In the late 1980s, 56% of high-school students reported engaging in sexual activity (intercourse), but in the early 2000s, the percentage had dropped to 46% (CDC, 2004). Although the early 2000s marked a decrease in teenage sexual activity, there were still about 20% of 14-year-olds who were sexually active (L. Ali & Scelfo, 2002). In the late 1980s and 1990s, teenage boys reported earlier and more sexual activity than teenage girls, but by the early 2000s, gender differences no longer existed (Wells & Twenge, 2005). Between the late 1980s and early 2000s, the number of teenagers who reported NOT having sexual intercourse rose about 10% (CDC, 2004).

4 PIAGET'S STAGES: CONTINUED

1. Sensorimotor
2. Preoperational
3. Concrete
4. Formal

According to Piaget's theory, children pass through four different cognitive stages—(1) sensorimotor, (2) preoperational, (3) concrete operations, and (4) formal operations—in that order but at different rates. With each stage, the child adds a new and qualitatively different kind of thinking or reasoning skill that helps the child make better sense of the world. Adolescents are entering Piaget's fourth stage, called the formal operations stage, which begins at about age 12 and extends through adulthood. During this stage, adolescents develop the abilities to think about abstract or hypothetical concepts, to consider an issue from another's viewpoint, and to solve cognitive problems in a logical way. These cognitive abilities are very useful during adulthood.

5 BRAIN DEVELOPMENT: REASON & EMOTION

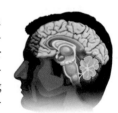

Researchers are finding that the adolescent's brain has an underdeveloped prefrontal cortex or executive officer but a well-developed limbic system or emotional center (L. Steinberg, 2004). This combination of a weak executive officer and a strong emotional center results in many of the unthinking, irresponsible, and irritating behaviors of adolescents. For example, the lack of a strong executive officer (prefrontal cortex) explains why adolescents engage in risky behaviors, switch moods suddenly, and act impulsively. As one researcher summarized, "Good judgment is learned but you can't learn it if you don't have the necessary hardware (neural development)" (Yurgelun-Todd, 1999, p. 48).

6 KOHLBERG'S THEORY OF MORAL REASONING

Kohlberg hypothesized that everyone goes through three levels of moral reasoning. Level 1, the preconventional level, involves stage 1 (fear of punishment) and stage 2 (self-interest). Level 2, the conventional level, involves stage 3 (conforming to the standards of others) and stage 4 (conforming to the standards of society). Level 3, the postconventional level, has only stage 5 (balancing human rights and society's laws). There is support for Kohlberg's assumption that individuals progress through the stages in order and that not everyone reaches the higher stages (Damon, 1999). Since Kohlberg's time, researchers have found several brain or neural factors (prefrontal cortex, emotional areas) that play a role in making moral decisions.

We'll discuss some of the cognitive changes that make people realize that they're not kids anymore.

Beyond Adolescence

In your 20s and 30s, cognitive abilities are usually at their peak.

In your 40s and 50s, memory problems usually begin and continue.

In your 60s, 70s, and 80s, there's slowing in cognitive processes.

As teenagers enter their 20s, they face a number of major changes, such as deciding about going to college, leaving home for perhaps the first time, choosing a career or major, entering the job market, and searching for a serious relationship (Arnett, 2000b). The 20s are a time when executive abilities (thinking, planning, deciding, remembering) are sharp, partly because the brain's prefrontal cortex is now more fully developed. Cognitive or executive abilities usually remain sharp through the 30s. But beginning in the 40s and continuing through the 50s and 60s, there is a gradual decline in some cognitive abilities, especially in the ability to remember things. We'll discuss some changes in cognitive abilities as we age.

Changes in Cognitive Speed

Why is my golf game slowing down?

From about ages 20 to 40, cognitive skills remain relatively stable. However, between 40 and 80, there is a general slowing of some cognitive processes. Beginning in the late 50s, there is a slowing of three cognitive processes:

1 There is a slowing in *processing speed,* which is the rate at which we encode information into long-term memory or recall or retrieve information from long-term memory.

2 There is a slowing in *perceptual speed,* which is the rate at which we can identify a particular sensory stimulus.

3 There is a slowing in *reaction time,* which is the rate at which we respond (see, hear, move) to some stimulus.

This slowing in processing, perceiving, and reacting partly explains why older people react more slowly when driving a car or playing golf and are slower to make decisions or understand and follow instructions. For example, partly because of the slowdown in these processes, there is a professional golf tour for seniors only (over 50); they can no longer keep up with younger golfers.

Besides a slowing in cognitive speed, older adults experience a problem in remembering things.

Changes in Memory

Beginning in the 40s and continuing into old age, most people complain about not remembering things. Researchers concluded that older adults have no trouble remembering the big picture (name of a movie) but do forget many of the small details (who played the starring role). In comparison, young adults easily remember the big picture plus all the details (Schacter, 2001). So as people move into their 50s, 60s, and 70s, their complaints are true: They do forget details (names, places, groceries) that may be bothersome but are usually unimportant.

Am I losing my memory?

Memory differences. Differences between 20-year-olds and 50-year-olds are that young adults excel at encoding (storing) and recalling vast amounts of detail but are not as good at making sense of what all the details mean. In comparison, mature adults excel at making sense of information but forget much of the detail.

Brain changes. Researchers report that decreases in memory skills result from the slowing down of memory abilities, reasoning processes, and focusing of attention. Brain scans show that these kinds of problems, which occur throughout normal aging, result from the normal loss of brain cells in the prefrontal cortex (Milham et al., 2002).

Memory-enhancing products. Americans spend billions on memory-enhancing products, such as a supplement called ginkgo biloba, which researchers found did NOT improve memory or concentration in healthy adults (Solomon et al., 2002). Memory experts advise the best way to combat age-related memory difficulties is to exercise physically (have a regular exercise program) and mentally (engage in cognitive activities like reading, doing crosswords) (G. Cohen, 2006).

Next, we'll learn about how the brain changes for the better as we age.

Resiliency

Recent findings indicate that as we age, our brains become more flexible and adaptable. Though brain cells may lose processing speed, their connections to other brain cells multiply and they form more meaningful neural connections as a result of more life experience. Also, the brain's left and right hemispheres become better integrated during middle age. This means that brains of older adults can compensate for age-related cognitive declines by expanding their neural network to include both brain hemispheres (G. Cohen, 2006). For instance, by using brain scans (pp. 70–71), researchers found that older adults who used both brain hemispheres during a memory task performed better than older adults who used only one brain hemisphere (Cabeza et al., 2002). As brains become more flexible and adaptable, they also manage emotions better.

Emotions

Older adults have a "positivity bias," which means they pay less attention to negative information and more to positive information. Research found that the part of the brain responsible for strong negative emotions (amygdala) becomes less active with age. This focus on the positive explains why older adults have better mental health than younger adults, who mostly focus on negative emotions (Cabeza, 2006; Carstensen, 2006).

Next, we turn to changes in personality and social development.

C. Personality & Social Changes

Definition

Who am I? We have discussed many of the major changes that occur during adolescence. One more change is that adolescents develop a sense of who they are, which involves personality and social development.

Personality and *social development* refer to how a person develops a sense of self or self-identity, develops relationships with others, and develops the skills useful in social interactions.

Like it or not, this is the real me!

For example, the teenager in the left photo shows her independence and what she believes is her real identity by having a very noticeable hairstyle and piercings.

Personal identity or *self-identity* refers to how we describe ourselves and includes our values, goals, traits, perceptions, interests, and motivations.

Personal identity grows and changes as adolescents acquire many new values, goals, beliefs, and interests (Bandura, 1999). A major influence on the kind of identity teenagers develop is how they feel about themselves, which is called self-esteem.

Development of Self-Esteem

What influences self-esteem? Throughout this module, we have discussed 12-year-old Branndi, who, like other teenagers, has many beliefs and goals, such as being proud to be Black and female, having high hopes for her future, and wanting to be a role model. How Branndi perceives herself, which is called self-esteem, has a significant influence on her developing personality.

Self-esteem is how much we like ourselves and how much we value our self-worth, importance, attractiveness, and social competence.

I'm proud to be Black and female.

For example, in adolescents, self-esteem is influenced by a number of factors, including how *physically attractive* and how *socially competent* they appear to their peers (DuBois et al., 2000). As teenagers develop sexually mature bodies, they wonder how physically attractive they are; as teenagers begin dating, they wonder how socially skilled they are. Researchers measure changes in adolescents' self-esteem by using longitudinal studies that begin in adolescence and continue through adulthood, such as measuring self-esteem at ages 14, 18, and 23. We'll discuss three different patterns of self-esteem development in adolescents (M. A. Zimmerman et al., 1997).

High Self-Esteem—develop and maintain high levels. A large percentage of adolescents (about 60%) develop and maintain a strong sense of self-esteem through junior high school. These individuals do well in school, develop rewarding friendships, participate in social activities, and are described as cheerful, assertive, emotionally warm, and unwilling to give up if frustrated.

Low Self-Esteem—develop and maintain low levels. A small percentage of adolescents (about 15%) develop and maintain a chronically low sense of self-esteem that continues through junior high school. These adolescents usually have continuing personal and social problems (shy, lonely, depressed) that have been present for some time and contribute to this low self-esteem.

Reversals—reverse levels. A moderate percentage of adolescents (about 25%) show dramatic reversals in self-esteem, either from high to low or from low to high. For example, some boys change from being stern, unemotional, and lacking social skills into being open and expressive. Researchers think that reversals in self-esteem may result from changes in peer groups, personal attractiveness, or parental relationships.

Next, we'll describe some influences on the development of self-esteem.

Forces shaping self-esteem. The development of self-esteem in adolescents involves many factors, such as physical attractiveness, acceptance by peers, parental support, media influences, and academic ability (Connor et al., 2004). However, boys and girls respond to different forces.

In girls, self-esteem is especially dependent on body image and perception of parental support (Polce-Lynch et al., 2001). In boys, self-esteem is especially dependent on looking cool in public, which means not letting stress or anxiety make them look bad (Block & Robins, 1993). The majority of studies show that girls report lower self-esteem than boys during adolescence, and some research finds that over time girls tend to report even lower levels of self-esteem while boys are more likely to show increasing or high levels (Connor et al., 2004).

Importance of self-esteem. Self-esteem is one of the most frequently studied characteristics in psychology because it has been linked to important positive and negative outcomes. For example, having high self-esteem is associated with positive outcomes, such as being cheerful and happy, having healthy social relationships, and promoting personal adjustment, while having low self-esteem is associated with negative outcomes, such as depression, anxiety, antisocial behavior, and poor personal adjustment (S. L. Murray, 2005; Trzesniewski et al., 2006). Generally, self-esteem is not very stable in childhood, is somewhat stable in adolescence, is much more stable in young adulthood, and becomes less stable again in midlife and old age (Trzesniewski et al., 2003). Thus, self-esteem is important because it influences many aspects of one's personality (Roberts et al., 2002). We'll discuss all aspects and theories of personality in Modules 19 and 20.

There's nothing wrong with us!

One theory of how self-esteem and personal identity develop is found in Erikson's psychosocial stages.

Adulthood: Erikson's Psychosocial Stages

What will I have to deal with?

At the beginning of this module, we described how Susan went from teenage prom queen to middle-aged adult. Along the way, she dealt with dating, going to college, getting married, having children, getting divorced, finding a job, and losing her son. How dealing with these life events might affect Susan's social and personality development was something that Erik Erikson (1982) tried to explain. As you may remember from Module 17, Erikson divided life into eight *psychosocial stages,* each of which contained a unique psychosocial conflict, such as intimacy versus isolation. If Susan successfully solved each psychosocial conflict, she would develop a healthy personality; if unsuccessful in solving these conflicts, she might develop an unhealthy personality and future psychological problems. In Module 17, we discussed Erikson's stages related to childhood; now, we'll discuss stages related to adolescence and adulthood.

What happened to all my dreams?

Stage 5 Identity versus Role Confusion

Period. Adolescence (12–20)

Potential conflict. Adolescents need to leave behind the carefree, irresponsible, and impulsive behaviors of childhood and develop the more purposeful, planned, and responsible behaviors of adulthood. If adolescents successfully resolve this problem, they will develop a healthy and confident sense of *identity.* If they are unsuccessful in resolving the problem, they will experience *role confusion,* which results in their having low self-esteem and becoming unstable or socially withdrawn.

Stage 6 Intimacy versus Isolation

Period. Young adulthood (20–40)

Potential conflict. Young adulthood is a time for finding intimacy by developing loving and meaningful relationships. On the positive side, we can find *intimacy* in caring relationships. On the negative side, without intimacy we will have a painful feeling of *isolation*, and our relationships will be impersonal.

Stage 7 Generativity versus Stagnation

Period. Middle adulthood (40–65)

Potential conflict. Middle adulthood is a time for helping the younger generation develop worthwhile lives. On the positive side, we can achieve *generativity* through raising our own children. If we do not have children of our own, we can achieve generativity through close relationships with children of friends or relatives. Generativity can also be achieved through mentoring at work and helping others. On the negative side, a lack of involvement leads to a feeling of *stagnation,* of having done nothing for the younger generation.

Stage 8 Integrity versus Despair

Period. Late adulthood (65 and older)

Potential conflict. Late adulthood is a time for reflecting on and reviewing how we met previous challenges and lived our lives. On the positive side, if we can look back and feel content about how we lived and what we accomplished, we will have a feeling of satisfaction or *integrity.* On the negative side, if we reflect and see a series of crises, problems, and bad experiences, we will have a feeling of regret and *despair.*

Conclusions. Erikson believed that achieving a personally satisfying identity was the very heart and soul of an adolescent's development. As adolescents developed into adults and reached middle adulthood (stage 7), Erikson described a shift from concerns about identity to concerns about being productive, creative, and nurturing (Coles, 2000).

Researchers have found evidence that we do go through a sequence of psychosocial stages and that how we handle conflicts at earlier stages affects our personality and social development at later stages (Van Manen & Whitbourne, 1997).

Personality Change

How much will I change?

When Mick Jagger, lead singer of the Rolling Stones, was in his early 20s (below), he boasted, "I'd rather be dead than sing 'Satisfaction' when I'm 45." Now at age 63, Jagger (right) has changed his tune; he and the Stones recently completed a world tour and sang "Satisfaction" dozens of times (L. Ali, 2005; Pareles, 2005). As Jagger found out, some of the things that we say and do at 20 may seem stupid at 60. The differences in Jagger at 20 and 60 raise an interesting question: How much do our personalities change and how much do they remain the same?

Researchers answer such questions with longitudinal studies, which measure personality development across time in the same group of individuals. One study found that from adolescence to middle adulthood, individuals became more trusting and intimate and developed a better sense of control and identity. Researchers also found that possessing certain personality traits as a

In his 20s, he said he'd rather be dead than singing at 45.

Now in his 60s, Jagger is still touring and singing.

young adult (early 20s) led to developing related traits in middle adulthood (middle 40s). For example, individuals with a high level of identity in their early 20s showed more independence, warmth, and compassion later on in their mid-40s (Vandewater et al., 1997). From these kinds of longitudinal studies researchers draw these conclusions: First, from the end of adolescence through middle adulthood, there are less dramatic but still continuing changes in personality traits, such as becoming more trusting and intimate. Second, possessing certain personality traits in early adulthood is the foundation for developing related traits later on (Roberts et al., 2002). Third, adults appear to pass through psychosocial stages and face conflicts in personality development similar to those proposed by Erikson (Van Manen & Whitbourne, 1997). We'll discuss personality more fully in Modules 19 and 20.

One of the major social and personality changes that women and men go through involves gender roles.

D. Gender Roles, Love & Relationships

Why couldn't women be firefighters?

As boys and girls grow to become men and women, they acquire a set of behavioral and cognitive rules called gender roles.

Gender roles are traditional or stereotypic behaviors, attitudes, values, and personality traits that society says are how males and females are to think and behave.

You can become aware of gender roles by noticing how differently males and females dress, behave, think, and express emotions. For example, gender roles played a major part in whether firefighters could be women. For as long as people could remember, firefighters had always been men because they were considered strong and cool in the face of danger, while women were considered weak and nervous. In the

Women fought for 20 years to become firefighters.

1970s, when women applied to become firefighters, a local paper warned against the city's "futile exercise in trying to fit women into jobs which common sense tells us are best filled by men." Only after 20 years of heated political and legal battles were gender roles changed and women, found to be strong and cool under pressure, were allowed to become firefighters (Kershaw, 2006).

During the past years, there have been some changes in gender roles in the United States. For example, women can now enter careers traditionally reserved for men, such as firefighters, doctors, police officers, senators, astronauts, and soldiers. Similarly, men can now enter careers traditionally reserved for women, such as nurses, single parents, and grade-school teachers. We'll discuss some of the issues surrounding current gender roles and their functions.

Current Gender Roles: U.S. and Worldwide

Each of us acquired a male or female gender role with little conscious effort or awareness, and we often don't notice the effect of gender roles on the development of our personality and social behaviors (Prentice & Carranza, 2002).

U.S. gender roles. The influence of gender roles on personality became clear when researchers asked U.S. college students to describe the traits of a typical female and a typical male. Students generally agreed the female gender role included being caring, insecure, emotional, social, and shy. In comparison, students said the male gender role included being arrogant, self-confident, aggressive, ambitious, not emotional, and dominant (Helgeson, 1994).

The influence of gender roles in the work setting is also undeniably evident. For instance, although an increasing number of women are graduating from top business schools, women fill less than 2% of chief executive jobs at Fortune 500 companies (Creswell, 2006). Also, although about half of all law degrees are granted to women, only 22% of U.S. District Court judges and 26% of Circuit Court judges are women (ABA, 2005). Researchers do not expect gender equality in high-rank positions to occur any time soon (Kinsman, 2006).

Worldwide gender roles. Not only U.S. college students but also students from around the world agreed that the male gender role included being ambitious, dominant, and independent, while the female gender role included being submissive, affectionate, and emotional (J. E. Williams & Best, 1990). Researchers concluded that differences in gender roles are clearly defined because society (family, peers, bosses, and colleagues) encourages and rewards behaviors and thoughts that match expected gender roles and discriminates against those that don't fit in (Eckes & Trautner, 2000).

Changes. In the United States, women have struggled to broaden their gender role by assuming traits, behaviors, and occupations traditionally associated with the male gender role. Although women are trying to assume some of the traits traditionally associated with the male gender role (ambitious, dominant, assertive, confident), males have been less eager to take on traits traditionally associated with the female gender role (caring, emotional, helpful, nurturing) (Twenge, 1997).

Why do gender roles develop worldwide, and what are their functions?

caring
insecure
helpful
emotional
social
shy

Gender Roles: Development and Function

The question of why gender roles develop in every culture has two different but related answers.

Evolutionary psychology theory. One answer from *evolutionary psychology theory* emphasizes genetic and biological forces and says that current gender differences are a continuation of the behaviors that evolved from early men and women who adapted these different behaviors to survive the problems of their time (Buss, 1999; Kenrick et al., 2004). According to evolutionary theory, men increased their chances for reproduction by being dominant, controlling, and aggressive. In comparison, women increased their chances of raising children by being concerned, sensitive, and nurturing.

Social role theory. A different but related answer comes from *social role theory,* which emphasizes social and cultural influences and states that gender differences between males and females arise from different divisions of labor (Eagly et al., 2004).

These two theories do not disagree but rather emphasize either biological or psychological factors. Differences in male and female gender roles do not mean one role is better or worse or that any differences may be used to condone discriminatory practices (Zemore et al., 2000).

Next, you'll see that gender roles affect our expectations about relationships.

arrogant
confident
aggressive
ambitious
unemotional
dominant

Did Susan recognize Mr. Right?

As we acquire a male or female gender role, we also develop expectations about who we would like for an intimate relationship (Fletcher, 2002; Fletcher & Simpson, 2000). For example, here are the expectations of Susan, the high-school prom queen.

"When I went away to college, I was a very sensible, logical, and levelheaded person. That's probably why the first person I dated was very much like me. We had wonderful serious talks, read poetry, discussed philosophy, but never had much passion. After we broke up, a friend of mine fixed me up

Susan's expectations changed.

with Charlie, who was a fun-loving, arrogant, cocky, abrasive basketball player and my complete opposite. We dated, got engaged, and about a year later were married. Oh, yes, I knew we were complete opposites, but I passionately loved Charlie and knew he was the one" (Wallechinsky, 1986).

Susan's first choice for someone to love was someone like her, but it didn't last. Then she chose someone very different from her and decided he was the right one to marry. After five years of marriage, she got divorced. Susan's experience brings up three issues: kinds of love, choosing a partner, and what makes a relationship a success or failure.

Kinds of Love

Which kind of love are you in?

Earlier researchers had thought love too mysterious for scientific study, but current researchers have begun to classify love into various components. As a starting point, researchers distinguish between passionate and companionate love (Rapson & Hatfield, 2005).

Passionate love involves continuously thinking about the loved one and is accompanied by warm sexual feelings and powerful emotional reactions.

Companionate love involves having trusting and tender feelings for someone whose life is closely bound up with one's own.

For example, when people fall madly in love, it's usually passionate love. When mature couples talk about enjoying each other's company, it's usually companionate love, which may or may not involve sexual behaviors. Thus, love is more complex than many think. One of the better known theories of love is Robert Sternberg's (1999) triangular theory of love.

Commitment
Intimacy
Love Triangle
Passion

Three components of love

The *triangular theory of love* has three components: passion, intimacy, and commitment. *Passion* is feeling physically aroused and attracted to someone. *Intimacy* is feeling close and connected to someone; it develops through sharing and communicating. *Commitment* is making a pledge to nourish the feelings of love and to actively maintain the relationship.

What makes you feel in love is the component of passion, which rises quickly and strongly influences and biases your judgment. What makes you want to share and offer emotional and material support is the component of intimacy. What makes you want to form a serious relationship, such as getting married, and to promise support through difficult times is the component of commitment. Sternberg believes that the kind of love most of us strive for is complete or consummate love, which is a balanced combination of all three components—passion, intimacy, and commitment.

Sternberg (1999) uses his triangular theory to answer some of the most commonly asked questions about love.

Is there love at first sight?
Love at first sight occurs when we are overwhelmed by passion, without any intimacy or commitment. Sternberg calls this *infatuated love,* which can arise in an instant, involves a great deal of physiological arousal, and lasts varying lengths of time. Because there is no intimacy or commitment, infatuated love is destined to fade away.

Why do some people get married so quickly?
Sternberg calls this *Hollywood love,* which is a combination of passion and commitment but without any intimacy. In Hollywood love, two people make a commitment based on their passion for each other. Unless they develop intimacy over time, the relationship is likely to fail.

Can there be love without sex?
Sternberg calls love without sex *companionate love,* which is a combination of intimacy and commitment without any sexual passion. An example of companionate love is a married couple who are committed to each other and share their lives but whose physical attraction has waned.

Why doesn't romantic love last?
Romantic love, which is a combination of intimacy and passion, usually doesn't last because there is no commitment. As soon as the passion dies and the intimacy fades, the individuals no longer feel in love and go their separate ways.

Brain in Love

Researchers took brain scans of college coeds who had been with their "one true love" for between 2 and 17 months and topped the charts on the passionate love scale (constantly think about their partners, can't sleep, feel euphoric). The coeds were shown photos of their loved ones interspersed with familiar but emotionally neutral faces. Only in response to seeing their loved ones did their brain's *reward/pleasure center* (p. 330) show increased activity, similar to the activity seen in cocaine-produced euphoria. The brains' activity patterns were similar in men and women with one difference: An area in men's brains that is involved in penile erections also showed increased activity (Helmuth,

2003a). In comparison, brain scans of partners who had been in longer relationships (average 2 years) indicated activity in additional emotional areas (insula, anterior cingulate) (Fisher, 2003). Researchers concluded that infatuated love primarily activates the brain's reward/pleasure center and the resulting euphoria lasts for a relatively limited time. In comparison, a more committed love activates additional emotional brain areas, which contributes to forming a longer-lasting relationship (Carey, 2002).

After choosing a partner and falling in love, the next step is to develop a long-term relationship, which is our next topic.

D. Gender Roles, Love & Relationships

Choosing a Partner

What am I looking for?

The fact that about 90% of adults in the United States marry means that most of us will eventually select a partner for a long-term relationship. However, the fact that 40 to 60% of new marriages and an even higher percentage of second marriages end in divorce means that selecting the right partner can be a very difficult, demanding, and somewhat mysterious process (K. S. Peterson, 2001).

Researchers suggest that one way we choose a partner for a long-term relationship is by finding someone who closely matches our ideal-partner schema (Fletcher & Simpson, 2000).

A *schema* is an organized mental or cognitive list that includes characteristics, facts, values, or beliefs about people, events, or objects.

An ideal-partner schema is a mental list of the most desirable characteristics that we are seeking. For instance, an ideal-partner schema in order of preference for unmarried college students (averaged for men and women) is shown above (Buss, 1994). Researchers concluded that men and women form ideal-partner schemas with two major differences: Men rank physical attractiveness as more important, and women

> **IDEAL PARTNER**
> 1. kind/understanding
> 2. exciting
> 3. intelligent
> 4. physically attractive (men rank higher)
> 5. healthy
> 6. easygoing
> 7. creative
> 8. wants children
> 9. good earning potential (women rank higher)

Looking for partner with good earning potential

rank good earning capacity higher (Buss, 1995, 2003).

One reason we date different people is to find the ideal partner who best matches the traits on our ideal-partner schema list. However, when we become passionately attracted to a person, our brain's reward/pleasure center is activated and we lose the ability to rationally decide whether a person really has the traits on our list. In this passionate state, we see our person through euphoric, rose-colored lenses that make disagreeable traits temporally disappear. However, such traits will reappear when the euphoric state fades, as it always does (Fisher, 2002).

After Mr. or Ms. Right is chosen, the couple is ready to make a commitment, such as getting married or living together. In the United States, the number of unmarried couples living together increased from 1 million in 1960 to 10 million in 2000 (Jayson, 2005). Researchers believe one reason for this increase is that high housing costs and tight budgets make living with a dating partner desirable (Smock, 2005). In any case, what happens during the next 7–10 years usually determines the success or failure of a long-term relationship (K. S. Peterson, 2001).

Looking for partner who is physically attractive

Long-Term Relationship: Success or Failure?

Why do marriages last?

To find out why some marriages succeed but about 40 to 60% fail, researcher John Gottman analyzed videotapes of couples' social interactions and physiological responses (heart rates) over 14 years. From these data, Gottman's predictions of which couples would stay together and which would divorce were 91% accurate (Gottman, 2003).

Critical factors. As Gottman analyzed couples' social interactions, he found that couples who later divorced had four major problems: One or both partners spent too much time criticizing the other; one or both partners became too defensive when one of their faults was criticized; one or both partners showed contempt for the other, especially during disagreements; and one or both partners, usually the male, engaged in stonewalling or being unwilling to talk about some problem (Gottman, 2000). The continual stress arising from these four problems—criticism, defensiveness, contempt, and stonewalling—resulted in couples becoming more unhappy and distressed through the years. Also, couples who were happily married and stayed together sent at least five times more affectionate signals than negative or hostile ones. In comparison, couples who grew more unhappy and later divorced had about the same number of positive and negative experiences (Gottman, 2003).

In some cases, couples in unhappy relationships may not know what's wrong or may not have the necessary social or communication skills. Couples who participated in programs on how

to manage conflicts and learn effective communication skills showed lower rates of both divorce and domestic violence (Prince & Jacobson, 1997).

Happy relationships. Couples in successful marriages find a way to deal with the four major problems—criticism, defensiveness, contempt, and stonewalling. For example, successful couples learn to confront and deal with stonewalling by settling disagreements in an open, straightforward way; try to be less defensive about negative feedback; criticize their partners less and try to be more supportive; and agree to overlook small problems they are unlikely to change (one partner is messy and one is neat) (Gottman, 1999). In addition, relationships are more likely to succeed if both partners are on the same emotional wavelength, such as both have positive outlooks (C. P. Anderson, 2003; Kosch, 2004).

Happiness graph. Every couple knows there are ups and downs in marital happiness (right graph). The lowest point in happiness is when adolescent children are learning to be independent, which involves many conflicts over parental rules (Benin & Robinson, 1997). One of the high points occurs when the children leave home and parents can again share peaceful times together.

Research on married couples reveals that falling in love is grand but achieving long-term success takes considerable work (Gottman, 2003).

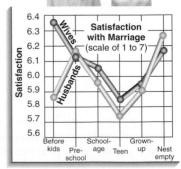

Satisfaction with Marriage (scale of 1 to 7)

✔ Concept Review

1. Puberty is accompanied by a number of biological and physical changes, which are triggered by male or female (a)_____. These chemicals result in the development of male and female secondary (b)_____ characteristics and, for females, their first menstrual cycle, which is called (c)_____.

2. The idea that adolescent development consists of a number of cognitive, sexual, social, and personality changes that occur simultaneously is called the _____ model.

3. Piaget hypothesized that cognitive development is made up of four distinct stages of reasoning, each of which is qualitatively different from and more advanced than the previous one. According to Piaget, from adolescence through adulthood, we are at the _____ stage, which involves the ability to think about hypothetical concepts, consider an issue from another's viewpoint, and solve abstract problems in a logical manner.

4. New findings indicate that teenagers do not yet have a fully developed part of their brains, called the (a)_____, which has (b)_____ functions, such as thinking, planning, and making decisions.

5. One reason adolescents engage in more risky behaviors is that they have an underdeveloped (a)_____ but a fully functioning emotional center, called the (b)_____.

6. The idea that moral reasoning can be classified into three distinct levels and that everyone goes through these levels in order is a theory of moral development proposed by (a)_____. The level of moral reasoning based primarily on punishment is called (b)_____; the one based on conforming to laws and society is called (c)_____; and the one based on balancing rights and laws is called (d)_____. Most research supports Kohlberg's idea that people do go through (e)_____ of moral development but not everyone reaches the higher stages.

7. Making impersonal moral decisions, such as keeping the money found in a stranger's wallet, involves areas of the brain associated with retrieving (a)_____. In comparison, making personal moral decisions, such as keeping the money found in a fellow worker's wallet, involves areas of the brain associated with (b)_____.

8. The development of independence and achievement during adolescence is shaped by a number of different parenting styles—in particular, (a)_____, (b)_____, and (c)_____—each of which has different costs and benefits to parents and adolescents.

9. In late adulthood, individuals experience a decline in three cognitive processes: an increase in the time required to respond to some sensory stimulus, which is called the (a)_____; a decrease in the rate at which we identify some sensory stimulus as different from other stimuli, which is called the (b)_____; and a decrease in the rate at which we encode information into long-term memory or retrieve it, which is called the (c)_____ speed.

Am I losing my memory?

What happened to all my dreams?

10. According to Erik Erikson, across our lifetimes we proceed through eight (a)_____, each of which presents a particular kind of personality or social problem. For adolescents, stage 5 is most relevant and involves (b)_____ versus role confusion. Finding one's identity has many aspects; the aspect that involves how much we like ourselves and our feelings of worth, attractiveness, and social competence is called (c)_____. Erikson believed that the most important part of personality development for an adolescent was to achieve a satisfying sense of (d)_____, while adults are more concerned about being (e)_____.

11. Males and females think, act, and behave in different ways, and these are called _____, which are enforced by expectations of parents and peers and by society rewarding traditional roles and punishing roles that are different.

12. One way we select a partner is by forming a mental list of characteristics and then looking for someone who matches our mental list, which is called a _____.

13. The theory of love that has three components—passion, intimacy, and commitment—is called the _____.

14. Infatuated love primarily activates the brain's reward/pleasure center and causes feelings of (a)_____. In comparison, a more committed love activates additional emotional brain areas, which help in forming a longer-lasting (b)_____.

15. Couples are more likely to have successful long-term relationships if they learn to deal with (a)_____ in a straightforward way and have at least five times more positive (b)_____ than negative ones.

Answers: 1. (a) hormones, (b) sexual, (c) menarche; 2. BioPsychoSocial; 3. formal operations; 4. (a) prefrontal cortex, (b) executive; 5. (a) prefrontal cortex, (b) limbic system; 6. (a) Kohlberg, (b) preconventional, (c) conventional, (d) postconventional, (e) stages; 7. (a) information, (b) emotions; 8. (a) authoritarian, (b) authoritative, (c) permissive; 9. (a) reaction time, (b) perceptual speed, (c) processing; 10. (a) psychosocial stages, (b) identity, (c) self-esteem, (d) identity, (e) productive, creative, nurturing; 11. gender roles; 12. schema; 13. triangular theory; 14. (a) euphoria, (b) relationship; 15. (a) conflicts, (b) experiences

E. Research Focus: Happy Marriages

PowerStudy 4.0™

Module 4
E. Limbic System: Old Brain

What's the key to a successful relationship?

Imagine being a researcher who wants to predict one of the most complex human behaviors: Which couples will succeed and which will fail in long-term relationships? The fact that 40 to 60% of marriages fail indicates that something is leading to success or failure. How would you design a "love lab," or a research program to figure out what that "something" is?

Every research program aims for the same four goals, which are to describe, explain, predict, and control behavior. The first two goals—describe and explain—are relatively easy. However, the last two goals—predict and control—are very difficult because many human behaviors are so complex that they cannot be completely explained, much less predicted or controlled. Now, along

comes psychologist and researcher John Gottman, who claims that not only can he explain the "something" but he can also predict with 91% accuracy which marriages will succeed or fail (Gottman et al., 2006). Since very few human behaviors can be predicted with 91% accuracy, his claim is nothing but amazing.

In the past, researchers used primarily self-reports or questionnaires to study the success or failure of long-term relationships. However, self-reports and questionnaires are not totally reliable, since marriage partners could knowingly (out of embarrassment) or unknowingly (out of defensiveness) bias their answers. Gottman's breakthrough in studying and predicting the success or failure of long-term relationships was to develop a better research method that goes by the zany name of "Love Lab."

Method

In the Love Lab, one partner sits facing the other (photos below). For 15 minutes they discuss a topic that is a known sore point while their facial and physiological responses are recorded.

Facial responses. The advantage of recording each of the partners' nonverbal facial responses is that facial responses reflect a wide range of emotional expressions (surprise, interest, anger, disgust, contempt) that one or both partners may be unaware of or try to deny. Nonverbal behaviors are very important ways of communicating in real life. For example, it's not uncommon for one partner to notice the other partner's facial expression and ask, "What's bothering you?" By recording nonverbal facial cues, which are difficult to hide or fake by normal (untrained) individuals, Gottman can reliably determine whether certain kinds of social interactions cause problems for the partners.

Physiological responses. Gottman also wants to know how long the emotional feelings last. He measures the duration of emotional feelings by recording physiological responses (heart and breathing rate, sweating). These responses reflect the start and duration of increased physiological or emotional arousal, which one or both partners may be unaware of or try to deny. For example, if one or both partners experience frequent and long-lasting bad feelings, it often signals that the marriage is in trouble (Gottman, 1999).

Longitudinal method. So far, you can see that Gottman's Love Lab solved the problem of how to reliably measure a couple's emotional responses and feelings. But how would he know if these measures predicted a marriage's success or failure? To answer this question, Gottman used the longitudinal research method, which means he retested the same couples regularly during 14 years. By retesting the same couples over time, he could determine whether a couple's social interactions and emotional responses recorded during early sessions could be used to predict with 91% accuracy whether this particular marriage would succeed or fail.

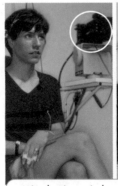

In the Love Lab, a video camera (circled) records facial expressions, and white bands of wires (visible on her fingers and his wrist) record various physiological responses.

Results and Conclusions

After retesting the same 79 couples for 14 years, Gottman (1999) reported that he could predict, based on previous observations in the Love Lab, which of the marriages would succeed or fail. Here are some of the findings that allowed him to predict with such accuracy.

Unsuccessful relationships. We have already discussed the four major problems that couples experience early on and that, if not dealt with successfully, predict failure in long-term relationships. These four problems are giving too many ***criticisms,*** becoming too ***defensive,*** showing ***contempt*** of a partner, and ***stonewalling*** or refusing to settle disagreements in an open, straightforward discussion.

Successful relationships. There are several things that predict successful relationships. First, happy marriages had ***husbands*** who were good at not immediately rejecting their wives' advice but either accepted it or found something reasonable in it. In contrast, unhappy marriages had husbands who were autocratic, failed to listen, and dismissed their wives' advice.

Second, happy marriages had ***wives*** who were careful to express their complaints and advice in gentle, soothing ways, which were easier for their husbands to accept. In contrast, unhappy marriages had wives who phrased their complaints and advice in angry, fighting words that, in turn, triggered equally angry replies from their husbands.

Advice. Gottman's advice is for couples to behave like good friends, which means their relationship should be based on respect, affection, and empathy, and for couples to manage conflicts in gentle, positive ways (Gottman et al., 2006).

Although in the United States most people marry for love, that's not true in other cultures.

F. Cultural Diversity: Preferences for Partners

Can 9,000 people agree?

Imagine being born and raised in a country different from your own, such as Nigeria, Germany, China, Iran, Brazil, Japan, France, or India. Now imagine being asked to list, in order, those traits that you consider most desirable in a potential partner. How much would your culture influence the order of desirable traits? To answer this

What if you were born in Egypt?

question, researchers surveyed more than 9,000 young adults (men and women), all in their 20s, who lived in 37 different countries (Buss, 1994; Buss et al., 1990). Subjects were given a list of 32 traits and asked to rank the traits from most to least desirable in a potential partner. The results indicate that 9,000 individuals from many different cultures seemed to agree reasonably well in ranking traits.

Desirable Traits

What is considered desirable in a potential partner? The list on the near right shows the most desirable traits for potential partners averaged across cultures. Men and women have similar lists of desirable traits, as indicated by a high correlation of +0.87 between lists. The numerous similarities between men's and women's lists indicate similar cultural influences.

The list on the far right shows that there were also some interesting differences between men and women. Men almost always ranked physical appearance in a partner higher, while women almost always ranked earning potential in a partner higher.

Average ranking of desirable traits
1 Kind and understanding
2 Intelligent
3 Exciting personality
4 Healthy
5 Emotionally stable and mature
6 Dependable character
7 Pleasing disposition

Differences in desirable traits
8 Good looks (ranked higher by men)
9 Good financial prospect (ranked higher by women)
10 Virginity (ranked higher by men)

How much is virginity valued around the world? In two-thirds of all the cultures measured, men desired virginity or chastity (the lack of previous sexual intercourse) in marriage partners more than women did; there were no cultures where women valued virginity in a prospective partner more than men did (Buss, 1994). For example, in China, virginity is indispensable in a partner; marrying a nonvirgin is simply out of the question (Buss, 1994). People in India, Taiwan, and Iran also placed great value on virginity, while people in the Netherlands, Sweden, and Norway placed little value on virginity in a prospective partner. These differences in the value placed on the virginity of women indicate how cultural influences can raise or lower the desirability of certain traits in potential marriage partners.

Reasons for Marrying

How much is love valued? As the figure on the right shows, cultures in different countries place different values on marrying for love. In the United States and other Western countries, marrying for love is highly valued, but it is valued less in some Middle East, Asian, and African nations.

How do women decide? Some anthropologists have argued that women, who invest more time in caring for offspring, would adopt more discriminating standards for potential mates than would men, who invest less time in rearing children. Thus, women would be more careful in deciding whom to marry. This proved true: In nearly every culture, women expressed more stringent standards across a wide range of characteristics (Buss, 1994).

How Citizens in Different Nations Ranked the Importance of Love in Choosing a Spouse

United States: Love ranked **FIRST**, that is, love was the most important factor in choosing a spouse.

Iran: Love ranked **THIRD**, while ranked higher were education, ambition, chastity.

Nigeria: Love ranked **FOURTH**, while ranked higher were good health, refinement, neatness, desire.

China: Love ranked **SIXTH**, while ranked higher were health, chastity, homemaker.

Zulu: Love ranked **SEVENTH**, while ranked higher were mature, emotionally stable, dependable.

How do men decide? Across cultures, men generally decide to marry younger women who are physically attractive. In those societies where men purchase their wives, younger women command a higher bride price. Also, across cultures, the most common reason that men use to dissolve marriages is infertility, or the inability to have children (Buss, 1994).

From surveys of desirable traits in marriage partners, researchers found many similarities across cultures, but they found considerable differences among cultures in reasons for getting married.

We have primarily discussed development in adolescents and young to middle-aged adults. Next, we'll examine the physical changes that come with aging.

G. Physical Changes: Aging

Kinds of Aging

Why do we grow old? As you look at the photo on the right, the difference you see between grandmother and granddaughter is an example of normal aging, which is very different from pathological aging.

Normal aging is a gradual and natural slowing of our physical and psychological processes from middle through late adulthood.

Pathological aging may be caused by genetic defects, physiological problems, or diseases, such as Alzheimer's (p. 47), all of which accelerate the aging process.

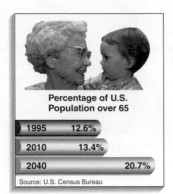

Percentage of U.S. Population over 65

1995	12.6%
2010	13.4%
2040	20.7%

Source: U.S. Census Bureau

One goal of the study of aging, which is called *gerontology*, is to separate the causes of normal aging from those of pathological aging. The percentage of people in the United States over 65 is expected to almost double by the year 2040 (left graph). Life expectancy in the United States was 45 years in 1945 but is now a record 78 years (NCHS, 2006). In the 1920s, there were only 2,300 people in the United States who were over 100, but currently there are about 40,000 over that age (women outnumber men 4 to 1) (K. Wright, 2003).

We'll examine two related questions about aging: Why do our bodies age? How do our bodies and behaviors change with age?

Aging and Physiological Changes

So far, the oldest people on record have lived from 113 to 122 years. How long you will live and how fast your body will age depend about 50% on heredity (genes) and 50% on other factors, such as diet, exercise, lifestyle, and diseases (K. Wright, 2003). In the past decades, the steady increases in life expectancy came primarily from improved public health and new cures for diseases. But, advances in controlling diseases are slowing and researchers believe that even with major improvements in geriatric care, the average life expectancy will not go beyond 85 years (J. Olshansky, 2003). Instead, researchers believe that large increases in life expectancy must now come from slowing the aging process itself (R. Miller, 2003).

The *aging process* is caused by a combination of certain genes and proteins that interfere with organ functioning and by the natural production of toxic molecules (free radicals), which in turn cause random damage to body organs and DNA (the building blocks of life). Such damage eventually exceeds the body's ability to repair itself and results in greater susceptibility to diseases and death (J. Olshansky et al., 2002).

Researchers recently found that stress—like that caused by job loss or divorce—results in the aging of DNA, and they plan to study the effects meditation and psychotherapy may have on slowing the aging of DNA (Epel & Blackburn, 2004). Animal studies have identified dozens of genes that extended the life span by 200 to 600% (Arantes-Oliveria et al., 2003; Sinclair & Guarente, 2006). Also, human studies have identified a half-dozen genetic factors in the very old (average age 98) that seemed to have slowed the aging process (K. Wright, 2003). Although such practices as having a good diet, exercising, reducing stress, and taking vitamins or antioxidants may improve quality of life and help one live into the 100s, none of these things alone has been shown to slow the aging process and allow humans to live to 130 or beyond (J. Olshansky, 2003).

As the population grows older, people are searching for and buying antiaging products. However, no antiaging remedies have proved to slow aging (J. Olshansky et al., 2002).

As our bodies age, they experience many physiological changes.

Physiological Changes: Early Adulthood

The finding that most athletes peak in their 20s indicates that this is a period of maximum physical ability and capacity. For example, tennis champions reach their peak at about 25 years, baseball players are best at about 27, Olympic runners at about 25, and Olympic swimmers at about 20 (Schulz & Curnow, 1988). In our early to middle 20s, our immune system, senses, physiological responses, and mental skills are at their peak efficiency.

Middle Adulthood

In our 30s and 40s, we usually gain weight, primarily because we are less active. By the late 40s, there is a slight decrease in a number of physiological responses, including heart rate, lung capacity, muscle strength, kidney function, and eyesight.

Late Adulthood

In our 50s and 60s, we may experience a gradual decline in height because of loss of bone, a further decrease in output of lungs and kidneys, an increase in skin wrinkles, and a deterioration in joints. Sensory organs become less sensitive, resulting in less acute vision, hearing, and taste. The heart, which is a muscle, becomes less effective at pumping blood, which may result in as much as a 35% decrease in blood flow through the coronary arteries. A general decrease occurs in both the number and diameter of muscle fibers, which may explain some of the slowing in motor functions that usually accompanies old age.

Very Late Adulthood

In our 70s and 80s, we undergo further decreases in muscle strength, bone density, speed of nerve conduction, and output of lungs, heart, and kidneys. More than 10% have Parkinson's or Alzheimer's disease. The oldest living persons ranged in age from 113 to 122.

As many of the body's physical responses slow down with aging, there are corresponding decreases in related behaviors. Earlier in this module we discussed decreases in memory with aging (p. 415), and now we'll discuss decreases in sexual behavior.

How does sex change with aging?

Surveys of sexual behavior, which usually sample people between ages 17 and 59, generally report that single men have more sex partners, experience orgasm more frequently, and masturbate more frequently than single women and that about one-third of married couples have sex two or three times a week (Crooks & Baur, 2002). People in late adulthood (60–80) are often not included in these surveys because of the common stereotype that they no longer have any interest in sexual activity or that it is inappropriate for them to engage in sex. However, a national survey of men and women over age 60 found that about 50% were sexually active (M. Dunn & Cutler, 2000). This survey indicates that adults can enjoy sexual activity well into their later years, especially if they know how sexual responses change and learn ways to deal with these changes. We'll discuss some of the normal changes in sexual responses that accompany aging.

Sexual Changes in Women

The most significant effect on women's sexual behavior in later adulthood is menopause. *Menopause* occurs in women at about age 50 (range 35–60) and involves a gradual stoppage in secretion of the major female hormone (estrogen), which in turn results in cessation of both ovulation and the menstrual cycle.

Menopause is not the end of sexual behavior.

Over the next 20 years, approximately 40 million baby boomers will enter menopause, and most can expect to live nearly one-third of their lives after menopause (Brewster et al., 1999). During and immediately after menopause, about 15% of women experience physical symptoms severe enough to require medical help; 65% of women experience mild symptoms that do not require medical help; and 20% of women have few if any physical symptoms (Hooyman & Niyak, 1999).

PHYSICAL SYMPTOMS

Most women experience hot flashes, some sleep disturbance, and dryness of the vagina, which results from a decrease and eventual stoppage in the secretion of the female hormone estrogen. A lack of estrogen results in thinning of the vaginal wall and reduction of lubrication during arousal. However, there is little or no change in the ability to become sexually aroused or to reach orgasm. Potential problems with lack of lubrication or painful intercourse may be treated with hormone replacement therapy, which has benefits and risks (L. Nathan & Judd, 2007; Reed & Sutton, 2006), or the use of vaginal creams. Because researchers find no correlation between decreased levels of hormones and sexual activity, women's continued sexual activity after menopause is affected primarily by psychological rather than physiological factors (Crooks & Baur, 2002; Potter, 2006).

PSYCHOLOGICAL SYMPTOMS

Researchers followed more than 400 healthy women through menopause and observed many psychological changes. They found that women did report psychological symptoms, such as moodiness, depression, anxiety, and anger. However, these symptoms were related to other stressful issues—for example, growing older in a society that glorifies being young—rather than to the physical symptoms of menopause. In addition, women's expectations greatly influenced their psychological outlook during menopause. Women with positive expectations about what they hope to accomplish have few psychological symptoms, compared to women who expect their lives to be over and thus feel depressed and angry during menopause (Dennerstein et al., 1997; Neugarten, 1994).

SEXUAL ACTIVITIES

Some older women think sexual activity is appropriate only for young people. Others expect sexual activity to be just like it was during their young adulthood, and they may have difficulty accepting the inevitable changes that occur as they age. Some aging couples report sexual relationships become more satisfying over time, but others report sexual activity becomes boring and predictable. Overall, about half of women age 50 and older are at least as satisfied with their sex life as during their younger years (Potter, 2006).

It is interesting that women in cultures where menopause results in increased social status look forward to menopause and have fewer symptoms than women in the United States (Richters, 1997).

Sexual Changes in Men

As men reach late adulthood (60s, 70s, and 80s), they may experience some physiological changes that decrease sexual responsiveness.

SEXUAL RESPONDING

Because many of the body's physiological responses slow down, older men may require more time and stimulation to have an erection and to reach orgasm. Upon ejaculation, there may be a reduction in the force and amount of fluid. However, healthy men usually have no difficulty in becoming sexually aroused or reaching orgasm. Some men worry that their decreased ability to have an erection or reach orgasm means an end to their sexuality (Masters & Johnson, 1981). Currently, there are a few drugs (such as Viagra, p. 356) approved for the treatment of impotency, which is the inability to have an erection. These drugs help about 70% of men who have impotency problems (Berenson, 2005).

PSYCHOLOGICAL PROBLEMS

Some things may take longer but that's OK.

Although older men are generally more sexually active than older women, their decreased sexual abilities can make them uncomfortable and threaten their self-esteem. However, having longer periods of stimulation, improving intimate communication, and using more imaginative sexual activity can usually compensate for men's decreased self-confidence (Bartlik & Goldstein, 2001). Health experts counsel that as we grow older, we should learn new skills, such as being more understanding and sensitive to our partner's needs, which will help maintain sexual enjoyment (Crooks & Baur, 2005).

Next, we'll discuss a serious problem that is shared by both adolescents and seniors, a high rate of suicide.

H. Application Suicide

What is the third leading cause of death?

In the United States, a person dies by suicide every 17 minutes and someone attempts suicide every minute (CDC, 2006d; Ezzell, 2003). Among teenagers and young adults (ages 15–24), the suicide rate is 10.4 per 100,000, making it their third leading cause of death. The suicide rate for people 25–64 years old is 14.4 per 100,000. People over 65 have a higher rate of suicide (16.5 per 100,000) (CDC, 2006d; Sharp, 2003).

We'll first discuss issues related to teenage/young adult suicide and then look at suicide in the elderly. We'll begin with four real-life teenage examples that illustrate how complex the issues and causes are. In a span of five weeks, four teenage boys—one a straight-A student, one the class clown, one deeply religious person, and one very troubled boy—committed suicide in the small southern town of Sheridan, Arkansas (adapted from *People*, May 21, 1990, pp. 56–59). Here are their sad and tragic stories.

1 March 28, 1990: Raymond, 17 Years Old

According to the police chief, Ray had threatened to kill himself in the past, but the threats were considered teenage histrionics. He had a drinking problem, had been arrested for drunken driving, and had been sent to a rehabilitation center for several weeks. Before Ray shot himself, however, his life seemed to be improving, and he had made plans to go to college. A suicide note to his girlfriend said, "Don't blame yourself. It's nobody's fault."

2 April 30, 1990: Tommy, 16 Years Old

His teenage peers considered Tommy a clown, but his best friend, Rhonda, didn't believe that. She thought Tommy's clever wit and clowning were a mask for his insecurity. On April 29, Tommy called Rhonda, which he did regularly, and told her that he was going to kill himself. Certain he would not carry out his threat, she made him promise to come to school the next day. Tommy came to school, and in one of his classes he got up and stated that he had two things to say. He said that he loved Rhonda, although they had never dated. "The other thing," he said, "is this." He pulled out a pistol and shot himself.

3 April 30, 1990: Thomas, 19 Years Old

Thomas was a straight-A student who liked to read, listen to oldies, and hunt and fish. He did not drink, smoke, or swear. He lived too far out of town to have many buddies. His father had died when he was 9. Two years earlier, his grandfather, who had terminal cancer, committed suicide with a pistol to his head. Tommy had shot himself in the afternoon, and that very night Thomas did the same. In his suicide note he said, "Where shall I begin? I really don't know. It's hard to say what's going on anymore. A long time now I have felt like I am on the edge and slipping fast. I guess I've finally slipped over the edge."

4 May 2, 1990: Jerry, 17 Years Old

Jerry's suicide was the last of the four and the most troubling. He was popular, gregarious, good-looking, and so deeply religious that he was nicknamed "preacher boy." The night after Tommy's suicide he told his mother, "I can't understand how anyone would commit suicide—that was the coward's way." That same night he called his girlfriend and said, "I love you. I'll talk to you tomorrow." The next day he stayed home from school, and around noon he shot himself in the head. The family insists that Jerry's death was accidental.

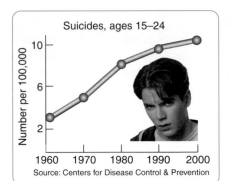

Suicides, ages 15–24

Number per 100,000

Source: Centers for Disease Control & Prevention

Why do teens take their own lives?

Notice that in the above examples, family and friends could not believe that two of the four adolescents would ever even think of committing suicide. That's because one was a straight-A student and the other was very popular and deeply religious. In the other two cases, one adolescent had said he was thinking about suicide and one had made a previous attempt. Thus, if and when adolescents talk about committing suicide, parents and friends need to take such talk seriously. In other cases, the problems, symptoms, or events leading up to or triggering suicide may be difficult to recognize. However, clinicians find that the following problems may lead to or trigger suicide attempts.

Problems: helplessness, depression, drugs

Problems and symptoms. The most common *psychological problems* include depression, feelings of helplessness, and drug-related problems, such as Raymond's alcohol problem. Usually these problems have persisted for some time (Haliburn, 2000). The most common *behavioral symptoms* include decline in school performance; social isolation and withdrawal; intense difficulties with parents, siblings, and peers; and antisocial behavior (Mayo Clinic, 2006b). For example, Thomas's suicide note says, "A long time now I have felt like I am on the edge and slipping fast."

Precipitators. In most cases, there are *precipitators* of suicide, which may be certain events, feelings, or situations. For example, common precipitators include problems with relationships, bouts of depression, drinking problems, and relatively ordinary stressors, such as difficulties with dating, parents, or school. A high percentage of victims had either expressed the wish to die or threatened suicide, as was true for both Raymond and Tommy (Mayo Clinic, 2006).

One reason parents and friends are shocked by a teenager's or young adult's suicide is that the problems or precipitators may be hard to spot.

How can suicide be prevented?

Even though rates of youth suicide in the United States have declined in the past decade (Lubell et al., 2004), there are still 2 million youth who attempt suicide each year (Weller et al., 2001). While more teenage females than males attempt suicide, males' attempts are 5 to 7 times more likely to end in death (R. N. Anderson & Smith, 2003; NIMH, 2003). Therapists have proposed a three-step program to help identify risk factors and ultimately prevent suicide.

Identify Risk Factors

The first step is to identify the risk factors, which include mood disorders, drug abuse, previous suicide attempt, suicide of a friend, and major life stressors, such as family turmoil or parental separation. A youth with one or more of these risk factors is considered to be in great danger of committing suicide (Mayo Clinic, 2006b). Identifying risk factors may involve reports from peers, programs on suicide prevention in schools, 24-hour hot lines, or concerned family members (Garland & Zigler, 1993).

Psychiatric Evaluation and Psychosocial Intervention

After parents, peers, or teachers identify one or more risk factors, the next step is a thorough medical and psychological evaluation of the individual as well as interviews with the individual's family members—with each family member being assured of complete confidentiality (Weller et al., 2001). Based on such information, a treatment plan is developed. In the short term, (1) a contract is negotiated so that the person will not harm him- or herself, (2) lethal means are removed from the home (guns and drugs), and (3) support and a 24-hour contact are provided. In the long term, the individual's personal problems are addressed, which may include help with improving his or her self-image and developing better interpersonal skills and functioning. Because most suicidal teenagers/young adults also have serious psychological problems (depression, loneliness, anxiety), psychotherapy and psychiatric medication are usually needed. Thus, this kind of psychosocial intervention involves family support and treatment of underlying mental problems (Fristad & Shaver, 2001).

Although teenagers/young adults have a relatively high rate of suicide, the highest rate is found in a group of people you might never expect: the retired, 65-and-over group.

Suicide in the Elderly

Why are rates so high?

Suicide rates in the elderly increase with age, from 13 per 100,000 for individuals aged 65–74 to as high as 59 per 100,000 for those 85 and older (NIMH, 2003; Sharp, 2003). Suicide rates in the elderly are expected to rise as a larger percentage of the population reaches age 65. Several risk factors contribute to this high rate of suicide.

Risk factors. The common risk factors for suicide among the elderly include serious health problems, stressful life events, loneliness, and especially depression, which is present in about 90–95% of those who commit suicide (Cavanagh et al., 2003). There is also a growing trend of murder-suicide, in which one member of an elderly couple kills the other and then takes his or her own life. Murder-suicides in the elderly account for about 2,500 deaths a year (Sharp, 2003).

"I have six months to live and I'm in constant pain."

Assisted suicide. Recent polls indicated that although only 12% of those surveyed said suicide was morally acceptable (Sharp, 2003), 46% said that a doctor should be allowed to help a person "commit suicide" provided that person has a painful and incurable disease (Grossman & Nichols, 2006). In the late 1990s, Oregon voters twice approved an assisted suicide law, which currently allows a mentally competent patient to request a lethal dose of drugs if at least two doctors determine that the person has less than six months to live. By 2005, 326 people had obtained lethal prescriptions and, of these, 208 people (about equal numbers of men and women), most suffering from cancer, took their own lives as allowed by Oregon's assisted suicide law (Grossman & Nichols, 2006). Assisted suicide is currently legal in the Netherlands, Belgium, and Switzerland (CBC News, 2004).

Opponents of Doctor-Assisted Suicide

Opponents include religious groups that believe taking one's life should never be sanctioned, others who think doctors should not be involved in helping people take their own lives, and those who fear caretakers may coerce vulnerable people into assisted suicide to reduce the financial burden of caring for them (CBC News, 2004; Verhovek, 2002). For example, making assisted suicide easier may increase the chances that people who are suffering from mental problems or temporary emotional difficulties will take their own lives without exploring other possibilities for living. Others argue that when people are distressed, they are unlikely or unable to think clearly or make a rational decision about committing suicide (Clay, 1997).

Proponents of Doctor-Assisted Suicide

Proponents explain that each of us has the moral right to end our life if we decide that life has become unbearable for health reasons (CBC News, 2004). The *New England Journal of Medicine* published an article by a group of doctors who proposed a policy of legalized physician-assisted death with safeguards to protect patients, preserve the integrity of physicians, and ensure that voluntary physician-assisted death occurs only as a last resort (F. G. Miller et al., 1994). Researchers reviewed the effects of Oregon's assisted suicide law and concluded that there have not been any of the abuses or problems feared by opponents and that most of the individuals who chose doctor-assisted suicide were well-educated, mostly elderly cancer patients who had health insurance and were concerned about loss of bodily functions and increasing pain (Wineberg & Werth, 2003).

The pros and cons of doctor-assisted suicide will continue to be debated, especially since the elderly population will almost double in the next 35 years.

Summary Test

A. Puberty & Sexual Behavior

1. Girls and boys experience three major bio-logical changes as they go through a period called (a)_____. For both girls and boys, one of these changes is the development of (b)_____ maturity, which for girls includes the first menstrual cycle, called (c)_____, and for boys includes the production of sperm. These physical changes in girls and boys are triggered by a portion of the brain called the (d)_____. A second change is the development of (e)_____ sexual characteristics, such as pubic hair and gender-specific physical changes. A third change is a surge in (f)_____ growth, especially height. The changes for girls tend to start about a year earlier than those for boys.

B. Cognitive & Emotional Changes

2. Piaget's fourth cognitive stage, which begins in adolescence and continues into adulthood, is called the (a)_____ stage. During this stage, adolescents and adults develop the ability to think about (b)_____ concepts, plan for the future, and solve abstract problems. One reason adolescents engage in more risky behaviors is that they have an underdeveloped (c)_____ but a fully functioning emotional center, called the (d)_____.

3. According to Kohlberg's theory, moral reason-ing can be classified into three distinct levels, and everyone progresses through the levels in the same order. However, not all adults reach the higher levels. The first level, the (a)_____ level, has two stages. In stage 1, moral decisions are determined primarily through fear of punishment, while at stage 2 they are guided by satisfying one's self-interest. The second level, the (b)_____ level, also has two stages. In the first of these, stage 3, people conform to the standards of others they value; in stage 4, they conform to the laws of society. In the third level, the (c)_____ level, moral decisions are made after thinking about all the alternatives and strik-ing a balance between human rights and the laws of society.

4. Making impersonal moral decisions, such as keeping the money found in a stranger's wallet, involves areas of the brain associated with retrieving (a)_____. In comparison, making personal moral decisions, such as keeping the money found in a fellow work-er's wallet, involves areas of the brain associated with (b)_____.

5. Parenting styles affect many aspects of adolescents' development. Parents who attempt to shape and control their children in accordance with a set standard of conduct are termed (a)_____. Par-ents who attempt to direct their children's activities in a rational and intelligent way and are supportive, loving, and committed are called (b)_____. Parents who are less controlling and behave with a nonpunishing and accepting attitude toward their children's impulses are called (c)_____.

C. Personality & Social Changes

6. How you describe yourself, including your values, goals, traits, interests, and motivations, is a function of your sense of (a)_____, which is part of the problem to be faced in stage 5 of Erikson's eight (b)_____ stages. Those who are unsuccessful in resolving the problems of this stage will experi-ence (c)_____, which results in low self-esteem, and may become socially withdrawn.

7. An adolescent's feeling of worth, attrac-tiveness, and social competence is called _____, which is influenced particularly by physical appearance, social acceptability, and management of public behaviors (anxiety and stress).

8. The challenges of adulthood are covered in the last three of Erikson's eight (a)_____ stages. According to his theory, in stage 6, young adults face the problems of intimacy versus (b)_____. In stage 7, middle adults face problems of generativity versus (c)_____. In stage 8, older adults reflect on their lives; if they feel positive and content about how they lived and what they accomplished, they will have a feeling of satis-faction or (d)_____; if not, they will have a feeling of regret and (e)_____.

D. Gender Roles, Love & Relationships

9. During childhood and adolescence, males and females experience pressures and expectations from parents, peers, and society to behave in different ways. These expected patterns of behavior and thought, called _____, influence cogni-tive, personality, and social development.

10. The kind of love that involves continually thinking about the loved one and is accompanied by sexual feelings and pow-erful emotional reactions is called (a)_____ love. The kind of love that involves trusting and tender feelings for someone whose life is closely bound up with one's own is called (b)_____ love. Sternberg's triangular theory of love has three components: feeling physiological aroused and attracted is (c)_____, feeling close and committed is (d)_____, and pledging to nourish feelings is (e)_____. Infatuated love primarily activates the brain's (f)_____ and causes feelings of euphoria. In comparison, a more committed love activates additional (g)_____ brain areas, which help in forming a longer-lasting relationship.

11. One way that we select a mate is by developing an organized mental list of desirable characteristics and then looking for someone who matches this mental list, which is called a _____.

E. Research Focus: Happy Marriages

12. Gottman identified four problems that can result in the failure of a long-term relationship: these problems involve (a)_____, _____, _____, and _____. In successful marriages, wives learn to express their (b)_____ in gentle ways so their husbands are more likely to listen and accept, and husbands learn not to reject their wives' (c)_____ without listening and finding something reasonable in it.

F. Cultural Diversity: Preferences for Partners

13. People's lists of desirable traits for a mate show remarkable similarity across cultures. However, there are some differences in ranking between the genders; for example, men rank (a)_____ higher than women do, and women rank (b)_____ higher than men do. Also, different cultures place different values on the desirability of marrying someone who is a (c)_____ and marrying someone primarily because of being in (d)_____.

United States: **Love** ranked **FIRST**, that is, love was the most important factor in choosing a spouse.

Iran: **Love** ranked **THIRD**, while ranked higher were education, ambition, chastity.

G. Physical Changes: Aging

14. The gradual and natural slowing of our physical and psychological processes from middle through late adulthood is called (a)_____ aging. This process occurs when certain (b)_____ and_____ interfere with organ functioning and when the natural production of toxic (c)_____ (free radicals) causes random damage to body organs and to DNA (the building blocks of life). This aging process, which decreases the effectiveness of sensory and body organs,

eventually exceeds the body's ability to repair itself and results in greater susceptible to (d)_____.

15. If the aging process is caused by genetic defects, physiological problems, or diseases, it is called _____ aging, an example of which is Alzheimer's disease.

16. In later adulthood (about age 50), women experience a gradual reduction in the secretion of estrogen, which results in cessation of ovulation and the menstrual cycle; this is called (a)_____. In late adulthood (60–80), men do not stop producing testosterone, but they may experience a decrease in sexual responsiveness due to (b)_____ changes.

H. Application: Suicide

17. A number of factors have been found to be related to teenage suicide. Before committing suicide, adolescents usually have a number of (a)_____ problems, such as depression, feelings of helplessness, or drug-related problems; adolescents also show a number of (b)_____ symptoms, such as falling grades, social isolation and withdrawal, difficulties with family and peers, and antisocial behavior. Usually, suicide is preceded by events or feelings called (c)_____; these may include problems with relationships or bouts of depression or drinking.

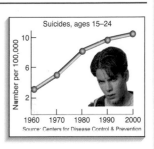

Suicides, ages 15–24

Number per 100,000

1960 1970 1980 1990 2000

Source: Centers for Disease Control & Prevention

18. Among the risk factors for suicide in the elderly are depression and loneliness, but the major contributing cause is (a)_____ problems. Currently, there is considerable discussion in the United States over the right of a person with a terminal disease to end his or her life through (b)_____ suicide.

Answers: *1. (a) puberty, (b) sexual, (c) menarche, (d) hypothalamus, (e) secondary, (f) physical; 2. (a) formal operations, (b) abstract or hypothetical, (c) prefrontal cortex, (d) limbic system; 3. (a) preconventional, (b) conventional, (c) postconventional; 4. (a) information, (b) emotions; 5. (a) authoritarian, (b) authoritative, (c) permissive; 6. (a) identity or self, (b) psychosocial, (c) identity confusion; 7. self-esteem; 8. (a) psychosocial, (b) isolation, (c) stagnation, (d) integrity, (e) despair; 9. gender roles; 10. (a) passionate, (b) companionate, (c) passion, (d) intimacy, (e) commitment, (f) reward/pleasure center, (g) emotional; 11. schema; 12. (a) criticism, defensiveness, contempt, stonewalling, (b) complaints, (c) advice; 13. (a) good looks, virginity, (b) financial prospects, (c) virgin, (d) love; 14. (a) normal, (b) genes, proteins, (c) molecules, (d) disease and death; 15. pathological; 16. (a) menopause, (b) physiological; 17. (a) psychological, (b) behavioral, (c) precipitators; 18. (a) health or medical, (b) assisted*

Critical Thinking

Are Teens Too Young to Drive?

Questions

1. Besides traffic accidents, what are other costs or dangers of teen driving?

2. What immature teen characteristics may contribute to their irresponsible driving?

3. What other irresponsible teen behaviors may be a result of an "executive branch" that is not yet fully developed?

Car crashes are the No. 1 cause of death for teens, killing about 6,000 a year and injuring 300,000 more. Teenage drivers are about four times more likely to crash than older drivers and three times more likely to die in a crash. The risk of crashes is highest for 16-year-olds; one in five will have a car crash within the first year of driving.

The possibility of raising the legal driving age has been receiving increasing attention. Proponents argue that teens are too immature to handle the responsibility of driving. In fact, a recent national survey found that nearly two-thirds (61%) of people believe that a 16-year-old is too young to have a driver's license and more than half (53%) think teens should be at least 18 to obtain a driver's license. Opponents of raising the legal driving age argue that responsible teen drivers should not be punished for the mistakes of careless teens causing accidents.

The opinion of the majority of Americans about teens being too young to drive is supported by scientific findings. Brain researchers report the "executive branch" of the teen brain—the part that considers risks and consequences, makes judgments, and controls impulsive behavior—is not fully developed until age 25 and is far less developed in 16-year-olds than in older teens. Driving is especially dangerous because the teenage years are filled with a huge rush of hormones that encourage thrill-seeking and risk-taking behaviors. For instance, when a teen drives 15–20 mph over the speed limit, the part of the brain that processes a thrill works fine, but the part that warns of dangerous consequences is essentially useless. Psychologist Laurence Steinberg describes the dangers of teen driving by saying, "It's like turning on the engine of a car without a skilled driver at the wheel" (Wallis & Dell, 2004).

Several states have already imposed restrictions on 16-year-old drivers, such as prohibiting late-night driving and limiting the number of passengers they are allowed to have in their car. But, how far should lawmakers go to reduce the dangers of teen drivers? Jeffrey Runge, an emergency room doctor, has treated many teen crash victims and makes it clear that lawmakers should take the dangers of teenage drivers very seriously: "If we had any other disease that was wiping out our teenagers at the rate of thousands per year, there would be no end to what we would do as a society to stop that" (Stafford, 2005). (Adapted from Associated Press, 2006; Brophy, 2006; R. Davis, 2005; Henderson, 2006; O'Donnell, 2005; Stafford, 2005; Wallis & Dell, 2004; Williamson, 2005)

4. What part of the brain is responsible for thrill-seeking and risk-taking behaviors?

5. Are stricter laws the solution to reducing the great dangers of teen driving?

1. Typical families with teen drivers spend $20,000 total during the first three years of teen driving, and if their teen crashes, the amount increases to $25,000. Teen crashes result in a hefty economic cost of over $40 billion a year. Also, let's not forget the thousands of innocent drivers and passengers who die or get injured as a result of careless teen driving.

2. Teenagers are known to make poor judgments, act impulsively, and take great risks. Common immature teen characteristics include excessive socializing, feelings of invulnerability, and a susceptibility to get easily distracted, all of which may contribute to reckless driving.

3. Some irresponsible teen behaviors that result from an underdeveloped executive branch include using drugs, having unprotected sex, bullying or fighting, stealing, not wearing a seat belt, and dropping out of school.

4. Sex hormones secreted during puberty increase the growth of the limbic system, which is believed to account for teenagers' thrill-seeking and risk-taking behaviors, as well as their moodiness.

5. Stricter restrictions on teen driving can help only so much because the brains of teens are simply not mature yet. Still, laws that impose strict conditions for a teen to obtain a driver's license can reduce fatal crashes involving 16-year-olds by up to 21%.

Links to Learning

Key Terms/Key People

Learning Activities

- **POWERSTUDY FOR INTRODUCTION TO PSYCHOLOGY 4.0**

  by Tom Doyle and Rod Plotnik

  Check out the quizzes and learning activities for "Adolesence & Adulthood" on **PowerStudy** and:
  - Test your knowledge using an interactive version of the Summary Test on pages pages 428 and 429. Also access related quizzing—true/false, multiple choice, and matching.
  - Explore an interactive version of the Critical Thinking exercise "Are Teens Too Young to Drive?" on page 430.
  - You will also find key terms, a chapter outline including a chapter abstract, and a special extended list of hotlinked websites that correlate to this module.

- *CengageNOW*
  academic.cengage.com/login

  Need help studying? This site is your one-stop study shop. Take a Pre-Test and CengageNOW will generate a Personalized Study Plan based on your test results. The Study Plan will identify the topics you need to review and direct you to online resources to help you master those topics. You can then take a Post-Test to determine the concepts you have mastered and what you still need to work on.

- **INTRODUCTION TO PSYCHOLOGY BOOK COMPANION WEBSITE**
  academic.cengage.com/psychology/plotnik

  Visit your book companion website where you will find more resources to help you study. At this site, you will find Learning Objectives, Internet Exercises, quizzing, flash cards, and a pronunciation glossary.

- *STUDY GUIDE and WEBTUTOR*

  Check the corresponding module in your Study Guide for effective student tips and help learning the material presented. Also go to **academic.cengage.com/webtutor** for an interactive version of the Study Guide features.

Study Questions

*A. **Puberty & Sexual Behavior**—How are the sexual concerns of adolescents and senior adults similar but also different? (**Suggested answer page 631**)

B. **Cognitive & Emotional Changes**—If you heard an adolescent discussing politics with her grandfather, what cognitive differences between them would you notice?

*C. **Personality & Social Changes**—If you become a parent, what special concerns might you have when your own children go through adolescence? (**Suggested answer page 631**)

D. **Gender Roles, Love & Relationships**—If you are beginning a long-term relationship, what two things should you and your partner do to ensure success?

E. **Research Focus: Happy Marriages**—What is different about the interactions of couples who are happy from those of couples who are unhappy?

F. **Cultural Diversity: Preferences for Partners**—What are the advantages and disadvantages of having parents arrange marriages for their children?

G. **Physical Changes: Aging**—Of two people who are both 65, why might one seem much older and the other much younger?

*H. **Application: Suicide**—If your grandmother had incurable cancer and unbearable pain and asked you to help her commit suicide, would you do it? (**Suggested answer page 631**)

*These questions are answered in Appendix B.

MODULE 19
Freudian & Humanistic Theories

Personality

How did he become a deceiver and a liar?

Ted Haggard founded New Life Church in the basement of his house 25 years ago and became a prominent author and national evangelical Christian leader with a congregation of 14,000 worshippers in the largest church in Colorado. He is married with five children and has boyish dimples and a warm smile.

In 2006, at the peak of his career, a male prostitute accused Haggard of having a three-year sexual affair with him and of using drugs. This accusation was alarming not only because Haggard was a married pastor, but also because he publicly supported a constitutional amendment banning gay marriage.

When the accusations were first broadcast on the news, Haggard confessed to church officials, saying, "Ninety-eight percent of what you know of me was the real me. Two percent of me would rise up, and I couldn't overcome it" (Haggard, 2006a).

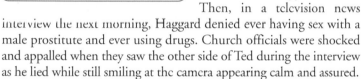

At the height of his career, Ted Haggard, well-known pastor, confessed to "sexual immorality."

Then, in a television news interview the next morning, Haggard denied ever having sex with a male prostitute and ever using drugs. Church officials were shocked and appalled when they saw the other side of Ted during the interview as he lied while still smiling at the camera appearing calm and assured.

As evidence of Haggard having sexual encounters with a male prostitute and using drugs continued to build, he made the following public confession: "The fact is that I am guilty of sexual immorality . . . I'm a deceiver and a liar. There is part of my life that is so repulsive and dark that I've been warring against it all of my adult life" (Haggard, 2006a). Haggard resigned as president of the 30-million-member National Association of Evangelicals and was dismissed as senior pastor of New Life Church. In less than 24 hours, everything Haggard had worked so hard for during the past 25 years quickly slipped away from him. Haggard may have been successful at battling evil on earth, but he lost the battle against evil within himself.

Figuring someone out involves examining the puzzling, fascinating, and complex components of our innermost selves, our personalities. *Personality* refers to a combination of long-lasting and distinctive behaviors, thoughts, motives, and emotions that typify how we react and adapt to other people and situations.

Haggard's moral public persona and dark private self raise a number of questions about personality: How does personality develop? Why do personalities differ? How well do we know ourselves? These kinds of questions are explored by theories of personality.

A *theory of personality* is an organized attempt to describe and explain how personalities develop and why personalities differ.

On the one hand, personality theories try to explain why Haggard's personality ended his career as an evangelical pastor. On the other hand, personality theories also try to explain why some individuals have personalities that help them overcome horrendous problems and achieve personal success. One such individual is Charles Dutton.

Changing Personality

How did he change from a criminal to an actor?

Charles Dutton had been in and out of reform schools since he was 12 years old and was finally sent to prison for manslaughter and illegal possession of a firearm. While in prison, he got into trouble for being a ringleader of a riot and was punished with solitary confinement. To pass his time, he took along a friend's book of plays by black authors. Dutton was so moved by the plays' messages that for the first time he thought about channeling his rage and anger into acting.

At one point he spent more than 60 painful days in the prison hospital after a fellow inmate had plunged an ice pick through his neck. During those long days in the hospital, Dutton decided that it was time to put his life in order and accomplish something worthwhile during his remaining time in prison. He obtained a high school equivalency certificate and then a two-year college degree, read dozens of plays, and even started a prison theater. After his parole, he attended college and got his B.A. in drama. His high point came when he was accepted into Yale drama school.

By the early 1990s, ex-problem boy, ex-con, ex-prisoner Charles Dutton (right photo) had turned into a very successful actor and starred in his own television series. He has since gone on to star in and direct movies (S. King, 1991; *San Diego Union-Tribune*, 2003). Dutton's story is an emotionally painful search for identity, culminating in the discovery and development of his acting potential. We'll discuss a theory of personality that emphasizes the development of our full potential.

Charles Dutton, formerly a convict and violent prisoner, became a respected actor and director.

What's Coming

We'll discuss two very different theories of personality: Sigmund Freud's psychodynamic theory emphasizes unconscious forces, irrational thoughts, and the lasting impressions of childhood experiences, whereas humanistic theories emphasize our rational processes and our natural striving to reach our true potentials.

We'll begin with a look at Ted Haggard's problems and where his inner demons came from.

A. Freud's Psychodynamic Theory

Why sexual immorality at age 50?

Freud's theory of personality begins with a controversial assumption that is an important key to unlocking the secrets of personality. To understand how Freud found this key idea, we'll journey back in time to the late 1800s.

At that time, Freud was wondering why several of his women patients had developed very noticeable physical symptoms, such as losing all sensation in their hands or being unable to control the movements of their legs. What most puzzled Freud, who was a medical doctor, was that despite these obvious physical complaints, he could not identify a single physical cause for these symptoms. Somehow, Freud's brilliant mind solved this problem and, in so doing, found an important key to unlocking the secrets of personality. Freud reasoned that since there were no observable physical or neurological causes of the women's physical symptoms, the causes must come from unconscious psychological forces (Westen & Gabbard, 1999).

In the 1800s, Freud's belief that human behavior was influenced by unconscious psychological forces was revolutionary, and it led to his equally revolutionary theory of personality.

Freud's psychodynamic theory of personality **emphasizes the importance of early childhood experiences, unconscious or repressed thoughts that we cannot voluntarily access, and the conflicts between conscious and unconscious forces that influence our feelings, thoughts, and behaviors.**

Freud believed not only that unconscious psychological forces

Freud would say childhood experiences and unconscious forces played a role in Ted Haggard's "sexual immorality."

had a powerful influence on personality but also that these forces originated in early childhood. If Freud were alive today, he would look for reasons behind Ted Haggard's self-confessed "sexual immorality" at age 50 by searching through Ted's childhood and his unconscious thoughts and forces. Here's what Freud would find.

Background. Ted Haggard was raised in a very religious family with a born-again father and a mother who counted the days to Sunday to help get Ted and his siblings excited about church. Ted remembers dressing in starched shirts and clip-on ties, clipping his nails just before church, and never missing a service. Ted wanted to attend journalism school, but his father pushed him to attend a Christian college. Soon after, Ted recalls receiving a calling from God to become a pastor (Asay, 2007; *Colorado Springs Gazette*, 2002). Even though Ted believes God wanted him to become a pastor, he admits to battling dark sexual desires throughout his adult life, which finally made him behave in inappropriate ways (Haggard, 2006a).

Freud might point to Ted's childhood, which was full of religious pressure, as greatly affecting his personality development and causing problems that eventually overwhelmed Ted. To explain the complex development of someone's personality, such as Ted Haggard's, is such a difficult task that only a dozen or so psychologists have tried. One of the best-known attempts to explain personality is included in Sigmund Freud's (1901/1960, 1924, 1940) overall theory of psychoanalysis, which includes two related theories: a method of psychotherapy, which we'll discuss in Module 24, and a theory of personality development, which we'll focus on here.

We'll begin with Freud's controversial and revolutionary assumption that unconscious psychological forces influence behavior.

Conscious Versus Unconscious Forces

Why was Ted Haggard fighting his dark side?

Ted Haggard's life was full of inconsistencies. His public behaviors as a pastor and husband were moral and respectable, but his private behaviors of having sexual relations with a male escort were immoral and degrading to his character: "The public person I was wasn't a lie; it was just incomplete . . . the darkness increased and finally dominated me. As a result, I did things that were contrary to everything I believe" (Haggard, 2006a).

Ted indicated that just as he had preached all along, he believed homosexual acts were immoral and lying about a sexual affair was equivalent to "the stinking garbage of a rotting sin" (Haggard, 2006b). In doing so, he was expressing conscious thoughts.

Conscious thoughts **are wishes, desires, or thoughts that we are aware of, or can recall, at any given moment.**

However, Freud theorized that our conscious thoughts are only a small part of our total mental activity, much of which involves unconscious thoughts or forces (Adler, 2006; McCrae & Costa, 2003).

Unconscious forces **represent wishes, desires, or thoughts**

that, **because of their disturbing or threatening content, we automatically repress and cannot voluntarily access.**

Did Ted have sexual relations with a male escort because of some unconscious forces that he was unaware of and had repressed? According to Freud, although repressed thoughts are unconscious, they may influence our behaviors through unconscious motivation.

Unconscious motivation **is a Freudian concept that refers to the influence of repressed thoughts, desires, or impulses on our conscious thoughts and behaviors.**

Freud used unconscious forces and motivation to explain why we say or do things that we cannot explain or understand. Once he assumed that there were unconscious forces and motivations, Freud needed to find ways to explore the unconscious.

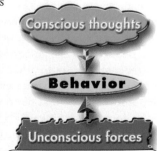

Freud would say that unconscious thoughts, desires, and feelings influence behaviors.

What was in Ted Haggard's unconscious?

It was one thing for Freud to propose the existence of powerful unconscious psychological forces and motivations, but it was quite another thing for him to show that such unconscious forces actually existed. For example, were there any signs that unconscious psychological forces were making Ted Haggard act out his sexual desires that were contrary to his conscious beliefs?

Ted's very strong religious upbringing and pressure from his father to attend a Christian college may have been too much for Ted to cope with as he was growing up. These early experiences may have served as unconscious forces that led him to act out against his Christian values, such as by having an affair with a male escort even though he was a married pastor with five children. Also, in contrast to his homosexual desires and his long-term relationship with a male escort is his strong public advocacy to ban gay marriages. The inconsistency between the values Ted learned while growing up and his sexual desires during adulthood undeniably led to Ted feeling anxious and guilty. As a way of coping with his anxiety and guilt, Ted actively condemned gay marriages, a behavior that is directly opposite to his own unacceptacle thoughts and wishes.

Freud proposed ways to unlock unconscious wishes and feelings.

Because neither Ted nor any of us can easily or voluntarily reveal or talk about our unconscious thoughts and desires, Freud needed to find ways for his patients to reveal their unconscious thoughts and desires, some of which may be psychologically threatening or disturbing. From observing his patients during therapy, Freud believed he had found three techniques that uncovered, revealed, or hinted at a person's unconscious wishes and desires.

Three techniques. Freud's three techniques to uncover the unconscious were free association, dream interpretation, and analysis of slips of the tongue (commonly known as Freudian slips) (Grunbaum, 2006).

Free Association

One of Freud's techniques for revealing the unconscious was to encourage his patients to relax and to sit back or lie down on his now-famous couch and talk freely about anything. He called this process free association.

Free association is a Freudian technique in which clients are encouraged to talk about any thoughts or images that enter their head; the assumption is that this kind of free-flowing, uncensored talking will provide clues to unconscious material.

Free association, which is one of Freud's important discoveries, continues to be used today by some therapists (Lothane, 2006b). However, not all therapists agree that free associations actually reveal a client's unconscious thoughts, desires, and wishes (Grunbaum, 1993).

Dream Interpretation

Freud listened to and interpreted his patients' dreams because he believed that dreams represent the purest form of free association and a path to the unconscious.

Exploring the unconscious with free association, dreams, and slips of the tongue

Dream interpretation, a Freudian technique of analyzing dreams, is based on the assumption that dreams contain underlying, hidden meanings and symbols that provide clues to unconscious thoughts and desires. Freud distinguished between the dream's obvious story or plot, called manifest content, and the dream's hidden or disguised meanings or symbols, called latent content.

For example, Freud interpreted the hidden meaning of dreams' objects, such as sticks and knives, as being symbols for male sexual organs and interpreted other objects (such as boxes and ovens) as symbols for female sexual organs. The therapist's task is to look behind the dream's manifest content (bizarre stories and symbols) and interpret the symbols' hidden or latent content, which provides clues to a person's unconscious wishes, feelings, and thoughts (Lothane, 2006a).

Freudian Slips

At one time or another, most of us, according to Freud, unintentionally reveal some unconscious thought or desire by making what is now called a Freudian slip (Grunbaum, 2006).

Freudian slips are mistakes or slips of the tongue that we make in everyday speech; such mistakes, which are often embarrassing, are thought to reflect unconscious thoughts or wishes.

For example, a colleague was lecturing on the importance of regular health care. She said, "It is important to visit a veterinarian for regular checkups." According to Freud, mistakes like substituting *veterinarian* for *physician* are not accidental but rather "intentional" ways of expressing unconscious desires. As it turns out, our colleague, who is in very good health, was having serious doubts about her relationship with a person who happened to be a veterinarian.

Freud assumed that free association, dream interpretation, and slips of the tongue share one thing in common: They are all mental processes that are the least controlled by our conscious, rational, and logical minds. As a result, he believed that these three techniques allowed uncensored clues to slip out and reveal our deeper unconscious wishes and desires (Grunbaum, 2006).

According to Freud's theory, there is a continuing battle going on in our minds between conscious thoughts and unconscious forces. How our minds fight these battles is perhaps one of Freud's best-known theories, and you'll easily recognize many of the terms, including id, ego, and superego.

B. Divisions of the Mind

What was in his apology letter?

Ted Haggard wrote an apology letter that was read to his congregation. Ted's letter revealed some of his problems and internal struggle. Here is an excerpt from his letter (Haggard, 2006a): "For extended periods of time, I would enjoy victory and rejoice in freedom. Then, from time to time, the dirt that I thought was gone would resurface, and I would find myself thinking thoughts and experiencing desires that were contrary to everything I believe and teach."

Freud might say that Haggard's immoral acts result from inner conflicts between his id and superego.

The above excerpt and other quotes you've read earlier in this module suggest Ted was fighting a number of psychological and emotional battles. After years of maintaining his privacy, Ted's problems became public when he confirmed that accusations of him having sexual relations with a male escort were true. According to Freud's theory, some of Ted's driving forces were rising from unconscious battles among three separate mental processes, which you know as the id, ego, and superego.

Iceberg example. To understand how the id, ego, and superego interact, imagine an iceberg floating in the sea. The part of the iceberg that is above water represents conscious forces of which we are aware, while parts below the water indicate unconscious forces of which we are not aware.

Freud divided the mind into three separate processes, each with a different function. Because of their different functions, Freud believed that interactions among the id, ego, and superego would result in conflicts (Jacobs, 2003).

Please begin at the top left with number **1**, the id.

1 Id: Pleasure Seeker

Freud believed that mental processes must have a source of energy, which he called the id.

The *id,* which is Freud's first division of the mind to develop, contains two biological drives—sex and aggression—that are the source of all psychic or mental energy; the id's goal is to pursue pleasure and satisfy the biological drives.

Freud assumed that the id operated at a totally unconscious level, which is analogous to an iceberg's massive underwater bulk. The id operates according to the pleasure principle.

The *pleasure principle* operates to satisfy drives and avoid pain, without concern for moral restrictions or society's regulations.

You can think of the id as a spoiled child who operates in a totally selfish, pleasure-seeking way without regard for reason, logic, or morality. Simply following the pleasure principle leads to conflict with others (parents), and this conflict results in the development of the ego.

2 Ego: Executive Negotiator between Id and Superego

As infants discover that parents put restrictions on satisfying their wishes, infants learn to control their wishes through the development of an ego.

The *ego,* which is Freud's second division of the mind, develops from the id during infancy; the ego's goal is to find safe and socially acceptable ways of satisfying the id's desires and to negotiate between the id's wants and the superego's prohibitions.

Freud said that a relatively large part of the ego's material is conscious (iceberg above water), such as information that we have gathered in adapting to our environments. A smaller part of the ego's material is unconscious (below water), such as threatening wishes that have been repressed. In contrast to the id's pleasure principle, the ego follows the reality principle.

The *reality principle* has a policy of satisfying a wish or desire only if there is a socially acceptable outlet available.

You can think of the ego as an executive negotiator that operates in a reasonable, logical, and socially acceptable way in finding outlets for satisfaction. The ego works to resolve conflicts that may arise because of different goals of the id and superego.

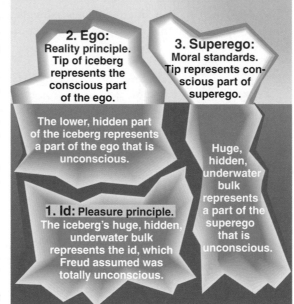

2. Ego: Reality principle. Tip of iceberg represents the conscious part of the ego.

The lower, hidden part of the iceberg represents a part of the ego that is unconscious.

3. Superego: Moral standards. Tip represents conscious part of superego.

Huge, hidden, underwater bulk represents a part of the superego that is unconscious.

1. Id: Pleasure principle. The iceberg's huge, hidden, underwater bulk represents the id, which Freud assumed was totally unconscious.

3 Superego: Regulator

As children learn that they must follow rules and regulations in satisfying their wishes, they develop a superego.

The *superego,* which is Freud's third division of the mind, develops from the ego during early childhood; the superego's goal is to apply the moral values and standards of one's parents or caregivers and society in satisfying one's wishes.

Think of the iceberg's visible tip as representing that part of the superego's moral standards of which we are conscious or aware and the huge underwater bulk as representing the part of the superego's moral standards that are unconscious or outside our awareness.

A child develops a superego through interactions with the parents or caregivers and by taking on or incorporating the parents' or caregivers' standards, values, and rules. The superego's power is in making the person feel guilty if the rules are disobeyed. Because the pleasure-seeking id wants to avoid feeling guilty, it is motivated to listen to the superego. You can think of a superego as a moral guardian or conscience that is trying to regulate or control the id's wishes and impulses.

Disagreements. Freud believed that in some situations there is little or no disagreement between the goals of the id and superego, which means a person experiences little if any conflict. However, in other situations, there could be disagreements between the goals of the id and superego, which result in the ego (executive negotiator) trying to mediate this conflict. Freud describes a number of mental processes that the ego uses to mediate conflicts between the id and superego. We'll next discuss these mental processes, called defense mechanisms.

Why do you feel anxious? Suppose you know that you should study for tomorrow's exam but at the same time you want to go to a friend's party. Freud explained that in this kind of situation there is a conflict between the desires of the pleasure-seeking id and the goals of the conscience-regulating superego, and this conflict causes anxiety.

Anxiety, in Freudian theory, is an uncomfortable feeling that results from inner conflicts between the primitive desires of the id and the moral goals of the superego.

For example, the study-or-party situation sets up a conflict between the pleasure-seeking goal of the id, which is to go to the party, and the conscience-keeping goal of the superego, which is to stay home and

study. Caught in the middle of this id–superego conflict is the ego, which, like any good executive, tries to negotiate an acceptable solution. However, this id–superego conflict along with the ego's continuing negotiations to resolve this conflict causes anxious feelings. Freud suggested that the ego, as executive negotiator, tries to reduce the anxious feelings by using a number of mental processes, which he called defense mechanisms (Cramer, 2006).

What happens if you want to party but know you should study?

Defense Mechanisms

Have you ever rationalized? In trying to decide whether to go to a friend's party or stay home and study for an important exam, a student would experience increasing levels of anxiety. Freud reasoned that anxiety is a sure sign of the id–superego inner conflict and that in order to reduce levels of anxiety, the ego may use defense mechanisms (Cramer, 2003, 2006).

Defense mechanisms are Freudian processes that operate at unconscious levels and that use self-deception or untrue explanations to protect the ego from being overwhelmed by anxiety.

According to Freud, a student's ego has two ways to reduce anxiety over deciding whether to party or study. The student's ego can take realistic steps to reduce anxiety, such as motivating or convincing the student to stay home and study. Or the student's ego can use a number of defense mechanisms, which reduce anxiety by deceiving the student to think it's OK to party and then study tomorrow. Here is a brief summary of some of Freud's more popular defense mechanisms (Durand & Barlow, 2006).

Rationalization involves covering up the true reasons for actions, thoughts, or feelings by making up excuses and incorrect explanations.

A student may rationalize that by going to a party tonight he or she will feel more motivated to study for the exam tomorrow, even if he or she will be very tired and in no mood or condition to study tomorrow.

Denial is refusing to recognize some anxiety-provoking event or piece of information that is clear to others.

Heavy smokers would be using denial if they disregarded the scientific evidence that smoking increases the risk of lung cancer and cardiovascular disease and in addition would be using rationalization if they say they can quit any time they want.

Repression involves blocking and pushing unacceptable or threatening feelings, wishes, or experiences into the unconscious.

Having feelings of jealousy about your best friend's academic success might be threatening to your self-concept, so you unknowingly block these unwanted feelings by also unknowingly pushing them into your unconscious.

Defense mechanisms function like a mental traffic cop trying to reduce conflict and anxiety.

Projection falsely and unconsciously attributes your own unacceptable feelings, traits, or thoughts to individuals or objects.

A student who refuses to accept responsibility for cheating during exams may look at other students and decide that they are cheating.

Reaction formation involves substituting behaviors, thoughts, or feelings that are the direct opposite of unacceptable ones.

A person who feels guilty about engaging in sexual activity may use reaction formation by joining a religious group that bans sex.

Displacement involves transferring feelings about, or response to, an object that causes anxiety to another person or object that is less threatening.

If you were anxious about getting angry at your best friend, you might unknowingly displace your anger by picking an argument with a safer individual, such as a salesclerk, waiter, or stranger.

Sublimation, which is a type of displacement, involves redirecting a threatening or forbidden desire, usually sexual, into a socially acceptable one.

For instance, a person might sublimate strong sexual desires by channeling that energy into physical activities.

Conclusions. Freud believed that defense mechanisms are totally unconscious, which means that, if a best friend or spouse points out that you are being defensive, you will absolutely deny it. We all use defense mechanisms at some time and they can be helpful or harmful. For example, the occasional use of defense mechanisms is normal and helps reduce conflict and anxiety so that we can continue to function as we work on the real cause of our anxiety. However, the overuse of defense mechanisms may prevent us from recognizing or working on the real causes of our anxiety. There is growing scientific evidence that we do indeed use unconscious defense mechanisms much as Freud theorized, which is to reduce anxiety and conflict. In fact, many of us have a dominant or most-often-used defense mechanism, which may be effective in reducing short-term but not necessarily long-term anxiety (Cramer, 2003, 2006).

We have discussed the three divisions of the mind—id, ego, and superego—and how the ego may use defense mechanisms to reduce anxiety. Now we'll turn to how one's ego and personality develop.

C. Developmental Stages

What shaped Ted's personality?

Imagine a theory so broad that it is able to describe almost exactly how and why your personality developed the way it did and why you did or did not develop certain personality problems along the way. Such is Sigmund Freud's personality theory, which can give a complex description of how each of us develops a different personality.

Case study. For example, let's return to the case of Ted Haggard. He was raised in a strong Christian family that never missed a Sunday service, and his father encouraged him to attend a Christian college. He got married and had five children while becoming the founder of the largest church in Colorado. Ted's life also had a dark side consisting of infidelity, lies, and hypocrisy, all of which made him feel anxious and guilty. He preached one thing and did the opposite behind everyone's back. When his immoral acts were discovered, he confessed to church officials but then went on a television news broadcast smiling happily and denying all accusations.

Psychosexual stages. According to Freud, the development of Ted's personality, such as being all smiles on the outside but feeling anxious and guilty internally, was primarily influenced by how he dealt with the five different kinds of conflicts that occurred at five different times or stages. According to Freud (1940), our personality develops as we pass through and deal with potential conflicts at five psychosexual stages.

According to Freud, Haggard's personality developed as he passed through five psychosexual stages.

Psychosexual stages are five developmental periods—oral, anal, phallic, latency, and genital stages—each marked by potential conflict between parent and child. The conflicts arise as a child seeks pleasure from different body areas that are associated with sexual feelings (different *erogenous zones*). Freud emphasized that the child's first five years were most important in personality development.

You can think of each psychosexual stage as being a source of potential *conflict* between the child's id, which seeks immediate gratification, and the parents, who place restrictions on when, where, and how the gratification can take place. For example, the child may want to be fed immediately, while the parent may wish to delay the feeding to a more convenient time. The kind of interactions that occur between parent and child in satisfying these psychosexual needs and the way a child learns to deal with psychosexual conflicts, especially during breast feeding or toilet training, will greatly influence the personality development as well as future problems and social interactions.

One of Freud's controversial ideas is the relationship between early psychosexual stages and development of later personality, social, and emotional problems. Here is Freud's explanation of how different problems may arise.

Why did Ted develop problems?

Freud explained that the way a person deals with early psychosexual conflicts lays the groundwork for personality growth and future problems. This means that, to a large extent, Ted's later personality problems grew out of early childhood experiences. Freud would say that Ted's problems in finding his identity began in childhood, likely as a result of having a specific need or wish that was either undergratified or overgratified.

Fixation. As an adult, there were times when Ted was happy, but at other times he was anxious and guilt-ridden. The problem for any theory of personality is to explain how problems and contradictions in personality occur. For example, why did Ted preach in front of 14,000 worshippers and become politically active, yet engage in immoral sexual conduct and then lie about it? Freud would explain that the development of Ted's personality depended, to a large extent, on the way he dealt with early psychosexual conflicts. One way a child can deal with or resolve these conflicts—wanting to satisfy all desires but not being allowed to by the parents—is to become fixated at a certain stage.

Healthy personality involves resolving conflicts during psychosexual stages.

Fixation, which can occur during any of the first three stages—oral, anal, or phallic—refers to a Freudian process through which an individual may be locked into a particular psychosexual stage because his or her wishes were either overgratified or undergratified.

For example, if a person were fixated at the oral stage because of *too little* gratification, he might go through life trying to obtain oral satisfaction through eating too much, boasting too much, or focusing on other oral behaviors. If fixation had occurred at the oral stage because of *too much* gratification, he might focus on seeking oral gratification while neglecting to develop other aspects of his personality.

Next, we'll summarize Freud's psychosexual stages, focusing on possible parent–child conflicts, problems from fixation, and implications for future personality and social development.

Fixation at one psychosexual stage could cause sexual problems.

What happens during the stages?

According to Freud, every child goes through certain situations, such as nursing, bottle feeding, and toilet training, that contain potential conflicts between the child's desire for instant satisfaction or gratification and the parents' wishes, which may involve delaying the child's satisfaction. How these conflicts are resolved and whether a child becomes fixated at one stage because of too much or too little satisfaction greatly influence development of personality and onset of future problems.

1 Oral Stage

Time. Early infancy: first 18 months of life.

Potential conflict. The *oral stage* lasts for the first 18 months of life and is a time when the infant's pleasure seeking is centered on the mouth.

Pleasure-seeking activities include sucking, chewing, and biting. If we were locked into or fixated at this stage because our oral wishes were gratified too much or too little, we would continue to seek oral gratification as adults. *Fixation* at this stage results in adults who continue to engage in oral activities, such as overeating, gum chewing, or smoking; oral activities can be symbolic as well, such as being overly demanding or "mouthing off."

2 Anal Stage

Time. Late infancy: $1\frac{1}{2}$ to 3 years.

Potential conflict. The *anal stage* lasts from the age of about $1\frac{1}{2}$ to 3 and is a time when the infant's pleasure seeking is centered on the anus and its functions of elimination.

Fixation at this stage results in adults who continue to engage in activities of retention or elimination. Retention may take the form of being very neat, stingy, or behaviorally rigid (thus the term *anal retentive*). Elimination may take the form of being generous, messy, or very loose or carefree.

3 Phallic Stage

Time. Early childhood: 3 to 6 years.

Potential conflict. The *phallic (FAL-ik) stage* lasts from the age of about 3 to 6 and is a time when the infant's pleasure seeking is centered on the genitals.

Freud theorized that the phallic stage is particularly important for personality development because of the occurrence of the Oedipus complex (named for Oedipus, the character in Greek mythology who unknowingly killed his father and married his mother).

The *Oedipus (ED-ah-pus) complex* is a process in which a child competes with the parent of the same sex for the affections and pleasures of the parent of the opposite sex.

According to Freud, the Oedipus complex causes different problems for boys and girls.

Boys. When a boy discovers that his penis is a source of pleasure, he develops a sexual attraction to his mother. As a result, the boy feels hatred, jealousy, and competition toward his father and has fears of castration. The boy resolves his Oedipus complex by identifying with his father. If he does not resolve the complex, fixation occurs and he may go through life trying to prove his toughness.

Girls. When a girl discovers that she does not have a penis, she feels a loss that Freud called *penis envy*. Her loss makes her turn against her mother and develop sexual desires for her father. A girl resolves her Oedipus complex, sometimes called the Electra complex (for Electra, a woman in Greek mythology who killed her mother), by identifying with her mother. If this complex is not resolved, fixation occurs and the woman may go through life feeling inferior to men.

Over the years, the idea of the Oedipus complex has waned in popularity and credibility, both within psychoanalysis and within the culture at large. That's because there's almost no way to scientifically test this idea. Also, Freud's assertion that the Oedipus complex occurs universally is not supported by data from other cultures (Crews, 1996).

1. Oral
2. Anal
3. Phallic
4. Latency
5. Genital

Freud would say that Ted's personality depended to a large extent on what happened during five psychosexual stages.

4 Latency Stage

Time. Middle and late childhood: 6 to puberty.

Potential conflict. The *latency stage,* which lasts from about age 6 to puberty, is a time when the child represses sexual thoughts and engages in nonsexual activities, such as developing social and intellectual skills.

At puberty, sexuality reappears and marks the beginning of a new stage, called the genital stage.

5 Genital Stage

Time. Puberty through adulthood.

Potential conflict. The *genital stage* lasts from puberty through adulthood and is a time when the individual has renewed sexual desires that he or she seeks to fulfill through relationships with other people.

How a person meets the conflicts of the genital stage depends on how conflicts in the first three stages were resolved. If the individual is fixated at an earlier stage, less energy will be available to resolve conflicts at the genital stage. If the individual successfully resolved conflicts in the first three stages, he or she will have the energy to develop loving relationships and a healthy and mature personality.

Summary. Freud's psychodynamic theory of personality development made a number of assumptions that, at the time, were revolutionary. His assumptions included the influence of unconscious forces; the division of the mind into the id, ego, and superego; the importance of resolving conflicts at five psychosexual stages; the importance of fixation; and the importance of the first five years to personality development.

Next, we'll discuss what Freud's critics have had to say about his theory and assumptions.

D. Freud's Followers & Critics

What did they argue about?

Because Freud's theory was so creative and revolutionary for its time, it attracted many followers, who formed a famous group called the Vienna Psychoanalytic Society. However, it was not long before members of the society began to disagree over some of Freud's theories and assumptions, such as whether Freud placed too much emphasis on biological urges (sex and aggression), psychosexual stages, and importance of early childhood experience in personality development (Horgan, 1996). We'll focus on three influential followers who eventually broke with Freud's theory.

Carl Jung

Jung disagreed on the importance of the sex drive.

Why did Freud's "crown prince" stop talking to him?

In 1910 Carl Jung, with the wholehearted support of Sigmund Freud, became the first president of the Vienna Psychoanalytic Society. Freud said that Jung was to be his "crown prince" and personal successor. However, just four years later, Jung and Freud ended their personal and professional relationship and never again spoke to each other.

The main reason for the split was that Jung disagreed with Freud's emphasis on the sex drive. Jung believed the collective unconscious—and not sex—was the basic force in the development of personality.

The *collective unconscious,* according to Jung, consists of ancient memory traces and symbols that are passed on by birth and are shared by all peoples in all cultures.

Jung's theory of collective unconscious and his elaborate theory of personality, called *analytical psychology,* had more influence on the areas of art, literature, philosophy, and counseling/therapy than on current areas of psychology.

Alfred Adler

Adler disagreed on the importance of biological urges.

Why did one of the society's presidents resign?

Alfred Adler was another contemporary of Freud's who later became president of the Vienna Psychoanalytic Society. However, after Adler voiced his disagreement with Freud at one of the society's meetings, he was so badly criticized by the other members that he resigned as president.

Like Jung, Adler disagreed with Freud's theory that humans are governed by biological and sexual urges. Adler believed that the main factors influencing a child's development were sibling influences and child-rearing practices.

In contrast to Freud's biological drives, Adler proposed that humans are motivated by *social urges* and that each person is a social being with a unique personality. Adler formed his own group, whose philosophy became known as *individual psychology.* In contrast to Freud's emphasis on unconscious forces that influence our behaviors, Adler suggested that we are aware of our motives and goals and have the capacity to guide and plan our futures.

Karen Horney

Horney disagreed on the importance of penis envy.

What would a woman say about penis envy?

Karen Horney was trained as a psychoanalyst; her career reached its peak shortly after Freud's death in 1939. For many years, Horney was dean of the American Institute of Psychoanalysis in New York.

Horney strongly objected to Freud's view that women were dependent, vain, and submissive because of biological forces and childhood sexual experiences. She especially took issue with Freud's idea that penis envy affects girls' development.

In contrast to Freud's psychosexual conflicts, Horney insisted that the major influence on personality development, whether in women or men, can be found in child–parent *social interactions.* Unlike Freud, who believed that every child must experience child–parent conflicts, Horney theorized that such conflicts are avoidable if the child is raised in a loving, trusting, and secure environment. Karen Horney would now be called a feminist and is credited with founding the psychology of women.

Karen Horney is sometimes referred to as a *neo-Freudian* because she changed and renovated Freud's original theory. One of the best-known neo-Freudians was Erik Erikson, who formulated his own theory of personality development, which we discussed in Modules 17 and 18. Erikson proposed that everyone goes through a series of *psychosocial* stages, rather than the *psychosexual* stages proposed by Freud.

Neo-Freudians generally agreed with Freud's basic ideas, such as the importance of the unconscious; the

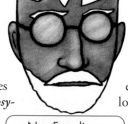

Neo-Freudians focused on social and cultural factors.

division of the mind into the id, ego, and superego; and the use of defense mechanisms to protect the ego. However, they mostly disagreed with Freud's placing so much emphasis on biological forces, sexual drives, and psychosexual stages. The neo-Freudians turned the emphasis of Freud's psychodynamic theory away from biological drives toward psychosocial and cultural influences (Plante, 2005).

From early on, followers of Freud criticized his theory and, as you'll see, criticisms continue to the present day.

What is the current status of Freud's theory?

In 1993, *Time* magazine's cover featured a picture of Sigmund Freud with the question "Is Freud Dead?" Answering this question with a loud "Yes" are several scholarly books that seriously question Freud's theory and all its assumptions (Crews, 1996, 1999). Answering this question with a loud "No" are hundreds of members of the American Psychological Association's psychoanalysis division and many neuroscientists who meet the attacks on Freud with equally strong defenses (Horgan, 1996; Solms, 2006). To give you an idea of where Freud's theory stands today, we'll focus on four questions: How valid is Freud's theory? How important are the first five years? Are there unconscious forces? What was the impact of Freud's theory?

1 HOW VALID IS FREUD'S THEORY?

Too comprehensive. Freud's psychodynamic theory, which includes how the mind develops (id, ego, and superego), how personality develops (psychosexual stages), and how to do therapy (psychoanalysis), is so comprehensive that it can explain almost any behavior. For example, Freud's theory predicts that fixation at the anal stage may result in a person being at one extreme very messy and at the other extreme very neat. Advocates of Freud's theory state that it is a coherent and sophisticated view of the mind, while critics argue that Freud's theory is too comprehensive to be useful in explaining or predicting behaviors of specific individuals (Horgan, 1996; Kandel, 2006).

Difficult to test. Current followers agree that some of Freud's concepts, such as the id being the source of energy, the importance of the Oedipus complex in personality development, and basic drives limited to sex and aggression, have been difficult to test or verify and are now out of date. The same followers add that other Freudian concepts, such as the influence of unconscious forces, long-term effects of early childhood patterns, and existence of defense mechanisms and conflicting cognitive processes, have been experimentally tested and received support (Fotopoulou, 2006; Ramachandran, 2006; Westen & Gabbard, 1999).

Must be updated. However, if psychoanalysis or psychodynamic theory is to survive in the 2000s, Freud's theory must continue to be tested experimentally and updated with findings from other areas of psychology. For example, Freud's theory needs to include how *genetic factors* account for 20 to 50% of a wide range of behaviors and explain how *brain development*, which is not complete until early adulthood, is associated with and necessary for the development of related behaviors, thoughts, and feelings (Westen, 1998). Currently, neuroscientists are examining many of Freud's questions about the mind and hope to build upon his theory (Solms, 2006).

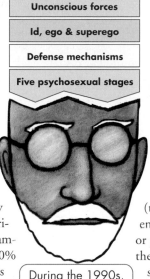

Theory of Personality

Unconscious forces

Id, ego & superego

Defense mechanisms

Five psychosexual stages

During the 1990s, Freud's theory had several major revisions.

3 ARE THERE UNCONSCIOUS FORCES?

One of Freud's major assumptions was that unconscious or repressed forces influence our conscious thoughts and behaviors. In contrast to Freud's theory of the repressed unconscious forces, cognitive neuroscientists developed a different concept, called implicit or nondeclarative memory (Frensch & Runger, 2003; Solms, 2006).

Implicit or *nondeclarative memory* means learning without awareness, such as occurs in experiencing emotional situations or acquiring motor habits. Although we are unaware of such learning, it can influence our conscious feelings, thoughts, and behaviors.

Examples of what goes into implicit memory include procedural memories (p. 246), such as motor skills and habits (typing), and classical or conditioned emotional responses, such as irrational fears or phobia. Thus, there is strong evidence for the *influence of unconscious forces* on conscious thoughts, feelings, and behaviors, but these forces are part of a cognitive-emotional system rather than Freud's battleground for conflicts among the id, ego, and superego (Guterl, 2002).

2 HOW IMPORTANT ARE THE FIRST FIVE YEARS?

Based on observations of his patients, Freud concluded that personality development is essentially complete after the first five years. However, Freud never did systematic research or collected longitudinal observations to support his hypothesis that personality development is fixed during a child's first five years (Bruer, 1999). In fact, there are two lines of research showing the opposite. First, our earlier discussion of *resilient children* (p. 394) indicated that the occurrence of serious psychological and physical problems during the first five years does not necessarily stunt or inhibit personality development, as Freud predicted. Many children who had experienced poverty, the death of or separation from their parents, or a poor home life developed into healthy, mature adults provided the children had a loving caregiver (E. E. Werner & Smith, 2001).

Second, a number of *longitudinal studies* that followed children into adulthood indicate that personality development is not complete in the first five years but rather continues well into middle adulthood (Caspi & Roberts, 1999). For these reasons, current psychologists question Freud's idea that personality development is complete in the first five years.

4 WHAT WAS FREUD'S IMPACT?

Freud's theory has had an enormous impact on society, as can be seen in the widespread use of Freudian terms *(ego, id, rationalization)* in literature, art, and our everyday conversations. Freud's theory also has had a great impact on psychology: Many of his concepts have been incorporated into the fields of personality, development, abnormal psychology, and psychotherapy. However, as we have discussed, some of Freud's terms are out of date *(Oedipus complex)* and Freud's psychoanalytic theory was modified in the 1990s (Guterl, 2002; Westen & Gabbard, 1999).

Unlike Freud's psychodynamic theory, which paints a picture of humans filled with irrational and unconscious forces with little free choice, we next discuss a family of theories—humanistic theory—that is almost the direct opposite of Freud's theory.

E. Humanistic Theories

How did he develop his real potential?

At the beginning of this module, we told you about two very different people. One was evangelical Christian leader Ted Haggard, who struggled with numerous personal problems. At age 50, as a husband, father, and national evangelical leader, he confessed to having sexual relations with a male escort and purchasing drugs.

The other person was Charles Dutton, who had been in and out of reform schools since he was 12 years old, was sent to prison on charges of manslaughter, and spent time in solitary confinement for his ringleader role in a prison riot. Just when most people would have given up on reforming Dutton, he began to reform himself. Inspired by reading a book of plays, he began to channel his rage against society into becoming a student and then an actor. After leaving prison, Charles Dutton (right photo) worked hard to change his life and became a very successful theater, television, and movie actor and director (Brantley, 2003).

What Dutton and Haggard shared in common as young men was that neither showed particular evidence of having special talents or great potentials. Few people would have predicted that Ted Haggard, who as a teen wanted to pursue journalism, would become a nationally recognized Christian pastor. No one would have predicted that angry, tough, mean Charles Dutton would discover, of all things, acting and would channel his anger into becoming a very successful professional actor. The lives of these two men demonstrate the difficulty in predicting someone's potential and whether he or she will develop it. Developing our potential is at the heart of humanistic theory.

Humanistic theories **emphasize our capacity for personal growth, development of our potential, and freedom to choose our destiny.**

Humanistic theories reject the biological determinism and the irrational, unconscious forces of Freud's psychodynamic theory. Humanistic theories emphasize freely choosing to go after one's dream and to change one's destiny, as Michelle Wie is doing.

> When most would have given up, Charles Dutton turned his life around.

Three Characteristics of Humanistic Theories

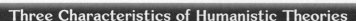

What was her goal?

Michelle Wie's goal since childhood has been to become a professional golfer and to graduate from Stanford University. Michelle started golfing at the young age of 4, and by age 11, she was winning amateur tournaments. Her countless hours of practicing, training, and pushing herself to the limits helped her to become the youngest female professional golfer (age 17) and to be accepted to Stanford University, her dream school (Gyr, 2007; Mario, 2006).

Michelle Wie's life illustrates the humanists' emphasis on developing fully one's potential to lead a rich and meaningful life and becoming the best person one can become (Moss, 2002). Michelle's drive to reach her lifelong dream exemplifies the three characteristics that distinguish humanistic theory from other theories of personality. We'll describe each of the three characteristics unique to humanistic theory: a phenomenological perspective, a holistic view, and a goal of self-actualization (Clay, 2002).

1 Humanistic theories stress learning about the world through personal experiences, which illustrates the phenomenological *(feh-nom-in-no-LODGE-uh-cal)* perspective.

The *phenomenological perspective* **means that your perception or view of the world, whether or not it is accurate, becomes your reality.**

For instance, Michelle's phenomenological perspective of how she perceived her golfing abilities may or may not have been accurate. However, because she believed so strongly that she had the abilities, this perception became her reality. Other examples of phenomenological perspectives are long-held beliefs that women could not perform certain jobs—for example, police officer, doctor, plumber, truck driver, or lawyer. Since women have demonstrated that they can perform these jobs, this particular perception has been proven false. As a result, people (especially men) have developed a new perspective and accepted the reality of what women can accomplish.

> Michelle's life dreams include becoming a professional golfer and a Stanford graduate.

2 Humanistic theories emphasize looking at the whole situation or person, which illustrates the holistic *(hole-LIS-tick)* view.

The *holistic view* **means that a person's personality is more than the sum of its individual parts; instead, the individual parts form a unique and total entity that functions as a unit.**

For example, the holistic view would explain that Michelle became the youngest female golfer to turn professional because of her unique combination of many traits—discipline, ability, motivation, persistence, desire—rather than any single trait.

3 Humanistic theories highlight the idea of developing one's true potential, which is called self-actualization.

Self-actualization **refers to our inherent tendency to develop and reach our true potentials.**

By becoming a professional golfer and being admitted to Stanford University, Michelle is a wonderful example of someone who is developing and reaching her true potential and thus is getting closer to achieving a high level of self-actualization. According to humanists, each of us has the capacity for self-actualization and for reaching our own potential. Humanists believe that one's self-esteem, self-expression, belonging, creativity, and love are as important to human life as the biological needs of food and water (Rabasca, 2000a).

The beginning of humanistic theory in the 1960s can be traced to two psychologists—Abraham Maslow and Carl Rogers. They had surprisingly different backgrounds but arrived at the same uplifting ideas.

Why did a behaviorist become a humanist?

We can trace the official beginning of the humanistic movement to the early 1960s and the publication of the *Journal of Humanistic Psychology*. One of the major figures behind establishing this journal was Abraham Maslow. Interestingly enough, Maslow was trained as a behaviorist, but along the way he felt there was too much emphasis on rewards and punishments and observable behaviors and too little emphasis on other

important aspects of human nature, such as feelings, emotions, and beliefs. For these reasons, Maslow (1968) broke away from the reward/punishment/observable behavior mentality of behaviorism and developed his humanistic theory, which emphasized two things: our capacity for growth, or self-actualization, and our desire to satisfy a variety of needs, which he arranged in a hierarchy.

Maslow's Hierarchy of Needs

Maslow's Hierarchy of Needs

Level 5
Self-actualization: fulfillment of one's unique potential

Level 4
Esteem needs: achievement, competency, gaining approval and recognition

Level 3
Love and belonging needs: affiliation with others and acceptance by others

Level 2
Safety needs: protection from harm and concern about safety and survival

Level 1
Physiological needs: hunger, thirst, sex, and sleep

For just a moment, think of all the needs that you try to meet each day: eating, having a safe place to live, talking to your friends, perhaps working at a part-time job, caring for loved ones, and studying for exams. Maslow believed that you satisfy these needs in a certain order. As you may remember from Module 15 (p. 333), Maslow arranged all human needs into a hierarchy of five major needs.

Maslow's hierarchy of needs arranges needs in ascending order (figure on left), with biological needs at the bottom and social and personal needs at the top. Only when needs at a lower level are met can we advance to the next level.

According to Maslow's hierarchy, you must satisfy your biological and safety needs before using energy to fulfill your personal and social needs. Finally, you can devote time and energy to reaching your true potential, which is called self-actualization, your highest need.

Maslow divided our needs into two general categories: deficiency and growth needs.

Deficiency needs are physiological needs (food, sleep) and psychological needs (safety, love, esteem) that we try to fulfill if they are not met.

Growth needs are those at the higher levels and include the desire for truth, goodness, beauty, and justice.

According to Maslow, we must satisfy our deficiency needs before we have the time and energy to satisfy our growth needs and move toward self-actualization.

Self-Actualization

One of the major characteristics of the humanistic movement is the emphasis on a process called self-actualization.

Self-actualization refers to the development and fulfillment of one's unique human potential.

Maslow (1971) developed the concept of self-actualization after studying the lives of highly productive and exceptional people, such as Abraham Lincoln, Albert Einstein, and Eleanor Roosevelt. Maslow believed that these individuals had been able to reach the goal of self-actualization because they had developed the following personality characteristics.

Characteristics of Self-Actualized Individuals

- They perceive reality accurately.
- They are independent and autonomous.
- They prefer to have a deep, loving relationship with only a few people.
- They focus on accomplishing their goals.
- They report peak experiences, which are moments of great joy and satisfaction.

Maslow believed that, although very few individuals reach the level of self-actualization, everyone has a self-actualizing tendency. This tendency motivates us to become the best kind of person we are capable of becoming.

Civil rights leader Martin Luther King, Jr., is an example of a self-actualized person.

There is no doubt that Maslow would also have considered Martin Luther King, Jr., an example of a self-actualized person. Martin Luther King, Jr., devoted his life to achieving civil rights for all people. Here he delivers his famous "I Have a Dream" speech at a civil rights rally in Washington, D.C. He was awarded the Nobel Prize for peace at age 35. He was gunned down by an assassin's bullet at age 39. King's achievements exemplify the humanistic idea of self-actualization.

About the same time that Maslow was making this journey from behaviorism to humanism and developing the concept of self-actualization, another psychologist by the name of Carl Rogers was developing a different but related humanistic theory.

E. Humanistic Theories

Rogers: Self Theory

What are the two most important concepts?

Carl Rogers was initially trained in the psychodynamic approach, which he used in his practice as a clinical psychologist. However, Rogers began to feel that Freud placed too much emphasis on unconscious, irrational forces and on biological urges, and too little emphasis on human potential for psychological growth. As a result, Rogers gradually abandoned the psychodynamic approach in favor of a new theory of personality that he developed in the 1960s. Rogers's new humanistic theory is often called self theory because of his emphasis on the self or self-concept.

Self theory, also called *self-actualization theory,* **is based on two major assumptions: that personality development is guided by each person's unique self-actualization tendency, and that each of us has a personal need for positive regard.**

Rogers's first major assumption about self-actualization is similar but slightly different from Maslow's use of the term.

Rogers's self-actualizing tendency **refers to an inborn tendency for us to develop all of our capacities in ways that best maintain and benefit our lives.**

The self-actualizing tendency relates to *biological functions,* such as meeting our basic need for food, water, and oxygen, as well as *psychological functions,* such as expanding our experiences, encour-

Because of different experiences, the girl in the wheelchair will likely develop a different concept of self than the other girl.

aging personal growth, and becoming self-sufficient. The self-actualizing tendency guides us toward positive or healthful behaviors rather than negative or harmful ones. For example, one of the two girls in the photo below has lost the use of her legs and must use a wheelchair. Part of her self-actualizing process will include learning to deal with her disability, engaging in positive healthful behaviors, and getting to know herself.

Self or *self-concept* **refers to how we see or describe ourselves. The self is made up of many self-perceptions, abilities, personality characteristics, and behaviors that are organized and consistent with one another.**

Because of very different experiences, the girl in the wheelchair will develop a self-concept different from that of her friend who has normal use of her legs. According to Rogers (1980), self-concept plays an important role in personality because it influences our behaviors, feelings, and thoughts. For example, if you have a *positive self-concept,* you will tend to act, feel, and think optimistically and constructively; if you have a *negative self-concept,* you will tend to act, feel, and think pessimistically and destructively.

Sometimes a person may be undecided about his or her real self. As we discover our real self, we may undergo a number of changes in personality.

Real Self Versus Ideal Self

Who is the real Sean Combs?

We all change how we see ourselves but probably not as much as hip-hop star Sean Combs, who, through the years, has radically changed his appearance and even his name. For example, at the start of his career, Combs was known as "Puff Daddy" and his appearance (top photo) and behaviors (legal problems) might have been described as pushing some of society's limits. Now, however, Combs is known as "Diddy" and has a rather conventional appearance (bottom photo). He has become a huge donor to charities, and he recently attempted to release a gospel album, unlike his other albums that all require a "Parental Advisory" warning. The question is: Which is Combs's real self?

Carl Rogers said that his clients often asked questions related to their selves: "How do I find myself?" "Why do I sometimes feel that I don't know myself?" "Why do I say or do things that aren't really me?" Rogers developed a clever answer to these relatively common and perplexing questions. He said there are two kinds of selves: a real self and an ideal self.

The *real self,* according to Rogers, **is based on our actual experiences and represents how we really see ourselves.**

The *ideal self,* according to Rogers, **is based on our hopes and wishes and reflects how we would like to see ourselves.**

My ideal self is based on my hopes and wishes.

My real self is based on my actual experience.

In some cases, the hopes and wishes of one's ideal self may contradict the abilities and experiences of the real self. For example, a student's ideal self may be someone who is very responsible and studies hard, but the real self may be someone who puts things off and studies less than is required.

Contradiction between ideal and real self. According to Rogers, a glaring contradiction between the ideal and real selves can result in personality problems. Rogers suggested that we can resolve contradictions between our ideal and real selves by paying more attention to our actual experiences, working to have more positive experiences, and paying less attention to the expectations of others. In working out discrepancies between our ideal and real selves, we may undergo a variety of changes in our appearance and behaviors, such as Sean Combs experienced.

Now that you know what the self is, here's how Rogers says that it develops.

Why are there millions of dog owners?

One reason I'm (R.P.) one of the millions of dog owners is that my dog Bear shows great happiness at seeing me, no matter how grouchy, distracted, or sad I may feel or act. In fact, researchers find that because people perceive their pets as showing appreciation, being supportive, and giving pleasure, pets are helpful in reducing stressful feelings and lowering blood pressure (K. Allen, 2003; Stich, 2003). The healing power of pets can be so strong that patients with heart failure report having less anxiety and stress when visited in the hospital by dogs rather than people (Song, 2005).

The need to feel appreciated is so important that in the United States we have a number of days throughout the year that are officially designated for appreciation, such as

> It's so nice you're always glad to see me.

Mother's, Father's, Grandparent's, and Secretary's days, as well as birthdays and the heartfelt Valentine's Day.

The creation of appreciation days and the popularity of pets illustrate the second assumption of Carl Rogers's self theory, which is that we have a need for receiving something called positive regard.

Positive regard **includes love, sympathy, warmth, acceptance, and respect, which we crave from family, friends, and people important to us.**

Rogers believed that positive regard was essential for the healthy development of one's self as well as for successful interpersonal relationships (Liebert & Spiegler, 1994). When we are children, positive regard comes mainly from our parents, siblings, or grandparents. But as we become adults, we learn to provide some of our own positive regard.

Conditional and Unconditional Positive Regard

What's a big problem for teenagers?

Unlike friends and family, pets never pass judgment; they provide endless amounts of positive regard no matter how their owners look, feel, dress, or talk. In contrast, friends and family can be very judgmental and may give only conditional positive regard.

Conditional positive regard **refers to the positive regard we receive if we behave in certain acceptable ways, such as living up to or meeting the standards of others.**

For instance, one way teenagers display their newly developed independence is by choosing different (radical, awful, outrageous) hairstyles and fashions. In this case, if the teenagers receive only conditional positive regard based on conforming to the more traditional fashion standards of their parents, they may develop a negative self-concept or feel bad or worthless because they displeased or disappointed their parents. Rogers believed that the development of a healthy and positive self-concept depends

on receiving as much unconditional positive regard as possible.

Unconditional positive regard **refers to the warmth, acceptance, and love that others show you because you are valued as a human being even though you may disappoint people by behaving in ways that are different from their standards or values or the way they think.**

No matter how she dresses, she hopes to get unconditional positive regard.

Parents who provide love and respect, even if a teenager does not always abide by their fashion standards, are showing unconditional positive regard, which will foster the development of a healthy self-concept. However, in real life, receiving unconditional positive regard appears to be more the exception, while receiving conditional positive regard appears to be more the rule (Culp et al., 1991).

Importance of Self-Actualization

What does it take to reach your potential?

Carrie Underwood was the winner of the fourth season of "American Idol" and has since become a multi-platinum-selling recording artist winning countless awards and prestigious recognitions. For instance, her debut album, *Some Hearts,* was the fastest-selling female country album ever, and she was voted Female Vocalist of the Year at the 40th Annual Country Music Association Awards in 2006.

The life of Carrie Underwood is a case study in self-actualization. Her dream since childhood was to become a profes-

> I never gave up on my dream to be a singer.

sional singer, and despite years of disappointing attempts to establish a singing career, she never lost sight of her dream. Rogers would explain that Underwood persisted in singing because of the tendency for self-actualization, which provides direction and motivation to develop one's potential.

Rogers recognized that our tendency for self-actualization may be hindered, tested, or blocked by a variety of situational hurdles or personal difficulties, as happened to Underwood. But like Underwood, Rogers believed that we will experience the greatest self-actualization if we work hard and diligently to remove situational problems, resolve our personal problems, and, hopefully, receive tons of unconditional positive regard.

Humanistic theories contain powerful positive messages, but how do these uplifting messages work in real life?

E. Humanistic Theories

What problems do at-risk students face?

Unlike almost every other theory of personality, humanism holds that people are basically good and can achieve their true potentials if the roadblocks placed by society, poverty, drugs, or other evil influences are removed (Megargee, 1997). One of the primary goals of the humanistic approach is to find ways of removing blocking influences so people can grow and self-actualize.

In 1998, a racially diverse group of 150 high-school seniors walked across a graduation stage, an event few people expected to ever happen. These teenagers grew up in rough neighborhoods, witnessing and, for many, being victims of gun shootings. At the start of high school these students made it clear they hated school and had no desire to learn. Thus, they were labeled "unteachable, at-risk" students. So, how did these 150 disadvantaged students overcome the many roadblocks on the path to graduating from high school?

Helping these students overcome roadblocks was Erin Gruwell, a dedicated teacher and role model. Erin encouraged students to think beyond the negative expectations others had of them and to actively set life goals. By believing in each of her students, Erin helped them develop and reach their own potentials. At the heart of Erin's

The Freedom Writers shattered stereotypes because of the positive regard received from their teacher, Erin Gruwell.

teaching was providing positive regard, including warmth, acceptance, and respect, to show them that someone truly cares.

With Erin's support, these students shattered stereotypes by not only graduating from high school but also going on to earn undergraduate and graduate degrees. The lives of these students had been transformed and it did not stop at their education. These 150 students are now known as the "Freedom Writers," and their mission is to teach tolerance and inspire others through their success. The Freedom Writers shared their story in a book they wrote together *The Freedom Writers Diary*. More recently, a Hollywood movie was made about their amazing success, *Freedom Writers* (The Freedom Writers, 1999; Gruwell, 2007).

In the United States, there are many mentoring programs, such as Big Brothers/Big Sisters of America, that instill a sense of pride and self-confidence and give children the motivation to achieve success. Children who participated in mentoring programs reported significantly higher self-confidence, grades, and social skills than children without mentors (Vredenburgh, 2007). Thus, applying humanistic principles helped improve the self-confidence, grades, and social skills of children who came from problem families or neighborhoods.

Next, we'll review the important humanistic concepts and discuss what critics have to say about humanistic theories.

How popular is humanism?

Perhaps the main reason humanistic theories, such as those of Maslow and Rogers, continue to be popular is that they view people as basically good and believe that people can develop their true potentials (Clay, 2002). However, these optimistic views of human nature have triggered a number of criticisms.

Impact

In the case of the Freedom Writers described above, the self-worth of at-risk students skyrocketed when their teacher and successful role model, Erin Gruwell, provided lots of positive regard. This program illustrates the humanistic theories' emphasis on building self-worth through positive regard. In a real sense, Erin Gruwell removed roadblocks so that students could find a path to their true potential through a process called self-actualization (Schneider et al., 2002).

Humanistic theories have had their greatest impact in counseling, clinical settings, and personal growth programs, where ideas like self-concept, self-actualization, and self-fulfillment have proven useful in developing healthy personalities and interpersonal relationships (Rabasca, 2000a; Soyez & Broekaert, 2005). Compared to Freud's idea that we are driven by unconscious irrational forces, humanism says we are driven by positive forces that point us toward realizing our good and true selves.

Criticisms

Humanistic theories have come under considerable criticism because Rogers and Maslow provided little or no scientific evidence that an inherent (biological) tendency to self-actualization really exists. Because the major assumption of self-actualization and other humanistic concepts, such as positive regard and self-worth, are difficult to demonstrate experimentally, critics argue that humanistic theories primarily describe how people behave rather than explain the causes of their behaviors. For these reasons, critics regard humanistic theories more as a wonderfully positive view of human nature or a very hopeful philosophy of life rather than as a scientific explanation of personality development (Burger, 2004). Critics note that because humanistic concepts are too descriptive and limited in scope, humanistic theories have had less impact on mainstream psychology and more on humanities. Another major problem is that humanistic theories generally ignore research showing that 20 to 60% of the development of intellectual, emotional, social, and personality traits comes from genetic factors (Jang, 2005; McClearn et al., 1997; Parens et al., 2006). This means that genetic factors must be considered when discussing a person's true potential or a person's ability to achieve self-actualization.

Maslow hoped that humanistic theories would become a major force in psychology, along with behavioral and psychoanalytic theories. Although the humanistic approach has not achieved Maslow's goal, humanism's ideas inspired the human potential movements in the 1960s–1970s and have been integrated into approaches for counseling, psychotherapy, and, as we learned with the Freedom Writers, education (Clay, 2002).

✔ Concept Review

1. The combination of long-lasting and distinctive behaviors, thoughts, and emotions that are typical of how we react and adapt to other people and situations forms our _____.

2. Freud's theory of personality, which emphasizes the importance of early childhood experiences and of conflicts between conscious thoughts and unconscious forces, is called a _____ theory.

3. Freud developed three techniques for probing the unconscious. A technique that encourages clients to talk about any thoughts or images that enter their head is called (a)_____. A technique to interpret the hidden meanings and symbols in dreams is called (b)_____. With a third technique, the therapist analyzes the mistakes or (c)_____ that the client makes in everyday speech.

4. Freud considered the mind to have three major divisions. The division that contains the biological drives and is the source of all psychic or mental energy is called the (a)_____. This division operates according to the (b)_____ principle, which demands immediate satisfaction. The division that develops from the id during infancy and whose goal is finding safe and socially acceptable ways of satisfying the id's desires is called the (c)_____. This division operates according to the (d)_____ principle, which involves satisfying a wish only if there is a socially acceptable outlet. The division that develops from the id during early childhood and whose goal is applying the moral values and standards of one's parents and society is called the (e)_____.

5. Conflicts between the id and the superego over satisfaction of desires may cause the ego to feel threatened. When threatened, the ego generates an unpleasant state that is associated with feelings of uneasiness, apprehension, and heightened physiological arousal; this unpleasant state is called (a)_____. Freud suggested that the ego may reduce anxiety by using unconscious mechanisms that produce self-deception; these are called (b)_____.

6. Freud proposed that the major influence on personality development occurs as we pass through five developmental periods that he called the (a)_____ stages, each of which results in conflicts between the child's wishes and parents' restrictions. The result of a person's wishes being overgratified or undergratified at any one of the first three stages is called (b)_____.

7. Personality theories that emphasize our capacity for personal growth, the development of our potential, and freedom to choose our destinies are referred to as _____ theories.

8. Humanistic theories have three characteristics in common. They take the perspective that our perception of the world, whether or not it is accurate, becomes our reality; this is called the (a)_____ perspective. Humanistic theories see personality as more than the sum of individual parts and consider personality as a unique and total entity that functions as a unit; this is the (b)_____ view of personality. Humanistic theories point to an inherent tendency that each of us has to reach our true potential; this tendency is called (c)_____.

9. The idea that our needs occur in ascending order, with biological needs at the bottom and social and personal needs toward the top, and that we must meet our lower-level needs before we can satisfy higher ones is called (a)_____. Our physiological needs (food, sleep) and psychological needs (safety, belongingness, esteem) are called (b)_____ needs because we try to fulfill them if they are not met. The highest need of self-actualization, which includes the desire for truth, goodness, beauty, and justice, is called a (c)_____ need.

10. Carl Rogers's self theory of personality makes two basic assumptions. The first is that personality development is guided by an inborn tendency to develop our potential; this idea is called (a)_____. The second assumption is that each of us has a personal need for acceptance and love, which Rogers called (b)_____. According to Rogers, it is important that we receive love and acceptance despite the fact that we sometimes behave in ways that are different from what others think or value; this type of acceptance is called (c)_____.

11. Rogers proposes that we have two kinds of selves: the self that is based on real-life experiences is called the (a)_____ self; the self that is based on how we would like to see ourselves is called the (b)_____ self.

Answers: 1. personality; 2. psychodynamic; 3. (a) free association, (b) dream interpretation, (c) Freudian slips or slips of the tongue; 4. (a) id, (b) pleasure, (c) ego, (d) reality, (e) superego; 5. (a) anxiety, (b) defense mechanisms; 6. (a) psychosexual, (b) fixation; 7. humanistic; 8. (a) phenomenological, (b) holistic, (c) self-actualization; 9. (a) Maslow's hierarchy of needs, (b) deficiency, (c) growth; 10. (a) self-actualization, (b) positive regard, (c) unconditional positive regard; 11. (a) real, (b) ideal

Boat People: Remarkable Achievement

What was different about these children?

We have always been puzzled by why students with similar academic skills perform so differently: some do well on our exams, while others do poorly. A humanist would look at the same differences and ask, "Why are some students developing their potential, while others are not?" One answer comes from studying thousands of Indo-Chinese refugees, known as the boat people, who were allowed to resettle in the United States in the 1970s and 1980s.

On their arrival in America, the boat people's only possessions were the clothes they wore. They knew virtually no English, had almost no knowledge of Western culture, and had no one to turn to for social or financial support. In spite of horrendous difficulties, refugee children achieved such remarkable academic success that American educators were scratching their heads and asking why.

Background. Researchers set out to discover why these refugee children had achieved astonishing scholastic success against overwhelming odds (N. Caplan et al., 1992). The researchers selected a random sample of 200 Indo-Chinese refugee families with a total of

Refugee boat people's children, who first had to learn English, went on to achieve remarkable academic success.

536 school-age children. The children had been in the United States for an average of $3\frac{1}{2}$ years. They had generally lived in low-income metropolitan areas with troublesome neighborhoods and rundown schools that were plagued with problems and not known for their high academic standards. Despite all these problems, the children of the boat people performed remarkably well in school. Here's what researchers found.

Amazing success. The researchers computed the mean grade point average for the 536 children, who were fairly evenly distributed among grades 1 to 12. They found that 27% of the children had a grade point average (GPA) in the A range, 52% had a GPA in the B range, 17% in the C range, and only 4% had a GPA below C. Equally noteworthy was the children's overall performance in math: almost 50% of the children earned A's, while another 33% earned B's. On national math tests, the Indo-Chinese children's average scores were almost three times higher than the national norm.

After analyzing all these data, researchers were able to identify several reasons immigrant Indo-Chinese students achieved such high grades.

Values and Motivation

What were their values?

Although Indo-Chinese refugee children had been in the United States for an average of only $3\frac{1}{2}$ years, they were doing better in math than 90% of their peers. It could not be the quality of their schools, which were average, undistinguished low-income schools in metropolitan areas. But clearly there were powerful factors helping these children overcome the problems of learning a second language and adapting to a new culture. Researchers located these powerful factors in the values of the Asian family.

The *primary values* held by the Indo-Chinese families were that parents and children have mutual respect, cooperate freely, and are committed to accomplishment and achievement. A clear example of commitment to accomplishment is the amount of time Indo-Chinese children spend doing homework: They average about 3 hours a day, while

Parental values on the importance of education motivated the children.

American students average about $1\frac{1}{2}$ hours. Thus, among refugee families, doing homework, not watching television, is the main activity; the older children help the younger children.

Another primary value is that parents were very involved in their children's education: Over 50% of parents read aloud and helped with homework. When children were asked, "What accounts for your academic success?" the children most often checked the category "having a love of learning." Love of learning was one of the values nourished and passed on from parent to child. When children were asked, "How much do you choose your own destiny?" the children answered that they did not trust luck or fate but were the masters of their own destinies.

Parental Attitudes

How did parents help?

One reason Indo-Chinese children earned great academic success was the personal and cultural values transmitted by their parents, who were committed to help their children succeed through educational performance. After studying the immigrant parents' values and how they instilled these values in their children, researchers concluded that for American schools to succeed, parents must become more committed to the education of their children. In this case, Americans can truly learn from the values of these refugees.

In explaining the immigrant children's wonderful academic achievement, humanists would emphasize how parental values served to remove mental roadblocks that otherwise might have hindered their children from developing their true potentials and reaching self-fulfillment.

Next, we turn to a relatively common personality problem, shyness, and discuss how different theories of personality explain its causes.

G. Research Focus: Shyness

What Is Shyness and What Causes It?

What's it like to be shy?

It's one thing to discuss Freud's psychodynamic theory of personality but it's another to see it in action, in this case, to treat shyness.

At some time and in some situations, we have all felt a little shy. However, there are degrees of shyness, and a high degree of shyness can interfere with enjoying personal and social interactions. For example, when Alan was a child, he would walk home from school through alleys to avoid meeting any of his classmates. Although he received a perfect math score on his SAT, he dropped out of the University of Texas because he always felt like a stranger and was continually frustrated by not being able to reach out and make contact with people. He was so shy that he could not even use the Internet. Finally, feeling so lonely, Alan sought help at the Shyness Clinic, which was founded in the 1970s by well-known shyness researcher, Philip Zimbardo of Stanford University (Noriyuki, 1996).

Shyness is a feeling of distress that comes from being tense, stressed, or awkward in social situations and from worrying about and fearing rejection.

20–60% are shy.

Surveys indicate that about 40% of adults report mild but chronic shyness and, although they are good at hiding their shyness, internally they feel distress. About 20% report more severe shyness and are unable to hide their pain and distress (Chavira et al., 2002). The cause and treatment for shyness depend partly on which theory of personality guides our thinking. We'll contrast answers from two different theories: Freud's psychodynamic theory and social cognitive theory.

Psychodynamic Approach

Is shyness due to unresolved conflicts?

As a practicing psychoanalyst, Donald Kaplan (1972) uses his clinical experience and psychodynamic concepts to answer the question, What causes shyness? Kaplan traces the causes of shyness back to *unresolved conflicts* at one or more of Freud's psychosexual stages. For example, one very shy client reported that his mother constantly fed him so that he would never cry or whimper. As a result, Kaplan suggests that this client's unresolved conflict during the oral stage resulted in his feelings of inadequacy and shyness in later social interactions.

According to Kaplan, the symptoms of shyness include both conscious fears, such as having nothing to say, and unconscious fears of being rejected. Shy people may deal with these anxieties by using *defense mechanisms*; for example, one client reduced his anxiety through displacement, by changing his fears of being rejected into opposite feelings of self-righteousness and contempt.

One *advantage* of the psychodynamic approach is that it suggests that a number of causes, such as conscious and unconscious fears as well as unresolved psychosexual conflicts, are involved in shyness.

One *disadvantage* of the psychodynamic approach is that Freudian concepts (unconscious fears, unresolved psychosexual stages) are difficult to verify by experimental methods (Torrey, 2005). For example, saying that being fixated at the oral stage may result in a person becoming a shy adult is mostly a descriptive guess rather than a testable hypothesis.

A very different account of what causes shyness comes from the social cognitive theory of personality.

The cause and treatment for shyness depend partly on which theory of personality the therapist follows.

Social Cognitive Theory

What are the three factors?

Unlike the Freudian approach, which relies primarily on therapists' personal observations, social cognitive theory uses primarily experimental studies to answer questions about personality. Social cognitive theory breaks shyness down into three measurable or observable components—cognitive, behavioral, and environmental—which can be studied using the experimental method described in Module 2 (Chavira et al., 2002). For example, in a series of longitudinal studies, researchers found that about 10–15% of the population have a shy personality that, to a large extent, comes from *genetic factors*—for example, inheriting a nervous system that is easily aroused by novel stimuli (Battaglia, 2005; Kagan, 2003a). By observing the social interactions (the behavioral component) of shy people, researchers found that shy people have too few social and communication skills and, as a consequence, they are continually punished during social interactions (Gabrieli, 2005; Putnam, 2005). By giving personality tests (the cognitive component), researchers found that shy people are overly self-conscious, which leads to worrisome thoughts and irrational beliefs that interfere with social functioning (Romney & Bynner, 1997). Therapies based on social cognitive theory (Module 20) have proved successful in helping shy individuals decrease their anxiety in social situations, develop better social and communication skills, and decrease levels of shyness (Greco & Morris, 2001; Kluger, 2005).

One *advantage* of social cognitive theory is that it breaks shyness down into three measurable or observable components, which can be experimentally studied and appropriate treatments developed.

One *disadvantage* of this approach is that researchers may overlook certain influences that we are neither conscious nor aware of, such as conditioned emotional responses, that can also trigger shy behaviors (Westen, 1998).

Our discussion of shyness raises the interesting question of how psychologists measure or assess personality traits, such as shyness.

H. Application Assessment—Projective Tests

Definition of Projective Tests

How did friends describe Ted's personality?

At the beginning of this module, we discussed Ted Haggard, the 50-year-old pastor, who at the height of his career confessed to committing infidelity with a male prostitute. When a close friend described Haggard's personality, he said that Ted was a family man who followed God's word (top photo) (Goodstein & Banerjee, 2006). Before the accusations against Ted were made, none of his family, friends, or colleagues described him as a deceitful, dishonest, or immoral individual (bottom photo). When friends were describing Ted's personality, they were making a kind of psychological assessment.

Psychological assessment refers to the use of various tools, such as psychological tests and/or interviews, to measure various characteristics, traits, or abilities in order to understand behaviors and predict future performances or behaviors.

Psychological tests are usually divided into ability tests and personality tests, which differ considerably. For example,

Was Ted Haggard generally an honest, righteous man or a deceitful, immoral one?

when people enter a psychological or drug treatment program, they are most likely given personality tests to identify their personal problems.

Personality tests are used to measure observable or overt traits and behaviors as well as unobservable or covert characteristics. Personality tests are used to identify personality problems and psychological disorders as well as to predict how a person might behave in the future.

Although you may not have taken a personality test, you certainly have taken many ability tests, such as exams.

Ability tests include achievement tests, which measure what we have learned; aptitude tests, which measure our potential for learning or acquiring a specific skill; and intelligence tests, which measure our general potential to solve problems, think abstractly, and profit from experience (R. M. Kaplan & Saccuzzo, 2005).

The primary tools of assessment are tests of ability and personality. There are two kinds of personality tests. We'll now focus on one kind, projective personality tests, and later (p. 474) discuss objective personality tests. Personality assessment is a $400-million-a-year industry (Gladwell, 2004).

Examples of Projective Tests

In describing Haggard's personality, we can identify observable behaviors, such as happy, family-oriented, and friendly, as well as unobservable behaviors, such as anxious, guilt-ridden, and deceitful. In Freud's psychodynamic theory, observable behaviors reflect conscious wishes, desires, and thoughts, while unobservable behaviors may reflect unconscious forces. Freud developed three techniques for revealing unconscious forces—free association, dream interpretation, and interpretation of slips of the tongue. We now add a fourth technique to reveal hidden or unconscious forces: projective tests.

Projective tests require individuals to look at some meaningless object or ambiguous photo and describe what they see. In describing or making up a story about the ambiguous object, individuals are assumed to project both their conscious and unconscious feelings, needs, and motives.

Although projective tests were not developed by Freud, they are assumed to reveal unconscious thoughts (Groth-Marnat, 2003). We'll examine the two most widely used projective tests—Rorschach *(ROAR-shock)* inkblot test and Thematic Apperception Test (TAT).

Rorschach Inkblot Test

What do you see in this inkblot?

The Rorschach inkblot test, which was published in the early 1920s by a Swiss psychiatrist, Hermann Rorschach (1921/1942), contains five inkblots printed in black and white and five that have color (the inkblot shown on the left is similar to but is not an actual Rorschach inkblot).

The *Rorschach inkblot test* is used to assess personality by showing a person a series of ten inkblots and then asking the person to describe what he or she thinks an image is.

This test is used primarily in the therapeutic setting to assess personality traits and identify potential problems of adolescents and adult clients (Mestel, 2003b).

What might this be?

Thematic Apperception Test (TAT)

What's happening in this picture?

A person would be shown a picture like the one on the right and asked to make up a plot or story about what the young man is thinking, feeling, or doing. This is an example but not a real TAT card.

The *Thematic Apperception Test,* or *TAT,* involves showing a person a series of 20 pictures of people in ambiguous situations and asking the person to make up a story about what the people are doing or thinking in each situation.

The TAT, which was developed by Henry Murray (1943), is used to assess the motivation and personality characteristics of normal individuals as well as clients with personality problems (R. M. Kaplan & Saccuzzo, 2005).

Before we discuss how well the Rorschach inkblot test and the TAT assess personality traits and identify potential problems, we'll look at another personality test that you have probably heard of: handwriting analysis. How much can someone learn from just your handwriting?

What's happening in this picture?

Two Characteristics

What does handwriting show?

Handwriting analysts (graphologists) charge about $75 an hour to do personality assessments that they claim reveal a person's strengths and weaknesses, which are important in selecting job applicants and identifying people who may not be trusted (M. C. Healy, 2005; Scanlon & Mauro, 1992).

However, researchers report that handwriting analysis is no better than chance at assessing personality characteristics, rating the success of job applicants, or identifying one's profession (M. C. Healy,

so confident
so sensitive
so impatient

Which handwriting reveals an honest and sincere person?

2005; Tripician, 2000). In order for handwriting analysis or any personality assessment test to be an effective personality assessment tool, it must have two characteristics validity and reliability. Handwriting analysis is no better than chance in assessing personality because it lacks validity.

Validity

Handwriting analysis is fun but no better than chance as a personality test because it lacks validity.

Validity **means that the test measures what it says it measures or what it is supposed to measure.**

For example, for a personality test to be valid, it must measure personality traits specific to the person rather than general traits that apply to almost everyone. Handwriting analysis does not measure, identify, or predict traits specific to an individual, so it has no validity as a personality test (M. C. Healy, 2005; Tripician, 2000).

In addition to validity, a good personality test must also have a second characteristic, reliability.

Reliability

In judging the usefulness of any personality test, the major question is always the same: How good are the test's validity and reliability?

Reliability **refers to having a consistent score at different times. A person who takes a test at one point in time should receive the same score on a similar test taken at a later time.**

For example, handwriting analysis may have good reliability provided your handwriting remains about the same across time. But, even if handwriting analysis has good reliability, it is still no better than chance at assessing or predicting an individual's personality traits because graphology lacks the important characteristic of validity.

This means that the usefulness of projective personality tests, such as the Rorschach test and TAT, depends on their validity and reliability.

Usefulness of Projective Tests

Are they valid and reliable?

Projective tests, such as the Rorschach inkblot test, have been used for over 80 years. However, there is still a debate between therapists, who report that projective tests are useful in assessing

personality traits and problems, and researchers, who continue to disagree about the reliability and validity of projective tests (Mestel, 2003b; Society for Personality Assessment, 2005). This debate involves the advantages and disadvantages of projective tests.

Advantages

Individuals who take projective tests do not know which are the best, correct, or socially desirable answers to give because the stimuli—the inkblot or the TAT picture—are ambiguous and have no right or wrong answers. Thus, one advantage of projective tests such as the Rorschach and the TAT is that they are difficult to fake or bias, since there are no correct or socially desirable answers.

When clients respond to Rorschach's meaningless inkblots or make up stories about what is happening in TAT's ambiguous pictures, clinicians assume that clients will project their hidden feelings, thoughts, or emotions onto these ambiguous stimuli. Based on this assumption, some clinicians believe that a second advantage of projective tests is that they are another method for assessing a client's hidden and unconscious thoughts and desires of which he or she is normally unaware (Groth-Marnat, 2003). Other researchers suggest that the Rorschach test is useful as an interview technique in eliciting unique information about the person (Aronow et al., 1995). Thus, the Rorschach test's advantage is obtaining information about the person in a setting where there are no right or wrong answers.

Clinician's experience affects reliability and validity of projective tests.

Disadvantages

One disadvantage of projective tests comes from their use of ambiguous stimuli to which there are no right or wrong answers. The current method of scoring the Rorschach is based on analyzing and making judgments about so many different variables (such as content, theme, color, and detail of the cards) that disagreements often arise over interpretations and classifications (Mestel, 2003b). For example, there are several studies using the Rorschach in which clinicians scored and interpreted the results as indicating that perfectly normal individuals were classified as psychologically disordered (J. M. Wood et al., 2003). Although the Rorschach is one of the more popular personality assessment tests and some studies show it has high reliability and validity, there are other studies that point to serious problems in scoring and interpreting responses and making assessments based on the Rorschach test (Society for Personality Assessment, 2005; J. M. Wood et al., 2003).

In spite of criticisms, some experienced clinicians report that projective tests can provide reliable and valid information about a client's personality and problems, especially when combined with other assessment techniques (Exner & Erdberg, 2005). Thus, a clinician's training and experience play a major role in the accuracy of assessing a client's personality and problems using projective tests (R. M. Kaplan & Saccuzzo, 2005).

Summary Test

A. Freud's Psychodynamic Theory

1. The lasting behaviors, thoughts, and emotions that typify how we react and adapt to other people and situations make up our (a)_____. An organized attempt to explain how personalities develop and why they differ is called a (b)_____ of personality.

2. Freud's approach, which emphasizes the importance of early childhood experiences and conflicts between conscious and unconscious forces, is called a (a)_____ theory of personality. According to Freud, those wishes, desires, or thoughts of which we are aware or that we can readily recall are (b)_____; those that we automatically repress because of their disturbing or threatening content are (c)_____.

3. Freud's technique of encouraging clients to talk about any thoughts or images that enter their heads is called (a)_____. His assumption that dreams provide clues to unconscious thoughts and desires gave rise to his technique of (b)_____. Mistakes that we make in everyday speech that are thought to reflect unconscious thoughts or wishes are called (c)_____.

B. Divisions of the Mind

4. According to Freud, the biological drives of sex and aggression are the source of all psychic or mental energy and give rise to the development of the (a)_____. Because this division of the mind strives to satisfy drives and avoid pain without concern for moral or social restrictions, it is said to be operating according to the (b)_____. During infancy, the second division of the mind develops from the id; it is called the (c)_____. The goal of this second division is to find safe and socially acceptable ways of satisfying the id's desires. The ego follows a policy of satisfying a wish or desire only if a socially acceptable outlet is available; thus it is said to operate according to the (d)_____. During early childhood, the third division of the mind develops from the id; it is called the (e)_____. The goal of this division is to apply the moral values and standards of one's parents and society in satisfying one's wishes.

5. When the id, ego, and superego are in conflict, an unpleasant state of uneasiness, apprehension, and heightened physiological arousal may occur; this is known as (a)_____. The Freudian processes that operate at unconscious levels to help the ego reduce anxiety through self-deception are called (b)_____; they can be helpful or harmful, depending on how much we rely on them.

C. Developmental Stages

6. The essence of Freud's theory of personality development is a series of five developmental stages, called (a)_____, during which the individual seeks pleasure from different parts of the body. The stage that lasts for the first 18 months of life is called the (b)_____ stage. It is followed by the (c)_____ stage, which lasts until about the age of 3. The next stage, until about the age of 6, is called the (d)_____ stage. The stage that lasts from about 6 to puberty is called the (e)_____ stage; it is followed by the (f)_____ stage, which lasts through adulthood.

7. The resolution of the potential conflict at each stage has important implications for personality. A Freudian process through which individuals may be locked into earlier psychosexual stages because their wishes were overgratified or undergratified is called _____; it can occur at any of the first three stages.

D. Freud's Followers & Critics

8. Jung believed that the basic force is not the sex drive, as Freud believed, but ancient memory traces and symbols shared by all peoples in all cultures, called the (a)_____. According to Adler's philosophy, each person is a social being with a unique personality and is motivated by (b)_____. Karen Horney disagreed with Freud's emphasis on biological urges and insisted that the major influence on personality development was (c)_____ between parents and child.

9. Those who generally agreed with Freud's basic ideas but disagreed with his emphasis on biological forces, sexual drives, and psychosexual stages are referred to as _____; they turned the emphasis of psychodynamic theory to psychosocial and cultural influences.

10. Criticisms of Freud's psychodynamic theory include that it is so comprehensive that it is not very useful for explaining or predicting behaviors of a specific (a)_____; that some Freudian ideas (Oedipal complex) are out of date because they could not be (b)_____; that psychodynamic theory must be updated with findings about (c)_____ factors and the association between (d)_____ development and related behaviors.

E. Humanistic Theories

11. Humanistic theories emphasize our capacity for personal growth, development of our potential, and freedom to choose our (a)_____. They stress that our perception of the world becomes our reality; this is called the (b)_____ perspective. These theories emphasize that one's personality is unique, functions as a unit, and is more than the sum of individual parts; together these ideas make up the (c)_____ view. These theories also highlight the idea of an inherent tendency to reach our true potentials, which is called (d)_____.

12. According to Maslow, our needs are arranged in a hierarchy with (a)_____ at the bottom and (b)_____ toward the top.

13. How we see or describe ourselves, including how we perceive our abilities, personality characteristics, and behaviors, is referred to as our (a)_____. According to Carl Rogers, the development of self-concept depends on our interactions with others. If we receive (b)_____ positive regard even when our behavior is disappointing, we will develop a positive self-concept and tend to act, feel, and think optimistically and constructively.

F. Cultural Diversity: Unexpected High Achievement

14. Indo-Chinese children overcame problems of language and culture and excelled in American schools in part because of the _____ held by their families, including mutual respect, cooperation, parental involvement, and the belief that they, not fate, controlled their destinies.

© Jason Goltz

G. Research Focus: Shyness

15. As a practicing psychoanalyst, Donald Kaplan traces the causes of shyness back to unresolved conflicts at one or more of Freud's

(a)_____. The Freudian approach primarily uses therapists' (b)_____ to answer questions about personality. In comparison, social cognitive theory breaks shyness down into three measurable or observable components that can be investigated using (c)_____.

H. Application: Assessment—Projective Tests

16. Tests that are used to measure observable traits and behaviors as well as unobservable characteristics of a person and to identify personality problems and psychological disorders are called _____ tests.

17. Achievement tests measure what we have learned; aptitude tests measure our potential for learning or acquiring a specific skill; and intelligence tests measure our general potential to solve problems, think abstractly, and profit from experience. Collectively, these are called _____ tests.

18. For a test to be useful, it must have two characteristics. First, a test must measure what it is supposed to measure; this is called (a)_____. Second, a person's score on a test at one point in time should be similar to the score obtained by the same person on a similar test at a later point in time; this is called (b)_____.

19. Typically, a combination of tests is used to assess personality. Tests that involve presenting an ambiguous stimulus and asking the person to describe it are called (a)_____ tests. A test used to assess personality in terms of how the subject interprets a series of inkblots is called the (b)_____ test. A test in which the subject is to make up a story about people shown in ambiguous situations is called the (c)_____.

Answers: *1. (a) personalities, (b) theory; 2. (a) psychodynamic, (b) conscious thoughts, (c) unconscious forces or thoughts; 3. (a) free association, (b) dream interpretation, (c) slips of the tongue or Freudian slips; 4. (a) id, (b) pleasure principle, (c) ego, (d) reality principle, (e) superego; 5. (a) anxiety, (b) defense mechanisms; 6. (a) psychosexual stages, (b) oral, (c) anal, (d) phallic, (e) latency, (f) genital; 7. fixation; 8. (a) collective unconscious, (b) social urges, (c) social interactions; 9. neo-Freudians; 10. (a) individual or person, (b) tested or verified, (c) genetic, (d) brain; 11. (a) destinies, (b) phenomenological, (c) holistic, (d) self-actualization; 12. (a) biological needs, (b) social and personal needs; 13. (a) self or self-concept, (b) unconditional; 14. primary values; 15. (a) psychosexual stages, (b) personal observations, (c) experimental studies; 16. personality; 17. ability; 18. (a) validity, (b) reliability; 19. (a) projective, (b) Rorschach inkblot, (c) Thematic Apperception Test (TAT)*

Critical Thinking

Can Personality Explain Obesity?

Questions

1. Which part of Freud's psychodynamic theory might explain why Peter could not control his eating?

2. What roles might the Freudian concepts of the id, ego, and super-ego have had in Peter becoming so obese that he could not walk?

3. Following Freud's psychodynamic theory, what kinds of questions might you ask or what techniques might you use to understand Peter's overeating behavior?

About two of every three American adults are overweight or obese. Peter Herida is one of the very few who is medically defined as "super massive morbid obese." As a 10–12-year-old child, Peter already weighed 179 pounds. At age 46, his weight reached an astonishing 863 pounds (right photo). His grocery bill was nearly $400 a week and he ate over 3,000 calories at each meal. Peter took 14 different medications four times a day because of the life-threatening health damage caused by his extreme morbid obesity. Some of Peter's medical problems included heart failure, diabetes, and difficulty breathing during sleep. He became so heavy he could not walk, which resulted in him being housebound for 20 years. His mobility became so limited that a trip to the doctor's office required a wheelchair van, two fire truck crews, and one ambulance crew to transport him.

During one doctor's visit, Peter was told that unless he took radical measures to lose weight quickly, he would die soon. Peter chose to undergo gastric bypass surgery, a risky procedure that promised to make his stomach smaller so he would feel full after eating much less food. His doctor warned him that because of his weight and health problems, the operation carried a 60% chance of death. So, when Peter woke up after surgery, he promised himself, "I'm going to try and make this thing work, as I now was given a second chance at life!" (Herida, 2003).

Peter knew the operation was the easy part and the challenging part would be to make long-term lifestyle changes. After not having moved his body for 20 years, Peter spent his first 3 months learning how to walk again. He exercised and dieted for years afterward. At age 49, he swims a mile a day and works out daily. His health improved so much he takes only two medications a day compared to the 14 he took before. He is no longer a diabetic, he sleeps without difficulty breathing, and his heart is functioning better.

Peter's efforts helped him to lose a whopping 560 pounds during the first 10 months after surgery. His self-esteem skyrocketed and he rewarded himself by purchasing his dream car, a mint-condition 1982 Mercedes sedan, which he says "beats the heck out of a wheelchair van and emergency vehicle motorcade" (Herida, 2005). Peter became a motivational speaker to encourage others to strive to reach their potential just as he did. (Adapted from Herida, 2003, 2005; "Incredible weight loss stories," 2007; Taneeru, 2006)

4. What psychological impulses or conflicts may have made losing weight difficult for Peter?

5. How might humanistic theories explain Peter's obesity and then the dramatic changes he made in his life?

1. The part of Freud's psychodynamic theory that focuses on the development of personality involves how a person goes through the five psychosexual stages and whether fixation occurs. For example, Peter may have become fixated at the oral stage, resulting in the inability to control his eating.

2. Peter's id, which follows the pleasure principle, wanted to eat all the time. Peter's superego, which contains moral standards, would argue against overeating as it jeopardizes health and well-being. Peter's ego, which follows the reality principle, would try to find a socially acceptable outlet for the id's desires. In Peter's case, the id's desires apparently won out.

3. Since Freud believed that most personality development and seeds of problems occurred during the first five years, you would ask questions about his early childhood, especially his relationship with his parents. To reveal Peter's unconscious forces, you might use free association and dream interpretation.

4. Psychological impulses or conflicts that may have led to Peter's overeating and may make losing weight challenging include anxiety, tension, worry, and insecurity. Also, overeating was likely a means of achieving pleasure, gratification, and excitement.

5. Humanistic theories are best at describing positive human growth. However, a humanist might say that because Peter had not received enough love or unconditional positive regard, he developed a poor or negative self-concept, which interfered with his self-actualization and instead led him to overeat. A humanist would also say that we all have the capacity for self-actualization and reaching our own potential, which for Peter was achieving a healthy weight and lifestyle.

Links to Learning

Learning Activities

- **POWERSTUDY FOR INTRODUCTION TO PSYCHOLOGY 4.0**
by Tom Doyle and Rod Plotnik
Check out the quizzes and learning activities for "Freudian & Humanistic Theories" on **PowerStudy** and:
  - Test your knowledge using an interactive version of the Summary Test on pages 452 and 453. Also access related quizzing—true/false, multiple choice, and matching.
  - Explore an interactive version of the Critical Thinking exercise "Can Personality Explain Obesity?" on page 454.
  - You will also find key terms, a chapter outline including a chapter abstract, and a special extended list of hotlinked websites that correlate to this module.

- **CengageNOW**
academic.cengage.com/login
Need help studying? This site is your one-stop study shop. Take a Pre-Test and CengageNOW will generate a Personalized Study Plan based on your test results. The Study Plan will identify the topics you need to review and direct you to online resources to help you master those topics. You can then take a Post-Test to determine the concepts you have mastered and what you still need to work on.

- **INTRODUCTION TO PSYCHOLOGY BOOK COMPANION WEBSITE**
academic.cengage.com/psychology/plotnik
Visit your book companion website where you will find more resources to help you study. At this site, you will find Learning Objectives, Internet Exercises, quizzing, flash cards, and a pronunciation glossary.

- **STUDY GUIDE and WEBTUTOR** WebTUTOR
Check the corresponding module in your Study Guide for effective student tips and help learning the material presented. Also go to **academic.cengage.com/webtutor** for an interactive version of the Study Guide features.

Study Questions

*A. Freud's Psychodynamic Theory—According to Freud, why do some students plan to study on the weekend but end up partying? (**Suggested answer p. 632**)

B. Divisions of the Mind—Sheryl wears sexy clothes but claims to be a feminist. How would Freud explain that?

C. Developmental Stages—How would Freud's theory explain why you are neat and outspoken while your sister is messy and demanding and feels inferior?

D. Freud's Followers & Critics—Which factors in the development of your personality support Freud's theory and which do not?

E. Humanistic Theories—How would humanistic theories explain why many students change their majors three to five times during their college careers?

*F. Cultural Diversity: Unexpected High Achievement—If you were the principal of a grade school, what might you do to improve overall student performance? (**Suggested answer p. 632**)

G. Research Focus: Shyness—Carl says that he's always been shy and it can't be helped. Would a Freudian respond to Carl's problem in the same way as a cognitive behaviorist?

*H. Application: Assessment—Projective Tests—How useful would projective tests be for identifying students who are most likely to cheat on exams? (**Suggested answer p. 632**)

*These questions are answered in Appendix B.

MODULE 20
Social Cognitive & Trait Theories

Courtesy of Sony Electronics, Inc.

Power of Beliefs

Why did she get threatened, clubbed, and jailed?

She chose to be tortured and jailed rather than change her major beliefs.

Wangari Maathai *(wan-GAH-ree mah-DHEYE)* was born in Kenya into a family of peasant farmers. She grew up in a beautiful countryside filled with many varieties of shrubs and trees. Water cascaded down to streams where she drank to quench her thirst. According to Kenyan tradition, as the oldest daughter, Maathai spent most of her days side by side with her mother, helping her and learning from her. She later made a bold decision to break with cultural expectations and study in the United States, where she earned both bachelor's and master's degrees. Upon returning home, Maathai yet again challenged cultural expectations by becoming the first woman in Kenya to earn a Ph.D. and later the first female professor at the University of Nairobi.

When Maathai returned to Kenya she realized there were fewer and fewer of the magnificent trees that once filled the region. One day she went to her yard and planted a tree, and it was then that she founded the Green Belt Movement, an organization that helps conserve the environment, educates people about environmental issues, and trains women to have jobs as nursery managers and forest rangers. Maathai empowered women by letting them plant their own trees and make profits from the products (nuts, fruits) to support their children's education and household needs.

As Maathai began her efforts to restore nature, she quickly realized that the government in Kenya was corrupt and was largely responsible for the deforestation by illegally selling land and trees to make room for buildings. The Green Belt Movement challenged the government's abuse of power, corruption, and destruction of the environment. Maathai initiated sit-ins and a hunger strike but was attacked with tear gas and viciously clubbed by police. On one occasion she was beaten unconscious. She received many death threats, was arrested more than a dozen times, and once even went into hiding.

Despite the brutality she experienced time and time again, Maathai persisted in her struggle for human rights and environmental conservation. Today, the Green Belt Movement has planted 30 million trees in Kenya and provided work for tens of thousands of women. Her unwavering dedication, absolute selflessness, and inspiring courage led her to receive many honors. In 2004, Maathai became the first African woman to win the Nobel Peace Prize (adapted from Maathai, 2004, 2005, 2006; Mjøs, 2004).

What were the forces that shaped Maathai's personality and gave her the strength and motivation to persist in the face of overwhelming adversity? In this module, we'll discuss some forces that shape and mold our personalities.

In a different nation, an ocean away, Beverly Harvard waged her own personal struggle against forces that said no African American woman should be doing what she wanted to do.

Determination

What's unusual about this woman?

In the 1970s, Beverly Harvard, an African American woman in a southern city (Atlanta, Georgia), was trying to become a police officer. In those days, female police recruits, Black or White, faced rejection, discrimination, and harassment by their male peers, who believed strongly that women had neither the physical strength nor the mental toughness to be police officers (C. Fletcher, 1995). From the 1970s through the 1980s, there were intense legal and political battles in the United States, in which women had to prove that they have what it takes to be good cops. Their struggle is slowly paying off: In the early 2000s, nearly 12% of this country's police officers were women.

With incredible determination, Beverly Harvard (photo below) worked her way up through the Atlanta police ranks. She put up with the male officers' sarcastic, hurtful, and discriminatory comments and concentrated on doing the best possible job. Finally, after struggling for almost 20 years, she was appointed head of the Atlanta police department. Her appointment in 1994 marked the first time an African American woman had headed a police department in a major city. She had 1,700 police officers under her command, and her motto is "You can talk about what's wrong with the world or help fix it" (Eddings, 1994, p. 87).

For her beliefs, Beverly Harvard fought against sex discrimination for 20 years.

Beverly Harvard, like thousands of female police officers around the country, has shown that women make good cops, partly because of their particular personality traits: women are less authoritarian, more open, better listeners, and less likely to trigger showdowns than are their male counterparts (Lonsway et al., 2003; Munoz, 2003). Apparently, what women may lack in sheer muscle power, they make up for in a winning combination of personality traits.

In this module, we'll discuss personality traits, which are powerful motivating forces that we all have, cannot live without, like to talk about, may be critical of, and are often asked to change but find it difficult to do so.

What's Coming

We'll discuss two theories of personality, each with a different emphasis. The first is social cognitive theory (previously called social learning theory), which stresses the influences of cognitive, learning, and social processes on personality development. The second is trait theory, which focuses on measuring traits and describing how traits make up our different personalities and influence our behaviors.

We'll begin with three social cognitive forces that helped shape Wangari Maathai's personality.

A. Social Cognitive Theory

What shaped her personality?

How many of us would still have fought to protect the environment after being beaten repeatedly, having our life threatened, and being imprisoned more than a dozen times, as Maathai did? What forces shaped Maathai's personality and gave her such courage, self-confidence, and perseverance? In Module 19, we discussed two approaches to this question: Freud's psychodynamic theory and humanistic theories.

Freud's psychodynamic theory said that our personality is shaped primarily by our inborn biological urges, especially sex and aggression, and by how we resolve conflicts during the psychosexual stages, especially during the first five years.

Humanistic theories, such as those of Abraham Maslow and Carl Rogers, assume that we are basically

Maathai won honors because of her unwavering courage.

good and that our personality is shaped primarily by our inborn tendency for self-actualization or self-fulfillment, which includes both biological and psychological factors.

Now we discuss two more answers: first, social cognitive theory and, later, trait theory.

Social cognitive theory **says that personality development is shaped primarily by three forces: environmental conditions (learning), cognitive-personal factors, and behavior, which all interact to influence how we evaluate, interpret, organize, and apply information.**

Social cognitive theory grew out of the research of a number of psychologists, especially Albert Bandura (1986, 2001a). According to social cognitive theory, we are neither good nor bad but shaped primarily by three influential factors.

Interaction of Three Factors

For about 30 years, Wangari Maathai has been fighting for human rights and environment conservation. During this time, she has suffered tremendous personal hardships, including being beaten and imprisoned. You can't help wondering what shaped her personality and gave her the strength, determination, and character to sacrifice

1 Cognitive factors
2 Behaviors
3 Enviromental factors

YOU

so much to reach her goals of preserving the environment and empowering women. According to social cognitive theory, Maathai's personality was influenced and shaped by the interactions among three significant forces—namely, cognitive-personal, behavioral, and environmental factors.

Cognitive-Personal Factors

Maathai was born to a family of peasant farmers and grew up during a time when Kenya had an abundance of greenery. Her childhood experiences taught her the beauty of nature's wonders. Her family encouraged her to be self-confident, ambitious, and determined to achieve her dreams. Being born into a farming family and being taught to value nature are examples of cognitive-personal factors that helped shape Maathai's personality.

Cognitive factors include our beliefs, expectations, values, intentions, and social roles. Personal factors include our emotional makeup and our biological and genetic influences.

Maathai plants trees because of cognitive-personal factors.

Cognitive factors guide personality development by influencing the way we view and interpret information. For example, Maathai views the world from the standpoint of someone whose livelihood depended on nature. These kinds of beliefs (cognitions) give Maathai the strength and determination to fight to plant more trees. Thus, cognitive-personal factors influence our personalities by affecting what we think, believe, and feel, which in turn affect how we act and behave.

Behaviors

For the past 30 years, Maathai has spoken forcefully against deforestation, founded the Green Belt Movement, and empowered women by involving them in restoring the environment. These are examples of the kinds of behaviors that also shaped her personality.

Behaviors include a variety of personal actions, such as the things we do and say.

In Maathai's case, the political and social behaviors that she engaged in to help preserve the environment in turn strengthened her belief that the government's actions to replace greenery with buildings was morally and politically wrong.

Just as behavior influences our beliefs, so too does our environment influence both.

Environmental Factors

Maathai lived in Kenya at a time of political oppression, which resulted in harsh beatings, imprisonment, and sometimes death when speaking out against the government's corrupt actions. These environmental factors certainly affected Maathai's personality development.

Environmental factors **include our social, political, and cultural influences, as well as our particular learning experiences.**

Just as our cognitive factors influence how we perceive and interpret our environment, our environment in turn affects our beliefs, values, and social roles.

We can assume that living in such an oppressive environment strengthened Maathai's determination to get a Ph.D. and to devote her life to restoring trees and empowering women.

According to Bandura (2001a), personality development is influenced by the interactions among these three factors. He especially focused on cognitive-personal factors.

Bandura's Social Cognitive Theory

Why are beliefs important?

Albert Bandura (1986, 2001a) originally called his theory of personality development the social learning theory. However, to emphasize the importance of cognitive factors in personality development, he has changed the name to the social cognitive theory.

Bandura's social cognitive theory assumes that personality development, growth, and change are influenced by four distinctively human cognitive processes: highly developed language ability, observational learning, purposeful behavior, and self-analysis.

Bandura believes that these four cognitive processes

Cognitive factors—beliefs, values, and goals—influence their personalities.

reach their highest level of functioning in humans and that much of human personality and behavior is shaped by our own thoughts and beliefs.

For example, the people in the photo on the left are members of Wangari Maathai's international Green Belt Movement. Maathai founded this organization 30 years ago to help restore the environment all over the world while helping to empower women by getting them actively involved in the organization. According to Bandura's social cognitive theory, the personalities of these members will, to a large extent, be molded by cognitive factors such as the beliefs, values, and goals of the Green Belt Movement. We'll briefly explain each of Bandura's cognitive factors.

Four Cognitive Factors

At the heart of Bandura's social cognitive theory is the idea that much of personality development is shaped and molded by cognitive processes that influence how we view and interpret the world. And, in turn, how we view and interpret the world influences how we behave. Here's how Bandura's cognitive processes apply to Green Belt Movement members.

1 Language ability. This is a powerful tool for processing and understanding information that influences personality development. We turn this information into ideas, beliefs, values, and goals, which shape, guide, and motivate our behaviors. For example, the Green Belt Movement teaches and values restoring the environment and empowering women, which helps motivate members to be more nurturing, giving, and self-confident.

2 Observational learning. Almost all of us "people watch"; we observe parents, brothers, sisters, peers, friends, and teachers; by doing so, we learn a great deal. Observational learning involves watching, imitating, and modeling. Most of the time, the observer provides his or her own reward for developing some belief or performing some behavior. For example, observational learning allows the members of the Green Belt Movement to imitate and model the personality characteristics of Wangari Maathai.

3 Purposeful behavior. Our capacity to anticipate events, plan ahead, and set goals influences our personality development, growth, and change. For instance, in working to restore the environment, members of the Green Belt Movement organize and plan ways to plant more trees and speak firmly against deforestation, which encourages them to become responsible, confident, and passionate about their cause.

4 Self-analysis. This is an internal process that allows us to monitor our own thoughts and actions. By deciding to change our goals or values, we can affect our personality development. For instance, members of the Green Belt Movement may use self-analysis to check their personality progress and to reward themselves for meeting the organization's goals.

According to Bandura's social cognitive theory, these four cognitive processes influence our personality development, growth, and change.

To make the relationship between cognitive factors and personality more concrete, we'll focus on three specific beliefs: locus of control (this page), delay of gratification, and self-efficacy (next page).

Locus of Control

Can you control when you'll graduate?

This is the kind of question that intrigued Julian Rotter (1990), who was interested in how social cognitive theory applied to human behavior. Rotter developed a well-known scale to measure a person's expectancies about how much control he or she has over situations, which Rotter called the locus of control.

Can you control when you will graduate?

Locus of control refers to our beliefs about how much control we have over situations or rewards. We are said to have an *internal locus of control* if we believe that we have control over situations and rewards. We are said to have an *external locus of control* if we believe that we do not have control over situations and rewards and that events outside ourselves (fate) determine what happens. People fall on a continuum between internal and external locus of control.

For example, if you believe that when you graduate depends primarily on your motivation and determination, then you have more of an internal locus of control. If you believe that when you graduate depends mostly on chance or things outside your control, then you have more of an external locus of control. Having more of an internal locus of control is an advantage because hundreds of studies report a positive correlation (0.20 to 0.30) between internal locus of control and mental health and psychological functioning (Burger, 2004). For example, people with an internal locus of control are generally higher achievers, cope better with chronic illness, report less stress, and are less depressed than those with an external locus of control (Burger, 2004; Livneh et al., 2004; Spector et al., 2001).

These findings indicate that a specific belief, such as how much control you believe you have, influences how you perceive your world; and this, in turn, affects how you behave. Next, we'll examine two other beliefs that influence behavior.

A. Social Cognitive Theory

Delay of Gratification

Get it now or wait for better things? Many young children have a difficult time not grabbing their favorite candy from the low-lying shelves at checkouts in spite of parents promising they'll get candy when they get home. Likewise, adults may see something they didn't intend to buy but do so on impulse, not always getting the best product or deal. These are common examples of a cognitive concept or belief called delay of gratification.

Delay of gratification **refers to not taking an immediate but less desirable reward and instead waiting and pursuing an object or completing a task that promises a better reward in the future.**

Although related to the ideas of self-control, impulsiveness, and will power, delay of gratification is defined so that it can easily be studied in the laboratory (Mischel et al., 1989). One technique to measure delay of gratification was to show children two objects, one less preferred (a single marshmallow) and one more preferred (two marshmallows). The children were told that to obtain the more preferred reward they had to wait until the experimenter, who had to leave the room, returned after some delay (about 15 minutes). Children were free to end the waiting period by ringing a bell, but then they would get only the less preferred reward. Thus, the child had a real conflict: Accept immediate gratification and take the less preferred reward, or delay gratification and obtain the more preferred reward. How long children could wait depended upon what they attended to. If they pictured the marshmallows in their minds, they could wait about 15 minutes, but if the marshmallows were right in front of them, they waited only 6 minutes (Mischel et al., 1989).

Should I take one marshmallow now or wait and get two later?

Important to delay gratification? Researchers found that the ability to delay gratification influenced many behaviors. For example, 4-year-old children good at delaying gratification tended to be more intelligent, to have greater social responsibility, and to strive for higher achievement. When these very same 4-year-old children were later retested at age 14, they were rated by parents as more competent, more intelligent, and better able to concentrate than those children who were not good at delaying gratification. NOT being able to delay gratification has been linked to a variety of self-regulatory problems, including impulsive violence, eating disorders, abusing drugs, having unprotected sex, and unwanted pregnancies (Peake et al., 2002). All of these studies make an important point: Developing the beliefs and cognitive processes involved in the ability to delay gratification can influence a variety of personal behaviors and social interactions in either positive or negative ways (Peake et al., 2002).

Another cognitive process that affects personality and behavior is how much we believe in our own capabilities.

Self-Efficacy

Can I get better grades? Students often ask about how to improve their grades. According to Albert Bandura (1999), one reason students differ in whether they receive high or low grades is related to self-efficacy.

Self-efficacy **refers to the confidence in your ability to organize and execute a given course of action to solve a problem or accomplish a task.**

For example, saying "I think that I am capable of getting a high grade in this course" is a sign of strong self-efficacy. You judge your self-efficacy by combining four sources of information (Bandura, 1999; B. J. Zimmerman, 2000):

1. You *use previous experiences* of success or failure on similar tasks to estimate how you will do on a new, related task.
2. You *compare* your capabilities with those of others.
3. You *listen* to what others say about your capabilities.
4. You *use feedback* from your body to assess your strength, vulnerability, and capability.

Why do my friends say that I should be getting better grades?

You would rate yourself as having strong self-efficacy for getting good grades if you had previous success with getting high grades, if you believe you are as academically capable as others, if your friends say you are smart, and if you do not become too stressed during exams. Twenty years of research show that students' levels of self-efficacy are good predictors of their motivation and learning during college (B. J. Zimmerman, 2000).

Influence of self-efficacy. According to Bandura's self-efficacy theory, your motivation to achieve, perform, and do well in a variety of tasks and situations is largely influenced by how strongly you believe in your own capabilities. Some people have a strong sense of self-efficacy that applies to many situations (academic settings, sports, and social interactions), others have a strong sense that applies to only a few situations (computers but not social interactions), while still others have a weak sense of self-efficacy, which predicts having less success in many of life's tasks (Eccles & Wigfield, 2002). For example, people with higher self-efficacy had greater success at stopping smoking, losing weight, overcoming a phobia, recovering from a heart attack, performing well in school, adjusting to new situations, coping with job stress, playing video games, and tolerating pain (Bandura, 2000; Joseph et al., 2003; Luszczynska & Sutton, 2006). These findings indicate that having either high or low self-efficacy can increase or decrease your performance and success in a variety of tasks and personal behaviors.

Conclusion. So far we have discussed three important beliefs: whether you have an internal or external locus of control, how much you can delay gratification, and whether you have high or low self-efficacy. Research on these three beliefs supports the basic assumption of social cognitive theory, which is that cognitive factors influence personality development, which in turn affects performance and success in a variety of tasks and situations.

Where does he get his courage? Sometimes a person's experience better illustrates the power and importance of beliefs than all the research in the world. Such an experience is that of Michael J. Fox, a talented actor who has starred in popular TV shows, such as "Spin City," and movies, including the *Back to the Future* trilogy. At age 30, Michael was diagnosed with young-onset Parkinson's disease (see p. 60), which began with a twitch in his left pinkie and led to relentless tremors in his arms and legs. Acting was his livelihood, but the progression of his symptoms made it increasingly difficult for him to act, even with the use of powerful medications to help control his tremors (Dudley, 2006; Fox, 2002).

The worsening of his symptoms forced Michael to make a key life decision: Would he allow his disease to lower his life's ambitions *or* would he believe in his ability to fight harder than ever before to reach his life's goals? Michael was unwilling to allow Parkinson's disease to take over his life. He began fighting against the disease and did so in incredible ways. Michael has continued to act by guest starring in television shows, such as "Boston Legal." Also, by starting his own charitable foundation, which has become a leader in Parkinson's disease research, and speaking in favor of stem cell research, he has taken an active and aggressive role in discovering a cure for Parkinson's disease.

In his memoir titled *Lucky Man* (Fox, 2002), Michael speaks of the pleasure he has had in increasing public awareness of Parkinson's disease: "The ten years since my diagnosis have been the best ten years of my life, and I consider myself a lucky man." Michael's story illustrates a major assumption of social cognitive theory: Beliefs have a great influence on personality, motivation, and behavior.

We'll evaluate social cognitive theory's approach to personality development and compare it with other theories.

1 Comprehensive Approach

Social cognitive theory focuses on the interaction of three primary forces in the development of personality: cognitive-personal factors, which include beliefs, expectations, social roles, and genetic influences; behaviors, which include actions, conversations, and emotional expressions; and environmental influences, such as social, political, and cultural forces.

> I believe I can continue to act.

Bandura (2001a) points out that other theories of personality tend to focus on one or two of these factors but neglect the interaction among all three factors. For example, Freudian and humanistic theories emphasize the effects of personal and cognitive forces on personality development but neglect the significant behavioral, learning, and environmental influences. Thus, one advantage of social cognitive theory is that its approach to personality development is more comprehensive and includes more influential factors than other theories.

2 Experimentally Based

Many of the concepts used in social cognitive theory have been developed from, and based on, objective measurement, laboratory research, and experimental studies. Because social cognitive theory's concepts—such as locus of control, delay of gratification, and self-efficacy—are experimentally based, they can be manipulated, controlled, and tested and are less subject to error and bias.

In comparison, many concepts from Freudian and humanistic theories of personality were developed from clinical interviews and practice and, for that reason, these concepts (oral stage, Oedipal complex, self-actualization, positive regard) are more difficult to test and validate and more open to error and bias.

3 Programs for Change

Because many of the concepts of social cognitive theory are experimentally based and objectively defined (observational learning, self-reward, modeling behavior, self-analysis, and planning), these concepts have been used to develop very successful programs for changing behavior and personality. For example, we earlier discussed two behavioral change programs that were based on social cognitive theory. In one study, individuals who had developed an intense fear of snakes showed decreased fear after observing a fearless model touching and handling a snake (p. 225); in another study, children who had observed an adult's aggressive behaviors imitated and performed similar aggressive behaviors when given an opportunity (p. 224). These are just two examples of behavioral changes that occurred after applying concepts based on social cognitive theory (Bandura, 2001a).

4 Criticisms and Conclusions

Critics say that because social cognitive concepts focus on narrowly defined behaviors, such as self-efficacy, locus of control, and delay of gratification, social cognitive theory is a somewhat piecemeal explanation of personality development. They add that social cognitive theory needs to combine these objectively but narrowly defined concepts into a more integrated theory of personality. Finally, critics contend that social cognitive theory pays too little attention to the influence of genetic factors, emotional influences, and childhood experiences on personality development (Bouchard & Loehlin, 2001; Loehlin et al., 2003).

Despite these criticisms, social cognitive theory has had a profound impact on personality theory by emphasizing the objective measurement of concepts, the influence of cognitive processes, and the application of concepts to programs for behavioral change.

Next, we'll discuss an interesting theory of personality that emphasizes describing and assessing differences between individuals and explaining why we do not always act in a consistent way.

B. Trait Theory

Do women make better cops?

At the beginning of this module, we told you about Beverly Harvard (photo below), who in 1994 became the first African American woman appointed to head a police department in a major city (Atlanta, Georgia). In 1992, Elizabeth Watson was the first Caucasian woman to head a major metropolitan police force (Houston, Texas).

Throughout the 1970s, 1980s, and 1990s, women had to fight discrimination and harassment from male police officers who believed that women did not have the physical or mental strength to be police officers (Copeland, 1999). However, a number of studies have shown that women do make good police officers and, in situations involving domestic abuse, they are more successful than policemen because policewomen have better interpersonal skills than men (Lonsway et al., 2003).

Which traits of policewomen make them better at keeping the peace?

Peacekeeper. For example, police officer Kelly, who is female, patrols an area known for problems with street thugs. Although we may think that the best way to control thugs is with threat or force, Kelly rarely uses either. Kelly readily admits that her physical strength cannot always match that of some of the macho males she encounters. "Coming across aggressively doesn't work with gang members," Kelly explains. "If that first encounter is direct, knowledgeable, and made with authority, they respond. It takes a few more words but it works" (McDowell, 1992, p. 70). As another woman police officer said, "We've been learning our whole lives how to deal with things without having to resort to physical strength and physical violence" (Munoz, 2003, p. B2). These examples suggest that, in some situations, women make better and more effective cops than men because they have different personality traits.

Men. Traits of male officers include being assertive, aggressive, and direct, which help them act as enforcers.

Women. Traits of female officers include being compassionate, sympathetic, and diplomatic, which help them act as peacekeepers.

The reason female police officers act more as peacekeepers and male police officers act more as enforcers may be explained by trait theory.

Trait theory **is an approach for analyzing the structure of personality by measuring, identifying, and classifying similarities and differences in personality characteristics or traits.**

The basic unit for measuring personality characteristics is the trait.

A *trait* **is a relatively stable and enduring tendency to behave in a particular way.**

For example, traits of female police officers include being compassionate, sympathetic, and diplomatic, which help them function as peacekeepers, while traits of male police officers include being assertive, aggressive, and direct, which help them function as enforcers. Determining exactly how many traits are needed to describe someone's personality took psychologists almost 60 years.

How to describe these five persons?

How would you describe the personalities of a criminal, clown, graduate, nun, and beauty queen? This seemingly impossible task was the major goal of personality researchers. They were determined to find a list of traits whose two characteristics seemed mutually exclusive: The list had to contain very few traits but at the same time be able to describe differences among anyone's and everyone's personality, from avocado grower to zookeeper. The search for this elusive list began in the 1930s with, of all things, a dictionary.

Which . . .

How many traits can there be?

In the 1930s, Gordon Allport and an associate went through the dictionary and selected every term that could distinguish differences among personalities (Allport & Odbert, 1936). They found about 18,000 terms that dealt with all kinds of personality differences; of these, about 4,500 were considered to fit their definition of personality traits. Allport defined *traits* as stable and consistent tendencies in how an individual adjusts to his or her environment. The advantage of Allport's list was that it was comprehensive enough to describe anyone's and everyone's personality. The disadvantage was that it was incredibly long and thus impractical to use in research.

. . . five . . .

Allport's search for a list of defining traits set the stage for future research. However, his list of thousands of traits needed to be organized into far fewer basic traits. This task fell to Raymond Cattell.

. . . traits . . .

Aren't some traits related?

In the 1940s, Raymond Cattell (1943) took Allport's list of 4,500 traits and used factor analysis to reduce the list to the most basic traits.

Factor analysis **is a complicated statistical method that finds relationships among many different or diverse items and allows them to be grouped together.**

Cattell used factor analysis to search for *relationships* among hundreds of traits on Allport's list so that the original list could be reduced to 35 basic traits, which Cattell called *source traits.* He claimed that these 35 basic traits could describe all differences among personalities. Although Cattell's achievement was remarkable, his list of 35 traits—and even

. . . describe . . .

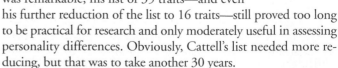

. . . each of these five different personalities?

his further reduction of the list to 16 traits—still proved too long to be practical for research and only moderately useful in assessing personality differences. Obviously, Cattell's list needed more reducing, but that was to take another 30 years.

Can it be done with just five?

From the 1960s to the early 1990s, about a dozen researchers in several countries were using factor analysis to find relationships among lists of adjectives that described personality differences. Doing the impossible, researchers reduced the list of 35 traits to only 5, which make up the five-factor model of personality (Burger, 2004; Durrett & Trull, 2005).

The *five-factor model* organizes personality traits and describes differences in personality using five categories, which are *openness, conscientiousness, extraversion, agreeableness,* and *neuroticism.*

These five factors became known as the *Big Five* and are easy to remember if you note that their first letters make the acronym OCEAN. Each of the five factors actually represents a continuum of behavior, as briefly described in the figure below.

Openness

| Is open to novel experiences. | Has narrow interests. |

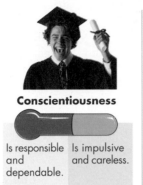

Conscientiousness

| Is responsible and dependable. | Is impulsive and careless. |

Extraversion

| Is outgoing and decisive. | Is retiring and withdrawn. |

Agreeableness

| Is warm and good-natured. | Is unfriendly and cold. |

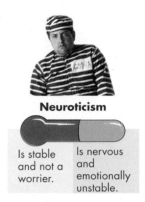

Neuroticism

| Is stable and not a worrier. | Is nervous and emotionally unstable. |

Hot and cold. You can think of each Big Five factor as a *supertrait* because each factor's thermometer includes dozens of related traits at the hot and cold ends. For example, conscientiousness, at the hot end, includes the traits of being dependable, responsible, deliberate, hardworking, and precise; at the cold end are the traits of being impulsive, careless, late, lazy, and aimless. Although it took 30 years of research, coming up with the Big Five means that trait theory finally achieved its major goal, which was to describe and organize personality characteristics using the fewest number of traits (McCrae & Costa, 2003).

Importance of the Big Five

Unlike earlier attempts to identify traits, there is now convincing evidence that the Big Five or five-factor theory can indeed describe personality differences among many thousands of individuals by using only five categories or traits. For example, the personalities of children and adults in the United States as well as in six other very different cultures or countries (Germany, Portugal, Israel, South Korea, Japan, and Philippines) were described by using the Big Five traits (Katigbak et al., 2002).

Big question. Since the five-factor model has been replicated in many different countries, researchers asked if the structure of personality was shaped primarily by different *cultural factors* (child-rearing practices, religious and moral values, language similarities) or primarily by differences in the *basic human ways* of acting and experiencing that are universal, or similar across all peoples and countries.

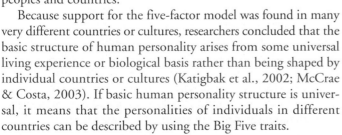

Each letter in the word OCEAN is the first letter of one of the Big Five traits.

Because support for the five-factor model was found in many very different countries or cultures, researchers concluded that the basic structure of human personality arises from some universal living experience or biological basis rather than being shaped by individual countries or cultures (Katigbak et al., 2002; McCrae & Costa, 2003). If basic human personality structure is universal, it means that the personalities of individuals in different countries can be described by using the Big Five traits.

Big Five in the Real World

When you describe a friend's personality, what you are doing (usually without knowing) is using the five supertraits described in the Big Five or five-factor theory. Because personality similarities and differences can be described by five categories, questionnaires based on the five-factor theory can more accurately assess personality and personality problems, which is one of the major tasks of therapists, clinicians, and psychologists.

Although the five-factor theory has proven very useful in describing and organizing personality traits, this theory does not explain how these traits develop across one's lifetime or account for people's behavior in unusual situations, such as risking one's life to climb Mount Everest (McCrae & Costa, 2003).

For instance, the Big Five traits can be used to describe differences between male and female police officers. Compared with policemen, policewomen are generally more agreeable (sympathetic, friendly, helpful), more open (insightful, intelligent), and more extraverted (sociable, talkative). These kinds of traits result in policewomen being less authoritarian, more diplomatic, and better at defusing potentially dangerous situations (Spillar & Harrington, 2000).

Researchers generally agree that the five-factor theory is a giant leap forward in trait theory and is a useful tool for defining personality structures and differences, predicting behaviors, and identifying personality problems (Burger, 2004; McCrae & Costa, 2003).

Although each of us possesses at least five relatively enduring supertraits that push us to behave in a stable way, why do we sometimes contradict ourselves and behave differently in different situations?

B. Trait Theory

How does private life compare to public life?

The best-known right-wing talk-radio host is Rush Limbaugh, who broadcasts his conservative law-and-order views to 20 million fans five days a week. For example, when Grateful Dead guitarist Jerry Garcia died in 1995, Limbaugh said, "When you strip it all away, Jerry Garcia destroyed his life on drugs. And yet he's being honored, like some godlike figure. Our priorities are out of whack, folks" (Laurence, 2003, p. F7). Talking about drug users, Limbaugh said, ". . . too many whites are getting away with drug use . . . The answer is to go out and find the ones who are getting away with it, convict them and send them up the river, too" (Laurence, 2003, p. F7).

Then, on October, 16, 2003, the *National Enquirer* headline read, "Rush Limbaugh caught in a drug ring." According to several other respected news accounts, Limbaugh had become a narcotic addict (pain pills). His maid claimed that for three years she had

Limbaugh preached law and order in public but in private he was a drug addict.

bought enough "baby blues" (OxyContin pills) to "kill an elephant." According to police, Limbaugh obtained 2,000 pain pills during only a six-month period. Limbaugh admitted to being a drug addict, turned himself in, and went into a drug rehab program (Campo-Flores & Thomas, 2006; E. Thomas, 2003).

The observation that, like Rush Limbaugh, individuals often behave differently in different situations questions one of the basic assumptions of trait theory, which is that traits create tendencies to behave in certain consistent ways. Psychologist Walter Mischel (1968) was one of the first to conduct a series of classic experiments on why traits fail to predict the behavior of people across different situations.

Experiment: Person-Situation

To test trait theory's basic assumption that people behave consistently across situations, Walter Mischel and Philip Peake (1982) asked college students, "How conscientious are you?" If students answer that they are "very conscientious," trait theory predicts that they will behave conscientiously in many different situations. Mischel then observed how conscientious college students behaved across 19 very different situations, such as attending classes, getting homework in on time, and keeping their rooms neat.

Students who rated themselves as very conscientious behaved that way day after day in similar situations. However, these same students did not behave conscientiously across all 19 conditions. For example, very conscientious students might clean their rooms daily but not get their homework in on time, or they might attend all their classes but not clean their rooms. Researchers concluded that, as trait theory predicted, students behaved with great consistency in the *same* situation, but contrary to trait theory's prediction, students behaved *differently* or with low consistency across different situations. This finding led to what is now called the person-situation interaction.

The *person-situation interaction* means that a person's behavior results from an interaction between his or her traits and the effects of being in or responding to cues from a particular situation.

The person-situation interaction explains that even if you were an extravert, you would behave differently at a wedding than at a funeral because each of these situations creates different cues to which you respond (Mischel & Shoda, 1995). Similarly, the person-situation interaction describes how Rush Limbaugh could be righteous in criticizing Jerry Garcia's drug use while being a drug addict himself.

The person-situation interaction says that to understand or predict a person's behavior across situations, we must consider both the person's traits and the powerful cues that come from being in each different situation (Malle et al., 2000).

If you are open to new experiences, would you try this? Do you see the dog?

Conclusions

There is no question that humans have stable and consistent parts of their personalities, which are called traits. There is no question that personality differences can be accurately described by using the Big Five traits. However, people may act inconsistently or contradictorily because traits interact with and are partly dependent upon situational cues. Thus, even though you consider yourself open to new experiences, you might very well draw the line and say "NO!" to potentially dangerous rock climbing (below left photo). Although researchers have found that traits are not consistent across all situations, the concept of traits is still useful for two reasons (G. Matthews et al., 2003).

Descriptions. First, traits are useful because they provide a kind of shorthand method for describing someone's personality. In fact, if we asked you to describe your best friend, you would essentially list this person's traits.

Predictions. Second, traits are useful because they help predict someone's behavior in future situations. However, you must keep in mind the person-situation interaction, which means you must take into account how the person's traits will interact with the situation's cues. For example, my friends would predict that I (R.P.) generally try to watch my weight but they also know that when placed in front of a dessert counter, I can easily consume my weight in chocolate. However, researchers found it is possible to significantly increase the accuracy of predicting a person's behaviors across situations if that person is actually observed in a number of different settings (G. Matthews et al., 2003).

Conclusion. Most personality researchers agree that traits, such as the Big Five, are useful in describing our stable and consistent behavioral tendencies, yet they warn that traits may not predict behaviors across different situations (Malle et al., 2000; G. Matthews et al., 2003).

Does saying that traits are stable and consistent mean that one's personality gradually becomes fixed?

How changeable are your traits?

If you are now 16, 18, 20, 25, or 30, what will your personality be like when you're 40, 50, 60, 70, or 80? The question of how much your personality traits remain the same and how much they change is answered by using a research approach called the longitudinal method.

Longitudinal method means that the same group of individuals is studied repeatedly at many different points in time.

For example, if you asked your parents to list your personality traits at age 3, would these traits match your traits at age 21? In other words, how changeable or fixed are your personality traits?

3 to 21 Years Old

To answer the question of how much personality traits change or remain the same, researchers did a longitudinal study on 1,000 children, whose traits were assessed at age 3 and then reassessed when the same children were 21 years old. Based on their assessment, the personality traits of 3-year-old children were divided into five different personality groups that were labeled undercontrolled, inhibited, confident, reserved, and well-adjusted (Caspi, 2000).

Will this 3-year-old child's personality traits . . .

. . . be similar to those he has at 21 years old?

Consistency. Researchers found significant consistencies between traits assessed at 3 years and at 21 years old. For example, traits of 3-year-old children in the *undercontrolled group* included being impulsive, restless, and distractible. When these 3-year-old children were retested at age 21, their traits were similar and included being reckless, careless, and favoring dangerous and exciting activities. In comparison, traits of 3-year-old children in the *well-adjusted group* included being confident, having self-control, and easily adjusting to new or stressful situations. When these 3-year-old children were retested at age 21, their traits were similar and included being in control, self-confident, and all-around well-adjusted and normal adults. Researchers concluded that the origin or development of a person's more stable personality traits begins around age 3. This means that traits observed at age 3 predict personality traits observed later in the same young adults (Caspi, 2000).

Change. Although there were remarkable consistencies in personality traits between age 3 and age 21, researchers point out that there are often major changes in emotional traits during adolescence. During adolescence, individuals may become less responsible, less cautious, and more moody or impulsive (Caspi & Roberts, 1999).

What happens to personality development after age 21, and does personality ever stop changing?

22 to 80 Years Old

If you are 18, 20, 25, or 30 now, what will your personality be like at 50, 60, 70, or 80? Answers come from a series of longitudinal studies, which reached the following conclusions (Caspi et al., 2005; McCrae & Costa, 1999; McCrae et al., 2000; Roberts et al., 2002; Trzesniewski et al., 2003):

1 Major changes in personality occur during childhood, adolescence, and young adulthood. Between 22 and 30, both men and women become less emotional, less likely to be thrill seekers, and somewhat more likely to be cooperative and self-disciplined. These personality changes are often associated with becoming more mature.

2 In fact, longitudinal studies find that most major changes in personality occur before the age of 30 because adolescents and young adults are more willing to adopt new values and attitudes or revise old ones.

3 Personality traits are relatively fixed by age 30, after which changes in personality are few and small. However, after 30, adults continue to grow in their ideas, beliefs, and attitudes as they respond to changing situations and environments. For example, an eager tennis player may, with age, become an eager gardener, but an eager liberal is unlikely to become an eager conservative.

4 Men and women, healthy and sick people, and Blacks and Whites all show the same stable personality pattern after age 30. Because personality is stable, it is somewhat predictable. However, individuals may struggle to overcome or change certain traits (become less shy, more confident), which brings up the question of how much personality changes during adulthood.

5 When middle-aged and older adults were asked to describe the course of their personality development, they all described increases in desirable traits (energetic, realistic, intelligent) as they grew older. But on objective tests, these same individuals showed little or no change in these same traits. These findings indicate that as people grow older, they tend to report more socially desirable or stereotypic responses rather than what actually has occurred.

Conclusions. Your personality is more likely to change the younger you are, but after age 30, personality traits are relatively stable and fixed. However, depending upon situations, stressors, and challenges, some change can occur throughout adulthood (Kluger, 2006a). Thus, personality has the interesting distinction of being both stable and changeable (up to a point). One reason personality traits remain relatively stable across time is that they are influenced by genetic factors, which we'll discuss next.

Before age 30, personality may go through major changes, but . . .

. . . after age 30, personality is relatively fixed and difficult to change.

C. Genetic Influences on Traits

Behavioral Genetics

Why are twins so similar?

Jim Lewis (left photo) and Jim Springer (right photo) drove the same model blue Chevrolet, chain-smoked the same brand of cigarettes, owned dogs named Toy, held jobs as deputy sheriff, enjoyed the same woodworking hobby, and had vacationed on the same beach in Florida. When they were given personality tests, they scored almost alike on traits of flexibility, self-control, and sociability. The two Jims are identical twins who were separated four weeks after birth and reared separately. When reunited at age 39, they were flabbergasted at how many things they had in common (Leo, 1987).

These surprising coincidences come from an ongoing University of Minnesota project on genetic factors (Bouchard, 1994; Bouchard & Loehlin, 2001). One of the project's major questions is whether the similarities between the two Jims are simply coincidence or reflect the influence of genetic factors on personality traits.

Most of us grew up hearing one or both of these phrases: "You're acting just like your father" or "You're behaving just like your mother." What these phrases suggest is that genetic factors that we inherited from our parents are influencing our behaviors. Psychologists have only recently recognized the importance and influence of

Why did they drive the same kind of car, smoke the same cigarettes, hold the same kind of job, and both name their dogs Toy?

genetic factors, which have resulted in a new area called behavioral genetics.

Behavioral genetics **is the study of how inherited or genetic factors influence and interact with psychological factors to shape our personality, intelligence, emotions, and motivation and also how we behave, adapt, and adjust to our environments.**

Many of us have a difficult time accepting the idea of genetic influences because we equate genetic with *fixed*. However, genetic factors do not fix behaviors but establish a range for a behavior, which environmental factors foster or impede. For example, genetic factors set a range for our height and weight. But our actual height and weight will also depend on how genetic factors interact with environmental influences, such as whether we have a good diet and exercise program.

As we discuss studies showing that genetic factors influence and set a range for development of various personality traits, please remember that our actual traits result from the interaction between genetic factors and environmental influences.

Studying Genetic Influences

What's in the genes?

Few studies have made as great an impact on beliefs about what shapes personality and behavior as the twin study at the University of Minnesota. Until the early 1990s, most psychologists recognized the existence of genetic factors in shaping personality but believed that genetic factors had much less impact than environmental factors. Then in 1990, Thomas Bouchard and his colleagues (1990) published the first study to simultaneously compare four different groups of twins: identical twins reared together, identical twins reared apart, fraternal twins reared together, and fraternal twins reared apart. Remember that identical twins share 100% of their genes, while fraternal twins share only 50% of their genes and thus are no more genetically alike than ordinary brothers and sisters. This study allowed researchers to separate genetic factors (identical versus fraternal twins) and environmental factors (reared together versus reared apart).

We're identical twins, and we share 100% of our genes.

This is a piece of the genetic code, which uses a chemical alphabet (A, C, G, T) to write instructions that influence the development of personality traits.

More than 100 sets of twins in the United States, Great Britain, and many other countries participated in this initial study. Each participant was given over 50 hours of medical and psychological assessment, including four different tests to measure personality

traits. Those identical and fraternal twins who were reared apart were adopted shortly after birth and had not met their twin until this study brought them together for testing. The measure that researchers use to estimate genetic influences is called heritability.

Heritability **is a statistical measure that estimates how much of some cognitive, personality, or behavioral trait is influenced by genetic factors.**

Heritability is expressed on an increasing scale of influence from 0.0 to 1.0. That is, if genetic factors have no influence, the heritability is 0.0, having half the influence is indicated by 0.5, and having total control over behavior is indicated by 1.0. For example, heritability of IQ is about 50% (p. 292), which means that about 50% of an individual's IQ score is explained by genetic factors; heritability of mental disorders is about 40–70% (pp. 533–539); and, as we'll discuss next, heritability estimates for personality traits are about 40–50%. However, keep in mind that genetic factors interact with environmental factors, which explain about 40–60% of the development of IQs, mental disorders, and personality traits.

We're fraternal twins, and we share only 50% of our genes.

Do genes influence the Big Five?

Identical twins Jim Lewis and Jim Springer (photos opposite page) were subjects in the now famous Minnesota twin study. Their scores were similar on personality tests that measured the Big Five traits—openness, conscientiousness, extraversion, agreeableness, and neuroticism. (Note that by taking the first letter of each Big Five trait, you make the word OCEAN.) One reason the two Jims' scores on personality tests were so similar was that their genetic factors were identical.

There are now many studies on thousands of twins, both identical and fraternal, who were reared together and apart and whose data were analyzed by different groups of researchers. Results from earlier studies and two large and recent studies are shown in the graph below (Bouchard & Loehlin, 2001). Researchers estimate the heritability of personality traits ranges from 0.41 to about 0.51, which means that genetic factors contribute about 40 to 50% to the development of an individual's personality traits (Bouchard, 2004).

Even though genetic factors are responsible for about half of each of the Big Five personality traits we develop, that still leaves about half coming from environmental factors. We'll describe two kinds of environmental factors—shared and nonshared—that influence personality development.

Heritability of Big Five Personality Traits	
Earlier twin studies	0.51
Loehlin twin studies	0.42
Minnesota twin studies	0.41

What shapes personality?

As I (R.P.) was growing up, I remember hearing my parents talking (when they thought I wasn't listening) about how different I was from my older brother and sister. My parents questioned how my brother and sister and I could be so (very) different even though we had the same parents, lived in the same house in the same town, and even went to the same school and church. One reason that brothers and sisters develop such different personalities is that 50% of their genes are different (and 50% are shared). And another important reason that brothers and sisters develop different personalities is that each brother's or sister's unique set of genetic factors interacts differently with his or her environment. Researchers have broken down the contributions to personality development into the following four factors.

40% Genetic Factors

The fingerprints of the two Jims were almost identical because they shared 100% of their genes, and genetic factors contribute 97% to the development of ridges on finger tips (Bouchard et al., 1990). In comparison, the two Jims' scores were similar but not identical on personality traits of self-control, flexibility, and sociability because, although they share 100% of their genes, genetic factors contribute about 40 to 50% to the kind of personality traits they developed. While genetic factors contribute about half to the development of certain personality traits, the next biggest factor is something of a surprise.

27% Nonshared Environmental Factors

Although we know that the two Jims show remarkable similarities in personality, they also display unique differences. Jim Lewis (left photo)

says that he is more easygoing and less of a worrier than his identical twin, Jim Springer (right photo). When the twins get on a plane, Jim Springer worries about the plane being late, while Jim Lewis says that there is no use worrying (*San Diego Tribune*, November 12, 1987). One of the reasons that the two Jims developed different personality traits is that about 27% of the influence on personality development comes from how each individual's genetic factors react and adjust to his or her own environment. These factors are called *nonshared environmental factors* because they involve how each individual's genetic factors react and adjust to his or her particular environment.

26% Error

About 26% of the influence on personality development cannot as yet be identified and is attributed to errors in testing and measurement procedures. As methodology improves, this error percentage will decrease and other factors will increase.

7% Shared Environmental Factors

About 7% of the influence on personality development comes from environmental factors that involve parental patterns and shared family experiences. These factors are called *shared environmental factors* because they involve how family members interact and share experiences. One of the major surprises to come out of the twin studies was how little impact parental practices and shared family experiences have on personality development. Researchers concluded that being raised in the same family contributes little (about 7%) to personality development. Far more

important for personality development are nonshared environmental factors (27%), which refer to how each child's unique genetic factors react and adjust to being in that family (Bouchard & Loehlin, 2001; De Fruyt et al., 2006). You can think of genetic factors as pushing and pulling personality development in certain directions, while environmental factors join in to push and pull it in the same or different directions.

Next, we'll take a last look at the impact of trait theory.

D. Evaluation of Trait Theory

Could we live without traits? It would be very difficult to live without traits because you use them constantly, usually without knowing it. For example, whenever you describe someone, or predict how he or she will behave, your descriptions of personality and predictions of behaviors are based almost entirely on knowing the person's

Personal Want Ad

Personal ads are based on traits.

traits. Newspapers are full of personal ads, which are essentially a list of most-desired traits.

Although traits are very useful as a shorthand to describe a person's personality and predict a person's behaviors, critics raise three major questions about traits: How good is the list? Can traits predict? What influences traits? We'll discuss each issue in turn.

How Good Is the List?

The Big Five or five-factor trait theory assumes that all similarities and differences among personalities can be described by an amazingly short but comprehensive list of five traits—openness, conscientiousness, extraversion, agreeableness, and neuroticism (OCEAN). Each of the *Big Five traits* has two poles or two dimensions, which include dozens of related traits. The Big Five traits' ability to describe personality has now been verified in many different countries, with different populations and age groups (John, 1990; McCrae & Allik, 2002).

The Big Five traits have the ability to describe personalities of children and adults in many different countries.

Critics of the five-factor model point out that the data for the model came from questionnaires that may be too structured to give real and complete portraits of personalities. As a result, data from questionnaires may paint too simplistic a picture of human personality and may not reflect its depth and complexity (Block, 1995). Critics also point out that traits primarily describe a person's personality rather than explain or point out its causes (Digman, 1997).

In defense of the five-factor theory, researchers have shown that the Big Five traits provide a valid and reliable way to describe personality differences and consistencies in our own lives and in our social interactions with others (McCrae & Costa, 2003).

Can Traits Predict?

One of the more serious problems faced by early trait theory involved the assumption that, since traits are consistent and stable influences on our behaviors, traits should be very useful in predicting behaviors.

Rush Limbaugh preached law and order on his talk-radio show but was a drug addict in private.

But how does trait theory explain why Rush Limbaugh behaved so inconsistently? He preached law and order and right-wing conservative moral standards on his radio talk show, but in his private life he had become a drug addict and was allegedly having his maid buy drugs on the black market.

One explanation is that Limbaugh did behave in a consistent moral way in public situations (radio talk shows). However, in other situations, such as his private life, he had become a drug addict. This problem of predicting behavior across situations is known as the *person-situation interaction.* Researchers found that situations may have as much influence on behavior as traits do, so situational influences must be taken into account when predicting someone's behavior (G. Matthews et al., 2003). Researchers found that traits could better predict behaviors if traits were measured under different conditions and situations.

Currently, the Big Five traits are considered useful concepts for describing consistent and stable behavioral tendencies in similar situations, but traits do not necessarily predict behaviors across different situations.

What Influences Traits?

One major surprise coming from twin studies was how relatively little effect parental practices or shared family experiences have on personality development (graph below). Researchers concluded that parental practices or *shared factors* contributed only about 7% to personality development. In contrast, how each child personally reacts or adjusts to parental or family practices, called *nonshared factors*, contributed about 27% to personality development (Bouchard & Loehlin, 2001; Plomin & Crabbe, 2000). This finding questioned a major belief of developmental psychologists, who hold that sharing parental or family environment greatly influences personality development among the siblings (brothers and sisters). Instead, twin research suggests that psychologists need to look more closely at each child's reactions to his or her family environment as a major influence on personality development.

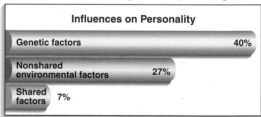

Influences on Personality

Genetic factors	40%
Nonshared environmental factors	27%
Shared factors	7%

Personality development depends more on genetic and nonshared factors (child's individual reactions) than on shared parental influences.

According to behavioral geneticists, the idea of genes influencing complex human behaviors was unthinkable as recently as 15 years ago. Today, however, there is convincing evidence that genetic factors exert a considerable influence on many complex human behaviors, including intelligence, mental health, and personality traits (Bouchard, 2004). Yet these same researchers warn that *genetic influences* on human behavior should not be blown out of proportion. Because heritability scores generally do not exceed 50%, this means the remaining 50% or more involves *environmental influences,* especially nonshared environmental influences.

✔ Concept Review

1. Social cognitive theory says that personality development is primarily shaped by three interacting forces: _____, _____, and _____.

2. The above three forces all interact to influence how we evaluate, interpret, and organize _____ and apply such knowledge to ourselves and others.

3. An example of the social cognitive approach is Bandura's social cognitive theory, which says that personality development, growth, and change are influenced by four distinctively human cognitive processes: highly developed (a)_____ ability, (b)_____ learning, (c)_____ behavior, and (d)_____.

4. Three different beliefs based on social cognitive theory have been shown to influence personality development and behavior. Rotter referred to beliefs concerning how much control we have over situations or rewards. If we believe that we have control over situations and rewards, we are said to have an (a)_____. If we believe that we do not have control over situations and rewards and that events outside ourselves (fate) determine what happens, we are said to have an (b)_____.

5. According to Bandura, our personal beliefs regarding how capable we are of exercising control over events in our lives—for example, carrying out certain tasks and behaviors—is called (a)_____, which, in turn, affects our performance on a wide variety of behaviors. Mischel devised ways of measuring our ability to voluntarily postpone an immediate reward and persist in completing a task for the promise of a future reward, which is called (b)_____.

> Should I take one marshmallow now or wait and get two?

6. The approach to describe the structure of personality that is based on identifying and analyzing ways in which personalities differ is known as _____ theory.

7. A relatively stable and enduring tendency to behave in a particular way is called a (a)_____. A statistical procedure that may be used to find relationships among many different or diverse items, such as traits, and form them into selected groups is called (b)_____.

OCEAN

8. The model that organizes all personality traits into five categories that can be used to describe differences in personality is called the (a)_____ model. This model uses the Big Five traits, which are (b)_____, _____, _____, _____, and _____.

9. Research supports the five-factor model and the Big Five traits. Each of the Big Five traits has two poles or dimensions and represents a wide range of _____.

10. Walter Mischel said that to predict a person's behavior we must take into account not only the person's traits but also the effects of the situation; this became known as the (a)_____. According to this idea, a person's behavior results from an (b)_____ between his or her traits and the effects of being in a particular situation.

11. To investigate whether personality changes as people grow older, psychologists study the same individuals at different times; this is called a (a)_____ study. In general, studies have shown that personality is more likely to change if a person is under (b)_____ years old. After that, changes usually involve variations on the same behavioral theme or accompany changes in social roles.

12. The field that focuses on how inherited or genetic factors influence and interact with psychological factors is called (a)_____. A statistical measure that estimates how much of some behavior is due to genetic influences is called (b)_____.

13. Studies have found that about 40% of the influence on personality development comes from (a)_____; about 27% comes from how each person adjusts to his or her own environment, which is called (b)_____; and about 7% comes from parental patterns and family experiences, which are called (c)_____.

Answers: *1. cognitive-personal factors, behavior, environmental influences; 2. information; 3. (a) language, (b) observational, (c) purposeful, (d) self-analysis; 4. (a) internal locus of control, (b) external locus of control; 5. (a) self-efficacy, (b) delay of gratification; 6. trait; 7. (a) trait, (b) factor analysis; 8. (a) five-factor, (b) openness, conscientiousness, extraversion, agreeableness, neuroticism; 9. behaviors; 10. (a) person-situation interaction, (b) interaction; 11. (a) longitudinal, (b) 30; 12. (a) behavioral genetics, (b) heritability; 13. (a) genetic factors, (b) nonshared environmental factors, (c) shared environmental factors*

E. Research Focus: 180-Degree Change

What triggers a major change?

Sometimes researchers study unusual behaviors that seem to contradict what is known. For example, anyone who has ever tried to change some behavior finds it difficult because traits are relatively stable and enduring. For this reason, it's difficult to believe people who claim to have totally changed their personalities in minutes, hours, or a single day. Researchers call these sudden, dramatic changes quantum personality changes (W. R. Miller & C'de Baca, 1994, 2001).

A *quantum personality change* refers to making a very radical or dramatic shift in one's personality, beliefs, or values in minutes, hours, or a day.

For example, here's the quantum personality change of Bill Wilson, who cofounded

How much could you change in one day?

Alcoholics Anonymous (AA). He was in the depths of alcoholic despair and depression when he suddenly saw his room lit with a bright light. In his mind's eye, he saw himself on a mountaintop and felt that spirit winds were blowing through him. Then, suddenly, a simple but powerful thought burst upon him: he was a free man (E. Kurtz, 1979). This dramatic experience changed Wilson's personality 180 degrees as he went from being a desperate and hopeless drunk to being a sober and dedicated worker who devoted his life to helping others overcome alcoholism.

Reports of sudden and major changes in personality challenge two well-established findings: First, personality traits are stable and enduring tendencies that may change gradually but rarely undergo sudden and dramatic changes; and second, even when people want to change their personalities, as in therapy, it doesn't happen overnight but takes considerable time and effort. Then how can quantum personality changes occur, often in a single day? To answer this question, researchers first had to develop a method to study quantum changes.

Method

Researchers found people who had experienced a quantum personality change through a feature story in the local paper (Albuquerque, New Mexico). Researchers asked for volunteers who, in a relatively short period of time, had experienced a transformation in their basic values, feelings, attitudes, or actions. Out of a total of 89 people who responded, 55 were found acceptable. These 55 subjects were given a series of personality tests and structured interviews (average length 107 minutes).

Structured interviews involve asking each individual the same set of relatively narrow and focused questions so that the same information is obtained from everyone.

During structured interviews, all subjects were asked the same detailed questions about the what, when, and where of the unusual experiences that had apparently transformed their personalities so completely.

Structured interviews use the subjects' self-reports to provide information about subjective thoughts, feelings, and experiences, which are most often unobservable cognitive and emotional processes.

Results

Researchers used a variety of personality tests to make sure the subjects (31 women and 24 men) performed within the normal range on personality tests, had no strange problems, and showed no striking or unusual things in common. In fact, based on the battery of personality tests and interviews, all the subjects seemed to be normal, ordinary individuals who had had extraordinary experiences (W. R. Miller & C'de Baca, 1994). Here are some of the study's major findings:

■ A majority of subjects (58%) could specify the date and time of day when the quantum experience occurred even though the experience had occurred, on average, 11 years earlier.

As if struck by light or hearing a voice → Quantum personality change

■ A majority of subjects (75%) reported that the quantum experience began suddenly and took them by surprise. For some the experience lasted only minutes (13%), and for most it was over within 24 hours (64%). The actual experiences included being struck by an intense thought, making a total commitment, hearing a voice, and hearing God's voice.

■ A majority of subjects (56%) reported a high level of emotional distress and a relatively high level of negative life experiences in the year before the quantum experience.

■ Most (96%) reported that the quantum experience had made their lives better, and most (80%) stated that the changes had lasted.

■ Most (87%) said that, during the quantum experience, an important truth was revealed to them; 78% said that they were relieved of a mental burden; and 60% said that they felt completely loved.

All of these 55 individuals reported that they had, in a single day or less, experienced a 180-degree change in personality. For the vast majority, the quantum change in personality seems to have resulted from or been triggered by a period of bad times. After the quantum change, subjects reported that their lives had improved.

Conclusions

Researchers concluded that the quantum personality changes reported by the subjects were dramatically larger than are ordinarily observed, occurred in a shorter period of time than is normally reported, and lasted for years (W. R. Miller & C'de Baca, 1994).

For most of the subjects, the changes represented an increased sense of meaning, happiness, and satisfaction; some reported a sense of closeness to God. This study suggests that quantum changes in personality do occur and may be one way a person solves some long-standing and stressful personal problem.

In many cases, people who experienced quantum personality changes also reported subsequent changes in behavior.

As you'll see next, how much personality influences behavior is partly dependent on one's culture.

F. Cultural Diversity: Suicide Bombers

Why was Arien the exception?

One of the most difficult and tragic issues for Westerners to understand is the reasons behind suicide bombers. Recently, a young woman agreed to tell her story of how she became a suicide bomber (Bennet, 2002).

Arien Ahmed (right photo) was a 20-year-old Palestinian student of business administration at Bethlehem University. Five days after she had volunteered to become a suicide bomber, she was pulled out of a marketing lecture and shown

> I believe Israeli forces killed my fiancé and I want to avenge his death.

how to trigger a bomb inside a backpack. She got into a old car with another would-be killer and went on her mission dressed as an Israeli woman. As she walked through an Israeli town carrying a heavy backpack containing a bomb surrounded with nails, she began to have second thoughts. She described a kind of awakening and remembered a childhood belief "that nobody has the right to stop anybody's life." At that moment she decided not to go through with the bombing. She was later arrested by Israeli police (Bennet, 2002). Arien was a rare exception, since suicide bombers almost never fail to complete their deadly missions.

Cultural & Personal Reasons

After Arien was arrested, she said that she agreed to tell her story to discourage other Palestinians from becoming suicide bombers and to gain sympathy for herself. The Israeli Security Agency, which allowed Arien to be interviewed by newspaper reporters, appeared eager to show how easily militants manipulate susceptible people and send them to kill and die (Bennet, 2002).

What conditions lead to suicide attacks? In the mid-1990s, there were more than 20 suicide attacks throughout Turkey. The attacks have since stopped because the Turkish government undertook steps to satisfy the rebel forces' demands. Before 1990, there were no suicide attacks in Chechnya. Since then suicide attacks have begun as Chechnyans fight to win their independence from Russia. For example, in 2003, there were at least seven suicide attacks in Chechnya that killed 165 people. All but one of the Chechnyan suicide bombers were women (Zakaria, 2003). From 1993 to 2003, there were almost 200 Palestinian suicide bomb attacks in Israel, which killed and wounded many hundreds of citizens.

What motivates a suicide bomber? Arien appeared to have been motivated by both personal and cultural reasons. As she told Israeli security agents, her strong

There were 200 suicide bombings in Israel.

personal reason was that she wanted to avenge the death of her fiancé, whom she believed had been killed by Israeli forces (who said that her fiancé accidentally blew himself up). After his death, she said, "So I lost all my future." Arien's recruiters told her that dying as a suicide attacker would earn her the reward of rejoining her slain fiancé in paradise. Even though Arien now calls her attempt to be a suicide bomber a mistake, she said she understood it. "It's a result of the situation we live in. There are also innocent people killed on both sides" (Bennet, 2002, p. A1).

There are also strong Muslim *cultural influences* that encourage women, such as Arien, to become suicide bombers. For example, during the past several years, women have been increasingly involved in Palestinian terrorism largely because their involvement is unsuspected by others and their actions receive heightened media attention. The use of women as suicide bombers is also thought to convey the seriousness of the threat and to make the men involved act more aggressively (Berko & Erez, 2006; Bloom, 2005). Jyad Sarraj, a Palestinian psychiatrist, states he cannot criticize the suicide bombers because their culture considers them to be martyrs and martyrs are considered prophets, who are revered (Sarraj, 2002). Other experts state the increasinging numbers of women who are becoming suicide bombers shows that women are taking a step forward in achieving status equal to men (Bloom, 2005).

Do suicide bombers share certain traits? Almost all of the suicide bombers have been Muslim, relatively young, single (one was the mother of a 3-year-old), varying in education, with some knowledge of political causes and terror tactics (Bennet, 2002; Zakaria, 2003). These traits tend to be general, however, and apply to many Palestinians who do not become suicide bombers. Israel's national security force studied suicide bombers, and their results are puzzling. They didn't find any specific personality profile or traits that differentiated suicide bombers from nonbombers. However, as in Arien's case, some powerful, tragic emotional event, such as the death of her fiancé, may be the final hurt that, combined with cultural forces, led her to become a suicide bomber.

What does the future hold? Because of strong Muslim cultural influences, such as suicide bombers being considered martyrs, some Palestinians hope their own children will be suicide bombers and thus become martyrs. There are others who oppose suicide attacks, such as the group of 55 Palestinian intellectuals who issued a public plea to halt the suicide bombing attacks on innocent Israeli civilians. Government officials believe that suicide attacks will continue until there is a peace settlement in the Middle East. Until then, violent Muslim groups will continue to use suicide bombers because they have widespread cultural approval and are an effective method of killing, instilling fear, and spreading their political message (Bennet, 2002).

Next, we'll briefly review the four major theories of personality to help you understand their major points.

G. Four Theories of Personality

Freud's psychodynamic theory, which was developed in the early 1900s, grew out of his work with patients.

Freud's *psychodynamic theory of personality* emphasizes the importance of early childhood experiences, the importance of repressed thoughts that we cannot voluntarily access, and the conflicts between conscious and unconscious forces that influence our thoughts and behaviors. (Freud used the term *dynamic* to refer to mental energy force.)

Conscious thoughts are wishes, desires, or thoughts that we are aware of or can recall at any given moment.

Unconscious forces represent wishes, desires, or thoughts that, because of their disturbing or threatening content, we automatically repress and cannot voluntarily access.

Freud believed that a large part of our behavior was guided or motivated by unconscious forces.

Unconscious motivation is a Freudian concept that refers to the influence of repressed thoughts, desires, or impulses on our conscious thoughts and behaviors.

Freud developed three methods to uncover unconscious processes: *free association, dream interpretation,* and *slips of the tongue* (Freudian slips).

Divisions of the Mind

Freud divided the mind into three divisions: id, ego, and superego.

The first division is the *id,* which contains two biological drives—sex and aggression—that are the source of all mental energy. The id follows the pleasure principle, which is to satisfy the biological drives.

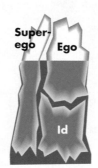

The second division is the *ego,* whose goal is to find socially acceptable ways of satisfying the id's desires within the range of the superego's prohibitions. The ego follows the reality principle, which is to satisfy a wish or desire only if there is a socially acceptable outlet available.

The third division is the *superego,* whose goal is to apply the moral values and standards of one's parents or caregivers and society in satisfying one's wishes.

Psychosexual Stages

Freud assumed that our personality develops as we pass through a series of *five psychosexual stages.*

During these developmental periods—the *oral, anal, phallic, latency,* and *genital stages*—the individual seeks pleasure from different areas of the body associated with sexual feelings. Freud emphasized that the child's first five years were the most important in personality development.

Humanistic theories emphasize our capacity for personal growth, development of our potential, and freedom to choose our destiny. *Humanistic theories* stress three major points—phenomenological perspective, holistic view, and self-actualization.

The *phenomenological perspective* means that our perception of the world, whether or not it is accurate, becomes our reality.

The *holistic view* means that a person's personality is more than the sum of its individual parts; instead, the individual parts form a unique and total entity that functions as a unit.

Self-actualization refers to our inherent tendency to reach our true potentials.

Humanistic theories reject the biological determinism and the irrational, unconscious forces of Freud's psychodynamic theory. Humanistic theories emphasize freely choosing to go after one's dream and change one's destiny.

The beginning of humanistic theory can be traced to two psychologists: Abraham Maslow, who rejected behaviorism's system of rewards and punishment, and Carl Rogers, who rejected Freud's psychodynamic theory with its emphasis on unconscious forces.

Abraham Maslow

Maslow (1968) broke away from the reward/punishment/observable behavior mentality of behaviorism and developed his humanistic theory. *Maslow's humanistic theory* emphasized two things: our capacity for growth or self-actualization and our desire to satisfy a variety of needs.

Maslow's hierarchy of needs arranges needs in ascending order, with biological needs at the bottom and social and personal needs toward the top; as needs at one level are met, we advance to the next level.

Carl Rogers's Self Theory

Carl Rogers rejected the psychodynamic approach because it placed too much emphasis on unconscious, irrational forces. Instead, Rogers developed a new humanistic theory, which is called self theory. *Rogers's self theory,* also called self-actualization theory, has two primary assumptions: Personality development is guided by each person's unique self-actualization tendency, and each of us has a personal need for positive regard.

Rogers said that the *self* is made up of many self-perceptions, abilities, personality characteristics, and behaviors that are organized and consistent with one another.

Freud's *psychodynamic theory*, developed in the early 1900s, grew out of his work with patients. Humanistic theories were developed in the 1960s by an ex-Freudian (Carl Rogers) and an ex-behaviorist (Abraham Maslow), who believed that previous theories had neglected the positive side of human potential, growth, and self-fulfillment.

In comparison, *social cognitive theory*, which was developed in the 1960s and 1970s, grew out of a strong research background, unlike the way humanistic and Freudian psychodynamic theories were developed. Social cognitive theory emphasized a more rigorous experimental approach to develop and test concepts that could be used to understand and explain personality development.

Social cognitive theory says that personality development is primarily shaped by three factors: environmental conditions (learning), cognitive-personal factors, and behavior. *Behavior* includes a variety of actions, such as what we do and say. *Environmental influences* include our social, political, and cultural influences as well as our particular learning experiences. Just as our cognitive factors influence how we perceive and interpret our environment, our environment in turn affects our beliefs, values, and social roles. *Cognitive-personal factors* include our beliefs, expectations, values, intentions, and social roles as well as our biological and genetic influences. Thus, what we think, believe, and feel affects how we act and behave.

Bandura's Social Cognitive Theory

Perhaps the best example of the social cognitive approach is Bandura's social cognitive theory, which he developed in the 1970s. *Bandura's social cognitive theory* says that personality development, growth, and change are influenced by four distinctively human cognitive processes: highly developed language ability, observational learning, purposeful behavior, and self-analysis.

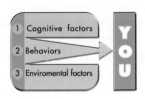

Should I take one marshmallow now or wait and get two?

Bandura's theory emphasizes *cognitive factors*, such as personal values, goals, and beliefs. Three particular beliefs have been shown to influence personality development: *locus of control*, which refers to how much control we think we have over our environment; *delay of gratification*, which involves our voluntarily postponing an immediate reward for the promise of a future reward; and *self-efficacy*, which refers to our personal beliefs of how capable we are in performing specific tasks and behaviors.

One of the *basic assumptions* of social cognitive theory is that our beliefs, values, and goals influence the development of our personalities, which, in turn, affects how we behave.

For over 50 years, a *major goal* of personality researchers was to find a way to define the structure of personality with the fewest possible traits. The search for a list of traits that could describe personality differences among everyone, including criminals and nuns, began in the 1930s with a list of about 4,500 traits and ended in the 1990s with a list of only 5 traits.

In the 1990s, trait theory developed the five-factor model, which is based on laboratory research, especially questionnaires and statistical procedures. *Trait theory* refers to an approach for analyzing the structure of personality by measuring, identifying, and classifying similarities and differences in personality characteristics or traits. The basic unit for measuring personality characteristics is the trait. *Traits* are relatively stable and enduring tendencies to behave in particular ways, but behavior is not always the same across different situations.

Trait theory says relatively little about the development or growth of personality but instead emphasizes measuring and identifying differences among personalities.

Five-Factor Model

The *five-factor model* organizes all personality traits into five categories—openness, conscientiousness, extraversion, agreeableness, and neuroticism (OCEAN). These traits, which are referred to as the *Big Five traits,* raise three major issues.

First, although traits are stable tendencies to behave in certain ways, this stability does not necessarily apply across situations. According to the *person-situation interaction,* you may behave differently in different situations because of the effects of a particular situation.

Second, personality traits are both *changeable and stable:* Most change occurs before age 30 because adolescents and young adults are more willing to adopt new values and attitudes or revise old ones; most stability occurs after age 30, but adults do continue to grow in their ideas, beliefs, and attitudes.

Third, *genetic factors* have a considerable influence on personality traits and behaviors. Genetic factors push and pull the development of certain traits, whose development may be helped or hindered by environmental factors.

Traits are useful in that they provide shorthand descriptions of people and predict certain behaviors.

H. Application: Assessment—Objective Tests

Definition

Why are traits big business?

The study of traits has become big business because traits are used in constructing personality tests. For example, if you're applying for a fast-food job, you may be asked to fill out a written questionnaire, which is really a honesty test. The employer knows that about 62% of fast-food workers steal money or give away food to friends and hopes this honesty test will help select a honest employee (K. R. Murphy, 1993). To help employers make hiring decisions, about 6,000 companies administer honesty tests to weed out dishonest job applicants each year (Cullen, 2006). Honesty tests, which are the most frequently administered psychological tests in the United States, are examples of objective personality tests (Mumford et al., 2001).

Objective personality tests, also called *self-report questionnaires,* consist of specific written statements that require individuals to indicate, for example, by checking "true" or "false," whether the statements do or do not apply to them.

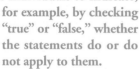

I would never give free drinks to my friends—it's against the rules.

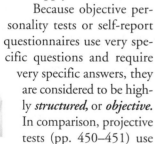

Because objective personality tests or self-report questionnaires use very specific questions and require very specific answers, they are considered to be highly *structured,* or *objective.* In comparison, projective tests (pp. 450–451) use ambiguous stimuli (inkblots or photos), have widely varying responses, and are considered to be *unstructured,* or *projective,* personality tests.

It is most likely that, as part of a job interview, you will be asked to take a variety of self-report questionnaires. That's because employers, clinicians, researchers, and government and law enforcement agencies use self-report questionnaires to identify and differentiate personality traits.

The basic assumption behind self-report questionnaires brings us back to the definition of traits. We defined traits as stable and enduring tendencies to behave in certain ways. Self-report questionnaires identify traits, which employers use to predict how prospective employees will behave in particular jobs or situations (D. J. Ozer, 1999).

Before we discuss how valid and reliable self-report questionnaires are in predicting behavior, we'll examine two of the more popular self-report questionnaires.

Examples of Objective Tests

How honest are most employees?

Objective personality tests are used in both business and clinical settings. In business settings, self-report questionnaires are often used in selecting employees for certain traits, such as being honest and trustworthy, which is why integrity tests are often used (Cullen & Sackett, 2003).

INTEGRITY TESTS

Integrity or honesty tests are supposed to assess whether individuals have high levels of the trait of honesty. Questions asked on honesty tests are similar to the following (Lilienfeld, 1993):

1. Have you ever stolen merchandise from your place of work?

2. Have you ever been tempted to steal a piece of jewelry from a store?

3. Do you think most people steal money from their workplace every now and then?

4. A person has been a loyal and honest employee at a firm for 20 years. One day, after realizing that she has neglected to bring lunch money, she takes $10 from her workplace but returns it the next day. Should she be fired?

Would you buy a gold watch from this man?

People strong in the trait of honesty answer: (1) no, (2) no, (3) no, (4) yes.

Notice that some self-report questionnaires, such as the integrity test, focus on measuring a single personality trait, in this case honesty. The next self-report questionnaire, called the MMPI-2, is used primarily in clinical settings and measures a number of traits and personality problems.

MINNESOTA MULTIPHASIC PERSONALITY INVENTORY-2

Suppose a parole board needed to decide if a convicted murderer had changed enough in prison to be let out on parole. To help make this decision, they might use a test that identifies the range of normal and abnormal personality traits, such as the well-known Minnesota Multiphasic Personality Inventory-2 (MMPI-2).

The *Minnesota Multiphasic Personality Inventory-2 (MMPI-2)* is a true-false self-report questionnaire that consists of 567 statements describing a wide range of normal and abnormal behaviors. The purpose of the MMPI-2 is to measure the personality style and emotional adjustment in individuals with mental illness.

The MMPI-2 asks about and identifies a variety of specific personality traits, including depression, hostility, high energy, and shyness, and plots whether these traits are in the normal or abnormal range. A few of the 567 statements used in the MMPI-2 are given below:

■ I do not tire quickly.
■ I am worried about sex.
■ When I get bored, I like to stir up some excitement.
■ I believe I am being plotted against.

One advantage of this test is that it contains three kinds of scales: *validity scales,* which assess whether the client was faking good or bad answers; *clinical scales,* which identify psychological disorders, such as depression, paranoia, or schizophrenia; and *content scales,* which identify specific areas, such as the anger scale, whose content includes references to being irritable and hotheaded and to difficulties controlling anger (R. M. Kaplan & Saccuzzo, 2005).

Could a test show if a person were ready for parole?

The MMPI-2 is commonly used to assess a wide range of personality traits, numerous behaviors, health and psychosomatic symptoms, and many well-known psychotic symptoms (Graham, 2005). The MMPI-2 and the integrity questionnaire are examples of objective tests used to identify personality traits.

Another method that claims to identify your particular traits involves astrology.

How do horoscopes work?

About 78% of women and 70% of men read horoscopes, and many believe that they are so correct that they were written especially for them (Halpern, 1998). As you read the horoscope on the right, note how many traits apply to you. Because horoscopes contain general traits, people believe horoscopes were written especially for them, a phenomenon called the Barnum principle (C. R. Snyder et al., 1977).

The *Barnum principle* (named after the famous circus owner P. T. Barnum) refers to the method of listing many general traits so that almost everyone who reads the horoscope thinks that these traits apply specifically to him or her. But, in fact, these traits are so general that they apply to almost everyone.

Astrologers claim they can identify your personality traits by knowing the sign under which you were born. However, researchers found that horoscopes do not assess personality traits for a particular individual, which means horoscopes lack one of the two characteristics of a good test—validity (Hartmann, 2006).

SCORPIO
Oct. 24th to
Nov. 21st

You are bright, sincere, and likable but can be too hard on yourself.

VALIDITY

Students claim that the Scorpio horoscope, which I (R. P.) wrote, is accurate for them. The reason I can write "accurate" horoscopes is that I use the *Barnum principle,* which means that I state personality traits in a general way so that they apply to everyone.

I read my horoscope every day, and it's always right on the mark.

Validity **means that the test measures what it claims or is supposed to measure.**

A personality test that has no validity is no better than chance at describing or predicting a particular individual's traits. For example, researchers found that the 12 zodiac signs were no better than chance at identifying traits for a particular individual (Svensen & White, 1994). Because horoscopes cannot identify or predict traits for a particular person, horoscopes lack validity. The reason horoscopes remain popular and seem to be "accurate" is that astrologers essentially use the Barnum principle, which means their horoscopes are "accurate" for almost everyone. In comparison, integrity tests generally have low validity, while the MMPI-2 has good validity, which means it can describe and predict behaviors for particular individuals (R. M. Kaplan & Saccuzzo, 2005). In addition to validity, a good personality test must also have reliability.

RELIABILITY

Even though horoscopes lack validity, they may actually have the second characteristic of a good personality test, reliability.

Reliability **refers to consistency: A person's score on a test at one point in time should be similar to the score obtained by the same person on a similar test at a later point in time.**

Horoscopes may be reliable if the astrologer remains the same. Integrity tests and the MMPI-2 have good reliability. However, the MMPI-2 is better than integrity tests because the MMPI-2 has both good validity and reliability, while the integrity test has good reliability but low validity (R. M. Kaplan & Saccuzzo, 2005).

Is a monk or a devil more honest?

Self-report questionnaires and objective personality tests are popular and widely used because they assess information about traits in a structured way so that such information can be compared with others who have taken the same tests. For example, employers and government and law enforcement agencies use objective personality tests, such as integrity tests, to compare and select certain traits in job applicants (Cullen, 2006). Researchers use objective personality tests to differentiate between people's traits. Counselors and clinicians use objective personality tests, such as the MMPI-2, to identify personality traits and potential psychological problems (Graham, 2005). We'll discuss the disadvantages and advantages of objective personality tests.

DISADVANTAGES

One disadvantage of objective personality tests is that their questions and answers are very structured, and critics from the psychodynamic approach point out that such structured tests may not assess deeper or unconscious personality factors. A second disadvantage comes from the straightforward questions, which often allow people to figure out what answers are most socially desirable or acceptable and thus bias the test results. For example, one problem with integrity tests is that the answers can be faked so that the person appears more trustworthy (compare the devil's and monk's responses on the right) (Cullen, 2006). Third, many self-report questionnaires measure specific traits, which we know may predict behavior in the same situations but not across situations. This means a person may behave honestly with his or her family but not necessarily with his or her employer.

Of course I'm a very, very honest person.

ADVANTAGES

One advantage of objective personality tests is that they are easily administered and can be taken individually or in groups. A second advantage is that, since the questions are structured and require either a true-false or yes-no answer, the scoring is straightforward. Third, many of the self-report questionnaires have good reliability. For example, the reliability of the MMPI-2 ranges from 0.70 to 0.85 (1.0 is perfect reliability) (R. M. Kaplan & Saccuzzo, 2005). Fourth, the validity of self-report questionnaires varies with the test; it ranges from poor to good. For example, the validity of integrity tests appears to be poor: In one study, a group of monks and nuns scored "more dishonest" than a group of prisoners in jail (Rieke & Guastello, 1995). In comparison, many studies on the MMPI-2 indicate its validity is good (R. M. Kaplan & Saccuzzo, 2005).

I'm not as honest as I should be.

Which of these two would you trust?

Because objective personality tests and projective personality tests (pp. 450–451) have different advantages and disadvantages, counselors and clinical psychologists may use a combination of both to assess a client's personality traits and problems.

Summary Test

A. Social Cognitive Theory

1. One theory says that personality development is shaped primarily by environmental conditions (learning), cognitive-personal factors, and behavior, which all interact to influence how we evaluate, interpret, and organize information and apply that information to ourselves and others; this is called the _____ theory.

2. Albert Bandura called the version of his original social learning theory the (a)_____ theory. Bandura's theory assumes that four distinctively human cognitive processes—highly developed language ability, observational learning, purposeful behavior, and self-analysis—influence the growth, development, and change in (b)_____.

3. Our highly developed (a)_____ ability provides us with a tool for processing and understanding information, which is critical to personality development. Our capacity for (b)_____ learning allows us to learn through watching, without observable behavior or a reinforcer. Our capacity for forethought enables us to plan ahead and set goals—to perform (c)_____ behavior. Finally, the fact that we can monitor our thoughts and actions as well as set and change goals and values gives us the capacity for (d)_____.

4. The power of beliefs and ideas to change the way that we interpret situations and events is one of the basic assumptions of social cognitive theories. Rotter developed a scale to measure our belief about how much control we have over situations or rewards; he called this belief (a)_____. If we believe that we have control over situations and rewards, we are said to have an (b)_____ locus of control. In contrast, if we believe that we do not have control over situations and rewards and that events outside ourselves determine what happens, we are said to have an (c)_____ locus of control.

5. According to Bandura, our personal belief regarding how capable we are of exercising control over events in our lives is called (a)_____. According to Mischel, our voluntary postponement of an immediate reward and persistence in completing a task for the promise of a future reward is called delay of (b)_____.

B. Trait Theory

6. A relatively stable and enduring tendency to behave in a particular way is called a (a)_____. An approach to understanding the structure of personality by measuring, identifying, and analyzing differences in personality is called (b)_____ theory. In attempting to pare down a list of traits by finding relationships among them, researchers have used a statistical method called (c)_____.

7. The model that organizes all personality traits into five categories is called the (a)_____. These five categories, known as the Big Five, are (b)_____, _____, _____, _____, and _____; their initial letters spell out the word OCEAN.

8. Mischel questioned the basic assumption of trait theory, saying that, if traits represent consistent behavioral tendencies, they should predict behaviors across many different (a)_____. Instead, he found that people behaved with great consistency in the same situation but behaved with low consistency across different situations. Mischel pointed out that predicting a person's behavior must take into account not only the person's traits but also the effects of the situation; this idea became known as the (b)_____ interaction.

C. Genetic Influences on Traits

9. How inherited or genetic factors influence and interact with psychological factors—for example, the ways we behave, adapt, and adjust to our environments—is the focus of the field of behavioral (a)_____. Current thinking about genetic factors is that they do not fix behaviors but rather set a range for behaviors. Researchers estimate genetic influences with a measure that estimates how much of some behavior is due to genetic influences; this measure is referred to as (b)_____.

10. Considering the various influences on personality development, researchers estimated that about 40% of the influence comes from (a)_____, which are inherited. About 27% of the influence on personality development comes from environmental factors that involve how each individual reacts and adjusts to his or her own environment; these are called (b)_____ factors. About 7% of the influence on personality development comes from environmental factors that involve parental patterns and shared family experiences; these are called (c)_____ factors. The remaining 26% of the influence on personality development cannot as yet be identified and is attributed to errors in testing and measurement procedures.

D. Evaluation of Trait Theory

11. Trait theory assumes that differences among personalities can be described by a short but comprehensive list of traits. Critics of the current list, known as the (a)_____, point out that the data for the model may paint too simplistic a picture of human personality and may not reflect its depth and complexity. Trait theory assumes that traits are consistent and stable influences on our (b)_____, but critics argue that when traits are measured in one situation, they do not necessarily predict behaviors in other situations.

OCEAN

12. The biggest changes in personality occur during childhood, adolescence, and young adulthood because young men and women are somewhat more likely to be open to new ideas. Personality is less likely to change after age (a)_____. Observations from over 10,000 pairs of twins indicate that (b)_____ factors significantly influence personality traits. Critics warn that inherited factors should not be exaggerated because 50% or more of the influence on traits comes from (c)_____ influences.

E. Research Focus: 180-Degree Change

13. If you were to experience a sudden and radical or dramatic shift in personality, beliefs, or values, you would be said to have experienced a (a)_____ in personality. One way researchers studied these changes in personality was to ask each individual the same set of relatively narrow and focused questions so that the same information was obtained from everyone; this method is called the (b)_____.

F. Cultural Diversity: Suicide Bombers

14. Individuals who volunteer to become suicide bombers do so for both strong (a)_____ and _____ reasons. Personal reasons may include such things as wanting to avenge the death of a loved one. Almost all suicide bombers are raised in the Muslim culture, whose beliefs hold that individuals who die as suicide bombers are considered (b)_____, who are revered in this culture as prophets.

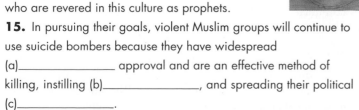

15. In pursuing their goals, violent Muslim groups will continue to use suicide bombers because they have widespread (a)_____ approval and are an effective method of killing, instilling (b)_____, and spreading their political (c)_____.

G. Four Theories of Personality

16. How does personality grow and develop? We discussed four different answers. The theory that emphasizes the importance of early childhood, unconscious factors, the three divisions of the mind, and psychosexual stages is called (a)_____. The theories that focus on the phenomenological perspective, a holistic view, and self-actualization are called (b)_____ theories.

The theory that says that personality development is shaped by the interaction among three factors—environmental conditions, cognitive-personal factors, and behavior—is called (c)_____ theory. The theory that emphasizes measuring and identifying differences among personalities is called (d)_____ theory.

H. Application: Assessment—Objective Tests

17. Self-report questionnaires, which consist of specific written statements that require structured responses—for example, checking "true" or "false"—are examples of _____ personality tests.

18. A true-false self-report questionnaire containing hundreds of statements that describe a wide range of normal and abnormal behaviors is called the (a)_____. The purpose of this test is to distinguish normal from (b)_____ groups.

19. The method of listing a number of traits in such a general way that almost everyone who reads a horoscope thinks that many of the traits apply specifically to him or her is called the _____ principle.

Answers: *1. social cognitive; 2. (a) social cognitive, (b) personality; 3. (a) language, (b) observational, (c) purposeful, (d) self-analysis; 4. (a) locus of control, (b) internal, (c) external; 5. (a) self-efficacy, (b) gratification; 6. (a) trait, (b) trait, (c) factor analysis; 7. (a) five-factor model, Big Five, (b) openness, conscientiousness, extraversion, agreeableness, neuroticism; 8. (a) situations, (b) person-situation; 9. (a) genetics, (b) heritability; 10. (a) genetic factors, (b) nonshared environmental, (c) shared environmental; 11. (a) Big Five, (b) behaviors; 12. (a) 30, (b) genetic, (c) environmental; 13. (a) quantum change, (b) structured interview; 14. (a) personal, cultural, (b) martyrs; 15. (a) cultural, (b) fear, (c) message; 16. (a) Freud's psychodynamic theory, (b) humanistic, (c) social learning, (d) trait; 17. objective; 18. (a) Minnesota Multiphasic Personality Inventory-2, or MMPI-2, (b) abnormal; 19. Barnum*

Critical Thinking

Personality Tests Help Employers Find Applicants Who Fit

Questions

1. Why do some employers use both interviews and objective personality tests in deciding whom to hire?

2. Why do companies look for certain traits in selecting employees, and why would Freud question the importance of selecting for traits?

3. If you were using the Big Five traits to design a test for salespeople who work as a team, which traits would you look for?

More and more job applicants are being required to take personality tests. Already, at least one-third of employers, ranging from governments to hospitals, retail stores to restaurants, and airlines to manufacturing plants, use personality tests in their hiring and promotion process.

There are many personality tests and each measures something different. For instance, the Myers-Briggs measures personality traits necessary for leadership and teamwork and is used by 89 of the Fortune 100 companies. The Minnesota Multiphasic Personality Inventory (p. 474), measures an individual's tendency toward substance abuse and psychopathology and is used by 60% of police departments as a way to screen applicants. Personality tests look at a variety of other characteristics such as thought processes, sociability, motivation, self-awareness, emotional intelligence, stress management, dependability, and work style.

Some experts believe personality tests are overused and overinterpreted, and caution employers about the potential negative impact the use of the tests may have on minority applicants. Others believe personality tests have an important place in the hiring process because the tests can predict how well an applicant "fits" with the job description. For instance, when hiring a salesperson, a company can have a list of the personality traits of successful salespeople and then match an applicant's test results against that standard.

Many companies that have used personality tests showed a decrease in

absenteeism and turnover, which means big savings for the company. By using personality tests, one California theme park increased levels of employee retention and customer satisfaction, and reduced levels of absenteeism and theft. Also, a bottling company in Milwaukee reduced the number of sick days in half and an airline reduced tardiness by one-third.

Personality tests are increasingly being used in the hiring process to supplement interviews and a resume review. So, how should you respond to test questions to be sure you get the job? Although ideal responses vary by job position and company, experts suggest that you not falsify your responses, as many personality tests have a sophisticated way of knowing if you're lying. Luis Valdes, an executive consultant, explains, "For any given character trait, say independence, there's an optimal amount. If a person seems to be really extreme, well, most people aren't that extreme, so it suggests they tried to answer all the questions in a positive but not very realistic way" (Valdes, 2006). In the case of personality tests, it appears that honesty is the best policy. (Adapted from Cha, 2005; Cullen, 2006; Frieswick, 2004; Gladwell, 2004; Gunn, 2006; C. Smith, 1997; Valdes, 2006; Wessel, 2003)

4. What are some objections to or disadvantages of using objective personality tests in the hiring process?

5. Which objective personality test has a scale to detect lying? Can objective personality tests prevent a person from "faking his or her character"?

Suggested Answers

1. Some employers believe that applicants may not always be truthful in interviews and that objective personality tests may be more difficult to fool.
2. Employers are looking for certain traits because, according to trait theory, traits are relatively stable and enduring tendencies to behave in certain ways and traits predict how people will behave in similar situations. Freud would point out that traits are important but that behaviors and feelings may be influenced by unconscious forces, of which applicants would not be aware and which are not easily measured by objective personality tests.
3. Salespeople who work as a team might be selected for being high in openness (open to new experiences), extraversion (outgoing

and decisive), agreeableness (warm and good-natured), and conscientiousness (responsible and dependable) but low in neuroticism (stable and not a worrier).
4. Since objective personality tests use very structured questions, simplified yes-no answers, and objective scoring, an applicant can sometimes figure out and give socially acceptable answers and thus bias the test in his or her favor. Also, some applicants, especially those already in upper management positions, find the use of personality tests during the hiring process to be off-putting.
5. The MMPI-2 has a scale to detect lying. To some degree, people may "fake their character" on objective personality tests provided they can figure out the socially acceptable or desirable answers while still being able to pass the test's lie detector.

Links to Learning

Learning Activities

- **POWERSTUDY FOR INTRODUCTION TO PSYCHOLOGY 4.0**
  by Tom Doyle and Rod Plotnik
  Check out the quizzes and learning activities for "Social Cognitive & Trait Theories" on **PowerStudy** and:
  - Test your knowledge using an interactive version of the Summary Test on pages pages 476 and 477. Also access related quizzing—true/false, multiple choice, and matching.
  - Explore an interactive version of the Critical Thinking exercise "Personality Tests Help Employers Find Applicants Who Fit" on page 478.
  - You will also find key terms, a chapter outline including a chapter abstract, and a special extended list of hotlinked websites that correlate to this module.

- *CengageNOW*
  academic.cengage.com/login
  Need help studying? This site is your one-stop study shop. Take a Pre-Test and CengageNOW will generate a Personalized Study Plan based on your test results. The Study Plan will identify the topics you need to review and direct you to online resources to help you master those topics. You can then take a Post-Test to determine the concepts you have mastered and what you still need to work on.

- **INTRODUCTION TO PSYCHOLOGY BOOK COMPANION WEBSITE**
  academic.cengage.com/psychology/plotnik
  Visit your book companion website where you will find more resources to help you study. At this site, you will find Learning Objectives, Internet Exercises, quizzing, flash cards, and a pronunciation glossary.

- **STUDY GUIDE and WEBTUTOR**
  Check the corresponding module in your Study Guide for effective student tips and help learning the material presented. Also go to **academic.cengage.com/webtutor** for an interactive version of the Study Guide features.

Study Questions

*A. Social Cognitive Theory—Why do students invest thousands of dollars and 4 to 6 years of hard work to obtain a college degree? (**Suggested answer p. 632**)

*B. Trait Theory—Would knowing about the Big Five traits help you write an ad to find the perfect roommate or life mate? (**Suggested answer p. 633**)

C. Genetic Influences on Traits—How is it possible that, in the same family, one child may be lively and outgoing and another may be shy and withdrawn?

D. Evaluation of Trait Theory—Why might newlyweds discover that the person they married is not the person they thought they knew?

E. Research Focus: 180-Degree Change—What are some of the reasons that we should be cautious in believing self-reports of dramatic behavioral changes?

F. Cultural Diversity: Suicide Bombers—Being familiar with Muslim cultural beliefs, what can the Israeli government do to stop suicide bombing in the Middle East?

G. Four Theories of Personality—Do you think that all four theories of personality could be or should be reduced to just one?

H. Application: Assessment—Objective Tests—A psychological test in a magazine promises to tell you what kind of mate is perfect for you. Can you believe it?

*These questions are answered in Appendix B.

MODULE 21
Health, Stress & Coping

 PowerStudy 4.0™ Complete Module

Introduction

Stress

Why does Luisa fear she will die?

One afternoon, Luisa, a 23-year-old college student, was walking on campus and she suddenly felt her heart rate rapidly accelerate, her throat tighten up, and her arms and legs tremble. She became so nauseous she almost vomited. Luisa felt she had no control over what was happening, and when she went to the doctor, she was told nothing was wrong. Still, she worried she might experience something like this again. Then, weeks later, while at the movies, she had another episode during which she experienced dizziness, chest pain, shortness of breath, and weakness in her legs and feet. She feared she was having a heart attack and might die, but after a series of tests, her doctors found no medical problem. About a month later, Luisa had her most serious attack while sitting in her physics class. This time she had a strong desire to leave the classroom, and as soon she got outside, her legs gave in and she fell to the floor. From then on, Luisa became fearful of places that were closed in or crowded, such as shopping malls, restaurants, theaters, and even classrooms. She avoided these places in fear she would have another crisis. After this most recent episode, she was diagnosed with panic disorder (adapted from Di Salvo, 2006).

23-year-old Luisa has severe anxiety.

Panic disorder **is characterized by recurrent and unexpected panic attacks (described below). The person becomes so worried about having another panic attack that this intense worrying interferes with normal psychological functioning (APA, 2000).**

The symptoms Luisa had while walking on campus, watching a movie, and sitting in class indicate she was having a *panic attack,* **a period of intense fear or discomfort in which four or more of the following symptoms are present: pounding heart, sweating, trembling, shortness of breath, feelings of choking, chest pain, nausea, dizziness, and fear of losing control or dying (APA, 2000).**

In any given year, about one-third of American adults have at least one panic attack, but most of these adults never develop repeated panic attacks. Like Luisa, about 4% of adults in the United States suffer from panic disorder (Halbreich, 2003). Also, as in Luisa's case, the onset of panic disorder typically occurs during late adolescence or early adulthood (Pine, 2000). Compared with most people who may experience only mild forms of anxiety, people who have panic attacks find their experiences to be very stressful.

Stress **is the anxious or threatening feeling that comes when we interpret or appraise a situation as being more than our psychological resources can adequately handle (Lazarus, 1999).**

The study of stress is very much the study of how the mind and body interact. In this module, you'll learn how your mind is involved in what happens to your body during stressful situations.

Just as we can use our mind to overreact to stress, we can also use it to cope with stress, which is something Sandra must do almost every minute of her life.

Coping

What's a day like for Sandra?

It's 6:30 A.M. With a groan Sandra slaps at the alarm, rolls out of bed, and stands grimacing at herself in the bathroom mirror. She ducks into the shower. A few minutes later she wakes Jesse, 5, and Caiti, 3, and the morning rush is on. She sits the kids down at the dinette for breakfast, packs their lunches, and reminds them Auntie Erika is picking them up after school today. She scoops up a stack of books, almost forgetting the 15-page religion paper she slaved over all weekend. She turns off the TV, bundles up the kids, and is out the door.

This is a normal day for Sandra Sullivan, a 27-year-old single mother of two wonderful kids. Sandra is a recovering drug addict and former homeless person. She is surviving without child support, needs food stamps to make ends meet, and is trying against all odds to go to college. And not just any college, but Wellesley, one of the most prestigious women's colleges in the nation.

The turning point for Sandra was the day she got the disappointing news that her husband had forged a check. She felt that she had come to the very end of her rope. She got down on her knees and prayed, and in a flash, it seemed that her old self had died and she was ready to make a new beginning. She swallowed her pride and made some very tough decisions. She left her husband, who had been in and out of jobs for five years, quit drugs, and

How does Sandra cope with being a single mother of two children and a college student?

moved with her babies into a homeless shelter. She decided to do something about her life and enrolled in a community college. She worked hard enough and did well enough to be accepted into Wellesley College (adapted from *Life,* April 1992, pp. 62–65).

For Sandra, every day is a series of nonstop potential stressors. To keep these stressors from growing out of control, she uses a variety of coping techniques. Some days she copes better than others, and she must continually guard against being overwhelmed by college, by kids, by duties, and by life. One of the interesting topics we'll discuss in this module is the different ways to cope with stressors.

What's Coming

We'll discuss how you decide something is stressful, your physiological and psychological responses to stress, how your immune system works, how you develop psychosomatic symptoms, which situational, personality, and social factors help or hinder your coping processes, and how you can develop your own stress management program.

We'll begin with how Luisa's mind can make her physical symptoms worse for no good reason.

A. Appraisal

What makes Luisa's symptoms so stressful?

Although Luisa believes she will die during a panic attack, in fact that is impossible ("Panic attacks," 2005). If there is no real threat to Luisa's survival, then why does she react so strongly to her physical symptoms (dizziness, trembling)? One explanation is she may misinterpret normal physical symptoms as serious problems, which can intensify the symptoms. For example, Luisa may be nervous about school grades or going on a date and experience that nervousness physiologically (sweating, racing heart). These symptoms can make her feel more anxious ("What is wrong with me?"), escalating the physical sensations into the chest pain of a heart attack (Ham, 2005). In this example, Luisa's initial interpretation of her physical symptoms is that a stressful situation is happening ("Something is wrong with me and I could die"). The initial interpretation of a potentially stressful situation is called a primary appraisal (Lazarus, 1999, 2000).

Luisa's mind creates her intense fear.

Primary appraisal refers to our initial, subjective evaluation of a situation, in which we balance the demands of a potentially stressful situation against our ability to meet these demands.

For example, there can be three different primary appraisals when experiencing a racing heart rate. If a doctor gives you medication to treat a painful headache and says you will initially feel your heart racing, your primary appraisal of your racing heart is that it is irrelevant (your real concern is your headache) and therefore mostly nonstressful. If you're running a marathon and feel your heart beating quickly, your primary appraisal is positive and mostly nonstressful because it makes you feel good. If you're trying to sleep or relax and your heart rate accelerates, your primary appraisal of this situation is stressful. Your primary appraisal that a situation is stressful involves three different interpretations: harm/loss, threat, or challenge.

Harm/Loss

If you broke your arm in a bike accident, you would know that you have suffered harm or loss.

Harm/loss appraisal

A *harm/loss appraisal* of a situation means that you have already sustained some damage or injury.

Because the harm/loss appraisal *elicits negative emotions,* such as fear, depression, fright, and anxiety, you will feel stressed; and the more intense your negative emotions are, the more stressful and overwhelming the situation will seem.

Threat

If you have a terrible fear of giving blood and are asked to do so, you would automatically interpret giving blood as a threat to your well-being.

Threat appraisal

A *threat appraisal* of a situation means that the harm/loss has not yet taken place but you know it will happen in the near future.

Because a threat appraisal also *elicits negative emotions,* such as fear, anxiety, and anger, the situation or event may seem especially stressful. In fact, just imagining or anticipating a threatening situation, such as giving blood or taking a final exam, can be as stressful as the actual event itself.

Challenge

If you are working hard in college but find that you have to take two more classes, you might interpret taking these classes as a way to achieve a major goal—that is, you use a challenge appraisal.

Challenge appraisal

A *challenge appraisal* of a situation means that you have the potential for gain or personal growth but you also need to mobilize your physical energy and psychological resources to meet the challenging situation.

Because a challenge appraisal *elicits positive emotions,* such as eagerness or excitement, it is usually less stressful than a harm/loss or a threat appraisal.

First reaction. Your first reaction to potentially stressful situations, such as waiting in line, dealing with a sloppy roommate, giving blood, making a public speech, dealing with a rude salesperson, taking an exam, seeing a vicious dog, or being in a car accident, is to appraise the situation in terms of whether it harms, threatens, or challenges your physical or psychological well-being.

Making primary appraisals about complex situations, such as whether to take a certain job, get married, or go on to graduate school, may require considerable time as you think over the different ways a situation will affect you. In comparison, making primary appraisals about very emotional situations, such as taking a surprise quiz, presenting a report in class,

This person made a primary appraisal that giving a speech was a threat to her self-esteem.

or getting into a car accident, may occur quickly, even automatically (Lazarus, 2000). However, not all appraisals neatly divide into harm/loss, threat, or challenge. Some primary appraisals are a combination of threat and challenge. For instance, if you are about to ask someone for a first date, you may feel threatened by the possibility of being rejected yet challenged by the chance to prove yourself.

Later in this module, we'll discuss how you can change a threat appraisal into more of a challenge appraisal and thus reduce your stressful feelings (N. Skinner & Brewer, 2002).

At this point, just keep in mind that making a primary appraisal is the first step in experiencing stress. Depending on the kind of primary appraisal, your level of stress may either increase or decrease.

Appraisal and Stress Level

Would it stress you to watch a bloody accident?

If you were asked to watch a film of bloody accidents caused by power saws, how much would your primary appraisal affect your level of stress? This is exactly what researchers asked subjects to do while they recorded a major sign of physiological arousal, called the galvanic skin response.

The *galvanic skin response* is a measure of how much a person's hand sweats due to physiological arousal and not to normal temperature changes.

As subjects watched the accident film, they were given instructions that would result in making a primary appraisal of challenge or threat. To encourage challenge appraisals, subjects were told to watch the film objectively, to consider how these accidents might be prevented, but not to identify with the injured. To encourage threat appraisals, subjects were told to put themselves in the place of men who accidentally cut off their fingers and imagine how they would feel.

As the graph below shows, subjects using threat appraisals showed significantly more physiological arousal—that is, higher levels of galvanic skin responses—than subjects using challenge appraisals (Dandoy & Goldstein, 1990). Researchers concluded that in threatening or disturbing situations, your feelings of stress increase with the kind of appraisal: Threat appraisals raise levels of stress more than challenge appraisals do. However, when people are asked to identify the cause of their stressful feelings, they usually—and often incorrectly—point to a particular situation rather than to their primary appraisals. As you'll see next, people often appraise the same situation in different ways.

Level of stress from watching a bloody accident depended on threat or challenge appraisal.

Average Physiological Arousal Scores

Threat appraisal	64
Challenge appraisal	24

Same Situation, Different Appraisals

How stressful is waiting in line?

When we ask our students, "What stresses you?" they always list a variety of situations, including many of those situations listed in the table below right. Notice especially how the same situation was stressful for some but not for others. For example, 65% said waiting for a late person was stressful, but 35% reported it wasn't. Similarly, 61% said waiting in line was stressful, but 39% said it wasn't. Because people don't agree on which situations are stressful, researchers concluded that level of stress depends not only on the kind of situation but also on the kind of *primary appraisal* one makes (C. Rasmussen et al., 2000). For example, you could appraise waiting in line to get your favorite beverage as a challenge, which elicits positive emotions and little stress. In contrast, you could appraise waiting in line as a threat or real test of your patience, which elicits negative emotions (growing impatient) and considerable stress. Thus, similar situations (waiting in line) can result in different levels of stress depending on your primary appraisals.

Why are 61% stressed by waiting in line while 39% are not?

Situation	Percentage rating it	
	stressful	not stressful
Waiting for someone who is late	65	35
Being caught in traffic	63	37
Waiting in line	61	39
Waiting in a doctor's office	59	41
Waiting for the government to act	51	49
Waiting for a repair person	46	54
Looking for a parking space	42	58
Waiting for an airplane to take off	26	74

Sequence: Appraisal to Arousal

How does stress start?

The first step in feeling stress depends on your primary appraisal, which can be one of harm/loss, threat, or challenge. In turn, harm/loss and threat appraisals elicit negative emotions, which, in turn, increase levels of stress. In comparison, challenge appraisals elicit positive emotions, which, in turn, decrease levels of stress. Thus, when you say that a situation is causing you stress, such as giving blood, taking an exam, making a public speech, changing your job, asking for a date, arguing with your boss, having to move, getting married, or arguing with your roommate, you are forgetting that part of the stress is coming from whether you make a harm/loss or threat appraisal versus a challenge appraisal (Lazarus, 2000).

The moment after you make an appraisal, especially a harm/loss or threat appraisal, your body changes from a generally calm state into one of heightened physiological arousal as it prepares to deal with the stressor, whether it involves a car accident, a mugger, a public speech, or giving blood. We'll look inside the body and see what happens when you are stressed.

Making a threat or harm/loss appraisal results in increased physiological arousal.

B. Physiological Responses

What happens when you're frightened?

Imagine giving a talk in class. As you look at everyone staring at you, you feel your heart pounding, mouth becoming dry, hands sweating, stomach knotting, and muscles tensing; you take in short, rapid breaths. Your body is fully aroused before you have spoken a single word (Tanouye, 1997). About 40% of adults report fear of speaking in public (A. Lewis, 2001).

Since speaking in public is no threat to your physical survival and you can neither fight nor flee, why is your body in this state of heightened physiological arousal? The answer is that once you make a primary appraisal that something is a threat—whether it's giving a speech or facing a mugger—these threatening and fearful thoughts automatically trigger one of the body's oldest physiological response systems, the fight-flight response (White & Porth, 2000).

The *fight-flight response* (a) directs great resources of energy to the muscles and the brain, (b) can be triggered by either physical stimuli that threaten our survival or psychological situations that are novel, threatening, or challenging, and (c) involves numerous physiological responses that arouse and prepare the body for action—fight or flight.

The fight-flight response helps us survive by preparing the body for action—fleeing or fighting.

We know that the fight-flight response is evolutionarily very old because it can be found in animals such as the alligator, which has been around for millions of years. We presume that our early ancestors evolved a similar fight-flight response to help them survive attacks by wild animals and enemies.

Physical stimuli. Today you have almost no need to fight wild animals or flee attacking enemies, so you rarely activate your fight-flight response for the reasons important to our early ancestors. However, you would activate the fight-flight response when faced with a potentially dangerous physical stimulus, such as a mugger, accident, police siren, snake, tornado, or other situation that threatened your physical survival.

Psychological stimuli. Today the most common reason you activate the fight-flight response is exposure to potentially bothersome or stressful psychological stimuli, such as worrying about exams, being impatient in traffic, having to wait in lines, getting angry over a putdown, or arguing with someone (Lazarus, 2000). We'll trace the sequence of how psychological or physical stimuli can trigger the fight-flight response and transform your body into a state of heightened physiological arousal (White & Porth, 2000).

Sequence for Activation of the Fight-Flight Response

1 Appraisal

A number of potentially dangerous physical stimuli, such as seeing a snake or being in an accident, can automatically trigger the fight-flight response. But much more common triggers of the fight-flight response are hundreds of psychological stimuli that you appraise as threatening, such as making a public speech or taking an exam. Thus, either *physically or psychologically threatening stimuli* can trigger the fight-flight response and negative emotional feelings (fear, rage).

2 Hypothalamus

If you appraise making a public speech as psychologically threatening, these thoughts activate a part of your brain called the *hypothalamus*. In turn, the hypothalamus simultaneously activates two stress-related responses: it triggers the pituitary gland to release a stress-fighting hormone called *ACTH* (adrenocorticotropic hormone); it also activates the sympathetic division of the autonomic nervous system.

3 Sympathetic Division

As we discussed earlier (p. 81), the autonomic nervous system has two divisions. The *sympathetic division,* which is activated by the hypothalamus, triggers a number of physiological responses that make up the fight-flight response, which prepares the body to deal with potentially threatening physical or psychological stimuli. In contrast, the *parasympathetic division,* also activated by the hypothalamus, returns the body to a more calm, relaxed state.

4 Fight-Flight Response

The sympathetic division triggers a very primitive *fight-flight response* (present in crocodiles), which causes great *physiological arousal* by increasing heart rate, blood pressure, respiration, secretion of excitatory hormones, and many other responses that prepare the body to deal with an impending threat, whether speaking in public or facing a mugger.

Next, we'll describe the many interesting physiological responses that literally transform the body into a powerful fighting or fleeing machine.

Physical or psychological stimuli can trigger the fight-flight response.

I hate to speak in public!

It is difficult to believe that the powerful fight-flight response can be triggered just as easily by potentially threatening psychological stimuli, such as speaking in public or taking exams, as by potentially threatening physical stimuli, such as seeing a rattlesnake. Although you rarely experience potentially threatening physical stimuli, such as meeting a snake, you do face many psychological situations that you appraise as threatening—"Let me tell you about my terrible day." As soon as you appraise a situation as threatening, specific parts of your brain start the fight-flight response, which in turn prepares your body for action (Cowley, 2003). We'll describe some of the major physiological changes triggered by the fight-flight response (S. Johnson, 2003).

1 A stress appraisal, especially if it involves something fearful or threatening, can instantly activate the *amygdala* (light blue), which functions like a threat detector (p. 363). In turn, the amygdala activates the *hypothalamus* (red), which functions like a switch to quickly and simultaneously trigger two systems that arouse the body for action (p. 81). One system involves the *pituitary gland* (p. 82), which triggers a release of the hormone ACTH (adrenocorticotropic hormone), which acts on part of the adrenal gland (adrenal cortex) to increase fuel for quick energy. A second system involves the *sympathetic division* of the autonomic nervous system (p. 72), which increases physiological arousal by automatically increasing heart rate, blood pressure, and other responses such as releasing powerful arousing hormones from the adrenal glands (see #7 on the right).

2 Respiration, which is increased by the sympathetic division, is more rapid and shallow so that there is a greater flow of oxygen into the body. However, if breathing is too rapid and shallow, we can feel light-headed or "spacey" from lack of oxygen.

3 Heart rate, which is increased by the sympathetic division, can rocket from a normal 70–90 beats per minute to an incredible 200–220 beats per minute. Rapid heart rate increases blood flow to muscles and vital organs (lungs, kidneys). Rapid heart rate during stressful experiences can lead to a "pounding heart" and, in extreme cases, result in heart attack and death.

4 Liver releases its stores of blood sugar (glycogen) to provide a ready source of energy during stress. After a stressful experience, we may feel fatigued because our supply of blood sugar is low.

Stomach and **intestinal activity** is reduced by the sympathetic division. During stressful experiences, the blood that is normally used by digestive organs is rerouted to muscles and vital organs. Because the sympathetic division shuts down the digestive system, people may experience problems with digestion, such as stomach pain, constipation, and diarrhea during stressful times.

Liver

Stomach

Fight-flight response prepares body for action.

5 Pupils are dilated by the sympathetic division. As a result, more light enters our eyes so we can see better if we have to fight or flee in dim light. One way to check for physiological arousal is to see how much a person's pupils are dilated: more dilation usually indicates more arousal (except in the case of drug use).

6 Hair stands up; this is called piloerection (goose bumps) and is more noticeable in dogs and cats. Piloerection, which occurs when we are stressed (frightened or angry) or cold (fluffy fur or hair conserves heat), is triggered by the sympathetic division, which also regulates sweating. The next time you are feeling stressed, look for piloerection and sweaty hands.

7 Adrenal glands, which are located above the kidneys, have an outside—adrenal cortex—and an inside—adrenal medulla. The *adrenal medulla,* which is activated by the sympathetic division, secretes two powerful activating hormones, epinephrine (adrenaline) and norepinephrine. These hormones increase heart rate, blood pressure, blood flow to muscles, and release of blood sugar (glucose) as a source of energy. Epinephrine and norepinephrine may be regarded as the body's own stimulants; they can result in euphoria, loss of appetite, and sleeplessness.

The *adrenal cortex,* which is activated by the pituitary gland's release of ACTH, secretes a group of hormones called corticoids, which regulate levels of minerals and increase fuel (glucose) for energy needed to take some action.

Kidney   Kidney

8 Muscle tension is increased during stressful experiences, so that we are better able to coordinate and move quickly if needed. However, if you are feeling stressed for long periods of time, you may end up with muscle aches and pains because of increased muscle tension throughout your body.

Male–female difference. The fight-flight response is automatically triggered to increase physiological arousal and prepare our bodies for action. However, researchers recently found that while men are more likely to fight or flee when stressed, women show a different response to stress, called tend and befriend, which involves nurturing (children) and seeking social support (S. E. Taylor, 2002). Researchers suggest that this male–female difference in responding to stress may have developed from evolutionary pressures on primitive men to fight and protect their families and on primitive women to nurture their children and seek help and social support for themselves and their families.

Although the fight-flight response is designed to aid survival in stressful situations, if the fight-flight response is continuously triggered over a period of time (days, weeks), you may develop painful physical problems, which we'll describe next.

B. Physiological Responses

Psychosomatic Symptoms

What causes stomach pains?

As a college freshman, Joan was stressed out from having too many classes, spending 28 hours a week on homework, working another 10 hours a week at a part-time job, and not getting enough sleep. Joan is one of the 30% of college students in the United States who reported feeling "frequently overwhelmed" by all they have to do (Sax, 2002). Women report more stress (37%) than men (17%), who seem to reduce stress by exercising, partying, and playing more video games than women (Deckro, 2002; Gallagher, 2002). If stress persists for weeks and months, there is a good possibility that you will develop one of a variety of unwanted psychosomatic (also called psychophysiological) symptoms (Kemeny, 2003; Selye, 1993).

Psychosomatic (SIGH-ko-so-MAH-tik) symptoms are real and sometimes painful physical symptoms, such as headaches, muscle pains, stomach problems, and increased susceptibility to colds and flu, that are caused by increased physiological arousal that results from psychological factors, such as worry, stress, and anxiety. (The word *psychosomatic* is derived from *psyche* meaning "mind" and *soma* meaning "body.")

"The fact is that we're now living in a world where our bodies aren't allowed a chance to rest . . . they're being driven by inadequate sleep, lack of exercise, by smoking, by isolation or frenzied competition" (McEwen, 2002). Although our bodies are cleverly designed to use the fight-flight response to deal with relatively infrequent stressors, our bodies do need time for rest and relaxation. However, for many, the busy and competitive world is filled with so many stressful situations that they are constantly appraising situations as threatening to their psychological survival and thus giving their bodies little chance to relax (Sapolsky, 2002). The result, as shown in the figure above, is that the constant use of threat appraisals continually triggers the fight-flight response. In turn, the fight-flight response produces a heightened state of physiological arousal that goes on and on and thus increases the risk of developing one or more *psychosomatic symptoms* (Kemeny, 2003).

We'll discuss different kinds of psychosomatic symptoms as well as why you may develop one symptom but not others.

Development of Symptoms

Do you have any of these symptoms?

Doctors estimate that 50–80% of patients seen in general medical practice have stress-related, psychosomatic symptoms (Wimbush & Nelson, 2000). For example, patients who had developed psychosomatic symptoms reported that they had experienced a serious stressor (breakup of a relationship, family member leaving home) during the previous six months (Creed, 1993). Some of the more common stress-related or psychosomatic symptoms are listed below. Our students (and each of us) usually report having developed at least one of these psychosomatic symptoms each semester.

Common Psychosomatic Symptoms

- **Stomach symptoms:** feelings of discomfort, pain, pressure, or acidity
- **Muscle pain and tension:** occurring in neck, shoulders, and back
- **Fatigue:** feeling tired or exhausted without doing physical activity
- **Headaches:** having either tension or migraine headaches
- **Intestinal difficulties:** having either constipation or diarrhea
- **Skin disorders:** exaggerated skin blemishes, pimples, oiliness
- **Eating problems:** feeling compelled to eat or having no appetite
- **Insomnia:** being unable to get to sleep or stay asleep
- **Asthmatic or allergic problems:** worsening of problems
- **High blood pressure or heart pounding**
- **Weak immune system and increased chances of getting a cold or flu**

DEVELOPMENT OF PSYCHOSOMATIC SYMPTOMS

Researchers find that whether one develops a psychosomatic symptom as well as the kind of symptom depends upon several different factors.

Genetic predisposition. Because of genetic predispositions, most of us inherit a tendency that targets a particular organ or bodily system for weakening or breaking down, such as the heart, blood vessels, stomach lining, or immune system. That's why different individuals who are in similar stressful situations experience different kinds of psychosomatic symptoms. For example, researchers found that some individuals inherit genes that protect their bodies from potentially harmful hormonal effects produced by frequent activation of the fight-flight response. As a result, these individuals may experience fewer psychosomatic symptoms (van Rossum et al., 2002).

Lifestyle. Some lifestyles, such as smoking, being overweight, not exercising, or taking little time for relaxing, promote poor health practices. Such lifestyles give the body little chance to relax and recover from the heightened state of physiological arousal that is produced when the fight-flight response is triggered.

Threat appraisals. Some of us are more likely to appraise situations as threatening, thus eliciting negative emotions, which automatically trigger the fight-flight response (Kiecolt-Glaser et al., 2002). One solution (discussed in the Application section) is to practice changing threat appraisals, which involve negative emotions, into challenge appraisals, which involve positive emotions (N. Skinner & Brewer, 2002).

But how can worrying cause my awful stomach pains?

Psychosomatic symptoms. The development of psychosomatic problems comes from poor lifestyles and too many threat appraisals, which in turn trigger many fight-flight responses, which can damage or break down body organs that may have already been weakened by genetic factors (Kemeny, 2003). Later we'll discuss how to prevent psychosomatic problems by developing an effective stress management programs.

Next, we'll examine in more detail how prolonged stressful experiences can affect and break down the body organs.

What does stress do?

One thing continued stress does is activate the fight-flight response. The continual activation of fight-flight responses results in what Hans Selye (1993) has described as the general adaptation syndrome.

The *general adaptation syndrome* (GAS) refers to the body's reaction to stressful situations during which it goes through a series of three stages—alarm, resistance, and exhaustion—that gradually increase the chances of developing psychosomatic symptoms.

Selye's general adaptation syndrome explains how coed Joan, who felt continually overwhelmed, developed a psychosomatic symptom, stomach pain.

1 Alarm Stage

Alarm: initial reaction

As sleep-deprived Joan worries about having too little time for all she has to do, she appraises that situation as a terrible threat to her well-being, which causes her body to be in the alarm stage.

The *alarm stage* is the initial reaction to stress and is marked by activation of the fight-flight response; in turn, the fight-flight response causes physiological arousal.

During stress, the body goes through 3 stages.

Your body may go into and out of the alarm stage (fight-flight response) many times during the day as stressful experiences come and go. Normally, you do not develop psychosomatic problems during the alarm stage because the fight-flight responses come and go. However, if stress continues for a longer period of time, your body goes into the resistance stage.

2 Resistance Stage

Resistance: fighting back

As the semester comes to an end, Joan's continual feelings of being overwhelmed cause almost continual fight-flight responses, which in turn cause her body to go into the resistance stage.

The *resistance stage* is the body's reaction to continued stress during which most of the physiological responses return to normal levels but the body uses up great stores of energy.

During the resistance stage, Joan's body will use up vital reserves of hormones, minerals, and glucose (blood sugar) because her body is almost continually in the fight-flight state. Joan doesn't realize that the resistance stage is taking a toll on her stomach by interfering with digestion and causing stomach pain, a psychosomatic symptom. If her stress continues, her body will go into the exhaustion stage and her psychosomatic symptom will worsen.

3 Exhaustion Stage

Exhaustion: breakdown in organs

As Joan's feeling of being overwhelmed continues over many weeks, her body may enter the exhaustion stage.

The *exhaustion stage* is the body's reaction to long-term, continuous stress and is marked by actual breakdown in internal organs or weakening of the infection-fighting immune system.

During the exhaustion stage, Joan's stomach problems may become more serious. Like Joan, extended periods of stress, such as during final exams, may cause your body to go into the stage of resistance or exhaustion. During this time you may develop a variety of psychosomatic symptoms, such as a cold, flu, cold sore, sore throat, allergy attack, aching muscles, or stomach problem. For example, researchers found that individuals who had prolonged and high levels of anger, signaling stages of resistance and exhaustion, were more likely to develop high blood pressure than those with normal levels (Jorgensen et al., 1996). As you'll see, psychosomatic symptoms develop because of a mind-body interaction.

Can your mind cause health problems?

At the beginning of this module, we learned how Luisa's mind can intensify the physical sensations she feels during a panic attack. This is a perfect example of the mind-body connection.

The *mind-body connection* refers to how your thoughts, beliefs, and emotions can produce physiological changes that may be either beneficial or detrimental to your health and well-being.

For example, the mind-body connection explains why, after a prolonged period of fearful or anxious thoughts that continually trigger the fight-flight response, there may be a breakdown in body organs and development of psychosomatic symptoms (Wimbush & Nelson, 2000). Researchers found that emotional stress, such as hearing the news of a death in the family, narrowly avoiding a car accident, or walking into a surprise party, can trigger a condition that mimics a massive heart attack. Doctors call this condition "broken-heart syndrome" and explain that when patients experience emotional shock, a sudden surge of stress hormones is released, overwhelming the heart. After the emotional stress subsides, the stress hormone levels return to normal and the heart functions properly again (Fackelmann, 2005).

Research on the importance and implications of the mind-body connection has given rise to mind-body therapy (Goleman & Gurin, 1993).

Mind-body therapy is based on the finding that thoughts and emotions can change physiological and immune responses. Mind-body therapy uses mental strategies, such as relaxation, meditation, and biofeedback, as well as social support groups to help individuals change negative beliefs, thoughts, and emotions into more positive ones.

At the end of this module, we'll discuss specific mind-body therapies, called stress management programs, which help people recognize and deal with stress overload and thus prevent or reduce psychosomatic symptoms.

Mind and body interact during times of stress.

The mind-body connection is involved in the prevention as well as the development and maintenance of psychosomatic symptoms. More unexpectedly, the mind-body connection is involved in the strengthening or weakening of our immune systems, which is the next topic.

B. Physiological Responses

Why did you get a cold?

How often have you gotten a cold, strep throat, or some other bacterial or viral infection when final exams were over? This rather common experience of "coming down with something" when exams are over indicates how prolonged stressful experiences can decrease the effectiveness of your immune system.

Getting a cold is partly due to how much stress you're under.

The *immune system* **is the body's defense and surveillance network of cells and chemicals that fight off bacteria, viruses, and other foreign or toxic substances.**

For many years, researchers believed that the immune system was a totally independent bodily system with no input from the brain and certainly not influenced by one's thoughts. However, in the mid-1970s, a psychologist and an immunologist found the first good evidence of a mind-body connection—that psychological factors, such as one's thoughts, influenced the immune system (R. Ader & Cohen, 1975). Their research led to the development of an entirely new area of medical science that is called psychoneuroimmunology *(SIGH-ko-new-row-im-you-NAWL-ah-gee),* which is a real example of the mind-body connection.

Psychoneuroimmunology

Researchers Ader and Cohen (1975) were trying to figure out why some of their rats were dying so young when they chanced upon one of the important scientific discoveries of the 1970s. For the previous 50 years, immunologists had believed that the immune system operated independently of psychological influences. To the surprise of all and disbelief of many, Ader and Cohen reported that psychological factors influenced the immune system's functioning, a finding that challenged 50 years of thinking. Today, no one doubts their findings, which launched the important field of psychoneuroimmunology (Fleshner & Laudenslager, 2004).

Psychoneuroimmunology **is the study of the relationship among three factors: the central nervous system (brain and spinal cord), the endocrine system (network of glands that secrete hormones), and psychosocial factors (stressful thoughts, personality traits, and social influences).**

For example, coming down with something (cold, flu) after a stressful period results from the interaction among three factors—central nervous system, endocrine system, and psychosocial factors. These three factors can suppress or strengthen the immune system and in turn make the body more or less susceptible to disease and infection (Kiecolt-Glaser et al., 2002). Researchers reported that taking exams suppressed the immune systems of students with high but not low anxiety. These results explain why some students, those highly anxious, are more likely to come down with something after exams or stressful events (Borella et al., 1999).

The immune system has several ways to kill foreign invaders. In the left photo, an immune system cell actually sends out a footlike extension to engulf and destroy the small green bacterial cell (inside white oval).

However, as you'll see next, the immune system's defenses can be weakened by psychosocial factors (Fleshner & Laudenslager, 2004).

An immune system cell sends out a footlike extension to destroy a bacterial cell (in white oval).

Evidence for Psychoneuroimmunology

Researchers were faced with a difficult question: Why doesn't everyone who is exposed to a disease virus or bacteria actually get the disease? They tackled this question head-on by giving the same amount of cold virus to 394 subjects, all of whom were quarantined for a week. During this period, the researchers checked for symptoms of colds and related the percentage of colds to the levels of stress that subjects had reported before they received the virus. As shown in the graph below, researchers found that those individuals who reported high levels of psychological stress were significantly more likely to develop colds than were those who reported low stress levels (S. Cohen, 2003; S. Cohen et al., 1997).

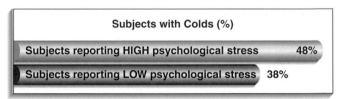

Subjects with Colds (%)

Subjects reporting HIGH psychological stress — 48%
Subjects reporting LOW psychological stress — 38%

Individuals who reported high levels of stress described their lives as somewhat unpredictable, uncontrollable, and overwhelming. Researchers concluded that, with every increase in psychological stress, there's an increased likelihood of developing a cold—provided we are exposed to the cold virus.

Fight-flight response. While short-term stress (such as exam stress or traffic) can weaken the immune system, chronic stress (such as relationship conflict or unemployment) has even more severe effects on our health (Segerstrom & Miller, 2004). People who experience chronic stress are more prone to illness because they are continually activating their fight-flight response. When the fight-flight response is activated, your body produces stress hormones, which suppress the immune system, and this suppression makes the body more susceptible to diseases, viruses, and other infections (Ebrecht et al., 2004).

Conclusion. Ader and Cohen's (1975) basic research on animals' immune systems resulted in the unexpected discovery that the immune system of humans is also influenced by psychosocial factors, such as the amount of stress in one's life—the more stress, the greater the risk of getting a cold (S. Cohen, 2003).

How psychological factors affect the immune system will become clearer as we next describe a really clever experiment.

Could artificial flowers make you sneeze?

There is an interesting story of a woman who was in therapy for having severe allergic reactions to flowers. The therapist was curious about what caused her allergic reaction. It could be caused either by organic factors, which refer to the physical properties of flowers, or by psychosomatic factors, which refer to thoughts, beliefs, or conditioned responses to flowers. To determine whether the cause was organic or psychosomatic, one day the therapist took a dozen red roses from under her desk, gave them to the woman, and asked her what the flowers reminded her of. The woman held them for a short time and then began to have allergic responses, including nasal congestion and tears. What the woman did not know was that the flowers were artificial.

Why do artificial flowers make my nose run?

The woman's allergic reaction to artificial flowers clearly demonstrated that the cause of her allergy was not physical but psychosomatic (caused by the woman's own thoughts). As the woman later explained, her husband had regularly given her flowers as a sign of affection, but now that he was seeking a divorce, the flowers had become a depressing or aversive stimulus. This means that, through classical conditioning, flowers had become conditioned stimuli capable of eliciting a conditioned response, in this case an allergic reaction (classical conditioning is discussed on pages 197–199). Just to be sure, researchers designed the following experiment that left no doubt that the immune system could be classically conditioned (Maier et al., 1994).

CLASSICAL CONDITIONING EXPERIMENT

If the immune system could be classically conditioned, it would clearly show the influence of psychological factors. As explained in Module 9, classical conditioning involves changing a neutral stimulus, such as a flashing light or a humming fan, into a conditioned stimulus so that it alone can elicit a conditioned response, in this case an allergic reaction in a rat. Here's how an immune response (allergic reaction) was classically conditioned in rats (MacQueen et al., 1989).

  Conditioned stimuli: flashing light and humming fan.

 **Unconditioned stimulus:** injection of a substance that produces allergy.

Unconditioned response: allergic reaction elicited by injected substance.

1 For the first three trials, each rat was first presented with two conditioned (neutral) stimuli, a light flashing and a fan humming. A short time later, each rat was given an injection of an allergy-producing substance, which was the unconditioned stimulus. In turn, the unconditioned stimulus elicited an allergic reaction, which was the unconditioned response.

2 On the fourth trial the animals were divided into two groups: control and experimental groups.

Control group received a trial with the regular sequence: flashing light and fan humming, then the injection of the substance, which elicited the allergic reaction.

Experimental group of rats received a different trial: Rats were exposed only to the conditioned stimuli of flashing light and fan humming, with no injection.

3 The *experimental group* of animals showed a conditioned response, which means that just being given or exposed to the conditioned stimuli (flashing light and humming fan) caused the allergic reaction, which is the *conditioned response.*

4 **Discussion.** During classical conditioning, animals or people learn that the neutral or conditioned stimulus signals or predicts what will happen next. In this study, rats learned that the flashing light and humming fan predicted an allergic reaction. And in fact, by the fourth trial, the conditioned stimuli (light and fan) alone elicited the allergic reaction—the conditioned response. Researchers concluded that psychological factors can trigger an allergic reaction in animals (MacQueen et al., 1989).

5 **Conclusion.** The amazing fact that immune responses can be conditioned demonstrates a method through which purely psychological or cognitive factors can affect immune function. Although the immune system was originally thought to act independently, it is now known that psychological factors influence the immune system in both animals and humans (F. Ader, 1999).

These findings in rats explain why the woman had an allergic reaction to artificial flowers: The artificial flowers had become conditioned stimuli that, by themselves, could elicit conditioned responses—in this case, allergic reactions of congestion and tearing eyes.

The history of psychoneuroimmunology reads like a mystery story. For 50 years, researchers had written in stone that the immune system was totally independent and only a fool would believe otherwise. In the early 1970s, Ader the psychologist and Cohen the immunologist were studying something entirely different (why animals were dying prematurely) when they discovered the reason was that the animals' immune systems had been weakened through classical conditioning (R. Ader & Cohen, 1975). This revolutionary finding meant the immune system could be influenced by psychological factors, and this led to the birth of a whole new field, called psychoneuroimmunology (F. Ader, 1999).

We have discussed how stressful experiences trigger the fight-flight response and affect the immune system. Next, we'll examine which situations are the most likely to become stressful.

C. Stressful Experiences

What are Sandra's stressors?

We began this module with a description of Sandra's busy day as a single mother and college student: She gets up at 6:30 A.M., wakes her two children, yells for them to get dressed, rushes to get her kids on the school bus, panics when she can't find her paper that's due today, and speeds out the door to make her first class. Every day of Sandra's life is filled with small annoyances that are called hassles, which can add up to make what she would probably call "a very bad day."

Besides dealing with daily hassles, Sandra has also gone through a number of major life changes: She left her husband, quit using

Sandra has dozens of hassles and had several major life changes.

drugs, began group therapy, did well in a community college, and went on to Wellesley College. Unlike hassles, which seem relatively small, major life events have had a significant impact on Sandra's life and can be very big stressors.

Both hassles and major life events have the potential to become stressful experiences that influence mood and development of psychosomatic problems.

Hassles

When someone asks, "And how was your day?" you usually reply with a list of hassles.

Hassles **are those small, irritating, frustrating events that we face daily and that we usually appraise or interpret as stressful experiences.**

For example, a nationwide survey of adults (ages 25–74) found that the most frequently reported daily hassles involved interpersonal tensions followed by work-related stressors. The most frequently reported appraisals involved danger (36%), loss (30%), or frustration (27%), and only 2% were appraised as representing opportunity or challenge. Generally, women reported the stressors as being more severe than did men. As the number of daily hassles increased, so too did the chance of developing psychosomatic problems or being in a bad mood (Almeida et al., 2002).

The opposite of a hassle is a good experience called an uplift.

Uplifts **are those small, pleasurable, happy, and satisfying experiences that we have in our daily lives.**

Daily hassles are related to having physical problems.

For many college students (and most adults), the daily hassles, which lead to having a "bad day," usually far outnumber the uplifts, which lead to having a "good day." For example, how often do you hear people say, "I had such a great day!" In contrast to hassles, daily uplifts are associated with less depression and better functioning (Macnee & McCabe, 2000).

Besides hassles, another source of stress involves major life events.

Major Life Events

Not only do hassles increase stress levels and predict daily mood and health, but so do major life events.

Major life events **are potentially disturbing, troubling, or disruptive situations, both positive and negative, that we appraise as having a significant impact on our lives.**

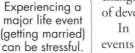

Experiencing a major life event (getting married) can be stressful.

Researchers measure life events using the Social Readjustment Rating Scale (below) (M. A. Miller & Rahe, 1997). The number after each event rates the impact that the event would have on one's life; death of one's spouse has the maximum rating (119). To obtain your score, add the numbers associated with each event you have experienced in the last year. The total reflects how much life change you have experienced. Researchers predicted that experiencing an increased number of life changes would increase levels of stress and, in turn, increase the chances of developing psychosomatic problems.

In the scale at the right, events in a six-month period that total over 300 and events in a one-year period that total over 500 indicate high recent life stress and a greatly increased risk of developing psychosomatic problems (M. A. Miller & Rahe, 1997). Researchers report a modest correlation (+0.20 to +0.30) between number of major life events experienced and development of psychosomatic symptoms (J. S. Werner & Frost, 2000).

One problem with the Social Readjustment Rating Scale is that it makes no distinction between appraisal of positive events (getting married) and negative events (getting divorced). More recent scales found that the appraisal of negative life events was more important in predicting illnesses or depression than were positive events (Dixon & Reid, 2000; Shimizu & Pelham, 2004). Both major life events and daily hassles are ways of assessing current level of stress, which contributes to our daily moods and chances of developing psychosomatic symptoms.

SOCIAL READJUSTMENT RATING SCALE	
Life event	**Mean value**
Death of spouse	119
Divorce	98
Death of close family member	92
Fired at work	79
Personal injury or illness	77
Death of a close friend	70
Pregnancy	66
Change in financial state	56
Change in work conditions	51
Marriage	50
Sex difficulties	45
Change in living conditions	42
Change in residence	41
Beginning or ending school	38
Great personal achievement	37
Change in school	35
Trouble with boss	29
Revision of personal habits	27
Change in sleeping habits	26
Vacation	25
Minor violations of the law	22

Female–male difference. Researchers found that females reported significantly more and intense stressful events and more symptoms of depression, anxiety, and psychosomatic problems than males. Researchers suggest that this female–male difference may result from females being socialized to be more sensitive and responsive to stressful and emotional events, while males are socialized to "grin and bear it" (M. C. Davis et al., 1999).

One characteristic of stressful events, such as major life events and hassles, is that they are generally frustrating experiences. We'll discuss frustration and its long-term effects.

What makes situations stressful?

We're going to examine three situations—being frustrated, feeling burned out, and experiencing interpersonal violence—that have the potential to be highly stressful. What can make these situations especially stressful is they can all elicit very negative emotions, which can greatly increase levels of stress.

Frustration

Being a pop music star is exhausting.

Several years ago, Mariah Carey (left photo), a Grammy-winning singer who has sold tens of millions of albums, cancelled all of her public appearances and checked herself into a hospital, complaining of "extreme exhaustion." She felt tremendous stress resulting from completing two movies while writing, recording, and producing an album ("Mariah in hospital," 2001). Mariah Carey's example illustrates the difficulties of having a job in which success is judged by how many albums you sell or the number of Grammy awards you win. Having low album sales or not winning an award can be very frustrating.

Frustration **is the awful feeling that results when your attempts to reach some goal are blocked.**

You may be blocked from reaching a goal because of *personal limitations,* such as losing your temper, making dumb mistakes on an exam, or not having the skills to pass a course. Or you may be blocked from reaching a goal because of *social* or *environmental limitations,* such as having to work 18-hour days. One reason frustrating situations are especially stressful is that they seem to be out of your control and they usually elicit *strong negative emotions,* such as anger or rage (Goldberger & Breznitz, 1993).

Monday versus Friday. One survey found that compared to Fridays, Mondays were more stressful and frustrating because of having to return to work, having too many things to do, not having enough time, and expecting but not getting as much done. The stress and frustration experienced on Mondays resulted in 33% more heart attacks than occurred on Fridays (Friend, 1994). This is an example of how stress and frustration can contribute to dangerous psychosomatic problems.

If frustration lasts for a long period of time, the result can be burnout.

Burnout

About 5 to 20% of nurses, lawyers, police officers, social workers, managers, counselors, teachers, medical residents, and others whose jobs demand intense involvement with people suffer from burnout (Farber, 2000a, 2000b).

Burnout **refers to being physically overwhelmed and exhausted, finding the job unrewarding and becoming cynical or detached, and developing a strong sense of ineffectiveness and lack of accomplishment in this particular job (Maslach, 2003).**

I'm burnt out after working 10 years in social services.

Burnout is accompanied by intense feelings and negative emotions that trigger the fight-flight response, keep the body in a continual state of heightened physiological arousal, and cause most of the psychosomatic symptoms we have discussed: sleep problems, stomach disorders, headaches, muscular pain (especially lower back and neck), and frequent and prolonged colds (Melamed et al., 2006).

One way to reduce the likelihood of burnout is to take a vacation. Research shows that time spent on vacation enhances people's well-being by decreasing their complaints about health problems and exhaustion (C. Fritz & Sonnentag, 2006).

Student burnout. College counselors report that burnout often causes students to drop out of college. Counselors suggest that before students decide to drop out, they should consider ways to reduce their work and class load so that school seems less overwhelming and more manageable (Schaufeli et al., 2002).

The next situation is so stressful that it leaves a terrible, lasting mark that may trigger years of problems.

Violence

Most people experience at least one violent or life-threatening situation during their life. For some people the experience is so stressful it results in posttraumatic stress disorder (E. J. Ozer et al., 2003).

Posttraumatic stress disorder, **or** *PTSD,* **is a disabling condition that results from personally experiencing an event that involves actual or threatened death or serious injury or from witnessing or hearing of such an event happening to a family member or close friend. People suffering from PTSD experience a number of psychological symptoms, including recurring and disturbing memories, terrible nightmares, and intense fear and anxiety (APA, 2000).**

For example, about 32% of women report having PTSD after being raped; about 15% of soldiers report having PTSD after serving in war; and about 15% of people report having PTSD after being in a natural disaster or serious car accident (Hidalgo & Davidson, 2000). These horrible memories and feelings of fear keep stress levels high and result in a wide range of psychosomatic symptoms, including sleep problems, pounding heart, high blood pressure, and stomach problems (Marshall et al., 2006; Schnurr et al., 2002).

I saw my best buddy blown apart.

Treatment. The treatment of posttraumatic stress disorder may involve drugs (SSRIs; p. 534), but some form of cognitive-behavioral therapy (p. 568) has proved more effective in the long term (Bolton et al., 2004). Cognitive-behavioral therapy provides emotional support so victims can begin the healing process, helps to slowly eliminate the horrible memories by bringing out the details of the experience, and gradually replaces the feeling of fear with a sense of courage to go on with life (Harvey et al., 2003; Marmar et al., 2002).

We'll examine two more situations with high potential for stress because they involve conflict or anxiety.

C. Stressful Experiences

Why are decisions so stressful?

Sometimes situations can be stressful because they involve making difficult decisions. For example, what decisions would you make in the following situations?

■ You can either go to a great party or see a good friend who is visiting town for just one day.

■ You can study for a psychology exam or write a paper for a history class.

■ You can ask a new acquaintance to have lunch, but

then you risk being rejected.

In making these kinds of decisions, you are most likely to feel stressed because each involves facing a different kind of conflict.

Conflict **is the feeling you experience when you must choose between two or more incompatible possibilities or options.**

The reason the situations put you in conflict is that, no matter which option you choose, you must give up something you really want to get or you must do something you really want to avoid. We'll describe three common kinds of conflicts—approach-approach, avoidance-avoidance, and approach-avoidance—and some of the ways of dealing with conflicts.

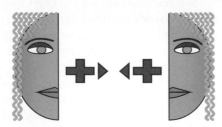

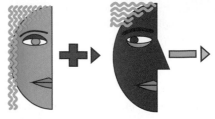

Approach-approach. Deciding between going to a party or seeing a friend involves choosing between two pleasurable options.

Approach-approach conflict **involves choosing between two situations that both have pleasurable consequences.**

At first it seems that approach-approach conflicts are the least stressful of the three kinds because, whichever option you choose, you will experience a pleasurable consequence. But on second thought, approach-approach conflicts can be the most stressful because you must give up one of the very pleasurable consequences. The result is that you will feel considerably stressed as you agonize over which one of the two great possibilities to give up.

Avoidance-avoidance. Deciding between studying for a psychology exam or writing a paper for a history class involves choosing between two undesirable options.

Avoidance-avoidance conflict **involves choosing between two situations that both have disagreeable consequences.**

In an avoidance-avoidance conflict, you may change your mind many times and wait until the last possible minute before making the final decision. You delay choosing as long as possible in trying to avoid the disagreeable or unpleasant outcome.

Approach-avoidance. Deciding between asking a new acquaintance to lunch and being afraid of being rejected involves a single situation that has both desirable and undesirable possibilities.

Approach-avoidance conflict involves a single situation that has both pleasurable and disagreeable aspects.

In this example, asking the person to lunch would make you feel good, but at the same time, being rejected is something you want to avoid because it makes you feel bad. Our lives are full of approach-avoidance conflicts, and trying to decide what to do about them can turn into very stressful experiences.

Five Styles of Dealing with Conflict

Researchers have identified five different styles of dealing with conflict, one of which may be similar to yours and one of which is better than the rest (R. J. Sternberg & Soriano, 1984).

1. Avoidance. These individuals find dealing with conflicts unpleasant. They hope that by avoiding or ignoring the conflict it will disappear or magically go away. Sadly, the conflict usually gets worse and will have to be dealt with eventually.

2. Accommodation. These individuals also hate conflicts and just give in to make the disagreement go away. They tend to please people and worry about approval. Unfortunately, giving in does not solve the problem, which in the long term will need to be solved.

3. Domination. In conflicts, these individuals go to any lengths to win, even if it means being aggressive and manipulative. However, aggressively solving conflicts results in hostility rather than intimate human relationships.

4. Compromise. These individuals recognize that others have different needs and try to solve conflicts through compromise. Unfortunately, they may use manipulation and misrepresentation to further their own goals, so compromise isn't always the best solution.

5. Integration. These individuals try to resolve conflicts by finding solutions to please both partners. They don't criticize the other person, they try to be open, and they emphasize similarities rather than differences.

Perhaps the best way to resolve relationship conflicts is to try to be as much of an integrator as possible because this style avoids criticism and has the best chance of pleasing both individuals (B. K. Williams & Knight, 1994).

Situations involving conflict can be very stressful because you must often make undesirable choices. The next situations are stressful because they involve anxiety.

What is the best way to settle conflicts?

This module began with two stories that involved anxiety. One story was about the sudden and intense panic attacks Luisa would have for no apparent reason. The other was about Sandra, who feared she did not have either the brains or the motivation to compete with all the excellent students who attend Wellesley College. Like Luisa's and Sandra's experiences, everyone at some time will feel the terrible grip of anxiety.

Anxiety is an unpleasant state characterized by feelings of uneasiness and apprehension as well as increased physiological arousal, such as increased heart rate and blood pressure.

Next, we'll learn three ways of developing anxiety: classical conditioning, observational learning, and unconscious conflict. We'll begin by sharing a personal story about how one of us (R.P.) developed a fear of blood.

Classical Conditioning

I developed anxiety through classical conditioning.

My fear of blood comes from a traumatic childhood incident: I had seen my father almost cut off his thumb. For me and about 76% of people surveyed, fear of blood began with a traumatic event that involved classical conditioning (Kleinknecht, 1994). In my case, the neutral stimulus was the sight of blood. It was paired with an unconditioned stimulus—seeing my father almost cut off his thumb—which caused an unconditioned response—anxiety, fear, and the fight-flight response. After this single pairing, the sight of blood became the conditioned stimulus, which now elicits the unconditioned response—great anxiety. My fear of blood is an example of a conditioned emotional response.

A conditioned emotional response results when an emotional response, such as fear or anxiety, is classically conditioned to a previously neutral stimulus.

A conditioned emotional response not only is highly resistant to extinction but can also cause stressful feelings (p. 201).

Observational Learning

One way that Sandra developed anxiety about being at Wellesley College was through observational learning on campus and in the classroom.

Observational learning, which is a form of cognitive learning, results from watching and modeling and does not require the observer to perform any observable behavior or receive a reinforcer.

In Sandra's case, her observations of younger and seemingly better prepared students made her feel anxious about being able to compete academically and socially. Her initial anxiety decreased somewhat as she earned good grades and made friends. Albert Bandura (2001b) believes that the majority of human learning, including feeling anxious in the classroom, occurs through observational learning (p. 225). However, having to compete will no doubt continue to make Sandra feel anxious, which in turn will keep her stress level high.

Sandra developed anxiety from observing competing students.

Unconscious Conflict

Luisa developed anxiety through unconscious conflict.

During her psychotherapy, Luisa discovered that the cause of her anxiety was she was giving up her lifelong dream of becoming a writer to respect her parents' wish for her to become a scientist.

Sigmund Freud hypothesized that there are three divisions of the mind—id, ego, and superego—that at times may be in conflict over how a need should be satisfied (p. 436). This unconscious conflict may result in feeling anxiety.

Anxiety, according to Freud, arises when there is an unconscious conflict between the id's and superego's desires regarding how to satisfy a need, with the ego caught in the middle. The ego's solution to this conflict is to create a feeling of anxiety.

According to Freud, we may try to decrease our anxiety by using a number of *defense mechanisms,* which are discussed below.

Luisa had been using the defense mechanism of repression to help manage her anxiety, but this did not solve her dilemma of which career to choose. As a result, her anxiety intensified and she began having panic attacks.

Next, we'll learn about the different ways to cope with anxiety.

Coping with Anxiety

We would use different methods to cope with anxiety, depending on whether it developed through classical conditioning, observational learning, or unconscious conflicts.

Extinction. If our anxious feelings were learned through classical conditioning or observational learning, we could use a number of extinction techniques discussed earlier (pp. 207, 233). As a quick review, these extinction methods include systematic desensitization and behavior modification, which are ways to unlearn responses. All extinction procedures involve actively working to change certain thoughts, behaviors, or physiological responses associated with our anxious feelings. These procedures might be characterized as *problem-focused, conscious coping techniques,* since they represent active attempts by us to deal with the problem itself.

Freudian defense mechanisms. In comparison to extinction procedures, which constitute conscious, problem-focused coping, Freud's defense mechanisms represent *emotion-focused, unconscious coping techniques.* As you may remember, defense mechanisms are processes that operate at unconscious levels to help the ego reduce anxiety through various forms of self-deception, such as denial, repression, rationalization, and projection (p. 437). Therefore, the defense mechanisms help manage a person's emotions rather than resolve the problem that is causing the anxiety.

Next, we'll examine how different kinds of personality variables can help or hinder our coping with anxiety and stress.

D. Personality & Social Factors

How does he cope with the stress of competition?

Shaun White, nicknamed the "Flying Red Tomato" for his long, curly red hair, has never been an ordinary athlete. At the age of 6, he began skateboarding on a ramp in his backyard, and he practiced snowboarding during family trips to the mountains. By the time Shaun was 13 years old, he became a pro skateboarder and snow-boarder. At age 19, he became the first athlete to compete in both the summer and winter X Games. Shaun always strives to do his very best, even under the most stressful situations. He does not allow the pressure of heated competition or the setback of an awkward landing to compromise his determination to win. Shaun's ability to handle extreme stress became most evident when he won an Olympic gold medal (Ruibal, 2006; "Shaun White," 2006).

How can Shaun White, the "Flying Red Tomato," perform so well in extremely stressful conditions?

Why is it that certain people, like Shaun White, seem to handle stressful situations better than others? This was exactly the question researchers asked as they studied the personality characteristics of middle- and upper-level executives and lawyers who had experienced considerable stress in the past three years (Kobasa, 1982; Kobasa et al., 1982a, 1982b). Researchers discovered that those executives and lawyers who stayed healthy in spite of stressful life situations had three personality traits, which, taken together, were labeled hardiness.

Hardiness is a combination of three personality traits—control, commitment, and challenge—that protect or buffer us from the potentially harmful effects of stressful situations and reduce our chances of developing psychosomatic illnesses.

Shaun White appears to be the perfect example of a hardy person who has the three Cs—control, commitment, and challenge. For example, his disciplined practicing shows he has *commitment* to his goal of being a snowboarding legend; his participation in the Olympics shows he likes a *challenge;* and his determination to come back more focused after even the slightest error indicates his desire to be in *control.*

Just as hardiness helps Shaun White deal with stress, research shows hardiness helps people cope in a wide range of stressful situations, such as nurses who work with dying patients and military personnel who experience life-threatening situations (Bartone, 1999; Maddi, 2002). Researchers also reported that hardiness helps college students cope by reducing the effects of daily frustrations (Beasley et al., 2003). Hardiness is a personality factor that increases protection against stress and decreases the chances of developing psychosomatic symptoms. Being hardy gives people a real edge in dealing with potentially stressful situations (Bonanno, 2004).

Next, we'll discuss what researchers have learned by studying control, one of the three traits in hardiness.

Why can waiting be such a hassle?

A daily hassle that most of us hate is having to wait for something or somebody. One reason waiting can be so stressful is that we have little or no control in this situation. How much control you feel you have over a situation is a personal belief that is called locus of control.

Locus of control represents a continuum: At one end is the belief that you are basically in control of life's events and that what you do influences the situation; this belief is called an internal locus of control. At the other end is the belief that chance and luck mostly determine what happens and that you do not have much influence; this belief is called an external locus of control.

Most of us lie somewhere along the locus of control continuum, rather than being at one end or the other (Carducci, 2006). For example, when students discuss how much their studying affects their grades, they are in part talking about their locus of control, which in turn affects their stress level.

> What's the use of studying when I do poorly on exams?

External locus of control. "No matter how much I study, it never seems to help," says the student with an external locus of control. This student will likely appraise exams and papers as less of a challenge and more of a threat, which in turn will generate negative emotions (fear, anxiety, anger) and increase stress levels.

Internal locus of control. "If I study hard and apply myself, I can get good grades," says the student with an internal locus of control. This student will likely appraise exams and papers less as threats and more as challenges, which in turn will generate positive emotions (excitement, enthusiasm) and decrease stress levels. This means that students with internal locus of control have lower levels of stress and, as a result, report fewer psychosomatic symptoms than those with external locus of control (Ruiz-Bueno, 2000).

A cross-cultural study comparing stress and coping styles among Japanese and British people revealed interesting results about stress and a sense of control. Though Japanese people reported having a lower sense of personal control, only British people reported that a lower sense of personal control results in increased stress. These results suggest that sense of control may be most important in Western cultures that emphasize autonomy and personal accomplishment (O'Connor & Shimizu, 2002).

Studies on locus of control show that our personality traits influence our appraisal (more or less challenging or threatening), which, in turn, increases or decreases our feelings of stress and our chances of developing psychosomatic symptoms (Kirkcaldy et al., 2002).

Another personality trait that can influence stress levels is how pessimistic or optimistic we generally are.

Optimism Versus Pessimism

Why is it better to be an optimist?

If you want to experience more positive than negative emotions and reduce your levels of stress, try being more optimistic.

Optimism **is a relatively stable personality trait that leads to believing and expecting that good things will happen.** *Pessimism* **is a relatively stable personality trait that leads to believing and expecting that bad things will happen.**

Optimists. One way optimists reduce stress is by focusing on the good things, a process called *positive reappraisal.* Forms of positive reappraisal include discovering new opportunities for personal growth, noticing actual personal growth, and seeing how your actions can benefit others. By using positive reappraisal, you can change the meaning or appraisal of situations to seem more positive and thus feel positive emotions (Folkman & Moskowitz, 2000). Researchers found that individuals who perceive themselves as in control—that is, have an internal locus of control—are more likely to

"I'm an optimist and believe that good things will happen."

have an optimistic attitude in dealing with stressors (C. T. F. Klein & Helweg-Larsen, 2002). Generally, optimists experience more positive emotions and report less stress and fewer psychosomatic symptoms (S. E. Taylor et al., 2000). Recent research shows that optimists may even live longer than pessimists (DeKeukelaere, 2006; B. R. Levy et al., 2002).

Pessimists. Because pessimists expect bad things to happen, they are likely to change the meaning or appraisal of situations to seem more negative and thus experience more negative emotions, such as anger, rage, fear, or anxiety, and are less able to ask for or receive social support. For example, researchers found that men with high levels of negative emotions, such as anger, were four times more likely to suffer sudden heart death. In comparison, optimistic patients who received heart transplants reported more positive emotions and dealt better with setbacks than patients with a pessimistic outlook (Leedham et al., 1995).

"I'm a pessimist and believe that bad things will happen."

Numerous studies associate pessimism and negative emotions with increasing stress levels, decreasing functioning of the immune system, and a wide range of psychosomatic symptoms such as high blood pressure, heart problems, headaches, allergies, and stomach problems (Vahtera et al., 2000).

Personality factors. During the past 10 years, a number of personality factors, such as optimism/pessimism, internal/external locus of control, and hardiness, have been associated with feeling more or less positive or negative emotions, which in turn are involved in increasing or decreasing stress levels and increasing or decreasing chances of developing psychosomatic symptoms (Salovey et al., 2000).

Next, we'll learn about a new direction in psychology that focuses on better understanding positive attitudes and happiness.

Positive Psychology

Why should I focus more on the positive?

Sherrod Ballentine has a stressful job as a court mediator, and although she's not clinically depressed, she wants to learn ways to improve her mood. She takes a class called "Authentic Happiness and How to Obtain It" and learns activities that will train her mind to focus more on the positive. One activity Sherrod learns is to write down three happy events and their causes at the end of each day for a week. After completing the class, she said, "I am happier. Every day, I feel so grateful to wake up this way" (Lemley, 2006). Sherrod's new learned skills are based on an area of interest called positive psychology.

Positive psychology **is the scientific study of optimal human functioning, focusing on the strengths and virtues that enable individuals and communities to thrive. It aims to better understand the positive, adaptive, and fulfilling aspects of human life.**

Positive psychology has three main concerns. The first is the study of *positive emotions,* such as happiness, hope, love, and contentment. The second is the study of *positive individual traits,* such as altruism, courage, compassion, and resilience. The third focus is *positive institutions,* which studies the strengths that promote better communities, such as justice, parenting, tolerance, and teamwork (Seligman, 2003).

One theoretical model states that positive emotions and positive traits enhance health by pushing away negative ones. For instance, it is difficult to be angry or bitter when one is showing compassion and love toward another person (N. B. Anderson, 2003).

There are many research examples showing that characteristics of positive psychology have a beneficial impact on mood and physical health. For example, a review of research data on altruism and its relationship to mental and physical health found volunteering and other supportive behaviors (such as providing emotional support to others) are associated with higher life satisfaction, as well as better physical and mental health (S. Post, 2005). Also, research on writing exercises, such as the one Sherrod did, show impressive results. One study found that after writing about positive experiences for 20 minutes each day for three consecutive days, college students reported improved mood and had fewer health center visits for illness in the months that followed (Burton & King, 2004).

One reason there is growing interest in positive psychology is that it provides a needed change from the tendency for psychological research to focus more on problems or weaknesses than on strengths and virtues. Because positive psychology is still a relatively new area of study, more time is needed to see the impact it will have on reshaping psychology's research interests.

Next, we'll examine two particular combinations of personality traits that have been labeled Type A and Type D behavior, which have been associated with increasing the chances of having a heart attack.

D. Personality & Social Factors

Is there such a thing as Type A behavior?

In the mid-1970s, a new expression—"You're a Type A person"—was coined when two doctors published the book *Type A Behavior and Your Heart* (M. Friedman & Rosenman, 1974). At that time, the best-known risk factors associated with developing heart disease were diet, exercise, and smoking. This book startled the medical world by describing a combination of personality traits that made up a psychological risk factor, which was called Type A behavior.

1970s: *Type A Behavior — Impatient, Hostile, Workaholic*

We'll begin with the original 1970s definition of Type A behavior (M. Friedman & Rosenman, 1974).

Impatient, hostile, and workaholic

Type A behavior referred to a combination of personality traits that included an overly competitive and aggressive drive to achieve, a hostile attitude when frustrated, a habitual sense of time urgency, a rapid and explosive pattern of speaking, and being a workaholic. *Type B behavior* was characterized by being easygoing, calm, relaxed, and patient.

The reason Type A behavior made such a big scientific splash was that compared to Type B's, Type A's were found to have experienced two to three times as many heart attacks. By 1978, Type A behavior was officially recognized as an independent risk factor for heart disease by a National Institutes of Health panel.

However, at about the same time that Type A behavior was declared a risk factor, researchers began having trouble replicating earlier findings and began to seriously question the definition of Type A behavior.

1980s–1990s: *Type A Behavior — Depressed, Angry*

Research in the 1980s that showed coronary disease was not associated with being impatient or a workaholic led to both traits being dropped from the new definition of Type A behavior (Booth-Kewley & Friedman, 1987; K. A. Matthews & Haynes, 1986).

Depressed and angry

Type A behavior was defined in the 1980s as being depressed, easily frustrated, anxious, and angry, or some combination of these traits.

Despite using this new and improved definition, a review of many studies between 1983 and 1992 led one researcher to conclude that the relationship between Type A behavior and cardiac disease is so low as to have no practical meaning and that Type A behavior is no longer a valid or useful concept (Myrtek, 1995). Because of the continuing failure to replicate the original relationship, researchers again redefined Type A behavior.

The 1990s definition of *Type A behavior* specifies an individual who feels angry and hostile much of the time but may or may not express these emotions publicly.

This definition made prolonged hostility or anger (felt or expressed) the major component of Type A behavior (Leventhal & Patrick-Miller, 2000). Research indicates that angry/hostile individuals are three times more likely to have heart attacks and individuals who are quick to anger under stress are five times more likely to develop a premature heart disease (D. Smith, 2003). Researchers concluded that individuals who either always *show* their anger/hostility or always *suppress* it have large increases in physiological arousal, which can have damaging effects on one's heart and one's health (Finney, 2003).

2000s: *Type D Behavior — Chronic Distress: Negative Affectivity, Social Inhibition*

What is Type D behavior?

In his work with cardiac patients, Johan Denollet, a psychologist, noticed that some heart-attack survivors remained happy and optimistic, while others became discouraged and pessimistic. He went on to describe a new set of behaviors he believed to be predictive of health risk (M. C. Miller, 2005b).

Type D behavior is defined as chronic distress in terms of two emotional states: negative affectivity (worry, irritability, gloom) and social inhibition (shyness, being reserved, lack of self-assurance).

Negative affectivity and social inhibition

People with Type D behavior tend to experience negative emotions and inhibit self-expression in social interactions. In terms of heath risk, Type D behavior is associated with greater cortisol reactivity to stress and consequently increased risk for coronary artery disease (Sher, 2004). Research on patients who had recently received stents to open their coronary arteries showed Type D patients were four times

as likely as others to have a heart attack or die within six to nine months of the procedure (M. C. Miller, 2005b).

Even though strong research supports the link between Type D behavior and health problems, recall that research on Type A behavior also began strong, and yet Type A behavior had to be redefined. Type D behavior is a relatively new concept and needs more research to better determine its impact on health conditions (M. C. Miller, 2005b).

In conclusion, research on Type A and Type D behavior shows certain personality traits, such as anger/hostility and negative affectivity/social inhibition, can increase the risks of cardiovascular diseases. This means that treatment for such diseases should include not only medical treatments but also behavioral therapy to decrease negative traits (Merz et al., 2002).

Besides personality factors, various social factors can also increase or decrease stress and affect one's health.

Do friends help you deal with stress?

We have told you how important findings are often discovered by chance. Here's a "chance" finding that began a new area of research.

In the small town of Roseto, Pennsylvania, people were relatively obese and ate a lot of animal fat. They smoked as much and exercised as little as residents of other neighboring towns. Despite the citizens' awful diet and lifestyle—obvious risk factors for developing heart disease—only one man in 1,000 died of a heart attack, compared with a national rate of 3.5 per 1,000, and the rates for women were even lower. Citizens of Roseto also had lower rates for ulcers and emotional problems compared with rates in the rest of the United States and their neighboring towns.

This puzzling question—why the citizens of Roseto should enjoy such good physical and mental health in the face of obvious risk factors—was answered by a study of the town's social order. "One striking feature did set Roseto apart from its neighbors," says Stewart Wolf, vice president for medical affairs at St. Luke's Hospital in Bethlehem, Pennsylvania, and a principal investigator of the Roseto phenomenon. "We found that family relationships were extremely close and mutually supportive, and this wonderful social support system extended to neighbors and to the community as a whole" (J. Greenberg, 1978, p. 378). But the story of Roseto does not have a happy ending.

As families of Roseto prospered, they moved into larger and finer homes in the countryside, and their social support system began to break down. Families no longer had helpful friends for neighbors, which meant fewer family and friendly get-togethers and far less social support. One of the most interesting and deadly findings was that with the breakdown in social support came an increase in heart attacks, especially in younger men. This study on families in Roseto was one of the first to suggest that dealing with stress and overcoming health risks were in large part aided by one's social support.

Social support refers to three factors: having a group or network of family or friends who provide strong social attachments; being able to exchange helpful resources among family or friends; and feeling, or making appraisals, that we have supportive relationships and behaviors.

Thirty years ago, no one would have thought that loneliness and lack of social support were major factors that contributed to becoming ill and developing psychosomatic symptoms. Today, social support is reported to be one of the most important coping methods that individuals use to decrease the effects of stressful situations and cope with psychosomatic problems (P. W. Underwood, 2000). We'll present studies that illustrate how social support buffers us from stress and helps maintain our mental health.

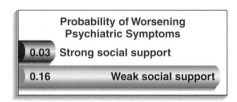

"We're always helping one another."

Social support reduces stress.

Buffer against Stress

Many of us have asked for help in solving a variety of problems, which range from feeling lonely to needing to borrow money. In these troublesome situations, social support helps us cope with stress by giving us confidence, raising our self-esteem, and increasing our feelings of self-worth, which in turn promote and maintain psychological adjustment.

For example, new cutting-edge research found that married women under extreme stress feel immediate relief upon holding their husband's hand (Carey, 2006). In this study, women were placed in an MRI machine and told they would periodically receive a mild electric shock. Brain scans showed heightened activity in areas involved in physical arousal and anticipating pain. As soon as husbands reached into the machine and touched their wife's hand, the activity levels in all brain areas responding to the stress dropped substantially. It is interesting

that, although a stranger's hand resulted in some drop in brain activity in areas responding to stress, the drop was not as substantial compared to the husband's touch. From this and other studies on social support and stress, researchers conclude that social support, such as help, advice, sympathy, and reassurance from family or friends, can decrease the effects of stressful experiences (P. D. Martin & Brantley, 2004).

Maintaining Mental Health

One reason we tell a friend or family member about how our day went and the problems we had is that the telling elicits support and sympathy, which make us feel better (Kowalski, 1996). Besides making us feel better, researchers wondered if social support would also help prevent individuals who already had mild psychiatric symptoms, such as anxiety or depression, from getting worse. In a 10-year study, researchers interviewed the same individuals several times to see how social support affected levels of anxiety or depression.

The graph below shows that individuals with a strong social support system had a low chance of worsening psychiatric symptoms even if they had faced two to six stressful life events in the past year. In comparison, individuals with a weak social support system had a significantly greater chance of worsening anxiety or depression. Researchers concluded that a good social support system, such as having one or more close friends or neighbors, decreases the effects of stressful life events, prevents the worsening of anxiety and depression, and thus helps maintain a person's mental health (Dalgard et al., 1995).

Probability of Worsening Psychiatric Symptoms

0.03	Strong social support
0.16	Weak social support

These kinds of studies indicate that, in a very real sense, a good social support system facilitates our maintaining good mental health and protects us from developing illnesses and psychosomatic symptoms (de Grott, 2002; Miyazaki et al., 2003). One of the important functions of a good social support system is to help us develop ways of coping with stress, which we'll discuss after the Concept Review.

Concept Review

1. The cognitive and behavioral efforts that we use to manage a situation that we have appraised as exceeding, straining, or taxing our personal resources are referred to as _____.

2. Our initial, subjective evaluation of a situation, in which we balance environmental demands against our ability to meet them, is referred to as _____. We may appraise the situation in three ways: as irrelevant, positive, or stressful.

3. If we appraise a situation as stressful, we go on to determine whether it represents (a)_____, _____, or _____. If our primary appraisal is one of harm/loss or threat, we will experience more (b)_____ than if our appraisal is one of challenge, because harm/loss or threat appraisals elicit (c)_____ emotions.

4. A combination of physiological responses that arouse and prepare the body for action is referred to as the (a)_____ response. This response begins in a part of the brain called the (b)_____, which triggers the (c)_____ division of the autonomic nervous system. This response is especially triggered by threat appraisals.

5. Real and painful physical symptoms that are caused by psychological factors, such as our reactions to stress, are called _____ symptoms.

6. A series of three stages—alarm, resistance, and exhaustion—that the body goes through in dealing with stress is referred to as the (a)_____. The alarm stage is our initial reaction to stress and is marked by activation of the (b)_____. The resistance stage is the body's reaction to continued stress and is marked by most physiological responses returning to (c)_____ levels. The exhaustion stage is the body's reaction to long-term, continuous stress and is marked by the actual breakdown or weakening of (d)_____.

7. The body's defense and surveillance network of cells and chemicals that fight off bacteria, viruses, and other foreign matter is called the _____ system.

8. The study of how three factors—the central nervous system, the endocrine system, and psychosocial factors—interact to affect the immune system is called _____.

9. Potentially disturbing, troubling, or disruptive situations—both positive and negative—that we appraise as having considerable impact on our lives are called (a)_____ events. In comparison, those small, irritating, frustrating events that we face in our daily lives are called (b)_____, and those small, pleasurable, daily experiences that make us feel happy are called (c)_____.

10. When our attempts to reach some goal are blocked, the feeling we have is called (a)_____. The feeling of doing poorly at one's job, physically wearing out, and becoming emotionally exhausted due to intense involvement with people is called (b)_____. The problem arising from direct personal experience of an event that involves actual or threatened death or serious injury or from witnessing such an event or hearing of such an event happening to a family member or close friend is called (c)_____.

11. There are three general kinds of conflict. A single situation that has both pleasurable and disagreeable aspects is called (a)_____ conflict; choosing between two options that both have pleasurable consequences is called (b)_____ conflict; choosing between two options that both have disagreeable consequences is called (c)_____ conflict.

12. We can become anxious in at least three different ways. If an emotional response is classically conditioned to a previously neutral stimulus, this procedure results in a (a)_____ response. If we become anxious through watching and do not perform any observable behavior or receive a reinforcer, this is called (b)_____ learning. If we become anxious because of unconscious conflicts between the id and the superego, this is (c)_____ explanation of anxiety.

13. A combination of three personality traits—control, commitment, and challenge—that protect or buffer us from the potentially harmful effects of stressful situations and reduce our chances of developing psychosomatic illness is referred to as (a)_____. The belief that you are basically in control of life's events and that what you do influences the situation is called an (b)_____ locus of control. The belief that chance and luck mostly determine what happens is called an (c)_____ locus of control.

14. If we have family or friends who provide strong social attachments, if we can exchange helpful resources among friends, and if we appraise our relationships as supportive, we would be said to have strong _____.

Answers: 1. stress or stressful; 2. primary appraisal; 3. (a) harm/loss, threat, challenge, (b) stress, (c) negative; 4. (a) fight-flight, (b) hypothalamus, (c) sympathetic; 5. psychosomatic; 6. (a) general adaptation syndrome, (b) fight-flight response, (c) normal, (d) internal organs or the immune system; 7. immune; 8. psychoneuroimmunology; 9. (a) major life, (b) hassles, (c) uplifts; 10. (a) frustration, (b) burnout, (c) posttraumatic stress disorder; 11. (a) approach-avoidance, (b) approach-approach, (c) avoidance-avoidance; 12. (a) conditioned emotional, (b) observational, (c) Freud's; 13. (a) hardiness, (b) internal, (c) external; 14. social support

Appraisal

Why is arguing stressful?

Sooner or later, every couple gets into an argument. In this case, Susan complained that Bill always got home late, but Bill had had a bad day and said that he didn't want to talk about it. Bill's reply angered Susan, who complained more, which made Bill quieter and madder. One reason Bill and Susan's argument quickly became very stressful was that each one made a *primary appraisal* of being threatened, which elicited negative emotions and triggered the fight-flight response, which in turn increased physiological arousal and further intensified their negative feelings. How Bill and Joan deal with their stressful situation depends on what kind of secondary appraisal they make next (Lazarus, 2000).

Secondary appraisal involves deciding to deal with a potential-ly stressful situation by using one or both of two different coping patterns: **problem-focused coping means doing something about the particular problem, while emotion-focused coping means dealing with one's negative feelings.**

Which coping strategy Bill and Susan use to deal with their stressful situation—that is, whether they use problem-focused or emotion-focused coping—will affect how their argument gets resolved and what happens to their levels of stress. We'll discuss how each coping strategy has both short- and long-term disadvantages and advantages.

How can they best end their argument?

Kinds of Coping

How to cope with arguing?

If Bill or Susan tried to decrease the stress by stopping arguing and making up, he or she would be using problem-focused coping.

Problem-focused coping **means we try to decrease stress by solving the problem through seeking information, changing our own behavior, or taking whatever action is needed to resolve the difficulty.**

For example, if Bill agreed to talk about ways of not being late, he would be using problem-focused coping. If Susan agreed to interpret Bill's being late as something he cannot always control and something not to get angry about, she would be using problem-focused coping. The *goal* of problem-focused coping is to reduce stress by solving the problem.

Another coping strategy that Bill and Susan might use to decrease stressful feelings is called emotion-focused coping.

Emotion-focused coping **means that we do things primarily to deal with our emotional distress, such as seeking support and sympathy or avoiding or denying the situation.**

These are the two kinds of coping strategies.

For example, Bill may use emotion-focused coping to get over his anger by going to a sports bar to drink and watch television with the "boys." Susan may use emotion-focused coping to deal with her hurt feelings by calling her friends to talk about what happened and get advice, sympathy, and support.

In the short term, emotion-focused coping may help Bill and Susan deal with their negative emotions, but it doesn't usually solve the basic stressful problem, which means that the problem will likely reoccur and cause more stress (Lazarus, 2000). In contrast, a big advantage of using problem-focused coping is that it's a long-term coping strategy, which can help identify and solve the underlying problem that is causing the stressful and negative emotional feelings. In addition, compared to using emotion-focused coping, using problem-focused coping is positively correlated with having and maintaining good physical and mental health (Penley et al., 2002).

Choosing a Coping Strategy

Which coping strategy to use?

Which coping strategy you choose depends partly on the situation and on your personality (Lazarus, 2000). For example, one *personality factor* that influences whether you use primarily problem-focused or emotion-focused coping is how much *control* you believe you have over the situation. If you appraise a situation (being late) as something under your control, you can use primarily problem-focused coping to solve this problem. On the other hand, if you appraise a situation (dealing with your partner's complaints) as being out of your control, you may first use emotion-focused coping to get over your negative emotions (anger). Once you calm down, you can use problem-focused coping to take some direct action to solve the basic problem (being late), which may involve changing some undesirable behavior (being disorganized). The more frustrating a situation is, the more likely you will need to use both emotion-focused coping and problem-focused coping (Lazarus, 2000).

Sex differences. Compared with men, women tend to use more coping strategies—problem-focused and emotion-focused—to deal with a wide range of stressors. In addition, compared with men, women are more likely to use emotion-focused coping to seek emotional support and advice from others about dealing with stressors. Compared with women, men are more likely to withdraw or avoid problems and not talk about or engage in emotion-focused coping, especially if problems involve relationship or health concerns (Tamres et al., 2002). Thus, women appear to use more coping strategies and are more willing to talk about solving problems, while men are more likely to keep silent or avoid certain problems.

To deal with stressors, emotion-focused coping is a useful short-term solution. Problem-focused coping is a long-term solution that involves changing our behaviors (Lazarus, 2000).

Women and men tend to use different kinds of coping strategies.

F. Research Focus:
Treatment for Panic Disorder

How is panic disorder best treated?

We have discussed stress and coping in general, and now we return to the case of Luisa, the 23-year-old college student with panic disorder. Remember Luisa had unexpected episodes in which she experienced rapid heart rate, a sense of suffocation, trembling of her arms and legs, dizziness, and chest pain. She felt so frightened by these episodes she worried she might die. Luisa's experience of having panic disorder is not uncommon. Many adults suffer from panic disorder, and fortunately there are treatment options available to them. Psychologists conduct research studies to learn which treatment or combination of treatments is most effective for problems such as panic disorder. Next, we'll discover which research method psychologists use to determine the effectiveness of treatments, as well as discuss research findings on the treatment of panic disorder.

1 Research Methods

In Module 2, we discussed several ways psychologists answer questions, including case studies and experiments, each of which has advantages and disadvantages.

A *case study* is an in-depth analysis of the thoughts, feelings, beliefs, or behaviors of an individual, without much ability to control or manipulate situations or variables.

For example, much of the initial information on how the brain functions came from case studies on individuals who had tumors, gunshot wounds, or accidental damage. Similarly, psychologists can learn about how individuals cope with panic disorder by observing and questioning them as they progress through treatment to identify how they cope and adjust to their condition.

When it is possible to control or manipulate situations or variables, the preferred choice of research method is an experiment.

An *experiment* is a method for identifying cause-and-effect relationships by following a set of guidelines that describe how to control, manipulate, and measure variables, while at the same time minimizing the possibility of error and bias.

Experiments permit great control over manipulating treatments and measuring subjects' responses. Also, they allow research data to be collected on a group of people, rather than on only one person, as in a case study, enabling the results to be more meaningful to a large group of people. Fortunately, psychologists can use experiments to compare the effectiveness of various treatments for panic disorder. We will learn about one such experiment, but before we do, let's learn about the most common treatments available for panic disorder.

2 How Can Panic Disorder Be Treated?

In Luisa's case, her treatment began with medication only, and a few months later she received a combination of medication and psychotherapy. Panic disorder is usually treated with drugs—benzodiazepines (tranquilizers, such as diazepam) or antidepressants (Prozac-like drugs, which are serotonin reuptake inhibitors or SSRIs)—and/or psychotherapy. Many more people with panic disorder receive drugs than psychotherapy, mostly because they seek treatment from their primary care physician rather than a psychologist. One popular type of psychotherapy used to treat panic disorder is cognitive-behavioral therapy or CBT (p. 559), which views the physiological arousal symptoms as a learned fear of certain bodily sensations and views the fear of being in closed or crowded situations as a behavioral response to expecting that the bodily sensations will intensify into a full-blown panic attack (Craske & Barlow, 2001). Given the various treatment options available for panic disorder, how do psychologists know for sure which treatment or combination of treatments is most effective?

Luisa received medication and psychotherapy.

3 Which Treatment Is Most Effective?

A comprehensive experiment including more than 300 people diagnosed with panic disorder used random assignment to place each participant in one of five treatment groups: drug only (a benzodiazepine), CBT only, placebo only, CBT plus drug, and CBT plus placebo (Craske & Barlow, 2001). The results showed that people who received drugs or CBT, as well as the combined treatments, showed more improvement than people in the placebo-only group. In regard to short-term treatment effects (measured after three months of treatment), CBT plus drugs was not better than CBT plus placebo, and people receiving combined treatments showed no more improvements than people receiving individual treatments. In regard to long-term treatment effects (six months after treatment had ended), many people in the drug-only group and CBT-plus-drug group relapsed. Thus, people treated with CBT alone or in combination with placebo did better than those who took medication. Though this study used only a benzodiazepine for drug treatment, similar research studies using an SSRI show comparable results. This suggests that CBT has a better long-term treatment benefit for panic disorder than medication.

4 Conclusions

By using an experiment, researchers found that the use of CBT and drugs, either individually or combined, worked about equally well in the short term. However, the use of CBT without drugs led to the best long-term treatment effects. It is well established that over 80% of people with panic disorder who receive CBT will be panic-free at the end of treatment, and they generally continue to show long-term treatment benefits (Craske & Barlow, 2001). Therefore, treatment for panic disorder should include CBT.

Next, we'll look at how some monks develop mind-over-body control.

G. Cultural Diversity: Tibetan Monks

Monks' Amazing Abilities

Tibetan monks claim that by meditating they can voluntarily control their autonomic nervous systems to perform a number of responses, such as warming their hands (graph below). Since many Western researchers believe that voluntary control of the autonomic nervous system is very, very difficult to learn, Western researcher Herbert Benson and his colleagues from Harvard Medical School have traveled to India to scientifically test and verify the monks' amazing claims (H. Benson et al., 1982, 1990).

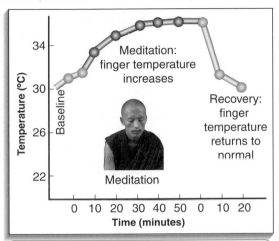

Tibetan monks use meditation to increase hand temperature, a response very difficult to control.

The *autonomic nervous system* has two divisions that are not usually under voluntary control: the sympathetic division causes physiological arousal by increasing heart rate, breathing, blood pressure, and secretion of hormones; the parasympathetic division calms and relaxes the body by decreasing physiological responses and stimulating digestion.

The only two responses of the autonomic nervous system that you can control *voluntarily* and *without practice* are breathing and eye blinking. All other responses of the autonomic nervous system, such as increasing or decreasing blood pressure, temperature, or heart rate and dilating or constricting blood vessels, are controlled automatically and, without considerable practice, are not under voluntary control.

If you want to voluntarily control one of your autonomic nervous system's responses, such as dilating blood vessels to warm your hands, sit quietly in a chair, close your eyes, and think relaxing thoughts. If you can think relaxing thoughts, they will activate your parasympathetic division, which will dilate blood vessels and result in warming your hands. However, the first time you try this, your hands will

probably become colder because by trying so hard to relax, you may be doing the reverse: activating your sympathetic system, which causes arousal and constricts the blood vessels in your fingers.

Westerners find it takes considerable practice to learn to warm our hands because we usually spend little time practicing how to produce relaxing thoughts. In comparison, certain Tibetan monks, through various forms of meditation, claim that they can warm their hands and bodies to such an extent that they can actually dry wet towels that are placed on their shoulders. This was exactly the kind of claim that excited and puzzled Benson's group of researchers.

Voluntary control—hand warming. Benson's group obtained permission from three monks at a monastery in India to measure skin temperature during heat meditation, or g Tum-mo yoga. The monks sat in the lotus position, closed their eyes, and began meditating. As shown in the left graph, within a short period of time, one monk had raised his finger temperature as much as 7–9°C or 9–12°F with no change in heart rate (H. Benson et al., 1982). The monks' success at warming their hands was about five times as great as Westerners, who had managed only 0.25–2°F (Freedman, 1991). However, only a small number of monks can produce this kind of hand and body warming and only after 10–20 years of practice.

Explanation. Westerner Benson gave a very scientific explanation: Monks are able to raise their hand temperature by using thoughts to deeply relax, which in turn activates the parasympathetic division, which dilates tiny blood vessels that lie near the surface of the skin. The Tibetan monks' explanation is much more mysterious: During their meditation, the monks gather winds that are scattered in consciousness and focus these winds into a "central channel" that can generate a great internal body heat (H. Benson et al., 1982).

Studying the mind's abilities. The monks' ability to voluntarily control their physiological responses clearly shows the mind-body interaction as they use their thoughts to influence the difficult-to-control and normally involuntary autonomic nervous system. Recently, Western scientists completed a study in which a group of Buddhist monks extensively trained in meditation and a group of volunteers without meditation experience were instructed to meditate on unconditional compassion while brain wave activity was recorded. The results clearly showed that meditation activated the minds of the trained monks very differently from those of the volunteers. The Buddhist monks had greater activation of fast-moving and powerful *gamma brain waves* (40 cycles per second—much faster than REM brain waves, p. 153). It is interesting that the highest gamma brain wave activity was recorded in the left prefrontal cortex, which is associated with happiness and positive thoughts. These findings suggest Buddhist monks can rid themselves of negative emotions through gamma brain wave activity occurring during meditation (M. Kaufman, 2005; Talan, 2006).

Although we are unlikely to ever achieve the monks' level of mind control, we'll next discuss several more easily learned techniques that can be used to reduce stress, decrease activation of the fight-flight response, and reduce the risk of developing psychosomatic symptoms.

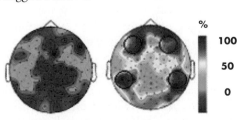

As shown in these head diagrams, volunteers (above left) had low gamma brain wave activity and the Buddhist monks (above right) had high gamma brain wave activity during the meditation task.

H. Stress Management Programs

Definition

How can I reduce my stress levels?

One reason 30% of college freshmen feel continuously overwhelmed is that their classes, exams, papers, personal problems, and part-time jobs combine to take more time and energy than they have (Duenwald, 2003). Being overwhelmed means increased levels of stress and increased risk of developing psychosomatic symptoms. One way to reduce levels of stress is with a stress management program.

*A **stress management program** uses a variety of strategies to reduce anxiety, fear, and stressful experiences by changing three different aspects of our lives: thoughts (appraisals), behaviors, and physiological responses.*

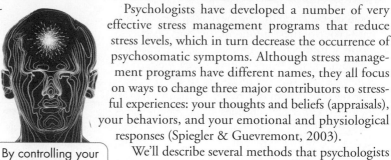

By controlling your thoughts you can control your body.

Psychologists have developed a number of very effective stress management programs that reduce stress levels, which in turn decrease the occurrence of psychosomatic symptoms. Although stress management programs have different names, they all focus on ways to change three major contributors to stressful experiences: your thoughts and beliefs (appraisals), your behaviors, and your emotional and physiological responses (Spiegler & Guevremont, 2003).

We'll describe several methods that psychologists have developed for effectively changing each of these three factors, beginning with changing your thoughts.

Changing Thoughts

Can you learn to think more positively?

Many daily hassles—dealing with long lines, slow traffic, rude people, loud neighbors, and sloppy roommates—can be made more or less stressful depending on how you appraise these situations. Since your appraisal of a situation as threatening or challenging is related to increasing or decreasing your stress levels, it follows that an effective way to decrease stressful experiences is to work at changing how you initially appraise a situation (Lazarus, 2000). We'll explain two effective strategies for changing your appraisals: thinking of potentially stressful situations as challenging rather than threatening, and changing negative self-statements into positive ones.

Use Challenge Appraisals

The reason you want to think or appraise potentially stressful situations as challenging rather than threatening is that threat appraisals elicit negative emotions (fear, anxiety, depression), which in turn raise stress levels, while challenge appraisals elicit positive emotions, which lower stress levels. For example, students who emphasize threat appraisals of exams, such as thinking they will not have time to study or expecting to do poorly, are more likely to experience negative emotions such as anxiety and fear (Shannon, 1994). In turn, anxiety and fear trigger the fight-flight response, which raises the level of stress and often leads to emotion-focused coping, such as complaining, seeking sympathy, or avoiding studying. However, emotion-focused coping does not usually motivate actions, such as studying, that are needed to prepare students for exams.

I see life as one big challenge!

In comparison, students who emphasize challenge appraisals of exams, such as wanting to do their best or to prove themselves, are more likely to experience positive emotions, such as excitement or eagerness, which decrease levels of stress. In turn, challenge appraisals are more likely to result in problem-focused coping, which means taking direct action to deal with the situation itself, such as developing a study program.

Thus, a good way to deal with potentially stressful situations is to focus on challenging rather than threatening appraisals (N. Skinner & Brewer, 2002).

Substitute Positive Self-Statements

Another way to prevent a situation, such as taking an exam, from becoming more stressful is to work at removing negative self-statements by substituting positive ones. Specifically, on one side of a sheet of paper write your negative self-statements; then next to them on the other side write the positive ones that you can substitute. The example below shows negative self-statements changed into positive ones.

Negative self-statements	Positive self-statements
"I know I'll do badly."	*"I know I can do OK."*
"I always get so anxious."	*"I'm going to stay calm."*
"I'm not smart enough."	*"I've got plenty of ability."*
"I'm never going to learn it."	*"I can learn the material."*

The reason you want to avoid making negative self-statements is that they elicit negative emotions (fear, anger, anxiety), which increase stress levels. By substituting positive self-statements, which elicit positive emotions, you can decrease stress levels. For example, each time you begin to think of a negative self-statement, stop yourself and substitute a positive one. For regularly occurring stressors, such as taking exams, waiting in lines, fighting with traffic, and dealing with rude people, it is best to have prepared a different list of self-statements to go with each different situation. Researchers found that a program of substituting positive self-statements proved very effective in helping people change their thought patterns and reduce their stress levels (Spiegler & Guevremont, 2003).

I believe I can. I believe I can. I believe I can.

Changing Behaviors

How do you get ready for an exam?

There are generally two different ways that students get ready for exams. Some students get ready for an exam by complaining about how much work there is, making excuses about not studying, or blaming the instructor for too much material. These behaviors involve *emotion-focused coping,* which in the short term serves to reduce stress by reducing negative emotional feelings. However, in the long run, students may need to change these behaviors and engage in *problem-focused coping,* which means developing a study plan (N. Skinner & Brewer, 2002).

Because some students are not aware of whether they use emotion-focused or problem-focused coping, stress management programs include an observation period of 1 to 2 weeks. During this time, a student observes or monitors his or her own behaviors to identify emotion-focused versus problem-focused behaviors. If a student is using primarily *emotion-focused coping* (making excuses, procrastinating, or blaming others), he or she will likely do poorly on exams. Instead, a student needs to start a program of *problem-focused coping* (making a study program, rewriting class notes) by using some of the self-reward and behavior modification techniques that we discussed in Module 10 (Spiegler & Guevremont, 2003). Thus, one way to reduce stress is to change your behaviors—that is, to emphasize problem-focused over emotion-focused activities.

> I'd rather complain than change.

Learning to Relax

How do you learn to relax?

Learning to relax at will is important for developing a stress management program because being able to relax is one way to turn off the fight-flight response and decrease your body's heightened arousal. But unless you practice one of the following methods, you will find it very difficult to relax at will. In fact, when someone says "Just relax," you usually get tenser because you don't know how to relax. We'll describe three techniques that have proved almost equally effective at getting you to relax, and each involves using your mind (brain) to control your body's responses (S. L. Shapiro et al., 2000).

Biofeedback

You could learn a relaxing response, such as decreasing muscle tension, by having small sensors placed on your forehead. The sensors are attached to a machine that records, amplifies, and displays changes in muscle tension. Each time you think thoughts or images that increase tension, you hear a high tone; if you decrease tension, you hear a low tone. This procedure is called biofeedback (Spiegler & Guevremont, 2003).

Biofeedback **refers to voluntarily learning to control physiological responses, such as muscle activity, blood pressure, or temperature, by recording and displaying these responses.**

After 12–30 biofeedback training sessions (about 20 minutes per session), most individuals have some success in turning on relaxing responses, especially after being stressed.

You could also learn to relax by using progressive relaxation.

> Choose any of these methods to learn to relax.

Progressive Relaxation

Progressive relaxation **involves practicing tensing and relaxing the major muscle groups of the body until you are able to relax any groups of muscles at will.**

With progressive relaxation, you usually begin by first tensing and relaxing your toes and then continuing up the body, tensing and relaxing the muscles of your calves, thighs, pelvis, stomach, shoulders, arms, hands, neck, face, and forehead. After several weeks of daily practice, about 20 minutes per session, you would be able to use this exercise to relax your body at will, especially immediately after being stressed.

You could also learn to relax by using a form of meditation.

Meditation

There are various kinds of meditation exercises. We'll describe three of the more popular ones.

Transcendental meditation **(TM) and yoga involve assuming a comfortable position, closing your eyes, and repeating a sound or concentrating on your breathing so that you clear your head of all thoughts, worrisome and otherwise.**

TM and yoga are Eastern forms of meditation. A Western and equally effective form is the relaxation response (H. Benson, 1975).

The *relaxation response* **involves sitting or lying in a comfortable position while silently repeating a sound over and over to rid oneself of anxious thoughts.**

Because meditation involves removing all worrisome or stressful thoughts and replacing them with peaceful ones, it can be a very effective method for relaxing and reducing stress. However, learning to use meditation to relax at will usually requires practicing about 20 minutes a day for many weeks (J. Stein, 2003).

Stopping Stress Responses

The next time some stressor triggers the fight-flight response, you can use some form of relaxation to stop or turn down the heightened arousal caused by the fight-flight response and thus reduce your stressful or negative feelings before they result in psychosomatic symptoms, such as a headache or stomach distress. Researchers report that most relaxation techniques, whether biofeedback, progressive relaxation, or various forms of meditation (Zen, yoga, TM), are about equally effective in producing relaxation and reducing stress (S. L. Shapiro et al., 2000). For example, different relaxation techniques were about equally effective in reducing anxiety and decreasing a variety of psychosomatic complaints, such as headaches, high blood pressure, insomnia, stomach pain, and intestinal problems (irritable bowel syndrome) (Spiegler & Guevremont, 2003). More important than which relaxation technique you choose is daily practice so that you can learn to relax at will. Being able to relax at will is vital to developing an effective stress management program (J. Stein, 2003; Walton et al., 2002).

Summary Test

A. Appraisal

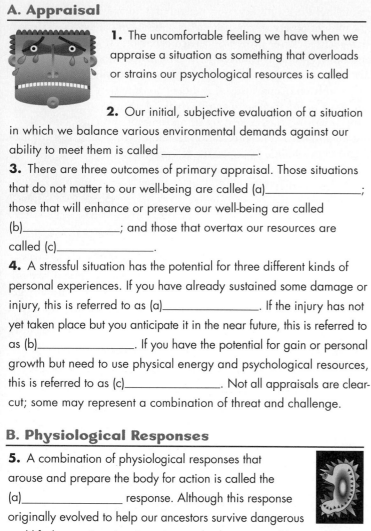

1. The uncomfortable feeling we have when we appraise a situation as something that overloads or strains our psychological resources is called _____.

2. Our initial, subjective evaluation of a situation in which we balance various environmental demands against our ability to meet them is called _____.

3. There are three outcomes of primary appraisal. Those situations that do not matter to our well-being are called (a)_____; those that will enhance or preserve our well-being are called (b)_____; and those that overtax our resources are called (c)_____.

4. A stressful situation has the potential for three different kinds of personal experiences. If you have already sustained some damage or injury, this is referred to as (a)_____. If the injury has not yet taken place but you anticipate it in the near future, this is referred to as (b)_____. If you have the potential for gain or personal growth but need to use physical energy and psychological resources, this is referred to as (c)_____. Not all appraisals are clear-cut; some may represent a combination of threat and challenge.

B. Physiological Responses

5. A combination of physiological responses that arouse and prepare the body for action is called the (a)_____ response. Although this response originally evolved to help our ancestors survive dangerous and life-threatening situations, it can also be triggered by psychological stimuli, such as our primary (b)_____ of a situation as harm/loss, threatening, or challenging.

6. Threat appraisals activate two brain areas, called the (a)_____ and _____, which trigger two responses simultaneously. The hypothalamus causes the (b)_____ gland to release ACTH, which acts on the adrenal cortex to secrete hormones that regulate levels of minerals and glucose in the body. It also triggers the (c)_____ division of the autonomic nervous system, which causes physiological arousal.

7. Our psychological reactions to stressful situations can result in real, painful, physical symptoms called (a)_____ symptoms. According to Selye, we develop psychosomatic symptoms because the body's response to stress involves going through three stages that he called the (b)_____ syndrome. The first is called the (c)_____ stage, which is our initial reaction to stress and is marked by physiological arousal. The second is called the (d)_____ stage, in which most physiological responses return to normal levels as the body uses up great stores of energy. The third is called the (e)_____ stage, which is marked by the actual breakdown in body organs or weakening of the infection-fighting immune system.

8. The body's network of cells and chemicals that automatically fight off bacteria, viruses, and other foreign matter is known as the (a)_____. The study of the relationship among the central nervous system, the endocrine system, and psychosocial factors is called (b)_____. The interaction among these factors affects the immune system and, in turn, makes the body more or less susceptible to disease and infection.

C. Stressful Experiences

9. Situations that are potentially disturbing or disruptive and that we appraise as having an impact on our lives are called (a)_____ events. Small, irritating daily events are called (b)_____, and small, pleasant daily experiences are called (c)_____. How we cope with hassles predicts our daily mood and the occurrence of psychosomatic symptoms.

10. The feeling that results when our attempts to reach some goal are blocked is called (a)_____. Feelings of wearing out or becoming exhausted because of too many demands on our time and energy are referred to as (b)_____. A direct personal experience of actual or threatened death or serious injury or witnessing such an event could result in terrible stress symptoms called (c)_____.

11. When we must decide between two or more incompatible choices, we are in (a)_____, which can include at least three possibilities. If we must choose between two options with pleasurable consequences, we experience (b)_____ conflict. If we must choose between two options that both have disagreeable consequences, we are in (c)_____ conflict. If a single situation has both pleasurable and disagreeable aspects, we are in (d)_____ conflict.

12. An unpleasant state in which we have feelings of uneasiness and apprehension as well as increased physiological arousal is called (a)_____. This feeling has at least three causes. One is classical conditioning of an emotional response to a previously neutral stimulus; the result is called a (b)_____ response. A second cause is a form of learning that develops through watching and does not require any observable behavior or reinforcer; this is called (c)_____ learning. According to Freud, anxiety arises when the id and superego disagree, leading to an (d)_____ conflict, which results in the ego producing a feeling of anxiety.

D. Personality & Social Factors

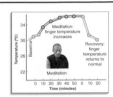

13. Three personality traits that decrease the potentially harmful effects of stressful situations are control, commitment, and challenge, which together are called _____.

14. If you believe that what you do influences what happens, you are said to have an (a)_____ of control. In contrast, if you believe that chance and luck mostly determine what happens and that you do not have much influence, you are said to have an (b)_____ of control. People with an external locus of control experience more negative emotions, higher levels of stress, and more psychosomatic symptoms than do those whose locus of control is internal.

15. Currently, the major components of Type A behavior are (a)_____ and _____. Individuals with these traits are many times more likely to have a (b)_____. Also, individuals who always show or always suppress anger and hostility have greater increases in (c)_____, which can have damaging effects one's heart and health.

16. One factor that buffers us from stressful experiences is having a group or network of family or friends who provide strong support; this is called _____.

E. Kinds of Coping

17. After we make a primary appraisal, we then must decide what action to take, which is called a (a)_____ appraisal. This involves two different kinds of coping. If we seek information about what needs to be done, change our own behavior, or take whatever action will solve the problem, we use (b)_____ coping. If we use our energies to deal with emotional distress caused by a harm or threat appraisal, we are using (c)_____ coping. Compared to emotion-focused coping, problem-focused coping is better at reducing long-term effects of stress because it solves the problem.

F. Research Focus: Treatment for Panic Disorder

18. Psychologists use a number of different research methods. One method is an in-depth analysis of the thoughts, feelings, beliefs, or behaviors of individuals; this is called the (a)_____. Another method identifies cause-and-effect relationships by following a set of guidelines that describe how to control and manipulate variables; this is called the (b)_____ method. Panic disorder is usually treated with (c)_____. By using an experiment, researchers found the use of cognitive-behavior therapy and drugs, either individually or combined,

worked equally well in terms of (d)_____ treatment effects. Research findings showed that the most effective long-term treatment for panic disorder is (e)_____.

G. Cultural Diversity: Tibetan Monks

19. Many of our physiological responses involved in relaxation (heart rate, blood pressure, temperature, and secretion of hormones) are not under voluntary control because they are regulated by the (a)_____ system. Researchers discovered that some monks have learned a method to voluntarily control temperature, which involves relaxation. This demonstrates that the (b)_____ can be used to control the (c)_____ physiological responses.

H. Application: Stress Management Programs

20. A program for reducing anxiety, fear, and stressful experiences by using a variety of strategies to change three different aspects of our lives— thoughts, behaviors, and physiological responses— is called a _____.

21. One component of a stress management program is learning to relax at will, which can be accomplished with three different methods. Recording and amplifying physiological signals from the body and displaying these signals so that we can learn to increase or decrease them is known as (a)_____. An exercise of tensing and relaxing the major muscle groups is called (b)_____. Meditation can take many forms. Sitting or lying in a comfortable position while repeating a meaningless sound over and over to rid oneself of anxious thoughts is called (c)_____ or the _____ response. Researchers have found that all three techniques are about equally effective in helping us to relax.

Answers: *1. stress; 2. primary appraisal; 3. (a) irrelevant, (b) positive, (c) stressful; 4. (a) harm/loss, (b) threat, (c) challenge; 5. (a) fight-flight, (b) appraisal; 6. (a) amygdala, hypothalamus, (b) pituitary, (c) sympathetic; 7. (a) psychosomatic, (b) general adaptation, (c) alarm, (d) resistance, (e) exhaustion; 8. (a) immune system, (b) psychoneuroimmunology; 9. (a) major life, (b) hassles, (c) uplifts; 10. (a) frustration, (b) burnout, (c) posttraumatic stress disorder; 11. (a) conflict, (b) approach-approach, (c) avoidance-avoidance, (d) approach-avoidance; 12. (a) anxiety, (b) conditioned emotional, (c) observational, (d) unconscious; 13. hardiness; 14. (a) internal locus, (b) external locus; 15. (a) hostility, anger, (b) heart attack, premature heart disease, (c) physiological arousal; 16. social support; 17. (a) secondary, (b) problem-focused, (c) emotion-focused; 18. (a) case study, (b) experimental or scientific, (c) drugs and/or psychotherapy, (d) short-term, (e) cognitive-behavior therapy; 19. (a) autonomic nervous or parasympathetic, (b) mind, (c) body's; 20. stress management program; 21. (a) biofeedback, (b) progressive relaxation, (c) transcendental meditation (TM), relaxation*

Critical Thinking

Coping with Cancer

Questions

1. After Lance noticed his right testicle was swollen, which Freudian defense mechanism does he use to deal with this potentially damaging news, and what is his primary appraisal of the situation?

2. Which kinds of personality traits would help Lance cope with the stress of knowing that he has cancer?

3. Why is it good news that his family and friends kept calling and visiting?

4. Which type of coping is Lance using by educating himself about cancer?

At age 25, world-renowned cyclist, Lance Armstrong, was training rigorously and cycling better than ever. His training schedule resulted in his legs, feet, back, neck, and just about every other body part being in pain. So, he didn't pay much attention when he noticed his right testicle was slightly swollen. Soon, he began to feel much more tired than usual. Then he began having vision trouble, and one morning he coughed up blood. He could no longer pretend something wasn't wrong.

Doctors diagnosed Lance with testicular cancer that had spread to his abdomen, lungs, and brain. When he first heard his doctor say "You have cancer," his fear became very real. Lance had third-degree testicular cancer (the most serious kind) and he was given less than a 40% chance of surviving. He would have surgery to remove his right testicle and brain lesions, followed by months of chemotherapy.

After leaving the doctor's office, Lance shared his diagnosis with family and friends. He received an overwhelming amount of support as his friends and family routinely called and visited. Lance also began learning as much as he could about cancer, what it is and how it is treated. He even began seeking second, third, and fourth medical opinions. Learning more about cancer provided him with some reassurance and comfort.

Lance felt so anxious about his diagnosis and treatment that he blocked out memory of what he thought and felt the morning of his risky brain surgery. In the midst of chemotherapy, he kept cycling, wanting to believe that if he could continue to cycle, then somehow he wouldn't be sick. Eventually, Lance became so weak from chemotherapy he could barely walk. Then, instead of feeling hopeless, he chose to believe in his doctors and in his treatment. He began to envision himself overcoming cancer.

Today, Lance Armstrong is a cancer survivor. He now seizes each day as an opportunity to enjoy his life. Since his recovery, he won the Tour de France, the 2,290-mile road race that's considered the single most grueling sporting event in the world, a record seven consecutive times. When asked about his trying experience with cancer, he said, "The truth is that cancer was the best thing that ever happened to me. I don't know why I got the illness, but it did wonders for me, and I wouldn't want to walk away from it. Why would I want to change, even for a day, the most important and shaping event in my life?" (p. 4). (Adapted from Armstrong, 2001)

5. Which Freudian defense mechanism(s) is Lance using during treatment?

6. How does Lance cope with cancer both near the end of his treatment and now that he has survived cancer?

Suggested Answers

1. Lance initially dismissed the problem, which is using the Freudian defense mechanism of denial to cope with the problem. However, after he had vision problems and coughed up blood, his primary appraisal changed to one of threat (Will the swollen testicle be cancerous?), which increased his level of stress.

2. Lance will be better able to cope with the news of having testicular cancer if he has the personality traits of hardiness (control, commitment, challenge), if he has an internal rather than an external locus of control, and if he has a more optimistic than pessimistic attitude toward life.

3. Lance is using emotion-focused coping to deal with his fear and anxiety by seeking support from his family and friends. Social support is a powerful way to reduce levels of stress as well as help prepare and be a buffer for future stressful situations.

4. Problem-focused coping is a long-term strategy to deal with the stressful problem itself, in this case learning more about cancer and his treatment options.

5. By blocking out memory of what he thought and felt before undergoing brain surgery, Lance was using the Freudian defense mechanism of repression to cope with his problem. He was using the Freudian defense mechanism of rationalization by convincing himself that by continuing to cycle, he would not have cancer.

6. Lance began to have an optimistic attitude about having cancer and his chances of overcoming it. Being optimistic can help lower stress levels and improve mood.

Links to Learning

Learning Activities

- **POWERSTUDY FOR INTRODUCTION TO PSYCHOLOGY 4.0**  by Tom Doyle and Rod Plotnik

  SuperModule: Check out "Health, Stress & Coping" on **PowerStudy.** It includes complete paragraph-by-paragraph explanations of all content using fully-narrated animations and graphics. An onscreen toolbar allows immediate access to text, text outline, and module glossary with notetaking and printing capabilities. This module also includes:

  - Videos—Imbedded videos explore the effects of support groups for women with breast cancer, the links between stress and your immune system, and between emotion and physical health.
  - A test of your knowledge using an interactive version of the Summary Test on pages 504 and 505. Also access related quizzing—true/false, multiple choice, and matching.
  - An interactive version of the Critical Thinking exercise "Coping with Cancer" on page 506.
  - Key terms, a chapter outline including chapter abstract, and a special extended list of hotlinked websites that correlate to this module.

- **CengageNOW**
  academic.cengage.com/login

  Need help studying? This site is your one-stop study shop. Take a Pre-Test and CengageNOW will generate a Personalized Study Plan based on your test results. The Study Plan will identify the topics you need to review and direct you to online resources to help you master those topics. You can then take a Post-Test to determine the concepts you have mastered and what you still need to work on.

- **INTRODUCTION TO PSYCHOLOGY BOOK COMPANION WEBSITE**
  academic.cengage.com/psychology/plotnik

  Visit your book companion website where you will find more resources to help you study. At this site, you will find Learning Objectives, Internet Exercises, quizzing, flash cards, and a pronunciation glossary.

- **STUDY GUIDE and WEBTUTOR**

  Check the corresponding module in your Study Guide for effective student tips and help learning the material presented. Also go to **academic.cengage.com/webtutor** for an interactive version of the Study Guide features.

Study Questions

*A. **Appraisal**—Sue says that some situations always cause her stress, but John says it's how she thinks about them. Who's right? (**Suggested answer p. 633**)

B. **Physiological Responses**—Why are people so very reluctant to admit that some painful physical symptoms can be caused by their thoughts?

C. **Stressful Experiences**—Why does Sally always feel a little anxious when she goes to parties where she doesn't know anyone?

D. **Personality & Social Factors**—Greg did great in high school, so why is he doing poorly in his first year of college, away from home?

E. **Kinds of Coping**—How would you cope with finding out that, because of major differences, you must break off your current relationship?

F. **Research Focus: Treatment for Panic Disorders**—Why do you think most people with panic disorder respond better to CBT than to medication in the long term?

G. **Cultural Diversity: Tibetan Monks**—Why is it so much easier for most of us to use our minds to trigger the fight-flight response than to calm or relax our bodies?

*H. **Application: Stress Management Programs**—Why is it better to cope with stress by changing three things—thoughts, behaviors, and physiological responses—rather than just one? (**Suggested answer p. 634**)

*These questions are answered in Appendix B.

MODULE 22
Assessment & Anxiety Disorders

 PowerStudy 4.0™ Complete Module

Introduction

Mental Disorder

How did a serial killer go unnoticed?

He was a loving husband, devoted father, respected church elder, and straight-laced county official. He also worked for a home security company, where he would help individuals protect themselves from dangerous people. Until the day he was caught, he blended into the Wichita community as an average next-door neighbor. But over a period of 17 years, Dennis Rader planned and carried out the cruel murders of 10 people. He became known as the "BTK killer," which stands for Bind, Torture, and Kill, describing the methods he used with his victims.

In a very real sense, Rader led two different lives. In public, Rader seemed like a quiet, law-abiding guy who helped to protect the safety of others. However, in private, Rader would break into people's homes, hide, and then sneak up on his victims. He would proceed to tie them up, callously strangle them, and eventually murder them.

Dennis Rader, who murdered 10 people, fits the pattern of serial killers.

Although no two serial killers are alike, Rader fits the typical pattern. Serial killers usually look like ordinary people, often with families and good jobs. Many serial killers have experienced a traumatic childhood event and have serious personality defects, such as low self-esteem and a lifelong sense of loneliness. They are obsessed with control, manipulation, and dominance and often con their victims into agreeing to their requests. Most serial killers enjoy not the actual killing, but the ruthless torturing of their victims. This explains why serial killers feel special when their victims suffer and plead for help, and why Rader became sexually aroused as he strangled each of his victims (Hickey, 2006; Mann, 2005).

When Rader's trial began, his defense attorneys had to decide if they wanted to claim he was legally insane when he committed the murders. You are probably thinking that a person who cold-heartedly plans and carries out 10 violent murders must certainly be insane, but let's consider what it means to be insane.

Insanity, according to its legal definition, means not knowing the difference between right and wrong.

As inhumane as Rader's behaviors may seem, his defense did not claim he was insane. Based on Rader's testimony, it was clear he knew all along that his actions were wrong and conducted for his own selfish interests. In 2005, thirty-one years after the first BTK attacks, Rader was charged with 10 counts of first-degree murder for which he must serve 10 life sentences (Davey, 2005; O'Driscoll, 2005; Wilgoren, 2005).

When mental health professionals examine Rader's behaviors, they are trying to identify his particular mental disorder.

A *mental disorder* is generally defined as a prolonged or recurring problem that seriously interferes with an individual's ability to live a satisfying personal life and function adequately in society.

Deciding whether a person has a mental disorder can be difficult because so many factors are involved in defining what is abnormal. As you'll learn in this module, someone's behavior may be described as abnormal but the person may or may not have a mental disorder.

Phobia

What's so scary about flying?

There is no doubt that Dennis Rader's murder and mutilation of 10 individuals indicate extremely abnormal behavior and a severe mental disorder (Hickey, 2005). In other cases, mental disorders may involve a relatively common behavior or event that, through some learning, observation, or other process, has the power to elicit tremendous anxiety and becomes a phobia (Rowa et al., 2006).

A *phobia (FOE-bee-ah)* is an anxiety disorder characterized by an intense, excessive, and irrational fear that is out of all proportion to the danger elicited by the object or situation.

Kate Premo's phobia of flying began in her childhood, when she experienced a turbulent flight that left her scared and anxious. Later, as a young adult, her fear of flying was worsened by memories of the 1988 terrorist bombing of Pan Am flight 103, which killed several of her fellow students from Syracuse University. After that incident, her phobia of flying kept her from visiting friends and family. She would try to fly and even make reservations but always cancel them at the last minute.

Kate Premo is trying to overcome her phobia of flying.

An estimated 25 million Americans have a similar irrational and intense fear of flying, which is called *aviophobia;* they refuse to get on a plane. Another 30 million Americans report moderate to high degrees of anxiety when they fly (Wilhelm & Roth, 1997). To treat her phobia, Kate Premo (photo above) took part in a weekend seminar that included actually flying in a plane. We'll tell you about Kate's phobia and treatment later in this module.

These two examples of Dennis Rader and Kate Premo raise a number of questions about mental disorders: How do they develop? How are they diagnosed? How are they treated? We'll answer these three questions as we discuss mental disorders.

What's Coming

In this module, we'll discuss three approaches to understanding mental disorders. We'll explain how mental disorders are assessed and diagnosed and go into some specific examples of mental disorders, such as generalized anxiety, phobias, obsessive-compulsive behaviors, and somatoform disorders. Finally, we'll discuss how common phobias, such as fear of flying, are treated.

We'll begin with the different factors that are involved in defining, explaining, and treating mental disorders, such as that of Dennis Rader.

509

A. Factors in Mental Disorders

Causes of Abnormal Behavior

Explanations for the causes of mental disorders have changed dramatically through the centuries. In the Middle Ages, mental disorders were thought to be the result of demons or devils who inhabited individuals and made them do strange and horrible things. In the 1600s, mental disorders were thought to involve witches, who were believed to speak to the devil. This was the case in Salem, Massachusetts, in 1692, where, in a short span of four months, 14 women and 5 men were hanged as witches on the testimony of young girls and God-fearing adults (L. Shapiro, 1992).

In the 1960s, one major cause of mental disorders was thought to be environmental factors, such as stressful events. In the 1990s came advances in studying genetic factors as well as new methods to study the structures and functions of living brains (p. 70). As a result, current researchers and clinicians believe that mental disorders, such as that of Dennis Rader, result from a number of factors, which include biological, cognitive-emotional-behavioral, and environmental influences (Hersen & Thomas, 2006).

Biological Factors

Biological influences include genetic or inherited factors and various neurological factors that influence how the brain functions.

Genetic factors. As an infant, Joan would cry, show great fear, and try to avoid new or novel objects or situations. Because Joan showed great fear as an infant, researchers concluded that her fearfulness was primarily due to genetic factors (Kagan, 2003a).

Genetic factors that contribute to the development of mental disorders are unlearned or inherited tendencies that influence how a person thinks, behaves, and feels.

Genetic factors operate by affecting the developing brain and/or the neurotransmitters that the brain uses for communication. Researchers estimate that genetic factors contribute from 30 to 60% to the development of mental disorders, such as depression, schizophrenia, and anxiety disorders (Rutter & Silberg, 2002).

Neurological factors. Joan, who had started life as a fearful infant, had developed a serious mental disorder called a social phobia (p. 518) by the time she was 20. Researchers believed that one reason she developed a social phobia was that her brain's emotional detector, called the amygdala (p. 362), was overactive and too often identified stimuli as threatening when they were only new or novel. In fact, when researchers measured the activity (fMRI) of Joan's amygdala, they found that her amygdala overreacted when she looked at new or novel faces, something that did not happen in the amygdalas of individuals who did not have social phobias (C. E. Schwartz et al., 2003). In a related study, individuals who had developed social phobias, like Joan, showed far more amygdala activity when looking at angry, fearful, or disgusted faces than did individuals without social phobias (Luan et al., 2006). The studies illustrate neurological factors, such as having an overactive brain structure that contributes to the development of a mental disorder by causing a person to see the world in a biased or distorted way and to see threats when none really exist.

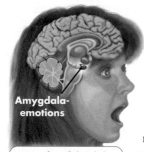

Amygdala-emotions

Very fearful adults had more activity in the amygdala.

Although these studies show that biological factors—genetic and neurological—can contribute to the development of mental disorders, not everyone with an overactive amygdala develops a mental disorder. This means that other factors are also involved in the development of mental disorders.

Cognitive-Emotional-Behavioral & Environmental Factors

Because biological factors themselves do not always explain why people develop mental disorders, psychologists point to various cognitive-emotional-behavioral factors that interact with and contribute to developing mental disorders.

Cognitive-emotional-behavioral and environmental factors that contribute to the development of mental disorders include deficits in cognitive processes, such as having unusual thoughts and beliefs; deficits in processing emotional stimuli, such as under- or overreacting to emotional situations; behavioral problems, such as lacking social skills; and environmental challenges, such as dealing with stressful situations.

Unusual thoughts, emotions, behaviors, or events contribute to developing mental disorders.

For example, Dennis Rader was a shy and polite child who preferred to spend time alone. As a boy, he recalls watching his grandparents strangle chickens at their farm, and by the time he reached high school, he was strangling cats and dogs. Rader's hobby during childhood was looking at pictures of women in bondage. By his teens, he fantasized about tying up, controlling, and torturing women. He was becoming increasingly bothered by murderous impulses but did not know how to tell anyone about it (Ortiz, 2005; Singular, 2006). Rader's many maladaptive thoughts, emotions, and behaviors interacted with his biological factors and resulted in his serious mental disorder.

Environmental factors. In some cases, traumatic events, such as being in a war, having a serious car accident, watching some horrible event (a dog attacking and killing a child), or being brutally mugged, assaulted, or raped, can result in a long-lasting emotional disorder called posttraumatic stress disorder, or PTSD. As we discussed earlier (p. 491), a person with PTSD may relive the terrible event through memories and nightmares and have serious emotional problems that often require professional help (Durand & Barlow, 2006). Experiencing PTSD is an example of how traumatic environmental factors can contribute to developing a serious mental disorder.

Many factors. The answer to why Joan developed a social phobia, or Dennis Rader became a serial killer, or a family member, friend, or relative developed a mental disorder involves a number of factors—genetic, neurological, cognitive-emotional-behavioral, and environmental. As several or more of these factors interact, the result in some cases can be the development of one of the mental disorders that we'll discuss in this and the next module.

Is Mr. Thompson abnormal?

In some cases, such as Dennis Rader's murder and mutilation of 10 individuals, we have no doubt that he demonstrated an extremely abnormal behavior pattern. In other cases, such as Kate Premo's phobia of flying, we would probably say that most of her life appears to be normal except for a small piece—fear of flying in airplanes—that is abnormal. In still other cases, such as that of 54-year-old Richard Thompson (right photo), it is less clear what is abnormal behavior.

Is it abnormal to live in a storm drain if you don't bother anyone?

The City of San Diego evicted Thompson and all his belongings from his home. His belongings included shirts, pants, dozens of shoes, several Bibles, a cooler, a tool chest, lawn chairs, a barbecue grill, tin plates, bird cages, two pet rats, and his self-fashioned bed. For the previous nine months, Thompson had lived happily and without any problems in a downtown storm drain (sewer). Because the city does not allow people to live in storm drains, however, Thompson was evicted from his underground storm-drain home and forbidden to return. Although Thompson later lived in several care centers and mental hospitals, he much preferred the privacy and comfort of the sewer (Grimaldi, 1986).

There are three different ways to decide whether Richard Thompson's behavior—living in the sewer—was abnormal.

Statistical Frequency

Although Thompson caused no problems to others except to violate a city law against living in a storm drain, his preferred living style could be considered abnormal according to statistical frequency.

According to statistical frequency, living in a monastery is abnormal.

The *statistical frequency approach* says that a behavior may be considered abnormal if it occurs rarely or infrequently in relation to the behaviors of the general population.

By this definition, Thompson's living in a storm drain would be considered very abnormal since, out of over 300 million people in the United States, only a very few prefer his kind of home. This illustrates that even though statistical frequency is a relatively precise measure, it is not a very useful measure of abnormality. By this criterion, getting a Ph.D., being president, living in a monastery, and selling a million records are abnormal, although some of these behaviors would be considered very desirable by most people. In fact, *Guinness World Records* (2007) lists thousands of people who have performed some statistically abnormal behaviors and are very proud of them. We would not consider any of these individuals to necessarily have mental disorders.

As all these examples demonstrate, the statistical frequency definition of abnormality has very limited usefulness.

Deviation from Social Norms

Thompson's behavior—preferring to live in a sewer—could also be considered abnormal based on social norms.

The *social norms approach* says that a behavior is considered abnormal if it deviates greatly from accepted social standards, values, or norms.

Thompson's decision to live by himself in a storm drain greatly deviates from society's norms about where people should live. However, a definition of abnormality based solely on deviations from social norms runs into problems when social norms change with time. For example, 25 years ago, very few males wore earrings, while today many males consider earrings very fashionable. Similarly, 40 years ago, a woman who

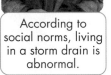

According to social norms, living in a storm drain is abnormal.

preferred to be very thin was considered to be ill and in need of medical help. Today, our society pressures women to be thin like the fashion models in the media.

Thus, defining abnormality on the basis of social norms can be risky, as social norms may, and do, change over time. The definition of abnormality most used by mental health professionals is the next one.

Maladaptive Behavior

The major problem with the first two definitions of abnormal behavior—statistical frequency and deviation from social norms—is that they don't say if a particular behavior is psychologically damaging or maladaptive.

The *maladaptive behavior approach* defines a behavior as psychologically damaging or abnormal if it interferes with the individual's ability to function in his or her personal life or in society.

For example, being terrified of flying, hearing voices that dictate dangerous acts, feeling compelled to wash one's hands for hours on end, starving oneself to the point of death (anorexia nervosa), and Dennis Rader's strangling of animals and humans and committing serial murders would all be considered maladaptive and, in that sense, abnormal.

However, Thompson's seemingly successful adaptation to living in a sewer may not be maladaptive for him and certainly has no adverse consequences to society.

Most useful. Of the three definitions discussed here, mental health professionals find the most useful definition of abnormal behaviors is the one based on the maladaptive definition—that is, whether a particular behavior or behavior

According to the maladaptive definition, some behavior is abnormal if it interferes with a person's ability to function.

ior pattern interferes with a person's ability to function normally (Durand & Barlow, 2006).

However, you'll see that deciding if behavior is truly maladaptive is not always so easy.

B. Assessing Mental Disorders

How do you find out what's wrong?

In some cases, it's relatively easy to identify what's wrong with a person. For example, it's clear that Dennis Rader was a serial killer and that Kate Premo has an intense and irrational fear of flying. But in other cases, it's more difficult to identify exactly what the person's motivation and mental problem are. Take the tragic case of Susan Smith.

Susan Smith appeared on the "Today" show, crying for the return of her two little boys (right photo), Michael, 3 years old, and Alex, 14 months old, who, she said, had been kidnapped. She begged the kidnapper to feed them, care for them, and please, please, return them. And then, nine days later, after a rigorous investigation turned up doubts about the kidnapping story, the police questioned Susan again. Not only did she change her story, but she made the teary confession that she had killed her two children. She said that she had parked her car by the edge of the lake, strapped her

Susan first said her sons were kidnapped but later confessed that she had drowned them.

two children into their car seats, shut the windows and doors, got out of the car, walked to the rear, and pushed the car into the lake. She covered her ears so she couldn't hear the splash. The car disappeared under the water. The two little boys, strapped into their seats, drowned.

Susan's confession stunned the nation as everyone asked, "How could she have killed her own children?" "What's wrong with Susan?" To answer these questions, mental health professionals evaluated Susan's mental health with a procedure called the clinical assessment (J. M. Wood et al., 2002).

A *clinical assessment* **involves a systematic evaluation of an individual's various psychological, biological, and social factors, as well as identifying past and present problems, stressors, and other cognitive or behavioral symptoms.**

A clinical assessment is the first step in figuring out which past or current problems may have contributed to Susan killing her own children (Begley, 1998b). We'll discuss how a clinical assessment is done.

How was Susan evaluated?

After Susan's arrest, mental health professionals did clinical assessments to try to discover what terrible forces pushed her over the edge. Depending on their training, mental health professionals use one or more of three major techniques—clinical interviews, psychological tests, and neurological exams—to do clinical assessments.

Neurological Tests

We can assume that Susan was given a number of *neurological tests* to check for possible brain damage or malfunction. These tests might include evaluating reflexes, brain structures (MRI scans), and brain functions (fMRI scans—p. 70).

Neurological exams are part of a clinical assessment because a variety of abnormal psychological symptoms may be caused by tumors, diseases, or infections of the brain.

Did Susan have neurological problems?

Neurological tests are used to distinguish physical or organic causes (tumors) from psychological ones (strange beliefs) (Zillmer et al., 2007). Susan was reported to have no neurological problems.

Clinical Interview

As part of her clinical assessment, several psychiatrists spent many hours interviewing Susan. This method is called a clinical interview (Craig, 2004).

The *clinical interview* **is one method of gathering information about a person's past and current behaviors, beliefs, attitudes, emotions, and problems. Some clinical interviews are unstructured, which means they have no set questions; others are structured, which means they follow a standard format of asking a similar set of questions.**

During the clinical interview, Susan would have been asked about the history of her current problems, such as when they started and what other events accompanied them. The focus of the interview would have been on Susan's current problem, killing her children, especially on the details of the

What are Susan's past and current psychological problems?

symptoms that led up to the killing. The clinical interview is perhaps the primary technique used to assess abnormal behavior (Durand & Barlow, 2006).

Based on 15 hours of interviews, Dr. Seymour Halleck testified that Susan was scarred by her father's suicide and her stepfather sexually abusing her, which led to periods of depression, her current problem (Towle, 1995).

Psychological Tests

As part of her assessment, psychologists may have given Susan a number of personality tests (pp. 450, 474).

Personality tests **include two different kinds of tests: objective tests (self-report questionnaires), such as the MMPI, which consist of specific statements or questions to which the person responds with specific answers, and projective tests, such as the Rorschach inkblot test, which have no set answers but consist of ambiguous stimuli that a person interprets or makes up a story about.**

As we also discussed in Modules 19 and 20, personality tests help clinicians evaluate a person's traits, attitudes, emotions, and beliefs.

Purpose. A major goal of doing a clinical assessment is to decide which mental health disorder best accounts for a client's symptoms. For example, based on her symptoms, Susan was described as having a mood disorder, which you'll see next is one of many possible mental health problems.

C. Diagnosing Mental Disorders

How many mental disorders?

In criminal trials that involve questions of mental health, the defense and prosecution usually hire their own psychiatrists or psychologists because they are looking for different problems or symptoms. In Susan's case, at least two psychiatrists did clinical assessments to answer a number of questions: What are her current symptoms? What past events and situations caused these symptoms? What role did her symptoms play in the killing of her children?

Her Past

During clinical interviews, the psychiatrist found that when Susan was 8 years old, her father shot himself. When she was 13, psychologists wanted to admit her to a hospital to treat her depression, but her mother and stepfather refused to cooperate. Later, when Susan was 15, her stepfather sexually molested her, but her mother refused to press charges. When she was in high school, she had periods of depression and attempted suicide. However, she did well academically, was an honor student and a member of the math club, and was voted the "friendliest female" in the class of 1989. She married David in 1991, but one year after the birth of their second son, their marriage fell apart and they filed for divorce (Bragg, 1995).

Dr. Seymour Halleck testified that Susan was scarred by her father's suicide, her stepfather's sexual abuse, and her periods of depression, which contributed to her current difficulties (Towle, 1995).

Susan's clinical assessment revealed a disturbed person. She is being led away to serve a life sentence.

Her Present

The psychiatrist found that Susan's present problems included becoming depressed after being rejected by her current boyfriend. She confessed to being so lonely in the months before the killings that she had multiple sexual encounters: with her stepfather, who had molested her as a teenager; with her estranged husband, whom she was divorcing; with her current boyfriend, who later wrote a good-bye letter; and with her boyfriend's father. In addition, Susan was drinking heavily during this period.

Dr. Halleck testified that Susan suffered from severe depression, drinking, and an adjustment disorder that caused her to have a heightened emotional reaction to stress (D. Morgan, 1995).

In just $2\frac{1}{2}$ hours, the jury decided that Susan Smith was guilty of murder. She was led from the courthouse (upper left photo) to serve a life sentence.

As a result of her clinical assessment, Susan was diagnosed as having a mood disorder and was treated in prison with antidepressants.

A clinical assessment is a method of identifying a client's symptoms, which are used to make a diagnosis. Making a diagnosis requires matching the symptoms to a particular disorder, which involves using the DSM-IV-TR.

How many mental disorders?

Those who knew Susan tried to diagnose the problem that led to her tragic crime.

"Maybe Susan was just plain crazy." "Maybe she was too depressed to know what she was doing." "Maybe she had bad genes." "Maybe something bad happened to her as a child."

Using a more rigorous method, mental health professionals conduct clinical assessments to identify symptoms, which are then used to make a clinical diagnosis.

A *clinical diagnosis* is a process of matching an individual's specific symptoms to those that define a particular mental disorder.

Making a clinical diagnosis was very difficult prior to the 1950s because there was no uniform code or diagnostic system. However, since 1952, the American Psychiatric Association (APA) has been developing a uniform diagnostic system, whose most recent version is known as the *Diagnostic and Statistical Manual of Mental Disorders*-IV-Text Revision, abbreviated as DSM-IV-TR (American Psychiatric Association, 2000).

The *Diagnostic and Statistical Manual of Mental Disorders-IV-Text Revision, or DSM-IV-TR,* describes a uniform system for assessing specific symptoms and matching them to almost 300 different mental disorders.

With each revision of the DSM, there have been improvements in diagnosing mental disorders. For example, the DSM-II (1968) gave only general descriptions of mental problems because it was based on Sigmund Freud's general concepts of *psychoses* (severe mental disorders, such as schizophrenia) and *neuroses* (less severe forms of psychological conflict, such as anxiety). Using only general descriptions caused disagreements in diagnosing problems. The DSM-III (1980) dropped Freudian terminology and instead listed specific symptoms and criteria for mental disorders. However, these criteria were based primarily on clinical opinions, not research, so disagreements continued. A major improvement in the current DSM-IV-TR is that it establishes criteria and symptoms for mental disorders based more on research findings than on clinical opinions (Clark et al., 1995). When the next DSM comes out, likely in 2011, mental health experts predict that it will use new findings from genetics and neuroscience to better identify the underlying causes of mental disorders (First, 2007).

Interestingly, the first *Diagnostic and Statistical Manual of Mental Disorders* (1952) described about 100 mental disorders, as compared to almost 300 in the most recent DSM-IV-TR (right figure).

We'll use the cases of Dennis Rader (serial killer), Susan Smith (murderer), and Kate Premo (phobia of flying) to show how mental health professionals use the DSM-IV-TR to make a diagnosis.

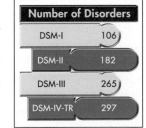

Number of Disorders

DSM-I	106
DSM-II	182
DSM-III	265
DSM-IV-TR	297

C. Diagnosing Mental Disorders

How do we make a diagnosis? In making a clinical diagnosis, a mental health professional first assesses the client's specific symptoms and then matches these symptoms to those described in the DSM-IV-TR. The DSM-IV-TR has five major dimensions, called *axes,* which serve as guidelines for making decisions about symptoms. We'll first describe Axis I and show how it can be used to diagnose the very different problems of Susan Smith and Kate Premo. (The numbered items below and on the opposite page are based on the *Diagnostic and Statistical Manual of Mental Disorders*-IV-Text Revision [2000], American Psychiatric Association.)

Axis I: Nine Major Clinical Syndromes

Axis I contains lists of symptoms and criteria about the onset, severity, and duration of these symptoms. In turn these lists of symptoms are used to make a clinical diagnosis of the following nine major clinical syndromes.

1. Disorders usually first diagnosed in infancy, childhood, or adolescence.

This category includes disorders that arise before adolescence, such as attention-deficit disorders, autism, mental retardation, enuresis, and stuttering (discussed in Modules 1, 2, and 13).

2. Organic mental disorders.

These disorders are temporary or permanent dysfunctions of brain tissue caused by diseases or chemicals, such as delirium, dementia (Alzheimer's—p. 50), and amnesia (p. 265).

3. Substance-related disorders.

This category refers to the maladaptive use of drugs and alcohol. Mere consumption and recreational use of such substances are not disorders. This category requires an abnormal pattern of use, as with alcohol abuse and cocaine dependence (pp. 188–189).

4. Schizophrenia and other psychotic disorders.

The schizophrenias are characterized by psychotic symptoms (for example, grossly disorganized behavior, delusions, and hallucinations) and by over six months of behavioral deterioration. This category, which also includes delusional disorder and schizoaffective disorder, will be discussed in Module 23.

5. Mood disorders.

The cardinal feature is emotional disturbance. Patients may or may not have psychotic symptoms. These disorders, including major depression, bipolar disorder, dysthymic disorder, and cyclothymic disorder, are discussed in Module 23. Susan Smith is an example of a person with a mood disorder.

Susan Smith: Diagnosis—Mood Disorder

From childhood on, Susan's symptoms include being depressed, attempting suicide, seeking sexual alliances to escape loneliness, drinking heavily, and having feelings of low self-esteem and hopelessness, all of which match the DSM-IV-TR's list of symptoms for a mood disorder. In Susan's case, the specific mood disorder most closely matches major depressive disorder but without serious thought disorders and delusions.

Diagnosis: Mood disorder

In diagnosing major depression, the DSM-IV-TR distinguishes between early (before age 21) and late onset depression—Susan would be early, and between mild and severe depression, as judged by how many episodes of depression she had and whether she showed a decreased capacity to function normally, such as the inability to work or care for children. Susan's ability to hold a job and care for her children suggest mild depression. This example shows how the guidelines of Axis I are used to arrive at one of nine major clinical syndromes—in this case, major depression.

6. Anxiety disorders.

These disorders are characterized by physiological signs of anxiety (for example, palpitations) and subjective feelings of tension, apprehension, or fear. Anxiety may be acute and focused (phobias) or continual and diffuse (generalized anxiety disorder). An example of an anxiety disorder is that of Kate Premo.

Kate Premo: Diagnosis—Specific Phobia

Kate Premo's symptoms include having an intense fear of flying, knowing that her fear is irrational and that she can't control it, going out of her way to avoid flying, and making reservations that she later cancels. Kate's symptoms most closely match the DSM-IV-TR's list of symptoms for an anxiety disorder called a specific phobia. The DSM-IV-TR's symptoms for a specific phobia match those of Premo—experiencing intense and irrational fear when exposed to a feared situation (flying) and having to avoid that situation at all costs, which interferes with part of her normal activities (going to meetings).

Diagnosis: Specific phobia (aviophobia)

7. Somatoform disorders.

These disorders are dominated by somatic symptoms that resemble physical illnesses. These symptoms cannot be accounted for by organic damage. There must also be strong evidence that these symptoms are produced by psychological factors or conflicts. This category, which includes somatization and conversion disorders and hypochondriasis, will be discussed in this module.

8. Dissociative disorders.

These disorders all feature a sudden, temporary alteration or dysfunction of memory, consciousness, identity, and behavior, as in dissociative amnesia and multiple personality (discussed in Module 23).

9. Sexual and gender-identity disorders.

There are three types of disorders in this category: gender-identity disorders (discomfort with identity as male or female), paraphilias (preference for unusual acts to achieve sexual arousal), and sexual dysfunctions (impairments in sexual functioning) (discussed in Module 15).

We have explained how Axis I is used to make clinical diagnoses of such mental disorders as major depression (mood disorder) and specific phobias (fear of flying). Now, we'll briefly describe how the other four axes are used in diagnosing problems.

Axis II: Personality Disorders

This axis refers to disorders that involve patterns of personality traits that are long-standing, maladaptive, and inflexible and involve impaired functioning or subjective distress. Examples include borderline, schizoid, and antisocial personality disorders. Personality disorders will be discussed in Module 23. An example of a personality disorder is that of Rader.

Dennis Rader: Diagnosis—Antisocial Personality Disorder

Diagnosis: Antisocial personality disorder

Dennis Rader's symptoms include torturing and killing 10 individuals, feeling no guilt or remorse, and exhibiting this behavior over a considerable period of time. Rader's symptoms may indicate a combination of mental disorders, but here we'll focus on only one from the DSM-IV-TR, a personality disorder. According to DSM-IV-TR, the essential features of an antisocial personality disorder are the existence of strange inner experiences that differ greatly from the expectations of one's culture, that lead to significant impairment in personal, occupational, or social functioning, and that form a pattern of disregard for, and violation of, the rights of others. This list of symptoms from DSM-IV-TR matches those of Rader.

Axis III: General Medical Conditions

This axis refers to physical disorders or conditions, such as diabetes, arthritis, and hemophilia, that have an influence on someone's mental disorder.

Axis IV: Psychosocial and Environmental Problems

This axis refers to psychosocial and environmental problems that may affect the diagnosis, treatment, and prognosis of mental disorders in Axes I and II. A psychosocial or environmental problem may be a negative life event (experiencing a traumatic event), an environmental difficulty or deficiency, a familial or other interpersonal stress, an inadequacy of social support or personal resources, or another problem that describes the context in which a person's difficulties have developed (PTSD was discussed on p. 491).

Axis V: Global Assessment of Functioning Scale

This axis is used to rate the overall psychological, social, and occupational functioning of the individual on a scale from 1 (severe danger of hurting self) to 100 (superior functioning in all activities).

Using all five axes. Mental health professionals use all five axes to make a clinical diagnosis. For example, to make a clinical diagnosis of Dennis Rader, his unusual sexual symptoms may match those of a sexual disorder in *Axis I.* His other maladaptive symptoms match those of an antisocial personality disorder in *Axis II.* Rader apparently had no related medical conditions listed in *Axis III.* Rader was a loner with poor self-esteem and struggled with his schoolwork, which match some of the psychological, social, and environmental factors listed in *Axis IV.* Amazingly, Rader functioned well enough to hold a job and go unnoticed in his neighborhood, which would be used to rate his general functioning listed in *Axis V.* As you can see, each of the five axes in DSM-IV-TR focuses on a different factor that contributes to making an overall clinical diagnosis of a person's mental health.

USEFULNESS OF DSM-IV-TR

The figure below shows the steps in making a clinical diagnosis. Mental health professionals begin by using three different methods to identify a client's symptoms, a process called clinical assessment. Next, the client's symptoms are matched to the five axes in the DSM-IV-TR to arrive at a diagnosis of each client's particular mental disorder.

1. Clinical interview
2. Personality tests
3. Neurological tests

Clinical assessment: identify symptoms

DSM-IV-TR: Use symptoms to diagnose mental disorder

For mental health professionals, there are three advantages of using DSM-IV-TR's uniform system to diagnose and classify mental disorders (Widiger & Clark, 2000).

First, mental health professionals use the classification system to communicate with one another and discuss their clients' problems.

Second, researchers use the classification system to study and explain mental disorders.

Third, therapists use the classification system to design their treatment program so as to best fit a particular client's problem.

Although using the DSM-IV-TR system to diagnose mental problems has advantages, it also has a number of potential problems. For example, mental health professionals do not always agree on whether a client fits a particular diagnosis. In addition, there may be social, political, and labeling problems, which we'll discuss next.

C. Diagnosing Mental Disorders

Potential Problems with Using the DSM-IV-TR

Is labeling a problem? It's not uncommon to hear people use labels, such as "Jim's really anxious," "Mary Ann is compulsive," or "Vicki is schizophrenic." Although the goal of the DSM-IV-TR is to give mental disorders particular diagnostic labels, once a person is labeled, the label itself may generate a negative stereotype. In turn, the negative stereotype results in negative social and political effects, such as biasing how others perceive and respond to the labeled person (Greatley, 2004).

Labeling Mental Disorders

David Oaks, a sophomore at Harvard University, was having such fearful emotional experiences that he was examined by a psychiatrist. Although David believed that he was having a mystical experience, the psychiatrist interpreted and labeled David's fearful experiences as indicating a kind of short-term schizophrenic disorder (Japenga, 1994). This mental health professional made a clinical diagnosis that resulted in giving a label to David's problem.

Labeling refers to identifying and naming differences among individuals. The label, which places individuals into specific categories, may have either positive or negative associations.

At first David felt relieved to know that his problem had a diagnosis or label. Later he realized that his new label was changing his life for the worse. People no longer responded to him as David-the-college-sophomore but as David-with-schizophrenic-disorder.

As David's case shows, the **advantage** of diagnostic labels is their ability to summarize and communicate a whole lot of information in a single word or phrase. But, the **disadvantage** is that if the label has negative associations—for example, mentally ill, retarded, schizo—the very label may elicit negative or undesirable responses. For this reason, mental health professionals advise that we not respond to people with mental disorders by their labels and instead respond to the person behind the label (Albee & Joffe, 2004).

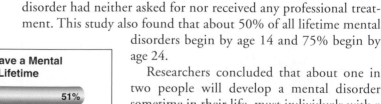

Some labels (anxious, depressed) have negative stereotypes.

Social and Political Implications

Diagnostic labels, such as anxious, compulsive, or mentally ill, can change how an individual is perceived and thus have important political and social implications. For instance, in the early 1970s, gays protested that homosexuality should not be included in DSM-I and II as a mental disorder. When studies found that homosexuals were no more or less mentally healthy than heterosexuals, homosexuality as a mental disorder was eliminated from DSM-III. Dropping this label had a powerful social and political effect because no longer would being homosexual be considered a mental disorder.

In the 1980s, women protested the DSM label of self-defeating personality disorder because this disorder applied primarily to women who were said to make destructive life choices, such as to stay in abusive relationships (Japenga, 1994). This label was dropped from DSM-IV because it suggested that women were deliberately choosing bad relationships, which wasn't true (P. Caplan, 1994).

Japan has a special problem with labels: Mental disorder labels have very negative connotations, which discourages Japanese from seeking professional help for mental disorders. One result of avoiding labels is that although Japan has half the population of the United States, it has more suicides. That's because one risk for suicide is depression, a label that Japanese avoid and thus they do not get timely treatment. In comparison, in the United States, the label of depression is widely accepted and more likely to be treated, even by doctors in general practice (Pomerantz, 2005).

These examples illustrate the social and political implications of labeling individuals with mental disorders. One advantage of the current DSM-IV-TR is that its labels or diagnostic categories are based on objective empirical findings, which reduces their potential for having a negative connotation or bias (Widiger & Clark, 2000).

Frequency of Mental Disorders

Although labels are a fact of life, researchers and clinicians try to apply the DSM labels as fairly as possible. Researchers interviewed a national sample of 9,282 noninstitutionalized civilians aged 18 and older and diagnosed their problems using the DSM's diagnostic system. As the graph at the right shows, based on those surveyed, 51% of people will develop at least one disorder during their lifetime (Kessler et al., 2005). The most common mental disorder was anxiety, followed by mood disorders and substance abuse, especially problems with

Percentage Who Will Have a Mental Disorder in Their Lifetime

Any disorder	51%
Anxiety disorders	32%
Mood disorders	28%
Alcohol use disorders	15%
Drug use disorders	9%

alcohol. What was surprising was that 59% of those with a mental disorder had neither asked for nor received any professional treatment. This study also found that about 50% of all lifetime mental disorders begin by age 14 and 75% begin by age 24.

Researchers concluded that about one in two people will develop a mental disorder sometime in their life, most individuals with a mental disorder do not seek treatment, and there is a need to understand how to best treat mental disorders in youth.

Next, we'll examine the symptoms and treatment of specific disorders, beginning with anxiety.

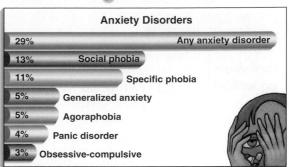

Anxiety Disorders

29%	Any anxiety disorder
13%	Social phobia
11%	Specific phobia
5%	Generalized anxiety
5%	Agoraphobia
4%	Panic disorder
3%	Obsessive-compulsive

How common is anxiety?

The most common mental disorder reported by adults in the United States is any kind of anxiety disorder (right graph) (Kessler et al., 2005). We have already discussed one serious anxiety problem, posttraumatic stress disorder (PTSD) (p. 491). Here we'll discuss six of the more common forms of anxiety: generalized anxiety disorder, panic disorder, three kinds of phobias, and obsessive-compulsive disorders.

Generalized Anxiety Disorder

During his initial therapy interview, Fred was sweating, fidgeting in his chair, and repeatedly asking for water to quench a never-ending thirst. From all indications, Fred was visibly distressed and extremely nervous. At first, Fred spoke only of his dizziness and problems with sleeping. However, it soon became clear that he had nearly always felt tense. He admitted to a long history of difficulties in interacting with others, difficulties that led to his being fired from two jobs. He constantly worried about all kinds of possible disasters that might happen to him (Davison & Neale, 1990). Fred's symptoms showed that he was suffering from generalized anxiety disorder.

Generalized anxiety disorder **(GAD) is characterized by excessive or unrealistic worry about almost everything or feeling that something bad is about to happen. These anxious feelings occur on a majority of days for a period of at least six months (American Psychiatric Association, 2000).**

About 5% of adults are reported to have GAD, but almost twice as many adult women (6.6%) report GAD as do men (3.6%). Researchers suggest that these differences may be related to women's greater worries related to getting or being pregnant, giving birth, and raising children (Halbreich, 2003).

SYMPTOMS

Generalized anxiety disorder includes both psychological and physical symptoms. Psychological symptoms include being irritable, having difficulty concentrating, and being unable to control one's worry, which is out of proportion to the actual event. Constant worrying causes significant distress or impaired functioning in social, occupational, and other areas. Physical symptoms include restlessness, being easily fatigued, sweating, flushing, pounding heart, insomnia, headaches, and muscle tension or aches (American Psychiatric Association, 2000).

TREATMENT

Generalized anxiety disorder is commonly treated with psychotherapy (see Module 24), with or without drugs. The drugs most frequently prescribed are tranquilizers such as alprazolam and diazepam, which belong to a group known as the *benzodiazepines (ben-zoh-die-AS-ah-peens)*. One of the limitations of these drugs is that at high doses they are addicting and interfere with the ability to remember newly learned information (Rivas-Vazquez, 2003). Antidepressant drugs are also used to treat GAD and have fewer side effects and a lower risk of addiction (Holmes & Newman, 2006).

Researchers found that about 40 to 50% of clients treated for generalized anxiety disorder with either psychotherapy (cognitive-behavioral) or drugs (tranquilizers) were free of symptoms six months to one year later (Arntz, 2003; Holmes & Newman, 2006).

Anxiety can be treated with drugs and psychotherapy.

Panic Disorder

Karen went down the street to Antoine's Beauty Shop to have her hair set. As she was sitting under the dryer, a sudden feeling swept over her. She thought she was losing her mind. Her heart started beating fast, her legs felt weak, and her body trembled. As a wave of fear spread over her, she wanted to scream. Suddenly Karen jumped up with all the pins still in her hair, slapped a $5 bill on the counter, and ran all the way home (*Los Angeles Times,* December 13, 1981). Karen's symptoms indicate that she had a panic disorder.

Panic disorder **is characterized by recurrent and unexpected panic attacks (described below). The person becomes so worried about having another panic attack that this intense worrying interferes with normal psychological functioning (American Psychiatric Association, 2000).**

Like Karen, about 4% of adults in the United States suffer from panic disorder, and women are 2 to 3 times more likely to report it than are men (Halbreich, 2003). People who suffer from panic disorder have an increased risk of alcohol and other drug abuse, an increased incidence of suicide, decreased social functioning, and less marital happiness. About half suffer from depression (Smits et al., 2006).

SYMPTOMS

Karen's symptoms in the beauty shop indicate that she was having a panic attack, which may occur in several different anxiety disorders but is the essential feature of panic disorder.

A *panic attack* **is a period of intense fear or discomfort in which four or more of the following symptoms are present: pounding heart, sweating, trembling, shortness of breath, feelings of choking, chest pain, nausea, feeling dizzy, and fear of losing control or dying (American Psychiatric Association, 2000).**

TREATMENT

Panic disorders are usually treated with drugs—benzodiazepines, antidepressants (Prozac-like drugs, which are selective serotonin reuptake inhibitors or SSRIs)— and/or psychotherapy. Research indicates psychotherapy is at least as effective as drug therapy and drug therapy alone increases the risk of clients relapsing after treatment ends (Smits et al., 2006). Researchers found that, one year after treatment with a combination of psychotherapy and drugs, about 30 to 50% of clients were symptom-free (Page, 2002).

Another kind of anxiety disorder that is relatively common involves different kinds of phobias.

D. Anxiety Disorders

Can fear go wild?

When common fears of seeing blood, spiders, or mice, having injections, meeting new people, speaking in public, flying, or being in small places turn into very intense fears, they are called phobias (over 500 phobias are listed on www.phobialist.com).

A phobia (FOE-bee-ah) is an anxiety disorder characterized by an intense and irrational fear that is out of all proportion to the possible danger of the object or situation. Because of this intense fear, which is accompanied by increased physiological arousal, a person goes to great lengths to avoid the feared event. If the feared event cannot be avoided, the person feels intense anxiety.

Reseachers report that because many individuals with phobias trace their onset to specific traumatic events, phobias are learned through conditioning or observing a person showing fear of something. Research also points to genetic and environmental causes of phobias. Thus, different pathways may lead to people developing phobias (Rowa et al., 2006).

We discussed blood injection phobias earlier (pp. 201, 487). Here we'll discuss three more common phobias—social phobias, specific phobias, and agoraphobia (graph above) (Durand & Barlow, 2006).

Common Phobias	
Social phobia	13%
Specific phobia	11%
Agoraphobia	5%

Social Phobias

Why didn't Billy speak up in class?

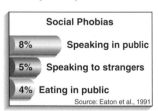

In junior high school, Billy never, never spoke up in class or answered any questions. The school counselor said that Billy would be sick to his stomach the whole day if he knew that he was going to be called on. Billy began to hide out in the restrooms to avoid going to class. Billy's fear of speaking up in class is an example of a social phobia (Durand & Barlow, 2006).

Social phobias are characterized by irrational, marked, and continuous fear of performing in social situations. The individuals fear that they will humiliate or embarrass themselves (American Psychiatric Association, 2000).

Social Phobias	
8%	Speaking in public
5%	Speaking to strangers
4%	Eating in public

Source: Eaton et al., 1991

As a fearful social situation approaches (graph above), anxiety builds up and may result in considerable bodily distress, such as nausea, sweating, and other signs of heightened physiological arousal. Although a person with a social phobia realizes that the fear is excessive or irrational, he or she may not know how to deal with it, other than by avoiding the situation.

Specific Phobias

Why couldn't Kate get on a plane?

In the beginning of this module, we told you about Kate Premo (photo below),  whose traumatic childhood and adult experiences with flying turned into a phobia of flying, which is called a specific phobia.

Specific phobias, formerly called simple phobias, are characterized by marked and persistent fears that are unreasonable and triggered by anticipation of, or exposure to, a specific object or situation (flying, heights, spiders, seeing blood) (American Psychiatric Association, 2000).

Specific Phobias	
Bugs, snakes, etc.	23%
Heights	22%
Water	13%
Closed places	10%

Source: Eaton et al., 1991

Among the more common specific phobias seen in clinical practice (graph above) are fear of animals (zoophobia), fear of heights (acrophobia), fear of confinement (claustrophobia), fear of injury or blood, and fear of flying (Durand & Barlow, 2006).

The content and occurrence of specific phobias vary with culture. For example, fears of spirits or ghosts are present in many cultures but become specific phobias only if the fear turns excessive and irrational (American Psychiatric Association, 2000).

Agoraphobia

Why couldn't Rose leave her house?

Fear trapped Rose in her house for years. If she thought about going outside to do her shopping, pain raced through her arms and chest. She grew hot and perspired. Her heart beat rapidly and her legs felt like rubber. She said that thinking about leaving her house caused stark terror, sometimes lasting for days. This 39-year-old mother of two is one of millions of Americans suffering from an intense fear of being in public places, which is called agoraphobia (*Los Angeles Times,* October 19, 1980).

Agoraphobia is characterized by anxiety about being in places or situations from which escape might be difficult or embarrassing (graph below) if a panic attack or paniclike symptoms (sudden dizziness or onset of diarrhea) were to occur (American Psychiatric Association, 2000).

Agoraphobia arises out of an underlying fear of either having a full-blown panic attack (discussed on the previous page) or having a sudden and unexpected onset of paniclike symptoms.

Agoraphobia	
Public transport	13%
Tunnels or bridges	8%
Crowds	7%
Going out by oneself	4%

Source: Eaton et al., 1991

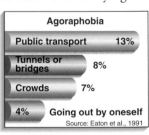

After any of these phobias are established, they are extremely persistent and may continue for years if not treated (Coles & Horng, 2006). We'll discuss drug and psychological treatments for phobias later in this module—in the Application section.

Next, we'll look at another form of anxiety that can be very difficult to deal with—obsessive-compulsive disorders.

Why was Shirley always late?

Shirley was an outgoing, popular high-school student with average grades. Her one problem was that she was late for school almost every day. Before she could leave the house in the morning, she had to be very sure that she was clean, so she needed to take a shower that lasted a full 2 hours. After her 2-hour shower, she spent a long time dressing, because for each thing she did, such as putting on her stockings, underclothes, skirt, and blouse, she had to repeat each act precisely 17 times. When asked about her washing and counting, she said she knew that it was crazy but that she just had to do it and couldn't explain why. She said that she had struggled against this problem for three years without success (Rapoport, 1988). Shirley's symptoms would be diagnosed as indicative of an anxiety problem called an obsessive-compulsive disorder.

An *obsessive-compulsive disorder* consists of obsessions, which are persistent, recurring irrational thoughts, impulses, or images that a person is unable to control and that interfere with normal functioning, and compulsions, which are irresistible impulses to perform over and over some senseless behavior or ritual (hand washing, checking things, counting, putting things in order) (American Psychiatric Association, 2000).

Obsessive-compulsive disorder or OCD was once considered relatively rare, but now it is known to affect about 3% of adults in the United States (graph above) (Riggs & Foa, 2006). We'll discuss OCD's symptoms, causes, and treatments.

Anxiety Disorders

Social phobia — 13%
5% Agoraphobia
3% Obsessive-compulsive

Symptoms and Causes

Shirley's symptoms included both obsession—her need to be very clean and careful about dressing—and compulsions—her need to take 2-hour showers and to perform each act of dressing precisely 17 times. Some individuals have obsessions (irrational, recurring thoughts) without compulsions. Because compulsions are usually very time consuming, they often take an hour or more to complete each day. Although doing the compulsive behaviors may help individuals reduce their anxiety in the short term, in the long term the compulsive behaviors interfere with normal daily functioning.

WASH WASH WASH WASH WASH WASH

Repeating an act 17 times is a sign of OCD.

The most common compulsions involve cleaning, checking, and counting; the less common include buying, hoarding, and putting things in order. For example, individuals obsessed with being dirty or contaminated reduce their anxiety by washing their hands until their skin is raw, while those obsessed with leaving a door unlocked may be driven to check the lock every few minutes (American Psychiatric Association, 2000). These kinds of obsessive-compulsive behaviors interfere with normal functioning and make holding a job or engaging in social interactions difficult.

Researchers report that OCD has both genetic (runs in families) and neurological (overactive anterior cingulate cortex) causes (Plomin & McGuffin, 2003; Ursu et al., 2003). Because of these underlying genetic and neurological factors, OCD can be a chronic problem that requires treatment with drugs, psychotherapy, or some combination (Riggs & Foa, 2006).

Treatment

Shirley's compulsive behaviors are thought to be one way that she reduces or avoids anxiety—in her case, anxiety associated with feeling dirty. In the late 1980s, obsessive-compulsive disorder was thought to be an incurable disorder. Currently, however, about half the patients with OCD report improvement after being treated with drugs or exposure therapy (Franklin et al., 2002).

Exposure therapy involves gradually exposing the person to the actual anxiety-producing situations or objects that he or she is attempting to avoid and continuing the exposure treatments until the anxiety decreases.

For example, a client like Shirley with obsessive-compulsive disorder (OCD) could be exposed over and over to her fearful objects (dirt or dirty things) until such exposures elicit little or no anxiety. Exposure therapy may involve 15 two-hour sessions over the course of a month. However, Shirley refused to try exposure therapy and instead was given antidepressant drugs.

Antidepressant drugs. Clients like Shirley, who cannot tolerate or are not motivated to undergo exposure therapy, may be given antidepressant drugs. For example, after taking an antidepressant drug for about three weeks, Shirley's urges to wash and count faded sufficiently that she could try exposure therapy (Rapoport, 1988). However, about one-third of clients with OCD are not helped by antidepressant drugs, even the newer class of such drugs that are called selective serotonin reuptake inhibitors (SSRIs, such as Prozac, Paxil, or Zoloft) (Riggs & Foa, 2006).

Effectiveness. For individuals with OCD, including those not helped with antidepressant drugs, the treatment of choice is exposure therapy. In most cases, exposure therapy proved the best treatment for OCD because it reduced symptoms more and lasted longer compared to clients who took antidepressant drugs. In addition, exposure therapy has none of the unwanted side effects of drugs (such as inhibiting liver enzymes) (McDonough & Kennedy, 2002).

Next, we'll discuss how people can create real physical symptoms that interfere with normal functioning.

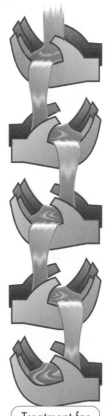

Treatment for obsessive-compulsive behavior is psychotherapy and/or antidepressant drugs.

E. Somatoform Disorders

Imagine someone whose whole life centers around physical symptoms, some that are imagined and others that appear real, such as developing paralysis in one's legs. This intense focus on imagined, painful, or uncomfortable physical symptoms is characteristic of individuals with somatoform disorders.

Somatoform (so-MA-toe-form) disorders **are marked by a pattern of recurring, multiple, and significant bodily (somatic) symptoms that extend over several years. The bodily symptoms (pain, vomiting, paralysis, blindness) are not under voluntary control, have no known physical causes, and are believed to be caused by psychological factors (American Psychiatric Association, 2000).**

Although not easily diagnosed, somatoform disorders are among the most common health problems seen in general medical practice (Wise & Birket-Smith, 2002). The DSM-IV-TR lists seven kinds of somatoform disorders. We'll discuss two of the more common forms—somatization and conversion disorders.

SOMATIZATION DISORDER

One kind of somatoform disorder, which was historically called hysteria, is now called somatization disorder and is relatively rare (2.7% of the population).

Somatization disorder **begins before age 30, lasts several years, and is characterized by multiple symptoms—including pain, gastrointestinal, sexual, and neurological symptoms—that have no physical causes but are triggered by psychological problems or distress (American Psychiatric Association, 2000).**

This disorder is reported in most cultures and women are five times more likely to report it than men (Gureje et al., 1997). Those who have somatization disorder use health services frequently and tend to have many hospitalizations and surgeries (De Gucht & Fischler, 2002).

A psychologically distressed individual may have painful physical symptoms that have no physical causes.

Somatization disorders are apparently a means of coping with a stressful situation, indicating distress, or obtaining attention (Durand & Barlow, 2006; Hurwitz, 2003).

CONVERSION DISORDER

Sometimes individuals report serious physical problems, such as blindness, which have no physical causes and are examples of a somatoform disorder called conversion disorder.

A *conversion disorder* **refers to changing anxiety or emotional distress into real physical, motor, sensory, or neurological symptoms (headaches, nausea, dizziness, loss of sensation, paralysis) for which no physical or organic cause can be identified (American Psychiatric Association, 2000).**

Usually the symptoms of a conversion disorder are associated with psychological factors, such as depression, concerns about health, or the occurrence of a stressful situation. Recent research examining the brains of people with medically unexplainable paralysis has shown that when patients try to move their paralyzed limbs, the emotional areas of the brain are activated inappropriately and may inhibit the functioning of the motor cortex, leaving the patients unable to move their paralyzed limbs (Kinetz, 2006). The development of such physical symptoms gets the person attention, removes the person from threatening or anxiety-producing situations, and thus reinforces the occurrence and maintenance of the symptoms involved in the conversion disorder (Durand & Barlow, 2006). Researchers found that in some cultures, bodily complaints (somatoform disorders) are used instead of emotional complaints to express psychological problems (Lewis-Fernandez et al., 2005).

The same kind of painful or uncomfortable physical symptoms observed in somatoform disorders are observed in individuals suffering from mass hysteria.

As more than 500 students from various schools began to give a choir and orchestra concert, they suddenly began to complain of headaches, dizziness, weakness, abdominal pain, and nausea. These symptoms spread rapidly until about half the students developed one or more of the symptoms. Students who became ill were most often those who saw someone near them take ill. Students from one school, particularly girls in the soprano section, experienced the highest rate of symptoms. Younger members reported more symptoms than older ones, and girls (51%) reported more symptoms than boys (41%). At first, someone thought that a gas line had broken, but no one in the audience developed any symptoms. There was no ruptured gas line. The students' symptoms resulted from mass hysteria (G. W. Small et al., 1991).

Mass hysteria **is a condition experienced by a group of people who, through suggestion, observation, or other psychological processes, develop similar fears, delusions, abnormal behaviors, or physical symptoms.**

In this case, several of the most popular and visible girls complained of feeling dizzy and nauseous (they had been standing for hours). Soon, other students were complaining about having similar physical symptoms until over 200 students eventually developed these same symptoms. A similar case of mass hysteria was reported in a group of teenage girls in Vietnam, 50 of whom were hospitalized due to sudden fainting after watching one girl collapse and be carried away by medical personnel (IANS, 2006).

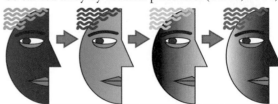

Individuals who are emotionally aroused in a group may experience similar physical symptoms.

In the Middle Ages, hysteria was attributed to possession by evil spirits or the devil. Today, mass hysteria is known to involve members of a group who experience and share emotional arousal or excitement, which spreads through the group and results in its members developing *real physical symptoms* with no known physical causes (Barlow & Durand, 2002). Mass hysteria is another example of somatoform disorders.

After the Concept Review, we'll discuss how symptoms of mental disorders can vary among cultures, as we examine a disorder that seems to be unique to Asian cultures, especially Japan.

✔ Concept Review

1. A prolonged or recurring problem that seriously interferes with the ability of an individual to live a satisfying personal life and function in society is called a _____.

2. Mental disorders arise from the interaction of a number of factors. Biological factors include inherited behavioral tendencies, which are called (a)_____ factors. These factors contribute from 30 to 60% to the development of mental disorders. Biological factors also include the overreaction of brain structures to certain stimuli, which are called (b)_____ factors. Other factors that contribute to the development of mental disorders, such as deficits or problems in thinking, processing emotional stimuli, and social skills, are called (c)_____ factors. Being in or seeing a traumatic event, which is called an (d)_____ factor, can contribute to developing a mental disorder such as PTSD.

3. There are three definitions of abnormality. A behavior that occurs infrequently in the general population is abnormal according to the (a)_____ definition. A behavior that deviates greatly from accepted social norms is abnormal according to the (b)_____ definition. Behavior that interferes with the individual's ability to function as a person or in society is abnormal according to the (c)_____ definition, which is used by most mental health professionals.

4. When performed by a mental health professional, a systematic evaluation of an individual's various psychological, biological, and social factors that may be contributing to his or her problem is called a clinical (a)_____. A mental health professional who determines whether an individual's specific problem meets or matches the standard symptoms that define a particular mental disorder is doing a clinical (b)_____. One of the primary techniques used to gather an enormous amount of information about a person's past behavior, attitudes, and emotions and details of current problems is the clinical (c)_____.

5. The manual that describes the symptoms for almost 300 different mental disorders is called the (a)_____. The manual's primary goal is to provide mental health professionals with a means of (b)_____ mental disorders and (c)_____ that information in a systematic and uniform way. The DSM-IV-TR has five major dimensions, called (d)_____, which serve as guidelines for making decisions about symptoms.

Number of Disorders	
DSM-I	106
DSM-II	182
DSM-III	265
DSM-IV-TR	297

6. There are several kinds of anxiety disorders. An anxiety disorder that is characterized by excessive and/or unrealistic worry or feelings of general apprehension about events or activities, when those feelings occur on a majority of days for a period of at least six months, is called (a)_____ disorder. An anxiety disorder marked by the presence of recurrent and unexpected panic attacks, plus continued worry about having another panic attack, when such worry interferes with psychological functioning, is called a (b)_____ disorder. Suppose a person has a period of intense fear or discomfort during which four or more of the following symptoms are present: pounding heart, sweating, trembling, shortness of breath, feelings of choking, chest pain, nausea, feeling dizzy, and fear of losing control or dying. That person is experiencing a (c)_____.

7. An anxiety disorder characterized by an intense and irrational fear and heightened physiological arousal that is out of all proportion to the danger elicited by the object or situation is called a (a)_____, of which there are several kinds. Unreasonable, marked, and persistent fears that are triggered by anticipation of, or exposure to, a specific object or situation are called a (b)_____. An anxiety that comes from being in places or situations from which escape might be difficult or embarrassing if a panic attack or paniclike symptoms were to occur is called (c)_____. Irrational, marked, and continuous fear of performing in social situations and feeling humiliated or embarrassed is called a (d)_____.

8. A disorder that consists of persistent, recurring irrational thoughts, impulses, or images that a person is unable to control and irresistible impulses to perform over and over some senseless behavior or ritual is called (a)_____ disorder. A nondrug treatment for this disorder, which consists of gradually exposing the person to the real anxiety-producing situations or objects that he or she is attempting to avoid, is called (b)_____ therapy.

9. When something happens to a group of people so that all share the same fears or delusions or develop similar physical symptoms, it is called (a)_____. There is a disorder that involves a pattern of recurring, multiple, and significant bodily complaints that have no known physical causes. This is called (b)_____ disorder, and one of its more common forms is somatization disorder.

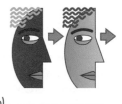

Answers: *1. mental disorder; 2. (a) genetic, (b) neurological, (c) cognitive-emotional-behavioral, (d) environmental; 3. (a) statistical, (b) social norms, (c) maladaptive; 4. (a) assessment, (b) diagnosis, (c) interview; 5. (a) Diagnostic and Statistical Manual of Mental Disorders-IV-TR, (b) diagnosing, (c) communicating, (d) axes; 6. (a) generalized anxiety, (b) panic, (c) panic attack; 7. (a) phobia, (b) specific phobia, (c) agoraphobia, (d) social phobia; 8. (a) obsessive-compulsive, (b) exposure; 9. (a) mass hysteria, (b) somatoform*

521

F. Cultural Diversity: An Asian Disorder

Taijin Kyofusho, or TKS

Can a culture create a disorder?

Anxiety is a worldwide concern and is the second most common mental disorder in the United States and several Asian nations, notably Japan. We have described how the symptoms of one kind of anxiety disorder, somatoform disorder, occur in very similar form in many cultures around the world (Lewis-Fernandez et al., 2005). However, it's also true that the unique cultural values of some countries, such as Japan, can result in the development of a unique anxiety order not found in Western cultures, such as the United States.

If you had a *social phobia* in the United States, it would usually mean that you had a great fear or were greatly embarrassed about behaving or performing in social situations, such as making a public speech. But if you had a social phobia in several Asian cultures, especially Japan and somewhat in Korea, it might mean that you had a very different kind of fear or embarrassment, called taijin kyofusho, or TKS (Tarumi et al., 2004).

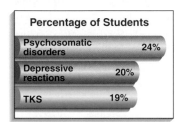

In Japan, the fear of offending others (by staring) is considered a kind of social phobia.

Taijin kyofusho (tie-GIN quo-FOO-show), **or TKS, is a kind of social phobia characterized by a terrible fear of offending others through awkward social or physical behavior, such as staring, blushing, giving off an offensive odor, having an unpleasant facial expression, or having trembling hands (Dinnel et al., 2002).**

Although many Westerners are also concerned or embarrassed about offending others through staring, having offensive body odors, or blushing, TKS is different in that it is an intense, irrational, morbid fear—in other words, a true phobia. In desperately trying to avoid TKS symptoms, Asians may try to avoid social interactions altogether. The Japanese word *taijin-kyofu* literally means "fear of interpersonal relations."

Occurrence. The graph below shows that TKS is the third most common psychiatric disorder treated in Japanese college students (Kirmayer, 1991). TKS is more common in males than in females, with a ratio of about 5:4. Most patients have a primary

Percentage of Students

Psychosomatic disorders	24%
Depressive reactions	20%
TKS	19%

symptom, which has changed during the past 40 years. Initially, fear of blushing was the primary symptom, but it has been replaced by fear of making eye contact or staring (Yamashita, 1993). In comparison, making eye contact is very common in Western cultures; if you do not make eye contact in social interactions, you may be judged as shy or lacking in social skills.

TKS begins around adolescence, when interpersonal interactions play a big role in one's life. TKS is rarely seen after the late 20s because, by then, individuals have learned the proper social behaviors. TKS seems to develop from certain cultural influences that are unique to Japan.

Cultural values. The Japanese culture places great emphasis on the appropriate way to conduct oneself in public, which means a person should avoid making direct eye contact, staring, blushing, having trembling hands, or giving off offensive odors. To emphasize the importance of avoiding these improper behaviors, mothers often use threats of abandonment, ridicule, and embarrassment as punishment. Through this process of *socialization,* the child is made aware of the importance of avoiding improper public behaviors, which result in a loss of face and reflect badly on the person's family and social group. Thus, from early on, Japanese children are strongly encouraged to live up to certain cultural expectations about avoiding improper public behaviors, especially staring and blushing, which are considered to be rude and disgraceful.

Social Customs

In Japan, individuals are expected to know the needs and thoughts of others by reading the emotional expressions of faces rather than asking direct questions, which is considered rude social behavior. In contrast, Westerners may ask direct questions to clarify some point and often use direct eye contact to show interest. Individuals in Japan who make too much eye contact or ask too direct questions are likely to be viewed as insensitive to others, unpleasantly bold, or aggressive. In fact, Japanese children are taught to fix their gaze at the level of the neck of people they are talking to. This Japanese social custom that emphasizes not making eye contact, blushing, or having trembling hands or offensive body odors during social interactions results in about 20% of Japanese teenagers and young adults developing the intense, irrational fear called TKS. This social phobia is so common in Japan that there are special clinics devoted only to treating TKS. The Japanese TKS clinics are comparable in popularity to the numerous weight-loss clinics found in the United States. Interestingly, TKS is a kind of social phobia that doesn't occur in Western cultures (Dinnel et al., 2002; Tarumi et al., 2004).

Cultural differences. Although people in many cultures report anxiety about behaving or performing in public, the particular fears that they report may depend on their own culture's values. For example, TKS is unique to Asian cultures and unknown in Western cultures. Japanese who are especially at risk for developing TKS are those who score low on independence and high on interdependence, two traits found in traditional Japanese cultural values (Dinnel et al., 2002). Clinicians emphasize the importance of taking cultural values, influences, and differences into account when diagnosing behaviors across cultures (Fernando, 2002).

In Japan, it is very important to know and show the proper public behaviors.

Next, we'll discuss a very serious problem in the U.S. culture: school shootings.

E. Research Focus: School Shootings

What is their problem? Sometimes researchers are faced with answering tragic questions, such as why teenage boys had taken guns to schools and shot and killed at least 40 and wounded another 79, including students and teachers. Everyone wondered what had turned these adolescents into killers. In some cases, but not all, these adolescents might be clinically diagnosed with conduct disorder.

School shootings average about 2 per year.

Conduct disorder **refers to a repetitive and persistent pattern of behaving that has been going on for at least a year and that violates the established social rules or the rights of others. Problems may include aggressive behaviors such as threatening to harm people, abusing or killing animals, destroying property, being deceitful, or stealing.**

The diagnosis of conduct disorder seems to apply to Kipland Kinkel, age 15, who was charged with firing 50 rounds from a semiautomatic rifle into the school cafeteria, killing 2 students and injuring 22. Those who knew him said that Kinkel had a violent temper and a history of behavioral problems, which included killing his cat by putting a firecracker in its mouth, blowing up a dead cow, stoning cars from a highway overpass, and making bombs (Witkin et al., 1998). In trying to answer the question, Why did these adolescents shoot their fellow students and teachers, mental health professionals have primarily used the case study approach.

A *case study* **is an in-depth analysis of the thoughts, feelings, beliefs, experiences, behaviors, and problems of a single individual.** We'll give brief case studies of two school shooters and then examine some factors that put a student at risk for becoming a shooter.

Case Studies

The first school shooting that received national attention occurred in Moses Lake, Washington, on February 2, 1996. On that date, Barry Loukaitis, 14, fired on his algebra class, killing three and wounding one. He said that he wanted to get back at a popular boy who had teased him. Loukaitis shot that boy dead. Since then, school shootings have continued, averaging about two per year. As of this writing, there have been at least 23 adolescent boys and 1 girl who took guns to their schools, fired over 100 shots, killed at least 40 teachers and students, and wounded 79 more (IANSA, 2006; *New York Times*, 2003).

One such shooter was 16-year-old Evan Ramsey (below photo), who is now serving a 210-year sentence in a maximum-security cell, which is next door to the cell in which his father served 10 years (Roche, 2001). Ramsey grew up in a remote town in Alaska. He came from a broken family and was considered an outcast by his peers. He was slightly built, shy, and recalls, "I got stuff thrown at me, I got spit on, I got beat up. Sometimes I fought back, but I wasn't that good at fighting" (Jerome, 2001, p. 56). As his peers continued to pick on him, Ramsey reported them to the teachers, who initially punished his tormentors. "After a while, [the principal] told me to just start ignoring everybody. But then you can't take it anymore." Ramsey later shot dead the principal and a star basketball player.

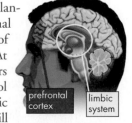

"I felt a sense of power with a gun. It was the only way to get rid of the anger."

However, very, very few students who are picked on and bullied commit violent acts, such as shooting teachers and students. We'll examine some of the factors that put students as risk for committing violent acts.

Risks Shared by Adolescent School Shooters

Although there are differences among school shooters, researchers have identified a number of risk factors that these boys shared (FBI, 2001; R. Lee, 2005; Verlinden et al., 2000).

■ Most of the boys (shooters) showed uncontrolled anger and depression, blaming others for problems and threatening violence. Most had poor coping skills, discipline problems at school or home, access to weapons, and a history of drug use.

■ Half of the boys had been given little parental supervision, had troubled family relationships, and perceived themselves as receiving little support from their families. Most of the boys had recently experienced the breakup of a relationship, a stressful event, or loss of status.

■ Most of the boys were generally isolated and rejected by their peers in school. Most had poor social skills and felt picked on, bullied, and persecuted and made friends who were also antisocial. The most commonly stated motives for shootings were to mete out justice to peers or adults who the teenage shooters believed had wronged them and to obtain status or importance among their peers. Most teenage shooters gave warning signs of their violent intentions that were not taken seriously.

Neurological factors. Although coming from a broken home, being bullied, and dealing with various life stressors are risk factors for adolescents committing violent acts, another important risk factor is inside an adolescent's brain. Everyone gets angry and has felt rage and the desire to get revenge, but most of us are able to control these violent impulses. This control involves the prefrontal cortex (p. 411), which has executive functions, such as planning, making decisions, and controlling strong emotional and violent impulses that arise from a very primitive part of the brain called the limbic system (p. 411) (right figure). At birth, the prefrontal cortex is immature, and it takes years to develop effective executive powers to inhibit and control the emotional and potentially violent impulses of the limbic system. The prefrontal cortex in the adolescent brain is still immature and may not reach complete maturity until the early 20s. For this reason, adolescents are especially at risk for committing all kinds of impulsive and violent behaviors and, in extreme cases, even school shootings (Luna, 2006).

prefrontal cortex   limbic system

Gathering data about what motivates school shooters is an example of using the case study method. Next, we turn to explaining several ways of treating two relatively common anxiety disorders—social and specific phobias.

H. Application Treating Phobias

Specific Phobia: Flying

At the beginning of this module, we told you about Kate Premo (right photo), who developed a phobia of flying. In some cases, people don't remember what caused their phobias, but Premo remembers exactly when her phobia began. Her fear began as a child when she was on a very turbulent and stressful flight. Her fear was further intensified by her memories of the terrorist bombing of Pan Am flight 103, which killed several of her fellow students. After that incident, her fear of flying turned into a real phobia that kept her from flying to visit friends and family. An estimated 25 million Americans have a phobia of flying called aviophobia, which may include fear of flying,

Kate is undergoing exposure therapy for fear of flying.

crashing, heights, being in small enclosed spaces, or not having control of the situation (Van Gerwen et al., 1997).

Most phobias do not disappear without some treatment, and on the few occasions that Premo was forced to fly, she dosed herself with so much alcohol and tranquilizers that she was groggy for days. Finally, she joined a weekend seminar that helps people overcome their fears of flying (M. Miller, 2003). Treatment for phobias can involve psychotherapy or drugs, or some combination of them. We'll discuss psychotherapy and drug treatment, beginning with cognitive-behavioral and exposure therapy.

Cognitive–Behavioral Therapy

Kate's phobia of flying involves fearful and irrational thoughts, which in turn cause increased physiological arousal. She can learn to reduce her irrational and fearful thoughts and reduce her arousal through cognitive-behavioral therapy (Singer & Dobson, 2006).

Cognitive-behavioral therapy involves using a combination of two methods: changing negative, unhealthy, or distorted thoughts and beliefs by substituting positive, healthy, and realistic ones; and changing limiting or disruptive behaviors by learning and practicing new skills to improve functioning.

Thoughts. Cognitive-behavioral therapy is useful in helping Kate control her fearful thoughts and eliminate dangerous beliefs about flying. For example, Kate had learned to fear various noises during flight, which she believed indicated trouble. To change these fearful thoughts, an airplane pilot explained the various noises, such as the thumps meant the landing gear was retracting after takeoff or being put down for landing. Thus, when Kate has a fearful thought, for example, "That noise must mean trouble," she immediately stops herself and substitutes a realistic thought, "That's just the landing gear."

Behaviors. Because Kate automatically gets nervous and fearful when just thinking about flying, she is instructed to do breathing, relaxation, and imagery exercises that will help her calm down. Deep and rhythmic breathing is an effective calming exercise because it distracts Kate from her fears and focuses her attention on a pleasant activity. Relaxing and tensing groups of muscles are also calming and help to decrease physiological arousal. Finally, imagery exercises are calming because focusing on pleasant images is a very powerful way of using her mind to control (relax) her body's fight-flight response.

Cognitive-behavioral methods have proved effective in treating a variety of phobias (Singer & Dobson, 2006). Sometimes cognitive-behavioral therapy is combined with another kind of therapy, called exposure therapy.

Exposure Therapy

For treating phobias, cognitive-behavioral therapy is often combined with exposure therapy. The most difficult part of Kate's phobia treatment is exposure therapy, when she must actually confront her most feared situation.

Exposure therapy consists of gradually exposing the person to the real anxiety-producing situations or objects that he or she is attempting to avoid and continuing exposure treatments until the anxiety decreases.

The first part of Kate's treatment involved cognitive-behavioral therapy, in which she learned how to control her irrational thoughts and acquire some basic relaxation techniques. The second part of her treatment involves exposure therapy, in which she is required to fly on a regularly scheduled airline, meaning that she will be exposed to her most feared situation. To help Kate deal with her fear of flying, Captain Michael Freebairn (photo below) sat next to Kate. Each time Kate tensed or looked fearful, the captain reassured Kate that all was normal and then reminded her to begin relaxation exercises (breathing

Kate smiles after successfully flying without feeling intense fear.

and relaxing muscles), to use pleasant images, and to substitute positive, healthy thoughts for negative, fearful ones. When the plane landed, Kate was all smiles (left photo) after realizing that exposure therapy had significantly reduced her fear or phobia of flying.

Programs that treat specific phobias, such as fear of flying, often use some combination of cognitive-behavioral and exposure therapy, which significantly reduces fear in the majority of clients (R. A. Friedman, 2006; M. Miller, 2003).

Clients not helped by cognitive-behavioral or exposure therapy may be given drug therapy (see next page) or may try virtual reality therapy.

Virtual reality therapy. Although clients never leave the ground, they sit in real airplane seats that vibrate to the sound of airplane engines. Clients wear head-mounted displays that surround them with 3-D experiences of "taking off" and "flying." Everything appears so real that clients who have a fear of flying begin to sweat and their hearts pound just as on real flights. Virtual reality therapy is a kind of exposure therapy, and it can be combined with relaxation exercises and thought substitution and be used to treat a variety of specific phobias, including fear of flying (Rothbaum et al., 2002).

Drug therapy for phobias involves tranquilizers or antidepressants.

When does a fear become a phobia?

Just as specific phobias can be successfully treated with psychotherapy, so too can social phobias, such as public speaking. Almost everyone is somewhat anxious about getting up and speaking in public. For a fear to become a full-blown phobia, however, the fear must be intense, irrational, and out of all proportion to the object or situation. For example, individuals with social phobias have such intense, excessive, and irrational fears of doing something humiliating or embarrassing that they will go to almost any lengths to avoid speaking in public. There are a number of very effective nondrug programs for treating social phobias (fear of speaking, performing, or acting in public). These programs combine cognitive-behavioral and exposure therapies and usually include the following four components (Coles & Horng, 2006).

1 Explain. Clinicians *explain* to the person that, since the fears involved in social phobias are usually learned, there are also methods to unlearn or extinguish such fears. The person is told how both thoughts and physiological arousal can exaggerate the phobic feelings and make the person go to any lengths to avoid the feared situation.

2 Learn and substitute. Clinicians found that some individuals needed to *learn* new social skills (initiating a conversation, writing a speech) so that they would function better in social situations. In addition, individuals were told to record their thoughts immediately after thinking about being in a feared situation. Then they were shown how to *substitute* positive and healthy thoughts for negative and fearful ones.

Treating social phobias involves four components.

3 Expose. Clinicians first used *imaginary exposure,* during which a person imagines being in the situation that elicits the fears. For example, some individuals imagined presenting material to their co-workers, making a classroom presentation, or initiating a conversation with the opposite sex. After imaginary exposure, clinicians used *real (in vivo) exposure,* in which the person gives his or her speech in front of a group of people or initiates conversations with strangers.

4 Practice. Clinicians asked subjects to *practice* homework assignments. For instance, individuals were asked to imagine themselves in feared situations and then to eliminate negative thoughts by substituting positive ones. In addition, individuals were instructed to gradually expose themselves to making longer and longer public presentations or having conversations with the opposite sex.

Researchers report that programs similar to the one above resulted in reduced social fears in about 56% of those who completed the program (Lincoln et al., 2003).

How effective are drugs?

Imagine being told to walk into a room and meet a group of strangers while you are stark naked. For most of us, this idea would cause such embarrassment, fear, and anxiety that we would absolutely refuse. This imagined situation is similar to the terrible kind of negative emotions that individuals with social phobia feel when they must initiate a conversation, meet strangers, or give a public presentation. As we have discussed, social phobias can be treated with cognitive-behavioral/exposure therapy. However, some individuals with social phobia do not choose to or are too fearful to complete a therapy program that includes exposure to the feared situation. Instead, these individuals may choose drug therapy, which may involve tranquilizers (benzodiazepines) or the increasingly prescribed antidepressants (Blanco et al., 2003; Coles & Horng, 2006).

The graphs below show the results of a double-blind study in which individuals with social phobia were given either a placebo or an antidepressant, in this case sertraline (Zoloft). After twenty weeks of treatment, individuals given antidepressants showed a significant clinical reduction in scores on both anxiety and fear tests, which means they were able to function relatively well in social situations (Van Ameringen et al., 2001). Although 34% of those on antidepressants showed a significant decrease in social anxiety, a remarkable 18% of those given placebos (sugar pills) showed a similar decrease. This means that the significant decrease in the social fears of almost one out of five individuals resulted from purely psychological factors, such as a client's expectations and beliefs ("The pill is powerful medicine and will reduce my fear").

Average Score on Fear Scale: Drug reduced fear more than placebo

Placebo	16
Drug	13

Average Score on Fear Scale: Drug reduced avoidance more than placebo

Placebo	16
Drug	13

Although drug treatments are effective in reducing social phobias, there are two potential problems. First, about 50–75% of individuals relapse when drugs are discontinued, which means that their original intense social phobic symptoms return. Second, long-term maintenance on drugs can result in tolerance and increases in dosage, which, in turn, can result in serious side effects, such as loss of memory (Stahl, 2000, 2002). Compared to drug treatment of phobias, psychotherapy programs have the advantages of no problems with tolerance and no unwanted physical side effects.

Which treatment to choose? Whether a client chooses psychotherapy or drug treatment for phobias depends to a large extent on the client's preference. That's because the treatment of different phobias, including specific phobias, social phobias, and agoraphobia, is about equally effective following either drug therapy (tranquilizers or antidepressants) or cognitive-behavioral/exposure therapy (Liebowitz et al., 1999).

✔ Summary Test

A. Factors in Mental Disorders

1. A prolonged or recurring problem that seriously interferes with an individual's ability to live a satisfying personal life and function in society is a _____. This definition takes into account genetic, behavioral, cognitive, and environmental factors, all of which may contribute to a mental disorder.

2. Mental disorders arise from the interaction of a number of factors. Biological factors include inherited behavioral tendencies, which are called (a)_____ factors. These factors contribute from 30 to 60% to the development of mental disorders. Biological factors also include the overreaction of brain structures to certain stimuli, which are called (b)_____ factors. Other factors that contribute to the development of mental disorders, such as deficits or problems in thinking, processing emotional stimuli, and social skills, are called (c)_____ factors. Being in or seeing a traumatic event, which is called an (d)_____ factor, can contribute to developing a mental disorder such as PTSD.

3. If a behavior is considered abnormal because it occurs infrequently in the general population, we are using a definition based on (a)_____ frequency. If a behavior is considered abnormal because it deviates greatly from what's acceptable, we are using a definition based on (b)_____. If a behavior is considered abnormal because it interferes with an individual's ability to function as a person or in society, we are using a definition based on (c)_____ behavior.

B. Assessing Mental Disorders

4. A systematic evaluation of an individual's various psychological, biological, and social factors that may be contributing to his or her problem is called a (a)_____. The primary method used in clinical assessments is to get information about a person's background, current behavior, attitudes, and emotions and also details of present problems through a (b)_____. A complete clinical assessment usually includes three major methods: (c)_____, _____, and _____.

5. Assessing mental disorders may be difficult because (a)_____ vary in intensity and complexity. The assessment must take into account past and present problems and current stressors. The accurate assessment of symptoms is important because it has significant implications for the kind of (b)_____ that the client will be given.

C. Diagnosing Mental Disorders

6. When mental health professionals determine whether an individual's specific problem meets or matches the standard symptoms that define a particular mental disorder, they are making a (a)_____. In trying to reach an agreement on the clinical diagnosis, mental health professionals use a set of guidelines developed by the American Psychiatric Association, which are called the (b)_____, abbreviated as DSM-IV-TR.

7. The DSM-IV-TR is a set of guidelines that uses five different dimensions or (a)_____ to diagnose mental disorders. The advantage of the DSM-IV-TR is that it helps mental health professionals communicate their findings, conduct research, and plan for treatment. One disadvantage of using the DSM-IV-TR to make a diagnosis is that it places people into specific categories that may have bad associations; this problem is called (b)_____.

D. Anxiety Disorders

8. A mental disorder that is marked by excessive and/or unrealistic worry or feelings of general apprehension about events or activities, when those feelings occur on a majority of days for a period of at least six months, is called _____. This anxiety disorder is treated with some form of psychotherapy and/or drugs known as benzodiazepines.

9. One mental disorder is characterized by recurring and unexpected panic attacks and continued worry about having another panic attack; such worry interferes with psychological functioning. This problem is called a _____ disorder.

10. Suppose you experience a period of intense fear or discomfort in which four or more of the following symptoms are present: pounding heart, sweating, trembling, shortness of breath, feelings of choking, chest pain, nausea, feeling dizzy, and fear of losing control or dying. You are having a (a)_____. Panic disorders are treated with a combination of benzodiazepines or antidepressants and (b)_____.

11. Another anxiety disorder characterized by increased physiological arousal and an intense, excessive, and irrational fear that is out of all proportion to the danger elicited by the object or situation is called a _____.

12. DSM-IV-TR divides phobias into three categories. Those that are triggered by common objects, situations, or animals (such as snakes or heights) are called (a)_____ phobias. Those that are brought on by having to perform in social situations and expecting to be humiliated and embarrassed are called (b)_____ phobias. Those that are characterized by fear of being in public places from which it may be difficult or embarrassing to escape if panic symptoms occur are called (c)_____. Once established, phobias are extremely persistent, continue for years, and may require professional treatment.

13. Persistent, recurring irrational thoughts that a person is unable to control and that interfere with normal functioning are called (a)_____. Irresistible impulses to perform some ritual over and over, even though the ritual serves no rational purpose, are called (b)_____. A disorder that consists of both of these behaviors and that interferes with normal functioning is called (c)_____. The most effective nondrug treatment for obsessive-compulsive disorder is (d)_____ therapy.

E. Somatoform Disorders

14. The appearance of real physical symptoms and bodily complaints that are not under voluntary control, have no known physical causes, extend over several years, and are believed to be caused by psychological factors is characteristic of (a)_____ disorders. DSM-IV-TR lists seven kinds of somatoform disorders. The occurrence of multiple symptoms—including pain, gastrointestinal, sexual, and neurological symptoms—that have no physical causes but are triggered by psychological problems or distress is referred to as (b)_____ disorder; a disorder characterized by unexplained and significant physical symptoms or deficits that affect voluntary motor or sensory functions and that suggest a real neurological or medical problem is called a (c)_____ disorder. A recent survey reported that somatoform disorders occur worldwide, although their symptoms may differ across cultures.

F. Cultural Diversity: An Asian Disorder

15. A social phobia found in Asia, especially Japan, that is characterized by morbid fear of making eye-to-eye contact, blushing, giving off an offensive odor, having an unpleasant or tense facial expression, or having trembling hands is called _____. This phobia appears to result from Asian cultural and social influences that stress the importance of showing proper behavior in public.

Percentage of Students	
Psychosomatic disorders	24%
Depressive reactions	20%
TKS	19%

G. Research Focus: School Shootings

16. A method of investigation that involves an in-depth analysis of the thoughts, feelings, beliefs, experiences, behaviors, or problems of a single individual is called a (a)_____. This method was used to decide if teenage school shooters had repetitive and persistent patterns of behavior that had been going on for at least a year and involved threats or physical harm to people or animals, destruction of property, being deceitful, or stealing. These symptoms define a mental disorder that is called (b)_____.

H. Application: Treating Phobias

17. There are several different treatments for phobias. A nondrug treatment combines changing negative, unhealthy, or distorted thoughts and beliefs by substituting positive, healthy, and realistic ones and learning new skills to improve functioning; this treatment is called (a)_____ therapy. Another therapy that gradually exposes the person to the real anxiety-producing situations or objects that he or she has been avoiding is called (b)_____ therapy. Individuals who are unwilling or too fearful to be exposed to fearful situations or objects may choose drug therapy.

18. Social and specific phobias have been successfully treated with tranquilizers called (a)_____. Although these drugs are effective, they have two problems: when individuals stop taking these drugs, the original fearful symptoms may return, which is called (b)_____; and, if individuals are maintained on drugs for some length of time, they may develop tolerance, which means they will have to take larger doses, which in turn may cause side effects such as loss of (c)_____. Researchers found that drug therapy was about equally effective as cognitive-behavioral or exposure therapy in reducing both social and specific phobias, including agoraphobia.

Answers: 1. mental disorder; 2. (a) genetic, (b) neurological, (c) cognitive-emotional-behavioral, (d) environmental; 3. (a) statistical, (b) social norms, (c) maladaptive; 4. (a) clinical assessment, (b) clinical interview, (c) clinical interview, psychological tests, neurological tests; 5. (a) symptoms, (b) treatment; 6. (a) clinical diagnosis, (b) Diagnostic and Statistical Manual of Mental Disorders-IV-TR; 7. (a) axes, (b) labeling; 8. generalized anxiety; 9. panic; 10. (a) panic attack, (b) psychotherapy; 11. phobia; 12. (a) specific, (b) social, (c) agoraphobia; 13. (a) obsessions, (b) compulsions, (c) obsessive-compulsive disorder, (d) exposure; 14. (a) somatoform, (b) somatization, (c) conversion; 15. taijin kyofusho, or TKS; 16. (a) case study, (b) conduct disorder; 17. (a) cognitive-behavioral, (b) exposure; 18. (a) benzodiazepines, (b) relapse, (c) memory

Critical Thinking

Why Women Marry Killers behind Bars

Questions

1. How would clinicians decide if women who fall in love with killers have a mental disorder?

In 2004, Scott Peterson was convicted of murdering his wife and unborn child. Within an hour of being on Death Row, he received a marriage proposal from a woman he didn't even know. As if this proposal wasn't bizarre enough, on his first day at San Quentin State Prison the warden's office received calls from over 30 women desperate to make contact with the convicted killer, many of them believing they were in love with Peterson.

About a decade earlier, Doreen Lioy, a 41-year-old woman, fell in love with satanic serial killer Richard Ramirez, who was convicted of torturing, sexually abusing, and murdering 13 people. Lioy described her attraction to Ramirez beginning immediately upon seeing his mug shot on TV: "I saw something in his eyes. Something that captivated me" (Warrick, 1996, E-1). Lioy began sending Ramirez letters and visiting him behind bars, and soon after they married at the prison, even though Ramirez would eventually be executed. Lioy speaks about her complete devotion to her new husband: "Because of my love for Richard, I have given up my family, home, employment, and friends" (Warrick, 1996, E-1).

There is such a demand for prisoner romance that matchmaking websites, such as prisonpenpals.com, offer thousands of ads from inmates who want to find love outside of their cellblocks. Marriages in

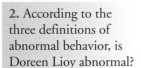

A woman fell in love with a convicted and jailed killer.

2. According to the three definitions of abnormal behavior, is Doreen Lioy abnormal?

prisons are common enough for each prison to have its own set of regulations for inmate marriages. Some of the rules for one California prison include: "No property will be exchanged and kept by inmate after the marriage ceremony. The marriage ceremony will be conducted in the visiting area with the glass separating the couple being married" ("Inmate marriages," 2007).

According to Sheila Isenberg, author of *Women Who Marry Men Who Kill*, women who pursue intimate relationships with killers are usually attractive, intelligent, and very well accomplished. Isenberg also says most of these women have come from loveless homes and have been abused by men earlier in their lives. Gilda Carle, a relationship adviser, explains that these women are attracted to the "bad boy syndrome" and they feel special when the man who has hurt and killed others, treats them with love, kindness, and respect. In fact, the most repugnant murderers receive the most attention from women.

Women in love with convicted killers find the danger, excitement, and drama of prison romance more arousing than the routine and predictability of romance outside prison. Having an intimate relationship with a man behind bars also makes the relationship exceptionally safe. (Adapted from Fimrite & Taylor, 2005; "Inmate marriages," 2007; Warrick, 1996, 1997; Wiltenburg, 2003)

3. According to Freud's psychodynamic theory of personality, why is it difficult to explain why women fall in love with and marry killers?

4. Which of the five axes in DSM-IV-TR best describes the problems these women share?

5. What are the advantages and disadvantages of labeling these women's problems?

Suggested Answers

1. Clinicians would use a clinical assessment (neurological and psychological/personality tests and interviews) to identify symptoms and then match symptoms to the mental disorders listed in the DSM-IV-TR.
2. A woman who falls in love with a convicted killer after seeing his mug shot and pursues him even though he will never be able to leave prison is certainly abnormal in terms of statistical frequency, in terms of deviation from social norms, and in terms of engaging in maladaptive behavior (giving up family, home, work, friends).
3. According to Freud's psychodynamic theory of personality,

women who fall in love with and marry killers are influenced by unconscious forces, wishes, and repressed desires, which are difficult to examine and understand because they are unconscious and not easily revealed or brought to the surface.
4. To identify potential problems of women who fall in love with killers, clinicians might use Axis II, which focuses on long-standing personality traits that are maladaptive or impair functioning.
5. One advantage in labeling these women's problem is that it may help decide which therapy is best. One disadvantage is that giving women a label may bias how others perceive and respond.

Links to Learning

Learning Activities

- **POWERSTUDY FOR INTRODUCTION TO PSYCHOLOGY 4.0**
by Tom Doyle and Rod Plotnik
SuperModule: Check out "Assessment & Anxiety Disorders" on **PowerStudy.** It includes complete paragraph-by-paragraph explanations of all content using fully-narrated animations and graphics. An onscreen toolbar allows immediate access to text, text outline, and module glossary with notetaking and printing capabilities. This module also includes:
  - Video—Imbedded videos discuss panic disorder and attacks, obsessive-compulsive disorder, and virtual reality therapy among other topics.
  - A test of your knowledge using an interactive version of the Summary Test on pages 526 and 527. Also access related quizzing-true/false, multiple choice, and matching.
  - An interactive version of the Critical Thinking exercise "Why Women Marry Killers behind Bars" on page 528.
  - Key terms, a chapter summary including chapter abstract, and a special extended list of hotlinked websites that correlate to this module.

- *CengageNOW*
academic.cengage.com/login
Need help studying? This site is your one-stop study shop.
Take a Pre-Test and CengageNOW will generate a Personalized Study Plan based on your test results. The Study Plan will identify the topics you need to review and direct you to online resources to help you master those topics. You can then take a Post-Test to determine the concepts you have mastered and what you still need to work on.

- **INTRODUCTION TO PSYCHOLOGY BOOK COMPANION WEBSITE**
academic.cengage.com/psychology/plotnik
Visit your book companion website where you will find more resources to help you study. At this site, you will find Learning Objectives, Internet Exercises, quizzing, flash cards, and a pronunciation glossary.

- *STUDY GUIDE and WEBTUTOR*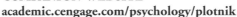
Check the corresponding module in your Study Guide for effective student tips and help learning the material presented. Also go to **academic.cengage.com/webtutor** for an interactive version of the Study Guide features.

Study Questions

*A. **Factors in Mental Disorders**—The night before a big exam, John gets drunk to relax. However, the next day he has a terrible hangover and does poorly on the exam. Is his behavior abnormal? (**Suggested answer p. 634**)

*B. **Assessing Mental Disorders**—Why must mental health professionals spend so much time and effort in assessing their clients' symptoms? (**Suggested answer p. 634**)

C. **Diagnosing Mental Disorders**—Why are negative attitudes or stereotypes associated with mental illness but not with physical illness?

D. **Anxiety Disorders**—Some of the things that make you anxious have no effect on other people. How do you explain this?

E. **Somatoform Disorders**—Why do you think some people express their psychological distress or emotional problems by exhibiting bodily symptoms?

F. **Cultural Diversity: An Asian Disorder**—What kind of cultural influences and pressures make the vast majority of us afraid to speak in public?

G. **Research Focus: School Shootings**—What are some characteristics that teenage school shooters have in common?

*H. **Application: Treating Phobias**—If you were very shy and uncomfortable about meeting strangers and talking to groups, what could you do about this problem? (**Suggested answer p. 634**)

*These questions are answered in Appendix B.

MODULE 23
Mood Disorders & Schizophrenia

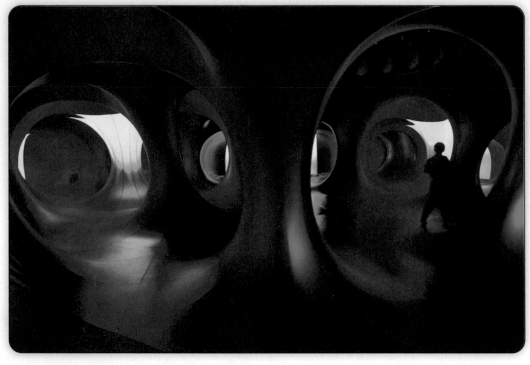

 PowerStudy 4.0™ Complete Module

Introduction

Mood Disorder

Why do his thoughts speed up?

Chuck Elliot (photo below) was checking out the exhibits at an electronics convention in Las Vegas when suddenly his mind seemed to go wild and spin at twice its regular speed. His words could not keep up with his thoughts, and he was talking in what sounded like some strange code, almost like rapid fire "dot, dot, dot." Then he stripped off all his clothes and ran stark naked through the gambling casino of the Hilton Hotel. The police were called and Chuck was taken to a mental hospital. After his symptoms were reviewed, Chuck was diagnosed with what was then called manic depression.

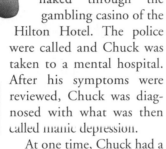

Chuck Elliot's mind spins and whirls out of contol. He was diagnosed with having bipolar I disorder.

At one time, Chuck had a very successful career. After taking postgraduate courses, he obtained a doctor of education degree (Ed.D.). He started and ran his own video production business while also designing computer software. But since that first strange episode at the computer electronics convention, Chuck has been hospitalized about twice a year when his mind races and spins wildly out of control in what are called manic episodes. He usually takes medication, but because the drug slows him down more than he likes, he stops taking his medication every so often. Without medication, his energy may come back with such force that it blasts him into superactive days and sleepless nights, and he often ends up in a psychiatric hospital.

His last regular job ended when he was in the middle of another manic attack. He was going on 100 hours without sleep when he went out to his car, grabbed a bunch of magazines, books, fruits, and vegetables, and piled them all on the desk in his office. When his boss came by and found a desk piled high with junk and Chuck sitting there with his mind spinning, the boss fired him on the spot (C. Brooks, 1994). Since that time, despite his very good academic, computer, and business qualifications, he has not been able to hold a steady job.

More recently, Chuck married a woman he had been dating for only ten days. She understands Chuck very well because she too is manic-depressive and has similar mental health problems. She hopes that they can care for each other. She says, "Chuck is the most brilliant man I have ever met. I am so lucky" (C. Brooks, 1994, p. 4).

In this module, we'll explain Chuck's illness, his treatment, and how he is dealing with his problem.

Schizophrenia

Why was he hearing voices?

When Michael McCabe was 18 years old, Marsha, his mother, thought that he was just about over his rebellious phase. She was looking forward to relaxing and enjoying herself. But then Michael said that he was hearing voices. At first Marsha thought that Michael's voices came from his smoking marijuana. But the voices persisted for two weeks, and Marsha checked Michael into a private drug treatment center. He left the center after 30 days and seemed no better off than he had been before. Several days later, Marsha found Michael in her parents' home, a couple of miles down the road from her own house. Michael was sitting on the floor, his head back, holding his throat and making grunting sounds like an animal. Marsha got really scared and called the police, but before they arrived, Michael ran off.

Michael spent time with his grandparents, who finally called Marsha and said that they couldn't take his strange behavior anymore. Once again Marsha called the police. Just as Michael (photo below) tried to run away, the police caught him and took him to the community psychiatric hospital.

Marsha received a call from a psychiatrist at the hospital, who explained that Michael had been diagnosed as having schizophrenia, a serious mental disorder that includes hearing voices and having disoriented thinking. A few days later, Michael escaped from the hospital. He was later returned by police, put into leather restraints, and given antipsychotic drugs that would also calm him down. Michael remained in the hospital and was treated with drugs for about a month, with little success.

Michael McCabe, 18 years old, began hearing voices and was diagnosed with having schizophrenia.

Just about the time Marsha was at her wits' end about what to do next, Michael was put on a new antipsychotic drug, clozapine. After about a month on the new drug, Michael improved enough to be discharged back into Marsha's care (C. Brooks, 1994, 1995a).

In this module, we'll explain what schizophrenia is, describe the drugs Michael was given, and report how his treatment is working.

What's Coming

We'll discuss several different mental disorders and their treatments. We'll explain mood disorders and their treatments, including the treatment of last resort for depression, electroconvulsive shock therapy. We'll also examine several personality disorders and different kinds of schizophrenia, along with old and new antipsychotic drugs. We'll end with a group of strange and unusual disorders, one of which is multiple personality.

We'll begin with Chuck Elliot's problem, which is an example of one kind of mood disorder.

A. Mood Disorders

How bad is it? Depression is not choosy; it happens to about 6 million Americans a year. Major depression is one example of a mood disorder.

A *mood disorder* **is a prolonged and disturbed emotional state that affects almost all of a person's thoughts, feelings, and behaviors.**

Most of us have experienced a continuum of moods, with depression on one end and elation on the other. However, think of the depression or blues that most of us feel as having a paper cut on our finger. Then major depression is more like having to undergo open-heart surgery. It's some of the worst news that you can get.

The DSM-IV-TR lists ten different mood disorders, but we'll focus on the symptoms of three of the more common forms: major depressive disorder, bipolar I disorder, and dysthymic disorder.

Major Depression

Popular singer-songwriter Sheryl Crow (photo below) says that she has battled major depression most of her life.

Major depressive disorder **is marked by at least two weeks of continually being in a bad mood, having no interest in anything, and getting no pleasure from activities. In addition, a person must have at least four of the following symptoms: problems with eating, sleeping, thinking, concentrating, or making decisions, lacking energy, thinking about suicide, and feeling worthless or guilty (American Psychiatric Association, 2000).**

Sheryl Crow says that she had been on a world tour with Michael Jackson, singing in front of 70,000 screaming fans. When the tour ended, she was back in her lonely apartment with the anxiety of having to get a record contract. All this stress triggered her first bout of depression, which resulted in her lying in bed, hardly able to move, going unshowered, stringy-haired, and ordering take-out for seven straight months (Hirshey, 2003). Like Crow, about 16% of U.S. adults reported at least one lifetime episode of major depression, with women outnumbering men by a ratio of 2 to 1 (Thase, 2006).

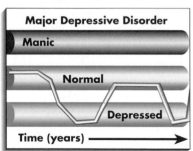

To help understand mood disorders, look at the left figure, which shows three general mood states. The top bar shows a manic episode or period of incredible energy and euphoria that we'll discuss later. The middle bar shows a normal period when a person's moods and emotions do not interfere with normal psychological functioning. However, like what happened to Crow, some event may cause a person to go from a normal period to a period of depression (bottom bar). Individuals may fluctuate between a normal period and a bout of severe depression. For example, Mike Wallace, television reporter for "60 Minutes," experienced three terrible bouts with depression, which he calls a crushing and paralyzing time of endless darkness, worse than death, a time of thinking about committing suicide (J. E. Brody, 1998).

Bipolar I Disorder

Unlike Sheryl Crow, who has a major depressive disorder, Chuck Elliot (right photo) fluctuates between two extreme moods of depression and mania; he has what is called bipolar I disorder.

Bipolar I disorder **is marked by fluctuations between episodes of depression and mania. A manic episode goes on for at least a week, during which a person is unusually euphoric, cheerful, and high and has at least three of the following symptoms: has great self-esteem, has little need for sleep, speaks rapidly and frequently, has racing thoughts, is easily distracted, and pursues pleasurable activities (American Psychiatric Association, 2000).**

About 1.3% of the population suffer from bipolar I disorder, and 1.6% suffer from only manic episodes (Rush, 2003).

Chuck Elliot has the typical pattern of bipolar I depression. As shown in the graph below, Elliot may have periods of being normal, which may turn into extreme manic episodes followed by periods of extreme depression.

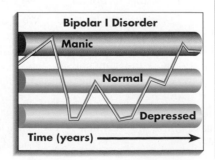

Dysthymic Disorder

Another mood disorder that is less serious than major depression is called dysthymic *(dis-THY-mick)* disorder.

Dysthymic disorder **is characterized by being chronically but not continuously depressed for a period of two years. While depressed, a person experiences at least two of the following symptoms: poor appetite, insomnia, fatigue, low self-esteem, poor concentration, and feelings of hopelessness (American Psychiatric Association, 2000).**

Individuals with dysthymic disorder, which affects about 6% of the population, are often described as "down in the dumps." Some of these individuals become accustomed to such feelings and describe themselves as "always being this way."

Besides these three mood disorders, we have also discussed another mood disorder, seasonal affective disorder, or SAD (p. 159). People with SAD become depressed as a result of a decrease in the number of sunny days, such as occurs in fall and winter months, and they recover with the arrival of summer.

Next, we'll examine some of the common causes of depression.

Causes of Mood Disorders

Sheryl Crow says that she has had a lifetime battle with mood disorders and, contrary to popular myths, when depressed she cannot make great music or work much at anything. Crow thought her depression was due to some

What caused Crow's depression?

chemical imbalance in her brain and that depression ran in families (partly inherited or genetic) because her father suffered from similar mood problems (Hirshey, 2003). Let's see if she's right.

Biological Factors

Using recently developed techniques for studying the living brain and information from mapping the genetic code (Human Genome Project—p. 68), researchers have been actively studying biological factors involved in mood disorders.

Biological factors underlying depression **are genetic, neurological, chemical, and physiological components that may predispose or put someone at risk for developing a mood disorder.**

Genetic factors. Sheryl Crow was right about depression having a genetic component. As shown in the graph below, if one identical twin has a bipolar disorder, the risk that the other twin will develop the disorder may be as high as 80%, while the chance of both fraternal twins developing this disorder is only 8–16% (Moldin et al., 1991). Researchers believe there is no single gene but rather a com-

Risk of Developing Bipolar Disorder

| Identical twins | 80% |
| Fraternal twins | 16% |

bination of genes that produce a risk, or predisposition, for developing a mood disorder (M. C. Miller, 2005a). One theory states that defects in specific genes affect our sensitivity to stress, which can result in depression (Weinberger, 2005). Genes play a role in developing a mood disorder because genes are involved in the regulation of the brain's neurotransmitter or chemical system used for communication (Charney, 2003).

Neurological factors. Sheryl Crow was also right about depression involving a chemical imbalance in her brain. A group of neurotransmitters, called the *monoamines* (serotonin, norepinephrine, and dopamine), are known to be involved in mood problems. Abnormal levels of certain neurotransmitters can interfere with the functioning of the brain's communication networks and, in turn, put individuals at risk for developing mood disorders (Gotlib & Hammen, 2002). More recently, researchers discovered that continued stress causes the brain and the body's stress management machinery (p. 485) to go into overdrive, which in turn alters hormonal and neurotransmitter levels and can trigger depression (Holden, 2003b).

Brain scans. Researchers took computerized photos of the structure and function of living brains and compared brains of depressed patients with those of individuals with normal moods. Researchers reported that a brain area called the anterior cingulate cortex (figure below) was overactive in very depressed patients. When the anterior cingulate cortex is overactive, it allows negative emotions to overwhelm thinking and mood. These same researchers cured two-thirds of a group of very depressed patients who had not benefitted from years of psychotherapy, drugs, or electroconvulsive therapy (p. 535) by electrically stimulating the brain, which led to reduced activity in the anterior cingulate cortex (Mayberg, 2006; Mayberg et al., 2005). This and other research examining the brains of depressed patients suggest that faulty brain structure or function contributes to the onset and/or maintenance of mood disorders (Thase, 2006).

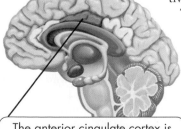

The anterior cingulate cortex is overactive in very depressed patients, which allows negative emotions to overwhelm thoughts and mood.

Psychosocial Factors

In addition to biological factors, an individual may be at risk for depression because of psychosocial factors.

Psychosocial factors, **such as personality traits, cognitive styles, social supports, and the ability to deal with stressors, interact with predisposing biological factors to put one at risk for developing a mood disorder.**

Stressful live events. Sheryl Crow says that her seven-month-long period of depression was triggered by the overwhelming stress of seeing a fantastic world tour end with her living in a lonely apartment, having to wait tables while struggling to get a record contact. Researchers found that stressful life events are strongly related to the onset of mood disorders such as depression (Kendler et al., 2004).

Negative cognitive style. There is considerable research to support Aaron Beck's (1991) idea that depression may result from one's perceiving the world in a negative way, which in turn leads to feeling depressed. We'll discuss Beck's theory later in the Application, but just note here that having a negative cognitive style or *negative way of thinking* and perceiving can put one at risk for developing a mood disorder such as depression.

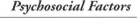

Certain personality factors increase risk for mood disorders.

Personality factors. Another psychosocial factor involves a person's personality traits. For example, individuals who are especially sensitive to and *overreact to negative events* (disappointments, rejections, criticisms) with feelings of fear, anxiety, guilt, sadness, and anger are at risk for developing a mood disorder (D. N. Klein et al., 2002). Researchers also found that individuals who make their self-worth primarily dependent on what others say or think have a kind of *socially dependent personality,* which puts them at risk for becoming seriously depressed when facing the end of a close personal relationship or friendship. Some individuals have a *need for control,* which puts them at risk for depression when they encounter uncontrollable stress or life events (Mazure et al., 2000).

The above psychosocial factors interact with underlying biological factors to increase one's risk of developing a mood disorder (Thase, 2006).

Next, we discuss the treatment for depression.

A. Mood Disorders

What's the treatment? Because the causes of depression include both biological and psychosocial causes, the treatment for depression, depending upon the diagnosis and severity, may include psychotherapy, antidepressant drugs, or both. We'll discuss the effectiveness of drugs and psychotherapy.

Major Depression and Dysthymic Disorder

After months of depression, Sheryl Crow's mother finally persuaded her (with threats of coming to haul her baby out of bed) to get professional treatment, which involved both psychotherapy and antidepressant drugs.

Treatment often requires professional help.

Antidepressant drugs act by increasing the levels of a specific group of neurotransmitters (monoamines—serotonin, norepinephrine, and dopamine) that are involved in the regulation of emotions and moods.

Selective serotonin reuptake inhibitors—SSRIs. About 80% of prescribed antidepressant drugs, such as Prozac and Zoloft, belong to a group of drugs called *SSRIs* (selective serotonin reuptake inhibitors) (Noonan & Cowley, 2002). The SSRIs work primarily by raising the level of the neurotransmitter serotonin. When the older antidepressant drugs (tricyclics) were compared with SSRIs, both groups of drugs proved effective, but the older drugs had more undesirable side effects than SSRIs (Faravelli et al., 2003). In 2005, 189 million prescriptions were written for antidepressants (Vedantam, 2006).

Effectiveness of antidepressants. When depressed patients use an antidepressant, which may take up to 8 weeks to work, symptoms for only one-third of the patients will go away (comparable to the recovery rate for a placebo) (Berenson, 2006). Often, patients must try a second or third antidepressant until they find one that works well. Between 50 and 67% of depressed patients benefit from trying additional drugs, while the remaining 33 to 50% receive little or no benefit (Rush, 2006a, 2006b).

Psychotherapy. Researchers compared patients who had received antidepressant drugs, psychotherapy, or a combination of drugs and psychotherapy to treat major depression. For patients with less severe depression, psychotherapy was as effective as antidepressant drugs. For patients with more severe depression, a combination of antidepressant drugs (SSRIs) and psychotherapy was more effective than either treatment alone (Hollon et al., 2002). Interestingly, 25–60% of depressed patients may have significantly reduced symptoms when treated with only placebos (patients believed the placebos were antidepressant drugs) (Leuchter et al., 2002).

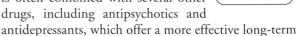

Antidepressants and psychotherapy are about equally effective.

Relapse. When patients who had recovered were followed for 18 months, the results were discouraging because, within that time, 70% of the patients had relapsed, which means they became depressed again and required additional treatment. Of those who maintained their recovery and were doing well, 30% had been treated with psychotherapy, 20% with antidepressant drugs, and 20% with placebos. Thus, patients treated with psychotherapy were somewhat less likely to relapse than those treated with drugs or placebos (Shea et al., 1992).

Because 70% of patients treated for depression relapse within 18 months and 82% relapse during the first five years, clinicians concluded that major depression is a long-term or chronic disorder that may require further treatments during the patient's lifetime (Moran, 2004; Vos et al., 2004).

Bipolar I Disorder

Unlike Sheryl Crow's problem, which is major depressive disorder, Chuck Elliot has bipolar I disorder, which means that he cycles between episodes of depression and mania. For example, one of Elliot's manic episodes lasted four days, during which he was in almost constant motion and did not sleep. Several times, when he lost control, he screamed at his wife and ripped the blinds from the windows. His wife called the police, who handcuffed Elliot (right photo) and drove him to a psychiatric hospital for drug treatment.

Bipolar I is treated with lithium and other drugs.

Treatment. In the past, the drug of choice to treat bipolar I disorder was a mood stabilizer called lithium *(LITH-ee-um)*. Although still used today as the drug of choice, lithium is often combined with several other drugs, including antipsychotics and antidepressants, which offer a more effective long-term treatment program (C. F. Newman, 2006).

Lithium is thought to prevent manic episodes by preventing neurons from being overstimulated (Lenox & Hahn, 2000). When Elliot takes medication, he functions well enough that he has enrolled in law school and is working toward his degree. The problem arises when Elliot doesn't take lithium. When patients with bipolar I disorder stop taking lithium (and combined drugs), about 50% experience a manic episode (Keck & McElroy, 2003). In terms of effectiveness, 50% of bipolar patients are greatly helped with a combined drug program (lithium plus other drugs), 30% are partially helped, and 20% get little or no help (F. K. Goodwin, 2003).

Mania. Lithium has been found to be effective in treating individuals with *mania*—that is, experiencing manic episodes without the depression (F. K. Goodwin, 2003). Because lithium prevents mania, patients may stop taking it to experience the euphoria they miss, as Elliot did several times.

Relapse. For both major depression and bipolar I disorder, 10–30% of patients receive no help from current drugs and 30–70% initially improve but later relapse. Researchers are constantly searching for new ways to treat mood disorders and prevent relapse.

For individuals with major depression who are not helped by drugs, there is something called the treatment of last resort.

B. Electroconvulsive Therapy

Definition and Usage

What's it like to get ECT?

Because the use of shock as therapy has often been wrongly portrayed in the media, it helps to see the treatment from the eyes of an actual patient.

". . . As far as manic-depressive tales go, my stories are typical. My illness went undiagnosed for a decade, a period of euphoric highs and desperate lows highlighted by $25,000 shopping sprees, impetuous trips to Tokyo, Paris, and Milan, drug and alcohol binges. . . . After seeing eight psychiatrists, I finally received a diagnosis of bipolar disorder on my 32nd birthday. Over the next year and a half, I was treated unsuccessfully with more than 30 medications. My suburban New Jersey upbringing, my achievements as a film major at Wesleyan, and a thriving career in public relations couldn't help me. . . . As a last resort, I'm admitted to the hospital

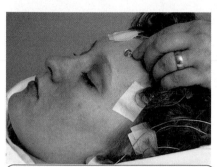

Electrodes on this patient's forehead will carry electricity through the brain and cause a major seizure.

for ECT, electroconvulsive therapy, more commonly known as electroshock. . . . The doctor presses a button. Electric current shoots through my brain for an instant, causing a grand-mal seizure for 20 seconds. . . . I wake up 30 minutes later and think I'm in a hotel room in Acapulco. My head feels as if I've just downed a frozen margarita too quickly. . . . After four treatments, there is marked improvement. No more egregious highs or lows. But there are huge gaps in my memory. I avoid friends and neighbors because I don't know their names anymore. I can't remember the books I've read or the movies I've seen. I have trouble recalling simple vocabulary. I forget phone numbers. . . . But I continue treatment because I'm getting better. . . . On the one-year anniversary of my first electroshock treatment, I'm clearheaded and even-keeled. I call my doctor to announce my 'new and improved' status. . . . Two and a half years later, I still miss ECT. But medication keeps my illness in check, and I'm more sane than I've ever been" (Behrman, 1999, p. 67).

This patient received electroconvulsive therapy (ECT).

Electroconvulsive therapy, or *ECT,* involves placing electrodes on the skull and administering a mild electric current that passes through the brain and causes a seizure. Usual treatment consists of a series of 10–12 ECT sessions, at the rate of about three per week.

Usage. Because antidepressants fail to decrease depression in up to 30% of patients in the United States, the only other available treatment is ECT—the last resort. As shown in the right graph, ECT's use has been increasing since 1980 and is currently estimated at 100,000 patients per year (*Newsweek*, 2006). ECT is used primarily to treat mood disorders (84%), especially depression.

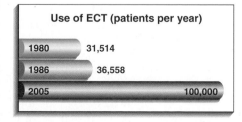

Use of ECT (patients per year)

1980	31,514
1986	36,558
2005	100,000

We'll discuss the pros and cons of electroconvulsive therapy.

Effectiveness of ECT

Why is ECT considered the last resort?

Because antidepressants had not worked, the patient we just described agreed to ECT. The reason ECT is the last resort for treating depression is that ECT produces major brain seizures and may cause varying degrees of memory loss. However, even as a treatment of last resort, ECT is effective in reducing depressive symptoms in about 60–80% of patients (Sackeim et al., 2000). For example, the graph below shows the results for eight out of nine seriously depressed patients who had received no help from antidepressants. After a series of ECT treatments, they showed a dramatic reduction in depressive symptoms and remained symptom-free after one year (Paul et al., 1981). However, the average

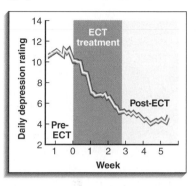

relapse rate after ECT treatment exceeds 50%, which means patients may need antidepressant therapy following ECT treatment or additional ECT treatments for depression (Nemeroff, 2007). Researchers are not sure how ECT works but suggest that it may temporarily reduce blood flow to certain brain areas or change neurotransmitter levels (Nobler & Sackeim, 1998).

Modern ECT. Unlike patients who received ECT in the movie *One Flew Over the Cuckoo's Nest,* there is no evidence that modern ECT procedures cause brain damage or turn people into "vegetables" (Ende et al., 2000). Various modifications to modern ECT, including the proper placement of electrodes on the scalp and reduced levels of electric current, have lessened the risk for complications (Nemeroff, 2007; Sackeim et al., 2000).

Memory loss. A serious side effect of ECT is memory loss, which, similar to the patient we described on the left, may range from a persistent loss of memory for events experienced during the weeks of treatment to include events before and after treatment. Following ECT treatment, there is a gradual improvement in memory functions, and researchers have reported that long-term impairment of memory following ECT was minimal and returned to pretreatment levels within six months (Sackeim & Stern, 1997). In spite of the finding that some memories return, about 50% of patients given ECT reported considerable memory loss, more so for information about the world than about themselves (personal memories), as long as three years after treatment (Lisanby et al., 2000).

Mental health experts have cautiously endorsed the use of ECT as a treatment of last resort for some types of severe depression. However, experts add that every patient should be informed as fully as possible of the potential risks, such as memory loss (R. M. Glass, 2001; K. G. Rasmussen, 2003).

Next, we'll discuss a disorder shared by many serial killers.

C. Personality Disorders

What are serial killers like?

We have all heard the expression "Don't judge a book by its cover." That advice proved absolutely true when we heard what their friends and neighbors said about the following individuals.

A high-school classmate of Joel Rifkin said that he was "quiet, shy, not the kind of guy who would do something like this." Rifkin confessed to killing 17 prostitutes.

His boss said David Berkowitz was "quiet and reserved and kept pretty much to himself. That's the way he was here, nice—a quiet, shy fellow." Berkowitz, known as "Son of Sam," was convicted of killing 6 people.

A neighbor of Westley Allan Dodd said that he "seemed so harmless, such an all-around, basic good citizen." Dodd was executed for kidnapping, raping, and murdering 3 small boys.

A neighbor said John Esposito "was such a quiet, caring person. He was a very nice person." Esposito was charged with kidnapping a young girl and keeping her in an underground bunker for 16 days.

A friend said Jeffrey Dahmer "didn't have much to say, was quiet, like the average Joe." Dahmer confessed to killing and dismembering 15 people (*Time*, July 12, 1993, p. 18).

Why do friends describe serial killers as quiet, nice, and caring?

Notice how friends and neighbors judged all these cold-blooded killers to be "quiet" and "nice" and even "caring" individuals. However, while these individuals appeared very ordinary in public appearance and behavior, each was hiding a deep-seated, serious, and dangerous personality disorder (Hickey, 2006).

A *personality disorder* **consists of inflexible, long-standing, maladaptive traits that cause significantly impaired functioning or great distress in one's personal and social life (American Psychiatric Association, 2000).**

Personality disorders are found in about 9% of the adult population in the United States, affecting men and women equally, although gender may influence which personality disorder a person develops (Kluger, 2003). Of the ten different personality disorders described in DSM-IV-TR, here are six of the more common types.

■ *Paranoid personality disorder* **is a pattern of distrust and suspiciousness and perceiving others as having evil motives (0.5–2.5% of population).**

■ *Schizotypal personality disorder* **is characterized by an acute discomfort in close relationships, distortions in thinking, and eccentric behavior (3–5% of population).**

■ *Histrionic personality disorder* **is characterized by excessive emotionality and attention seeking (2% of population).**

■ *Obsessive-compulsive personality disorder* **is an intense interest in being orderly, achieving perfection, and having control (4% of population).**

■ *Dependent personality disorder* **refers to a pattern of being submissive and clingy because of an excessive need to be taken care of (2% of population).**

■ *Antisocial personality disorder* **refers to a pattern of disregarding or violating the rights of others without feeling guilt or remorse (3% of population, predominantly males) (American Psychiatric Association, 2000).**

Individuals with personality disorders often have the following characteristics: troubled childhoods, childhood problems that continue into adulthood, maladaptive or poor personal relationships, and abnormal behaviors that are at the extreme end of the behavioral continuum. Their difficulties arise from a combination of genetic, psychological, social, and environmental factors (Vargha-Khadem, 2000).

We'll focus on one particular personality disorder, the antisocial personality, because it is the one most mentioned by the media.

The five "nice," "quiet" killers we described would probably be diagnosed as having antisocial personality disorder or some combination of personality disorders. Between 50 and 80% of prisoners meet the criteria for a diagnosis of antisocial personality disorder (Ogloff, 2006). But, not all people diagnosed with antisocial personality disorder are alike, and the diagnostic symptoms vary on a continuum. At one end of the continuum are the chronic delinquents, bullies, and lawbreakers; at the other end are the serial killers.

Delinquent. An example of someone on the delinquent end of the continuum is Tom, who always seemed to be in trouble. As a child, he would steal items (silverware) from home and sell or swap them for things he wanted. As a teenager, he skipped classes in school, set deserted buildings on fire, forged his father's name on checks, stole cars, and was finally sent to a federal institution. After Tom served his time, he continued to break the law, and by the age of 21, he had been arrested and imprisoned 50–60 times (Spitzer et al., 1994).

Serial killer. At the other end of the psychopathic continuum is serial killer Jeffrey Dahmer, who would pick up young gay men, bring them home, drug them, strangle them, have sex with their corpses, and then, in some cases, eat their flesh. As Dahmer said in an interview, "I could completely control a person—a person that I found physically attractive, and keep them with me as long as possible, even if it meant just keep a part of them" (Gleick et al., 1994, p. 129).

Jeffrey Dahmer was diagnosed as having an antisocial personality disorder.

Two characteristics. One characteristic of people with antisocial personality disorder is their consistent pattern of disregard for or violation of the rights or properties of others; they may steal, harass, or beat people, destroy property, kidnap, or kill. Another characteristic is their dishonesty, lying, or deceitful manipulation of others. The combination of these two groups of characteristics makes these individuals potentially dangerous to deal with and, as you'll see, very difficult to treat or change into more responsible individuals.

Antisocial Personality Disorder: Causes and Treatment

How does one become antisocial?

Researchers have found genetic and neurological factors that may predispose individuals for developing an antisocial personality, which involves behaving irresponsibly, being a habitual and convincing liar, having no guilt or remorse, being impulsive and reckless, and failing to learn from experience (C. E. Lewis, 1991). Antisocial personality disorder is three times more common in men than in women. These individuals usually have a number of other related problems, such as substance abuse and other personality disorders (American Psychiatric Association, 2000; K. N. Levy & Scott, 2006). We'll discuss the causes and treatment of antisocial personality disorder.

Causes

Antisocial personality disorder involves complex psychosocial and biological factors (Moffitt, 2005).

Psychosocial factors. To identify psychosocial factors, researchers followed more than 500 cases of children who had been referred for behavioral problems (Robins et al., 1991). Many of these problem children, who later developed antisocial personality disorder, had originally been brought to the clinic because of aggressive and antisocial behaviors, such as truancy, theft, disobeying their parents, and frequent lying with no remorse. Thus, an aggressive and antisocial child whom parents find almost impossible to control is at risk for developing an antisocial personality (Morey, 1997).

Another psychosocial factor that may contribute to developing an antisocial personality is physical or sexual abuse in childhood. People with an antisocial personality are more likely than others to have been abused as children (D. Black, 2006). However, since many abused children do not develop an antisocial personality, it is difficult to determine how much childhood abuse contributes to the development of antisocial personality disorders.

Biological factors. Many parents reported that, from infancy on, their children had temper tantrums, became furious when frustrated, bullied other children, did not respond to punishment, and were generally unmanageable. Researchers suggest that the early appearance of serious behavioral problems indicates that underlying biological factors, both genetic and neurological, may predispose or place a child at risk for developing antisocial personality disorders.

Evidence for *genetic factors* comes from twin and adoption studies that show that genetic factors contribute 30–50% to the development of antisocial personality disorders (Thapar & McGuffin, 1993). Evidence for *neurological factors* comes from individuals with brain damage and from MRI studies on the brains of individuals with antisocial personality disorder.

For example, researchers found that early brain damage to the *prefrontal cortex* (shown below) resulted in two children who did not learn normal social and moral behaviors and showed no empathy, remorse, or guilt as adults. In addition, MRI scans (p. 70) indicated

Prefrontal cortex

that individuals diagnosed with antisocial personality disorder had 11% fewer brain cells in their prefrontal cortex (A. Raine et al., 2000). Since the prefrontal cortex is known to be involved in important executive functions, such as making decisions and planning, researchers suggest that damage to or maldevelopment of the prefrontal cortex predisposes or increases the risk of an individual developing an antisocial personality disorder. Researchers believe that biological factors can predispose individuals to act in certain ways but that the interaction between biological and psychosocial factors results in the development and onset of personality disorders (A. B. Morgan & Lilienfeld, 2000).

Treatment

Psychotherapy has not proved very effective in treating people with antisocial personality disorder because these individuals are guiltless, mistrusting, irresponsible, and practiced liars, who fail to see that many of their behaviors are antisocial and maladaptive. As a result, psychotherapists have a very difficult time modifying or changing their behavior (Bateman & Fonagy, 2000).

People with antisocial personality disorder do not want to change their behaviors.

Because of the relative ineffectiveness of psychotherapy, clinicians have tried various drugs, including antidepressants, that act to raise levels of serotonin in the brain. Researchers believe that some abnormality in the brain's serotonin system may underlie the impulsive and aggressive behaviors observed in personality disorders (D. Black, 2006).

Drug That Increases Serotonin

(graph: Aggression score vs. Weeks — Baseline, 2, 4, 8)

As shown in the left graph, patients who took a serotonin-increasing drug (sertraline) reported significant decreases in their aggressive behaviors across eight weeks of treatment. However, researchers caution that aggressive behaviors may return once patients stop taking these serotonin-increasing drugs (Coccaro & Kavoussi, 1997). Other research shows the use of antipsychotic medication (p. 541) can decrease impulsivity, hostility, aggressiveness, and rage in patients with antisocial personality disorder (C. Walker et al., 2003).

A major question is whether people with antisocial personality disorder improve over time. Researchers did a 29-year follow-up of 71 men who had been treated for antisocial personality disorder. They found that only 31% continued to show improvement; the remaining 69% either showed no improvement or relapsed (D. W. Black et al., 1995). Researchers concluded that, for 69% of the patients, antisocial personality disorder is an ongoing, relatively stable, long-term problem that needs continual treatment (Parker, 2000).

Next, we'll examine one of the most tragic mental disorders—schizophrenia.

D. Schizophrenia

What if you lose touch with reality?

At the beginning of this module, we described 18-year-old Michael McCabe (photo below), who said that his mind began to weaken during the summer of 1992. "I totally hit this point in my life where I was so high on life, it was amazing. I had this sense of independence. I was 18 and turning into an adult. Next thing I knew I got this feeling that people were trying to take things from me. Not my soul, but physical things from me. I couldn't sleep because they [his mother and sister] were planning to do something to me. I think there was a higher power inside the 7-Eleven that was helping me out the whole time, just bringing me back to a strong mental state" (C. Brooks, 1994, p. 9). Michael was diagnosed as having schizophrenia *(skit-suh-FREE-nee-ah)*.

Schizophrenia is a serious mental disorder that lasts for at least six months and includes at least two of the following symptoms: delusions, hallucinations, disorganized speech, disorganized behavior, and decreased emotional expression. These symptoms interfere with personal or social functioning (American Psychiatric Association, 2000).

Michael has a number of these symptoms, including delusions (higher power inside the 7-Eleven), hallucinations (hearing voices), and disorganized behavior. Schizophrenia affects about 0.2–2% of the adult population, or about 4.5 million people (equal numbers of men and women) in the United States (American Psychiatric Association, 2000). Of the inpatients in mental hospitals, about 30% are there because of schizophrenia, and this percentage is the highest of any mental disorder (Robins & Regier, 1991).

Michael McCabe had many of the symptoms described on the right.

SUBCATEGORIES OF SCHIZOPHRENIA

Michael's case illustrates some of the symptoms that occur in schizophrenia. In fact, no two patients have exactly the same set of symptoms, which are described in the list on the right. The DSM-IV-TR describes five different subcategories of schizophrenia, each of which is characterized by different symptoms. We'll briefly describe three of the more common schizophrenia subcategories.

Paranoid schizophrenia **is characterized by auditory hallucinations or delusions, such as thoughts of being persecuted by others or thoughts of grandeur.**

Disorganized schizophrenia **is marked by bizarre ideas, often about one's body (bones melting), confused speech, childish behavior (giggling for no apparent reason, making faces at people), great emotional swings (fits of laughing or crying), and often extreme neglect of personal appearance and hygiene.**

Catatonic schizophrenia **is characterized by periods of wild excitement or periods of rigid, prolonged immobility; sometimes the person assumes the same frozen posture for hours on end.**

Differentiating between types of schizophrenia can be difficult because some symptoms, such as disordered thought processes and delusions, are shared by all types.

CHANCE OF RECOVERY

Chances of recovery are dependent upon a number of factors, which have been grouped under two major types of schizophrenia (Crow, 1985).

Type I schizophrenia **includes having positive symptoms, such as hallucinations and delusions, which are a distortion of normal functions. In addition, this group has no intellectual impairment, good reaction to medication, and thus a good chance of recovery.**

Type II schizophrenia **includes having negative symptoms, such as dulled emotions and little inclination to speak, which are a loss of normal functions. In addition, this group has intellectual impairment, poor reaction to medication, and thus a poor chance of recovery.**

According to this classification system, the best predictor of recovery for a person with schizophrenia is his or her symptoms: those with positive symptoms have a good chance of recovery, while those with negative symptoms have a poor chance (Dyck et al., 2000).

Next, we'll describe the major symptoms of schizophrenia.

Schizophrenia is a serious mental disorder that lasts for at least six months and includes at least two of the following symptoms:

1 Disorders of thought.
These are characterized by incoherent thought patterns, formation of new words (called *neologisms*), inability to stick to one topic, and irrational beliefs or *delusions*. For example, Michael believed that his mother and sister were plotting against him.

2 Disorders of attention.
These include difficulties in concentration and in focusing on a single chain of events. For instance, one patient said that he could not concentrate on television because he couldn't watch and listen at the same time.

3 Disorders of perception.
These include strange bodily sensations and hallucinations.

Hallucinations **are sensory experiences without any stimulation from the environment.**

From 50 to 75% of schizophrenics report hearing voices that sound real and talk either to them (steal brain cells) or about them (mostly negative things, like "you have a cancer") (Goode, 2003a).

4 Motor disorders. These include making strange facial expressions, being extremely active, or (the opposite) remaining immobile for long periods of time.

5 Emotional (affective) disorders. These may include having little or no emotional responsiveness or having emotional responses that are inappropriate to the situation—for example, laughing when told of the death of a close friend.

The cause of these schizophrenia symptoms involves the interaction among biological, neurological, and environmental factors.

Marsha tries to help her son, Michael, who has schizophrenia.

When Michael was in the hospital, his mother, Marsha (photo below), began going to a support group to get help and find out about schizophrenia. At one meeting, Marsha said, "I haven't been doing very well with this, to be perfectly honest. How in the hell were we dealt this hand?" (C. Brooks, 1994, p. 8).

The psychiatrist who led Marsha's group answered that about 1 in 100 people get schizophrenia but the odds increase to 1 in 10 if it's already in the family. If a person inherits a predisposition for schizophrenia, any number of things—such as drugs, a death in the family, growing-up problems—can trigger its onset (C. Brooks, 1994). The psychiatrist was pointing out three major factors—biological, neurological, and environmental—that interact in the development of schizophrenia. We'll begin with biological factors, specifically genetic causes.

GENETIC PREDISPOSITION

In 1930, the birth of four identical baby girls (quadruplets) was a rare occurrence (1 in 16 million) and received great publicity. By the time the girls had reached high school, all four were labeled "different."

All four of these identical quadruplets developed schizophrenia.

They sometimes broke light bulbs, tore buttons off their clothes, complained of bones slipping out of place, and had periods of great confusion. By young adulthood, all four girls, who are called the Genain quadruplets and share 100% of their genes, were diagnosed with schizophrenia (Mirsky & Quinn, 1988). The finding that all four Genain quadruplets (above photo) developed schizophrenia indicates that increased genetic similarity is associated with increased risk for developing schizophrenia and suggests that a person inherits a *predisposition* for developing the disorder. Support for a genetic predisposition also comes from twin studies.

GENETIC MARKERS

Because researchers knew that schizophrenia might have a genetic factor, they compared rates of schizophrenia in identical twins, who share 100% of their genes, with rates in fraternal twins and siblings (brothers and sisters), who share only 50% of their genes. The right graph shows the risk of developing schizophrenia for individuals who share different percentages of genes and thus have different degrees of genetic similarity. Notice that if one identical twin has schizophrenia, there is a 48–83% chance that the other twin will also develop the disorder. In comparison, if one brother or sister (sibling or

fraternal twin) has schizophrenia, there is only about a 10–17% chance that the other will develop the disorder (Gottesman, 2001). Because genetic factors are involved in developing schizophrenia, researchers are searching for the location of specific genes involved in schizophrenia; such genes are called genetic markers (Levinson, 2003).

A *genetic marker* refers to an identifiable gene or number of genes or a specific segment of a chromosome that is directly linked to some behavioral, physiological, or neurological trait or disease.

During the past ten years, researchers have reported about ten genetic markers for schizophrenia, but none proved valid because none could be repeated or replicated by other laboratories (Wade, 2006). Researchers now believe that schizophrenia depends on a combination of genes and that no one gene by itself has a strong genetic influence.

Breakthroughs. There have been several reports of major breakthroughs in identifying genetic markers for schizophrenia. Most recently, researchers found evidence of a slight excess of a protein in the prefrontal cortex of people with schizophrenia, resulting from a variation in a gene they believe may explain common symptoms of the disorder (Law & Weinberger, 2006). In another study, researchers identified two genes that, if they occur together, greatly increase the risk of developing schizophrenia (D. Cohen, 2002). These two genes interfere with the normal action of an important neurotransmitter (glutamate), and this disruption can result in confused thinking and hallucinations, two symptoms of schizophrenia. Other researchers found a gene linked to negative symptoms of schizophrenia (p. 541), which suggests that researchers should seek genes responsible for specific symptoms (Fanous et al., 2005). Researchers believe genetic factors are most likely to act during the 9th to 15th week of the fetal stage, when brain cells (neurons) undergo a rapid rate of development (Waddington et al., 2000). Taken together, recent genetic studies plus earlier studies on identical twins indicate that schizophrenia has a genetic factor.

Environmental factors. However, genetic factors alone cannot completely explain why some individuals develop schizophrenia. Studies on identical twins indicate if one identical twin develops schizophrenia, then there is a 17–52% chance the other twin will NOT develop schizophrenia. As we'll discuss later, this means environmental factors, such as a stressful life event, interact with genetic factors in the development of schizophrenia (Mueser et al., 2006).

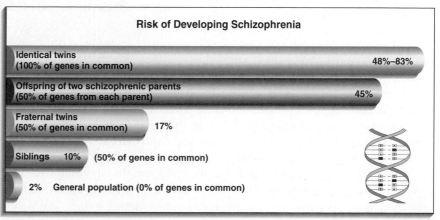

Risk of Developing Schizophrenia

Identical twins (100% of genes in common)	48%–83%
Offspring of two schizophrenic parents (50% of genes from each parent)	45%
Fraternal twins (50% of genes in common)	17%
Siblings 10% (50% of genes in common)	
2% General population (0% of genes in common)	

D. Schizophrenia

Is the brain different?

New techniques for studying the structures and functions of the living brain (MRI and fMRI—p. 70) reveal major differences between brains of schizophrenics and brains of mentally healthy individuals. We'll discuss two reliable differences—larger ventricles and decreased activity in the prefrontal cortex.

VENTRICLE SIZE

Most us of don't realize that our brains have four fluid-filled cavities called ventricles (left figure). The fluid in these cavities helps to cushion the brain against blows and also serves as a reservoir of nutrients and hormones for the brain. One reliable finding is that in up to 80% of the brains of schizophrenics, the ventricles are larger than normal (Niznikiewicz et al., 2003). Using brain scans (MRIs), researchers studied 15 pairs of identical twins; one was diagnosed with schizophrenia, while the other was mentally healthy (normal). The brains of twins with schizophrenia had *larger ventricles* than the brains of the mentally healthy twins (left figures) (Suddath et al., 1990). However, not all brains of people with schizophrenia have larger ventricles or an overall decrease in brain size. Also, the enlarged ventricles in some schizophrenics may remain the same over the course of their illness, while the size of ventricles may change over time for others (DeLisi et al., 2004). Researchers conclude that some people with schizophrenia have abnormally large ventricles, which results in a reduction in brain size and in turn may contribute to the development of schizophrenia (I. C. Wright et al., 2000).

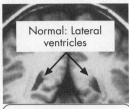

Normal: Lateral ventricles

Fluid-filled ventricles in normal brains

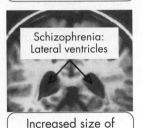

Schizophrenia: Lateral ventricles

Increased size of fluid-filled ventricles in brains of schizophrenics

FRONTAL LOBE: PREFRONTAL CORTEX

Another brain structure involved in many executive functions, such as reasoning, planning, remembering, paying attention, and making decisions, is the prefrontal cortex (figure below). Researchers report that in pairs of identical twins where one twin has schizophrenia and the other does not, the brain of the twin with schizophrenia was characterized by significantly *less activation of the prefrontal cortex* (Torrey et al., 1994). This decreased prefrontal lobe activity is consistent with the deficits in many executive functions observed in schizophrenics, such as disorganized thinking, irrational beliefs, and lack of concentration (Niznikiewicz et al., 2003).

Other researchers report that in the brains of people with schizophrenia, the frontal and temporal lobes are smaller because there are fewer brain cells (neurons—p. 50) and fewer connections (axons—p. 50) among neurons (K. Davis, 2003; Pantelis et al., 2003). Fewer neurons with fewer connections cause deficits in transmitting information, which in turn may underlie problems in executive functions, such as disorganized thinking and reasoning, which are major symptoms of patients diagnosed with schizophrenia (Holden, 2003a).

Prefrontal cortex

These studies point to neurological factors, such as abnormal brain structures and functions, that researchers believe underlie and contribute to the development of schizophrenia and make it so difficult to treat (Holden, 2003a).

Besides genetic and neurological factors, there are also environmental factors involved in developing schizophrenia.

Can stress act as a trigger?

If biological or neurological factors explained why people develop schizophrenia, then the risk for developing schizophrenia in identical twins would be 100% rather than 48 to 83%. Because biological and neurological factors alone cannot explain the development of schizophrenia, researchers look at the influence of environmental factors, such as the incidence of stressful events and how individuals cope. For example, when Michael McCabe (right photo) was 18, he began to develop symptoms of schizophrenia. The onset of these symptoms occurred after the death of his father and during the well-known potentially stressful period of adolescence.

Stressful events may have led to his onset of schizophrenia.

Stressful events, such as hostile parents, poor social relations, the death of a parent or loved one, and career or personal problems, can contribute to the development and onset of schizophrenia. This relationship between stress and the onset of schizophrenia is called the diathesis stress theory (Durand & Barlow, 2006).

The *diathesis (die-ATH-uh-sis) stress theory* of schizophrenia says that some people have a genetic predisposition (a diathesis) that interacts with life stressors to result in the onset and development of schizophrenia.

The diathesis stress theory assumes that biological or neurological factors have initially produced a *predisposition for schizophrenia*. If a person already has a predisposition for schizophrenia, then being faced with stressful environmental factors can increase the risk and vulnerability for developing schizophrenia as well as trigger the onset of schizophrenia symptoms (S. R. Jones & Fernyhough, 2006). Thus, the diathesis stress theory says that biological and neurological factors first create a predisposition, such as overreacting to stressful situations, that then makes a person vulnerable or at risk for developing schizophrenia.

Now we'll examine the drugs used to treat schizophrenia.

How is Michael treated?

After Michael (right photo) was taken to the psychiatric hospital, his symptoms were assessed and he was diagnosed with schizophrenia. Schizophrenia symptoms are commonly divided into positive and negative symptoms.

Positive symptoms of schizophrenia reflect a distortion of normal functions: distorted thinking results in delusions; distorted perceptions result in hallucinations; distorted language results in disorganized speech.

Negative symptoms of schizophrenia reflect a decrease in or loss of normal functions: decreased range and intensity of emotions,

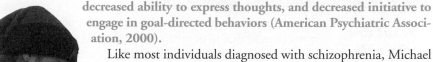

Michael was given a neuroleptic drug to treat his schizophrenia.

decreased ability to express thoughts, and decreased initiative to engage in goal-directed behaviors (American Psychiatric Association, 2000).

Like most individuals diagnosed with schizophrenia, Michael had both positive symptoms, such as delusions that people were going to steal from him, and negative symptoms, such as loss of emotional expression. To reduce these symptoms, he was given haloperidol, which is an example of an antipsychotic or neuroleptic (meaning "taking hold of the nerves") drug.

Neuroleptic drugs, also called *antipsychotic drugs,* are used to treat serious mental disorders, such as schizophrenia, by changing the levels of neurotransmitters in the brain.

There are two kinds of neuroleptic drugs: typical and atypical.

Typical Neuroleptics

Typical neuroleptics: decrease dopamine

Typical neuroleptics were discovered in the 1950s and were the first effective medical treatment for schizophrenia.

Typical neuroleptic drugs primarily reduce levels of the neurotransmitter dopamine. These drugs mainly reduce positive symptoms and have little effect on negative symptoms (Reus, 2006). Because typical neuroleptics reduce levels of dopamine, their action supports the dopamine theory of schizophrenia (Mueser et al., 2006).

The *dopamine theory* says that in schizophrenia, the dopamine neurotransmitter system is somehow overactive and gives rise to a wide range of symptoms.

The dopamine theory focuses on neurons in a group of brain structures called the *basal ganglia* (right figure). Typical neuroleptics block dopamine usage in the basal ganglia, which reduces communication among these neurons and in turn reduces some of the symptoms of schizophrenia. However, because 20% of people with schizophrenia are not helped by typical neuroleptics and because recent findings point to the involvement of several nondopamine neurotransmitters (serotonin and glutamate), the dopamine theory will need revision to include other neurotransmitter systems.

Basal ganglia

Using typical neuroleptics to treat schizophrenia is being challenged by newer drugs, called atypical neuroleptics.

Atypical Neuroleptics

In Michael's case and for about 20% of all schizophrenics, typical neuroleptic drugs (phenothiazines, such as haloperidol or Thorazine) have little or no effect on their symptoms. Many of these patients are being helped by newer atypical neuroleptic drugs.

Atypical neuroleptic drugs (clozapine, risperidone) lower levels of dopamine and also reduce levels of other neurotransmitters, especially serotonin. These drugs primarily reduce positive symptoms, may reduce negative symptoms, and prevent relapse (Burton, 2006; Tuunainen et al., 2002).

Atypical neuroleptics: decrease dopamine & serotonin

The first atypical neuroleptic, clozapine, was approved for use in schizophrenia in 1990. Since then, a number of atypical neuroleptics have proven effective in decreasing symptoms of schizophrenia, especially in patients who were not helped by typical neuroleptics (W. Carpenter, 2003).

Michael, for example, showed little improvement with typical neuroleptics (haloperidol). However, the atypical neuroleptic clozapine reduced his positive symptoms to the point that he was allowed to leave the psychiatric hospital and return home. A year later, Michael is still taking clozapine and is making slow progress in overcoming his symptoms, such as paranoia.

On most days, Michael comes home from group therapy and job-training classes, puts on a Bob Marley record, and sits and listens, afraid to do much else. As Michael explains, "I can't go out and skate or do anything because I'm afraid I'm going to have a paranoia attack" (C. Brooks, 1995b, p. D-3). His mother and sister (right photo) provide Michael

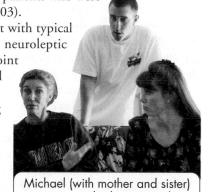

Michael (with mother and sister) was switched to atypical neuroleptics, which reduced his symptoms.

(standing in back) with financial and social support but wish Michael would take greater initiative to improve his own life. Michael, as well as others with schizophrenia, face a daily struggle to overcome their symptoms, which points to the need for continued social support and psychotherapy (Bustillo et al., 2001).

Current treatment. Compared to older typical neuroleptics, newer atypical neuroleptics are currently the preferred treatment because they are at least as effective in reducing positive symptoms, more effective in reducing negative symptoms, better at preventing relapse, and helpful for those patients who showed no improvement with typical neuroleptics (Burton, 2006; J. M. Davis et al., 2003).

Although the discoveries of typical neuroleptics in the 1950s and atypical neuroleptics in the 1990s represented major advances in treating schizophrenia, both can produce significant and undesirable side effects, which we'll discuss next (Talan, 2005).

D. Schizophrenia

Evaluation of Neuroleptic Drugs

What are the side effects? The major advantage of neuroleptic drugs is that they effectively reduce positive symptoms so that many patients can regain some degree of normal functioning. However, neuroleptics also have two potentially serious disadvantages: They may produce undesirable side effects, and they may decrease but not prevent relapse or return of the original symptoms of schizophrenia.

NEUROLEPTICS

Typical: decrease dopamine	Atypical: decrease dopamine & serotonin

Typical Neuroleptics

Side effects. One group of typical neuroleptics, called the phenothiazines *(pheen–no–THIGH–ah–zines),* is widely prescribed to treat schizophrenia. Phenothiazines can produce unwanted motor movements, which is a side effect called tardive dyskinesia (Reus, 2006).

Tardive dyskinesia (TARD-if dis-cah-KNEE-zee-ah) **involves the appearance of slow, involuntary, and uncontrollable rhythmic movements and rapid twitching of the mouth and lips, as well as unusual movements of the limbs. This condition is associated with the continued use of typical neuroleptics.**

As shown in the right graph, the risk for developing tardive dyskinesia increases with use: After three months, 16% developed this side effect; after ten years, 40% developed it (Sweet et al., 1995). About 30% of patients with tardive dyskinesia will experience a reduction in symptoms if they are taken off typical neuroleptics, but the remaining 70% may continue to have the problem when the drug therapy is stopped (Roy-Byrne & Fann, 1997).

Effectiveness. Researchers have completed several long-term follow-up studies on patients who were treated for schizophrenia with typical neuroleptics. They found that, 2–12 years after treatment, about 20–30% of patients showed a good outcome, which means they needed no further treatment and had no relapse; about 40–60% continued to suffer some behavior impairment and relapse, although their symptoms reached a plateau in about 5 years and did not worsen after that; and about 20% were not helped by these drugs.

Relapse. The basic problem with taking patients off typical neuroleptics is that they may relapse. For example, after an average of about one year, 60% of patients taken off a typical neuroleptic experienced a relapse as compared to a relapse rate of 34% for those who were maintained on an atypical neuroleptic (Csernansky et al., 2002). Next, we'll learn about the side effects and effectiveness of the newer atypical neuroleptics.

Risk of Developing Tardive Dyskinesia

3 months	16%
3–12 months	29%
1–10 years	30%
More than 10 years	40%

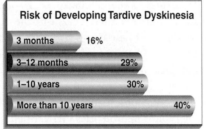

Unwanted motor movements (lip smacking) are a side effect of typical neuroleptics but less so with atypical neuroleptics.

Atypical Neuroleptics

Side effects. One advantage of atypical neuroleptics (especially newer ones—risperidone, olanzapine) is that they cause tardive dyskinesia in only about 5% of patients, compared to 1–29% of patients given typical neuroleptics (Caroff et al., 2002). However, atypical neuroleptics can cause side effects, the most serious being increased levels of cholesterol and glucose or blood sugar (hyperglycemia), excessive weight gain, and onset of or worsening of diabetes (Burton, 2006; Talan 2005). Thus, typical and atypical neuroleptics may produce serious side effects.

Effectiveness and relapse. From the 1950s through the middle of the 1990s, the drugs of choice for treating schizophrenia were typical neuroleptics. Beginning in the late 1990s and continuing to the present, there has been a general switch to atypical neuroleptics. That's because, compared to typical neuroleptics, atypical neuroleptics have generally proved to be as effective in reducing positive symptoms, more effective in reducing negative symptoms, less likely to cause tardive dyskinesia, and more effective in preventing relapse, the recurrence of schizophrenia symptoms (Burton, 2006; J. M. Davis et al., 2003). For example, one study found that patients with schizophrenia who took an atypical drug experienced a greater reduction in symptoms, less tardive dyskinesia, and lower rates of relapse compared to patients who took a typical drug (Csernansky et al., 2002). However, another study found the use of typical and atypical drugs led to about equal improvement in patients with schizophrenia and similar rates of movement-related side effects, such as tardive dyskinesia (J. A. Lieberman, 2005b). Due to these inconsistencies, clinicians must carefully consider which type of drug to prescribe to their patients.

Different nervous systems, different drugs. Two strange, recurring findings in the treatment of mental disorders are that the same drug may help one patient but not another, and in 20% of patients drugs cause no improvement at all. One reason drugs don't always work is that mental disorders, like schizophrenia, may have different causes (genetic, neurological, environmental) that may require a combination of different drugs and/or psychotherapy. Another reason drugs don't always work is that each person's nervous system functions differently and has a different level of neurotransmitters (Niznikiewicz et al., 2003). This explains why the same drug may cause various types and severities of side effects for different people. Overall, about three-quarters of patients with schizophrenia stop taking their medication because it did not work well or caused intolerable side effects (J. A. Lieberman, 2005a). Thus, clinicians often try different drugs or a combination of drugs to find the best one to treat a patient's symptoms (Bright, 2003).

Researchers do find that, for the majority of patients, schizophrenia is a chronic or life-long problem with a high risk for relapse. Thus, in addition to drug treatment, patients need psychotherapy and social support to improve their social interactions, work at an acceptable job, and maintain their quality of life (Mueser et al., 2006).

After the Concept Review, we'll discuss a disorder that has a very strange symptom—the person does not know who he or she is.

✔ Concept Review

1. A prolonged emotional state that affects almost all of a person's thoughts and behaviors is called a _____ disorder.

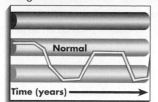

2. The most common form of mood disorder is marked by at least two weeks of daily being in a bad mood, having no interest in anything, and getting no pleasure from activities and having at least four of these additional symptoms: problems with weight or appetite, insomnia, fatigue, difficulty thinking, and feeling worthless and guilty. This problem is called _____ disorder.

3. Another depressive disorder is characterized by being chronically depressed for many but not all days over a period of two years and having two of the following symptoms: poor appetite, insomnia, fatigue, low self-esteem, and feelings of hopelessness. This problem is called _____ disorder.

4. Another mood disorder is characterized by a fluctuation between a depressive episode and a manic episode that lasts about a week, during which a person is unusually euphoric, cheerful, or high, speaks rapidly, feels great self-esteem, and needs little sleep. This problem is called _____ disorder.

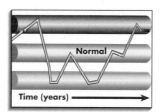

5. Underlying genetic, neurological, chemical, or physiological components may predispose a person to developing a mood disorder. Together, these components are called _____ factors.

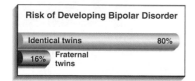

6. Factors such as dealing with stressors and stressful life events are believed to interact with predisposing biological factors and contribute to the development, onset, and maintenance of mood disorders. These are called _____ factors.

7. One treatment for major depression involves placing electrodes on the skull and administering a mild electric current that passes through the brain and causes a seizure. Usual treatment consists of a series of 10–12 such sessions, at the rate of about three per week. This treatment is called _____.

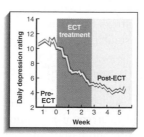

8. Certain psychoactive drugs act by increasing levels of a specific group of neurotransmitters (monoamines, such as serotonin) that are believed to be involved in the regulation of emotions and moods. These are called (a)_____ drugs. A mood stabilizer that is used to treat bipolar I disorder is called (b)_____, and it's often combined with antidepressants and antipsychotics.

9. A person who has inflexible, long-standing, maladaptive traits that cause significantly impaired functioning or great distress in his or her personal and social life is said to have a (a)_____ disorder. Examples of this disorder include a pattern of distrust and suspiciousness and perceiving others as having evil motives, which is called a (b)_____ personality disorder; a pattern of being submissive and clingy because of an excessive need to be taken care of, which is called a (c)_____ personality disorder; and a pattern of disregarding or violating the rights of others without feeling guilt or remorse, which is called an (d)_____ personality disorder.

10. A serious mental disturbance that lasts for at least six months and that includes at least two of the following persistent symptoms—delusions, hallucinations, disorganized speech, grossly disorganized behavior, and decreased emotional expression—is called (a)_____. There are subcategories of this disorder: the one characterized by auditory hallucinations or delusions, such as thoughts of being persecuted by others or thoughts of grandeur, is called (b)_____ schizophrenia.

11. Drugs that are used to treat schizophrenia and act primarily to reduce levels of dopamine are called (a)_____ drugs. Drugs that are used to treat schizophrenia and reduce levels of dopamine and levels of serotonin are called (b)_____ drugs, which are generally more effective than (c)_____ drugs. The theory that, in schizophrenia, the dopamine neurotransmitter system is somehow overactive and gives rise to many of the symptoms observed in schizophrenics is called the (d)_____ theory, which is supported by the actions of (e)_____ drugs but not by the actions of (f)_____ drugs.

| decrease dopamine | decrease dopamine & serotonin |

Answers: 1. mood; 2. major depressive; 3. dysthymic; 4. bipolar I; 5. biological; 6. psychosocial; 7. electroconvulsive therapy, or ECT; 8. (a) antidepressant, (b) lithium; 9. (a) personality, (b) paranoid, (c) dependent, (d) antisocial; 10. (a) schizophrenia, (b) paranoid; 11. (a) typical neuroleptic, (b) atypical neuroleptic, (c) typical neuroleptic, (d) dopamine, (e) typical neuroleptic, (f) atypical neuroleptic

E. Dissociative Disorders

What if you became someone else?

You have probably had the experience of being so absorbed in a fantasy, thought, or memory that, for a short period of time, you cut yourself off from the real world. However, if someone calls your name, you quickly return and explain, "I'm sorry, I wasn't paying attention. I was off in my own world." This is an example of a normal "break from reality," or dissociative experience, which may occur when you are self-absorbed, hypnotized, or fantasizing (Kihlstrom et al., 1994). Now

What if you had a split or breakdown in your self?

imagine a dissociative experience so extreme that your own self splits, breaks down, or disappears.

A *dissociative disorder* is characterized by a person having a disruption, split, or breakdown in his or her normal integrated self, consciousness, memory, or sense of identity. This disorder is relatively rare and unusual (American Psychiatric Association, 2000).

We'll discuss three of the five more common dissociative disorders listed in the DSM-IV-TR. These are dissociative amnesia (Who am I?), dissociative fugue (Where am I?), and dissociative identity disorder (formerly called multiple personality disorder).

Dissociative Amnesia

Mark is brought into the hospital emergency room by police. He looks exhausted and is badly sunburned. When questioned, he gives the wrong date, answering September 27th instead of October 1st. He has trouble answering specific questions about what happened to him. With much probing, he gradually remembers going sailing with friends on about September 25th and hitting bad weather. He cannot recall anything else; he doesn't know what happened to his friends or the sailboat, how he got to shore, where he has been, or where he is now. Each time he is told that it is really October 1st and he is in a hospital, he looks very surprised (Spitzer et al., 1994). Mark is suffering from dissociative amnesia.

Dissociative amnesia is characterized by the inability to recall important personal information or events and is usually associated with stressful or traumatic events. The importance or extent of the information forgotten is too great to be explained by normal forgetfulness (American Psychiatric Association, 2000).

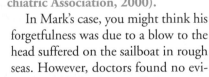

What if you forgot a month in your life?

In Mark's case, you might think his forgetfulness was due to a blow to the head suffered on the sailboat in rough seas. However, doctors found no evidence of head injury or neural problems. To recall the events between September 25th and October 1st, Mark was given a drug (sodium amytal) that helps people relax and recall events that may be blocked by stressful experiences. While under the effect of the drug, Mark recalled a big storm that washed his companions overboard but spared him because he had tied himself to the boat. Thus, Mark did suffer from dissociative amnesia, which was triggered by the stressful event of seeing his friends washed overboard (Spitzer et al., 1994). In dissociative amnesia, the length of memory loss varies from days to weeks to years and is often associated with a series of stressful events (Eich et al., 1997).

As we'll see next, a person may forget who he or she is.

Dissociative Fugue

A 40-year-old man wanders the streets of Denver with $8 in his pocket. He asks people to help him figure out who he is and where he lives. He feels lost, alone, anxious, and desperate to learn his identity. He appears on news shows pleading for help: "If anybody recognizes me, knows who I am, please let somebody know" (Ingram, 2006). After his parents and fiancé see him on television, they contact the police, informing them that the man's name is Jeffrey Ingram and that he lives in Seattle. Upon reuniting with his fiancé and family, Jeffrey fails to recognize their faces. He also cannot recall anything about his past (Woodward, 2006). Jeffrey Ingram had experienced dissociative fugue.

Who am I? What's my name?

Dissociative fugue is a disturbance marked by suddenly and unexpectedly traveling away from one's home or place of work and being unable to recall one's past. The person may not remember his or her identity or may be confused about his or her new assumed identity (American Psychiatric Association, 2000).

Before clinicians diagnosed Jeffrey as suffering from dissociative fugue, they ruled out drugs, medications, and head injuries. His fiancé explained that Jeffrey had been on his way to Canada to visit his best friend who was dying of cancer. She believes the stress and sadness of seeing his best friend dying led him to an amnesia state. Jeffrey's history is especially fascinating because he had experienced a similar dissociative fugue in 1995, when he disappeared during a trip to the grocery store and wasn't found until 9 months later. His mother said he never fully regained his memory after the first episode.

As Jeffrey's case illustrates, the onset of dissociative fugue is related to stressful or traumatic life events. Usually, fugue states end quite suddenly, and the individual recalls most or all of his or her identity and past.

In other cases, a person's self seems to split into two or more "true" selves or identities. This condition is called dissociative identity disorder.

Is it really true?

The idea that one individual could possess two or more "different persons" who may or may not know one another and who may appear at different times to say and do different things describes one of the more remarkable and controversial mental disorders (Eich et al., 1997). Previously this disorder was called multiple personality disorder, but now it's called dissociative identity disorder. We'll discuss a real case of dissociative identity disorder and its possible causes.

Definition

Mary noticed something very peculiar about her car's gas gauge. Each night when she returned home from work, the gauge registered a nearly full tank of gas. However, when she got in to drive to work the next morning, the gauge registered about half full. Thinking that something suspicious was going on, she noted the mileage on the odometer each evening and compared it with the morning's reading. Someone was driving her car between 50 and 100 miles each night, and she had no idea who it was.

During a hypnotic treatment for pain, the physician asked Mary about the mileage someone was putting on her car. Suddenly a different voice answered, "It's about time you knew about me." This new voice said that her name was Marian and that she drove the car around at night to work out difficulties. Marian was as hostile and unfriendly as Mary was pleasing and sociable. During the course of therapy, six other personalities came out, some of whom were independent and aggressive, while others were dependent and submissive. At times, the different personalities fought for control; each reported different memories. As a child, Mary had been physically and sexually abused by her father (Spitzer et al., 1994). The physician diagnosed Mary as suffering from dissociative identity disorder.

Dissociative identity disorder (formerly called multiple personality disorder) is the presence of two or more distinct identities or personality states, each with its own pattern of perceiving, thinking about, and relating to the world. Different personality states may take control of the individual's thoughts and behaviors at different times (American Psychiatric Association, 2000).

As in Mary's case, the personalities are usually quite different and complex, and the original personality is seldom aware of the others. After four years of psychotherapy, Mary managed to integrate the personalities into just two, which continued to fight with each other (Spitzer et al., 1994).

How common is dissociative identity disorder, and what causes it?

Formerly called multiple personality, dissociative identity disorder is said to have two very different causes.

Occurrence and Causes

As shown in the right graph, the worldwide occurrence of dissociative identity disorder was very rare before 1970, with only 36 cases reported. However, an "epidemic" occurred in the 1970s and 1980s, with estimates ranging from 300 to 2,000 cases (Spanos, 1994). Reasons for the upsurge include incorrect diagnosis, renewed professional interest, the trendiness of the disorder, and therapists' (unknowing) encouragement of patients to play the roles. Whatever the reasons, the vast majority (70–80%) of mental health professionals are skeptical about the upsurge in occurrence of dissociative identity disorder (Lilienfeld et al., 1999). The patients most often diagnosed with dissociative identity disorder (DID) are females, who outnumber males by 8:1. In addition, patients with DID usually have a history of other mental disorders.

Explanations. There are two opposing explanations for DID. One is that DID results from the severe trauma of childhood abuse, which causes a mental splitting or dissociation of identities as one way to defend against or cope with the terrible trauma. In one study, 89% of patients diagnosed with DID were women, and of these, 98% reported having been physically or sexually abused during childhood (Ellason & Ross, 1997). A second explanation is that DID has become commonplace because of cultural factors, such as DID becoming a legitimate way for people to express their frustrations or to manipulate or gain personal rewards (Lilienfeld et al., 1999). These opposing explanations reflect the current controversy about why so many patients have been diagnosed with DID.

Treatment. Patients diagnosed with DID may also have problems with depression, anxiety, interpersonal relationships, and substance abuse. As a result, treatment for DID involves helping patients with these related problems as well as helping them integrate their various personalities into one unified self, which may take years. For example, after two years of treatment, patients diagnosed with DID who showed the greatest improvement were those who showed the greatest ability to integrate or bring together and resolve the differences of their separate selves and see themselves as a person with a single self. Clinicians concluded that treatment for DID is a long-term process that usually involves some form of psychotherapy (Chu et al., 2005).

Worldwide Cases of Dissociative Identity Disorder

1971–1988

1874–1920: 28
1921–1970: 8
1971–1988: 300

F. Cultural Diversity: Interpreting Symptoms

Spirit Possession

How does the world view mental disorders?

Imagine being a clinician and interviewing a 26-year-old female client who reports the following symptoms: "Sometimes a spirit takes complete control of my body and mind and makes me do things and say things that I don't always remember. The spirit is very powerful and I never know when it will take control. The spirit first appeared when I was 16 and has been with me ever since."

As a clinician, you would of course conduct a much more in-depth clinical interview and administer a number of psychological tests. But on the basis of these symptoms alone, would you say that she has delusions and hallucinations and possibly schizophrenia or that she has multiple identities and possibly dissociative identity disorder? In this case, both diagnoses would be incorrect. This female client comes from a small village in Northern Sudan,

About 45% of the women in Northern Sudan report spirit possession, which is part of their culture.

where spirit possession is part of their culture and about 45% of married women over 15 years of age report spirit possession (Boddy, 1988). While in the United States symptoms of spirit possession would probably be interpreted as delusional and abnormal, in Northern Sudan spirit possession is interpreted as a normal behavior and an expression of the women's culture. To deal with possible cultural differences, the DSM-IV-TR now includes an appendix that describes how to diagnose symptoms within the context of a person's culture (American Psychiatric Association, 2000).

Spirit possession is an example of how cultural factors determine whether symptoms are interpreted as normal or abnormal. Researchers are also finding that cultural factors influence the occurrence of certain other kinds of mental disorders (Chin & Kameoka, 2006). We'll examine how cultural factors influence their occurrence.

Cultural Differences in Occurrence

Just as there is a manual to guide the diagnosis of mental disorders in the United States, the *Diagnostic and Statistical Manual*-IV-Text Revision (DSM-IV-TR), there is also a worldwide classification system, called the *International Classification of Disease and Related Health Problems,* 10th revision (ICD-10) (World Health Organization, 1993). Since 1970, the ICD-10 has been used to make uniform, worldwide diagnoses of mental disorders. Using this worldwide diagnostic system, clinicians report remarkable differences in the frequencies of certain mental disorders.

■ Since 1970, the United States recorded the greatest increase in dissociative identity disorders (DIDs), while DIDs are rarely diagnosed in France, Great Britain, Russia, Japan, or Switzerland (Spanos, 1994).

■ Paranoid schizophrenia is 50% more common in developed countries. Catatonic schizophrenia, which has almost disappeared in developed nations, is 60% more common in developing countries (Kleinman & Cohen, 1997).

■ The suicide rate in China is about twice the rate in the United States and is highest among rural women. In the United States, the suicide rate is highest among White men (Kleinman & Cohen, 1997).

Although we know that biological factors play a role in the development of mental disorders, the examples above show the importance of cultural factors in the development of mental disorders.

Cultural factors influence not only the occurrence of disorders but also the rates of occurrence in males and females.

Cultural Differences in Gender Roles

Many mental disorders in the United States, such as bipolar I disorder and personality disorders, are reported about equally by women and men (Kluger, 2003; C. E. Newman, 2006). However, as shown in the graph below, disorders such as major depression and dysthymic disorders are reported significantly more frequently by women than by men in the United States as well as in many other countries around the world (Kessler, 2003; Thase, 2006).

Major Depression and Dysthymic Disorder

Women	67%
Men	33%

Compared with men, twice as many women report problems with depression.

Some clinicians attribute the higher percentage of women reporting depression to cultural differences in gender roles. For example, the stereotypic gender role for men is to be independent and assertive and to take control, which tends to reduce levels of stress. In comparison, the stereotypic gender role for women is to be dependent, passive, and emotionally sensitive, which reinforces women's feelings of being dependent, not having control, and being helpless, and increases levels of stress and puts women at greater risk for developing depression (Durand & Barlow, 2006). Some researchers suggest that biological (hormonal changes) and psychosocial (concerns over having and raising children) factors may also contribute to women's higher rate of depression (NIMH, 2005a).

Cultural differences in the United States may play a role in the use of antidepressants. For example, Utah had the highest number of prescriptions for antidepressants: 2 times the national average, 2 times that of California, and 3 times that of New York and New Jersey (Cart, 2002; Walch, 2006). Researchers haven't identified which cultural differences are involved in the different rates of antidepressant usage among states.

Next, we'll look at a very simple yet effective treatment for depression.

G. Research Focus: Exercise Versus Drugs

Choices of Therapy for Depression

Can exercise help?

What would you think if you were in the middle of feeling very depressed and someone recommended running three times a week as a good treatment? It seems hard to believe that something as simple as exercising could be as effective as antidepressants. Remember that major depression is not how you feel from having a bad day or doing poorly on an exam. Major depression must meet the following definition.

Major depressive disorder is marked by at least two weeks of continually being in a bad mood, having no interest in anything, and getting no pleasure from activities.

Can depressed people get help from walking?

In addition, a person must have at least four of the following symptoms: problems with eating, sleeping, thinking, concentrating, or making decisions, lacking energy, thinking about suicide, and feeling worthless or guilty (American Psychiatric Association, 2000).

We have already discussed how psychotherapy, antidepressants, and a combination of the two have proven effective in treating major depression (Goode, 2003b). Now researchers are asking if regular exercise can also be effective in treating major depression.

This Research Focus shows how scientists used the experimental approach to answer a question that potentially has very practical or applied benefits.

Exercise Experiment: Seven Rules

METHOD AND RESULTS

You may remember that there are seven rules for doing an experiment (pp. 36–37). We'll review these seven rules by showing how researchers followed them in their study (Babyak et al., 2000).

Rule 1: Ask. Every experiment asks a specific question that is changed into a hypothesis or educated guess. In this study, the *hypothesis* is that exercise will be as effective a treatment for major depression as are antidepressants.

Rule 2: Identify. Researchers *identify* the treatment, which is called the *independent variable* because researchers are able to control or administer it to the subjects. Here, the independent variable has three levels of treatments: first level is 30 minutes of exercise (stationary bike or walking/jogging) 3 times a week; second level is taking antidepressants (Zoloft); and third level is a combination of exercising and taking antidepressants.

Zoloft

Antidepressants: independent variable

Exercise: independent variable

Next, researchers *identify* the behavior(s), called the *dependent variable,* which depends on the treatment, and measure its effectiveness. In this study, the dependent variable is a scale (Hamilton rating scale for depression) that measures increases or decreases in subjects' depression.

Scale to measure depression: dependent variable

Rule 3: Choose. Researchers *choose* subjects, who in this study are 156 adult volunteers (50 years or older) who have been diagnosed with major depression (according to the above definition).

Rule 4: Assign. The chosen patients are *randomly assigned* to groups, which means that each of the 156 patients has an equal chance of being assigned to one of the three treatment groups.

Rule 5: Manipulate. Researchers administer or *manipulate* the three levels of the treatment by giving one level of treatment to each of the three groups of patients.

Rule 6: Measure. After 4 months of treatments, researchers use the depression scale to *measure* how effective each one of the three levels of treatment was in decreasing the patients' depression.

Rule 7: Analyze. Researchers found that about 60% of patients in the exercise group had greatly improved, compared with 66% of subjects taking antidepressants and 69% of those who combined exercise and antidepressants. Although these percentages look different, *statistical analysis* indicated that the three treatments were equally effective. This means that exercise alone was as effective in reducing depression as were antidepressants or the combination, which supports the researchers' original hypothesis.

RELAPSE

We discussed how, after treatment for a mental disorder, a certain percentage of patients relapse or again return to having serious symptoms. Of the 60 to 69% of patients in each of the three treatment groups who

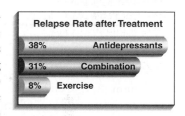

Relapse Rate after Treatment	
38%	Antidepressants
31%	Combination
8%	Exercise

showed significant improvement (few if any depressive symptoms), some patients had relapsed during the 6-month period following treatment. Researchers reported (above graph) that 38% of patients who had received antidepressants had relapsed and 31% of patients who had received both exercise and antidepressants had relapsed. However, a major finding was that only 8% of patients relapsed who were in the exercise-only treatment.

CONCLUSIONS

Researchers found that after 4 months of treatment for major depression, patients in all three treatment groups showed significant improvement. However, when patients were retested 6 months later, those who had received exercise only showed significantly less relapse. Researchers suggest that exercise helps patients develop a sense of personal mastery and positive self-regard, which helps patients get over being depressed and also decreases the risk of future relapse (Babyak et al., 2000). Other research found that depressed patients who exercised 30 minutes, 3 to 5 times a week, reported a 50% reduction in symptoms of depression after 12 weeks (A. L. Dunn et al., 2005). As a treatment for depression, exercise is effective, inexpensive, and without unwanted physical side effects.

Next, we'll discuss several ways to overcome mild depression.

H. Application: Dealing with Mild Depression

Mild Versus Major Depression

How does depression differ?

There is a big difference between mild and major depression. Earlier, we discussed singer Sheryl Crow, who experienced major depressive disorder. Symptoms of major depressive disorder include being in a bad mood for at least two weeks, having no interest in anything, and getting no pleasure from activities. Additionally, to be diagnosed with major depression, a person must have at least two of the following problems: difficulty in sleeping, eating, thinking, and making decisions or having no energy and feeling continually fatigued. Compared with the symptoms of major depressive disorder, the symptoms of mild depression are milder and generally have less impact on a person's functioning. For example, take the case of Janice, who has what is often called the sophomore blues.

There is a big difference between the symptoms of major and mild depression.

"At first I was excited about going off to college and being on my own," explains Janice. "But now I feel worn out from the constant pressure to study, get good grades, and scrape up enough bucks to pay my rent. I've lost interest in classes, I have trouble concentrating, I'm doing poorly on exams, and I'm thinking about changing my major—again. And to make everything even more depressing, my boyfriend just broke up with me. I sit around wondering what went wrong or what I did or why he broke it off. What did I do that was so bad? My friends are tired of my moping around and complaining, and I know they are starting to avoid me. Yeah, everyone says that I should just get over him and get on with my life. But exactly what do I do to get out of my funk?"

Continuum. Some researchers have argued that the kind of depression reported by college students is related more to general distress and does not represent any of the particular symptoms and feelings found in major depression (Coyne, 1994). However, other researchers find that depression is best thought of as on a continuum. At one end of the continuum is mild depression, such as that experienced by college students, which is basically similar in quality but just a milder form of major depression, which is at the other end of the continuum (Flett et al., 1997).

Similarities. There are a number of similarities between the symptoms of mild and major depression that support the idea of depression being on a continuum. For example, about 40–60% of individuals with major depression report thinking about suicide; similarly, about 50% of depressed college students also report thinking about suicide (A. B. Hill et al., 1987). In fact, thinking about suicide is 50% more common among college students than among nonstudents of the same age, and suicide is estimated to be the second leading cause of death among college students (Vredenburg et al., 1994). College students also experience almost all the major stressors of adulthood, including coping with a new environment, dealing with academic pressures, trying to establish intimate personal relationships, experiencing financial difficulties, and trying to achieve some independence from parents and family (Pennebaker et al., 1990).

Vulnerability. There are three major factors that increase an individual's vulnerability or risk for developing mild depression. The first factor is being a young adult who is facing new, challenging, and threatening situations, events, and feelings. The second factor is having a high and chronic level of troubling or negative life events. Since college students experience both of these factors, they are at high risk for developing mild depression in college, which may lead to a more serious or a major depressive disorder later in life. The third factor involves an individual's pattern of thinking, which is the basis for Beck's theory of depression.

Beck's Theory of Depression

How much do thoughts matter?

Janice thinks that her depression is caused by outside forces, such as academic pressures, financial concerns, personal difficulties, and family pressures. There is no question that stressful events or negative situations can depress Janice's mood. However, another factor that Janice may not be aware of and that may contribute to her depression is a particular pattern of thinking, which is described by Aaron Beck's (1991) cognitive theory of depression.

Beck's cognitive theory of depression says that when we are feeling down, automatic negative thoughts that we rarely notice occur continually throughout the day. These negative thoughts distort how we perceive and interpret the world and thus influence our behaviors and feelings, which in turn contribute to our feeling depressed.

Often these automatic negative thoughts are centered on personal inadequacies, such as thinking one is a failure, is not liked, or never gets anything done. Beck has identified a number of *specific negative, maladaptive thoughts* that he believes contribute to developing anxiety and depression. For example, thinking "I'm a failure" after doing poorly on one test is an example of *overgeneralization*—that is, making a blanket judgment about yourself based on a single incident. Thinking "People always criticize me" is an example of *selective attention*—that is, focusing on one detail so much that you do not notice other positive events, such as being complimented. Beck believes that maladaptive thought patterns cause a distorted view of oneself and one's world, which in turn may lead to various emotional problems, such as depression. Thus, one of the things that Janice must work on to get out of her depressed state is to identify and change her negative, maladaptive thoughts.

We'll discuss how negative thoughts and two other factors maintain depression, as well as ways to change them.

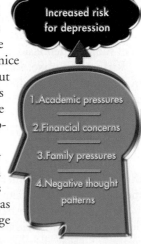

Increased risk for depression

1. Academic pressures
2. Financial concerns
3. Family pressures
4. Negative thought patterns

What can one do? Once we get "down in the dumps," we are likely to stay there for some time unless we work at changing certain thoughts and behaviors, such as improving social skills, increasing social support, and eliminating negative thoughts. We'll describe several ways to "get out of the dumps" and overcome mild depression.

Improving Social Skills

Problem. In some cases, a person may feel mildly depressed because he or she has poor social skills, which lead to problems in having good social interactions.

For example, researchers found that depressed teenagers and college students may be overly dependent, competitive, aggressive, or mistrustful, which in turn caused problems in developing and maintaining close social relationships (M. K. Reed, 1994). If part of being depressed involves poor social skills, a person can learn new ways of interacting with friends.

Program. As with every behavioral change program, the first step is to monitor our social interactions to notice what we are doing wrong, such as complaining too much and irritating our friends. Once we're aware of our bad habits, such as being negative, not asking questions or showing interest, and not being sympathetic, we can begin to take positive steps. That means making a real effort to stop complaining and to show more interest in our friends' activities and to be more sensitive to their feelings. By proceeding in gradual steps, we can learn to improve our social skills and get more rewards from social interactions, which in turn will make us feel better and help us get over our mild depression (Hokanson & Butler, 1992).

Poor social skills can increase chances of feeling depressed.

Problem. Researchers find that individuals often become and remain mildly depressed because they do not give themselves credit for any success (however small), make every situation (however small) into a bad or unpleasant experience, and constantly blame themselves for every failure, which makes them more depressed and thus elicits more negative reactions from friends (Nurius & Berlin, 1994).

Program. The first step in increasing our self-esteem is to become aware of self-blame by monitoring our thoughts and noticing all the times we blame ourselves for things, no matter how small. Once we become aware of self-blame, we can substitute thoughts of our past or recent accomplishments, no matter how small. By substituting thoughts of accomplishment and focusing on recent successes, we will gradually improve our self-esteem. As our self-esteem improves, we will slowly get a more positive attitude, which increases the social support of our friends (Granvold, 1994).

Learning to take credit for our actions can help overcome feelings of mild depression.

Eliminating Negative Thoughts

Problem. According to Beck's theory of depression, a depressed person thinks negative, maladaptive thoughts, which in turn cause the person to pay attention to, perceive, and remember primarily negative and depressing situations, events, and conversations (A. T. Beck, 1991). Thus, besides improving social skills and increasing social support, depressed individuals also need to stop the automatic negative thought pattern that maintains depression.

Researchers found that depressed individuals have a tendency to select and remember unhappy, critical, or depressing thoughts, events, or remarks, remember fewer good things than bad things, and take a more pessimistic view of life (Corey, 2005). Although discussed later (pp. 574–575), here's a brief description of a program for changing negative thought patterns.

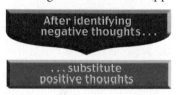

After identifying negative thoughts...

...substitute positive thoughts

Program. The first step is to monitor the occurrence of negative, depressive thoughts. The second step is to eliminate depressive thoughts by substituting positive ones. This second step is difficult because it requires considerable effort to stop thinking negative thoughts ("I really am a failure") and substitute positive ones ("I've got a lot going for me"). With practice, we can break the negative thought pattern by stopping negative thoughts and substituting positive ones. These kind of "talk" programs can help a person overcome mild depression and enjoy life more (Freeman et al., 2004). One reason "talk" programs can help as much as antidepressants is that "talk" programs and antidepressants produce strikingly similar changes in the brain.

Power of Positive Thinking

Everyone has heard about the power of positive thinking and now researchers have found a concrete example. It began with the interesting and reliable finding that psychotherapy ("talk" therapy) can often reduce depressive symptoms as much as antidepressants can (Rupke et al., 2006). Wondering why psychotherapy was as powerful as drugs, researchers took brain scans (pp. 70–71) of patients diagnosed with depression before and after 12 weeks of treatment with either psychotherapy or antidepressants. The result was that both treatments, psychotherapy and antidepressants, decreased depression. But the surprising finding was that both psychotherapy and antidepressants produced similar changes in the brain, one of which was to decrease the abnormally high activity of the prefrontal cortex (right figure) (A. L. Brody et al., 2001).

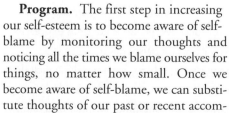

Prefrontal cortex

Several studies have now reported similar results: Talk therapy can and does alter brain functioning (Roffman et al., 2005). This means that the next time you are down in the dumps, try the power of positive thinking to change your brain functioning. You may be pleasantly surprised by the happy results.

✔ Summary Test

A. Mood Disorders

1. A prolonged emotional state that affects almost all of a person's thoughts and behaviors is called a _____ disorder.

Risk of Developing Bipolar Disorder

Identical twins — 80%

16% Fraternal twins

2. One mood disorder is marked by being in a daily bad mood, having no interest in anything, getting no pleasure from activities, and having at least four of the following symptoms: problems with weight, appetite, sleep, fatigue, thinking, or making decisions and having suicidal thoughts. This is called (a)_____ disorder, which is the most common form of mood disorder. Another mood disorder is characterized by being chronically depressed for many but not all days over a long period of time and having two of the following symptoms: problems with appetite and sleep, fatigue, low self-esteem, and feelings of hopelessness. This is called (b)_____ disorder.

3. A mood episode that is characterized by a distinct period, lasting at least a week, during which a person is unusually euphoric, cheerful, or high and has at least three of the following symptoms— has great self-esteem, needs little sleep, speaks rapidly and frequently, experiences racing thoughts, is easily distracted—is called a (a)_____ episode. A disorder characterized by periods of fluctuation between episodes of depression and mania is called (b)_____ disorder.

4. Underlying genetic, neurological, or physiological components may predispose a person to developing a mood disorder. These components are called (a)_____ factors. Factors such as dealing with stressors and stressful life events are believed to interact with predisposing biological influences and contribute to the development, onset, and maintenance of mood disorders. These are called (b)_____ factors.

5. Some drugs increase levels of neurotransmitters (serotonin, norepinephrine, dopamine) and are called (a)_____. These drugs, which are involved in the regulation of emotions and moods, such as major depression, are called (b)_____ and may take up to 8 weeks before they begin to work. The newer and more popular antidepressants (Prozac) are called (c)_____, or SSRIs, and are not more effective but have fewer unwanted (d)_____ than older antidepressants. However, about 33–50% of patients receive little or no benefit from antidepressants.

6. A mood stabilizer used to treat bipolar I disorder is called (a)_____, and it's often combined with antidepressants and antipsychotics. This drug is also used to treat euphoric periods without depression; this disorder is called (b)_____.

B. Electroconvulsive Therapy

7. If antidepressant drugs fail to treat major depression, the treatment of last resort involves placing electrodes on the skull and administering a mild electric current that passes through the brain and causes a seizure. This treatment is called (a)_____ therapy. A potentially serious side effect of this treatment is impairment or deficits in (b)_____, which usually affects events experienced during the weeks of treatment as well as events before and after treatment. However, following ECT treatment, there is a gradual improvement in memory functions.

C. Personality Disorders

8. A disorder that involves inflexible, long-standing, maladaptive traits that cause significantly impaired functioning or great distress in one's personal and social life is called a (a)_____ disorder. Ten of these disorders are listed in the DSM-IV-TR, including: a pattern of being submissive and clingy because of an excessive need to be taken care of, which is called a (b)_____ disorder; and a pattern of disregarding or violating the rights of others without feeling guilt or remorse, which is called an (c)_____ disorder. There is evidence that personality disorders develop from an interaction of (d)_____ and _____ factors.

9. Evidence that genetic factors influence personality disorders comes from studies on _____, which show that genetic factors contribute 30–50% to the development of these personality disorders.

D. Schizophrenia

NEUROLEPTICS

Typical: decrease dopamine | Atypical: decrease dopamine & serotonin

10. Schizophrenia is a serious mental disturbance that lasts for at least six months and includes at least two of the following persistent symptoms: delusions, hallucinations, disorganized speech, grossly disorganized behavior, and decreased emotional expression. These symptoms interfere with personal or social _____.

11. DSM-IV-TR lists five categories of schizophrenia, which include the following three. A category characterized by bizarre ideas, confused speech, childish behavior, great emotional swings, and often extreme neglect of personal appearance and hygiene is called (a)_____ schizophrenia. Another form marked by periods of wild excitement or periods of rigid, prolonged immobility is called (b)_____ schizophrenia. A third form characterized by thoughts of being persecuted or thoughts of grandeur is called (c)_____ schizophrenia.

12. Researchers have searched for an identifiable gene or a specific segment of a chromosome that is directly linked to developing schizophrenia. This genetic link is called a _____.

13. Two kinds of neuroleptic drugs are used to treat schizophrenia symptoms by changing levels of neurotransmitters in the brain. Drugs that act primarily to reduce levels of the neurotransmitter dopamine are called (a)_____ neuroleptics. An example is the phenothiazines. Drugs that lower levels of dopamine but, more important, also reduce levels of other neurotransmitters, especially serotonin, are called (b)_____ neuroleptics. These drugs are generally more effective in reducing schizophrenia symptoms and better at preventing (c)_____.

14. One side effect of the continued use of phenothiazines is the appearance of slow, involuntary, and uncontrollable rhythmic movements and rapid twitching of the mouth and lips, as well as unusual movements of the limbs. This side effect is called _____.

15. One theory of schizophrenia says that it develops when the (a)_____ neurotransmitter is overactive. Another related theory says that some people have a genetic predisposition, called a (b)_____, that interacts with life stressors to result in the onset and development of schizophrenia.

E. Dissociative Disorders

16. A dissociative disorder is characterized by a (a)_____ in a person's normally integrated functions of memory, identity, or perception of the environment. The DSM-IV-TR lists five types of dissociative disorder, which include the following three. If a person is unable to recall important personal information or events, usually in connection with a stressful or traumatic event, and the information forgotten is too important or lengthy to be explained by normal forgetfulness, it is called (b)_____. If a person suddenly and unexpectedly travels away from home or place of work and is unable to recall the past and may assume a new identity, it is called (c)_____. If a person experiences the presence of two or more distinct identities or personality states, each with its own pattern of perceiving, thinking about, and relating to the world, it is called (d)_____ disorder.

17. One theory says that dissociative identity disorder (DID) develops as a way to cope with the severe trauma of childhood (a)_____. A second explanation is that DID has become

a culturally approved way for people to express their (b)_____ or to control others or gain personal rewards.

F. Cultural Diversity: Interpreting Symptoms

18. Spirit possession is one example of how cultural factors determine whether symptoms are interpreted as (a)_____ or _____. An example of how cultural factors may increase the risk for development of mood disorders can be traced to the differences in assigned (b)_____ roles: males are expected to be independent and in control, and females are expected to be dependent and not have control.

G. Research Focus: Exercise Versus Drugs

19. After three different treatments, including exercise only, researchers found that at least 60% of patients diagnosed with (a)_____ showed significant improvement. Another finding was that when patients were retested 6 months later, those who had received exercise only showed significantly less (b)_____. Researchers suggest that (c)_____ helps patients develop a sense of personal mastery and positive self-regard, which helps prevent relapse.

H. Application: Dealing with Mild Depression

20. Beck's cognitive theory of depression says that when we are depressed, we have automatically occurring (a)_____, which center around being personally inadequate. In turn, these negative thoughts (b)_____ how we perceive and interpret the world and thus influence our behaviors and feelings. There are effective programs for developing better social skills and eliminating negative thoughts. Psychotherapy and antidepressant drugs both reduced depression and both produced similar changes in how the (c)_____ functions.

Answers: *1. mood; 2. (a) major depressive, (b) dysthymic; 3. (a) manic, (b) bipolar I; 4. (a) biological, (b) psychosocial; 5. (a) monoamines, (b) antidepressants, (c) selective serotonin reuptake inhibitors, (d) side effects; 6. (a) lithium, (b) mania; 7. (a) electroconvulsive, (b) memory; 8. (a) personality, (b) dependent, (c) antisocial, (d) biological, psychological; 9. twins; 10. functioning; 11. (a) disorganized, (b) catatonic, (c) paranoid; 12. genetic marker; 13. (a) typical, (b) atypical, (c) relapse; 14. tardive dyskinesia; 15. (a) dopamine, (b) diathesis; 16. (a) disruption, split, breakdown, (b) dissociative amnesia, (c) dissociative fugue, (d) dissociative identity; 17. (a) physical or sexual abuse, (b) frustrations, fears; 18. (a) normal, abnormal, (b) gender; 19. (a) major depression, (b) relapse, (c) exercise; 20. (a) negative thoughts, (b) bias or distort, (c) brain*

Critical Thinking

What Is a Psychopath?

1. According to the three definitions of abnormal behavior (p. 511), are Dahmer and Rader abnormal?

2. What objective test can be used to best assess for these psychopathic personality traits?

3. Which trait theory can explain how an individual can display such drastically inconsistent behaviors?

Jeffrey Dahmer would pick up young gay men, bring them home, drug them, strangle them, have sex with their corpses, and then, in some cases, eat their flesh.

Dennis Rader would break into people's homes, tie them up, strangle them, and eventually murder them. His murder method earned him the name "BTK killer," which stands for Bind, Torture, and Kill.

Dahmer and Rader share much in common. They are superficially charming, unemotional, impulsive, and self-centered. They are pathological liars who constantly manipulate others. Also, both men completely lack remorse, guilt, and empathy. Finally, they have low self-esteem, a strong desire to be in control, and a lifelong sense of loneliness. Dahmer, for example, felt so lonely that he admitted to killing people for company. Together, the above characteristics define a psychopath.

What may seem surprising is that psychopaths can love their parents, spouses, and children, but have great difficulty loving the rest of the world. Rader, for instance, was a loving husband and father. Yet, he seemed completely devoid of humanity as he plainly recounted the details of how he murdered his many victims.

Some of the fascinating characteristics and behaviors of psychopaths may be explained by biological and neurological factors. For example, some psychopaths have abnormalities in their limbic system, which is responsible for motivational behaviors, such as eating and sex, as well as emotional behaviors, such as fear, anger, and aggression. Also, some psychopaths have a disruption in the communication between the hippocampus and the prefrontal cortex, which is believed to contribute to their lack of control, inability to regulate aggression, and insensitivity to cues that predict they will get caught and punished. Interestingly, psychopaths also have lower autonomic arousal and consequently experience less distress when exposed to threats.

The life histories of psychopaths often include a chaotic upbringing, lack of parental attention, parental substance abuse, and child abuse. These life experiences may interact with biological or neurological factors linked to psychopathic behaviors. For instance, children may have genes for psychopathic behaviors that get activated only under stress; if they are raised in a nurturing environment, they may very well develop into well-behaved, moral adults. In other words, at least for some children, the consequences of having a stressful childhood can be deadly. (Adapted from B. Bower, 2006b; Crenson, 2005; C. Goldberg, 2003; Hickey, 2006; Larsson et al., 2006; Martens, 2002; A. Raine et al., 2004; Wilgoren, 2005; Yang et al., 2005b)

4. What part of the limbic system explains how psychopaths can be so cold and fearless?

5. How would a psychopath do on a lie detector test?

6. What is it called when someone has inherited a gene for psychopathic behaviors but develops those behaviors only if he or she has a stressful childhood?

1. Dahmer and Rader's serial killing behaviors are certainly abnormal in terms of statistical frequency, in terms of deviation from social norms, and in terms of being maladaptive (p. 511).
2. The Minnesota Multiphasic Personality Inventory-2 (MMPI-2) (p. 474) is an objective personality test that assesses a range of personality traits, including anger, truthfulness, self-esteem, friendliness, and seriously deviant behaviors.
3. The person-situation interaction (p. 464) explains how a person's behavior results from an interaction between his or her traits and the effects of being in a particular situation. It explains how psychopaths, such as Dahmer and Rader, can be loving people with their families, but cold-blooded, heartless serial killers in the community.
4. The amygdala (pp. 80, 362) is the structure located in the limbic system that is responsible for evaluating whether stimuli have positive

(happy) or negative (fearful, threatening) emotional significance for our survival. Damage to the amygdala explains how psychopaths can completely lack empathy and not learn to fear and avoid dangerous situations, such as cues that predict they will get caught.

5. A lie detector test (pp. 370–371) measures involuntary physiological responses and is based on the theory that if a person lies, he or she will feel guilt or fear, which will result in an increase in the galvanic skin response (sweating) and other physiological responses. But, because psychopaths do not feel guilt or fear and do not sweat easily due to lower autonomic arousal, psychopaths should pass a lie detector test with flying colors.
6. Having biological or neurological factors for psychopathic behaviors produces a *predisposition* (p. 540) for psychopathic behaviors, which increases the risk or vulnerability of developing such behaviors.

Links to Learning

Learning Activities

● ***POWERSTUDY FOR INTRODUCTION TO PSYCHOLOGY 4.0***

by Tom Doyle and Rod Plotnik

SuperModule: Check out "Mood Disorders & Schizophrenia" on **PowerStudy.** It includes complete paragraph-by-paragraph explanations of all content using fully-narrated animations and graphics. An onscreen toolbar allows immediate access to text, text outline, and module glossary with notetaking and printing capabilities. This module also includes:

- Video—Imbedded videos cover a wide range of topics such as major depression, bipolar disorder, personality disorders, and schizophrenia.
- A multitude of animations designed to help you understand each section of your text. For example, animated charts and menus to help you learn about mood disorders, a drag-and-drop exercise explores personality disorders, and an interactive exercise about schizophrenia reinforces your understainding of the symptoms.
- A test of your knowledge using an interactive version of the Summary Test on pages 550 and 551. Also access related quizzing—true/false, multiple choice, and matching.
- An interactive version of the Critical Thinking exercise "What Is a Psychopath?" on page 552.
- Key terms, a chapter outline including chapter abstract, and a special extended list of hotlinked websites that correlate to this module.

● *CengageNOW*

academic.cengage.com/login

Need help studying? This site is your one-stop study shop. Take a Pre-Test and CengageNOW will generate a Personalized Study Plan based on your test results. The Study Plan will identify the topics you need to review and direct you to online resources to help you master those topics. You can then take a Post-Test to determine the concepts you have mastered and what you still need to work on.

● ***INTRODUCTION TO PSYCHOLOGY BOOK COMPANION WEBSITE***

academic.cengage.com/psychology/plotnik

Visit your book companion website where you will find more resources to help you study. At this site, you will find Learning Objectives, Internet Exercises, quizzing, flash cards, and a pronunciation glossary.

● *STUDY GUIDE and WEBTUTOR*

webTUTOR

Check the corresponding module in your Study Guide for effective student tips and help learning the material presented. Also go to **academic.cengage.com/webtutor** for an interactive version of the Study Guide features.

Study Questions

*A. Mood Disorders—A student is brought in to the health clinic for being depressed and having attempted suicide. What will be her treatment program? (**Suggested answer p. 635**)

*B. Electroconvulsive Therapy—How would you compare the effectiveness and side effects of electroconvulsive shock therapy with those of antidepressant drugs? (**Suggested answer p. 635**)

C. Personality Disorders—A teenager is arrested by police for maliciously breaking car windows. How would you determine if this teenager is a potential psychopath?

D. Schizophrenia—Why do you think that drugs are more effective than psychotherapy in treating schizophrenia?

*These questions are answered in Appendix B.

E. Dissociative Disorders—How would you decide whether someone really has dissociative fugue or is just faking it to avoid dealing with stressful life events?

F. Cultural Diversity: Interpreting Symptoms—What differences in our cultural gender roles contribute to men's reporting significantly more alcohol abuse than women?

G. Research Focus: Exercise Versus Drugs—How might a brain image of a person with a mental disorder differ from an image of a person without a mental disorder?

*H. Application: Dealing with Mild Depression—When some people get depressed, why do they prefer to spread their gloom rather than do something to get over it? (**Suggested answer p. 635**)

MODULE 24
Therapies

Beginning of Psychoanalysis

Why couldn't she drink a glass of water?

It is the late 1800s, and we are listening to a young, intelligent woman named Anna O. She explains that she was perfectly healthy until she was 21 years old, when she began to experience strange physical symptoms. She developed a terrible squint that blurred her vision, a gagging feeling when she tried to drink a glass of water, and a paralysis in her right arm that would spread down her body. These symptoms occurred at about the time her father developed a serious illness and she felt the need to care for him by spending endless hours at his bedside. When her symptoms persisted, she consulted her doctor, Joseph Breuer.

Dr. Breuer takes up Anna's story and explains that, during some of her visits, she would sit in a trancelike state and talk uninhibitedly of her past experiences. One time Anna related a childhood incident in which she had watched her governess's dog drink out of a glass. The experience was disgusting to her because she disliked both the governess and the dog. At the time of the incident, Anna had shown no emotional reaction. But as she retold her story, she let out strong emotional reactions that had been locked inside. After releasing these pent-up emotional feelings, she was once again able to drink a glass of water without gagging.

Breuer explains that sometimes hypnosis helped Anna recall painful past experiences. She told of sitting by her father's sickbed, falling asleep, and having a horrifying dream in which a snake attacked him. She could not reach out and stop the snake because her arm had fallen asleep from hanging over the chair. As Anna relived her powerful guilt feelings of not being able to protect her father, the paralysis of her right arm disappeared. Breuer describes how, each time Anna recalled a past traumatic experience, a physical symptom associated with that trauma would vanish. Breuer would often discuss Anna's case with his friend and colleague, Sigmund Freud.

Dr. Freud interpreted Anna's symptoms as being caused by strong, primitive forces, probably related to unconscious sexual desires (Breuer & Freud, 1895/1955). The case of Anna O. is important because it played a role in the development of Freud's system of psychoanalysis, which was the start of what we currently call psychotherapy.

Just as psychoanalysis had its beginning with Anna O., another very different kind of therapy had its beginning with Little Albert.

Her right arm became paralyzed with no physical or neurological cause.

Beginning of Behavior Therapy

Why was Albert afraid of a white rat?

It was the early 1900s when John Watson, an up-and-coming behaviorist, showed 9-month-old Albert a number of objects to see if any caused fear. Little Albert looked at a white rat, rabbit, dog, monkey, several masks, pieces of wool, and burning newspapers without showing the slightest sign of fear.

Later, when Albert was about 11 months old, Watson retested Albert. This time, as Albert sat on a mattress, Watson suddenly took a white rat out of a basket and showed it to Albert. At the very moment

Albert touched the animal, another experimenter standing behind Albert struck a steel bar with a hammer. The sudden loud noise made Albert jump violently and fall forward into the mattress. Five more times Watson showed Albert the white rat and each time a loud sound rang out from behind. Finally, Watson showed Albert the rat but there was no loud sound. The instant the rat appeared, Albert began to cry and turn away from the rat. From this demonstration, Watson concluded that he had shown, for the first time, that an emotional reaction—in this case, fear—could be conditioned to any stimulus (Watson & Rayner, 1920).

This white rat caused no fear until . . .

The case of Little Albert could be considered the starting point for a very different kind of psychotherapy, known as behavior therapy. Behavior therapists believe that emotional problems may arise through conditioning and thus may be treated—or unconditioned—by using other principles of learning.

The cases of Little Albert and Anna O. illustrate two very different assumptions about how psychotherapy works. According to behavior therapy, emotional problems are learned and thus can be unlearned through conditioning techniques. According to psychoanalysis, emotional problems arise from unconscious fears, which can be uncovered and revealed only with special techniques. We'll discuss these two assumptions along with those of several other therapies as well as whether different therapies produce different results.

. . . Little Albert was classically conditioned.

What's Coming

In this module we'll discuss the history of psychotherapy and how current therapists are trained. We'll explain Freud's psychoanalysis, and how those who disagreed with Freud developed their own kinds of therapies. We'll discuss three of the more popular forms of psychotherapy: behavior therapy, cognitive therapy, and humanistic therapy. Finally, we'll answer one of the most interesting questions: Do therapies differ in their effectiveness?

Let's begin with how psychotherapy came about and how it has developed into a multibillion-dollar business.

A. Historical Background

Today, there are over 400 different forms of psychotherapy, some of them tested and some based purely on personal beliefs. For example, some states do not require the licensing of therapists; almost anyone can hang out a sign and go into practice (M. T. Singer & Lalich, 1997). The remaining states require licensing and training of therapists. There are about a dozen tested psychotherapies that may differ in assumptions and methods but generally share the following three characteristics.

Psychotherapy has three basic characteristics: verbal inter-

action between therapist and client(s); the development of a supportive relationship in which a client can bring up and discuss traumatic or bothersome experiences that may have led to current problems; and analysis of the client's experiences and/or suggested ways for the client to deal with or overcome his or her problems.

We'll discuss the major changes in treating mental disorders, including early inhumane treatments, the breakthrough in the use of drugs, and the development of modern forms of psychotherapy.

Early Treatments

Why did hospitals sell tickets?

From 1400 to 1700, people who today would be diagnosed as schizophrenics were considered insane and called lunatics. They were primarily confined to asylums or hospitals for the mentally ill, where the treatment was often inhumane and cruel. For example, patients were treated by being placed in a hood and straitjacket, chained to a cell wall, swung back and forth until they were quieted, strapped into a chair (right drawing), locked in handcuffs, hosed down with water until they were exhausted, or twirled until they passed out.

In the late 1700s, Dr. Benjamin Rush, who is considered the father of American psychiatry, developed the "tranquilizing chair" (bottom drawing). A patient was strapped into this chair and remained until he or she seemed calmed down. Dr. Rush believed that mental disorders were caused by too much blood in the brain. To cure this problem, he attempted to treat patients by withdrawing huge amounts of blood, as much as six quarts over a period of months. Dr. Rush also tried to cure patients with fright, such as putting them into coffins and convincing them they were about to die. Despite these strange and inhumane treatments, Dr. Rush encouraged his staff to treat patients with kindness and understanding (Davison & Neale, 1994).

Early treatment was to be strapped to a chair.

In the 1700s, some hospitals even sold tickets to the general public. People came to see the locked-up "wild beasts" and to laugh at the tragic and pathetic behaviors of individuals with severe mental disorders. However, in the late 1700s and early 1800s, a few doctors began to make reforms by removing the patients' chains, forbidding physical punishment, and using a more psychological approach to treat mental disorders (J. C. Harris, 2003).

Early treatment was to sit in a "tranquilizing chair."

Reform Movement

What did she change?

In the 1800s, a Boston schoolteacher named Dorothea Dix (right photo below) began to visit the jails and poorhouses where most of the mental patients in the United States were kept. Dix publicized the terrible living conditions and the lack of reasonable treatment of mental patients. Her work was part of the reform movement that emphasized moral therapy.

Moral therapy, which was popular in the early 1800s, was the belief that mental patients could be helped to function better by providing humane treatment in a relaxed and decent environment.

During the reform movement, pleasant mental hospitals were built in rural settings so that moral therapy could be used to treat patients. However, these mental hospitals soon became overcrowded, the public lost interest, funds became tight, and treatment became scarce.

Dorothea Dix began the humane treatment of the mentally ill.

By the late 1800s, the belief that moral therapy would cure mental disorders was abandoned. Mental hospitals began to resemble human snake pits, in which hundreds of mental patients, in various states of dress or undress, milled about in a large room while acting out their symptoms with little or no supervision. Treatment went backward, and once again patients were put into straitjackets, handcuffs, and various restraining devices (Routh, 1994).

By the early 1900s, Sigmund Freud had developed psychoanalysis, the first psychotherapy. Psychoanalysis eventually spread from Europe to the United States and reached its peak of popularity in the 1950s. However, psychoanalysis was more effective in treating less serious mental disorders (neuroses) than in treating the serious mental disorders (psychoses) that kept people in mental hospitals.

Freud developed first psychotherapy.

Thus, the wretched conditions and inhumane treatment of patients with serious mental disorders persisted until the early 1950s. By then, more than half a million patients were locked away. But in the mid-1950s, two events dramatically changed the treatment of mental patients: one was the discovery of antipsychotic drugs, and the other was the development of community mental health centers.

What was the first break-through?

The discovery of drugs for treating mental disorders often occurs by chance. Such was the case in the 1950s as a French surgeon, Henri Laborit, searched for a drug that would calm down patients before surgery without causing unconsciousness. He happened to try a new drug on a woman about to have surgery and who was also schizophrenic. To the doctor's great surprise, the drug not only calmed the woman down but also decreased her schizophrenic symptoms. This is how the drug, chlorpromazine, was discovered to be a treatment for schizophrenia. Chlorpromazine *(klor-PRO-ma-zeen)* belongs to a group of drugs called phenothiazines.

Phenothiazines (fee-no-THIGH-ah-zeens), **which were discovered in the early 1950s, block or reduce the effects of the neurotransmitter dopamine and reduce schizophrenic symptoms, such as delusions and hallucinations.**

After 200 years of often cruel and inhumane treatments for mental disorders, chlorpromazine was the first drug shown to be effective in reducing severe mental symptoms, such as delusions and hallucinations. For this reason, the discovery of chlorpromazine is considered the first revolution in the drug treatment of mental disorders. Earlier we discussed the phenothiazines, now called typical neuroleptics, as well as the newer discovery of atypical neuroleptics (p. 541), which are used in the treatment of schizophrenia.

In 1954, one of the phenothiazines, chlorpromazine (trade name: Thorazine), reached the United States and had two huge effects. First, it stimulated research on neurotransmitters and on the development of new drugs to treat mental disorders. Second, chlorpromazine reduced severe mental symptoms such as delusions and hallucinations to the point that patients could function well enough to be released from mental hospitals, a policy called deinstitutionalization.

Deinstitutionalization **refers to the release of mental patients from mental hospitals and their return to the community to develop more independent and fulfilling lives.**

In 1950, before the discovery of phenothiazines, there were 550,000 patients in mental hospitals in the United States. After the use of phenothiazines and deinstitutionalization, the number of patients in mental hospitals had dropped to about 150,000 in 1970 and to about 80,000 in 2000 (Manderscheid & Sonnenschein, 1992). However, deinstitutionalization has created a related problem.

Homeless. The goal of deinstitutionalization, which is to get patients back into the community, has been only partly realized. Some former mental patients do live in well-run halfway houses (F. R. Lipton et al., 2000). However, recent investigations have found that some halfway houses are poorly maintained, use untrained staff, and provide little or no treatment for the residents. The major problems are lack of funding and poor supervision of halfway houses.

About 25–80% of the homeless have some degree of mental problems.

Because there are not enough good halfway houses, many deinstitutionalized patients end up on the streets and homeless. The result is that about 25–80% of today's homeless individuals have serious mental disorders and receive little or no treatment (Hartwell, 2003; Sosin, 2003). To provide mental health treatment for the homeless as well as those released from hospitals or too poor to pay for services, there is another place to receive help, community mental health centers.

Where can they go for treatment?

There is a need for treatment of mental disorders in the homeless, county prisoners, those released from mental hospitals, as well as about 20% of Americans who experience a mental disorder in the course of a year (NIMH, 2005b). Some of these individuals may have less serious mental disorders that require professional help but not hospitalization. One way to provide professional help to individuals with less serious mental disorders is through community mental health centers.

Community mental health centers **offer low-cost or free mental health care to members of the surrounding community, especially the underprivileged. The services may include psychotherapy, support groups, and telephone crisis counseling.**

Therapist is treating a client in a community mental health center, which helps those who need care but can't afford it.

Just as the 1950s saw the introduction of a new drug treatment for mental disorders (phenothiazines), the 1960s saw the growing availability of new treatment facilities, community mental health centers. The goal of these centers as well as other outpatient centers is to provide treatment for the poor and those who have no other forms of treatment for their mental health problems (Olfson et al., 2002). These kinds of mental health centers provide briefer forms of therapy that are needed in emergencies and focus on the early detection and prevention of psychological problems (Barlow & Durand, 2005). To meet these ambitious goals required an enormous increase in mental health personnel.

In the 1960s, *psychiatrists* provided the majority of psychological services, which consisted of mainly psychoanalysis and served individuals in the middle and upper social classes who were not very seriously disturbed. Because of the limited number of psychiatrists, community mental health centers turned to *clinical psychologists* and *social workers* to provide the new mental health services. This demand increased the number of clinical and counseling psychologists and social workers and stimulated the development of new therapy approaches (Garfield & Bergin, 1994).

Before discussing specific psychotherapies, we'll answer four general questions about psychotherapy.

A. *HISTORICAL BACKGROUND* **557**

B. Questions about Psychotherapy

What do I need to know? If you or a family member, friend, relative, or acquaintance has a mental health problem, there are at least four questions that you might ask about seeking professional help or psychotherapy: Do I need professional help? Are there different kinds of therapists? What are the different approaches? How effective is psychotherapy? We'll answer each question in turn.

Do I Need Professional Help?

Each year, more than 30 million Americans need help in dealing with a variety of mental disorders (American Psychological Association, 2004a). For example, a person may feel overwhelmed by a sense of sadness, depression, or helplessness so that he or she cannot form a meaningful relationship. A person may worry or expect such terrible things to happen that he or she cannot concentrate or carry out everyday activities. A person may become so dependent on drugs that he or she has difficulty functioning in personal, social, or professional situations. If these problems begin to interfere with daily functioning in social, personal, business, academic, or professional interactions and activities, then a person may need help from a mental health professional (Satcher, 2000).

Each year, about 30 million Americans need help in dealing with mental disorders.

One reason individuals do not seek professional help involves the social stigma attached to having a mental disorder. For example, in an earlier module, we discussed how well-known singer-songwriter Sheryl Crow suffered from major depression for several years before being persuaded by her mother to seek professional help (p. 532). Although still present, the stigma of having a mental disorder is decreasing as people recognize the need for professional treatment (Elswick, 2004).

Another reason individuals do not seek professional help is that they don't realize they need it. In an earlier module, we discussed the case of Michael McCabe, who heard voices and believed people were going to steal things from him (schizophrenia); and in another case, Chuck Elliot went sleepless for four nights and had trouble controlling his behavior (bipolar I disorder) (p. 531). Although both of these individuals needed professional treatment, neither wanted or asked for it. Thus, in some cases, individuals with serious mental disorders may not be able to decide what is best, and their friends or family may need to help them get professional help.

Currently, there are a number of different kinds of mental health professionals who may provide a drug or nondrug treatment program or some combination.

Are There Different Kinds of Therapists?

We'll discuss three of the more common kinds of therapists: psychiatrists, clinical psychologists, and counseling psychologists, each of whom receives a different kind of training in psychotherapy techniques.

Psychiatrists **go to medical school, receive an M.D. degree, and then take a psychiatric residency, which involves additional training in pharmacology, neurology, psychopathology, and psychotherapeutic techniques.**

Psychiatrists focus on biological factors and usually prescribe drugs to treat mental health disorders. Psychiatrists who receive additional training in psychoanalytic institutes are called ***psychoanalysts***.

Clinical psychologists **go to graduate school in clinical psychology and earn a doctorate degree (Ph.D., Psy.D., or Ed.D.). This training, which includes one year of work in an applied clinical setting, usually requires five to six years of work after obtaining a college degree.**

Clinical psychologists who receive additional training in psychoanalytic institutes can also practice psychoanalysis. Clinical psychologists focus on psychosocial and environmental factors and use psychotherapy to treat mental health disorders. They generally cannot prescribe drugs. However, in a trial program, clinical psychologists were trained in prescribing drugs for a variety of mental disorders. Evaluators of this program concluded that, with proper training, clinical psychologists can provide safe and high-quality drug treatment for their patients (Dittmann, 2003). Since then, New Mexico and Louisiana have passed laws that allow psychologists with advanced medical training to prescribe medications for patients with mental disorders (Levin, 2005). At least 12 other states are considering passing similar laws (Dittmann, 2003). For political and financial reasons, psychiatrists oppose laws that allow specially trained psychologists to prescribe drugs (Munsey, 2006; R. J. Sternberg, 2003c).

Counseling psychologist has a Ph.D., Psy.D., or Ed.D. and counseling experience.

Clinical psychologist has a Ph.D., Psy.D., or Ed.D. and clinical experience.

College degree

Psychiatrist has an M.D. and psychiatric residency.

Counseling psychologists **go to graduate school in psychology or education and earn a doctorate degree (Ph.D., Psy.D., or Ed.D). This training, which includes work in a counseling setting, usually requires about four to six years after obtaining a bachelor's degree.**

Counseling psychologists receive training similar to that of clinical psychologists but with less emphasis on research and more emphasis on counseling in real-world settings. Counseling psychologists, who function in settings such as schools, colleges, industry, and private practice, generally deal more with problems of living than with the mental disorders that are treated by clinical psychologists.

In addition, other mental health professionals, such as ***clinical social workers*** and ***psychiatric nurses***, also provide mental health services.

Just as there are different kinds of therapists, there are also different kinds of therapeutic approaches from which to choose.

What Are the Different Approaches?

If you were to seek professional help for a mental problem, you could choose from a number of different therapeutic approaches: Some use primarily psychotherapy, some use primarily drugs, and others use a combination of psychotherapy and drugs. These different therapies can be divided into three groups: insight therapy, cognitive-behavioral therapy, and medical therapy.

With *insight therapy,* the therapist and client talk about the client's symptoms and problems with the goal of reaching or identifying the cause of the problem. Once the client has an insight into the cause of the problem, possible solutions can be discussed with the therapist.

The classic example of insight therapy is psychoanalysis, whose goal is to help clients get insights into their problems. But because psychoanalysis requires hundreds of sessions, it is very costly; and because it is no more effective than other, briefer therapies, its popularity has significantly decreased since the 1950s. The next kind of therapy, called cognitive-behavioral therapy, combines some features of insight therapy with a much more directive approach.

Here's my problem . . .

There are several kinds of drug and nondrug therapies for mental disorders.

***Cognitive-behavioral therapy* involves the application of principles of learning that were discussed in Modules 9 and 10. The therapist focuses on the client's problem, identifies specific thoughts and behaviors that need to be changed, and provides techniques based on learning principles to make desired changes.**

Unlike psychoanalysis, which focuses on insight and gives little direction for change, cognitive-behavioral therapy focuses on changing specific undesirable or problematic thoughts and behaviors. This approach combines techniques and ideas from cognitive therapy (p. 565) and behavior therapy (p. 566). Cognitive-behavioral therapy is an example of the most popular approach, which is used by 25–33% of therapists and is called the eclectic approach (Norcross, 2005).

The *eclectic (ee-KLEK-tik) approach* involves combining and using techniques and ideas from many different therapeutic approaches.

For example, a therapist using an eclectic approach might combine some of the nondirective techniques from psychoanalysis with more directive techniques from cognitive-behavioral therapy. Unlike insight and cognitive-behavioral approaches, which focus on psychosocial factors, the next kind of therapy focuses on changing biological factors.

***Medical therapy* involves the use of various psychoactive drugs to treat mental disorders by changing biological factors, such as the levels of neurotransmitters in the brain.**

In Modules 22 and 23, we discussed medical therapies and how various psychoactive drugs are used to treat a wide variety of mental disorders, including anxiety, mood disorders, and schizophrenia. Unlike medical therapies, in which drugs may have undesirable physical side effects, no undesirable side effects are associated with psychotherapy. In this module, we'll focus on several psychotherapies, specifically insight and cognitive-behavioral approaches.

A number of different drugs (neuroleptics, antidepressants) may be used to treat more serious mental disorders.

With so many different therapeutic approaches, is one kind of psychotherapy more effective than another?

How Effective Is Psychotherapy?

Sometimes when we have a problem, we might say, "I'll just wait and maybe the problem will go away by itself." This kind of remark raises a major question: Is psychotherapy more effective than just waiting for problems to go away? To answer this question and determine the effectiveness of psychotherapy, researchers have used a complex statistical procedure called meta-analysis.

***Meta-analysis* is a powerful statistical procedure that compares the results of dozens or hundreds of studies to determine the effectiveness of some variable or treatment examined in these studies.**

Researchers have done meta-analysis on over 1,500 studies that examined the effects of psychotherapy on a variety of problems, such as depression, anxiety disorders, family problems, eating disorders, and headaches (A. C. Butler et al., 2006; Luborsky et al., 2002; P. E. Nathan et al., 2000). We'll discuss three of the major findings:

■ Psychotherapy was effective in relieving a wide variety of psychological and behavioral symptoms in comparison with control groups who were on a waiting list to receive therapy or who received no systematic treatment.

Psychotherapy has proved effective for a wide variety of mental disorders.

■ There was little or no significant difference in effectiveness between the approaches used by different therapies. In other words, the same psychological or behavioral symptoms were, in most cases, treated effectively with different approaches.

■ The vast majority of patients (75%) showed measurable improvement by the end of six months of once-a-week psychotherapy sessions (24 sessions).

Thus, based on data from thousands of patients, psychotherapy has proved effective in treating many mental and behavioral problems, and the greatest improvement occurs in a relatively brief time (13 to 18 sessions) (M. J. Lambert et al., 2004). Almost 10 million individuals seek psychotherapy each year, and of these about 10–20% experience great improvement, about 30–50% receive some improvement, and about 10–30% show little or no improvement (Olfson et al., 2002). Thus, although psychotherapy has proved to be an effective treatment, the amount of improvement varies across patients (G. S. Brown et al., 2005; Sotsky et al., 2006).

Although many different therapies have been shown to be about equally effective, we'll discuss how some therapeutic approaches are preferred for certain problems and how some clients may prefer one approach over another (Chambless & Ollendick, 2001).

We'll begin with one of the oldest and best-known therapy approaches—Freud's system of psychoanalysis.

C. Insight Therapies

Psychoanalysis

What happens in psychoanalysis?

One reason almost everyone knows the name Freud is that he constructed one of the first amazingly complete and interesting descriptions of personality development, mental disorder, and treatment, which was a monumental and revolutionary accomplishment at the time. In fact, Sigmund Freud's theory of psychoanalysis includes two related theories. The first is his comprehensive theory of personality development (id, ego, superego, and psychosexual stages), which we discussed in Module 19. His second theory involves the development and treatment of various mental disorders, which we'll examine here.

Psychoanalysis focuses on the idea that each of us has an unconscious part that contains ideas, memories, desires, or thoughts that have been hidden or repressed because they are psychologically dangerous or threatening to our self-concept. To protect our self-concept from these threatening thoughts and desires, we automatically build a mental barrier that we cannot voluntarily remove. However, the presence of these threatening thoughts and desires gives rise to unconscious conflicts, which, in turn, can result in psychological and physical symptoms and mental disorders.

Freud's psychoanalysis searches for unconscious conflicts that result in psychological problems.

Freud began developing the theory of psychoanalysis in the late 1800s. From 1902 onward, a number of young doctors and interested laypersons gathered around Freud to learn the principles and practice of psychoanalysis. In 1908, Freud was invited to America to discuss his approach, which reached the height of its popularity in the 1950s. Psychoanalysis makes three major assumptions (Arlow, 2005; Corey, 2005).

1 Freud believed that *unconscious conflicts* were the chief reason for the development of psychological problems (such as paranoia) and physical symptoms (such as loss of feeling in a hand). To overcome psychological and physical problems, patients needed to become aware of, and gain insight into, their unconscious conflicts and repressed thoughts.

2 Freud developed *three techniques*—free association, dream interpretation, and analysis of slips of the tongue—that he believed provide clues to unconscious conflicts and repressed thoughts.

3 Freud found that at some point during therapy the patient would react to the therapist as a substitute parent, lover, sibling, or friend and, in the process, project or *transfer* strong emotions onto the therapist.

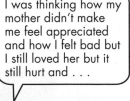

I was thinking how my mother didn't make me feel appreciated and how I felt bad but I still loved her but it still hurt and . . .

One of Freud's techniques was the use of free association.

Freud developed these three assumptions gradually, over a period of about ten years, when he was treating patients for a variety of psychological problems and physical symptoms.

We'll explain how Freud used these three assumptions to develop the therapy he called psychoanalysis.

Therapy session. To give you an appreciation of what happens during psychoanalysis, we'll begin with an excerpt from a therapy session and then explain what goes on between client and psychoanalyst.

Henry is in his mid-forties and is well advanced in treatment. As he arrives, he casually mentions his somewhat late arrival at the analyst's office, which might otherwise have gone unnoticed.

"You will think it is a resistance," Henry remarked sarcastically, "but it was nothing of the kind. I had hailed a taxi that would have gotten me to the office on time. However, the traffic light changed just before the cab reached me, and someone else got in instead. I was so annoyed that I yelled 'F___ you!' after the cab driver."

A brief pause ensued, followed by laughter as Henry repeated "F___ you!"—this time clearly directed to the analyst.

The analyst interpreted this interaction to mean that the cabbie had represented the analyst in the first place. Henry's anger at the analyst was relieved by the opportunity to curse out the analyst (cabbie).

After another brief pause, it was the analyst who broke the silence and injected his first and only interpretation of the 50-minute session. He asserted that Henry seemed to be angry about a previously canceled therapy session.

Henry was furious over the interpretation. "Who are you that I should care about missing that session?" he stormed.

Henry paused again, and then reflected more tranquilly, "My father, I suppose."

This time it was the word *father* that served as the switch word to a new line of thought.

"My father was distant, like you," he began. "We never really had a conversation" (adapted from S. D. Lipton, 1983).

ROLE OF ANALYST

This brief excerpt from a psychoanalytic session illustrates the basic assumptions of psychoanalysis.

■ **Free association.** Notice that the patient is encouraged to free-associate or say anything that comes into his mind, while the analyst makes few comments.

■ **Interpretation.** When the analyst does comment, he or she interprets or analyzes something the patient says, such as the meaning of the anger at the cab driver.

■ **Unconscious conflicts.** By analyzing the client's free associations, the analyst hopes to reveal the client's unconscious and threatening desires, which are causing unconscious conflicts that, in turn, cause psychological problems.

We'll examine two of Freud's therapy techniques in more detail.

One of Freud's major challenges was to find ways to uncover unconscious conflicts, which, he believed, led to psychological problems that he labeled neuroses.

Neuroses, according to Freud, are maladaptive thoughts and actions that arise from some unconscious thought or conflict and indicate feelings of anxiety.

In order to treat neuroses or neurotic symptoms, such as phobias, anxieties, and obsessions, Freud wanted to discover what was in the patient's unconscious. To do this, he developed two major techniques: free association and dream interpretation. To show how these techniques work, we'll describe two of Freud's most famous cases, Rat Man and Wolf-Man.

Rat Man: Free Association

Freud encouraged patients to relax, sit back, or lie down on his now-famous couch and engage in something called free association.

Free association is a technique that encourages clients to talk about any thoughts or images that enter their heads; the assumption is that this kind of free-flowing, uncensored talking will provide clues to unconscious material.

Rat Man believed that rats would destroy his father and lover.

For example, here is how Freud described a session with one of his most famous patients, a 29-year-old lawyer later named the Rat Man because of his obsession that rats would destroy his father and lover.

Freud writes, "The next day I made him [Rat Man] pledge himself to submit to the one and only condition of the treatment—namely, to say everything that came into his head even if it was *unpleasant* to him, or seemed *unimportant* or *irrelevant* or *senseless.* I then gave him leave to start his communications with any subject he pleased" (Freud, 1909/1949, p. 297; italics in the original).

Freud is actually telling Rat Man to free-associate. By this means, Freud uncovered a number of Rat Man's repressed memories, such as how Rat Man, as a child, would get into rages and bite people, just like a rat.

Free association was one of Freud's important methodological discoveries. Psychoanalysts still use this technique today to probe a client's unconscious thoughts, desires, and conflicts (Corey, 2005).

Wolf-Man: Dream Interpretation

Freud listened to and interpreted his patients' dreams because he believed that dreams represent the purest form of free association.

Dream interpretation is a psychoanalytic technique based on the assumption that dreams contain underlying, hidden meanings and symbols that provide clues to unconscious thoughts and desires.

For example, here is one of the best-known dreams in psychoanalytic literature. This dream was told to Freud by a 23-year-old patient who was later named Wolf-Man because he had a phobia of wolves and other animals (Buckley, 1989).

Wolf-Man dreamed wolves were sitting in the tree outside his room.

"I dreamt that it was night and that I was lying in my bed. Suddenly the window opened of its own accord, and I was terrified to see that some white wolves were sitting on the big walnut tree in front of the window. There were six or seven of them. The wolves were quite white, and looked more like foxes or sheep-dogs, for they had big tails like foxes and they had their ears pricked like dogs when they are attending to something. In great terror, evidently of being eaten up by the wolves, I screamed and woke up . . . I was 3, 4, or at most 5 years old at the time. From then until my 11th or 12th year I was always afraid of seeing something terrible in my dreams" (Freud, 1909/1949, p. 498).

Freud's interpretation of this dream was that, as a young boy, Wolf-Man was "transformed" into a wolf and had witnessed his parents' sexual intercourse (looking through the bedroom window). Later, sexual fears created unconscious conflicts and resulted in a phobia of wolves and other animals.

As Freud demonstrates, the psychoanalyst's task is to look behind the dream's often bizarre disguises and symbols and decipher clues to unconscious, repressed memories, thoughts, feelings, and conflicts (R. Greenberg & Perlman, 1999).

Case Studies: Anna O., Rat Man, and Wolf-Man

Case studies, such as those of Rat Man, Wolf-Man, and Anna O., whom we discussed at the beginning of the module, were very important because from these Freud developed the major concepts of psychoanalysis. For example, from cases like that of Anna O., who had physical symptoms (paralyzed arm, blurred vision) but no apparent physical causes, Freud developed the idea that repressed feelings and unconscious conflicts could affect behavior but that the person would have no awareness of this happening. In support of Freud's belief that unconscious forces were causing Anna O.'s physical problems, each

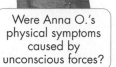

Were Anna O.'s physical symptoms caused by unconscious forces?

time she let out some apparently repressed emotional experience, one of her physical symptoms disappeared.

Freud's case studies read like mystery stories with Freud being the master detective who searches for psychological clues that will reveal the person's repressed feelings and unconscious conflicts. At the time, Freud's assumptions and theories, such as repressed feelings and unconscious motivation, were revolutionary. However, as we'll discuss later, Freud's theories and assumptions have been very difficult to verify or prove with experimental methods (Grunbaum, 1993).

Besides developing methods to reveal unconscious thoughts and conflicts, Freud discovered two other concepts that are central to psychoanalysis.

C. Insight Therapies

Why did clients get angry?

Freud was the first to notice that, during therapy, his clients became somewhat hostile toward him, a problem he called transference. He also found that patients became very resistant about dealing with their feelings. Freud believed that how these two problems, called transference and resistance, were handled determined how successful therapy would be. We'll explain these two concepts by using the cases of Rat Man and Wolf-Man.

Rat Man: Transference

Freud describes a patient, later labeled Rat Man, as expressing powerful, aggressive feelings toward him. For example, Rat Man refused to shake hands with Freud, accused Freud of

During therapy, Rat Man called Freud a "filthy swine," which Freud believed resulted from transference.

picking his nose, called Freud a "filthy swine," and said that Freud needed to be taught some manners (Freud, 1909/1949).

According to Freud, Rat Man was projecting negative traits of his own very controlling mother onto Freud, who became a "substitute mother." This process of transferring feelings to the therapist is called transference.

Transference **is the process by which a client expresses strong emotions toward the therapist because the therapist substitutes for someone important in the client's life, such as the client's mother or father.**

Freud believed that the main part of therapy involved working through the transference—that is, resolving the emotional feelings that the client has transferred to the therapist. Freud said that if the feelings involved in transference were not worked out, therapy would stall and treatment would not occur. For this reason, Freud believed that one of the major roles of the analyst was to help the client deal with, work through, and resolve the transferred feelings. Identifying the process of transference, which occurs in many therapeutic relationships, is considered one of Freud's greatest insights (Eagle, 2000).

Wolf-Man: Resistance

For most patients, working out transference and achieving insight into their problems are long and difficult processes. One reason for the difficulty is that the client has so many defenses against admitting repressed thoughts and feelings into consciousness. These defenses lead to resistance.

Resistance **is characterized by the client's reluctance to work through or deal with feelings or to recognize unconscious conflicts and repressed thoughts.**

Resistance may show up in many ways: clients may cancel sessions or come late, argue continually, criticize the analyst, or develop physical problems. For example, the patient named Wolf-Man constantly complained of severe constipation. Freud said that Wolf-Man used constipation as an obvious sign that he was resisting having to deal with his feelings (Freud, 1909/1949).

Freud overcame Wolf-Man's resistance by promising that his constipation would disappear with continued therapy, and it did (Buckley, 1989). Freud cautioned that the analyst must use tact and patience to break down the client's resistance so that the client faces his feelings.

During therapy, Wolf-Man complained of constipation, which Freud believed indicated resistance.

A necessary role of the analyst is to overcome the client's resistance so that the therapy can proceed and stay on course (Arlow, 2005).

Short-Term Dynamic Psychotherapy

The cases of Rat Man and Wolf-Man illustrate two problems that psychoanalysts must solve before their clients can get better. One problem involves the strong emotional feelings that occur with transference, which must be resolved before therapy can succeed. The second problem is helping clients overcome their resistance so they can begin to deal with threatening or undesirable feelings. Resolving the problems of transference and resistance may take 200–600 sessions across several years of traditional psychoanalysis. However, there is currently a strong push toward shorter versions of psychotherapy, in large part because current health insurance coverage typically pays for only 20–30 sessions. As a result, therapists have developed a briefer version of psychoanalysis, which is called short-term dynamic psychotherapy (Prochaska & Norcross, 2007).

Shorter versions of traditional psychoanalysis have proved effective.

How long will it take for me to get over my fears?

Short-term dynamic psychotherapy **emphasizes a limited time for treatment (20–30 sessions) and focuses on limited goals, such as solving a relatively well-defined problem. Therapists take a more active and directive role by identifying and discussing the client's problems, resolving issues of transference, interpreting the patient's behaviors, and offering an opportunity for the patient to foster changes in behavior and thinking that will result in more active coping and an improved image of oneself.**

Several forms of short-term dynamic psychotherapy have recently become more popular than long-term traditional psychoanalysis. Short-term dynamic psychotherapy, which incorporates techniques of traditional psychoanalysis, has proven effective for treating a number of problems, including anxiety, drug abuse, eating disorders, depression, and several personality disorders (Leichsenring et al., 2004; Milrod et al., 2007).

Next, we'll evaluate the current importance of psychoanalysis.

Psychoanalysis: Evaluation

The 50th anniversary of Sigmund Freud's death (1939) was marked by a series of articles in *Psychoanalytic Quarterly* titled, "Is There a Future for American Psychoanalysis?" One author said that such a question was unheard of in the 1950s, when psychoanalysis was at the height of its popularity (Kirsner,

1990). However, following the 1950s, there was a decline in the popularity of psychoanalysis (Bornstein, 2001). Now, 150 years after Freud's birth (1856), many articles are reporting that some of his ideas are returning in popularity and describe his influence as an "inescapable force" (Adler, 2006). We'll discuss the decline in popularity of psychoanalysis following the 1950s as well as its current status.

Decline in Popularity

How did it happen that psychoanalysis, the number one therapy in the 1950s, lost its popularity and is now struggling to compete with other therapies? Here are some of the reasons according to its own members (Wallerstein & Fonagy, 1999; Westen & Gabbard, 1999).

■ **Lack of research.** In the 1970s, critics pointed out that almost no research had been done on whether the psychoanalytic process was an effective form of therapy. For example, psychoanalysts were very slow to analyze their own profession in terms of education—how best to train analysts—and to conduct research into what goes on during analysis and how to make it more effective. This criticism, which questioned the effectiveness of psychoanalysis, contributed to its decline in popularity.

■ **Competing therapies.** Perhaps the major reason for the decrease in popularity of psychoanalysis was that, beginning in the 1970s, a number of competing psychotherapies (discussed later in this module) were developed that proved to be equally effective but had a great advantage in that they are much quicker and far less costly. For example, psychoanalysis may require 200–600 sessions (2–4 per week for several years) versus about 25 for other therapies. This last point is particularly important, since most major health insurance plans limit either the amount of money or the number of sessions (usually about 25) for treatment of psychological problems. Because of this policy, health plans would not pay the costs of therapy for patients choosing psychoanalysis.

■ **Psychoactive drugs.** Another reason for the decline of psychoanalysis was the discovery of many new psychoactive drugs that proved effective in treating many of the problems formerly dealt with in psychoanalysis, such as anxiety and mood disorders. Some patients preferred drugs to psychoanalysis.

All of the above factors—lack of research on its effectiveness, development of new and less costly therapies, and discovery of psychoactive drugs—resulted in psychoanalysis experiencing a great decline from its peak popularity in the 1950s.

Is it true that there have been some changes to my theory?

Freud's method of psychoanalysis has declined in popularity, but his ideas have been incorporated into other therapies.

Current Status

Beginning in the 1980s and continuing to the present, there has been a major effort by psychoanalytic societies and their members to encourage research on the methods, concepts, and outcomes of therapy. This shift toward research indicates a major turning point in psychoanalysis. Previously, psychoanalysts almost exclusively reported individual case studies; they rarely studied the psychoanalytic process or its effectiveness using the experimental approach that had been adopted by newly developed and competing therapies. For example, when compared with different kinds of long-term psychotherapies, researchers found that psychoanalysis was just as successful in improving patients' mental status (Blomberg et al., 2001). This is one example of the current efforts to test, compare, and show that long-term psychoanalysis can produce results as successful as those found with other therapies.

Freudian concepts. Current followers agree that some of Freud's concepts, such as the id being the source of energy, the importance of the Oedipus complex in personality development, and basic drives limited to sex and aggression, have proved difficult to verify and are now out of date. The same followers add that other Freudian concepts, such as the influence of unconscious forces, long-term effects of early childhood patterns, and existence of defense mechanisms, have been experimentally tested and supported (Fotopoulou, 2006; Ramachandran, 2006). For example, researchers discovered that we do have memories, called procedural or nondeclarative (p. 246), that are outside our awareness (unconscious) but affect a variety of behaviors, such as acquiring strong emotional responses (fears and phobias) through classical conditioning (Mayes, 2000).

Thus, two basic concepts underlying psychoanalysis—the influence of unconscious forces and the use of defense mechanisms—have received support (Solms, 2006).

According to recent surveys, Freud's influence is very much alive in today's culture. Forty-three percent of adults in the United States believe dreams reflect unconscious desires, and nearly 30% believe that an adult's psychological problems can be traced back to his or her childhood (Adler, 2006).

Conclusion

Through the years, many ideas from Freud's classical psychoanalysis have been used to develop a kind of therapy called the psychodynamic approach. Although sharing some of its concepts with classical psychoanalysis, the psychodynamic approach has the therapist taking a more directive role that reduces the number of sessions but seems equally effective. One example of this newer approach is short-term dynamic therapy (p. 562) (Piper et al., 2002).

Next, we'll discuss an approach developed by a clinician who had been using Freud's psychoanalytic approach but became very displeased with it.

C. Insight Therapies

What is a therapist's role?

As a therapist, Carl Rogers used the most popular therapy in his time, which was Freud's psychoanalytic approach. However, before long Rogers became dissatisfied with Freud's view that human nature was dependent on biological urges and instincts—sex and aggression—and that psychological problems arose from unconscious thoughts and desires that threatened one's self-concept. Rogers also disagreed with Freud's belief that the analyst—and not the client—was responsible for the client's progress. Instead, Rogers said that clients themselves have the capacity and are responsible for change. Using these ideas, Rogers developed client-centered therapy (C. R. Rogers, 1951, 1986).

Client-centered therapy (also called **person-centered therapy**) assumes that each person has an actualizing tendency, which is a tendency to develop one's full potential. The therapist's task is to be nondirective and show compassion and positive regard in helping the client reach his or her potential.

Rogers believed that each person has a tendency to develop his or her potential.

In client-centered therapy, Rogers changed the therapist's role from that of an all-knowing expert to a helper or facilitator, whose personal characteristics would foster growth and change (C. R. Rogers, 1986).

Therapy session. To illustrate some of the differences between psychoanalysis and client-centered therapy, here is a brief excerpt of a client-centered therapy session where a mother is talking about her problems with letting her daughter be more independent.

Client: I'm having a lot of problems dealing with my daughter. She's 20 years old; she's in college; I'm having a lot of trouble letting her go . . . And I have a lot of guilt feelings about her; I have a real need to hang on to her. And it's very hard with a lot of empty places now that she's not with me.

Rogers: The old vacuum, sort of, when she's not there.

Client: Yes, yes. I also would like to be the kind of mother that could be strong and say, you know, "go and have a good life," and it's really hard for me to do that.

Rogers: It's very hard to give up something that's been so precious in your life, but also something that I guess has caused you pain when you mentioned guilt.

Client: Yeah, and I'm aware that I have some anger toward her that I don't always get what I want. I have needs that are not met. And, uh, I don't feel I have a right to those needs. You know . . . she's a daughter; she's not my mother—though sometimes I feel as if I'd like her to mother me . . . It's very difficult for me to ask for that and have a right to it.

Rogers: So it may be unreasonable, but still, when she doesn't meet your needs, it makes you mad.

Client: Yeah. I get very angry, very angry with her. *(pause)*

Rogers: You're also feeling a little tension at this point, I guess.

Client: Yeah, yeah. A lot of conflict . . .

Rogers: A lot of pain.

Client: A lot of pain.

Rogers: A lot of pain. Can you say anything more what that's about? (adapted from C. R. Rogers, 1989).

Client-centered approach. In this brief excerpt, you can see two of the hallmarks of client-centered therapy. First, Rogers avoids giving any suggestions, advice, or disapproval and primarily shows the client that he understands what the client is feeling. Second, one technique Rogers uses for showing understanding is *reflecting* or restating the client's concerns. Reflecting the client's feelings is one of the basic techniques of the person-centered approach. In addition, humanistic therapists believe that clients have the capacity to discover and reach their true potential and it is the therapist's role to help and remove any roadblocks in their paths (Prochaska & Norcross, 2007).

THERAPIST'S TRAITS

Rogers believed that personal characteristics of the therapist—empathy, positive regard, genuineness—would bring about the client's change. *Empathy* is the ability to understand what the client is saying and feeling. *Positive regard* is the ability to communicate caring, respect, and regard for the client. *Genuineness* is the ability to be real and nondefensive in interactions with the client. Rogers and his followers assumed that a therapist with these three characteristics would be able to help a client change and grow (Raskin & Rogers, 2005).

However, numerous studies have shown that these three characteristics are not always related to successful outcomes (C. E. Hill & Nakayama, 2000). The success of client-centered therapy appears to be due more to developing a good working client–therapist partnership and to the client's attitudes of wanting to and working hard to change (Prochaska & Norcross, 2007).

What's blocking my path to developing my true potential?

EFFECTIVENESS

Client-centered therapy has been found to be effective in producing significant changes in clients in comparison with no-treatment control groups, but no more or less effective than other forms of therapy (C. E. Hill & Nakayama, 2000). According to client-centered therapy, the client–therapist relationship is the main reason the approach is effective (Kirschenbaum & Jourdan, 2005). Some studies, however, report that client-centered therapists who are very reflective and give very little direction are less effective than therapists who make more suggestions and give more direction (L. S. Greenberg & Rice, 1997).

Although very few therapists currently identify themselves as primarily client-centered in their approach, the principles of client-centered therapy have greatly contributed to making therapists aware of the importance of and the need to develop a positive working relationship with their clients (Kirschenbaum & Jourdan, 2005).

The therapist takes a much more directive role in the next kind of insight therapy, called cognitive therapy.

Do negative thoughts get you down?

Similar to Carl Rogers's experience, Aaron Beck was also trained in psychoanalytic techniques and used them to treat patients, many of whom were suffering from depression. When he asked them to free-associate, he noticed that depressed patients often expressed negative or distorted thoughts about themselves—"I'm a failure, no one likes me, nothing turns out right." What really caught his attention was how patients would express a string of negative thoughts almost automatically, without paying much attention. Beck reasoned that these automatically occurring negative thoughts had a great impact on the patients' lives, such as by lowering their self-esteem and encouraging self-blame and self-criticism. Beck developed his form of cognitive therapy to stop these thoughts and so treat depression and other problems (A. T. Beck, 1976, 1991).

Cognitive therapy, as developed by Aaron Beck, assumes that we have automatic negative thoughts that we typically say to ourselves without much notice. By continually repeating these automatic negative thoughts, we color and distort how we perceive and interpret our world and influence how we behave and feel.

Negative things we say to ourselves—for example, "Nothing ever goes right," "I'm a failure," or "Everybody criticizes me"—can bias and distort our thoughts and feelings. Cognitive therapy was developed to make a person aware of, and stop, negative self-statements.

Therapy session. To give you an idea of how negative thoughts occur, here is a brief excerpt from one of Dr. Beck's sessions.

The client is a 26-year-old graduate student who has bouts of depression.

Client: I get depressed when things go wrong. Like when I fail a test.

Therapist: How can failing a test make you depressed?

Client: Well, if I fail, I'll never get into law school.

Therapist: Do you agree that the way you interpret the results of the test will affect you? You might feel depressed, you might have trouble sleeping, not feel like eating, and you might even wonder if you should drop out of the course.

Client: I have been thinking that I wasn't going to make it. Yes, I agree.

Why do I keep thinking all those negative thoughts?

Therapist: Now what did failing mean?

Client: *(tearful)* That I couldn't get into law school.

Therapist: And what does that mean to you?

Client: That I'm just not smart enough.

Therapist: Anything else?

Client: That I can never be happy.

Therapist: And how do these thoughts make you feel?

Client: Very unhappy.

Therapist: So it is the meaning of failing a test that makes you very unhappy. In fact, believing that you can never be happy is a powerful factor in producing unhappiness. So, you get yourself into a trap—by definition, failure to get into law school equals "I can never be happy" (A. T. Beck et al., 1979, pp. 145–146).

Cognitive approach. Notice how the client tries to avoid admitting that her thoughts influence her feelings. Also notice her negative self-statements, such as "I'm just not smart enough" and "I can never be happy." Beck believes that these kinds of negative self-statements will influence this client's thoughts and feelings and contribute to her major symptom, depression.

IMPORTANT FACTORS

Beck identified a number of specific maladaptive thoughts that contribute to various symptoms, such as anxiety and depression. Thus, thinking "I'm a failure" after doing poorly on one test is an example of *overgeneralization*, which is making blanket judgments about yourself on the basis of a single incident. Thinking "Most people don't like me" is an example of *polarized thinking*, which is sorting information into one of two categories, good or bad. Thinking "People always criticize me" is an example of *selective attention*, which is focusing on one detail so much that you do not notice other events, such as being complimented. Beck believes that maladaptive thought patterns cause a distorted view of oneself and one's world, which in turn may lead to various emotional problems. Thus, the primary goals of cognitive therapy are to identify and change maladaptive thoughts.

Cognitive techniques. Beck's approach, which is an example of cognitive therapy, works to change thought patterns, which, in turn, play a critical role in influencing behavior and emotions. In cognitive therapy, clients are told how their maladaptive thoughts and irrational beliefs can result in feelings of depression, anxiety, or other symptoms. Clients are shown how to monitor their thoughts and beliefs, how to recognize maladaptive thought patterns, such as overgeneralization and polarized thinking, and how to substitute rational thought patterns (A. T. Beck & Weishaar, 2005). In the Application section (p. 574), we'll give several examples of specific techniques for stopping negative thoughts and substituting positive ones.

EFFECTIVENESS

Cognitive therapy has proved effective in treating a variety of symptoms. For example, it is as effective as various drugs in treating depression, general anxiety, agoraphobia, panic attacks, smoking, anger, and eating disorders (Deffenbacher et al., 2000; DeRubeis et al., 2005; Dobson & Khatri, 2000; Rupke et al., 2006). The benefits of cognitive therapy extend beyond the end of treatment (Hollon et al., 2005). In some cases, the benefits are longer lasting than those of other forms of therapy (Hollon, 2003).

Increasingly, methods of cognitive therapy are combined with those of the next approach, behavioral therapy. The result is a very popular approach called cognitive-behavioral therapy. However, before explaining cognitive-behavioral therapy, we'll need to discuss behavior therapy, which is our next topic.

Overgeneralization → EMOTIONAL PROBLEMS

Polarized thinking →

Selective attention →

D. Behavior Therapy

PowerStudy 4.0™

Module 9
F. Research Focus:
Conditioning Little Albert
Module 10
I. Application: Behavior
Modification

Definition

What's so important about Little Albert?

The 1950s was the time Carl Rogers developed client-centered therapy and Aaron Beck developed cognitive therapy. Both were motivated to develop new approaches because they had become disillusioned with the techniques and results of the psychoanalytic approach, which they had used in clinical practice.

This was also the time Joseph Wolpe (1958, 1990), a physician in South Africa, became disillusioned with psychoanalysis and developed a new, quicker, and more effective procedure to reduce fear and anxiety.

Through classical conditioning, this pet rat . . .

At the beginning of this module, we told you about Little Albert, who initially wanted to touch and play with a white rat but, after being conditioned, came to fear it (Watson & Rayner, 1920). This demonstration, which occurred in the 1920s, showed that emotional responses could be conditioned. But it was not until the 1950s that a clinician developed a procedure to unlearn emotional responses.

In a real sense, Wolpe finished what John Watson had started: Watson had conditioned Little Albert to fear an object, while Wolpe conditioned patients to be less fearful. Wolpe's procedure was the first experimental demonstration of reducing fear through conditioning and gave a real jump-start to the development of behavior therapy (Persons, 1997).

. . . came to be feared by Little Albert.

Behavior therapy, **also called behavior modification, uses the principles of classical and operant conditioning to change disruptive behaviors and improve human functioning. It focuses on changing particular behaviors rather than the underlying mental events or possible unconscious factors.**

We'll first give you an example of a behavior therapy session and then describe Wolpe's conditioning procedure to reduce fear.

Therapy session. In this session, the therapist is talking to a woman who feels bad because she has great difficulty being assertive.

Client: The basic problem is that I have the tendency to let people step all over me. I don't know why, but I just have difficulty in speaking my mind.

Therapist: So you find yourself in a number of different situations where you don't respond the way you would really like to and you would like to learn how to behave differently.

Client: Yes. But you know, I have tried to handle certain situations differently, but I just don't seem to be able to do so.

Therapist: Well, maybe you tried to do too much or didn't quite know the right technique. For example, imagine yourself at the bottom of a staircase, wanting to get to the top. It's too much to ask to get there in one gigantic leap. Perhaps a better way to go about changing your reaction in these situations is to take it one step at a time.

Client: That would seem to make sense, but I'm not sure if I see how it could be done.

Therapist: Well, there are probably certain situations in which it would be less difficult for you to assert yourself, such as telling your boss that he forgot to pay you for the past four weeks.

Client: *(laughing)* I guess in that situation, I would say something. Although I must admit, I would feel uneasy about it.

Therapist: But not as uneasy as if you went in and asked him for a raise.

Client: No. Certainly not.

Therapist: So, the first situation would be low on the staircase, whereas the second would be higher up. If you can learn to handle easier situations, then the more difficult ones would present less of a problem. And the only way you can really learn to change your reactions is through practice.

Client: In other words, I really have to go out and actually force myself to speak up more, but taking it a little bit at a time?

Therapist: Exactly. And it's easier and safer to run through some of these situations here because you can't really get into trouble if you make a mistake. Once you learn different ways to speak your mind, you can try them out in the real world (adapted from Goldfried & Davison, 1976).

Behavioral approach. Notice that the behavior therapist does not encourage the client to free-associate, which is a major technique of psychoanalysis. The behavior therapist does not repeat or reflect what the client says, which is a major technique of client-centered therapy. The behavior therapist does not discuss the client's tendency to automatically think negative thoughts, which is a major technique of cognitive therapy.

Instead, the behavior therapist quickly identifies the specific problem, which is the woman's tendency to be unassertive when she really wants to speak her mind. Next, the behavior therapist will discuss a program for behavioral change that will help this woman learn to behave more assertively.

Two goals. Behavior therapy has two goals. The first is to modify undesirable behaviors, using many of the principles of operant conditioning, and teach the client how to perform new behaviors, which for this woman involves learning ways to be more assertive. The second goal of behavior therapy is to help the client meet specific behavioral goals through constant practice and reward (Spiegler & Guevremont, 2003). For example, this woman would be asked to practice initiating conversations and stating her opinions, perhaps beginning in the safety of the therapist's office and gradually practicing these new assertive behaviors in the more threatening situations of the real world.

Why do I let people walk all over me?

The next example of behavior therapy illustrates a specific technique that is used to help clients overcome phobias.

Systematic Desensitization

CASE STUDY

Jack had developed a phobia of blood that interfered with his plans. He was a high-school senior who wanted to be an ambulance driver. But the problem was that he passed out at the sight or discussion of blood. He had been afraid of blood for years and had fainted about 20 times in science and biology classes. He even felt queasy when bloody accidents or operating-room scenes were shown on television. If his supervisor found out about his phobia, Jack might lose his chance to be an ambulance driver. Except for his phobia, Jack was happy at school, rarely became depressed, and was generally easygoing (Yule & Fernando, 1980).

Jack's fear of blood interfered with his being an ambulance driver.

Some therapies for phobias might require years of treatment; for instance, a psychoanalyst would search for unconscious conflicts causing the phobia. In contrast, behavior therapists would take a direct approach to the treatment, requiring 5–30 sessions. The technique used today by behavior therapists is based on the one that Wolpe (1958) developed in the 1950s and is called systematic desensitization.

Systematic desensitization is a technique of behavior therapy in which the client is gradually exposed to the feared object while simultaneously practicing relaxation. Desensitization involves three steps: learning to relax, constructing a hierarchy with the least feared situation on the bottom and the most feared situation at the top, and being progressively exposed to the feared situation.

Behavior therapists assume that since Jack's phobia was acquired through a conditioning process, his phobia can be unconditioned by gradually exposing him to the feared object through the process of systematic desensitization.

1 Relaxation

Jack, whose phobia was a fear of blood, underwent systematic desensitization, a very effective treatment for phobias (Cormier & Nurius, 2003). In the first step, Jack learned to relax by practicing progressive relaxation. This method involves tensing and relaxing various muscle groups, beginning with the toes and working up to the head. With this procedure, Jack learned how to put himself into a relaxed state. For most individuals, learning progressive relaxation requires several weeks with at least one 15-minute session every day.

2 Stimulus Hierarchy

The second step was for Jack to make a *stimulus hierarchy,* which is a list of feared stimuli, arranged in order from least to most feared. With the help of his therapist, Jack made the stimulus hierarchy shown on the right, which lists various situations associated with blood. A rating of 1 indicates little fear if confronted by this stimulus, while a rating of 7 indicates that he would probably pass out from this stimulus.

MOST STRESSFUL
7. Needle drawing blood
6. Finger dripping blood
5. Seeing someone cut
4. Needle entering arm
3. Watching blood on TV
2. Cutting own finger
1. Seeing word "blood"

Stimulus hierarchy ranks fearful situations from least (1) to most (7).

3 Exposure

Systematic desensitization training means that, after successfully completing steps 1 and 2, Jack was ready for step 3, which was to systematically desensitize himself by exposing himself to the fear stimuli. Desensitization occurs through relaxing while simultaneously imagining the feared stimuli.

A necessary part of therapy is exposure to the feared situation.

Jack put himself into a relaxed state and then imagined the first or least feared item in his hierarchy, seeing the word *blood.* He tried to remain in a relaxed state while vividly imagining the word *blood.* He repeated this procedure until he felt no tension or anxiety in this situation. At this point, he went on to the next item in his hierarchy. Jack repeated the procedure of pairing relaxation with images of each feared item until he reached the last and most feared item.

Through the desensitization program described here, Jack's blood phobia was treated in five one-hour sessions. A follow-up five years later indicated that Jack was still free of his blood phobia, had not developed any substitute symptoms, and was training to be an ambulance driver (Yule & Fernando, 1980).

4 Exposure: Imagined or In Vivo

Systematic desensitization appears to be most effective if, instead of just imagining the items on the list, which is called *imagined exposure,* clients gradually expose themselves to the actual situation, which is called *in vivo exposure* (the phrase *in vivo* is Latin for "in real life") (G. T. Wilson, 2005). For example, in Module 22 we described the case of Kate Premo (right photo), who signed up for a treatment course that used in vivo exposure to treat her lifetime phobia of flying. In her case, a modified systematic desensitization program included in vivo exposure, which meant taking an actual flight while doing the breathing and relaxation exercises that she had learned. The in vivo exposure worked for Premo, who was able to overcome her phobia of flying.

Clinicians also found that in vivo exposure was a very effective treatment for about 85% of obsessive-compulsives, who were once viewed as having chronic, incurable problems (Kozak et al., 2000). Thus, systematic desensitization has proved to be a very effective treatment for a variety of anxiety disorders, especially when combined with in vivo exposure (Emmelkamp, 2004).

The next therapy is actually a combination of behavior and cognitive therapies.

Kate is being exposed to the actual situation (in vivo) that causes her fear, flying in an airplane.

D. Behavior Therapy

Why combine two different therapies? As psychoanalysis reached its peak of popularity in the 1950s, a number of clinicians and researchers were becoming dissatisfied with its procedures, which were time-consuming, costly, and useful for treating only a limited number of clients with relatively minor problems (Franks, 1994).

At this same time, there was a great increase in the popularity of learning principles that came from Pavlov's work on classical conditioning and Skinner's work on operant conditioning. Researchers and clinicians began to apply these learning principles to change human behavior with methods based on a strong experimental foundation rather than Freud's unverified beliefs about unconscious conflicts. Both behavior and cognitive therapies developed out of dissatisfaction with psychoanalysis and the belief that learning principles would provide more effective methods of changing human behavior than would the concepts of psychoanalysis.

Combining therapies. One of the interesting developments in therapy has been occurring since the late 1970s as both behavior and cognitive therapies have become increasingly popular. The major difference between them is that *behavior therapy* focuses on identifying and changing specific behaviors, while *cognitive therapy* focuses on identifying and changing specific maladaptive thought patterns. Beginning in the early 1990s, researchers and clinicians began combining methods of behavior and cognitive therapies into what is now called cognitive-behavioral therapy (Grant et al., 2005).

Cognitive-behavioral therapy **combines the cognitive therapy technique of changing negative, unhealthy, or distorted thought patterns with the behavior therapy technique of changing maladaptive or disruptive behaviors by learning and practicing new skills to improve functioning.**

Currently, the difference between cognitive therapy and behavior therapy has become blurred as techniques from these two approaches are combined into what has become a very popular therapy that is commonly called cognitive-behavioral therapy (A. C. Butler et al., 2006; Dobson & Khatri, 2000).

I need to stop thinking all those negative thoughts.

Cognitive-behavioral techniques. Cognitive-behavioral therapists combine a number of techniques that are designed to change both thoughts and behaviors and thus improve a person's psychological functioning. These techniques include monitoring one's own thoughts and behaviors; identifying thoughts and behaviors that need to be changed; setting specific goals that increase in difficulty; learning to reinforce oneself for reaching a goal; imitating or modeling new behaviors; substituting positive for negative thoughts; and doing homework, which involves practicing new behaviors in a safe setting before performing them in the real world (A. T. Beck & Weishaar, 2005). These cognitive-behavioral techniques are the basis for almost all *self-help programs,* which may be completed without the assistance of a therapist. For more serious problems or additional support, the aid and help of a therapist may be needed.

Who can be helped? Throughout this text, we have discussed how behavior therapy, cognitive therapy, and the popular cognitive-behavioral therapy have been used to treat the following problems:

■ **Insomnia:** cognitive-behavioral program was as effective as drugs in helping people get to sleep (p. 162).

■ **Conditioned nausea:** individuals undergoing chemotherapy developed conditioned nausea and were treated with behavior therapy (p. 207).

■ **Noncompliance in children:** behavior therapy, also called behavior modification, was used to treat young children who refused to eat healthy foods (p. 230).

■ **Autistic children:** behavior modification helped some autistic children develop sufficient academic and social skills to enter public schools and function very well (p. 232).

■ **Psychosomatic problems:** behavior therapy (biofeedback) helped people decrease stress-related symptoms by reducing headaches and physiological arousal (p. 233).

I need to learn assertive behaviors.

■ **Abusive parents:** cognitive-behavioral therapy that involved training in social skills helped parents deal with their own personal problems as well as daily difficulties related to caring for demanding children (p. 401).

■ **Stress management:** cognitive-behavioral techniques are basic to all programs for reducing stress (p. 502).

■ **Phobias:** various phobias, such as fear of specific situations (flying, public speaking) or objects (snakes, bugs, blood), were treated with cognitive-behavioral techniques (pp. 225, 524, 525).

We'll also discuss several other examples of cognitive-behavioral techniques in the upcoming Application section.

Effectiveness. Cognitive-behavioral therapy is currently being used to treat a wide variety of problems, including eating disorders, marital problems, anxiety and phobias, depression, and sexual dysfunction. Programs based on cognitive-behavioral therapy are widely used to help people stop smoking, become more assertive, improve communication and interpersonal skills, manage stress, and control anger. Researchers report that cognitive-behavioral therapy was significantly more effective in treating this wide variety of problems than were control procedures (A. C. Butler et al., 2006; Dobson & Khatri, 2000; Hollon, 2003). And in some cases, cognitive-behavioral therapy was as effective as drugs in treating some forms of anxiety, phobia, depression, and compulsive behavior (A. C. Butler et al., 2006; Spiegler & Guevremont, 2003).

After the Concept Review, we'll review and compare the development, techniques, and effectiveness of all the major therapies that we have discussed.

1. If you first trained as a physician and then went into a psychiatric residency, which involves additional training in pharmacology, neurology, and psychotherapeutic techniques, you would be a (a)_____. If you completed a Ph.D. program in psychology, including one year of work in a clinical setting, you would be a (b)_____. If you completed a Ph.D. program in psychology or education, including work in a counseling setting, you would be a (c)_____.

2. A process characterized by verbal interaction between therapist and client and the development of a supportive relationship, during which a therapist may analyze or suggest ways for the client to deal with and overcome his or her problems, is called _____.

3. One approach to therapy is characterized by the idea that we have an unconscious part whose activities and thoughts are hidden behind a mental barrier that we cannot voluntarily remove. Behind this barrier are repressed and psychologically dangerous thoughts that give rise to unconscious conflicts, which, in turn, can result in psychological and physical symptoms. This approach is called _____.

4. Freud developed two techniques to uncover unconscious thoughts. One was to encourage clients to talk about any thoughts or images that entered their heads, which is called (a)_____. The second technique was based on the assumption that dreams contain hidden meanings and symbols and the therapist's role was to (b)_____ these dream symbols.

5. Freud said that, during therapy, a patient may respond as if the therapist were a father or mother and project strong feelings toward the therapist. This process is called (a)_____. Also during therapy, a patient may be reluctant to work through feelings or to recognize unconscious conflicts and repressed thoughts; this is called (b)_____.

6. The popular approach to therapy shares many of the features of psychoanalysis—for example, discussing the client's feelings, breaking down the client's defenses and resistances, and interpreting the client's behaviors—but may not necessarily use free association or agree that many problems result from unconscious sexual conflicts. This approach, which takes less time than psychoanalysis, is called _____ psychotherapy.

7. One approach to therapy assumes that each person has an actualizing tendency—that is, a tendency to develop his or her full potential. In this approach, the therapist's task is to show compassion and positive regard in helping the client reach his or her potential. This approach was developed by (a)_____ and is called (b)_____ therapy.

8. Another approach to therapy assumes that we have automatic negative thoughts that we usually say to ourselves without much notice. By continually repeating these automatic negative thoughts, we color and distort how we perceive and interpret our world and influence how we behave and feel. This approach to therapy was developed by (a)_____ and is called (b)_____ therapy.

9. One approach to therapy primarily uses the principles of classical and operant conditioning to change disruptive behaviors and improve human functioning. This approach, which focuses on changing particular behaviors rather than on the underlying mental events or possible unconscious factors, is called _____ therapy.

10. One approach combines changing negative, unhealthy, or distorted thoughts and beliefs by substituting positive, healthy, and realistic ones and changing one's undesirable or disruptive behaviors by learning and practicing new skills to improve functioning. This approach, which combines two therapies, is called _____ therapy.

11. There is a technique of behavior therapy in which the client is gradually exposed to the feared object while simultaneously practicing relaxation. This technique, which involves three steps—learning to relax, constructing a hierarchy with the least feared situation on the bottom and the most feared situation at the top, and being progressively exposed to the feared situation—is called _____.

12. Because of its effectiveness, cognitive-behavioral therapy has become the basis for many self-help programs to stop smoking, reduce insomnia, decrease conditioned nausea, help autistic children develop academic and social skills, and reduce intense and irrational fears called _____.

Answers: *1. (a) psychiatrist, (b) clinical psychologist, (c) counseling psychologist; 2. psychotherapy; 3. psychoanalysis; 4. (a) free association, (b) interpret; 5. (a) transference, (b) resistance; 6. psychodynamic; 7. (a) Carl Rogers, (b) client-centered; 8. (a) Aaron Beck, (b) cognitive; 9. behavior; 10. cognitive-behavioral; 11. systematic desensitization; 12. phobias*

E. Review: Evaluation of Approaches

Background, Assumptions, and Techniques

How do they differ?

We have discussed five different approaches to psychotherapy, including psychoanalysis, client-centered therapy, cognitive therapy, behavior therapy, and the increasingly popular cognitive-behavioral therapy. We'll briefly review the different backgrounds, assumptions, and techniques for four of these approaches, and then discuss their effectiveness.

PSYCHOANALYSIS

Background. Psychoanalysis, which was developed by Sigmund Freud in the late 1800s and early 1900s, marked the beginning of psychotherapy. Freud gradually developed his major assumptions from treating patients for a variety of symptoms and problems. Thus, Freud's assumptions are based on case studies rather than on experimental data.

Basic assumption. Freud believed that unacceptable or threatening thoughts were repressed and unavailable to conscious recall. Repressed thoughts could produce unconscious conflicts that, in turn, could result in feelings of anxiety and a variety of psychological and emotional problems.

Techniques. Freud developed two techniques for uncovering and revealing unconscious thoughts: free association and dream interpretation. Freud was also the first to identify and recognize the importance of transference and resistance during therapy. He believed that patients overcame their problems by bringing up and dealing with underlying unconscious conflicts.

CLIENT-CENTERED THERAPY

Background. In the late 1940s and early 1950s, Carl Rogers became disillusioned with the psychoanalytic role of the therapist as expert and in charge of changing the client. To give the client a greater role in making decisions and changes, he developed his client-centered approach.

Basic assumption. Rogers assumed that the client has the capacity to actualize and reach his or her full potential and the client, not the therapist, is responsible for change. He believed that, although the client had the major role in making changes, there were certain characteristics of the therapist that helped the client change.

Techniques. The client-centered therapist uses the technique of repeating or reflecting what the client says and thereby showing interest and understanding. Rogers believed that therapists would be effective if they had three characteristics: empathy, positive regard, and genuineness. These characteristics produced a warm and supportive atmosphere in which the client felt comfortable and could better deal with solving his or her problems.

COGNITIVE THERAPY

Background. In the late 1960s and early 1970s, Aaron Beck became dissatisfied with the psychoanalytic assumption that unconscious conflicts were the chief cause of psychological problems. As Beck treated patients, he noticed that they would often repeat a string of negative statements, almost without notice. Beck believed that these automatic, negative self-statements played a major role in emotional problems.

Basic assumption. Beck pointed out that our automatic, irrational thoughts and beliefs can color our feelings and actions, distort our perceptions, and result in various psychological and emotional problems. He assumed that these irrational self-statements, such as polarized thinking, needed to be changed.

Techniques. The techniques of cognitive therapy include having the client monitor and identify his or her automatic, negative, irrational thoughts and replace them with positive ones. Thus, clients deal with and solve their problems by gradually substituting positive thoughts for distorted self-statements.

BEHAVIOR THERAPY

Background. Developed in the 1950s, behavior therapy was based on principles of learning from classical and operant conditioning. Behavior therapy was a reaction against psychoanalysis, whose emphasis was on unconscious and unobservable conflicts and whose concepts lacked a scientific foundation.

Basic assumption. Behavior therapy assumes that just as emotional reactions can be learned or conditioned, so too can they be unlearned using the same principles of learning. Behavior therapy focuses on observable behaviors, while cognitive-behavioral therapy also emphasizes changing thought patterns.

Techniques. The behavior therapist identifies specific behaviors that need to be changed and provides the client with particular methods for carrying out the changes. Specific behavioral techniques include self-observation, self-reward, modeling, and role playing. For treatment of anxiety, fears, and phobias, systematic desensitization combined with in vivo exposure has proved effective.

Currently, techniques of cognitive and behavior therapies are combined into *cognitive-behavioral therapy*, which has proved effective for treating a variety of psychological problems and self-help programs.

Because these four approaches differ in their assumptions and techniques, is one approach more effective than another?

Effectiveness of Psychotherapy

How helpful is psycho-therapy?

Nearly 20% of the adult population in the United States seek help and treatment for mental illness from various mental services, such as community mental health centers (Adler, 2006). However, about half of all individuals who have a serious mental health problem do not seek treatment because they want to avoid the stigma that many in our society attach to mental illness (Satcher, 2000). Mental health professionals have tried to erase this stigma by explaining that mental illness is not a character flaw but a real health problem that can often be successfully treated with therapy programs that may involve drug, nondrug, or a combination of therapies.

For only a small percentage (10–20%) of individuals with psychological problems, simply waiting for the problem to go away will work. However, clinicians do not know how to identify these individuals beforehand and give them the option of waiting. For a very large percentage (80–90%) of individuals with psychological problems, simply waiting is not effective and their problems may either continue or worsen (Eysenck, 1994). For these individuals with psychological problems, professional help is the better choice.

How do I know if I need therapy for my problem?

A person needs therapy for a problem if that problem begins to interfere with the person's social interactions, relationships, work, career, or daily functioning.

Researchers have analyzed over 1,500 studies that examined the effects of psychotherapy on a variety of problems, such as depression, various kinds of anxieties, phobias, family problems, interpersonal difficulties, and eating disorders. Researchers found that psychotherapy was more effective in relieving a wide variety of psychological and behavioral symptoms than were control procedures such as being on a waiting list to receive therapy or just being in a group that received no systematic treatment. In addition, most improvement occurs in a relatively short period of time, about 25 to 40 sessions (Shadish et al., 2000).

Knowing that psychotherapy is an effective treatment brings us to the second question: Is one kind of psychotherapy more effective than another?

Common Factors

Is one approach more effective?

If you lived fifty years ago and needed professional help for a mental illness, your only choice was psychoanalysis, which was very time-consuming and expensive. In contrast, if you need professional help today, you can choose from a number of different therapies, which are available at a variety of mental health facilities. However, because the current therapy approaches begin with different assumptions and use different methods, you might wonder if one therapy is more effective than another. In answer to this question, researchers have consistently found that there is very little, if any, difference in effectiveness among various therapies (Drisko, 2004; Luborsky et al., 2002). However, for a small number of specific disorders, including *panic attacks, phobias, generalized anxiety, obsessive-compulsions, insomnia,* and *depression,* cognitive-behavior-type therapies have generally been shown to be more effective than traditional talk therapies, such as the psychodynamic approaches (A. C. Butler et al., 2006; Dobson & Khatri, 2000).

I need professional help, but I don't know which therapy to choose.

It may seem surprising that therapies with such different assumptions and techniques have been found to be equally effective. One reason different therapies using different techniques can achieve the same results is that they all share common factors (Luborsky et al., 2002).

Common factors are a basic set of procedures and experiences that different therapies share and that explain why different approaches are equally effective. Common factors include the growth of a supportive and trusting relationship between therapist and client and the development of an accepting atmosphere, in which the client feels willing to admit problems and is motivated to work on changing.

The fact that the above common factors are basic to all approaches explains why different assumptions and different techniques can be effectively combined to develop the several different current forms of psychotherapy, all of which are about equally effective (Luborsky et al., 2002).

I found out that many of the therapies are about equally effective.

For example, one common factor—development of a warm, trusting, and accepting relationship between client and therapist—has been shown to play a major role in helping clients work out their problems and change their behaviors (Drisko, 2004). Since the client–therapist relationship is important in influencing the effectiveness of treatment, researchers suggest that a client select a therapist to whom he or she can relate (Ackerman & Hilsenroth, 2003).

The client-consumer should know that psychotherapy is generally effective and that (except for depression and anxiety disorders, such as phobias and obsessive-compulsive behavior) the particular therapy approach does not matter as much as do the common factors.

Common factors may also explain why the next treatment, which seems very strange to Westerners, has proved effective.

Case Study: Young Woman

What was her problem? In Bali, which is a province of Indonesia, as well as in parts of Africa, China, and Fiji Islands, many psychological problems that Western clinicians would diagnose as anxiety, mood disorders, or schizophrenia are believed to be caused by possession by evil spirits (McGrath, 2003; Straker, 1994). For example, take the case of Putu, a young unmarried woman, who was about 20 years old.

Putu lived with her family in a small village on the beautiful island of Bali. Putu's family had made her break off her loving relationship with one man and become engaged to another, whom she did not want to marry. Since her new engagement, Putu had lost all interest in things around her, ate very little, and did not take part in normal activities or conversation. Putu was taken to the local nurse, who gave an injection of multivitamins to treat her low energy level and general apathy. The injection did not help and the nurse recommended that the family take Putu to a local witch doctor or healer, who could use special rituals to cure Putu (Connor, 1982).

In Western terminology, clinicians would say that Putu was suffering from depression, which was most certainly brought on by having to break off her loving relationship and being forced by her family to become engaged to someone she did not like. Western therapists would have treated her depression with some form of psychotherapy and, if possible, would have brought the whole family in for therapy. However, in Bali, Putu was believed to be the victim of witchcraft, which could be cured by taking her to a traditional healer, who is called a *balian*.

Healer's Diagnosis and Treatment

What is healing smoke? The family took the depressed Putu to a well-respected healer or balian, a woman named Jero. Balians, such as Jero, believe their powers come from supernatural forces. The balians often undergo periods of fasting and isolation that induce trances through which the spirits speak to them. Balians are considered special healers who are asked to help individuals with a variety of personal and mental problems (Keeney, 2004).

In Putu's case, Jero located a small pulsation beneath Putu's jawbone that indicated the presence of an evil wind spirit. The rejected lover had placed the evil spirit into Putu's body, and there was now a great danger that this evil spirit might travel throughout her body: If it reached Putu's ears, she would go deaf; if it reached her brain, she would become violent and insane. Jero (right photo) said that she would mix a special medicine and that the family should return in two days for an exorcism of the evil wind spirit.

As part of the exorcism rites, two small human effigies, a male and a female, were made out of cooked rice and were set on the ground

> You are possessed of an evil wind spirit.

Indonesian healers, called balians, function like Western therapists.

to the south of the girl. When the evil spirit was driven out of Putu's body by smoke, the evil spirit would be attracted to the effigies, which would then be broken to destroy the spirit.

In the morning, Jero asked Putu to stand in the middle of healing smoke. After about 40 minutes, the evil wind spirit left Putu's body and entered the small male and female rice figures, which were broken and thrown away. Then Putu's body was purified with holy water. During the course of the afternoon, Putu began to talk, show interest in food and things around her, and generally get over her former apathy.

For two more weeks, Putu stayed with Jero, who continued to perform purification ceremonies and drive away any lingering evil wind spirits. As part of the purification ceremonies, Putu was asked to take part in everyday activities, such as gathering and making food, engaging in normal conversations, washing clothes, and doing other chores. Through this process, Putu was helped and encouraged to resume her normal duties and take part in social activities.

Healers Versus Western Therapists

Is a balian a therapist? The case of Putu shows that the beliefs and treatments used in the traditional healing practices of African and Asian balians or healers are very different from those used by Western therapists to treat psychological problems. But notice that the balian's exorcism rites, purification rituals, and herbal medicines did reduce Putu's depression. In many parts of Asia, China, Africa, Fiji Islands, and Indonesia, healers use herbal medicines, exorcism, and purification rituals to successfully treat a variety of psychological problems (McGrath, 2003; Sue & Sue, 2003).

There are two explanations of why a balian's potions and rituals are effective treatments for various mental and physical problems. First, studies on Western patients find that many patients suffering from a variety of psychological and physical problems show remarkable improvement after receiving placebo treatments (Wampold et al., 2005). The balian's rituals and herbs may function like Western placebos (p. 111), which create positive beliefs and expectations to help individuals recover from a variety of physical and psychological problems. Second, the balian's purification ceremonies involve the development of a close relationship with the sufferer, and this relationship may involve common factors similar to those found effective in Western therapy. Thus, placebos and psychotherapy's common factors may explain the success of balians in treating a variety of mental problems in different cultures.

Next, we'll discuss treatment of one of the more difficult psychological problems, getting over a terrible and traumatic situation.

Does EMDR Stop Traumatic Memories?

What is EMDR?

In the early 1990s a new kind of psychotherapy appeared that was unlike any we have discussed. After only a few sessions, clients reported a decrease in traumatic memories, a problem very difficult to treat. This therapy was called Eye Movement Desensitization and Reprocessing (F. Shapiro, 2002).

Eye Movement Desensitization and Reprocessing, or *EMDR,* essentially involves having the client talk about or imagine a troubling traumatic memory while visually focusing on and following the

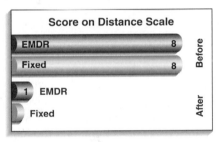

Can watching a moving hand reduce terrible memories?

back-and-forth movement of a therapist's hand. This process usually continues for several 90-minute sessions, after which the traumatic memories are greatly reduced or eliminated.

Francine Shapiro (1991) discovered EMDR after noticing that her own troubling thoughts disappeared after she associated them with her back-and-forth eye movements. Because EMDR's method and claims were so unusual, researchers wondered if it really worked.

Evidence from Case Studies

All of the early support for the effectiveness of EMDR came from testimonials and case studies, many of them as dramatic as the following:

After one individual lost both arms and hearing in a tragic fire and explosion, he experienced terrible flashbacks and nightmares for the next six years. When he finally consulted a psychiatrist, he was desperate and agreed to try the then-new EMDR procedure. During the EMDR procedure, he vividly recalled the fire, the shouts of the employees, and other terrible images, while visually following the back-and-forth movement of the therapist's hand. However, as he continued imagining terrible images and following the therapist's hand movements, he began to feel a flowing sensation of peace. Following a number of sessions, he was reported to be free of flashbacks and nightmares, had taught himself to drive a car, and had joined a group that helps children who need artificial limbs (Wartik, 1994).

Dramatic cases like this suggested that EMDR was a very simple yet effective treatment for getting rid of traumatic memories, one of the most difficult problems therapists face. In explaining how EMDR worked, Shapiro (1991) hypothesized that the eye movements during EMDR aided information processing to somehow reduce the distress accompanying traumatic events and images.

During EMDR, a client talks about a painful memory while watching a therapist's moving hand.

Although the effectiveness of EMDR was supported by case studies and testimonials, we must remember that such methods have great potential for error and bias and cannot demonstrate cause and effect. Thus, to evaluate the effectiveness of EMDR, researchers used a more scientific approach, the experimental method (p. 36).

Evidence from Experiments

Does EMDR work? We have discussed many examples of so-called "medical treatments" (bear gallbladders, rhino horns, fake pills and injections) that, according to 30–80% of users' testimonials, reduced pain, increased sexual stamina, or cured various physical problems (pp. 31, 111) (Talbot, 2000). These "medical treatments" are examples of the well-known *placebo effect,* which can have a powerful influence and may explain why EMDR works. For over a decade, researchers have studied EMDR therapy and generally concluded that it was not simply a placebo effect but was effective in reducing traumatic memories, such as occur in posttraumatic stress disorder or PTSD (p. 491). So our first question, Does EMDR work? has been answered positively (R. Shapiro, 2005; Silver et al., 2005).

However, wondering if eye movement was the critical feature of EMDR therapy, researchers compared clients who moved their eyes with those who stared straight ahead. As shown in the right graph, subjects who made eye movements (EMDR) and who fixed their stare both showed

Score on Distance Scale		
EMDR	8	Before
Fixed	8	Before
EMDR	1	After
Fixed		After

significant reductions in distress (Renfrey & Spates, 1994). Researchers now know that different kinds of stimulation (eye movements, fixed staring, hand taps) are effective as long as such stimulation occurs while clients are recalling their traumatic memories (May, 2005; F. Shapiro & Maxfield, 2002).

How does EMDR work? This question has not yet been answered. What is known is that, during EMDR, clients are recalling and confronting their most feared feelings, images, or situations, an established method of exposure therapy (p. 567). Thus, researchers suggest that EMDR may be another form of exposure therapy, which has been proven very effective for reducing fearful thoughts, images, and situations (Devilly, 2002). What is not known is why other stimulation, such as eye movement, seems to speed up the treatment process. At this point there are three therapies—EMDR, exposure therapy, and cognitive-behavioral therapy (p. 568)—that have been shown to be effective treatments for posttraumatic stress disorder (F. Shapiro, 2002).

Why is EMDR controversial? Some of the reasons EMDR has been so controversial are that it seems too unusual, too simple, and too quick. However, research has shown that EMDR is one of three therapies that is effective for treating a notoriously difficult and unusually persistent problem—the occurrence of traumatic memories (Marsa, 2002; R. Shapiro, 2005).

Next, we'll review several cognitive-behavioral techniques that have proven effective in treating some relatively common psychological problems.

H.  Application: Cognitive-Behavioral Techniques

Thought Problems

What's a common problem?

There are a number of psychological/behavioral problems that are not usually considered serious mental disorders but that can be very bothersome and interfere with our functioning normally.

For example, if you happened to do poorly on an exam, were criticized by someone important to you, broke up with someone, or had an accident, you may find it difficult to stop worrying and thinking about the troubling event. Researchers find a gender difference in worrying: Compared to men, women report more worrying and more recurring negative thoughts (Robichaud et al., 2003). Although it's good advice to "Just stop

How do I battle crazy thoughts?

worrying about it," such advice is often very difficult to follow. The harder you try to stop worrying about something, the more you may worry about it.

Fortunately, clinicians have developed a number of helpful cognitive-behavioral techniques that can be used to solve a variety of psychological or behavior problems. We'll discuss programs to stop recurring and troubling thoughts, to change negative thoughts into positive ones, and to deal with mild insomnia.

Thought-Stopping Program

Could you not think about a white bear?

Researchers asked college students to try very hard to suppress or stop any thoughts having to do with a large white bear. But researchers found that no matter how hard students tried to suppress worrisome negative thoughts, they kept coming back (Borton, 2002). These kinds of recurring and unwanted thoughts are called intrusive thoughts.

Intrusive thoughts **are thoughts that we repeatedly experience, are usually unwanted or disruptive, and are very difficult to stop or eliminate.**

Researchers found that just trying to stop thinking about something, called *thought suppression*, is not very effective, especially when the thoughts involve emotional situations and especially if you are under a lot of stress (G. J. Beck et al., 2006; Wenzlaff & Luxton, 2003). Instead of using thought suppression (trying not to think that thought), which is not effective, researchers suggest using a mental program that either distracts us or helps us change our goals (Wenzlaff & Wegner, 2000). For example, we'll describe a cognitive-behavioral program to identify and change intrusive thoughts. This program can be carried out on one's own or with the help and support of a therapist.

Here's a real-life example of Carol, who couldn't stop thinking about her former boyfriend, Fred, with whom she had just broken up. No matter how much she tried, she thought about Fred almost every day, and her thinking about breaking up with Fred triggered a chain of other negative thoughts about herself: "I feel that I am a failure. I feel ugly and useless. I keep thinking about not being able to have a relationship. I feel really depressed and I

How do I stop thinking of my former boyfriend?

don't want to do anything" (G. L. Martin, 1982).

Carol's problem is that she has been unable to stop the intrusive thoughts about Fred, which results in her feeling depressed. An effective cognitive-behavioral technique for stopping intrusive thoughts has three steps.

1 Self-Monitoring

In all behavior-changing procedures, the first step is *self-monitoring,* which is observing one's own behavior without making any changes. In Carol's case, it meant that for one week she wrote down all depressing thoughts about Fred that lasted for more than a couple of minutes. In addition, the therapist asked Carol to bring in pictures of herself that showed her in pleasurable activities. These pictures would provide cues for thinking rational thoughts.

2 Thought Stopping

Each time Carol began to experience a disturbing thought, she would stop what she was doing, clasp her hands togther, close her eyes, silently yell "Stop!" to herself, and silently count to ten. This was the *thought-stopping procedure.*

3 Thought Substitution

After counting silently to ten, she would open her eyes and take five photographs out of her purse. She would look at each photograph and read what she had written on the back. For example, one photograph showed her about to board an airplane for a trip. On the back she had written, "I'm my own boss. My life is ahead of me. I can do what I want to do." Carol would then think about the trip and how much she liked to travel. She would do the same for all five photographs.

This *thought-substituting procedure* took 1–2 minutes. After that, she would return to whatever she had been doing.

During Carol's first week of self-monitoring, she thought about Fred constantly and spent from 15 minutes to an hour each day crying. However, after using the thought-stopping and thought-substituting procedures for eight weeks, Carol had reduced the time thinking about Fred to the point that she rarely cried or was depressed. A follow-up interview four months after therapy revealed that Carol was no longer having intrusive thoughts about Fred, was no longer depressed, had developed no new symptoms, and had a new boyfriend (G. L. Martin, 1982).

In Carol's case, thought suppression alone (trying not to think that thought) did not stop intrusive thoughts about Fred. What Carol and most individuals with this problem need is a thought-stopping plus a substitution program, which together are very effective (Borton, 2002).

As you'll see next, thought substitution is a very useful technique for a number of problems, including fear and anxiety.

How can I change fearful thoughts?

For many years Rose was trapped in her house by intrusive thoughts that resulted in an intense fear of going out into public places, which is called *agoraphobia*. If she even thought about going outside to do her shopping, she felt pain in her arms and chest, she began to perspire, her heart beat rapidly, and her feet felt like rubber. However, after cognitive-behavioral therapy, she overcame her agoraphobia.

As part of the overall therapy program, a cognitive therapist asked Rose a number of questions to identify her irrational thoughts. For example, she may have overgeneralized, thinking, "The last time I went out I was terrified; it's sure to happen again." Or Rose may have engaged in polarized thinking: "All my happiness is right here in this house; nothing outside could give me any pleasure." Her thinking might have been distorted by selective attention, such as remembering all those activities outside the house that terrified her and forgetting all those activities that she had once found pleasurable, such as shopping and going to movies.

Rose was asked to make a list of all her irrational thoughts on one side of a sheet of paper. Then, next to each irrational thought, she was asked to write down a rational response that could be substituted for the irrational one. Here are some examples:

IRRATIONAL THOUGHTS

Thought substitution

- I am much safer if I stay at home.
- I feel more protected if I do not have to walk through crowds.
- I think something awful will occur if I go to a supermarket.
- I can't bear the thought of going to a movie theater.

RATIONAL THOUGHTS

- Rarely has anything bad happened when I have gone out.
- I have never been harmed by a crowd of people.
- Thousands of people go to supermarkets and do their shopping unharmed.
- Many people enjoy going to movies.

Like Rose, you can follow the same three steps of the thought-substitution program, which is a very effective technique for changing feelings and behaviors.

1 Through self-monitoring, write down as many irrational thoughts as possible. If you are in a habit of thinking irrational thoughts, it may require special attention to identify them.

How do I change my fearful thoughts so I can go out in public?

2 Next to the column of irrational thoughts, compose a matching list of rational thoughts. The rational thoughts should be as detailed or specific as possible.

3 Begin to practice substituting rational thoughts for irrational ones. Each time you make a substitution, give yourself a mental reward for your effort.

One reason therapists give clients homework, such as using thought substitution in daily life, is to encourage clients to practice thinking rationally (A. T. Beck & Weishaar, 2005). Cognitive-behavioral therapists see irrational thoughts and beliefs as the primary causes of emotional and behavioral problems (A. R. Singer & Dobson, 2006).

Worrisome, annoying, and irrational thoughts are one of the major causes of insomnia, which can also be treated with a cognitive-behavioral program.

How can I get to sleep?

Two major causes of insomnia are excessive worry and tension. There are several nondrug treatments for insomnia that differ in method, but all have the same goal: to stop the person from excessive worrying and reduce tension. One proven cognitive-behavioral method to reduce insomnia is to establish an optimal sleep pattern (Bootzin & Rider, 1997; Means & Edinger, 2006).

Establishing an Optimal Sleep Pattern

Cognitive-behavioral program for insomnia

By following the eight steps below, your sleep pattern will become more regular and efficient and help reduce insomnia.

1. Go to bed only when you are *sleepy*, not by convention (it's time for bed) or habit.

2. Put the *light out* immediately when you get into bed.

3. *Do not read or watch television* in bed, since these are activities that you do when awake.

4. If you are not asleep within *20 minutes*, get out of bed and sit and relax in another room until you are *sleepy and tired* again. Relaxation can include tensing and relaxing one's muscles or using *visual imagery*, which involves closing one's eyes and concentrating on some calm scene or image for several minutes.

5. *Repeat step 4* as often as required and also if you wake up for any long periods of time.

6. *Set the alarm to the same time each morning* so that your time of waking is always the same. This step is very important because oversleeping or sleeping in is one of the primary causes of insomnia the next night.

7. *Do not nap during the day* because it will throw off your sleep schedule that night.

8. *Follow this program* rigidly for several weeks to establish an efficient and regular pattern of sleep.

Results. Nondrug treatment programs, such as the eight-step program described here, were among the most effective programs for significantly decreasing insomnia (Means & Edinger, 2006).

We have discussed several cognitive-behavioral techniques that can be used on one's own or with the aid of a therapist. These techniques are effective for treating a wide range of mild to severe mental problems (A. R. Singer & Dobson, 2006).

✔ Summary Test

A. Historical Background

1. In the early 1800s, the popular belief that mental patients could be helped to function better by providing humane treatment in a relaxed and decent environment was called (a)_____. In the early 1950s, the first drugs to reduce schizophrenic symptoms were discovered. These drugs, called (b)_____, reduced the effects of the neurotransmitter (c)_____.

2. Following the use of phenothiazines, many mental patients were released from mental hospitals and returned to the community to develop more independent and fulfilling lives; this process was called (a)_____. People with mental disorders that do not require hospitalization often seek treatment in (b)_____ centers.

B. Questions about Psychotherapy

3. If you go to medical school, receive an M.D. degree, and then take a psychiatric residency, you can become a (a)_____. If you go to graduate school in clinical psychology and complete a Ph.D. program, including at least one year of work in a clinical setting, you can become a (b)_____. If you go to graduate school in psychology or education and complete a Ph.D. program, including work in a counseling setting, you can become a (c)_____.

4. Therapy in which the therapist and client talk about the client's symptoms and problems with the goal of reaching or identifying the cause of the problem is called (a)_____ therapy. Therapy that involves the application of learning principles and focuses on identifying and changing specific behaviors is called (b)_____ therapy. Therapy that involves the use of various psychoactive drugs, such as tranquilizers and neuroleptics, to treat mental disorders is called (c)_____ therapy.

C. Insight Therapies

5. Freud developed one of the first forms of insight therapy, which he called (a)_____. At the core of psychoanalysis is the idea that psychological and physical symptoms arise from (b)_____ that a person cannot voluntarily uncover or recall.

6. Freud developed two techniques that he believed provide clues to unconscious thoughts and conflicts: when clients are encouraged to talk about any thoughts or images that enter their heads, this is called (a)_____; when a therapist looks for hidden meanings and symbols in dreams, this is called (b)_____.

7. During the course of therapy, a patient will project conflict-ridden emotions onto the therapist; this process is called (a)_____. Working through transference is one of the two essential requirements for improvement in psychoanalysis; the other is that the patient achieves (b)_____ into the causes of his or her problem. A patient's reluctance to work through feelings or recognize unconscious conflicts and repressed thoughts is called (c)_____.

8. Increasing pressure to use briefer versions of psychotherapy resulted in a shortened form of traditional psychoanalysis. This new version uses some of the same principles, such as dealing with transference, but has the therapist taking a more active role and dealing with a more specific problem; this approach is called _____ psychotherapy.

9. A form of insight therapy developed by Carl Rogers emphasizes our creative and constructive tendencies and the importance of building caring relationships. This is called (a)_____ therapy. One of its basic techniques is to restate or (b)_____ the client's concerns and feelings.

10. Rogers believed that the therapist's characteristics foster growth and change. The therapist needs to have the ability to understand what the client is saying and feeling, a trait called (a)_____; the ability to communicate caring, respect, and regard for the client, called (b)_____; and the ability to be real and nondefensive in interactions with the client, called (c)_____.

11. Another form of insight therapy is the cognitive therapy developed by Aaron Beck. The basic assumption of Beck's cognitive theory is that our (a)_____ negative thoughts distort how we perceive and interpret things, thus influencing our behaviors and feelings. For example, making blanket judgments about yourself on the basis of a single incident is called (b)_____. Sorting information into one of two categories is (c)_____. Focusing on one detail so much that you do not notice other events is using (d)_____. Beck believes that maladaptive thought patterns cause a distorted view of one's world, which in turn may lead to various emotional problems.

12. Cognitive therapy has been shown to have approximately the same effectiveness as do drugs in treating major _____ and has been used effectively to treat other psychological problems.

D. Behavior Therapy

13. Therapy that emphasizes treatment of specific behaviors and working toward specific goals without focusing on mental events or underlying unconscious factors is known as _____ therapy. This form of therapy is based on classical and operant conditioning principles.

14. A technique of behavior therapy in which the client is gradually exposed to the feared object while simultaneously practicing relaxation is called (a)_____. As part of this technique, the client must prepare a list of feared stimuli, arranged in order from least to most feared; this is called a (b)_____ hierarchy. Another technique is for the client to be gradually exposed to the actual feared or anxiety-producing situation; this is called (c)_____ exposure.

15. One form of therapy combines two methods: changing negative thoughts by substituting positive ones, and changing unwanted or disruptive behaviors by learning and practicing new skills to improve functioning. This approach is called _____ therapy.

E. Review: Evaluation of Approaches

16. Sigmund Freud developed psychoanalysis, whose basic assumption is that emotional problems are caused by underlying (a)_____. Techniques used to uncover unconscious conflicts include (b)_____ and _____.

17. Carl Rogers developed (a)_____ therapy, whose basic assumption is that the client is responsible for change and has the capacity to grow and reach his or her full potential. Techniques include (b)_____ the client's concerns; therapists must also show the characteristics of empathy, positive regard, and genuineness.

18. Aaron Beck's cognitive theory assumes that automatic, negative, and irrational (a)_____ can color our feelings and actions, distort our perceptions, and result in various problems. Its techniques include recognizing negative thoughts and (b)_____ positive ones.

19. An approach to therapy based on learning principles is called (a)_____ therapy, whose basic assumption is that emotional problems are (b)_____ and thus can be unlearned by using learning principles. Its techniques include systematic desensitization, role-playing, imitation, and modeling.

20. Despite differences in approaches and techniques, the five most popular forms of psychotherapy differ little in (a)_____, except for a small number of disorders, such as phobias, panic attacks, and depression, in which (b)_____ therapy is found more effective. Most improvement in therapy occurs in a relatively short period of (c)_____.

21. One reason therapies tend to be equally effective is that they all share _____. For example, the development of a supportive and trusting relationship between therapist and client results in an accepting atmosphere in which the client feels willing to admit problems and is motivated to work on changing.

F. Cultural Diversity: Different Healer

22. In many cases, the healers in Asia and Africa are as effective as Western therapists. One explanation is that these healers may rely on the (a)_____ effect, which is found to produce significant improvement in 10–30% of Western patients. Another is that the healers' ceremonies may involve some of the (b)_____ that underlie the effectiveness of Western therapy.

G. Research Focus: EMDR—New Therapy

23. Researchers have shown that three different therapies are effective ways to reduce the distress, anxiety, and traumatic memories in individuals suffering from (a)_____ or PTSD. These three therapies are (b)_____ or EMDR, (c)_____ and _____. Researchers believe that EMDR may work because it is similar to another therapy called (d)_____.

H. Application: Cognitive-Behavioral Techniques

24. Behavior or cognitive-behavioral therapy usually involves three steps in changing thought patterns. The first step is observing one's own behavior without making any changes; this is called (a)_____. The second step is to identify those (b)_____ thoughts that need to be changed. The third step is to (c)_____ a positive thought for a negative one. Another step that is sometimes included is to actively stop (d)_____ thoughts.

Thought substitution

Answers: 1. (a) moral therapy, (b) phenothiazines, (c) dopamine; 2. (a) deinstitutionalization, (b) community mental health; 3. (a) psychiatrist, (b) clinical psychologist, (c) counseling psychologist; 4. (a) insight, (b) behavior, (c) medical; 5. (a) psychoanalysis, (b) unconscious conflicts; 6. (a) free association, (b) dream interpretation; 7. (a) transference, (b) insight, (c) resistance; 8. short–term dynamic; 9. (a) client-centered, (b) reflect; 10. (a) empathy, (b) positive regard, (c) genuineness; 11. (a) automatic, (b) overgeneralization, (c) polarized thinking, (d) selective attention; 12. depression; 13. behavior; 14. (a) systematic desensitization, (b) stimulus, (c) in vivo; 15. cognitive-behavioral; 16. (a) unconscious conflicts, (b) free association, dream interpretation; 17. (a) client-centered, (b) reflecting or restating; 18. (a) thoughts, (b) substituting; 19. (a) behavior, (b) learned; 20. (a) effectiveness, (b) behavior or cognitive-behavioral, (c) time; 21. common factors; 22. (a) placebo, (b) common factors; 23. (a) posttraumatic stress disorder, (b) Eye Movement Desensitization and Reprocessing, (c) exposure therapy, cognitive–behavioral therapy, (d) exposure; 24. (a) self-monitoring, (b) negative or automatic, (c) substitute, (d) intrusive or annoying

Critical Thinking

What Is Exorcism?

Questions

1. Besides the United States, what other country did we discuss in which people believe that they can be possessed by evil spirits?

2. Do you think exorcism and its related problems are listed in the American Psychiatric Association's official guide to mental disorders, called the DSM-IV-TR?

A deep growling sound came from Karen, a 42-year-old medical student. The terrible voice said it was a demon who had entered Karen and forced her to have evil sex and would continue to use her as it wanted. An evangelical minister, holding a Bible in one hand, shouted, "Witchcraft, face me! We break every curse! I now call down to you the wrath of God. Go now to the pit!" (Watanabe, 2000, p. A1). Immediately Karen's contorted face relaxed and she called out thanks to Jesus. Later, Karen said her demons were "completely gone." What Karen experienced is called *exorcism,* which is a ritual for banishing evil demons or devils that are believed to have entered and caused a person to experience or perform terrible or sinful behaviors.

Fordham University Associate Professor Michael W. Cuneo, author of a book on exorcism, believes that recent interest in exorcism can be traced partly to the very popular movie *The Exorcist,* which first appeared in 1973 and was re-released in 2000, and to the appearance of exorcists on many popular TV talk shows and the Internet. Currently, there are about 600 charismatic and evangelical Protestant ministries devoted to exorcism. The Roman Catholic Church has increased the number of exorcists in the United States from one in 1990 to about 15–20 today.

Along with exorcism's rise in popularity has come a heated debate over whether a person's problems come from possession by devils and whether these problems can be erased through exorcism. The Catholic Church allows exorcism only after all physical and psychological causes for the person's problems have been ruled out. In other ministries, a variety of personal and social behaviors may be taken as evidence of possession by devils. For example, Karen (described above) underwent exorcism because she had apparently been forced (by the demon) to engage in evil sex.

Albert Landry, a lay pastor at the Harvest Rock Church (Pasadena, CA), looks at whether the possessed person had traumatic childhood experiences, which he believes can create Satan's strongholds and cause anger, bitterness, and lack of forgiveness. Landry explains that initially when devils were cast out, they returned and caused more problems. Now, he combines exorcism with counseling to get at the root of the person's problems.

In some cases, exorcisms are performed out of spiritual compassion to help troubled individuals, while in other cases, there have been reports of beatings and in one case death. "And experts say the psychological dangers of what some see as playing with people's minds and telling them they are possessed can be great" (Watanabe, 2000, p. A16). (Adapted from Watanabe, 2000)

3. Can exorcism be considered a kind of psychotherapy?

4. In what ways do Landry and Freud give similar explanations of what causes mental illness?

5. What big problem can result from telling people that their mental problems are caused by demons?

1. Earlier (p. 546) we explained that about 45% of the married women in Northern Sudan complain of being possessed by spirits that can make the women do and think strange things.

2. The American Psychiatric Association's official guide to mental disorders (DSM-IV-TR) (p. 514) does not list exorcism as a mental disorder. However, the DSM-IV-TR has an appendix that discusses a variety of mental illnesses that are found in particular cultures. For example, members of some American Indian tribes report ghost sickness, which includes various psychological problems such as hallucinations, fear, anxiety, and confusion.

3. Besides the three or four major therapy approaches discussed in this module, there are hundreds of other kinds of psychotherapy. Almost any approach, even exorcism, could be called a therapy, since exorcism is a ritual that is reported to treat mental illnesses.

However, unlike many exorcists, mental health professionals first do a careful evaluation of the client's problems and only then develop a program for therapy. In addition, mental health professionals use therapy approaches whose effectiveness has been investigated and evaluated through systematic research.

4. Both Landry and Freud suggest that early traumatic childhood experiences can make a lasting impact and contribute to the future development of mental health problems. However, the similarity ends when Landry talks of "Satan's strongholds."

5. Telling people that their mental problems are caused by devil possession may create a self-fulfilling prophecy (p. 30) in which the person not only believes the prophecy ("I'm possessed by devils") but then acts to fulfill the prophecy by developing a variety of undesirable symptoms for which they take no responsibility.

Links to Learning

Key Terms/Key People

agoraphobia, 575

agoraphobia: treatment, 575

Beck, Aaron, 565

behavior therapy, 566

behavior therapy: basic
  assumptions, 570

behavior therapy: techniques, 570

client-centered therapy, 564

client-centered therapy: basic
  assumptions, 570

client-centered therapy:
  techniques, 570

clinical psychologists, 558

cognitive-behavioral therapy:
  techniques, 568

cognitive-behavioral
  therapy, 559, 568

cognitive therapy, 565

cognitive therapy: basic
  assumptions, 570

cognitive therapy: techniques, 570

common factors, 571

community mental health
  centers, 557

counseling psychologists, 558

deinstitutionalization, 557

dream interpretation, 561

eclectic approach, 559

effectiveness of
  psychotherapy, 571

exorcism, 578

Eye Movement Desensitization and
  Reprocessing, or EMDR, 573

free association, 561

Freud, Sigmund, 560

healers versus Western
  therapists, 572

imagined exposure, 567

insight therapy, 559

insomnia: treatment, 575

intrusive thoughts, 574

in vivo exposure, 567

medical therapy, 559

meta-analysis, 559

moral therapy, 556

neuroses, 561

phenothiazines, 557

psychiatrists, 558

psychoanalysis, 560

psychoanalysis: basic
  assumptions, 570

psychoanalysis: evaluation, 563

psychoanalysis: techniques, 570

psychotherapy, 556

resistance, 562

Rogers, Carl, 564

self-monitoring, 574

short-term dynamic
  psychotherapy, 562

stimulus hierarchy, 567

systematic desensitization, 567

thought stopping, 574

thought substitution, 574, 575

transference, 562

Learning Activities

- **POWERSTUDY FOR INTRODUCTION
TO PSYCHOLOGY 4.0**
by Tom Doyle and Rod Plotnik
Check out the quizzes and learning activities for "Therapies" on **PowerStudy**
and:
  - Test your knowledge using an interactive version of the Summary Test on pages 576 and 577. Also access related quizzing—true/false, multiple choice, and matching.
  - Explore an interactive version of the critical thinking exercise "What Is Exorcism?" on page 578.
  - You will also find key terms, a chapter outline including chapter abstract, and a special extended list of hotlinked websites that correlate to this module.

- *CengageNOW*
academic.cengage.com/login
Need help studying? This site is your one-stop study shop.
Take a Pre-Test and CengageNOW will generate a Personalized Study Plan based on your test results. The Study Plan will identify the topics you need to review and direct you to online resources to help you master those topics. You can then take a Post-Test to determine the concepts you have mastered and what you still need to work on.

- **INTRODUCTION TO PSYCHOLOGY BOOK
COMPANION WEBSITE**
academic.cengage.com/psychology/plotnik
Visit your book companion website where you will find more resources to help you study. Resources include Learning Objectives, Internet Exercises, quizzing, flash cards, and a pronunciation glossary.

- **STUDY GUIDE and WEBTUTOR**
Check the corresponding module in your Study Guide
for effective student tips and help learning the material presented. Also go to **academic.cengage.com/webtutor** for an interactive version of the Study Guide features.

Study Questions

*A. **Historical Background**—Should our major cities spend more money to develop care and treatment programs for the homeless? (**Suggested answer p. 635**)

B. **Questions about Psychotherapy**—Suppose your friend or loved one has a relatively serious psychological problem. Should you suggest that he or she get professional help?

C. **Insight Therapies**—Several computer programs have been written to "do psychotherapy." Could a computer program be written to "do psychoanalysis"?

*D. **Behavior Therapy**—Susan complains of having terrible test anxiety. What would a behavior therapist do to help her? (**Suggested answer p. 636**)

E. **Review: Evaluation of Approaches**—Janice has a phobia of going out in public. Which approach would be most effective for treating her problem?

F. **Cultural Diversity: Different Healer**—If a Westerner believed that he or she was possessed by the devil, would therapy or an exorcism ritual be the more effective treatment?

G. **Research Focus: EMDR—New Therapy**—Why do you think that people are often more convinced by dramatic case studies than by sound experimental evidence?

*H. **Application: Cognitive-Behavioral Techniques**—Frank has very little self-confidence and self-esteem. What is one way that he could work on raising them? (**Suggested answer p. 636**)

*These questions are answered in Appendix B.

MODULE 25
Social Psychology

Introduction

Stereotypes

Why did he take a $90,000 pay cut?

Lawrence Graham wanted to get a job at a country club and had phoned numerous clubs to set up personal interviews. Here's what happened when he arrived for one of his interviews.

"We don't have any job openings—and if you don't leave the building, I will have to call security," the receptionist said at the first club Graham visited.

"But I just spoke to Donna, your dining manager, and she said to come by and discuss the waiter job."

"Sorry, but there are no jobs and no one here named Donna" (Graham, 1995, p. 4).

Graham finally got two job offers and decided on the exclusive Greenwich Country Club. This club had been in existence for 100 years and was *the* country club in the very affluent, prestigious, and White town of Greenwich, Connecticut. The club's members included a former president, a number of high-ranking government officials, and dozens of *Fortune* 500 executives, bankers, and Wall Street lawyers.

A posh country club would offer Graham only the job of a busboy.

Although Graham wanted a job as a waiter, he was hired to be a busboy. Except when one of the members wanted something and deliberately looked for him, Graham's job as a busboy made him quite invisible and able to overhear members' conversations.

"Here, busboy. Here, busboy," a woman called out. "Busboy, my coffee is cold. Give me a refill."

"Certainly, I would be happy to," said Graham.

Before he returned to the kitchen, Graham heard the woman say to her companion, "My goodness. Did you hear that? That busboy has diction like an educated White person" (Graham, 1995, p. 12).

In real life, Lawrence Graham was a Harvard Law School graduate, had a job as an associate in a New York law firm, and earned $105,000 a year. Although he was ready to move up the social ladder, Graham, who is African American, received no invitations to join a country club, as his White associates did. So to find out what goes on in country clubs that do not admit African Americans, he got in the only way he could, as a busboy making $7 an hour.

Graham's example points out how people often make judgments about others on the basis of physical appearance and accompanying stereotypes, which are both major topics of social psychology.

Social psychology is a broad field whose goals are to understand and explain how our thoughts, feelings, perceptions, and behaviors are influenced by the presence of, or interactions with, others.

One relatively new, rapidly growing, and important subarea of social psychology is cognitive social psychology.

Cognitive social psychology is a subarea of social psychology that focuses on how cognitive processes, such as perceiving, retrieving, and interpreting information about social interactions and events, affect emotions and behaviors and how emotions and behaviors affect cognitions (Roese, 2001).

Social psychologists study how we form impressions and perceive others, how we form attitudes and stereotypes, how we evaluate social interactions, and why racism exists—all of which are involved in Lawrence Graham's story.

Another major topic of social psychology is how people behave in groups.

Behavior in Groups

Why did the girls turn violent?

The touch football game had been going on for years and was considered a rite of passage for incoming seniors. During the game, some minor hazing usually took place, such as senior girls dumping various kinds of food (ketchup, whipped cream, syrup) on junior girls. For this game, the time and place were kept secret from school administrators. Also, several parents arranged to have kegs at their homes so that the underage girls could drink beer before going to the game.

About 10 minutes into the junior-senior touch football game, something happened and the game turned ugly and violent. The senior girls started to act in violent ways that just happened to be videotaped by another student. Later, as CNN played the tape over and over, everyone wondered how these particular senior girls, who came from a well-to-do Chicago suburb and went to a good high school, could have done such disgusting things.

Senior girls engage in violent hazing of juniors while about 100 watch.

According to the video (above illustration) and police reports, junior girls were beaten, slapped, kicked, splattered in the eyes with Tabasco sauce and vinegar, hit with buckets, covered with animal intestines and urine, and smeared with blood, fish guts, mud, and feces. Five girls ended up in the hospital, some requiring stitches. During the violent hazing, about a hundred students just stood and watched, not trying to stop the brawl (L. Black & Flynn, 2003). What kind of group pressure causes normal people to submit to being hazed, and what kind of group pressure turns normal people into violent and ugly hazers?

What's Coming

We'll discuss how we perceive people, how we explain the causes of our behaviors, why we develop attitudes, and how we respond to persuasion. We'll also explore a variety of social influences and group behaviors, such as what makes hazing so popular, how we respond to group pressures, what motivates us to help others, and why we behave aggressively.

We'll begin with Graham's story, which raises the question of how we form impressions of others.

A. Perceiving Others

Person Perception

How do you form first impressions?

Compare the photo of Lawrence Graham on the left with that on the right. In the left photo, your first impression is that Graham is a busboy or waiter, while in the right photo, your first impression is that Graham is a confident businessman or professional. Your first impressions, which were formed in seconds, with little conscious thought, and were biased by your past experiences, are part of person perception.

Person perception refers to seeing someone and then forming impressions and making judgments about that person's likability and the kind of person he or she is, such as guessing his or her intentions, traits, and behaviors.

At country clubs, Graham was offered jobs as a busperson.

Graham was actually a graduate of Harvard Law School.

As you formed a first impression of Graham from each photo, four factors influenced your judgment (L. S. Newman, 2001).

1 Physical appearance. Your initial impressions and judgments of a person are influenced and biased by a person's physical appearance. For example, Graham makes a very different first impression when he looks like a busboy or a professional.

2 Need to explain. You don't just look at a person, but rather you try to explain why he looks, dresses, or behaves in a certain way. You might explain that Graham-as-busboy is working his way through college, while Graham-as-professional is successfully developing his career.

3 Influence on behavior. Your first impressions will influence how you would like or interact with a person. For example, if your first impression of Graham is as a $7-an-hour busboy, you would interact very differently than if your impression of him was as a $105,000-a-year professional working for a large corporation.

4 Effects of race. Researchers found that members of one race generally recognize faces of their own race more accurately than faces of other races (Ferguson et al., 2001). This means we may perceive faces that are racially different from our own in a biased way because they do not appear as distinct as faces from our own race. Further evidence of racial bias occurring in first impressions is found in research showing that the area of the brain associated with emotional vigilance becomes more activated when White people view photos of unfamiliar Black, as compared to unfamiliar White, faces (Fiske, 2006).

Researchers report that first impressions, such as the one you make of Graham, usually occur automatically and function to influence or bias future social interactions in a positive or negative direction (Andersen et al., 2007; L. S. Newman, 2001). One factor that plays a major role in person perception, especially forming first impressions, is physical attractiveness.

Physical Appearance

What makes a face attractive?

Researchers found that, for better or worse, a person's looks matter, since people who are judged more physically attractive generally make more favorable impressions (D. K. Marcus & Miller, 2003). To determine why a face is judged attractive, researchers created faces by combining and averaging physical features taken from different faces. Researchers could make faces more or less attractive by averaging more (32) or fewer (16) faces (Langlois et al., 1994). For example, the face in the left photo, which was rated very attractive, was actually created by averaging thousands of faces (Johnston, 2000). When faces of attractive women were shown to heterosexual men, the men's brain scans showed that looking at attractive faces activated the brain's reward/pleasure center (p. 330), the same center that is activated by food, sex, and drugs (cocaine) (Aharon et al., 2001).

How attractive is this woman?

Somewhat surprisingly, researchers found that both within and across cultures, there is strong agreement (correlation about 0.90) among Whites, African Americans, Asians, and Hispanics about which faces of adults and children are and are not attractive (Langlois et al., 2000). According to evolutionary psychologists, judging and valuing attractiveness may have evolved and become a kind of "built-in" ability because attractiveness was a visible sign of a person being fit, healthy, and a potentially good mate (Fink & Penton-Voak, 2002).

Next, we'll learn about how our social interactions affect our brain.

Social Neuroscience

What happens in our brains as we perceive others?

As we learned already, the area of the brain associated with emotional vigilance becomes activated when White people view unfamiliar Black faces, and the brain area associated with reward and pleasure becomes activated when heterosexual men view faces of attractive women. These research findings are examples of social neuroscience.

Social neuroscience refers to an emerging area of research that examines social behavior, such as perceiving others, by combining biological and social approaches. In other words, it focuses on understanding how social behavior influences the brain, as well as how the brain influences social behavior (Cacioppo & Berntson, 2002).

Perhaps the most fascinating research has been identifying brain cells that are responsible for human empathy (mirror neurons). Researchers found that empathizing with a friend activates our brains in the same way as the friend's brain, so we feel the same emotional pain. Other research found that being rejected activates a part of the brain that responds to physical pain, and receiving support from a loved one reduces activity in our brain area that produces stress hormones (A. Underwood, 2006).

One reason our first impressions, such as those we made of Graham, occur quickly and automatically is we often base them on stereotypes, which we'll discuss next (Andersen et al., 2007).

What could bias medical treatment?

On the right are photos of actors who played the roles of patients complaining of chest pains. While describing their symptoms, the actor-patients were videotaped. These videotapes were shown to over 700 physicians who were asked to recommend treatments. Because the actor-patients all described the same physical symptoms, all the physicians should have generally recommended the same treatments. However, physicians recommended different treatments that depended on the physicians' particular sexual and racial stereotypes (Schulman et al., 1999).

Stereotypes are widely held beliefs that people have certain traits because they belong to a particular group. Stereotypes are often inaccurate and frequently portray the members of less powerful, less controlling groups more

Which of these individuals received the best treatment for heart problems?

negatively than members of more powerful or more controlling groups.

Stereotypes played an important role in the study we just described. Although the actor-patients reported the same symptoms and should have received about the same kinds of treatment, physicians were 40% less likely to recommend sophisticated medical tests for women and African Americans compared to White men (Schulman et al., 1999). More recent research also found that African Americans were less likely than Whites to receive expensive medical procedures (*USA Today*, 2005).

These studies show that racial and sexual stereotypes, which may occur automatically and without awareness, may bias the physicians' perceptions and judgments (Andersen et al., 2007). As you'll see next, once negative stereotypes are formed, they are difficult to change.

Development of Stereotypes

Psychologists believe that we develop stereotypes when parents, peers, co-workers, teachers, and others reward us with social approval for holding certain attitudes and beliefs. There are also cultural pressures to adopt certain values and beliefs about members of different groups. For example, in the weight-conscious culture of the United States, there is an emphasis on being thin (see Module 15), so we might expect a negative stereotype to apply to women who are overweight (Sands et al., 1997).

To test this idea, researchers asked subjects to watch videotapes of job applicants and decide if they would hire them. The applicants were professional male and female actors made up to appear normal weight or overweight (about 28–35 pounds heavier). When asked to make hiring decisions, subjects showed a significant bias against hiring overweight applicants, especially overweight women

Why do you think I wasn't hired?

(Pingitore et al., 1994). This bias against hiring overweight women is an example of a negative stereotype, which is often accompanied by prejudice and discrimination.

Prejudice refers to an unfair, biased, or intolerant attitude toward another group of people.

An example of prejudice is believing that overweight women are not as intelligent, competent, or capable as women of normal weight.

Discrimination refers to specific unfair behaviors exhibited toward members of a group.

An employer's bias against hiring overweight applicants is an example of discrimination.

The history of the United States provides many examples of racist and sexist cultural stereotypes, such as beliefs that women are not smart enough to vote and that African Americans are inferior to Whites (Swim et al., 1995). Research shows that some stereotypes, including racial prejudice, are so much a part of our society that they begin developing as early as 6 years of age (Baron & Banaji, 2006).

One reason we frequently use stereotypes to make judgments about people is that stereotypes save us thinking time.

Functions of Stereotypes

Social cognitive psychologists suggest that, just as we have developed physical tools, such as hammers and saws, to help us build things more efficiently, we have also developed cognitive tools, such as stereotypes, to help us think and make decisions more efficiently. For example, instead of having to analyze in detail the person in the right photo, you immediately notice the person's unique characteristics, assign the person to a social group, such as teenage-punker, and use the information stored in your "teenage-punker" stereotype: disregards standard social customs and fashions, is independent, dislikes authority, goes to rave parties, experiments with drugs, and so on. This example shows that stereotypes are frequently used because they serve at least two major functions (Banaji, 2005; Schneider, 2004).

Why don't adults like me?

Thought-saving device. Stereotypes help to conserve time and energy when making decisions in social situations. By using stereotypes, you make quick (and sometimes inaccurate) decisions and thus save time and energy by not having to analyze an overwhelming amount of personal and social information.

Alertness and survival. Recent neurological research found that the sight of a stranger of another race leads to heightened physiological arousal, which likely reflects unconscious biases and a natural awareness of individuals of unfamiliar groups (such as race) (Olsson et al., 2005). Thus, one function of stereotypes is to make us alert and cautious around members of an unfamiliar group.

However, a major problem with stereotypes is they are very difficult to change because they occur automatically and without our awareness of having used them to make judgments (Schneider, 2004). Another reason stereotypes are difficult to change is that we often dismiss information that contradicts or doesn't fit our stereotypes (Banaji, 2006). This means biased stereotypes can live on and lead to inaccurate judgments and decisions in social situations.

Another view of stereotypes is they are like having information categories in the brain, which are called schemas, our next topic.

A. Perceiving Others

Schemas

How are schemas like social filters?

When Dr. Fran Conley reached her goal of becoming a board-certified neurosurgeon, she was one of only two female board-certified neurosurgeons in the United States. With such exceptional accomplishments, Dr. Conley was surprised and disappointed by her male colleagues' sexist attitudes. For example, as a young neurosurgeon, she was repeatedly propositioned by fellow doctors in front of others, primarily for effect. Dr. Conley admits that she tolerated this kind of behavior because she wanted to advance in her profession and be accepted by her colleagues. However, even after Dr. Conley had achieved the status of a full professor at Stanford Medical Center (right photo), the sexism continued. For instance, whenever Dr. Conley disagreed with male colleagues, they would jokingly attribute her lack of agreement to a difficult menstrual period. But disagreements between male colleagues were viewed as honest differences of opinion (Manning,

Why did fellow neurosurgeons show her less respect?

1998). One reason male colleagues responded to Dr. Conley in sexist ways is that they had developed mental categories, called schemas.

Schemas are mental categories that, like computer files, contain knowledge about people, events, and concepts. Because schemas affect what we attend to and how we interpret things, schemas can influence, bias, and distort our thoughts, perceptions, and social behaviors.

Sexist schemas of women working in scientific fields put women, such as Dr. Conley, at a clear disadvantage compared to their male colleagues (Dean, 2006). The social relationships between Dr. Conley and her male colleagues show how schemas, in this case sexist, served at least three functions (Higgins, 2000).

Functions. Schemas provided male colleagues with *information* about social stimuli, such as because Dr. Conley was a woman, she was inferior to men. Schemas influenced what male colleagues pay *attention* to, such as noticing when Dr. Conley disagreed with a male colleague. Schemas influenced how some male colleagues *responded* to women, such as making sexual advances to Dr. Conley. Thus, schemas contain files of information that influence our thoughts, behaviors, and feelings toward others (J. E. Young et al., 2006).

Kinds of Schemas

Schemas are part of *social cognition*, which studies how and what people learn about social relationships. Schemas, which are like hundreds of different information files in your brain, are generally divided into four types: person, role, event, and self schemas.

Person schemas include our judgments about the traits that we and others possess.

For example, when meeting someone new, we may rely on person schemas to provide general information about that person. Person schemas that contain general information about people who have membership in groups are *stereotypes* (Wyer, 2007).

Role schemas are based on the jobs people perform or the social positions they hold.

The reason you often ask "What do you do?" is so you can use your role schemas to provide any missing information about the person and provide mental shortcuts about what you might say or how you might act in social situations.

Event schemas, also called scripts, contain behaviors that we associate with familiar activities, events, or procedures.

The event schema for graduation is to celebrate getting your degree. In contrast, the event schema for a college class is to be silent, pay attention, and take notes. Event schemas help us know what to expect and provide guidelines on how to behave in different kinds of situations.

Self schemas contain personal information about ourselves, and this information influences, modifies, and distorts what we perceive and remember and how we behave.

What's interesting about our self schemas is that they overemphasize our good points, which explains why being criticized in public easily hurts our feelings.

We especially look for information or feedback to support our schemas and tend to disregard information that doesn't (Wyer, 2007). For this reason, once schemas are formed, they are difficult to change (J. E. Young et al., 2006).

Person schema has information on how to act with a new date.

Event schema has information on how to act at graduation.

Advantages and Disadvantages

There are two *disadvantages* of schemas. The first is that schemas may *restrict, bias,* or *distort* what we attend to and remember and thus cause us to overlook important information (Devine et al., 1994). For example, if your self schema is being a good student, you may not pay attention to suggestions from parents, teachers, or friends that may make you a better student.

The second disadvantage of schemas is that they are highly *resistant to change* because we generally select and attend to information that supports our schemas and deny any information that is inconsistent with them (Macrae & Bodenhausen, 2000). For example, you might pay attention to positive written comments on a class paper and reject any constructive suggestions about ways to improve your writing skills.

Schemas also have *advantages.* For example, if someone says "I'm a freshman," you use your "freshman schema," which contains *information* about how freshmen think and behave, to help you analyze and respond appropriately in this particular social situation. Schemas also provide *guidelines* for how to behave in various social events (event schemas) and help us explain the social behavior of others (role schemas) (Howard & Renfrow, 2006). Explaining social behavior is one of the most intriguing areas of social cognition, and it's our next topic.

Your person schema may cause you to reject valid criticisms of your work.

Definition

What is unusual about this umpire?

After 13 seasons and 2,000 games in the minor leagues, this umpire was passed over for promotion to the major leagues and released. An evaluation report by the Office for Umpire Development claimed that this umpire's work had "deteriorated in areas of enthusiasm and execution," even though earlier in the season the rating had been "better than average." What is unusual about this umpire is that she is a woman. Pam Postema (right photo) claims the reason she was passed over for promotion and released was that she was a woman and there are no female

Because I'm a woman, I wasn't promoted.

umpires in major league baseball. She filed a sex discrimination suit because, as Pam says, "Baseball wasn't ready for a woman umpire no matter how good she was" (S. Reed & Stambler, 1992).

Most sports fans would have an explanation as to why Pam Postema was not promoted to be an umpire in major league baseball. These kinds of explanations are called attributions.

Attributions are things we point to as the causes of events, other people's behaviors, and our own behaviors.

If you had to explain why there are no female umpires in major league baseball, you would choose between internal and external attributions.

Internal Versus External

A famous social psychologist, Fritz Heider (1958), believed that we all function to some extent like social psychologists as we try to explain everyday behaviors. Heider was the first to distinguish between internal and external causes or attributions for behaviors.

Internal attributions are explanations of behavior based on the internal characteristics or dispositions of the person performing the behavior. They are sometimes referred to as dispositional attributions.

For example, if you used internal attributions to explain why Postema was not made a major league umpire, you would point to her personal characteristics or dispositions, such as saying that she was not a good judge of balls and strikes.

External attributions are explanations of behavior based on the external circumstances or situations. They are sometimes called situational attributions.

If you used external attributions to explain why Postema was not promoted, you would point to external circumstances, such as saying that major league baseball is run by men, and they do not want to have a woman umpire.

Thus, making internal or external attributions has important implications for personal and social behaviors (Derlaga et al., 2005). For example, if you use internal attributions, you would say that Postema does not have the skill or talent to be a major league umpire. If you use external attributions, you would say that, although she has the skills, the league discriminated against her because she is a woman. How people make the distinction between internal and external attributions is a rather complicated process.

Kelley's Model of Covariation

How do we decide whether Pam was passed over for promotion because of dispositional or situational factors? To answer this question, social psychologist Harold Kelley (1967) developed the covariation model.

The *covariation model,* developed by Harold Kelley, says that, in making attributions, we should look for factors that are present when the behavior occurs and factors that are absent when the behavior does not occur.

Kelley proposed that, in explaining someone's behavior, we should look for information about three factors: consensus, consistency, and distinctiveness (Forster & Liberman, 2007).

Consensus means determining whether other people engage in the same behavior in the same situation.

Consistency means determining whether the person engages in this behavior every time he or she is in a particular situation.

Distinctiveness means determining how differently the person behaves in one situation when compared to other situations.

In the examples on the left, we have applied the three factors in

How do you decide if internal or external attributions apply to Pam?

Kelley's covariation model to Pam Postema's situation. Notice that high consistency, low distinctiveness, and low consensus result in an internal, or dispositional, attribution (fired because she's a poor umpire). But high consistency, high distinctiveness, and high consensus result in an external or situational attribution (fired because of sexual discrimination). Thus, Kelley's covariation model helps us determine if Postema's firing was due to internal or external attributions (Ployhart et al., 2005). However, if we don't follow Kelley's model, we make errors in attributing causes. We'll discuss three errors in making attributions—that is, in deciding what caused what.

---

1. HIGH CONSISTENCY
Pam performs about the same every time.

2. LOW DISTINCTIVENESS
Pam makes good decisions in calling strikes but not in calling base runners out.

3. LOW CONSENSUS
Pam does not show the same skills as other umpires.

INTERNAL ATTRIBUTION
Pam's lack of promotion is due to her poor umpiring skills.

1. HIGH CONSISTENCY
Pam performs about the same every time.

2. HIGH DISTINCTIVENESS
Pam makes good decisions in all aspects of the game.

3. HIGH CONSENSUS
Pam shows the same skills as other umpires.

EXTERNAL ATTRIBUTION
Pam's lack of promotion is due to discrimination by the league.

B. Attributions

Can we make the wrong attributions?

Most people have heard the term *glass ceiling,* which refers to a real but invisible barrier that keeps women and people of color from reaching the top positions in a business or organization. Evidence that there is a very thick glass ceiling is clear because only 9 (less than 2%) of *Fortune* magazine's top 500 chairpersons are women and 95% of the senior managers are White men (Creswell, 2006). One woman who was successful in breaking the glass ceiling is Carol Bartz (right photo), who at age 43 became one of the first women to head a large organization. Through perseverance, hard work, and a winning personality, she broke through the glass ceiling by becoming chief executive officer at Autodesk and making the company an international leader in software.

Breaking through the glass ceiling involves decisions about attributions. Do women and people of color fail to be appointed to senior-level positions because they lack skills and intelligence, which is an internal or dispositional attribution, or because they

> I broke through the glass ceiling.

face discrimination from senior-level White males, which is an external or situational attribution? Although Kelley's covariation model would help decide this issue, many want a quicker way and use the cognitive miser model (S. E. Taylor, 1981).

The *cognitive miser model* says that, in making attributions, people feel they must conserve time and effort by taking cognitive shortcuts.

We have already discussed several cognitive shortcuts that we use in selecting, gathering, remembering, and using information—for example, relying on stereotypes and schemas. Besides these, researchers have identified a number of other cognitive shortcuts that we frequently use in making attributions (Forgas et al., 2003; Weiner & Graham, 1999). Although these cognitive shortcuts save mental time and effort, they may result in biased or incorrect attributions.

We'll discuss three of the most common biases in making attributions: the fundamental attribution error, the actor-observer effect, and the self-serving bias.

Fundamental Attribution Error

If you believe that women and people of color cannot break through the glass ceiling because they lack the skills and intelligence to do so, you may be making the fundamental attribution error (Langdridge & Butt, 2004).

The *fundamental attribution error* refers to our tendency, when we look for causes of a person's behavior, to focus on the person's disposition or personality traits and overlook how the situation influenced the person's behavior.

> When you explain someone's behavior, you may be wrong.

An example of the *fundamental attribution error* would be to conclude that women and people of color cannot break through the glass ceiling because of personal or dispositional factors, such as a lack of assertiveness or intelligence. However, the real reason may be not personal or dispositional factors but the situation: 95% of senior management in *Fortune*'s 1,000 top companies are White men who may want to keep the status quo and use subtle discriminatory hiring practices to keep out women and people of color.

Actor-Observer Effect

John angrily explains that he got to his car to put more money in the meter just as the police officer was driving away. John adds that he's very responsible and the ticket was bad luck because he was only 45 seconds late. John says he got the ticket because the police officer was just being mean. John's explanation is a good example of the actor-observer effect (Malle, 2006).

The *actor-observer effect* refers to the tendency, when you are behaving (or acting), to attribute your own behavior to situational factors. However, when you are observing others, you attribute another's behavior to his or her personality traits or disposition.

In the parking ticket example, John, the *actor*, attributes his getting the ticket to situational factors, just having bad luck, rather than to his own behavior, being late. In addition, John, the *observer*, explains that the police officer ticketed him because of a dispositional or personality factor—the officer was mean (Liberman et al., 2007). The actor-observer error is very common. You can tell if you're making it by putting yourself in the position of the one you are observing (S. R. Wilson et al., 1997).

Self-Serving Bias

When we look for the causes of our own behaviors, such as why we received a good or bad grade on a test, we may make errors because of the self-serving bias (Fiedler, 2007; Mcallister et al., 2002).

The *self-serving bias* refers to explaining our successes by attributing them to our dispositions or personality traits and explaining our failures by attributing them to the situations.

The self-serving bias can be considered another part of the actor-observer effect. According to the self-serving bias, if you get an A on an exam, you tend to attribute your success to your personality traits or disposition, such as intelligence and perseverance. However, if you get a D on an exam, you tend to attribute your failure to the situation, such as a difficult test or unfair questions. Thus, according to the *self-serving bias*, we try to keep ourselves in the best possible light by making different and even opposite attributions, depending on whether we have performed well or poorly (Mcallister et al., 2002).

> I didn't do well on this exam because the text was confusing.

The three errors that we just discussed show the need to be on guard so that these errors don't bias our attributions (Kenworthy & Miller, 2002).

Although biased attributions can create problems, they can also be an advantage when they help us change our behaviors, as we'll discuss next.

C. Research Focus: Attributions & Grades

What problems do freshmen face?

Perhaps 20% of the students we counsel tell us about getting poor grades in their freshman year, and their reasons are very similar. Either they didn't develop good study habits in high school so they weren't academically prepared for college or they spent too much time partying or dealing with stressful personal, social, or financial difficulties. What is interesting is that some of the freshmen who got poor grades their

I'm having problems with my grades and wonder if I should drop out.

first year were able to bounce back academically their second year, while others became discouraged and dropped out of college. Researchers discovered many differences in students' attributions—that is, how students explained why they bounced back or dropped out. Because one goal of psychology is to apply scientific findings to real-world problems, researchers used findings on attributions to develop a program for improving grades and lowering the dropout rate (T. D. Wilson & Linville, 1982). Here's what actually happened.

Kinds of Attributions

In explaining why a freshman is having academic problems, researchers may point to personal or dispositional attributions, such as the lack of necessary academic skills. Or researchers may point to external or situational attributions, such as pressures to party rather than study. Once a freshman has developed a pattern of getting poor grades, another question is whether the causes are permanent or temporary. For example, if freshmen attributed their academic problems to relatively permanent conditions, such as poor abilities, they would have little motivation and would expect little improvement. In addition, poor academic performance would make new students worried and anxious, which in turn would interfere with their ability to study.

However, if freshmen attributed their academic problems to temporary conditions, such as poor study habits, they could expect to improve if they developed better study skills. Researchers thought that if they could change students' attributions about poor academic performance and help them realize that it was a temporary rather than a permanent state, students could improve their grades.

Method: Changing Attributions

I did terribly my freshman year but I got my act together and didn't drop out.

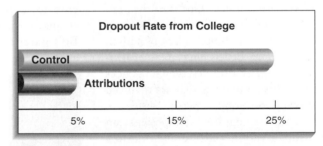

Researchers recruited freshmen who were having academic problems, such as scoring poorly on exams, not keeping up with assignments, and considering dropping out of college. These students were randomly divided into two different groups.

Students in the ***experimental group*** (attributions group) were given a number of procedures that changed their attributions about poor academic performance from a permanent cause to only a temporary condition. For example, students in the experimental group read a booklet about previous freshmen who had similar academic problems but showed improvement later in college. These subjects watched videotapes of previous students who described very convincingly how their grade point averages had risen after their freshman year. Next, these subjects were asked to write down all the reasons they could think of why grade point averages might increase after the freshman year.

The other group of freshmen with academic problems did not receive any of this information and served as a ***control group***.

Results and Conclusions

Researchers found that changing students' attributions for poor academic performance from permanent to temporary had two significant positive effects.

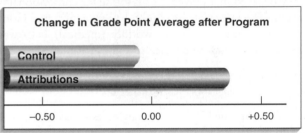

Change in Grade Point Average after Program

| Control | |
| Attributions | |

−0.50   0.00   +0.50

First, in the graph above, notice that freshmen who were told how to attribute their academic problems to temporary conditions (attributions group) had a significant improvement in grade point averages one year after the completion of this program.

Second, as shown in the graph below, only 5% of freshmen who changed their attributions for poor academic performance from permanent to temporary dropped out of college, while 25% of those in the control group dropped out.

Dropout Rate from College

| Control | |
| Attributions | |

5%   15%   25%

From these data, researchers reached two important conclusions. First, it is possible to change students' attributions and expectations about academic performance. Second, changing students' attributions and expectations actually improved academic performance and reduced the dropout rate (T. D. Wilson & Linville, 1982). This study illustrates how social psychologists used the concept of attribution to solve a real-world problem (Covington, 2000).

Next, we'll discuss one of the most active areas of social cognition—forming and changing attitudes.

D. Attitudes

Definition

How much power do attitudes have?

The media regularly report on people's attitudes toward a wide range of hot topics, such as politics, religion, drug use, abortion, and sports. The concept of attitude, which in the 1930s was called the single most indispensable term in social psychology (Allport, 1935), continues to be one of the most studied concepts (Maio et al., 2006).

An *attitude* is any belief or opinion that includes an evaluation of some object, person, or event along a continuum from negative to positive and that predisposes us to act in a certain way toward that object, person, or event.

Attitudes can have a significant impact on behavior, as happened in the tragic death of a 11-year-old boy named Bo. An autopsy showed that Bo had died of complications from diabetes. After suffering painful symptoms for seven days, he went into a coma and died. At the time, he was 15–20 pounds underweight. Bo's parents were members of the Followers of Christ Church in Oregon, and they believed that prayer is a substitute for conventional medical treatment. The leader of the church had preached that God would heal and that anyone seeking worldly (medical) help was weak and lacked faith in God. Because of these attitudes, Bo received no

They believed God healed and prayer was the only treatment.

medical treatment for his diabetes, which doctors said was an easily treatable problem. Records showed that as many as 25 children in the congregation had died in the past 20 years because they were treated with prayers instead of conventional medical help.

In most states, immunity from prosecution is granted to parents whose children sicken and die if the parents' religious beliefs permit only faith healing and not conventional medical treatment. Since Bo's death, Oregon changed its law so that parents who use religious beliefs to withhold medical treatment and allow their children to die of a treatable medical illness can face criminal charges (Hamilton, 2005; Reaves, 2001).

Bo's case, as well as our earlier discussion of suicide bombers (p. 471), is an example of attitudes that have the power to influence life-and-death decisions. Attitudes influence a wide range of behaviors and that is one reason billions of dollars are spent each year trying to measure and change attitudes and get people to buy certain products or vote for particular candidates. Attitudes, which can have very powerful influences on our lives, have three components.

Components of Attitudes

If we closely examined Bo's parents' attitudes toward faith healing and conventional medical treatment, we would find that attitudes influence their thoughts (cognitive component), feelings (affective component), and behaviors (behavioral component) (Huskinson & Haddock, 2006; Maio & Haddock, 2007).

1 Cognitive Component

Bo's parents did not approve of conventional medical treatment for their son because they believed that only prayers were needed since God does the healing (if that is His/Her will) and that seeking medical treatment indicated a lack of faith in God. The parents' beliefs illustrate the ***cognitive component*** of attitudes, which includes both thoughts and beliefs that are involved in evaluating some object, person, or idea.

An attitude's cognitive component can range from a very negative evaluation to a very positive one. For example, Bo's parents have a very positive belief in faith healing and a very negative evaluation of conventional medical treatment.

We have many attitudes that show our likes and dislikes, and often these attitudes are ***automatically*** triggered, without conscious thought on our part (Fabrigar et al., 2005).

2 Affective Component

Bo's parents were fearful of seeking conventional medical treatment because it meant going against God's will. The parents' fearful feelings illustrate the ***affective component*** of attitudes, which involves emotional feelings that can be weak or strong, positive or negative. For example, Bo's parents had strong positive feelings about using only prayers to treat their son's medical problem and strong fearful or negative feelings about seeking conventional medical treatment.

Researchers found that both ***beliefs*** and ***feelings*** are involved in how we form attitudes (Maio et al., 2006). For example, beliefs may be more important in forming political attitudes, such as whom to vote for, while feelings may be more important in forming dietary attitudes, such as deciding to eat dog or horse meat, which is considered very appetizing in some cultures.

3 Behavioral Component

The parents' positive attitude toward using prayer alone and their negative attitude toward seeking conventional medical treatment resulted in their not calling a medical doctor. The parents' refusal to call a medical doctor illustrates the ***behavioral component*** of attitudes, which involves performing or not performing some behavior.

In some cases, engaging in some behavior can influence the formation of an attitude (Maio et al., 2006). For example, having a good or bad experience in doing something (snowboarding, sky diving, using drugs, going to concerts) may result in a positive or negative attitude toward that activity.

Attitudes can have weak to strong and positive to negative influences on our behaviors and, as you'll see next, can also serve other important functions.

What if attitudes collide?

Shannon Faulkner (right photo, front) had an attitude about going to college that set off an enormous personal and legal struggle. In the early 1990s, she applied to and was accepted at the Citadel, a military college in Charleston, South Carolina. But almost immediately, she was rejected because officials discovered that Shannon was a woman (she had eliminated all references to gender on her application). During the next two years, there was a battle of attitudes between the Citadel, which wanted to continue its 150-year-old tradition as a male-only college, and Shannon, who wanted to be given the same opportunities as males. She challenged the Citadel's all-male attitude and policy on legal grounds: Since the Citadel received 28% of its financial support from the state's tax dollars, it should be open to all the state's residents, male or female.

Shannon's attitude—that she be allowed to attend the Citadel—elicited death threats, hate mail, harassing phone calls, and hissing in restaurants. However, after two years of legal battles, the court ruled that the Citadel had to admit Shannon, and she was escorted into the Citadel by her parents and federal marshals.

But her first week at the Citadel, which is called hell week because of the terrible harassment new cadets must endure, was triple hell for Shannon. Not a single male cadet, new or old, would speak to her or offer any support (S. Reed & Esselman, 1995).

Shannon's struggle to become the first female cadet at the all-male Citadel resulted in a fierce battle between opposing attitudes. We'll use Shannon's experience to illustrate three general functions of attitudes: how they affect our predispositions, interpretations, and evaluations (Ajzen, 2001).

1 *Predispose*

Shannon had heard about the Citadel in her senior year of high school and said, "There was just something inside of me that wanted to do this" (Baum, 1994, p. 4). As Shannon's battle dragged on for two years, she explained, "It really has been a long struggle. When I started this lawsuit, I was told I would *never* enter the Citadel" (S. Reed & Esselman, 1995, p. 44). However, Shannon's attitude that women must be given the same opportunities as men predisposed her to behave in a certain way.

The *predisposing function* of attitudes means that they guide or influence us to behave in specific ways.

Shannon's attitude predisposed her to apply to the Citadel, so that she could obtain the same education and profit from the same network as males.

Because attitudes predispose us to behave in specific ways, attitudes are often used to predict behavior. A meta-analysis of 88 studies on how attitudes predispose behavior reported that attitudes significantly and substantially predicted future behaviors (Kraus, 1995). The fact that attitudes can and do predispose us to behave in certain ways is the primary reason that politicians survey voters' attitudes and manufacturers measure consumers' attitudes.

Although attitudes predispose us to behave in specific ways, they do not force us to do so, which explains why voters don't always vote as they say and consumers don't always buy what they say they like (Maio et al., 2006).

2 *Interpret*

New cadets' first week at the Citadel is called hell week because they endure constant harassment—for example, being yelled at for almost everything or being punished by having to take scalding showers until they throw up (Peyser et al., 1995). One reason cadets endure such harassment is that their attitudes influence how they interpret this cruel treatment.

The *interpreting function* of attitudes means that they provide convenient guidelines for interpreting and categorizing objects and events and deciding whether to approach or avoid them.

Cadets with very positive attitudes toward the Citadel's proud traditions will interpret hell week's harassment as one way to prove themselves. In contrast, cadets with less positive attitudes may question and rebel against such cruel harassment. Although Shannon had fought hard to enter the Citadel, she decided to drop out during hell week, as did 24 male cadets.

3 *Evaluate*

During the two years Shannon fought for admission to the Citadel, garbage was heaped on her car, hate mail called her every ugly name, and she was jeered and hissed at in restaurants. One reason Shannon put up with this harassment was that attitudes help us evaluate situations and stand up for our beliefs.

The *evaluative function* of attitudes means that they help us stand up for those beliefs and values that we consider very important to ourselves.

For example, Shannon's strong attitude that women should have equal opportunities for education, especially in publicly supported institutions, helped her endure two years of harassment and struggle.

The evaluative function of attitudes explains why people with strong attitudes about equal rights, the homeless, religion, freedom, abortion, gays, and politics often endure great personal hardships in standing up and fighting for their beliefs.

Although Shannon dropped out of the Citadel in 1995, four more women entered the Citadel in 1996. Although the Citadel promised to halt harassment, two of the four women dropped out because of excessive harassment (having their clothes set on fire, made to drink iced tea until they vomited). The Citadel officially punished 10 cadets for excessive hazing (Gleick, 1997). One reason male cadets continue to harass female cadets is that the Citadel knowingly or unknowingly has fostered negative attitudes toward women cadets. However, despite negative attitudes, 6% of all cadets enrolled at the Citadel are currently women and the numbers are expected to rise (Grinalds, 2002).

Researchers have found that strong negative attitudes are very difficult to change (Petty et al., 2007). Changing attitudes is our next topic.

D. Attitudes

What made a skinhead reform?

At one time, Floyd Cochran (right photo) was an out-and-out hatemonger who was a leader of the Neo-Nazi group, Aryan Nation, in Idaho. His goal was to exterminate everyone who wasn't White. He constantly preached hatred, and he recruited many White youths to help him "spread the hate like a disease" (Cochran, 2007). Then, as he was preparing for the annual Hitler Youth Festival, a group of White supremacists told him that his 4-year-old son must be euthanized because he was born with a birth defect. Floyd found himself caught between his own years of preaching hate and members of

I was a racist until my values hurt my son.

Aryan Nation hating the son he loved. Floyd resolved his personal dilemma by renouncing his White supremacist values and abandoning the hate organizations. He now speaks out against hate and racism (Charmoli, 2006).

Why did Floyd radically change his attitudes, from preaching hate and racism to denouncing these beliefs? We'll discuss two popular theories that explain why people change their attitudes: the theory of cognitive dissonance and self-perception theory (Harmon-Jones & Harmon Jones, 2002; Petty et al., 1997).

Cognitive Dissonance

After a group of White supremacists told him his son must be euthanized, Floyd's life became one big conflict. He had spent most of his adult life practicing racism and hate, but now his own personal values were causing him great anguish. Floyd found himself in the middle of a very troubling inconsistency, which Leon Festinger (1957) called cognitive dissonance.

Cognitive dissonance **refers to a state of unpleasant psychological tension that motivates us to reduce our cognitive inconsistencies by making our beliefs more consistent with each other.**

There are two main ways to reduce cognitive dissonance—that is, to make our beliefs and attitudes consistent with our behavior (Andersen et al., 2007).

Adding or changing beliefs. We can reduce cognitive dissonance by adding new beliefs or changing old beliefs and making them consistent with our behavior. In Floyd's case, cognitive dissonance was created by the conflict between being told the son he loved must be euthanized and his own racist and hate-filled beliefs. To decrease his cognitive dissonance, Floyd renounced his hateful beliefs so that his attitudes became consistent with his behavior, which was loving his son regardless of his birth defect.

Counterattitudinal behavior. Another way we can reduce cognitive dissonance is by engaging in opposite or counterattitudinal behavior (Leippe & Eisenstadt, 1994).

Counterattitudinal behavior **involves taking a public position that runs counter to your private attitude.**

Did he change his racist attitudes to resolve his cognitive dissonance?

A classic study by Festinger and Carlsmith (1959) illustrates how counterattitudinal behavior works. In this study, subjects were asked to do an extremely boring task, such as turning pegs in a board. At the end of the task, the experimenter asked the subjects to help out by telling the next group of subjects how interesting the task was. Subjects were asked to lie about the task and say it was interesting, which is engaging in counterattitudinal behavior. For saying the task was interesting, some subjects received $1 and some received $20. Sometime later, the original subjects were asked how much they had liked the boring task. A curious finding emerged. Subjects paid just $1 had a more favorable attitude about the boring task than those who were paid $20. That's because subjects paid $20 felt they were paid well for lying. Subjects paid $1 had no good reason for lying, and so, to resolve the cognitive dissonance between what they'd said (it was interesting) and what they felt (it was boring), they convinced themselves that the task was somewhat interesting. This shows that engaging in opposite or counterattitudinal behaviors can change attitudes. However, there's a different explanation for this experiment's results.

Self-Perception Theory

Perhaps subjects in the previous experiment came to believe their own lies (task was interesting) after engaging in counterattitudinal behavior not to reduce cognitive dissonance but because of changing their own self-perceptions.

Self-perception theory **says that we first observe or perceive our own behavior and then, as a result, we change our attitudes.**

Daryl Bem (1967), who developed self-perception theory, would explain that subjects paid only $1 for lying would recall their behavior and conclude that they would never have lied for only $1, so the task must have actually been interesting.

At first glance, cognitive dissonance theory and self-perception theory seem to be similar, since they both indicate that if we say something, it must be true. However, each theory points to a different reason. According to **cognitive dissonance theory**, the belief "if I said it, it must be true" occurs because we are trying to reduce the inconsistency in our beliefs and behaviors. In comparison, according to **self-perception theory**, concluding "if I said it, it must be true" simply reflects another way of explaining our own behaviors.

Self-perception theory also challenges the traditional assumption that attitudes give rise to behavior. According to self-perception theory, behaviors give rise to attitudes. For example, after Floyd began speaking out against racism, his attitudes changed radically. Researchers have

Did he change his racist attitudes because he spoke against racism?

shown that behavior can influence attitudes (Leippe & Eisenstadt, 1994; Van Laar et al., 2005).

We may change our own attitudes in response to cognitive dissonance or self-perception. However, others are continually trying to change our attitudes through various forms of persuasion, our next topic.

Political candidates spend much of their time, energy, and money trying to persuade people to vote for them. What politicians have to decide is whether to use an intellectual or emotional appeal, how to appear honest, and what arguments to use. We'll begin with choosing between two different routes—central or peripheral (Maio & Haddock, 2007; Petty & Cacioppo, 1986).

Central Route

If the audience is interested in thinking about the real issues, a politician might best use the central route.

The *central route for persuasion* presents information with strong arguments, analyses, facts, and logic.

A political candidate using the central route for persuasion should present clear and detailed information about his or her views and accomplishments, should appear *honest* and *credible* by demonstrating knowledge and commitment to the issues and pointing out the opponents' records (Priester & Petty, 1995).

Politicians should choose the central route when they are trying to persuade voters who have a high need to know the facts and issues (Cacioppo & Petty, 1982). The central route for persuasion works with people who think about and analyze the issues. However, not all voters can be persuaded by the central route. For some, a peripheral route for persuasion proves the better method.

> I think logical arguments and hard facts work best.

> I think emotional and personal appeals work best.

Peripheral Route

If the audience is more interested in the candidate's personality or image, a politician might seek votes using the peripheral route.

The *peripheral route for persuasion* emphasizes emotional appeal, focuses on personal traits, and generates positive feelings.

The peripheral route assumes that not all voters will spend the time and energy to digest or discuss the issues. Instead, some audiences are more interested in the candidate's ability to generate excitement and support by giving an *energetic* and *enthusiastic speech* (Priester & Petty, 1995). This route involves bands, banners, parties, and personal appearances, which build an inviting and exciting image and create a positive attitude toward the candidate. If audiences like the candidate's image, they will more likely agree with the candidate's views (J. M. Carlson, 1990).

The peripheral route is more concerned with style and image, and the central route is more concerned with substance and ideas. Researchers generally find that the central route produces more enduring results, while the peripheral route produces more transient results (Maio & Haddock, 2007; Perloff, 2002). Whether the central or peripheral route is used, a number of specific elements are important in persuasion.

Elements of Persuasion

Figuring out which elements are important in persuading people was begun in the 1950s by the Yale Communication Program, which is still considered one of the best models. This communication program identified a number of important elements in persuasion, including the source, message, and audience (Jacks & Cameron, 2003; Petty et al., 1997).

Source. One element in persuading someone to adopt your point of view involves the *source of the message.* We are more likely to believe sources who have a sense of authority, appear honest and trustworthy, have expertise and credibility, and are attractive and likable (Priester & Petty, 1995). For example, researchers found that good-looking TV fundraisers generated nearly twice as many donations as did less attractive fundraisers (Cialdini, 2001). The source element explains why national and cable TV newscasters and anchorpersons are usually physically attractive, likable, and believable.

Message. Another element of persuasion involves the *content of the message.* If the persuader is using the *central route,* the messages will contain convincing and understandable facts. If the facts are complicated, a written message is better than a spoken one (Chaiken & Eagly, 1976).

If the persuader is using the *peripheral route,* the messages should be designed to arouse emotion, sentiment, and loyalty. Television infomercials use the peripheral approach by having an attractive and likable demonstrator show how you will look or feel better by buying and using a particular product. However, using fearful messages to persuade people, such as showing blackened lungs to get smokers to quit, may not be effective because arousing fear may interfere with and distract people from hearing and taking precautionary measures to stop unhealthy practices (Ruiter et al., 2001).

One- versus two-sided messages. Some messages are better presented as *one-sided;* that is, you present only the message that you want accepted. Other messages are better presented as *two-sided;* that is, you include both the message and arguments against any potential disagreements (Jacks & Cameron, 2003). Thus, a persuader will select the best route (central or peripheral) and also the kind of message (one- or two-sided) (Jacks & Devine, 2000).

> Why is "The Daily Show" newscaster Jon Stewart worth millions?

Audience. Another element of being an effective persuader involves knowing the *characteristics of the audience.* For example, audiences who are interested in facts are best persuaded using the central route, while audiences interested in personal traits are best persuaded using the peripheral route. If the audience is leaning toward the persuader, a one-sided message is best; if an audience is leaning away from the persuader, a two-sided message is best.

Thus, persuasion is a complicated process that involves the source's traits, using the central or peripheral route, and judging the audience's characteristics. Good persuaders may combine central and peripheral routes to win over the audience to their viewpoints (Cialdini, 2003).

Besides the above components, persuasion also involves social forces, which we'll discuss next.

E. Social & Group Influences

Why did the seniors haze the juniors?

At the beginning of this module, we discussed a hazing incident (right photo) in which senior girls beat, slapped, and kicked junior girls, hit them with buckets, and smeared them with blood, fish guts, mud, and feces. Five of the junior girls ended up in the hospital, some requiring stitches. Especially troubling was that these students, who came from a well-to-do Chicago suburb, attended a very good high school, and went on to attend college, would engage in such ugly and violent hazing behaviors (L. Black & Flynn, 2003).

Hazing may be part of a group's initiation ritual during which individuals are subjected to a variety of behaviors that range from humiliating and unpleasant to potentially dangerous both physically and psychologically.

In the United States, about 48% of high school and college students involved in a group activity (clubs, sports) report being hazed, and nearly everyone who gets hazed is humiliated (Lipkins, 2006). When students were asked why they agreed to be hazed, many answered they did so because it made them feel part of the group (Hoover & Pollard, 2000). "Going along" with the group is an example of conformity (J. M. Levine & Kerr, 2007).

Conformity refers to any behavior you perform because of group pressure, even though that pressure might not involve direct requests.

Hazing has changed to include potentially dangerous behaviors.

Normally, most students (and most of us) would never conform or agree to be publicly humiliated. Yet, reacting to strong group pressures, 48% of high school and college students who participate in groups activities conform and agree to be hazed, which means humiliation and possible injury.

There are many examples of conforming, such as wearing clothes that are in style, adopting the "in" slang phrases, and buying the currently popular products. A recent example of conformity in the United States began in the late 1990s, when it became popular to carry your own bottle of water. This practice has grown in popularity, fueled by the idea that bottled water was pure but also that it was healthy and perhaps necessary to drink at least "8 glasses of water a day." When a researcher looked into the evidence behind "8 glasses a day" (about half a gallon), he discovered that this idea was based on opinion, not any scientific evidence. The researcher concluded that it's safe for healthy people to drink considerably less, since we obtain fluids from a variety of foods and beverages (G. Reynolds, 2006). The water bottle phenomenon is a modern example of conformity and, as one researcher put it, perhaps a new kind of adult security blanket (Valtin, 2002).

We'll discuss group pressures and why people conform and obey, beginning with a classic experiment in social psychology.

ASCH'S EXPERIMENT

A classic experiment is one that causes us to change the way we think about something—in this case, how social pressures can influence conformity (Blakeslee, 2005; Stasser & Dietz-Uhler, 2003). Solomon Asch's (1958) classic experiment showed very clearly how an individual can be pressured to conform to a group's standards. As we describe Asch's experiment, imagine that you are a subject and guess how you might have behaved.

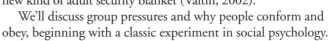

Procedure	*Results*

You are seated at a round table with five others and have been told that you are taking part in a visual perception experiment. Your group is shown a straight line and then is instructed to look at three more lines of different lengths and pick out the line equal in length to the original one. The three choices are different enough that it is not hard to pick out the correct one. Each person at the round table identifies his or her choice out loud, with you answering next to last. When you are ready to answer, you will have heard four others state their opinions. What you do not know is that these four other people are the experimenter's accomplices. On certain trials, they will answer correctly, making you feel your choice is right. On other trials, they will deliberately answer incorrectly, much to your surprise. In these cases you will have heard four identical incorrect answers before it is your turn to answer. You will almost certainly feel some group pressure to conform to the others' opinion. Will you give in?

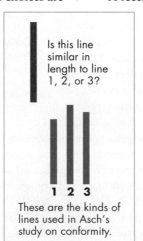

Is this line similar in length to line 1, 2, or 3?

1 2 3

These are the kinds of lines used in Asch's study on conformity.

Out of 50 subjects in Asch's experiment, 75% conformed on some of the trials, but no one conformed on all the trials; 25% never conformed. These data indicate that the desire to have your attitudes and behaviors match those of others in a group can be a powerful force.

A recent study used fMRI brain scans (p. 70) to record brain activity during an Asch-type research design to examine whether social pressure changes people's perceptions or people who give in to the group do so knowing their answers are wrong (Berns, 2005). Results showed that when people went along with the group on wrong answers, activity in the brain area associated with spatial awareness and perception increased. But, when people resisted group pressure and gave a correct answer, activity in the brain area associated with strong emotions increased. These results suggest that information provided by others may actually change what we see and that going against the group can be a very unpleasant experience.

Asch's study is considered a classic because it was the first to clearly show that group pressures can influence conformity. However, we may conform publicly but disagree privately, and this is an example of compliance.

Compliance

Were the subjects just pretending?

One interpretation of Asch's data is that subjects were not really changing their beliefs but rather just pretending to go along with the group. For example, when subjects in Asch's experiment privately recorded their answers, conforming drastically declined. This decline indicated that subjects were conforming but not really changing their beliefs, which is one kind of compliance.

Compliance is a kind of conformity in which we give in to social pressure in our public responses but do not change our private beliefs.

For example, you may conform to your instructor's suggestions on rewriting a paper although you do not agree with the suggestions. In this case, you would be complying with someone in authority.

One particular technique of compliance is used by salespeople, who know that if they get the customer to comply with a small request (get a foot in the door), the customer is more likely to comply with a later request to buy the product (Cialdini & Goldstein, 2004).

The *foot-in-the-door technique* refers to the technique of starting with a little request to gain eventual compliance with a later request.

A common example of the foot-in-the-door technique is telemarketers who first get you to answer a simple question such as "How are you today?" so that you'll stay on the phone and answer their other questions. The foot-in-the-door technique is one successful way to obtain compliance (Rodafinos et al., 2005).

Salespeople use the foot-in-the-door technique.

If you are officially or formally asked to comply with a request, such as "Take a test on Friday," your compliance is called obedience.

Obedience

Do you run red lights?

When it comes to signs, laws, rules, and regulations, such as speed limits, traffic lights, smoking restrictions, parental requests, instructors' assignments, and doctors' orders, people differ in what they choose to obey.

Obedience refers to performing some behavior in response to an order given by someone in a position of power or authority.

A serious problem in states across the country is drivers who run red lights and cause accidents. To increase obedience, cameras automatically take photos of drivers who run red lights, and these drivers are mailed tickets with expensive fines ($270 in California). Here's a case of using punishment to decrease accidents by increasing obedience (up to 96% reduction in running red lights) (Copeland, 2007).

Most of us obey orders, rules, and regulations that are for the general good. But what if the orders or rules are cruel or immoral?

MILGRAM'S EXPERIMENT

Stanley Milgram's (1963) experiment on obedience is a classic experiment in social psychology because it was the first to study whether people would obey commands that were clearly inhumane and immoral (A. Miller, 2005). As we describe this famous experiment, imagine being the "teacher" and consider whether you would have obeyed the experimenter's commands.

The Setup

Imagine that you have volunteered for a study on the effects of punishment on learning. After arriving in the laboratory at Yale University, you are selected to be the "teacher" and another volunteer is to be the "learner." What you don't know is that the *learner* is actually an accomplice of the experimenter. As the *teacher,* you watch the learner being strapped into a chair and having electrodes placed on his wrists. The electrodes are attached to a shock generator in the next room. You and the researcher then leave the learner's room, close the door, and go into an adjoining room.

The researcher gives you a list of questions to ask the learner over an intercom, and the learner is to signal his answer on a panel of lights in front of you. For each wrong answer, you, the teacher, are to *shock the learner* and to increase the intensity of the shock by 15 volts for each succeeding wrong answer. In front of you is the shock machine, with 30 separate switches that indicate increasing intensities. The first switch is marked "15 volts. Slight shock," and the last switch is marked "XXX 450 volts. Danger: Severe shock." You begin to ask the learner questions, and as he misses them, you administer stronger and stronger shocks.

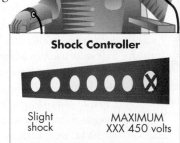

Whenever you make a mistake, you'll receive an electric shock.

Shock Controller

Slight shock   MAXIMUM XXX 450 volts

The Conflict

As the teacher, you give the learner shocks that increase in intensity up to 300 volts, when the learner pounds on the wall. You continue and after the next miss, you give the learner a 315-volt shock, after which the learner pounds on the wall and stops answering any more questions. Although you plead with the researcher to stop the experiment, the researcher explains that, as the teacher, you are to continue asking questions and shocking the learner for incorrect answers. Even though the learner has pounded on the wall and stopped answering questions after a 315-volt shock, would you continue the procedure until you deliver the **XXX 450 volts**?

What you, the teacher, didn't know is that the learner is part of the experiment and acts like being shocked but never received a single one. The teacher was misled into believing that he or she was really shocking the learner. The question was whether a teacher would continue and deliver the maximum shock.

E. Social & Group Influences

How many obeyed?

The scary question was how many "teachers" (subjects) would deliver the maximum intensity shock to the "learner."

0.12% When psychiatrists were asked to predict how many subjects would deliver the full range of shocks, including the last 450 volts, they estimated that only 0.12% of the subjects would do so.

2% When members of the general public were asked the same question, they predicted that only 2% of the subjects would deliver the maximum 450 volts.

65% To the surprise and dismay of many, including Milgram, 65% of the subjects (no difference between males and females) delivered the full range of shocks, including the final XXX 450 volts.

When Stanley Milgram conducted these studies on obedience in the early 1960s, they demonstrated that people will obey inhumane orders simply because they are told to do so. This kind of unthinking obedience to immoral commands was something that psychiatrists, members of the general population, and Milgram had not predicted. Milgram (1974) repeated variations of this experiment many times and obtained similar results. Additionally, Milgram's experiment was repeated in various parts of the world with similar results (T. Blass, 2000).

The results of these experiments helped answer a question people had asked since World War II: Why had Germans obeyed Hitler's commands? And why do students follow group leaders and engage in hazing, with sometimes dangerous consequences? According to Milgram's experiments, social situations that involve power and authority greatly increase obedience to the point that a large percentage of people will obey orders even if they are clearly unreasonable and inhumane.

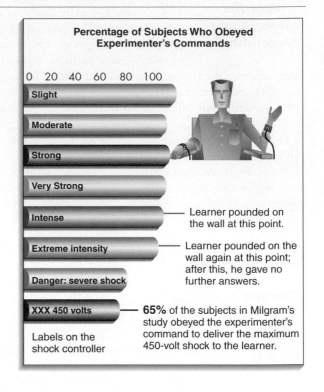

Percentage of Subjects Who Obeyed Experimenter's Commands

0 20 40 60 80 100

- Slight
- Moderate
- Strong
- Very Strong
- Intense —— Learner pounded on the wall at this point.
- Extreme intensity —— Learner pounded on the wall again at this point; after this, he gave no further answers.
- Danger: severe shock
- XXX 450 volts —— **65%** of the subjects in Milgram's study obeyed the experimenter's command to deliver the maximum 450-volt shock to the learner.

Labels on the shock controller

Why Do People Obey?

Psychologists have suggested several reasons about 65% of the subjects in Milgram's experiment agreed to deliver the maximum shock to learners. Perhaps the major reason is that people have learned to follow the orders of **authority figures,** whether they are religious leaders, army commanders, doctors, scientists, or parents. However, people are more likely to obey authority figures when they are present. In one of his follow-up studies, Milgram (1974) found that when subjects received their instructions over the telephone, they were more likely to defy authority than when they received their instructions in person. This also explains why patients don't follow doctors' orders once they leave their offices.

People also obey because they have **learned to follow orders** in their daily lives, whether in traffic, on the job, or in personal interactions. However, people are more likely to obey if an authority figure is present (police officer, boss, or parent). What Milgram's study showed was that blind obedience to unreasonable authority or inhumane orders is more likely than we think.

> Why do some show blind obedience to immoral orders?

Were Milgram's Experiments Ethical?

Although the Milgram experiments provided important information about obedience, the study could not be conducted under today's research guidelines. As we discussed (p. 40), all experiments today, especially those with the potential for causing psychological or physical harm, are carefully screened by research committees, a practice that did not exist at the time of Milgram's research. When there is a possibility of an experiment causing **psychological harm,** the researchers must propose ways to eliminate or counteract the potential harmful effects. This is usually done by thoroughly debriefing the subjects.

Debriefing occurs after an experimental procedure and involves explaining the purpose and method of the experiment, asking the subjects their feelings about being in the experiment, and helping the subjects deal with possible doubts or guilt arising from their behaviors in the experiment.

Although Milgram's subjects were debriefed, critics doubted that the question of whether any psychological harm had been done to the subjects was resolved. Because the potential for psychological harm to the subjects was so great in Milgram's studies, any related research had to pass very strict ethical standards. Jerry Burger, a researcher at Santa Clara University, designed a study replicating as much of Milgram's study as possible while complying with current ethical standards (Burger, 2007a, 2007b). Subjects were an ethnically diverse group of 18 men and 22 women. The setup and conflict procedures were mostly the same as in Milgram's study except that, due to ethical standards, the maximum shock the subjects could administer was 150 volts, compared to the 450 volts used in Milgram's study. Results showed that 70% of subjects (equal percentages of men and women) pressed the button for the highest, most dangerous shock possible (150 volts). Thus, ordinary people, even in today's society, are capable of hurting others despite hearing the person begging them to stop, as long as they are ordered by an authority figure to do so.

Next, we'll turn to another interesting question: Why do people help?

Would you help an accident victim?

About 60 people had gathered around a serious car crash in a downtown area. They were talking about the accident and pointing at the victims, but no one was helping. One of the victims was a woman, obviously pregnant and unconscious. One person in the crowd, Ken Von, came forward and tried to save the woman with cardiopulmonary and mouth-to-mouth resuscitation that he had learned by watching television. He kept her alive until paramedics arrived (*San Diego Tribune*, September 9, 1983). Ken's quick action is an example of helping, or prosocial behavior.

Prosocial behavior, which is also called *helping*, is any behavior that benefits others or has positive social consequences.

In our society, professionals, such as paramedics, are trained and paid to provide help. However, in Ken's case, he was the only one of 60 onlookers who came forward to help the unconscious accident victim. Ken's helping may be described as altruistic, since he expected no external reward.

> I donated most of my life savings for student scholarships.

Altruism is one form of helping or doing something, often at a cost or risk, for reasons other than the expectation of a material or social reward.

Altruistic people often do things that touch our hearts. Consider 87-year-old Osceola McCarty (left photo), who handwashed clothes most of her life for grateful clients. When she finally retired at age 86, she donated most of her life savings, an amazing $150,000, to the University of Southern Mississippi to finance scholarships for the area's African American students. "I want them to have an education," said McCarty, who never married and has no children of her own. "I had to work hard all my life. They can have the chance that I didn't have" (Plummer & Ridenhour, 1995, p. 40). As these examples show, some people help in emergencies, and others help by donating time or money. What motivates people to help others?

Why People Help

Would you help?

Why did Osceola McCarty, who spent her life washing clothes, donate most of her hard-earned life savings to finance scholarships instead of using her savings to make her retirement more comfortable? Researchers suggest at least three different motivations—empathy, personal distress, and norms and values—to explain why people, like McCarty, are altruistic and help others without thought of rewards (Batson, 1998; Schroeder et al., 1995):

■ We may help because we feel *empathy*—that is, we identify with what the victim must be going through. Osceola McCarty may have donated her life savings for scholarships because she felt empathy for other African American students.

■ We may help because we feel *personal distress*—that is, we have feelings of fear, alarm, or disgust from seeing a victim in need. Osceola said that she didn't want other young African American people to have to go through the hard times that she had faced.

■ We may help because of our *norms* and *values*—that is, we may feel morally bound or socially responsible to help those in need.

Researchers have combined these three motivations along with several other ideas to construct two different theories of why people come out of a crowd and help perfect strangers. We can use these two theories to explain why Ken Von was the only person in a crowd of 60 spectators to help a pregnant woman who was seriously injured in a car accident.

DECISION-STAGE MODEL

Ken may have decided to help after going through five stages, which involved making five different decisions.

> Why did only one man from a crowd of 60 come forward to help a pregnant accident victim?

The *decision-stage model of helping* says that you go through five stages in deciding to help: (1) you notice the situation; (2) you interpret it as one in which help is needed; (3) you assume personal responsibility; (4) you choose a form of assistance; and (5) you carry out that assistance.

According to the decision-stage model, Ken helped because he went through all five stages. Most onlookers stopped at stage 3 and decided it was not their responsibility; so they did not help. This model explains that people may recognize a situation as an emergency (stages 1 and 2) yet fail to help because they do not take personal responsibility for the situation (Latané & Darley, 1970).

AROUSAL-COST-REWARD MODEL

Ken also may have helped the pregnant woman because he thought about the costs and rewards.

The *arousal-cost-reward model of helping* says that we make decisions to help by calculating the costs and rewards of helping.

For example, seeing an accident may cause you to be unpleasantly and emotionally *aroused*, which you wish to reduce. In deciding how to reduce these unpleasant feelings, you calculate the *costs* and *rewards* of helping. For example, those who decided not to help may have felt that the costs of helping, such as getting involved in a potentially dangerous situation, outweighed the rewards (Piliavin et al., 1982).

According to these two models, Ken experienced five stages (five decisions) and then decided to help, or Ken possibly considered the costs and rewards of reducing his unpleasant emotional feelings and then decided to help. Although the arousal-cost-reward model and the decision-stage model focus on different factors, they are not mutually exclusive.

Next, we'll explain how social forces influence people in groups.

E. Social & Group Influences

What happens in groups?

When you're with family, friends, or co-workers, you may or may not be aware of the numerous group influences that can greatly change how you think, feel, and behave.

Groups are collections of two or more people who interact, share some common idea, goal, or purpose, and influence how their members think and behave.

To illustrate the powerful influences of groups, we'll describe the case of Dennis Jay, who almost died in a drunken coma and later heard that his fraternity brothers had lied about the initiation that had almost killed him.

Group Cohesion and Norms

As a pledge at a fraternity initiation party, Dennis Jay and 19 others submitted to hazing: They were forced to drink from a "beer bong," a funnel into which beer was poured; the beer ran down a plastic hose placed in the mouth (left photo). The rule was that once you threw up, you could stop drinking from the beer bong. Because he did not throw up, Jay was given straight shots of whiskey until he fell on his face. By the time his frat brothers got Jay to the hospital, he was in a coma and barely breathing. His blood alcohol content was 0.48, and a level of 0.50 is usually fatal (legally drunk in many states is 0.08).

> My fraternity brothers lied about why I was in a coma.

At first, Jay refused to describe what happened because he wanted to be loyal to his fraternity. Then he heard that the fraternity brothers had lied and said that he had stumbled drunk into their frat house and that they had brought him to the emergency ward just to help out. The fraternity brothers' lies made Jay angry and he told the truth (Grogan et al., 1993). As discussed earlier, one reason individuals like Jay endure harmful and humiliating hazing rites is because they wish to become a member of a desired group.

Social psychologists would explain that the fraternity lied about what happened to Jay because of two powerful group influences: group cohesion and group norms.

Group cohesion **is group togetherness, which is determined by how much group members perceive that they share common attributes.**

One reason many groups have some form of initiation rites and rituals is to have all members share a common experience and thus increase group cohesion.

Group norms **are the formal or informal rules about how group members should behave.**

Group norms, written or unwritten, can exert powerful influences, both good and bad, on group members' behaviors (Hewstone et al., 2002). For example, because of powerful group norms to stick together to preserve their group, these fraternity members were willing to lie about what really happened to Jay.

Group Membership

In his hierarchy of human needs (see p. 333), humanistic psychologist Abraham Maslow identified *the need for love and belonging* as fundamental to human happiness (Maslow, 1970). One way to satisfy this social need is by joining a group, which helps individuals feel a sense of belonging, friendship, and support. The need for belonging carries into adulthood as individuals join various community and business organizations. According to Maslow's theory, the social need to belong points to a *motivational reason* for joining groups. At about the same time Maslow published his work on the hierarchy of motivation, Leon Festinger (1954) offered another reason for joining groups, based on the social comparison theory.

Social comparison theory **says that we are driven to compare ourselves to others who are similar to us, so that we can measure the correctness of our attitudes and beliefs. According to Festinger, this drive to compare ourselves motivates us to join groups.**

According to Festinger's theory, the drive to compare and judge our attitudes and beliefs against those of others who are similar to us points to a *cognitive reason* for joining groups.

An additional reason for forming groups is that we can accomplish things in groups that we simply cannot do alone. For example, students form study groups because they want academic help, social support, and motivation. However, there are two kinds of study groups, each with different goals: task-oriented and socially oriented groups (Burn, 2004).

In a *task-oriented group,* **members have specific duties to complete.**

In a *socially oriented group,* **the members are primarily concerned about fostering and maintaining social relationships among the members of the group.**

For example, a task-oriented group helps members achieve certain academic, business, political, or career goals, while a socially oriented group primarily provides a source of friends, fun activities, and social support.

Group membership **can have a powerful influence on many social interactions, such as deciding with whom to**

A group of young Mormons in training

socialize, whom to discriminate against, which principles to follow, and whom to battle, psychologically and physically (Simon & Sturmer, 2003). An example of how group membership influences members' views and behaviors occurs during national elections, when Republicans and Democrats wage hard-fought political and personal battles for money, votes, and power.

Next, we'll discuss how groups and crowds can influence our behaviors.

How do you behave in a crowd?

You may not notice, but being in a crowd can cause you to think and behave differently than when you're alone. A *crowd,* which is a large group of persons who are usually strangers, can facilitate or inhibit certain behaviors. For example, we'll discuss how being in a crowd can increase or decrease personal performance, encourage individuals to engage in antisocial behaviors, such as riots, or cause individuals to refuse to help to someone in need.

Facilitation and Inhibition

Performing before a large crowd can facilitate or inhibit behaviors.

If a runner has a history of successful competition, he may turn in a better performance in front of a large crowd as a result of social facilitation.

Social facilitation is an increase in performance in the presence of a crowd.

In contrast, if a runner has a spotty history in competition, he may turn in a worse performance in front of a large crowd because of social inhibition.

Social inhibition is a decrease in performance in the presence of a crowd.

Whether we show facilitation or inhibition depends partly on our previous experience. Generally, the presence of others will facilitate well-learned, simple, or reflexive responses but will inhibit new, unusual, or complex responses. An example of social facilitation occurs during championship games when a player is awarded the title of "most valuable player." An example of social inhibition also occurs during championship games when a star player, who is expected to do great, instead feels anxiety about performing and plays poorly or "chokes" (Baumeister, 1995). Thus, the presence of a crowd can either facilitate or inhibit behaviors, depending on the situation (Burn, 2004).

Deindividuation in Crowds

During the Los Angeles riots in the early 1990s, people were arrested for looting, setting fires, and beating others. Individuals in a crowd are more likely to commit such antisocial acts because being in a crowd conceals the person's identity, a process called deindividuation.

Deindividuation refers to the increased tendency for subjects to behave irrationally or perform antisocial behaviors when there is less chance of being personally identified.

Looting is more likely to occur in a crowd because of deindividuation.

Researchers believe deindividuation occurs because being in a crowd gives individuals anonymity and reduces guilt and self-awareness, so that people are less controlled by internal standards and more willing to engage in deviant or antisocial roles (Silke, 2003; Zimbardo, 1970). Support for this explanation of deindividuation comes from competitive sporting events in which spectators turned into violent individuals (Postmes & Spears, 1998).

Another situation where deindividuation occurs and people feel anonymous is on the Internet. For instance, teens are willing to disclose sexual information when their anonymity is ensured on the Internet (Chiou, 2006).

The Bystander Effect

As a person lies unconscious on a city sidewalk, dozens or hundreds of people may walk by without helping. There are several reasons no one stops to help, including fear of the person's reactions, inexperience with providing help, and the bystander effect.

The *bystander effect* says that an individual may feel inhibited from taking some action because of the presence of others.

Data from over 50 studies indicate that 75% of people offer assistance when alone, but fewer than 53% do so when in a group (Latané & Nida, 1981). There are two explanations for the bystander effect.

The *informational influence theory* says that we use the reactions of others to judge the seriousness of the situation.

If other bystanders are taking no action, we conclude that no emergency exists and we do nothing to offer help or aid (Burn, 2004).

The *diffusion of responsibility theory* says that, in the presence of others, individuals feel less personal responsibility and are less likely to take action in a situation where help is required (Latané, 1981).

Recent survey results report that 77% of Americans want to help victims of disasters such as hurricanes and earthquakes, but when it comes to volunteering, many will not because they believe the whole country is already helping (Marchetti & Bunte, 2006). Thus, an individual may feel less responsibility to offer help or aid.

The presence of others also influences how we make decisions, which we'll examine next.

Just being in the presence of other strangers can inhibit an individual from helping someone in need.

E. Social & Group Influences

Does being in a group affect thinking?

All of us have been in groups—families, fraternities, sororities, various social or business clubs. What you may not realize is that being in a group creates social pressures that influence how you think and make decisions. We'll discuss two interesting factors in making decisions: group polarization and groupthink.

Group Polarization

Imagine that a young lawyer is trying to decide between two job offers. The first offer is from a large, well-established firm that promises more security, financial opportunities, and prestige. However, it has a poor record as an equal opportunity employer of women and currently has no women partners. The second offer is from a small, recently established firm that can promise little security or prestige. However, this firm is doing well and has an excellent record in promoting women as partners. Which offer should the lawyer accept? Using dilemmas such as this, researchers compared the recommendations from individuals in a group with those made by the group after it had engaged in discussion (Gigone & Hastie, 1997; Pruitt, 1971). Group discussions change individuals' judgments, such as when a group urges a more risky recommendation than do individuals. This phenomenon became known as the *risky shift.*

Researchers later discovered that the direction of a group's risky shift depends on how conservative or liberal the group was to begin with. If a group's members are initially more conservative, group discussion will shift its decision to an even more conservative one. If a group's members are initially more liberal, group discussion will shift its decision to an even more liberal one.

The group's shift to a more extreme position is called polarization (Fiedler, 2007).

Group polarization **is a phenomenon in which group discussion reinforces the majority's point of view and shifts that view to a more extreme position.**

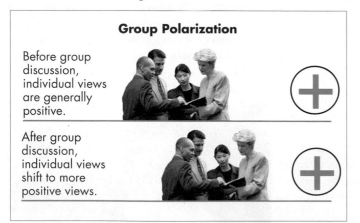

Group Polarization

Before group discussion, individual views are generally positive.

After group discussion, individual views shift to more positive views.

Whether this group polarization (figure above) is in a liberal or conservative direction depends on the initial leanings of the group's members. Researchers also found that the more the group repeated each other's arguments, the more polarized the group became (Burn, 2004). Thus, repetition of the same arguments resulted in stronger formation of attitudes and more group polarization.

Groupthink

In the early 1960s, President John F. Kennedy took the world to the brink of nuclear war when he ordered the invasion of Cuba. This invasion, which occurred at the Bay of Pigs, was a terrible decision and a well-remembered failure. Researchers have analyzed group decision-making processes involved in bad decisions, such as the Bay of Pigs, the escalation of war in Vietnam, the Watergate cover-up, and the *Challenger* disaster, as well as flawed group decisions in business and other organizations. One reason that groups made bad decisions in the above examples is a phenomenon called groupthink (Janis, 1989; Vallacher & Nowak, 2007).

Groupthink **refers to a group making bad decisions because the group is more concerned about reaching agreement and sticking together than gathering the relevant information and considering all the alternatives (right figure).**

Groupthink

What's most important is that we stick together.

Groupthink. According to psychologist Irving Janis (1989), groupthink has a number of clearly defined characteristics: Discussions are limited, few alternatives are presented, and there is increased pressure to conform. For example, the group usually has a member that Janis calls a ***mindguard,*** whose job is to discourage ideas that might be a threat to the group's unity. In addition, groupthink results in viewing the world in very simple terms: There is the *ingroup,* which includes only the immediate members of the group, versus the *outgroup,* which includes everyone who is not a part of the group. When a group adopts the ingroup–outgroup attitude and mentality, the result is that it strengthens groupthink by emphasizing the protection of the group's members over making the best decisions.

Avoiding groupthink. One authority on groupthink recommends using a method, called vigilant decision making, that helps a group avoid falling into groupthink and thus leads to better decisions (Janis, 1989). Major elements of ***vigilant decision making*** include the following: doing a thorough, open, and unbiased information search; evaluating as many alternative ideas as possible; and having an impartial leader who allows the members to freely and openly express differing opinions without being criticized or being considered a threat to the group. Researchers found that the vigilant decision-making method does result in better and more successful group decisions, although it is criticized for being very time-consuming (Burn, 2004).

After the Concept Review, we'll discuss a potentially very disruptive social behavior—aggression.

✔ Concept Review

1. A broad field that studies how our thoughts, feelings, perceptions, and behaviors are influenced by interactions with others is called (a)_____. A major branch of this field that studies how people perceive, store, and retrieve information about social interactions is called (b)_____.

2. Making judgments about the traits of others through social interactions and gaining knowledge from our social perceptions are called _____.

3. Widely held beliefs that people have certain traits because they belong to a particular group are known as (a)_____. An unfair, biased, or intolerant attitude toward another group of people is called (b)_____. Specific unfair behaviors exhibited toward members of a group are known as (c)_____.

4. Cognitive structures that represent an organized collection of knowledge about people, events, and concepts are called _____. They influence what we perceive and remember and how we behave.

5. The process by which we look for causes to explain a person's behavior is known as (a)_____. If we attribute behavior to the internal characteristics of a person, we are attributing the behavior to the person's (b)_____. If we attribute behavior to the external circumstances or context of that behavior, we are attributing the behavior to the (c)_____.

6. If we attribute the cause of a behavior to a person's disposition and overlook the demands of the environment or situation, we are committing the (a)_____ error. If we attribute our own behavior to situational factors but the behaviors of others to their disposition, we are committing the (b)_____ error. If we attribute success to our disposition and failure to the situation, we are using the (c)_____ bias.

7. Beliefs or opinions that include a positive or negative evaluation of some target (object, person, or event) and that predispose us to act in a certain way toward the target are called _____.

8. There are two different theories about why we change our attitudes. One theory says that experiencing cognitive inconsistencies produces psychological tension that we try to reduce by making our beliefs more consistent. This is called (a)_____ theory. If we take a public position that is counter to our private attitude, we are engaging in (b)_____ behavior.

9. Another theory of attitude change says that we first observe our own behaviors, which in turn causes us to change our attitudes. This is called _____ theory.

10. If a politician tries to get votes by presenting information with strong arguments, analyses, facts, and logic, he or she is using the (a)_____ route of persuasion. If a politician seeks votes by emphasizing emotional appeals, focusing on personal accomplishments, and generating positive feelings, he or she is using the (b)_____ route of persuasion.

11. Persuasion involves at least three elements: We are likely to believe a (a)_____ who appears honest and trustworthy; if we disagree with the message, it is better if the persuader presents a (b)_____ message; if the (c)_____ is less interested in issues, the peripheral route is more effective.

12. Any behavior we perform because of social influences or group pressure, even if that pressure involves no direct requests, is called (a)_____. A kind of conformity in which we give in to social pressure in our public responses but do not change our private beliefs is called (b)_____. Any behavior performed in response to an order given by someone in a position of authority is called (c)_____.

13. An increase in performance in the presence of a crowd is called social (a)_____; a decrease in performance in the presence of a crowd is called social (b)_____. An increased tendency for individuals to behave irrationally or perform antisocial behaviors if there is less chance of being personally identified is called (c)_____. Being socially inhibited to take some action, such as helping, because of the presence of others is called the (d)_____ effect.

14. A collection of two or more people who interact and share some common attribute or attributes is called a (a)_____. Togetherness, which is determined by how much group members perceive that they share common attributes, is called group (b)_____.

15. The phenomenon by which group discussion reinforces the majority's point of view and shifts that view to a more extreme position is called group (a)_____. If a group makes bad decisions because it is more concerned about reaching an agreement and sticking together than gathering the relevant information and considering all the alternatives, it is referred to as (b)_____.

Answers: 1. (a) social psychology, (b) social cognition; 2. person perception; 3. (a) stereotypes, (b) prejudice, (c) discrimination; 4. schemas; 5. (a) attribution, (b) disposition, (c) situation; 6. (a) fundamental attribution, (b) actor-observer, (c) self-serving; 7. attitudes; 8. (a) cognitive dissonance, (b) counterattitudinal; 9. self-perception; 10. (a) central, (b) peripheral; 11. (a) source, (b) two-sided, (c) audience; 12. (a) conformity, (b) compliance, (c) obedience; 13. (a) facilitation, (b) inhibition, (c) deindividuation, (d) bystander; 14. (a) group, (b) cohesion; 15. (a) polarization, (b) groupthink

Shock Controller

Slight shock — MAXIMUM XXX 450 volts

F. Aggression

PowerStudy 4.0™

Module 3
E. Transmitters
Module 4
A. Genes & Evolution

Genes and Environment

Is aggression in a person's genes?

Drive-by shootings, gang fights and killings, spouse and child abuse, school shootings, hate crimes, revenge-shooting by angry workers, bullying, road rage, and extreme forms of hazing are all examples of aggression.

Aggression **is any behavior directed toward another that is intended to cause harm.**

Animal aggression is largely regulated by genetic factors.

There is no single reason someone turns into a child bully or an aggressive adult but rather three major components: genetic and environmental influences, social cognitive and personality traits, and situational cues (Baron & Richardson, 2004; B. Bower, 2006a; Kalat & Shiota, 2007). We'll begin with genetic or hereditary influences.

Genetic influences in animals. You can clearly see that genetic influences can regulate aggression by watching the behavior of animals. Ethologists, who study animal behavior in natural settings, have identified numerous social signals that animals have evolved to regulate aggression. For example, the photo below shows a dominant wolf standing above a submissive wolf. The submissive wolf avoids being attacked by lying down and rolling over to expose its vulnerable belly. Many of the dominant and submissive gestures observed in animals are largely programmed by genetic factors and help animals avoid potentially damaging aggressive attacks and improve their chances of survival. Compared with animals, reasons for aggressive acts in humans are much more complicated.

Animals use built-in social signals to threaten or to avoid aggression.

Genetic influences in humans. We all begin life with a different set of genes (pp. 68, 378) that contain chemical instructions that regulate the manufacture and assembly of the many thousands of parts that make up our body and brain. In earlier modules, we discussed how genetic factors contribute 30–70% to the development of many human behaviors, such as personality traits, temperament, intelligence, emotions, motivation, and various mental health problems (Hamer, 2002). Similarly, genetic factors also play an important role in the development of human aggression.

Researchers studied levels of aggression in twins and adopted children to gauge how much genetic factors influence human aggression. If genetic factors influence aggression in humans, then identical twins, who share 100% of their genes, should be more alike in committing aggressive behaviors than fraternal twins, who share only 50% of their genes. Also, if genetic factors influence human aggression, then children from aggressive biological parents should be more aggressive, even if adopted by nonaggressive parents. Researchers analyzed over 50 twin and adoption studies and found that genetic factors accounted for about 34% of the total

factors that were responsible for developing aggressive/antisocial behaviors (Rhee & Waldman, 2002). These studies show that genetic influences may partly predispose a person to develop aggressive behaviors, but whether this actually occurs depends upon the interaction with potentially powerful good or bad environmental influences.

Human aggression is regulated by the interaction of three major components.

Genes interact with good/bad environments. The evidence for the interaction of genetic and environmental factors in aggressive behavior is abundant. Researchers found that a specific gene variation influences brain development to make someone more prone to engage in impulsive violence, but only when the gene variation is combined with environmental stress. Other researchers reported that this same gene variation results in neurotransmitter imbalances, unusually small brain structures associated with emotions, and minimal activity in the prefrontal lobe, which result in poor impulse control and problems regulating emotions (Meyer-Lindenberg, 2006; Mullin & Hinshaw, 2007).

Researchers have also studied the interaction of genetic and environmental factors by following boys who had inherited potentially "bad genes" from their criminally inclined biological parents. Some of these boys were adopted by noncriminal parents and raised in good environments, while others were raised in "bad environments" by criminally inclined adoptive parents. Results showed the combination of "bad genes" interacting with "bad environments" resulted in a large percentage of boys going on to commit criminal acts. However, results also showed that good environments can, to a large extent, compensate for inheriting "bad genes" and can override the development of aggressive or antisocial behaviors (A. Raine, 2002).

Genes interact with child abuse. A tragic and unexplained question is why some children who suffer physical, sexual, or emotional abuse go on to become violent adults, while others do not. Researchers studied a group of severely abused boys who were also found to have a gene that creates abnormal levels of neurotransmitters in the brain. Boys who had the combination of being abused and having this particular gene were twice as likely to have been diagnosed with conduct disorder as a child and three times more likely to have been convicted of a violent crime by age 26. However, if boys who had this particular gene were not abused as children, they weren't any more likely to be antisocial or violent. Researchers concluded that this particular gene did not lead to developing antisocial behaviors unless an individual had also experienced a particular environmental influence—being abused as a child.

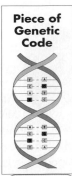

Piece of Genetic Code

Genes regulate chemicals in the brain.

The above studies show how genes and environmental factors combine, interact, and influence each other to increase or decrease antisocial or aggressive behaviors (B. Bower, 2006a; Stokstad, 2002).

Next, we'll examine specific environmental factors and situations that are involved in aggression.

Social Cognitive and Personality Factors

We have discussed how genetic factors may predispose a person to be aggressive, but whether this actually occurs depends upon the interaction with various environmental factors, such as one's learning experiences and personality traits. One theory that explains how people learn to be aggressive is Bandura's (2001a) social cognitive theory.

Social cognitive theory says that much of human behavior, including aggressive behavior, may be learned through watching, imitating, and modeling and does not require the observer to perform any observable behavior or receive any observable reward.

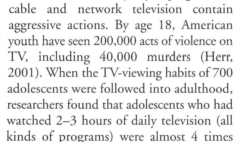

I like to bully kids and make them do things.

Support for social cognitive theory comes from laboratory and naturalistic studies. A classic laboratory study by Bandura (1965) found that children who observed a model's aggressive behaviors performed similar aggressive behaviors (p. 224). Children who were exposed to aggressive models, such as seeing parents use physical punishment, were reported to show increased aggression with their peers, parents, and dating partners (C. A. Anderson & Huesmann, 2003). These studies show that individuals predisposed to be aggressive are more likely to become so after observing aggressive role models in their families, on television, or in video games (Eron, 1990).

Television/video games. Children have ample opportunity to see, model, and imitate aggressive adults, since the majority of programs on

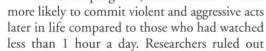

TV watching was linked to later aggressive acts.

cable and network television contain aggressive actions. By age 18, American youth have seen 200,000 acts of violence on TV, including 40,000 murders (Herr, 2001). When the TV-viewing habits of 700 adolescents were followed into adulthood, researchers found that adolescents who had watched 2–3 hours of daily television (all kinds of programs) were almost 4 times more likely to commit violent and aggressive acts later in life compared to those who had watched less than 1 hour a day. Researchers ruled out neglect, poverty, and bad neighborhoods and concluded that frequent TV viewing correlated with committing violent acts later in life (J. G. Johnson et al., 2002). However, it's also possible that aggressive-prone adolescents prefer to watch TV rather than engage in other activities.

Model of aggression. One model of how children develop aggressive behaviors points to an interaction among *genetic/environmental factors,* which can predispose individuals to develop an irritable or angry temperament and become more or less aggressive depending upon the environment; *social cognitive factors*, which involve imitating and modeling the aggressive behaviors observed on television and in video games; and *personality factors*, such as being impulsive, having little empathy, and wanting to dominate others. According to this model, the interaction of these three factors increases the chances of a child developing into an aggressive adolescent and an aggressive adult (C. A. Anderson & Bushman, 2002; Tisak et al., 2006).

There are also situational factors that can increase or trigger aggressive behaviors.

Situational Cues

A number of situational cues have been linked to increased aggression, including hot weather (above 90°F), the presence of or easy access to guns, and exposure to violent TV shows and video games (C. A. Anderson & Bushman, 2002). In recent years, another situational cue made the news when more and more drivers became so frustrated and angry by other drivers' annoying driving habits that they responded by aggressively pursuing, ramming, fighting, and even shooting another driver (Galovski et al., 2006). The press labeled this aggressive action by frustrated drivers *road rage,* which shows how frustration can trigger aggression.

The *frustration-aggression hypothesis* says that when our goals are blocked, we become frustrated and respond with anger and aggression.

However, researchers soon discovered that although frustration may lead to aggression, the link between the two is not absolute. Leonard Berkowitz (1989) reviewed the research on the frustration-aggression hypothesis and concluded the following:

- Frustration doesn't always lead to aggression.
- Social rules may inhibit aggression.
- Frustration may result in behaviors other than aggression.
- Cognitive factors can override aggression.

Thus, Berkowitz (1993) modified the original hypothesis.

The *modified frustration-aggression hypothesis* says that although frustration may lead to aggression, a number of situational and cognitive factors may override the aggressive response.

Although our daily lives are often filled with frustrations, we usually find ways to control our frustrations and don't express them in anger, violence, or

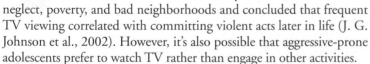

A citizen slyly shows her frustrated feelings toward police.

road rage. However, a child is more likely to react to frustration with violence if he or she has observed and imitated the aggressive behaviors of adults (Osofsky, 1995). Similarly, adults with a personality trait to be impulsive or a genetic tendency to be aggressive are more likely to react to frustration with aggression (Lindsay & Anderson, 2000).

Summary. We have discussed a number of recent studies on aggression that show how genetic influences interact with environmental factors and how neurotransmitters' levels in the brain affect aggressive behavior (B. Bower, 2006; R. Raine, 2002). Earlier, we also discussed how the decision-making area of the brain (prefrontal cortex—p. 411) doesn't develop until early adulthood, which explains why adolescents are likely to engage in impulsive and dangerous actions. All these studies point to the importance of biological influences and emphasize that any explanation of human aggression must consider the interaction among three major factors—genes and environment, social cognitive learning and personality traits, and situational cues.

One terrifying and degrading form of aggression is sexual aggression, which we'll examine next.

F. Aggression

Why do men rape? According to a recent National Crime Victimization Survey of U.S. citizens aged 12 and older, there were 191,670 reported rapes and sexual assaults in 2005 (Catalano, 2006). Because only about one-third of rape victims report their attacks to the police, the total number of sexual assaults may be closer to 600,000 annually (AAUW, 2007a). About 51% of rape victims were under 18 years old, and of those, 85% were raped by either a relative or an acquaintance.

National surveys of female college students report that about 20–27% of college women experience either rape or attempted rape, and about 42% experience forced sexual encounters, some of which lead to nonconsensual sexual intercourse (AAUW, 2007a; Flores, 1999).

Most researchers agree that the primary motivation for

In the United States, a woman is raped about every 3 minutes.

rape is not sexual but rather a combination of aggression, power, and control (Polaschek et al., 1997). For example, in interviews with ten convicted rapists, nine said that sex was of secondary importance and that either anger or the need to dominate was the most important factor to them (S. Levine & Koenig, 1980).

Another form of aggression is sexual harassment. Researchers found that sexual harassment is widespread and was reported by 40–70% of women and 10–20% of men in occupational settings and by 62% of female and 61% of male college students. Although sexual harassment produces psychological and physical effects in most of the victims, less than 10% of victims file formal complaints (AAUW, 2007a, 2007b; ACA Group, 2004).

Here, we'll focus on rape and sexual assault and begin by describing the common types of rapists.

Characteristics and Kinds of Rapists

Psychologists have identified several developmental factors that are associated with men who rape: They often come from broken homes, did not have a loving caregiver, were sexually or physically abused, were neglected, and spent time in penal institutions (Polaschek et al., 1997). However, these factors alone do not produce rapists; other men who have suffered similar development problems do not become rapists. At present, there is no generally accepted theory of what turns men into rapists.

Researchers have interviewed rapists to understand the motivation behind their sexual aggression. Rapists reported different degrees and combinations of anger, sexual violence, power, and control. Here are descriptions of four types of rapists (Knight, 1992).

The most common rapist is a man who wants to possess his victim.

■ The *power rapist*, who commits 70% of all rapes, is not out to hurt physically but to possess. His acts are premeditated and are often preceded by rape fantasies. He may carry a weapon, not to hurt but to intimidate the victim.

■ The *sadistic rapist* accounts for fewer than 5% of rapes, but he is the most dangerous because for him sexuality and aggression have become fused, and using physical force is arousing and exciting.

■ For the *anger rapist*, rape is an impulsive, savage attack of uncontrolled physical violence. The act is of short duration, accompanied by abusive language, and the victim usually suffers extensive physical trauma, such as broken bones and bruises.

■ The *acquaintance* or *date rapist* knows his victim and uses varying amounts of verbal or physical coercion to force his partner to engage in sexual activities.

These examples indicate that men rape for a number of or a combination of reasons, such as to exercise power and control, express anger, and become sexually aroused.

Other factors that contribute to rape are the false beliefs, called rape myths, that some men hold about women.

Rape Myths

One consistent finding about rapists is that they hold negative and demeaning attitudes toward women. For example, here are some of their negative beliefs:

■ Healthy women cannot be raped against their will.
■ Women often falsely accuse men of rape.
■ Rape is primarily a sex crime committed by sex-crazed maniacs.
■ Only bad girls get raped.
■ If a girl engages in petting and lets things get out of hand, it is her own fault if her partner forces sex on her.

Some men mistakenly believe that only bad women get raped.

These kinds of statements are called rape myths (Buddie & Miller, 2002; Greensite, 2007).

Rape myths **are misinformed, false beliefs about women, and these myths are frequently held by rapists.**

Men who believe in rape myths tend to have a more traditional view of sex roles and hold more negative attitudes toward women. Although researchers found that acceptance of rape myths is more common among men who have raped, rape myths are also held by men in general. For example, one survey of male college students reported that from 17 to 75% of students agreed with one or more of nine rape myths (Giacopassi & Dull, 1986). This association between rape myths and rapists illustrates how negative beliefs and attitudes can contribute to sexual aggression (DeGue & DiLillo, 2005).

In the United States, it is estimated that during their lifetime 20–30% of women will be victims of some type of sexual aggression. Researchers are developing a number of rape prevention programs to both prevent rape and stop the perpetuation of rape myths, and these programs are becoming increasingly common on college campuses (DeGue & DiLillo, 2005; Schewe, 2002). We'll discuss ways to prevent rape in the upcoming Application section.

Next, we'll discuss how cultures differ in their attitudes toward beauty, organ transplants, and women's rights.

G. Cultural Diversity: National Attitudes & Behaviors

Nigeria: Beauty Ideal

How do Nigerians judge beauty?

One reason that the concept of attitude has been so dominant in social psychology is that our attitudes push or predispose us to think and behave in certain ways. What we often don't realize is how much our culture shapes our attitudes. For example, in the United States, the current attitude, especially among the middle and upper classes, is that for a woman to be attractive, she should be slender. This thin-is-beautiful attitude can pressure women to behave in certain ways, such as to constantly worry about their weight and go on strict diets, which in some cases may result in eating disorders (Heatherton et al., 1997).

But thin is not always beautiful. For example, in Nigeria, Africa, a small group of young women were discussing who had the most beautiful body. They all agreed on Monique, age 15,

Beauty in Nigeria is to be heavy.

because she was already heavy for her age and on her way to being very rotund. As one woman said, "I want to gain weight like Monique. I don't want to be thin" (Onishi, 2001, p. A4). Before getting married, young brides-to-be are sent to so-called fattening rooms, where the goal is to eat as much as they can to get fat and round so that the bride will be admired for her fullness.

However, in 2001, a slim, 6-foot-tall Nigerian became Miss World. This was the first time in 51 years that a Nigerian woman had won this title. Since most Nigerians over 40 consider beautiful women to have ample backsides and bosoms, they thought the new trim Miss World was not particularly beautiful. But many of the younger Nigerians took notice of Miss World's dimensions and have begun to change their attitudes and adopt Western beauty standards that value being slim (Onishi, 2002). This difference in beauty attitudes between America and Africa clearly shows how cultural values not only shape attitudes but also predispose us to behave in certain ways.

A different debate over attitudes is going on in Japan.

Japan: Organ Transplants

What is the Japanese attitude on death?

Miss Wakana Kume, who lives in Japan, was going to die unless she received a liver transplant. However, since 1968, it has been illegal in Japan to transplant organs from donors who are brain-dead. Like all Japanese, Miss Kume grew up with the attitude that brain-dead was not really dead, so she was very reluctant to get a transplant from a brain-dead donor. But because of the seriousness of her condition, Miss Kume flew to Australia, where she underwent a liver transplant. In a very real sense, Miss Kume engaged in counterattitudinal behavior by doing a behavior opposite of what she believed—getting a transplanted organ. Since her lifesaving transplant, Miss Kume has changed her attitude toward organ transplants and now approves of them. This is a real example of changing attitudes by engaging in counterattitudinal behavior.

The reason there were about 24,000 organ transplants in the

Organ transplants are now more common in Japan.

United States in 1997 but none in Japan is that cultures have different definitions of death. In the United States, death is defined as brain death—when a person's brain no longer shows electrical activity, even though the heart is still beating. In Japan, however, death was defined as the moment a person's heart stops beating, and donor organs could be removed only after the heart stops. But to be useful, donor organs must be removed when a person's heart is still beating. In 1997, Japan passed a law allowing organs to be donated by an individual who is brain-dead under certain strict conditions. Because brain death has been legalized in Japan, organ transplants are now possible and many Japanese have changed their attitudes toward death and accept organ transplants (Ling & Ming, 2006; McNeill & Coonan, 2007).

A debate over attitudes and behaviors is also going on in Egypt.

Egypt: Women's Rights

How do Egyptians view women?

Since the early 1900s, Egyptian women have been fighting for their sexual, political, and legal rights in a society that is dominated by Muslim religious principles, which grant women few rights. For example, while women are supposed to wear veils to preserve their dignity, a husband may strike his wife as long as he doesn't hit her in the face and hits lightly. Many women are not given birth certificates, which means that they cannot vote, get a passport, or go to court. Although genital cutting (p. 346) is illegal in Egypt, virtually all women in certain areas have been subjected to it. There are no public hotlines

Egyptian women fight for equal rights.

to help battered women and no statistics on rape, although both are common in certain areas. Although Egyptian women are currently fighting for equal rights, such as not wearing veils in public (photo below) and getting good jobs, they are having limited success because these traditional attitudes are backed by powerful social forces, including political, cultural, and religious institutions (Ezzat, 2004; Tolson, 2003). In getting Egyptians to change their attitudes toward women, advocates will need to use some of the methods that we have discussed, such as using trustworthy and honest sources, presenting one- or two-sided arguments, and, depending on the audience, using either the central or the peripheral route for persuasion.

Next, we'll examine programs psychologists have developed to change attitudes toward aggression.

H. Application Controlling Aggression

Why did only one of six children develop into a violent adult?

In a family of six children, one was so bad he was nicknamed Monster Kody. He became a gang member and shot his first victim at age 11. Kody continued his violent and aggressive ways until he was arrested, convicted, and sentenced to jail for robbery. When he wrote his autobiography from his prison cell, he blamed his problems and violent behavior on his parents' poverty and destitution and on his belonging to a violent gang. But as it turned out,

Monster Kody had three brothers and two sisters who grew up in the same poverty and destitution but developed into law-abiding citizens who are leading very productive lives (Azar & Sleek, 1994).

Out of six children raised in the same environment, only one, Monster Kody, became an aggressive adult. This shows that the development of aggressive behavior depends on the interaction of the three factors that we have discussed: genetic and environmental, social cognitive, and personality factors. Because genetic and environmental factors are sometimes difficult to change, recent programs focus on social cognitive factors to reduce and control aggression.

Controlling Aggression in Children

Most children have occasional outbursts of anger and aggression, but if these outbursts become frequent, young children may develop a pattern of using aggressive behaviors to deal with problems (Lemerise & Dodge, 2000). Researchers found that, unless treated, an aggressive child will surely become an aggressive adolescent and adult and develop later problems, such as substance abuse, criminality, and mental health disorders (Broidy et al., 2003). Researchers have discovered that aggressive children have a number of cognitive-behavioral deficits that make them perceive, remember, and react to a world that appears more hostile than it really is. We'll first discuss these cognitive-behavioral deficits and then a treatment program.

Aggressive children usually become aggressive adolescents and adults.

COGNITIVE-BEHAVIORAL DEFICITS

Parents and teachers need to realize that an aggressive child or teenager does not perceive the world, take feedback, or act as regular nonaggressive children do. Here are some of the ways that aggressive children differ (Lochman et al., 2006; Spielman & Staub, 2000):

■ An aggressive child *does not accurately perceive or recall social cues.* For example, the aggressive child selectively attends to aggressive or hostile actions and overlooks positive social cues. When an aggressive child is asked to recall what happened that day, the child tends to remember all the hostile actions rather than any friendly cues.

■ An aggressive child *does not make accurate explanations* or attributions of the situation. For instance, aggressive children tend to attribute hostile actions to other children when, in fact, other children are not behaving in an aggressive or hostile way.

■ An aggressive child *does not have many adaptive solutions* to problems. This means aggressive children tend to use hostile and aggressive actions to solve many of their problems rather than using nonhostile or verbal solutions.

■ An aggressive child *is reinforced for aggressive behaviors* rather than for positive social behaviors. That's because aggressive children get their way by using hostile actions, which in turn are reinforced. Aggressive children *have poor social skills*, which means they rarely solve problems in nonaggressive ways, such as by discussion.

Because of these cognitive-behavioral deficits, aggressive children perceive a more hostile world and respond with more aggressive behaviors (Lochman et al., 2006). There are programs that teach children how to control their aggression.

You know I've got a quick temper, so don't make me angry!

PROGRAMS TO CONTROL AGGRESSION

Children who engage in antisocial and aggressive behaviors are usually described by the term *conduct disorder,* which is one of the most frequent reasons for referral to treatment programs (Ollendick et al., 2006). We'll discuss two successful programs for treating conduct disorder.

Cognitive problem-solving skills training. A well-researched treatment program involves helping aggressive children overcome the deficits in cognitive-behavioral skills that we just discussed. For example, because an aggressive child does not know how to stop thinking and acting in aggressive ways, therapists teach the child specific rules, such as no matter how angry the child gets, he or she must not hit, yell, or kick. The child receives special reinforcement for obeying these rules. The child learns to use self-statements to inhibit impulsive behavior, including "I can stop myself." The child learns to use alternative, nonaggressive solutions when frustrated. These might be hand clapping, scribbling on a sheet of paper, or tensing and relaxing muscles. Cognitive programs have reduced the aggression of children in both home and school (Nangle et al., 2002; C. R. Thomas, 2006).

Parent Management Training (PMT). An effective treatment program for conduct disorder is called Parent Management Training, or PMT (Mash & Wolfe, 2007). In this program, a therapist teaches parents how to use specific procedures in the home to alter angry interactions with their child, to decrease deviant behaviors, and, very important, to promote positive or prosocial behaviors. For example, parents learn to not reinforce aggressive behaviors that a child uses to get his or her way, to establish and enforce reasonable rules, and to reinforce appropriate behaviors. PMT has proven very effective in decreasing aggressive behaviors in the home and school (C. R. Thomas, 2006).

Now, we'll examine methods of controlling aggression in adults.

Controlling Anger in Adults

How do I stop being angry?

You've probably known people who get mad, rant and rave, and then take their anger out on whoever happens to be near. Then, after their violent outbursts, they may apologize, say they're sorry, or explain that they have to let out their angry feelings or they'll explode. Is it true that "letting it all out" is a good way to deal with anger?

Catharsis

A popular idea for reducing and controlling aggression involves catharsis.

Catharsis **is a psychological process through which anger or aggressive energy is released by expressing or letting out powerful negative emotions.**

According to the concept of catharsis, a good way to deal with anger or aggression is to "let off steam," which means expressing strong negative emotions by yelling, arguing, hitting, or kicking something.

Sigmund Freud used the term *catharsis* to mean that one should let frustration and anger out so that they don't build up and explode in an aggressive rage. However, most research does not support Freud's conclusion about the usefulness of catharsis. For example, after college students were made angry, some were told to punch a bag while thinking about the person who made them angry (catharsis group), while others were told only to sit quietly for 2 minutes (control group). Afterward, students in the catharsis group, who vented their anger, rated their anger higher than those in the control group, who did nothing to let it out. The researcher concluded that venting to let anger out (catharsis group) was like pouring gasoline on a fire; it only adds fuel and makes the anger worse. Accordingly, it's bad to vent one's anger by punching a pillow, since it seems to only make the anger worse (Bushman, 2002). A better way to deal with anger, at the job, school, home, or on the road, is to use a cognitive-relaxation program.

I'll get you for cutting me off, you dumb . . . !

Cognitive-Relaxation Program

At the urging of his wife, Rob came to therapy because he's prone to angry outbursts, especially when driving. He says things like, "I'm not doing anything unsafe; it's that jerk in front of me who's going too slow." Rob admits to getting angry at one thing or another many times a day (Holloway, 2003). Rob can learn to gain control over his anger with an anger management program.

One such successful program is the cognitive-relaxation program. It begins by having Rob observe and later write down his behaviors (feeling tense) and anger-producing thoughts ("That guy's a jerk") during several days of driving. This process is called self-monitoring and helps Rob make a record of the anger-producing thoughts and behaviors that he may not have been aware of and that trigger and maintain his anger. Next, Rob learns a method to quickly relax himself on cue (progressive relaxation—p. 503) so that he will be able to reduce his body tension and arousal. He also makes a list of positive thoughts ("That guy's a careful driver," "That guy is trying to avoid an accident") that he can substitute for his anger-producing ones ("That driver's a jerk"). Once Rob has learned to relax on cue and has his list of positive thoughts, he's ready to begin driving while substituting positive for negative thoughts and relaxing on cue whenever he begins to feel tense or angry. Being able to relax on cue is important because it's very hard to get angry if you're relaxed. Researchers found that this cognitive-relaxation program has proved very effective in helping individuals reduce and control their anger (Deffenbacher, 2003, 2005).

Controlling Sexual Coercion

What are the risks?

Several studies have found that from 42 to 78% of college women report sexual coercion, which includes men using social pressure, verbal coercion, lies, alcohol or drugs, emotional manipulation, or threat of force to have sexual contact with women (Struckman-Johnson et al., 2003). Part of the socialization of males involves seeing situations that may reinforce and increase their risk of using sexual coercion. For example, the media (movies, videos, songs) portray situations in which men believe that using sexual coercion does no harm and may even be arousing to their partners, or may be necessary to achieve their goals (Lonsway & Fitzgerald, 1994). These media portrayals reinforce the idea that sexual coercion is acceptable and even arousing to women and increase the risk that men will be sexually coercive and not be perceptive and responsive to a woman's wishes or refusals.

Somehow the socialization creates a difference between men who are sexually coercive and those who are not. For example, men who report higher levels of sexual coercion also perceived

One problem is that males do not take "NO!" for an answer.

women as showing higher levels of sexual interest in nonsexual, mundane situations (having a conversation). Researchers concluded that, in these cases, it is not the women's behaviors that put them at risk for sexual coercion but rather it is that sexually coercive men misperceive women as showing sexual interest when they are not (Bondurant & Donat, 1999). These researchers suggest that prevention programs need to educate sexually coercive men about how they may misperceive the sexual interest of women, even in very mundane situations like ordinary conversations.

According to researchers, one way to avoid sexual coercion on a date is for men and women to know the risk factors. For women, these include the heavy use of alcohol or other drugs that dull reason and perception. For men, these include overuse of drugs, thinking that paying the expenses entitles him to sex, misperceiving his date's sexual interest, and not recognizing that "NO" means "NO!" (Struckman-Johnson et al., 2003).

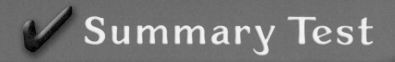

A. Perceiving Others

1. How our thoughts, feelings, perceptions, and behaviors are influenced by interactions with others is studied in the field of (a)_____ psychology. A branch of this field studies how people perceive, store, and retrieve information about social interactions; this branch is called social (b)_____.

2. Making judgments about the traits of others through social interactions and gaining knowledge from our social perceptions are part of person (a)_____. This process is aided by a wealth of social information that is stored in our memories. However, some memories can bias our perceptions. Widely held beliefs that people have certain traits because they belong to a particular group are called (b)_____. Negative beliefs that are often accompanied by an unfair, biased, or intolerant attitude toward another group of people are called (c)_____. Specific unfair behaviors exhibited toward members of a group are called (d)_____.

3. Cognitive structures that represent an organized collection of knowledge about people, events, and concepts are called _____. They help us select and interpret relevant information from a tremendous amount of incoming social information and provide guidelines for how we should behave in different situations.

4. There are different kinds of schemas: Those that include our judgments about the traits that we and others possess are called (a)_____ schemas; those that are based on the jobs people perform or the social positions they hold are called (b)_____ schemas; those that contain behaviors that we associate with familiar activities, events, or procedures are called (c)_____ schemas, or scripts.

B. Attributions

5. The factors or events that we point to as causes or explanations for people's behavior are called (a)_____. If we attribute behavior to the internal characteristics of the person performing the behavior, we are using (b)_____ explanations; if we attribute behavior to the circumstances or context of that behavior, we are using (c)_____ explanations.

6. Harold Kelley proposed that in deciding between dispositional and situational explanations, we should look for factors that change along with the behavior we are trying to explain; this is called the _____ model. To decide between dispositional and situational explanations, we should look for consensus, consistency, and distinctiveness.

7. An error that we make by attributing the cause of a behavior to a person's disposition and overlooking the demands of the environment or situation is the (a)_____ attribution error. If we attribute our own behavior to situational factors but others' behaviors to their dispositions, we fall prey to the (b)_____ effect. If we attribute success to our disposition and failure to the situation, we use the (c)_____ bias.

C. Research Focus: Attributions & Grades

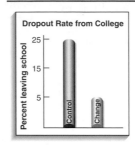

Dropout Rate from College

Percent leaving school — 25, 15, 5 — Control, Change

8. Researchers found that freshmen who were encouraged to attribute their academic problems to _____ conditions, such as poor study habits, showed a significant improvement in grade point average and were less likely to drop out than were students who continued to attribute their poor performance to permanent factors.

D. Attitudes

9. Beliefs or opinions that include a positive or negative evaluation of an object, person, or event and that predispose us to act in a certain way are called (a)_____. General attitudes are convenient guidelines for interpreting and categorizing objects and events and deciding whether to approach or avoid them. Attitudes have three components: beliefs and ideas make up the (b)_____ component; emotions and feelings make up the (c)_____ component; and predispositions make up the (d)_____ component.

10. A state of unpleasant psychological tension that motivates us to reduce our inconsistencies and return to a more consistent state is called (a)_____. To reduce this tension and return to a more consistent state, we may add or change (b)_____ or take a public position that is counter to our private attitude, which is called engaging in (c)_____ behavior. According to Daryl Bem's theory, we first observe or perceive our own behavior and then infer attitudes from that behavior; this is called (d)_____ theory.

11. One method of persuasion presents information with strong arguments, analyses, facts, and logic; this is the (a)_____ route, which works primarily on the cognitive component of our attitudes. Another route emphasizes emotional appeal, focuses on personal traits, and generates positive feelings; this is called the (b)_____ route and works primarily on the affective or feeling component. Three factors to consider in persuasion are the source, (c)_____, and (d)_____.

E. Social & Group Influences

12. If you perform a behavior because of group pressure, you are exhibiting (a)_____. Giving in to social pressure in your public responses but not changing your private beliefs is called (b)_____. A sales technique that relies on the increased probability of getting a second request if you obtain compliance with a small first request is called the (c)_____ technique. Performing a behavior in response to an order given by someone in authority is called (d)_____.

13. Any behavior that benefits others or has positive social consequences is called (a)_____ behavior. A form of helping that involves doing something, often at a cost or risk, for reasons other than the expectation of a material or social reward is called (b)_____. Two different models explain how we make our decisions to help. The model that frames our decision as a five-stage process is called the (c)_____ model. According to another model, we make decisions to help by calculating the costs and rewards of helping; this is called the (d)_____ model.

14. A collection of two or more people who interact and share some common attribute or attributes is called a (a)_____. How much group members perceive that they share common attributes determines group (b)_____. The formal or informal rules about how group members should behave are called group (c)_____. According to Leon Festinger's (d)_____ theory, we compare ourselves to others who are similar to us so that we can measure the correctness of our attitudes and beliefs.

15. If the presence of a crowd increases performance, it is called social (a)_____; if it decreases performance, it is called social (b)_____. If people in a crowd take on antisocial roles because they cannot be identified easily, it is called (c)_____. If an individual in a crowd is inhibited from helping someone in need, it is called the (d)_____ effect.

16. The effect in which a group discussion reinforces the majority's point of view and shifts that view to a more extreme position is called (a)_____. If a group makes a bad decison because it emphasizes sticking together over gathering data and considering all the alternatives, that is called (b)_____.

F. Aggression

17. The findings that identical twins are more alike in aggression and that not all abused children become aggressive are evidence for (a)_____ influences on aggression. The finding that people can learn aggressive behavior through observation, imitation, and self-reinforcement supports the influence of (b)_____ factors. The finding that frustration may lead to or trigger aggression supports the influence of (c)_____ factors. Unlike humans, aggression in animals is primarily influenced by (d)_____ factors.

18. The primary motivation for rape is not sexual but a combination of (a)_____, _____, and _____. The misinformed beliefs that are frequently held by rapists and that are contributing factors to rape are called (b)_____.

G. Cultural Diversity: National Attitudes & Behaviors

19. National attitudes are important because they predispose citizens to (a)_____ in certain ways. For example, compared to the West, traditional Nigerian attitudes are for a woman to become beautiful by (b)_____ a lot. One reason Egyptian women are having such difficulty changing (c)_____ toward them is that these discriminatory policies are backed by social, political, and religious forces.

H. Application: Controlling Aggression

20. An aggressive child perceives and reacts to a world that appears more hostile than normal because this child has a number of (a)_____ deficits. Children can learn to control their aggressive behavior by being reinforced for obeying certain (b)_____. Freud believed that adults should release frustration by acting out, which reduces anger and is called (c)_____. Freud's idea is not supported by modern research. A successful anger management program for adults is called the (d)_____ program.

Answers: 1. (a) social, (b) cognition; 2. (a) perception, (b) stereotypes, (c) prejudice, (d) discrimination; 3. schemas; 4. (a) person, (b) role, (c) event; 5. (a) attributions, (b) internal (dispositional), (c) external (situational); 6. covariation model; 7. (a) fundamental, (b) actor-observer, (c) self-serving; 8. temporary; 9. (a) attitudes, (b) cognitive, (c) affective, (d) behavioral; 10. (a) cognitive dissonance, (b) beliefs, (c) counterattitudinal, (d) self-perception; 11. (a) central, (b) peripheral, (c) message, (d) audience; 12. (a) conformity, (b) compliance, (c) foot-in-the-door, (d) obedience; 13. (a) prosocial or helping, (b) altruism, (c) decision-stage, (d) arousal-cost-reward; 14. (a) group, (b) cohesion, (c) norms, (d) social comparison; 15. (a) facilitation, (b) inhibition, (c) deindividuation, (d) bystander; 16. (a) group polarization, (b) groupthink; 17. (a) genetic and environmental, (b) social cognitive, (c) situational, (d) genetic; 18. (a) power, aggression, control, (b) rape myths; 19. (a) behave, (b) eating, (c) attitudes; 20. (a) cognitive-behavioral, (b) rules, (c) catharsis, (d) cognitive-relaxation

Critical Thinking

Why the Debate over Teen Vaccination?

Questions

1. What role does brain development play in adolescents' likelihood of having safe sex to reduce the chances of getting infected with HPV?

2. How do the three components of attitude apply to the conservatives' position?

3. Why has preaching abstinence not been more successful in preventing girls from getting HPV?

What if modern medicine could prevent three-quarters of the occurrences of a leading cause of cancer in women and save almost 300,000 lives across the world each year? A major public health breakthrough makes this possible. The first vaccine to protect women against cervical cancer is now available, but it comes with much controversy.

Cervical cancer is caused by HPV (human papillomavirus), the most common sexually transmitted infection in the United States. Cervical cancer usually strikes when a woman is young, often before she has had children, and the treatment for cervical cancer may cause infertility. Because cervical cancer is the leading cause of cancer death in women and its treatment has very serious risks, prevention is essential.

A vaccine that prevents infection of four types of HPV and comes with minimal side effects is now available. The vaccine is 100% effective in targeting certain causes of cervical cancer that together comprise about three-quarters of all cervical cancer cases. Despite its effectiveness and safety, the use of the vaccine has provoked considerable social controversy.

Because many teens contract HPV within only a few years after their first sexual experience, it is recommended that the vaccine be administered to girls during their early teens. Some conservative officials and parents oppose vaccinating teen girls, stating the vaccine undermines their value of abstinence being the best

method to avoid getting HPV. These same opponents fear that vaccinating young teens against a sexually transmitted infection, such as HPV, conveys approval to be sexually promiscuous.

Alan Kaye, the executive director of the National Cervical Cancer Coalition, disagrees with opponents who worry the vaccination will result in girls becoming sexually promiscuous. He responds to these moral objections by comparing the vaccine to wearing a seat belt: "Just because you wear a seat belt doesn't mean you're seeking out an accident" (R. Stein, 2005). Others argue the cervical cancer vaccine is no different from routine vaccines that protect children from diseases, such as measles, polio, or chicken pox.

Texas Governor Rick Perry boldly decided the benefits of the vaccine outweighed the moral concerns. Texas became the first state to require girls to be immunized before entering the 6th grade, and at least 17 other states are considering similar school mandates.

In addition to the HPV vaccine targeting the major causes of cervical cancer, it protects against the causes of 90% of all genital warts cases. Consequently, another social debate is deciding whether boys should be vaccinated as well. (Adapted from Associated Press, 2005; Bosch, 2002; FDA, 2006; Gostout, 2007; Hitti, 2006; M. Kaufman, 2006; MSNBC, 2006; Peterson, 2007; R. Rubin, 2007; R. Stein, 2005b)

4. Which group attitudes or norms do the members of the conservative side share? How does a group benefit by sharing norms?

5. What type of persuasion are advocates of the vaccine mostly using to pass legislation?

6. What needs to happen for a parent opposed to vaccinating a teen to change his or her attitude toward teens getting vaccinated?

Suggested Answers

1. The executive functions in the adolescent's brain are not yet fully developed, which helps explain an adolescent's tendency to take risks (p. 411). Adolescents simply do not have the neural bases to carefully analyze risks and make intelligence decisions, such as to always use protection when having sex.

2. **Cognitive component:** believe in abstinence and negatively evaluate vaccinating teen girls. **Affective component:** have strong feelings about abstinence being the best course of action and fear that vaccination may send the wrong message to teens. **Behavioral component:** refuse to allow teens to receive the vaccine.

3. The problem is that changing attitudes and beliefs is difficult, especially in this case, when national surveys report that about 50% of teenagers have sex by age 17. In attempts to change attitudes through persuasion, many factors are involved: whether to use facts and logic, the central route, or use emotional appeals, the peripheral route; whether a one-sided or a two-sided message will be more effective; and who will be the

most believable and trusted source of the message: the parents, teachers, minister, peers, or boyfriends.

4. One of the main attitudes or norms conservatives share is that abstinence, especially for teenagers, is the best policy to avoid getting HPV. The group comes together and develops group cohesion by sharing common attitudes or norms.

5. Advocates are using strong arguments, facts, and logic to persuade others to permit teen girls to receive the vaccine, which indicates they are using the central route for persuasion.

6. Parents who oppose vaccinating teens expect their daughter to abstain from sex. But, if their daughter does not abstain from sex and gets cervical cancer, these parents will develop conflicting beliefs (the vaccine is immoral, but it can help save lives) that would cause cognitive dissonance. They might resolve this dissonance by changing their belief or engaging in counterattitudinal behavior.

Links to Learning

Learning Activities

- **POWERSTUDY FOR INTRODUCTION TO PSYCHOLOGY 4.0**
by Tom Doyle and Rod Plotnik
Check out the quizzes and learning activities for "Social Psychology" on **PowerStudy** and:
  - Test your knowledge using an interactive version of the Summary Test on pages 606 and 607. Also access related quizzing—true/false, multiple choice, and matching.
  - Explore an interactive version of the critical thinking exercise "Why the Debate over Teen Vaccination?" on page 608.
  - You will also find key terms, a chapter outline including chapter abstract, and a special extended list of hotlinked websites that correlate to this module.

- *CengageNOW*
academic.cengage.com/login
Need help studying? This site is your one-stop study shop. Take a Pre-Test and CengageNOW will generate a Personalized Study Plan based on your test results. The Study Plan will identify the topics you need to review and direct you to online resources to help you master those topics. You can then take a Post-Test to determine the concepts you have mastered and what you still need to work on.

- **INTRODUCTION TO PSYCHOLOGY BOOK COMPANION WEBSITE**
academic.cengage.com/psychology/plotnik
Visit your book companion website where you will find more resources to help you study. At this site, you will find Learning Objectives, Internet Exercises, quizzing, flash cards, and a pronunciation glossary.

- **STUDY GUIDE and WEBTUTOR**
WebTUTOR
Check the corresponding module in your Study Guide for effective student tips and help learning the material presented. Also go to **academic.cengage.com/webtutor** for an interactive version of the Study Guide features.

Study Questions

*A **Perceiving Others**—Mark says that he doesn't make snap judgments but waits until he knows people. Do you think Mark does what he claims? (**Suggested answer p. 636**)

*B. **Attributions**—What should you be aware of when you try to explain the behaviors of your friend or mate? (**Suggested answer p. 636**)

C. **Research Focus: Attributions & Grades**—As a senior in college, what advice would you give to your younger brother or sister who is an incoming freshman?

D. **Attitudes**—You are trying to persuade your loved one to be more neat and tidy around the house. How would you do this?

*These questions are answered in Appendix B.

E. **Social & Group Influences**—A family of five is trying to decide where to go on vacation. What problems might arise?

*F. **Aggression**—One of your friends says, "Getting angry and being aggressive are just part of human nature." What would you reply? (**Suggested answer p. 637**)

G. **Cultural Diversity: National Attitudes & Behaviors**—In changing national attitudes, do you think the central or peripheral route for persuasion is more effective?

H. **Application: Controlling Aggression**—Why do you think that about 4 million women each year are victims of domestic violence initiated by their spouses?

Appendix A

STATISTICS IN PSYCHOLOGY

Descriptive Statistics

Frequency Distributions
Measures of Central Tendency
Measures of Variability

Inferential Statistics

Chance and Reliability
Tests of Statistical Significance
Analysis of Variance
Chi-Square

Descriptive Statistics

Do numbers speak for themselves?

Suppose you are curious about how many people are capable of being hypnotized. You read up on how to induce hypnosis and put together a list of five things that people under hypnosis have been known to do, such as feeling no pain when a finger is pricked, being unable to bend an arm when told that the arm will remain stiff, and acting like a young child when told to regress to infancy.

You next persuade 20 people to participate in a little test. You attempt to hypnotize them and then ask them to do each of the things on your list. Of your 20 subjects, 2 follow none of your suggestions, 4 follow only one, 7 go along with two suggestions, 4 go along with three, 2 go along with as many as four, and only 1 follows all five.

The next day, a friend asks you how your study worked out. How would you make generalizations about your findings?

To answer this type of question, psychologists rely on *statistics*. Although you often hear that numbers "speak for themselves," this is not really true. Numbers must be sorted, organized, and presented in a meaningful fashion before they tell us much.

Statistics **are the tools researchers use to analyze and summarize large amounts of data.**

If the very word *statistics* brings to mind complex formulas you think you could never master, you may be surprised to realize how much you already use statistics in your everyday life. When you hear that a ball player has a batting average of .250 and you know this means he has gotten one hit in every four times at the plate, you are using statistics. When you understand that a rise in the median income means that people, on average, are earning more money, you are understanding statistics. When you know that scoring in the 90th percentile on a final exam means you did better than nine out of ten of your classmates, you are showing a grasp of statistics—specifically, descriptive statistics.

Descriptive statistics **are numbers used to present a collection of data in a brief yet meaningful form.**

One important part of descriptive statistics is presenting distributions of measurements and scores.

FREQUENCY DISTRIBUTIONS

Individual differences show up in everything that can be measured. There are no measurements—whether of height, heart rate, memory capability, shyness, or political opinion—that do not show individual variation.

The *frequency distribution* **is the range of scores we get and the frequency of each one when we measure a sample of people regarding some trait.**

Frequency distributions are often presented in graphic form so their patterns can be seen at a glance. We'll discuss two of these distributions, normal and skewed.

What is a normal distribution?

For many traits in a large population, the frequency distribution has a characteristic pattern. For instance, if you measured the height of 500 students chosen at random from your school, you would find a few very short people and a few very tall people, while the height of the majority of students would be somewhere in the middle. Height, like weight, IQ, years of education, and many other characteristics, has what is known as a *normal distribution.* When graphed, a normal distribution produces a normal curve.

A *normal curve* **is a graph of a frequency distribution in which the curve tapers off equally on either side of a central high point.**

This characteristic bell shape (Figure A.1) shows that most of the measurements fall near the center, with as many falling to one side as to the other. When you measure a trait that is distributed normally throughout a population, your measurements should produce an approximately normal curve, provided that your sample is large enough.

What is a skewed distribution?

Not all traits are distributed normally.

Skewed distributions **are distributions in which more data fall toward one side of the scale than toward the other.**

When plotted on a graph, skewed distributions do not have a symmetrical shape. Instead, they have a "tail" on one end, which shows that relatively fewer frequencies occur on that side of the horizontal scale. When the tail is on the right, as in Figure A.2, we say

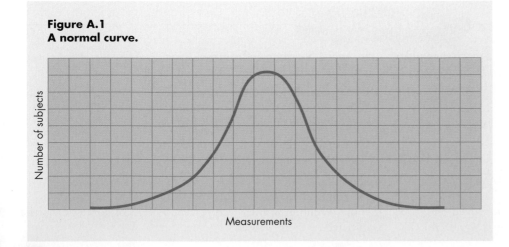

Figure A.1
A normal curve.

Number of subjects

Measurements

the distribution is skewed to the right, or has a *positive skew* (there are fewer frequencies at the higher end of the horizontal scale). When the tail is on the left, as in Figure A.3, we say the distribution is skewed to the left, or has a *negative skew* (there are fewer frequencies at the lower end of the horizontal scale).

The data you collected about susceptibility to hypnosis present a skewed distribution. If you plotted them on a graph, with score along the horizontal axis and number of people along the vertical one, the curve would be skewed to the right. This would show at a glance that more people in the sample fell at the low end of your hypnotic susceptibility scale than fell at the high end.

In fact, your sample is fairly representative of the general population. About twice as many people are poor hypnotic subjects as are excellent ones. But note that to be assured of obtaining the true distribution in a large population, you would usually have to test quite a large representative sample.

MEASURES OF CENTRAL TENDENCY

Suppose you want to summarize in a few words the average height of people, the typical susceptibility to hypnosis, or the most common performance on an IQ test. For this you would need another kind of descriptive statistic, called a **measure of central tendency.** There are three measures of central tendency: the mean, the median, and the mode. Each is a slightly different way of describing what is "typical" within a given distribution.

The *mean* **is the arithmetic average of all the individual measurements in a distribution.**

Suppose that ten students in a seminar took an exam. Their scores were 98, 96, 92, 88, 88, 86, 82, 80, 78, and 72. You would find the mean by adding all the scores and dividing the sum by the total number of scores. In this case, the sum of all the scores is 860; dividing this by 10 gives a mean of 86.

The *median* **is the score above and below which half the scores in the distribution fall.**

If you took our ten test results and arranged them in order from highest to lowest, the median would be the point right in the middle, between the fifth and sixth scores on the list. That would be 87.

The *mode* **is the most frequent measurement in a distribution.**

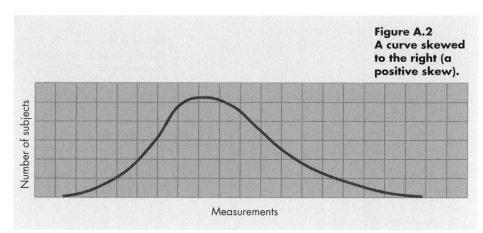

Figure A.2
A curve skewed to the right (a positive skew).

Number of subjects

Measurements

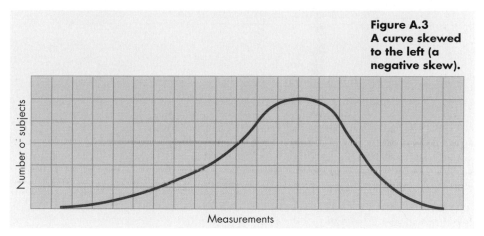

Figure A.3
A curve skewed to the left (a negative skew).

Number of subjects

Measurements

In this group of scores, the mode, the score that occurs most often, is 88.

In the example just given, the mean, median, and mode are very close together, but this is not always true. In some distributions, particularly those that are strongly skewed, these three measures of central tendency may be quite far apart. In such cases, all three of the measures may be needed to give a complete understanding of what is typical.

For instance, look at the graph in Figure A.4, which shows the distribution of income in an imaginary company. The mean income of its 50 employees is $30,600 a year. But look at the distribution. The president of the company earns $140,000, three other executives earn $80,000, and another four earn $60,000 a year. There are also six lower-level managers at $40,000, six salespeople at $30,000, and ten foremen at $25,000. The rest of the employees, the 20 people who keep the company records and run the machines, earn only $12,000 each. Thus, the mean of $30,600 does not really give an accurate indication of a typical income of an employee at this firm.

Appendix A

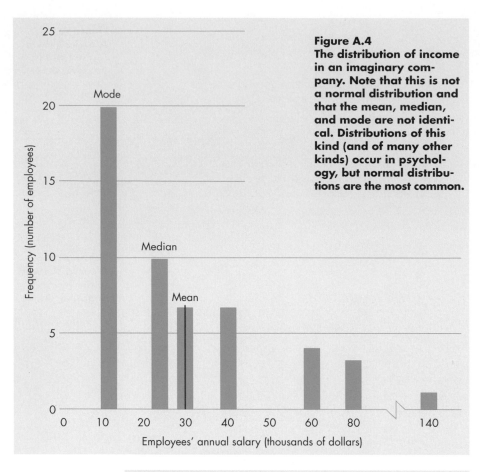

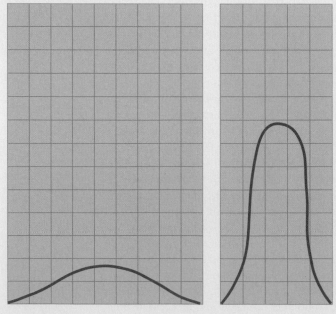

Figure A.4
The distribution of income in an imaginary company. Note that this is not a normal distribution and that the mean, median, and mode are not identical. Distributions of this kind (and of many other kinds) occur in psychology, but normal distributions are the most common.

Figure A.5
At left, a distribution with a great deal of variability. At right, a distribution with little variability.

A better measure of central tendency in this instance is probably the median, or $25,000. It tells us that half the people at the company earn no more than this amount. Also revealing is the mode, or most common salary; it is only $12,000 a year. As you can see, the mean, median, and mode can provide us with very different figures.

MEASURES OF VARIABILITY

If you get an A in a course and are told that the grades ranged from A to F, you will feel a greater sense of accomplishment than if the grades ranged only from A to B. Why this difference in how you perceive a grade? The answer is that it is often important to take into account the extent to which scores in a distribution are spread out. In other words, it is often informative to have a measure of variability.

A *measure of variability* is an indication of how much scores vary from one another.

On a graph, scores that vary greatly produce a wide, flat curve; scores that vary little produce a curve that is narrow and steep. Figure A.5 illustrates these two patterns.

One measure of variability is the range.

The *range* consists of the two most extreme scores at either end of a distribution.

Another measure is the standard deviation.

The *standard deviation* shows how widely all the scores in a distribution are scattered above and below the mean.

If scores cluster closely around the mean, the standard deviation will be small; if scores are dispersed widely from the mean, the standard deviation will be large. Thus, the standard deviation is an indication of how representative the mean is. If the standard deviation is small, we know that the mean is representative of most scores in the distribution. Conversely, if the standard deviation is large, we know that many scores are quite far from the mean.

Figure A.6 shows that the standard deviation divides a normal curve into several portions, each of which has a certain percentage of the total distribution. As you can see, 68.2% of all scores fall somewhere between the mean and one standard deviation to either side of it. If you move two standard deviations to either side of the mean, you will take in 95.4% of all the scores in the distribution. Finally, 99.8% of all the scores

Finding the standard deviation of a distribution is not difficult, although it is tedious without the aid of a calculator. To compute the standard deviation, follow these five steps:

1. Determine the mean of all the measurements in the distribution.
2. Subtract the mean from each measurement and square the difference. (Squaring the difference eliminates the negative signs that result when dealing with measurements that fall below the mean.)
3. Add the squares together.
4. Divide the sum of the squares by the number of measurements.
5. Take the square root of the value you obtained in step 4. This figure is the standard deviation.

will fall between the mean and three standard deviations from it. Only a scant 0.2% fall beyond three standard deviations.

Knowing the mean and the standard deviation of any normal distribution allows you to determine just how "average" any given score is. For instance, suppose you take a difficult test consisting of 100 questions and receive a score of 80. How well did you perform? If you learn that the mean is 60 and the standard deviation is 8, you know that your score of 80 is very good indeed. The overwhelming majority of people—95.4%—scored no better than 76, or two standard deviations above the mean. Thus, relative to what most others have done, an 80 is excellent. By the same token, a 40 is not very good at all; 95.4% of people scored 44 or higher on this test. Thus, if you received a 40 you are near the bottom of the distribution and had better start studying much harder.

Inferential Statistics

Can scientists be 100% certain?

In the mid-1970s, many Americans were puzzled to learn that a distinguished panel of scientists could not determine with absolute certainty whether the artificial sweetener called cyclamate posed a risk of cancer. The scientists announced that, after months of research, costing millions of dollars, they could be only 95% sure that cyclamate was safe. Why this

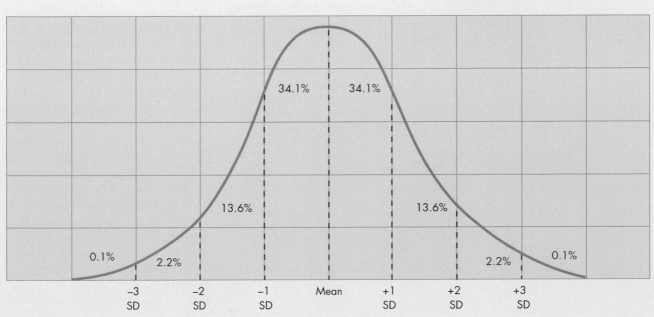

Figure A.6
A normal distribution showing the percentage of measurements that fall within one, two, or three standard deviations from the mean.

34.1%   34.1%
13.6%   13.6%
0.1%   2.2%   2.2%   0.1%

−3 SD   −2 SD   −1 SD   Mean   +1 SD   +2 SD   +3 SD

Appendix A

remaining margin of doubt? Why can't a team of highly skilled researchers, backed by government funds, manage to tell us absolutely if a substance is hazardous to our health?

CHANCE AND RELIABILITY

No one can totally eliminate the influence of chance on scientific findings. Even when you randomly select groups of subjects, there is always the possibility that, just by chance, those groups will differ slightly in ways that affect your experiment. This is why scientists must rely on statistics to tell them the likelihood that a certain set of results could have happened purely by chance. If this likelihood is small—5% or less—the researchers are justified in rejecting the chance explanation and in concluding instead that their findings are probably reliable. *Reliable* means that the investigators would probably obtain similar results if they repeated their study over and over with different groups of subjects.

Determining the reliability of experimental findings is a major way in which psychologists use inferential statistics.

Inferential statistics are a set of procedures for determining what conclusions can be legitimately inferred from a set of data.

These procedures include what are called *tests of statistical significance.* Tests of statistical significance were used to determine the 95% certainty of the finding that cyclamate is safe to eat. Different tests of statistical significance are needed for different kinds of data.

TESTS OF STATISTICAL SIGNIFICANCE

Suppose you are an educational psychologist who has put together a special program to raise the IQ levels of children with learning disabilities. You expose one group of children with learning deficits to the special program and another group, with equal learning deficits, to the standard curriculum. At the end of a year, you give all the subjects an IQ test. Those in the special program score an average of ten points higher than those in the standard curriculum. Is this enough of a difference to reject the chance explanation and conclude that the program was a success? The procedure most frequently used to answer questions like this is a test of statistical significance called the *t* test.

What is a t *test?*

The *t test* **is an estimate of reliability that takes into account both the size of the mean difference and the variability in distributions.** The *greater* the mean difference and the *less* the variability, the less the likelihood that the results happened purely by chance.

Imagine that the results of your experiment looked like the ones in Figure A.7. The mean IQs of the two groups differ by ten points: 75 for the experimental subjects and 65 for the controls. But look at the variability in the two distributions: there is almost none. All the children in the experimental group received a score within five points of 75; all the children in the control group received a score within five points of 65. It seems that some genuine effect is at work here. The IQ patterns in the two groups are distinctly different and are not the kinds of differences usually caused by chance.

Unfortunately, the results of most experiments are not this clear-cut. Far more often, the distributions look more like those in Figure A.8. In this figure, you can see that the mean difference in scores is still ten points, but now there is a sizable amount of variability in the two groups. In fact, some of the experimental subjects are doing no better than some of the

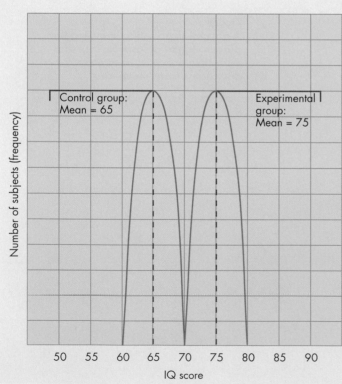

Figure A.7
In this distribution of IQ scores, the control group has a mean of 65; the experimental group, a mean of 75. When distributions in a study show this little variability and no overlap between the two curves, they are not very likely to have happened purely by chance.

controls, while some of the controls are scoring higher than some of those in the experimental program. Is a mean difference of ten points in this case large enough to be considered reliable?

When should you use a t test?

The *t* test also considers how many subjects are included in the study. You should not put much faith in a comparison of educational programs that tries out each approach on only two or three children. There is too great a likelihood that such samples are not representative of the larger population from which they are drawn. Let's say that, in the hypothetical experiment we have been describing, you included 100 randomly selected children in each of the two groups. It is much less likely that samples of this size would be biased enough to distort the research's findings.

To learn the steps involved in actually performing the *t* test, please read the accompanying box.

ANALYSIS OF VARIANCE

Not all data lend themselves to a *t* test, however. Often researchers want to compare the mean scores of more than two groups, or they want to make comparisons among groups that are classified in more than one way. (For instance, does age or sex have an effect on how much children benefit from our special education program?) In such cases another test of statistical significance is needed. This test is

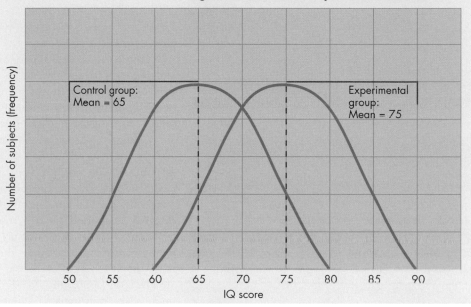

Figure A.8
This set of distributions is much more likely than the one in Figure A.7. The mean is still 65 for the control group and 75 for the experimental group. But now the variability of the distributions is substantially greater. There is also substantial overlap between the two curves. Is the mean difference in this case statistically significant? A *t* test can provide the answer.

called an ***analysis of variance,*** or *ANOVA* for short. An analysis of variance is rather like a more complex *t* test. To learn more about the ANOVA technique, consult any introductory statistics text.

How to Perform the t Test

The *t* test is an estimate of how reliable the difference between two means is. To determine the likelihood that the outcome occurred by chance, you first need to know the size of the mean difference (mean 1 minus mean 2). In general, the larger the mean difference, the less likely that it happened by chance alone. You also need to know the variance within each group.

The *variance* is a measure of the variability within the two distributions.

In general, the lower the variance, the less likely that chance alone caused the results. Finally, you need to know how many subjects are in the random samples. In general, the larger the samples, the less the likelihood of a purely chance explanation.

To calculate the *t* test just follow these steps:

1. Determine the mean of the scores for each group and subtract one from the other.
2. Go back to the box on standard deviation and work through that calculation for each of your distributions, stopping at step 4. This gives you the variance of each distribution.
3. Add the two variances.
4. Add the total number of subjects minus 2 (in our example 200 − 2 = 198).
5. Divide the summed variances by the number obtained in step 4 and take the square root.
6. Divide the mean difference between the two groups by the square root from step 5.

If the samples add up to more than 50 individuals, any value of *t* over 2 is statistically reliable more than 95% of the time.

Appendix A

CHI-SQUARE

Sometimes the data psychologists collect do not consist of sets of scores with means or averages. Instead, the researchers have recorded who does what, or who falls into which of several categories. For instance, psychologists have found that chess players are more apt to be introverts than they are to be extroverts. Is this just a chance association? To answer such questions, statisticians often use the *chi (ky) square,* a test of statistical significance.

Suppose you are a psychologist and you want to study the usefulness of fear tactics in changing people's behavior. You randomly select 200 habitual smokers who are willing to participate in an experiment. You expose half to a 20-minute talk on the known health hazards of smoking, complete with graphic illustrations of diseased lungs and hearts. You expose the rest to a 20-minute talk on the history of tobacco. After the talks, the members of each group are given the opportunity to sign up for a free "quit smoking" clinic. Some people from each group sign up for the clinic; some do not. The easiest way to present their choices is with a 2 × 2 table, like the one set up in Table A.1.

Table A.2 shows how the distribution worked out in your study. Of the 100 subjects in your experimental group (the ones exposed to the fear tactics), 60 signed up for the quit-smoking clinic and 40 did not. Of the 100 subjects in the control group, 40 signed up for the free clinic and 60 did not. Is this difference in the distribution of choices statistically significant? The chi-square can be used to estimate the reliability of this difference.

The *chi-square* is a test of statistical significance that compares the actual observed distribution of people (or events) among various categories with the distribution expected purely on the basis of chance.

If people had made their decisions purely by chance—for instance, by the toss of a coin—the same number of people would be expected to sign up for the clinic in each of the two groups. The accompanying box gives a step-by-step description of how to do the chi-square calculation.

Table A.1: The Format of a 2 × 2 Table

Talk heard	Signed up for clinic	Didn't sign up	Row total
Fear tactics			100
No fear tactics			100
Column totals			200 (grand total)

Table A.2: Study Results in Our Example

Talk heard	Signed up for clinic	Didn't sign up	Row total
Fear tactics	60	40	100
No fear tactics	40	60	100
Column totals	100	100	200 (grand total)

How to Calculate Chi-Square

Chi-square (χ^2) is an estimate of how sure we can be that a distribution of events or of people did not happen just by chance. In our example, chi-square calculates the *expected* number of people that a chance distribution would place in each of the categories represented by the four cells in the table. This expected number is then compared with the actual *observed* number of people in each of these categories, shown by cells (the data presented in Table A.2). If the difference between the expected and observed numbers is large enough, the distribution is not likely to have happened by chance alone.

Here are the steps in making the chi-square calculation:

1. Figure out how many people, by chance alone, would be likely to fall into the upper-left cell. To do this, multiply the first row total by the first column total (100×100) and divide by the grand total (200). The expected number is 50.

2. Subtract the expected number (50) from the observed number in the upper-left cell (60). The difference is 10 ($60 - 50 = 10$). Square the difference to eliminate negative signs ($10 \times 10 = 100$) and divide the result by the expected number: $100 \div 50 = 2$.

3. Repeat steps 1 and 2 for each of the four cells. In this example, the expected values are the same for each cell, but that won't always be true.

4. Add the four values you get from calculating the difference between the expected and observed number for each cell. This is the chi-square.

The reliability of the chi-square value must be looked up in a table. In this example, the fear-tactic subjects signed up for the clinic so much more often than the control subjects did that this distribution could have occurred by chance only two times in a hundred.

✔ Summary Test

Descriptive Statistics

1. The tools that researchers use to analyze and summarize large amounts of data are called (a)_____. Numbers that are used to present a collection of data in a brief yet meaningful form are (b)_____ statistics, which are often used to present distributions of measurements and scores. The range of scores and the frequency of each one are called the (c)_____; this is often presented in graphic form so the patterns can be seen at a glance.

2. When graphed, a normal distribution produces a curve that tapers off equally on either side from a central high point; this is called a (a)_____ curve. This curve has the characteristic shape of a (b)_____ and shows that most of the measurements fall near the center, with as many falling to one side as to the other. However, not all traits are distributed normally. If more data fall toward one side of the scale than toward the other, it is called a (c)_____ distribution. Such distributions do not have symmetrical shapes when plotted; instead, they have a "tail" on one end. When there are fewer frequencies at the higher end of the horizontal scale (the tail is on the right), we say the distribution is skewed to the right or has a (d)_____ skew. When there are fewer frequencies at the lower end of the horizontal scale (the tail is on the left), we say the distribution is skewed to the left or has a (e)_____ skew.

3. Ways of describing what is "typical" within a given distribution are called measures of (a)_____. The arithmetic average of all the individual measurements in a distribution is the (b)_____. The score above and below which half the scores in the distribution fall is the (c)_____. The measurement that occurs most often in a distribution is the (d)_____.

4. The extent to which scores in a distribution are spread out—in other words, how much scores vary from one another—is the measure of (a)_____. The two most extreme scores at either end of a distribution indicate the range. The measure of variability that shows how widely all the scores in a distribution are scattered above and below the mean is called the (b)_____.

Inferential Statistics

5. Because the influence of chance on scientific findings cannot be completely avoided, procedures are necessary to determine what conclusions can be properly inferred from a set of data; these procedures are called (a)_____ statistics. If the likelihood that the results could have occurred purely by chance is small, researchers can reject the chance explanation and conclude that their findings are probably (b)_____; that is, they would probably obtain similar results if they repeated the study over and over with different groups.

6. Different kinds of data require different tests of statistical significance. An estimate of reliability that takes the size of the mean difference and the variability in distributions into account is called the (a)_____; it estimates how reliable the difference between two means is. In general, the larger the difference between (b)_____, the less likely that it happened by chance alone.

7. A measure of the variability within two distributions is called the (a)_____. In general, the lower the variance, the less likely that chance alone caused the results. An analysis of variance, or (b)_____ test, is similar to, but more complex than, the *t* test.

8. How sure we can be that a distribution of events or of people did not happen just by chance is measured by another test of statistical significance, called the _____.

Answers: *1. (a) statistics, (b) descriptive, (c) frequency distribution; 2. (a) normal, (b) bell, (c) skewed, (d) positive, (e) negative; 3. (a) central tendency, (b) mean, (c) median, (d) mode; 4. (a) variability, (b) standard deviation; 5. (a) inferential, (b) reliable; 6. (a) t test, (b) mean difference; 7. (a) variance, (b) ANOVA; 8. chi-square*

CRITICAL THINKING STUDY QUESTIONS WITH ANSWERS

Why Answer the Critical Thinking Study Questions?

As you read and study a module, you will learn new concepts, terms, and theories. We hope you will think about how you can apply these concepts to your own lives and to the problems and events in your own environment. To give you some practice, we have included answers to some of the Critical Thinking study questions that appear at the end of each module. Other kinds of questions may have a single correct answer, but study questions are open to a variety of interpretations. Answering them will help you learn to think about and discuss issues in greater depth.

Just as you must put extra effort into acquiring any complex skill, from tennis to algebra, you will have to exert yourself mentally to answer the study questions. To make the task easier, we have provided possible answers for selected questions. The first study question in each module is discussed in considerable detail to give you a strategy for answering other questions. Remember that our answers are only suggestions; you may think of other, equally good responses. If you use our answers as examples when you answer study questions on your own, you will acquire the very important skill of knowing how to apply concepts, terms, and theories to significant questions that often have no single correct answer. In fact, you will discover that many of the issues you face in the real world are very similar to the ones included here. When you have practiced answering our study questions, you will be better equipped to respond to related questions in your own life.

In this appendix we answer three to four study questions from each module. We always include a detailed response to the first question in each module and then suggest briefer answers to the following questions. As a result, you have an opportunity both to study a model for answering questions and to practice answering them more fully on your own.

At first you may find it difficult to answer study questions by yourself, but with practice you'll get the knack and actually find it fun to apply the concepts that you have learned. Remember, the more you stretch your mind by answering study questions, the bigger and stronger your mind will become. Unlike a balloon that bursts when expanded too far, your mind loves to be stretched and will never explode.

Rod Plotnik
Katie Townsend-Merino

Module 1
DISCOVERING PSYCHOLOGY

A. Definition & Goals

STUDY QUESTION: How would you rank the four goals of psychology in terms of importance?

1. Need to Know: What specific information do I need to answer this question?

I need to know the four goals of psychology: **describe, explain, predict,** and **control.**

2. Defining Terms: Do I need to use my own words to define or review any terms?

I need to define each of the four goals.

Describe: Psychologists want to describe in detail the particular behavior. What is the organism doing?

Explain: Psychologists want to explain why organisms behave in a particular way. What causes this behavior to occur?

Predict: Psychologists want to make predictions about how organisms will behave in the future. If I know something about the causes of a particular behavior, I can predict who will demonstrate that behavior.

Control: Psychologists want to control the behavior of an organism. This may allow for positive change in an individual's behavior.

3. Identify Key Words: Which words in the question hold the key to the best answer?

The key words are "rank" and "importance." Both are dependent on the nature of a *particular* question. For example, if you are trying to understand what *causes* schizophrenia, the goals **describe** and **explain** would be ranked 1 and 2. However, if you want to *treat* or *prevent* schizophrenia, the goals **predict** and **control** would be ranked 1 and 2. Keep in mind, though, that it is impossible to predict and control without first describing and explaining!

D. Cultural Diversity: Early Discrimination

STUDY QUESTION: Why would discriminatory practices exist in psychology, an area devoted to studying human behavior?

Possible Answer: In our culture people can be privileged in a number of ways. Privilege by race (White), gender (male), and class (upper) are among the most common types of special status. Historically, advantaged groups have had a difficult time seeing that status differences are real, or they have attributed them to differences in abilities. The founders of psychology were themselves privileged and saw no harm in their beliefs regarding women and minorities. For example, being Black and female in the early days of psychology meant that you were doubly disadvantaged. Disadvantages took a number of forms: difficulties for a minority member in obtaining an education, problems finding work in academia, and discrimination in employment as a clinical psychologist.

H. Application: Study Skills

STUDY QUESTION: What changes would you make to study most efficiently?

Possible Answer: There is no simple relationship between the amount of time spent studying and the grades one receives. Study time is judged by its *quality* rather than its *quantity.*

In-class time must not be wasted. To make the most of it, I must keep my attention focused. I will ask myself questions during class, or I will participate in discussion when the opportunity arises. Note-taking in my own words demands more attention than direct dictation.

Good planning is the key to using study time efficiently. My plan will include specific goal setting, a realistic time schedule, and self-reinforcement. Such planning is *present-oriented* because it emphasizes getting down to work right away on tasks that will result in my meeting short-term goals. When I think, "How will I ever graduate?!" I'm looking beyond the here and now to do some rather destructive "global worrying."

When learning, I will focus on specific material and concepts, dividing the course into manageable chunks. I will do the self-tests that are contained in the text.

Module 2
PSYCHOLOGY & SCIENCE

A. Answering Questions

STUDY QUESTION: Which method would you use to find out if caffeine improves memory?

1. Need to Know: What specific information do I need to answer this question?

I need to know the methods for answering questions: **survey, case study,** and **experiment.**

I need to know the **advantages** and **disadvantages** of each method.

2. Defining Terms: Do I need to use my own words to define or review any terms? Do I know the advantages and disadvantages of each?

I need to define each of the methods and list the advantages and disadvantages.

Survey: This is a way to get information by asking people directly to respond to a set of questions. This can be done in person, over the phone, or through the mail. An advantage is that you can easily get a lot of information relatively quickly, but it may be biased in accord with the beliefs and truthfulness of the respondents.

Case study: This is a way to get information by studying a particular individual in depth. You get a lot of information about one person, but this information may not apply to anyone else.

Experiment: This is a way to get information in a controlled environment so you can systematically manipulate treatments and measure their effects on behavior. You can identify cause-and-effect relationships, but information gained in a controlled environment may not apply in the real world.

Appendix B

3. *Identify Key Words:* Which words in the question hold the key to the best answer?

The key terms are "caffeine" and "improves memory." Although you might get interesting stories using the survey approach, your data would not be particularly valuable: it would be distorted by error and bias. That is, the placebo effect might be strong in this case. If you used the case-study method, you would learn a lot about the relationship between one individual's memory response and caffeine. But you would not know whether that information applied to anyone else. The best method of assessing cause-and-effect relationships ("Does caffeine cause memory improvement?") is to do an experiment. You could have two groups of students tested on the same material. Before the test, one group would drink a cup of caffeinated coffee and the other would drink one cup of decaffeinated coffee. You would then compare their test performances. This method would provide the most accurate answer to this question.

D. Cultural Diversity: Use of Placebos

STUDY QUESTION: Why do Americans think it strange that Asians use rhino horn as medicine?

Possible Answer: Belief is the most important factor in generating the placebo effect. In some Asian cultures there is a strong belief that rhino horn is an aphrodisiac and a potent medicine. Therefore, there is a high incidence of rhino horn treatments available in those countries. In the United States, we hold no beliefs about the medicinal value of rhino horn and recognize it as a placebo. Therefore, we regard those who use rhino horn as strange! But Americans do not regard taking vitamin C as unusual because we believe it has medicinal value.

F. Decisions about Doing Research

STUDY QUESTION: Which research techniques and settings would you use to study mental problems in the homeless?

Possible Answer: To decide on the best way of answering this question, let's look at each of the methods at our disposal and assess their utility.

Questionnaires and interviews. We could interview people who live in homeless shelters or on the street about their mental conditions. We could also talk to people who work with the homeless, asking their opinions about mental illness and the homeless.

Standardized tests. We could administer tests designed to detect different kinds of mental illness to homeless individuals. This might give us information about the prevalence and type of mental illness in that population.

Laboratory experiment: behaviors. It would be impossible to do a true experiment on this question. You cannot randomly assign someone to homelessness or mental illness. It would be difficult to get homeless people to a laboratory setting. You could possibly assess the effects of treatments for mental illness on the homeless.

Laboratory experiment: physiological and genetic techniques. Again, it may be difficult to get homeless individuals to a laboratory. If you could, you might be able to compare brain structure and function in the mentally ill and the non-mentally ill homeless.

Module 3
BRAIN'S BUILDING BLOCKS

A. Overview: Human Brain

STUDY QUESTION: Why is it really smart to drive a car only if it is equipped with driver- and passenger-side airbags?

1. *Need to Know:* What specific information do I need to answer this question?

I need to know the advantages of airbags and to relate them to the information regarding the brain provided in this module.

2. *Defining Terms:* Do I need to use my own words to define or review any terms?

I need to know that airbags reduce the incidence of head injury in auto accidents.

3. *Identify Key Words:* Which words in the question hold the key to the best answer?

The key words are "really smart to drive . . . only." In the context of the current module, we should focus on the fact that airbags can help prevent head injuries during auto accidents. Severe blows to the head during a traffic accident can damage neurons in the brain and spine. Because mature primate brains are capable of very little growth of new neurons, such damage is usually permanent.

This is very serious because the brain controls almost all of our most important functions. So airbags are advantageous because they might help prevent irreversible damage to the brain.

D. Sending Information

STUDY QUESTION: How are the structure and function of the axon like those of a battery?

Possible Answer: Both batteries and neurons must generate electrical impulses. They both achieve this by transforming chemical energy into electrical energy. Like batteries, neurons get their potential to generate electrical impulses from an imbalance between positive and negative charges. When the barrier between these charges is removed, positive and negative charges are attracted to each other like opposite poles of magnets. In a battery, a built-up charge is released when a connection is made between the negative and positive terminals. In the axon, the barrier between positive and negative ions is broken when the axon membrane becomes permeable.

Once the charge has been spent, both batteries and neurons must be recharged. For the neuron, this involves pumping the positively charged sodium ions back outside the axon membrane, which returns to its semipermeable state.

H. Cultural Diversity: Plants & Drugs

STUDY QUESTION: What are the different ways that drugs can affect neurotransmitters?

Possible Answer: Some of the ways drugs can affect neurotransmitters are by blocking reuptake, blocking receptors, and mimicking neurotransmitters. A drug like cocaine blocks the process of reuptake, so that the neurotransmitter stays in the synapse and continues to activate the receiving neuron. Other drugs block the receptors on the receiving neuron by occupying the receptor sites, which prevents the neurotransmitter from relaying its message. Finally, some drugs, such as mescaline, actually mimic one of the brain's natural neurotransmitters. These drugs bind to receptor sites, thereby activating neurons.

Module 4
INCREDIBLE NERVOUS SYSTEM

A. Genes & Evolution

STUDY QUESTION: If a species of humans with 5-pound brains was discovered, would their behavior differ from ours?

1. Need to Know: What specific information do I need to answer this question?

I need to know how much an average human brain weighs. Furthermore, I must know how much our ancestors' brains weighed on average.

2. Identify Key Words: Which words in the question hold the key to the best answer?

The key words are "would their behavior differ from ours?" In the context of the current module, we see that our brain has already tripled in size since the time of our earliest known ancestors. It is believed that these early humans did not make tools, make fire, or use language. Later, humans with a brain twice as large as our earliest ancestors' walked upright and made precise tools. By the time the human brain was as large as ours today, our ancestors were growing crops, living in communities, developing language, and painting representations of animals and humans. It seems that large changes in brain size are associated with large changes in human capabilities and behaviors. If we had 5-pound brains, our behavior would probably be very different. *How* different is impossible to predict. Much science fiction has been written on this topic.

B. Studying the Living Brain

STUDY QUESTION: How would you know if a professional boxer had brain damage?

Possible Answer: If the behavior or capabilities of this boxer have changed in ways that make us suspect brain damage, we could examine the brain using one or more imaging techniques.

Computerized axial tomography—CAT scan. We could take a sophisticated x-ray of the patient's brain to check for possible abnormalities. This would give us video images that represented slices of the brain. In this way, we could penetrate brain tissue to search for possible causes of the changes in the boxer's behavior.

Magnetic resonance imaging—MRI. We could penetrate farther into the boxer's brain with a device that sends nonharmful magnetic fields and radio frequencies through it. This gives us more detailed and clearer pictures and, unlike the CAT scan, does not expose the patient to radiation.

Positron emission tomography—PET scan. PET scans allow us to analyze brain function by providing a video image whose colors correspond to various levels of brain activity and abnormality. In our diagnosis of the boxer, we could compare these images to PET scans of age- and gender-matched controls to see if there are any *functional* differences.

H. Cultural Diversity: Brain Size & Racial Myths

STUDY QUESTION: Why is there a continuing interest in whether a bigger brain is more intelligent?

Possible Answer: Scientists might hope for a relationship between brain size and intelligence for a number of reasons. First of all, brain size is measurable, and thus we would have another quantifiable indicator of intelligence, of which there are precious few. Second, individuals' brain sizes can be quite easily compared. Group comparisons of intelligence have always intrigued science, though their usefulness to society has been questioned.

Other reasons have more to do with historical sociology than psychology. For example, Marx might have said that finding consistent differences in brain size that correlate with intelligence would be of interest to the ruling class, as a means of maintaining the status quo. An individual's ticket to aristocracy would be an MRI.

Finally, racism and sexism may play a part in the continuing interest in establishing differences. If such a measure were found to be reliably true, some would argue that, because their brains are somewhat smaller, women cannot be regarded as men's equal in intelligence.

Module 5
SENSATION

A. Eye: Vision

STUDY QUESTION: What kinds of problems in the visual system could result in some form of blindness?

1. Need to Know: What specific information do I need to answer this question?

I need to know: the structure and function of the parts of the eye; how light gets to the retina; how the light is transformed into a neural message; and the pathway that the neural message takes to the brain.

2. Identify Key Words: Which words in the question hold the key to the best answer?

The key words are "problems in the visual system" and "result in . . . blindness." In order to effectively answer this question, we need to examine the entire process of normal vision and to imagine all the possible ways that this process could be interrupted.

Let's examine the structure and function of the eye. First, we see that if the cornea or lens is damaged or occluded, the light waves cannot reach the retina, and vision cannot occur. If the retina or any of its cells are damaged, the light waves cannot be transformed into neural messages that are sent to the brain; in other words, there can be no vision.

Second, if any part of the optic nerve is damaged, the neural messages cannot be sent to the brain. Damage to the part of the thalamus responsible for sending messages about vision to the occipital lobe would also cause blindness.

Appendix B

Finally, if an individual sustains damage to the primary visual cortex or the association cortex, either total or partial blindness would occur.

B. Ear: Audition

STUDY QUESTION: What kinds of problems in the auditory system could result in some form of deafness?

Possible Answer: If we examine the structure of the auditory system, we can see where problems could occur that would result in some form of deafness. First, if the tympanic membrane lost flexibility (as sometimes occurs in children with frequent ear infections), the vibrations could lose strength and fail to be transmitted to the ossicles, which would prevent those sound vibrations from reaching the cochlea. Second, if any of the ossicles became calcified or fused together, sound vibrations would again be stopped before reaching the cochlea. These types of damage result in conduction deafness.

In the event of damage to any part of the cochlea, particularly the hair cells, the vibrations would not be changed into nerve impulses that are sent to the brain. Consequently, no sound would be heard. If there is any damage to the auditory nerve, the primary auditory cortex, or the auditory association areas, various types of nerve deafness will occur.

D. Chemical Senses

STUDY QUESTION: How might a master chef's chemical senses differ from yours?

Possible Answer: It makes sense that a master chef would have a particularly acute sense of taste. The number of taste buds on the human tongue varies widely from individual to individual. Very likely, the tongue of a master chef would have more taste buds than the average person's. Also, because flavor is actually the combination of taste and smell, a master chef might have a very sensitive sense of smell (olfaction). It's reasonable to guess that a master chef could distinguish very subtle differences in flavor that the average person could not.

Module 6
PERCEPTION

A. Perceptual Thresholds

STUDY QUESTION: How does Weber's law apply to how old you perceive someone to be?

1. *Need to Know:* What specific information do I need to answer this question?

I need to know what Weber's law states and what a "just noticeable difference" is.

2. *Defining Terms:* Do I need to use my own words to define or review any terms?

I need to define *just noticeable difference* and Weber's law.

Just noticeable difference (JND): The smallest increase or decrease in the intensity of a stimulus that a person can manage to detect.

Weber's law: This law states that the amount of increase in a stimulus needed to provide a just noticeable difference grows with the intensity of the stimulus.

3. *Identify Key Words:* Which words in the question hold the key to the best answer?

The key words are "how old you perceive someone to be." When people are babies, just a few months make a huge difference in how old we perceive them to be. As humans age, the increase in time before someone looks older becomes longer; it may even be many years. For example, it might take five or more years before someone of 60 looks older to us, while if we saw a child at 3 it might take only six months before the child looks different. This follows directly from Weber's law. If the person's age is the stimulus, Weber's law says that the change in the person's age that we are able to notice increases with increase in intensity of the stimulus—that is, as the person gets older.

B. Sensation Versus Perception

STUDY QUESTION: What would your life be like if your brain could receive sensations but could not assemble them into perceptions?

Possible Answer: Sensations are just the bits of information that we first become aware of from an outside stimulus. The receptors have transformed the stimulus into a neural impulse that the brain can understand. However, without perception, those neural impulses have *no meaning*. For example, if you had no ability to form visual perceptions, you would be aware that something was out there in the environment, but you would not be able to know or to tell anyone what it was.

If you lost *all* your perceptual abilities, you would be extremely disadvantaged; in fact, the world would cease to have meaning. You would be unable to form a relationship with the world.

H. Cultural Diversity: Influence on Perceptions

STUDY QUESTION: When foreigners visit the United States, what do you think they perceive differently?

Possible Answer: It is very difficult to answer this question because the way we perceive our own world is invisible to us. However what is normal in one culture may be abnormal in another. For example, it may seem weird to us that women in India cover their heads. But, to Indians, it is the custom. So to answer this question, we have to step outside ourselves and our culture.

The new visitor might notice that American teenagers are more heavily monitored by their parents than are teenagers in Europe. It is normal in many European countries for adolescents of 16 to smoke, drink, and dance the night away (with no curfew) at the local discos.

Module 7
SLEEP & DREAMS

A. Continuum of Consciousness

STUDY QUESTION: How many different states of consciousness have you been in today?

1. *Need to Know:* What specific information do I need to answer this question?

I need to know what the different states of consciousness are.

The states of consciousness include controlled processes, automatic processes, daydreaming, altered states of consciousness, sleep and dreams, the unconscious, and unconsciousness.

2. *Defining Terms:* Do I need to use my own words to define or review any terms?

I need to define each of the states of consciousness.

Controlled processes: These activities require our full awareness and concentration to complete. Usually we cannot perform other tasks at the same time.

Automatic processes: These tasks (eating, driving, listening to the radio) are performed on autopilot and can be done in conjunction with other activities.

Daydreaming: This occurs with very low levels of awareness and often *during* automatic processes. In this state, we are fantasizing or imagining while we are awake.

Altered states of consciousness: We experience these states under the influence of an external source or technique, such as meditation, psychoactive drugs, sleep deprivation, or hypnosis.

Sleep and dreams: During **sleep**, we go through five different stages of awareness and consciousness. When we **dream**, we experience visual and auditory images, both in black and white and in color.

The unconscious: Freud's theory of the unconscious says that when we experience something threatening (sexual or aggressive events or thoughts), we put these in a place in our mind that cannot be accessed during ordinary recall. The updated theory of the **cognitive unconscious** says that a mental structure of which we are unaware influences our conscious behaviors and thoughts.

Unconsciousness: This refers to a state in which we are completely unaware and unresponsive, most often as a result of a head injury, disease, or surgical anesthesia.

3. *Identify Key Words:* Which words in the question hold the key to the best answer?

The key words are "How many . . . states . . . have you been in today?" Simply review what you have learned about the different states and apply it to what you have experienced so far today.

D. Research Focus: Circadian Preference

STUDY QUESTION: What kind of problems might arise if a morning person married an evening person?

Possible Answer: The lifestyles of these two people are likely to be quite different. The morning person would wake up early and get a number of things accomplished in the morning. She or he would eat a large breakfast before beginning the day. The evening partner would probably be annoyed by all this early activity. She or he would wake up later, skip breakfast (or eat lightly), and not feel like beginning the day's activities until the afternoon or evening. During the evening, when the night owl still had energy to spare, the early bird would be wound down and ready for bed. This couple would need to understand that their differences in this regard are innate and that

one style is not superior to the other. They would need to compromise and have realistic expectations (which is difficult for any of us!).

F. Cultural Diversity: Incidence of SAD

STUDY QUESTION: What cultural values might New Hampshire residents have that contribute to their incidence of SAD?

Possible Answer: This question is difficult to answer for those of us who have never been to New Hampshire. The answer given here is based purely on film and TV portrayals of New Hampshirites, which are probably full of stereotypes.

Icelanders appear to have lower expectations of the good life than do New Hampshirites. When New Hampshirites' expectations are not met, depression may be one outcome. Also, the text reports that Icelanders tend not to complain. In New Hampshire, complaining is more socially acceptable and, in fact, may be a lifestyle itself. Complaining may cause New Hampshirites to dwell on problems that might trigger SAD. Further, if New Hampshirites have fewer support systems than do Icelanders, that would also contribute to the higher incidence of SAD. (It also seems possible that there could be fewer people who are susceptible to SAD in Iceland—from an evolutionary perspective.)

Module 8
HYPNOSIS & DRUGS

A. Hypnosis

STUDY QUESTION: A student has great test anxiety, which is interfering with his success in college. Would hypnosis help?

1. *Need to Know:* What specific information do I need to answer this question?

I need to know what type of hypnotic tool I could use and whether hypnosis helps with relaxation.

I could give the student a posthypnotic suggestion to be relaxed during test taking.

2. *Identify Key Words:* Which words in the question hold the key to the best answer?

The key words are "would hypnosis help [with test anxiety]?" I know from the text that I can give a posthypnotic suggestion, and the text further reports that hypnosis appears to relieve tension. So, in this case hypnosis might be worth a try—if my student is susceptible.

F. Alcohol

STUDY QUESTION: If researchers know who has an increased risk for alcoholism, at what age should such a person be told?

Possible Answer: Before we tell people that they are at increased risk for any condition, we must have clear evidence that a risk exists. What is the evidence that we can confidently predict increased risk for alcoholism when someone is still in childhood?

Environmental and genetic risk factors can be reliably identified in childhood. For example, an adoption study has shown that babies born to alcoholic parents are three or four times more likely to become

Appendix B

alcoholics than are babies born to nonalcoholics. There are also some environmental risk factors associated with growing up in a home in which the parents are alcoholic: specifically, children can learn to turn to alcohol as a way of coping with problems. In addition, they may learn different norms regarding how much alcohol consumption is appropriate, or where and when it is appropriate to consume alcohol.

What are the possible benefits of telling children that they are at risk? It might act as an early warning, alerting children that they should exercise extreme caution when consuming alcohol. This might reduce the likelihood that they will become alcoholics.

Are there any reasons why we shouldn't tell children that they are at risk? We should bear in mind that children of different ages have different levels of comprehension. Our warning would be lost on young children, who could not understand the notion of a risk much later in their lives. Adolescents might benefit from the warning, but we would have to be careful not to make the risk seem thrilling. Telling some people that they are at risk for something actually increases the likelihood that they will bring it on; the warning becomes a self-fulfilling prophecy. We would also have to be careful to accompany our warning with clear advice on how the risk can be lowered.

Given all this, we can state the following guidelines about informing children of their risk for alcoholism. Don't bring up the idea before the child is old enough to understand the notion of long-term risk. If talking with adolescents, don't make the notion of risk sound attractive to thrill seekers. Finally, be sure to accompany the warning with clear advice regarding how the risk can be reduced.

H. Marijuana

STUDY QUESTION: A regular user of marijuana says that he can drive just fine after smoking. Would you ride with him?

Possible Answer: Only if I was driving. Otherwise, *no way!*

This person is overlooking a number of factors. The most obvious is that marijuana acts as a depressant: it decreases reaction time, judgment, and the use of peripheral vision. In addition, larger dosages can produce time and perceptual distortions and hallucinations, none of which are conducive to the safe operation of heavy machinery, such as a car.

Module 9
CLASSICAL CONDITIONING

A. Three Kinds of Learning

STUDY QUESTION: Can you recall situations in which you have experienced each of the three kinds of learning?

1. Need to Know: What specific information do I need to answer this question?

I need to know what the three types of learning are.

They are classical conditioning, operant conditioning, and cognitive learning.

2. Defining Terms: Do I need to use my own words to define or review any terms?

Classical conditioning: This kind of learning involves *involuntary* responses. A neutral stimulus is paired with an unconditioned stimulus, so that the response that occurred to the unconditioned stimulus now occurs to what was the neutral stimulus (which is now called the conditioned stimulus).

Operant conditioning: This kind of learning involves *voluntary* behavior. The responses that follow a behavior will either increase or decrease the likelihood of that behavior's recurrence.

Cognitive learning: This kind of learning involves our mental processes. A behavior can be learned through observation or imitation.

3. Identify Key Words: Which words in the question hold the key to the best answer?

The key words are "you have experienced." Since we all have learned something in these three ways, you just need to come up with a personal example for each learning method.

B. Procedure: Classical Conditioning

STUDY QUESTION: How do you explain why your heart pounds when you hear the words "There will be a test next class"?

Possible Answer: In this example, the pounding heart would be considered a *conditioned response*. (In fact, it's a *conditioned emotional response*.) The heart is stimulated to beat faster by the sympathetic nervous system when danger is perceived. In this case, the teacher's words are perceived to be anxiety provoking (or "dangerous") because of learning that has taken place via classical conditioning.

The words "There will be a test next time" constitute the conditioned stimulus. We know this is a conditioned stimulus because words are not inherently dangerous. Also, someone who has never taken a test and, therefore, has had no opportunity to be conditioned would not experience the same change in heart rate.

H. Application: Conditioned Fear & Nausea

STUDY QUESTION: How would systematic desensitization be used to help reduce a student's test anxiety?

Possible Answer: I would use the three steps of the systematic desensitization procedure to help reduce the test anxiety in a student. (To avoid the complication of saying "he or she," I'll assume, arbitrarily, that the student is female.) First, she must learn how to relax intentionally. I would teach her to tense and relax all the muscles in her body from her toes to her head. The student must practice this for 15–20 minutes every day for several weeks before we could proceed. The second step would be for this student to make up a list of 7–12 stressful situations associated with test taking and to rank them from least to most stressful. Finally, my student friend would put herself in a deeply relaxed state and vividly imagine the least stressful situation. At the first sign of stress, I would stop her and have her put herself in a deeply relaxed state again. She would then begin imagining the situation again until she could continue without becoming stressed. When she had mastered that stressful situation, we would move up the hierarchy to the next stressful scenario. In this way, she would move all the way up her hierarchy until she could actually take a test with reduced anxiety.

Module 10
OPERANT & COGNITIVE APPROACHES

A. Operant Conditioning

STUDY QUESTION: How do you explain why your significant other sulks every time something is wrong even though you've told him or her that it bugs you?

1. *Need to Know:* What specific information do I need to answer this question?

I need to know why people persist in a particular behavior.

BICOC: behavior is contingent on consequences. This is the essence of operant conditioning.

2. *Defining Terms:* Do I need to use my own words to define or review any terms?

BICOC: This means that someone performs or does not perform a specific behavior because of the consequences that will follow. If the consequence is a reinforcer, the person will likely repeat the behavior. If the consequence is a punisher, the person will not repeat that behavior.

Operant conditioning: This kind of learning involves voluntary behavior. The responses that follow a behavior will either increase or decrease the likelihood of that behavior's recurrence.

3. *Identify Key Words:* Which words in the question hold the key to the best answer?

The key words are "explain why [the person] sulks." From an understanding of the concepts involved, it is clear that whatever I am doing when my partner sulks is reinforcing that behavior. I need to change my behavior before my partner's behavior will change.

B. Reinforcers

STUDY QUESTION: How would you use operant conditioning to change a rude friend into a more likable and friendly person?

Possible Answer: This question asks me to design a program that **shapes** my friend toward a desired **goal**, that of polite behavior. In order to do this operantly, I must find a relevant reinforcer for my friend. If my friend does not like people very much, that might be difficult. However, I'll assume that anyone likes the company of another as long as it is pleasant and the attention the person receives is positive.

This means that the reinforcer in this case will be that positive attention my friend receives from others. One way to accomplish this is to enlist the help of my other friends. I'll tell them to give this positive attention in the form of smiles, compliments, and general concerned attention whenever my friend exhibits the desired behaviors.

If I'm going to shape my friend, then I will have to move him or her gradually away from rude behavior toward more polite, likable behavior. I cannot simply wait for the desired final behavior before giving any reinforcement. In the beginning of the program, my other friends must be instructed to provide reinforcement whenever my problematic friend is in their company and not being rude. This might mean reinforcing him or her for just standing quietly.

From there, my friends must become more particular in the criteria they use for giving reinforcement. They will wait until the friend does or says something that is polite or pleasant. For example, if the friend asks someone how she is today, the person must respond very positively and ask after his or her welfare as well. If the friend offers to get someone a cup of coffee or help carry something, that must be reinforced strongly as well.

If this program works, my friend will learn that rude behavior gets him or her ignored, whereas polite, considerate behavior leads to social rewards in the form of pleasant attention from others. This program won't be easy to put into practice, because rude behavior is hard to ignore, and it makes people less interested in persevering to find polite behavior in the person. Still, people can be shaped by the social reinforcement they receive.

H. Cultural Diversity: East Meets West

STUDY QUESTION: Why do the same principles of learning work in very different cultures?

Possible Answer: Actually, this shows that learning principles come close to being laws of human nature, just like the laws of physics or chemistry. There is no reason why these principles *should* be different in other cultures. What is learned varies—for example, using a fork and knife or using chopsticks. It is also true that what an individual perceives as a reinforcer or punisher varies between cultures. However, once we know what is reinforcing to an individual, we can use that reinforcer to increase the likelihood that a response will occur again. Social mores are culturally dependent; the principles of learning are not.

Module 11
TYPES OF MEMORY

A. Three Types of Memory

STUDY QUESTION: Why does seeing an ambulance speed by remind you of your father's heart attack and his trip to the hospital?

1. *Need to Know:* What specific information do I need to answer this question?

I need to know what processes are involved in memory formation and retrieval.

The basic process is sensory memory to short-term memory to long-term memory.

2. *Defining Terms:* Do I need to use my own words to define or review any terms?

Sensory memory: Visual images are stored here for a quarter of a second or more, and auditory images last for about 2 seconds.

Short-term memory: If we attend to information, we can hold it for about 30 seconds in the working memory.

Long-term memory: Unlimited amounts of information can be held here for an unlimited amount of time. This information can go back and forth between long-term memory and short-term memory.

3. *Identify Key Words:* Which words in the question hold the key to the best answer?

The key words are "why does seeing an ambulance . . . remind

Appendix B

you?" The visual and probably also auditory image of the ambulance was put into my short-term memory and, while exploring ambulance-related thoughts from my long-term memory, I stumbled upon an emotional memory related to my father's heart attack.

F. Encoding: Transferring

STUDY QUESTION: Why is it important that teachers make learning interesting and meaningful?

Possible Answer: Most of what you learn and need to remember from teachers requires that you use **effortful encoding.** You have to work hard to transfer information from short-term to long-term memory either by using **maintenance rehearsal** or by making new associations. We know from research that simple maintenance rehearsal results in reduced retention and retrieval. When teachers make material *interesting* to you, you pay attention, which in itself makes it more likely you will remember—because the information got through the first process in memory. When teachers make the material *meaningful,* it means something to you individually, and you can connect this information to other information in your memory. By **making associations** between this new learning and previous learning, you will process this meaningful information at the deepest **level of processing.** Thus, you will have the best retention and recall for information learned in this manner.

H. Cultural Diversity: Oral Versus Written

STUDY QUESTION: How might playing video games affect a child's encoding process?

Possible Answer: The text points out that we in the United States spend most of our time encoding information with words—by reading and writing—and that we excel at retrieving information in that form. But individuals in cultures with a strong oral tradition excel at retrieval of information that they have heard. This suggests that using a particular form of encoding over a period of time may improve your recall for information encoded in that way. Video games are organized around visual images. Children who play them get a lot of practice at encoding visual-spatial images. It seems likely that children who play video games would have better recall for visual-spatial information than do children (or adults) who do not play video games.

Module 12
REMEMBERING & FORGETTING

A. Organization of Memories

STUDY QUESTION: How would your memory be affected if you accidentally took a drug that prevented the formation of any new nodes?

1. *Need to Know:* What specific information do I need to answer this question?

I need to know what a node is and how it relates to memory formation.

2. *Defining Terms:* Do I need to use my own words to define or review any terms?

Node: A node is a memory file in which information is organized around a specific topic.

Memory process and nodes: Nodes are linked to one another in a hierarchy.

3. *Identify Key Words:* Which words in the question hold the key to the best answer?

The key words are "memory be affected" and "prevented the formation of any new nodes." Probably the nature of the memory damage would be related to the age at which I took this drug. Presuming I'm an adult when this happens, I would appear normal much of the time because I would already have had time to form many hundreds (thousands) of nodes. But I would be unable to learn any new concepts. I would have to try and fit any new information into an already existing node. This would greatly impair the sophistication of my network hierarchy.

D. Biological Bases of Memory

STUDY QUESTION: If a virus suddenly destroyed your hippocampus, what effect would it have on your performance in college?

Possible Answer: The hippocampus is crucial for transferring semantic information and episodic information from short-term to long-term memory. However, it is not involved in the processing of procedural information—for example, motor skills.

Therefore, my performance in English would be impaired because I would not be able to encode details from what I read into long-term memory. Thus, it would be impossible for me to discuss a novel I read because I could not remember its plot. I would also have great difficulty in mathematics. The rules for solving quadratic equations or finding the area under a curve wouldn't be in long-term memory when I needed them.

My physical education class would be a slightly different story. I would not lose my motor skills, so if I had been a talented athlete before losing my hippocampus, I would still be one after losing it. My coordination would not be affected. However, if I had played a sport in which there were any rule changes after my hippocampus had been destroyed, I would have to be reminded of them all the time because I would not be able to encode them.

H. Application: Eyewitness Testimony

STUDY QUESTION: If you were on a jury, what concerns would you have when listening to eyewitness testimony?

Possible Answer: Most jurors regard eyewitness testimony as a very important form of evidence, yet it is prone to biases and errors. If I were on a jury, I would listen carefully to the way the lawyers phrased their questions to the witnesses because, as the textbook points out, this phrasing can influence the witnesses' testimony.

I would remember that witnesses are often not completely sure of the accuracy of their accounts. This makes them susceptible to influence. So if the lawyer used an especially strong verb, such as "smashed," to describe a collision, the witness might tend to give a higher estimate of the vehicle's speed. The lawyer can also introduce potentially false information as background to a question, so that the witness will verify that information at a later time.

Witnesses are often trying to recall events they experienced under considerable emotional duress. Thus, encoding the information must have been difficult in the first place. Now, under more duress on the witness stand, the person is expected to recall with accuracy something that occurred as an emotional blur perhaps six months or a year ago.

Finally, I would try hard to remember that there is no correlation between the accuracy of an eyewitness's testimony and the person's confidence in that accuracy. So when a lawyer asks a witness if she is sure she is right, the fact that the witness answers yes does not verify the accuracy of the testimony.

Module 13
INTELLIGENCE

A. Defining Intelligence

STUDY QUESTION: How intelligent was Ray Kroc, who never finished high school but started the world-famous McDonald's hamburger chain?

1. Need to Know: What specific information do I need to answer this question?

I need to know the different ways intelligence is defined.

Intelligence has been defined in three ways: using a two-factor approach; using Gardner's theory of multiple intelligences; and using Sternberg's triarchic theory.

2. Defining Terms: Do I need to use my own words to define or review any terms?

Two-factor theory: This theory of intelligence says that there is a general factor, *g,* that represents a person's ability to perform complex mental functions. Standard IQ tests are presumed to measure *g.*

A second factor, *s,* measures specific mental skills such as mathematical skills and verbal skills.

Theory of multiple intelligences: This theory concludes that there are seven kinds of intelligence: verbal, musical, logical-mathematical, spatial, body movement, understanding oneself, and understanding others.

Triarchic Theory: This theory concludes that there are three kinds of intelligence: analytical and logical thinking; the ability to deal creatively with new situations and learn from experience; and the ability to use practical skills to adjust to one's sociocultural environment.

3. Identify Key Words: Which words in the question hold the key to the best answer?

The key words are "how intelligent was Ray Kroc?" The answer to this question lies in the way we define intelligence. We could try comparing Ray Kroc to Albert Einstein using each approach.

Two-factor approach: There are two basic tenets to this approach. First, intelligence can be quantified in the form of tests, most notably the IQ test. Second, there is a general trait called intelligence, *g,* that is supplemented by a few specific abilities, *s.* In this approach, if Albert Einstein scored higher on an IQ test than Ray Kroc, he would be considered more intelligent.

Multiple-intelligence approach: Gardner also considers intelligence to be quantifiable, but not into one composite score. Instead, he considers intelligence to be multidimensional: there are many different kinds of intelligence. It may be that Ray Kroc would have scored very high on measures of insight about others and verbal skills, whereas Einstein would have scored higher on math skills. Using this approach, we would not talk about one person being more intelligent than another; rather (provided some skills were demonstrated), we'd say the individuals had different kinds of intelligence.

Triarchic approach: According to this approach, intelligence should not be defined by how much you know, but by how you came to know it. In other words, *thinking skills*—logic, problem-solving, and practicality—are the hallmark of intelligence. It could be assumed that both Kroc and Einstein had impressive problem-solving skills, though some might want to debate which man was working on the more complex problems. Certainly, it is hard to build a business empire without some ability to think practically. Einstein's thinking could stay at a very abstract level, which does not necessitate practicality. Again, this approach does not make comparisons between people in terms of a global trait called intelligence. Rather, the emphasis is on the way the person thinks.

D. Potential Problems of IQ Testing

STUDY QUESTION: Should we use IQ scores to assign the growing number of students from different cultures to grade levels?

Possible Answer: First of all, unless IQ tests were also being used to assess nonminority students' grade levels (which they are not), the possibility should not even be considered. However, for the sake of discussion, let's assume that IQ tests are used to place children into grade levels. Given that, the question is whether IQ tests are a good means of deciding at which grade level a child should be placed.

Experience (for example, the story of Larry described in the text) leads us to predict that if IQ tests were used as the sole criterion for placement, minority students would be overrepresented at the lower levels and underrepresented at the upper levels. This would mean that, at each grade level, the average age of minority children would be higher than that of nonminority children. This is due, in no small part, to the **cultural bias** in most IQ tests.

The problem, then, is that IQ tests are not valid criteria for placement; rather, they are *discriminatory*. The conclusion would be to avoid the use of IQ tests as the sole criterion for placement. Perhaps the best strategy is to use a number of criteria, including past academic performance and the child's behaviors both in and out of the classroom.

H. Application: Intervention Programs

STUDY QUESTION: Since Head Start fails to raise IQ scores over the long run, should its financial support be reduced?

Possible Answer: This is another question that probes the value of IQ scores in decision-making—in this case, in evaluating the efficacy of the intervention program Head Start.

It is true that Head Start has not yielded long-term changes in children's IQs. However, research quite clearly indicates other very

Appendix B

tangible benefits of the program. The text cites research demonstrating that the Head Start children were less likely to repeat classes and less likely to show antisocial or delinquent behavior. People who had been in the Head Start program were more likely to be holding jobs.

Research has also shown that the program has benefited other family members. Mothers of children who had been in the program reported fewer psychological symptoms, greater feelings of mastery, and greater current life satisfaction.

Given all the problems in assessing what an IQ score really means, it should not be used as the sole measure of a program's success. The Head Start program should not be dropped.

Module 14
THOUGHT & LANGUAGE

A. Forming Concepts

STUDY QUESTION: Why is it difficult to explain to your younger sister or brother that a whale is a mammal and not a fish?

1. *Need to Know:* What specific information do I need to answer this question?

I need to know how people form concepts like "fish" and "mammal."

The two theories of concept formation are **definition theory** and **prototype theory**.

2. *Defining Terms:* Do I need to use my own words to define or review any terms?

Definition theory: This theory suggests that we make a concept by listing all the properties that define it.

Prototype theory: This theory says we form a concept by forming a prototype, which is a mental picture of an average example of the thing we are defining.

3. *Identify Key Words:* Which words in the question hold the key to the best answer?

The key words are "difficult to explain . . . that a whale is a mammal and not a fish." The answer to this question lies in the way we form concepts. Let's look at the two different approaches in terms of whales.

Definition theory helps us understand why your younger sister (provided she is quite young) might have difficulty understanding that a whale is not a fish. The problem is that a whale and a fish share many common **defining properties**: they both swim in water; they both have similar shapes; they have similar tails; and so on. In fact, the property that defines a whale as a mammal—the fact that it gives birth to its young—is not readily apparent to a young child.

You might have more success taking a **prototype** approach. With this approach, you would show the child a picture of a typical whale—one that was an average of most whale types. Perhaps a killer whale would be a good prototype. This would lead the child to the rather straightforward and often-correct conclusion that whales are larger than fish. The disadvantage, of course, is that you haven't really taught the child what a mammal is.

F. Reason, Thought & Language

STUDY QUESTION: What problems might result when heads of government speak through translators?

Possible Answer: The text explores the different ways a person can think depending on which language the person is using. This reminds us that there is more to language than mere words; language is inextricably tied to culture. Not only are there words that exist in one language but not in another; there are also *ideas* that are not shared across cultures. This means that *literal translations* often lack clarity and, in fact, can be misunderstood.

To be a translator is difficult, therefore, when words and concepts encountered in one language do not have equivalents in another. For example, to call someone "a character" in English does not translate well into French. The French might use a word like "type" (pronounced "teep") to describe an unusual or eccentric person. In English we would use "type" to describe certain personalities, like "the nervous type" or "the outgoing type."

We can see how potentially dangerous translation can become when applied to something as important as diplomatic relations and communication. Translators must have a very good working knowledge of the nuances of both languages and the way words are used in each cultural context.

H. Cultural Diversity: Influences on Thinking

STUDY QUESTION: What kinds of social problems can arise from finding differences between male and female brains?

Possible Answer: In an ideal world, the fact that there are gender differences in the brain should not cause any social dissension. Historically, though, we have seen that differences (for example, in skin color, genitalia, presumed brain size, IQ) have been used to imply that one is better than another. So, instead of a "different but equal" philosophy, we see attitudes that "mine is better than yours" or "you can't play with me."

One problem is that when most people hear about gender differences, they assume that all males are different from all females, when, in fact, there is a huge overlap. For example, there is a gender difference in height, but this *doesn't* mean that all males are taller than all females. These false beliefs may translate into social policy that would unfairly discriminate against people because of their gender and not because of their individual abilities. A woman who is applying to be an air traffic controller might be told, "Well, women have a smaller amount of brain area devoted to visual-spatial skills than men do, so we don't want to hire you."

These findings may be used to enforce a difference in status between men and women in our social structure.

Module 15
MOTIVATION

A. Theories of Motivation

STUDY QUESTION: Which theory best explains why students work hard to get good grades?

1. *Need to Know:* What specific information do I need to answer this question?

I need to know the various theories regarding human motivation.

The four theories of motivation are **instinct theory, drive-reduction theory, incentive theory,** and **cognitive theory.**

2. *Defining Terms:* Do I need to use my own words to define or review any terms?

Instinct theory: This theory suggests that there are innate, inborn forces that cause us to behave in certain ways or inborn forces that cause a particular behavior when we are faced with a specific environmental condition.

Drive-reduction theory: This theory states that a biological need produces a drive to fill that need. To bring our body back to homeostasis, we are motivated to produce a particular need-reducing behavior.

Incentive theory: This theory suggests that we are motivated to behave in certain ways by external and environmental factors (rewards, money, and other reinforcers).

Cognitive theory: This theory proposes that our beliefs can influence our behavior and that our motivation is intrinsic: we engage in particular behaviors because we find them personally rewarding or because they fulfill our beliefs and expectations.

3. *Identify Key Words:* Which words in the question hold the key to the best answer?

The key words are "which theory *best explains?*" I need to evaluate each of the theories in terms of its account of why students work hard to get good grades. Then I can decide which is the best explanation.

Instinct theory: It is unlikely that a student's hard work is purely instinctual: we are not born with the biological determination to study and attain good grades. You might want to say that a desire for survival motivates students, but it would be much easier to argue that notion from a cognitive, rather than instinctual, point of view.

Drive-reduction theory: This approach is also too biological to explain something as cognitively based as studying in college. Some students might tell you that if they don't get good grades, their parents will stop sending them money and so they will go hungry! Nevertheless, the brain does not monitor *homeostasis* in terms of grade maintenance, and so if students are driven, it is not likely to be because of biological necessity.

Incentive theory: Now we come to a perspective that will help us explain the hard work of college students. People with college degrees tend to have higher salaries than those without such degrees, and money can be translated into other material incentives, such as clothes, a nice apartment, and a Ford Explorer. Beyond material incentives, there are also social incentives, such as praise and status. Just having a college degree confers status in our culture.

Cognitive theory: The focus here is on intrinsic motivators. In a humanistic sense, students might think that they have the potential to excel academically, and they believe that the best way to reach that potential is by getting good grades. In those terms, they get considerable satisfaction from their success. This means that some

students do not need praise or encouragement from others, nor do they need the promise of a big salary at the end of their studies. Their motivation is self-determined and independent of these external factors. If these students decide to go into academic life, they are well advised to be motivated by cognitive, rather than external, factors.

B. Biological & Social Needs

STUDY QUESTION: How would your needs change if you won a $20-million lottery?

Possible Answer: We have all heard the cliché "Money can't buy happiness." Money can help us satisfy some, but not all, of our needs. After winning a lottery, I should be able to look after most *biological needs*, unless I become ill or am physically threatened (for instance, kidnapped for ransom). Money can also help with the attainment of *social needs*, to the extent that it allows the person to meet others, be generous, and just plain have fun.

However, money might be less helpful in my attempt to satisfy my need to achieve. Getting $1 million per year would eliminate the need to work for a living, but many people satisfy most of their achievement needs at work. I could travel the world; I could have servants, expensive cars, and wild parties; but boredom might set in anyway because I would not be *achieving* anything through all this. Such lack of self-actualization might explain why people's lives don't change as much as they expect when they win large sums of money.

Another problem in terms of social needs is that an abrupt change in financial status might bring about an unwelcome change in my friendship network. I might like to continue as always with my friends, but they now perceive me to be rich and, therefore, different from them.

H. Application: Eating Problems & Treatments

STUDY QUESTION: Would you believe an ad that promised you could "lose weight easily and quickly without dieting or exercise by practicing self-hypnosis"?

Possible Answer: A good starting question would be, "What is the physiological basis for weight loss via hypnosis?" Since the only known means of losing weight are reducing consumption of certain foods and increasing metabolism, usually by exercise, it is hard to imagine that a hypnosis program could work without at least one of those components.

Another question, therefore, would be, "What is the content of the hypnotic suggestion?" A strong hunch would be that it would involve repressing urges to eat by desensitizing us to external food cues. That might be all right, depending on the answers to the next questions.

"How quickly will I lose weight with this program, and what long-term coping strategies does it include?" If the hypnosis provides little more than the means to survive a crash diet, it isn't a good idea. Staying within healthy weight limits involves controlling aspects of one's *lifestyle*. Self-hypnosis can play a part in this, especially with confidence building and relaxation (since some people eat more when anxious), but people should probably be skeptical of "lose-weight-quick" schemes that rely on self-hypnosis. In fact, any plan to lose weight quickly should be given careful scrutiny.

Appendix B

Module 16
EMOTION

A. Peripheral Theories

STUDY QUESTION: Does someone with many facial expressions experience more emotions than someone with few facial expressions?

1. Need to Know: What specific information do I need to answer this question?

I need to know what facial expressions have to do with emotions. Specifically, what is facial feedback theory?

2. Defining Terms: Do I need to use my own words to define or review any terms?

Facial feedback theory: This theory suggests that sensations or feedback from the movement of the facial muscles are interpreted as emotions.

3. Identify Key Words: Which words in the question hold the key to the best answer?

The key words are "experience more emotions." The answer to this question lies in the validity of facial feedback theory.

At first glance, the answer would seem to be yes. If facial feedback theory is correct, the individual with few expressions is having fewer emotions than is the individual with a lot of facial expressions. But the text reports that facial feedback theory has not been demonstrated to be correct. A relationship has, however, been found between facial expression and the *intensity* of our subjective emotional experience. So, the person with a lot of facial expressions would be having more *intense* experiences than would someone with fewer expressions, but not *more* emotions.

E. Function of Emotions

STUDY QUESTION: Why might people who are madly in love have difficulty making the right decisions?

Possible Answer: When individuals are madly in love, they are in a state of high physiological arousal. According to the Yerkes-Dodson law, high levels of arousal improve our performance on easy tasks but impair performance on difficult tasks. When we are making an important decision (which is certainly a difficult task), it's best to be in a relaxed state of low arousal. If we are in a heightened state of arousal, the decision that we make at this time—for example, "Should I marry this person?"—might not be the best one for us.

I. Application: Lie Detection

STUDY QUESTION: Would it be fair to use lie detector tests to identify students who are suspected of cheating on exams?

Possible Answer: Let's start with the assumption that your students did not, in fact, cheat on the exams. Can you prove their innocence via the polygraph? Putting the question another way, could an innocent person fail a lie detector test?

The answer to this question appears to be yes. The text points out that such tests lead to false conclusions from 5 to 75% of the time. There are many reasons for this. The most important follows from the fundamental assumptions of the lie detector test—that lying is accompanied by guilt, and guilt yields arousal.

No one has doubted that a polygraph can detect physiological arousal. The problem is in the interpretation of that arousal. Your students might respond with arousal to a critical question about the exam because they know that they are under suspicion and the exam is very relevant to that suspicion. Perhaps they saw someone who seemed to be cheating during the exam, and the mention of that makes them anxious. In short, there are many reasons why the students might show a positive response to the critical question.

It would be extremely unfair to use the lie detector to assess guilt (or innocence) of cheating.

Module 17
INFANCY & CHILDHOOD

A. Prenatal Influences

STUDY QUESTION: A pregnant woman asks, "Why do I have to worry about ingesting chemicals, since my unborn child has a separate blood supply?" What is your response?

1. Need to Know: What specific information do I need to answer this question?

I need to know whether fetuses in fact have their own blood supply.

2. Identify Key Words: Which words in the question hold the key to the best answer?

The key words are "separate blood supply." To answer this question, I must establish whether the blood supplies of mother and fetus are shared.

This pregnant woman is wrong. The blood supplies of mother and fetus are connected via the **placenta,** which is the life-support system for the fetus. In fact, the chemicals that this woman injects might very well be **teratogens**—agents that can cause birth defects. Here is some evidence that the mother's bloodstream can supply teratogens to the fetus.

Heavy maternal drinking during pregnancy results in **fetal alcohol syndrome,** which is characterized by a number of physical and psychological defects. Mothers who smoke heavily during pregnancy have a higher rate of stillbirths and premature births and have babies with significantly lower birth weight. Finally, pregnant women who are cocaine and heroine addicts experience problems such as the premature birth, lower birth weight, and smaller head circumference of babies. These babies are also born with dependencies on the drugs and must go through drug withdrawal after birth.

D. Research Focus: Temperament

STUDY QUESTION: Marcie and Jeff love their 6-month-old son but find that he is easily irritated and frightened. What should they do?

Possible Answer: Marcie and Jeff should be told that, for reasons that have nothing to do with parenting, children differ in the early emotional patterns they display. Their son would fit into a category called **inhibited children.** Inhibited children show reluctance, anxiety, and fear when approaching a strange child, exploring new objects, playing with peers, or speaking to adults.

Once they know they have not done anything wrong, Marcie and Jeff can be told that there are things they can do that might reduce their son's relatively high fear response. They need to be caring and supportive and to consistently help their child with minor stressors. Marcie and Jeff should also avoid becoming too anxious, overprotective, or angry at their child's fearfulness. If they can provide their infant son with the love and support he needs, this inhibited baby will have a better chance of becoming less and less fearful as he approaches adolescence. Parents can help their shy or fearful child become more expressive and outgoing.

F. Social Development

STUDY QUESTION: How would Freud's and Erikson's theories apply to a 3-year-old child whose parents are getting divorced?

Possible Answer: Let's consider Freud's and Erikson's approaches in turn.

Freud. Freud would probably say that the parents' separation will cause more problems when the child approaches puberty than at age 3. The child had both parents around when he or she was going through some of the early stages that Freud considered vital—breast feeding and toilet training. The next critical stage will be near puberty, when the child begins to develop subconscious sexual urges. Freud believed that, for a boy, these subconscious urges are directed at the mother, and that the father is then seen as a rival. (For a girl, the parents' roles are reversed.) All of this arouses subconscious guilt in the child. With one of the parents missing, this process will be disrupted. (This Oedipal analysis is presented later in the text.)

Erikson. In Erikson's view, this 3-year-old is making a transition between stages 2 and 3 in terms of psychosocial development. This means that the child might be working to establish autonomy over shame and initiative over guilt. The parents can play an important role in the resolution of both these conflicts. If they encourage the child to try things on his or her own—for example, getting dressed in the morning—the child is more likely to develop autonomy. If they also encourage the child to take on appropriate challenges—for example, building things or cleaning up his or her room—the child will develop initiative.

The problem is that both these processes require parental presence. The parents must take the time to encourage and praise the child when he or she shows autonomy and initiative. Unfortunately, divorce often becomes the focus of the parents' attention. In addition, the child might feel partly to blame for the parents' difficulties, which makes shame and guilt more likely.

Module 18
ADOLESCENCE & ADULTHOOD

A. Puberty & Sexual Behavior

STUDY QUESTION: How are the sexual concerns of adolescents and senior adults similar but also different?

1. Need to Know: What specific information do I need to answer this question?

I need to know what the sexual concerns of adolescents and senior adults are.

2. Identify Key Words: Which words in the question hold the key to the best answer?

The key words are "similar but also different." To answer this question, I need to examine the sexual concerns of people in these age groups.

One of the biggest concerns for teenagers is whether to become sexually active. And there is considerable peer pressure for them to do so. Once they have decided to be sexually active, avoiding pregnancy and sexually transmitted diseases is of great concern. Many teens are not viewed as sexually active by adults, in the same way that senior adults are not viewed as sexually active. Senior adults are often confused by the physical changes in their bodies (just like teens!) that make sex different than it once was. Seniors have to fight the stereotype that they are asexual: research indicates that many senior couples are happier with their sex lives now than when they were individuals in the singles scene.

C. Personality & Social Changes

STUDY QUESTION: If you become a parent, what special concerns might you have when your own children go through adolescence?

Possible Answer: According to the text, one of the primary tasks an adolescent has is to develop a **self-identity** and **self-esteem**. This also corresponds to Erikson's **stage 5: identity versus role confusion.** Erikson suggests that if teens do not develop a purposeful life, they will experience **identity confusion** and they will be unstable or socially withdrawn. So I would be concerned about their successful development of self-identity.

A parent might not only want teenagers to be happy with their self-identity but also hope that they will find productive work that they love and form deep and lasting relationships with their family and friends. Safety is another concern: can the teenagers explore their developing selves without getting AIDS, having bad experiences with drugs, or becoming enmeshed in unhealthy relationships with other people?

H. Application: Suicide

STUDY QUESTION: If your grandmother had incurable cancer and unbearable pain and asked you to help her commit suicide, would you do it?

Possible Answer: Here is what I would do for my grandmother. Other people might have different responses.

I would not get angry with her or say that her desire to end her life was silly or selfish. Instead, I would say that her wishes were perfectly understandable. Then I would suggest that we find a hospice facility willing to do its utmost to reduce her pain and allow her to retain her dignity.

If, in the hospice, she found that the pain was still intolerable, I would have to face the moral dilemma of whether to help her commit suicide. Probably, I would first try to convince her caregivers to let her end her life peacefully and with dignity. I could not actively kill my grandma but, if it came to it, I would help her to do what it takes to commit suicide—to gather pills, and so on.

Appendix B

Module 19
FREUDIAN & HUMANISTIC THEORIES

A. Freud's Psychodynamic Theory

STUDY QUESTION: According to Freud, why do some students plan to study on the weekend but end up partying?

1. Need to Know: What specific information do I need to answer this question?

I need to know what Freud's psychodynamic theory of personality is.

It is a theory about our personality development that emphasizes early childhood experiences, the importance of repressed thoughts that we can't access, and conflicts between our conscious and our unconscious desires. These conflicts are used to explain why we do things that we don't intend.

2. Defining Terms: Do I need to use my own words to define or review any terms?

Conscious thoughts: These are wishes and desires that we can express at any time.

Unconscious thoughts: These are our wishes and desires that are repressed because of their disturbing content. We cannot access them.

3. Identify Key Words: Which words in the question hold the key to the best answer?

The key words are "plan to study . . . but end up partying." This question asks us to explain why we do things we don't intend to do.

Our conscious desire is to study. But every weekend we end up partying and don't understand why. Freud would say that we had an unconscious desire to seek pleasure (remember Module 17?) in the form of partying. We aren't aware that we desire to party every weekend (this wish is repressed), because to recognize that we'd rather party than graduate from college threatens our sense of who we are. The unconscious desire is winning over our conscious desire.

F. Cultural Diversity: Unexpected High Achievement

STUDY QUESTION: If you were the principal of a grade school, what might you do to improve overall student performance?

Possible Answer: The experiences of Indochinese immigrants outlined in the text suggest that you must pay attention to particular **primary values** in order to improve overall student performance at your school. These primary values include mutual respect, cooperation, a love of learning, a commitment to accomplishment and achievement, and the belief that you cannot let fate or luck control your life. Instead, students must believe that they are the masters of their own destiny.

Parental involvement appears to be vital. Over half the Indochinese parents read aloud to their children. Parents at your school should be encouraged to make homework a family activity. This doesn't mean that parents do their children's homework. Instead, it means that, each night, every family member has something to do that enhances his or her learning. This makes it clear that all family members are committed to accomplishment and achievement. Students should be expected to do more homework than the national average, perhaps as much as three hours per night, to the

exclusion of television. You should also encourage strong family ties, so that parents and children feel mutual respect and obligation, and family members strive to maintain cooperation and harmony.

All of this would be very difficult to achieve because, as principal, you are going beyond the principles of pedagogy; you are attempting to make changes to our culture by borrowing from the strengths of another.

H. Application: Assessment—Projective Tests

STUDY QUESTION: How useful would projective tests be in identifying students who are most likely to cheat on exams?

Possible Answer: Strong proponents of projective tests might claim that they have this type of predictive power. Others would suggest that projective tests can provide insights into general personality traits or more global behavioral tendencies but that they could not be used to predict a behavior as specific as cheating on exams. Still others would argue that projective tests are too open to interpretation by the clinician to be predictive of anything.

If projective tests were to be used in this way, many different testings would have to be conducted with a variety of projective tests. If a student showed consistent trends indicative of extreme mark anxiety, external pressure, poor moral development, or perhaps an animosity toward the instructor or toward authority in general, we could perhaps infer that this student would be more likely to cheat than would students who do not show these tendencies. Of course, the problem comes in ascertaining these tendencies from the open-ended responses of the student.

Module 20
SOCIAL COGNITIVE & TRAIT THEORIES

A. Social Cognitive Theory

STUDY QUESTION: Why do students invest thousands of dollars and 4 to 6 years of hard work to obtain a college degree?

1. Need to Know: What specific information do I need to answer this question?

I need to know what social cognitive theory says about our behaviors—in this case, going to college.

Social cognitive theory suggests that our beliefs and feelings influence our behavior. What beliefs (cognitive factors) might be related to our behavior of going to college?

2. Defining Terms: Do I need to use my own words to define or review any terms?

Cognitive factors: Four cognitive factors are important, according to social cognitive theory. Specifically, there are three important beliefs: locus of control, self-efficacy, and delay of gratification.

3. Identify Key Words: Which words in the question hold the key to the best answer?

The key word is "why?" We are asked to examine what motivates a person to go to college, from a social cognitive perspective. Let's look at the relevant cognitive factors.

One important belief that would help explain students' desire to attain a university degree is their **locus of control**. Most people who put out considerable effort and resources to attain a goal believe that its attainment is within their control. In other words, they have an *internal locus of control*.

Students' sense of **self-efficacy** refers to their beliefs regarding how capable they are of achieving their goals. Individuals who have a history of success in similar tasks, who feel they are as good as or better than others, and who have received positive feedback about their capabilities will have a high sense of self-efficacy. Students generally come to university with a fairly high sense of self-efficacy, since they were successful in high school. However, university presents new challenges that might make immediate success difficult. The danger, therefore, is that students' self-efficacy will drop dramatically in their first year. This can start a damaging cycle for them, in which they do not succeed because they feel they can't. In turn, their lack of success reinforces their low self-efficacy.

Students who invest all this money and effort must be willing to **delay gratification** for long periods of time. While some of their friends have full-time jobs that allow them to buy new cars and stereos, students live in residence halls or noisy apartments and drive beaters. To be successful students, they must persist at a number of difficult tasks for the promise of future reward.

B. Trait Theory

STUDY QUESTION: Would knowing about the Big Five traits help you write an ad to find the perfect roommate or life mate?

Possible Answer: This question is as concerned with attraction and compatibility as it is with trait theory. The literature on attraction makes it quite clear that similarity is a stronger unifying force than is dissimilarity, or complementary differences. Given that, it would be reasonable to assume that you are better advised to look for a roommate or a life partner who is similar to you.

Remember also that the definition of personality includes behavioral tendencies. Indeed, personality theorists assume that it is our personalities that predispose us to act in certain ways. This means that compatible personalities will engage in similar behaviors, such as keeping the apartment tidy, going to bed at similar times, and respecting other people's privacy. Similarity in these behaviors reduces the likelihood of conflict.

Knowing how you measure in the Big Five traits—openness, conscientiousness, extraversion, agreeableness, and neuroticism—might help you in finding someone who is more similar than different to share your apartment. Of course, this assumes that you can measure these traits in ways that will predict behavior in this particular situation (living together). To do this with some reliability, you must have made observations in related contexts.

It seems unlikely that you could find a life partner from a simple ad in the paper using the Big Five traits. You could find someone who appears to be very similar to you on a paper-and-pencil test but have no interpersonal or sexual attraction to that person.

Module 21
HEALTH, STRESS & COPING

A. Appraisal

STUDY QUESTION: Sue says that some situations always cause her stress, but John says it's how she thinks about them. Who's right?

1. *Need to Know:* What specific information do I need to answer this question?

I need to know what the research indicates about how situations cause stress.

2. *Identify Key Words:* Which words in the question hold the key to the best answer?

The key words are "some situations always cause her stress" and "how she thinks about them." The question is asking if the way we think about situations can change the amount of stress we feel in reaction to the situation.

According to the text, any situation (even a nonthreatening one) can cause stress through a process called **primary appraisal.** This is our first evaluation of the situation and how it relates to us. We may appraise the situation in one of three ways: as *irrelevant*, which means that the situation doesn't affect us at all; as *positive*, meaning that the situation will benefit us in some way; or as *stressful*, meaning that it overtaxes our resources. This would indicate that John is right and that how we appraise, or think about, the situation greatly affects whether or not we feel stressed.

The text also reports that in an experimental setting, the type of appraisal that individuals gave a stressful situation (whether they were told to view an industrial accident film objectively or to think about how they would feel) changed the physiological reaction to the stress. Subjects who were told to think about how they would feel in an industrial accident demonstrated higher physiological stress responses. This also supports John's position that how Sue thinks about a situation causes (or increases) her stress.

H. Application: Stress Management Programs

STUDY QUESTION: Why is it better to cope with stress by changing three things—thoughts, behaviors, and physiological responses—rather than just one?

Possible Answer: Our thoughts, behaviors, and physiological reactions all contribute to our feelings of stress. So it makes sense that the *best* way to reduce or manage stress is by changing all three factors. We can make our acid stomach better by popping antacids, thereby reducing the physiological reaction, but this is only temporary and doesn't change our reactions to stress.

Changing our thoughts means, for example, appraising events as a challenge rather than a threat and substituting positive self-statements when we notice ourselves making negative self-statements. Changing our behaviors means taking a problem-solving approach (taking action) rather than using emotion-focused temporary solutions to our stressors. Finally, changing our physiological reaction to stress means learning how to relax. Relaxation methods can include biofeedback, progressive relaxation, or meditation. Successful long-term stress management involves changing all three of the factors affecting our stress levels.

Appendix B

Module 22
ASSESSMENT & ANXIETY DISORDERS

A. Factors in Mental Disorders

STUDY QUESTION: The night before a big exam, John gets drunk to relax. However, the next day he has a terrible hangover and does poorly on the exam. Is his behavior abnormal?

1. *Need to Know:* What specific information do I need to answer this question?

I need to know how *abnormal* is defined.

Abnormality can be defined by three different methods: statistical frequency, deviation from the social norm, and maladaptive behavior.

2. *Defining Terms:* Do I need to use my own words to define or review any terms?

Statistical frequency: This method defines behavior as abnormal if it occurs rarely in the population as a whole.

Deviation from social norm: Behavior is considered abnormal if it differs greatly from the prevailing social standards.

Maladaptive behavior: Behavior is regarded as abnormal if it interferes with an individual's ability to function in society and as a person.

3. *Identify Key Words:* Which words in the question hold the key to the best answer?

The key words are "is his behavior abnormal?" If we look at John's behavior in the context of each method of defining what is abnormal, we will be able to answer the question.

If we use the statistical frequency approach and compare John's behavior to the general population of college students, his behavior would probably be considered abnormal. Most college students do not get so drunk before an exam that they are hung over.

On the basis of deviation from social norms, we would call John's behavior abnormal. It is not socially acceptable to drink so much that it interferes with your ability to take a test. However, it is probably more acceptable among young college students than in the population at large.

On the basis of the maladaptive behavior approach, we would say that if this is an isolated incident, John's behavior is not abnormal and will not greatly interfere with his responsibilities. However, if this behavior were to increase in frequency, it would interfere with his ability to function as a person and in society and would thus be considered abnormal.

B. Assessing Mental Disorders

STUDY QUESTION: Why must mental health professionals spend so much time and effort in assessing their clients' symptoms?

Possible Answer: There are a number of reasons why a detailed and usable diagnosis of mental disorders is essential to the understanding of mental health and the treatment of those disorders. Here are some of them.

Human behavior covers an extremely broad range. Because people are capable of so many different behaviors, it can be difficult to determine which are normal and which are abnormal. It might be that a behavior is infrequent and unusual but not maladaptive. Also, the possible range of abnormal behaviors is very broad, and it takes a great deal of time and experience to put names to each type.

The consequences of diagnosis are considerable. Passing diagnosis on a person carries considerable implications for that person. It could mean the difference between a prison term and psychiatric treatment, for example, or the difference between getting a job and being passed over. For this reason, the classification system must be detailed enough to gain diagnosticians' confidence. Also, diagnoses of mental disorders often carry a social stigma. This stigma can be reduced if the language is carefully chosen; for example, "antisocial personality disorder" sounds less condemning than "psychopath."

Treatment depends on classification. As with any intervention, the type of treatment is determined by the diagnosis.

H. Application: Treating Phobias

STUDY QUESTION: If you were very shy and uncomfortable about meeting strangers and talking to groups, what could you do about this problem?

Possible Answer: A number of cognitive-behavioral programs could help me. These programs use four components that I can try on my own. First, I would try to understand and believe that, since social fears are learned, they can be unlearned; after reading all the modules so far, this is easy to believe. I need to understand that I avoid meeting people and talking to groups of people in order to avoid the thoughts and physiological arousal that I experience in these situations.

Second, I would learn and substitute new social skills. I would carefully watch individuals who successfully meet others, so as to learn what the appropriate behaviors are. I would begin to write down my thoughts when I think about a group social situation or when I am in one. Then I would write a list of positive and healthy thoughts that I can use instead.

Third, I would begin to imagine myself successfully meeting others and talking to groups of strangers, until I am comfortable with these thoughts. Then I would begin actually to participate in these social situations.

Finally, I would continue doing homework by imagining these situations and also actually participate in group situations. If I was unable to treat myself to my satisfaction, I would get a referral to a therapist.

Module 23
MOOD DISORDERS & SCHIZOPHRENIA

A. Mood Disorders

STUDY QUESTION: A student is brought in to the health clinic for being depressed and having attempted suicide. What will be her treatment program?

1. *Need to Know:* What specific information do I need to answer this question?

I need to know what treatments are usually given for severe depression.

According to the text, the usual treatment consists of antidepressant drug therapy and/or psychotherapy.

2. *Identify Key Words:* Which words in the question hold the key to the best answer?

The key words are "what will be her treatment program?" The treatment options for major depression that are discussed in this section are antidepressant drug therapy and psychotherapy.

Generally, someone who has just attempted suicide is hospitalized for two reasons. First, constant monitoring will ensure the safety of the individual while he or she is deeply depressed. Second, this student will immediately begin a regimen of antidepressant drugs, as well as intensive psychotherapy. After the individual is no longer a suicide risk and if the depression has remitted somewhat, he or she will be released. It is important to continue the drug treatment and/or psychotherapy in order to prevent relapse.

B. Electroconvulsive Therapy

STUDY QUESTION: How would you compare the effectiveness and side effects of electroconvulsive shock therapy with those of antidepressant drugs?

Possible Answer: The text notes that about half of those patients for whom antidepressant drugs were initially prescribed quit because of the negative side effects. So there are obviously some significant side effects. Of those who remain on the drugs, about 30% show no benefit from the treatment; they still have major depression.

The question for those with unremitting depression is Are the side effects and risks of ECT worth the benefits? One of the side effects of ECT is significant memory impairment. Consequently, ECT should not be undertaken without first attempting to treat the depression with several different antidepressants under the direction of qualified therapists. However, the effectiveness rate of ECT is 60–80%. This is very high, considering that only the most depressed people ever get ECT. It may be that ECT is worth the risks when all else fails.

H. Application: Dealing with Mild Depression

STUDY QUESTION: When some people get depressed, why do they prefer to spread their gloom rather than do something to get over it?

Possible Answer: The essential problem is that those who are mildly depressed are used to this condition and often do not know that help is available. What's more, the state of depression leaves a person without the motivation or energy to do anything. Taken together, these problems mean that depressed people are unlikely to get unsolicited help or to help themselves. So where does the impetus to get help come from?

People with mild depression get caught in a cycle that cuts off social contact. It usually begins with deficiencies in social behavior, such as overdependence or general mistrust of others. Not surprisingly, people react negatively to depressed individuals, who interpret this to mean that they are right about themselves: they are worthless. In addition, friends tend to withdraw social support. This deepens the person's depressed state, which makes it less likely that the person will try to do anything to remedy the situation. Often, it takes a persistent, true friend to start the change, by getting the depressed person to seek professional help.

Module 24
THERAPIES

A. Historical Background

STUDY QUESTION: Should our major cities spend more money to develop care and treatment programs for the homeless?

1. *Need to Know:* What specific information do I need to answer this question?

I need to know why the homeless would need care and treatment programs.

According to the text, one of the results of deinstitutionalization has been that many former mental patients are no longer able to get the care and medication that they need. It is estimated that 25–50% of the current homeless population have serious mental disorders.

2. *Identify Key Words:* Which words in the question hold the key to the best answer?

The key words are "should our major cities spend more money?" This is a question of personal values. What do I think government should do?

Many homeless individuals are actually very ill and are untreated. In some cases, good treatment might be able to rehabilitate an individual as a functioning member of society. In other cases, even though treatment would improve the quality of an individual's life, he or she would never become an independent, functioning member of society. I think that it is important to deliver humane psychological and medical care and housing to individuals in *both* cases. How we choose to spend our money reflects what we value.

D. Behavior Therapy

STUDY QUESTION: Susan complains of having terrible test anxiety. What would a behavior therapist do to help her?

Possible Answer: A behavior therapist would look at **behaviors** that are causing Susan's problems, with the hope of replacing these with new **target behaviors.** The therapist would also look at **stimuli** that might be eliciting these unwanted responses, with the hope of desensitizing Susan so that the stimuli no longer bring on the unwanted response. For example, Susan might feel her heart pound before an exam. She might shake and feel nauseated. She might avoid studying because it is associated with the test; she goes jogging or hits the fridge instead. The therapist would like Susan to remain relaxed

Appendix B

when she thinks about her exam and when she approaches the exam room. This will allow her to concentrate when she studies and when she takes the exam. After identifying which behaviors to change and which new ones to replace them with, the therapist could use **desensitization** to help Susan overcome her test anxiety. The steps of systematic desensitization include relaxation, stimulus hierarchy, and desensitization training. Susan and the therapist together would design a stimulus hierarchy. The therapist would slowly take Susan through each step, making sure that she is fully relaxed and comfortable before proceeding to the next level of the hierarchy. This might take weeks, but the end result would be a reduction in Susan's test anxiety.

H. Application: Cognitive-Behavior Techniques

STUDY QUESTION: Frank has very little self-confidence and self-esteem. What is one way that he could work on raising them?

Possible Answer: There are a few cognitive-behavior techniques that can be practiced without the assistance of a therapist. Two very good strategies are called **thought stopping** and **thought substitution.**

Thought stopping has two basic components. In the first step, Frank must close his eyes each time he has a thought that is self-deprecating, silently yell "Stop!" and then silently count to ten. In the second step, Frank uses a collection of five photographs that he has pulled from albums. These photos show Frank having a good time with friends. On the back of each photo, he has written positive self-statements—for example, "I am a good person with good friends" or "My life is under my control. " He thinks about each picture for a moment, then turns over the photo, and repeats the sentence to himself. The entire process takes from one to two minutes.

Frank can follow up on this by making plans to improve his self-confidence. He can engage in activities for which he has some ability. Also, he can make a list of the irrational thoughts that have accompanied these activities—for example, "I can never do well" or "People will hate me if I don't do well. " These can be replaced with positive statements like those on the back of his photos. He must also be willing to reinforce himself when he succeeds. This can take the form of self-praise or tangible reinforcers—things he likes to eat and do.

Module 25
SOCIAL PSYCHOLOGY

A. Perceiving Others

STUDY QUESTION: Mark says that he doesn't make snap judgments but waits until he knows people. Do you think Mark does what he claims?

1. *Need to Know:* What specific information do I need to answer this question?

I need to know how we normally form first impressions.

Normally, our first impression of an individual is shaped by the person's physical appearance; our need to explain why the individual looks, dresses, or behaves as he or she does, and the person's race. Our first impression is formed in seconds, and it influences how we interact with that person.

2. *Identify Key Words:* Which words in the question hold the key to the best answer?

The key words are "do you think Mark does what he claims?" The question is asking whether or not anyone can stop making first impressions.

Mark might reserve judgment about people until he gets to know them better. If so, he's in a very small minority. Most of us do form judgments about others on meeting them. Let's look at some of the reasons why we form these first impressions.

As the text points out, making judgments about others has *social consequences:* the behavior we exhibit toward another person is guided by our impressions of that person. It is very difficult to treat someone in an entirely neutral way; our behavior can be placed on a continuum of friendliness, or of patience, tolerance, and so on. In order for Mark to reserve judgment, he must treat everyone *the same way* until he makes a judgment that helps dictate how he will treat the person. While this is possible, it is not the way most people operate.

Another factor is that, in order to avoid forming first impressions, Mark will have to either ignore some very salient social data or store it in memory without acting upon it. He must remain totally uninfluenced by appearance, accent, nonverbal behavior, and the first things a person says to him. Again, if Mark can do this, he has set himself apart from most of us, who pay quite close attention to these things.

In summary, Mark will have to control powerful motivational and cognitive factors in order to avoid these snap judgments. It's unlikely that he does so. Perhaps a more realistic goal is to admit to making first impressions but to allow for changes in them as you get to know a person better.

B. Attributions

STUDY QUESTION: What should you be aware of when you try to explain the behaviors of your friend or your mate?

Possible Answer: This question requires a knowledge of biases and errors in attribution. Let's look at each of the three discussed in the text and see how they can be avoided.

Fundamental attribution error. According to fundamental attribution error, we place inordinate weight on dispositional factors when making attributions. This means that we fail to appreciate the power that a situation can exert on behavior. For example, when someone does poorly on a test, we think the person isn't very smart, rather than thinking that the person might have been prevented from studying by a family crisis. To avoid this error, we must force ourselves to look at the situations in which people find themselves and acknowledge that they can have a strong influence on behavior.

Actor-observer effect. The actor-observer effect describes our tendency to attribute our own behavior to the situation and other people's behavior to their dispositions. We have eliminated some fundamental attribution error by gaining an appreciation of how the situation can influence our own behavior, but we still are insensitive to the effect the situation can have on the behavior of others. To avoid this effect requires that we show *empathy* for other people when they are in situations that bring out behavior that is less than their best. It also requires that we realize how favorable situations can sometimes make other people look better than they really are.

Self-serving bias. As its name implies, self-serving bias applies to our explanations of our own behavior. This isn't directly relevant to explanations of your friend's behavior, but it is worth reviewing as an addendum to the question.

We attribute our successes to our dispositions and our failures to the situation. In so doing, we protect our self-esteem. Though this protection has benefits as a short-term strategy, it does little to help us reduce the likelihood of failure in the future. If we were to be truly honest with ourselves, we would admit that some of our success is due to good fortune and the hard work of others, both of which are situational factors. Also, we would acknowledge that some of our failures could have been avoided if we had worked harder or if we had the talent to do better.

On the other hand, this honesty is not necessarily the best way to improve ourselves. A large body of research indicates that attributing all our outcomes to our own effort is most likely to result in self-improvement and high motivation.

F. Aggression

STUDY QUESTION: One of your friends says, "Getting angry and being aggressive are just part of human nature." What would you reply?

Possible Answer: The key phrase in my friend's sentence is "human nature." This term implies that being aggressive is inborn and that nothing can be done to change aggressive behavior. Although there is research suggesting that some aggressive behavior is related to neurotransmitter levels and thus is inborn, much more evidence points to external contributors to aggressive behavior, such as social learning and environmental factors. If all anger (an emotion that probably is inborn) were expressed aggressively, there would be even more world wide cross-cultural aggression than we see now.

I would further suggest to my friend that his belief is more likely to cause his own anger to be expressed as aggression. Research has shown that cognitive factors can override aggression and also indicates that social rules can inhibit aggression. If we have rules that say aggressive behavior is unacceptable, we are less likely to experience aggression.

Glossary

ability tests Achievement tests, which measure what we have learned; aptitude tests, which measure our potential for learning or acquiring a specific skill; and intelligence tests, which measure our general potential to solve problems, think abstractly, and profit from experience.

absolute threshold The intensity level of a stimulus such that a person has a 50% chance of detecting it.

accommodation The process by which a person changes old methods to deal with or adjust to new situations.

achievement need The desire to set challenging goals and to persist in pursuing those goals in the face of obstacles, frustrations, and setbacks.

acquired immune deficiency syndrome *See* AIDS.

action potential A tiny electric current that is generated when the positive sodium ions rush inside the axon. The enormous increase of sodium ions inside the axon causes the inside of the axon to reverse its charge: The inside becomes positive, while the outside becomes negative.

activation-synthesis theory of dreams The idea that dreaming represents the random and meaningless activity of nerve cells in the brain. According to this theory, the pons, an area in the brain, sends millions of random nerve impulses to the cortex; in turn, the cortex tries to make sense of these signals by creating the feelings, imagined movements, perceptions, changing scenes, and meaningless images that we define as dreams.

actor-observer effect Our tendency, when we are behaving (or acting), to attribute our own behavior to situational factors but, when we are observing, to attribute another person's behavior to his or her personality traits or disposition.

acupuncture An ancient Chinese procedure for the relief of pain, in which a trained practitioner inserts thin needles into various points on the body's surface, often far from the site of the pain, and then manually twirls or electrically stimulates the needles.

adaptation The decreasing response of the sensory organs as they are exposed to a continuous level of stimulation.

adaptation level theory The idea that we quickly become accustomed to receiving some good fortune (money, job, car, degree). We take the good fortune for granted within a short period of time and, as a result, the initial impact of our good fortune fades and contributes less to our long-term level of happiness.

adaptive theory A theory suggesting that sleep evolved as a survival mechanism, since it prevented early humans and animals from wasting energy and exposing themselves to the dangers of nocturnal predators.

adaptive value The usefulness of certain abilities or traits that have evolved in animals or humans that tend to increase their chances of survival, such as the ability to find food, acquire mates, and avoid illness and injury.

addiction A behavioral pattern of drug abuse that is marked by an overwhelming and compulsive desire to obtain and use the drug. Even after stopping, the addict has a tendency to relapse and begin using the drug again.

adolescence A developmental period, lasting from about the ages of 12 to 18, that marks the end of childhood and the beginning of adulthood; it is a transitional period of considerable biological, cognitive, social, and personality changes.

adrenal glands Structures in the endocrine system. The adrenal cortex (outer part) secretes hormones that regulate sugar and salt balances and help the body resist stress; they are also responsible for the growth of pubic hair, a secondary sexual characteristic. The adrenal medulla (inner part) secretes two hormones that arouse the body to deal with stress and emergencies: epinephrine (adrenaline) and norepinephrine (noradrenaline).

affective neuroscience approach The study of the underlying neural bases of mood and emotion by focusing on the brain's neural circuits that evaluate stimuli and produce or contribute to experiencing and expressing different emotional states.

afferent neurons Neurons that carry information from the senses to the spinal cord; also called sensory neurons.

afterimage A visual image that continues after the original stimulus is removed.

age regression In hypnosis, the suggestion that subjects regress, or return, to an earlier time in their lives—for example, to early childhood.

aggression Any behavior directed toward another that is intended to cause harm.

aging process Changes caused by a combination of certain genes and proteins that interfere with organ functioning and by the natural production of toxic molecules (free radicals) that, in turn, cause random damage to body organs and to DNA (the building blocks of life). Such damage eventually exceeds the body's ability to repair itself and results in greater susceptibility to diseases and death.

agoraphobia An anxiety about being in places or situations from which escape might be difficult or embarrassing if a panic attack or paniclike symptoms (sudden dizziness or onset of diarrhea) were to occur.

AIDS (acquired immune deficiency syndrome) A life-threatening condition that, by the latest definition, is present when the individual is HIV positive and has a level of T-cells (CD4 immune cells) of no more than 200 per cubic milliliter of blood (one-fifth the level of a healthy person) or has developed one or more of 26 specified illnesses (including recurrent pneumonia and skin cancer).

alarm stage In the general adaptation syndrome, our initial reaction to stress, marked by activation of the fight-flight response, which causes physiological arousal.

alcohol (ethyl alcohol) A psychoactive drug classified as a depressant; it depresses activity of the central nervous system. Alcohol causes friendliness and loss of inhibitions at low doses, impairs drinkers' social judgment and understanding at medium doses, and seriously impairs motor coordination, cognitive abilities, decision making, and speech at higher doses. Very high doses may result in coma and death.

alcoholism A problem involving addiction to alcohol. An alcoholic is a person who has drunk heavily for a long period of time, is addicted to and has an intense craving for alcohol, and, as a result, has problems in two or three major life areas (social, personal, and financial areas, for example).

algorithms Rules that, if followed correctly, will eventually lead to the solution of a problem.

all-or-none law The fact that, once a nerve impulse starts in a small segment at the very beginning of the axon, it will continue at the same speed, segment by segment, to the very end of the axon.

alpha stage In sleep, a stage marked by feelings of being relaxed and drowsy, usually with the eyes closed. Alpha waves have low amplitude and high frequency (8–12 cycles per second).

altered state of consciousness An awareness that differs from normal consciousness; such awareness may be produced by using any number of procedures, such as meditation, psychoactive drugs, hypnosis, or sleep deprivation.

altered state theory of hypnosis The idea that hypnosis is not a trancelike state but rather an altered state of consciousness, during which a person experiences different sensations and feelings. No physiological measures have been found to indicate that a person is in a trance. For another view of hypnosis, see the sociocognitive theory of hypnosis.

altruism Helping or doing something, often at a cost or risk, for reasons other than the expectation of a material or social reward.

Alzheimer's disease A disorder that usually begins after people reach age 50 and is always fatal; it results from widespread damage to the brain, including the hippocampus, and produces deterioration in personality, emotions, cognitive processes, and memory.

Ames room A viewing environment, designed by Albert Ames, that demonstrates how our perception of size may be distorted by manipulating our depth cues.

amnesia Memory loss that may occur after damage to the brain (temporary or permanent), following drug use, or after severe psychological stress.

amniocentesis A medical test performed between weeks 14 and 20 of pregnancy. A long needle is inserted through the mother's abdominal muscles into the amniotic fluid surrounding the fetus. By withdrawing and analyzing fetal cells in the fluid, doctors can identify a number of genetic problems.

amygdala A structure in the limbic system that is located in the tip of the temporal lobe and is involved in forming, recognizing, and remembering emotional experiences and facial expressions.

anal stage Freud's second psychosexual stage, lasting from the age of about $1\frac{1}{2}$ to 3. In this stage, the infant's pleasure seeking is centered on the anus and its functions of elimination.

analogy A strategy for finding a similarity between a new situation and an old, familiar situation.

androgens Male sex hormones.

anencephaly The condition of being born with little or no brain. If some brain or nervous tissue is present, it is totally exposed and often damaged because the top of the skull is missing. Survival is usually limited to days; the longest has been 2 months.

animal model An approach to studying some human problem, situation, or disease by observing, testing, and measuring animals' behavioral, physiological, or neurological changes under conditions that closely approximate it.

anorexia nervosa A serious eating disorder characterized by refusing to eat and not maintaining weight at 85% of what is expected, having an intense fear of gaining weight or becoming fat, and missing at least three consecutive menstrual cycles. Anorexics also have a disturbed body image: They see themselves as fat even though they are very thin.

anterior pituitary The front part of the pituitary gland, a key component of the endocrine system. It regulates growth through the secretion of growth hormone and produces hormones that control the adrenal cortex, pancreas, thyroid, and gonads.

anticipatory nausea Feelings of nausea that are elicited by stimuli associated with nausea-inducing chemotherapy treatments. Patients experience nausea after treatment but also in anticipation of their treatment. Researchers believe that anticipatory nausea occurs through classical conditioning.

antidepressant drugs Drugs used to combat depression. They act by increasing levels of a specific group of neurotransmitters (monoamines, such as serotonin) that is believed to be involved in the regulation of emotions and moods.

antipsychotic drugs *See* neuroleptic drugs.

antisocial personality disorder A pattern of disregarding or violating the rights of others without feeling guilt or remorse. It is found in 3% of the population, predominantly in males.

anxiety An unpleasant state that is associated with feelings of uneasiness, apprehension, and heightened physiological arousal, such as increased heart rate and blood pressure. According to Freud, it arises when there is an unconscious conflict between the id's and superego's desires regarding how to satisfy a need; the ego, caught in the

middle, reacts by creating a feeling of anxiety. More modern theories of anxiety are based on conditioned emotional responses and observational learning.

apparent motion An illusion that a stimulus or object is moving in space when, in fact, it is stationary. This illusion is created by rapidly showing a series of stationary images, each of which has a slightly different position or posture than the one before.

approach-approach conflict Having to choose between two situations that both have pleasurable consequences.

approach-avoidance conflict The conflict that arises in a single situation that has both pleasurable and disagreeable aspects.

arousal-cost-reward model of helping The idea that we make decisions to help by calculating the costs and rewards of helping.

assimilation The process by which a child uses old methods or experiences to deal with new situations and then incorporates the new information into his or her existing knowledge.

atmospheric perspective In three-dimensional vision, a monocular depth cue that comes into play in the presence of dust, smog, or water vapor. Hazy objects are interpreted as being farther away.

attachment A close fundamental emotional bond that develops between the infant and his or her parent or caregiver.

attention-deficit/hyperactivity disorder (ADHD) A condition diagnosed on the basis of the occurrence of certain behavioral problems, rather than medical tests. A child must have six or more symptoms of inattention (such as making careless mistakes in schoolwork) and six or more symptoms of hyperactivity (such as fidgeting or talking excessively). These symptoms should have been present from an early age, persisted for at least six months, and contributed to maladaptive development.

attitude Any belief or opinion that includes a positive or negative evaluation of some object, person, or event and that predisposes us to act in a certain way toward that object, person, or event.

attributions Our explanations of the causes of events, other people's behaviors, and our own behaviors.

atypical neuroleptic drugs Neuroleptics that somewhat lower levels of dopamine but, more important, reduce levels of other neurotransmitters, especially serotonin. One group of these drugs is the benzamides, such as clozapine. These drugs primarily reduce positive symptoms and may slightly improve negative symptoms.

auditory association area An area directly below the primary auditory cortex that receives and transforms meaningless auditory sensations into perceptions or meaningful sounds, such as melodies or words.

auditory canal A long tube in the ear that funnels sound waves down its length so that the waves

strike a thin, taut membrane-the eardrum, or tympanic membrane.

auditory nerve A band of fibers that carries impulses (electrical signals) from the cochlea to the brain, resulting in the perception of sounds.

authoritarian parents Parents who attempt to shape, control, and evaluate the behavior and attitudes of their children in accordance with a set standard of conduct, usually an absolute standard that comes from religious or respected authorities.

authoritative parents Parents who attempt to direct their children's activities in a rational and intelligent way. They are supporting, loving, and committed, encourage verbal give-and-take, and discuss their rules and policies with their children.

autism A condition marked by especially abnormal or impaired development in social interactions, spoken language, and sensory-motor systems. Autistics characteristically have few activities or interests and spend long periods of time repeating the same ritualistic physical behaviors. Signs of autism begin in a child's first three years.

automatic encoding The transfer of information from short-term into long-term memory without any effort and usually without any awareness.

automatic processes Activities that require little awareness, take minimal attention, and do not interfere with other ongoing activities.

autonomic nervous system That portion of the peripheral nervous system that regulates heart rate, breathing, blood pressure, digestion, hormone secretion, and other functions, as well as maintains the body in a state of optimal balance, or homeostasis. It usually functions without conscious effort, which means that only a few of its responses, such as breathing, can also be controlled voluntarily. Its two subdivisions are the sympathetic division and the parasympathetic division.

availability heuristic A rule of thumb by which we rely on information that is more prominent or easily recalled and overlook other information that is available but less prominent or notable.

avoidance-avoidance conflict Having to choose between two situations that both have disagreeable consequences.

axon A single threadlike structure within the neuron. It extends from, and carries signals away from, the cell body to neighboring neurons, organs, or muscles.

axon membrane The axon wall, which contains chemical gates that may be opened or closed to control the inward and outward flow of electrically charged particles called ions.

babbling The first stage in acquiring language, in which infants, at an age of about 6 months, begin to make one-syllable sounds such as "deedeedee" or "bababa." Many of these sounds are common across languages.

Bandura's social cognitive theory A personality theory that assumes that personality development, growth, and change are influenced by

Glossary

four distinctively human cognitive processes: highly developed language ability, observational learning, purposeful behavior, and self-analysis. Bandura emphasizes the importance of learning through observation, imitation, and self-reward in the development of social skills, interactions, and behaviors. He contends that we can learn new social skills without performing any observable behaviors or receiving any external rewards. *See also* social cognitive theory.

Barnum principle A technique used in horoscopes and elsewhere, in which a number of traits are listed in such a general way that almost everyone who reads them thinks that these traits apply specifically to him or her. This technique was named after circus owner P. T. Barnum.

basal ganglia A group of structures in the center of the brain that are involved in regulating movements. To function properly, neurons in the basal ganglia must have a sufficient supply of the neurotransmitter dopamine.

basic rules of grammar Rules for combining nouns, verbs, and other parts of speech into meaningful sentences.

basilar membrane A membrane within the cochlea that contains the auditory receptors, or hair cells.

Beck's cognitive theory of depression The idea that when we are depressed, automatic negative thoughts that we rarely notice occur continually throughout the day. These negative thoughts distort how we perceive and interpret the world and thus influence our behaviors and feelings, which in turn contribute to our feeling depressed.

Beck's cognitive therapy *See* cognitive therapy.

behavior modification A treatment or therapy that changes or modifies problems or undesirable behaviors by using learning principles based on operant conditioning, classical conditioning, and social cognitive learning.

behavior therapy A form of psychotherapy in which disruptive behaviors are changed and human functioning is improved on the basis of principles of classical and operant conditioning. It focuses on changing particular behaviors rather than on the underlying mental events or possible unconscious factors. Sometimes called behavior modification or cognitive-behavioral therapy.

behavioral approach A psychological viewpoint that analyzes how organisms learn new behaviors or modify existing ones, depending on whether events in their environments reward or punish these behaviors. Historically, as founded by John B. Watson, the behavioral approach emphasized the objective, scientific analysis of observable behaviors.

behavioral genetics The study of how inherited or genetic factors influence and interact with psychological factors to shape our personality, intelligence, emotions, and motivation and also how we behave, adapt, and adjust to our environment.

benzodiazepines Minor tranquilizers (Librium, Valium, Xanax, Dalmane, Halcion) that reduce anxiety and stress. They are frequently prescribed

for the short-term (3–4 weeks) treatment of insomnia. Side effects associated with high doses or prolonged use include daytime drowsiness, loss of memory, tolerance, and dependency.

Binet-Simon Intelligence Scale The world's first standardized intelligence test, containing items arranged in order of increasing difficulty. The items measured vocabulary, memory, common knowledge, and other cognitive abilities.

binocular depth cues In three-dimensional vision, depth cues that depend upon the movement of both eyes (*bi* means "two"; *ocular* means "eye").

biofeedback A training procedure through which a person is made aware of his or her physiological responses, such as muscle activity, heart rate, blood pressure, or temperature, and then tries to increase or decrease these physiological responses.

biological approach A psychological viewpoint that examines how our genes, hormones, and nervous systems interact with our environments to influence learning, personality, memory, motivation, emotions, coping techniques, and other traits and abilities.

biological clock The body's internal timing device that is genetically set to regulate various physiological responses for certain periods of time.

biological factors Innate tendencies or predispositions that may either facilitate or inhibit certain kinds of learning.

biological hunger factors Physiological changes in blood chemistry and signals from digestive organs that provide feedback to the brain, which, in turn, triggers us to eat or stop eating.

biological needs Physiological requirements that are critical to our survival and physical wellbeing.

biological psychology *See* psychobiology.

biological sex factors The action of sex hormones, which is involved in secondary sexual characteristics (facial hair, breasts), sexual motivation (more so in animals than in humans), and the development of ova and sperm.

BioPsychoSocial model The representation of adolescent development as a process that occurs simultaneously on many levels and includes sexual, cognitive, social, and personality changes that interact and influence each other.

biosocial theory A theory that emphasizes social and cultural forces; it says that differences in sexual activities and values for selecting mates developed from traditional cultural divisions of labor: Women were primarily childbearers and homemakers, while men were primarily providers and protectors.

bipolar I disorder A mood disorder characterized by fluctuations between episodes of depression and mania. A manic episode goes on for at least a week, during which a person is unusually euphoric, cheerful, and high and has at least three of the following symptoms: has great self-esteem, has little need of sleep, speaks rapidly and frequently, has racing thoughts, is easily distracted, and pursues pleasurable activities. Formerly called manic-depressive illness.

bisexual orientation A pattern of sexual arousal by persons of either sex.

brightness constancy Our tendency to perceive brightness as remaining the same in changing illumination.

Broca's aphasia An inability to speak in fluent sentences while retaining the ability to understand written or spoken words. It is caused by damage to Broca's area.

Broca's area An area usually located in the left frontal lobe that is necessary for combining sounds into words and arranging words into meaningful sentences. *See* Broca's aphasia.

bulimia nervosa An eating disorder characterized by a minimum of two binge-eating episodes per week for at least three months; fear of not being able to stop eating; regularly engaging in vomiting, use of laxatives, or rigorous dieting and fasting; and excessive concern about body shape and weight.

burnout Feelings of doing poorly at one's job, physically wearing out, and becoming emotionally exhausted due to intense involvement with people who demand too much of one's time and energy and provide too little reward or satisfaction.

bystander effect The phenomenon in which an individual feels inhibited from taking some action because of the presence of others.

caffeine A mild stimulant that produces dilation of blood vessels, increased secretion of stomach acid, and moderate physiological arousal. Psychological effects include a feeling of alertness, decreased fatigue and drowsiness, and improved reaction times. Caffeine, which is present in coffee, tea, chocolate, and other foods, can be addictive, especially in higher doses.

case study An in-depth analysis of the thoughts, feelings, beliefs, experiences, behaviors, or problems of an individual. This research method offers little opportunity to control or manipulate situations or variables.

catatonic schizophrenia A subcategory of schizophrenia characterized by periods of wild excitement or periods of rigid, prolonged immobility; sometimes the person assumes the same frozen posture for hours on end.

catharsis A psychological process through which anger or aggressive energy is released by expressing or letting out powerful negative emotions. Freud's view that catharsis can be helpful in reducing aggression is not supported by most research.

cell body For neurons, a relatively large, egg-shaped structure that provides fuel, manufactures chemicals, and maintains the entire neuron in working order; also called the soma.

central cues Hunger cues associated with the activity of chemicals and neurotransmitters in different areas of the brain.

central nervous system Neurons located in the brain and spinal cord. From the bottom of the brain emerges the spinal cord, which is made up of neurons and bundles of axons and dendrites that carry information back and forth between the brain and the body. Neurons in the central nervous system normally have almost no capacity to regrow or regenerate if damaged or diseased.

central route for persuasion Presenting information with strong arguments, analyses, facts, and logic.

cephalocaudal principle The rule that parts of the body closer to the infant's head develop before parts closer to the feet.

cerebellum A region of the hindbrain that is involved in coordinating movements but not in initiating voluntary movements. It is also involved in cognitive functions, such as short-term memory, following rules, and carrying out plans. Surprising new evidence suggests that the cerebellum is also involved in learning to perform timed motor responses, such as those required in playing games or sports.

challenge appraisal Our conclusion that we have the potential for gain or personal growth in a particular situation but that we also need to mobilize our physical energy and psychological resources to meet the challenging situation.

chi-square A test of statistical significance that compares the actual observed distribution of people (or events) among various categories with the distribution expected purely on the basis of chance.

child abuse and neglect Inadequate care or acts by the parent(s) (physical or emotional abuse) that put a child in danger, cause physical harm or injury, or involve sexual molestation.

Chomsky's theory of language The idea that all languages share a common universal grammar and that children inherit a mental program to learn this universal grammar. This theory includes the concepts of deep structure and surface structure and of transformational rules to convert from one to the other.

chromosome A hairlike structure that contains tightly coiled strands of deoxyribonucleic acid (DNA). Each cell of the human body (except for the sperm and egg) contains 46 chromosomes, arranged in 23 pairs.

chunking Combining separate items of information into a larger unit, or chunk, and then remembering chunks of information rather than individual items. A technique of memory enhancement.

circadian rhythm A biological clock that is genetically programmed to regulate physiological responses within a time period of 24 or 25 hours (about a day); one example is the sleep-wake cycle.

clairvoyance The ability to perceive events or objects that are out of sight.

classical conditioning A kind of learning in which a neutral stimulus acquires the ability to produce a response that was originally produced by a different stimulus.

client-centered therapy An approach developed by Carl Rogers that assumes that each person has an actualizing tendency—that is, a tendency to develop his or her own potential; the therapist's task is to show compassion and positive regard in helping the client reach his or her potential. Also called person-centered therapy.

clinical assessment A systematic evaluation of an individual's various psychological, biological, and social factors, as well as the identification of past and present problems, stressors, and other cognitive and behavioral symptoms.

clinical diagnosis A process of determining how closely an individual's specific symptoms match those that define a particular mental disorder.

clinical interview In assessment, a method of gathering information about relevant aspects of a person's past as well as current behaviors, attitudes, emotions, and details of present difficulties or problems. Some clinical interviews are unstructured, which means that they have no set questions; others are structured, which means that they follow a standard format of asking the same questions.

clinical psychologist An individual who has a Ph.D., has specialized in the clinical subarea, and has spent an additional year in a supervised therapy setting to gain experience in diagnosing and treating a wide range of abnormal behaviors. To train as a clinical psychologist usually requires 4–6 years of work after obtaining a college degree.

closure rule A perceptual rule stating that, in organizing stimuli, we tend to fill in any missing parts of a figure and see the figure as complete.

cocaine A stimulant produced from the leaves of the coca plant. Its physiological and behavioral effects are very similar to those of amphetamine: It produces increased heart rate and blood pressure, enhanced mood, alertness, increased activity, decreased appetite, and diminished fatigue. At higher doses, it can produce anxiety, emotional instability, and suspiciousness.

cochlea A coiled, fluid-filled structure in the inner ear that contains the receptors for hearing. Its function is transduction—transforming vibrations into nerve impulses that are sent to the brain for processing into auditory information.

cochlear implant A miniature electronic device that is surgically implanted into the cochlea to restore hearing in those with neural deafness. It converts sound waves to electrical signals, which are fed into the auditory nerve and hence reach the brain for processing.

cognitive appraisal theory The idea that our interpretation or appraisal of a situation is often the primary cause of emotions.

cognitive approach See cognitive psychology.

cognitive—behavioral therapy A treatment for phobias and other mental disorders based on a combination of two methods: changing negative, unhealthy, or distorted thoughts and beliefs by substituting positive, healthy, and realistic ones; and changing limiting or disruptive behaviors by learning and practicing new skills to improve functioning. Sometimes called behavior therapy.

cognitive development How a person perceives, thinks, and gains an understanding of his or her world through the interaction and influence of genetic and learned factors.

cognitive developmental theory The idea that, as they develop mental skills and interact with their environments, children learn one set of rules for male behavior and another set of rules for female behavior.

cognitive dissonance A state of unpleasant psychological tension that motivates us to reduce our cognitive inconsistencies by making our beliefs more consistent with one another.

cognitive—emotional—behavioral and environmental factors The factors that contribute to the development of mental disorders, including deficits in cognitive processes, such as having unusual thoughts and beliefs; deficits in processing emotional stimuli, such as under- or overreacting to emotional situations; behavioral problems, such as lacking social skills; and environmental challenges, such as dealing with stressful situations.

cognitive factors According to social cognitive theory, factors that include our beliefs, expectations, values, intentions, and social roles—all of which help to shape our personalities.

cognitive factors in motivation The influence of individuals' evaluations or perceptions of a situation on their willingness to work.

cognitive interview A technique for questioning eyewitnesses and others by having them imagine and reconstruct the details of an event, report everything they remember without holding anything back, and narrate the event from different viewpoints.

cognitive learning A kind of learning that involves mental processes, such as attention and memory; may proceed through observation or imitation; and may not involve any external rewards or require the person to perform any observable behaviors.

cognitive map A mental representation of the layout of an environment and its features.

cognitive miser model The idea that, in making attributions, people feel they must conserve time and effort by taking cognitive shortcuts.

cognitive neuroscience An approach to studying cognitive processes that involves taking pictures of the structures and functions of the living brain during the performance of a wide variety of mental or cognitive processes, such as thinking, planning, naming, and recognizing objects.

cognitive perspective The theory that an organism learns a predictable relationship between two stimuli such that the occurrence of one stimulus (neutral stimulus) predicts the occurrence of another (unconditioned stimulus). In other words, classical conditioning occurs because the organism learns what to expect. Formerly called information theory.

cognitive psychology The study of how we process, store, retrieve, and use information and how cognitive processes influence what we attend to, perceive, learn, remember, believe, feel, and do.

Glossary

cognitive social psychology A subarea of social psychology that focuses on how cognitive processes, such as perceiving, retrieving, and interpreting information about social interactions and events, affect emotions and behaviors and how emotions and behaviors affect cognitions.

cognitive therapy An approach to therapy that focuses on the role of thoughts in our emotions and actions. The widely used version developed by Aaron Beck assumes that we have automatic negative thoughts that we typically say to ourselves without much notice. By continuously repeating these automatic negative thoughts, we color and distort how we perceive and interpret the world and influence how we behave and feel. The goal of the therapy is to change these automatic negative thoughts.

collective unconscious According to Jung, ancient memory traces and symbols that are passed on by birth and are shared by all people in all cultures.

color blindness Inability to distinguish between two or more shades in the color spectrum. There are several kinds of color blindness. *See* monochromats and dichromats.

color constancy Our tendency to perceive colors as remaining stable despite differences in lighting.

commitment In Sternberg's triangular theory of love, the component of love associated with making a pledge to nourish the feelings of love and to actively maintain the relationship.

common factors A basic set of procedures and experiences shared by different therapies that account for those therapies' comparable effectiveness despite their different fundamental principles and techniques. Common factors include the growth of a supportive and trusting relationship between therapist and client and the accompanying development of an accepting atmosphere in which the client feels willing to admit problems and is motivated to work on changing.

communication The ability to use sounds, smells, or gestures to exchange information.

community mental health centers Government-sponsored centers that offer low-cost or free mental health care to members of the surrounding community, especially the underprivileged. The services may include psychotherapy, support groups, or telephone crisis counseling.

companionate love A condition associated with trusting and tender feelings for someone whose life is closely bound up with one's own.

compliance A kind of conformity in which we give in to social pressure in our public responses but do not change our private beliefs.

concept A way to group objects, events, or characteristics on the basis of some common property they all share.

conception The process in which one of the millions of sperm penetrates the ovum's outside membrane; also called fertilization. After penetration, the outside membrane changes and becomes impenetrable to the millions of remaining sperm.

concrete operations stage The third of Piaget's cognitive stages, lasting from about the age of 7 to 11 years. During this stage, children can perform a number of logical mental operations on concrete objects that are physically present.

conditional positive regard Positive regard that depends on our behaving in certain ways—for example, living up to or meeting others' standards.

conditioned emotional response The feeling of some positive or negative emotion, such as happiness, fear, or anxiety, when experiencing a stimulus that previously accompanied a pleasant or painful event. This is an example of classical conditioning.

conditioned response (CR) A response elicited by the conditioned stimulus; it is similar to the unconditioned response but not identical in magnitude or amount.

conditioned stimulus (CS) A formerly neutral stimulus that has acquired the ability to elicit a response previously elicited by the unconditioned stimulus.

conduct disorder A repetitive and persistent pattern of aggressive behavior that has been going on for at least a year and that violates the established social rules or the rights of others. Problems may include threatening to harm people, abusing or killing animals, destroying property, being deceitful, or stealing.

conduction deafness Deafness caused by wax in the auditory canal, injury to the tympanic membrane, or malfunction of the ossicles.

cones Photoreceptors that contain three chemicals called opsins, which are activated in bright light and allow us to see color. Unlike rods, cones are wired individually to neighboring cells; this one-on-one system of relaying information allows us to see fine details.

conflict The feeling we experience when we must decide between two or more incompatible choices.

conformity Any behavior you perform because of group pressure, even though that pressure might not involve direct requests.

conscious thoughts Wishes, desires, or thoughts that we are aware of, or can recall, at any given moment.

consciousness An individual's different levels of awareness of his or her thoughts and feelings. Creating images in the mind, following thought processes, and having unique emotional experiences are all part of consciousness.

consensus In making attributions, determining whether other people engage in the same behavior in the same situation.

conservation The idea that even though the shape of some object of substance is changed, the total amount remains the same.

consistency In making attributions, determining whether an individual engages in a certain behavior every time he or she is in a particular situation.

contiguity theory The view that classical conditioning occurs because two stimuli (the neutral stimulus and the unconditioned stimulus) are paired close together in time (are contiguous). Eventually, as a result of this contiguous pairing, the neutral stimulus becomes the conditioned stimulus, which elicits the conditioned response.

continuity rule A perceptual rule stating that, in organizing stimuli, we tend to favor smooth or continuous paths when interpreting a series of points or lines.

continuous reinforcement The simplest reinforcement schedule, in which every occurrence of the operant response results in delivery of the reinforcer.

continuum of consciousness The wide range of human experiences, from being acutely aware and alert to being totally unaware and unresponsive.

control group In an experiment, subjects who undergo all the same procedures as the experimental subjects do, except that the control subjects do not receive the treatment.

Control Question Technique A lie-detection procedure in which the examiner asks two kinds of questions: neutral questions that elicit little emotional response and critical questions that are designed to elicit greater emotional responses. The person answers only "Yes" or "No" to the questions and, if guilty, is expected to show a greater emotional response to the critical questions than to the neutral questions.

controlled processes Activities that require full awareness, alertness, and concentration to reach some goal. Because of the strongly focused attention they require, controlled processes often interfere with other ongoing activities.

conventional level Kohlberg's intermediate level of moral reasoning. It consists of two stages: At stage 3, moral decisions are guided most by conforming to the standards of others we value; at stage 4, moral reasoning is determined most by conforming to the laws of society.

convergence In three-dimensional vision, a binocular cue for depth perception based on signals sent from the muscles that turn the eyes. To focus on near or approaching objects, these muscles turn the eyes inward, toward the nose. The brain uses the signals sent by these muscles to determine the distance of the object.

convergent thinking Beginning with a problem and coming up with a single correct solution.

conversion disorder A type of somatoform disorder characterized by unexplained and significant physical symptoms—headaches, nausea, dizziness, loss of sensation, paralysis—that suggest a real neurological or medical problem but for which no physical or organic cause can be identified. Anxiety or emotional distress is apparently converted to symptoms that disrupt physical functioning.

cornea The rounded, transparent covering over the front of the eye. As the light waves pass through the cornea, its curved surface bends, or focuses, the waves into a narrower beam.

correlation An association or relationship between the occurrence of two or more events.

correlation coefficient A number that indicates the strength of a relationship between two or more events. The closer the number is to -1.00 or +1.00, the greater is the strength of the relationship.

cortex A thin layer of cells that essentially covers the entire surface of the forebrain. The cortex consists of the frontal, parietal, occipital, and temporal lobes, whose control centers allow us to carry out hundreds of cognitive, emotional, sensory, and motor functions.

counseling psychologist An individual who has a Ph.D. in psychology or education and whose training included work in a counseling setting. Counseling psychologists generally have a less extensive research background than clinical psychologists and work in real-world settings, such as schools, industry, and private practice. Whereas clinical psychologists treat mental disorders, counseling psychologists deal largely with problems of living. To train as a counseling psychologist generally takes 4–6 years after obtaining a bachelor's degree.

counterattitudinal behavior Taking a public position that runs counter to your private attitude.

covariation model A model developed by Harold Kelley that may be used in deciding between internal and external attributions. The model says that, in determining attributions, we should look for factors that are present when the behavior occurs and factors that are absent when the behavior does not occur.

creative individual Someone who regularly solves problems, fashions products, or defines new questions that make an impact on his or her society.

creative thinking A combination of flexibility in thinking and reorganization of understanding to produce innovative ideas and new solutions.

critical language period A period of time from infancy to adolescence when language is easiest to learn; in the period after adolescence through adulthood, language is more difficult to learn.

critical period In imprinting, a relatively brief time during which learning is most likely to occur. Also called the sensitive period.

cross-cultural approach A psychological viewpoint that studies the influence of cultural and ethnic similarities and differences on psychological and social functioning.

cross-sectional method A research design in which several groups of different-aged individuals are studied at the same time.

crowd A large group of persons, most of whom are unacquainted.

cultural bias In testing, the situation in which the wording of the questions and the experiences on which they are based are more familiar to members of some social groups than to others.

cultural-familial retardation Mental retardation that results from greatly impoverished environments, with no evidence of genetic or brain damage.

cultural influences Pervasive pressures that encourage members of a particular society or ethnic group to conform to shared behaviors, values, and beliefs.

cumulative record A continuous written record that shows an organism's responses and reinforcements.

curare A drug that enters the bloodstream, reaches the muscles, and blocks receptors on the muscles. As a result, acetylcholine, the neurotransmitter that normally activates muscles, is blocked, and the muscles are paralyzed.

DARE (Drug Abuse Resistance Program) A drug awareness program taught in the classroom by trained, uniformed police officers. It is based on the idea of using social influence and role-playing to discourage adolescents from starting drug use and to encourage them to refuse drugs in the future.

daydreaming An activity that requires a low level of awareness, often occurs during automatic processes, and involves fantasizing or dreaming while awake.

debriefing A procedure administered to subjects after an experiment to minimize any potential negative effects. It includes explaining the purpose and method of the experiment, asking the subjects their feelings about having been in the experiment, and helping the subjects deal with possible doubts or guilt that arises from their behaviors in the experiments.

decibel A unit to measure loudness. The human range for hearing is from 0 decibels, which is absolutely no sound, to 140 decibels, which can produce pain and permanent hearing loss.

decision-stage model of helping The idea that we go through five stages in deciding to help: (1) we notice the situation; (2) we interpret it as one in which help is needed; (3) we assume personal responsibility; (4) we choose a form of assistance; and (5) we carry out that assistance.

declarative memory Memories of facts or events, such as scenes, stories, words, conversations, faces, or daily events. We are aware of these kinds of memories and can retrieve them.

deep structure According to Chomsky, a sentence's underlying meaning that is not spoken but is present in the mind of the listener.

defense mechanisms Freudian processes that operate at unconscious levels to help the ego reduce anxiety through self-deception.

deficiency needs Physiological needs (food and sleep) and psychological needs (safety, belongingness, and esteem) that we try to fulfill if they are not met.

deindividuation The increased tendency for subjects to behave irrationally or perform antisocial behaviors when there is less chance of being personally identified.

deinstitutionalization The release of mental patients from mental hospitals and their return to the community to develop more independent and fulfilling lives.

delay of gratification Voluntarily postponing an immediate reward to persist in completing a task for the promise of a future reward.

dendrites Branchlike extensions that arise from the cell body; they receive signals from other neurons,

muscles, or sense organs and pass them to the cell body.

denial Refusal to recognize some anxiety-provoking event or piece of information.

dependency A change in the nervous system such that a person addicted to a drug now needs to take it to prevent the occurrence of painful symptoms.

dependent personality disorder A pattern of being submissive and clingy because of an excessive need to be taken care of. It is found in 2% of the population.

dependent variable In an experiment, one or more of the subjects' behaviors that are used to measure the potential effects of the treatment or independent variable.

depth perception In visual perception, the ability of the eye and brain to add a third dimension, depth, to visual perceptions, even though the images projected on our retina have only two dimensions, height and width.

descriptive statistics Numbers used to present a collection of data in a brief yet meaningful form.

designer drugs Manufactured or synthetic drugs designed to resemble already existing illegal psychoactive drugs and to produce or mimic their psychoactive effects.

developmental norms The average ages at which children perform various skills or exhibit particular abilities or behaviors.

developmental psychologists Psychologists who study a person's biological, emotional, cognitive, personal, and social development across the life span, from infancy through late adulthood.

developmental psychology The study of moral, social, emotional, and cognitive development throughout a person's entire life.

Diagnostic and Statistical Manual of Mental Disorders-IV-Text Revision (DSM-IV-TR) The 2000 edition of the American Psychiatric Association's uniform diagnostic system for assessing specific symptoms and matching them to almost 300 different mental disorders. The DSM-IV-TR has five major dimensions, or axes.

diathesis stress theory of schizophrenia The idea that some people have a genetic predisposition (a diathesis) that interacts with life stressors to result in the onset and development of schizophrenia.

dichromats People who have trouble distinguishing red from green because their eyes have just two kinds of cones. This is an inherited condition, found most often in males, that results in seeing mostly shades of green, but it differs in severity.

diffusion of responsibility theory The idea that, in the presence of others, individuals feel less personal responsibility and are less likely to take action in a situation where help is required.

direction of a sound The brain determines the direction of a sound by calculating the slight difference in time that it takes sound waves to reach the two ears, which are about 6 inches apart.

discrimination In classical conditioning, the tendency for some stimuli but not others to elicit a conditioned response. In operant conditioning,

Glossary

the tendency for a response to be emitted in the presence of a stimulus that is reinforced but not in the presence of unreinforced stimuli. In social psychology, specific unfair behaviors exhibited toward members of a group.

discriminative stimulus In conditioning, a cue that behavior will be enforced.

disgust A universal facial expression—closing the eyes, narrowing the nostrils, curling the lips downward, and sometimes sticking out the tongue—that indicates the rejection of an item of food.

disorganized schizophrenia A subcategory of schizophrenia marked by bizarre ideas, often about one's body (bones melting), confused speech, childish behavior (giggling for no apparent reason, making faces at people), great emotional swings (fits of laughing or crying), and often extreme neglect of personal appearance and hygiene.

displacement Transferring feelings from their true source to another source that is safer and more socially acceptable.

display rules Specific cultural norms that regulate when, where, and how much emotion we should or should not express in different situations.

dispositional attributions *See* internal attributions.

dissociative amnesia A dissociative disorder characterized by the inability to recall important personal information or events and usually associated with stressful or traumatic events. The importance of the information forgotten or the duration of the memory lapse is too great to be explained by normal forgetfulness.

dissociative disorder A disorder characterized by a disruption, split, or breakdown in a person's normally integrated and functioning consciousness, memory, sense of identity, or perception.

dissociative fugue A disturbance in which an individual suddenly and unexpectedly travels away from home or place of work and is unable to recall his or her past. The person may not remember his or her identity or may be confused about his or her new, assumed identity.

dissociative identity disorder The presence in a single individual of two or more distinct identities or personality states, each with its own pattern of perceiving, thinking about, and relating to the world. Different personality states may take control of the individual's thoughts and behaviors at different times. Formerly called multiple personality disorder.

distinctiveness In making attributions, determining how differently the person behaves in one situation in comparison with other situations.

divergent thinking Beginning with a problem and coming up with many different solutions.

dopamine theory The idea that, in schizophrenia, the dopamine neurotransmitter system is somehow overactive and gives rise to a wide range of symptoms.

double-blind procedure An experimental design in which neither the researchers nor the subjects know which group is receiving which treatment. This design makes it possible to separate the

effects of medical treatment from the participants' beliefs or expectations about the treatment.

double standard for sexual behavior A set of beliefs, values, and expectations that subtly encourages sexual activity in men but discourages the same behavior in women.

Down syndrome A genetic disorder that results from an extra 21st chromosome and causes abnormal physical traits (a fold of skin at the corner of each eye, a wide tongue, heart defects) and abnormal brain development, resulting in degrees of mental retardation.

dream interpretation A Freudian technique of dream analysis, based on the assumption that dreams contain underlying, hidden meanings and symbols that provide clues to unconscious thoughts and desires. Freud distinguished between a dream's manifest content—the plot of the dream at the surface level—and its latent content—the hidden or disguised meaning of the plot's events.

dreaming A unique state of consciousness in which we are asleep but we experience a variety of images, often in color. People blind from birth have only auditory or tactile dreams, while sighted people have dreams with astonishing visual, auditory, and tactile images.

Drug Abuse Resistance Program *See* DARE.

DSM-IV-TR *See Diagnostic and Statistical Manual of Mental Disorders*-IV-Text Revision.

dyslexia An unexpected difficulty learning to read despite intelligence, motivation, and education. Causes of dyslexia include genetic factors (defects in neural circuitry) and environmental factors (disadvantaged schooling).

dysthymic disorder A mood disorder characterized by feeling chronically but not continuously depressed for a period of two years. While depressed, a person experiences at least two of the following symptoms: poor appetite, insomnia, fatigue, low self-esteem, poor concentration, and feelings of hopelessness.

eardrum *See* tympanic membrane.

echoic memory A form of sensory memory that holds auditory information for 1–2 seconds.

eclectic approach An approach to therapy in which the psychotherapist combines techniques and ideas from many different schools of thought.

ecstacy *See* MDMA.

ECT *See* electroconvulsive therapy.

efferent neurons Neurons that carry information away from the spinal cord to produce responses in various muscles and organs throughout the body. Also called motor neurons.

effortful encoding The transfer of information from short-term into long-term memory either by working hard to repeat or rehearse the information or by making associations between new and old information.

ego Freud's second division of the mind, which develops from the id during infancy; its goal is to find safe and socially acceptable ways of satisfying the id's desires and to negotiate between the id's wants and the superego's prohibitions.

egocentric thinking Seeing and thinking of the world only from your own viewpoint and having difficulty appreciating someone else's viewpoint.

eidetic imagery The ability to examine a picture or page for 10–30 seconds and then retain a detailed visual image of the material for several minutes. Eidetic memory is found in a small percentage of children and almost always disappears around adolescence.

elaborative rehearsal Making meaningful associations between information to be learned and information already learned. An effective strategy for encoding information into long-term memory.

Electra complex *See* Oedipus complex.

electroconvulsive therapy (ECT) A treatment for depression in which electrodes are placed on the skull and a mild electric current is administered. As it passes through the brain, the current causes a seizure. Usual treatment consists of 10 to 12 ECT sessions, at the rate of about three per week.

embryonic stage The second stage of the prenatal period, spanning the 2–8 weeks that follow conception; during this stage, cells divide and begin to differentiate into bone, muscle, and body organs.

EMDR *See* Eye Movement Desensitization and Reprocessing.

emotion A response consisting of four components: interpreting or appraising a stimulus (event, object, or thought) in terms of one's well-being; having a subjective feeling, such as happiness or sadness; experiencing physiological responses, such as changes in heart rate or breathing; and possibly showing overt behaviors, such as smiling or crying.

emotion-focused coping Making some effort to deal with the emotional distress caused by a harm/loss or threat appraisal. These efforts include seeking support and sympathy, avoiding or denying the situation, and redirecting our attention.

emotional development The process in which genetic factors, brain changes, cognitive factors, coping abilities, and cultural factors influence and interact in the development of emotional behaviors, expressions, thoughts, and feelings.

emotional intelligence The ability to perceive and express emotion, understand and reason with emotion, and regulate emotion in oneself and others.

encoding Placing or storing information—such as images, events, or sounds (music, noise, speech)—in memory by making mental representations.

end bulbs Bulblike swellings at the extreme ends of axons' branches that store chemicals called neurotransmitters, which are used to communicate with neighboring cells.

endocrine system Numerous glands, located throughout the body, that secrete various chemicals called hormones, which affect organs, muscles, and other glands in the body.

endorphins Chemicals produced by the brain and secreted in response to injury or severe physical or psychological stress. Their powerful pain-reducing properties are similar to those of morphine.

environmental factors Our social, political, and cultural influences as well as our particular learning experiences.

environmental language factors Interactions that children have with parents, peers, teachers, and others whose feedback rewards and encourages language development; these interactions also provide opportunities for children to observe, imitate, and practice language skills.

episodic memory A type of declarative memory, consisting of knowledge about one's personal experiences (episodes) or activities, such as naming or describing favorite restaurants, movies, songs, habits, or hobbies.

ESP *See* extrasensory perception.

estrogen One of the major female hormones. At puberty, estrogen levels increase eightfold and stimulate the development of both primary and secondary sexual characteristics.

ethologists Behavioral biologists who observe and study animal behavior in the animal's natural environment or under relatively naturalistic conditions.

evaluative function The role of our attitudes in helping us to stand up for those beliefs and values that we consider very important to ourselves.

evening persons People who prefer to get up late, go to bed late, and engage in afternoon or evening activities. *See* morning persons.

event schemas Social schemas containing behaviors that we associate with familiar activities, events, or procedures. Also called scripts.

evolution *See* theory of evolution.

evolutionary theory of emotions The theory that says one function of emotions is to help a person evaluate objects, people, and situations in terms of how good or bad they are for the individual's well-being and survival.

evolutionary theory (of gender differences) The idea in sociobiology, which emphasizes genetic and biological forces, that current behavioral and cognitive differences between men and women can be traced back to different survival problems faced by early women and men and the different behaviors they adapted to survive.

exemplar model The idea that a person forms a concept of an object, event, animal, or person by defining or making a mental list of the essential characteristics of that particular thing.

exhaustion stage The third stage in the general adaptation syndrome. In reaction to long-term, continuous stress, there is actual breakdown in internal organs or weakening of the infection-fighting immune system.

experiment A method for identifying cause-and-effect relationships by following a set of rules and guidelines that minimize the possibility of error, bias, and chance occurrences. *See also* laboratory experiment.

experimental group In an experiment, the subjects who receive the treatment.

experimental psychology The study of sensation, perception, learning, human performance, motivation, and emotion in carefully controlled laboratory conditions, with both animal and human subjects.

exposure therapy A treatment for anxiety in which the person is gradually exposed to the real anxiety-producing situations or objects that he or she is attempting to avoid; exposure treatment is continued until the anxiety decreases.

extensions of waking life theory of dreams The theory that our dreams reflect the same thoughts, fears, concerns, problems, and emotions that we have when awake.

external attributions Explanations of behavior based on the external circumstances or situations. Also called situational attributions.

external ear An oval-shaped structure that protrudes from the side of the head. Its function is to pick up sound waves and send them along the auditory canal.

extinction In classical conditioning, the reduction in a response when the conditioned stimulus is no longer followed by the unconditioned stimulus. As a result, the conditioned stimulus tends to no longer elicit the conditioned response. In operant conditioning, the reduction in the operant response when it is no longer followed by the reinforcer.

extrasensory perception (ESP) A group of psychic experiences that involve perceiving or sending information (images) outside normal sensory processes or channels. ESP includes four general abilities: telepathy, precognition, clairvoyance, and psychokinesis.

extrinsic motivation Engaging in certain activities or behaviors that either reduce our biological needs or help us obtain incentives or external rewards.

Eye Movement Desensitization and Reprocessing (EMDR) A new technique in which the client focuses on a traumatic memory while visually following the back-and-forth movement of a therapist's hand or pen. The process usually continues for several 90-minute sessions, after which the traumatic memories are greatly reduced or eliminated.

eyewitness testimony Recollection or recognition of a suspect observed during a possibly disruptive emotional situation that may have interfered with accurate remembering.

facial expressions Social signals that accompany emotions and express the state of our personal feelings; they provide social signals that elicit a variety of responses from those around us.

facial feedback theory The idea that sensations or feedback from the movement of facial muscles and skin are interpreted by your brain as emotional feelings.

factor analysis A complicated statistical method that finds relationships among different or diverse items and allows them to be grouped together.

farsightedness A visual acuity problem that may result when the eyeball is too short, so that

objects are focused at a point slightly behind the retina. The result is that distant objects are clear, but near objects are blurry.

FAS *See* fetal alcohol syndrome.

fat cells Cells that store body fat. The number of fat cells in the body is primarily determined by heredity. They do not normally multiply except when we become obese. Fat cells shrink as we give up fat and lose weight and greatly enlarge as we store fat and gain weight.

fear of failure A tendency to avoid failure by choosing easy, nonchallenging tasks where failure is unlikely or difficult.

female hypothalamus Because of neural programming in the womb, the hypothalamus, a structure in the brain that controls the endocrine system, functions differently in the male and female. The female hypothalamus triggers a cyclical release of estrogens from the ovaries. The increased estrogen level is responsible for female secondary sexual characteristics, such as pubic hair, breast development, and widening of the hips. The cyclic release of hormones (estrogen and progesterone) also regulates the menstrual cycle.

female secondary sexual characteristics Sexual characteristics whose development in the female is triggered by the increased secretion of estrogen during puberty; they include the growth of pubic hair, development of breasts, and widening of hips.

fertilization *See* conception.

fetal alcohol syndrome (FAS) A condition caused by heavy maternal drinking during pregnancy. It results in a combination of physical changes, such as short stature, flattened nose, and short eye openings, and psychological defects, such as degrees of mental retardation and hyperactivity.

fetal stage The third stage in prenatal development, beginning two months after conception and lasting until birth.

fight-flight response A state of increased physiological arousal that (a) directs great resources of energy to the muscles and brain; (b) can be triggered by either physical stimuli that threaten our survival or psychological situations that are novel, threatening, or challenging; and (c) involves numerous physiological responses that arouse and prepare the body for action-fight or flight. Caused by the activation of the sympathetic nervous system, it helps us to cope with, and survive, threatening situations.

figure-ground rule A perceptual rule stating that, in organizing stimuli, we tend to automatically distinguish between a figure and a ground: The figure, with more detail, stands out against the background, which has less detail.

five-factor model An approach to personality in which all traits are organized into five categories—openness, conscientiousness, extraversion, agreeableness, and neuroticism—that are used to describe differences in personality.

fixation A Freudian process through which an individual may be locked into any one of the

Glossary

three psychosexual stages—oral, anal, or phallic—because his or her wishes were either over-gratified or undergratified in that stage.

fixed action pattern An innate biological force that predisposes an organism to behave in a fixed way in the presence of a specific environmental condition. Previously called instinct.

fixed-interval schedule In conditioning, a schedule in which a reinforcer occurs following a subject's first response after a fixed interval of time.

fixed-ratio schedule In conditioning, a schedule in which a reinforcer occurs only after a fixed number of responses by the subject.

flashbulb memories Vivid recollections, usually in great deal, of dramatic or emotionally charged incidents, which are encoded effortlessly and may last for long periods of time.

flavor What we experience when we combine the sensations of taste and smell.

fMRI See functional magnetic resonance imaging.

food-entrainable circadian clock A sort of timing device that regulates eating patterns in people and animals and might be responsible for late-night eating in people.

foot-in-the-door technique A method of persuasion that relies on the increased probability of compliance to a second request if a person complies with a small first request.

forebrain The largest part of the brain, consisting of left and right hemispheres, which are connected by a wide band of fibers, the corpus callosum. The hemispheres are responsible for a vast array of responses, including learning and memory, speaking and language, emotional responses, experiencing sensations, initiating voluntary movements, planning, and making decisions.

forgetting Inability to retrieve, recall, or recognize information that was stored or is still stored in long-term memory.

forgetting curve A graph measuring the amount of previously learned information that subjects can recall or recognize across time.

formal operations stage Piaget's fourth cognitive stage, lasting from about 12 years of age through adulthood. During this stage, adolescents and adults develop the ability to think about abstract or hypothetical concepts, to consider an issue from another person's viewpoint, and to solve cognitive problems in a logical manner.

fragile X syndrome A defect in the X chromosome that can result in physical changes such as a relatively large head with protruding ears, as well as mild to profound mental retardation.

fraternal twins Twins who develop from separate eggs and share 50% of their genes.

free association A Freudian technique in which clients are encouraged to talk about any thoughts or images that enter their heads; the assumption is that this kind of free-flowing, uncensored talking will provide clues to unconscious material.

frequency distribution The range of scores we get and the frequency of each one, when we measure a sample of people (or objects) regarding some trait.

frequency theory In pitch perception, the idea that, for low-frequency sound waves (1,000 cycles or less), the rate at which nerve impulses reach the brain determines how low a sound is. A rate of 50 impulses per second is interpreted as a lower sound than a rate of 200 impulses per second.

Freudian slips Mistakes or slips of the tongue that we make in everyday speech; such mistakes are thought to reflect unconscious thoughts or wishes.

Freud's psychodynamic theory of personality A personality theory that emphasizes the importance of early childhood experiences; repressed thoughts that we cannot voluntarily access; and the conflicts between conscious and unconscious forces that influence our thoughts and behaviors. See also psychoanalytic approach.

Freud's theory of dreams A theory that says we have a "censor" that protects us from realizing threatening and unconscious desires or wishes, especially those involving sex or aggression, by transforming them into harmless symbols that appear in our dreams and do not disturb our sleep or conscious thoughts.

Freud's theory of the unconscious The idea that, when faced with very threatening—especially sexual or aggressive—wishes or desires, we automatically defend our self-esteem by placing these psychologically dangerous thoughts into a mental place, the unconscious, that is sealed off from voluntary recall.

frontal lobe An area in the front part of the brain that includes a huge area of cortex. The frontal lobe is involved in many functions: performing voluntary motor movements, interpreting and performing emotional behaviors, behaving normally in social situations, maintaining a healthy personality, paying attention to things in the environment, making decisions, and carrying out plans.

frontal lobotomy A surgical procedure in which about one-third of the front part of the frontal lobe is separated from the rest of the brain.

frustration The feeling that results when our attempts to reach some goal are blocked.

frustration-aggression hypothesis The idea that, when our goals are blocked, we become frustrated and respond with anger and aggression. See also modified frustration-aggression hypothesis.

functional fixedness A mental set characterized by the inability to see an object as having a function different from its usual one.

functional magnetic resonance imaging (fMRI) A brain scan that measures the activity of specific neurons that are functioning during cognitive tasks such as thinking, listening, or reading.

functionalism An early school of psychological thought that emphasized the function rather than the structure of consciousness and was interested in how our minds adapt to our changing environment.

fundamental attribution error Our tendency, when we look for causes of a person's behavior, to focus on the person's disposition or personality traits and overlook how the situation influenced the person's behavior.

galvanic skin response Changes in sweating of the fingers (or palms) that accompany emotional experiences and are independent of perspiration under normal temperatures.

Ganzfeld procedure A controlled method for eliminating trickery, error, and bias while testing telepathic communication between two people.

Gardner's multiple-intelligence theory The idea that, instead of one kind of general intelligence, there are at least seven different kinds: verbal intelligence, musical intelligence, logical-mathematical intelligence, spatial intelligence, body movement intelligence, intelligence to understand oneself, and intelligence to understand others.

GAS See general adaptation syndrome.

gate control theory The idea that nonpainful nerve impulses compete with pain impulses as they enter the spinal cord, creating a neural gate through which only the nonpainful impulses pass; the pain impulses do not reach the brain. Thus, we can reduce feelings of pain by rubbing an injured area or becoming absorbed in other activities.

gender identity The individual's subjective experience and feelings of being either a male or a female; formerly called sexual identity.

gender identity disorder Commonly referred to as transsexualism, an individual's strong desire or feeling of wanting to be the opposite sex, discomfort with being one's assigned sex, and the wish to live as a member of the other sex.

gender roles Traditional or stereotypic behaviors, attitudes, and personality traits that parents, peers, and society designate as masculine or feminine. Gender roles affect how we think and behave; formerly called sex roles.

gender schemas Sets of information and rules organized around how either a male or a female should think and behave.

gene A specific segment on the strand of DNA (the chromosome) that contains instructions for making proteins, the chemical building blocks from which all the parts of the brain and body are constructed.

general adaptation syndrome (GAS) According to Selye, a series of three stages—alarm, resistance, and exhaustion—that correspond to the three different reactions of the body to stressful situations and that gradually increase the chances of developing psychosomatic symptoms.

generalization In classical conditioning, the tendency for a stimulus that is similar to the original conditioned stimulus to elicit a response that is similar to the conditioned response. Usually, the more similar the new stimulus is to the original conditioned stimulus, the larger will be the conditioned response. In operant conditioning, the situation in which an animal or a person emits the same response to similar stimuli.

generalized anxiety disorder A psychological disorder primarily characterized by excessive and/or unrealistic worry or feelings of general apprehension about events or activities. These anxious feelings occur on a majority of days for a period of at least six months.

genetic factors (in mental disorders) Unlearned or inherited tendencies that influence how a person thinks, behaves, and feels.

genetic hunger factors Inherited instructions found in our genes that influence our hunger; these instructions may determine our number of fat cells or our metabolic rate of burning off the body's fuel, for example, and push us toward being normal, overweight, or underweight.

genetic marker An identifiable gene or number of genes or a specific segment of a chromosome that is directly linked to some behavioral, physiological, or neurological trait or disease.

genetic sex factors Inherited instructions for the development of sexual organs, the secretion of sex hormones, and the wiring of the neural circuits that control sexual reflexes.

genital cutting The practice of cutting away the female's external genitalia, usually including her clitoris and surrounding skin (labia minora). The remaining edges are sewn together, which leaves only a small opening for urination and menstruation.

genital stage Freud's fifth, and final, psychosexual stage, lasting from puberty through adulthood. In this stage, the individual has renewed sexual desires that he or she seeks to fulfill through relationships with other people.

germinal stage The first stage of prenatal development, lasting two weeks from the moment of conception.

Gestalt approach An older theoretical approach that emphasized the idea that perception is more than the sum of its parts. In contrast to the structuralists, the Gestalt psychologists believed that perceptions are formed by the brain on the basis of a set of rules that specify how individual elements may be organized to form a meaningful pattern—that is, a perception.

gifted A term applied to an individual (usually to a child) who has above-average intelligence as well as some superior talent or skill. A moderately gifted child is usually defined by an IQ score between 130 and 150; a profoundly gifted child has an IQ score of 180 or above.

glial cells Cells in the nervous system that have at least three functions: They provide scaffolding to guide the growth of developing neurons and support mature neurons; they wrap themselves around neurons and form a kind of insulation to prevent interference from other electrical signals; and they release chemicals that influence a neuron's growth and function.

gonads Glands—the ovaries in females and the testes in males—that produce hormones to regulate sexual development, ovulation or sperm production, and the growth of sex organs. They are part of the endocrine system.

grammar A set of rules for combining words into phrases and sentences to express an infinite number of thoughts that can be understood by others.

group A collection of two or more people who interact and share some common attribute or purpose. A group also influences how its members think and behave.

group cohesion Group togetherness, which is determined by how much group members perceive that they share common attributes.

group norms Formal or informal rules about how group members should behave.

group polarization The phenomenon in which group discussion reinforces the majority's point of view and shifts that view to a more extreme position.

groupthink Poor group decision making that occurs when group discussions emphasize cohesion and agreement rather than critical thinking and the best possible outcome.

growth needs According to Maslow, higher-level needs that are not essential to existence, such as the desire for truth, goodness, beauty, and justice.

hair cells The auditory receptors. These miniature hair-shaped cells rise from the basilar membrane in the cochlea.

hallucinations Sensory experiences without any stimulation from the environment. Common symptoms of schizophrenia, hallucinations may be auditory, such as hearing voices, or may include distorted perceptions, such as feeling that parts of one's body are too small or too large.

hallucinogens Psychoactive drugs that can produce hallucinations—strange perceptual, sensory, and cognitive experiences that the person sees or hears but knows are not occurring in reality. Such unreal experiences are called hallucinations.

happiness A mental state that includes three components: feeling positive emotions, being satisfied with one's life, and not experiencing negative emotions.

hardiness A combination of three personality traits—control, commitment, and challenge—that protect or buffer us from the potentially harmful effects of stressful situations and reduce our chances of developing psychosomatic illness.

harm/loss appraisal Our conclusion that we have already sustained some damage or injury in a particular situation.

hassles Small, irritating, frustrating events that we face daily and that we usually appraise as stressful experiences.

hazing Part of a group's initiation ritual during which individuals are subjected to a variety of behaviors that range from humiliating and unpleasant to potentially dangerous both physically and psychologically.

helping *See* prosocial behavior.

heritability A statistical measure that estimates the amount or proportion of some ability, characteristic, or trait that can be attributed to genetic factors.

heterosexual orientation A pattern of sexual arousal by persons of the opposite sex.

heuristics Rules of thumb that reduce the number of operations or allow us to take shortcuts in solving problems.

hierarchy of needs *See* Maslow's hierarchy of needs.

high need for achievement A tendency to persist longer at tasks; show better performance on tasks, activities, or exams; set challenging but realistic goals; compete with others to win; and be attracted to careers that require initiative.

hindbrain An area at the base of the brain that is involved in sleeping, waking, coordinating body movements, and regulating vital reflexes (heart rate, blood pressure, and respiration).

hippocampus A curved structure within the temporal lobe that is involved in transforming many kinds of fleeting memories into permanent storage. It forms part of the limbic system.

histrionic personality disorder A disorder characterized by excessive emotionality and attention seeking. It is found in 2% of the population.

HIV positive Having HIV antibodies, which implies infection by the human immunodeficiency virus (HIV).

holistic view The idea, emphasized in humanistic theories, that a person's personality is more than the sum of its individual parts; instead, the individual parts form a unique and total entity that functions as a unit.

homeostasis The tendency of the sympathetic and parasympathetic divisions of the autonomic nervous system to work together to maintain the body's level of arousal in balance for optimum functioning.

homosexual orientation A pattern of sexual arousal by persons of the same sex.

humanistic approach A psychological viewpoint emphasizing that each individual has great freedom in directing his or her future, considerable capacity for achieving personal growth, intrinsic worth, and enormous potential for self-fulfillment.

humanistic theories *See* humanistic approach.

hypnosis A situation or set of procedures in which a researcher, clinician, or hypnotist suggests to another person that he or she will experience various changes in sensation, perception, cognition, or control over motor behaviors.

hypnotic analgesia Reduction in pain reported by clients after undergoing hypnosis and receiving suggestions that reduced anxiety and promoted relaxation.

hypnotic induction Various methods of inducing hypnosis, such as asking subjects to close their eyes and go to sleep, having them fix their attention on an object (for example, a watch), and instructing them to go into deep relaxation.

hypothalamus A structure of the limbic system that is located near the bottom middle of the brain

Glossary

and regulates many motivational and emotional behaviors. It controls much of the endocrine system by regulating the pituitary gland.

hypothesis An educated guess about some phenomenon, stated in precise, concrete language so as to rule out any confusion or error in the meaning of its terms.

iconic memory A form of sensory memory that holds visual information for about a quarter of a second or longer. (The word *icon* means "image.")

id Freud's first division of the mind, which contains two biological drives—sex and aggression—that are the source of all psychic or mental energy. The id's goal is to pursue pleasure and satisfy the biological drives.

ideal self According to Rogers, the self that is based on our hopes and wishes and reflects how we would like to see ourselves; its complement is the real self.

ideal weight *See* optimal weight.

identical twins Twins who develop from a single egg and thus have exactly the same genes.

identity How we describe ourselves, including our values, goals, traits, interests, and motivations.

illusion Perception of an image so distorted that, in reality, it cannot and does not exist. An illusion is created when space, size, and depth cues are manipulated so that our brains can no longer correctly interpret them.

imagined perception In hypnosis, the subject's willingness, at the hypnotist's suggestion, to respond to nonexistent stimuli and imaginary perceptions. It can also include bizarre behaviors, such as imitating Elvis Presley in public.

immune system The body's defense and surveillance network of cells and chemicals that fight off bacteria, viruses, and other foreign or toxic substances.

implicit or nondeclarative memory Mental and emotional processes that we are unaware of but that bias and influence our conscious feelings, thoughts, and behaviors. *See* procedural memory.

impossible figure A perceptual experience in which a drawing seems to defy basic geometric laws.

imprinting Inherited tendencies or responses that are displayed by newborn animals when they encounter certain stimuli in their environment.

incentives Environmental factors, such as external stimuli, reinforcers, or rewards, that motivate our behavior.

independent variable In an experiment, a treatment or something else that the researcher controls or manipulates.

inferential statistics A set of procedures for determining what conclusions can be legitimately inferred from a set of data.

informational influence theory The theory that we use the reactions of others to judge the seriousness of the situation.

inhibited/fearful children Kagan's term for children who show reluctance, anxiety, or fear (measured by motor activity, fretting, or crying) when approaching a strange child, exploring novel objects, playing with a peer, or talking to an unfamiliar adult. In addition, inhibited children show increased physiological arousal to novel or strange situations.

inhibited female orgasm A persistent delay or absence of orgasm after becoming aroused and excited.

innate language factors Genetically programmed physiological and neurological features of the brain and vocal apparatus that facilitate our making speech sounds and learning language skills.

insanity According to the legal definition, not knowing the difference between right and wrong.

insecure attachment An emotional bond characteristic of infants who avoid, or show ambivalence toward, their parents.

insight A mental process marked by the sudden and unexpected solution to a problem; a phenomenon often called the "ah-ha!" experience.

insight therapy An approach in which the therapist and client talk about the client's symptoms and problems, with the goal of identifying the cause of the problem. Once the client has an insight into the cause of the problem, possible solutions can be discussed with the therapist.

insomnia Difficulties in going to sleep or in staying asleep through the night. Associated daytime complaints include fatigue, impairment of concentration, memory difficulty, and lack of well-being. About 33% of adult Americans report some type of insomnia.

instincts According to McDougall (1908), innate tendencies or biological forces that determine behavior; now used as a synonym for fixed action pattern.

intelligence quotient (IQ) A measure of intelligence computed by dividing a child's mental age, as measured in an intelligence test, by the child's chronological age and multiplying the result by 100.

interactive model of sexual orientation The theory that genetic and biological factors, such as genetic instructions and prenatal hormones, interact with psychological factors, such as the individual's attitudes, personality traits, and behaviors, to influence the development of sexual orientation.

interference The forgetting process in which the recall of some particular memory is blocked or prevented by new information that overwrites or interferes with it. *See also* proactive interference and retroactive interference.

internal attributions Explanations of behavior on the basis of the internal characteristics (or dispositions) of the person performing the behavior. Also called dispositional attributions.

interneuron A relatively short neuron whose primary task is to make connections between other neurons.

interposition In three-dimensional vision, a monocular depth cue that comes into play when objects overlap. The overlapping object appears closer, and the object that is overlapped appears to be farther away.

interpreting function The role played by our attitudes in providing convenient guidelines by means of which we can interpret and categorize objects and events and decide whether to approach or avoid them.

interval timing clock A sort of timing device, located in the basal ganglia of the brain, that gauges the passage of seconds, minutes, or hours and helps creatures know when to start or stop doing some activity.

intervention program A program for disadvantaged children that creates an environment offering increased opportunities for intellectual, social, and personality-emotional development while ensuring good physical health.

interview A technique for obtaining information by asking questions, ranging from open-ended to highly structured, about a subject's behaviors and attitudes, usually in a one-on-one situation.

intestines The body organ that responds to the presence of food, especially fats, by secreting a hormone called CCK (cholecystokinin), which inhibits eating.

intimacy In Sternberg's triangular theory of love, the component of love associated with feeling close and connected to someone; it develops through sharing and communicating.

intrinsic motivation Engaging in certain activities or behaviors because they are personally rewarding or because we are fulfilling our beliefs or expectations.

introspection A method of exploring conscious mental processes adopted by the structuralists; subjects were asked to look inward and report their sensations and perceptions.

intrusive thoughts Thoughts that we repeatedly experience, that are usually unwanted or disruptive, and that are very difficult to stop or eliminate.

Inuit beliefs about dreams The Inuit, or Eskimo people, like other isolated indigenous people, believe that dreams are ways to enter the spiritual world, where the souls of departed animals, supernaturals, and relatives are made known.

ions Electrically charged chemical particles, which obey the rule that opposite charges attract and like charges repel.

IQ *See* intelligence quotient.

iris A circular muscle that surrounds the pupil and controls the amount of light that enters the eye. In dim light, the iris relaxes, allowing more light to enter—the pupil dilates; in bright light, the iris constricts, allowing less light to enter—the pupil constricts. The iris muscle contains the pigment that gives the eye its characteristic color.

James-Lange theory The idea that our brains interpret specific physiological changes as feelings or emotions and that there is a different physiological pattern underlying each emotion.

jet lag A condition in which travelers' internal circadian rhythm is out of step, or synchrony, with the external clock time at their new location. They experience fatigue, disorientation, lack of concentration, and reduced cognitive skills.

It takes about one day to reset the circadian clock for each hour of time change.

just noticeable difference (JND) The smallest increase or decrease in the intensity of a stimulus that a person can manage to detect.

labeling A process of identifying differences among individuals and placing them into specific categories, which may have either positive or negative associations.

laboratory experiment A technique to gather information by studying behavior in a controlled environment that permits the careful manipulation of some treatment and the measurement of the treatment's effects on behavior.

laboratory setting An environment in which individuals may be studied under systematic and controlled conditions, thus eliminating many of the real-world influences.

language A form of communication in which we learn and use complex rules to form and manipulate symbols (words or gestures) that are used to generate an endless number of meaningful sentences.

language stages Four different periods in a child's acquisition of language and grammar: babbling, single words, two-word combinations, and sentences. In each subsequent stage, a child displays new and more complex language skills.

latency stage The fourth of Freud's psychosexual stages, lasting from the age of about 6 years to puberty. In this stage, the child represses sexual thoughts and engages in nonsexual activities, such as developing social and intellectual skills.

lateral hypothalamus A group of brain cells that regulates hunger by creating feelings of being hungry.

law of effect The principle that behaviors followed by positive (pleasurable) consequences are strengthened (and thus will likely occur in the future), while behaviors followed by negative consequences are weakened.

learning A relatively permanent change in behavior (both unobservable mental events and observable responses) associated with specific stimuli and/or responses that change as a result of experience.

learning-performance distinction The idea that learning may occur but may not always be measured by, or immediately evident in, performance.

lens A transparent, oval structure in the eye whose curved surface functions to bend and focus light waves into an even narrower beam. The lens is attached to muscles that adjust the curve of the lens, which, in turn, adjusts the focusing.

levels-of-processing theory The theory that memory depends on how well information is encoded in the mind. Information is encoded at a shallow level if we simply pay attention to its basic features but is encoded at a deep level if we form new associations with existing information. According to the theory, poor memory corresponds to information encoded at a shallow level, and good memory to information encoded at deep levels.

lie detector tests *See* polygraph tests.

light and shadow A monocular depth cue; brightly lit objects appear closer, while objects in shadows appear farther away.

light therapy The use of bright, artificial light to reset circadian rhythms and so combat the insomnia and drowsiness that plague shift workers and jet-lag sufferers; it is also used to help people with sleeping disorders in which the body fails to stay in time with the external environment.

limbic system A group of about half a dozen interconnected structures in the core of the forebrain that are involved in many motivational behaviors, such as obtaining food, drink, and sex; organizing emotional behaviors such as fear, anger, and aggression; and storing memories. It is sometimes referred to as our primitive, or animal, brain because the same structures are found in the brains of animals that are evolutionarily very old.

linear perspective In three-dimensional vision, a monocular depth cue associated with the convergence of parallel lines in the far distance.

linguistic relativity *See* theory of linguistic relativity.

liver The body organ that monitors nutrients, especially the level of glucose (sugar) in the blood. When the level of glucose falls, the liver signals hunger; when the level of glucose rises, the liver signals fullness.

lobes The four areas into which the brain's cortex is divided.

locus of control Our beliefs concerning how much control we have over situations or rewards. For each of us, these beliefs lie somewhere on a continuum between internal and external locus of control. We have an internal locus of control if we believe that we have control over situations and rewards and an external locus of control if we believe that we do not have control over situations and rewards and that events outside ourselves (fate) determine what happens.

long-term memory The process that can store almost unlimited amounts of information over long periods of time.

long-term potentiation (LTP) The increased sensitivity of a neuron to stimulation after it has been repeatedly stimulated. Neuroscientists believe that the LTP process may be the basis for learning and memory in animals and humans.

longitudinal method A research design in which the same group of individuals is studied repeatedly at many different points in time.

loudness Our subjective experience of a sound's intensity, which is determined by the height (amplitude) of the sound wave. The brain calculates loudness from the rate of nerve impulses that arrive in the auditory nerve.

LSD (*d*-lysergic acid diethylamide) A very potent hallucinogen. Very small doses can produce experiences such as visual hallucinations, perceptual distortions, increased sensory awareness, and emotional responses that may last 8–10 hours.

LTP *See* long-term potentiation.

magnetic resonance imaging (MRI) A technique for studying the structure of the living brain. Nonharmful radio frequencies are passed through the brain, and a computer measures their interaction with brain cells and transforms this interaction into an incredibly detailed image of the brain (or body).

maintenance rehearsal The practice of intentionally repeating or rehearsing information (rather than forming any new associations) so that it remains longer in short-term memory.

major depressive disorder A mood disorder marked by at least two weeks of continually being in a bad mood, having no interest in anything, and getting no pleasure from activities. In addition, a person must have at least four of the following symptoms: problems with eating, sleeping, thinking, concentrating, or making decisions; lacking energy; thinking about suicide; and feeling worthless or guilty. Also called unipolar depression.

major life events Potentially disturbing, troubling, or disruptive situations, both positive and negative, that we appraise as having a significant impact on our lives.

maladaptive behavior approach In defining abnormality, the idea that a behavior is psychologically damaging or abnormal if it interferes with the individual's ability to function in one's personal life or in society.

male hypothalamus Because of neural programming in the womb, the hypothalamus, a structure in the brain that controls the endocrine system, functions differently in the male and female. The male hypothalamus triggers a continuous release of androgens, such as testosterone, from the testes. The increased androgen level is responsible for male secondary sexual characteristics, such as facial and pubic hair, muscle growth, and lowered voice.

male secondary sexual characteristics Sexual characteristics whose development in the male is triggered by the increased secretion of testosterone during puberty; they include the growth of pubic hair, muscle development, and a change (deepening) of the voice.

marijuana A psychoactive drug whose primary active ingredient is THC (tetrahydrocannabinol), which is found in the leaves of the cannabis plant. Low doses produce mild euphoria; moderate doses produce perceptual and time distortions; and high doses may produce hallucinations, delusions, and distortions of body image.

Maslow's hierarchy of needs An ascending order, or hierarchy, in which biological needs are placed at the bottom and social needs at the top. As needs at lower levels are met, we advance to the next higher level. This hierarchy indicates that we satisfy our biological needs before we satisfy our social needs.

mass hysteria A condition experienced by a group of people who, through suggestion, observation, or other psychological processes, develop similar

Glossary

fears, delusions, abnormal behaviors, and, in some cases, physical symptoms.

maturation The succession of developmental changes that are genetically or biologically programmed rather than acquired through learning or life experiences.

MDMA Also called ecstasy, this drug resembles both mescaline (a hallucinogen) and amphetamine (a stimulant). It heightens sensations, gives a euphoric rush, raises body temperature, and creates feelings of warmth and empathy.

mean The arithmetic average of all the individual measurements in a distribution.

measure of variability An indication of how much scores in a distribution vary from one another.

median The score above and below which half the scores in the distribution fall.

medical therapy Any approach that uses psychoactive drugs, such as tranquilizers and neuroleptics, to treat mental disorders by changing biological factors, such as the levels of neurotransmitters in the brain.

medulla An area in the hindbrain, located at the top of the spinal cord, that includes a group of cells that control vital reflexes, such as respiration, heart rate, and blood pressure.

melatonin A hormone secreted by the pineal gland, an oval group of cells in the center of the human brain. Melatonin secretion, controlled by the suprachiasmatic nucleus, increases with darkness and decreases with light; thus, it plays a role in the regulation of circadian rhythms and in promoting sleep.

memory The ability to retain information over time through the processes of encoding, storing, and retrieving. Memories are not copies but representations of the world that vary in accuracy and are subject to error and bias.

menarche The first menstrual period; it is a signal that ovulation may have occurred and that the girl may have the potential to conceive and bear a child.

Meniere's disease Sudden attacks of dizziness, nausea, vomiting, and head-splitting buzzing sounds that result from a malfunction of the semicircular canals in the vestibular system.

menopause A gradual stoppage in the secretion of the major female hormone (estrogen). This process, which occurs in women at about age 50 (range 35–60), results in the cessation of ovulation and the menstrual cycle.

mental age The estimation of a child's intellectual progress, which is calculated by comparing the child's score on an intelligence test with the scores of average children of the same age.

mental disorder A prolonged or recurring problem that seriously interferes with an individual's ability to live a satisfying personal life and function adequately in society.

mental retardation Substantial limitation in present functioning, characterized by significantly subaverage intellectual functioning along with related limitations in two of ten areas, including communication, self-care, home living, social skills, and safety.

mescaline The active ingredient in the peyote cactus. At high doses, mescaline produces physiological arousal and very clear, colorful, and vivid visual hallucinations. It primarily increases the activity of the neurotransmitters norepinephrine and dopamine. Mescaline does not impair the intellect or cloud consciousness.

meta-analysis A powerful statistical procedure that compares the results of dozens or hundreds of studies to determine the effectiveness of some variable or treatment examined in those studies (for example, a type of therapy).

metabolic rate The efficiency with which the body breaks food down into energy and the speed with which the body burns off that fuel. An inherited trait, it can be raised by exercise or smoking.

methamphetamine (D-methamphetamine) A stimulant similar to amphetamine in both its chemical makeup and its physical and psychological effects. It causes marked increases in blood pressure and heart rate and feelings of enhanced mood, alertness, and energy. Methamphetamine, whose street names are meth, speed, crank, crystal, and ice, produces an almost instantaneous high when smoked and is highly addictive.

method of loci A mnemonic device, or encoding technique, that improves encoding by creating visual associations between memorized places and new items to be memorized.

midbrain The part of the brain that contains the reward/pleasure center, which is stimulated by food, sex, money, music, attractive faces, and some drugs (cocaine); contains areas for visual and auditory reflexes, such as automatically turning your head toward a noise; and holds the reticular formation, which arouses the forebrain so that it is ready to process information from the senses.

middle ear A bony cavity that is sealed at each end by a membrane. The two membranes are connected by three small bones, collectively called ossicles. Because of their shapes, these bones are referred to as the hammer, anvil, and stirrup. The ossicles act like levers that greatly amplify vibrations from the eardrum and transmit them to the oval window and inner ear.

mind-body connection The ability of our thoughts, beliefs, and emotions to produce physiological changes that may be either beneficial or detrimental to our health and well-being.

mind-body question The debate about how complex mental activities, such as feeling, thinking, learning, imagining, and dreaming, can be generated by the brain's physical membranes, fluids, and chemicals.

mind-body therapy An approach to healing based on the finding that thoughts and emotions can change physiological and immune responses. It attempts to increase physical and mental well-being by means of mental strategies, such as relaxation, meditation, and biofeedback, as well as social support groups.

Minnesota Multiphasic Personality Inventory-2 (MMPI-2) A true-false self-report questionnaire that consists of 567 statements describing a wide range of normal and abnormal behaviors. The purpose of MMPI-2 is to help distinguish normal from abnormal groups.

mnemonic methods Very effective ways to improve encoding and create better retrieval cues by forming vivid associations or images that facilitate recall and decrease forgetting.

mode The most frequent measurement in a distribution.

modified frustration-aggression hypothesis The idea that although frustration may lead to aggression, a number of situational and cognitive factors may override the aggressive response.

monochromats Individuals who have total color blindness; their world looks like a black-and-white movie. This kind of color blindness is rare and results from individuals having only rods or only one kind of functioning cone instead of three.

monocular depth cues In three-dimensional vision, depth cues produced by signals from a single eye. They are most commonly determined by the way objects are arranged in the environment.

mood disorder A prolonged and disturbed emotional state that affects almost all of a person's thoughts and behaviors.

moral therapy The belief that mental patients could be helped to function better by receiving humane treatment in a relaxed and decent environment. This approach was fundamental to the reform movement of the early 1800s.

morning persons People who prefer to get up early, go to bed early, and engage in morning activities. *See* evening persons.

morphemes The smallest meaningful combination of sounds in a language.

morphology A system that we use to group phonemes—consonants and vowels—into meaningful combinations of sounds and words.

motion parallax In three-dimensional vision, a monocular depth cue based on the speed of moving objects: Objects that appear to be moving at high speed are interpreted as closer to us than those moving more slowly.

motion sickness Feelings of nausea and dizziness experienced in a moving vehicle when information from the vestibular system (that your head is bouncing around) conflicts with information reported by your eyes (that objects in the distance look fairly steady).

motivation Various physiological and psychological factors that cause us to act in a specific way at a particular time.

motor cortex A narrow strip of cortex that is located on the back edge of the frontal lobe and extends down its side. It is involved in the initiation of all voluntary movements. The right motor cortex controls muscles on the left side of the body and vice versa.

motor development The stages of motor skills that all infants pass through as they acquire the muscular control necessary for making coordinated movements.

motor neurons *See* efferent neurons.

MRI *See* magnetic resonance imaging.

multiple-intelligence theory *See* Gardner's multiple-intelligence theory.

multiple sclerosis A disease that attacks the myelin sheaths that wrap around and insulate cells in the central nervous system. Because of this damage, messages between the brain and other parts of the body are disrupted, often causing problems in motor coordination, strength, and sensation.

myelin sheath A tubelike structure of fatty material that wraps around and insulates an axon, preventing interference from electrical signals generated in adjacent axons.

narcolepsy A relatively rare, chronic disorder marked by excessive sleepiness, usually in the form of sleep attacks or short periods of sleep throughout the day. The sleep attacks are accompanied by brief periods of REM sleep and loss of muscle control (cataplexy), which may be triggered by big emotional changes.

naturalistic setting A relatively normal environment in which researchers gather information by observing individuals' behaviors without attempting to change or control the situation.

nature-nurture question The debate concerning the relative contribution of genetic factors (nature) and environmental factors (nurture) to a person's intelligence as well as to his or her biological, emotional, cognitive, personal, and social development.

nearsightedness A visual acuity problem that may result when the eyeball is too long, so that objects are focused at a point slightly in front of the retina. The result is that near objects are clear, but distant objects appear blurry.

negative punishment Removal of a reinforcing stimulus (for example, taking away a child's allowance) after a response. This removal decreases the chances that the response will recur.

negative reinforcement The occurrence of an operant response that either stops or removes an aversive stimulus. Removal of the aversive stimulus increases the likelihood that the response will occur again.

negative symptoms of schizophrenia Symptoms that reflect a decrease in or loss of normal functions: decreased range and intensity of emotions, decreased ability to express thoughts, and decreased initiative to engage in goal-directed behaviors.

neglect syndrome The failure of a patient to see objects or parts of the body on the side opposite the brain damage when the damage is to an association area, usually in occipital and parietal lobes, and usually in the right hemisphere.

nerve impulse A series of separate action potentials that take place, segment by segment, as they move down the length of an axon.

nerves Stringlike bundles of axons and dendrites that are held together by connective tissue. Nerves in the peripheral nervous system have the ability to regrow, regenerate, or reattach if severed or damaged. They carry information from the senses, skin, muscles, and the body's organs to and from the spinal cord.

network hierarchy In the network theory of memory, the arrangement of nodes or categories so that concrete ideas are at the bottom of the hierarchy and are connected to more abstract ideas located above them. The most abstract ideas are at the top of the hierarchy.

network theory The theory that we store related ideas in separate memory categories, or files, called nodes. As we make associations between information, we create links among thousands of nodes, which make up a gigantic interconnected network for storing and retrieving information.

neural assemblies Groups of interconnected neurons whose activation allows information or stimuli to be recognized and held briefly and temporarily in short-term memory.

neural deafness Deafness caused by damage to the auditory receptors (hair cells), which prevents the triggering of impulses, or by damage to the auditory nerve, which prevents impulses from reaching the brain. *See also* cochlear implant.

neuroleptic drugs Drugs that change the levels of neurotransmitters in the brain. They are used to treat serious mental disorders, such as schizophrenia. Also called antipsychotic drugs.

neurons Cells that have specialized extensions for the reception and transmission of electrical signals.

neuroses According to Freud, maladaptive thoughts and actions that arise from some unconscious thought or conflict and indicate feelings of anxiety.

neurotransmitters About a dozen different chemicals that are made by neurons and then used for communication between neurons during the performance of mental or physical activities.

neutral stimulus A stimulus that causes a sensory response, such as being seen, heard, or smelled, but does not produce the reflex being tested.

nicotine A stimulant; it first produces arousal but then produces calming. Present in cigarettes, nicotine increases both heart rate and blood pressure. It improves attention and concentration, may improve short-term memory, but may interfere with complex processing. Regular use of nicotine causes addiction, and stopping leads to withdrawal symptoms.

night terrors Sleep disruptions in children that occur during stage 3 or stage 4 (delta) sleep. They usually start with a piercing scream, after which the child wakes suddenly in a fearful state, with rapid breathing and increased heart rate. The next morning, the child has no memory of the frightening experience.

nightmares Dreams that contain frightening and anxiety-producing images. They usually involve great danger—being attacked, injured, or pursued. Upon awakening, the dreamer can usually describe the nightmare in considerable detail. Nightmares occur during REM sleep.

nodes Memory files that contain related information organized around a specific topic or category.

non-REM sleep Stages 1–4 of sleep, in which rapid eye movement does not occur; it makes up about 80% of sleep time.

nonbenzodiazepines Drugs, such as Ambien and Sonata, that are becoming popular sleeping pills because they are rapid acting, are of short duration, and have few cognitive side effects.

noncompliance In children, refusal to follow directions, carry out a request, or obey a command given by a parent or caregiver. Noncompliance is one of the most common complaints of parents in general and the most frequent problem of parents who bring their children to clinics for treatment of behavioral problems.

nonintellectual factors Factors such as attitude, experience, and emotional functions that may help or hinder an individual's performance on intelligence tests.

normal aging A gradual and natural slowing of our physical and psychological processes from middle through late adulthood.

normal curve A graph of a frequency distribution in which the curve tapers off equally on either side of a central high point—in other words, a graph of a normal distribution.

normal distribution A bell-shaped frequency distribution curve. The scores are arranged symmetrically so that the vast majority fall in the middle range, with fewer scores near the two extreme ends of the curve.

obedience Behavior performed in response to an order given by someone in a position of authority.

obesity A body weight 30% or more above the ideal value.

object permanence The understanding that objects or events continue to exist even if they can no longer be heard, touched, or seen.

objective personality tests Tests consisting of specific written statements that require individuals to indicate—for example, by checking "true" or "false"—whether the statements do or do not apply to them; also called self-report questionnaires.

observational learning *See* social cognitive learning.

obsessive-compulsive disorder An anxiety disorder consisting of obsessions, which are persistent, recurring, irrational thoughts, impulses, or images that a person is unable to control and that interfere with normal functioning; and compulsions, which are irresistible impulses to perform over and over some senseless behavior or ritual (hand washing, checking things, counting, putting things in order).

obsessive-compulsive personality disorder A personality disorder characterized by an intense interest in being orderly, achieving perfection, and having control. It is found in 4% of the population.

Glossary

occipital lobe A region at the very back of the brain that is involved in processing visual information, which includes seeing colors and perceiving and recognizing objects, animals, and people.

Oedipus complex According to Freud, a process in which a child competes with the parent of the same sex for the affections and pleasures of the parent of the opposite sex; called the Electra complex in girls.

olfaction The sense of smell. Its stimuli are various chemicals that are carried by the air.

olfactory cells The receptors for smell, located in the uppermost part of the nasal passages. As volatile molecules dissolve in the mucus covering the cells, they stimulate the receptors, which send nerve impulses to the brain.

operant conditioning A kind of learning in which the consequences—reward or punishment—that follow some behavior increase or decrease the likelihood of that behavior's occurrence in the future. Also called instrumental conditioning.

operant response A response that can be modified by its consequences. Operant responses offer a way of dividing ongoing behavior into meaningful and measurable units.

opiates Drugs derived from the opium poppy, including opium and morphine, which is chemically altered to make heroin. All opiates have three primary effects: analgesia (pain reduction); opiate euphoria, which is often described as a pleasurable state between waking and sleeping; and constipation. Continued use of opiates results in tolerance, physical addiction, and an intense craving for the drug.

opponent-process theory A theory of color vision suggesting that ganglion cells in the retina and cells in the thalamus respond to two pairs of colors: red-green and blue-yellow. When these cells are excited, they respond to one color of the pair; when inhibited, they respond to the complementary pair.

optimal weight The body weight resulting from an almost perfect balance between how much food an organism eats and how much it needs to meet its body's energy needs; also called ideal weight.

optimism A relatively stable personality trait that leads one to believe and expect that good things will happen. It is one of the personality factors associated with lower stress levels and fewer chances of developing psychosomatic symptoms. *See* pessimism.

oral stage Freud's first psychosexual stage, which lasts for the first 18 months of life. In this stage, the infant's pleasure seeking is centered on the mouth.

organic factors Medical conditions or drug or medication problems that lead to sexual difficulties.

organic retardation Mental retardation that results from genetic problems or brain damage.

ossicles *See* middle ear.

outer ear Three structures important to the hearing process: the external ear, auditory canal, and tympanic membrane (eardrum).

overgeneralization A common error during language acquisition, in which children apply a grammatical rule to cases where it should not be used.

overweight A body weight 20% over the ideal value.

ovulation The release of an ovum, or egg cell, from a woman's ovaries.

pain Sensations caused by various stimuli that activate the pain receptors, free nerve endings. Nerve impulses from these pain receptors travel to the somatosensory and limbic areas of the brain, where they are transformed into pain sensations. Pain is essential for survival: It warns us to avoid or escape dangerous situations or stimuli and makes us take time to recover from injury.

pancreas An organ that regulates the level of sugar in the bloodstream by secreting insulin. It forms part of the endocrine system.

panic attack A period of intense fear or discomfort in which four or more of the following symptoms are present: pounding heart, sweating, trembling, shortness of breath, feelings of choking, chest pain, nausea, feeling dizzy, and fear of losing control or dying.

panic disorder A mental disorder characterized primarily by recurrent and unexpected panic attacks, plus continued worry about having another attack; such worry interferes with psychological functioning.

paranoid personality disorder A pattern of distrust and suspiciousness and perceiving others as having evil motives. It is found in 0.5–2.5% of the population.

paranoid schizophrenia A subcategory of schizophrenia characterized by auditory hallucinations or delusions, such as thoughts of being persecuted by others or delusions of grandeur.

paraphilias Repetitive or preferred sexual fantasies involving nonhuman objects, such as sexual attractions to particular articles of clothing (shoes, underwear); commonly called sexual deviations.

parasympathetic division The subdivision of the autonomic nervous system that decreases physiological arousal and helps return the body to a calmer, more relaxed state. It also stimulates digestion during eating.

parentese A way of speaking to young children in which the adult speaks in a voice that is slower and higher than normal, emphasizes and stretches out each word, uses very simple sentences, and repeats words and phrases. Formerly known as motherese.

parietal lobe An area of the cortex located directly behind the frontal lobe. Its functions include: processing sensory information from body parts, which includes touching, locating positions of limbs, and feeling temperature and pain; and carrying out several cognitive functions, such as attending to and perceiving objects.

Parkinson's disease A condition caused by the destruction of neurons that produce the neurotransmitter dopamine. Symptoms include tremors and

shakes in the limbs, a slowing of voluntary movements, and feelings of depression. As the disease progresses, patients develop a peculiar shuffling walk and may suddenly freeze in space for minutes or hours at a time.

partial reinforcement A schedule of reinforcement in which the response is reinforced only some of the time.

passion In Sternberg's triangular theory of love, the component of love associated with feeling physically aroused and attracted to someone.

passionate love A condition that is associated with continuously thinking about the loved one and is accompanied by warm sexual feelings and powerful emotional reactions.

pathological aging Acceleration of the aging process, which may be caused by genetic defects, physiological problems, or diseases.

peg method A mnemonic device, or encoding technique, that creates associations between number-word rhymes and items to be memorized.

perception The experience of a meaningful pattern or image that the brain assembles from thousands of individual meaningless sensations; a perception is normally changed, biased, colored, or distorted by a person's unique set of experiences.

perceptual constancy Our tendency to perceive sizes, colors, brightness, and shapes as remaining the same even though their physical characteristics are constantly changing.

perceptual sets Learned expectations that are based on our personal, social, or cultural experiences. These expectations automatically add information, meaning, or feelings to our perceptions and thus change or bias our perceptions.

perceptual speed The rate at which we can identify a particular sensory stimulus; this rate slows down noticeably after age 60.

peripheral cues Hunger cues associated with changes in blood chemistry or signals from digestive organs.

peripheral nervous system All the nerves that extend from the spinal cord and carry messages to and from various muscles, glands, and sense organs located throughout the body. It has two divisions: the somatic nervous system and the autonomic nervous system.

peripheral route for persuasion Approaches to persuasion that emphasize emotional appeal, focus on personal traits, and generate positive feelings.

peripheral theories of emotions Theories that attribute our subjective feelings primarily to our body's physiological changes.

permissive parents Parents who are less controlling and behave with a nonpunishing and accepting attitude toward their children's impulses, desires, and actions. They consult with their children about policy decisions, make few demands, and tend to use reason rather than direct power.

person perception The process by which we form impressions of, and make judgments about, the traits and characteristics of others.

person schemas Social schemas including our judgments about the traits that we and others possess.

person-situation interaction The interaction between a person's traits and the effects of being in a particular situation, which, according to Mischel, determines the person's behavior.

personal factors According to social cognitive theory, factors that include our emotional makeup and our biological and genetic influences and that help to shape our personalities.

personal identity *See* identity.

personality A combination of long-lasting and distinctive behaviors, thoughts, motives, and emotions that typify how we react and adapt to other people and situations. *See also* theory of personality.

personality development *See* social development.

personality disorder Any psychological disorder characterized by inflexible, long-standing, maladaptive traits that cause significantly impaired functioning or great distress in one's personal and social life.

personality psychology The study of personality development, personality change, assessment, and abnormal behaviors.

personality tests Tests used to measure a person's observable traits and behaviors and unobservable characteristics. In addition, some are used to identify personality problems and psychological disorders, as well as to predict how a person might behave in the future. Objective personality tests (self-report questionnaires), such as the MMPI, consist of specific statements or questions to which the person responds with specific answers; projective tests, such as the Rorschach inkblot test, have no set answers but consist of ambiguous stimuli that a person interprets or makes up stories about.

pessimism A relatively stable personality trait that leads one to believe and expect that bad things will happen. It is one of the personality factors associated with increased stress levels and chances of developing psychosomatic symptoms. *See* optimism.

PET *See* positron emission tomography.

phallic stage Freud's third psychosexual stage, lasting from the ages of about 3 to 6 years. In this stage, the infant's pleasure seeking is centered on the genitals.

phantom limb The experience of sensations and feelings coming from a limb that has been amputated. The sensations and feelings are extremely vivid, as if the amputated limb were still present.

phenomenological perspective The idea that our perspective of the world, whether or not it is accurate, becomes our reality. This idea is stressed in humanistic theories.

phenothiazines The first group of drugs to reduce schizophrenic symptoms, such as delusions and hallucinations. Discovered in the early 1950s, the phenothiazines operate by blocking or reducing the effects of the neurotransmitter dopamine.

phi movement The illusion that stationary lights are moving. The illusion of movement—today called apparent motion—is created by flashing closely positioned stationary lights at regular intervals.

phobia An anxiety disorder characterized by an intense and irrational fear that is out of all proportion to the danger elicited by the object or situation. In comparison, fear is a realistic response to a threatening situation.

phonemes The basic sounds of consonants and vowels.

phonology Rules specifying how we make the meaningful sounds used by a particular language.

photographic memory The ability to form sharp, detailed visual images after examining a picture or page for a short period of time and to recall the entire image at a later date. Photographic memory is similar to eidetic imagery but occurs in adults.

physiological psychology *See* psychobiology.

Piaget's cognitive stages Four different stages—the sensorimotor, preoperational, concrete operations, and formal operations stages—each of which is more advanced than the preceding stage because it involves new reasoning and thinking abilities.

pica A behavioral disorder in which individuals eat inedible objects or unhealthy substances. Pica can lead to serious physical problems, including lead poisoning, intestinal blockage, and parasites, and is most often seen in individuals with mental retardation.

pitch Our subjective experience of how low or high a sound is. The brain calculates pitch from the speed (frequency) of the sound waves. The frequency of sound waves is measured in cycles, which refers to how many sound waves occur in 1 second.

pituitary gland A key component of the endocrine system, which hangs directly below the hypothalamus, to which it is connected by a narrow stalk. Its anterior section regulates growth and controls much of the endocrine system, while its posterior section regulates water and salt balance.

place theory The theory that the brain perceives the pitch of a sound by receiving information about where on the basilar membrane a given sound vibrates the most; it applies to medium and higher pitches.

placebo An intervention—taking a pill, receiving an injection, or undergoing an operation—that resembles medical therapy but that, in fact, has no medical effects.

placebo effect A change in the patient's illness that is attributable to an imagined treatment rather than to a medical treatment.

placenta An organ that connects the blood supply of the mother to that of the fetus. The placenta acts like a filter, allowing oxygen and nutrients to pass through while keeping out certain toxic or harmful substances.

pleasure principle The satisfaction of drives and avoidance of pain, without concern for moral restrictions or society's regulations. According to Freud, this is the id's operating principle.

polygraph tests Tests based on the theory that, if a person tells a lie, he or she will feel some emotion, such as guilt or fear. Feeling guilty or fearful will usually be accompanied by involuntary physiological responses, which are difficult to suppress or control and can be measured with a machine called a polygraph.

pons A bridge that connects the spinal cord with the brain and parts of the brain with one another. Cells in the pons manufacture chemicals involved in sleep.

positive psychology The scientific study of optimal human functioning, focusing on the strengths and virtues that enable individuals and communities to thrive. It aims to better understand the positive, adaptive, and fulfiling aspects of human life.

positive punishment The presentation of an aversive stimulus (for example, spanking) after a response. The aversive stimulus decreases the chances that the response will recur.

positive regard Love, sympathy, warmth, acceptance, and respect, which we crave from family, friends, and people important to us.

positive reinforcement The presentation of a stimulus that increases the probability of a behavior's recurrence.

positive reinforcer A stimulus that increases the likelihood that a response will occur again.

positive symptoms of schizophrenia Symptoms that reflect a distortion of normal functions. Distorted thinking results in delusions; distorted perceptions result in hallucinations; and distorted language results in disorganized speech.

positron emission tomography (PET) A technique to measure the function of the living brain. A slightly radioactive solution is injected into the blood and the amount of radiation absorbed by the brain cells is measured. Very active brain cells—neurons—absorb more radioactive solution than less active ones. A computer transforms the different levels of absorption into colors that indicate the activity of neurons. The colors red and yellow indicate maximum activity of neurons; blue and green indicate minimal activity.

postconventional level Kohlberg's highest level of moral reasoning, at which moral decisions are made after carefully thinking about all the alternatives and striking a balance between human rights and the laws of society.

posterior pituitary The rear part of the pituitary gland, a key component of the endocrine system. It regulates water and salt balance.

Glossary

posthypnotic amnesia Inability to remember what happened during hypnosis, prompted by a specific suggestion from the hypnotist.

posthypnotic suggestion A suggestion given to the subject during hypnosis about performing a particular behavior, in response to a predetermined cue, when the subject comes out of hypnosis.

posttraumatic stress disorder (PTSD) A disabling condition that results from direct personal experience of an event that involves actual or threatened death or serious injury or from witnessing such an event or hearing that such an event has happened to a family member or close friend.

precognition The ability to foretell events.

preconventional level Kohlberg's lowest level of moral reasoning. It consists of two stages: At stage 1, moral decisions are based primarily on fear of punishment or the need to be obedient; at stage 2, moral reasoning is guided most by satisfaction of one's self-interest, which may involve making bargains.

predisposing function The role of our attitudes in guiding or influencing us to behave in specific ways.

prejudice An unfair, biased, or intolerant attitude toward another group of people.

premature ejaculation Persistent or recurrent absence of voluntary control over ejaculation, in that the male ejaculates with minimal sexual stimulation before, upon, or shortly after penetration and before he wishes to; also called rapid ejaculation.

prenatal period The period from conception to birth, which lasts about 266 days (about nine months). It is divided into three phases: germinal, embryonic, and fetal. During the prenatal period, a single cell will divide and grow to form 200 billion cells.

preoperational stage The second of Piaget's cognitive stages, lasting from the ages of about 2 to 7 years. During this stage, children learn to use symbols (such as words or mental images) to think about things that are not present and to help them solve simple problems.

preparedness The innate or biological tendency of animals and humans to recognize, attend to, and store certain cues over others, as well as to associate some combinations of conditioned and unconditioned stimuli more easily than others. Also called prepared learning.

primacy effect Better recall, or improvement in retention, of information presented at the beginning of a task.

primacy-recency effect Better recall of information presented at the beginning and end of a task.

primary appraisal Our initial, subjective evaluation of a situation, in which we balance the demands of a potentially stressful situation against our ability to meet them.

primary auditory cortex An area at the top edge of the temporal lobe that transforms nerve impulses (electrical signals) into basic auditory sensations, such as meaningless sounds and tones of varying pitch and loudness. Next, it sends impulses (sensations) to the auditory association areas.

primary reinforcer A stimulus, such as food, water, or sex, that is innately satisfying and requires no learning on the part of the subject to become pleasurable.

primary visual cortex A small area, located at the back of each occipital lobe, that receives electrical signals from receptors in the eyes and transforms these signals into meaningless, basic visual sensations, such as lights, lines, shadows, colors, and textures.

principle of bidirectionality The idea that a child's behaviors influence how his or her parents respond and, in turn, the parents' behaviors influence how the child responds.

proactive interference A forgetting process in which information that we learned earlier blocks or disrupts the retrieval of related information that was learned later.

problem-focused coping Solving a problem by seeking information, changing our own behavior, or taking whatever action is necessary.

problem solving Searching for some rule, plan, or strategy in order to reach a certain goal that is currently out of reach.

procedural memory Memories of performing motor or perceptual tasks (playing sports), carrying out habitual behaviors (brushing teeth), and responding to stimuli because of classical conditioning (fearing spiders). We cannot retrieve these memories and are not conscious of them.

processing speed The rate at which we encode information into long-term memory or recall or retrieve information from long-term memory; this rate slows down after age 60.

procrastination The tendency to always put off completing a task to the point of feeling anxious or uncomfortable about one's delay.

prodigy A child who shows unusual talent, ability, or genius at a very early age and does not have mental retardation. A small percentage of autistic children, who have some degree of mental retardation, may also show unusual artistic or mathematical abilities; they are called savants.

progressive relaxation An exercise in which the major muscle groups of the body are tensed and relaxed repeatedly until the individual can relax any group of muscles at will.

projection Unconsciously transferring unacceptable traits to others.

projective tests Tests in which the subject is presented with some type of ambiguous stimulus—such as a meaningless object or ambiguous photo— and then asked to make up a story about the stimulus. The assumption is that the person will project conscious or unconscious feelings, needs, and motives in his or her responses.

prosocial behavior Any behavior that benefits others or has positive social consequences. Also called helping.

prototype theory The idea that we form a concept by first constructing a prototype of an object— that is, a mental image based on its average characteristics. Once we have formed a set of prototypes, we identify new objects by matching them against our prototypes.

proximity rule A perceptual rule stating that, in organizing stimuli, objects that are physically close to one another will be grouped together.

proximodistal principle The rule that parts closer to the center of the infant's body develop before parts that are farther away.

psi The processing of information or transfer of energy by methods that have no known physical or biological mechanisms and that seem to stretch the laws of physics.

psilocybin A hallucinogen, the active ingredient in magic mushrooms. Low doses produce pleasant and relaxed feelings; medium doses produce distortions in the perception of time and space; and high doses produce distortions in perceptions and body image and sometimes hallucinations.

psychiatrist A medical doctor (M.D.) who has taken a psychiatric residency, which involves additional training in pharmacology, neurology, psychopathology, and therapeutic techniques. In diagnosing the possible causes of abnormal behaviors, psychiatrists focus on biological factors; they tend to view mental disorders as diseases and to treat them with drugs. Psychiatrists who receive additional training in psychoanalytic institutes are called psychoanalysts.

psychoactive drugs Chemicals that affect the nervous system and, as a result, may alter consciousness and awareness, influence sensations and perceptions, and modify moods and cognitive processes. Some are legal (coffee, alcohol, and tobacco) and some are illegal (marijuana, heroin, cocaine, and LSD).

psychoanalysis A form of psychotherapy based on the idea that each of us has an unconscious part that contains ideas, memories, desires, or thoughts that have been hidden or repressed because they are psychologically dangerous or threatening to our self-concept. To protect our self-concept, we automatically build a mental barrier that we cannot voluntarily remove. But the presence of these thoughts and desires gives rise to unconscious conflicts, which, in turn, can result in psychological and physical symptoms and mental disorders.

psychoanalyst *See* psychiatrist.

psychoanalytic approach A psychological viewpoint that stresses the influence of unconscious fears, desires, and motivations on thoughts and behaviors and also the impact of childhood experiences on the development of later personality traits and psychological problems. As applied to mental disorders, this approach traces their origin to unconscious conflicts or problems with unresolved conflicts at one or more of Freud's psychosexual stages. Treatment of mental disorders, in this approach, centers on the therapist's helping the patient to identify and resolve his or her unconscious conflicts.

psychobiological approach *See* biological approach.

psychobiology The scientific study of the physical and chemical changes that occur during stress, learning, and emotions, as well as how our genetic makeup and nervous system interact with our environments and influence our behaviors.

psychodynamic theory of personality *See* Freud's psychodynamic theory of personality.

psychokinesis The ability to exert mind over matter—for example, by moving objects without touching them.

psychological assessment The use of various tools—including psychological tests and interviews—to measure characteristics, traits, or abilities in order to understand behavior and predict future performance or behavior.

psychological factors Performance anxiety, sexual trauma, guilt, or failure to communicate, all of which may lead to sexual problems.

psychological sex factors Factors involved in the development of a gender identity, gender role, and sexual orientation, as well as in difficulties in sexual performance or enjoyment.

psychologist An individual who has completed four to five years of postgraduate education and has obtained a Ph.D. in psychology; in some states, an individual with a master's degree.

psychology The systematic, scientific study of behaviors and mental processes.

psychometric approach An approach to the assessment of intelligence that measures or quantifies cognitive abilities or factors that are thought to be involved in intellectual performance.

psychometrics A subarea of psychology concerned with the development of tests to assess an individual's abilities, skills, intelligence, personality traits, and abnormal behaviors in a wide range of settings—school, the workplace, or a clinic.

psychoneuroimmunology The study of the relationship among the central nervous system, the endocrine system, and psychosocial factors such as cognitive reactions to stressful events, the individual's personality traits, and social influences.

psychosexual stages According to Freud, five developmental periods—the oral, anal, phallic, latency, and genital stages—each marked by potential conflict between parent and child. The conflicts arise as the child seeks pleasure from different bodily areas associated with sexual feelings (different erogenous zones). Freud emphasized that the child's first five years were most important in social and personality development.

psychosocial factors Underlying personality traits, amount of social support, and ability to deal with stressful life events—these factors are believed to combine and interact with predisposing biological factors to either increase or decrease a person's vulnerability to the development and maintenance of a mood disorder.

psychosocial hunger factors Learned associations between food and other stimuli, such as snacking while watching television; sociocultural influences, such as pressures to be thin; and various personality problems, such as depression, dislike of body image, or low self-esteem.

psychosocial stages According to Erikson, eight developmental periods during which an individual's primary goal is to satisfy desires associated with social needs: The eight periods are associated, respectively, with issues of trust, autonomy, initiative, industry, identity, intimacy, generativity, and ego integrity.

psychosomatic symptoms Real, physical, and often painful symptoms, such as headaches, muscle pain, and stomach problems, that are caused by psychological factors, such as worry, tension, and anxiety.

psychotherapy Approaches to treating psychological problems that share three characteristics: verbal interaction between therapist and client(s); the development of a supportive relationship during which a client can bring up and discuss traumatic or bothersome experiences that may have led to current problems; and analysis of the client's experiences and/or suggested ways for the client to deal with or overcome his or her problems.

puberty A developmental period, corresponding to the ages of 9 to 17 years, when the individual experiences significant biological changes and, as a result, develops secondary sexual characteristics and reaches sexual maturity.

punishment A consequence that occurs after behavior and decreases the likelihood that that behavior will recur.

pupil The round opening at the front of the eye that allows light waves to pass through into the eye's interior.

quantum personality change A sudden and radical or dramatic shift in personality, beliefs, or values.

questionnaire A method for obtaining information by asking subjects to read a list of written questions and to check off, or rate their preference for, specific answers.

random selection A research design such that each subject in a sample population has an equal chance of being selected to participate in the experiment.

range The two most extreme scores at either end of a distribution.

rape myths Misinformed false beliefs about women that are frequently held by rapists as well as by other men.

rationalization Inventing acceptable excuses for behaviors that make us feel anxious.

reaction formation Turning unacceptable wishes into acceptable behaviors.

reaction range The extent to which traits, abilities, or IQ scores may increase or decrease as a result of interaction with environmental factors.

reaction time The rate at which we respond (see, hear, move) to some stimulus; this rate slows down noticeably after age 60.

reactive attachment disorder A psychiatric illness characterized by serious problems in emotional attachments to others, beginning before age 5. Symptoms include resisting comfort and affection by parents, being superficially engaging and overly friendly with strangers, having poor peer relationships, and engaging in destructive behaviors.

real motion Our perception of any stimulus or object that actually moves in space; the opposite of apparent motion.

real self According to Rogers, the self that is based on our actual experiences and represents how we really see ourselves; its complement is the ideal self.

reality principle A policy of satisfying a wish or desire only if a socially acceptable outlet is available. According to Freud, this is the ego's operating principle.

recall Retrieval of previously learned information without the aid of or with very few external cues.

recency effect Better recall, or improvement in retention, of information presented at the end of a task.

recognition The identification of previously learned information with the help of external cues.

reflex An unlearned, involuntary reaction to some stimulus. The neural connections of the network underlying a reflex are prewired by genetic instructions.

reinforcement A consequence that occurs after behavior and increases the likelihood that that behavior will recur.

relative size In three-dimensional vision, a monocular depth cue that results when we expect two objects to be the same size and they are not. In that case, the larger of the objects will appear closer, and the smaller will appear to be farther away.

relaxation response A physiological response induced by sitting or lying in a comfortable position while repeating a meaningless sound over and over to drive out anxious thoughts.

reliability The extent to which a test is consistent: A person's score on a test at one point in time should be similar to the score obtained by the same person on a similar test at a later point in time.

REM behavior disorder A disorder, usually found in older people, in which the voluntary muscles are not paralyzed during REM sleep; sleepers can and do act out their dreams.

REM (rapid eye movement) sleep The stage of sleep in which our eyes move rapidly back and forth behind closed eyelids. This stage makes up 20% of our sleep time; in a normal night, we experience five or six periods of REM sleep, each one lasting 15–45 minutes. REM brain waves, which have a high frequency and a low amplitude, look very similar to the beta waves that are recorded when we are wide awake and alert; the body's voluntary muscles, however, are paralyzed. Dreams usually occur during REM sleep.

REM rebound The tendency of individuals to spend proportionately longer in the REM stage after they have been deprived of REM sleep on previous nights.

Glossary

repair theory A theory of sleep suggesting that activities during the day deplete key factors in the brain or body that are replenished or repaired by sleep.

repression According to Freud, a mental process that automatically hides emotionally threatening or anxiety-producing information in the unconscious. Repressed information cannot be retrieved voluntarily, but something may cause it to be released and to reenter the person's consciousness at a later time.

resiliency Various personal, family, or environmental factors that compensate for increased life stresses so that expected problems do not develop.

resistance In psychotherapy, especially psychoanalysis, the client's reluctance to work through or deal with feelings or to recognize unconscious conflicts and repressed thoughts.

resistance stage The second stage in the general adaptation syndrome. In reaction to continued stress, most physiological responses return to normal levels, but the body uses up great stores of energy.

resting state A condition in which the axon, like a battery, has a charge, or potential, because the axon membrane separates positive ions on the outside from negative ions on the inside.

reticular formation A column of brain cells that arouses and alerts the forebrain and prepares it to receive information from all the senses. It plays an important role in keeping the forebrain alert and producing a state of wakefulness. Animals or humans whose reticular formation is seriously damaged lapse into permanent unconsciousness or coma.

retina A thin film, located at the very back of the eyeball, that contains cells, called photoreceptors, that are extremely sensitive to light. The retina consists of three layers, the third and deepest of which contains two kinds of photoreceptors, rods and cones, that perform transduction—that is, they change light waves into nerve impulses.

retinal disparity A binocular depth cue that depends on the distance between the two eyes. Because of their different positions, the two eyes receive slightly different images. The difference between these images is the retinal disparity. The brain interprets large retinal disparity to mean a close object and small retinal disparity to mean a distant object.

retrieval cues Mental reminders that we create by forming vivid mental images of information or associating new information with information that we already know. Forgetting can result from not taking the time to create effective retrieval cues.

retrieving The process of getting or recalling information that has been placed into short-term or long-term storage.

retroactive interference A forgetting process in which information that we learned later blocks or disrupts the retrieval of related information that was learned earlier.

reuptake The process by which some neurotransmitters, such as dopamine, are removed from the synapse by being transported back into the end bulbs.

reward/pleasure center The part of the brain that includes the nucleus accumbens and ventral tegmental area and involves several neurotransmitters, especially dopamine. Combined with other brain areas, it forms a neural circuit that produces rewarding and pleasurable feelings.

rods Photoreceptors containing the chemical rhodopsin, which is activated by small amounts of light. Because rods are extremely light sensitive, they allow us to see in dim light but to see only black, white, and shades of gray.

role schemas Social schemas based on the jobs people perform or the social positions they hold.

Rorschach inkblot test A projective test used to assess personality in which a person is shown a series of ten inkblots and then asked to describe what he or she sees in each.

rules of organization Rules identified by Gestalt psychologists that specify how our brains combine and organize individual pieces or elements into a meaningful whole—that is, a perception.

SAD *See* seasonal affective disorder.

savants Autistic individuals who show some incredible memory, music, or drawing talent. They represent about 10% of the total number of autistics.

schedule of reinforcement In conditioning, a program or rule that determines how and when a response will be followed by a reinforcer.

schemas Mental categories that, like computer files, contain knowledge about people, events, and concepts. Because schemas influence which stimuli we attend to, how we interpret stimuli, and how we respond to stimuli, they can bias and distort our thoughts, perceptions, and behaviors. *See also:* event schemas; gender schemas; person schemas; role schemas; and self schemas.

schizophrenia A serious mental disturbance that lasts at least six months and includes at least two of the following symptoms: delusions, hallucinations, disorganized speech, grossly disorganized behavior, and decreased emotional expression. These symptoms interfere with personal or social functioning. *See also* Type I and Type II schizophrenia.

schizotypical personality disorder A disorder characterized by acute discomfort in close relationships, distortions in thinking, and eccentric behavior. It is found in 3–5% of the population.

scientific method A general approach to gathering information and answering questions so that errors and biases are minimized.

scripts *See* event schemas.

seasonal affective disorder (SAD) A pattern of depressive symptoms that cycle with the seasons, typically beginning in fall or winter. The depression is accompanied by feelings of lethargy, excessive sleepiness, overeating, weight gain, and craving for carbohydrates.

secondary appraisal Deciding what we can do to deal with a potentially stressful situation. We can choose some combination of problem-focused coping, which means doing something about the problem, and emotion-focused coping, which means dealing with our emotions.

secondary reinforcer Any stimulus that has acquired its reinforcing power through experience; secondary reinforcers are learned, for example, by being paired with primary reinforcers or other secondary reinforcers.

secure attachment An emotional bond characteristic of infants who use their parent as a safe home base from which they can wander off and explore their environments.

self How we see or describe ourselves; also called self-concept. The self is made up of many self-perceptions, abilities, personality characteristics, and behaviors that are organized so as to be consistent with one another.

self-actualization Our inherent tendency to reach our true potentials. The concept of self-actualization, developed by Maslow, is central to humanistic theories.

self-actualization theory *See* self theory.

self-actualizing tendency An inborn tendency for us to develop all of our capacities in ways that best maintain and benefit our lives.

self-concept *See* self.

self-efficacy Our personal beliefs regarding how capable we are of exercising control over events in our lives, such as completing specific tasks and behaviors.

self-esteem How much an individual likes himself or herself; it includes feelings of self-worth, attractiveness, and social competence.

self-fulfilling prophecy A situation in which a person has a strong belief or makes a statement (prophecy) about a future behavior and then acts, usually unknowingly, to fulfill or carry out that behavior.

self-handicapping A tendency to adopt tactics that are prone to failure and then to use those tactics as excuses for failures in performance, activities, or achieving goals.

self-identity *See* identity.

self-injurious behavior A behavior pattern in which an individual inflicts serious and sometimes life-threatening physical damage on his or her own body; this may take the form of body or head banging, biting, kicking, poking ears or eyes, pulling hair, or intense scratching.

self-perception theory The idea, developed by Daryl Bem, that we first observe or perceive our own behavior and then, as a result, change our attitudes.

self-report questionnaires *See* objective personality tests.

self schemas Social schemas containing personal information about ourselves. They can influence how we behave as well as what we perceive and remember.

self-serving bias Attributing our successes to our dispositions or personality traits and our failures to the situations.

self theory Rogers's humanistic theory, based on two major assumptions: that personality development is guided by each person's unique self-actualization tendency; and that each of us has a personal need for positive regard.

semantic memory A type of declarative memory consisting of factual knowledge about the world, concepts, word definitions, and language rules.

semantics A set of rules that specify the meanings of words or phrases when they appear in various sentences or contexts.

sensation Our first awareness of some outside stimulus; relatively meaningless bits of information that result when the brain processes electrical signals that come from the sense organs.

sensitive period *See* critical period.

sensorimotor stage The first of Piaget's cognitive stages, lasting from birth to about age 2 years. During this stage, infants interact with and learn about their environments by relating their sensory experiences (such as hearing and seeing) to their motor actions (mouthing and grasping).

sensory memory An initial memory process that receives and holds environmental information in its raw form for a brief period of time, from an instant to several seconds.

sensory neurons *See* afferent neurons.

sentence stage The fourth stage in acquiring language, which begins at about 4 years of age. Sentences range from three to eight words in length and indicate a growing knowledge of the rules of grammar.

separation anxiety An infant's distress—as indicated by loud protests, crying, and agitation—whenever his or her parents temporarily leave.

set point A certain level of body fat (adipose tissue) that our body strives to maintain constant throughout our lives; the set point is an inherited characteristic.

sex chromosome The sperm or the egg. Each contains only 23 chromosomes, on which are the genes bearing the instructions that determine the sex of the child.

sex (gender) differences in the brain Structural or functional differences in cognitive, behavioral, or brain processes that arise from being male or female.

sex hormones Chemicals, secreted by glands, that circulate in the bloodstream and influence the brain, other body organs, and behaviors. The major male sex hormones secreted by the testes are androgens, such as testosterone; the major female sex hormones secreted by the ovaries are estrogens.

sexual dysfunctions Problems of sexual arousal or orgasm that interfere with adequate functioning during sexual behavior.

sexual orientation A person's pattern of primary sexual arousal: by members of his or her own sex, the opposite sex, or both sexes; also called sexual preference.

shape constancy Our tendency to see an object as remaining the same shape when viewed at different angles—that is, despite considerable change in the shape of its image on the retina.

shaping In operant conditioning, a procedure in which an experimenter successively reinforces behaviors that lead up to or approximate the desired behavior.

short-term dynamic psychotherapy A shortened version of psychoanalysis. It emphasizes a limited time for treatment (20–30 sessions) and focuses on limited goals, such as solving a relatively well-defined problem. Therapists take an active and directive role by identifying and discussing the client's problems, resolving issues of transference, interpreting the patient's behaviors, and offering an opportunity for the patient to foster changes in behavior and thinking that will result in more active coping and an improved self-image.

short-term memory A process that can hold a limited amount of information—an average of seven items—for a short time (2–30 seconds), which can be lengthened if you rehearse the information. Sometimes called working memory.

shyness The tendency to feel tense, worried, or awkward in social situations.

similarity rule A perceptual rule stating that, in organizing stimuli, elements that appear similar are grouped together.

simplicity rule A perceptual rule stating that stimuli are organized in the simplest way possible.

single-word stage The second stage in acquiring language, which begins when the child is about 1 year old. Infants say single words that usually refer to what they can see, hear, or feel.

situational attributions *See* external attributions.

size constancy Our tendency to perceive objects as remaining the same size even when their images on the retina are continually growing or shrinking.

skewed distributions Distributions in which more data fall toward one side of the scale than toward the other.

sleep A condition in which we pass through five different stages, each with its own level of consciousness, awareness, responsiveness, and physiological arousal. In the deepest stage of sleep, we enter a state that borders on unconsciousness.

sleep apnea A condition characterized by a cycle in which a sleeper stops breathing for intervals of 10 seconds or longer, wakes up briefly, resumes breathing, and returns to sleep. This cycle can leave apnea sufferers exhausted during the day but oblivious to the cause of their tiredness. It is more common among habitual snorers.

sleepwalking Walking or carrying out behaviors while still asleep. Sleepwalkers generally are clumsy and have poor coordination but can avoid objects; they can engage in very limited conversations. Sleepwalking behaviors can include dressing, eating, performing bathroom functions, and even driving a car. Sleepwalking usually occurs in stage 3 or stage 4 (delta) sleep.

social cognitive learning A form of learning that results from watching, imitating, and modeling and does not require the observer to perform any observable behavior or receive any observable reward. Formerly called observational learning.

social cognitive theory The theory that grew out of the research of a number of psychologists—Rotter, Bandura, and Mischel—that says that personality development is primarily shaped by three forces: environmental conditions, cognitive-personal factors, and behavior, which all interact to influence how we evaluate, interpret, organize, and apply information. *See also* Bandura's social cognitive theory.

social comparison theory The idea that we are driven to compare ourselves to others who are similar to us, so that we can measure the correctness of our attitudes and beliefs. According to Festinger, this drive motivates us to join groups.

social development How a person develops a sense of self or self-identity, develops relationships with others, and develops the skills useful in social interactions.

social facilitation An increase in performance in the presence of a crowd.

social inhibition A decrease in performance in the presence of a crowd.

social needs Needs that are acquired through learning and experience.

social neuroscience An emerging area of research that examines social behavior by combining biological and social approaches. It focuses on understanding how social behavior influences the brain, and vice versa.

social norms approach Relating to abnormality, the idea that a behavior is considered abnormal if it deviates greatly from accepted social standards, values, or norms.

social phobias Irrational, marked, and continuous fear of performing in social situations. The individuals fear that they will humiliate or embarrass themselves.

social psychology A broad field whose goals are to understand and explain how our thoughts, feelings, perceptions, and behaviors are influenced by interactions with others. It includes the study of stereotypes, prejudices, attitudes, conformity, group behaviors, and aggression.

social role theory The theory that emphasizes the importance of social and cultural influences on gender roles and states that gender differences between males and females arise from different divisions of labor.

social support A stress-reducing factor that includes three components: having a group or network of family or friends who provide strong social attachments; being able to exchange helpful resources among family or friends; and feeling, or making appraisals, that we have supportive relationships or behaviors.

Glossary

socially oriented group A group in which members are primarily concerned about fostering and maintaining social relationships among the members of the group.

sociobiology theory *See* evolutionary theory.

sociocognitive theory of hypnosis The idea that the impressive effects of hypnosis are due to social influences and pressures as well as the subject's personal abilities. For another view, see altered state theory of hypnosis.

sodium pump A chemical transport process that picks up any sodium ions that enter the axon's chemical gates and returns them back outside. In this way, the sodium pump is responsible for keeping the axon charged by returning and keeping sodium ions outside the axon membrane.

somatic nervous system A network of nerves that are connected either to sensory receptors or to muscles that you can move voluntarily, such as muscles in your limbs, back, neck, and chest. Nerves in the somatic nervous system usually contain two kinds of fibers: afferent, or sensory, fibers that carry information from sensory receptors in the skin, muscles, and other organs to the spinal cord and brain; and efferent, or motor, fibers that carry information from the brain and spinal cord to the muscles.

somatization disorder A somatoform disorder that begins before age 30, lasts several years, and is characterized by multiple symptoms—including pain, gastrointestinal, sexual, and neurological symptoms—that have no physical causes but are triggered by psychological problems or distress.

somatoform disorder A pattern of recurring, multiple, and significant bodily (somatic) complaints that extend over several years. The physical symptoms (pain, vomiting, paralysis, blindness) are not under voluntary control, have no known physical causes, and are believed to be caused by psychological factors.

somatosensory cortex A narrow strip of the cortex that is located at the front edge of the parietal lobe and extends down its side. It processes sensory information about touch, location of limbs, pain, and temperature. The right somatosensory cortex receives information from the left side of the body, and vice versa.

sound waves The stimuli for hearing, or audition. Similar to ripples on a pond, sound waves travel through space with varying heights and speeds. Height, or amplitude, is the distance from the bottom to the top of a sound wave; speed, or frequency, is the number of sound waves that occur within 1 second.

source misattribution A memory error that results when a person has difficulty in deciding which of two or more sources a memory came from: Was the source something the person saw or imagined, or was it a suggestion?

Spearman's *g* *See* two-factor theory.

specific phobias Unreasonable, marked, and persistent fears triggered by anticipation of, or exposure to, a specific object or situation (flying, heights, spiders, seeing blood); formerly called simple phobias.

split-brain operation A procedure for moderating severe, uncontrollable seizures by cutting the corpus callosum, a wide band of nerve fibers that connects the right and left hemispheres.

spontaneous recovery In classical conditioning, the temporary occurrence of the conditioned response to the presence of the conditioned.

stimulus In operant conditioning, a temporary recovery in the rate of responding.

stage 1 In sleep, a stage lasting 1–7 minutes in which the individual gradually loses responsiveness to stimuli and experiences drifting thoughts and images. This stage marks the transition from wakefulness to sleep and is characterized by the presence of theta waves, which are lower in amplitude and lower in frequency (3–7 cycles per second) than alpha waves.

stage 2 In sleep, the stage that marks the beginning of what we know as sleep; subjects awakened in stage 2 report having been asleep. EEG tracings show high-frequency bursts of brain activity called sleep spindles.

stages 3 and 4 About 30–45 minutes after drifting off to sleep, we pass rapidly through stage 3 and enter stage 4 sleep, a stage characterized by delta waves, which have very high amplitude and very low frequency (less than 4 cycles per second). Stage 4 is often considered the deepest stage of sleep because it is the most difficult from which to be awakened. During stage 4, heart rate, respiration, temperature, and blood flow to the brain are reduced, and there is a marked secretion of growth hormone, which controls many aspects of metabolism, physical growth, and brain development. This stage is also called slow-wave or delta sleep.

stages of sleep Distinctive changes in the electrical activity of the brain and accompanying physiological responses of the body that occur as we pass through different stages of sleep. *See also* stage 1, stage 2, stages 3 and 4.

standard deviation A statistic indicating how widely all the scores in a distribution are scattered above and below the mean.

standardized test A technique to obtain information by administering a psychological test that has been standardized, which means that the test has been given to hundreds of people and shown to reliably measure thought patterns, personality traits, emotions, or behaviors.

state-dependent learning The idea that we recall information more easily when we are in the same physiological or emotional state or setting as when we originally encoded the information.

statistical frequency approach In defining abnormality, the idea that a behavior may be considered abnormal if it occurs rarely or infrequently in relation to the behaviors of the general population.

statistical procedures In experiments, procedures to determine whether differences observed in dependent variables (behaviors) are due to independent variables (treatment) or to error or chance occurrence.

statistics Tools researchers use to analyze and summarize large amounts of data.

stem cells Cells formed in the embryo that have the amazing capacity to change into any of the 220 cells that make up a human body, including skin, heart, liver, bones, and neurons.

stereotaxic procedure A method used for introducing material at a precise location within the brain. The patient's head is fixed in a holder, and a small hole is drilled through the skull. The holder has a syringe that can be precisely guided to a predetermined location in the brain.

stereotypes Widely held beliefs that people have certain traits because they belong to a particular group. Stereotypes are often inaccurate and frequently portray the members of less powerful, less controlling groups more negatively than members of more powerful, more controlling groups.

Sternberg's triangular theory of love The idea that love has three components: passion, intimacy, and commitment. Passion is feeling physically aroused and attracted to someone; intimacy is feeling close and connected to someone, through sharing and communicating; and commitment is pledging to nourish the feelings of love and actively maintain the relationship.

Sternberg's triarchic theory The idea that intelligence can be divided into three ways of gathering and processing information (*triarchic* means "three"): using analytical or logical thinking skills that are measured by traditional intelligence tests; using problem-solving skills that require creative thinking, the ability to deal with novel situations, and the ability to learn from experience; and using practical thinking skills that help a person adjust to, and cope with, his or her sociocultural environment.

stimulants Drugs, such as cocaine, amphetamines, caffeine, and nicotine, that increase activity in the nervous system and result in heightened alertness, arousal, and euphoria and decreased appetite and fatigue.

stimulus substitution The theory that, in classical conditioning, a neural bond or association is formed between the neutral stimulus and unconditioned stimulus. After repeated trials, the neutral stimulus becomes the conditioned stimulus, which, in turn, substitutes for the unconditioned stimulus. Thereafter, the conditioned stimulus elicits a response similar to that of the unconditioned stimulus.

stomach The body organ that monitors the amount and kinds of nutrients our body needs to restore our depleted stores of fuel. In addition, after we eat a meal, the stomach's walls are distended and their stretch receptors signal fullness or time to stop eating.

storing The process of placing encoded information into relatively permanent mental storage for later recall.

stress The anxious or threatening feeling that comes when we interpret or appraise a situation as being more than our psychological resources can adequately handle.

stress management program A program to reduce anxiety, fear, and stressful experiences by using a variety of strategies to change three different aspects of our lives: thoughts (appraisals), behaviors, and physiological responses.

structuralism An early school of psychological thought that emphasized the study of the basic elements—primarily sensations and perceptions—that make up conscious mental experiences. Structuralists argued that we can understand how perceptions are formed by breaking them down into smaller and smaller elements. Then we can analyze how these basic elements are recombined to form a perception. They believed that a perception is simply the sum of its parts.

structured interviews A research technique in which each individual is asked the same set of relatively narrow and focused questions, so that the same information is obtained from everyone.

subgoals In problem solving, a strategy by which the overall problem is broken into separate parts that, when completed in order, will result in a solution.

sublimation A type of displacement in which threatening or forbidden desire, usually sexual, is redirected into socially acceptable forms.

subliminal messages Brief auditory or visual messages that are presented below the absolute threshold, so that their chance of perception is less than 50%.

subliminal stimulus A stimulus whose intensity is such that a person has a less than 50% chance of detecting it.

substance abuse A maladaptive pattern of frequent and continued usage of a substance—a drug or medicine—that results in significant problems, such as failing to meet major obligations and having multiple legal, social, family, health, work, or interpersonal difficulties. These problems must occur repeatedly during a single 12-month period to be classified as substance abuse.

superego Freud's third division of the mind, which develops from the ego during early childhood; its goal is to apply the moral values and standards of one's parents or caregivers and society in satisfying one's wishes.

superstitious behavior In operant conditioning, any behavior that increases in frequency because its occurrence is accidentally paired with the delivery of a reinforcer.

suprachiasmatic nucleus A sophisticated biological clock, located in the hypothalamus, that regulates a number of circadian rhythms, including the sleep-wake cycle. Suprachiasmatic cells are highly responsive to changes in light.

surface structure According to Chomsky, the actual wording of a sentence, as it is spoken.

survey A way to obtain information by asking many individuals—person to person, by telephone, or by mail—to answer a fixed set of questions about particular subjects.

sympathetic division The subdivision of the autonomic nervous system that is triggered by threatening or challenging physical or psychological stimuli, increasing the body's physiological arousal and preparing the body for action.

synapse An infinitely small space (20–30 billionths of a meter) between an end bulb and its adjacent body organ, muscle, or cell body; it is a space over which chemical messages are transmitted.

syntax *See* grammar.

systematic desensitization A technique of behavior therapy, based on classical conditioning, in which a person is gradually and progressively exposed to fearful or anxiety-evoking stimuli while practicing deep relaxation. Systematic desensitization is a form of counterconditioning because it replaces, or counters, fear and anxiety with relaxation.

t test An estimate of reliability that takes into account both the size of the mean difference and the variability in distributions.

taijin kyofusho (TKS) A mental disorder found only in Asian cultures, particularly Japan. This social phobia is characterized by a morbid fear of offending others through awkward social or physical behavior, such as making eye-to-eye contact, blushing, giving off an offensive odor, having an unpleasant or tense facial expression, or having trembling hands.

tardive dyskinesia A condition characterized by the appearance of slow, involuntary, and uncontrollable rhythmic movements and rapid twitching of the mouth and lips, as well as unusual movements of the limbs. This condition is a side effect of the continued use of typical neuroleptics.

task-oriented group A group in which members have specific duties to complete.

taste A chemical sense that makes use of various chemicals or stimuli.

taste-aversion learning The association of a particular sensory cue (smell, taste, sound, or sight) with an unpleasant response, such as nausea or vomiting, resulting in future avoidance of that particular sensory cue.

taste buds Onion-shaped structures on the tongue that contain the receptors for taste.

TAT *See* Thematic Apperception Test.

telegraphic speech A distinctive speech pattern observed during language acquisition in which the child omits articles, prepositions, and parts of verbs.

telepathy The ability to transfer thoughts to another person or to read the thoughts of others.

temperament An individual's distinctive pattern of attention, arousal, and reactivity to new or novel situations. This pattern appears early, is relatively stable and long-lasting, and is influenced in large part by genetic factors.

temporal lobe A segment of the brain located directly below the parietal lobe that is involved in hearing, speaking coherently, and understanding verbal and written material.

teratogen Any agent that can harm a developing fetus (causing deformities or brain damage). It might be a disease (such as genital herpes), a drug (such as alcohol), or another environmental agent (such as chemicals).

test anxiety A combination of physiological, emotional, and cognitive components that are caused by the stress of taking exams and that may interfere with a student's ability to think, reason, and plan.

testimonial A statement in support of a particular viewpoint based on personal experience.

testosterone The major male hormone, which stimulates the growth of genital organs and the development of secondary sexual characteristics.

texture gradient In three-dimensional vision, a monocular depth cue: Areas with sharp, detailed texture are interpreted as being closer, and those with less sharpness and detail as more distant.

thalamus A structure of the limbic system that is located in the middle of the forebrain and is involved in receiving sensory information, doing some initial processing, and then relaying the sensory information to appropriate areas of the cortex, including the somatosensory cortex, primary auditory cortex, and primary visual cortex.

Thematic Apperception Test (TAT) A personality test in which subjects are asked to look at pictures of people in ambiguous situations and to make up stories about what the characters are thinking and feeling and what the outcome will be.

theory of evolution Darwin's theory that different species arose from a common ancestor and that those species survived that were best adapted to meet the demands of their environments.

theory of linguistic relativity Whorf's theory that the differences among languages result in differences in the ways people think and perceive the world.

theory of personality An organized attempt to describe and explain how personalities develop and why personalities differ.

thinking Mental processes by which we form concepts, solve problems, and engage in creative activities. Sometimes referred to as reasoning.

threat appraisal Our conclusion that harm or loss has not yet taken place in a particular situation but we anticipate it in the near future.

threshold A point above which a stimulus is perceived and below which it is not perceived. *See also* absolute threshold.

thyroid A gland located in the neck that regulates metabolism through secretion of hormones. It forms part of the endocrine system.

time-out In training children, a form of negative punishment in which reinforcing stimuli are removed after an undesirable response. This removal decreases the chances that the response will

Glossary

recur. In time-out, the child is told to sit quietly in the corner of a room or put in some other situation where there is no chance to obtain reinforcers or engage in pleasurable behaviors.

tip-of-the-tongue phenomenon The situation in which, despite making a great effort, we are temporarily unable to recall information that we absolutely know is in our memory.

TKS *See* taijin kyofusho.

tolerance The reaction of the body and brain to regular drug use, whereby the person has to take larger doses of the drug to achieve the same behavioral effect.

touch The skin senses, which include temperature, pressure, and pain. Touch sensors change mechanical pressure or changes in temperature into nerve impulses that are sent to the brain for processing.

trait A relatively stable and enduring tendency to behave in a particular way.

trait theory An approach for analyzing the structure of personality by measuring, identifying, and classifying similarities and differences in personality characteristics or traits.

transcendental meditation (TM) A meditation exercise in which individuals assume a comfortable position, close their eyes, and repeat and concentrate on a sound to clear their head of all thoughts (worrisome and otherwise).

transduction The process by which a sense organ changes, or transforms, physical energy into electrical signals that become neural impulses, which may be sent to the brain for processing.

transference In psychotherapy, the process by which a client expresses strong emotions toward the therapist because the therapist substitutes for someone important in the client's life, such as the client's mother or father. Freud first developed this concept.

transformational rules According to Chomsky, procedures by which we convert our ideas from surface structures into deep structures and from deep structures back into surface structures.

transmitter A chemical messenger that transmits information between nerves and body organs, such as muscles and heart. *See also* neurotransmitters.

transsexualism *See* gender identity disorder.

triangular theory of love *See* Sternberg's triangular theory of love.

triarchic theory *See* Sternberg's triarchic theory.

trichromatic theory The idea that there are three different kinds of cones in the retina, and each cone contains one of three different light-sensitive chemicals, called opsins. Each opsin is most responsive to wavelengths that correspond to each of the three primary colors—blue, green, and red—from which all other colors can be mixed.

two-factor theory A theory of intelligence proposed by Spearman, according to which a general mental ability factor, *g*, represents a person's ability to

perform complex mental work, such as abstract reasoning and problem solving, while many specific factors, *s*, represent a person's specific mental abilities, such as mathematical, mechanical, or verbal skills. Thus, *g* is constant across tests, while *s* may vary across tests.

two-word combinations The third stage in acquiring language, which begins at about 2 years of age. The infant says strings of two words that express various actions ("Me play," "See boy") or relationships ("Hit ball," "Milk gone").

tympanic membrane The thin, taut membrane, commonly called the eardrum, that is the boundary between the outer ear and middle ear. Struck by sound waves, it vibrates and passes the vibrations to the ossicles.

Type A behavior A combination of personality traits that may be a risk factor for coronary heart disease. According to the original (1970s) definition, these traits included an overly competitive and aggressive drive to achieve, a hostile attitude when frustrated, a habitual sense of time urgency, a rapid and explosive pattern of speaking, and workaholic tendencies; in contrast, type B behavior was easygoing, calm, relaxed, and patient. In the 1980s, the list of traits was reduced to being depressed, aggressively competitive, easily frustrated, anxious, and angry. In the 1990s, the list was reduced again, to frequent feelings of anger and hostility, which may or may not be publicly expressed. Currently, researchers conclude that individuals who either always show their anger and hostility or always suppress it have large increases in physiological arousal, which can have damaging effects on one's heart and health.

Type D behavior Behavior characterized by chronic distress in terms of two emotional states: negative affectivity (worry, irritability, gloom) and social inhibition (shyness, being reserved, lack of self-assurance).

Type I schizophrenia A type of schizophrenia characterized by positive symptoms, such as hallucinations and delusions, which are distortions of normal functions. Individuals diagnosed with Type I schizophrenia have no intellectual impairment, good reaction to medication, and thus a good chance of recovery.

Type II schizophrenia A type of schizophrenia characterized by negative symptoms, such as dulled emotions and little inclination to speak, which are a loss of normal functions. Individuals diagnosed with Type II schizophrenia have intellectual impairment, poor reaction to medication, and thus a poor chance of recovery.

typical neuroleptic drugs Neuroleptics that primarily reduce the levels of the neurotransmitter dopamine. Two of the more common are phenothiazines (for example, Thorazine) and butrophenones (for example, haloperidol). These drugs primarily reduce positive symptoms but have little or no effects on negative symptoms.

unconditional positive regard The warmth, acceptance, and love that others show us because we are valued human beings even though we may behave in ways that disappoint them because they differ from their standards and values or the way they think.

unconditioned response (UCR) An unlearned, innate, involuntary physiological reflex that is elicited by the unconditioned stimulus.

unconditioned stimulus (UCS) A stimulus that triggers or elicits some physiological response, such as salivation or eye blink.

unconscious forces Wishes, desires, or thoughts that, because of their disturbing or threatening content, we automatically repress and cannot voluntarily access.

unconscious motivation A Freudian concept that refers to the influence of repressed thoughts, desires, or impulses on our conscious thoughts and behaviors.

unconsciousness Total loss of awareness and responsiveness to the environment. It may be due to disease, trauma, a blow to the head, or general medical anesthesia.

underachievers Individuals who score relatively high on tests of ability or intelligence but perform more poorly than their scores would predict.

unipolar depression *See* major depressive disorder.

universal emotional expressions A number of specific inherited facial patterns or expressions that signal specific feelings or emotional states, such as a smile signaling a happy state.

uplifts Small, pleasurable, happy, and satisfying experiences that we have in our daily lives.

validity The extent to which a test measures what it is supposed to measure.

variable-interval schedule A conditioning schedule such that the time between the response and the subsequent reinforcer is variable.

variable-ratio schedule A conditioning schedule in which the subject must make a different number of responses for the delivery of each reinforcer.

variance A measure of the variability within two distributions.

ventrolateral preoptic nucleus (VPN) A group of cells in the hypothalamus that acts like a master switch for sleep. Turned on, the VPN secretes a neurotransmitter (GABA) that turns off areas that keep the brain awake; turned off, the VPN causes certain brain areas to become active and we wake up.

ventromedial hypothalamus A group of brain cells that regulates hunger by creating feelings of satiety, or fullness.

vertigo Feelings of dizziness and nausea resulting from malfunction of the semicircular canals in the vestibular system.

vestibular system Three semicircular canals in the inner ear that sense the position of the head, keep the head upright, and maintain balance. Fluid in the semicircular canals moves in response to movements of the head, and sensors (hair cells) in the canals respond to the movement of the fluid.

virtual reality A perceptual experience—of being inside an object, moving through an environment, or carrying out some action—that is, in fact, entirely simulated by a computer.

visible spectrum The one particular segment of electromagnetic energy that we can see because these waves are the right length to stimulate receptors in the eye.

visual acuity The ability to see fine details.

visual agnosia A condition caused by damage to the visual association area. An individual with visual agnosia is unable to recognize some object, person, or color and yet is able to see and even describe parts of some visual stimulus.

visual association area An area of the brain, located next to the primary visual cortex, that transforms basic sensations, such as lights, lines, colors, and textures, into complete, meaningful visual perceptions, such as persons, objects, or animals.

visual cliff A glass tabletop with a checkerboard pattern over part of its surface; the remaining surface consists of clear glass with a checkerboard pattern several feet below, creating the illusion of a clifflike drop to the floor.

VPN *See* ventrolateral preoptic nucleus.

vulnerability Psychological or environmental difficulties that make children more at risk for developing later personality, behavioral, or social problems.

Weber's law A psychophysics law stating that the increase in intensity of a stimulus needed to produce a just noticeable difference grows in proportion to the intensity of the initial stimulus.

Wechsler Adult Intelligence Scale (WAIS-III) and Wechsler Intelligence Scale for Children (WISC-III) Intelligence tests that are divided into various subtests. The verbal section contains a subtest of general information, a vocabulary subtest, and so forth. The performance section contains a subtest that involves arranging pictures in a meaningful order, one that requires assembling objects, and one that involves using codes. The verbal and performance scores are combined to give a single IQ score.

weight-regulating genes Genes that play a role in influencing appetite, body metabolism, and secretion of hormones (such as leptin) that regulate fat stores.

Wernicke's aphasia Difficulty in understanding spoken or written words and in putting words into meaningful sentences, as a result of injury to Wernicke's area in the brain.

Wernicke's area An area usually located in the left temporal lobe that plays a role in understanding speech and speaking in coherent sentences. *See* Wernicke's aphasia.

withdrawal symptoms Painful physical and psychological symptoms that occur when a drug-dependent person stops using a drug.

word An arbitrary pairing between a sound or symbol and a meaning.

working memory *See* short-term memory.

Yerkes-Dodson law The principle that performance on a task is an interaction between the level of physiological arousal and the difficulty of the task. For difficult tasks, low arousal results in better performance; for most tasks, moderate arousal helps performance; and for easy tasks, high arousal may facilitate performance.

zygote The cell that results when an egg is fertilized. It contains 46 chromosomes, arranged in 23 pairs.

References

AAUW (American Association of University Women). (2007a). *Sexual assault on campus* [On-line]. Available: http://www.aauw.org/laf/library/assault_stats.cfm

AAUW. (2007b). *Sexual harassment on campus* [On-line]. Available: http://www.aauw.org/laf/library/harassment_stats.cfm

ABA (American Bar Association). (2005). A current glance at women in the law, 2005. *American Bar Association Commission on Women in the Profession.* Chicago: Author.

ABC News. (2004, September 22). *Alcohol-poisoned teen's parents speak out* [On-line]. Available: http://www.abcnews.go.com/GMA/story?id=127571&page=1

Abelson, R. (2002, June 14). Limits on residents' hours worry teaching hospitals. *New York Times*, A16.

Abernethy, B., Neal, R. J., & Koning, P. (1994). Visual-perceptual and cognitive differences between expert, intermediate, and novice snooker players. *Applied Cognitive Psychology, 8,* 185–211.

Abrahamsson, K. H., Berggren, U., Hallberg, L. R. M., & Carlsson, S. G. (2002). Ambivalence in coping with dental fear and avoidance: A qualitative study. *Journal of Health Psychology, 7,* 653–665.

Abrams, M. (2002, June). Sight/Unseen. *Discover,* 54–59.

Abrams, R. L., & Greenwald, A. G. (2000). Parts outweigh the whole (word) in unconscious analysis of meaning. *Psychological Science, 11,* 118–124.

Abu-Lughod, L. (1986). *Veiled sentiments.* Berkeley: University of California Press.

ACA Group. (2004). *Preventing sexual harassment: It's the law in California* [On-line]. Available: http://www.theacagroup.com/harassmentarticle.htm

ACF (Administration for Children & Families). (2006, March). *Head Start program fact sheet* [On-line]. Available: http://www.acf.hhs.gov/programs/hsb/research/2006.htm

Ackerman, S. J., & Hilsenroth, M. J. (2003). A review of therapist characteristics and techniques positively impacting the therapeutic alliance. *Clinical Psychology Review, 23,* 1–33.

ACS (American Cancer Society). (2005, June). *Nausea and vomiting: Treatment guidelines for patients with cancer.* National Comprehensive Cancer Network and the American Cancer Society.

Adam, D. (2005, February 17). Ecstasy trials for combat stress. *The Guardian.*

Adams, W. L. (2006, March/April). The truth about photographic memory. *Psychology Today.*

Adan, A. (1992). The influence of age, work schedule and personality on morningness dimensions. *International Journal of Psychophysiology, 12,* 95–99.

Ader, F. (1999, June). Cited in B. Azar, Father of PNI reflects on the field growth. *Monitor: American Psychological Association,* 18.

Ader, R., & Cohen, N. (1975). Behaviorally conditioned immunosuppression. *Psychosomatic Medicine, 37,* 333–340.

Adler, J. (2006, March 27). Freud in our midst. *Newsweek,* 42–51.

Adolphs, R. (2004). Processing of emotional and social information by the human amygdala. In M. S. Gazzaniga (Ed.), *The cognitive neurosciences III* (pp. 1017–1031). Cambridge, MA: MIT Press.

Aharon, I., Etcoff, N., Ariely, D., Chabris, C. F., O'Connor, E., & Breiter, H. C. (2001). Beautiful faces have variable reward value: fMRI and behavioral evidence. *Neuron, 30,* 537–551.

Ainsworth, M. D. S. (1979). Infant-mother attachment. *American Psychologist, 34,* 932–937.

Ainsworth, M. D. S. (1989). Attachments beyond infancy. *American Psychologist, 44,* 709–716.

Ajzen, I. (2001). Nature and operation of attitudes. *Annual Review of Psychology, 52,* 27–58.

Albee, G. W., & Joffe, J. M. (2004). Mental illness is not "an illness like any other." *The Journal of Primary Prevention, 24,* 419–436.

Albert, M. L., Connor, L. T., & Obler, L. K. (2000). Brain, language, and environment. *Brain and Language, 71,* 4–6.

Albright, T. D., Dixon, J. E., Gage, F. H., & Macagno, E. R. (2005, May 26). A promise for future of medicine. *The San Diego Union-Tribune,* B11.

Ali, L. (2005, August 12). Satisfaction guaranteed. *Newsweek,* 44–46.

Ali, L., & Scelfo, J. (2002, December 9). Choosing virginity. *Newsweek,* 61–64.

Ali, S. I., & Begum, S. (1994). Fabric softeners and softness perception. *Ergonomics, 37,* 801–806.

Alivisatos, B., & Petrides, M. (1997). Functional activation of the human brain during mental rotation. *Neuropsychologia, 35,* 111–118.

Allen, J. E. (2000, May 8). How do you know if it's attention deficit/hyperactivity disorder? *Los Angeles Times,* S3.

Allen, K. (2003). Are pets a healthy pleasure? The influence of pets on blood pressure. *Current Directions in Psychology, 12,* 236–239.

Allgood, W. P., Risko, V. J., Alvarez, M. C., & Fairbanks, M. M. (2000). Factors that influence study. In R. F. Flippo & D. C. Caverly (Eds.), *Handbook of college reading and study strategy research.* Mahwah, NJ: Lawrence Erlbaum.

Allport, G. W. (1935). Attitudes. In C. Murchison (Ed.), *Handbook of social psychology* (Vol. 2). Worcester, MA: Clark University Press.

Allport, G. W., & Odbert, H. S. (1936). Trait-names: A psycho-lexical study. *Psychological Monographs, 47* (Whole No. 211).

Almeida, D. M., Wethingon, E., & Kessler, R. C. (2002). The daily inventory of stressful events. *Assessment, 9,* 41–55.

Alonso-Zaldivar, R. (2006, February 12). Panel calls for ADHD drug effect warning. *Contra Costa Times,* Health 14–15.

Altermatt, E. R., & Pomerantz, E. M. (2003, March/April). Why girls worry about school performance. *Principal, 67*–68.

Althof, S. E. (1995). Pharmacologic treatment of rapid ejaculation. *The Psychiatric Clinics of North America, 18,* 85–94.

Alzheimer's Association. (2005). *About Alzheimer's disease: Causes.* Available: http://www.alz.org/AboutAD/causes.asp

Amabile, T. M. (1985). Motivation and creativity: Effects of motivational orientation on creative writers. *Journal of Personality and Social Psychology, 48,* 393–399.

Amass, L. (2003, June). Cited in E. Benson, A new treatment for addiction. *Monitor on Psychology,* 18–20.

American Psychiatric Association. (2000). *Diagnostic and statistical manual of mental disorders* (4th ed., text revision). Washington, DC: Author.

American Psychological Association. (2000). Demographic characteristics of APA members by membership status, 2000. *2000 APA directory survey.* Washington, DC: Author.

American Psychological Association. (2002). *Ethical principles of psychologists and code of conduct.* Washington, DC: Author.

American Psychological Association. (2004a). *Finding help: How to choose a psychotherapist.* Washington, DC: Author.

American Psychological Association. (2004b). Race/ethnicity of newly enrolled students in doctoral- and master's-level departments of psychology: 2002–03. *2004 Graduate study in psychology.* Washington, DC: Author.

American Psychological Association, Division of Psychological Hypnosis. (1993). Hypnosis. *Psychological Hypnosis, 2*(3).

Anastasi, A., & Urbina, S. (1997). *Psychological testing.* Upper Saddle River, NJ: Prentice-Hall.

Andersen, S. M., Moskowitz, G. B., Blair, I. V., & Nosek, B. A. (2007). Automatic thought. In A. W. Kruglanski & E. T. Huggins, *Social psychology: Handbook of basic principles* (2nd ed., pp. 138–175). New York: Guilford Press.

Andershed, A. (2005). *In sync with adolescence: The role of morningness-eveningness in development.* New York: Springer.

Anderson, C. A., & Bushman, B. J. (2002). Human aggression. *Annual Review of Psychology, 53,* 27–51.

Anderson, C. A., & Huesmann, L. R. (2003). Human aggression: A social-cognitive view. In M.A. Hogg & J. Cooper (Eds.), *The Sage handbook of social psychology* (pp. 296–323). Thousand Oaks, CA: Sage.

Anderson, C. P. (2003, June 23). Cited in D. P. Lange, Couples on the same emotional wavelengths are likelier to succeed. *Los Angeles Times,* F2.

Anderson, J. (2005, May 27). Bionic vision: Rare operation brings sight to a blind woman. *Dobelle Institute,* KSDK-TV.

Anderson, K. J. (1994). Impulsivity, caffeine, and task difficulty: A within-subjects test of the Yerkes-Dodson law. *Personality and Individual Differences, 16,* 813–819.

Anderson, M. C., Ochsner, K. N., Kuhl, B., Cooper, J., Robertson, E., Gabrieli, S. W., Glover, G. H., & Gabrieli, J. D. E. (2004). Neural systems underlying the suppression of unwanted memories. *Science, 303,* 232–235.

Anderson, N. B. (2003). *Emotional longevity: What really determines how long you live.* New York: Viking.

Anderson, R. N., & Smith, B. L. (2003). Deaths: Leading causes for 2001. *National Vital Statistics Report, 52,* 1–86.

Anderson, S. (2004, May). *How many languages are there in the world?* [On-line]. Available: http://www.lsadc.org

Anderson, S. E., Dallal, G. E., & Must, A. (2003). Relative weight and race influence average age at menarche: Results from two nationally representative surveys of U.S. girls studied 25 years apart. *Pediatrics, 111,* 844–850.

Andrews, B., Brewin, C. R., Ochera, J., Morton, J., Bekerian, D. A., Davies, G. M., & Mollon, P. (2000). The timing, triggers and qualities of recovered memories in therapy. *British Journal of Clinical Psychology, 39,* 11–26.

Angelo, B. (1991, November 4). Life at the end of the rainbow. *Time.*

Angier, N. (2003, February 25). Not just genes: Moving beyond nature vs. nurture. *New York Times,* D1.

Animal training at SeaWorld. (2002). Busch Entertainment Corporation [On-line]. Available: http://www.seaworld.org/infobooks/Training/home.html. Accessed October 19, 2006.

Anrep, H. M. (1920). Pitch discrimination in the dog. *Journal of Physiology, 53,* 367–385.

Anstett, P. (2006, January 12). In these SAD times of the year, follow the sun. *USA Today,* 4D.

Aqua facts: Training marine mammals. (2006, October 19). Vancouver Aquarium [On-line]. Available: http://www.vanaqua.org/education/trainingmarinemammals.html. Accessed October 19, 2006.

Arantes-Oliveria, N., Berman, J. R., & Kenyon, C. (2003). Healthy animals with extreme longevity. *Science, 302,* 611.

Ariely, D., & Wertenbroch, K. (2002). Procrastination, deadlines, and performance: Self-control by precommitment. *Psychological Science, 13,* 219–224.

Arlow, J. A. (2005). Psychoanalysis. In R. J. Corsini & D. Wedding, *Current psychotherapies* (7th ed., pp. 15–51). Belmont, CA: Brooks/Cole–Thomson Learning.

Armbruster, B. B. (2000). Taking notes from lectures. In R. F. Flippo & D. C. Caverly (Eds.), *Handbook of college reading and study strategy research*. Mahwah, NJ: Lawrence Erlbaum.

Armstrong, L. (2001). *It's not about the bike*. New York: Berkley Publishing.

Arnedt, J. T., Owens, J., Crouch, M., Stahl, J., & Carskadon, M. A. (2005). Neurobehavioral performance of residents after heavy night call vs. after alcohol ingestion. *The Journal of the American Medical Association, 294,* 1025–1033.

Arnett, J. J. (2000a). Adolescent storm and stress, reconsidered. *American Psychologist, 54,* 317–326.

Arnett, J. J. (2000b). Emerging adulthood. *American Psychologist, 55,* 469–480.

Arnold, D. H., & Doctoroff, G. L. (2003). The early education of socioeconomically disadvantaged children. *Annual Review of Psychology, 54,* 517–545.

Arntz, A. (2003). Cognitive therapy versus applied relaxation as treatment for generalized anxiety disorder. *Behaviour Research and Therapy, 41,* 633–646.

Aronow, E., Reznikoff, M., & Moreland, K. L. (1995). The Rorschach: Projective technique or psychometric test? *Journal of Personality Assessment, 64,* 213–218.

Aronson, E., Wilson, T. D., & Akert, R. M. (2004). *Social psychology* (5th ed.). Upper Saddle River, NJ: Prentice Hall.

Asay, P. (2007, January 7). "There are no secrets." *Colorado Springs Gazette.*

Asch, S. E. (1958). Effects of group pressure upon modification and distortion of judgments. In E. E. Maccoby, T. M. Newcomb & E. L. Hartley (Eds.), *Readings in social psychology* (3rd ed.). New York: Holt, Rinehart & Winston.

Aserinsky, E., & Kleitman, N. (1953). Regularly occurring periods of eye motility, and concomitant phenomena during sleep. *Science, 118,* 273–274.

Assanangkornchai, S., Noi-pha, K., Saunders, J. G., & Ralanachaiyavong, S. (2003). Aldehyde dehydrogenase 2 genotypes, alcohol flushing, symptoms and drinking patterns in Thai men. *Psychiatry Research, 118,* 9–17.

Associated Press. (2002, November 18). Loss of McNabb overshadows win. *Los Angeles Times,* D8.

Associated Press. (2004, October 27). *Sleep interns make more medical mistakes* [On-line]. Available: http://msnbc. msn.com/id/6346069/

Associated Press. (2005a, March 28). *Docs: Schiavo videos misleading* [On-line]. Available: http://www. foxnews.com/story/0,2933,151662m00.html

Associated Press. (2005, June 13). *More than a million in U.S. live with HIV* [On-line]. Available: http:// www.newsmax.com/archives/articles/2005/6/13/202448.html

Associated Press. (2005b, June 15). *Schiavo autopsy shows irreversible brain damage* [On-line]. Available: http://www.msnbc.msn.com/id/8225637/

Associated Press. (2005, October 7). More evidence supports cervical cancer vaccine. *MSNBC* [On-line]. Available: http://www.msnbc.com/id/9609603/

Associated Press. (2005, December 16). *Report: Cell phone talking while driving on the rise* [On-line]. Available: http://www.cnn.com/2005/TEACH/ptech/12/16/cell.phone.drivers.ap/

Associated Press. (2006, January 4). R.I. legalizes medical marijuana. *The San Diego Union-Tribune,* A6.

Associated Press. (2006, March 7). *Some coffee drinkers risk a real jolt* [On-line]. Available: http://msnbc. msn.com/id/11713660/

Associated Press. (2006, July 2). More restrictions on teen drivers result in less accidents, study shows. *USA Today.*

Associated Press. (2006, October 4). *Japanese man recites first 100,000 digits of pi* [On-line]. Available: http://www.foxnews.com

Associated Press. (2006, October 27). *Immigrant father on trial for genital cutting* [On-line]. Available: http://www.msnbc.msn.com/id/15447708/

Atkinson, J. W. (1964). *An introduction to motivation.* Princeton, NJ: Van Nostrand Reinhold.

Atkinson, J. W. (Ed.). (1958). *Motives in fantasy, action and society.* Princeton, NJ: Van Nostrand Reinhold.

Atkinson, J. W., & Raynor, J. O. (Eds.). (1974). *Motivation and achievement.* Washington, DC: V. H. Winston.

Atkinson, R. C., & Shiffrin, R. M. (1968). Human memory: A proposed system and its control processes. In K. W. Spence & J. T. Spence (Eds.), *The psychology of learning and motivation: Advances in research and theory* (Vol. 2). New York: Academic Press.

Audrain, J. E., Klesges, R. C., & Klesges, L. M. (1995). Relationship between obesity and the metabolic effects of smoking in women. *Health Psychology, 14,* 116–123.

Austrian, S. G. (Eds.). (2002). *Developmental theories through the life cycle.* New York: Columbia University.

Axelsson, J., Stefansson, J. G., Magnusson, A., Sigvaldason, H., & Karlsson, M. M. (2002). Seasonal affective disorders: Relevance of Icelandic and Icelandic-Canadian evidence to etiological hypotheses. *Canadian Journal of Psychiatry, 47,* 153–158.

Azar, B. (1997, August). *When research is swept under the rug.* APA Monitor.

Azar, B., & Sleek, S. (1994, October). *Do roots of violence grow from nature or nurture?* APA Monitor.

Babyak, M., Blumenthal, J. A., Herman, S., Khatri, P., Doraiswamy, M., Moore, K., Craighead, W. E., Baldewicz, T. T., & Krishnan, K. R. (2000). Exercise treatment for major depression: Maintenance of therapeutic benefit at 10 months. *Psychosomatic Medicine, 62,* 633–638.

Bacchelli, E., & Maestrini, E. (2006). Autism spectrum disorders: Molecular genetic advances. *American Journal of Medical Genetics, 15,* 13–23.

Baddeley, A. (2004). *Your memory: A user's guide.* Buffalo, NY: Firefly.

Baddeley, A. (2006). Working memory: An overview. In S. J. Pickering (Ed.), *Working memory and education.* Burlington, MA: Elsevier.

Baer, J. S., Sampson, P. D., Barr, H. M., Connor, P. D., & Streissguth, A. P. (2003). A 21-year longitudinal analysis of the effects of prenatal alcohol exposure on young adult drinking. *Archives of General Psychiatry, 60,* 377–385.

Bahrick, H. P. (2000). Long-term maintenance of knowledge. In E. Tulving & F. M. Craik (Eds.), *The Oxford handbook of memory.* New York: Oxford University Press.

Bahrick, H. P., Bahrick, P. O., & Wittlinger, R. P. (1975). Fifty years of memory for names and faces. *Journal of Experimental Psychology: General, 104,* 54–75.

Bahrick, H. P., Hall, L. K., & Berger, S. A. (1996). Accuracy and distortion in memory for high school girls. *Psychological Science, 7,* 265–271.

Bailenson, J. N., Shum, M. S., & Uttal, D. H. (2000). The initial segment strategy: A heuristic for route selection. *Memory & Cognition, 28,* 306–318.

Bailes, E., Gao, F., Bibollet-Ruche, F., Courgnaud, V., Peeters, M., Marx, P. A., Hahn, B. H., & Sharp, P. M. (2003). Hybrid origin of SIV in chimpanzees. *Science, 200,* 1713.

Bailey, J. M., Dunne, M. P., & Martin, N. G. (2000). Genetic and environmental influences on sexual orientation and its correlates in an Australian twin sample. *Journal of Personality and Social Psychology, 78,* 524–536.

Bailey, J. M., & Zucker, H. J. (1995). Childhood sex-typed behavior and sexual orientation: A conceptual analysis and quantitative review. *Developmental Psychology, 31,* 43–55.

Baillargeon, R. (2002). Gender differences in physical aggression at 17 months of age: Results from the longitudinal study of child development in Quebec. In S. Cote (Chair), *Sex differences and similarities in aggression: Correlates and consequences from infancy to mid-life.* Symposium conducted at the 15th world meeting of the International Society for Research on Aggression, Montreal, Canada.

Bakalar, N. (2005, September 27). Many don't wash hands after using the bathroom. *The New York Times,* D7.

Baker, C. (2004). *Behavioral genetics: An introduction to how genes and environments interact through development to shape differences in mood, personality, and intelligence.* Washington, DC: American Association for the Advancement of Science.

Baker, M. C. (2002, January 15). Cited in B. Fowler, Expert says he discerns "hard-wired" grammar rules. *New York Times,* D5.

Baldwin, J. D., & Baldwin, J. I. (1997). Gender differences in sexual interest. *Archives of Sexual Behavior, 26,* 181–210.

Balter, M. (2002). What made humans modern? *Science, 295,* 1219–1225.

Balzar, J. (1997, March 8). A passion for canines, cold winds. *Los Angeles Times.*

Banaji, M. R. (2005, August 2). Cited in B. Carey, Neurology study uncovers a tendency to learn racial bias. *The New York Times,* D4.

Banaji, M. R. (2006, June). Cited in S. Lehrman, The implicit prejudice. *Scientific American,* 32–33.

Banay, S. (2006, February 3). *Most expensive perfumes* [On-line]. Available: http://www.forbes.com/lifestyle/2006/02/03/most-expensive-perfumes-ex_sb_0203 fashion3_ls.html

Bancroft, J. (2002). Biological factors in human sexuality. *The Journal of Sex Research, 39,* 15–21.

Bandura, A. (1965). Influence of models' reinforcement contingencies on the acquisition of imitative responses. *Journal of Personality and Social Psychology, 1,* 589–596.

Bandura, A. (1986). *Social foundations of thought and action: A social cognitive theory.* Englewood Cliffs, NJ: Prentice-Hall.

Bandura, A. (1999). Social cognitive theory of personality. In L. A. Pervin & O. P. John (Eds.), *Handbook of personality: Theory and research* (2nd ed.). New York: Guilford.

Bandura, A. (2000). Exercise of human agency through collective efficacy. *Current Directions in Psychological Science, 9,* 75–78.

Bandura, A. (2001a). Social cognitive theory: An agentic perspective. *Annual Review of Psychology, 52,* 1–26.

Bandura, A. (2001b). Social cognitive theory of personality. In L. A. Pervin & O. P. John (Eds.), *Handbook of personality: Theory and research* (2nd ed.). New York: Guilford Press.

Bandura, A., Blanchard, E. B., & Ritter, B. (1969). Relative efficacy of desensitization and modeling approaches for inducing behavioral, affective and attitudinal changes. *Journal of Personality and Social Psychology, 13,* 173–179.

Bandura, A., Ross, D., & Ross, S. A. (1963). Imitation of film-mediated aggressive models. *Journal of Abnormal and Social Psychology, 66,* 3–11.

Barinaga, M. (1996). Backlash strikes at affirmative action programs. *Science, 271,* 1908–1910.

Barinaga, M. (2000). Family of bitter taste receptors found. *Science, 287,* 2133–2135.

Barinaga, M. (2002). How the brain's clock gets daily enlightenment. *Science, 295,* 955–957.

References

Barinaga, M. (2003). Newborn neurons search for meaning. *Science, 299,* 32–34.

Barlow, D. H., & Durand, V. M. (2002). *Abnormal psychology* (3rd ed.). Belmont, CA: Thomson Wadsworth.

Barlow, D. H., & Durand, V. M. (2005). *Abnormal psychology* (4th ed.). Belmont, CA: Thomson Wadsworth.

Barnard, N. D., & Kaufman, S. R. (1997, February). Animal research is wasteful and misleading. *Scientific American,* 80–82.

Baron, A. S., & Banaji, M. R. (2006). The development of implicit attitudes: Evidence of race evaluations from ages 6 and 10 and adulthood. *Psychological Science, 17,* 53–58.

Baron, R. A., & Richardson, D. R. (2004). *Human aggression* (2nd ed.). New York: Springer.

Bartels, A. (2002, December 16). Cited in C. Carey, The brain in love. *Los Angeles Times,* F1.

Bartlett, N. H., Vasey, P. L., & Bukowski, W. M. (2000, December). Is gender identity disorder in children a mental disorder? *Sex Roles, 43,* 753–775.

Bartlik, B., & Goldstein, M. Z. (2001). Men's sexual health after midlife. *Psychiatric Services, 52,* 291–306.

Bartone, P. T. (1999). Hardiness protects against war-related stress in Army Reserve forces. *Consulting Psychology Journal, 51,* 72–82.

Bartoshuk, L. M. (1997). Cited in K. Fackelmann, The bitter truth. *Science News, 152,* 24–25.

Basbaum, A. I., & Julius, D. (2006, June). Toward better pain control. *Scientific American,* 60–67.

Bashore, T. R., & Rapp, P. E. (1993). Are there alternatives to traditional polygraph procedures? *Psychological Bulletin, 113,* 3–22.

Basil, R. (1989). Graphology and personality: Let the buyer beware. *Skeptical Inquirer, 13,* 241–248.

Bateman, A. W., & Fonagy, P. (2000). Effectiveness of psychotherapeutic treatment of personality disorder. *British Journal of Psychiatry, 177,* 138–143.

Bates, B. L. (1994). Individual differences in response to hypnosis. In J. W. Rhue, S. J. Lynn & I. Kirsch (Eds.), *Handbook of clinical hypnosis.* Washington, DC: American Psychological Association.

Bates, J. (2004). Temperament as an emotion construct: Theoretical and practical issues. In M. Lewis & J. M. Haviland-Jones (Eds.), *Handbook of emotions* (2nd ed.). New York: Guilford Press.

Bateson, P. (1991). Is imprinting such a special case? In J. R. Krebs & G. Horn (Eds.), *Behavioural and neural aspects of learning and memory.* Oxford: Oxford University Press.

Batson, C. D. (1998). Who cares? When? Where? Why? How? *Contemporary Psychology, 43,* 108–109.

Battaglia, M. (2005, April 4). Cited in J. Kluger, Secrets of the shy. *Time,* 50–52.

Battles, J. (2004, February 8). Virtual reality limbs for amputees. *The Times of London.*

Bauer, P. J. (2002). Long-term recall memory: Behavioral and neuro-developmental changes in the first 2 years of life. *Current Directions in Psychological Science, 11,* 139–140.

Baum, G. (1994, February 13). Storming the Citadel. *Los Angeles Times.*

Baumeister, R. F. (1995). Disputing the effects of championship pressures and home audiences. *Journal of Personality and Social Psychology, 68,* 644–648.

Baumrind, D. (1991). Effective parenting during the early adolescent transition. In P. A. Cowan & E. M. Hetherington (Eds.), *Advances in family research.* Hillsdale, NJ: Erlbaum.

Baumrind, D. (1993). The average expectable environment is not good enough: A response to Scarr. *Child Development, 64,* 1299–1317.

Baumrind, D. (1995). Commentary on sexual orientation: Research and social policy implications. *Developmental Psychology, 31,* 130–136.

Baumrind, D., Larzelere, R. E., & Cowan, P. A. (2002). Ordinary physical punishment: Is it harmful? Comment on Gershoff (2002). *Psychological Bulletin, 128,* 580–589.

Baylen, C. A., & Rosenberg, H. (2006). A review of the acute subjective effects of MDMA/ecstasy. *Addiction, 101,* 933.

Bayley, P. J., Gold, J. J., Hopkins, R. O., & Squire, L. R. (2005). The neuroanatomy of remote memory. *Neuron, 46,* 799–810.

Bayley, P. J., Hopkins, R. O., & Squire, L. R. (2003). Successful recollection of remote autobiographical memories by amnesic patients with medial temporal lobe lesions. *Neuron, 38,* 135–144.

BBC News. (2003, January 11). Clue to Mystery Viagra deaths.

BCSSE (Board on Behavioral, Cognitive, and Sensory Sciences and Education). (2002). *Mental retardation: Determining eligibility for Social Security benefits.* Washington, DC: National Academy Press.

Bear, M. F., Connors, B. W., & Paradiso, M. A. (1996). *Neuroscience: Exploring the brain.* Baltimore, MD: Williams & Wilkins.

Beasley, M., Thompson, T., & Davidson, J. (2003). Resilience in response to life stress: The effects of coping style and cognitive hardiness. *Personality and Individual Differences, 34,* 77–95.

Beck, A. T. (1976). *Cognitive therapy and the emotional disorders.* New York: International Universities Press.

Beck, A. T. (1991). Cognitive therapy: A 30-year retrospective. *American Psychologist, 46,* 368–375.

Beck, A. T., Rush, A. J., Shaw, B. F., & Emery, G. (1979). *Cognitive therapy of depression.* New York: Guilford.

Beck, A. T., & Weishaar, M. E. (2005). Cognitive therapy. In R. J. Corsini & D. Wedding, *Current psychotherapies* (7th ed., pp. 238–268). Belmont, CA: Brooks/Cole–Thomson Learning.

Beck, G. J., Gudmundsdottir, B., Palyo, S. A., Miller, L. M., & Grant, D. D. (2006). Rebound effects following deliberate thought suppression: Does PTSD make a difference? *Behavior Therapy, 37,* 170–180.

Becker, A., Burwell, R. A., Gilman, S. E., Herzog, D. B., & Hamburg, P. (2002). Eating behaviours and attitudes following prolonged exposure to television among ethnic Fijian adolescent girls. *British Journal of Psychiatry, 10,* 509–514.

Begley, S. (1998a, January 19). Aping language. *Newsweek.*

Begley, S. (1998b, January 26). Is everybody crazy? *Newsweek,* 51–55.

Begley, S. (2001, February 12). How it all starts inside your brain. *Newsweek,* 40–43.

Behrman, A. (1999, January 27). Electroboy. *New York Times Magazine,* 67.

Bekoff, M. (2001). Social play behavior: Cooperation, fairness, trust, and the evolution of morality. *Journal of Consciousness Studies, 8,* 81–90.

Bem, D. (1967). Self-perception: An alternative interpretation of cognitive dissonance phenomena. *Psychological Review, 74,* 183–200.

Bem, D. J., & Honorton, C. (1994). Does psi exist? Replicable evidence for an anomalous process of information transfer. *Psychological Bulletin, 115,* 4–18.

Bem, S. L. (1981). Gender schema theory: A cognitive account of sex-typing. *Psychological Review, 88,* 354–364.

Bem, S. L. (1985). Androgyny and gender schema theory: Conceptual and empirical integration. In T. B. Sonderegger (Ed.), *Nebraska symposium on motivation.* Lincoln: University of Nebraska Press.

Bendersky, M., & Lewis, M. (1999). Prenatal cocaine exposure and neonatal condition. *Infant Behavior & Development, 22,* 353–366.

Bendsen, E., Byskov, A. G., Andersen, C. Y., & Westergaard, L. G. (2006). Number of germ cells and somatic cells in human fetal ovaries during the first weeks after sex differentiation. *Human Reproduction, 21,* 30–35.

Benin, M. H., & Robinson, L. B. (1997, August 25). Marital happiness across the family life cycle: A longitudinal analysis. Cited in *Time,* 24.

Benjamin, L. T., Jr. (2000). The psychology laboratory at the turn of the 20th century. *American Psychologist, 55,* 318–321.

Benjet, C., & Kazdin, A. E. (2003). Spanking children: The controversies, findings, and new directions. *Clinical Psychology Review, 23,* 197–224.

Bennet, J. (2002, June 21). Rash of new suicide bombers showing no pattern or ties. *New York Times,* A1.

Ben-Shakhar, G., & Elaad, E. (2003). The validity of psychophysiological detection of information with the guilty knowledge test: A meta-analysis review. *Journal of Applied Psychology, 88,* 131–151.

Benson, E. (2003a, February). Intelligent intelligence testing. *Monitor on Psychology,* 48–51.

Benson, E. (2003b, February). Intelligence across cultures. *Monitor on Psychology,* 56–58.

Benson, H. (1975). *The relaxation response.* New York: Morrow.

Benson, H., Lehmann, J. W., Malhotra, M. S., Goldman, R. F., Hopkins, P. J., & Epstein, M. D. (1982). Body temperature changes during the practice of g Tum-mo yoga. *Nature, 295,* 234–235.

Benson, H., Malhotra, M. S., Goldman, R. F., Jacobs, G. D., & Hopkins, P. J. (1990). Three case reports of the metabolic and electroencephalographic changes during advanced Buddhist meditation techniques. *Behavioral Medicine, 16,* 90–95.

Berenson, A. (2005, December 4). Sales of impotence drugs fall, defying expectations. *The New York Times.*

Berenson, A. (2006, January 1). Antidepressants seem to cut suicide risk in teenagers and adults, study says. *The New York Times,* 14.

Berg, C. A. (2000). Intellectual development in adulthood. In R. J. Sternberg (Ed.), *Handbook of intelligence.* New York: Cambridge University Press.

Berger, J., & Cunningham, C. (1994). Active intervention and conservation: Africa's pachyderm problem. *Science, 263,* 1241–1242.

Bergfield, C. (2006, July 26). *War vets get a dose of virtual reality* [On-line]. Available: http://www.msnbc.msn.com/id/14048170/print/1/displaymode/1098/

Berk, L. B., & Patrick, C. F. (1990). Epidemiologic aspects of toilet training. *Clinical Pediatrics, 29,* 278–282.

Berko, A., & Erez, E. (2006, December 6). Women in terrorism: A Palestinian feminist revolution or gender oppression? *Institute for Counter-Terrorism* [On-line]. Available: http://www.ict.org.il/apage/9102.php

Berkowitz, L. (1989). Frustration-aggression hypothesis: Examination and reformulation. *Psychological Bulletin, 106,* 59–73.

Berkowitz, L. (1993). *Aggression: Its causes, consequences, and control.* New York: McGraw-Hill.

Berlinger, N. T. (2006). Robotic surgery—Squeezing into tight places. *The New England Journal of Medicine, 354,* 2099–2101.

Berns, G. (2005, June 28). Cited in S. Blakeslee, What other people say may change what you see. *The New York Times,* D3.

Berns, G. S., Chappelow, M. C., Zink, C. F., Pagnoni, G., & Martin-Skurski, M. E. (2005, May 5). Neurobiological substrates of dread. *Science, 312,* 754–758.

Bernstein, D. A. (1993, March). Excuses, excuses. *APS Observer.*

Bernstein, D. M., Laney, C., Morris, E. K., & Loftus, E. F. (2005, September 27). False beliefs about fattening foods can have healthy consequences. Proceedings of the *National Academy of Sciences, 102,* 13724–13731.

Berntsen, D., & Thomsen, D. K. (2005). Personal memories for remote historical events: Accuracy and clarity of flashbulb memories related to World War II. *Journal of Experimental Psychology: General, 134,* 242–257.

Berridge, K. C. (2003). Comparing the emotional brains of human and other animals. In R. J. Davidson, K. R. Scherer & H. H. Goldsmith (Eds.), *Handbook of affective sciences.* New York: Oxford University Press.

Berry, H. (2002). *Halle Berry: 2002 Oscar acceptance address for best actress.* Available: http://www.americanrhetoric.com/speeches/halleberryoscarspeech.htm

Berson, D. M. (2003). Strange vision: Ganglion cells as circadian photoreceptors. *Trends in Neurosciences, 26,* 314–320.

Best, D. L., & Thomas, J. J. (2004). Cultural diversity and cross-cultural perspectives. In A. H. Eagly, A. E. Beall, & R. J. Sternberg (Eds.), *The psychology of gender* (2nd ed., pp. 296–327). New York: Guilford Press.

Betancourt, H., & Lopez, S. R. (1993). The study of culture, ethnicity, and race in American psychology. *American Psychologist, 48,* 629–637.

Bever, T., & Montalbetti, M. (2002). Noam's ark. *Science, 298,* 1565.

Bhattacharya, S. (2003, February 17). *"Supertasters" diet raises cancer risk* [On-line]. Available: http://www.newscientist.com/article.ns?id=dn3396& print=true

Bibikova, A., & Kotcinikov, V. Managing cross-cultural differences. www.1000ventures.com/business_guide/crosscuttings/cross-cultural_differences.html

Biello, D. (2006, May 24). Large study finds no link between marijuana and lung cancer. *Scientific American.*

Billingsley, J. (2005, November 30). *Coffee perks up short-term memory* [On-line]. Available: http://health. msn.com/healthnews/articlepage. aspx? cp-documentid=100119786

Billy, J. O. G., Tanfer, K., Grady, W. R., & Klepinger, D. H. (1993). The sexual behavior of females in the United States. *Family Planning Perspectives, 25,* 52–60.

Binet, A., & Simon, T. (1905). Methodes nouvelles pour le diagnostic du niveau intellectuel des anormaux. *L'Annee Psychologique, 11,* 191–244.

Bishop, E. G., Cherny, S. S., Corley, R., Plomin, R., DeFries, J. C., & Hewitt, J. K. (2003). Development genetic analysis of general cognitive ability from 1 to 12 years in a sample of adoptees, biological siblings, and twins. *Intelligence, 31,* 31–49.

Bjorklund, D. F. (2005). *Children's thinking: Cognitive development and individual differences.* Belmont, CA: Wadsworth/Thomson.

Black, D. (2006, December 12). What causes antisocial personality disorder? *PsychCentral* [On-line]. Available: http://psychcentral.com/lib/2006/12/what-causes-antisocial-personality-disorder/

Black, D. W., Baumgard, C. H., & Bell, S. E. (1995). A 16- to 45-year follow-up of 71 men with antisocial personality disorder. *Comprehensive Psychiatry, 36,* 130–140.

Black, L., & Flynn, C. (2003, May 7). Glenbrook North, cops investigate brawl at hazing; 5 girls are hurt during "initiation." *Chicago Tribune,* 1.

Blakely, M. R. (1994, May 15). A place of belonging. *Los Angeles Times Magazine.*

Blakemore, J. E. O. (2003). Children's beliefs about violating gender norms: Boys shouldn't look like girls, and girls shouldn't act like boys. *Sex Roles, 48,* 411–419.

Blakeslee, S. (2000, January 12). Researchers developing bold new theories to explain autism. *San Diego Union-Tribune.*

Blakeslee, S. (2002, November, 11). A boy, a mother and a rare map of autism's world. *New York Times,* D1.

Blakeslee, S. (2005, June 28). What other people say may change what you see. *The New York Times,* D3.

Blakeslee, S. (2006, May 5). Study points to a solution for dread: Distraction. *The New York Times,* A18.

Blanco, C., Schneier, F. R., Schmidt, A., Blanco-Jerez, C., Marshall, R. D., Sanchez-Lacay, A., & Liebowitz, M. R. (2003). Pharmacological treatment of social anxiety disorder: A meta-analysis. *Depression & Anxiety, 18,* 29–40.

Blass, E. M., & Camp, C. A. (2001). The ontogeny of face recognition: Eye contact and sweet taste induce face preference in 9- and 12-week-old human infants. *Developmental Psychology, 37,* 762–774.

Blass, T. (Ed.). (2000). *Obedience to authority.* Mahwah, NJ: Lawrence Erlbaum.

Block, J. (1995). Going beyond the five factors given: Rejoinder to Costa & McCrae (1995) and Goldberg & Saucier (1995). *Psychological Bulletin, 117,* 226–229.

Block, J., & Robins, R. W. (1993). Longitudinal study of consistency and change in self-esteem from early adolescence to early adulthood. *Child Development, 64,* 909–923.

Blomberg, J., Lazar, A., & Sandell, R. (2001). Long-term outcome of long-term psychoanalytically oriented therapies: First findings of the Stockholm outcome of psychotherapy and psychoanalysis study. *Psychotherapy Research, 11,* 361–382.

Blood, A. J., & Zatorre, R. J. (2001). Intensely pleasurable responses to music correlate with activity in brain regions implicated in reward and emotion. *Proceedings of the National Academy of Sciences, 98,* 11818–11823.

Bloom, M. M. (2005). *Dying to kill: The allure of suicide terror.* New York: Columbia University Press.

Blum, N. (2003, April 14). Cited in B. Carey, Ready or not. *Los Angeles Times,* F2.

Blum, R. (2002, September 5). Cited in D. J. Schemo, Mothers of sex-active youths often think they're virgins. *New York Times,* A14.

Blunt, A. K., & Pychyl, T. A. (2000). Task aversiveness and procrastination: A multi-dimensional approach to task aversiveness across stages of personal projects. *Personality and Individual Differences, 28,* 153–167.

Boddy, J. (1988). Spirits and selves in northern Sudan: The cultural therapeutics of possession and trance. *American Ethnologist, 15,* 4–27.

Boden, M. A. (1994). Précis of the creative mind: Myths and mechanisms. *Behavioral and Brain Sciences, 17,* 519–570.

Bogaert, A. F. (2006a, June 26). Cited in R. E. Schmid, *Men with older brothers more likely to be gay* [On-line]. Available: http://abcnews.go.com/Health/wireStory?id=2119484

Bogaert, A. F. (2006b, July 11). Biological versus nonbiological older brothers and men's sexual orientation. *Proceedings of the National Academy of Sciences, 103,* 10771–10774.

Bolton, E. E., Lambert, J. F., Wolf, E. J., Raja, S., Varra, A. A., & Fisher, L. M. (2004). Evaluating a cognitive-behavioral group treatment program for veterans with posttraumatic stress disorder. *Psychological Services, 1,* 140–146.

Bonanno, G. A. (2004). Loss, trauma, and human resilience. *American Psychologist, 59,* 20–28.

Bondurant, B., & Donat, P. L. N. (1999). Perceptions of women's sexual interest and acquaintance rape. *Psychology of Women Quarterly, 23,* 691–705.

Bonnet, M. H. (2005). Acute sleep deprivation. In M. H. Kryger, T. Roth, & W. C. Dement (Eds.), *Principles and practice of sleep medicine* (4th ed., pp. 51–66). Philadelphia: Elsevier Saunders.

Booth-Kewley, S., & Friedman, H. S. (1987). Psychological predictions of heart disease: A quantitative review. *Psychological Bulletin, 101,* 343–362.

Bootzin, R. R., & Rider, S. P. (1997). Behavioral techniques and biofeedback for insomnia. In M. R. Pressman & W. C. Roo (Eds.), *Understanding sleep: The evaluation and treatment of sleep disorders.* Washington, DC: American Psychological Association.

Borella, P., Bargellini, A., Rovesti, S., Pinelli, M., Vivoli, R., Solfrini, V., & Vivoli, G. (1999). Emotional stability, anxiety, and natural killer activity under examination stress. *Psychoneuroendocrinology, 224,* 613–627.

Born, J., Lange, T., Hansen, K., Molle, M., & Fehm, H. L. (1997). Effects of sleep and circadian rhythm on human circulating immune cells. *Journal of Immunology, 158,* 4454–4464.

Bornstein, R. F. (2001). The impending death of psychoanalysis. *Psychoanalytic Psychology, 18,* 3–20.

Borton, J. L. D. (2002). The suppression of negative self-referent thoughts. *Anxiety, Stress, and Coping, 15,* 31–46.

Bosch, F. X., Lorincz, A., Munoz, N., Meijer, C. J. L. M., & Shah, K. V. (2002). The causal relation between human papillomavirus and cervical cancer. *Journal of Clinical Pathology, 55,* 244–265.

Botting, J. H., & Morrison, A. R. (1997, February). Animal research vital to medicine. *Scientific American,* 83–85.

Bouchard, T. J., Jr. (1994). Genes, environment, and personality. *Science, 264,* 1700–1701.

Bouchard, T. J., Jr. (1995). Breaking the last taboo. *Contemporary Psychology, 40,* 415–418.

Bouchard, T. J., Jr. (1997). IQ similarity in twins reared apart: Findings and responses to critics. In R. J. Sternberg & E. Grigorenko (Eds.), *Intelligence, heredity, and environment.* New York: Cambridge University Press.

Bouchard, T. J., Jr. (2004). Genetic influence on human psychological traits. *Current Directions in Psychological Science, 13,* 148–151.

Bouchard, T. J., Jr., & Loehlin, J. C. (2001). Genes, evolution, and personality. *Behavior Genetics, 31,* 243–273.

Bouchard, T. J., Jr., Lykken, D. T., McGue, M., Segal, N. L., & Tellegen, A. (1990). Sources of human psychological differences: The Minnesota study of twins reared apart. *Science, 250,* 223–228.

Bouchard, T. J., & McGue, M. (1981). Familial studies of intelligence: A review. *Science, 212,* 1055–1059.

Bower, B. (1993a). Sudden recall. *Science News, 144,* 184–186.

Bower, B. (1993b). Flashbulb memories: Confident blunders. *Science News, 143,* 166–167.

Bower, B. (1996). Creatures in the brain. *Science News, 149,* 234–235.

Bower, B. (1997). Forbidden flavors. *Science News, 151,* 198–199.

Bower, B. (2001). Brains in dreamland. *Science News, 160,* 90–92.

Bower, B. (2002a). Chromosome study homes in on Alzheimer's disease. *Science News, 161,* 116–117.

Bower, B. (2002b, November 2). Neural shape-up: Brain anticipates object perception. *Science News, 162,* 275.

Bower, B. (2003a, January 11). Speech veers left in babies' brains. *Science News, 163,* 30.

Bower, B. (2003b). Words get in the way. *Science News, 163,* 250–251.

Bower, B. (2005, April 23). Mood brighteners: Light therapy gets nod as depression buster. *Science News, 167,* 261–262.

References

Bower, B. (2006a, May 27). Violent developments. Disruptive kids grow into their behavior. *Science News, 169,* 328–329.

Bower, B. (2006b, December 9). The predator's gaze. *Science News, 170,* 379?381.

Bower, F. (1997). The power of limited thinking. *Science News, 152,* 334–335.

Bower, F. (2000). Building blocks of talk. *Science News, 157,* 344–346.

Bower G. H. (2005). A brief history of memory research. In E. Tulving & F. M. Craik (Eds.), *The Oxford handbook of memory.* New York: Oxford University Press.

Bowlby, J. (1969). *Attachment and loss: Vol. 1. Attachment.* New York: Basic Books.

Bowman, L. (2005, December 1). *Caffeine can improve short-term memory* [On-line]. Available: http://seattlepi.nwsource.com/health/250310_cofee01.html

Boyce, N. (2002, October 7). Chips vs. the chess masters. *U.S. News & World Report,* 70–71.

Bradley, R., Greene, J., Russ, E., Dutra, L., & Westen, D. (2005). A multidimensional meta-analysis of psychotherapy for PTSD. *American Journal of Psychiatry, 162,* 214–227.

Bragg, R. (1995, July 16). In South Carolina, a mother's defense, and life, could hinge on 2 choices. *New York Times.*

Brantley, B. (2003, February 7). Old Blues, new riffs. *New York Times,* B1.

Brasic, J. R. (2005). Pervasive developmental disorder: Autism. In C. D. Berkowitz, R. Konop, D. Pataki, C. Sylvester & M. M. Kappelman (Eds.), *Pediatrics.* Available: http://www.emedicine.com/ped/topic180.htm

Braun, A. R., Balkin, T. J., Wesensten, N. J., Gwadry, F., Carson, R. E., Varga, M., Baldwin, P., Belenky, G., & Herscovitch, P. (1998). Dissociated pattern of activity in visual cortices and their projections during human rapid eye movement sleep. *Science, 279,* 91–95.

Braun, J., Kahn, R. S., Froehlich, T., Auinger, P., & Lanphear, B. P. (2006, October 7). Cited in B. Harder, Cigarettes and lead linked to attention disorder. *Science News, 170.*

Brecher, E. M. (1972). *Licit and illicit drugs.* Boston: Little, Brown.

Breckler, S. J. (2006, February). The IRB problem. *Monitor on Psychology, 37,* 21.

Breiter, H. C., Aharon, I., Kahneman, D., Dale, A., & Shizgal, P. (2001). Functional imaging of neural responses to expectancy and experience of monetary gains and losses. *Neuron, 30,* 619–639.

Brendza, R. P., Bacskai, B. J., Cirrito, J. R., Simmons, K. A., Skoch, J. M., Klunk, W. E., Mathis, C. A., Bales, K. R., Paul, S. M., Hyman, B. T., & Holtzman, D. M. (2005). Anti-Aß1 antibody treatment promotes the rapid recovery of amyloid-associated neuritic dystrophy in PDAPP transgenic mice. *Journal of Clinical Investigation, 115,* 428–433.

Brennan, J. (1997, September 28). This 1,800-pound bear is no 800-pound gorilla. *Los Angeles Times/Calendar.*

Breuer, J., & Freud, S. (1895; reprinted 1955). Studies on hysteria. In J. Strachey (Ed. and Trans.), *The standard edition of the complete psychological works of Sigmund Freud.* London: Hogarth.

Brewster, W., DiSaia, P., & Grosen, E. (1999). An experience with estrogen replacement therapy in breast cancer survivors. *International Journal of Fertility, 44,* 186–192.

Brickman, P., Coates, D., & Janoff-Bulman, R. (1978). Lottery winners and accident victims: Is happiness relative? *Journal of Personality and Social Psychology, 36,* 917–927.

Bridges, A. (2006, March 24). Gov't advisers reject strong ADHD warnings. *U.S. News & World Report.*

Briggs, J. L. (1970). *Never in anger: Portrait of an Eskimo family.* Cambridge, MA: Harvard University Press.

Bright, J. (2003, May 20). Cited in E. Goode, Leading drugs for psychosis come under new scrutiny. *New York Times,* A1.

Broad, W. J. (2002, October 9). Lie-detector tests found too flawed to discover spies. *New York Times,* A1.

Brody, A. L., Saxena, S., Stoessel, P., Gillies, L. A., Fairbanks, L. A., Alborzian, S., Phelps, M. E., Huang, S. C., Wu, H. M., Ho, M. L., Ho, M. K., Scott, C., Maidment, K., & Baxter, L. R., Jr. (2001). Regional brain metabolic changes in patients with major depression treated with either paroxetine or interpersonal therapy. *Archives of General Psychiatry, 58,* 631–640.

Brody, J. E. (1998, January 6). Depression: 2 famous men tell their stories. *San Diego Union-Tribune.*

Brody, J. E. (2000a, April 25). Memories of things that never were. *New York Times,* D8.

Brody, J. E. (2000b, October 17). One-two punch for losing pounds: Exercise and careful diet. *New York Times,* D6.

Brody, J. E. (2002, September 17). Sleep apnea, a noisy but often invisible threat. *New York Times,* D7.

Brody, J. E. (2003, August 18). Skipping a college course: Weight gain 101. *New York Times,* D7.

Brody, N. (1992). *Intelligence.* New York: Academic Press.

Brody, N. (1997). Intelligence, schooling, and society. *American Psychologist, 52,* 1046–1050.

Brody, N. (2000). Theories and measurements of intelligence. In R. J. Sternberg (Ed.), *Handbook of intelligence.* New York: Cambridge University Press.

Brody, N. (2003). What Sternberg should have concluded. *Intelligence, 31,* 339–342.

Brodzinsky, S. (2006, July 25). *Columbia cracks down on drug cash* [On-line]. Available: http://www.usatoday.com/news/world/2006-07-25-columbia-smuggling_x.htm

Broidy, L. M., Nagin, D. S., Tremblay, R. E., Bates, J. E., Brame, B., Dodge, K. A., Fergusson, D., Horwood, J. K., Loeber, R., Laird, R., Lynam, D. R., Moffitt, T. E., Pettit, G. S., & Vitaro, F. (2003). Developmental trajectories of childhood disruptive behaviors and adolescent delinquency: A six-site cross-national study. *Developmental Psychology, 39,* 222–245.

Brooks, C. (1994, February 27). Breakdown into the shadows of mental illness. Special report. *San Diego Union-Tribune.*

Brooks, C. (1995a, February 27). Shadowlands: Three profiled in mental illness series are striving to improve their conditions. *San Diego Union-Tribune.*

Brooks, C. (1995b, June 5). Rod Steiger is powerful voice for mentally ill. *San Diego Union-Tribune.*

Brooks, D. C. (2000). Recent and remote extinction cues reduce spontaneous recovery. *Quarterly Journal of Experimental Psychology, 53B,* 25–58.

Brooks, R., & Goldstein, S. (2002). *Raising resilient children.* New York: McGraw-Hill/Contemporary Books.

Brooks-Gunn, J. (2006, November 26). Cited in P. Tough, What it takes to make a student. *The New York Times Magazine.*

Brophy, B. (2006, December 25). Give your teen more driving time. *U.S. News & World Report,* 71.

Brown, G. S., Lambert, M. J., Jones, E. R., & Minami, T. (2005, August). Identifying highly effective psychotherapists in a managed care environment. *The American Journal of Managed Care, 11,* 513–520.

Brown, R., & Kulik, J. (1977). Flashbulb memories. *Cognition, 5,* 73–99.

Brown, S. A. (1996, May 13). Talent for living. *People,* 85–86.

Brown, S. C., & Craik, F. I. M. (2005). Encoding and retrieval of information. In E. Tulving & F. M. Craik (Eds.), *The Oxford handbook of memory.* New York: Oxford University Press.

Brown, W. A. (1997, January). The placebo effect. *Scientific American,* 90–95.

Brownlee, C. (2005, September 3). Food fix. *Science News,* 155–156.

Brownlee, C. (2006, August 12). Scientists find midnight-snack center in brain. *Science News, 170,* 109–110.

Brownlee, S. (1997, February 3). The case for frivolity. *U.S. News & World Report.*

Bruer, J. T. (1999). *The myth of the first three years.* New York: Free Press.

Bruner, J. (1997). Celebrating divergence: Piaget and Vygotsky. *Human Development, 40,* 63–73.

Brzezinski, A. (1997). Melatonin in humans. *New England Journal of Medicine, 336,* 186–195.

Buck, L. (1999). Cited in J. Travis, Making sense of scents. *Science News, 155,* 236–238.

Buckley, P. (1989). Fifty years after Freud: Dora, the Rat Man, and the Wolf-Man. *American Journal of Psychiatry, 146,* 1394–1403.

Buckout, R. (1980). Nearly 2,000 witnesses can be wrong. *Bulletin of the Psychonomic Society, 16,* 307–310.

Buddie, A. M., & Miller, A. G. (2002). Beyond rape myths: A more complex view of perceptions of rape myths. *Sex Roles, 45,* 139–160.

Buehler, R., Griffin, D., & Ross, M. (1994). Exploring the "planning fallacy": Why people underestimate their task completion times. *Journal of Personality and Social Psychology, 67,* 366–381.

Bugental, B. B., & Goodnow, J. J. (1998). Socialization processes. In W. Damon & N. Eisenberg (Eds.), *Handbook of child psychology (5th ed.).* New York: John Wiley & Sons.

Bulik, C. M. (2006, March 15). In T. Whitmire, Study: Genes may cause risk for anorexia. *USA Today.*

Bulik, C. M., Sullivan, P. F., & Kendler, K. S. (2003). Genetic and environmental contributions to obesity and eating. *International Journal of Eating Disorders, 33,* 293–298.

Bunting, M. (2006). Proactive interference and item similarity in working memory. *Journal of Experimental Psychology: Learning, Memory, and Cognition, 32,* 183–196.

Buonomano, D. V., & Merzenich, M. M. (1995). Temporal information transformed into a spatial code by a neural network with realistic properties. *Science, 267,* 1028–1030.

Burge, D., Hammen, C., Davila, J., Daley, S. E., Paley, B., Herzberg, D., & Lindberg, N. (1997). Attachment cognitions and college and work functioning two years later in late adolescent women. *Journal of Youth and Adolescence, 26,* 285–301.

Burger, J. M. (2004). *Personality* (6th ed.). Belmont, CA: Wadsworth.

Burger, J. M. (2007a). Cited in C. Borge, Basic instincts: The science of evil. *ABC News* [On-line]. Available: http://abcnews.go.com/Primetime/print?id=2765416

Burger, J. M. (2007b). *Replicating Milgram: Would people still obey today?* Manuscript submitted for publication.

Burn, S. M. (2004). *Groups: Theory and practice.* Belmont, CA: Wadsworth/Thomson.

Burton, C. M., & King, L. A. (2004). The health benefits of writing about intensely positive experiences. *Journal of Research in Personality, 38,* 150–163.

Burton, S. (2006). Symptom domains of schizophrenia: The role of atypical antipsychotic agents. *Journal of Psychopharmacology, 20,* 6–20.

Bushman, B. J. (2002). Does venting anger feed or extinguish the flame? Catharsis, rumination, distraction, anger, and aggressive responding. *Personality and Social Psychology Bulletin, 28,* 724–731.

Business Week Online. (2004, May 24). *Michael J. Fox's take on stem cells.* Available: http://www.businessweek.com/magazine/content/04_21/b3884010_mz001.htm

Buss, D. M. (1994). Mate preferences in 37 cultures. In W. J. Lonner & R. Malpass (Eds.), Psychology and culture. Boston: Allyn & Bacon. Buss, D. M. (1995). Psychological sex differences. American Psychologist, 50, 164–168.

Buss, D. M. (1999). Human nature and individual differences: The evolution of human personality. In L. A. Pervin & O. P. John (Eds.), Handbook of personality (2nd ed.). New York: Guilford.

Buss, D. M. (2003). The evolution of desire: Strategies of human mating. New York: Basic Books.

Buss, D. M., & Schmitt, D. P. (1993). Sexual strategies theory: An evolutionary perspective on human mating. Psychological Review, 100, 204–232.

Buss, D. M., Abbott, M., Angleitner, A., Asherian, A., Biaggio, A., Blanco-VillaSenor, A., Bruchon-Schweitzer, M., Ch'u, H. Y., Czapinski, J., DeRaad, B., Ekehammar, B., Fioravanti, M., Georgas, J., Gjerde, P., Guttman, R., Hazan, F., Iwawaki, S., Janakiramaiah, H., Khosroshani, F., Kreitler, S., Lachenicht, L., Lee, M., Liik, K., Little, B., Lohamy, N., Makun, S., Mika, S., Moadel-Shahid, M., Moane, G., Montero, M., Mundy-Casde, A. C., Niit, T., Nsenduluka, E., Peltzer, K., Pienkowski, R., Pirttila-Backman, A., Ponce De Leon, J., Rousseau, J., Runco, M. A., Safir, M. P., Samuels, C., Sanitioso, R., Schweitzer, B., Serpell, R., Smid, N., Spencer, C., Tadinac, M., Todorova, E. N., Troland, K., Van den Brande, L., Van Heck, G., Van Langenhove, L., & Yang, K. S. (1990). International preferences in selecting mates. Journal of Cross-Cultural Psychology, 21, 5–47.

Bustillo, J. R., Lauriello, J., Horan, W. P., & Keith, S. J. (2001). The psychosocial treatment of schizophrenia: An update. American Journal of Psychiatry, 158, 163–175.

Butler, A. C., Chapman, J. E., Forman, E. M., & Beck, A. T. (2006). The empirical status of cognitive-behavioral therapy: A review of meta-analyses. Clinical Psychology Review, 26, 17–31.

Butler, K. (1994, June 26). A house divided. Los Angeles Times Magazine.

Byne, W. (1997). Why we cannot conclude that sexual orientation is primarily a biological phenomenon. Journal of Homosexuality, 34, 73–80.

Byrne, R. (2003, March 2). When man pulled ahead of machine, albeit briefly. New York Times, 12.

Cabeza, R. (2006, January 16). Cited in G. Cohen, The myth of the midlife crisis. Newsweek, 82–87.

Cabeza, R., Anderson, N. D., Locantore, J. K., & McIntosh, A. R. (2002). Aging gracefully: Compensatory brain activity in high-performing older adults. NeuroImage, 17, 1394–1402.

Cabeza, R., & Nyberg, L. (2003). Special issue of functional neuroimaging of memory. Neuropsychologia, 41, 241–244.

Cacioppo, J. T. (2002). Social neuroscience: Understanding the pieces fosters understanding the whole and vice versa. American Psychologist, 57, 819–831.

Cacioppo, J. T., & Berntson, G. G. (2002). Social neuroscience. In J. T. Cacioppo, G. G. Berntson, R. Adolphs, C. S. Carter, R. J. Davidson, M. K. McClintock, B. S. McEwen, M. J. Meaney, D. L. Schacter, E. M. Sternberg, S. S. Suomi, & S. E. Taylor (Eds.), Foundations of social neuroscience (pp. 1–9). Cambridge, MA: MIT Press.

Cacioppo, J. T., Berntson, G. G., Larsen, J. R., Poehlmann, K. M., & Ito, T. A. (2000). The psychophysiology of emotion. In M. Lewis & J. M. Haviland-Jones (Eds.), Handbook of emotions (2nd ed., pp. 173–191). New York: Guilford.

Cacioppo, J. T., Berntson, G. G., Lorig, T. S., Norris, C. J., Rickett, E., & Nusbaum, H. (2003). Just because you're imaging the brain doesn't mean you can stop using your head: A primer and set of first principles. Journal of Personality and Social Psychology, 85, 650–661.

Cacioppo, J. T., Klein, D. J., Berntson, G. G., & Hatfield, E. (1993). The psychophysiology of emotion. In M. Lewis & J. M. Haviland (Eds.), Handbook of emotions. New York: Guilford.

Cacioppo, J. T., & Petty, R. E. (1982). The need for cognition. Journal of Personality and Social Psychology, 42, 116–131.

Cahill, L. (2005). His brain, her brain. Scientific American, 292, 40–47.

Cahill, L., Prins, B., Weber, M., & McGaugh, J. L. (1994). B-adrenergic activation and memory for emotional events. Nature, 371, 702–704.

Cahill, L., Uncapher, M., Kilpatrick, L., Alkire, M. T., & Turner, J. (2004). Sex-related hemispheric lateralization of amygdala function in emotionally influenced memory: An fMRI investigation. Learning & Memory, 11, 261–266.

Caldwell, J. C., Orubuloye, I. O., & Caldwell, P. (1997). Male and female circumcision in Africa from a regional to a specific Nigerian examination. Social Science & Medicine, 44, 1181–1193.

Callahan, C. M. (2000). Intelligence and giftedness. In R. J. Sternberg (Ed.), Handbook of intelligence. New York: Cambridge University Press.

Calle, E. E., Rodriguez, C., Walker-Thurmond, K., & Thun, M. J. (2003). Overweight, obesity, and mortality from cancer in a prospectively studied cohort of U.S. adults. New England Journal of Medicine, 348, 1625–1638.

Calvo, M. G., & Carreiras, M. (1993). Selective influence of test anxiety on reading processes. British Journal of Psychology, 84, 375–388.

Camelot Press Office (CPO). (2006). 2,000 millionaires: The national lottery millioinaire survey [On-line]. Available: www.camelotgroup.co.uk/2000Millionaires MORISurvey.pdf

Camp, G. C. (1994). A longitudinal study of correlates of creativity. Creativity Research Journal, 7, 125–144.

Campbell, D. (2003, May 2). With pot and porn outstripping corn, America's black economy is flying high. The Guardian.

Campbell, F. A., Pungello, E. P., Miller-Johnson, S., Burchinal, M., & Ramey, C. T. (2001). The development of cognitive and academic abilities: Growth curves from an early childhood educational experiment. Developmental Psychology, 37, 231–242.

Campo-Flores, A., & Thomas, E. (2006, May 8). Rehabbing Rush. Newsweek, 26–29.

Canfield, R. L. (2003, August 5). Cited in J. E. Brody, Even low lead levels pose perils for children. New York Times, D7.

Canli, T., Desmond, J. E., Zhao, Z., & Gabrieli, J. D. E. (2002). Sex differences in the neural basis of emotional memories. Proceedings of the National Academy of Sciences, 99, 10789–10794.

Capello, E., Saccardi, R., Murialdo, A., Gualandi, F., Pagliai, F., Bacigalupo, A., Marmont, A., Uccello, A., Inglese, M., Bruzzi, P., Sormani, M. P., Cocco, E., Meucci, G., Massacesi, L., Bertolotto, A., Lugaresi, A., Merelli, E., Solari, A., Filippi, M., Mancardi, G. L., & the Italian GITMO-Neuro Intergroup on ASCT for Multiple Sclerosis. (2005). Intense immunosuppression followed by autologous stem cell transplantation in severe multiple sclerosis. Neurological Sciences, 26, 200–203.

Caplan, N., Choy, M. H., & Whitmore, J. K. (1992). Indochinese refugee families and academic achievement. Scientific American, 266, 36–42.

Caplan, P. (1994, June 5). Cited in A. Japenga, DMS. Los Angeles Times Magazine.

Caporael, L. R. (2001). Evolutionary psychology: Toward a unifying theory and a hybrid science. Annual Review of Psychology, 52, 607–628.

Carducci, B. J. (2006). Psychology of personality. Boston: Blackwell Publishing.

Carey, B. (2002, December 16). The brain in love. Los Angeles Times, F1.

Carey, B. (2004, December 27). Autism therapies still a mystery, but parents take a leap of faith. The New York Times, A1, A14.

Carey, B. (2006, January 31). Holding loved one's hand can calm jittery neurons. The New York Times, D7.

Cariaga, D. (1995, April 9). The return of the prodigy. Los Angeles Times/Calendar, 54–55.

Carlin, A. (2000, July 4). Cited in J. Robbins, Virtual reality finds a real place as a medical aid. New York Times, D6.

Carlson, J. M. (1990). Subjective ideological similarity between candidates and supporters: A study of party elites. Political Psychology, 11, 485–492.

Carlson, N. R. (1998). Physiology of behavior (6th ed.). Boston: Allyn & Bacon.

Carne, R. P., Vogrin, S., Litewka, L., & Cook, M. J. (2006). Cerebral cortex: An MRI-based study of volume and variance with age and sex. Journal of Clinical Neuroscience, 13, 60–72.

Caroff, S. N., Mann, S. C., Campbell, E. C., & Sullivan, K. A. (2002). Movement disorders associated with atypical antipsychotic drugs. Journal of Clinical Psychiatry, 63 (supplement 4), 12–19.

Carpenter, S. (2001, February). Of mice (and rats and birds) and amendments. Monitor on Psychology, 32.

Carpenter, W. (2003, May 20). Cited in E. Goode, Leading drugs for psychosis come under new scrutiny. New York Times, A1.

Carskadon, M. A. (2006). The sleep of America's children [On-line]. Available: http://www.sleepfoundation.org/hottopics/index.php?secid=11&id=82. Accessed October 5, 2006.

Carstensen, L. (2006, January 31). Cited in T. Valeo, The aging brain puts accent on the positive. St. Petersburg Times.

Cart, J. (2002, February 20). Study finds Utah leads nation in antidepressant use. Los Angeles Times, A6.

Carter, O. L., Pettigrew, J. D., Hasler, F., Wallis, G. M., Liu, G. B., Hell, D., & Vollenweider, F. X. (2005). Modulating the rate and rhythmicity of perceptual rivalry alterations with the mixed 5-HT2A and 5-HT1A agonist psilocybin. Neuropsychopharmacology, 30, 1154–1162.

Cartwright, R. (1988, July–August). Cited in Psychology Today.

Cartwright, R. (2002, July 15). Cited in M. H. Gossard, Taking control. Newsweek, 47.

Caspi, A. (2000). The child is father of the man: Personality continuities from childhood to adulthood. Journal of Personality and Social Psychology, 78, 158–172.

Caspi, A., & Roberts, B. W. (1999). Personality continuity and change across the life course. In L. A. Pervin & O. P. John (Eds.), Handbook of personality (2nd ed.). New York: Guilford.

Caspi, A., Roberts, B. W., & Shiner, R. L. (2005). Personality development: Stability and change. Annual Review of Psychology, 453–484.

Cassady, J. C., & Johnson, R. E. (2002). Cognitive test anxiety and academic performance. Contemporary Educational Psychology, 27, 270–295.

Casselman, A. (2006, January). Blinking flips an off switch in brain. Discover, 42.

Catalano, S. M. (2006, September). National crime victimization survey: Criminal victimization, 2005. Bureau of Justice Statistics Bulletin, 1–12.

Cattell, R. B. (1943). The description of personality: Basic traits resolved into clusters. Journal of Abnormal and Social Psychology, 38, 476–506.

References

Cavanagh, J. T. O., Carson, A. J., Sharpe, M., & Lawrie, S. M. (2003). Psychological autopsy studies of suicide: A systematic review. *Psychological Medicine, 33,* 395–405.

CBS News. (2004, June 16). *Tony Hawk takes off* [On-line]. Available: http://www.cbsnews.com/stories/ 2002/12/ 10/60II/main532509.shtml

CBS News. (2004, September 24). *Assisted suicide* [On-line]. Available: http://www.cbs.ca/includes/ printablestory.jsp

CDC (Centers for Disease Control and Prevention). (2000). Declines in lung cancer rates? California, 1988–1997. *Morbidity and Mortality Weekly Report, 49,* 1066–1069.

CDC. (2004, December). Teenagers in the United States: Sexual activity, contraceptive use, and childbearing, 2002. *Vital Health Statistics, 23*(24).

CDC. (2006a). Cited in Associated Press, CDD report finds obesity rates rising in American youths, men. *The San Diego Union-Tribune,* A7.

CDC. (2006b). Cited in K. Tumulty, The politics of fat. *Time,* 40–43.

CDC. (2006c). *Overweight and obesity: An overview* [On-line]. Available: http://cdc.gov/nccdphp/dnpa/ obesity/contributing_factors.htm

CDC. (2006d). Preventing suicide. *Program Activities Guide.* Atlanta, GA: Author.

Ceci, S. J. (2000, April 25). Cited in J. E. Brody, Memories of things that never were. *New York Times,* D8.

Ceci, S. J., Rosenblum, T., de Bruyn, E., & Lee, D. Y. (1997). A bio-ecological model of intellectual development: Moving beyond h2. In R. J. Sternberg & E. Grigorenko (Eds.), *Intelligence, heredity, and environment.* New York: Cambridge University Press.

Ceniceros, S., & Brown, G. R. (1998). Acupuncture: A review of its history, theories, and indications. *Southern Medical Journal, 91,* 1121–1125.

Cerone, D. (1989, October 22). How to train an 1,800-pound star. *Los Angeles Times/Calendar.*

Cha, A. E. (2005, March 27). Employers replying on personality tests to screen applicants. *Washington Post,* A1.

Chaiken, S., & Eagly, A. H. (1976). Communication modality as a determinant of message persuasiveness and message comprehensibility. *Journal of Personality and Social Psychology, 34,* 605–614.

Chambless, D. L., & Ollendick, T. H. (2001). Empirically supported psychological interventions: Controversies and evidence. *Annual Review of Psychology, 52,* 685–716.

Chance, P. (2006). *Learning & behavior* (5th ed.). Belmont, CA: Thomson Wadsworth.

Chapell, M. S., Blanding, Z. B., Silverstein, M. E., Takahashi, M., Newman, G., Gubi, A., & McCann, N. (2005). Test anxiety and academic performance in undergraduate and graduate students. *Journal of Educational Psychology, 97,* 268–274.

Charkalis, D. M. (2005, December 22). Delayed diagnosis: Dyslexia. *USA Today,* 8D.

Charmoli, R. (2006, May 13). Former Spokesman for Aryan Nations speaks about hate groups. *Cadillac News.*

Charney, D. (2003). Cited in C. Holden, Future brightening for depression treatment. *Science, 302,* 810–813.

Chasnoff, I. (1997, December). Cited in B. Azar, Researchers debunk myth of the "crack baby." *APA Monitor.*

Chaudri, O., Small, C., & Bloom, S. (2006). Gastrointestinal hormones regulating appetite. *Philosophical Transactions of the Royal Society of London. Series B, Biological Sciences, 29,* 1187–1209.

Chavez, S. (1994, January 3). Tough stand on attendance pays off at South Gate High. *Los Angeles Times.*

Chavira, D. A., Stein, M. B., & Malcarne, V. L. (2002). Scrutinizing the relationship between shyness and social phobia. *Anxiety Disorders, 16,* 585–598.

Check, E. (2003). Battle of the mind. *Nature, 422,* 370–372.

Chellappah, N. K., Viegnehas, H., Milgrom, P., & Lo, B. L. (1990). Prevalence of dental anxiety and fear in children in Singapore. *Community Dentistry Oral Epidemiology, 18,* 269–271.

Chemers, M. M., Hu, L., & Garcia, B. F. (2001). Academic self-efficacy and first-year college student performance and adjustment. *Journal of Educational Psychology, 93,* 55–64.

Chiavegatto, S., & Nelson, R. J. (2003). Interaction of nitric oxide and serotonin in aggressive behavior. *Hormones and Behavior, 44,* 233–241.

Chin, D., & Kameoka, V. A. (2006). Sociocultural influences. In M. Hersen & J. C. Thomas (Eds.), *Comprehensive handbook of personality and psychopathology: Adult psychopathology* (Vol. 2, pp. 67–84). Hoboken, NJ: John Wiley & Sons.

Chiou, W. (2006). Adolescents' sexual self-disclosure on the Internet: Deindividuation and impression management. *Adolescence, 41,* 547–561.

Chokroverty, S. (2000). *Sleep disorders medicine* (2nd ed.). Boston: Butterworth-Heinemann.

Chomsky, N. (1957). *Syntactic structures.* The Hague: Mouton.

Christensen, D. (2001). Medicinal mimicry. *Science News, 159,* 74–75.

Christensen, D. (2003). Dietary dilemmas. *Science News, 163,* 88–90.

Christman, M. F. (2006, April 18). Common genetic link to obesity is discovered. *The New York Times,* O4.

Chu, J. A., Loewenstein, R., Dell, P. F., Barach, P. M., Kluft, R. P., Gelinas, D. J., Van der Hart, O., Dalenberg, C. J., Nijenhuis, E. R. S., Bowman, E. S., Boon, S., Goodwin, J., Jacobson, M., Ross, C. A., Sar, V., Fine, C. G., Frankel, A. S., Coons, P. M., Courtois, C. A., Gold, S. N., & Howell, E. J. (2005). Guidelines for treating dissociative identity disorder in adults. *Journal of Trauma & Dissociation, 6,* 69–149.

Chua, H. F., Boland, J. E., & Nisbett, R. E. (2005). Cultural variation in eye movements during scene perception. *Proceedings of the National Academy of Sciences, 102,* 12629–12633.

Chumlea, W. C., Schubert, C. M., Roche, A. F., Kulin, H. E., Lee, P. A., Himes, J. H., & Sun, S. S. (2003). Age at menarche and racial comparisons in U.S. girls. *Pediatrics, 111,* 110–113.

Chwalisz, K., Diener, E., & Gallagher, D. (1988). Autonomic arousal feedback and emotional experience: Evidence from the spinal cord injury. *Journal of Personality and Social Psychology, 54,* 820–828.

Cialdini, R. B. (2001). *Influence: Science and practice* (4th ed.). New York: Allyn & Bacon.

Cialdini, R. B. (2003, February). The science of persuasion. *Scientific American,* 76–81.

Cialdini, R. B., & Goldstein, N. J. (2004). Social influence: Compliance and conformity. *Annual Review of Psychology, 55,* 591–621.

Clark, L. A., Watson, D., & Reynolds, S. (1995). Diagnosis and classification of psychopathology: Challenges to the current system and future directions. *Annual Review of Psychology, 46,* 121–153.

Clarke, A. M., & Clarke, A. D. B. (1989). The later cognitive effects on early intervention. *Intelligence, 13,* 289–297.

Clausen, L. (2004). Review of studies evaluating psychotherapy in bulimia nervosa: The influence of research methods. *Scandinavian Journal of Psychology, 45,* 247–252.

Clay, R. A. (1997, April). Is assisted suicide ever a rational choice? *APA Monitor.*

Clay, R. A. (2002, September). A renaissance for humanistic psychology. *Monitor on Psychology,* 42–43.

Clements, A. M., Rimbrodt, S. L., Abel, J. R., Blankner, J. G., Mostofsky, S. H., Pekar, J. J., Denckla, M. B., & Cutting, L. E. (2006). Sex differences in cerebral laterality of language and visuospatial processing. *Brain & Language, 98,* 150–158.

Cleveland, H. H., Jacobson, K. C., Lipinski, J. J., & Rose, D. C. (2000). Genetic and shared environmental contributions to the relationship between the home environment and child and adolescent achievement. *Intelligence, 28,* 69–86.

Cloud, J. (2002, November 4). Is pot good for you? *Time,* 62–66.

Coates, T. P. (2006, May 8). When parents are the threat. *Time,* 181–182.

Coccaro, E. F., & Kavoussi, R. J. (1997). Fluoxetine and impulsive aggressive behavior in personality-disordered subjects. *Archives of General Psychiatry, 54,* 1081–1088.

Cochran, F. (2007, February 16). *About Floyd Cochran* [On-line]. Available: http://www.geocities.com/ onemansmind/hg/Cochran.html

Cohen, D. (2002). Cited in B. Bower, Psychotic biology, *Science News, 162,* 195–196.

Cohen, D. B. (1979). *Sleep and dreaming: Origins, nature and functions.* New York: Pergamon Press.

Cohen, G. (2006, January 16). The myth of the midlife crisis. *Newsweek,* 82–87.

Cohen, J. S. (2001). Comparison of FDA reports of patient deaths associated with sildenafil and with injectable alprostadil. *The Annals of Pharmacotherapy, 35,* 285–288.

Cohen, N. J. (1984). Preserved learning capacity in amnesia: Evidence for multiple memory systems. In L. R. Squire & N. Butters (Eds.), *Neuropsychology of memory.* New York: Guilford.

Cohen, S. (2003). Social stress, social support, and the susceptibility to the common cold. *American Psychological Society, 16,* 13.

Cohen, S., Tyrrell, D. A. J., & Smith, A. P. (1997). Psychological stress in humans and susceptibility to the common cold. In T. W. Miller (Ed.), *Clinical disorders and stressful life events.* Madison, CT: International Universities Press.

Cohen, S. L. (2000, March 22). Hi, I'm your doctor. I haven't slept in 36 hours. *USA Today,* 29A.

Coie, J. D., & Dodge, K. A. (1998). Aggression and antisocial behavior. In W. Damon & R. M. Lerner (Eds.), *Handbook of child psychology* (Vol. 1). New York: John Wiley & Sons.

Colangelo, N. (1997). The "termites" grow up and grow old. *Contemporary Psychology, 42,* 208–209.

Cole, S. O. (2005). An update on the effects of marijuana & its potential medical use: Forensic focus. *The Forensic Examiner, 14.3,* 14.

Coles, M. E., & Horng, B. (2006). Social anxiety disorder. In M. Hersen & J. C. Thomas (Eds.), *Comprehensive handbook of personality and psychopathology: Adult psychopathology* (Vol. 2, pp. 138–153). Hoboken, NJ: John Wiley & Sons.

Coles, R. (Ed.). (2000). *The Erik Erikson reader.* New York: W. W. Norton & Company.

Collings, S., & King, M. (1994). Ten-year follow-up of 50 patients with bulimia nervosa. *British Journal of Psychiatry, 164,* 80–87.

Collins, W. A., Maccoby, E. E., Steinberg, L., Hetherington, E. M., & Bornstein, M. H. (2000). Contemporary research on parenting. *American Psychologist, 55,* 218–232.

Colom, R., Juan-Espinosa, M., Abad, F., & Garcia, L. F. (2000). Negligible sex differences in general intelligence. *Intelligence, 28,* 57–68.

Colorado Springs Gazette. (2002, December 22). Reality stems from pastor's vision.

Comarow, A. (2001, April 23). Scary news, soothing numbers. *U.S. News & World Report*, 74.

Condor, B. (2004, October 18). Living well: Let moderation be the guide to caffeine enjoyment [On-line]. Available: http://seattlepi.nwsource.com/health/195442_condor18.html

Conners, C. K., March, J. S., Frances, A., Wells, K. C., & Ross, R. (2001). Treatment of attention deficit-hyperactivity disorder: Expert consensus guidelines. *Journal of Attention Disorders, 4*, 7–128.

Connor, J. M., Povrazli, S., Ferrer-Wreder, L., & Grahame, K. M. (2004). The relation of age, gender, ethnicity, and risk behaviors to self-esteem among students in nonmainstream schools. *Adolescence, 39*, 457–473.

Connor, L. (1982). In A. J. Marsella & G. M. White (Eds.), *Cultural conceptions of mental health and therapy*. Boston: D. Reidel.

Cook, G. (2002, January 2). Aha! Eureka moments start with confusion and end with discovery. *San Diego Union Tribune*, F1.

Cooper, M. J. (2005). Cognitive theory in anorexia nervosa and bulimia nervosa: Progress, development and future directions. *Clinical Psychology Review, 25*, 511–531.

Cooper, P. J., Zheng, Y., Richard, C., Vavrik, J., Heinrichs, B., & Siegmund, G. J. (2003). The impact of hands-free message reception response on driving task performance. *Accident Analysis and Prevention, 35*, 23–35.

Cooper, R. T. (1999, April 14). Head Start's fresh start. *Los Angeles Times*, B2.

Copeland, L. (1999, December 16). Meet South's new sheriffs. *USA Today*, A1.

Copeland, L. (2007, February 14). Research: Red-light cameras work. *USA Today*.

Coren, S., & Ward, L. M. (1993). *Sensation and perception* (4th ed.). San Diego: Harcourt Brace Jovanovich.

Corey, G. (2005). *Theory and practice of counseling and psychotherapy* (7th ed.). Belmont, CA: Brooks/Cole–Thomson Learning.

Cormier, S., & Nurius, P. S. (2003). *Interviewing and change strategies for helpers: Fundamental skills and cognitive behavioral interventions* (5th ed.). Pacific Grove, CA: Brooks/Cole.

Courchesne, E., Carper, R., & Akshoomoff, N. (2003). Evidence of brain overgrowth in the first year of life in autism. *Journal of the American Medical Association, 290*, 337–344.

Covington, M. V. (2000). Goal theory, motivation, and school achievement: An integrative review. *Annual Review of Psychology, 51*, 171–200.

Cowings, P. S., Toscano, W. B., Timbers, A., Casey, C., & Hufnagel, J. (2005). Autogenic feedback training exercise: A treatment for airsickness in military pilots. *International Journal of Aviation Psychology, 15*, 395–412.

Cowley, G. (2000a, April 24). Looking beyond Viagra. *Newsweek*, 77–78.

Cowley, G. (2000b, July 31). Understanding autism. *Newsweek*, 46–55.

Cowley, G. (2002, June 24). The disappearing mind. *Newsweek*, 42–50.

Cowley, G. (2003, February 24). Our bodies our fears. *Newsweek*, 42–49.

Coyne, J. C. (1994). Self-reported distress: Analog or ersatz depression? *Psychological Bulletin, 116*, 29–45.

Craig, R. J. (2004). *Clinical and diagnostic interviewing* (2nd ed.). Lanham, MD: Jason Aronson.

Craik, F. I. M., & Lockhart, R. S. (1972). Levels of processing: A framework for memory research. *Journal of Verbal Learning and Verbal Behavior, 11*, 671–684.

Craik, F. I. M., & Tulving, E. (1975). Depth of processing and the retention of words in episodic memory. *Journal of Experimental Psychology: General, 104*, 268–294.

Cramer, P. (2003). Defense mechanisms and physiological reactivity to stress. *Journal of Personality, 71*, 221–244.

Cramer, P. (2006). *Protecting the self: Defense mechanisms in action*. New York: Guilford Press.

Craske, M. G., & Barlow, D. H. (2001). Panic disorder and agoraphobia. In D. H. Barlow (Ed.), *Clinical handbook of psychological disorders* (3rd ed.). New York: Guilford Press.

Crawford, H. J., Gur, R. C., Skolnick, B., Gur, R. E., & Benson, D. M. (1993). Effects of hypnosis on regional cerebral blood flow during ischemic pain with and without suggested hypnotic analgesia. *International Journal of Psychophysiology, 15*, 181–195.

Crawford, M., & Popp, D. (2002). Sexual double standards: A review and methodological critique of two decades of research. *The Journal of Sex Research, 40*, 13–26.

Crea, J. (2003, September 26). *Meth dealer details D.C. drug scene* [On-line]. Available: http://www.washblade.com/print.cfm?content_id= 1177

Creed, F. (1993). Stress and psychosomatic disorders. In L. Goldberger & S. Breznitz (Eds.), *Handbook of stress: Theoretical and clinical aspects* (2nd ed.). New York: Free Press.

Crenson, M. (2005, September 11). What makes a sexual predator? *North County Times*.

Creswell, J. (2006, December 17). How suite it isn't: A dearth of female bosses. *The New York Times*, 3.

Crews, F. (1996). The verdict on Freud. *Psychological Science, 7*, 63–68.

Crews, F. (Ed.). (1999). *Unauthorized Freud: Doubters confront a legend*. New York: Penguin.

Crews, F. (2001, January 2). Cited in M. Crenson, Brain growth gets blame for turbulent teen years. *USA Today*, 6D.

Crews, F. (2006, July 9). Cited in K. Butler, Alcohol harder on teen brains than thought. *The San Francisco Chronicle*, B1.

Crick, F. (2002, November 17). Cited in M. A. Hiltzik, Nobel Laureate Francis H.C. Crick discovered DNA. Now he's hunting for the very essence of our being—the course of conscious thought. *Los Angeles Times Magazine*, 12–15.

Crooks, R., & Baur, K. (2002). *Our sexuality* (8th ed.). Pacific Grove, CA: Wadsworth.

Crooks, R., & Baur, K. (2005). *Our sexuality* (9th ed.). Belmont, CA: Thomson Wadsworth.

Crow, T. J. (1985). The two syndrome concept: Origins and current status. *Schizophrenia Bulletin, 11*, 471–486.

Crowder, R. G. (1992). Eidetic imagery. In L. R. Squire (Ed.), *Encyclopedia of learning and memory*. New York: Macmillan.

Csernansky, J. G., Mahmoud, R., & Brenner, R. (2002). A comparison of risperidone and haloperidol for the prevention of relapse in patients with schizophrenia. *The New England Journal of Medicine, 346*, 16–23.

Cuijpers, P. (2003). Three decades of drug prevention research. Drugs: Education, *Prevention and Policy, 10*, 7–20.

Cull, W. L., & Zechmeister, E. B. (1994). The learning ability paradox in adult metamemory research: Where are the metamemory differences between good and poor learners? *Memory & Cognition, 22*, 249–257.

Cullen, L. T. (2006, April 3). SATS for J-O-B-s. *Time*, 89.

Cullen, M. J., & Sackett, P. R. (2003). Integrity testing in the workplace. In J. C. Thomas & M. Hersen (Eds.), *Comprehensive handbook of psychological assessment, industrial and organizational assessment* (pp. 149–165). Hoboken, NJ: John Wiley & Sons.

Culp, R. E., Culp, A. M., Osofsky, J. D., & Osofsky, H. J. (1991). Adolescent and older mothers' interaction patterns with their six-month-old infants. *Journal of Adolescence, 14*, 195–200.

Cummings, B. J., Uchida, N., Tamaki, S. J., Salazar, D. L., Hooschmand, M., Summers, R., Gage, F. H., & Anderson, A. J. (2005). Human neural stem cells differentiate and promote locomotor recovery in spinal cord-injured mice. *Proceedings of the National Academy of Sciences of the United States of America, 102*, 14069–14074.

Cunningham, F. G., Hauth, J. C., Leveno, K. J., Gilstrap, L., III, Bloom, S. L., & Wenstrom, K. D. (Eds.). (2005). *Williams obstetrics* (22nd ed.). New York: McGraw-Hill.

Curtiss, S. (1977). *Genie: A psycholinguistic study of a modern-day "wild child."* New York: Academic Press.

Czeisler, C. A. (1994). Cited in R. Nowak, Chronobiologists out of sync over light therapy patents. *Science, 263*, 1217–1218.

Czeisler, C. A., Duffy, J. F., Shanahan, T. L., Brown, E. N., Mitchell, J. F., Rimmer, D. W., Ronda, J. M., Siva, E. J., Allan, J. S., Emens, J. S., Dijk, K., & Kronauer, R. E. (1999). Stability, precision, and near-24-hour period of the human circadian pacemaker. *Science, 284*, 2177–2181.

Czeisler, C. A., Shanahan, T. L., Klerman, E. B., Martens, H., Brotman, D. J., Emens, J. S., Klein, T., & Rizzo, J. F. (1995). Suppression of melatonin secretion in some blind patients by exposure to bright light. *New England Journal of Medicine, 332*, 6–11.

Czeisler, C. A., Winkelman, J. R., & Richardson, G. S. (2006). Sleep disorders. In S. L. Hauser (Ed.), *Harrison's neurology in clinical medicine* (pp. 169–183). New York: McGraw-Hill.

Dackis, C. A., & O'Brien, C. P. (2001). Cocaine dependence: A disease of the brain's reward center. *Journal of Substance Abuse Treatment, 21*, 111–117.

Dackis, C. A., & O'Brien, C. P. (2003). Glutamatergic agents for cocaine dependence. *Annals of the New York Academy of Sciences, 1003*, 325–345.

Dalgard, O. S., Bjork, S., & Tambs, K. (1995). Social support, negative life events and mental health. *British Journal of Psychiatry, 166*, 29–34.

Dallman, M. F., Pecoraro, N. C., & la Fleur, S. E. (2005). Chronic stress and comfort foods: Self-medication and abdominal obesity. *Brain, Behavior, and Immunity, 19*, 275–280.

Damasio, A. (1999, October 19). Cited in S. Blakeslee, Brain damage during infancy stunts moral learning, study finds. *Los Angeles Times*, A1.

Damasio, A. (2006, August 7). Cited in D. Vergano, Study: Ask with care. *USA Today*, 5D.

Damasio, H., Brabowski, T., Frank, R., Galaburda, A. M., & Damasio, A. R. (1994). The return of Phineas Gage: Clues about the brain from the skull of a famous patient. *Science, 264*, 1102–1105.

Dambro, M. R. (Ed.). (2006). *Griffith's 5-minute clinical consult* (14th ed.). Philadelphia: Lippincott Williams & Wilkins.

Damon, W. (1999, August). The moral development of children. *Scientific American*, 73–78.

Dandoy, A. C., & Goldstein, A. G. (1990). The use of cognitive appraisal to reduce stress reactions: A replication. *Journal of Social Behavior and Personality, 5*, 275–285.

Daniszewski, J. (1997, June 25). Female circumcision ban nullified. *Los Angeles Times*, A4.

Dapretto, M., Davies, M. S., Pfeifer, J. H., Scott, A. A., Sigman, M., Bookheimer, S. Y., & Iacoboni, M. (2006). Understanding emotions in others: Mirror neuron dysfunction in children with autism spectrum disorders. *Nature Neuroscience, 9*, 28–30.

References

DARE (Drug Abuse Resistance Education). (2006a). *What is D.A.R.E.?* [On-line]. Available: http://www.dare.com/home/Curriculum/what_is_DARE.asp

DARE. (2006b). *About D.A.R.E.* [On-line]. Available: http://www.dare.com/home/about_dare.asp

Darwin, C. (1859). *The origin of species by means of natural selection or the preservation of favored races in the struggle for life.* London: John Murray.

Darwin, C. (1872; reprinted 1965). *The expression of the emotions in man and animals.* Chicago: University of Chicago Press.

Davey, M. (2005, March 6). Suspect in 10 Kansas murders lived an intensely ordinary life. *The New York Times,* 1.

Davidson, P. S. R., & Glisky, E. L. (2002). Is flashbulb memory a special instance of source memory? Evidence from older adults. *Memory, 10,* 99–111.

Davies, I. R. L., & Corbett, G. G. (1997). A cross-cultural study of colour grouping: Evidence for weak linguistic relativity. *British Journal of Psychology, 88,* 493–517.

Davis, J. (2003, May 23). Cited in K. S. Peterson, Sexually active teens also are often clueless. *USA Today,* 8D.

Davis, J. (2005, August). The straight dope on cannabis-inspired meds. *Popular Science,* 44.

Davis, J. L., & Petretic-Jackson, P. A. (2000). The impact of child sexual abuse on adult interpersonal functioning: A review and synthesis of the empirical literature. *Aggression and Violent Behavior, 5,* 291–328.

Davis, J. M., Chen, N., & Glick, I. D. (2003). A meta-analysis of the efficacy of second-generation antipsychotics. *Archives of General Psychiatry, 60,* 553–564.

Davis, K. (2003). Cited in C. Holden, Deconstructing schizophrenia. *Science, 299,* 333–335.

Davis, M. C., Matthews, K. A., & Twamley, E. W. (1999). Is life more difficult on Mars or Venus? A meta-analytic review of sex differences in major and minor life events. *Annals of Behavioral Medicine, 21,* 83–97.

Davis, R. (2005, March 2). Is 16 too young to drive a car? *USA Today.*

Davison, G. C., & Neale, J. M. (1990). *Abnormal psychology* (3rd ed.). New York: Wiley.

Davison, G. C., & Neale, J. M. (1994). *Abnormal psychology* (6th ed.). New York: Wiley.

Dawood, K., Pillard, R. C., Horvath, C., Revelle, W., & Bailey, J. M. (2000). Familial aspects of male homosexuality. *Archives of Sexual Behavior, 29,* 155–163.

Dawson, G., Carver, L., Meltzoff, A. N., Panagiotides, H., McPartland, J., & Webb, S. J. (2002). Neural correlates of face and object recognition in young children with autism spectrum disorders, developmental delay, and typical development. *Child Development, 73,* 700–717.

De Fruyt, F., Bartels, M., Van Leeuwen, K. G., Clercq, B. D., Decuyper, M., & Mervielde, I. (2006). Five types of personality continuity in childhood and adolescence. *Journal of Personality and Social Psychology, 91,* 538–552.

de Grott, J. M. (2002). The complexity of the role of social support in relation to the psychological distress associated with cancer. *Journal of Psychosomatic Research, 52,* 277–278.

De Gucht, V., & Fischler, B. (2002). Somatization: A critical review of conceptual and methodological issues. *Psychosomatics, 43,* 1–9.

De Martino, B. (2006a, August 3). *Cited in University College London Media Relations, Irrational decisions driven by emotions* [On-line]. Available: http://ucl.ac.uk/media/library/decisionbrain

De Martino, B. (2006b, August 7). Cited in D. Vergano, Study: Ask with care. *USA Today,* 6D.

De Martino, B., Kumaran, D., Seymour, B., & Dolan, R. J. (2006, August). Frames, biases, and rational decision-making in the human brain. *Science, 313,* 684–687.

de Rivera, J. (1997). The construction of false memory syndrome: The experience of retractors. *Psychological Inquiry, 8,* 271–292.

de Waal, F. B. M. (2002). Evolutionary psychology: The wheat and the chaff. *Current Directions in Psychological Science, 11,* 187–190.

Dean, C. (2006, September 19). Bias is hurting women in science, panel reports. *The New York Times,* A20.

DeAngelis, T. (1966, March). Women's contributions large; recognition isn't. *Monitor American Psychological Association.*

DeAngelis, T. (1994, February). People's drug of choice offers potent side effects. *APA Monitor.*

DeAngelis, T. (2002, March). Binge-eating disorder: What's the best treatment? *Monitor on Psychology,* 30–32.

deCharms, R. (1980). The origins of competence and achievement motivation in personal causation. In L. J. Fyans, Jr. (Ed.), *Achievement motivation.* New York: Plenum Press.

deCharms, R. C., Maeda, F., Glover, G. H., Ludlow, D., Pauly, J. M., Soneji, D., Gabrieli, J. D. E., & Mackey, S. C. (2005). Control over brain activation and pain learned by using real-time functional MRI. *Proceedings of the National Academy of Sciences, 102,* 18626–18631.

Deci, E. L., Koestner, R., & Ryan, R. M. (1999). A meta-analytic review of experiments examining the effects of extrinsic rewards on intrinsic motivation. *Psychological Bulletin, 125,* 627–668.

Deci, E. L., & Moller, A. C. (2005). The concept of competence. In A. J. Elliot & C. S. Dweck (Eds.), *Handbook of competence and motivation* (pp. 579–597). New York: Guilford Press.

Deci, E. L., & Ryan, R. M. (1985). *Intrinsic motivation and self-determination in human behavior.* New York: Plenum Press.

Deckro, G. R. (2002, September 11). Cited in M. Duenwald, Students find another staple of campus life: Stress. *New York Times,* D5.

Deffenbacher, J. (2003, March). Cited in J. D. Holloway, Advances in anger management. *Monitor on Psychology,* 54–55.

Deffenbacher, J. (2005, June). Cited in M. Dittmann, Anger on the road. *Monitor on Psychology, 36,* 26.

Deffenbacher, J. L., Dahlen, E. R., Lynch, R. S., Morris, C. D., & Gowensmith, W. N. (2000). An application of Beck's cognitive therapy to general anger reduction. *Cognitive Therapy and Research, 24,* 689–697.

DeGue, S., & DiLillo, D. (2005). "You would if you loved me": Toward an improved conceptual and etiological understanding of nonphysical male sexual coercion. *Aggression and Violent Behavior, 10,* 513–532.

Dehaene-Lambertz, G., Dehaene, S., & Hertz-Pannier, L. (2002). Functional neuroimaging of speech perception in infants. *Science, 298,* 2013–2015.

DeKeukelaere, L. (2006, February/March). Optimism prolongs life. *Scientific American Mind, 17,* 7.

DeLisi, L. E., Sakuma, M., Maurizio, A. M., Relja, M., & Hoff, A. L. (2004). Cerebral ventricular change over the first 10 years after the onset of schizophrenia. *Psychiatric Research: Neuroimaging, 130,* 57–70.

Dement, W. C. (1999). *The promise of sleep.* New York: Random House.

Dement, W. C., & Kleitman, N. (1957). The relation of eye movements during sleep to dream activity: An objective method for the study of dreaming. *Journal of Experimental Psychology, 53,* 339–346.

Dennerstein, L., Dudley, E., & Burger, H. (1997). Well-being and the menopausal transition. *Journal of Psychosomatic Obstetrics and Gynecology, 18,* 95–101.

Denworth, L. (2006, April 10). The sun has finally come out for Alex. *Newsweek,* 26.

DePetrillo, P. (2003, September 8). Cited in J. Ewers, Drinking in your genes. *U.S. News & World Report,* 44.

Deregowski, J. B. (1980). *Illusions, patterns and pictures: A crosscultural perspective.* Orlando, FL: Academic Press.

Derlega, V. J., Winstead, B. A., & Jones, W. H. (2005). *Personality: Comtemporary theory and research* (3rd ed.). Belmont, CA: Thomson Wadsworth.

DeRubeis, R. J., Hollon, S. D., Amsterdam, J. D., Shelton, R. C., Young, P. R., Salomon, R. M., O'Reardon, J. P., Lovett, M. L., Gladis, M. M., Brown, L. L., & Gallop, R. (2005). Cognitive therapy vs. medications in the treatment of moderate to severe depression. *Archives of General Psychiatry, 62,* 409–416.

Despopoulos, S., & Silbernagl. S. (2003). *Color atlas of physiology* (5th ed.). New York: Thieme Medical.

Devilly, G. J. (2002). Eye movement desensitization and reprocessing. *The Scientific Review of Mental Health Practice, 1*(2).

Devine, P. G., Hamilton, D. L., & Ostrom, T. M. (Eds.). (1994). *Social cognition: Impact on social psychology.* New York: Academic Press.

Di Salvo, S. (2006, August 25). *The story of Luisa: A case of panic attack disorder* [On-line]. Available: http://www.depression-panic.org

Diamond, M., & Sigmundson, H. K. (1997). Sex reassignment at birth. *Archives of Pediatric & Adolescent Medicine, 151,* 298–304.

Dickens, W. T., & Flynn, J. R. (2006). Black Americans reduce the racial IQ gap: Evidence from standardization samples. *Psychological Science, 17,* 913–920.

Diener, E., & Diener, C. (1996). Most people are happy. *Psychological Science, 7,* 181–185.

Diesendruck, G., & Shatz, M. (2001). Two-year-olds' recognition of hierarchies: Evidence from their interpretation of the semantic relation between object labels. *Cognitive Development, 16,* 577–594.

Dietrich, K. (2003, August 5). Cited in J. E. Brody, Even low lead levels pose perils for children. *New York Times,* D7.

Digman, J. M. (1997). Higher-order factors of the Big Five. *Journal of Personality and Social Psychology, 73,* 1246–1256.

DiIulio, R. (2004, October 2). Is time on mammography's side? *Medical Imaging.*

DiLalla, L. F. (2002). Behavior genetics of aggression in children: Review and future directions. *Developmental Review, 22,* 593–622.

Dingfelder, S. F. (2006, March). Fear itself. *Monitor on Psychology, 37,* 22.

Dinnel, D. L., Kleinknecht, R. A., & Tanaka-Matsumi, J. (2002). A cross-cultural comparison of social phobia symptoms. *Journal of Psychopathology and Behavioral Assessment, 24,* 75–84.

Dittmann, M. (2003, February). Psychology's first prescribers. *Monitor on Psychology,* 36–39.

Dittman, M. (2005). Attracting minority students early: Psychology faculty and undergraduates reach out to minority high school students. *Monitor on Psychology, 36,* 30–34.

Dityatev, A. E., & Bolshakov, V. Y. (2005). Amygdala, long-term potentiation, and fear conditioning. *Neuroscientist, 11,* 75–88.

Dixon, W. A., & Reid, J. K. (2000). Positive life events as a moderator of stress-related depressive symptoms. *Journal of Counseling & Development, 78,* 343–347.

Dobbs, D. (2006, February/March). Mastery of emotions. *Scientific American Mind,* 44–49.

Dobelle, W. (2000, January 17). Cited in M. Ritter, Camera wired to brain provides some useful vision for blind man. *San Diego Union-Tribune*, A6.

Dobson, K. S., & Khatri, N. (2000). Cognitive therapy: Looking backward, looking forward. *Journal of Clinical Psychology, 56*, 907–923.

Dolan, M. (1995, February 11). When the mind's eye blinks. *Los Angeles Times*.

Dolan, M. (2002, June 7). Fatherhood transcends biology, high court says. *Los Angeles Times*, A1.

Dolan, R. J. (2002). Emotion, cognition, and behavior. *Science, 298*, 1191–1194.

Doland, A. (2006, February 7). Frenchwoman mauled by dog shows partial face transplant. *The San Diego Union-Tribune*, A10.

Domhoff, G. W. (2003). *The scientific study of dreams*. Washington, DC: American Psychological Association.

Domhoff, G. W. (2005a). The content of dreams: Methodologic and theoretical implications. In M. H. Kryger, T. Roth & W. C. Dement (Eds.), *Principles and practice of sleep*. Philadelphia: Elsevier Saunders.

Domhoff, G. W. (2005b). Refocusing the neurocognitive approach to dreams: A critique of the Hobson versus Solms debate. *Dreaming, 15*, 3–20.

Domino, G. (1994). Assessment of creativity with the ACL: An empirical comparison of four scales. *Creativity Research Journal, 7*, 21–33.

Donderi, D. C. (2006). Visual complexity: A review. *Psychological Bulletin, 132*, 73–97.

Dorman, M. F. (2003, January 14). Cited in E. Nagourney, Experts urge early ear implants. *New York Times*, D6.

Dorn, L. D., Susman, E. J., & Ponirakis, A. (2003). Pubertal timing and adolescent adjustment and behavior: Conclusions vary by rater. *Journal of Youth and Adolescence, 32*, 157–167.

Doty, R. L. (2001). Olfaction. *Annual Review of Psychology, 52*, 423–452.

Douglas, E. M., & Finkelhor, D. (2005). *Childhood sexual abuse fact sheet* [On-line]. Available: http://www.unh.edu/ccrc/factsheet/pdf/CSA-FS20.pdf

Dowling, C. G. (2000, August, 14). Mistaken identity. *People*, 50–55.

Drisko, J. W. (2004). Common factors in psychotherapy outcome: Meta-analytic findings and their implications for practice and research. *Families in Society, 85*, 81–90.

Drolet, G., Dumont, E. C., Gosselin, I., Kinkhead, R., Laforest, S., & Trottier, J. F. (2001). Role of endogenous opioid system in the regulation of the stress response. *Progress in Neuro-Psychopharmacology & Biological Psychiatry, 25*, 729–741.

Dronkers, N. F., Wilkins, D. P., & Van Valin, R. D., Jr. (2004). Lesion analysis of the brain areas involved in language comprehension. *Cognition, 92*, 145–177.

Drummond, S. P. A. (2000). Cited in B. Bower, Sleepyheads' brains veer from restful path. *Science News, 157*, 103.

DuBois, D. L., Tevendale, H. D., Burk-Braxton, C., Swenson, L. P., & Hardesty, J. L. (2000). Self-system influences during early adolescence: Investigation of an integrative model. *Journal of Early Adolescence, 20*, 12–43.

Dudley, D. (2006, January/February). Impact awards 2006 honorees. *AARP: The Magazine*.

Duenwald, M. (2003, June 17). More Americans seeking help for depression. *New York Times*, A1.

Duffy, J. (2002, April). Cited in M. Weinstock, Night owls vs. early birds. *Discover*, 11.

Dugatkin, L. E., & Bekoff, M. (2003). Play and the evolution of fairness: A game theory model. *Behavioural Processes, 60*, 209–214.

Dunn, A. L., Trivedi, M. H., Kampert, J. B., Clark, C. G., & Chambliss, H. O. (2005). Exercise treatment for depression. Efficacy and dose response. *American Journal of Preventive Medicine, 28*, 1–8.

Dunn, J. (2003). Emotional development in early childhood: A social relationship perspective. In R. J. Davidson, K. R. Scherer, & H. H. Goldsmith (Eds.), *Handbook of affective sciences*. New York: Oxford University Press.

Dunn, M., & Cutler, N. (2000). Sexual issues in older adults. *AIDS Patient Care and STDs, 14*, 67–69.

Durand, V. M., & Barlow, D. H. (2006). *Essentials of abnormal psychology* (4th ed.). Belmont, CA: Thomson Wadsworth.

Durrett, C., & Trull, T. J. (2005). An evaluation of evaluative personality terms: A comparison of the big seven and five-factor model in predicting psychopathology. *Psychological Assessment, 17*, 359–368.

Durso, F. T., Rea, C. B., & Dayton, T. (1994). Graph-theoretic confirmation of restructuring during insight. *Psychological Science, 5*, 94–98.

Duyme, M. (1999). Cited in B. Bower, Kids adopted late reap IQ increases. *Science News, 156*, 54–55.

Dyck, D. G., Short, R. A., Hendryx, M. S., Norell, D., Myers, M., Patterson, T., McDonell, M. G., Voss, W. D., & McFarlane, W. R. (2000). Management of negative symptoms among patients with schizophrenia attending multiple-family groups. *Psychiatric Services, 51*, 513–519.

Eagle, M. N. (2000). A critical evaluation of current conceptions of transference and countertransference. *Psychoanalytic Psychology, 17*, 24–37.

Eagly, A. H., & Karau, S. J. (2002). Role congruity theory of prejudice toward female leaders. *Psychological Review, 109*, 573–598.

Eagly, A. H., Wood, W., & Diekman, A. B. (2000). Social role theory of sex differences and similarities: A current appraisal. In T. Eckes & H. M. Trautner (Eds.), *The developmental social psychology of gender*. Mahwah, NJ: Lawrence Erlbaum.

Eagly, A. H., Wood, W., & Johannesen-Schmidt, M. C. (2004). Social role theory of sex differences and similarities. In A. H. Eagly, A. E. Beall, & R. J. Sternberg (Eds.), *The psychology of gender* (2nd ed., pp. 269–295). New York: Guilford Press.

Easterlin, R. A. (2003). Explaining happiness. *Proceedings of the National Academy of Sciences, 100*, 11176–11183.

Ebbinghaus, H. (1885; reprinted 1913). *Memory: A contribution to experimental psychology* (H. A. Ruger & C. E. Bussenius, Trans.). New York: Teachers College Press.

Ebrecht, M., Hextall, J., Kirtley, L. G., Taylor, A., Dyson, M., & Weinman, J. (2004). Perceived stress and cortisol levels predict speed of wound healing in healthy male adults. *Psychoneuroimmunology, 29*, 798–809.

Eccles, J. S. (2005). Subjective task value and the Eccles et al. model of achievement-related choices. In A. J. Elliot & C. S. Dweck (Eds.), *Handbook of competence and motivation* (pp. 105–121). New York: Guilford Press.

Eccles, J. S., & Wigfield, A. (2002). Motivational beliefs, values and goals. *Annual Review of Psychology, 53*, 109–132.

Eckes, T., & Trautner, H. M. (2000). *The developmental social psychology of gender*. Mahwah, NJ: Lawrence Erlbaum.

Eddings, J. (1994, December 26). Atlanta's new top cop makes her mark. *U.S. News & World Report*.

Edelman, G. M. (2003). Naturalizing consciousness: A theoretical framework. *Proceedings of the National Academy of Sciences, 100*, 5520–5524.

Eden, G. (2003, July 28). Cited in C. Gorman, The new science of dyslexia. *Time*, 52–59.

Edenberg, H. J., & Foroud, T. (2006). The genetics of alcoholism: Identifying specific genes through family studies. *Addictive Biology, 11*, 386–396.

Edinger, J. D., Wohlgemuth, W. K., Radtke, R. A., Marsh, G. F., & Quillian, R. E. (2001). Cognitive behavioral therapy for treatment of chronic primary insomnia. *Journal of the American Medical Association, 285*, 1856–1864.

Egan, T. (1999, February 28). The war on crack retreats, still taking prisoners. *New York Times*, 1.

Eggen, D. (2005, August 31). 400 arrests in U.S. methamphetamine raids. *The Washington Post*, A2.

Eibl-Eibesfeldt, I. (1973). The expressive behavior of the deaf-and-blind-born. In M. von Cranach & I. Vine (Eds.), *Social communication and movement*. San Diego, CA: Academic Press.

Eich, E., Macaulay, D., Loewenstein, R. J., & Dihle, P. H. (1997). Memory, amnesia, and dissociative identity disorder. *Psychological Science, 8*, 417–422.

Eichenbaum, H. (2004). An information processing framework for memory representation by the hippocampus. In M. S. Gazzaniga (Ed.), *The cognitive neurosciences III*. Cambridge, MA: MIT Press.

Eikeseth, S. (2001). Recent critiques of the UCLA Young Autism Project. *Behavioral Interventions, 16*, 249–264.

Eisen, M. R. (1994). Psychoanalytic and psychodynamic models of hypnoanalysis. In J. W. Rhue, S. J. Lynn & I. Kirsch (Eds.), *Handbook of clinical hypnosis*. Washington, DC: American Psychological Association.

Eisenberg, D. (2005, April 4). Lessons of the Schiavo battle: What the bitter fight over a woman's right to live or die tells us about politics, religion, the courts and life itself. *Time*, 22–30.

Eisenberger, R., & Armeli, S. (1997). Can salient reward increase creative performance without reducing intrinsic creative interest? *Journal of Personality and Social Psychology, 72*, 652–663.

Eisenberger, R., Pierce, W. D., & Cameron, J. (1999). Effects of reward on intrinsic motivation—negative, neutral, and positive: Comment on Deci, Koestner, and Ryan (1999). *Psychological Bulletin, 125*, 677–691.

Ekman, P. (2003). *Emotions revealed: Recognizing faces and feelings to improve communication and emotional life*. New York: Times Books.

Ekman, P. (2006, October/November). Cited in S. Schubert, A look tells all. *Scientific American Mind*, 26–31.

Ekman, P., & Rosenberg, E. L. (Eds.). (2005). *What the face reveals: Basic and applied studies of spontaneous expression using the facial action coding system* (FACS). New York: Oxford University Press.

Elias, M. (1989, August 9). With guidance, a child can control negative traits. *USA Today*.

Elias M. (2005a, August 22). ADHD haunts children into adulthood, study shows. *USA Today*, 5D.

Elias, M. (2005b, August 22). Critical, demanding parents can damage gifted children. *USA Today*, 5D.

Ellason, J. W., & Ross, C. A. (1997). Two-year follow-up of inpatients with dissociative identity disorder. *American Journal of Psychiatry, 154*, 832–839.

Elliot, A. J., & Church, M. A. (2003). A motivational analysis of defensive pessimism and self-handicapping. *Journal of Personality, 71*, 370–396.

Elliott, D. (1995, March 20). The fat of the land. *Newsweek*.

Ellison, P. T. (2002). Puberty. In N. Cameron (Ed.), *Human growth and development* (pp. 65–84). New York: Academic Press.

Ellsworth, P. C., & Scherer, K. R. (2003). Appraisal processes in emotion. In R. J. Davidson, K. R. Scherer & H. H. Goldsmith (Eds.), *Handbook of affective sciences*. New York: Oxford University Press.

References

Elswick, J. (2004, June 15). Americans seek mental health care as old stigmas subside. *Employee Benefit News.*

Emery, R. E., & Laumann-Billings, L. (1998). An overview of the nature, causes, and consequences of abusive family relationships. *American Psychologist, 53,* 121–135.

Emmelkamp, P. M. G. (2004). Behavior therapy with adults. In M. J. Lambert (Ed.), *Bergin and Garfield's handbook of psychotherapy and behavior change* (pp. 393–446). New York: Wiley.

Ende, G., Braus, D. F., Walter, S., Weber-Fahr, W., & Henn, R. A. (2000). The hippocampus in patients treated with electroconvulsive therapy. *Archives of General Psychiatry, 57,* 937–943.

Endler, N. S., Kantor, L., & Parker, J. D. A. (1994). State-trait coping, state-trait anxiety and academic performance. *Personality and Individual Differences, 16,* 663–670.

Engeler, E. (2006, November 22). Global epidemic of the AIDS virus grows, U.N. says. *The San Diego Union-Tribune,* A3.

Ennett, S. T., Rosenbaum, D. P., Flewelling, R. L., Bieler, G. S., Ringwalt, C. L., & Bailey, S. L. (1994). Long-term evaluation of drug abuse resistance education. *Addictive Behaviors, 19,* 113–125.

Epel, E., & Blackburn, E. (2004, November 30). Cited in B. Carey, Stress and distress may give your genes gray hair. *The New York Times,* D5.

Epley, N., Savitsky, K., & Kachelski, R. A. (1999, September/October). What every skeptic should know about subliminal persuasion. *Skeptical Inquirer,* 40–45.

Epstein, R. (2006, April/May). Sexuality and choice. *Scientific American Mind,* 16–17.

Erber, J. T. (2005). *Aging & older adulthood.* Belmont, CA: Thomson/Wadsworth.

Erickson, M. H. (1980/1941). Hypnosis: A general review. In E. L. Rossie (Ed.), *The collected papers of Milton H. Erickson on hypnosis* (Vol. 30). New York: Irvington.

Erikson, E. H. (1963). *Childhood and society.* New York: Norton.

Erikson, E. H. (1982). *The life cycle completed: Review.* New York: Norton.

Eron, L. D. (1990). Understanding aggression. *Bulletin of the International Society for Research on Aggression, 12,* 5–9.

Esch, T., & Stefano, G. B. (2005). The neurobiology of love. *Neuroendocrinology Letters, 26,* 175–192.

Espiard, M., Lecardeur, L., Abadie, P., Halbecq, I., & Dollfus, S. (2005). Hallucinogen persisting perception disorder after psilocybin consumption: A case study. *European Psychiaatry, 20,* 458–460.

Evans, R. B. (1999, December). A century of psychology. *Monitor on Psychology.*

Everson, H. T., Smodlaka, I., & Tobias, S. (1994). Exploring the relationship of test anxiety and metacognition on reading test performance: A cognitive analysis. *Anxiety, Stress, and Coping, 7,* 85–96.

Exner, J. E., Jr., & Erdberg, P. (2005). *The Rorschach, advanced interpretation* (3rd ed.). Hoboken, NJ: John Wiley & Sons.

Eysenck, H. J. (1994). The outcome problem in psychotherapy: What have we learned? *Behaviour Research and Therapy, 32,* 477–495.

Ezzat, D. (2004, June 17–23). Fortifying women's rights. *Al-Ahram Weekly,* 695.

Ezzell, C. (2003, February). Why? The neuroscience of suicide. *Scientific American,* 45–51.

Fabrigar, L. R., MacDonald, T. K., & Wegener, D. T. (2005). The structure of attitudes. In D. Albarracin, B. T. Johnson & M. P. Zanna (Eds.), *The handbook of attitudes.* Mahwah, NJ: Erlbaum.

Fackelmann, K. (2005, January 13). Sleepy medical interns become medical hazards. *USA Today,* 9D.

Fackelmann, K. (2005, February 10). "Broken-heart syndrome" has medical link. *USA Today,* 8D.

Fackelmann, K. A. (1993). Marijuana and the brain. *Science News, 143,* 88–94.

Falcon, M. (2002, April 22). Montel Williams fights MS with fitness. *USA Today.*

Faller, A., Schunke, M., & Shunke, G. (2004). *The human body: An introduction to structure and function.* New York: Thieme Medical.

Fanous, A. H., van den Oordm, E. J., Riley, B. P., Aggen, S. H., Neale, M. D., O'Neill, F. A., Walsh, D., & Kendler, K. S. (2005). Relationship between a high-risk haplotype in the DTNBP1 (dysbindin) gene and clinical features of schizophrenia. *American Journal of Psychiatry, 162,* 1824–1832.

Faravelli, C., Cosci, F., Ciampelli, M., Scarpareo, M. A., Spiti, R., & Ricca, V. (2003). A self-controlled, naturalistic study of selective serotonin reuptake inhibitors versus tricyclic antidepressants. *Psychotherapy and Psychosomatics, 72,* 95–101.

Farber, B. A. (2000a). Introduction: Understanding and treating burnout in a changing culture. *Journal of Clinical Psychology/In Session, 56,* 589–594.

Farber, B. A. (2000b). Treatment strategies for different types of teacher burnout. *Journal of Clinical Psychology/In Session, 56,* 675–689.

Fayek, A. (2005). The centrality of the system Ucs in the theory of psychoanalysis: The nonrepressed unconscious. *Psychoanalytic Psychology, 22,* 524–543.

FBI (Federal Bureau of Investigation). (2001, March 5). *Cited in CNN, Risk factors for school violence* [On-line]. Available: http://archives.cnn.com/2001/US/03/05/fbi. shooter.profile/index.html

FDA (Food and Drug Administration). (2006, June 8). *FDA licenses new vaccine for prevention of cervical cancer and other diseases in females caused by human papilomavirus* [On-line]. Available: http://www.fda.gov/bbs/topics/NEWS/2006/NEW01385.html

Fechner, G. T. (1860). *Elemente der Psychophysik* (Vol. 1). Leipzig: Brietkopf and Marterl (H. E. Alder, D. H. Howes & E. G. Boring, Trans.). New York: Holt, Rinehart & Winston.

Feingold, B. R. (1975). Hyperkinesis and learning disabilities linked to artificial food flavors and colors. *American Journal of Nursing, 75,* 797–803.

Fenly, L. (2006, January 18). Autistic expert feels bond with animals. *The San Diego Union-Tribune,* F1.

Ferguson, D. P., Rhodes, G., Lee, K., & Sriram, N. (2001). "They all look alike to me"; Prejudice and cross-race face recognition. *British Journal of Psychology, 92,* 567–577.

Fergusson, D. M., Horwood, L. J., & Ridder, E. M. (2005). Tests of causal linkages between cannabis use and psychotic symptoms. *Addiction, 100,* 354–366.

Fernald, A. (1992). Human maternal vocalizations to infants as biologically relevant signals: An evolutionary perspective. In J. H. Barkow, L. Cosmides & J. Tooby (Eds.), *The adapted mind: Evolutionary psychology and the generation of culture.* New York: Oxford University Press.

Fernando, S. (2002). *Mental health, race, and culture* (2nd ed.). New York: Palgrave Macmillan.

Ferrari, J. R., & Tice, D. M. (2000). Procrastination as a self-handicap for men and women: A task-avoidance strategy in a laboratory setting. *Journal of Research in Personality, 34,* 73–83.

Ferster, D., & Spruston, N. (1995). Cracking the neuronal code. *Science, 270,* 756–757.

Festinger, L. (1954). A theory of social comparison processes. *Human Relations, 7,* 117–140.

Festinger, L. (1957). *A theory of cognitive dissonance.* Palo Alto, CA: Stanford University Press.

Festinger, L., & Carlsmith, J. M. (1959). Cognitive consequences of forced compliance. *Journal of Abnormal and Social Psychology, 58,* 203–210.

Fiedler, K. (2007). Information ecology and the explanation of social cognition and behavior. In A. W. Kruglanski & E. T. Higgins, *Social psychology: Handbook of basic principles* (2nd ed., pp. 176–200). New York: Guilford Press.

Fiedler, K., Schmid, J., & Stahl, T. (2002). What is the current truth about polygraph lie detection? *Basic and Applied Social Psychology, 24,* 313–324.

Fields, H. (2006, February 13). More sleep–and more oxygen. *U.S. News & World Report,* 58.

Fields, R. D. (2005, February). Making memories stick. *Scientific American,* 75–81.

Fields, R. D., & Stevens-Graham, B. (2002). New insights into neuron-glial communication. *Science, 298,* 556–562.

Fillmore, M. T., Roach, E. L., & Rice, J. T. (2002). Does caffeine counteract alcohol-induced impairment? The ironic effects of expectancy. *Journal of Studies on Alcohol, 63,* 745–754.

Fimrite, P., & Taylor, M. (2005, March 27). No shortage of women who dream of snaring a husband on Death Row. Experts ponder why deadliest criminals get so many proposals. *San Francisco Gate.*

Fink, B., & Penton-Voak, I. (2002). Evolutionary psychology of facial attractiveness. *Current Directions in Psychological Science, 11,* 154–158.

Finke, R. A. (1993). Mental imagery and creative discovery. In B. Roskos-Ewoldsen, M. J. Intons-Peterson & R. E. Anderson (Eds.), *Imagery, creativity, and discovery: A cognitive perspective.* Amsterdam: North Holland.

Finkelhor, D. (2002, December 3). Cited in L. Villarosa, To prevent sexual abuse, abusers step forward. *New York Times,* D5.

Finn, J. D., & Rock, D. A. (1997). Academic success among students at risk for school failure. *Journal of Applied Psychology, 82,* 221–234.

Finney, M. L. (2003, March). Cited in D. Smith, Angry thoughts, at-risk hearts. *Monitor on Psychology,* 46–47.

First, M. B. (2007, January 24). *A research agenda for DSM-V: Summary of the DSM-V preplanning white papers published in May 2002* [On-line]. Available: http://www.dsm5.org/whitepapers.cfm

Fischer, J. S. (1999, September 13). From Romania, a lesson in resilience. *U.S. News & World Report.*

Fischman, J. (2006, February 20). Fixing your brain: When pills fail, electrical implants can mend brains damaged by Parkinson's, stroke, and depression. *U.S. News & World Report.*

Fisher, H. (2002, December 16). Cited in B. Carey, The brain in love. *Los Angeles Times,* F1.

Fisher, H. (2003). Cited in L. Helmuth, Caudate-over-heels in love. *Science, 302,* 1320.

Fishman, S. (1988). *A bomb in the brain.* New York: Scribner's.

Fiske, S. (2006, January 2). Cited in Don't race to judgment. *U.S. News & World Report,* 90–91.

FitzGerald, G. J. (1993). The reproductive behavior of the stickleback. *Scientific American, 268,* 80–85.

Flagg, E. J., Cardy, J. E., Roberts, W., & Roberts, T. P. (2005). Language lateralization development in children with autism: Insights from the late field magnetoencephalogram. *Neuroscience Letters, 386,* 82–87.

Fleshner, M., & Laudenslager, M. L. (2004). Psychoneuroimmunology: Then and now. *Behavioral and Cognitive Neuroscience Reviews, 3,* 114–130.

Fletcher, C. (1995). *Breaking and entering: Women cops talk about life in the ultimate men's club.* New York: HarperCollins.

Fletcher, G. (2002). *The new science of intimate relationships.* Malden, MA: Blackwell Publishing.

Fletcher, G. J. O., & Simpson, J. A. (2000). Ideal standards in close relationships: Their structure and functions. *Directions in Psychological Science, 9,* 102–105.

Flett, G. L., Vredenburg, K., & Krames, L. (1997). The continuity of depression in clinical and nonclinical samples. *Psychological Bulletin, 121,* 395–416.

Flippo, R. F., Becker, M. J., & Wark, D. M. (2000). Preparing for and taking tests. In R. F. Flippo & D. C. Caverly (Eds.), *Handbook of college reading and study strategy research.* Mahwah, NJ: Lawrence Erlbaum.

Flippo, R. F., & Caverly, D. C. (Eds.). (2000). *Handbook of college reading and study strategy research.* Mahwah, NJ: Lawrence Erlbaum.

Flor, H., Elbert, T., Knecht, S., Wienbruch, C., Pantev, C., Birbaumer, N., Larbig, W., & Taub, E. (1995). Phantom-limb pain as a perceptual correlate of cortical reorganization following arm amputation. *Nature, 375,* 482–483.

Flores, S. A. (1999). Attributional biases in sexually coercive males. *Journal of Applied Social Psychology, 29,* 2425–2442.

Fogel, D. B. (2000, July 25). Cited in J. Glanz, It's only checkers, but the computer taught itself. *New York Times,* D1.

Folkman, S., & Moskowitz, J. T. (2000). Stress, positive emotion, and coping. *Current Directions in Psychological Science, 9,* 115–118.

Fombonne, E. (2005). Epidemiology of autistic disorder and other pervasive developmental disorders. *Journal of Clinical Psychiatry, 66,* 3–8.

Forero, J. (2006, August 19). Colombia's coca survives U.S. plan to uproot it. *The New York Times,* A1, A7.

Forgas, J. P., Williams, K. D., & Von Hippel, W. (Eds.). (2003). *Social judgments: Implicit and explicit processes.* Cambridge, UK: Cambridge University Press.

Forster, J., & Liberman, N. (2007). Knowledge activation. In A. W. Kruglanski & E. T. Higgins, *Social psychology: Handbook of basic principles* (2nd ed., pp. 201–231). New York: Guilford Press.

Fotopoulou, A. (2006, April/May). Cited in M. Solms, Freud returns. *Scientific American Mind,* 28–34.

Foulkes, D. (2003). Cited in C. W. Domhoff, Making sense of dreaming. *Science, 299,* 1987–1988.

Foulks, E. G. (1992). Reflections on dream material from arctic native people. *Journal of the American Academy of Psychoanalysis, 20,* 193–203.

Fox, J. (2005, December 4). "Robots helped treat my prostate cancer" [On-line]. Available: http://edition.cnn.com/2005/ TECH/12/02/ john.fox/index.html

Fox, M. J. (2002). *Lucky man: A memoir.* New York: Hyperion.

Foxhall, K. (2001, June). Preventing relapse. *Monitor on Psychology,* 46–47.

Frank, D. A., Augustyn, M., Knight, W. G., Pell, T., & Zuckerman, B. (2001). Growth, development, and behavior in early childhood following prenatal cocaine exposure. *Journal of the American Medical Association, 285,* 1613–1625.

Franklin, M. E., Abramowitz, J. S., Bux, D. A., Jr., Zoellner, L. A., & Feeny, N. C. (2002). Cognitive-behavioral therapy with and without medication in the treatment of obsessive-compulsive disorder. *Professional Psychology: Research and Practice, 33,* 162–168.

Franks, C. M. (1994). Behavioral model. In V. B. Van Hasselt & M. Hersen (Eds.), *Advanced abnormal psychology.* New York: Plenum Press.

Franz, V. H., Gegenfurtner, K. R., Bulthoff, H. H., & Fahle, M. (2000). Grasping visual illusions: No evidence for a dissociation between perception and action. *Psychological Science, 11,* 20–25.

Frazier, K. (2003, January/February). National Academy of Science report says polygraph testing too flawed for security screening. *Skeptical Inquirer,* 5–6.

Fredrickson, M., Hursti, T., Salmi, P., Borjeson, S., Furst, C. J., Peterson, C., & Steineck, G. (1993). Conditioned nausea after cancer chemotherapy and autonomic nervous system conditionability. *Scandinavian Journal of Psychology, 34,* 318–317.

Freedman, R. R. (1991). Physiological mechanisms of temperature biofeedback. *Biofeedback and Self-Regulation, 16,* 95–115.

Freedom Writers. (1999). *The Freedom Writers diary.* New York: Broadway Books.

Freeman, A., Pretzer, J., Fleming, B., & Simon, K. M. (2004). *Clinical applications of cognitive therapy* (2nd ed.). New York: Springer.

Frensch, P. A., & Runger, D. (2003). Implicit learning. Current *Directions in Psychological Science, 12,* 13–18.

Freud, S. (1900; reprinted 1980). *The interpretation of dreams* (J. Strachey, Ed. and Trans.). New York: Avon.

Freud, S. (1901; reprinted 1960). The psychopathology of everyday life. In J. Strachey (Ed. and Trans.), *The standard edition of the complete psychological works of Sigmund Freud* (Vol. 6). London: Hogarth.

Freud, S. (1905; reprinted 1953). Three essays on the theory of sexuality. In J. Strachey (Ed. and Trans.), *The standard edition of the complete psychological works of Sigmund Freud* (Vol. 7). London: Hogarth.

Freud, S. (1909; reprinted 1949). Notes upon a case of obsessional neurosis. In *Collected papers* (Vol. 3), (Alix and James Strachey, Trans.). London: Hogarth.

Freud, S. (1924). *A general introduction to psychoanalysis.* New York: Boni & Liveright.

Freud, S. (1940; reprinted 1961). An outline of psychoanalysis. In J. Strachey (Ed. and Trans.), *The standard edition of the complete psychological works of Sigmund Freud* (Vol. 23). London: Hogarth.

Freudenheim, M. (2003, June 18). Employers plan obesity fight, citing $12-billion-a-year cost. *New York Times,* C2.

Freyd, J. J. (1994). Circling creativity. *Psychological Science, 5,* 122–126.

Frick, W. B. (2000). Remembering Maslow: Reflections on a 1968 interview. *Journal of Humanistic Psychology, 40,* 128–147.

Friedman, J. M. (2003). A war on obesity, not the obese. *Science, 299,* 856–858.

Friedman, M., & Rosenman, R. (1974). *Type A behavior and your heart.* New York: Knopf.

Friedman, R. (2006, January 5). *TV psychic misses mark on miners* [On-line]. Available: http://www.foxnews.com/story/0,2933,180681,00.html

Friedman, R. A. (2006, September 18). For fearful fliers, a guide to easing the jitters. *The New York Times,* 11.

Friedman, S., & Stevenson, M. (1980). Perception of movements in pictures. In M. Hagen (Ed.), *Perception of pictures, Vol. 1: Alberti's window: The projective model of pictorial information.* Orlando, FL: Academic Press.

Friend, T. (1994, July 19). Monday just got worse: It's a coronary day. *USA Today,* D1.

Friend, T. (1997, December 9). The race to save the wild tiger from extinction. *USA Today.*

Friend, T. (2003, March 27). A wartime first: Dolphins called to clear mines. *USA Today,* 8D.

Frieswick, K. (2004, July 1). Casting to type. *CFO Magazine.*

Frijda, N. S. (2000). The psychologists' point of view. In M. Lewis & J. M. Haviland-Jones (Eds.), *Handbook of emotions* (2nd ed.). New York: Guilford.

Fristad, M. A., & Shaver, A. E. (2001). Psychosocial interventions for suicidal children and adolescents. *Depression and Anxiety, 14,* 192–197.

Fritz, C., & Sonnentag, S. (2006). Recovery, well-being, and performance-related outcomes: The role of workload and vacation experiences. *Journal of Applied Psychology, 91,* 936–945.

Fritz, S. (1995, June). Found: Wonders in a secret cave. *Popular Science.*

Fryer, R. (2005, November 29). Cited in J. Tierney, Got each other's backs, or holding each other back? The *New York Times,* A27.

Fuller, R. K., & Hiller-Sturmhofel, S. (1999). Alcoholism treatment in the United States. *Alcohol Research and Health, 23,* 69–77.

Furumoto, L. (1989). The new history of psychology. In I. S. Cohen (Ed.), *The G. Stanley Hall lecture series* (Vol. 9). Washington, DC: American Psychological Association.

Furumoto, L., & Scarborough, E. (1986). Placing women in the history of psychology. *American Psychologist, 41,* 35–42.

Gabrieli, J. (2005, April 4). Cited in J. Kluger, Secrets of the shy. *Time,* 50–52.

Gaetani, S., Cuomo, V., & Piomelli, D. (2003). Anandamide hydrolysis: A new target for anti-anxiety drugs? *Trends in Molecular Medicine, 9,* 474–478.

Gage, F. H. (2003, September). Brain, repair yourself. *Scientific American,* 47–53.

Gaillard, R., Naccache, L., Pinel, P., Clemenceau, S., Volle, E., Hasboun, D., Dupont, S., Baulac, M., Dehaene, S., Adam, C., & Cohen, L. (2006). Direct intracranial, fMRI, and lesion evidence for the causal role of left inferotemporal cortex in reading. *Neuron, 50,* 191–204.

Gallagher, R. P. (2002, September 11). Cited in M. Duenwald, Students find another staple of campus life: Stress. *New York Times,* D5.

Galliano, G. (2003). *Gender crossing boundaries.* Belmont, CA: Wadsworth/Thomson Learning.

Gallopin, T., Luppi, P. H., Cauli, B., Urade, Y., Rossier, J., Hayaishi, O., Lambolez, B., & Fort, P. (2005). The endogenous somnogen adenosine excites a subset of sleep-promoting neurons via A2A receptors in the ventrolateral preoptic nucleus. *Neuroscience, 134,* 1377–1390.

Galovski, T. E., Malta, L. S., & Blanchard, E. B. (2006). *Road rage: Assessment and treatment of the angry, aggressive driver.* Washington, DC: American Psychological Association.

Galton, F. (1888). Head growth in students at the University of Cambridge. *Nature, 38,* 14–15.

Gangestad, S. W., & Simpson, J. A. (2000). Trade-offs, the allocation of reproductive effort, and the evolutionary psychology of human mating. *Behavioral and Brain Sciences, 23,* 624–644.

Ganong, W. F. (2005). *Review of medical physiology* (22nd ed.). New York: McGraw-Hill.

Garbarini, N. (2006, December). Blinking turns off the brain. *Scientific American Mind.*

Garcia, J., Ervin, F. R., & Koelling, R. A. (1966). Learning with prolonged delay of reinforcement. *Psychonomic Science, 5,* 121–122.

Garcia, J., Hankins, W. G., & Rusinak, K. W. (1974). Behavioral regulation of the milieu interne in man and rat. *Science, 185,* 824–831.

Garcia-Rill, E., Wallace, T., & Good, C. (2006). Neuropharmacology of sleep and wakefulness. In T. L. Lee-Chiong (Ed.), *Sleep: A comprehensive handbook* (pp. 63–72). Hoboken, NJ: John Wiley & Sons.

Gardner, A. (2005, November 4). *Peyote use by Native Americans doesn't damage brain* [On-line]. Available: http://www.hom.ch/News/HSN/528941.html

Gardner, B. T., & Gardner, R. A. (1975). Evidence for sentence constituents in the early utterances of child and chimpanzee. *Journal of Experimental Psychology: General, 104,* 244–267.

References

Gardner, H. (1976). *The shattered mind.* New York: Vintage Books.

Gardner, H. (1993). *Creating minds.* New York: Basic Books.

Gardner, H. (1995, November). Reflections on multiple intelligences. *Phi Delta Kappan.*

Gardner, H. (1999). *Intelligence reframed.* New York: Basic Books.

Gardner, H. (2003). Three distinct meanings of intelligence. In R. J. Sternberg, J. Lautrey & T. I. Lubart (Eds.), *Models of intelligence.* Washington, DC: American Psychological Association.

Gardner, H. (2006a). *Changing minds.* Boston: Harvard Business School Publishing.

Gardner, H. (2006b). *Multiple intelligences: New horizons.* New York: Basic Books.

Gardner, R., III, Ford, D. Y., & Miranda, A. H. (2001). The education of African American students: The struggle continues. *The Journal of Negro Education, 70,* 241–242.

Garfield, S. L., & Bergin, A. E. (1994). Introduction and historical overview. In A. E. Bergin & S. L. Garfield (Eds.), *Handbook of psychotherapy and behavior change* (4th ed.). New York: Wiley.

Garland, A. R., & Zigler, E. (1993). Adolescent suicide prevention. *American Psychologist, 48,* 169–182.

Garry, M., Sharman, S. J., Feldman, J., Marlatt, G. A., & Loftus, E. (2002). Examining memory for heterosexual college students' sexual experiences using an electronic mail diary. *Health Psychology, 21,* 629–634.

Gazzaniga, M. S. (1998, July). The split brain revisited. *Scientific American,* 50–55.

Gazzaniga, M. S. (2000). Cerebral specialization and interhemispheric communication: Does the corpus callosum enable the human condition? *Brain, 123,* 1293–1326.

Gazzaniga, M. S. (Ed.). (2004). *The cognitive neurosciences* (3rd ed.). Cambridge, MA: MIT Press.

Gazzaniga, M. S. (2005). Forty-five years of split-brain research and still going strong. *Nature Review Neuroscience, 6,* 653–659.

Gazzaniga, M. S., Bogen, J. E., & Sperry, R. W. (1962). Some functional effects of sectioning the cerebral commissures in man. *Proceedings of the National Academy of Science, 48,* 1765–1769.

Geiger, D. (2002). Cited in K. Cobb, Sleepy heads. *Science News, 162,* 38.

Gelder, T. V. (2005). Beyond the mind-body problem. In C. E. Erneling & D. M. Johnson (Eds.), *The mind as a scientific object: Between brain and culture* (pp. 457–470). New York: Oxford University Press.

Geliebter, A., Ladell, T., Logan, M., Schweider, T., Sharafi, M., & Hirsch, J. (2006). Responsivity to food stimuli in obese and lean binge eaters using functional MRI. *Appetite, 46,* 31–35.

Geller, L. (1982). The failure of self-actualization theory: A critique of Carl Rogers and Abraham Maslow. *Journal of Humanistic Psychology, 22,* 56–73.

George, K. I. (1995, December 6). Driver gets children to mind pizzas and Qs. *USA Today.*

Gerlach, D. (2006, May 15). Cited in D. Jefferson, How AIDS changed America. *Time,* 36–41.

Gershoff, E. T. (2002). Corporal punishment by parents and associated child behaviors and experiences: A meta-analytic and theoretical review. *Psychological Bulletin, 128,* 539–579.

Gerwig, M., Dimitrova, A., Kolb, F. P., Maschke, M., Brol, B., Kunnel, A., Boring, D., Thilmann, A. F., Forsting, M., Diener, H. C., & Timmann, D. (2003). Comparison of eyeblink conditioning in patients with superior and posterior inferior cerebellar lesions. *Brain, 126,* 71–94.

Giacopassi, D. J., & Dull, R. T. (1986). Gender and racial differences in the acceptance of rape myths within a college population. *Sex Roles, 15,* 63–75.

Giannotti, F., Cortesi, F., Sebastiani, T., & Ottaviano, S. (2002). Circadian preference, sleep and daytime behaviour in adolescence. *Journal of Sleep Research, 11,* 191–199.

Gibbons, A. (2002). In search of the first hominids. *Science, 295,* 1214–1219.

Gibbs, N. (1993, July 19). In whose best interest? *Time.*

Gibbs, N. (1995, October 2). The EQ factor. *Time,* 60–68.

Gibson, B. M., & Kamil, A. C. (2001). Tests for cognitive mapping in Clark's nutcrackers. *Journal of Comparative Psychology, 115,* 403–417.

Gibson, E. J., & Walk, R. (1960). The visual "cliff." *Scientific American, 202,* 64–71.

Giedd, J. (1999, August 9). Cited in S. Brownlee, Inside the teen brain. *U.S. News & World Report,* 45–54.

Gigone, D., & Hastie, R. (1997). Proper analysis of the accuracy of group judgments. *Psychological Bulletin, 121,* 149–167.

Gilbert, K. (2006, July/August). Your personal time zone. *Psychology Today.*

Giles, J. (2006). Scans suggest IQ scores reflect brain structure. *Nature, 440,* 588–589.

Gilligan, C. (1982). *In a different voice: Psychological theory and women's development.* Cambridge, MA: Harvard University Press.

Giorgi, A. (2005). Remaining challenges for humanistic psychology. *Journal of Humanistic Psychology, 45,* 204–216.

Gladwell, M. (2004, September 20). Personality plus. *The New Yorker,* 42–48.

Glantz, M. D., & Hartel, C. R. (1999). *Drug abuse: Origins & interventions.* Washington, DC: American Psychological Association.

Glanzer, M., & Cunitz, A. R. (1966). Two storage mechanisms in free recall. *Journal of Verbal Learning and Verbal Behavior, 5,* 351–360.

Glass, R. M. (2001). Electroconvulsive therapy. *Journal of the American Medical Association, 285,* 1346–1348.

Glass, S. (1998, March 5). Truth & D.A.R.E. *Rolling Stone,* 42–43.

Glasser, M., Kolvin, I., Campbell, D., Glasser, A., Leitch, I., & Farrelly, S. (2001). Cycle of child sexual abuse: Links between being a victim and becoming a perpetrator. *British Journal of Psychiatry, 179,* 482–494.

Gleick, E. (1997, January 27). And then there were two. . . . *Time,* 38–39.

Gleick, E., Alexander, B., Eskin, L., Pick, G., Skolnik, S., Dodd, J., & Sugden, J. (1994, December 12). The final victim. *People.*

Glenberg, A. M., Sanocki, T., Epstein, W., & Morris, C. (1987). Enhancing calibration of comprehension. *Journal of Experimental Psychology: General, 116,* 119–136.

Gliatto, T. (2006). Black. White. *People,* 37.

Goetz, C. G. (Ed.). (2003). *Textbook of clinical neurology* (2nd ed.). Philadelphia: W. B. Saunders.

Goin-Kochel, R. P., & Myers, B. J. (2005). Congenital versus regressive onset of autism spectrum disorders: Parents' beliefs about causes. *Focus on Autism and Other Developmental Disabilities, 20,* 169–179.

Gold, S. N., Hughes, D., & Hohnecker, L. (1994). Degrees of repression of sexual abuse memories. *American Psychologist, 49,* 441–442.

Goldberg, C. (1998, May 31). Acceptance of gay men and lesbians is growing, study says. *New York Times,* 15.

Goldberg, C. (2003, July 15). *Inside the psychopath: Moving ahead on diagnosis and possible treatment* [On-line]. Available: http://hubel.sfasu.edu/courseinfo/articles/physio_psychopathology.html

Goldberg, E. (2001). *The executive brain: Frontal lobes and the civilized mind.* New York: Oxford University Press.

Goldberg, E., Bilder, R. M., Hughes, J. E., Antin, S. P., & Mattis, S. (1989). A reticulofrontal disconnection syndrome. *Cortex, 25,* 687–695.

Goldberg, R. (2004). *Taking sides: Clashing views on controversial issues in drugs and society.* Guilford, CT: McGraw-Hill.

Goldberg, R. (2006). *Drugs across the spectrum* (5th ed.). Belmont, CA: Wadsworth/Thomson Learning.

Goldberger, L., & Breznitz, S. (Eds.). (1993). *Handbook of stress: Theoretical and clinical aspects.* New York: Free Press.

Goldfried, M. R., & Davison, G. C. (1976). *Clinical behavior therapy.* New York: Holt, Rinehart & Winston.

Goldsmith, H. H. (2003). Introduction: Genetics and development. In R. J. Davidson, K. B. Scherer & H. H. Goldsmith (Eds.), *Handbook of affective sciences.* New York: Oxford University Press.

Goldsmith, L. A. (2003). Disorders of the eccrine sweat glands. In I. M. Freeberg, A. Z. Eisen, K. Wolff, K. F. Austen, L. A. Goldsmith & S. I. Katz (Eds.), *Fitzpatrick's dermatology in general medicine* (6th ed.). New York: McGraw Hill.

Goldstein, E. B. (2005). *Cognitive psychology.* Belmont, CA: Thomson Wadsworth.

Goldstein, E. B. (2007). *Sensation & perception* (7th ed.). Belmont, CA: Thomson Wadsworth.

Goleman, D. (1995). *Emotional intelligence: Why it can matter more than IQ.* New York: Bantam Books.

Goleman, D. (2005). *Emotional intelligence. The tenth anniversary edition.* New York: Bantam Dell.

Goleman, D. (2006a, October 23). Cited in A. Underwood, How to read a face. *Newsweek,* 65.

Goleman, D. (2006b, September 22). Cited in W. Herbert, The power of two. *Psychological Science.*

Goleman, D. (2006c, September 6). Cited in R. Karir, Gandhi "offers a model for social intelligence." *Deutsche Presse Agentur* [On-line]. Available: http://rawstory.com/news/2006/Gandhi_offers_a_model_for_social_in_09062006.html

Goleman, D., & Gurin, J. (1993). *Mind/body medicine: How to use your mind for better health.* New York: Consumer Reports.

Golub, A., Johnson, B. D., Sifaneck, S. J., Chesluk, B., & Parker, H. (2001). Is the U.S. experiencing an incipient epidemic of hallucinogen use? *Substance Use & Misues, 36,* 1699–1729.

Gomes, H., Sussman, E., Ritter, W., Kurtzberg, D., Cowan, N., & Vaughan, H. G., Jr. (1999). Electrophysiological evidence of developmental changes in the duration of auditory sensory memory. *Developmental Psychology, 35,* 299–302.

Goode, E. (2002, March 12). The uneasy fit of the precocious and the average. *New York Times,* D1.

Goode, E. (2003a, May 14). Trying to silence the voices of illness. *San Diego Union-Tribune,* F10.

Goode, E. (2003b, May 20). Leading drugs for psychosis come under new scrutiny. *New York Times,* A1.

Goodstein, L., & Banerjee, N. (2006, November 4). Minister admits buying drug but denies tryst. *The New York Times.*

Goodwin, F. K. (2003). Rationale for long-term treatment of bipolar disorder and evidence for long-term lithium treatment. *Journal of Clinical Psychiatry, 64* (supplement 6), 5–12.

Goodwin, I. (2003). The relevance of attachment theory to the philosophy, organization, and practice of adult mental health care. *Clinical Psychology Review, 23,* 35–36.

Goodwin, J. (2006, June). Forget me not. *Reader's Digest,* 124–131.

Gordon, R. G., Jr. (Ed.). (2005). *Ethnologue: Languages of the world* (15th ed.). Dallas, TX: SIL International.

Gore, R. (1997, February). The first steps. *National Geographic,* 72–99.

Gorman, C. (2003, July 28). The new science of dyslexia. *Time,* 52–59.

Gorman, C. (2005a, January 17). The importance of resilience. *Time,* 52–55.

Gorman, C. (2005b, December 12). A transplant first. *Time,* 58.

Gorman, C. (2006, June 5). What alcohol does to a child. *Time,* 76.

Gostout, B. (2007, January 22). *Cervical cancer vaccine: Who needs it, how it works* [On-line]. Available: http://www.mayoclinic.com/print/ccrvical-cancer-vaccine/WO00120

Gotlib, I. H., & Hammen, C. L. (Eds.). (2002). *Handbook of depression.* New York: Guilford Press.

Gottesman, I. I. (2001). Psychopathology through a lifespan-genetic prism. *American Psychologist, 56,* 867–877.

Gottfredson, L. S. (2002). Where and why *g* matters: Not a mystery. *Human Performance, 15,* 24–46.

Gottfredson, L. S. (2003). Dissecting practical intelligence theory: Its claims and evidence. *Intelligence, 31,* 342–397.

Gottman, J. M. (2003, May 1). Cited in B. Carey, For better or worse: Marriage by the numbers. *Los Angeles Times,* F1.

Gottman, J. M. (1999). *Seven principles for making marriage work.* New York: Three Rivers Press.

Gottman, J. M. (2000, September 14). Cited in K. S. Peterson, "Hot" and "cool" phases could predict divorce. *USA Today,* 9D.

Gottman, J. M., Gottman, J. S., & DeClaire, J. (2006). *10 lessons to transform your marriage.* New York: Crown Publishers.

Gould, R. A. (1969). Subsistence behaviour among the Western Desert Aborigines of Australia. *Oceania, 39,* 253–274.

Gould, S. J. (1981). *The mismeasure of man.* New York: Norton.

Gould, S. J. (1994, November). The geometer of race. *Discover.*

Gould, S. J. (1996). *The mismeasure of man* (revised and expanded). New York: Norton.

Graham, J. R. (2005). *MMPI-2: Assessing personality and psychopathology* (4th ed.). New York: Oxford University Press.

Graham, L. O. (1995). *Member of the club.* New York: HarperCollins.

Gramling, C. (2006, March 4). Gender gap: Male-only gene affects men's dopamine levels. *Science News, 169,* 132–133.

Grandin, T. (1992). Calming effects of deep touch pressure in patients with autistic disorder, college students, and animals. *Journal of Child and Adolescent Psychopharmacology, 2,* 63–72.

Grandin, T. (2002, May 6). Myself. *Time,* 56.

Grant, P., Young, P., & DeRubeis, R. (2005). Cognitive behavioral therapy. In G. O. Gabbard, J. S. Beck & J. Holmes (Eds.), *Oxford textbook of psychotherapy.* New York: Oxford University Press.

Granvold, D. K. (Ed.). (1994). *Cognitive and behavioral treatment.* Pacific Grove, CA: Brooks/Cole.

Gray, J. R., Braver, T. S., & Raichle, M. E. (2002). Integration of emotion and cognition in the lateral prefrontal cortex. *Proceeding of the National Academy of Sciences, 99,* 4115–4120.

Greatley, A. (2004, June 13). Cited in BBC News, *Bid to end mental health stigma* [On-line]. Available: http://news.bbc.co.uk/go/pr/-/2/hi/health/ 3798593.stm

Greco, L. A., & Morris, T. L. (2001). Treating childhood shyness and related behavior: Empirically evaluated approaches to promote positive social interactions. *Clinical Child and Family Psychology Review, 4,* 299–318.

Green, J. P., & Lynn, S. J. (2000). Hypnosis and suggestion-based approaches to smoking cessation: An examination of the evidence. *International Journal of Clinical and Experimental Hypnosis, 48,* 195–224.

Greenberg, J. (1978). The americanization of Roseto. *Science News, 113,* 378–382.

Greenberg, L. S., & Rice, L. N. (1997). Humanistic approaches to psychotherapy. In P. L. Wachtel & S. B. Messer (Eds.), *Theories of psychotherapy: Origins and evolution.* Washington, DC: American Psychological Association.

Greenberg, R., & Perlman, C. A. (1999). The interpretation of dreams: A classic revisited. *Psychoanalytic Dialogues, 9,* 749–765.

Greene, B., & Winfrey, O. (1996). *Make the connection.* New York: Hyperion.

Greene, J. D., Nystrom, L. E., Engell, A. D., Darley, J. M., & Cohen, J. D. (2004). The neural bases of cognitive conflict and control in moral judgment. *Neuron, 44,* 389–400.

Greenfield, P. M. (2003, February). Cited in E. Benson, Intelligence across cultures. *Monitor on Psychology,* 56–58.

Greenfield, P. M. (1997). You can't take it with you. *American Psychologist, 52,* 1115–1124.

Greensite, G. (2007, February 17). Myths and facts: Rape myths. *California Coalition Against Sexual Assault* [On-line]. Available: http://www.calcasa.org/34,0,html

Greer, M. (2005). Structural malformations. In L. P. Rowland (Ed.), *Merritt's neurology* (pp. 587–600). Philadelphia: Lippincott Williams & Wilkins.

Gregory, R. L. (1974). Recovery from blindness: A case study. In R. L. Gregory (Ed.), *Concepts and mechanisms of perception.* London: Gerald Duckworth.

Gresham, F. M., Beebe-Frankenberger, M. E., & MacMillan, D. L. (1999). A selective review of treatments for children with autism: Description and methodological considerations. *School Psychology Review, 28,* 559–575.

Grigorenko, R. (2006, April 1). Cited in B. Bower, Smarty brains: High-IQ kids navigate notable neural shifts. *Science News, 169,* 195.

Grimaldi, J. V. (1986, April 16). "The mole" evicted from sewer. *San Diego Tribune.*

Grimes, W. (2006, September 2). Tracing the strange history of a family with a mysterious, incurable disease. *The New York Times,* A20.

Grinalds, J. (2002, September 12). Cited in Fifty female cadets report to The Citadel. *Black Issues in Higher Education.*

Grogan, B., Shaw, B., Ridenhour, R., Fine, A., & Eftimiades, M. (1993, May). Their brothers' keepers? *People.*

Gron, G., Wunderlich, A. P., Spitzer, M., Tomczak, R., & Riepe, M. W. (2000). Brain activation during human navigation: Gender-different neural networks as substrate of performance. *Nature Neuroscience, 3,* 404–408.

Grossman, C. L., & Nichols, B. (2006, January 18). Some hope for more laws; others fear them. *USA Today,* 5A.

Groth-Marnat, G. (2003). *Handbook of psychological assessment* (4th ed.). Hoboken, NJ: John Wiley & Sons.

Gruen, J. R. (2005, November 5). Cited in B. Bower, Bad readout from DNA. *Science News, 168,* 292–293.

Grunbaum, A. (1993). *Validation in the clinical theory of psychoanalysis.* Madison, CT: International Universities Press.

Grunbaum, A. (2006). Is Sigmund Freud's psychoanalytic edifice relevant to the 21st century? *Psychoanalytic Psychology, 23,* 257–284.

Grundberg, A. (2006, March 8). Gordon Parks, photojournalist who showed dignity amid oppression, dies at 93. *The New York Times,* C16.

Gruwell, E. (2007). *Teach with your heart.* New York: Broadway Books.

Guilford, J. P. (1967). *The nature of human intelligence.* New York: McGraw-Hill.

Guinness world records 2007. (2007). London: Guinness.

Gunn, E. P. (2006, October 16). It is in your head. *U.S. News & World Report,* EE8–9.

Gupta, S. (2002, March 11). Is your doctor too drowsy? *Time,* 85.

Gupta, S. (2006, March 13). Sleep deprived. *Time.*

Gura, T. (1997). Obesity sheds its secrets. *Science, 275,* 751–753.

Gureje, O., Simon, G. E., Ustun, T. B., & Goldberg, D. P. (1997). Somatization in cross-cultural perspective: A World Health Organization study in primary care. *American Journal of Psychiatry, 154,* 989–995.

Gurung, R. A. R. (2005). How do students really study (and does it matter)? *Teaching of Psychology, 32,* 239–241.

Gustavson, C. R., Kelly, D. J., Sweeney, M., & Garcia, J. (1976). Prey-lithium aversion I: Coyotes and wolves. *Behavioral Biology, 17,* 61–72.

Guterl, F. (2002, November 11). What Freud got right. *Newsweek,* 50–51.

Gutgesell, M. E., & Payne, N. (2004). Issues of adolescent psychological development in the 21st century. *Pediatrics in Review, 25,* 79–85.

Guthrie, J. P., Ash, R. A., & Bendapudi, V. (1995). Additional validity evidence for a measure of morning-ness. *Journal of Applied Psychology, 80,* 186–190.

Guthrie, R. V. (1976). *Even the rat was white.* New York: Harper & Row.

Gwyer, P., & Clifford, B. R. (1997). The effects of the cognitive interview on recall, identification, confidence, and the confidence/accuracy relationship. *Applied Cognitive Psychology, 11,* 121–145.

Gyr, A. (2007, January 8). Wie set to attend Stanford. *The Stanford Daily.*

Haber, N. R. (1980, November). Eidetic images are not just imaginary. *Psychology Today.*

Hadders-Algra, M. (2002). Variability in infant motor behavior: A hallmark of the healthy nervous system. *Infant Behavior & Development, 2,* 433–451.

Haessler, A., & Rosenthal, M. B. (2003). Psychological aspects of obstetrics & gynecology. In A. H. DeCherney & L. Nathan (Eds.), *Current obstetric & gynecologic diagnosis & treatment* (9th ed.). New York: Lange Medical Books/McGraw-Hill.

Haggard, T. (2006a, November 5). Ted Haggard's letter to New Life Church. *Colorado Springs Gazette.*

Haggard, T. (2006b, November 19). Cited in L. Goodstein, Minister's own rules sealed his fate. *The New York Times,* 22.

Haislip, G. (2003, November 27). *Methylphenidate (Ritalin™) facts.* Office of Diversion Control, U.S. Drug Enforcement Agency, Washington, DC. Washington, DC: National Institute of Health.

Halbreich, U. (2003). Anxiety disorders in women: A developmental and lifecycle perspective. *Depression and Anxiety, 17,* 107–110.

References

Haliburn, J. (2000). Reasons for adolescent suicide attempts. *Journal of the American Academy of Child and Adolescent Psychiatry, 29*, 13.

Halpern, D. (2003, May). Cited in K. Kersting, Cognitive sex differences: A "political minefield." *Monitor on Psychology*, 54–55.

Halpern, D. F. (1998). Teaching critical thinking for transfer across domains. *American Psychologist, 53*, 449–455.

Halpern, D. F. (2000). *Sex differences in cognitive abilities* (3rd ed.). Hillsdale, NJ: Lawrence Erlbaum.

Ham, P. (2005, February 15). Treatment of panic disorder. *American Family Physician*.

Hamann, S. B., Ely, T. D., Hoffman, J. M., & Kilts, C. D. (2002). Ecstasy and agony: Activation of the human amygdala in positive and negative emotions. *Psychological Science, 13*, 135–141.

Hamer, D. (2002). Rethinking behavior genetics. *Science, 298*, 71–72.

Hamilton, B. (2004). *Soul surfer*. New York: Pocket Books.

Hamilton, M. A. (2005). *God vs. the gavel*. New York: Cambridge University Press.

Hamm, A. O., Schupp, H. T., & Weike, A. I. (2003). Motivational organization of emotions: Autonomic changes, cortical responses, and reflex modulation. In R. D. Lane & L. Nadel (Eds.), *Cognitive neuroscience of emotion*. New York: Oxford University Press.

Han, S., & Humphreys, G. W. (1999). Interactions between perceptual organization based on Gestalt laws and those based on hierarchical processing. *Perception & Psychophysics, 61*, 1287–1298.

Hancock, L. (1996, March 18). Mother's little helper. *Newsweek*.

Hansen, J. T. (2000). Psychoanalysis and humanism: A review and critical examination of integrationist efforts with some proposed resolutions. *Journal of Counseling and Development, 78*, 21–28.

Hanson, G. R., & Venturelli, P. J. (1998). *Drugs and society* (5th ed.). Boston: Jones and Bartlett.

Hanson, G. R., Venturelli, P. J., & Fleckenstein, A. E. (2002). *Drugs and society* (7th ed.). Boston: Jones and Bartlett.

Hanson, G. R., Venturelli, P. J., & Fleckenstein, A. E. (2006). *Drugs and society* (9th ed.). Sudbury, MA: Jones and Bartlett.

Hao, J., Li, K., Li, K., Zhang, D., Wang, W. M., Yang, Y., Yan B., Shan, B., & Zhou, X. (2005). Visual attention deficits in Alzheimer's disease: An fMRI study. *Neuroscience Letters, 385*, 18–23.

Harder, B. (2006, April 29). Brain delay: Air pollutants linked to slow childhood mental development. *Science News, 169*, 259–260.

Hardin, C., & Banaji, M. R. (1993). The influence of language on thought. *Social Cognition, 11*, 277–308.

Hardy, J. B., Welcher, D. W., Mellits, E. D., & Kagan, J. (1976). Pitfalls in the measurement of intelligence: Are standardized intelligence tests valid for measuring the intellectual potential of urban children? *Journal of Psychology, 94*, 43–51.

Hareli, S., & Weiner, B. (2002). Social emotions and personality inferences: A scaffold for a new direction in the study of achievement motivation. *Educational Psychologist, 37*, 183–193.

Hargreaves, D. A., & Tiggemann, M. (2006). Body image is for girls: A qualitative study of boys' body image. *Journal of Health Psychology, 11*, 567–576.

Harmon, A. (2006, June 15). That wild streak? Maybe it runs in the family. *The New York Times*, A19.

Harmon-Jones, E., & Harmon Jones, C. (2002). Testing the action-based model of cognitive dissonance: The effect of action orientation on postdecisional attitudes. *Personality and Social Psychology Bulletin, 28*, 711–723.

Harris, J. C. (1995). *Developmental neuropsychiatry* (Vol. 1). New York: Oxford University Press.

Harris, J. C. (2003). Pinel orders the chains removed from the insane at Bicetre. *Archives of General Psychiatry, 60*, 442.

Harris, J. M., & Dean, P. J. A. (2003). Accuracy and precision of binocular 3-D motion perception. *Journal of Experimental Psychology, 29*, 869–881.

Hart, B., & Risley, T. R. (2006, November 26). Cited in P. Tough, What it takes to make a student. *The New York Times Magazine*.

Hart, F., & Risley, T. (1996). Cited in B. Bower, Talkative parents make kids smarter. *Science News, 150*, 100.

Hartmann, P. (2006, May 21). Cited in D. Sefton, Sign language: Studies debunking astrology do little to deter followers. *The San Diego Union-Tribune*, E2.

Hartwell, S. (2003). Deviance over the life course: The case of homeless substance abusers. *Substance Use & Misuse, 38*, 475–502.

Harvey, G. A., Bryant, R. A., & Tarrier, N. (2003). Cognitive behaviour therapy for posttraumatic stress disorder. *Clinical Psychology Review, 23*, 501–522.

Harzem, P. (2004). Behaviorism for new psychology: What was wrong with behaviorism and what is wrong with it now? *Behavior and Philosophy, 32*, 5–12.

Haslinger, K. (2005). Placebo power. *Scientific American Mind, 16*, 31.

Hathaway, W. (2006, April 13). Teens lose out on ample hours of precious sleep. *Northwest Herald*.

Hauk, O., Johnstrude, I., & Pulvermuller, F. (2004). Somatotopic representation of action words in human motor and premotor cortex. *Neuron, 41*, 301–307.

Hauser, M. (2003, July 15). Cited in N. Wade, Early voices: The leap to language. *New York Times*, D1.

Hauser, S. L., & Beal, M. F. (2006). Introduction: Pathogenesis of neurological diseases. In S. L. Hauser (Ed.), *Harrison's neurology in clinical medicine* (pp. 3–13). New York: McGraw-Hill.

Hawk, T. (2002). *Tony Hawk: Professional skateboarder*. New York: HarperCollins.

Hayes, K. J., & Hayes, C. H. (1951). The intellectual development of a home-raised chimpanzee. *Proceedings of the American Philosophical Society, 95*, 105–109.

Hazeltine, E., & Ivry, R. B. (2002). Can we teach the cerebellum new tricks? *Science, 296*, 1979–1980.

Healy, B. (2006, September 4). Obesity gets an early start. *U.S. News & World Report*, 79.

Healy, M. (2000, November 29). Computer improves mammogram results. *USA Today*, 9D.

Healy, M. C. (2005, July/August). A cautionary note on using graphology for hiring and promoting employees. *Explorer* [On-line]. Available: http://www.rockethire.com/newsletter/2005/3/best.html

Healy, S. D., de Kort, S. R., & Clayton, N. S. (2005). The hippocampus, spatial memory and food hoarding: A puzzle revisited. *Trends in Ecology and Evolution, 20*, 17–22.

Heatherton, T. F., Mahamedi, F., Striepe, M., Gield, A. E., & Keel, P. (1997). A 10-year longitudinal study of body weight, dieting, and eating disorder symptoms. *Journal of Abnormal Psychology, 106*, 117–125.

Heatherton, T. F., Phelps, E. A., & Ledoux, J. E. (2004). Emotion and social neuroscience. Introduction. In M. S. Gazzaniga (Ed.), *The cognitive neurosciences III* (pp. 973–975). Cambridge, MA: MIT Press.

Hechtman, L., Abikoff, H., Klein, R. G., Weiss, G., Respitz, D., Kouri, J., Blum, C., Greenfield, B., Etcovitch, J., Fleiss, K., & Pollack, S. (2004). Academic achievement and emotional status of children with ADHD treated with long-term methylphenidate and multimodal psychosocial treatment. *Journal of the American Academy of Child and Adolescent Psychiatry, 43*, 812–819.

Heider, F. (1958). *The psychology of interpersonal relations*. New York: Wiley.

Heilman, K. M. (2000). Emotional experience: A neurological model. In R. D. Lane & L. Nadel (Eds.), *Cognitive neuroscience of emotion*. New York: Oxford University Press.

Heiman, J. R. (2002). Sexual dysfunction: Overview of prevalence, etiological factors, and treatments. *The Journal of Sex Research, 39*, 73–78.

Helgeson, V. S. (1994). Prototypes and dimensions of masculinity and femininity. *Sex Roles, 31*, 653–682.

Helmes, E., & Pachana, N. A. (2005). Professional doctoral training in psychology: International comparison and commentary. *Australian Psychology, 40*, 45–53.

Hellmich, N. (2000, March 29). One way to get to sleep: Get up. *USA Today*, 1A.

Hellmich, N. (2005, October 20). Bigger portions will get eaten. *USA Today*, 9D.

Hellmich, N. (2006a, September 14). Report pleads for a united front against childhood obesity. *USA Today*, 8D.

Hellmich, N. (2006b, October 23). Freshman 15 drops some pounds. *USA Today*.

Helmuth, L. (2002). Redrawing the brain's map of the body. *Science, 296*, 1587–1588.

Helmuth, L. (2003a). Caudate-over-heels in love. *Science, 302*, 1320.

Helmuth, L. (2003b). Fear and trembling in the amygdala. *Science, 300*, 568–569.

Helson, R. (1996). In search of the creative personality. *Creativity Research Journal, 9*, 295–306.

Helwig, C. C. (1997). Making moral cognition respectable (again): A retrospective review of Lawrence Kohlberg. *Contemporary Psychology, 42*, 191–195.

Helzer, J. E., & Canino, G. J. (Eds.). (1992). *Alcoholism in North America, Europe, and Asia*. New York: Oxford University Press.

Hemphill, J. F. (2003). Interpreting the magnitudes of correlation coefficients. *American Psychologist, 58*, 78–80.

Henderson, W. C. (2006, October 23). Putting limits on teen drivers. *Time*, 71–72.

Henker, B., & Whalen, C. K. (1989). Hyperactivity and attention deficits. *American Psychologist, 44*, 216–233.

Henry, T. (1999, September 15). Sex is No. 1 struggle, teen girls say. *USA Today*, 9D.

Herdt, G. (2004, January). Sexual development, social oppression, and local culture. *Sexuality Research & Social Policy, 1*, 39–62.

Hergenhahn, B. R. (2004). *An introduction to the history of psychology* (5th ed.). Belmont, CA: Wadsworth.

Herida, P. (2003). *Profile for Peter Herida* [On-line]. Available: http://obesityhelp.com/morbidobesity/members/profile.php?N=H982614091

Herida, P. (2005). *A survivor's story: He lost 500 pounds and gained a new life* [On-line]. Available: http://www.srhs.org/betterhealth_story. asp?Story ID=246

Herkenham, M. (1996, December 16). Cited in D. Ferrell, Scientists unlocking secrets of marijuana's effects. *Los Angeles Times*.

Herman, L. (1999, July 21). Cited in J. Mastro, Dialogue with a dolphin. *San Diego Union-Tribune*, E1.

Herman, L. (2006, November). Cited in M. J. Weiss, Animal Einsteins. *Reader's Digest*, 144–150.

Herman, W. E. (1990). Fear of failure as a distinctive personality trait measure of test anxiety. *Journal of Research and Development in Education, 23*, 180–185.

Herr, N. (2001). *The sourcebook for teaching science*. Australia: John Wiley & Sons.

Herrnstein, R. J., & Murray, C. (1994). *The bell curve*. New York: Free Press.

Hersen, M., & Thomas, J. C. (Eds.). (2006). *Comprehensive handbook of personality and psychopathology: Adult psychopathology* (Vol. 2). Hoboken, NJ: John Wiley & Sons.

Heussler, H. S. (2005). Common causes of sleep disruption and daytime sleepiness: Childhood sleep disorders II. *Medical Journal of Australia, 182,* 484–489.

Hewstone, M., Rubin, M., & Willis, H. (2002). Intergroup bias. *Annual Review of Psychology, 53,* 575–604.

Hickey, E. W. (2006). *Serial murderers and their victims* (4th ed.). Belmont, CA: Thomson Wadsworth.

Hickman, G., Bartholomae, S., & McKenry, P. C. (2000). Influence of parenting styles on the adjustment and academic achievement of traditional college freshmen. *Journal of College Student Development, 41,* 41–54.

Hidalgo, R. B., & Davidson, J. R. T. (2000). Posttraumatic stress disorder: Epidemiology and health-related considerations. *Journal of Clinical Psychiatry, 61 (supplement 7),* 5–13.

Higbee, K. L. (2001). *Your memory: How it works and how to improve it* (2nd ed.). New York: Marlowe & Company.

Higgins, E. T. (2000). Social cognition: Learning about what matters in the social world. *European Journal of Social Psychology, 30,* 3–39.

Higley, D. (2002, July). Cited in M. F. Small, Drunk monkeys. *Discover,* 41–44.

Hill, A., Niven, C. A., & Knussen, C. (1996). Pain memories in phantom limbs: A case study. *Pain, 66,* 381–384.

Hill, A. B., Kemp-Wheeler, S. M., & Jones, S. A. (1987). Subclinical and clinical depression: Are analogue studies justifiable? *Personality and Individual Differences, 8,* 113–120.

Hill, C. E., & Nakayama, E. Y. (2000). Client-centered therapy: Where has it been and where is it going? A comment on Hathaway (1948). *Journal of Clinical Psychology, 56,* 861–875.

Hill, D. E., Yeo, R. A., Campbell, R. A., Hart, B., Vigil, J., & Brooks, W. (2003). Magnetic resonance imaging correlates of attention-deficit/hyperactivity disorder in children. *Neuropsychology, 17,* 496–506.

Hill, J. O., Wyatt, H. R., Reed, G. W., & Peters, J. C. (2003). Obesity and the environment: Where do we go from here? *Science, 299,* 853–855.

Hilts, P. H. (1995). *Memory's ghost: The strange tale of Mr. M and the nature of memory.* New York: Simon & Schuster.

Hingson, R., & Winter, M. (2003). Epidemiology and consequences of drinking and driving. *Alcohol Research and Health, 27,* 63–78.

Hirshey, G. (2003, April). Songs from the heart. *Ladies Home Journal,* 122–123.

Hirshkowitz, M., Moore, C. A., & Minhoto, G. (1997). The basics of sleep. In M. R. Pressman & W. C. Orr (Eds.), *Understanding sleep: The evaluation and treatment of sleep disorders.* Washington, DC: American Psychological Association.

Hitti, M. (2006, June 8). What you need to know about Gardasil, the newly approved cervical cancer vaccine. *WebMD* [On-line]. Available: http://www.webmd.com/content/Article/123/115100.htm

Hobson, J. A. (2002). *Making sense of dreaming.* New York: Oxford University Press.

Hoff, E. (2005). *Language development* (3rd ed.). Belmont, CA: Thomson Wadsworth.

Hoffman, C., Lau, I., & Johnson, D. R. (1986). The linguistic relativity of person cognition: An English-Chinese comparison. *Journal of Personality and Social Psychology, 51,* 1097–1105.

Hoffman, G. A., Harrington, A., & Fields, H. L. (2005). Pain and the placebo: What we have learned. *Perspectives in Biology and Medicine, 48,* 248–265.

Hoffman, H. G. (2004, July 26). Virtual-reality therapy. *Scientific American.*

Hofmann, A. (1983). *LSD: My problem child.* Los Angeles: J. P. Tarcher.

Hokanson, J. E., & Butler, A. C. (1992). Cluster analysis of depressed college students' social behaviors. *Journal of Personality and Social Psychology, 62,* 273–280.

Holahan, C. K., & Sears, R. R. (1995). *The gifted group in later maturity.* Stanford, CA: Stanford University Press.

Holden, C. (1995). Sex and the granular layer. *Science, 268,* 807.

Holden, C. (1997). Thumbs up for acupuncture. *Science, 278,* 1231.

Holden, C. (2002). Versatile cells against intractable diseases. *Science, 297,* 500–502.

Holden, C. (2003a). Deconstructing schizophrenia, *Science, 299,* 333–335.

Holden, C. (2003b). Future brightening for depression treatment. *Science, 302,* 810–813.

Hollingworth, L. (2002, March 12). Cited in E. Goode, The uneasy fit of the precocious and the average. *New York Times,* D1.

Hollon, S. D. (2003). Does cognitive therapy have an enduring effect? *Cognitive Therapy and Research, 27,* 71–75.

Hollon, S. D., DeRubeis, R. J., Shelton, R. C., Amsterdam, J. D., Salomon, R. M., O'Reardon, J. P., Lovett, M. L., Young, P. R., Haman, K. L., Freeman, B. B., & Gallop, R. (2005). Prevention of relapse following cognitive therapy vs. medications in moderate to severe depression. *Archives of General Psychiatry, 62,* 417–422.

Hollon, S. D., Thase, M. E., & Markowitz, J. C. (2002). Treatment and prevention of depression. *Psychological Science (supplement), 3,* 39–77

Holloway, J. D. (2003, March). Advances in anger management. *Monitor on Psychology,* 54–55.

Holmes, M., & Newman, M. G. (2006). Generalized anxiety disorder. In M. Hersen & J. C. Thomas (Eds.), *Comprehensive handbook of personality and psychopathology: Adult psychopathology* (Vol. 2, pp. 101–120). Hoboken, NJ: John Wiley & Sons.

Holroyd, C. B., & Coles, M. G. H. (2002). The neural basis of human error processing: Reinforcement learning, dopamine, and the error-related negativity. *Psychological Review, 109,* 679–709.

Holt, J. (2005, May 8). Of two minds. *New York Times Magazine,* 11–13.

Honda, H., Shimizu, Y., & Rutter, M. (2005). No effect of MMR withdrawal on the incidence of autism: A total population study. *Journal of Child Psychology and Psychiatry, 46,* 572–579.

Honey, R. C. (2000). Associative priming in Pavlovian conditioning. *The Quarterly Journal of Experimental Psychology, 53B,* 1–23.

Hong, Y., Morris, M. W., Chiu, C., & Benet-Martinez, V. (2000). Multicultural minds. *American Psychologist, 55,* 709–720.

Honts, C. R. (1994). Psychophysiological detection of deception. *Current Directions in Psychological Science, 3,* 77–82.

Honts, C. R., Raskin, D. C., & Kircher, J. C. (1994). Mental and physical countermeasures reduce the accuracy of polygraph tests. *Journal of Applied Psychology, 79,* 252–259.

Hoover, N. C., & Pollard, N. J. (2000). Initiation rites in American high schools: A national survey. http://www.alfred.edu/news/html/hazing_study.html

Hooyman, N., & Niyak, H. (1999). *Social gerontology* (5th ed.). New York: Allyn & Bacon.

Horgan, J. (1996, December). Why Freud isn't dead. *Scientific American,* 106–111.

Horovitz, B. (2003, July 1). Under fire, food giants switch to healthier fare. *USA Today,* 1A.

Horowitz, J. M. (1999, March 22). Libido letdown. *Time,* 115.

Horsburgh, S., Biermann, R., & Howard, C. (2001, December 31). Going strong. *People,* 125–126.

Howard, J. A., & Renfrow, D. G. (2006). Social cognition. In J. Delamater (Ed.), *Handbook of social psychology* (pp. 259–281). New York: Springer.

Howard, M. S., & Medway, F. (2004). Adolescents' attachment and coping with stress. *Psychology in the Schools, 41,* 391–402.

Howe, M. L. (2003). Memories from the cradle. *Current Directions in Psychological Sciences, 12,* 62–65.

Howlin, P. (1997). Prognosis in autism: Do specialist treatments affect long-term outcome? *European Child & Adolescent Psychiatry, 6,* 55–72.

Hser, Y. I., Hoffman, V., Grella, C. E., & Anglin, D. (2001). A 33-year follow-up of narcotic addicts. *Archives of General Psychiatry, 58,* 503–508.

Hsu, C. (2006, January 14). Put down that fork. *Science News, 169,* 21.

Hubel, D. H., & Wiesel, T. N. (1979). Brain mechanisms of vision. *Scientific American, 241,* 150–162.

Huggins, L. E. (2005). *Drug war deadlock: The policy battle continues.* Stanford, CA: Hoover Institution Press.

Hui, K. K. S., Liu, J., Makris, N., Gollub, R. L., Chen, A. J. W., Moore, C. I., Kennedy, D. N., Rosen, B. R., & Kwong, K. K. (2000). Acupuncture modulates the limbic system and subcortical gray structures of the human brain: Evidence from fMRI studies in normal subjects. *Human Brain Mapping, 9,* 13–25.

Hulbert, A. (2005, November 20). The prodigy puzzle. *The New York Times Magazine,* 64.

Humane Society of the United States. (2006). *General information on animal research* [On-line]. Available: http://www.hsus.org/animals_in_research/general_information_on_animal_research/frequently_asked_questions_about_animals_in_research.html

Humphreys, G. W., & Forde, E. M. E. (2001). Category specificity in mind and brain. *Behavioral and Brain Sciences, 243,* 497–509.

Humphreys, G. W., & Muller, H. (2000). A search asymmetry reversed by figure-ground assignment. *Psychological Science, 11,* 196–210.

Hunt, M. (1993). *The story of psychology.* New York: Doubleday.

Hurwitz, T. A. (2003). Somatization and conversion disorder. *Canadian Journal of Psychiatry,* 172–178.

Huskinson, T. L. H., & Haddock, G. (2006). Individual differences in attitude structure and the accessibility of the affective and cognitive components of attitude. *Social Cognition, 24,* 453–468.

IANS (Indo-Asian News Service). (2006, December 16). *Over 50 Vietnamese girls faint due to mass "hysteria."* New Delhi, India: Author.

IANSA (International Action Network on Small Arms). (2006, March 13). *Number of children and adults killed and wounded in school shootings around the world since 1996.* London: Author.

Ignelzi, R. J. (2006a, January 31). So, if syrup is sullied, how do we conquer a cough? *The San Diego Union-Tribune,* E1.

Ignelzi, R. J. (2006b, May 9). Queasy rider: Motion sickness can make your travels a real trial *The San Diego Union-Tribune,* E1–E4.

IHGSC (International Human Genome Sequencing Consortium). (2004). Finishing the euchromatic sequence of the human genome. *Nature, 431,* 931–945.

Ilmberger, J., Rau, S., Noachtar, S., Arnold, S., & Winkler, P. (2002). Naming tools and animals: Asymmetries observed during direct electrical cortical stimulation. *Neuropsychologia, 40,* 695–700.

References

Incredible weight loss stories. (2007, January 10). [Online]. Available: http://www.oprah.com

Ingram, J. A. (2006, November 3). Cited in C. Woodward, Amnesiac can't return to his past to go into future. *The San Diego Union-Tribune*, A4.

Inmate marriages. (2007, January 27). County of Mendocino [On-line]. Available: http://www.co.mendocino.ca/us/sheriff/corrections/inmatemarriages.htm

Irwin, C. E., Burg, S. J., & Cart, C. U. (2002). America's adolescents: Where have we been, where are we going? *Journal of Adolescent Health, 31,* 91–123.

Isacson, O., Bjorklund, L. M., & Schumacher, J. M. (2003). Towards full restoration of synaptic and terminal function of the dopaminergic system in Parkinson's disease from regeneration and neuronal replacement by stem cells. *Annals of Neurology, 53,* 135–148.

Iversen, L. L. (2000). *The science of marijuana.* New York: Oxford University Press.

Izard, C. E. (1993). Four systems for emotion activation: Cognitive and noncognitive processes. *Psychological Review, 100,* 68–90.

Jackendoff, R. (1994). *Patterns in the mind. Language and human nature.* New York: Basic Books.

Jacks, J. Z., & Cameron, K. A. (2003). Strategies for resisting persuasion. *Basic and Applied Social Psychology, 25,* 145–161.

Jacks, J. Z., & Devine, P. G. (2000). Attitude importance, forewarning of message content, and resistance to persuasion. *Basic and Applied Social Psychology, 22,* 19–29.

Jackson, R. L. (1994, May 4). A false sense of sincerity: Some cases belie polygraph results. *Los Angeles Times.*

Jacob, T. J. C., Wang, L., Jaffer, S., & McPhee, S. (2006). Changes in the odor quality of androstadienone during exposure-induced sensitization. *Chemical Senses, 31,* 3–8.

Jacobi, C., Dahme, B., & Dittmann, R. (2002). Cognitive-behavioural, fluoxetine and combined treatment for bulimia nervosa: Short- and long-term results. *European Eating Disorders Review, 10,* 179–198.

Jacobs, M. (2003). *Sigmund Freud* (2nd ed.). Thousand Oaks, CA: Sage.

Jacobson, J. L., & Jacobson, S. W. (1999). Drinking moderately and pregnancy. *Alcohol Research and Health, 23,* 25–30.

Jaffee, S., & Hyde, J.S. (2000). Gender differences in moral orientation: A meta-analysis. *Psychological Bulletin, 126,* 703–726.

James, W. (1884; reprinted 1969). What is an emotion? In *William James: Collected essays and reviews.* New York: Russell & Russell.

James, W. (1890). *The principles of psychology.* New York: Dover.

Jamison, K. R. (1995). Manic-depressive illness and creativity. *Scientific American, 272,* 62–67.

Jang, K. L. (2005). *The behavioral genetics of psychopathology: A clinical guide.* Mahwah, NJ: Erlbaum.

Janis, I. L. (1989). *Crucial decisions: Leadership in policymaking and crisis management.* New York: Free Press.

Janofsky, M. (2000, September 16). Antidrug program's end stirs up Salt Lake City. *New York Times,* A8.

Janus, S. S., & Janus, C. L. (1993). *The Janus report on sexual behavior.* New York: John Wiley & Sons.

Japenga, A. (1994, June 5). Rewriting the dictionary of madness. *Los Angeles Times Magazine.*

Jarrett, C. (2006, March 3). Food, glorious food—Czech eating habits after 1989. *Radio Prague* [On-line]. Available: http://www.radio.cz/en/article/77368

Jarriel, T., & Sawyer, D. (1997, January 16). Romania: What happened to the children? *Turning point.* New York: ABC News.

Jauhar, S. (2001, May 6). Life out of balance. *New York Times Magazine,* 104–107.

Jayson, S. (2005, July 18). Cohabitation is replacing dating. *USA Today,* 6D.

Jefferson, D. J. (2005, August 8). America's most dangerous drug. *Newsweek,* 40–48.

Jensen, P. (1999). A 14-month randomized clinical trial of treatment strategies for attention-deficit/hyperactivity disorder. *Archives of General Psychiatry, 56,* 1073–1086.

Jensen, A. R. (2005). Mental chronometry and the unification of differential psychology. In R. J. Sternberg & J. E. Pretz (Eds.), *Cognition and intelligence* (pp. 26–50). New York: Cambridge University Press.

Jerome, R. (2001, June 4). Disarming the rage. *People,* 56–57.

John, O. P. (1990). The "big five" factor taxonomy: Dimensions of personality in the natural language and in questionnaires. In L. A. Pervin (Ed.), *Handbook of personality.* New York: Guilford.

Johnsen, B. H., Thayer, J. F., Laberg, J. C., Wormnes, B., Raadal, M., Skaret, E., Kvale, G., & Berg, E. (2003). Attentional and physiological characteristics of patients with dental anxiety. *Anxiety Disorders, 17,* 75–87.

Johnson, C. R., Hunt, F. M., & Siebert, J. J. (1994). Discrimination training in the treatment of pica and food scavenging. *Behavior Modification, 18,* 214–229.

Johnson, J. G., Cohen, P., Smailes, E. M., Kasen, S., & Brook, J. S. (2002). Television viewing and aggressive behavior during adolescence and adulthood. *Science, 295,* 2468–2471.

Johnson, K. (1999, April 5). Government agencies see truth in polygraphs. *USA Today,* 11A.

Johnson, L. C., Slye, E. S., & Dement, W. (1965). Electroencephalographic and autonomic activity during and after prolonged sleep deprivation. *Psychosomatic Medicine, 27,* 415–423.

Johnson, N. (2006, September 30). *Supporters: Med marijuana bill needed* [On-line]. Available: http://www.yankton.net/stories/093006/community_20060930030.shtml

Johnson, S. (2003, March). Brain and emotions: Fear. *Discover,* 32–39.

Johnston, V. (2000, February). Cited in B. Lemley, Isn't she lovely. *Discover,* 43–49.

Jones, E. (1953). *The life and work of Sigmund Freud* (3 vols.). New York: Basic Books.

Jones, E., & Berglas, S. (1978). Control of attributions about the self through self-handicapping strategies: The appeal of alcohol and the role of underachievement. *Personality and Social Psychology Bulletin, 4,* 200–206.

Jones, S. M., & Zigler, E. (2002). The Mozart effect: Not learning from history. *Applied Developmental Psychology, 23,* 355–372.

Jones, S. R., & Fernyhough, C. (2006). A new look at the neural diathesis-stress model of schizophrenia: The primacy of social-evaluative and uncontrollable situations. *Schizophrenia Bulletin.*

Jorgensen, R. S., Johnson, B. T., Kolodziej, M. E., & Schreer, G. D. (1996). Elevated blood pressure and personality: A meta-analytic review. *Psychological Bulletin, 120,* 293–320.

Joseph, S., Manafi, E., Iakovaki, A. M., & Cooper, R. (2003). Personality, smoking motivation, and self-efficacy to quit. *Personality and Individual Differences, 34,* 749–758.

Jusczyk, P. W., & Hohne, E. A. (1997). Infants' memory for spoken words. *Science, 277,* 1984–1986.

Kabot, S., Masi, W., & Segal, M. (2003). Advances in the diagnosis and treatment of autism spectrum disorders. *Professional Psychology, Research and Practice, 34,* 26–33.

Kagan, J. (1994). *The nature of the child* (10th anniversary edition). New York: Basic Books.

Kagan, J. (1998). Biology and the child. In W. Damon & R. M. Lerner (Eds.), *Handbook of child psychology* (Vol. 1). New York: John Wiley & Sons.

Kagan, J. (2003a). Behavioral inhibition as a temperamental category. In R. J. Davidson, K. R. Scherer & H. H. Goldsmith (Eds.), *Handbook of affective sciences.* New York: Oxford University Press.

Kagan, J. (2003b). Biology, context, and developmental inquiry. *Annual Review of Psychology, 54,* 1–23.

Kagan, J., Reznick, J. S., & Snidman, N. (1988). Biological bases of childhood shyness. *Science, 240,* 167–171.

Kagan, J., & Snidman, N. (1991). Temperamental factors in human development. *American Psychologist, 46,* 856–862.

Kagitcibasi, C., & Poortinga, Y. H. (2000). Cross-cultural psychology. *Journal of Cross-Cultural Psychology, 31,* 129–147.

Kalat, J. W. (2004). *Biological psychology* (8th ed.). Belmont, CA: Wadsworth.

Kalat, J. W. (2007). *Biological psychology* (9th ed.). Belmont, CA: Thomson/Wadsworth.

Kalat, J. W., & Shiota, M. N. (2007). *Emotion.* Belmont, CA: Thomson/Wadsworth

Kalb, L. M., & Loeber, R. (2003). Child disobedience and noncompliance: A review. *Pediatrics, 111,* 641–652.

Kalimo, R., Tenkanen, L., Harma, M., Poppius, E., & Heinsalmi, P. (2000). Job stress and sleep disorders: Findings from the Helsinki heart study. *Stress Medicine, 16,* 65–75.

Kamil, A. C., & Cheng, K. (2001). Way-finding and landmarks: The multiple-bearings hypothesis. *The Journal of Experimental Biology, 2043,* 103–113.

Kandel, E., & Abel, T. (1995). Neuropeptides, adenylyl cyclase, and memory storage. *Science, 268,* 825–826.

Kandel, E. R. (2006, April/May). Cited in M. Solms, Freud returns. *Scientific American Mind,* 28–34.

Kanner, L. (1943). Autistic disturbances in affective contact. *Nervous Child, 2,* 217–250.

Kantowitz, B. H., Roediger, H. L., III, & Elmes, D. G. (2005). *Experimental psychology: Understanding psychology research* (8th ed.). Belmont, CA: Wadsworth.

Kaplan, D. M. (1972). On shyness. *International Journal of Psycho-Analysis, 53,* 439–453.

Kaplan, R. M., & Saccuzzo, K. P. (2005). *Psychological testing: Principles, applications, and issues* (6th ed.). Belmont, CA: Thomson Wadsworth.

Kassebaum, N. L. (1994). Head start: Only the best for America's children. *American Psychologist, 49,* 123–126.

Katigbak, M. S., Church, A. T., Guanzon-Lapena, M. A., Carlota, A., & del Pilar, G. H. (2002). Are indigenous personality dimensions culture specific? Philippine inventories and the five-factor model. *Journal of Personality and Social Psychology, 82,* 89–101.

Kato, M., Phillips, B. G., Sigurdsson, G., Narkiewicz, K., Pesek, C. A., & Somers, V. K. (2000). Effects of sleep deprivation on neural circulatory control. *Hypertension, 35,* 1173–1175.

Katz, J. (1992). Psychophysiological contributions to phantom limbs. *Canadian Journal of Psychiatry, 37,* 282–298.

Kaufman, A. S. (2003, February). Cited in E. Benson, Intelligent intelligence testing. *Monitor on Psychology,* 48–51.

Kaufman, A. S. (2000). Tests of intelligence. In R. J. Sternberg (Ed.), *Handbook of intelligence.* New York: Cambridge University Press.

Kaufman, A. S., Reynolds, C. R., & McLean J. E. (1989). Age and WAIS-R intelligence in a national sample of adults in the 20 to 74 age range: A cross-sectional analysis with educational level controlled. *Intelligence, 13,* 235–253.

Kaufman, J., & Zigler, E. (1989). The intergenerational transmission of child abuse. In C. Cicchetti & V. Carlson (Eds.), *Child maltreatment: Theory and research on the causes and consequences of child abuse and neglect.* Cambridge, England: Cambridge University Press.

Kaufman, J. C., & Baer, J. (2002). I bask in dreams of suicide: Mental illness, poetry, and women. *Review of General Psychology, 6,* 271–286.

Kaufman, L. (2000). Cited in B. Bower, The moon also rises—and assumes new sizes. *Science News, 157,* 22.

Kaufman, M. (2005, January 3). Meditation gives brain a charge, study finds. *Washington Post,* A5.

Kaufman, M. (2006, June 9). FDA approves vaccine that should prevent most cervical cancers. *Washington Post,* A1.

Kaye, W. (2002, March). Cited in T. DeAngelis, Further gene studies show promise. *Monitor on Psychology,* 35.

Kearins, J. M. (1981). Visual spatial memory in Australian Aboriginal children of desert regions. *Cognitive Psychology, 13,* 434–460.

Keats, J. (2006, June). We see the future better than 20/20. *Popular Science,* 58–60.

Keck, G. C., & Kupecky, R. M. (1995). *Adopting the hurt child: Hope for families with special-needs children.* Colorado Springs, CO: Pinon Press.

Keck, P. E., & McElroy, S. L. (2003). New approaches in managing bipolar depression. *Journal of Clinical Psychiatry, 64 (supplement 6),* 13–18.

Keefe, F. J., Lumley, M. A., Buffington, A. L. H., Carson, W., Studts, J. L., Edwards, C. L., Macklem, D. J., Aspnes, A. K., Fox, L., & Steffey, D. (2002). Changing face of pain: Evolution of pain research in *Psychosomatic Medicine. Psychosomatic Medicine, 64,* 921–938.

Keel, P. K., & Mitchell, J. E. (1997). Outcome in bulimia nervosa. *The American Journal of Psychiatry, 154,* 313–321.

Keenan, K., & Shaw, D. (1997). Developmental and social influences on young girl's early problem behavior. *Psychological Bulletin, 121,* 95–113.

Keeney, B. (2004). *Balians: Traditional healers of Bali.* Creek, CT: Leete's Island Books.

Keiser, R. E., & Prather, E. N. (1990). What is the TAT? A review of ten years of research. *Journal of Personality Assessment, 55,* 800–803.

Keisler, B. D., & Armsey, T. D., II (2006). Caffeine as an ergogenic acid. *Current Sports Medicine Reports, 5,* 215–219.

Keller, H., & Greenfield, P. M. (2000). History and future of development in cross-cultural psychology. *Journal of Cross-Cultural Psychology, 31,* 52–62.

Kelley, H. H. (1967). Attribution theory in social psychology. In D. Levine (Ed.), *Nebraska symposium on motivation* (Vol. 15). Lincoln: University of Nebraska Press.

Kelley, W. M. (2002). Cited in J. Travis, The brain's funny bone. *Science News, 162,* 308–309.

Keltner, D., & Ekman, P. (2000). Facial expression of emotion. Cognitive and social construction in emotions. In M. Lewis & J. M. Haviland-Jones (Eds.), *Handbook of emotions* (2nd ed.). New York: Guilford.

Keltner, D., Ekman, P., Gonzaga, G. C., & Beer, J. (2003). Facial expression of emotion. In R. D. Lane & L. Nadel (Eds.), *Cognitive neuroscience of emotion.* New York: Oxford University Press.

Kemeny, M. C. (2003). The psychobiology of stress. *Current Directions in Psychological Science, 12,* 125–129.

Kendler, K. S., Aggen, S. H., Tambs, K., & Reichborn-Kjennerud, T. (2006). Illicit psychoactive substance use, abuse and dependence in a population-based sample of Norwegian twins. *Psychological Medicine, 36,* 955–962.

Kendler, K. S., Karkowski, L. M., Neale, M. C., & Prescott, C. A. (2000a). Illicit psychoactive substance use, heavy use, abuse, and dependence in a US population-based sample of male twins. *Archives of General Psychiatry, 57,* 261–269.

Kendler, K. S., Kuhn, J., & Prescott, C. A. (2004). The interrelationship of neuroticism, sex, and stressful life events in the prediction of episodes of major depression. *American Journal of Psychiatry, 161,* 631–636.

Kendler, K. S., Thornton, L. M., Gilman, S. E., & Kessler, R. C. (2000b). Sexual orientation in a U.S. National sample of twin and nontwin sibling pairs. *American Journal of Psychiatry, 157,* 1843–1846.

Kennedy, D. V., & Doepke, K. J. (1999). Multicomponent treatment of a test anxious college student. *Education and Treatment of Children, 22,* 203–217.

Kenrick, D. T., Trost, M. R., & Sundie, J. M. (2004). Sex roles as adaptations: An evolutionary perspective on gender differences and similarities. In A. H. Eagly, A. E. Beall, & R. J. Sternberg (Eds.), *The psychology of gender* (2nd ed., pp. 65–91). New York: Guilford Press.

Kenworthy, J. B., & Miller, N. (2002). Attributional biases about the origins of attitudes: Externality, emotionality, and rationality. *Journal of Personality and Social Psychology, 82,* 693–707.

Kershaw, S. (2006, January 23). On engine 22, it's women who answer the bell. *The New York Times,* A1.

Kershaw, T. C., & Ohlsson, S. (2004). Multiple causes of difficulty in insight: The case of the nine-dot problem. *Journal of Experimental Psychology: Learning, Memory, and Cognition, 30,* 3–13.

Kessler, R. C. (2003). Epidemiology of women and depression. *Journal of Affective Disorders, 74,* 25–33.

Kessler, R. C., Berglund, P., Demler, O., Jim, R., Merikangas, K. R., & Walters, E. E. (2005). Lifetime prevalence and age-of-onset distributions of DSM-IV disorders in the national comorbidity survey replication. *Archives of General Psychiatry, 62,* 593–602.

Kessler, R. C., McGonagle, K. A., Zhao, S., Nelson, C. B., Higher, M., Eshleman, S., Wittchen, H., & Kendler, K. S. (1994). Lifetime and 12-month prevalence of DSM-III-R psychiatric disorders in the United States. *Archives of General Psychiatry, 51,* 8–19.

Khantzian, E. J., & Mack, J. E. (1994). How AA works and why it's important for clinicians to understand. *Journal of Substance Abuse Treatment, 11,* 77–92.

Kiecolt-Glaser, J. K., McGuire, L., Robles, T. F., & Glaser, R. (2002). Emotions, morbidity, and mortality: New perspectives from psychoneuroimmunology. *Annual Review of Psychology, 53,* 83–107.

Kiedis, A. (2004). *Scar tissue.* New York: Hyperion.

Kihlstrom, J. F. (1993). The continuum of consciousness. *Consciousness and Cognition, 2,* 334–354.

Kihlstrom, J. F., Glisky, M. L., & Angiulo, M. J. (1994). Dissociative tendencies and dissociative disorders. *Journal of Abnormal Psychology, 103,* 117–124.

Kimball, D. R., & Holyoak, K. J. (2005). Transfer and expertise. In E. Tulving & F. M. Craik (Eds.), *The Oxford handbook of memory.* New York: Oxford University Press.

Kimura, D. (1992). Sex differences in the brain. *Scientific American, 267,* 119–125.

Kinetz, E. (2006, September 26). Is hysteria real? Brain images say yes. *The New York Times,* D1.

King, A. (1992). Comparison of self-questioning, summarizing, and notetaking-review as strategies for learning from lectures. *American Educational Research Journal, 29,* 303–323.

King, B. M. (2006). The rise, fall, and resurrection of the ventromedial hypothalamus in the regulation of feeding behavior and body weight. *Physiology & Behavior, 87,* 221–244.

King, F. A., Yarbrough, C. J., Anderson, D. C., Gordon, T. P., & Gould, K. G. (1988). Primates. *Science, 240,* 1475–1482.

King, M. C., & Motulsky, A. G. (2002). Mapping human history. *Science, 298,* 2342–2343.

King, S. (1991, August 25). From hard time to prime time. *Los Angeles Times/Calendar,* 3.

Kinsbourne, M. (1994). Sugar and the hyperactive child. *New England Journal of Medicine, 330,* 355–356.

Kinsey, A. C., Pomeroy, W. B., & Martin, C. E. (1948). *Sexual behavior in the human male.* Philadelphia: Saunders.

Kinsman, M. (2006, September 19). Businesswomen in California still hit glass ceiling. *The San Diego Union-Tribune,* H2.

Kirk, M. S. (1972, March). Head-hunters in today's world. *National Geographic.*

Kirkcaldy, B. D., Shephard, R. J., & Furnham, A. F. (2002). The influence of type A behaviour and locus of control upon job satisfaction and occupational health. *Personality and Individual Differences, 33,* 1361–1371.

Kirmayer, L. J. (1991). The place of culture in psychiatric nosology: Taijin kyofusho and DSM-III-R. *Journal of Nervous and Mental Disease, 179,* 19–28.

Kirp, D. L. (2004, November 11). Life way after Head Start. *The New York Times Magazine,* 32–38.

Kirsch, I. (1994). Cognitive-behavioral hypnotherapy. In J. W. Rhue, S. J. Lynn, & I. Kirsch (Eds.), *Handbook of clinical hypnosis.* Washington, DC: American Psychological Association.

Kirsch, I., & Braffman, W. (2001). Imaginative suggestibility and hypnotizability. *Current Directions in Psychological Sciences, 10,* 57–61.

Kirsch, I., & Lynn, S. J. (1995). The altered state of hypnosis. *American Psychologist, 50,* 846–858.

Kirsch, I., & Lynn, S. J. (1998). Dissociation theories of hypnosis. *Psychological Bulletin, 123,* 100–115.

Kirsch, I., Lynn, S. J., & Rhue, J. W. (1993). Introduction to clinical hypnosis. In J. W. Rhue, S. J. Lynn, & I. Kirsch (Eds.), *Handbook of clinical hypnosis.* Washington, DC: American Psychological Association.

Kirschenbaum, H., & Jourdan, A. (2005). The current status of Carl Rogers and the person-centered approach. *Psychotherapy: Theory, Research, Practice, Training, 42,* 37–51.

Kirsner, D. (1990). Is there a future for American psychoanalysis? *Psychoanalytic Review, 77,* 175–200.

Kitayama, N., Quinn, S., & Bremner, J. D. (2006). Smaller volume of anterior cingulated cortex in abuse-related posttraumatic stress disorder. *Journal of Affective Disorders, 90,* 171–174.

Kitayama, S., Duffy, S., Kawamura, T., & Larsen, J. T. (2003). Perceiving an object and its context in different cultures: A cultural look at new look. *Psychological Science, 14,* 201–206.

Kleijn, W. C., van der Ploeg, H. M., & Topman, R. M. (1994). Cognition, study habits, test anxiety, and academic performance. *Psychological Reports, 75,* 1219–1226.

Klein, C. T. F., & Helweg-Larsen, M. (2002). Perceived control and the optimistic bias: A meta-analytic review. *Psychology and Health, 17,* 437–446.

Klein, D. N., Durbin, C. E., Shankman, S. A., & Santiago, N. J. (2002). Depression and personality. In I. H. Gotlib & C. L. Hammen (Eds.), *Handbook of depression.* New York: Guilford Press.

Klein, R. (2002, August 15). Cited in N. Wade, Language gene is traced to emergence of humans. *New York Times,* A18.

Kleinknecht, R. A. (1994). Acquisition of blood, injury, and needle fears and phobias. *Behavior Research and Therapy, 32,* 817–823.

References

Kleinman, A., & Cohen, A. (1997, March). Psychiatry's global challenge. *Scientific American*, 86–89.

Klich, L. Z., & Davidson, G. R. (1983). A cultural difference in visual memory: On le voit, on ne le voit plus. *International Journal of Psychology, 18*, 189–201.

Klingberg, G., & Hwang, C. P. (1994). Children's dental fear picture test (CDFP): A projective test for the assessment of child dental fear. *Journal of Dentistry for Children, 62*, 89–96.

Klinger, E. (1987, October). The power of daydreams. *Psychology Today*.

Kluger, J. (2003, January 20). Masters of denial. *Time*.

Kluger, J. (2005, April 4). Secrets of the shy. *Time*, 50–52.

Kluger, J. (2006a, January 16). The surprising power of the aging brain. *Time*, 84–87.

Kluger, J. (2006b, July 10). The new science of siblings. *Time*, 46–55.

Kluger, J., & Masters, C. (2006, August 28). How to spot a liar. *Time*, 46–48.

Knight, R. A. (1992, July). Cited in N. Youngstrom, Rapist studies reveal complex mental map. *APA Monitor*.

Knutson, J. R. (1995). Psychological characteristics of maltreated children: Putative risk factors and consequences. *Annual Review of Psychology, 46*, 401–431.

Kobasa, S. C. (1982). Commitment and coping in stress resistance among lawyers. *Journal of Personality and Social Psychology, 42*, 707–717.

Kobasa, S. C., Maddi, S. R., & Kahn, S. (1982a). Hardiness and health: A prospective study. *Journal of Personality and Social Psychology, 42*, 168–177.

Kobasa, S. C., Maddi, S. R., & Puccetti, M. C. (1982b). Personality and exercise as buffers in the stress-illness relationship. *Journal of Behavioral Medicine, 5*, 391–404.

Kobayashi, M., Tomioka, N., Ushiyama, Y., & Ohhashi, T. (2003). Arithmetic calculation, deep inspiration or handgrip exercise-mediated pre-operational active palmer sweating responses in humans. *Autonomic Neuroscience: Basic and Clinical, 104*, 58–65.

Koch, D. D., & Harvey, T. M. (2006). Vision correction procedures. In R. E. Rakel & E. T. Bope (Eds.), *Conn's current therapy* (pp. 227–228). Philadelphia: Saunders.

Koch, W. (2000, June 16). Big tobacco tells Florida jury it has reformed. *USA Today*, 13A.

Koh, M. T., & Bernstein, I. L. (2005). Mapping conditioned taste aversion associations using c-Fos reveals a dynamic role for insular cortex. *Behavioral Neuroscience, 119*, 388–398.

Kohlberg, L. (1984). *The psychology of moral development: Essays on moral development* (Vol. 11). San Francisco: Harper & Row.

Köhler, W. (1917; reprinted 1925). *The mentality of apes* (E. Winter, Trans.). New York: Harcourt Brace & World.

Kohn, D. (2004, July 25). Ecstasy research looks for benefits. *Baltimore Sun*.

Koko's world. (2006, November 20). [On-line]. Available: http://www.koko.org/world/

Kolata, G. (2000a, May 15). Sharing of profits is debated as the value of tissue rises. *New York Times*, A1.

Kolata, G. (2000b, October 17). How the body knows when to gain or lose. *New York Times*, D1.

Kolata, G. (2001, March 8). Parkinson's research is set back by failure of fetal cell implants. *New York Times*, A1.

Kolata, G. (2003, February 25). Genetic revolution: How much, how fast? *New York Times*, D7.

Kolb, B., & Taylor, L. (2000). Facial expression, emotion and hemispheric organization. In R. D. Lane & L. Nadel (Eds.), *Cognitive neuroscience of emotion*. New York: Oxford University Press.

Kong, J., Gollub, R. L., Rosman, I. S., Webb, J. M., Vangel, M. G., Kirsch, I., & Kaptchuk, T. J. (2006). Brain activity associated with expectancy-enhanced placebo analgesia as measured by functional magnetic resonance imaging. *The Journal of Neuroscience, 26*, 381–388.

Koolman, J. (2005). *Color atlas of biochemistry* (2nd ed.). Stuttgart: Thieme Medical Publishers.

Koopman, J. M. (1995, February 20). Cited in M. Cimons & T. H. Maugh, II, New strategies fuel optimism in AIDS fight. *Los Angeles Times*.

Kopp, C. B., & Neufeld, S. J. (2003). Emotional development during infancy. In R. J. Davidson, K. R. Scherer & H. H. Goldsmith (Eds.), *Handbook of affective sciences*. New York: Oxford University Press.

Koppelstaetter, K., Siedentopf, C., Poeppel, T., Haala, I., Ischebeck, A., & Mottaghy, F. (2005, December 1). Influence of caffeine excess on activation patterns in verbal working memory. *Radiological Society of North America*, annual meeting, Chicago.

Koren, G. (2004). Special aspects of perinatal and pediatric pharmacology. In B. G. Katzung (Ed.), *Basic and Clinical Pharmacology* (9th ed., pp. 995–1006). New York: McGraw-Hill.

Koriat, A. (2005). Control processes in remembering. In E. Tulving & F. M. Craik (Eds.), *The Oxford handbook of memory*. New York: Oxford University Press.

Koriat, A., Goldsmith, M., & Pansky, A. (2000). Toward a psychology of memory accuracy. *Annual Review of Psychology, 51*, 481–537.

Kornack, D. R., & Rakic, P. (2001). Cell proliferation without neurogenesis in adult primate neocortex. *Science, 29*, 2127–2130.

Kosch, G. (2004, November 11). Cited in J. L. Davis, Want a happy marriage? Be nice, don't nitpick. *MedicineNet.com*.

Kotulak, R. (2006, June 22). Hormone that may launch puberty is discovered. *The San Diego Union-Tribune*, E1.

Kowalski, R. M. (1996). Complaints and complaining: Functions, antecedents, and consequences. *Psychological Bulletin, 119*, 179–196.

Kozak, J. M., Liebowitz, M. R., & Foa, E. B. (2000). Cognitive behavior therapy for obsessive-compulsive disorder: The NIMH sponsored collaborative study. In W. K. Goodman & M. V. Rudorfer (Eds.), *Obsessive-compulsive disorder: Contemporary issues in treatment. Personality and clinical psychology series* (pp. 501–530). Mahwah, NJ: Erlbaum.

Kramer, M. (2006). Psychology of dreaming. In T. L. Lee-Chiong (Ed.), *Sleep: A comprehensive handbook* (pp. 37–43). Hoboken, NJ: John Wiley & Sons.

Kraus, S. J. (1995). Attitudes and the prediction of behavior: A meta-analysis of the empirical literature. *Personality and Social Psychology Bulletin, 21*, 58–75.

Kreinin, T. (2003, May 23). Cited in K. S. Peterson, Sexually active teens also are often clueless. *USA Today*, 8D.

Kubovy, M., & Wagemans, J. (1995). Grouping by proximity and multistability in dot lattices: A quantitative Gestalt theory. *Psychological Science, 6*, 225–234.

Kugelmann, R. (1998). The psychology and management of pain: Gate control as theory and symbol. In S. J. Henderikus (Ed.), *The body and psychology*. London: Academy of Hebrew Language.

Kuhl, P. K., Andruski, J. E., Christovich, I. A., Christovich, L. A., Kolzhevnikova, E. V., Ryskina, V. L., Stolyarova, E. I., Sundberg, U., & Lacerda, F. (1997). Cross-language analysis of phonetic units in language addressed to infants. *Science, 277*, 684–687.

Kurtz, E. (1979). *Not-God: A history of Alcoholics Anonymous*. Center City, MN: Hazelden.

Kurtz, P. (1995, May/June). Is John Beloff an absolute paranormalist? *Skeptical Inquirer*.

Lacey, M. (2002, January 6). In Kenyan family, ritual for girls still divides. *New York Times*, 4.

Lacey, M. (2003, February 6). African women gather to denounce genital cutting. *New York Times*, A3.

LaFee, S. (1996, September 11). Fragile lives. *San Diego Union-Tribune*.

LaFee, S. (2000, March 29). Sight to behold. *San Diego Union-Tribune*, E12.

LaFrance, M., Hecht, M. A., & Paluck, E. L. (2003). The contingent smile: A meta-analysis of sex differences in smiling. *Psychological Bulletin, 129*, 305–334.

Lake, D. F., Briggs, A. D., & Akporiaye, E. T. (2004). Immunopharmacology. In B. G. Katzung (Ed.), *Basic and clinical pharmacology* (9th ed., pp. 931–957). New York: McGraw Hill.

Lalwani, A. K., & Snow, J. G., Jr. (2006). Disorders of smell, taste, and hearing. In S. L. Hauser (Ed.)., *Harrison's neurology in clinical medicine*. New York: McGraw-Hill.

Lamb, N. (1990). *Guide to teaching strings* (5th ed.). Dubuque, IA: William C. Brown.

Lamberg, L. (2004). Road to recovery for cocaine users can start in primary care setting. *Journal of the American Medical Association, 292*, 1807–1809.

Lamberg, L. (2006). Melatonin effective in totally blind people. *Psychiatric News, 41*, 26.

Lambert, G. W., Reid, C., Kaye, D. M., Jennings, G. L., & Ester, M. D. (2002). Effect of sunlight and season on serotonin turnover in the brain. *The Lancet, 360*, 1840–1842.

Lambert, M. J., Bergin, A. E., & Garfield, S. L. (2004). Introduction and historical overview. In M. J. Lambert (Ed.), *Bergin and Garfield's handbook of psychotherapy and behavior change*. New York: Wiley.

Lanfranco, F., Kamischke, A., Zitzmann, M., & Nieschlag, P. E. (2004). Klinefelter's syndrome. *Lancet, 364*, 273–284.

Langdridge, D., & Butt, T. (2004). The fundamental attribution error: A phenomenological critique. *British Journal of Social Psychology, 43*, 357–369.

Langleben, D. (2006, February 5). In R. M. Henig, Looking for the lie. *The New York Times Magazine*, 47–80.

Langlois, J. H., Kalakanis, L., Rubenstein, A. J., Larson, A., Hallam, M., & Smoot, M. (2000). Maxims or myths of beauty? A meta-analysis and theoretical review. *Psychological Bulletin, 136*, 390–423.

Langlois, J. H., Roggman, L. A., & Musselman, L. (1994). What is average and what is not average about attractive faces? *Psychological Science, 5*, 214–220.

Lanyado, M., & Horne, A. (Eds.). (1999). *The handbook of child and adolescent psychotherapy*. New York: Routledge.

Larivee, S., Normandeau, S., & Parent, S. (2000). The French connection: Some contributions of French-language research in the post-Piagetian era. *Child Development, 71*, 823–839.

Larsson, H., Andershed, H., & Lichtenstein, P. (2006). A genetic factor explains most of the variation in the psychopathic personality. *Journal of Abnormal Psychology, 115*, 221–230.

Latané, B. (1981). The psychology of social impact. *American Psychologist, 36*, 343–356.

Latané, B., & Darley, J. M. (1970). *The unresponsive bystander: Why doesn't he help?* New York: Appleton-Century-Crofts.

Latané, B., & Nida, S. (1981). Ten years of research on group size and helping. *Psychological Bulletin, 89*, 308–324.

Laumann, E., Michael, R. T., Gagnon, J. H., & Kolata, G. (1994). *The social organization of sexuality.* Chicago: University of Chicago Press.

Laumann, E. O., Nicolosi, A., Glasser, D. B., Paik, A., Gingell, C., Moreira, E., & Wang, T. (2005). Sexual problems among women and men aged 40–80 y: Prevalence and correlates identified in the Global Study of Sexual Attitudes and Behaviors. *International Journal of Impotence Research, 17,* 39–57.

Laurence, R. P. (2003, October 15). Now Limbaugh asks for a rush to change judgment of drug use. *San Diego Union-Tribune,* F7.

Law, A. J., & Weinberger, D. R. (2006, April 18). Cited in N. Wade, Schizophrenia as misstep by giant gene. *The New York Times,* D4.

Lazarus, R. S. (1999). *Stress and emotion.* New York: Springer.

Lazarus, R. S. (2000). Evolution of a model of stress, coping and discrete emotions. In V. R. Rice (Ed.), *Handbook of stress, coping and health.* Thousand Oaks, CA: Sage.

Lazarus, R. S. (2006). *Stress and emotion: A new synthesis.* New York: Springer.

Leaper, C. (2000). Gender, affiliation, assertion, and the interactive context of parent-child play. *Developmental Psychology, 36,* 381–393.

Leavy, J. (1996, March 18). With Ritalin, the son also rises. *Newsweek.*

LeBlanc, L. A., Hagopian, L. P., & Maglieri, K. A. (2000). Use of a token economy to eliminate excessive inappropriate social behavior in an adult with developmental disabilities. *Behavioral Interventions, 15,* 135–143.

LeDoux, J. (2003). Cited in L. Helmuth, Fear and trembling in the amygdala. *Science, 300,* 568–569.

Lee, M. R. (2005). Curare: The South American arrow poison. *Journal of the Royal College of Physicians of Edinburgh, 35,* 83–92.

Lee, R. (2005, April 15). "Boy code" a factor in fatal school shootings? *Washington Blade.*

Lee-Chiong, T., & Sateia, M. (2006). Pharmacologic therapy of insomnia. In T. L. Lee-Chiong (Ed.), *Sleep: A comprehensive handbook* (pp. 125–132). Hoboken, NJ: John Wiley & Sons.

Leedham, B., Meyerowitz, B. E., Muirhead, J., & Frist, W. H. (1995). Positive expectations predict health after heart transplantation. *Health Psychology, 14,* 74–79.

Legrand, L. N., Iacono, W. G., & McGue, M. (2005, March/April). Predicting addiction. *American Scientist, 93,* 140–147.

LeGrange, D. (2002, March). Cited in T. DeAngelis, Promising treatments for anorexia and bulimia. *Monitor on Psychology,* 38–41.

Lehrman, S. (2006, June). The implicit prejudice. *Scientific American,* 32–34.

Leibel, R. L., Rosenbaum, M., & Hirsch, J. (1995). Changes in energy expenditure resulting from altered body weight. *New England Journal of Medicine, 332,* 621–628.

Leichsenring, F., Rabung, S., & Leibing, E. (2004). The efficacy of short-term psychodynamic psychotherapy in specific psychiatric disorders. *Archives of General Psychiatry, 61,* 1208–1216.

Leinwand, D. (2000, May 9). Heroin's resurgence closes drug's traditional gender gap. *USA Today,* A1.

Leinwand, D. (2002, February 11). Ecstasy grows as danger to teens. *USA Today,* A1.

Leippe, M. R., & Eisenstadt, D. (1994). Generalization of dissonance reduction: Decreasing prejudice through induced compliance. *Journal of Personality and Social Psychology, 67,* 395–413.

Leland, J. (1994, February 14). Homophobia, *Newsweek.*

Leland, J. (1998, October 26). Not quite Viagra nation. *Newsweek,* 68.

Lemerise, E. A., & Dodge, K. A. (2000). The development of anger and hostile interactions. In M. Lewis & J. M. Haviland-Jones (Eds.), *Handbook of emotions* (2nd ed.). New York: Guilford.

Lemley, B. (2000, February). Isn't she lovely? *Discover,* 42–49.

Lemley, B. (2006, August). Shiny happy people: Can you reach nirvana with the aid of science? *Discover, 27,* 62–77.

Lemonick, M. D. (2006, January 16). Measuring IQ points by the cupful. *Time,* 94–95.

Lemonick, M. D., & Dorfman, A. (1999, August 23). Up from the apes. *Time,* 50–58.

Lenox, R. H., & Hahn, C. (2000). Overview of the mechanism of action of lithium in the brain: Fifty-year update. *Journal of Clinical Psychiatry, 2000 (supplement 9),* 5–15.

Leo, J. (1987, January 12). Exploring the traits of twins. *Time.*

Leonard, W. R. (2002, December). Food for thought. *Scientific American,* 106–115.

Lepper, M. R., Henderlong, J., & Gingras, I. (1999). Understanding the effects of extrinsic rewards on intrinsic motivation—Uses and abuses of meta-analysis: Comment on Deci, Koestner, and Ryan (1999). *Psychological Bulletin, 125,* 669–676.

Lerner, R. M., & Galambos, N. L. (1998). Adolescent development: Challenges and opportunities for research, programs, and policies. *Annual Review of Psychology, 49,* 413–446.

Lesch, K. P. (2005). Alcohol dependence and gene x environment interaction in emotion regulation: Is serotonin the link? *European Journal of Pharmacology, 526,* 113–124.

Leshner, A. I. (2001, June). What does it mean that addiction is a brain disease? *Monitor on Psychology,* 19.

Lessmoellmann, A. (2006, October). Don't count on it. *Scientific American Mind.*

Lester, B. M., LaGasse, L. L., & Seifer, R. (1998). Cocaine exposure and children: The meaning of subtle effects. *Science, 282,* 633–634.

Leuchter, A. F., Cook, I. A., Witte, E. A., Morgan, M., & Abrams, M. (2002). Changes in brain function of depressed subjects during treatment with placebo. *American Journal of Psychiatry, 159,* 122–129.

Leventhal, H., & Patrick-Miller, L. (2000). Emotions and physical illness: Causes and indicators of vulnerability. In M. Lewis & J. M. Haviland-Jones (Eds.), *Handbook of emotions* (2nd ed.). New York: Guilford.

Levin, A. (2005). Psychologists widen push for prescribing privileges. *Psychiatric News, 40,* 6.

Levine, J. M., & Kerr, N. L. (2007). Inclusion and exclusion: Implications for group processes. In A. W. Kruglanski & E. T. Higgins, *Social psychology: Handbook of basic principles* (2nd ed., pp. 759–784). New York: Guilford Press.

Levine, S., & Koenig, J. (Eds.). (1980). *Why men rape: Interviews with convicted rapists.* Toronto: Macmillan.

Levinson, D. F. (2003). Molecular genetics of schizophrenia: A review of the recent literature. *Current Opinion in Psychiatry, 16,* 157–170.

Levitsky, D. (2003, August 11). The "freshman." *U.S. News & World Report,* 54.

Levy, B. R., Slade, M. D., Kunkel, S. R., & Kasl, S. V. (2002). Longevity increased by positive self-perceptions of aging. *Journal of Personality and Social Psychology, 83,* 261–270.

Levy, J. (1985, May). Right brain, left brain: Fact and fiction. *Psychology Today.*

Levy, J., & Trevarthen, C. (1976). Metacontrol of hemispheric function in human split-brain patients. *Journal of Experimental Psychology: Human Perception and Performance, 2,* 299–312.

Levy, J., Trevarthen, C., & Sperry, R. W. (1972). Perception of bilateral chimeric figures following hemispheric deconnection. *Brain, 95,* 61–68.

Levy, K. N., & Scott, L. N. (2006). Other personality disorders. In M. Hersen & J. D. Thomas (Eds.), *Comprehensive handbook of personality and psychopathology: Adult psychopathology* (Vol. 2, pp. 316–336). Hoboken, NJ: John Wiley & Sons.

Lewis, A. (2001, March 26). Snakes scarier than public speaking. *USA Today,* A1.

Lewis, C. E. (1991). Neurochemical mechanisms of chronic antisocial behavior (psychopathy). *Journal of Nervous and Mental Disease, 179,* 720–727.

Lewis, J. W., Brefcynski, J. A., Phinney, R. E., Janik, J. J., & DeYoe, E. A. (2005). Distinct cortical pathways for processing tool versus animal sounds. *Journal of Neuroscience, 25,* 5148–5158.

Lewis, M. H., & Lazoritz, M. (2005). Psychopharmacology of autism spectrum disorders. *Psychiatric Times, 22.*

Lewis-Fernandez, R., Das, A. K., Alfonso, C., Weissman, M. M., & Olfson, M. (2005). Depression in U.S. Hispanics: Diagnostic and management considerations in family practice. *The Journal of the American Board of Family Practice, 18,* 282–296.

Li, T. K. (2000). Pharmacogenetics of responses to alcohol and genes that influence alcohol drinking. *Journal of Studies on Alcohol, 61,* 5–12.

Liberman, N., Trope, Y., & Stephan, E. (2007). Psychological distance. In A. W. Kruglanski & E. T. Higgins, *Social psychology: Handbook of basic principles* (2nd ed., pp. 353–383). New York: Guilford Press.

Lieber, J. (2002, August 12). Swimmer Coughlin may steal show at 2004 Athens Games. *USA Today,* 1C.

Lieberman, D. A. (2000). *Learning: Behavior and cognition* (3rd ed.). Belmont, CA: Wadsworth.

Lieberman, D. A. (2004). *Learning and memory.* Belmont, CA: Wadsworth/Thomson Learning.

Lieberman, J. A. (2005a). Cited in J. Talan, Schizophrenia drugs questioned. *Scientific American Mind, 16,* 8.

Lieberman, J. A. (2005b, September 25). Cited in B. Bower, Meds alert. *Science News, 168,* 195.

Liebert, R. M., & Spiegler, M. D. (1994). *Personality: Strategies and issues* (7th ed.). Pacific Grove, CA: Brooks/Cole.

Liebowitz, M. R., Heimberg, R. G., Schneier, F. R., Hope, D. A., Davies, S., Holt, C. S., Goetz, D., Juster, H. R., Lin, S. H., Bruch, M. A., Marshall, R. D., & Klein, D. F. (1999). Cognitive-behavioral group therapy versus phenelzine in social phobia: Long-term outcome. *Depression and Anxiety, 10,* 89–98.

Lilienfeld, S. O. (1993). Do "honesty" tests really measure honesty? *Skeptical Inquirer, 18,* 32–41.

Lilienfeld, S. O. (2003). When worlds collide. *American Psychologist, 7,* 176–188.

Lilienfeld, S. O., Kirsch, I., Sarbin, T. R., Lynn, S. J., Chaves, J. F., Ganaway, G. K., & Powell, R. A. (1999). Dissociative identity disorder and the sociocognitive model: Recalling the lessons of the past. *Psychological Bulletin, 125,* 507–523.

Lilly, J. C. (1972). *The center of the cyclone.* New York: Bantam.

Lincoln, T. M., Hahlweg, K., Frank, M., vonWitzleben, I., Schroeder, B., & Fiegenbaum, W. (2003). Effectiveness of an empirically supported treatment for social phobia in the field. *Behaviour Research and Therapy, 41,* 1251–1269.

References

Lindsay, J. J., & Anderson, C. A. (2000). From antecedent conditions to violent actions: A general affective aggression model. *Personality and Social Psychological Bulletin, 26,* 533–547.

Lindstrom, M. (2005). *Brand sense: Build powerful brands through touch, taste, smell, sight, and sound.* New York: Free Press.

Ling, G., & Ming, W. (2006, April 27). Japanese organ transplant agency: Chinese organ supplies will not decrease. *The Epoch Times.*

Linnet, K. M., Wisborg, K., Obel, C., Secher, N. J., Thomson, P. H., Agerbo, E., & Henriksen, T. B. (2005). Smoking during pregnancy and the risk for hyperkinetic disorder in offspring. *Pediatrics, 116,* 462–467.

Lipkin, R. (1995). Additional genes may affect color vision. *Science News, 147,* 100.

Lipkins, S. (2006). *Preventing hazing: How parents, teachers, and coaches can stop the violence, harassment, and humiliation.* San Francisco: Jossey-Bass.

Lipton, F. R., Siegel, C., Hannigan, A., Samuels, J., & Baker, S. (2000). Tenure in supportive housing for homeless persons with severe mental illness. *Psychiatric Services, 51,* 479–486.

Lipton, S. D. (1983). A critique of so-called standard psychoanalytic technique. *Contemporary Psychoanalysis, 19,* 35–52.

Lisanby, S. H., Maddox, J. H., Prudic, J., Devanand, D. P., & Sackeim, H. A. (2000). The effects of electroconvulsive therapy on memory of autobiographical and public events. *Archives of General Psychiatry, 57,* 581–590.

Liska, K. (1994). *Drugs & the human body* (4th ed.). New York: Macmillan.

Litt, M. D., Kalinowski, L., & Shafer, D. (1999). A dental fears typology of oral surgery patients: Matching patients to anxiety interventions. *Health Psychology, 18,* 614–624.

Liu, Z., Muehlbauer, K. R., Schmeiser, H. H., Hergenhahn, M., Belharazem, D., & Hollsetin, M. C. (2005). P53 mutations in a benzo(a)pyrene-exposed human p53 knock-in murine fibroblasts correlate with p53 mutations in human lung tumors. *Cancer Research, 65,* 2583–2587.

Livneh, H., Lott, S. M., & Antonak, R. F. (2004). Patterns of psychosocial adaptation to chronic illness and disability: A cluster analytic approach. *Psychology, Health, and Medicine, 9,* 411–430.

Lochman, J. E., Powell, N. R., Whidby, J. M., & Fitzgerald, D. P. (2006). Aggressive children: Cognitive-behavioral assessment and treatment. In P. C. Kendall (Ed.), *Child and adolescent therapy: Cognitive-behavioral procedures* (3rd ed., pp. 33–81). New York: Guilford Press.

Locke, E. A., & Latham, G. P. (2002). Building a practically useful theory of goal setting and task motivation. *American Psychologist, 57,* 705–717.

Loehlin, J. C. (2000). Group differences in intelligence. In R. J. Sternberg (Ed.), *Handbook of intelligence.* New York: Cambridge University Press.

Loehlin, J. C., Neiderhiser, J. M., & Reiss, D. (2003). The behavior genetics of personality and the NEAD study. *Journal of Research in Personality, 37,* 373–387.

Loftus, E. F. (1975). Leading questions and the eyewitness report. *Cognitive Psychology, 7,* 560–572.

Loftus, E. F. (1979). The malleability of memory. *American Scientist, 67,* 312–320.

Loftus, E. F. (1993). The reality of repressed memories. *American Psychologist, 48,* 518–537.

Loftus, E. F. (1997a, September). Creating false memories. *Scientific American,* 70–75.

Loftus, E. F. (1997b). Repressed memory accusations: Devastated families and devastated patients. *Applied Cognitive Psychology, 11,* 25–30.

Loftus, E. F. (1999). Repressed memories. *Forensic Psychiatry, 22,* 61–69.

Loftus, E. F. (2000, April 25). Cited in J. E. Brody, Memories of things that never were. *New York Times,* D8.

Loftus, E. F. (2003a, February 17). Cited in J. Gottlieb, Memories made to order at UCI. *Los Angeles Times,* 81.

Loftus, E. F. (2003b, November). Make-believe memories. *American Psychologist,* 867–873.

Loftus, E. F. (2005a, August 1). Cited in Today@UCI, *Power of suggestion may help diets avoid specific foods.* Available: http://today.uci.edu/ news/release_detail.asp-key=1360

Loftus, E. F. (2005b, December). Cited in A. Krauss, False memories. *Scientific American Mind,* 14–15.

Loftus, E. F., & Hoffman, H. G. (1989). Misinformation and memory: The creation of new memories. *Journal of Experimental Psychology: General, 118,* 409–420.

Loftus, E. F., & Loftus, G. R. (1980). On the performance of stored information in the human brain. *American Psychologist, 35,* 409–420.

Loftus, E. F., Miller, D. G., & Burns, H. J. (1978). Semantic integration of verbal information into a visual memory. *Journal of Experimental Psychology: Human Learning and Memory, 4,* 19–31.

Logue, A. W., Ophir, I., & Strauss, K. E. (1981). The acquisition of taste aversions in humans. *Behavior Research and Therapy, 19,* 319–335.

Lohman, D. F. (2000). Complex information processing and intelligence. In R. J. Sternberg (Ed.), *Handbook of intelligence.* New York: Cambridge University Press.

Long, J. D., Gaynor, P., Erwin, A., & Williams, R. L. (1994). The relationship of self-management to academic motivation, study efficiency, academic satisfaction, and grade point average among prospective education majors. *Psychology, A Journal of Human Behavior, 31,* 22–30.

Lonsway, K., Moore, M., Harrington, C. P., Smeal, E., & Spillar, K. (2003, Spring). Hiring & retaining more women: The advantages to law enforcement agencies. *National Center for Women & Policing,* 1–16.

Lonsway, K. A., & Fitzgerald, L. F. (1994). Rape myths: In review. *Psychology of Women Quarterly, 18,* 133–164.

Lord, C. (2002, October 22). Cited in L. Tarkan, Autism therapy is called effective, but rare. *New York Times,* D2.

Lorenz, K. (1952). *King Solomon's ring.* New York: Crowell.

Losen, D., & Orfield, G. (Eds.). (2002). *Racial inequity in special education.* Cambridge, MA: Harvard Education Publishing Group.

Lothane, Z. (2006a). Freud's legacy–Is it still with us? *Psychoanalytic Psychology, 23,* 285–301.

Lothane, Z. (2006b). Reciprocal free association. *Psychoanalytic Psychology, 23,* 711–727.

Lovaas, O. I. (1987). Behavioral treatment and normal educational and intellectual functioning in young autistic children. *Journal of Consulting and Clinical Psychology, 55,* 3–9.

Lovaas, O. I. (1993). The development of a treatment-research project for developmentally disabled autistic children. *Journal of Applied Behavior Analysis, 26,* 617–630.

Lovaas, O. I. (1999, September). Cited in H. McIntosh, Two autism studies fuel hope—and skepticism. *Monitor: American Psychological Association,* 28.

Lovaas, O. I., & Buch, G. (1997). Intensive behavioral intervention with young children. In N. N. Singh (Ed.), *Prevention and treatment of severe behavior problems.* Pacific Grove, CA: Brooks/Cole.

Loviglio, J. (2003, June 25). Scientists probing where untruths lie. *San Diego Union-Tribune,* F3.

Low, A., Bentin, S., Rockstroh, B., Silberman, Y., Gomolla, A., Cohen, R., & Elbert, T. (2003). Semantic categorization in the human brain: Spatiotemporal dynamics revealed by magnetoencephalography. *Psychological Science, 14,* 367–372.

Loy, I., & Hall, G. (2002). Taste aversion after ingestion of lithium chloride: An associative analysis. *The Quarterly Journal of Experimental Psychology, 55B,* 365–380.

Luan, P. K., Fitzgerald, D. A., Nathan, P. J., & Tancer, M. E. (2006). Association between amygdala hyperactivity to harsh faces and severity of social anxiety in generalized social phobia. *Biological Psychiatry, 59,* 424–429.

Lubell, K. M., Swahn, M. H., Crosby, A. E., & Kegler, S. R. (2004). Methods of suicide among persons aged 10–19 years—United States, 1992–2001. *Morbidity and Mortality Weekly Report, 53,* 471–473.

Luborsky, L., Rosenthal, R., Diguer, L., Andrusyna, T. P., Berman, J. S., Levitt, J. T., Seligman, D. A., & Krause, E. D. (2002). The dodo bird verdict is alive and well—mostly. *Clinical Psychology: Science and Practice, 9,* 2–12.

Luders, E., Narr, K. L., Thompson, P. M., Rex, D. E., Jancke, L., Steinmetz, H., & Toga, A. W. (2004). Gender differences in cortical complexity. *Nature Neuroscience, 7,* 799–800.

Luna, B. (2006, August/September). Cited in L. Sabbagh, Hard at work no, really. *Scientific American Mind,* 20–25.

Lupart, J. L., & Pyryt, M. C. (1996). "Hidden gifted" students: Underachiever prevalence and profile. *Journal for the Education of the Gifted, 20,* 36–53.

Luszczynska, A., & Sutton, S. (2006). Physical activity after cardiac rehabilitation: Evidence that different types of self-efficacy are important in maintainers and relapsers. *Rehabilitation Psychology, 51,* 314–321.

Lykken, D. T. (2003). Cited in D. Watson, Happiness is in your jeans. *Contemporary Psychology, 48,* 242–243.

Lynam, D. R., Milich, R., Zimmerman, R., Novak, S. P., Logan, T. K., Martin, C., Leukefeld, C., & Clayton, R. (1999). Project DARE: No effects at 10-year follow-up. *Journal of Counseling and Clinical Psychology, 67,* 590–593.

Lynn, S. J., Kirsch, I., Barabasz, A., Cardena, E., & Patterson, D. (2000). Hypnosis as an empirically supported clinical intervention: The state of the evidence and a look to the future. *International Journal of Clinical and Experimental Hypnosis, 48,* 239–259.

Lynn, S. J., Loftus, E. F., Lilienfeld, S. O., & Lock, T. (2003, July/August). Memory recovery techniques in psychotherapy. *Skeptical Inquirer,* 40–46.

Lyon, R. (1999, November 22). Cited in B. Kantrowitz & A. Underwood, Dyslexia and the new science of reading. *Newsweek,* 72–78.

Maathai, W. (2004, December 10). *Wangari Maathai? Nobel lecture* [On-line]. Available: http://nobelprize.org/nobel_prozes/peace/laureates/2004/maathai-lecture-text.html

Maathai, W. (2005, January 5). Cited in D. Gilson, *Root causes: An interview with Wangari Maathai* [On-line]. Available: http://www.motherjones.com/news/qa/2005/01/wangari_maathai.html

Maathai, W. (2006). *Unbowed.* New York: Alfred A. Knopf.

Maccoby, E. E. (1984). Socialization and developmental change. *Child Development, 55,* 317–328.

Macfarlane, A. J. (1975). Olfaction in the development of social preferences in the human neonate. *CIBA Foundation Symposium, 33,* 103–117.

MacInnis, L. (2006, June 2). Genital cutting's fatal results cited. *The San Diego Union-Tribune,* A16.

Mackenzie, D. (2000, July). Remote heart surgery. *Popular Science*, 65.

Maclachlan, M., Desmond, D., & Horgan, O. (2003). Psychological correlates of illusory body experiences. *Journal of Rehabilitation Research & Development, 40*, 59–66.

Maclachlan, M., McDonald, D., & Waloch, J. (2004). Mirror treatment of lower limb phantom pain: A case study. *Disability and Rehabilitation, 26*, 901–904.

Macnee, C. L., & McCabe, S. (2000). Microstressors and health. In V. R. Rice (Ed.), *Handbook of stress, coping and health*. Thousand Oaks, CA: Sage.

MacQueen, G., Marshall, J., Perdue, M., Siegel, S., & Biennenstock, J. (1989). Pavlovian conditioning of rat mucosal mast cells to secrete rat mast cell protease II. *Science, 243*, 83–85.

Macrae, C. N., & Bodenhausen, G. V. (2000). Social cognition: Thinking categorically about others. *Annual Review of Psychology, 51*, 93–120.

Maddi, S. R. (2002). The story of hardiness: Twenty years of theorizing, research, and practice. *Consulting Psychology Journal, 54*, 173–185.

Magidoff, R. (1973). *Yehudi Menuhin*. London: Robert Hale.

Magnier, M. (2000, March 25). Japanese on a fast track to addiction. *Los Angeles Times*, A2.

Magnusson, A. (2000). An overview of epidemiological studies on seasonal affective disorder. *Acta Psychiatrica Scandinavica, 101*, 176–184.

Magnusson, A., & Partonen, T. (2005). The diagnosis, symptomatology, and epidemiology of seasonal affective disorder. *CNS Spectrums, 10*, 625–634.

Mahoney, M. J. (2005). Suffering, philosophy, and psychotherapy. *Journal of Psychotherapy Integration, 15*, 337–352.

Mahowlad, M. (2003, February 2). Cited in C. Brown, The man who mistook his wife for a deer. *New York Times Magazine*, 34–41.

Maier, S. R., Watkins, L. R., & Fleshner, M. (1994). Psychoneuroimmunology. *American Psychologist, 49*, 1004–1007.

Maio, G. R., & Haddock, G. (2007). Attitude change. In A. W. Kruglanski & F. T. Higgins, *Social psychology: Handbook of basic principles* (2nd ed., pp. 565–586). New York: Guilford Press.

Maio, G. R., Olson, J. M., Bernard, M. M., & Luke M. A. (2006). Ideologies, values, attitudes, and behavior. In J. Delamater (Ed.), *Handbook of social psychology* (pp. 283–308). New York: Springer.

Maisto, S. A., Galizio, M., & Connors, G. J. (2004). *Drug use and abuse* (4th ed.). Belmont, CA: Wadsworth/Thomson Learning.

Maldonado, P. E., Godecke, I., Gray, C. M., & Bonhoffer, T. (1997). Orientation selectivity in pinwheel centers in cat striate cortex. *Science, 276*, 1551–1555.

Malle, B. F. (2006). The actor-observer assymmetry in attribution: A (surprising) meta-analysis. *Psychological Bulletin, 132*, 895–919.

Malle, B. F., Knobe, J., O'Lauglin, M. J., Pearce, G. E., & Nelson, S. E. (2000). Conceptual structure and social functions of behavior explanations: Beyond person-situation attributions. *Journal of Personality and Social Psychology, 79*, 309–326.

Malone, F. G., Canick, J. A., Ball, R. H., Nyberg, D. A., Comstock, C. H., Bukowski, R., Berkowitz, R. L., Gross, S. J., Dugoff, L., Craigo, S. D., Timor-Tritsch, I. E., Carr, S. R., Wolfe, H. M., Dukes, K., Bianchi, D. W., Rudnicka, A. R., Hacksaw, A. K., Lambert-Messerlian, G., Wald, N. J., & D'Alton, M. E. (2005). First-trimester or second-trimester screening, or both, for Down's syndrome. *The New England Journal of Medicine, 353*, 2001–2011.

Manderscheid, R. W., & Sonnenschein, M. A. (1992). *Mental health, United States, 1992*. Washington, DC: U.S. Department of Health and Human Services.

Mann, D. (2005, June 29). Portrait of a psychopath. *WebMD* [On-line]. Available: http://www.webmd.com/content/Article/108/108749.htm?pagenumber=1

Manning, A. (1998, February 23). Operating with sexism. *USA Today*, D1.

Mansvelder, D. D., De Rover, M., McGehee, D. S., & Brussaard, A. B. (2003). Cholinergic modulation of dopaminergic reward areas: Upstream and downstream targets of nicotine addiction. *European Journal of Pharmacology, 480*, 117–123.

Maratsos, M., & Matheny, L. (1994). Language specificity and elasticity: Brain and clinical syndrome studies. *Annual Review of Psychology, 45*, 487–516.

Marchetti, S., & Bunte, K. (2006). Retailers and banks leverage fundraising power, raising more than $139 million for hurricane relief. *Press room: American Red Cross* [On-line]. Available: http://redcross.org/pressrelease/0,1077,0_314_5172,00.htm

Marcus, D. K., & Miller, R. W. (2003). Sex differences in judgments of physical attractiveness: A social relations analysis. *Personality and Social Psychology Bulletin, 29*, 325–335.

Marcus, M. B. (2000, October 2). Don't let false alarms scare you off prenatal tests, but do get the facts first. *U.S. News & World Report*, 69–70.

Mareschal, D., & Quinn, P. C. (2001). Categorization in infancy. *Trends in Cognitive Science, 5*, 443–450.

"Mariah in hospital with 'exhaustion.'" (2001, July 27). *BBC News*.

Mario, J. (2006). *Michelle Wie: The making of a champion*. New York: St. Martin's Press.

Marklein, M. D. (2002, January 28). California rewrites college admissions. *USA Today*, D1.

Marmar, C. R., Neylan, T. C., & Schoenfeld, F. B. (2002). New directions in the pharmacotherapy of posttraumatic stress disorders. *Psychiatric Quarterly, 73*, 259–270.

Marsa, L. (2002, March 25). Trauma therapy's new focus. *Los Angeles Times*, S8.

Marsh, A. A., Elfenbein, A., & Ambady, N. (2003). Nonverbal "accents": Cultural differences in facial expressions of emotion. *Psychological Science, 14*, 373–376.

Marshall, G. N., Schell, T. L., Glynn, S. M., & Shetty, V. (2006). The role of hyperarousal in the manifestation of posttraumatic psychological distress following injury. *Journal of Abnormal Psychology, 115*, 624–628.

Martens, W. H. J. (2002, January). The hidden suffering of the psychopath. *Psychiatric Times*, 19.

Martin, A., Wiggs, C. L., Ungerfelder, L. G., & Haxby, J. V. (1996). Neural correlates of category-specific knowledge. *Nature, 379*, 649–652.

Martin, C. L. (2000). Cognitive theories of gender development. In T. Eckes & H. M. Trautner (Eds.), *The developmental social psychology of gender*. Mahwah, NJ: Lawrence Erlbaum.

Martin, C. L., Ruble, D. N., & Szrkrybalo, J. (2002). Cognitive theories of early gender development. *Psychological Bulletin, 128*, 903–933.

Martin, G. L. (1982). Thought-stopping and stimulus control to decrease persistent disturbing thoughts. *Journal of Behavior Therapy and Experimental Psychiatry, 13*, 215–220.

Martin, L. (1986). Eskimo words for snow: A case study in the genesis and decay of an anthropological example. *American Anthropologist, 88*, 418–423.

Martin, P. D., & Brantley, P. J. (2004). Stress, coping, and social support in health and behavior. In J. M. Raczynsky & L. C. Leviton (Eds.), *Handbook of clinical health psychology* (Vol. 2, pp. 233–267). Washington, DC: American Psychological Association.

Martins, S., Tramontina, S., Polanczyk, G., Eizirik, M., Swanson, J., & Rohde, L. A. (2004). Weekend holidays during methylphenidate use in ADHD children: A randomized clinical trial. *Journal of Child and Adolescent Psychopharmacology, 14*, 195–206.

Mash, E. J., & Wolfe, D. A. (2007). *Abnormal child psychology* (3rd ed.). Belmont, CA: Thomson Wadsworth.

Mashour, G. A., Walker, E. E., & Martuza, R. L. (2005). Psychosurgery: Past, present, and future. *Brain Research Reviews, 48*, 409–419.

Maslach, C. (2003). Job burnout: New directions in research and intervention. *Current Directions in Psychological Science, 12*, 189–192.

Maslow, A. H. (1968). *Toward a psychology of being* (2nd ed.). New York: Van Nostrand.

Maslow, A. H. (1970). *Motivation and personality*. New York: Harper & Row.

Maslow, A. H. (1971). *The farther reaches of human nature*. New York: Viking Press.

Mason, D. J., & Kohn, M. L. (2001). *The memory workbook*. New York: Harbinger Publications.

Mass, E., Lapidot, M., & Gadoth, N. (2005). Case report: Multiple endocrine neoplasia type 2B misdiagnosed as familial dysautonomia. *European Journal of Pediatric Dentistry, 6*, 48–50.

Masters, W. H., & Johnson, V. E. (1966). *Human sexual response*. Boston: Little, Brown.

Masters, W. H., & Johnson, V. E. (1970). *Human sexual inadequacy*. Boston: Little, Brown.

Masters, W. H., & Johnson, V. E. (1981). Sex and the aging process. *Journal of the American Geriatrics Society, 19*, 385–389.

Mastro, J. (1999, July 21). Dialogue with a dolphin. *San Diego Union-Tribune*, E1.

Matson, J. L., & Ollendick, T. H. (1977). Issues in toilet training normal children. *Behavior Therapy, 8*, 549–553.

Matsuda, L. A., Lolait, S. J., Brownstein, M. J., Young, A. C., & Bonner, T. I. (1990). Structure of a cannabinoid receptor and functional expression of the cloned cDNA. *Nature, 346*, 561–564.

Matsumoto, D., & Ekman, P. (1989). American-Japanese cultural differences in intensity ratings of facial expressions of emotion. *Motivation and Emotion, 13*, 143–157.

Matsumoto, D., Consolacion, T., Yamada, H., Suzuki, R., Franklin, B., Paul, S., Ray, R., & Uchida, H. (2002). American-Japanese cultural differences in judgments of emotional expression of different intensities. *Cognition and Emotion, 16*, 721–747.

Matthews, G., Deary, I. J., & Whiteman, M. C. (2003). *Personality traits* (2nd ed.). New York: Cambridge University Press.

Matthews, G., Zeidner, M., & Roberts, R. D. (2003). *Emotional intelligence: Science and myth*. Cambridge, MA.: MIT Press.

Matthews, K. A., & Haynes, S. G. (1986). Type A behavior pattern and coronary disease risk. *American Journal of Epidemiology, 123*, 923–960.

Mattson, S. N., Schoenfeld, A. M., & Riley, E. P. (2001). Teratogenic effects of alcohol on brain and behavior. *Alcohol Research and Health, 25*, 185–191.

Mauss, I. (2005). Control your anger! *Scientific American Mind, 16*, 64–71.

Max, D. T. (2001, May 6). To sleep no more. *New York Times Magazine*, 74–78.

May, R. (2005). How do we know what works? *Journal of College Student Psychotherapy, 19*, 69–73.

Mayberg, H. S. (2006, August/September). Cited in D. Dobbs, Turning off depression. *Scientific American Mind*, 26–31.

References

Mayberg, H. S., Lozano, A. M., Voon, V., McNeely, H. E., Seminowicz, D., Hamani, C., Schwalb, J. M., & Kennedy, S. H. (2005). Deep brain stimulation for treatment-resistant depression. *Neuron, 45,* 651–660.

Mayer, J. D., Salovey, P., & Caruso, D. (2000). Models of emotional intelligence. In R. J. Sternberg (Ed.), *Handbook of intelligence.* New York: Cambridge University Press.

Mayes, A. R. (2000). Selective memory disorders. In E. Tulving & F. M. Craik (Eds.), *The Oxford handbook of memory.* New York: Oxford University Press.

Mayes, A. R. (2005). Selective memory disorders. In E. Tulving & F. M. Craik (Eds.), *The Oxford handbook of memory.* New York: Oxford University Press.

Mayford, M., & Korzus, E. (2002). Genetics of memory in the mouse. In L. R. Squire & D. L. Schacter, *Neuropsychology of memory* (3rd ed.). New York: Guilford Press.

Mayo Clinic. (2006a). Cited in CNN.com, *Eating disorders* [On-line]. Available: http://www.cnn.com/HEALTH/library/DS/00194.html

Mayo Clinic. (2006b). *Suicide: Understanding causes, signs, and prevention* [On-line]. Available: http://www.mayoclinic.com/health/suicide/MH00053

Mayr, E. (2000, July). Darwin's influence on modern thought. *Scientific American,* 79–83.

Mazor, K. M., Clauser, B. E., Field, T., Yood, R. A., & Gurwitz, J. H. (2002). A demonstration of the impact of response bias on the results of patient satisfaction surveys. *Human Services Research, 37,* 1403–1417.

Mazure, C. M., Brude, M. L., Maciejewski, P. K., & Jacobs, S. C. (2000). Adverse life events and cognitive-personality characteristics in the prediction of major depression and antidepressant response. *American Journal of Psychiatry, 157,* 896–903.

Mazzoni, G., & Cornoldi, C. (1993). Strategies in study time allocation: Why is study time sometimes not effective? *Journal of Experimental Psychology: General, 122,* 47–60.

Mcallister, H. A., Baker, J. D., Mannes, C., Stewart, H., & Sutherland, A. (2002). The optimal margin of illusion hypothesis: Evidence from self-serving bias and personality disorders. *Journal of Social and Clinical Psychology, 21,* 414–426.

McCall, R. B. (1994). Academic underachievers. *Current Directions in Psychological Science, 3,* 15–19.

McCarry, J. (1996, May). Peru begins again. *National Geographic.*

McCarthy, T. (2005, October 24). Getting inside your head. *Time,* 95–97.

McClain, D. L. (2005, June 29). Machine clobbers man. *The New York Times,* B2.

McClearn, G. E., Johansson, B., Berg, S., Pedersen, N. L., Ahern, F., Petrill, S. A., & Plomin, R. (1997). Substantial genetic influence on cognitive abilities in twins 80 or more years old. *Science, 276,* 1560–1563.

McClelland, D. C. (1985). *Human motivation.* Glenview, IL: Scott, Foresman.

McClelland, D. C., Atkinson, J. W., Clark, R. W., & Lowell, E. L. (1953). *The achievement motive.* New York: Appleton-Century-Crofts.

McClelland, J. L. (2005). Connectionist models of memory. In E. Tulving & F. M. Craik (Eds.), *The Oxford handbook of memory.* New York: Oxford University Press.

McClure, S. M., Li, J., Tomlin, D., Cypert, K. S., Montague, L. M., & Montague, P. R. (2004a). Neural correlates of behavioral preference for culturally familiar drinks. *Neuron, 44,* 379–387.

McClure, S. M., Li, J., Tomlin, D., Cypert, K. S., Montague, L. M., & Montague, P. R. (2004b, October 25). In H. Fields, Coke vs. Pepsi: How does your brain react to soft drinks? *U.S. News & World Report.*

McConnell, E. S. (2006, February). DARE middle school program revamped. *Middle Ground,* 33–44.

McConnell, J. V., Cutler, R. L., & McNeil, E. B. (1958). Subliminal stimulation: An overview. *American Psychologist, 13,* 229–242.

McCrae, R. R., & Allik, J. (Eds.). (2002). *The five-factor model of personality across cultures.* New York: Springer.

McCrae, R. R., & Costa, P. T., Jr. (1999). A five-factor theory of personality. In L. A. Pervin & O. P. John (Eds.), *Handbook of personality* (2nd ed.). New York: Guilford.

McCrae, R. R., & Costa, P. T., Jr. (Eds.). (2003). *Personality in adulthood* (2nd ed.). New York: Guilford Press.

McCrae, R. R., Costa, P. T., Jr., Hrebickova, M., Osteandorf, F., Angleitner, A., Avia, M., Sanz, J., Sanchez-Bernardos, M. L., Kusdil, M. E., Woodfield, R., Saunders, P. R., & Smith, P. B. (2000). Nature over nurture: Temperament, personality and life-span development. *Journal of Personality and Social Psychology, 78,* 173–186.

McDaniel, M. A. (2005). Big-brained people are smarter: A meta-analysis of the relationship between in vivo brain volume and intelligence. *Intelligence, 33,* 337–346.

McDaniel, M. A., & Einstein, G. O. (1986). Bizarre imagery as an effective memory aid: The importance of distinctiveness. *Journal of Experimental Psychology: Learning, Memory and Cognition, 12,* 54–65.

McDonough, M., & Kennedy, N. (2002). Pharmacological management of obsessive-compulsive disorder: A review for clinicians. *Harvard Review of Psychiatry, 10,* 127–137.

McDougall, W. (1908). *Social psychology.* New York: Putnam.

McDowell, J. (1992, February 17). Are women better cops? *Time.*

McEachin, J. J., Smith, T., & Lovaas, O. I. (1993). Long-term outcome for children with autism who received early intensive behavioral interventions. *American Journal on Mental Retardation, 97,* 359–372.

McElrath, D. (1997). The Minnesota model. *Journal of Psychoactive Drugs, 29,* 141–144.

McEwen, B. S. (2002, December 17). Cited in E. Goode, The heavy cost of stress. *New York Times,* D1.

McGaugh, J. L. (1990). Significance and remembrance: The role of neuromodulatory systems. *Psychological Science, 1,* 15–25.

McGaugh, J. L. (1999, February). Cited in B. Azar, McGaugh blazes on down his own path to keys of memory. *APA Monitor,* 18.

McGrath, B. B. (2003). A view from the other side: The place of spirits in the Tongan social field. *Culture, Medicine and Psychiatry, 27,* 29–48.

McIntosh, A. R., & Lobaugh, N. J. (2003). When is a word not a word? *Science, 301,* 322–323.

McKay, A. (2005). Sexuality and substance use: The impact of tobacco, alcohol, and selected recreational drugs on sexual function. *The Canadian Journal of Human Sexuality, 14,* 47–56.

McKenna, K. (1994, November 13). He just did it. *Los Angeles Times Calendar.*

McKerracher, L., & Ellezam, B. (2002). Putting the brakes on regeneration. *Science, 296,* 1819–1820.

McKie, R. (2005, July 31). Chemical kiss turns kids into adolescents. *Observer.*

McKinley, J. C., Jr. (2001, May 9). Court opens door to data on eyewitness fallibility. *New York Times,* A27.

McNally, G. P., & Westbrook, R. F. (2006). Predicting danger: The nature, consequences, and neural mechanisms of predictive fear learning. *Learning & Memory, 13,* 245–253.

McNeill, D., & Coonan, C. (2006, April 2). Japanese flock to China for organ transplants. *Japan Focus.*

McRonald, F. E., & Fleisher, D. R. (2005). Anticipatory nausea in cyclical vomiting. *BMC Pediatrics,* 5.

McVeigh, K. (2006, August 24). Limiting expert's eyewitness-reliability testimony upends carjacking verdict. *Expert & Scientific Evidence Litigation Reporter,* 3.

McWhorter, J. H. (2000). *Losing the race.* New York: Free Press.

Means, M. K., & Edinger, J. D. (2006). Neuropharmacologic therapy for insomnia. In T. L. Lee-Chiong (Ed.), *Sleep: A comprehensive handbook* (pp. 133–136). Hoboken, NJ: John Wiley & Sons.

Mechelli, A., Crinion, J. T., Noppeney, U., O'Doherty, J., Ashburner, J., Frackowiak, R. S., & Price, C. J. (2004). Neurolinguistics: Structural plasticity in the bilingual brain. *Nature, 431,* 97.

Medical News Today. (2005, May 25). *$77 billion in lost income is attributed to ADHD annually in USA* [On-line]. Available: http://www.medicalnewstoday.com/medicalnews.php?newsid=24988

Medical robot succeeds in removing brain tumor. (2002, December). *Japan, Inc.*

Megargee, E. I. (1997). Internal inhibitions and controls. In R. Hogan, J. Johnson & S. Briggs (Eds.), *Handbook of personality psychology.* New York: Academic Press.

Melamed, S., Shirom, A., Toker, S., Berliner, S., & Shapira, I. (2006). Burnout and risk of cardiovascular disease: Evidence, possible causal paths, and promising research directions. *Psychological Bulletin, 132,* 327–353.

Melzack, R. (1989). Phantom limbs, the self and the brain. *Canadian Psychology, 30,* 1–16.

Melzack, R. (1997). Phantom limbs. *Scientific American, Special Issue,* 84–91.

Melzack, R., & Wall, P. D. (1983). *The challenge of pain.* New York: Basic Books.

Menaker, M. (2003). Circadian photoreception. *Science, 299,* 213–214.

Mendelson, J. H., Mello, N. K., Schuckit, M. A., & Segal, D. S. (2006). Cocaine, opioids, and other commonly abused drugs. In S. L. Hauser (Ed.), *Harrison's neurology in clinical medicine* (pp. 625–632). New York: McGraw-Hill.

Menon, V., & Desmond, J. E. (2001). Left superior parietal cortex involvement in writing: Integrating fMRI with lesion evidence. *Cognitive Brain Research, 12,* 337–340.

Mercuri, N. B., & Bernardi, G. (2005). The "magic" of L-dopa: Why is it the gold standard Parkinson's disease therapy? *Trends in Pharmacological Sciences, 26,* 341–344.

Merz, C. N. B., Dwyer, J., Nordstrom, C. K., Walton, K. G., Salerno, J. W., & Schneider, R. H. (2002). Psychosocial stress and cardiovascular disease: Pathophysiological links. *Behavioral Medicine, 27,* 141–147.

Messager, S. (2006). Kisspeptin and its receptors: New gatekeepers of puberty. *British Society for Neuroendocrinology,* 24.

Mestel, R. (1999, January). Sexual chemistry. *Discover,* 32.

Mestel, R. (2003a, April 15). Human Genome is completed: Now comes the hard part. *Los Angeles Times,* A18.

Mestel, R. (2003b, May 19). Rorschach tested. *Los Angeles Times,* F1.

Mesulam, M. (2005). Aphasia, memory loss, and other focal cerebral disorders. In D. L. Kasper, E. Braunwald, A. S. Fauci, S. L. Hauser, D. L. Longo, J. L. Jameson, & K. F. Isselbacher (Eds.), *Harrison's principles of internal medicine* (16th ed.). New York: McGraw-Hill.

Metrebian, N., Shanahan, W., Stimson, G. V., Small, C., Lee, M., Mtutu, V., & Wells, B. (2001). Prescribing drug of choice to opiate dependent drug users: A comparison of clients receiving heroin with those receiving injectable methadone at a West London drug clinic. *Drug and Alcohol Review, 20,* 267–276.

Meyer-Lindenberg, A. (2006, May 27). Cited in B. Bower, Violent developments. Disruptive kids grow into their behavior. *Science News, 169,* 328–329.

MFMER (Mayo Foundation for Medical Education and Research). (2005, August 8). *Adolescent sleep problems: Why is your teen so tired?* [On-line]. Available: http://www.mayoclinic.com/health/teens-health/CC00019

Mieda, M., Williams, S. C., Richardson, J. A., Tanaka, K., & Yanagisawa, M. (2006). The dorsomedial hypothalamic nucleus as a putative food-entrainable circadian pacemaker. *Proceedings of the National Academy of Sciences, 103,* 12150–12155.

Mignot, E. (2000, August 30). Cited in A. Manning, Narcolepsy is caused by loss of particular brain cells. *USA Today,* D10.

Mignot, E. (2002, January 8). Cited in D. Tuller, A quiet revolution for those prone to nodding off. *New York Times,* D7.

Milgram, N. A., Dangour, W., & Raviv, A. (1992). Situational and personal determinants of academic procrastination. *Journal of General Psychology, 119,* 123–133.

Milgram, S. (1963). Behavioral study of obedience. *Journal of Abnormal and Social Psychology, 67,* 371–378.

Milgram, S. (1974). *Obedience to authority.* New York: Harper & Row.

Milgrom, P., Mancl, L., Kng, B., & Weinstein, P. (1995). Origins of childhood dental fear. *Behaviour Research and Therapy, 33,* 313–319.

Milgrom, P., Quang, J. Z., & Tay, K. M. (1994). Cross-cultural validity of a parent's version of the Dental Fear Survey Schedule for children in Chinese. *Behavior Research and Therapy, 32,* 131–135.

Milgrom, P., Vigehesa, H., & Weinstein, P. (1992). Adolescent dental fear and control: Prevalence and theoretical implications. *Behavior Research and Therapy, 30,* 367–373.

Milham, M. P., Erickson, K. I., Banich, M. T., Kramer, A. F., Webb, A., Wszalek, T., & Cohen, H. J. (2002). Attentional control in the aging brain: Insights from an fMRI study of the Stroop task. *Brain and Cognition, 49,* 277–296.

Miller, A. (Ed.) (2005). *The social psychology of good and evil.* New York: Guilford Press.

Miller, F. G., Quill, T. E., Brody, H., Fletcher, J. C., Gostin, L. O., & Meier, D. E. (1994). Regulating physician-assisted death. *New England Journal of Medicine, 331,* 119–122.

Miller, G. (1956). The magical number seven, plus or minus two: Some limits on our capacity for information processing. *Psychological Review, 48,* 337–442.

Miller, G. (2003). Singing in the brain. *Science, 299,* 646–648.

Miller, J. (1995, April). Cited in T. DeAngelis, Research documents trauma of abuse. *APA Monitor.*

Miller, M. (2003, July 7). When anxiety runs sky-high. *Los Angeles Times,* F1.

Miller, M. A., & Rahe, R. H. (1997). Life changes scaling for the 1990s. *Journal of Psychosomatic Research, 43,* 279–292.

Miller, M. C. (2005a, Summer). Managing every shade of blue. *Newsweek,* 34–35.

Miller, M. C. (2005b, October 3). The dangers of chronic disease. *Newsweek,* 58–59.

Miller, R. (2003, November). Cited in K. Wright, Staying alive. *Discover,* 64–70.

Miller, W. R., & C'de Baca, J. (1994). Quantum change: Toward a psychology of transformation. In T. F. Heatherton & J. L. Weinberger (Eds.), *Can personality change?* Washington, DC: American Psychological Association.

Miller, W. R., & C'de Baca, J. (2001). *Quantum change.* New York: Guilford Press.

Millman, R. P., Working Group on Sleepiness in Adolescents/Young Adults, and APA Committee on Adolescence. (2005). Excessive sleepiness in adolescents and young adults: Causes, consequences, and treatment strategies. *Pediatrics, 115,* 1774–1786.

Milrod, B., Leon, A. C., Busch, F., Gudden, M., Schwalberg, M., Clarkin, J., Aronson, A., Singer, M., Turchin, W., Klass, E. T., Graf, E., Teres, J. J., & Shear, M. K. (2007). A randomized controlled clinical trial of psychoanalytic psychotherapy for panic disorder. *American Journal of Psychiatry, 164,* 265–272.

Miltenberger, R. G. (2004). *Behavior modification: Principles and procedures* (3rd ed.). Monterey, CA: Wadsworth.

Milton, J., & Wiseman, R. (1999). Does Psi exist? Lack of replication of an anomalous process of information transfer. *Psychological Bulletin, 125,* 387–391.

Milton, J., & Wiseman, R. (2001). Does Psi exist: Reply to Storm and Ertel (2001). *Psychological Bulletin, 127,* 434–438.

Minda, J. P., & Smith, J. D. (2001). Prototypes in category learning. The effects of category size, category structure, and stimulus complexity. *Journal of Experimental Psychology: Learning, Memory and Cognition, 27,* 775–799.

Mirsky, A. F., & Quinn, O. W. (1988). The Genain quadruplets. *Schizophrenia Bulletin, 14,* 595–612.

Mischel, W. (1968). *Personality and assessment.* New York: Wiley.

Mischel, W., & Peake, P. K. (1982). Beyond deja vu in the search for cross-situational consistency. *Psychological Review, 89,* 730–755.

Mischel, W., & Shoda, Y. (1995). A cognitive-affective system theory of personality: Reconceptualizing situations, dispositions, dynamics, and invariance of personality structure. *Psychological Review, 102,* 246–268.

Mischel, W., Shoda, Y., & Rodriguez, M. L. (1989). Delay of gratification in children. *Science, 244,* 933–937.

Miyazaki, T., Ishikawa, T., Iimori, H., Miki, A., Wenner, M., Fukunishi, I., & Kawawura, N. (2003). Relationship between perceived social support and immune function. *Stress and Health, 19,* 3–7.

Mjøs, O. D. (2004, December 10). *The Nobel Peace Prize 2004 presentation speech* [On-line]. Available: http://nobelprize.org/nobel_prizes/peace/laureates/2004/presentation-speech.html

Moe, K. A., & Son, M. H. (2005, July). Tradition or sideshow? *The Irrawaddy.*

Moffitt, T. E. (2005). The new look of behavioral genetics in development psychopathology: Gene-environment interplay in antisocial behaviors. *Psychological Bulletin, 131,* 533–554.

Mokdad, A. H., Marks, J. S., Stroup, D. F., & Gerberding, J. L. (2004). Actual causes of death in the United States, 2000. *Journal of the American Medical Association, 291,* 1238–1241.

Moldin, S. O., Reich, T., & Rice, J. P. (1991). Current perspectives on the genetics of unipolar depression. *Behavior Genetics, 21,* 211–242.

Money, J. (1987). Sin, sickness or status? *American Psychologist, 42,* 384–399.

Monk, T. H., Kennedy, K. S., Rose, L. R., & Linenger, J. M. (2001). Decreased human circadian pacemaker influence after 100 days in space. *Psychosomatic Medicine, 63,* 881–885.

Montgomery, G. H., & Bovbjerg, D. H. (1997). The development of anticipatory nausea in patients receiving adjuvant chemotherapy for breast cancer. *Physiology & Behavior, 61,* 737–741.

Montgomery, G. H., DuHamel, K. N., & Redd, W. H. (2000). A meta-analysis of hypnotically induced analgesia: How effective is hypnosis? *International Journal of Clinical and Experimental Hypnosis, 48,* 138–153.

Montoya, A. G., Sorrentino, R., Lukas, S. E., & Price, B. H. (2002). Long-term neuropsychiatric consequences of "ecstasy" (MDMA): A review. *Harvard Review of Psychiatry, 10,* 212–220.

Moore, D. W. (2005, June 16). Three in four Americans believe in paranormal. *Gallup Poll News Service.*

Moore, R. Y. (1997). Circadian rhythms: Basic neurobiology and clinical applications. *Annual Review of Medicine, 48,* 253–266.

Moore, R. Y. (2006). Biological rhythms and sleep. In T. L. Lee-Chiong (Ed.), *Sleep: A comprehensive handbook* (pp. 25–29). Hoboken, NJ: John Wiley & Sons.

Moran, M. (2004). Treating depression as chronic brings positive results. *Psychiatric News, 39,* 2.

Morey, L. C. (1997). Personality diagnosis and personality disorders. In R. Hogan, J. Johnson & S. Briggs (Eds.), *Handbook of personality psychology.* New York: Academic Press

Morgan, A. B., & Lilienfeld, S. O. (2000). A meta-analytic review of the relation between antisocial behavior and neuropsychological measures of executive function. *Clinical Psychology Review, 20,* 113–136.

Morgan, D. (1995, July 11). Cited in C. Sullivan, Mother called fit for trial in sons' deaths. *San Diego Union-Tribune.*

Morgan, M. (1985). Self-monitoring of attained subgoals in private study. *Journal of Educational Psychology, 77,* 623–630/

Morral, A. R., McCaffrey, D. F., & Paddock, S. M. (2002). Reassessing the marijuana gateway effect. *Addiction, 97,* 1493–1504.

Morrison, A. (1993). Cited in H. Herzog, Animal rights and wrongs. *Science, 262,* 1906–1908.

Morrongiello, B. A., & Hogg, K. (2004). Mother reactions to children misbehaving in ways that can lead to injury: Implications for gender differences in children's risk taking and injuries. *Sex Roles, 50,* 1003–1018.

Morse, J. (2002, April 1). Women on a binge. *Time,* 56–62.

Mortensen, E. L., Michaelsen, K. F., Sanders, S. A., & Reinisch, J. M. (2002). The association between duration of breastfeeding and adult intelligence. *The Journal of the American Medical Association, 287,* 2365–2371.

Morton, S. (2004, November 1). Rare disease makes girl unable to feel pain. *Associated Press.*

Mosconi, L., Tsui, W. H., De Danti, S., Li, J., Rusinek, H., Convit, A., Li, Y., Boppana, M., & de Leon, M. J. (2005). Reduced hippocampal metabolism in MCI and AD: Automated FDG-PET image analysis. *Neurology, 64,* 1860–1867.

Moseley, J. B., O'Malley, K., Petersen, N. J., Menke, T. J., Brody, B. A., Kuykendall, D. H., Hollingsworth, J. C., Ashton, C. M., & Wray, N. P. (2002). A controlled trial of arthroscopic surgery for osteoarthritis of the knee. The *New England Journal of Medicine, 347,* 81–88.

References

Mosher, W. D., Chandra, A., & Jones, J. (2005, September 15). Sexual behavior and selected health measures: Men and woman 15–44 years of age, United States, 2002. *Centers for Disease Control and Prevention: Advance data from vital and health statistics, 362.*

Moss, D. (2002). The roots and genealogy of humanistic psychology. In K. J. Schneider, J. F. T. Bugental, & J. F. Pierson (Eds.), *The handbook of humanistic psychology: Leading edges in theory, research, and practice.* Thousand Oaks, CA: Sage.

MSNBC. (2006, June 19). *Parents split on STD shot for preteens* [On-line]. Available: http://www.msnbc.com/id/12956410/

Mueser, K. T., Bolton, E., & McGurk, S. R. (2006). Schizophrenia. In M. Hersen & J. C. Thomas (Eds.), *Comprehensive handbook of personality and psychopathology: Adult psychopathology* (Vol. 2, pp. 262–277). Hoboken, NJ: John Wiley & Sons.

Mukerjee, M. (1997, February). Trends in animal research. *Scientific American,* 86–93.

Mullin, B. C., & Hinshaw, S. P. (2007). Emotion regulation and externalizing disorders in children and adolescents. In J. J. Gross (Ed.), *Handbook of emotion regulation* (pp. 523–541). New York: Guilford Press.

Mumford, M. D., Connelly, M. S., Helton, W. B., Strange, J. M., & Osburn, H. K. (2001). On the construct validity of integrity tests: Individual and situational factors as predictors of test performance. *International Journal of Selection and Assessment, 9,* 240–257.

Munoz, H. (2003, May 30). Working to get more female police officers. *Los Angeles Times,* B2.

Munsey, C. (2006, June 6). RxP legislation made historic progress in Hawaii. *Monitor on Psychology, 37,* 42.

Murat, I., Bekir, O., Selhan, K., Zuhal, Y., Bulent, O., Hasmet, H., & Mefkure, E. (2005). Destructive stereotaxic surgery for treatment of dystonia. *Surgical Neurology, 64,* 289–295.

Murnane, K., Phelps, M. P., & Malmberg, K. (1999). Context-dependent recognition memory: The ICE theory. *Journal of Experimental Psychology: General, 128,* 403–415.

Murphy, C., Schubert, C. R., Cruickshanks, K. J., Klein, B. E., Klein, R., & Nondahl, D. M. (2002). Prevalence of olfactory impairment in older adults. *Journal of the American Medical Association, 288,* 2307–2312.

Murphy, K. R. (1993). *Honesty in the workplace.* Pacific Grove, CA: Brooks/Cole.

Murray, D. J., Kilgout, A. R., & Wasykliw, L. (2000). Conflicts and missed signals in psychoanalysis, behaviorism, and Gestalt psychology. *American Psychologist, 55,* 422–426.

Murray, H. (1943). *Thematic Apperception Test manual.* Cambridge, MA: Harvard University Press.

Murray, J. P., Liotti, M., Ingmundson, P. T., Mayberg, H. S., Pu, Y., Zamarripa, F., Liu, Y., Woldorff, M. G., Gao, J., & Fox, P. T. (2006). Children's brain activations while viewing televised violence revealed by fMRI. *Media Psychology, 8,* 25–37.

Murray, S. L. (2005). Regulating the risks of closeness: A relationship specific sense of felt security. *Current Directions in Psychological Science, 14,* 74–78.

Murray, S. O., Kersten, D., Olhausen, B. A., Schrater, P., & Woods, D. L. (2002). Shape perception reduces activity in human primary visual cortex. *Proceedings of the National Academy of Sciences, 99,* 15164–15169.

Musto, D. F. (1996, April). Alcohol in American history. *Scientific American,* 78–83.

Musto, D. F. (1999). The impact of public attitudes on drug abuse research in the twentieth century. In M. D. Glantz & C. R. Hartel, (Eds.), *Drug abuse: Origins & interventions.* Washington, DC: American Psychological Association.

Mydans, S. (2003, March 11). Clustering in cities, Asians are becoming obese. *New York Times,* A3.

Myrtek, M. (1995). Type A behavior pattern, personality factors, disease, and physiological reactivity: A meta-analytic update. *Personality and Individual Differences, 18,* 491–502.

Nagarahole, E. L. (1994, March 28). Tigers on the brink. *Time.*

Nagtegaal, J. E., Laurant, M. W., Kerkof, G. A., Smits, M. G., van der Meer, Y. G., & Coenen, A. M. L. (2000). Effects of melatonin on the quality of life in patients with delayed sleep phase syndrome. *Journal of Psychosomatic Research, 48,* 45–50.

Naimi, T. S., Brewer, R. D., Mokdad, A., Denny, C., Serdula, M. K., & Marks, J. S. (2003). Binge drinking among U.S. adults. *Journal of the American Medical Association, 289,* 70–75.

NAMHC (National Advisory Mental Health Council). (1996). Basic behavioral science research for mental health: Perception, attention, learning, and memory. *American Psychologist, 51,* 133–142.

Nangle, D. W., Erdley, C. A., Carpenter, E. M., & Newman, J. E. (2002). Social skills training as a treatment for aggressive children and adolescents: A developmental-clinical integration. *Aggression and Violent Behavior, 7,* 169–199.

Nash, J. M. (2002, November 11). Inside the womb. *Time,* 68–78.

Nash, M. R. (2001, July). The truth and the hype of hypnosis. *Scientific American,* 47–55.

Nathan, L., & Judd, H. L. (2007). Menopause and postmenopause. In A. H. DeCherney, L. Nathan, T. M. Goodwin & N. Laufer (Eds.), *Current diagnosis & treatment obstetrics & gynecology* (10th ed.). New York: McGraw-Hill.

Nathan, P. E., Stuart, S. P., & Dolan, S. L. (2000). Research of psychotherapy efficacy and effectiveness: Between Scylla and Charybdis. *Psychological Bulletin, 126,* 964–981.

NCHS (National Center for Health Statistics). (2006, April 20). Cited in M. Stobbe, U.S. deaths dropped 2% during '04, report finds. *The San Diego Union-Tribune,* A1.

NCSDR (National Commission on Sleep Disorders Research). (1993). *Wake up America: A national sleep alert.* Washington, DC: Department of Health and Human Services.

Neath, I., & Suprenant, A. M. (2003). *Human memory* (2nd ed.). Belmont, CA: Wadsworth/Thomson Learning.

Neher, A. (1991). Maslow's theory of motivation: A critique. *Journal of Humanistic Psychology, 31,* 89–112.

Neisser, U., & Libby, L. K. (2000). Remembering life experiences. In E. Tulving & F. M. Craik (Eds.), *The Oxford handbook of memory.* New York: Oxford University Press.

Neisser, U., & Libby, L. K. (2005). Remembering life experiences. In E. Tulving & F. M. Craik (Eds.), *The Oxford handbook of memory.* New York: Oxford University Press.

Neitz, J., Neitz, M., & Kainz, P. M. (1996). Visual pigment gene structure and the severity of color vision defects. *Science, 274,* 801–803.

Neitz, M., & Neitz, J. (1995). Numbers and ratios of visual pigment genes for normal red-green color vision. *Science, 267,* 1013–1016.

Nelson, D. L. (2004). 5-HT5 receptors. *Current Drug Targets. CNS Neurological Disorders, 3,* 53–58.

Nelson, G., Westhues, A., & MacLeod, J. (2003). A meta-analysis of longitudinal research on preschool prevention programs for children. *Prevention & Treatment, 6,* 116–133.

Nelson, R. J., Demas, G. E., Huang, P. L., Fishman, M. C., Dawson, V. L., Dawson, T. M., & Snyder, S. H. (1995). Behavioural abnormalities in male mice lacking neuronal nitric oxide synthase. *Nature, 378,* 383–386.

Nemeroff, C. G. (2007). The burden of severe depression: A review of diagnostic challenges and treatment alternatives. *Journal of Psychiatric Research, 41,* 189–206.

Nestler, E. (2005, January 17). In M. D. Lemonick, The biology of joy. *Time,* 12–17.

Nestler, E. J., & Malenka, R. C. (2004, March). The addicted brain. *Scientific American,* 78–85.

Netting, J. (2001). Teams find probable gene for sweet sense. *Science News, 159,* 263.

Neugarten, B. (1994, May). Cited in B. Azar, Women are barraged by media on "the change." *APA Monitor.*

Neverlien, P. O., & Johnsen, T. B. (1991). Optimism-pessimism dimension and dental anxiety in children aged 10–12. *Community Dentistry Oral Epidemiology, 19,* 342–346.

New virtual reality surgery simulator hones surgeons' skills, improves patient safety. (2005, June 27). *Science Daily.* Available: http://www.sciencedaily.com/releases/2005/06/050627062144.htm

New York Times. (2003, April 25). Middle school boy shoots his principal then kills himself. A20.

New York Times. (2006, February 12). A surprising warning on stimulants, D13.

Newcombe, N. S. (2002). The nativist-empiricist controversy in the context of recent research on spatial and quantitative development. *Psychological Science, 13,* 395–401.

Newman, C. F. (2006). Bipolar disorder. In M. Hersen & J. C. Thomas (Eds.), *Comprehensive handbook of personality and psychopathology: Adult psychopathology* (Vol. 2, pp. 244–261). Hoboken, NJ: John Wiley & Sons.

Newman, L. S. (2001). A cornerstone for the science of interpersonal behavior? Person perception and person memory, past, present, and future. In G. B. Moskowitz (Ed.), *Cognitive social psychology.* Mahwah, NJ: Lawrence Erlbaum.

Newsweek. (2006, September 18). "I feel good, I feel alive," 62–63.

NHTA (National Highway Traffic Administration). (2003). New statistics from the National Highway Traffic Administration. *AIM Research Highlights,* 4.

NICHD (National Institute of Child Health & Human Development). (1997). The effects of infant child care on infant-mother attachment security: Results of the NICHD study of early child care. *Child Development, 68,* 860–879.

NICHD. (2001). Nonmaternal care and family factors in early development: An overview of the NICHD study of early child care. *Applied Developmental Psychology, 22,* 457–492.

NICHD. (2003). Does quality of child care affect child outcomes at age $4\frac{1}{2}$ *Developmental Psychology, 39,* 451–469.

NICHD. (2005). *Autism overview: What we know.* Available: http://www.nichd.nih.gov/publications/pubs/autism_overview_2005.pdf

Nichols, M. P. (2004). *Stop arguing with your kids.* New York: Guilford Press.

NIDA (National Institute on Drug Abuse). (2006a). Crack and cocaine. *NIDA InfoFacts.* Available: http://www.drugabuse.gov

NIDA. (2006b). High school and youth trends. *NIDA InfoFacts.* Available: http://www.drugabuse.gov

NIH (National Institutes of Health). (2005). *Alzheimer's disease: Fact sheet* (NIH Publication No. 03-3431). Washington, DC: U.S. Government Printing Office.

NIMH (National Institute of Mental Health). (2003). *In harm's way. Suicide in America.* Bethesda, MD: Author.

NIMH. (2005a). *Depression: What every woman should know.* Bethesda, MD: Author.

NIMH. (2005b). *The numbers count* [On-line]. Available: http://www.nimh.nih.gov

Nisbet, M. (1998, May/June). Psychic telephone networks profit on yearning, gullibility. *Skeptical Inquirer,* 5–6.

Nisbett, R. (2000, August 8). Cited in E. Goode, How culture molds habits of thought. *New York Times,* D1.

Nisbett, R. E., & Miyamoto, Y. (2005). The influence of culture: Holistic versus analytic perception. *Trends in Cognitive Sciences, 9,* 467–473.

Niznikiewicz, M. A., Kubicki, M., & Shenton, M. E. (2003). Recent structural and functional imaging findings in schizophrenia. *Current Opinion in Psychiatry, 16,* 123–147.

Nobler, M. S., & Sackeim, H. A. (1998). Mechanisms of action of electroconvulsive therapy: Functional brain imaging studies. *Psychiatric Annals, 28,* 23–29.

Noonan, D., & Cowley, G. (2002, July 15). Prozac vs. placebos. *Newsweek,* 48–49.

Norcross, J. C. (2005). A primer on psychotherapy integration. In J. C. Norcross & M. R. Goldfried (Eds.), *Handbook of psychotherapy integration* (2nd ed.). New York: Oxford University Press.

Norenzayan, A., & Nisbett, R. E. (2000). Culture and causal cognition. *Current Directions in Psychological Science, 9,* 132–135.

Noriyuki, D. (1996, February). Breaking down the walls. *Los Angeles Times,* E1.

Norman, D. A. (1982). *Learning and memory.* New York: Freeman.

Norungolo, D. (2005, January 19). Colleges and law enforcement work together to stop the "undetected rapist." *The Beat.* Available: http://www.metrobeat.net/Expedite/Content?oid=oid%3A175

Nosofsky, R. M., & Zaki, S. R. (2002). Exemplar and prototype models revisited: Response strategies, selective attention, and stimulus generalization. *Journal of Experimental Psychology: Learning, Memory and Cognition, 28,* 924–940.

Nour, N. (2000, July 11). Cited in C. Dreifus, A life devoted to stopping the suffering of mutilation. *New York Times,* D7.

Novak, V. (September 10, 2001). New Ritalin ad blitz makes parents jumpy. *Time,* 62–63.

Nowak, R. (1994). Chronobiologists out of sync over light therapy patents. *Science, 263,* 1217–1218.

NSF (National Science Foundation). (2003). *2003 Sleep in America poll.* Washington, DC: Author.

NSF. (2004). *Adolescent sleep needs and patterns: Research report and resource guide.* Washington, DC: Author.

NSF. (2005). *2005 Sleep in America poll.* Washington, DC: Author.

Nurius, P. S., & Berlin, S. S. (1994). Treatment of negative self-concept and depression. In D. K. Granvold (Ed.), *Cognitive and behavioral treatment: Methods and applications.* Pacific Grove, CA: Brooks/Cole.

NY Rock. (2002). *By the way? The Chilis are back: Interview with Anthony Kiedis of the Red Hot Chili Peppers* [On-line]. Available: http://www.nyrock.com/interviews/2002/chili_int2.asp

Nyberg, L., & Cabeza, R. (2005). Brain imaging of memory. In E. Tulving & F. M. Craik (Eds.), *The Oxford handbook of memory.* New York: Oxford University Press.

O'Callaghan, K. (2006, August). Is it okay to spank? *Parenting.*

O'Connor, D. B., & Shimizu, M. (2002). Sense of personal control, stress and coping style: A cross-cultural study. *Stress and Health: Journal of the International Society for the Investigation of Stress, 18,* 173–183.

O'Donnell, J. (2005, March 2). What other nations do. *USA Today.*

O'Driscoll, P. (2005, February 28). Wichita cheers arrest in "BTK" killings. *USA Today,* 3A.

Oesterle, S., Hill, K. G., Hawkins, J. D., Guo, J., Catalano, R. F., & Abbott, R. D. (2004). Adolescent heavy episodic drinking trajectories and health in young adulthood. *Journal on Studies of Alcohol, 65,* 204–212.

Offer, D., Kaiz, M., Howard, K. I., & Bennett, E. S. (2000). The altering of reported experiences. *Journal of the American Academy of Child and Adolescent Psychiatry, 39,* 735–742.

Ogden, C. L., Carroll, M. D., Curtin, L. R., McDowell, M. A., Tabak. C. J., & Flegal, K. (2006, April 5). Prevalence of overweight and obesity in the United States, 1999–2004. *The Journal of the American Medical Association, 295,* 1549–1555.

Ogloff, J. R. P. (2006). Psychopathy/antisocial personality disorder continuum. *Australian and New Zealand Journal of Psychiatry, 40,* 519–528.

Ohayon, M. M., & Guilleminault, C. (2006). Epidemiology of sleep disorders. In T. L. Lee-Chiong (Ed.), *Sleep: A comprehensive handbook* (pp. 73–82). Hoboken, NJ: John Wiley & Sons.

Ohayon, M. M., Lemine, P., Arnaud-Briant, V., & Dreyfus, M. (2002). Prevalence and consequences of sleep disorders in a shift worker population. *Journal of Psychosomatic Research, 53,* 577–583.

Ohman, A. (2002). Automaticity and the amygdala: Nonconscious responses to emotional faces. *Current Directions in Psychological Science, 11,* 62–66.

Ojeda, S. R., Lomniczi, A., Mastronardi, C., Heger, S., Roth, C., Parent, A. S., Matagne, V., & Mungenast, A. E. (2006). The neuroendocrine regulation of puberty: Is the time ripe for a systems biology approach? *Endocrinology, 147,* 1166–1174.

Oldenburg, A. (2002, December 11). Oprah pounds away. *USA Today,* D2.

Olfson, M., Marcus, S. C., Druss, F. B., Elinson, L., Tanielian, T., & Pincus, H. A. (2002). National trends in the outpatient treatment of depression. *Journal of the American Medical Association, 287,* 203–209.

Ollendick, T. H., King, N. J., & Chorpita, B. F. (2006). Empirically supported treatments for children and adolescents. In P. C. Kendall (Ed.), *Child and adolescent therapy: Cognitive-behavioral procedures* (3rd ed., pp. 492–520). New York: Guilford Press.

Olshansky, J. (2003, November). Cited in K. Wright, Staying alive. *Discover,* 64–70.

Olshansky, J., Hayflick, L., & Carnes, B. A. (2002, June). No truth to the fountain of youth. *Scientific American,* 92–95.

Olshansky, S. J. (2006, January 14). Put down that fork. *Science News, 169,* 21.

Olson, L., & Houlihan, D. (2000). A review of behavioral treatments used for Lesch-Nyhan syndrome. *Behavior Modification, 24,* 202–222.

Olsson, A., Ebert, J. P., Banaji, M. R., & Phelps, E. A. (2005). The role of social groups in the persistence of learned fear. *Science, 309,* 785–787.

Olsson, H., Wennerholm, P., & Lyxzen, U. (2004). Exemplars, prototypes, and the flexibility of classification models. *Journal of Experimental Psychology, 30,* 936–941.

ONDCP (Office of National Drug Control Policy). (2000). *What America's users spend on illegal drugs, 1988–1998.* Washington, DC: Author.

O'Neil, J. (2006, June 28). A warning on hazards of smoke secondhand. *The New York Times,* A14.

Onishi, N. (2001, February 12). On the scale of beauty, weight weighs heavily. *New York Times,* A4.

Onishi, N. (2002, October 3). Globalization of beauty makes slimness trendy. *New York Times,* A4.

Oostdam, R., & Meijer, J. (2003). Influence of test anxiety on measurement of intelligence. *Psychological Reports, 92,* 3–20.

O'Regan, J. K., Deubel, H., Clark, J. J., & Rensink, R. A. (2000). Picture changes during blinks: Looking without seeing and seeing without looking. *Visual Cognition, 7,* 191–211.

Ortiz, B. (2005, December 12). BTK thought police wouldn't lie to him. *Herald-Leader.*

Osofsky, J. D. (1995). The effects of exposure to violence on young children. *American Psychologist, 50,* 782–788.

Ost, L., Helstrom, K., & Kaver, A. (1992). One versus five sessions of exposure in the treatment of injection phobia. *Behavior Therapy, 23,* 263–282.

Owen, P. (2003). *Minnesota model: Description of counseling approach* [On-line]. Available: http://www.nida.nih.gov

Ozer, D. J. (1999). Four principles for personality assessment. In L. A. Pervin & O. P. John (Eds.), *Handbook of personality* (2nd ed.), New York: Guilford.

Ozer, E. J., Best, S. R., Lipsey, T. L., & Weiss, D. S. (2003). Predictors of posttraumatic stress disorder and symptoms in adults: A meta-analysis. *Psychological Bulletin, 129,* 52–71.

Paabo, S. (2003, July 15). Cited in N. Wade, Early voices: The leap to language. *New York Times,* D1.

Page, A. C. (2002). Nature and treatment of panic disorder. *Current Opinion in Psychiatry, 15,* 149–155.

Page, A. C. (2003). The role of disgust in faintness elicited by blood and injection stimuli. *Anxiety Disorders, 17,* 45–58.

Page, A. C., Bennett, K. S., Carter, O., Smith, M., & Woodmore, K. (1997). The blood-injection symptoms scale (BISS) assessing a structure of phobic symptoms elicited by blood and injections. *Behaviour Research and Therapy, 35,* 457–464.

Pahwa, R., & Lyons, K. E. (2003). Essential tremor: Differential diagnosis and current therapy. *The American Journal of Medicine, 115,* 134–142.

Palmer, S. E., Brooks, J. L., & Nelson, R. (2003). When does grouping happen? *Acta Psychologica, 114,* 311–330.

Palomares, R. (2003, February). Cited in E. Benson, Intelligent intelligence testing. *Monitor on Psychology,* 48–51.

"Panic attacks." (2005, February 15). *American Family Physician.*

Pantelis, C., Velakoulis, D., McGorry, P. D., Wood, S. J., Suckling, J., Phillips, L. J., Yung, A. R., Bullmore, E. T., Brewer, W., Soulsby, B., Desmond, P., & McGuire, P. K. (2003). Neuroanatomical abnormalities before and after onset of psychosis: A cross-sectional and longitudinal MRI comparison. *Lancet, 361,* 281–288.

Pareles, J. (2005, August 23). Rock's patriarchs open their tour, mixing old and new. *The New York Times,* B1.

Parens, E., Chapman, A. R., & Press, N. (Eds.). (2006). *Wrestling with behavioral genetics: Science, ethics, and public conversation.* Baltimore, MD: Johns Hopkins University Press.

Park, A. (2005, August 15). The mental diet. *Time.*

Parker, G. (2000). Personality and personality disorder: Current issues and directions. *Psychological Medicine, 30,* 1–9.

Parks, G. (1997). *Half past autumn.* New York: Bulfinch Press & Little, Brown & Company.

Parvizi, J., & Damasio, A. R. (2003). Neuroanatomical correlates of brainstem coma. *Brain, 126,* 1524–1536.

Pascalis, O., de Haan, M., & Nelson, C. A. (2002). Is face processing species-specific during the first year of life? *Science, 296,* 1321–1323.

References

Patel, M. R., Piazza, C. C., Martinez, C. J., Volkert, V. M., & Santana, C. M. (2002). An evaluation of two differential reinforcement procedures with escape extinctions to treat food refusal. *Journal of Applied Behavior Analysis, 35,* 363–374.

Patterson, D. R., & Jensen, M. P. (2003). Hypnosis and clinical pain. *Psychological Bulletin, 129,* 495–521.

Paul, S. M., Extein, I., Calil, H. M., Potter, W. Z., Chodoff, P., & Goodwin, F. K. (1981). Use of ECT with treatment-resistant depressed patients at the National Institute of Mental Health. *American Journal of Psychiatry, 138,* 486–489.

Payne, D. G., Toglia, M. P., & Anastasi, J. S. (1994). Recognition performance level and the magnitude of the misinformation effect in eyewitness memory. *Psychonomic Bulletin and Review, 1,* 376–382.

Payne, J. W. (2006, January 17). Cold advice: New guidelines: Don't bother with OTC cough meds. *Washington Post.*

Peake, P. K., Hebl, M., & Mischel, W. (2002). Strategic attention deployment for delay of gratification in working and waiting situations. *Developmental Psychology, 38,* 313–326.

Pear, R. (2000, June 11). Interns' long workdays prompt first crackdown. *New York Times,* D2.

Pearce, J. M., & Bouton, M. E. (2003). Theories of the associative learning in animals. *Annual Review of Psychology, 52,* 111–139.

Peele, S. (1997). Utilizing culture and behaviour in epidemiological models of alcohol consumption and consequences of western nations. *Alcohol & Alcoholism, 32,* 51–64.

Pelham, W. E., Manos, M. J., Ezzell, C. A., Tresco, K. T., Gnagy, E. M., Hoffman, M. T., Onyango, A. N., Fabiano, G. A., Lopez-Williams, A., Wymbs, B. T., Caserta, D., Chronis, A. M., Burrows-Maclean, L., & Morse, G. (2005). A dose-ranging study of a methylphenidate transdermal system in children with ADHD. *Journal of the American Academy of Child and Adolescent Psychiatry, 44,* 522–529.

Penley, J. A., Tomaka, J., & Wiebe, J. S. (2002). The association of coping to physical and psychological health outcomes: A meta-analytic review. *Journal of Behavioral Medicine, 25,* 551–603.

Penn, H. E. (2006). Neurobiological correlates of autism: A review of recent research. *Child Neuropsychology, 12,* 57–59.

Pennebaker, J. W., Colder, M., & Sharp, L. (1990). Accelerating the coping process. *Journal of Personality and Social Psychology, 58,* 528–537.

Peplau, L. A. (2003). Human sexuality: How do men and women differ? *Current Directions in Psychological Science, 12,* 37–40.

Perez-Pena, R. (2003, March 16). Broad movement is backing embryo stem cell research. *New York Times,* 18.

Perlis, M. L., Smith, M. T., Cacialli, D. O., Nowakowski, S., & Orff, H. (2003). On the comparability of pharmacotherapy and behavior therapy for chronic insomnia: Commentary and implications. *Journal of Psychosomatic Research, 54,* 51–59.

Perloff, R. M. (2002). *The dynamics of persuasion.* Mahwah, NJ: Erlbaum.

Perry, C. (1997). Admissibility and per se exclusion of hypnotically elicited recall in American courts of law. *International Journal of Clinical and Experimental Hypnosis, 45,* 266–279.

Persons, J. B. (1997). Dissemination of effective methods: Behavior therapy's next challenge. *Behavior Therapy, 28,* 465–471.

Pert, C. B., Snowman, A. M., & Snyder, S. H. (1974). Localization of opiate receptor binding in presynaptic membranes of rat brain. *Brain Research, 70,* 184–188.

Perusse, D., & Gendreau, P. L. (2005). Genetics and the development of aggression. In R. E. Tremblay, W. W. Hartup & J. Archer (Eds.), *Developmental origins of aggression* (pp. 223–241). New York: Guilford Press.

Pesonen, A. K., Raikkonen, K., Keskivaara, P., & Keltifkangas-Jarvinen, L. (2003). Difficult temperament in childhood and adulthood: Continuity from maternal perceptions to self-ratings over 17 years. *Personality and Individual Differences, 34,* 19–31.

Pessoa, L., & Ungerleider, L. G. (2004). Top-down mechanisms for working memory and attentional processes. In M. S. Gazzaniga (Ed.), *The cognitive neurosciences III.* Cambridge, MA: MIT Press.

Peterson, K. S. (2001, May 25). 43% of 1st marriages end in 15 years. *USA Today,* A2.

Peterson, L., & Brown, D. (1994). Integrating child injury and abuse-neglect research: Common histories, etiologies, and solutions. *Psychological Bulletin, 116,* 293–315.

Peterson, L. A. (2007, February 3). Texas gov. orders anti-cancer vaccine. *Yahoo! News.*

Peterson, L. R., & Peterson, M. J. (1950). Short-term retention of individual verbal terms. *Journal of Experimental Psychology, 58,* 193–198.

Petitto, L. A. (1997, December 11). Cited in R. L. Hotz, The brain: Designed to speak the mind. *Los Angeles Times.*

Petitto, L. A., & Marentette, P. F. (1991). Babbling in the manual mode: Evidence for the ontogeny of language. *Science, 251,* 1493–1496.

Petri, H. L., & Govern, J. M. (2004). *Motivation* (5th ed.). Belmont, CA: Wadsworth.

Petrides, K. V., Furnham, A., & Martin, G. N. (2004). Estimates of emotional and psychometric intelligence: Evidence for gender-based stereotypes. *The Journal of Social Psychology, 144,* 149–162.

Petrill, S. A. (2003). The development of intelligence: Behavioral genetic approaches. In R. J. Sternberg, J. Lautrey, & T. I. Lubart (Eds.), *Models of intelligence.* Washington, DC: American Psychological Association.

Petrovic, P., Kalso, E., Petersson, K. M., & Ingvar, M. (2002). Placebo and opioid analgesia—imaging a shared neuronal network. *Science, 295,* 1737–1740.

Petty, R. E., Brinol, P., Tormala, Z. L., & Wegener, D. T. (2007). The role of metacognition in social judgment. In A. W. Kruglanski & E. T. Higgins, *Social psychology: Handbook of basic principles* (2nd ed., pp. 254–284). New York: Guilford Press.

Petty, R. E., & Cacioppo, J. T. (1986). *Attitudes and persuasion: Classic and contemporary approaches.* Dubuque, IA: William C. Brown.

Petty, R. E., Tormala, Z. L., Briñol, P., & Jarvis, W. B. G. (2006). Implicit ambivalence from attitude change: An exploration of the PAST model. *Journal of Personality and Social Psychology, 90,* 21–41.

Petty, R. E., Wegener, D. T., & Fabrigar, L. R. (1997). Attitudes and attitude change. *Annual Review of Psychology, 46,* 609–647.

Peverly, S. T., Brobst, K. E., Graham, M., & Shaw, R. (2003). College adults are not good at self-regulation: A study on the relationship of self-regulation, note taking, and test taking. *Journal of Educational Psychology, 95,* 335–346.

Peyser, M., Biddle, N. A., Brant, M., Wingert, P., Hackworth, D. H., & O'Shea, M. (1995, August 28). Sounding retreat. *Newsweek.*

Pezdek, K. (1995, February 11). Cited in M. Dolan, When the mind's eye blinks. *Los Angeles Times.*

Phelps, E. A. (2004). The human amygdala and awareness: Interactions between emotion and cognition. In M. S. Gazzaniga (Ed.), *The cognitive neurosciences III* (pp. 1005–1030). Cambridge, MA: MIT Press.

Piaget, J. (1929). *The child's conception of the world.* New York: Harcourt Brace.

Picchioni, D., Goeltzenleucher, B., Green, D. N., Convento, M. J., Crittenden, R., Hallgren, M., & Hicks, R. A. (2002). Nightmares as a coping mechanism for stress. *Dreaming, 12,* 155–169.

Pierce, B. H. (1999). An evolutionary perspective on insight. In D. H. Rosen & M. D. Luebbert (Eds.), *Evolution of the psyche. Human evolution, behavior, and intelligence.* Westport, CT: Praeger/Greenwood Publishing.

Piliavin, J. A., Dovidio, J. F., Gaertner, S. L., & Clark, R. D. (1982). Responsive bystanders: The process of intervention. In V. J. Derlega & J. Grzelak (Eds.), *Cooperation and helping behavior.* Orlando, FL: Academic Press.

Pillard, R. C., & Bailey, M. J. (1995). A biologic perspective on sexual orientation. *The Psychiatric Clinics of North America, 18,* 71–84.

Pillemer, D. B. (1984). Flashbulb memories of the assassination attempt on President Reagan. *Cognition, 16,* 63–80.

Pincus, T., & Morley, S. (2001). Cognitive-processing bias in chronic pain: A review and integration. *Psychological Bulletin, 127,* 599–617.

Pine, D. S. (2000). Anxiety disorder: Clinical features. In B. J. Sadock & V. A. Sadock (Eds.), *Kaplan and Sadock's comprehensive textbook of psychiatry* (7th ed., Vol. 1, pp. 1476–1489). Philadelphia: Lippincott Williams & Wilkins.

Pingitore, R., Dugoni, B. L., Tindale, R. S., & Spring, B. (1994). Bias against overweight job applicants in a simulated employment interview. *Journal of Applied Psychology, 79,* 909–917.

Pinker, S. (1994). *The language instinct.* New York: William Morrow.

Pinker, S. (1995). Introduction. In M. S. Gazzaniga (Ed.), *The cognitive neurosciences.* Cambridge, MA: MIT Press.

Pinker, S. (2000, April 10). Will the mind figure out how the brain works? *Time,* 90–91.

Pinker, S. (2003). *The blank slate: The modern denial of human nature.* New York: Viking.

Piomelli, D. (1999). Cited in J. Travis, Marijuana mimic reveals brain role. *Science News, 155,* 215.

Piper, W. E., Joyce, A. S., McCallum, M., Azim, H. F., & Ogrodniczuk, J. S. (2002). *Interpretive and supportive psychotherapies.* Washington, DC: American Psychological Association.

Pisano, E. D., Gatsonis, C., Hendrick, E., Yaffe, M., Baum, J. K., Acharyya, S., Conant, E. F., Fajardo, L. L., Bassett, L., D'Orsi, C., Jong, R., & Rebner, M. (2005). Diagnostic performance of digital versus film mammography for breast-cancer screening. *The New England Journal of Medicine, 353,* 1773–1783.

Pi-Sunyer, X. (2003). A clinical view of the obesity problem. *Science, 299,* 859–860.

Pittman, J. F., & Buckley, R. R. (2006). Comparing maltreating fathers and mothers in terms of personal distress, interpersonal functioning, and perceptions of family climate. *Child Abuse & Neglect, 30,* 481–496.

Plante, T. (2005). *Contemporary clinical psychology.* Hoboken, NJ: John Wiley & Sons.

Pleuvry, B. J. (2005). Opioid mechanisms and opioid drugs. *Anaesthesia and Intensive Care Medicine, 6,* 30–34.

Ploghaus, A., Becerra, L., Borras, C., & Borsook, D. (2003). Neural circuitry underlying pain modulation: Expectation, hypnosis, placebo. *Trends in Cognitive Science, 7,* 197–200.

Plomin, R., & Crabbe, J. (2000). DNA. *Psychological Bulletin, 126,* 806–828.

Plomin, R., & McGuffin, P. (2003). Psychopathology in the postgenomic era. *Annual Review of Psychology, 54,* 205–228.

Plomin, R., & Petrill, S. A. (1997). Genetics and intelligence: What's new? *Intelligence, 24,* 53–77.

Plomin, R., & Spinath, F. M. (2004). Intelligence: Genetics, genes, and genomics. *Journal of Personality and Social Psychology, 86,* 112–129.

Ployhart, R. E., Ehrhart, K. H., & Hayes, S. C. (2005). Using attributions to understand the effects of explanations on applicant reactions: Are reactions consistent with the covariation principle? *Journal of Applied Social Psychology, 35,* 259–296.

Plumet, J., Gil, R., & Gaonac'h, D. (2005). Neuropsychological assessment of executive functions in women: Effects of age and education. *Neuropsychology, 19,* 566–577.

Plummer, W., & Ridenhour, R. (1995, August 28). Saving grace. *People.*

Polaschek, D. L. L., Ward, T., & Hudson, S. M. (1997). Rape and rapists: Theory and treatment. *Clinical Psychology Review, 17,* 117–144.

Polce-Lynch, M., Myers, B. J., Kliewer, W., & Kilmartin, C. (2001). Adolescent self-esteem and gender: Exploring relations to sexual harassment, body image, media influence, and emotional expression. *Journal of Youth and Adolescence, 30,* 225–244.

Poldrack, R. A., & Packard, M. G. (2003). Competition among multiple memory systems: Converging evidence from animal and human brain studies. *Neuropsychologia, 41,* 245–251.

Polivy, J., & Herman, C. P. (2002). Causes of eating disorders. *Annual Review of Psychology, 53,* 187–213.

Pollak, S. D., & Kistler, D. J. (2002). Early experience is associated with the development of categorical representations of facial expressions of emotion. *Proceedings of the National Academy of Sciences, 99,* 9072–9076.

Pomerantz, E. M., Altermatt, E. R., & Saxon, J. L. (2002). Making the grade but feeling distressed: Gender differences in academic performance and internal distress. *Journal of Educational Psychology, 94,* 396–404.

Pomerantz, J. M. (2005). Screening for depression in primary care. *Drug Benefit Trends, 17,* 273–274.

Popper, C. W., Gammon, G. D., West, S. A., & Bailey, C. E. (2003). Disorders usually diagnosed in infancy, childhood, or adolescence. In R. E. Hales & S. C. Yudofsky (Eds.), *Textbook of clinical psychiatry* (4th ed., pp. 833–974). Washington, DC: American Psychiatric Publishing.

Post, R. (1994). Creativity and psychopathology: A study of 291 world-famous men. *British Journal of Psychiatry, 165,* 22–34.

Post, S. (2005). Altruism, happiness, and health: It's good to be good. *International Journal of Behavioral Medicine, 2,* 66–77.

Postmes, T., & Spears, R. (1998). Deindividuation and antinormative behavior: A meta-analysis. *Psychological Bulletin, 13,* 238–259.

Potter, J. (2006). Female sexuality: Assessing satisfaction and addressing problems. In D. C. Dale & D. D. Federman (Eds.), *ACP Medicine.* New York: WebMD Professional Publishing.

Poulton, R., Thomson, W. M., Davies, S., Kruger E., Brown, R. H., & Silva, P. (1997). Good teeth, bad teeth, and fear of the dentist. *Behaviour Research and Therapy, 35,* 327–334.

Pratkanis, A. R. (1992). The cargo cult science of subliminal persuasion. *Skeptical Inquirer, 16,* 260–286.

Pray, W. S., & Pray, J. J. (2005). Meniere's disease. *U.S. Pharmacist, 7,* 19–24.

Prentice, D. A., & Carranza, E. (2002). What women and men should be, shouldn't be, are allowed to be, and don't have to be: The contents of prescriptive gender stereotypes. *Psychology of Women Quarterly, 26,* 269–281.

Priester, J. R., & Petty, R. E. (1995). Source attributions and persuasion: Perceived honesty as a determinant of message scrutiny. *Personality and Social Psychology Bulletin, 21,* 637–654.

Prince, S. E., & Jacobson, N. S. (1997). A review and evaluation of marital and family therapies for affective disorders. *Journal of Marital and Family Therapy, 21,* 377–402.

Prochaska, J. O., & Norcross, J. C. (2007). *Systems of psychotherapy* (6th ed.). Belmont, CA: Brooks/Cole–Thomson Learning.

Project Match Research Group. (1997). Matching alcoholism treatments to client heterogeneity: Project MATCH posttreatment drinking outcomes. *Journal of Studies on Alcohol, 58,* 7–29.

Pruitt, D. G. (1971). Choice shifts in group discussion: An introductory review. *Journal of Personality and Social Psychology, 20,* 339–360.

Pryor, J. (2006, September 10). Drug treatment for premature ejaculation is effective, researchers show. *Science Daily.*

Pullum, G. K. (1991). *The great Eskimo vocabulary hoax.* Chicago: University of Chicago Press.

Purves, D., Augustine, G. J., Fitzpatrick D., Hall, W. C., LaMantia, A., McNamara, J. O., & Williams, S. M. (Eds.). (2004). *Neuroscience* (3rd ed.). Sunderland, MA: Sinauer Associates.

Putnam, S. (2005, April 4). Cited in J. Kluger, Secrets of the shy. *Time,* 50–52.

Pychyl, T. A., Coplan, R. J., & Reid, P. A. M. (2002). Parenting and procrastination: Gender differences in the relations between procrastination, parenting style and self-worth in early adolescence. *Personality and Individual Differences, 33,* 271–285.

Querna, E. (2004, October 12). Teenagers and alcohol: Teen drinking linked to health problems in young adults. *U.S. News & World Report.*

Quinn, P. C. (2002). Category representation in young infants. *Current Directions in Psychological Science, 11,* 66–70.

Quinn, P. C., & Oates, J. (2004). Early category representation and concepts. In J. Oates & A. Grayson (Eds.), *Cognitive and language development in children* (pp. 21–60). Malden, MA: Blackwell Publishing.

Quinn, P. C., Ramesh, S. B., Brush, D., Grimes, A., & Sharpnack, H. (2002). Development of form similarity as a Gestalt grouping principle in infancy. *Psychological Science, 13,* 320–328.

Quirk, G. J. (2007). Prefrontal-amygdala interactions in the regulation of fear. In J. J. Gross (Ed.), *Handbook of emotion regulation* (pp. 27–46). New York: Guilford Press.

Rabasca, L. (1999, December). Not enough evidence to support "abstinence-only." *Monitor of American Psychological Association, 39.*

Rabasca, L. (2000a, March). Humanistic psychologists look to revamp their image. *Monitor on Psychology,* 54–55.

Rabasca, L. (2000b, November). In search of equality. *Monitor on Psychology,* 30–31.

Rabkin, S. W., Boyko, E., Shane, F., & Kaufert, J. (1984). A randomized trial comparing smoking cessation programs utilizing behavior modification, health education or hypnosis. *Addictive Behaviors, 9,* 157–173.

Rachman, S. (2002). Fears born and bred: Non-associative fear acquisitions. *Behaviour Research and Therapy, 40,* 121–126.

Rahman, Q., & Wilson, G. D. (2003). Born gay? The psychobiology of human sexual orientation. *Personality and Individual Differences, 34,* 1337–1382.

Raichle, M. E. (1994). Visualizing the mind. *Scientific American, 270,* 58–64.

Raine, A. (2002). Biosocial studies of antisocial and violent behavior in children and adults: A review. *Journal of Abnormal Child Psychology, 30,* 311–326.

Raine, A., Ishikawa, S. S., Arce, E., Lencz, T., Knuth, K. H., Bihrie, S., LaCasse, L., & Colletti, P. (2004). Hippocampal structural asymmetry in unsuccessful psychopaths. *Biological Psychiatry, 55,* 185–191.

Raine, A., Lencz, T., Bihrle, S., LaCasse, L., & Colletti, P. (2000). Reduced prefrontal gray matter volume and reduced autonomic activity in antisocial personality disorder. *Archives of General Psychiatry, 57,* 119–127.

Raine, A., Reynolds, C., Venables, P. H., & Mednick, S. A. (2002). Stimulation seeking and intelligence: A prospective longitudinal study. *Journal of Personality and Social Psychology, 82,* 663–674.

Raine, R. (2002, April 29). Cited in J. Foreman, Roots of violence may lie in damaged brain cells. *Los Angeles Times,* S1.

Rainville, P., Duncan, G. H., Price, D. D., Carrier, B., & Bushnell, M. C. (1997). Pain affect encoded in human anterior cingulated but not somatosensory cortex. *Science, 277,* 968–971.

Raloff, J. (2005, April 2). Still hungry? *Science News, 167,* 216–220.

Ramachandran, V. S. (2006, April/May). Cited in M. Solms, Freud returns. *Scientific American Mind,* 28–34.

Ramachandran, V. S., & Anstis, S. M. (1986). The perception of apparent motion. *Scientific American, 254,* 102–109.

Ramirez-Esparza, N., Gosling, S. D., Benet-Martinez, V., Potter, J. P., & Pennebaker, J. W. (2006). Do bilinguals have two personalities? A special case of cultural frame switching. *Journal of Research in Personality, 40,* 99–120.

Rao, S. M. (2002, September). Cited in K. Wright, Times of our lives. *Scientific American,* 59–65.

Rapoport, J. L. (1988). The neurobiology of obsessive-compulsive disorder. *Journal of the American Medical Association, 260,* 2888–2890.

Rapson, E., & Hatfield, R. L. (2005). *Love and sex: Cross-cultural perspectives.* Lanham, MD: University Press of America.

Ras-Work, B. (2006, June 2). Cited in L. MacInnis, Genital cutting's fatal results cited. *The San Diego Union-Tribune,* A16.

Raskin, N. J., & Rogers, C. R. (2005). Person-centered therapy. In R. J. Corsini & D. Wedding, *Current psychotherapies* (7th ed., pp. 130–165). Belmont, CA: Brooks/Cole–Thomson Learning.

Rasmussen, C., Knapp, T. J., & Garner, L. (2000). Driving-induced stress in urban college students. *Perceptual and Motor Skills, 90,* 437–443.

Rasmussen, K. G. (2003). Clinical applications of recent research on electroconvulsive therapy. *Bulletin of the Menninger Clinic, 67,* 18–31.

Ratcliff, R., & McKoon, G. (2005). Memory models. In E. Tulving & F. M. Craik (Eds.), *The Oxford handbook of memory.* New York: Oxford University Press.

Rauschecker, J. P., & Shannon, R. V. (2002). Sending sound to the brain. *Science, 295,* 1025–1029.

Reaves, J. (2001, February 21). Freedom of religion or state-sanctioned child abuse? *Time.*

Rechtschaffen, A. (1997, August). Cited in T. Geier, What is sleep for? *U.S. News & World Report.*

Reed, M. K. (1994). Social skills training to reduce depression in adolescents. *Adolescence, 29,* 293–302.

References

Reed, S., & Breu, G. (1995, June 6). The wild ones. *People*.

Reed, S., & Cook, D. (1993, April 19). Realm of the senses. *People*.

Reed, S., & Esselman, M. (1995, August 28). Catching hell. *People*.

Reed, S., & Free, C. (1995, October 16). The big payoff. *People*.

Reed, S., & Stambler, L. (1992, May 25). The umpire strikes back. *People*, 87–88.

Reed, S. D., & Sutton, E. L. (2006). Menopause. In D. C. Dale & D. D. Federman (Eds.), *ACP Medicine*. New York: WebMD Professional Publishing.

Reid, J. B., Taplin, P. S., & Lorber, R. (1981). A social interactional approach to the treatment of abusive families. In R. B. Stuart (Ed.), *Violent behavior: Social learning approaches to prediction, management and treatment*. New York: Brunner/Mazel.

Reisler, J. (2002, February 24). Technology; improving sound, easing fury. *Newsweek*, 16.

Reitman, V. (1999, February 22). Learning to grin—and bear it. *Los Angeles Times*, A1.

Renfrey, G., & Spates, C. R. (1994). Eye movement desensitization: A partial dismantling study. *Journal of Behavior Therapy and Experimental Psychiatry, 25*, 231–239.

Repanshek, K. (2006, January). Cell phones simulate premature aging. *Discover*, 67.

Rescorla, R. A. (1966). Predictability and number of pairings in Pavlovian fear conditioning. *Psychonomic Science, 4*, 383–384.

Rescorla, R. A. (1987). A Pavlovian analysis of goal-directed behavior. *American Psychologist, 42*, 119–129.

Rescorla, R. A. (1988). Pavlovian conditioning. *American Psychologist, 43*, 151–160.

Research Triangle Institute. (1994). *Past and future directions of the D.A.R.E. program: An evaluation review*. Washington, DC: National Institute of Justice.

Reus, V. I. (2006). Mental disorders. In S. L. Hauser (Ed.), *Harrison's neurology in clinical medicine* (pp. 589–613). New York: McGraw-Hill.

Rex, C. S., Lauterborn, J. C., Lin, C., Kramar, E. A., Rogers, G. A., Gall, C. M., & Lynch, G. (2006). Restoration of long-term potentiation in middle-aged hippocampus after induction of brain-derived neurotrophic factor. *Journal of Neurophysiology, 96*, 677–685.

Rey, G. (1983). Concepts and stereotypes. *Cognition, 15*, 237–262.

Reyner, L. A., & Horne, J. A. (2000). Early morning driver sleepiness: Effectiveness of 200 mg caffeine. *Psychophysiology, 7*, 251–256.

Reynolds, A. J., Temple, J. A., Robertson, D. L., & Mann, E. A. (2001). Long-term effects of an early childhood intervention on educational achievement and juvenile arrest. *Journal of the American Medical Association, 285*, 2339–2346.

Reyonds, G. (2006, June). Hydration angst. *Play*, 30–31.

Rhee, S. H., & Waldman, I. D. (2002). Genetic and environmental influences on antisocial behavior: A meta-analysis of twin and adoption studies. *Psychological Bulletin, 128*, 490–529.

Rhodewalt, F., & Vohs, K. D. (2005). Defensive strategies, motivation, and the self. In A. J. Elliot & C. S. Dweck (Eds.), *Handbook of competence and motivation* (pp. 548–565). New York: Guilford Press.

Ricaurte, G. A. (2003, September 6). Cited in D. G. McNeil, Jr., Report of ecstasy drug's risks is retracted. *New York Times*, A8.

Ricaurte, G. A., Yuan, J., Hatzidimitrious, G., Cord, B. J., & McCann, U. D. (2002). Severe dopaminergic neurotoxicity in primates after a common recreational dose regime of MDMA ("ecstasy"). *Science, 297*, 2260–2263.

Riccio, D. C., Millin, P. M., & Gisquet-Verier, P. (2003). Retrograde amnesia: Forgetting back. *Current Directions in Psychological Science, 12*, 41–44.

Richters, J. M. A. (1997). Menopause in different cultures. *Journal of Psychosomatic Obstetrics and Gynecology, 18*, 73–80.

Ridderinkhof, K. R., de Vlugt, Y., Bramlage, A., Spaan, M., Elton, M., Snel, J., & Band, G. P. H. (2002). Alcohol consumption impairs detection of performance errors in mediofrontal cortex. *Science, 298*, 2209–2211.

Riddle, E. L., Fleckenstein, A. E., & Hanson, G. R. (2006). Mechanisms of methamphetamine-induced dopaminergic neurotoxicity. *American Association of Pharmaceutical Scientists Journal, 8*, E413–418.

Rieke, M. L., & Guastello, S. J. (1995). Unresolved issues in honesty and integrity testing. *American Psychologist, 50*, 458–459.

Riggs, D. S., & Foa, E. B. (2006). Obsessive-compulsive disorder. In M. Hersen & J. C. Thomas (Eds.), *Comprehensive handbook of personality and psychopathology: Adult psychopathology* (Vol. 2, pp. 169–188). Hoboken, NJ: John Wiley & Sons.

Rimland, B. (1964). *Infantile autism*. New York: Appleton-Century-Crofts.

Rivas-Vazquez, R. A. (2003). Benzodiazepines in contemporary clinical practice. *Professional Psychology: Research and Practice, 34*, 324–328.

Rivera, C. (2000, June 9). Helping hands for mentally ill. *Los Angeles Times*, A1.

Rizzolatti, G., Fogassi, L., & Gallese, V. (2006, November). In the mind. *Scientific American*, 54–61.

Roan, S. (1998, March 16). A reason for hope. *Los Angeles Times*, S1.

Roan, S. (2002, June 17). A new way to treat alcoholism. *Los Angeles Times*, S1.

Robbins, J. (2000, July 4). Virtual reality finds a real place as a medical aid. *New York Times*, D6.

Roberts, B. W., Helson, R., & Klohnen, E. V. (2002). Personality development and growth in women across 30 years: Three perspectives. *Journal of Personality, 70*, 79–102.

Robichaud, M., Dugas, M. J., & Conway, M. (2003). Gender differences in worry and associated cognitive-behavioral variables. *Anxiety Disorders, 17*, 501–516.

Robins, L. N., & Regier, D. A. (Eds.). (1991). *Psychiatric disorders in America*. New York: Free Press.

Robins, L. N., Tipp, J., & Przybeck, T. (1991). Antisocial personality. In L. N. Robins & D. A. Regier (Eds.), *Psychiatric disorders in America*. New York: Free Press.

Robinson-Riegler, B., & McDaniel, M. A. (1994). Further constraints on the bizarreness effect: Elaboration at encoding. *Memory and Cognition, 22*, 702–712.

Rochat, P. (2003). Five levels of self-awareness as they unfold early in life. *Consciousness and cognition, 12*, 171–181.

Roche, T. (2001, May 28). Voices from the cell. *Time*, 29–38.

Rock, I., & Palmer, S. (1990). The legacy of Gestalt psychology. *Scientific American, 263*, 84–90.

Rodafinos, A., Vucevic, A., & Sideridis, G. D. (2005). The effectiveness of compliance techniques: Foot in the door versus door in the face. *The Journal of Social Psychology, 145*, 237–239.

Rodgers, J. E. (1982). The malleable memory of eyewitnesses. *Science*.

Rodriguez-Tome, H., Bariaud, F., Cohen-Zardi, M. F., Delmas, C., Jeanvoine, F., & Szylagyi, P. (1993). The effects of pubertal changes on body image and relations with peers of the opposite sex in adolescence. *Journal of Adolescence, 16*, 421–438.

Roediger, H. L., Gallo, D. A., & Geraci, L. (2002). Processing approaches to cognition: The impetus from the levels-of-processing framework. *Memory, 10*, 319–332.

Roediger, H. L., & McDermott, K. B. (2005). Distortions of memory. In E. Tulving & F. M. Craik (Eds.), *The Oxford handbook of memory*. New York: Oxford University Press.

Roese, N. J. (2001). The crossroads of affect and cognition: Counterfactuals as compensatory cognition. In G. B. Moskowitz (Ed.), *Cognitive social psychology*. Mahwah, NJ: Lawrence Erlbaum.

Roffman, J. L., Marci, C. D., Glick, D. M., Dougherty, D. D., & Rauch, S. L. (2005). Neuroimaging and the functional neuroanatomy of psychotherapy. *Psychological Medicine, 35*, 1385–1398.

Rogers, C. R. (1951). *Client-centered therapy: Its current practice, implications, and theory*. Boston: Houghton Mifflin.

Rogers, C. R. (1980). *A way of being*. Boston: Houghton Mifflin.

Rogers, C. R. (1986). Client-centered therapy. In I. L. Kutash & A. Wolf (Eds.), *Psychotherapists' casebook*. San Francisco: Jossey-Bass.

Rogers, C. R. (1989). Cited in N. J. Raskin & C. R. Rogers, Person-centered therapy. In R. J. Corsini & D. Wedding (Eds.), *Current psychotherapies* (4th ed.). Itasca, IL: F. E. Peacock.

Rogers, L. (2001). *Sexing the brain*. New York: Columbia University Press.

Rogers, P., & Morehouse, W., III. (1999, April 12). She's got it. *People*, 89.

Roitberg, B. Z., & Kordower, J. H. (2004). Brain implants and transplants. In *International Encyclopedia of the Social & Behavioral Sciences* (pp. 1345–1352). Burlington, MA: Elsevier Science & Technology.

Romney, D. M., & Bynner, J. M. (1997). A re-examination of the relationship between shyness, attributional style, and depression. *Journal of Genetic Psychology, 158*, 261–270.

Root, R. W., II, & Resnick, R. J. (2003). An update on the diagnosis and treatment of attention-deficit/hyperactivity disorders in children. *Professional Psychology: Research Practice, 34*, 34–41.

Ropper, A. H. (2006). Acute confusional states and coma. In S. L. Hauser (Ed.), *Harrison's neurology in clinical medicine* (pp. 103–114). New York: McGraw-Hill.

Ropper, A. H., & Brown, R. H. (2005). *Adams & Victors' principles of neurology* (8th ed.). New York: McGraw-Hill.

Rorschach, R. (1921; reprinted 1942). *Psychodiagnostics*. Bern: Hans Huber.

Rortvedt, A. K., & Miltenberger, R. G. (1994). Analysis of a high-probability instructional sequence and time-out in the treatment of child noncompliance. *Journal of Applied Behavior Analysis, 27*, 327–330.

Rosch, E. (1978). Principles of categorization. In E. Rosch & B. B. Lloyd (Eds.), *Cognition and categorization*. Hillsdale, NJ: Lawrence Erlbaum.

Rose, D. A., & Kahan, T. L. (2001). Melatonin and sleep qualities in healthy adults: Pharmacological and expectancy effects. *The Journal of General Psychology, 128*, 401–421.

Rosenbaum, J. E. (2006). Reborn a virgin: Adolescents' retracting of virginity pledges and sexual histories. *American Journal of Public Health, 96*, 1098–1103.

Rosenberg, K. P. (1994). Notes and comments: Biology and homosexuality. *Journal of Sex and Marital Therapy, 20*, 147–150.

Rosenberg, R. S. (2006). Operating and managing a sleep disorders clinic. In T. L. Lee-Chiong (Ed.), *Sleep: A comprehensive handbook* (pp. 1051–1054). Hoboken, NJ: John Wiley & Sons.

Rosenthal, E. (2006, June 2). Genital cutting raises by 50% likelihood mothers or their newborns will die, study finds. *The New York Times*, A10.

Rosenthal, L. (2006). Physiologic processes during sleep. In T. L. Lee-Chiong (Ed.), *Sleep: A comprehensive handbook* (pp. 19–23). Hoboken, NJ: John Wiley & Sons.

Rosenthal , R. (2003). Covert communication in laboratories, classrooms, and the truly real world. *Current Directions in Psychological Science, 12*, 151–154.

Rosenthal, S. L., Burklow, K. A., Lewis, L. M., Succop, P. A., & Biro, F. M. (1997). Heterosexual romantic relationships and sexual behaviors of young adolescent girls. *Journal of Adolescent Health, 21*, 238–243.

Ross, B. M., & Millsom, C. (1970). Repeated memory of oral prose in Ghana and New York. *International Journal of Psychology, 5*, 173–181.

Ross, H. E., & Plug, C. (2002). *The mystery of the moon illusion. Exploring size perception.* Oxford: Oxford University Press.

Ross, P. E. (1991). Hard words. *Scientific American, 264*, 138–147.

Ross, P. E. (2006, August). The expert mind. *Scientific American*, 64–71.

Rothbart, M. K., & Sheese, B. E. (2007). Temperament and emotion regulation. In J. J. Gross (Ed.), *Handbook of emotion regulation* (pp. 331–350). New York: Guilford Press.

Rothbaum, B. O., Hodges, L., Anderson, P. L., Price, L., & Smith, S. (2002). Twelve-month follow-up of virtual reality and standard exposure therapies for the fear of flying. *Journal of Counseling and Clinical Psychology, 70*, 428–432.

Rotter, J. B. (1990). Internal versus external control of reinforcement: A case history of a variable. *American Psychologist, 45*, 489–493.

Routh, D. K. (1994). *The founding of clinical psychology (1896) and some important early developments: Introduction.* New York: Plenum Publishing.

Rowa, K., McCabe, R. E., & Antony, M. M. (2006). Specific phobias. In M. Hersen & J. D. Thomas (Eds.), *Comprehensive handbook of personality and psychopathology: Adult psychopathology* (Vol. 2, pp. 154–168). Hoboken, NJ: John Wiley & Sons.

Rowan, A. N. (1997, February). The benefits and ethics of animal research. *Scientific American*, 79–94.

Roy-Byrne, P. P., & Fann, J. R. (1997). Psychopharmacologic treatments for patients with neuropsychiatric disorders. In S. C. Yudofsky & R. E. Hales (Eds.), *American Psychiatric Press textbook of neuropsychiatry* (3rd ed.). Washington, DC: American Psychiatric Press.

Rozin, P. (1986). One-trial acquired likes and dislikes in humans: Disgust as a U.S. food predominance, and negative learning predominance. *Learning and Motivation, 17*, 180–189.

Rozin, P. (2003). Introduction: Evolutionary and cultural perspectives on affect. In R. D. Lane & L. Nadel (Eds.), *Cognitive neuroscience of emotion.* Oxford: Oxford University Press.

Rozin, P., Haidt, J., & McCauley, C. R. (2000). Disgust. In M. Lewis & J. M. Haviland-Jones (Eds.), *Handbook of emotions* (2nd ed., pp. 637–653). New York: Guilford.

Rozin, P., Kabnick, K., Pete, E., Fischler, C., & Shields, C. (2003). The ecology of eating: Smaller portion sizes in France than in the United States help explain the French paradox. *Psychological Science, 14*, 450–454.

RSNA (Radiological Society of North America). (2005, November 30). Coffee jump-starts short-term memory. *RSNA 2005 Newsroom.* Available: http://www.rsna.org/rsna/media/pr2005/Coffee.cfm

Rubin, D. C., & Kozin, M. (1984). Vivid memories. *Cognition, 16*, 81–95.

Rubin, R. (2006, January 24). New drug treats the new face of addiction. *USA Today*, 1A.

Rubin, R. (2007, February 20). Merck drops its push for vaccine mandate. *USA Today.*

Ruble, D. N., Martin, C. L., & Berenbaum, S. A. (2006). Gender development. In N. Eisenberg, W. Damon & R. M. Lerner (Eds.), *Handbook of child psychology* (6th ed., pp. 858–932). Hoboken, NJ: John Wiley & Sons.

Rui, L. (2005, August 21). Leptin-signaling protein maintains normal body weight and energy balance in mice. *Science Daily.*

Ruibal, S. (2006, February 12). White a gold winner in halfpipe, Kass is second. *USA Today.*

Ruiter, R. A. C., Abraham, C., & Kok, G. (2001). Scary warnings and rational precautions: A review of the psychology of fear appeals. *Psychology and Health, 16*, 613–630.

Ruiz-Bueno, J. B. (2000). Locus of control, perceived control, and learned helplessness. In V. R. Rice (Ed.), *Handbook of stress, coping and health.* Thousand Oaks, CA: Sage.

Runco, M. A. (2004). Creativity. *Annual Review of Psychology, 55*, 657–687.

Rupke, S. J., Blecke, D., & Renfrow, M. (2006). Cognitive therapy for depression. *American Family Physician, 73*, 83–86.

Rush, A. J. (2003). Toward an understanding of bipolar disorder and its origins. *Journal of Clinical Psychiatry, 64 (supplement 6)*, 4–8.

Rush, A. J. (2006a, March 25). Cited in B. Bower, Mood meds' second wind. *Science News, 169*, 179–180.

Rush, A. J. (2006b, November 1). Cited in M. Marchione, Landmark govt. study examines depression. *ABC News* [On-line]. Available: http://abcnews.go.com/Health/print?id=2620203

Russell, S. (2005, March 23). The Terri Schiavo case: Her condition: Doctor explains the "persistent vegetative state." *San Francisco Chronicle.*

Rutherford, M. (2001, March). What did you say? *Time, Bonus Section Generations*, G8–9.

Rutter, M., & Silberg, J. (2002). Gene-environment interplay in relation to emotional and behavioral disturbance. *Annual Review of Psychology, 53*, 463–490.

Sackeim, H. A., & Stern, Y. (1997). Neuropsychiatric aspects of memory and amnesia. In S. C. Yudofsky & R. E. Hales (Eds.), *The American Psychiatric Press textbook of neuropsychiatry* (3rd ed.). Washington, DC: American Psychiatric Press.

Sackeim, H. A., Prudic, J., Devanand, D. P., Nobler, M. S., Lisanby, S., Peyser, S., Fitzsimons, L., Moody, B. J., & Clark, J. (2000). A prospective, randomized, double blind comparison of bilateral and right unilateral electroconvulsive therapy at different stimulus intensities. *Archives of General Psychiatry, 57*, 425–434.

Sacks, O. (1995). *An anthropologist on Mars.* New York: Alfred A. Knopf.

Sadock, B. J., & Sadock, V. A. (Eds.). (2005). *Kaplan & Sadock's comprehensive textbook of psychiatry.* Philadelphia: Lippincott Williams & Wilkins.

Salamon, E., Bernstein, S. R., Kim, S., Kim, M., & Stefano, G. B. (2003). The effects of auditory perception and musical preference on anxiety in naïve human subjects. *Medical Science Monitor, 9*, 396–399.

Salovey, P., & Mayer, J. D. (1990). Emotional intelligence. *Imagination, Cognition, and Personality, 9*, 185–211.

Salovey, P., & Pizarro, D. A. (2003). In R. J. Sternberg, J. Lautrey & T. I. Lubart (Eds.), *Models of intelligence.* Washington, DC: American Psychological Association.

Salovey, P., Rothman, A. J., Detweiller, J. B., & Steward, W. T. (2000). Emotional states and physical health. *American Psychologist, 55*, 110–121.

Samelson, F. (1980). J. B. Watson's little Albert, Cyril Burt's twins, and the need for a critical science. *American Psychologist, 35*, 619–625.

SAMHSA (Substance Abuse and Mental Health Services Administration). (2000). Heroin deaths. *Drug abuse warning network annual medical examiner data 1999.* DAWN series D-16, DHHS Publication No. (SMA) 01-3491. Rockville, MD: Author.

SAMHSA. (2005a). Annual causes of death in the United States. *Drug War Facts.* Available: http://www.drugwarfacts.org/causes.htm

SAMHSA. (2005b). *Results from the 2004 national survey on drug use and health: National findings.* Rockville, MD: Author.

SAMHSA. (2006). *Results from the 2005 national survey on drug use and health: National findings.* Office of Applied Studies, NSDUH Series H-30, DHHS Publication No. SMA 06-4194.

Samuel, D. (1996). Cited in N. Williams, How the ancient Egyptians brewed beer. *Science, 273*, 432.

San Diego Union-Tribune. (2003, April 27). "Gothika" a Montreal thriller for Dutton. F8.

Sanchez, R. (2001, August 26). West Coast meth lab operations reaching new levels, DEA says. *The Washington Post, 121*(35).

Sanders, M. R., Cann, W., & Markie-Dadds, C. (2003). Why a universal population-level approach to the prevention of child abuse is essential. *Child Abuse Review, 12*, 145–154.

Sands, R., Tricker, J., Sherman, C., Armatas, C., & Maschette, W. (1997). Disordered eating patterns, body image, self-esteem, and physical activity in preadolescent school children. *International Journal of Eating Disorders, 21*, 159–166.

Sang, F. Y. P., Billar, J., Gresty, M. A., & Golding, J. F. (2005). Effect of a novel desensitization training regime and controlled breathing on habituation to motion sickness. *Perceptual and Motor Skills, 101*, 244–256.

Sang, F. Y. P., Golding, J. F., & Gresty, M. A. (2003). Suppression of sickness by controlled breathing during mildly nauseogenic motion. *Aviation, Space, and Environmental Medicine, 74*, 998–1002.

Sapolsky, R. (2006, April). The 2% difference. *Discover*, 42–45.

Sapolsky, R. M. (2002, December 17). Cited in E. Goode, The heavy cost of stress. *New York Times*, D1.

Sarraj, I. (2002, June 21). Cited in J. Bennet, Rash of new suicide bombers showing no pattern or ties. *New York Times*, A1.

Satcher, D. (2000). Mental health: A report of the Surgeon General—executive summary. *Professional Psychology, Research and Practice, 31*, 5–13.

Saul, S. (2006, February 7). Record sales of sleep pills cause worry. *The New York Times*, A1, C4.

Savage-Rumbaugh, S. (1998, January 19). Cited in S. Begley, Aping language. *Newsweek.*

Savage-Rumbaugh, S., & Lewin, R. (1994). *Kanzi.* New York: Wiley.

Savic, I. (2005, May 10). Cited in N. Wade, For gay men, different scent of attraction. *The New York Times*, A1.

Savic, I., Berglund, H., & Lindstrom, P. (2005). Brain response to putative pheromones in homosexual men. *Proceedings of the National Academy of Sciences, 102*, 7356–7361.

References

Savin-Williams, R. (2005, October 10). Cited in J. Cloud, The battle over gay teens. *Time*, 42–51.

Sax, L. J. (2002, September 11). Cited in M. Duenwald, Students find another staple of campus life: Stress. *New York Times*, D5.

Saxbe, D. (2004, September/October). Placebo power: A mystery grows. *Psychology Today*.

Saxe, L. (1994). Detection of deception: Polygraph and integrity tests. *Current Directions in Psychological Science, 3*, 69–73.

Saywitz, K. J., Mannarino, A. P., Berliner, L., & Cohen, J. A. (2000). Treatment for sexually abused children and adolescents. *American Psychologist, 55,* 1040–1049.

Scanlon, M., & Mauro, J. (1992, November–December). The lowdown on handwriting analysis. *Psychology Today*.

Scarr, S., & Weinberg, R. A. (1976). IQ test performance of black children adopted by white families. *American Psychologist, 31,* 726–739.

Schachter, S., & Singer, J. (1962). Cognitive, social and physiological determinants of emotional state. *Psychological Review, 69,* 379–399.

Schacter, D. L. (1996). *Searching for memory*. New York: Basic Books.

Schacter, D. L. (1997, October). Cited in E. Yoffe, How quickly we forget. *U.S. News & World Report*.

Schacter, D. L. (2001). *The seven sins of memory: How the mind forgets and remembers*. New York: Houghton Mifflin.

Schacter, D. L., Wagner, A. D., & Buckner, R. L. (2005). Memory systems of 1999. In E. Tulving & F. M. Craik (Eds.), *The Oxford handbook of memory*. New York: Oxford University Press.

Schaufeli, W. B., & Peeters, M. C. W. (2000). Job stress and burnout among correctional officers: A literature review. *International Journal of Stress Management, 7,* 19–48.

Schenck, C. H. (2003, January 7). Cited in E. Goode, When the brain disrupts the night. *New York Times*, D1.

Schewe, P. (Ed.). (2002). *Preventing violence in relationships: Interventions across the life span*. Washington, DC: American Psychological Association.

Schiff, M., Duyme, M., Dumaret, A., & Tomkiewicz, S. (1982). How much could we boost scholastic achievement and IQ scores? A direct answer from a French adoption study. *Cognition, 12,* 165–196.

Schlaggar, B. L., Brown, T. T., Lugar, H. M., Visscher, K. M., Miezin, F. M., & Petersen, S. E. (2002). Functional neuroanatomical differences between adults and school-age children in the processing of single words. *Science, 296,* 1476–1479.

Schmid, R. E. (2002, June 1). Normal protein in brain possible cause of Parkinson's. *San Diego Union-Tribune*, A8.

Schmidt, M. (1997). In D. J. Cohen & F. R. Volkmar (Eds.), *Handbook of autism and pervasive developmental disorders* (2nd ed.). New York: John Wiley & Sons.

Schneider, D. J. (2004). *The psychology of stereotyping*. New York: Guilford Press.

Schneider, K. J., Bugental, J. F. T., & Pierson, J. F. (Eds.). (2002). *The handbook of humanistic psychology: Leading edges in theory, research, and practice*. Thousand Oaks, CA: Sage.

Schnurr, P. P., Friedman, M. J., & Bernardy, N. C. (2002). Research on posttraumatic stress disorder: Epidemiology, pathophysiology, and assessment. *Journal of Clinical Psychology/In Session: Psychotherapy in Practice, 58,* 877–889.

Schooler, J. W. (1994). Seeking the core: The issues and evidence surrounding recovered accounts of sexual trauma. *Consciousness and Cognition, 3,* 452–469.

Schooler, J. W., & Eich, E. (2005). Memory for emotional events. In E. Tulving & F. M. Craik (Eds.), *The Oxford handbook of memory*. New York: Oxford University Press.

Schroeder, D. A., Penner, L. A., Dovidio, J. F., & Piliavin, J. A. (1995). *The psychology of helping and altruism: Problems and puzzles*. New York: McGraw-Hill.

Schuckit, M. (2000). *Drug and alcohol abuse* (5th ed.). New York: Kluwer Academic.

Schuckit, M. (2002, June 17). Cited in S. Roan, A new way to treat alcoholism. *Los Angeles Times*, S1.

Schuckit, M. (2006). Alcohol and alcoholism. In S. L. Hauser (Ed.), *Harrison's neurology in clinical medicine* (pp. 617–624). New York: McGraw-Hill.

Schulman, K. A., Berlin, J. A., Harless, W., Kerner, J. F., Sistrunk, S., Gersh, B. J., Dube, R., Taleghani, C. K., Burke, J. E., Williams, S., Eisenberg, J. M., & Escarce, J. J. (1999). The effect of race and sex on physicians' recommendations for cardiac catheterization. *The New England Journal of Medicine, 340,* 618–626.

Schultz, R. T., Gauthier, I., Klin, A., Fulbright, R. K., Anderson, A. W., Volkmar, F. R., Schudlarski, P., Lacadie, C., Cohen, D. J., & Gore, J. C. (2000). Abnormal ventral temporal cortical activity during face discrimination among individuals with autism and Asperger syndrome. *Archives of General Psychiatry, 57,* 331–340.

Schulz, R., & Curnow, C. (1988). Peak performance and age among superathletes: Track and field, swimming, baseball, tennis, and golf. *Journal of Gerontology, 43,* 113–120.

Schwab, J., Kulin, H. E., Susman, E. J., Finkelstein, J. W., Chinchilli, V. M., Kunselman, S. J., Liben, L. S., D'Arangelo, M. R., & Demers, L. M. (2001). The role of sex hormone replacement therapy on self-perceived competence in adolescents with delayed puberty. *Child Development, 72,* 1439–1450.

Schwab, M. E. (2002). Repairing the injured spinal cord. *Science, 295,* 1029–1030.

Schwartz, B. L. (1999). Sparkling at the end of the tongue: The etiology of tip-of-the-tongue phenomenology. *Psychonomic Bulletin & Review, 6,* 379–393.

Schwartz, B., & Reisberg, D. (1991). *Learning and memory*. New York: Norton.

Schwartz, C. E., Wright, C. I., Shin, L. M., Kagan, J., & Rauch, S. L. (2003). Inhibited and uninhibited infants "grown up": Adult amygdalar response to novelty. *Science, 300,* 1952–1953.

Schwartz, N. (1999). Self-reports: How the questions shape the answers. *American Psychologist, 54,* 93–105.

Schweinhart, L. J., & Weikart, D. P. (1980). *Young children grow up: The effects of the Perry Preschool Program on youth through age 15* (Monograph No. 7). Ypsilanti, MI: High/Scope Educational Research Foundation.

Sciutto, M. J., Terjesen, M. D., & Bender Frank, A. S. (2000). Teacher's knowledge and misperceptions of attention-deficit/hyperactivity disorder. *Psychology in the Schools, 37,* 115–122.

Searles, J. (1998, September). Write on! Learn to read his handwriting and read his mind. *Cosmopolitan*, 310–311.

Segerstrom, S. C., & Miller, G. E. (2004). Psychological stress and the human immune system: A meta-analytic study of 30 years of inquiry. *Psychological Bulletin, 130,* 601–630.

Segurado, R., Convoy, J., Meally, E., Fitzgerald, M., Gill, M., & Gallagher, L. (2005). Confirmation of association between autism and the mitochondrial aspartate/glutamate carrier SLC25A12 gene on chromosone 2q31. *American Journal of Psychiatry, 162,* 2182–2184.

Seligman, M. E. P. (1970). On the generality of the laws of learning. *Psychological Review, 77,* 406–418.

Seligman, M. E. P. (2002, December 9). Cited in M. Elias, What makes people happy psychologists now know. *USA Today*, A1.

Seligman, M. E. P. (2003). The past and future of positive psychology. In C. L. M. Keyes & J. Daidt (Eds.), *Flourishing: Positive psychology and the life well-lived*. Washington, DC: American Psychological Association.

Selye, H. (1993). History of the stress concept. In L. Goldberger & S. Breznitz (Eds.), *Handbook of stress: Theoretical and clinical aspects* (2nd ed.). New York: Free Press.

Senden, M. von. (1960). *Space and sight: The perception of space and shape in the congenitally blind before and after operation* (P. Heath, Trans.). New York: Free Press.

Senécal, C., Koestner, R., & Vallerand, R. J. (1995). Self-regulation and academic procrastination. *Journal of Social Psychology, 135,* 607–619.

Seppa, N. (2005, December 10). Beyond hearing. *Science News*, 371–372.

Serpell, R. (2000). Intelligence and culture. In R. J. Sternberg (Ed.), *Handbook of intelligence*. New York: Cambridge University Press.

Serpell, R. (2003, February). Cited in E. Benson, Intelligence across cultures. *Monitor on Psychology*, 56–58.

Settineri, S., Tati, F., & Fanara, G. (2005). Gender differences in dental anxiety: Is the chair position important? *Journal of Contemporary Dental Practice, 6,* 115–122.

Seymour, N. E., Gallagher, A. G., Roman, S. A., O'Brien, M. K., Bansal, V. K., Andersen, D. K., & Satava, R. M. (2002). Virtual reality training improves operating room performances: Results of a randomized, double-blinded study. *Annals of Surgery, 236,* 458–464.

Shadish, W. R., Navarro, A. M., Matt, G. E., & Phillips, G. (2000). The effects of psychological therapies under clinically representative conditions: A meta-analysis. *Psychological Bulletin, 126,* 512–529.

Shanker, S. G., Savage-Rumbaugh, E. S., & Taylor, T. J. (1999). Kanzi: A new beginning. *Animal Learning & Behavior, 27,* 24–25.

Shannon, C. (1994). Stress management. In D. K. Granvold (Ed.), *Cognitive and behavioral treatment*. Pacific Grove, CA: Brooks/Cole.

Shapiro, C. M. (1981). Growth hormone sleep interaction: A review. *Research Communications in Psychology, Psychiatry and Behavior, 6,* 115–131.

Shapiro, F. (1991). Eye movement desensitization and reprocessing: From MD to EMD/R—A new treatment model for anxiety and related trauma. *Behavior Therapist, 14,* 133–135.

Shapiro, F. (2002). EMDR 12 years after its introduction: Past and future research. *Journal of Clinical Psychology, 58,* 1–22.

Shapiro, F., & Maxfield, L. (2002). Eye movement desensitization and reprocessing (EMDR): Information processing in the treatment of trauma. *Journal of Clinical Psychology, 58,* 933–948.

Shapiro, J. P. (1996, May 27). Beyond the rain man. *U.S. News & World Report*, 78–79.

Shapiro, J. P., Loeb, P., Bowermaster, D., Wright, A., Headden, S., & Toch, T. (1993, December 13). Special report. *U.S. News & World Report*.

Shapiro, L. (1992, August 31). The lesson of Salem. *Newsweek*.

Shapiro, R. (2005). Treating anxiety disorders with EMDR. In R. Shapiro, *EMDR solutions: Pathways to healing* (pp. 312–326). New York: W. W. Norton.

Shapiro, S. L., Shapiro, D. E., & Schwartz, G. E. R. (2000). Stress management in medical education: A review of the literature. *Academic Medicine, 75,* 748–759.

Sharp, D. (2000, August 10). Family embraces ear implants. *USA Today,* D9.

Sharp, D. (2003, February 20). Senior suicides to increase as U.S. ages. *USA Today,* A3.

Shaun White. (2006). [On-line]. Available: http://www.nbcolympics.com/athletes/5058606/detail.html

Shaw, P., Greenstein, D., Lerch, J., Clasen, L., Lenroot, R., Gogtay, N., Evans, A., & Giedd, J. (2006, March). Intellectual ability and cortical development in children and adolescents. *Nature, 440,* 676–679.

Shaywitz, B. A., Shaywitz, S., Pugh, K. R., Constable, R. T., Skudlarski, P., Fulbright, R. K., Bronen, R. A., Fletcher, J. M., Shankweiler, D. P., Katz, L., & Gore, J. C. (1995). Sex differences in the functional organization of the brain for language. *Nature, 373,* 607–609.

Shaywitz, B. A., Sullivan, C. M., Anderson, G. M., Gillespie, S. M., Sullivan, B., & Shaywitz, S. E. (1994). Aspartame, behavior, and cognitive function in children with attention deficit disorder. *Pediatrics, 93,* 70–75.

Shaywitz, S. E. (2003, July 28). Cited in C. Gorman, The new science of dyslexia. *Time,* 52–59.

Shaywitz, S. E., Shaywitz, B. A., Fulbright, R. K., Skudlarski, P., Mencl, W. E. Constable, R. T., Pugh, K. R., Holahan, J. M., Marchione, K. E., Fletcher, J. M., Lyon, G. R., & Gore, J. C. (2003). Neural systems for compensation and persistence: Young adult outcome of childhood reading disability. *Biological Psychiatry, 54,* 25–33.

Shea, M. T., Elkin, I., Imber, S. D., Sotsky, S. M., Watkins, J. T., Collins, J. F., Pilkonis, P. A., Beckham, E., Glass, D. R., Dolan, R. T., & Parloff, M. B. (1992). Course of depressive symptoms over follow-up: Findings from the National Institute of Mental Health Treatment of Depression Collaborative Research Program. *Archives of General Psychiatry, 49,* 782–787.

Sheaffer, R. (1997, May/June). Psychic departures and a discovery institute. *Skeptical Inquirer, 21.*

Shenour, E. A. (1990). Lying about polygraph tests. *Skeptical Inquirer, 14,* 292–297.

Sher, L. (2004). Type D personality, cortisol and cardiac disease. *Australian & New Zealand Journal of Psychiatry, 38,* 652–653.

Sherman, R. A. (1997). *Phantom pain.* New York: Plenum Press.

Shermer, M. (2002, December). Mesmerized by magnetism. *Scientific American,* 41.

Shetty, A. K., & Turner, D. A. (1996). Development of fetal hippocampal grafts in intact and lesioned hippocampus. *Progress in Neurobiology, 50,* 597–653.

Shilts, R. (1988). *And the band played on.* New York: Penguin.

Shimaya, A. (1997). Perception of complex line drawings. *Journal of Experimental Psychology: Human Perception and Performance, 23,* 25–50.

Shimizu, M., & Pelham, B. W. (2004). The unconscious cost of good fortune: Implicit and explicit self-esteem, positive life events, and health. *Health Psychology, 23,* 101–105.

Shizgal, P., & Arvanitogiannis, A. (2003). Gambling on dopamine. *Science, 299,* 856–857.

Shomstein, S., & Yantis, S. (2006). Parietal cortex mediates voluntary control of spatial and nonspatial auditory attention. *The Journal of Neuroscience, 26,* 435–439.

Shriver, M. (2005, April 7). Cited in C. Brownlee, Code of many colors: Can researchers see race in the genome? *Science News, 167,* 232–234.

Sibbitt, W. (2006, August 19). Cited in S. Vorenberg, Less fear is decorated needle's point. *The Albuquerque Tribune.*

Sidtis, J. J., Volpe, B. T., Wilson, D. H., Rayport, M., & Gazzaniga, M. S. (1981). Variability in right hemisphere language function after callosal section: Evidence for a continuum of generative capacity. *Journal of Neuroscience, 1,* 323–331.

Siebert, M., Markowitsch, H. J., & Bartel, P. (2003). Amygdala, affect, and cognition: Evidence from 10 patients with Urbach-Wiethe disease. *Brain, 126,* 2627–2637.

Siegal, M. (2005). Can we cure fear? *Scientific American Mind, 16,* 45–49.

Siegel, J. M. (2003, November). Why we sleep. *Scientific American,* 92–97.

Siegel, R. K. (1989). *Intoxication.* New York: Dutton.

Sigelman, C. K., & Rider, E. A. (2006). *Life-span human development* (5th ed.). Belmont, CA: Wadsworth/Thomson.

Silke, A. (2003). Deindividuation, anonymity, and violence: Findings from Northern Ireland. *Journal of Social Psychology, 143,* 493–499.

Sillery, B. (2002, June). At what level of the animal hierarchy do we find true sleep? *Popular Science,* 89.

Silver, J., & Miller, J. H. (2004). Regeneration beyond the glial scar. *Nature Reviews Neuroscience, 5,* 146–156.

Silver, S. M., Rogers, S., Knipe, J., & Colelli, G. (2005). EMDR therapy following the 9/11 terrorist attacks: A community-based intervention project in New York City. *International Journal of Stress Management, 12,* 29–42.

Simcock, G., & Hayne, H. (2002). Breaking the barrier? Children fail to translate their preverbal memories into language. *Psychological Science, 13,* 225–231.

Simeonova, D. I., Chang, K. D., Strong, C., & Ketter, T. A. (2005). Creativity in familial bipolar disorder. *Journal of Psychiatric Research, 39,* 623–631.

Simon, B., & Sturmer, S. (2003). Respect for group members: Intragroup determinants of collective identification and group-serving behavior. *Personality and Social Psychology Bulletin, 29,* 183–193.

Simonton, D. K. (2000). Creativity: Cognitive, personal, developmental, and social aspects. *American Psychologist, 55,* 151–158.

Simpson, J. A., & Tran, S. (2006). The needs, benefits, and perils of close relationships. In P. Noller & J. A. Feeney (Eds.), *Close relationships: Functions, forms, and processes* (pp. 3–24). Hove, England: Psychology Press/Taylor & Francis.

Sinclair, D. A., & Guarente, L. (2006, March). Unlocking the secrets of longevity genes. *Scientific American,* 48–57.

Singer, A. R., & Dobson, K. S. (2006). Cognitive behavioral treatment. In M. Hersen & J. C. Thomas (Eds.), *Comprehensive handbook of personality and psychopathology: Adult psychopathology* (Vol. 2, pp. 487–502). Hoboken, NJ: John Wiley & Sons.

Singer, M. T., & Lalich, J. (1997). *Crazy therapies: What are they? Do they work?* San Francisco: Jossey-Bass.

Singular, S. (2006). *Unholy messenger: The life and crimes of the BTK serial killer.* New York: Scribner.

Sinha, G. (2001, June). Out of control. *Popular Science,* 47–52.

Sivertsen, B., Omvik, S., Pallesen, S., Bjorvatn, B., Havik, O. E., Kvale, G., Nielsen, G. H., & Nordhus, I. H. (2006). Cognitive behavioral therapy vs. Zopiclone for treatment of chronic primary insomnia in older adults. *The Journal of the American Medical Association, 295,* 2851–2858.

Skaret, E., & Soevdsnes, E-K. (2005). Behavioral science in dentistry. The role of the dental hygienist in prevention and treatment of the fearful dental patient. *International Journal of Dental Hygiene, 3,* 2–6.

Skinner, B. F. (1938). *The behavior of organisms.* New York: Appleton-Century-Crofts.

Skinner, B. F. (1953). *Science and human behavior.* New York: Macmillan.

Skinner, B. F. (1989). The origin of cognitive thought. *American Psychologist, 44,* 13–18.

Skinner, N., & Brewer, N. (2002). The dynamics of threat and challenge appraisals prior to stressful achievement events. *Journal of Personality and Social Psychology, 83,* 678–692.

Skipp, C., & Johnson, D. (2003, October 5). Brianna: The little girl that could. *Newsweek.*

Skloot, R. (2006, January). Can memory manipulation change the way you eat? *Discover,* 30.

Slone, K. C. (1985). *They're rarely too young . . . and never too old "to twinkle."* Ann Arbor, MI: Shar Publications.

Small, D. (2001, August 29). Cited in Northwestern University, Measuring brain activity in people eating chocolate offers new clues about how the body becomes addicted. *Science Daily.* Available: http://www.sciencedaily.com/releases/2001/08/010829082943.htm

Small, G. W., Propper, M. W., Randolph, E. T., & Spencer, E. (1991). Mass hysteria among student performers: Social relationship as a symptom predictor. *American Journal of Psychiatry, 148,* 1200–1205.

Small, S. A., & Mayeux, R. (2005). Alzheimer's disease and related dementias. In L. P. Rowland & H. H. Merritt (Eds.), *Merritt's neurology* (11th ed., pp. 772–777). Philadelphia: Lippincott Williams & Wilkins.

Smith, A. (2005). Caffeine. In H. R. Lieberman, R. B. Kanarek & C. Prasad (Eds.), *Nutritional neuroscience: Nutrition, brain, and behavior* (pp. 341–361). Philadelphia: Taylor & Francis.

Smith, C. (1997, February 9). Companies using personality tests for making hires that fit. *The Los Angeles Times.*

Smith, D. (2002, June). Where are recent grads getting jobs? *Monitor on Psychology,* 28–32.

Smith, D. (2003, March). Angry thoughts, at-risk hearts. *Monitor on Psychology,* 46–47.

Smith, E. E. (2000). Neural bases of human working memory. *Current Directions in Psychological Science, 9,* 45–49.

Smith, M. (2005, August 2). *False memory may block unhealthy eating* [On-line]. Available: http://www.medpagetoday.com/PrimaryCare/DietNutrition/tb/1466?pfc=101&spc=

Smith, N. T. (2002). A review of the published literature into cannabis withdrawal symptoms in human users. *Addiction, 97,* 621–632.

Smith, P. (2003, February 19). First hand-transplant recipients progressing. *USA Today,* D5.

Smith, R. (2005, December 11). *Siemen Westinghouse science winners announced* [On-line]. Available: http://www.npr.org/templates/story/story.php?story1d=5039607

Smith, S. M., Gleaves, D. H., Pierce, G. H., Williams, T. L., Gilliland, T. R., & Gerkens, D. R. (2003). Eliciting and comparing false and recovered memories: An experimental approach. *Applied Cognitive Psychology, 17,* 251–279.

Smits, J. A. J., O'Cleirigh, C. M., & Otto, M. W. (2006). Panic and agoraphobia. In M. Hersen & J. C. Thomas (Eds.), *Comprehensive handbook of personality and psychopathology: Adult psychopathology* (Vol. 2, pp. 121–137). Hoboken, NJ: John Wiley & Sons.

Smock, P. (2005, July 18). Cited in S. Jayson, Cohabitation is replacing dating. *USA Today,* 6D.

Snyder, C. R., Shenkel, R. J., & Lowery, C. R. (1977). Acceptance of personality interpretations: The "Barnum effect" and beyond. *Journal of Consulting and Clinical Psychology, 45,* 104–114.

References

Snyder, S. (2002). Forty years of neurotransmitters. *Archives of General Psychiatry, 59*, 983–994.

Society for Personality Assessment. (2005). The status of the Rorschach in clinical and forensic practice: An official statement by the Board of Trustees of the Society for Personality Assessment. *Journal of Personality Assessment, 85*, 219–237.

Sohn, E. (2002, June 10). The hunger artists. *U.S. News & World Report*, 45–50.

Solms, M. (2006, April/May). Freud returns. *Scientific American Mind*, 28–34.

Solomon, P. R., Adams, F., Silver, A., Zimmer, J., & DeVeaux, R. (2002). Ginkgo for memory enhancement. *Journal of the American Medical Association, 288*, 835–840.

Solomon, P. R., & Murphy, C. A. (2005). Should we screen for Alzheimer's disease? A review of the evidence for and against screening for Alzheimer's disease in primary care practice. *Geriatrics, 60*(11), 26–31.

Sommer, I. E. C., Aleman, A., Bouma, A., & Kahn, R. S. (2004). Do women really have more bilateral language representation than men? A meta-analysis of functional imaging studies. *Brain 127*, 1845–1852.

Song, S. (2005, November 28). Pet Rx: Nothing to sniff at. *Time*, 83.

Song, S. (2006, July 14). The daily Rx. *Time*. Available: http://www.time.blogs.com/daily_rx/2006/07/childbehavior.html

Sonntag, K., Simantov, R., & Isacson, O. (2005). Stem cells may reshape the prospect of Parkinson's disease therapy. *Molecular Brain Research, 134*, 34–51.

Sosin, M. R. (2003). Explaining adult homeless in the US by stratification or situation. *Journal of Community & Applied Social Psychology, 13*, 91–104.

Sotsky, S. M., Glass, D. R., Shea, T., Pilkonis, P. A., Collins, F., Elkin, I., Watkins, J. T., Imber, S. D., Leber, W. R., Moyer, J., & Oliveri, M. E. (2006, April). Patient predictors of response to psychotherapy and pharmacotherapy: Findings in the NIMH treatment of depression collaborative research program. *Focus, 4*, 278.

Soyez, V., & Broekaert, E. (2005). Therapeutic communities, family therapy, and humanistic psychology: History and current examples. *Journal of Humanistic Psychology, 45*, 302–332.

Spanos, N. P. (1994). Multiple identity enactments and multiple personality disorder: A sociocognitive perspective. *Psychological Bulletin, 116*, 143–165.

Spanos, N. P. (1996). *Multiple identities and false memories: A sociocognitive perspective*. Washington, DC: American Psychological Association.

Spearman, C. (1904). "General intelligence" objectively determined and measured. *American Journal of Psychology, 15*, 201–293.

Spector, P. E., Cooper, C. L., Sanchez, J. I., O'Driscoll, M., Sparks, K., Bernin, P., Bussing, A., Dewe, P., Hart, P., Lu, L., Miller, K., de Moraes, R. F., Ostrognay, G. M., Pagon, M., Pitariu, H., Poelmans, S., Radhakrishnan, P., Russinova, V., Salamatov, V., Salgado, J., Shima, S., Siu, O. L., Stora, J. B., Teichmann, M., Theorell, T., Vlerick, P., Westman, M., Widerszal-Bazyl, M., Wong, P., & Yu, A. S. (2001). Do national levels of individualism and internal locus of control relate to well-being: An ecological level international study. *Journal of Organizational Behavior, 22*, 815–832.

Spencer, R. M. C., Zelaznik, H. N., Diedrichsen, J., & Ivry, R. B. (2003). Disrupted timing of discontinuous but not continuous movements by cerebellar lesions. *Science, 300*, 1437–1439.

Sperling, G. A. (1960). The information available in brief visual presentations. *Psychological Monographs, 74 (Whole No. 498)*.

Sperry, R. W. (1974). Lateral specialization in the surgically separated hemisphere. In R. O. Schmitt & F. G. Worden (Eds.), *The neurosciences: Third study program*. Cambridge, MA: MIT Press.

Sperry, R. W. (1993, August). Cited in T. Deangelis, Sperry plumbs science for values and solutions. *APA Monitor*.

Spiegal, D. (2005, November 22). Cited in S. Blakeslee, This is your brain under hypnosis. *The New York Times*, D1, D4.

Spiegal, K. (2006, April 1). In B. Harder, XXL from too few Zs? *Science News, 169*, 195–196.

Spiegler, M. D., & Guevremont, D. C. (2003). *Contemporary behavior therapy* (4th ed.). Belmont, CA: Wadsworth/Thomson Learning.

Spielman, D. A., & Staub, E. (2000). Reducing boys' aggression: Learning to fulfill basic needs constructively. *Journal of Applied Developmental Psychology, 21*, 165–181.

Spillar, K., & Harrington, P. (2000, February, 18). This is what you get when men rule the roost. *Los Angeles Times*, B7.

Spitz, H. H. (1997). Some questions about the results of the Abecedarian early intervention project cited by the APA task force on intelligence. *American Psychologist, 52*, 72.

Spitzer, R. L., Gibbon, M., Skodol, A. E., Williams, J. B. W., & First, M. B. (Eds.). (1994). *DSM-IV casebook*. Washington, DC: American Psychiatric Association.

Spitzer, R. L., Terman, M., Williams, J. B., Terman, J. S., Malt, U. F., Singer, F., & Lewy, A. J. (1999). Jet lag. *American Journal of Psychiatry, 156*, 1392–1396.

Springer, S. P., & Deutsch, G. (1997). *Left brain, right brain* (5th ed.). New York: Freeman.

Squire, L. R. (1994). Declarative and nondeclarative memory: Multiple brain systems supporting learning and memory. In D. L. Schachter & E. Tulving (Eds.), *Memory systems 1994*. Cambridge, MA: MIT Press.

Squire, L. R., Clark, R. E., & Bayley, P. J. (2004). Medial temporal lobe function and memory. In M. S. Gazzaniga (Ed.), *The cognitive neurosciences III*. Cambridge, MA: MIT Press.

Squire, L. R., & Knowlton, B. J. (1995). Memory, hippocampus, and brain systems. In M. S. Gazzaniga (Ed.), *The cognitive neurosciences*. Cambridge, MA: MIT Press.

Stafford, R. (2005, July 8). A family's painful lesson on the dangers of teen driving. *Dateline NBC* [On-line]. Available: http://www.msnbc.msn.com/id/8501174/print/1/displaymode/1098/

Stahl, S. M. (2000). *Essential psychopharmacology* (2nd ed.). New York: Cambridge University Press.

Stahl, S. M. (2002). Don't ask, don't tell, but benzodiazepines are still the leading treatments for anxiety disorder. *Journal of Clinical Psychiatry, 63*, 756–757.

Stasser, G., & Dietz-Uhler, B. (2003). Collective choice, judgment, and problem solving. In M. A. Hogg & S. Tindale (Eds.), *Blackwell handbook of social psychology: Group processes* (pp. 31–55). Malden, MA: Blackwell Publishing.

Stein, J. (2003, August 4). Just say Om. *Time*, 50–55.

Stein, L. M., & Memon, A. (2006). Testing the efficacy of the cognitive interview in a developing country. *Applied Cognitive Psychology, 20*, 597–605.

Stein, M. B., Goldin, P. R., Sareen, J., Zorrilla, L. T. E., & Brown, G. G. (2002). Increased amygdala activation to angry and contemptuous faces in generalized social phobia. *Archives of General Psychiatry, 59*, 1027–1034.

Stein, R. (2005a, October 9). Scientists finding out what losing sleep does to a body. *Washington Post*, A1.

Stein, R. (2005b, October 31). Cervical cancer vaccine gets injected with a social issue. *Washington Post*, A3.

Stein, R. (2006, September 7). U.S. breast cancer rate stabilizes. *Washington Post*, A3.

Steinberg, J. (2003, February 11). Flaws seen in campus policies replacing affirmative action. *New York Times*, A23.

Steinberg, L. (2004, May 10). Cited in C. Wallis & K. Dell, What makes teens tick. *Time*.

Steiner, R. (1989). Live TV special explores, tests psychic powers. *Skeptical Inquirer, 14*, 2–6.

Steptoe, A., & Wardle, J. (1988). Emotional fainting and the psychophysiologic response to blood and injury: Autonomic mechanisms and coping strategies. *Psychosomatic Medicine, 50*, 402–417.

Sternberg, R. J. (1995). For whom the Bell Curve tolls: A review of *The Bell Curve*. *Psychological Science, 6*, 257–261.

Sternberg, R. J. (1999). *Cupid's arrow: The course of love through time*. New York: Cambridge University Press.

Sternberg, R. J. (2001). What is the common thread of creativity? *American Psychologist, 56*, 360–362.

Sternberg, R. J. (2003a). Our research program validating the triarchic theory of successful intelligence: Reply to Gottfredson. *Intelligence, 31*, 399–413.

Sternberg, R. J. (2003b, June). It's time for prescription privileges. *Monitor on Psychology*, 5.

Sternberg, R. J., Lautrey, J., & Lubart, T. I. (Eds.). (2003a). *Models of intelligence*. Washington, DC: American Psychological Association.

Sternberg, R. J., Lautrey, J., & Lubart, T. I. (2003b). Where are we in the field of intelligence, how did we get here, and where are we going? In R. J. Sternberg, J. Lautrey, & T. I. Lubart (Eds.), *Models of intelligence*. Washington, DC: American Psychological Association.

Sternberg, R. J., & O'Hara, L. A. (2000). Intelligence and creativity. In R. J. Sternberg (Ed.), *Handbook of intelligence*. New York: Cambridge University Press.

Sternberg, R. J., & Soriano, L. J. (1984). Styles of conflict resolution. *Journal of Personality and Social Psychology, 47*, 115–126.

Sternberg, R. J., & Yang, S. (2003, February). Cited in E. Benson, Intelligence across cultures. *Monitor on Psychology*, 56–58.

Sternberg, S. (2002, November 27–28). Women now make up half of AIDS cases, U.N. study finds. *USA Today*, A1.

Sternberg, S. (2006, July 13). Once-a-day HIV drug cocktail–in one pill–wins FDA approval. *USA Today*, 6D.

Stetter, F., & Kupper, S. (2002). Autogenic training: A meta-analysis of clinical outcome studies. *Applied Psychophysiology and Biofeedback, 27*, 45–98.

Stice, E. (2002). Risk and maintenance factors for eating pathology: A meta-analytic review. *Psychological Bulletin, 128*, 825–848.

Stich, S. S. (2003, November). Animal attraction. *Time Bonus Section*, 34.

Stickgold, R. (2000, March 7). Cited in S. Blakeslee, For better learning, researchers endorse "sleep on it" adage. *New York Times*, D2.

Stickgold, R. (2005). Sleep-dependent memory consolidation. *Nature, 437*, 1272–1278.

Stix, G. (2006, June). A new assault on HIV. *Scientific American*, 76–79.

Stobbe, M. (2006, November 11). HIV patients' life expectancy put at 24 years. *The San Diego Union-Tribune*, A7.

Stokstad, E. (2002). Violent effects of abuse tied to gene. *Science, 297*, 752.

Stolberg, S. G. (2001, April 22). Science, studies and motherhood. *New York Times*, 3.

Stone, A. (2004, December 6). Cited in S. Roan, A better measure of true happiness. *The Los Angeles Times,* F1.

Stone, B. (2002, June 24). How to recharge the second sense. *Newsweek,* 54.

Storbeck, J., Robinson, M. D., & McCourt, M. E. (2006). Semantic processing precedes affect retrieval: The neurological case for cognitive primacy in visual processing. *Review of General Psychology, 10,* 41–55.

Strain, E. C., Mumford, G. K., Silverman, K., & Griffiths, R. R. (1994). Caffeine dependence syndrome. *Journal of the American Medical Association, 272,* 1043–1048.

Straker, G. (1994). Integrating African and Western healing practices in South Africa. *American Journal of Psychotherapy, 48,* 455–467.

Strange, B. A., Hurlemann, R., & Dolan, R. J. (2003, November 11). An emotion-induced retrograde amnesia in humans is amygdala- and β-adrenergic-dependent. *Proceedings of the National Academy of Sciences, 100,* 13626–13631.

Strauss, V. (2004, September 14). Can exam anxiety be overcome with effort? Teachers urged to address issues as test pressures grow. *Washington Post,* A12.

Streissguth, A. P., Barr, H. M., Bookstein, F. L., Sampson, P. D., & Olson, H. C. (1999). The long-term neurocognitive consequences of prenatal alcohol exposure: A 14-year study. *Psychological Science, 10,* 186–190.

Stromeyer, C. F., III. (1970, November). Eidetikers. *Psychology Today.*

Stromswold, K. (1995). The cognitive and neural bases of language acquisition. In M. S. Gazzaniga (Ed.), *The cognitive neurosciences.* Cambridge, MA: MIT Press.

Struckman-Johnson, C., Struckman-Johnson, D., & Anderson, P. B. (2003). Tactics of sexual coercion: When men and women won't take no for an answer. *The Journal of Sex Research, 40,* 76–86.

Stuss, D. T., & Levine, B. (2002). Adult clinical neuropsychology: Lessons from studies on the frontal lobes. *Annual Review of Psychology, 53,* 401–433.

Stutts, J. C., Wilkins, J. W., Osberg, J. S., & Vaughn, B. V. (2002). Driver risk factors for sleep-related crashes. *Accident Analysis & Prevention, 841,* 1–11.

Suddath, R. L., Christison, G. W., Torrey, E. F., Casanova, M. R., & Weinberger, D. R. (1990). Anatomical abnormalities in the brains of monozygotic twins discordant for schizophrenia. *New England Journal of Medicine, 322,* 789–794.

Sue, D. W., & Sue, D. (2003). *Counseling the culturally diverse: Theory and practice* (4th ed.). New York: Wiley.

Sullivan, R. M., Taborsky-Barba, S., Mendoza, R., Itano, A., Leon, M., Cotman, C. W., Payne, T. R., & Lott, I. (1991). Olfactory classical conditioning in neonates. *Pediatrics, 87,* 511–518.

Survey finds Americans still worry about medical errors (brief article). (2005). *Association of Operating Room Nurses Journal, 81,* 816.

Suzuki, S. (1998, January 27). Cited in Shinichi Suzuki: Started music classes for toddlers. *Los Angeles Times,* B8.

Svensen, S., & White, K. (1994). A content analysis of horoscopes. *Genetic, Social and General Psychology Monographs, 12,* 5–38.

Svirsky, M. A., Robbins, A. M., Kirk, K. I., Pisoni, D. B., & Miyamoto, R. T. (2000). Language development in profoundly deaf children with cochlear implants. *Psychological Science, 11,* 153–158.

Svitil, K. A. (2006, February). Why fat tastes so good. *Discover,* 13.

Sweet, R. A., Mulsant, B. H., Gupta, B., Rifai, A. H., Pasternak, R. E., McEachran, A., & Zubenko, G. S. (1995). Duration of neuroleptic treatment and prevalence of tardive dyskinesia in late life. *Archives of General Psychiatry, 52,* 478–486.

Swim, J. K., Aikin, K. J., Hall, W. S., & Hunter, B. A. (1995). Sexism and racism: Old-fashioned and modern principles. *Journal of Personality and Social Psychology, 68,* 199–214.

Sylvester, C. Y. C., Wager, T. D., Lacey, S. C., Hernandez, L., Nichols, T. E., Smith, E. E., & Jonides, J. (2003). Switching attention and resolving interference: fMRI measures of executive functions. *Neuropsychologia, 41,* 357–370.

Szabo, L. (2004, October 24). Spinal cord injury patients often succumb to bed sores. *USA Today.*

Szabo, L. (2006, April 24). Insomnia drugs: A wake-up call? *USA Today,* 8D.

Szyfelbein, S. K., Osgood, P. F., & Carr, D. B. (1985). The assessment of pain and plasma B-endorphin immunoactivity in burned children. *Pain, 22,* 173–182.

Taani, D. Q., El-Qaderi, S. S., & Abu Alhaija, E. S. J. (2005). Dental anxiety in children and its relationship to dental caries and gingival condition. *International Journal of Dental Hygiene, 3,* 83–87.

Taddese, A., Nah, S. Y., & McCleskey, E. W. (1995). Selective opioid inhibition of small nociceptive neurons. *Science, 270,* 1366–1369.

Talan, J. (2005). Schizophrenia drugs questioned. *Scientific American Mind, 16,* 8.

Talan, J. (2006, February/March). Spirituality. *Scientific American Mind, 17,* 39–41.

Talarico, J. M., & Rubin, D. C. (2003). Confidence, not consistency, characterizes flashbulb memories. *Psychological Science, 14,* 455–461.

Talbot, M. (2000, January 9). The placebo prescription. *New York Times Magazine,* 34.

Tallal, P. (1995, August 29). Cited in S. Begley, Why Johnny and Joanie can't read. *Newsweek.*

Tamis-LeMonda, C. S., Bornstein, M. H., & Baumwell, L. (2001). Maternal responsiveness and children's achievement of language milestones. *Child Development, 72,* 748–767.

Tamres, L. K., Janicki, D., & Helgeson, V. S. (2002). Sex differences in coping behavior: A meta-analysis review and an examination of relative coping. *Personality and Social Psychology Review, 6,* 2–30.

Taneeru, M. (2006, December 29). Obesity: A lurking national threat? *CNN* [On-line]. Available: http://www.cnn.com/2006/HEALTH.diet.fitness/03/24/hb.obesity.epidemic/index.html

Tang, Y., Shimizu, E., & Tsien, J. Z. (2001). Do "smart" mice feel more pain, or are they just better learners? *Nature Neuroscience, 4,* 453.

Tankova, I., Adan, A., & Buela-Casal, G. (1994). Circadian typology and individual differences. A review. *Personality and Individual Differences, 16,* 671–684.

Tannen, D. (1990). *You just don't understand: Women and men in conversation.* New York: William Morrow.

Tannen, D. (1994). *Talking from 9 to 5.* New York: William Morrow.

Tanner, L. (2000, May). Pediatrician guidelines issued to spot disorder. *San Diego Union-Tribune,* A1.

Tanouye, E. (1997, July 7). Got a big public speaking phobia? *San Diego Union-Tribune.*

Tao, K. (1987). Infantile autism in China. *Journal of Autism and Developmental Disorders, 2,* 289.

Tao, K. T., & Yang, X. L. (1997). China. In D. J. Cohen & F. R. Volkmar (Eds.), *Handbook of autism and pervasive developmental disorders* (2nd ed.). New York: John Wiley & Sons.

Tarkan, L. (2002, October 22). Autism therapy is called effective, but rare. *New York Times,* D2.

Tarumi, S., Ichimiya, A., Yamada, S., Umesue, M., & Kuroki, T. (2004). Taijin kyofusho in university students: Patterns of fear and predispositions to the offensive variant. *Transcultural Psychiatry, 41,* 533–546.

Tawa, R. (1995, March 12). Shattering the silence. *Los Angeles Times.*

Taylor, J., & Miller, M. (1997). When time-out works some of the time: The importance of treatment integrity and functional assessment. *School Psychology Quarterly, 12,* 4–22.

Taylor, S. E. (1981). The interface of cognitive and social psychology. In J. Harvey (Ed.), *Cognition, social behavior, and the environment.* Hillsdale, NJ: Erlbaum.

Taylor, S. E. (2002). *The tending instinct: How nurturing is essential to who we are and how we live.* New York: Times Books, Henry Holt and Company.

Taylor, S. E., Kemeny, M. E., Reed, G. M., Bower, J. E., & Gruenewald, T. L. (2000). Psychological resources, positive illusions, and health. *American Psychologist, 55,* 99–109.

Teicher, M. H. (2002, March). The neurobiology of child abuse. *Scientific American,* 68–75.

Temple, E., Deutsch, G. K., Poldrack, R. A., Miller, S. L., Tallal, P., Merzenich, M. M., & Gabrieli, J. D. E. (2003). Neural deficits in children with dyslexia ameliorated by behavioral remediation: Evidence from functional MRI. *Proceedings of the National Academy of Science, 100,* 2860–2865.

Terman, L. M. (1916). *The measurement of intelligence.* Boston: Houghton Mifflin.

Terman, L. M., & Oden, M. H. (1959). *The gifted group at mid-life* (Vol. 5). Stanford, CA: Stanford University Press.

Terrace, H. S. (1981). A report to an academy, 1980. *Annals of the New York Academy of Sciences, 364,* 94–114.

Thapar, A., & McGuffin, P. (1993). Is personality disorder inherited? An overview of the evidence. *Journal of Psychopathology and Behavioral Assessment, 15,* 325–345.

Thase, M. E. (2006). Major depressive disorder. In M. Hersen & J. C. Thomas (Eds.), *Comprehensive handbook of personality and psychopathology: Adult psychopathology* (Vol. 2, pp. 207–230). Hoboken, NJ: John Wiley & Sons.

Thelen, E. (1995). Motor development. *American Psychologist, 50,* 79–95.

Thomas, A., & Chess, S. (1977). *Temperament and development.* New York: Brunner/Mazel.

Thomas, C. R. (2006). Evidence-based practice for conduct disorder symptoms. *Journal of the American Academy of Child and Adolescent Psychiatry, 45,* 109–114.

Thomas, E. (2003, October 20). I am addicted to pain prescription medication. *Newsweek,* 43–47.

Thombs, D. L. (1995). Problem behavior and academic achievement among first-semester college freshmen. *Journal of College Student Development, 36,* 280–288.

Thompson, C., Cowan, T., & Frieman, J. (1993). *Memory search by a memorist.* Hillsdale, NJ: Lawrence Erlbaum.

Thompson, P. M., Cannon, T. D., Narr, K., van Erp, T., Poutamen, V. P., Huttunen, M., Loonqvist, J., Standertskjold-Nordenstam, C. G., Kaprio, J., Khaledy, M., Dail, R., Zoulmalan,, C. I., & Toga, A. W. (2001). Genetic influences on brain structure. *Nature Neuroscience, 4,* 1253–1258.

Thompson, R. A. (1998). Early sociopersonality development. In W. Damon, & R. M. Lerner (Eds.), *Handbook of child psychology* (Vol. 1). New York: John Wiley & Sons.

Thompson, R. A. (2006). The development of the person: Social understanding, relationships, conscience, self. In N. Eisenberg, W. Damon, & R. M. Lerner (Eds.), *Handbook of child psychology* (6th ed., pp. 24–98). Hoboken, NJ: John Wiley & Sons.

Thorndike, E. L. (1898). Animal intelligence: An experimental study of the associative process in animals. *Psychological Review Monograph Supplement, 2*(8).

References

Tierney, A. J. (2000). Egas Moniz and the origins of psychosurgery: A review commemorating the 50th anniversary of Moniz's Nobel Prize. *Journal of the History of the Neurosciences, 9*, 22–36.

Timmer, S. G., Urquiza, A. J., Zebell, N. M., & McGrath, J. M. (2005). Parent-child interaction therapy: Application to maltreating parent-child dyads. *Child Abuse & Neglect, 29*, 825–842.

Tisak, M. S., Tisak, J., & Goldstein, S. E. (2006). Aggression, delinquency, and morality: A social-cognitive perspective. In M. Killen & J. Smetana (Eds.), *Handbook of moral development* (pp. 611–629). Mahwah, NJ: Lawrence Erlbaum.

Tolman, D. L., Striepe, M. I., & Harmon, T. (2003). Gender matters: Constructing a model of adolescent sexual health. *Journal of Sex Research, 40*, 4–12.

Tolman, E. C. (1948). Cognitive maps in rats and men. *Psychological Review, 55*, 189–208.

Tolson, J. (2003, November 10). Faith & freedom. *U.S. News & World Report*, 60–62.

Tomes, H. (2000, July/August). Why did APA take so long? *Monitor on Psychology*, 57.

Tompkins, J. (2003a, June 16). A night owl resets his body clock. *Los Angeles Times*, F1.

Tompkins, J. (2003b, June 16). How light became a therapy. *Los Angeles Times*, F1.

Tonegawa, S., & Wilson, M. (1997). Cited in W. Roush, New knockout mice point to molecular basis of memory. *Science, 275*, 32–33.

Toner, M. (2006, January 29). Chimpanzees closer to humans than to other apes, study confirms. *The Sunday Times*, A10.

Tong, F. (2003). Primary visual cortex and visual awareness. *Nature Review Neuroscience, 4*, 219–229.

Torrey, E. F. (2005). Does psychoanalysis have a future? No. *Canadian Journal of Psychiatry, 50*, 743–744.

Torrey, F. E., Bowler, A. E., Taylor, E. H., & Gottesman, I. I. (1994). *Schizophrenia and manic-depressive disorder*. New York: Basic Books.

Tough, P. (2006, November 26). What it takes to make a student. *The New York Times Magazine*.

Towle, L. H. (1995, July 31). Elegy for lost boys. *Time*.

Townsend, E., Dimigen, G., & Fung, D. (2000). A clinical study of child dental anxiety. *Behaviour Research and Therapy, 38*, 31–46.

Tramer, M. R., Carroll, D., Campbell, F. A., Reynolds, D. J. M., Moore, R. A., & McQuay, H. J. (2001). Cannabinoids for control of chemotherapy induced nausea and vomiting: Quantitative systematic review. *British Medical Journal, 323*, 16–21.

Treffert, D. A., & Wallace, G. L. (2002, June). Island of genius. *Scientific American*, 76–85.

Tresniowski, A., & Bell, B. (1996, September 9). Oprah buff. *People*, 81.

Tresniowski, A., Harmel, K., & Matsushita, N. (2005, January 24). The girl who can't feel pain. *People*, 99–101.

Triandis, H. C., & Suh, E. M. (2002). Cultural influences on personality. *Annual Review of Psychology, 53*, 133–160.

Tripathi, H. L., Olson, K. G., & Dewey, W. L. (1993). Borphin response to endurance exercise: Relationship to exercise dependence. *Perceptual and Motor Skills, 77*, 767–770.

Tripician, R. J. (2000, January/February). Confessions of a (former) graphologist. *Skeptical Inquirer*, 44–47.

Trzesniewski, K. H., Donnellan, M. B., Moffitt, T. E., Robins, R. W., Poulton, R., & Caspi, A. (2006). Low self-esteem during adolescence predicts poor health, criminal behavior, and limited economic prospects during adulthood. *Developmental Psychology, 42*, 381–390.

Trzesniewski, K. H., Donnellan, M. B., & Robins, R. W. (2003). Stability of self-esteem across the life span. *Journal of Personality and Social Psychology, 84*, 205–220.

Tsien, J. Z. (2000). Building a brainier mouse. *Scientific American*, 62–68.

Tulving, E. (2002). Episodic memory: From mind to brain. *Annual Review of Psychology, 53*, 1–25.

Tulving E., & Craik, F. M. (Eds.). (2005). *The Oxford handbook of memory*. New York: Oxford University Press.

Turk, D. J. (2002). Cited in B. Bower, All about me: Left brain may shine spotlight on self. *Science News, 162*, 118.

Turner, J. A., Deyo, R. A., Loeser, J. D., Von Korff, M., & Fordyce, W. E. (1994). The importance of placebo effects in pain treatment and research. *Journal of the American Medical Association, 271*, 1609–1614.

Tuunainen, A., Wahlbeck, K., & Gilbody, S. (2002). Newer atypical antipsychotic medication in comparison to clozapine: A systematic review of randomized trials. *Schizophrenia Research 56*, 1–10.

Twenge, J. M. (1997). Changes in masculine and feminine traits over time: A meta-analysis. *Sex Roles, 36*, 305–325.

Tyack, P. L. (2000). Dolphins whistle a signature tune. *Science, 289*, 1310–1313.

Tyre, P. (2005, December 5). Fighting anorexia. No one to blame. *Newsweek*, 50–59.

Tyre, P. (2006, January 30). The trouble with boys. *Newsweek*, 44–52.

Ulett, G. A. (2003, March/April). Acupuncture, magic and make-believe. *Skeptical Inquirer*, 47–50.

Underwood, A. (2006, October 23). How to read a face. *Newsweek*, 65.

Underwood, P. W. (2000). Social support: The promise and the reality. In V. R. Rice (Ed.), *Handbook of stress, coping and health*. Thousand Oaks, CA: Sage.

UPI (United Press International). (2006, November 24). Chinese learn to smile for 2008 Olympics. *Science Daily*.

Ursu, S., Stenger, V. A., Shear, M. K., Jones, M. R., & Carter, C. S. (2003). Overactive action monitoring in obsessive-compulsive disorder: Evidence from functional magnetic resonance imaging. *Psychological Science, 14*, 347–353.

U.S. Department of Health and Human Services (USDHHS), Administration on Children, Youth, and Families. (2006). *Child maltreatment 2004: Reports from the states to the national child abuse and neglect data system* [On-line]. Available: http://www.acf.hhs.gov/programs/cb/pubs/cm04/index.htm

USDHHS. (2006). *The health consequences of involuntary exposure to tobacco smoke: A report of the surgeon general*. U.S. Department of Health and Human Services, Centers for Disease Control and Prevention, National Center for Chronic Disease Prevention and Health Promotion, Office on Smoking and Health. Washington, DC: Author

U.S. Department of Labor. Bureau of Labor Statistics. (2006). *Occupational outlook handbook*. Available: www.bls.gov

USA Today. (2005, August 18). Race disparities in health care persist, 5D.

Vahtera, J., Kivimaki, M., Uutela, A., & Pentti, J. (2000). Hostility and ill health: Role of psychosocial resources in two contexts of working life. *Journal of Psychosomatic Research, 48*, 89–98.

Valdes, L. (2006, October 16). Cited in E. P. Gunn, It is in your head. *U.S. News & World Report*, EE8–9.

Vallacher, R. R., & Nowak, A. (2007). Dynamical social psychology: Finding order in the flow of human experience. In A. W. Kruglanski & E. T. Higgins, *Social psychology: Handbook of basic principles* (2nd ed., pp. 734–758). New York: Guilford Press.

Valtin, H. (2002). "Drink at least eight glasses of water a day." Really? Is there scientific evidence for "8 x 8"? *American Journal of Physiology, 283*, R993–R1004.

Van Ameringen, M. A., Lane, R. M., Walker, J. R., Bowen, R. C., Chokka, P. R., Goldner, E. M., Johnston, D. G., Lavallee, Y., Nandy, S., Pecknold, J. C., Hadrava, V., & Swinson, R. P. (2001). Sertraline treatment for generalized social phobia: A 20-week, double-blind, placebo-controlled study. *American Journal of Psychiatry, 158*, 275–281.

Van de Castle, R. L. (1994). *Our dreaming mind*. New York: Ballantine.

van Derbur Atler, D. (1991, June). The darkest secret. *People*.

Van Esch, H. (2006). The fragile X permutation: New insights and clinical consequences. *European Journal of Medical Genetics, 49*, 1–8.

Van Gerwen, L. J., Spinhoven, P., Diekstra, R. F. W., & Van Dyck, F. (1997). People who seek help for fear of flying: Typology of flying phobics. *Behavior Therapy, 28*, 237–251.

Van Laar, C., Levin, S., Sinclair, S., & Sidanius, J. (2005). The effect of university roommate contact on ethnic attitudes and behavior. *Journal of Experimental Social Psychology, 41*, 329–345.

Van Manen, K., & Whitbourne, S. K. (1997). Psychosocial development and life experiences in adulthood: A 22-year sequential study. *Psychology and Aging, 12*, 239–246.

van Praag, H., Schinder, A. F., Christie, B. R., Toni, N., Palmer, T. D., & Gage, F. H. (2002). Functional neurogenesis in the adult hippocampus. *Nature, 415*, 1030–1034.

Van Rossum, E. F. C., Koper, J. W., Huizenga, N. A. T. M., Uitterlnden, A. G., Janssen, J. A. J. L., Brinkman, A. O., Grobee, D. E., de Jong, F. H., van Duyn, C. M., Pols, H. A. P., & Lamberts, S. W. J. (2002). A polymorphism in the glucocorticoid receptor gene, which decreases sensitivity to glucocorticoids in vivo, is associated with low insulin and cholesterol levels. *Diabetes, 51*, 3128–3134.

Vandewater, E. A., Ostrove, J. M., & Stewart, A. J. (1997). Predicting women's well-being in midlife: The importance of personality development and social role involvements. *Journal of Personality and Social Psychology, 72*, 1147–1160.

Vargas, J. S. (1991). B. F. Skinner: The last few days. *Journal of the Experimental Analysis of Behavior, 55*, 1–2.

Vargha-Khadem, F. (2000, November 20). Cited in J. Fischman, Seeds of a sociopath. *U.S. News & World Report*, 82.

Vastag, B. (2003). Addiction poorly understood by clinicians. *Journal of the American Medical Association, 290*, 1299–1303.

Vazsonyi, A. T., Hibbert, J. R., & Snider, J. B. (2003). Exotic enterprise no more? Adolescent reports of family and parenting processes from youth in four countries. *Journal of Research on Adolescence, 13*, 129–160.

Vecera, S. (2002, June). Cited in R. Adelson, Figure this: Deciding what's figure, what's ground. *Monitor on Psychology*, 44–45.

Vedantam, S. (2005, January 23). See no bias. *Washington Post*, W12.

Vedantam, S. (2006, March 23). Antidepressants don't help half of users, study finds. *The San Diego Union-Tribune*, A1.

Venter, J. C. (2000, August 22). Cited in N. Angier, Do races differ: not really, genes show. *New York Times,* D1.

Vergano, D. (2001, June 19). As many opinions as treatments in tobacco fight. *USA Today,* D8.

Vergano, D. (2006, August 7). Study: Ask with care. *USA Today,* 6D.

Verhovek, S. H. (2002, February 7). As suicide approvals rise in Oregon, half go unused. *New York Times,* A16.

Verlinden, S., Hersen, M., & Thomas, J. (2000). Risk factors in school shootings. *Clinical Psychology Review, 29,* 3–56.

Vernon, P. A., Wickett, J. C., Bazana, G. P., & Stelmack, R. M. (2000). The neuropsychology of human intelligence. In R. J. Sternberg (Ed.), *Handbook of intelligence.* New York: Cambridge University Press.

Vince G. (2005, January 17). First biological test for ADHD unveiled [On-line]. Available: http://www.newscientist.com/article.ns?id=dn6886

Vocci, F. J., Acri, J., & Elkashef, A. (2005). Medication development for addictive disorders: The state of the science. *American Journal of Psychiatry, 162,* 1432–1440.

Vogel, S. (1999, April). Why we get fat. *Discover,* 94–99.

Vogele, C., Coles, J., Wardle, J., & Steptoe, A. (2003). Psychophysiologic effects of applied tension on the emotional fainting response to blood and injury. *Behaviour Research and Therapy, 41,* 139–155.

Volkow, N. D. (2004, March 30). *Testimony: Measuring the effectiveness of drug addiction treatment—Testimony before the house committee on government reform subcommittee on criminal justice, drug policy, and human resources? U.S. House of Representatives* [On-line]. Available: http://www.drugabuse.gov/Testimony/3-30-04Testimony.html

Volkow, N. D., Chang, L., Wang, G., Fowler, J. S., Ding, Y., Sedler, M., Logan, J., Franceschi, D., Gatley, J., Hitzemann, R., Gifford, A., Wong, C., & Pappas, N. (2003). Low level of brain dopamine D2 receptors in methamphetamine abusers: Association with metabolism in the orbitofrontal cortex. *Focus, 1,* 150–157.

Vos, T., Haby, M. M., Barendregt, J. J., Kruijshaar, M., Corry, J., & Andrews, G. (2004). The burden of major depression avoidable by longer-term treatment strategies. *Archives of General Psychiatry, 61,* 1097–1103.

Vredenburg, K., Flett, G. L., & Krames, L. (1994). Analogue versus clinical depression: A critical reappraisal. *Psychological Bulletin, 113,* 327–344.

Vredenburgh, J. (2007). Cited in Big Brothers Big Sisters, *Our impact* [On-line]. Available: http://www.bbbs.org

Waddington, J. L., Lane, A., Scully, P., Meagher, D., Quinn, J., Larkin, C., & O'Callaghan, E. (2000). Early cerebro-craniofacial dysmorphogenesis in schizophrenia: A lifetime trajectory model from neurodevelopmental basis to "neuroprogressive" process. *Journal of Psychiatric Research, 33,* 477–489.

Wade, N. (2002, June 21). Stem cell progress reported on Parkinson's. *New York Times,* A18.

Wade, N. (2003a, February 25). Double helix leaps from lab into real life. *New York Times,* D1.

Wade, N. (2003b, July 15). Early voices: The leap to language. *New York Times,* A18.

Wade, N. (2005, May 10). For gay men, different scent of attraction. *The New York Times,* A1.

Wade, N. (2006, April 18). Schizophrenia as misstep by giant gene. *The New York Times,* D4.

Wakefeld, J. (2001, July). A mind for a consciousness. *Scientific American,* 36–37.

Walch, T. (2006, July 22). Why high antidepressant use in Utah? *Deseret News.*

Walker, A., & Parmar, P. (1993). *Warrior marks: Female genital mutilation and sexual blinding of women.* New York: Harcourt Brace.

Walker, C., Thomas, J., & Allen, T. S. (2003). Treating impulsivity, irritability, and aggression of antisocial personality disorder with quetiapine. *International Journal of Offender Therapy and Comparative Criminology, 47,* 556–567.

Wallace, S. G. (2004, April 21). Storm and stress? *SADD Op-eds* [On-line]. Available: http://sadd.org/oped/storm.htm

Wallechinsky, D. (1986). *Midterm report.* New York: Viking.

Wallerstein, R. S., & Fonagy, P. (1999). Psychoanalytic research and the IPA: History, present status and future potential. *International Journal of Psychoanalysis, 80,* 91–109.

Wallis, C. (2006, May 15). Inside the autistic mind. *Time,* 42–48.

Wallis, C., & Dell, K. (2004, May 10). What makes teen tick. *Time.*

Walsh, B. T., Kaplan, A. S., Attia, E., Olmsted, M., Parides, M., Carter, J. C., Pike, K. M., Devlin, M. J., Woodside, B., Roberto, C. A., & Rockert, W. (2006, June 14). Fluoxetine after weight restoration in anorexia nervosa. *The Journal of the American Medical Association, 295,* 2605–2612.

Walton, K. G., Schneider, R. H., Nidlich, S. I., Salerno, J. W., Nordstrom, C. K., & Merz, C. N. B. (2002). Psychosocial stress and cardiovascular disease part 2: Effectiveness of the transcendental meditation program in treatment and prevention. *Behavioral Medicine, 8,* 106–123.

Wampold, B. E., Minami, T., Tierney, S. C., Baskin, T. W., & Bhati, K. S. (2005). The placebo is powerful: Estimating placebo effects in medicine and psychotherapy from randomized clinical trials. *Journal of Clinical Psychology, 61,* 835–854.

Wand, G. (2005). The anxious amygdala: CREB signaling and predisposition to anxiety and alcoholism. *The Journal of Clinical Investigation, 115,* 2697–2699.

Wang, Q. (2003). Infantile amnesia reconsidered: A cross cultural analysis. *Memory, 11,* 65–80.

Wang, S., Baillargeon, R., & Paterson, S. (2005). Detecting continuity violations in infancy: A new account and new evidence from covering and tube events. *Cognition, 95,* 129–173.

Wang, S. C. (2000). In search of Einstein's genius. *Science, 289,* 1477.

Ward, A., Tiller, J., Treasure, J., & Russell, G. (2000). Eating disorders: Psyche or soma? *International Journal of Eating Disorders, 27,* 279–287.

Warden, C. H. (1997). Cited in J. Travis, Gene heats up obesity research. *Science News, 151,* 142.

Warrick, P. (1996, October 3). "I saw something … that captivated me." *The Los Angeles Times,* E1.

Warrick, P. (1997, January 23). Prisoners of love. *The Los Angeles Times.*

Wartik, N. (1994, August 7). The amazingly simple, inexplicable therapy that just might work. *Los Angeles Times.*

Watanabe, T. (2000, October 31). Exorcism flourishing once again. *Los Angeles Times,* A1.

Watson, J. B. (1924). *Behaviorism.* Chicago: University of Chicago Press.

Watson, J. B., & Rayner, R. (1920). Conditioned emotional reactions. *Journal of Experimental Psychology, 3,* 1–14.

Weaver, C. A., & Krug, K. S. (2004). Consolidation-like effects in flashbulb memories: Evidence from September 11, 2001. *American Journal of Psychology, 117,* 517–530.

Webb, T., Whittington, J., Holland, A. J., Soni, S., Boer, H., Clarke, D., & Horsthemke, B. (2006). CD36 expression and its relationship with obesity in blood cells from people with and without Prader-Willi syndrome. *Clinical Genetics, 69,* 26–32.

Webb, W. B. (1992). *Sleep: The gentle tyrant* (2nd ed.). Bolton, MA: Anker.

Weber, E. H. (1834). *De pulsu, resorptione, auditu et tactu: Annotationes anatomical et physiological.* Liepzig: Koehler.

Weil, E. (2006, March 12). A wrongful birth? *The New York Times,* 6–42.

Weinberg, R. A., Scarr, S., & Waldman, I. D. (1992). The Minnesota transracial adoption study: A follow-up of IQ test performance at adolescence. *Intelligence, 16,* 117–135.

Weinberger, D. R. (2005, May 14). Cited in B. Bower, DNA's moody temperament. *Science News, 167,* 308–309.

Weinberger, D. R., Goldberg, T. E., & Tamminga, C. A. (1995). Prefrontal leukotomy. *American Journal of Psychiatry, 152,* 330–331.

Weiner, B. (1991). Metaphors in motivation and attribution. *American Psychologist, 46,* 921–930.

Weiner, B., & Graham, S. (1999). Attribution in personality psychology. In L. A. Pervin & O. P. John (Eds.), *Handbook of personality* (2nd ed.). New York: Guilford.

Weinraub, B. (2000, May 24). Out of "Spin City" and onto a new stage. *New York Times,* B1.

Weisberg, R. W. (1993). *Creativity: Beyond the myth of genius.* New York: Freeman.

Weiss, K. R. (1997, January 13). Survey finds record stress in class of 2000. *Los Angeles Times.*

Weitzenhoffer, A. M. (2002). Scales, scales, and more scales. *American Journal of Clinical Hypnosis, 44,* 209–219.

Weller, E. B., Young, K. M., Rohrbaugh, A. H., & Weller, R. A. (2001). Overview and assessment of the suicidal child. *Depression and Anxiety, 14,* 157–163.

Wells, B. E., & Twenge, J. M. (2005). Changes in young people's sexual behavior and attitudes, 1943–1999: A cross-temporal meta-analysis. *Review of General Psychology, 9,* 249–261.

Wells, G. L., Malpass, R. S., Lindsay, R. C. L., Fisher, R. P., Turtle, J. W., & Fulero, S. M. (2000). From the lab to the police station. *American Psychologist, 55,* 581–598.

Wells, G. L., & Olson, E. A. (2003). Eyewitness testimony. *Annual Review of Psychology, 54,* 277–295.

Wenzlaff, R. M., & Luxton, D. D. (2003). The role of thought suppression in depressive rumination. *Cognitive Therapy and Research, 27,* 293–308.

Wenzlaff, R. M., & Wegner, D. M. (2000). Thought suppression. *Annual Review of Psychology, 51,* 59–91.

Werle, M. A., Murphy, T. B., & Budd, K. S. (1993). Treating chronic food refusal in young children: Home-based parent training. *Journal of Applied Behavior Analysis, 26,* 421–433.

Werner, E. E. (1989). Children of the garden island. *Scientific American, 260,* 106–111.

Werner, E. E. (1995). Resilience in development. *Current Directions in Psychological Science, 4,* 81–85.

Werner, E. E., & Smith, R. S. (2001). *Journeys from childhood to midlife: Risk, resilience and recovery.* Ithaca, NY: Cornell University Press.

Werner, J. S., & Frost, M. H. (2000). Major life stressors and health outcomes. In V. R. Rice (Ed.), *Handbook of stress, coping and health.* Thousand Oaks, CA: Sage.

Wessel, H. (2003, February 17). Big employers increasingly using personality tests before they hire. *The Milwaukee Journal Sentinel.*

Westen, D. (1998). Unconscious thought, feeling, and motivation: The end of a century-long debate. In R. F. Bornstein & J. M. Masling (Eds.), *Empirical perspectives on the psychoanalytic unconscious.* Washington, DC: American Psychological Association.

References

Westen, D. (2006a, January 24). *Political bias affects brain activity, study finds. MSNBC* [On-line]. Available: http://www.msnbc.com/id/11009379/

Westen, D. (2006b, July). The political brain. *Scientific American,* 36.

Westen, D., & Gabbard, G. O. (1999). Psychoanalytic approaches to personality. In L. A. Pervin & O. P. John (Eds.), *Handbook of personality* (2nd ed.), New York: Guilford.

Whalen, D. H., Benson, R. R., Richardson, M., Swainson, B., Clark, V. P., Lai, S., Mencl, W. E., Fulbright, R. K., Constable, R. T., & Liberman, A. M. (2006). Differentiation of speech and nonspeech processing within primary auditory cortex. *The Journal of the Acoustical Society of America, 119,* 575–581.

White, J. M., & Porth, C. M. (2000). Evolution of a model of stress, coping and discrete emotions. In V. R. Rice (Ed.), *Handbook of stress, coping and health.* Thousand Oaks, CA: Sage.

White, R. (2002). Memory for events after twenty years. *Applied Cognitive Psychology, 16,* 603–612.

Whorf, B. L. (1940). In J. B. Carroll (Ed.), *Language, thought, and reality: Selected writing of Benjamin Lee Whorf.* Cambridge, MA: MIT Press.

Whorf, B. L. (1956). *Language, thought, and reality.* New York: Wiley.

Widiger, T. A., & Clark, L. A. (2000). Toward DSM-V and the classification of psychopathology. *Psychological Bulletin, 126,* 946–963.

Wierson, M., & Forehand, R. (1994). Parent behavioral training for child noncompliance: Rationale, concepts, and effectiveness. *Current Directions in Psychological Science, 3,* 146–150.

Wilcoxon, H. C., Dragoin, W. B., & Kral, P. A. (1971). Illness-induced aversions in rat and quail: Relative salience of visual and gustatory cues. *Science, 171,* 826–828.

Wilgoren, J. (2005, August 19). 10 life terms for B.T.K. strangler as anguished families condemn him in court. *The New York Times,* A13.

Wilhelm, F. H., & Roth, W. T. (1997). Clinical characteristics of flight phobia. *Journal of Anxiety Disorders, 11,* 241–261.

Williams, B. K., & Knight, S. M. (1994). *Healthy for life.* Pacific Grove, CA: Brooks/Cole.

Williams, D. (1992). *Nobody nowhere.* New York: Times Books.

Williams, D. (1994). *Somebody somewhere.* New York: Times Books.

Williams, D. E., Kirkpatrick-Sanchez, S., & Iwata, B. A. (1993). A comparison of shock intensity in the treatment of longstanding and severe self-injurious behavior. *Research in Development Disabilities, 14,* 207–219.

Williams, J. E., & Best, D. L. (1990). *Measuring sex stereotypes* (Vol. 6, rev. ed.). Newbury Park, CA: Sage Publications.

Williams, L. M., Grieve, S. M., Whitford, T. J., Clark, C. R., Gur, R. C., Goldberg, E., Flor-Henry, P., Peduto, A. S., & Gordon, E. (2005). Neural synchrony and gray matter variation in human males and females: Integration of 40 Hz gamma synchrony and MRI measures. *Journal of Integrative Neuroscience, 4,* 77–93.

Williams, M. A., & Gross, A. M. (1994). Behavior therapy. In V. B. Hasselt & M. Hersen (Eds.), *Advanced abnormal psychology.* New York: Plenum Press.

Williams, M. A., & Mattingley, J. B. (2006, June 6). Do angry men get noticed? *Current Biology, 16,* R402.

Williamson, E. (2005, February 1). Brain immaturity could explain teen crash rate. *Washington Post.*

Wilson, G. T. (2005). Behavior therapy. In R. J. Corsini & D. Wedding, *Current psychotherapies* (7th ed., pp. 202–237). Belmont, CA: Brooks/Cole–Thomson Learning.

Wilson, G. T., Fairburn, C. C., Agras, W. S., Walsh, B. T., & Kramer, H. (2002). Cognitive-behavioral therapy for bulimia nervosa: Time course and mechanisms of change. *Journal of Consulting and Clinical Psychology, 20,* 267–274.

Wilson, S. R., Levine, K. J., Cruz, M. G., & Rao, N. (1997). Attribution complexity and actor-observer bias. *Journal of Social Behavior and Personality, 12,* 709–726.

Wilson, T. D., & Linville, P. W. (1982). Improving the academic performance of college freshmen: Attribution therapy revisited. *Journal of Personality and Social Psychology, 42,* 367–376.

Wiltenburg, M. (2003, August 7). Internet dating goes behind bars. *The Christian Science Monitor,* 15.

Wimbush, F. B., & Nelson, M. L. (2000). Stress, psychosomatic illness, and health. In V. R. Rice (Ed.), *Handbook of stress, coping and health.* Thousand Oaks, CA: Sage.

Wincze, J. P., & Carey, M. P. (1991). *Sexual dysfunction: A guide for assessment and treatment.* New York: Guilford.

Wineberg, H., & Werth, J. L., Jr. (2003). Physician-assisted suicide in Oregon: What are the key factors? *Death Studies, 27,* 501–518.

Wing, R. (2005, October 17). Cited in N. Hellmich, Weight war can be never-ending. *USA Today,* D1.

Wingert, P., & Brant, M. (2005, August 15). Reading your baby's mind. *Newsweek,* 32–39.

Winner, E. (2000). The origins and ends of giftedness. *American Psychologist, 55,* 159–169.

Winner, E. (2002, March 12). Cited in E. Goode, The uneasy fit of the precocious and the average. *New York Times,* D1.

Winograd, E., & Soloway, R. M. (1986). On forgetting the locations of things stored in special places. *Journal of Experimental Psychology: General, 115,* 366–372.

Winters, K. C., Stinchfield, R. D., Opland, E., Weller, C., & Latimer, W. W. (2000). The effectiveness of the Minnesota Model approach in the treatment of adolescent drug abusers. *Addiction, 95,* 601–612.

Wise, T. N., & Birket-Smith, M. (2002). The somatoform disorders for DSM-V: The need for changes in process and content. *Psychosomatics 43,* 437–440.

Witelson, S. F., Beresh, H., & Kigar, D. L. (2006). Intelligence and brain size in 100 postmortem brains: Sex, lateralization and age factors. *Brain, 129,* 386–398.

Witelson, S. F., Kigar, D. L., & Harvey, T. (1999). The exceptional brain of Albert Einstein. *Lancet, 353,* 2149–2153.

Witkin, G. (1995, November 13). A new drug gallops through the West. *U.S. News & World Report.*

Witkin, G., Tharp, M., Schrof, J. M., Toch, T., & Scattarella, C. (1998, June 1). Again. *U.S. News & World Report,* 16–18.

Wittman, J. (1994, January 5). Nausea, euphoria alternate marks of chemotherapy. *San Diego Union-Tribune.*

Wolf, T. H. (1973). *Alfred Binet.* Chicago: University of Chicago Press.

Wolpe, J. (1958). *Psychotherapy by reciprocal inhibition.* Stanford, CA: Stanford University Press.

Wolpe, J. (1990). *The practice of behavior therapy* (4th ed.). London: Pergamon Press.

Wolpe, J., & Lazarus, A. A. (1966). *Behavior therapy techniques.* London: Pergamon Press.

Wolters, C. A. (2003). Understanding procrastination from a self-regulated learning perspective. *Journal of Educational Psychology, 95,* 179–187.

Wong, A. M., Hodges, H., & Horsburg, K. (2005). Neural stem cell grafts reduce the extent of neuronal damage in a mouse model of global ischaemia. *Brain Research, 1063,* 140–150.

Wood, J. M., Garb, H. N., Lilienfeld, S. O., & Nezworski, M. T. (2002). Clinical assessment. *Annual Review of Psychology, 53,* 519–543.

Wood, J. M., Nezwoski, M. T., Lilienfeld, S. O., & Garb, H. N. (2003). *What's wrong with the Rorschach?* San Francisco: Jossey-Bass.

Wood, W., Christensen, P. N., Hebl, M. R., & Rothgerber, H. (1997). Conformity to sex-typed norms, affect and the self-concept. *Journal of Personality and Social Psychology, 73,* 523–535.

Wood, W., & Eagly, A. H. (2002). A cross-cultural analysis of the behavior of women and men: Implications for the origins of sex differences. *Psychological Bulletin, 128,* 699–727.

Woodard, C. (2005, April 15). Did domestication make dogs smarter? *The Chronicle of Higher Education.*

Woods, S. C., Schwartz, M. W., Baskin, D. G., & Seeley, R. J. (2000). Food intake and the regulation of body weight. *Annual Review of Psychology, 51,* 255–277.

Woodward, C. (2006, November 3). Amnesiac can't return to his past to go into future. *The San Diego Union-Tribune,* A4.

World Health Organization. (1993). *International classification of disease and related health problems* (10th rev.). Geneva: Author.

Wright, I. C., Rabe-Hesketh, S., Woodruff, P. W. R., David, A. S., Murray, R. M., & Bullmore, E. T. (2000). Meta-analysis of regional brain volumes in schizophrenia. *American Journal of Psychiatry, 157,* 16–25.

Wright, K. (2002, September). Times of our lives. *Scientific American,* 59–65.

Wright, K. (2003, November). Staying alive. *Discover,* 64–70.

Wyer, R. S., Jr. (2007). Principles of mental representation. In A. W. Kruglanski & E. T. Higgins, *Social psychology: Handbook of basic principles* (2nd ed., pp. 285–307). New York: Guilford Press.

Yamashita, I. (1993). *Taijin-kyofu or delusional social phobia.* Sapporo, Japan: Hokkaido University Press.

Yang, Y., Raine, A., Lencz, T., Bihrle, S., Lacasse, L., & Colletti, P. (2005a). Prefrontal white matter in pathological liars. *British Journal of Psychiatry, 187,* 320–325.

Yang, Y., Raine, A., Lencz, T., Bihrle, S., LaCasse, L., & Colletti, P. (2005b). Volume reduction in prefrontal gray matter in unsuccessful criminal psychopaths. *Biological Psychiatry, 57,* 1103–1108.

Yanoff, M., Duker, J. S., & Augsburger, J. J. (Eds.). (2003). *Ophthalmology* (2nd ed.). St. Louis: Elsevier Health Sciences.

Yasuda, S., & Matsuishi, T. (2002). Autism detection in children under 18 months—Sensitivity of medical exam screening in infancy and early childhood. *Journal of Disability, Medicine, and Education, 5,* 18–23.

Ybarra, M. J. (1991, September 13). The psychic and the skeptic. *Los Angeles Times.*

Yeargin-Allsop, M., Rice, C., Karapurkar, T., Doernberg, N., Boyle, C., & Murphy, M. (2003). Prevalence of autism in a US metropolitan area. *Journal of the American Medical Association, 289,* 49–55.

Yehuda, R. (2000, August 2). Cited in E. Goode, Childhood abuse and adult stress. *New York Times,* A14.

Yerkes, R. M. (1921). *Psychological examining in the United States Army (Memoir No. 15).* Washington, DC: National Academy of Sciences.

Yoffe, E. (1997, October). How quickly we forget. *U.S. News & World Report.*

Young, J. E., Klosko, J. S., & Weishaar, M. E. (2006). *Schema therapy: A practitioner's guide.* New York: Guilford Press.

Young, M. W. (2000, March). The tick-tock of the biological clock. *Scientific American,* 64–71.

Yule, W., & Fernando, P. (1980). Blood phobia: Beware. *Behavior Research and Therapy, 18,* 587–590.

Yurgelun-Todd, D. (1999, August 9). Cited in S. Brownlee, Inside the teen brain. *U.S. News & World Report,* 44–45.

Yurgelun-Todd, D. (2004, May 10). Cited in C. Wallis & K. Dell, What makes teens tick. *Time.*

Zajonc, R. B. (1984). On the primacy of affect. *American Psychologist, 39,* 117–123.

Zakaria, F. (2003, August 25). Suicide bombers can be stopped. *Newsweek,* 57.

Zaragoza, M. S., & Lane, S. M. (1994). Source misattributions and the suggestibility of eyewitness memory. *Journal of Experimental Psychology: Learning Memory, and Cognition, 20,* 934–935.

Zeidner, M. (1998). *Test anxiety: The state of the art.* New York: Plenum Press.

Zeidner, M., & Matthews, G. (2005). Evaluation anxiety. In A. J. Elliot & C. S. Dweck (Eds.), *Handbook of competence and motivation* (pp. 141–163). New York: Guilford Press.

Zeineh, M. M., Engel, S. A., Thompson, P. M., & Bookheimer, S. Y. (2003). Dynamics of the hippocampus during encoding and retrieval of face-name pairs. *Science, 299,* 577–580.

Zemore, S. E., Fiske, S. T., & Kim, H. (2000). Gender stereotypes and the dynamics of social interaction. In T. Eckes & H. M. Trautner (Eds.), *The developmental social psychology of gender.* Mahwah, NJ: Lawrence Erlbaum.

Zener, K. (1937). The significance of behavior accompanying conditioned salivary secretion for theories of the conditioned response. *American Journal of Psychology, 50,* 384–403.

Zernike, K. (2006, April 19). Study fuels a growing debate over changing police lineups. *The New York Times,* A1, A17.

Zhang, W., Oya, S., Kung, M. P., Hou, C., Maier, D. L., & Hung, H. F. (2005). F-18 silbenes as PET imaging agents for detecting beta-amyloid plaques in the brain. *Journal of Medicinal Chemistry, 48,* 5980–5988.

Zigler, E. (1995, January). Cited in B. Azar, DNA-environment mix forms intellectual fate. *APA Monitor.*

Zigler, E., & Seitz, V. (1982). Social policy and intelligence. In R. J. Sternberg (Ed.), *Handbook of human intelligence.* Cambridge, England: Cambridge University Press.

Zigler, E., & Styfco, S. J. (1994). Head start: Criticisms in a constructive context. *American Psychologist, 49,* 127–132.

Zigler, E., & Styfco, S. J. (2001). Extended childhood intervention prepares children for school and beyond. *Journal of the American Medical Association, 285,* 2378–2380.

Zillmer, E. A., Spiers, M. V., & Culbertson, W. C. (2007). *Principles of neuropsychology* (2nd ed.). Belmont, CA: Thomson Wadsworth.

Zimbardo, P. G. (1970). The human choice: Individuation, reason and order versus deindividuation, impulse and chaos. In W. J. Arnold & D. Levine (Eds.), *Nebraska symposium on motivation.* Lincoln: University of Nebraska Press.

Zimmerman, B. J. (2000). Self-efficacy: An essential motive to learn. *Contemporary Educational Psychology, 25,* 82–91.

Zimmerman, M. A., Copeland, L. A., Shope, J. T., & Gielman, T. E. (1997). A longitudinal study of self-esteem: Implications for adolescent development. *Journal of Youth and Adolescence, 26,* 117–141.

Zola, S. M., & Squire, L. R. (2005). The medial temporal lobe and the hippocampus. In E. Tulving & F. M. Craik (Eds.), *The Oxford handbook of memory.* New York: Oxford University Press.

Zubieta, J., Bueller, J. A., Jackson, L. R., Scott, D. J., Xu, Y., Koeppe, R. A., Nichols, T. E., & Stohler, C. S. (2005). Placebo effects mediated by endogenous opioid activity on u-opioid receptors. *The Journal of Neuroscience, 25,* 7754–7762.

Zucker, K. J. (1990). Gender identity disorders in children: Clinical descriptions and natural history. In R. Blanchard & B. W. Steiner (Eds.), *Clinical management of gender identity disorders in children and adults.* Washington, DC: American Psychiatric Press.

Photo Credits

This page constitutes an extension of the copyright page. We have made every effort to trace the ownership of all copyrighted material and to secure permission from copyright holders. In the event of any question arising as to the use of any material, we will be pleased to make the necessary corrections in future printings. Thanks are due to the following authors, publishers, and agents for permission to use the material indicated.

Front Matter

v: top right, © Russell Illig/Photodisc Blue/Getty Images **vi:** bottom left, Based an illustration in *Scientific American Mind*, April/May, 2006 pg. 18 by Jason Lee. By permission of Jason Lee. **viii:** top right, Craig McClain **ix:** top right, © George Frey **xi:** bottom right, © Michael Nichols/Magnum Photos **xii:** top left, PhotoDisc, Inc. **xii:** top right, © Kalahari Photo/Jamie-Andrea Yanak via AP Images **xiii:** bottom right, PhotoDisc, Inc. **xiii:** top right, PhotoDisc, Inc. **xiv:** top right, PhotoDisc, Inc. **xiv:** bottom right, PhotoDisc, Inc. **xvii:** top left, PhotoDisc, Inc. **xvii:** bottom left, © 2003 AP Images/Eduardo Di Baia **xxii:** © Digital Vision/Getty Images **xxiii:** (#1) © Kalahari Photo/Jamie-Andrea Yanak via AP Images **xxiii:** (#10) *Idaho Statesman*/© Tom Shanahan **xxiii:** (#11) © Kevin Peterson/Photodisc Green/Getty Images **xxiii:** (#5) © Photo24/Brand X Pictures/Getty Images **xxiii:** (#7) Digital Stock Corporation **xxiii:** (#8) © Topham/OB/The Image Works **xxiv:** top, James Bennet/ *The New York Times*/Redux Pictures **xxiv:** center, © AP Images/Raanan Cohen **xxvi:** © Andrew H. Walker/Getty Images **xxvii:** (#7) *People Weekly* © 1992 Taro Inc. Yamasaki **xxviii:** © 2005 Eric Larson/Light of Day **xxxii:** bottom left, © Alfred Pasika-SPL/Photo Researchers, Inc.

Module Openers

One, p. 2: © Alan Thornton/Getty Images **Two, p. 26:** © Firefly Productions/Corbis **Four, p. 66:** © Tom Barrick, Chris Clark, SGHMS / Photo Researchers, Inc. **Five, p. 92:** © Royalty-Free/Corbis **Six, p. 120:** © Digital Vision/Getty Images **Seven, p. 146:** © Louie Psihoyos/Getty Images **Eight, p. 168:** © Miquel Vidal /Reuters **Nine, p. 194:** © Dean Shalhoup/Nashua Telegraph, digital courtesy of AP Images **Ten, p. 212:** Photo by Robert Hanashiro. Copyright © 2006, USA TODAY. Reprinted by permission. **Eleven, p. 238:** © AP Images/Alastair Grant **Twelve, p. 260:** © Haig Kouyoumdjian **Thirteen, p. 280:** © Robert Essel/Corbis **Fourteen, p. 304:** © butterflyalphabet/ IndexStock Imagery **Fifteen, p. 328:** © Zia Soleil/ Iconica/Getty Images **Sixteen, p. 358:** © Manpreet Romana/AFP/Getty **Seventeen, p. 376:** © Oliviero Toscani for BENETTON **Eighteen, p. 406:** © Veronique Beranger/zefa/Corbis **Nineteen, p. 432:** © Bruce Dale/ National Geographic Society Collection **Twenty, p. 456:** Courtesy of Sony Electronics, Inc. **Twenty-one, p. 480:** Roy Toft/National Geographic/Getty Images **Twenty-two, p. 508:** © AP Images/Rodrigo Abd **Twenty-three, p. 530:** © AP Images/ Vincent Yu **Twenty-four, p. 554:** © Michael Freeman/Corbis **Twenty-five, p. 580:** © AP Images/Pankaj Nangia

Module 1

4: Courtesy of Doubleday/AB/Times Books/Random House, by permission of Donna Williams **5:** (#5) Jacket cover from *Somebody Somewhere* by Donna Williams. Used by permission of Times Books, a division of Random House, Inc. **7:** © Dana Fineman/Vistalux **10:** center, Jacket cover from *Somebody Somewhere* by Donna Williams. Used by permission of Times Books, a division of Random House, Inc. **13:** © Tony Freeman/PhotoEdit **14:** top, Courtesy, Margaret Clapp Library Archives, Wellesley College, photo by Patridge **14:** left, Robert Guthrie Collection, courtesy of Archives of the History of American Psychology, University of Akron **14:** right, The Institute of Texan Cultures, University of Texas, San Antonio **15:** (#1) Courtesy of Doubleday/AB/Times Books/Random House, by permission of Donna Williams **15:** (#11) © Tony Freeman/PhotoEdit **15:** (#4) © Dana Fineman/Vistalux **15:** (#7) Jacket cover from *Somebody Somewhere* by Donna Williams. Used by permission of Times Books, a division of Random House, Inc. **18:** left, © David Young-Wolff/Photo Edit **18:** center, © Lori Adamski Peek/Stone/Getty Images **19:** left, © Doug Menuez/Corbis - SABA **19:** right, © Odilon Dimier/ PhotoAlto/Getty Images **20:** © Hangarter/The Picture Cube/Index Stock **21:** © Gary Conner/IndexStock Imagery **22:** (#1) Courtesy of Doubleday/AB/Times Books/Random House, by permission of Donna Williams **22:** (#13) Courtesy, Margaret Clapp Library Archives, Wellesley College, photo by Patridge **23:** (#16) © Doug Menuez/Corbis - SABA **23:** (#18) © Hangarter/The Picture Cube/Index Stock **24:** Courtesy of Temple Grandin, Ph.D.

Module 2

27: right, © Joe McDonald/Animals, Animals **27:** top, © Jose Azel/Aurora Quanta Productions **28:** © Jose Azel/Aurora Quanta Productions **31:** (tiger) © Belinda Wright/DRK Photo **31:** left, © Joe McDonald/Animals, Animals **31:** center, © Peter Weimann/Animals, Animals **32:** © Jose Azel/Aurora Quanta Productions **33:** © Photodisc, Inc. **34:** bottom left, *People Weekly* © 1995 Alan S. Weiner **34:** bottom right, © Masterfile Royalty Free (RF) **34:** top right, © Russell Illig/Photodisc Blue/Getty Images **35:** © Michael McLaughlin **36:** top, (both) © Jose Azel/Aurora Quanta Productions **38:** (#1) © Jose Azel/Aurora Quanta Productions **38:** (#2) © Joe McDonald/Animals, Animals **38:** (#4) © Russell Illig/Photodisc Blue/Getty Images **39:** © Michael McLaughlin **40:** center, Craig McClain **40:** bottom, © Jack Hollingsworth/Photodisc Green/Getty **41:** Courtesy of the Foundation for Biomedical Research **42:** (#1) © Jose Azel/Aurora Quanta Productions **42:** (#4) © Joe McDonald/Animals, Animals **43:** (#14) Craig McClain **44:** © ImageSource/Getty Images

Module 3

47: © Melchior Digiacomo **48:** © Melchior Digiacomo **49:** Courtesy of Center on Aging and Department of Molecular and Medical Pharmacology, University of California, Los Angeles **50:** © Alfred Pasika-SPL/Photo Researchers, Inc. **51:** top right, AP Images/CHU de Lyon **51:** left, *People Weekly* © 1992 Taro Yamasaki **51:** bottom right, © AP Images/Jennifer Graylock **55:** bottom right, Courtesy of Johns Hopkins University, Office of Public Affairs **55:** top right, Courtesy of Miles Herkenham, Ph.D., Section of Functional Neuroanatomy, NIMH **58:** top, © AP Images/David Longstrength **59:** top, Adalberto Rios Szal Sol/PhotoDisc **59:** center, © Borys Malkin/Anthro-Photo **59:** bottom, © G.I. Bernard/Animals, Animals/Earth Sciences **60:** © Andrew H. Walker/Getty Images **62:** (#7) *People Weekly* © 1992 Taro Yamasaki **63:** (#13) © AP Images/David Longstrength

Module 4

67: center right, By courtesy and kind permission of Cynthia de Gruchy **67:** bottom left, © Patrick Farrell/ *Miami Herald* photo **67:** top right, © Peter A. Simon/Phototake, NYC **68:** bottom, By courtesy and kind permission of Cynthia de Gruchy **69:** bottom right, Craig McClain **70:** left, Digital Stock Corporation **70:** right, Graphic data courtesy of Dr. Ahmad Hariri **71:** bottom, (center and bottom right) Digital Stock Corporation **71:** top, Courtesy of Dr. Marcus Raichle, University of Washington **71:** top center, Courtesy of Dr. Marcus Raichle, University of Washington **72:** bottom right, © David Stewart/Stone/Getty Images **74:** top left, Wadsworth Thomson Collection **74:** right, © Patrick Farrell/ *Miami Herald* photo **75:** left, From: Damasio, H., Grabowski, T., Frank, R., Galaburda, A.M., Damasio, A.R.: The return of Phineas Gage: Clues about the brain from a famous patient. *Science*, 264:1102–1105, 1994. Department of Neurology and Image Analysis Facility, University of Iowa. Copyright © 1994 by the American Association for the Advancement in Science. Reprinted with permission of author and publisher. **76:** bottom, Courtesy of J.A. Fiez, Dept. of Neurology, Washington University School of Medicine **80:** top right, © Ron Dahlquist/Stone/Getty Images **80:** bottom left, © Topham/OB/The Image Works **81:** © David Stewart/Stone/Getty Images **83:** (#2) Digital Stock Corporation **83:** (#5 b) © David Stewart/Stone/Getty Images **85:** © PhotoDisc, Inc. **89:** (#16) © Ron Dahlquist/Stone/Getty Images

Module 5

93: (center #2) PhotoDisc, Inc. **98:** center, Digital Stock Corporation **99:** (top & right center) Normal and altered reproduction of Vincent van Gogh self portrait originally appearing in *Popular Science*, July 1995, p. 44, "Color for the Color Blind: Self Portrait of Van Gogh." **99:** bottom, Ishihara Tests for Colour Blindness, Courtesy of Graham-Field, Inc. **100:** top left, © 2002 AP Images/Wade Payne **100:** bottom left, © Tony Freeman/Photo Edit **104:** left, © M.P. Kahl/DRK Photo **104:** right, © Tony Freeman/Photo Edit **105:** PhotoDisc, Inc. **107:** © 1989 Jonathan Levine **108:** © 1986 Steven Green-Armytage/The Stock Market/Corbis **110:** right, Danielle Pellegrini/Photo Researchers, Inc. **110:** top, © Burt Glinn/Magnum Photos **110:** center, © Guy Mary-Rousseliere **110:** left, © Malcolm S. Kirk **110:** bottom, © Malcolm S. Kirk **112:** Digital Stock Corporation **113:** right, Photodisc, Inc. **113:** top, © AP Images/Aaron Harris **113:** bottom, © Leonard Freed/Magnum Photos **114:** © AP Images/Stephen Chernin **115:** © James M.

Kubus, Greensburg, PA **117:** (#17) © Danielle Pellegrini/Photo Researchers, Inc. **118:** © 2005 Eric Larson/Light of Day, Inc.

Module 6

121: © Howard Sochurek/The Stock Market/Corbis **122:** © Howard Sochurek/The Stock Market/Corbis **123:** left, © Al Francekevich/The Stock Market/Corbis **123:** bottom, © Pat Bruno/Positive Images **124:** bottom, Custom Medical Stock Photo **126:** Painting by Richard Haas, photo © Bill Horsman **127:** top, Painting by Richard Haas, photo © Bill Horsman **128:** right, © Pat Bruno/Positive Images **129:** center, Random House photo by Charlotte Green **130:** right, Digital Stock Corporation **130:** bottom left, © Bob Daemmrich/Stock, Boston **130:** top left, © Peter Turner **131:** bottom left, © Garry Gay **131:** top right, © Henry/Gamma Press **131:** bottom right, © Robert Holmes/Corbis **131:** top left, © Stephen Firsch/Stock, Boston **132:** right, © John Elk/Stock, Boston **132:** left, © Robert P. Comport/Animals, Animals/Earth Sciences **133:** center right, Craig McClain **133:** top left, © Baron Wolman/Woodfin Camp & Associates **134:** (# 13) © Garry Gay **134:** (#4) Painting by Richard Haas, photo © Bill Horsman **134:** (left #3) Custom Medical Stock Photo **135:** top right, PhotoDisc, Inc. **135:** center right, © Peter Glass/Alamy **136:** (dog) PhotoDisc, Inc. **136:** bottom, By courtesy of Takahiko Masuda and Dr. Richard Nisbett, University of Michigan **136:** center, Digital Stock Corporation **136:** top, © Ric Ergenbright/Corbis **137:** left, Digital Stock Corporation **137:** center, Digital Stock Corporation **137:** right, © Peter Beavis/ The Image Bank/Getty Images **138:** bottom, © Dana Fineman/Vistalux **139:** top right, Corel Gallery **140:** (runner) © Globus Brothers **140:** (sign) PhotoDisc, Inc. **140:** top right, © Gianni Dagli Orti/Corbis **141:** center, (Howard Stern) by Allen Tannenbaum/POLARIS Images. Photo illustration by Doug Stern. Copyright © 1997 *U. S. News & World Report*, L.P. Reproduced with permission. **141:** center, (Marilyn Monroe) © Doc Alain/Retna, Inc., (Julia Roberts) © Bill Davila/Retna, Inc., Photo illustrations by Doug Stern. Copyright © 1997 *U. S. News & World Report*, L.P. Reproduced with permission. **141:** bottom right, (Queen Elizabeth) Courtesy of *Colors Magazine*, Rome **141:** center right, (Schwarzenegger) Courtesy of *Colors Magazine*, Rome **141:** left, 2000 Computer Motion Photograph by Bobbi Bennett; altered by John MacNeill. Reprinted with permission from John MacNeill. **141:** top right, Ames Research Center/NASA, photo by Walt Sisler **142:** (#7) © Peter Turner **142:** (# 1) © Al Francekevich/The Stock Market/Corbis **143:** (#14) Ames Research Center/NASA, photo by Walt Sisler **144:** © Alyson Aliano

Module 7

147: right, © Alan Hobson/Science Source/Photo Researchers **147:** left, © Murrae Haynes **148:** (far left) © Michael S. Yamashita/Corbis **148:** center right, Craig McClain **148:** right, © David Stewart/Stone/Getty Images **148:** center left, © Tony Freeman/Photo Edit **149:** center, © Cesar Paredes **149:** left, © Robert E. Daemmrich **149:** right, © Tim Shaffer/Reuters/Corbis **150:** bottom right, © Burger/Phanie/Photo Researchers, Inc. **150:** top left, ©

Murrae Haynes **153:** © Alan Hobson/Science Source/Photo Researchers **158:** (#1) © Michael S. Yamashita/Corbis **159:** Digital Stock Corporation **161:** Craig McClain **162:** center, © Carol Fords/Stone/Getty Images **162:** left, © Rob Bartee/SuperStock **163:** right, © Dan McCoy/Rainbow **163:** bottom left, © GARO/PHANIE/Photo Researchers, Inc. **163:** center, © Louie Psihoyos **164:** (#1) © Michael S. Yamashita/Corbis **165:** (#17) © Rob Bartee/SuperStock **166:** © Luca DiCecco/Alamy

Module 8

169: left, Craig McClain **170:** Craig McClain **171:** bottom, Craig McClain **172:** top center, © Michael Salas **172:** right, © Myrleen Ferguson/Photo Edit **173:** Courtesy, Rainbow Babies and Children's Hospital, University Hospitals of Cleveland, Dr. Howard Hall. Photo © Joe Glick **174:** © James Porto **178:** top left, Craig McClain **179:** bottom, © Dr. Jeremy Burgess/Photo Researchers, Inc. **180:** bottom center, (psilocybe) © Joy Spurr/Bruce Coleman Inc. **180:** bottom left, © Andy Small/Corbis **180:** center left, © Michael and Patricia Fogden/Corbis **180:** top, © Robert Pickett/Corbis **181:** top, © David Muench/Corbis **181:** top left, © Joseph Sohm/Visions of America, LLC/Alamy **181:** center, © Scott Houston/Corbis Sygma **181:** bottom left, © Scott Houston/Corbis Sygma **182:** top, Courtesy, Joseph E. Seagram's and Sons, Inc. **182:** right, Craig McClain **183:** bottom, © Andrew Lichtenstein/Corbis Sygma **184:** (#1) Craig McClain **184:** (#10) Craig McClain **184:** (#2) Craig McClain **184:** (#4) © James Porto **184:** (#7) © Robert Pickett/Corbis **184:** (#8) © Scott Houston/Corbis Sygma **184:** (#9) © Dr. Jeremy Burgess/Photo Researchers, Inc. **185:** top, © Pat Bruno/Positive Images **185:** left, © Richard Kalvar/Magnum Photos **186:** © Brooks Kraft/Corbis Sygma **187:** Courtesy of D.A.R.E. America **188:** left, © Pat Bruno/Positive Images **188:** right, © Zigy Kaluzny/Stone/Getty Images **189:** © Pat Bruno/Positive Images **190:** (#1) Craig McClain **190:** (#13) © Dr. Jeremy Burgess/Photo Researchers, Inc. **190:** (#14) © Robert Pickett/Corbis **191:** (#19) © Brooks Kraft/Corbis Sygma **191:** (#20) Courtesy of D.A.R.E. America **192:** © Stockdisc/Getty Images

Module 9

195: bottom, Digital Stock Corporation **196:** right, Craig McClain **200:** bottom right, Courtesy of Professor Stuart Ellins, California State University, San Bernardino, CA **200:** top right, PhotoDisc, Inc. **201:** (center left & bottom right) © AP Images/Las Cruces Sun-News/Norm Dettlaff **201:** top left, Runk/Schoenberger/Grant Heilman Photography **201:** bottom left, © Christian Abraham **201:** top right, © Michael Stuckey/Comstock **202:** PhotoDisc, Inc. **204:** bottom right, (rabbit) PhotoDisc, Inc. **204:** (rat) PhotoDisc, Inc. **204:** (toddler smiling & yelling) Digital Stock Corporation **205:** © Royalty-Free/Corbis **206:** Digital Stock Corporation **207:** Digital Stock Corporation **209:** (rat) PhotoDisc, Inc. **209:** (toddler) Digital Stock Corporation

Module 10

213: right, © Evan Agostini/Getty Images **213:** left,

© George Frey **214:** right, (rat) PhotoDisc, Inc. **216:** top, Courtesy of Wurlitzer Jukebox Company **216:** left, © Peter Southwick/Stock, Boston **217:** (top and bottom) © George Frey **218:** left, © Savage Productions **219:** left, © Simon Belcher/Alamy **220:** top, © 1971 *Time*, Inc./Getty Images. Reprinted by permission. **221:** (Fixed interval) © Warren Bolster/Stone/Getty Images **221:** (Fixed ratio) © Andy Sacks/SaxPix **221:** (Variable ratio) © Michael P. Gadomski/Photo Researchers, Inc. **221:** top right, © 2003 AP Images/U.S. Navy, Brien Aho, HO **222:** top, © George Frey **222:** center, © George Frey **222:** left, © Stephen Kraseman/DRK Photo **223:** (rat) PhotoDisc, Inc. **223:** top, © Evan Agostini/Getty Images **225:** center, © Barry Lewis/Corbis Saba **225:** bottom left, © Jon Lowenstein/Aurora Photos **226:** left, (Sultan) From *The Mentality of Apes*, by Wolfgang Koehler, Routledge & Kegan Paul. Reproduced by permission of International Thomson Publishing Services, Ltd. **226:** left, (banana) Craig McClain **226:** (gun) PhotoDisc, Inc. **226:** right, (water glass) PhotoDisc, Inc. **227:** (#12) © Jon Lowenstein/Aurora Photos **227:** (#11) Craig McClain **227:** (#6) © Simon Belcher/Alamy **227:** (bear cub #8) © Stephen Kraseman/DRK Photo **228:** right, Photo by Ron Garrison, © Zoological Society of San Diego **228:** left, PhotoDisc, Inc. **228:** top, © Mitsuaki Iwago/National Geographic Society/Minden Pictures **229:** left, © Arthur C. Smith, III/Grant Heilman Photography **229:** right, © Kennan Ward Photography/Corbis **231:** (top & right) © Hiroji Kubota/Magnum Photos **233:** right, © 1998 Danny Gonzalez **233:** top, © Dan McCoy/Rainbow **234:** (bear cub #13) © Stephen Kraseman/DRK Photo **234:** (#11) © Michael P. Gadomski/Photo Researchers, Inc. **234:** (#8) © Simon Belcher/Alamy **235:** (#14) © Jon Lowenstein/Aurora Photos **235:** (#19) Photo by Ron Garrison, © Zoological Society of San Diego **235:** (#23) © Hiroji Kubota/Magnum Photos **236:** © AP Images/Amy Sancetta

Module 11

239: left, Courtesy of Rajan Mahadevan **240:** left, PhotoDisc, Inc. **241:** center, (eyes) PhotoDisc, Inc. **242:** (prefrontal cortex) From "A Head for Figures," by Brian Butterworth, *Science*, 284, p. 928. By permission of B. Butterworth. **243:** Courtesy of Rajan Mahadevan **244:** left, PhotoDisc, Inc. **244:** bottom, PhotoDisc, Inc. **245:** (bear) PhotoDisc, Inc. **245:** (frog) PhotoDisc, Inc. **245:** (owl) PhotoDisc, Inc. **246:** left, Digital Stock Corporation **246:** right, PhotoDisc, Inc. **247:** © AP Images/Kevork Djansezian **250:** top right, © AP Images/Al Francis **250:** top left, © John Harding **252:** (#13) © AP Images/Kevork Djansezian **252:** (#5) Courtesy of Rajan Mahadevan **252:** (#7) PhotoDisc, Inc. **253:** Bob Carey/*Los Angeles Times* Photo **254:** bottom, Courtesy of Prof. Ralph Norman Haber **254:** top, © Doug Levere **256:** (#5) PhotoDisc, Inc. **257:** (#13) © AP Images/Kevork Djansezian **257:** (#18) Bob Carey/*Los Angeles Times* Photo **258:** © Image Source/Alamy

Module 12

263: bottom, Digital Stock Corporation **264:** bottom, (faces in graph) PhotoDisc, Inc. **264:** top, © Laura Dwight

Photo Credits

267: bottom, © Topham/OB/The Image Works 268: center left, PhotoDisc, Inc. 268: right, PhotoDisc, Inc. 269: bottom, © Bill Ballenberg 270: (face #4) PhotoDisc, Inc. 272: (meeting) PhotoDisc, Inc. 272: top, © Tad Janocinski 273: © Peter M. Corr/Alamy 274: bottom left, UPI/Corbis Bettmann 274: bottom right, UPI/Corbis Bettmann 276: (#5 - faces in graph) PhotoDisc, Inc. 277: (#23) © Peter M. Corr/Alamy 277: (#22) Tad Janocinski 277:(#24 left) UPI/Corbis Bettmann 277: (#24 right) UPI/Corbis Bettmann 278: *People Weekly* © 1996 Adolphe Pierre Louis

Module 13

281: (Berry) © AP Images/Luis Martinez 281: (Gates) © AP Images /Cheryl Hatch 281: (Gregg Cox) © Stephen Ellison/Corbis Outline 281: (Midori) Photo by Brigitte Lacombe, courtesy of Cerritos Center for the Performing Arts, California 281: (Steve Lu) *Los Angeles Times* Photo by Bob Chamberlin 282: (Berry) © AP Images/Luis Martinez 282: (Gates) © AP Images/Cheryl Hatch 282: (Gregg Cox) © Stephen Ellison/Corbis Outline 282: (Midori) Photo by Brigitte Lacombe, courtesy of Cerritos Center for the Performing Arts, California 282: (Steve Lu) *Los Angeles Times* Photo by Bob Chamberlin 283: (Berry) © AP Images/Luis Martinez 283: (Midori) Photo by Brigitte Lacombe, courtesy of Cerritos Center for the Performing Arts, California 283: (analytical) PhotoDisc, Inc. 283: (practical) PhotoDisc, Inc. 283: (problem solving) PhotoDisc, Inc. 285: top, Corbis-Bettmann 285: left, PhotoDisc, Inc. 285: center, PhotoDisc, Inc. 286: top left, Courtesy, John Fitzgerald Kennedy Library/ Museum, # C283-51-63. 286: top center, Photo by Deborah Feingold, courtesy of *Parade Magazine* and Marilyn vos Savant. 286: top right, UPI-Bettmann Corbis 288: top left, Courtesy of Marian Burke. 288: top right, Photo by Deborah Feingold, courtesy of *Parade Magazine* and Marilyn vos Savant 289: top left, PhotoDisc, Inc. 289: right, PhotoDisc, Inc. 289: center left, © AP Images/Anne Ryan 291: right, PhotoDisc, Inc. 291: center, © Natalie Behring-Chisholm/Getty Images 292: top, Photo by Brigitte Lacombe, courtesy of Cerritos Center for the Performing Arts, California 292: center, © Myrleen Ferguson/PhotoEdit 293: left, PhotoDisc, Inc. 293: right, PhotoDisc, Inc. 293: top, © Anne Rippy 294: ("decided?") © Anthony Barboza 294: ("how") © Anthony Barboza 294: ("is") © Anthony Barboza 294: ("race") © Anthony Barboza 295: (#1) *Los Angeles Times* Photo by Bob Chamberlin 295: (#2) Photo by Brigitte Lacombe, courtesy of Cerritos Center for the Performing Arts, California 295: (#3) PhotoDisc, Inc. 295: (#4) PhotoDisc, Inc. 296: UPI-Bettmann/Corbis 297: top, Adapted from S. F. Witelson, D. L. Kigar, & T. Harvey, Fig. 2, *The Lancet*, 353, 1999, with permission of the authors. 297: bottom, Lateral prefrontal cortex: From "A Head for Figures," by Brian Butterworth, *Science*, 284, p. 928. By permission of B. Butterworth. 298: 1991 © Ira Block 299: inset, PhotoDisc, Inc. 299: top, © Jacques Chenet/Woodfin Camp & Associates 300: (#1) *Los Angeles Times* Photo by Bob Chamberlin 301: (#12) © Natalie Behring-Chisholm/Getty Images 301: (#14) UPI-Bettmann/Corbis 301: (#15) Adapted from S. F. Witelson, D. L. Kigar, & T. Harvey, Fig. 2, *The Lancet*, 353, 1999, with permission of the authors. 302: © Judy Griesedieck

Module 14

305: top right, © AP Images/Mark Lennihan 305: left, © Charles Allen 306: (Black Puli) © Animals/Animals 306: (Chihauhau) PhotoDisc, Inc. 306: (Dalmation) PhotoDisc, Inc. 306: (bassett hound) PhotoDisc, Inc. 306: (brown dog) PhotoDisc, Inc. 306: (rabbit) PhotoDisc, Inc. 306: (tabby cat) PhotoDisc, Inc. 307: (apple) PhotoDisc, Inc. 307: (clown) PhotoDisc, Inc. 307: (turtle) PhotoDisc, Inc. 307: top left, PhotoDisc, Inc. 308: bottom, PhotoDisc, Inc. 308: top, © Richard Pohle/Sipa Press 309: center, Craig McClain 310: top, © AP Images/Mark Lennihan 310: right, © The Gordon Parks, Courtesy of the Howard Greeenberg Gallery, NYC 311: top, Courtesy of and by permission of John Johnson, Ltd. on behalf of Stephen Wilshire 314: top, From Conel, J. L. 1939, 1941, 1959 *The Postnatal Development of the Human Cerebral Cortex*, 6 Volumes, Cambridge: Harvard 314: left, © Romilly Lockyer 314: right, © Royalty Free/Masterfile 315: ("two words") © Laura Dwight 315: (babbling) © Romilly Lockyer 315: (right & sentences) © Frank Bates 315: (single word) © Royalty Free/Masterfile 315: left, © Laura Dwight 316: center, Courtesy of Robert Zatorre, and Denise Klein, McGill University 316: bottom, PhotoDisc, Inc. 316: top, © Jeremy Horner/Corbis 317: (#8) © Romilly Lockyer 317: (#9) © Jeremy Horner/Corbis 317: (#4) Craig McClain 318: left, © AP Images/John Schultz 318: right, © Steve Pope/Landov 319: right, PhotoDisc, Inc. 319: left, © Hans Blohm/Masterfile 320: top, *Los Angeles Times* Photo by Brian Vander Brug 321: top, By courtesy of Takahiko Masuda and Dr. Richard Nisbett, University of Michigan 321: bottom, From Shaywitz, et al., 1995, "Sex differences in the functional organization of the brain for language," *Nature*, 373, 607–609. Courtesy of NMR Research/Yale Medical School 322: center, (dolphins) © 1989 Ed Kashi 322: top, Author's collection 323: center, Courtesy of Language Research Center, Georgia State University, Dr. Duane Rumbaugh, © 1991 Public Sphere 323: bottom, © Michael Nichols/Magnum Photos 323: top, © Ron Cohn/koko.org/The Gorilla Foundation 324: (#3) Craig McClain 324: (#7) Courtesy of and by permission of John Johnson, Ltd. on behalf of Stephen Wilshire 325: (#11) © Jeremy Horner/Corbis 325: (#17–18) Shaywitz, et al., 1995 Courtesy of NMR Research/Yale Medical School 325: (#19) © Michael Nichols/Magnum Photos 326: Digital Stock Corporation

Module 15

329: left, © Jay Mather/Corbis Sygma 329: right, © *San Diego Union-Tribune*/John McCutchen 330: left, © John Dominis/Time Life Pictures/Getty Images 330: top right, © Michael Melford 331: right, © Mike Malyszko/Stock, Boston 331: left, © Richard Sjoberg 332: center, PhotoDisc, Inc. 332: left, © William Campbell/*Time Magazine*/Getty Images 332: right, © PhotoDisc, Inc. 334: top, PhotoDisc, Inc. 334: center, © Les Stone/Corbis Sygma 335: © Kim Newton/Woodfin Camp & Associates 336: bottom, Courtesy of Jeffrey M. Friedman, Rockefeller University 336: top, © Cohen/Ostrow/Getty Images 337: center, © Guang Nu/Reuters Newmedia, Inc./Corbis 337: top, © Royalty Free/Masterfile 337: left, © image100/Alamy 338: © George B. Shaller/Bruce Coleman, Inc. 340: bottom, © George Simian/Corbis 340: center, © Tony Freeman/Photo Edit 341: top left, PhotoDisc, Inc. 341: top right, PhotoDisc, Inc. 341: bottom, © Left Lane Productions/Corbis 342: inset, (graph photos) PhotoDisc, Inc. 343: © Red Morgan/*Time Magazine*/Silver Image 345: S. Wanke/PhotoLink/PhotoDisc, Inc. 346: top, *Los Angeles Times* Photo by Gina Ferazzi 346: bottom, © Mariella Furrer/Corbis - SABA 347: (#1) © Michael Melford 347: (#15) S. Wanke/PhotoLink/PhotoDisc, Inc. 347: (#4) © Mike Malyszko/Stock, Boston 348: right, © AP Images/ Thomas Kienzle 348: top, © *San Diego Union-Tribune* John McCutchen 350: top, AP Images/Greg Kinch/Siemens Foundation 350: left, PhotoDisc, Inc. 350: right, PhotoDisc, Inc. 351: © 2006 Justine Kurland 352: top left, UPI/Bettmann/Corbis 352: center left, UPI/Bettmann/Corbis 352: center right, © AP Images/Charles Bennet 352: bottom, © L. Schwartzwald/Corbis Sygma 353: © Scott Goldsmith 354: (#1) © Richard Sjoberg 354: (#4) Courtesy of Jeffrey M. Friedman, Rockefeller University 355: (#13) © Mariella Furrer/Corbis SABA 355: (#14) PhotoDisc, Inc. 355: (#17) UPI/Bettmann/Corbis

Module 16

359: right, *Idaho Statesman*/© Tom Shanahan 359: left, © Kalahari Photo/Jamie-Andrea Yanak via AP Images. 360: (center right & bottom center) PhotoDisc, Inc. 361: (center left & bottom right) PhotoDisc, Inc. 361: (top and bottom left) *Idaho Statesman*/© Tom Shanahan 361: center right, PhotoDisc, Inc. 362: left, © Photo24/Brand X Pictures/Getty Images 363: center, (wolf) © Photo24/Brand X Pictures/Getty Images 364: center, (2nd down) Digital Stock Corporation 364: center, (3rd down) Digital Stock Corporation 364: center, (4th down) Digital Stock Corporation 364: top, Digital Stock Corporation 365: top left, Digital Stock Corporation 365: center, © Topham/OB/The Image Works 366: top left, *Idaho Statesman*/© Tom Shanahan 366: bottom left, PhotoDisc, Inc. 366: bottom right, PhotoDisc, Inc. 367: bottom right, PhotoDisc, Inc. 367: top right, © Burt Glinn/Magnum Photos 367: top, © Kevin Peterson/Photodisc Green/Getty Images 368: (#1) © Kalahari Photo/Jamie-Andrea Yanak via AP Images. 368: (#10) *Idaho Statesman*/© Tom Shanahan 368: (#11) © Kevin Peterson/Photodisc Green/Getty Images 368: (#5) © Photo24/Brand X Pictures/Getty Images 368: (#7) Digital Stock Corporation 368: (#8) © Topham/OB/The Image Works 369: © Carlo Allegri/Getty Images 370: bottom left, Photograph by Joel Reicherter, reprinted by permission and courtesy of the photographer. 370: top, © Luke Frazza/AFP/Getty Images 371: bottom, © Luke Frazza/AFP/Getty Images 372: (#5) © Photo24/Brand X Pictures/Getty Images 372: (#7) Digital Stock Corporation 373: (#11) *Idaho Statesman*/© Tom Shanahan 374: © Noburo Hashimoto/Corbis

Module 17

378: UPI-Bettmann Corbis **379:** left, © Pascal Goetgheluck/Photo Researchers, Inc. **379:** right, © Petit Format/Science Source/Photo Researchers, Inc. **380:** top, Lennart Nilsson, *The Incredible Machine*, National Geographic Society, by permission of Bokforlaget Bonnier Alba AB. **381:** center, PhotoDisc, Inc. **381:** right, © George Steinmetz **382:** center left, PhotoDisc, Inc. **382:** bottom left, PhotoDisc, Inc. **382:** right, PhotoDisc, Inc. **383:** center right, © Laura Dwight **383:** bottom, © Elyse Lewin/The Image Bank/Getty Images **383:** top, © Laura Dwight **384:** top center, (crying) © David M. Grossman/Photo Researchers, Inc. **384:** bottom, (happy) PhotoDisc, Inc. **384:** left, *People Weekly* © 1995 Taro Yamaski **386:** top, © Joseph Nettis/Stock, Boston **386:** bottom, © Kayoco/zefa/Corbis **387:** bottom right, © Joseph Nettis/Stock, Boston **387:** top, © Kayoco/zefa/Corbis **388:** top, PhotoDisc, Inc. **388:** center, PhotoDisc, Inc. **389:** left, © Doug Goodman/ Photo Researchers, Inc. **389:** right, Craig McClain **390:** PhotoDisc, Inc. **391:** left, Jean Piaget © Etienne Delessert **391:** right, © Doug Goodman/Photo Researchers, Inc. **392:** PhotoDisc, Inc. **393:** PhotoDisc, Inc. **394:** top, PhotoDisc,Inc. **394:** bottom, © Mike Teruya/Free Spirit Photography **395:** top, © Jon Feingersh **395:** right, © Charles Gupton/Flash! Light/Stock, Boston **395:** left, © Bob Daemmrich/Stock, Boston **396:** top left, PhotoDisc, Inc. **396:** top right, PhotoDisc, Inc. **396:** bottom left, © Topham/OB/The Image Works **397:** center left, PhotoDisc, Inc. **397:** center, PhotoDisc, Inc. **397:** bottom right, © Olivero Toscani for BENETTON **398:** (#10) PhotoDisc, Inc. **399:** right, © Lila Abu Lughod/AnthroPhoto **399:** left, © Steven Winn/ AnthroPhoto **400:** left, UPI-Bettmann Corbis **400:** right, © Christopher Little/Corbis Outline **401:** Private Collection **403:** (#17) PhotoDisc, Inc. **403:** (#22) Steven Winn/AnthroPhoto

Module 18

407: right, H. Armstrong Roberts/Robertstock.com **407:** left, *Los Angeles Times* Photo by Tammy Lechner **408:** center, © David Michael Kennedy **409:** © Lauren Greenfield/VII Picture Agency, LLC **410:** top, *Los Angeles Times* Photo by Tammy Lechner **410:** right, PhotoDisc, Inc. **411:** left, PhotoDisc, Inc. **411:** bottom, PhotoDisc, Inc. **411:** right, PhotoDisc, Inc. **413:** right, PhotoDisc, Inc. **413:** left, © David Michael Kennedy **414:** left, (#1 & #2) © David Michael Kennedy **414:** bottom left, © Lauren Greenfield/VII Picture Agency, LLC **414:** top, © Lawrence Manning/Corbis **415:** top left, PhotoDisc, Inc. **415:** top center, PhotoDisc, Inc. **415:** top right, PhotoDisc, Inc. **415:** center left, PhotoDisc., Inc. **415:** bottom, PhotoDisc., Inc. **416:** center, *Los Angeles Times* Photo by Tammy Lechner **416:** top, PhotoDisc, Inc. **416:** bottom, © David Michael Kennedy **417:** top left, H. Armstrong Roberts/Robertstock.com **417:** bottom left, © Bob Grant/Getty Images **417:** bottom right, © Mike Clarke/Getty Images **418:** top, *Los Angeles Times* photo by Dave Gatley **418:** left, PhotoDisc., Inc. **418:** right, PhotoDisc., Inc. **419:** H. Armstrong Roberts/ Robertstock.com **420:** (left, right & bottom) PhotoDisc, Inc. **421:** (#10) H. Armstrong Roberts/Robertstock.com **421:** (#11) PhotoDisc., Inc. **421:** (#8) PhotoDisc, Inc. **421:** (#9) PhotoDisc., Inc. **422:** © Andrew Brusso/Corbis Outline **423:** © Roger Wood/Corbis **424:** top, © David J. Sams/Stock, Boston **424:** center, © Werner Bokelberg. Photo altered by Doug Stern, Copyright © 1997 *U. S. News & World Report*, L.P. Reproduced with permission. **425:** left, PhotoDisc., Inc. **425:** right, PhotoDisc., Inc. **426:** (both) PhotoDisc, Inc. **427:** PhotoDisc, Inc. **428:** (#1) © Lawrence Manning/Corbis **428:** (#7) © David Michael Kennedy **428:** (#9) PhotoDisc, Inc. **429:** (#15) David J. Sams/Stock, Boston **429:** inset, (#17) PhotoDisc, Inc. **430:** © CLEO Freelance/Index Stock Imagery

Module 19

433: left, © Dennis Oda **433:** right, © Fox/Shooting Star **434:** © Kevin Moloney/Getty Images **436:** © Kevin Moloney/Getty Images **438:** top right, © Dennis Oda **438:** bottom right, © Kevin Moloney/Getty Images **439:** center, © Dennis Oda **440:** center, Courtesy, Adler School of Professional Psychology. Reproduced by permission of Kurt Adler. **440:** right, Courtesy, Association for the Advancement of Psychoanalysis. **440:** left, National Library of Medicine, Bethesda, MD **442:** bottom, © Dean Mouhtaropoulos/Getty Images **442:** top, © Fox/Shooting Star **443:** top, J. Howard Miller/National Archives/Bettman Corbis **443:** bottom, © Bob Adelman/Magnum Photos **444:** center, © AP Images/ Jim Cooper **444:** bottom, © Carlo Allegri/Getty Images **444:** top, © Laura Dwight/Corbis **445:** center, PhotoDisc, Inc. **445:** top, © Jose Azel/Woodfin Camp & Associates **445:** bottom, © Peter Kramer/Getty Images **446:** © AP Images/Mark J. Terrill **447:** (#10) © Jose Azel/ Woodfin Camp & Associates **448:** © Jason Goltz **449:** both, © Walter Wick/Telegraph Colour Library/FPG International/Getty Images **450:** top center, © Dennis Oda **450:** center, © Kevin Moloney/Getty Images **453:** (#15) © Walter Wick/Telegraph Colour Library/FPG International/Getty Images **453:** (#11) © AP Images/Mark J. Terrill **453:** (#14) © Jason Goltz

Module 20

457: right, © Alan Weiner **457:** left, © Siphwe Sibeko/Reuters/Landov **458:** bottom, © AP Images/Karel Prinsloo **458:** top, © Tor Richardsen/AFP/Getty Images **459:** center, PhotoDisc, Inc. **459:** top, © AP Images/ Sayyid Azim **460:** left, PhotoDisc, Inc. **460:** right, PhotoDisc, Inc. **461:** © Andrew H. Walker/Getty Images **462:** right, (beauty queen) © Joshua-Ets-Hokin/ PhotoDisc, Inc. **462:** right, (clown) PhotoDisc, Inc. **462:** right, (criminal) PhotoDisc, Inc. **462:** right, (graduate) PhotoDisc, Inc. **462:** right, (nun) PhotoDisc, Inc. **462:** top left, © Alan Weiner **462:** bottom left, © *Los Angeles Times* Photo by Lawrence K. Ho **463:** (beauty queen) © Joshua-Ets-Hokin/PhotoDisc, Inc. **463:** (clown) PhotoDisc, Inc. **463:** (criminal) PhotoDisc, Inc. **463:** (graduate) PhotoDisc, Inc. **463:** (nun) PhotoDisc, Inc. **464:** top, © AP Images/Joseph Kaczmarek **464:** bottom, © Galen Rowell/Corbis **465:** left, (adult) © Barbara Penoyar/PhotoDisc, Inc. **465:** left, (child) © Barbara Penoyar/PhotoDisc, Inc. **465:** right, © Werner Bokelberg. Photo altered by Doug Stern, Copyright © 1997 *U. S. News & World Report*, L.P. Reproduced with permission. **466:** bottom left, PhotoDisc, Inc. **466:** bottom right, PhotoDisc, inc. **466:** top, © Michael Nichols/Magnum Photos **467:** (left + center) © Michael Nichols/Magnum Photos **467:** right, PhotoDisc, Inc. **468:** © AP Images/Joseph Kaczmarek **469:** (#10) PhotoDisc, Inc. **469:** (#11) © Barbara Penoyar/PhotoDisc, Inc. **469:** right, (#11) © Barbara Penoyar/PhotoDisc, Inc. **469:** (#4) PhotoDisc, Inc. **469:** (#5) PhotoDisc, Inc. **469:** (#9) PhotoDisc, Inc. **471:** top, James Bennet/ *The New York Times* **471:** center, © AP Images/Raanan Cohen **472:** © Dean Mouhtaropoulos/Getty Images **473:** (criminal) PhotoDisc, Inc. **473:** (nun) PhotoDisc, Inc. **473:** bottom right, (twins w/dogs) © Michael Nichols/Magnum Photos **473:** bottom left, PhotoDisc, Inc. **473:** top left, © Tor Richardsen/AFP/Getty Images **474:** left, PhotoDisc, Inc. **474:** top right, PhotoDisc, Inc. **474:** bottom right, PhotoDisc, Inc. **475:** top, Corel Gallery **475:** top right, PhotoDisc, Inc. **475:** bottom right, PhotoDisc, Inc. **475:** left, Photodisc, Inc. **476:** (#6) © *Los Angeles Times* Photo by Lawrence K. Ho **477:** (#14) James Bennet/ *The New York Times* **477:** (#18) Corel Gallery **478:** PhotoDisc, Inc.

Module 21

481: right, © Arlene Gottfried **482:** left, PhotoDisc, Inc. **482:** right, PhotoDisc, Inc. **482:** center, PhotoDisc, Inc. **483:** left, PhotoDisc, Inc. **484:** top left, PhotoDisc, Inc. **484:** top right, PhotoDisc, Inc. **484:** right, © Ron Dahlquist/Stone/Getty Images **486:** bottom, PhotoDisc, Inc. **487:** top center, PhotoDisc, Inc. **488:** top, Digital Stock Corporation **488:** bottom left, © Lennart Nilsson, *The Incredible Machine*, National Geographic Society, by permission of Bokforlaget Bonnier Alba AB. **489:** top, © Royalty Free/Corbis **490:** top, © Arlene Gottfried **490:** center, © Christoph Wilhelm/Photodisc Red/Getty Images **490:** left, © Laryy Dale Gordon/The Image Bank/Getty Images **491:** center, PhotoDisc, Inc. **491:** bottom right, © 1991 David Turnley/Detroit Free Press/Corbis **491:** top left, © AP Images/Kristie Bull/Graylock.com **493:** left, PhotoDisc, Inc. **493:** center, © Arlene Gottfried **494:** right, PhotoDisc, Inc. **494:** left, © Joe Klamar/AFP/Getty Images **495:** left, (both) PhotoDisc, Inc. **497:** top, PhotoDisc, Inc.; **497:** bottom left, © Juan Silva/The Image Bank/Getty Images **498:** (#13) © Joe Klamar/AFP/Getty Images **498:** (#14) PhotoDisc, Inc.; **498:** (#9) © Laryy Dale Gordon/The Image Bank/Getty Images **499:** right, PhotoDisc, Inc. **499:** left, © R. W. Jones/Corbis **501:** inset, © Fredrik Renander/Alamy **501:** right, © Richard J. Davidson, Director, W.M. Kcck Laboratory for Functional Brain Imaging and Behavior **502:** top, PhotoDisc, Inc. **502:** left, PhotoDisc, Inc. **503:** (#20) PhotoDisc, Inc. **503:** right, © Benno de Wilde/Imageshop/Alamy **505:** (#17) PhotoDisc, Inc. **505:** inset, (#19) © Fredrik Renander/Alamy **505:** (#20) PhotoDisc, Inc. **506:** © Robert Laberge/Getty Images

Photo Credits

Module 22

509: right, © Elizabeth Roll **509:** left, © Larry W. Smith/AFP/Getty Images **510:** right, © Henrik Drescher **511:** (top and center) © *San Diego Union-Tribune*/Rick McCarthy **511:** left, PhotoDisc, Inc. **511:** bottom right, © Henrik Drescher **512:** bottom center, © AP Images/Tim Kimzey **512:** top, © William Cambell/*Time Magazine*/Getty Images **513:** © AP Images/Ruth Fremson **514:** top, © AP Images/Tim Kimzey **514:** right, © Elizabeth Roll **515:** © Larry W. Smith/AFP/Getty Images **518:** center, © Elizabeth Roll **520:** left, © Marvin Mattelson **521:** (#2) © Henrik Drescher **521:** (#3) © *San Diego Union-Tribune*/Rick McCarthy **521:** (#4) © AP Images/Tim Kimzey **522:** right, PhotoDisc, Inc. **522:** left, © David Young-Wolff/PhotoEdit **523:** bottom left, *People Weekly* © 2001 Axel Koester **524:** both, © Elizabeth Roll **526:** (#1) © *San Diego Union-Tribune*/Rick McCarthy **526:** (#4) ©AP Images/Ruth Fremson **527:** (#14) © Marvin Mattelson **528:** © GN/RCS Reuters

Module 23

531: left, © Robert Gauthier (originally appeared in *San Diego Union-Tribune* 2/27/94, p. 1) **531:** right, © Robert Gauthier (originally appeared in *San Diego Union-Tribune* 2/27/94, p. 12) **532:** left, © Evan Agostini/Getty Images **532:** center, © Robert Gauthier (originally appeared in *San Diego Union-Tribune*) **533:** top, © Evan Agostini/Getty Images **533:** right, © Matthew Klein/Corbis **534:** left, © Evan Agostini/Getty Images **534:** right, © Robert Gauthier (originally appeared in *San Diego Union-Tribune*) **535:** © Photo Researchers, Inc. **536:** © Reuters/Corbis **538:** © Robert Gauthier (originally appeared in *San Diego Union-Tribune*) **539:** center, Courtesy of Edna Morlok **539:** top, © Robert Gauthier (originally appeared in *San Diego Union-Tribune*) **540:** top left, Courtesy of Drs. E. Fuller Torrey & Daniel R. Weinberger, NIMH, Neuroscience Center, Washington D.C. **540:** right, © Robert Gauthier (originally appeared in *San Diego Union-Tribune*) **541:** top, © Robert Gauthier (originally appeared in *San Diego Union-Tribune* 2/27/94) **541:** right, © Robert Gauthier (originally appeared in *San Diego Union-Tribune*) **543:** (#10) © Robert Gauthier (originally appeared in *San Diego Union-Tribune*) **543:** (#9) © Reuters/Corbis **544:** © AP Images/ *The Denver Post*/Karl Gehring **545:** Craig McClain **547:** (top and left) PhotoLink/PhotoDisc, Inc. **550:** (#8) © Reuters/Corbis **551:** (#16) Craig McClain **551:** (#19) PhotoLink/PhotoDisc, Inc.

Module 24

555: right, Digital Stock Corporation **555:** left, Mary Evans/Sigmund Freud Copyrights/Sulloway **555:** top center, PhotoDisc, Inc. **556:** center left, National Library of Medicine neg# A-13392 **556:** bottom left, National Library of Medicine, neg# A-13394 **556:** right, Photo by Ken Smith of painting in Harrisburg State Hospital/LLR Collection **557:** left, © AP Images/Rusty Kennedy **557:** right, © Bernard Gotfryd/Woodfin Camp & Associates **558:** PhotoDisc, Inc. **559:** S. Wanke/PhotoLink/PhotoDisc, Inc. **561:** bottom, Mary Evans/Sigmund Freud Copyrights/Sulloway **563:** Image credit, © Zohar Lazar **566:** center, Digital Stock Corporation **566:** top left, PhotoDisc, Inc. **567:** © Elizabeth Roll **572:** © Roger Dashow/AnthroPhoto **573:** *Los Angeles Times* Photo by Al Seib **574:** top, PhotoDisc, Inc. **574:** bottom, PhotoDisc, Inc. **575:** © Rob Bartee/SuperStock **576:** (#1) National Library of Medicine neg# A-13392 **577:** (#22) © Roger Dashow/AnthroPhoto

Module 25

581: left, © Ted Hardin **582:** bottom left, By permission of Dr. Victor Johnston, author of *Why We Feel* **582:** top, (both) © Ted Hardin **583:** top, From "The Effect of Race and Sex on Physicians' Recommendations for Cardiac Catheterization" by K. A. Schulman et al., 1999, *The New England Journal of Medicine*, 2/5/99, pp. 621–622. Copyright © 1999, Massachusetts Medical Society. Reprinted by permission of publisher and Interactive Drama. **583:** left, PhotoDisc, Inc. **583:** right, PhotoDisc, Inc. **584:** left, PhotoDisc, Inc. **584:** bottom left, PhotoDisc, Inc. **584:** right, PhotoDisc, Inc. **584:** top, © James Wilson/Woodfin Camp & Associates **585:** right, PhotoDisc, Inc. **585:** top, © Robert Johnson **586:** left, PhotoDisc, Inc. **586:** right, PhotoDisc, Inc. **586:** top, ©AP Images/Autodesk/Court Mast **587:** top, PhotoDisc, Inc. **587:** left, PhotoDisc, Inc. **589:** © Wade Spees **590:** Courtesy of Floyd Cochran. **591:** bottom, © Scott Gries/Getty Images **591:** top, © Steve Pope/Landov Images **595:** top, © Alan Weiner **596:** right, Jim LoScalzo/ *U.S. News & World Report* **596:** left, *People Weekly* © 1993 Taro Yamasaki **597:** left, © Bill Ross/Woodfin Camp & Associates **597:** right, © Dan Miller/Woodfin Camp & Associates **597:** center, © Reuters/Corbis **598:** (all) PhotoDisc, Inc. **599:** (#1) © Ted Hardin **599:** (#11) © Steve Pope/Landov **599:** (#13) © Bill Ross/Woodfin Camp & Associates **599:** (#15) PhotoDisc, Inc. **599:** (#4) PhotoDisc, Inc. **599:** (#6) PhotoDisc, Inc. **599:** (#8) Courtesy of Floyd Cochran. **600:** top left, © Photo24/Brand X Pictures/Getty Images **600:** right, © Topham/OB/The Image Works **600:** center, © Zig Leszczynski/Animals, Animals **601:** top, PhotoDisc, Inc. **601:** left, PhotoDisc, Inc. **601:** right, © 2003 AP Images/Eduardo Di Baia **602:** (left and right) PhotoDisc, Inc. **602:** top, PhotoDisc, Inc. **603:** bottom, © Thomas Hartwell/Corbis - SABA **604:** center, PhotoDisc., Inc. **604:** right, © Topham/OB/The Image Works **606:** (#1) © James Wilson/Woodfin Camp & Associates **606:** (#5) PhotoDisc, Inc. **606:** (#9) © Steve Pope/Landov **607:** (#13) Jim LoScalzo/ *U.S. News & World Report* **607:** (#17) © Topham/OB/The Image Works **607:** (#20) PhotoDisc., Inc. **608:** © Bob Pardue/Alamy

Figure/Text Credits

This page constitutes an extension of the copyright page. We have made every effort to trace the ownership of all copyrighted material and to secure permission from copyright holders. In the event of any question arising as to the use of any material, we will be pleased to make the necessary corrections in future printings. Thanks are due to the following authors, publishers, and agents for permission to use the material indicated.

Front Matter

viii: (bottom left) Based on an illustration in *Scientific American Mind,* April/May, 2006, p. 18 by Jason Lee. By permission of Jason Lee.

Module 1

6: Graph data from "Arithmetic calculation, deep inspiration or handgrip exercise-mediated pre-operational active palmar sweating responses in humans," by Masayoshi Kobayashi, Noriko Tomioka, Yoshihisa Ushiyama and Toshio Ohhashi *Autonomic Neuroscience,* Volume 104, Issue 1, pp. 58–65. **17:** Pie chart data from "Psychological Science Around the World," by M. R. Rosenzweig, 1992, *American Psychologist, 47,* 718–22. **21:** Excuses list from "Excuses, Excuses," by D. A. Bernstein, 1993, *APS Observer,* March, 1993, Vol 6, No. 2, p. 4. Copyright © 1993 by the Association for Psychological Sciences. Reprinted by permission of the author.

Module 3

58: Based on an illustration in *Scientific American Mind,* April/May, 2006, p. 18 by Jason Lee. By permission of Jason Lee

Module 4

68: Chromosome drawing (right) redrawn by permission from an illustration on p. 126 by Michael Goodman in "DNA's New Twists," by John Rennie, *Scientific American,* March, 1993. All rights reserved. **79:** (bottom left) From "Language Specificity and Elasticity: Brain and Clinical Syndrome Studies," by M. Maratsos and L. Matheny, 1994, *Annual Review of Psychology, 45,* 487–516. **79:** (bottom right) Adapted from *Left Brain, Right Brain,* by S. P. Springer and G. Deutsch, 4/e, 1989. W. H. Freeman Company. **84:** (houses and letter L) Based on data from *Sex Differences in Cognitive Abilities,* by D. F. Halpern, 2000. Lawrence Erlbaum Associates.

Module 5

114: (top) Illustration based on K. Daniel Clark from "Newsfronts: Science & Technology," by Dawn Stover, *Popular Science,* August 1997 p. 29. Reprinted by permission.

Module 8

188: Adapted from "How AA Works and Why It's Important for Clinicians to Understand," by E. J. Khantzian and J. E. Mack, 1994, *Journal of Substance Abuse Treatment, 11,* 77–92.

Module 9

196: Bar graph data from "Pitch Discrimination in the Dog," by H. M. Anrep, 1920, *Journal of Physiology, 53,* 367–385. **206:** Graph adapted from "Emotional Fainting and the Psychophysiologic Response to Blood and Injury: Autonomic Mechanisms and Coping Strategies," by A. Steptoe and J. Wardle, 1988, *Psychosomatic Medicine, 50,* 402–417.

Module 10

214: Graph on right based on data from *Behavior of Organisms,* by B. F. Skinner, 1938. Appleton-Century-Crofts. **215:** Skinner box illustration from *Introduction to Psychology* by E. Bruce Goldstein, 1995. Brooks/Cole. **216:** Adapted from "Treating Chronic Food Refusal in Young Children: Home-Based Parent Training," by M. A. Werle, T. B. Murphy & K. S. Budd, 1993, *Journal of Applied Behavior Analysis, 26,* 421–433. **220:** Reinforcement diagram from *Psychology: Themes and Variations,* by Wayne Weiten, 2nd ed., figure 6.13. Copyright © 1992 by Wadsworth, Inc. Reproduced by permission. **221:** Based on data from the U.S. Department of the Navy and an illustration by Suzy Parker, *USA Today,* March 27, 2003, p. 8D. **225:** Bar graph data from "Relative Efficacy of Densensitization and Modeling Approaches for Inducing Behavior, Affective and Attitudinal Changes" by A. Bandura, E. B. Blanchard & B. Ritter, 1969, *Journal of Personality and Social Psychology, 13,* 173–179. **227:** (top, #1) Skinner box illustration from *Introduction to Psychology* by E. Bruce Goldstein, 1995. Brooks/Cole **230:** Graph from "Analysis of a High-Probability Instructional Sequence and Time-Out in the Treatment of Child Non-compliance," by A. K. Rortvedt and R. G. Miltenberger, 1994, *Journal of Applied Behavior Analysis, 27,* 327–330, figure 1a. Copyright © 1993 Society for the Experimental Analysis of Behavior. Reprinted by permission of the author. **234:** (#1 graph) Adapted from "Treating Chronic Food Refusal in Young Children: Home-Based Parent Training," by M. A. Werle, T. B. Murphy & K. S. Budd, 1993, *Journal of Applied Behavior Analysis, 26,* 421–433.

Module 11

253: Bar graph data from "Repeated Memory of Oral Prose in Ghana and New York," by B. M. Ross and C. Millson, 1970, *International Journal of Psychology, 5,* 173–181. **253:** Excerpt from *Remembering: A Study in Experimental and Social Psychology,* by F. C. Bartlett, p. 65, 1932. Cambridge University Press. Copyright © 1932. Reprinted with the permission of Cambridge University Press. **255:** Adapted from "Vivid Memories," by D. C. Rubin and M. Kozin, 1984, *Cognition, 16,* 81–95. Copyright © 1984 by Elsevier Science Publishers BV. Adapted by permission from Elsevier Science.

Module 12

261: Adapted from "Nearly 2,000 Witnesses Can Be Wrong," by R. Buckout, 1980, *Bulletin of the Psychonomic Society, 16,* 307–310. **262:** Memory figure based on Learning and Memory, by D. A. Norman, 1982. W. H. Freeman & Company. **263:** Network hierarchy based on "Retrieval time from semantic memory," by A.M. Colins and M. R. Quillian, 1969, *Verbal Learning and Verbal Behavior, 8,* 240–247. **270:** (#4) Graph data from "Fifty Years of Memory for Names and Faces," by H. P. Bahrick, P. O. Bahrick & R. P. Wittlinger, 1975, *Journal of Experimental Psychology: General, 104,* 54–75. **276:** (#5) Graph data from "Fifty Years of Memory for Names and Faces," by H. P. Bahrick, P. O. Bahrick & R. P. Wittlinger, 1975, *Journal of Experimental Psychology: General, 104,* 54–75.

Module 13

287: (center) Graphs Adapted from "Age and WAIS-R A Cross-Sectional Analysis with Educational Level Controlled, " by A. S. Kaufman, C. R. Reynolds & J. E. McLean, 1989, *Intelligence, 13,* pp. 246–247. Copyright © 1989 by Ablex Publishing Company. Adapted by permission. **294:** Figure adapted with the permission of The Free Press, a Division of Simon & Schuster Adult Publishing Group, from *The Bell Curve: Intelligence and Class Structure in America* by Richard E. Hernstein and Charles Murray, p. 279. Copyright © 1994 Richard J. Hernstein and Charles Murray. All rights reserved. **295:** (right, #7) Graph adapted from "Age and WAIS-R A Cross-Sectional Analysis with Educational Level Controlled," by A. S. Kaufman, C. R. Reynolds & J. E. McLean, 1989, *Intelligence, 13,* pp. 246–247. Copyright © 1989 by Ablex Publishing Company. Adapted by permission.

Module 14

309: (top left and p. **317**) Adapted from *Conceptual Blockbusting: A Guide to Better Ideas,* by James L. Adams, pp. 17–18. Copyright © 2001, 1974 by James L. Adams. Adapted by permission of Da Capo Press, a member of Perseus Books Group. **326:** Article adapted from "The Language of Learning," by Robert Lee Hotz, 1997, *Los Angeles Times,* Sept. 18, 1997, p. B2. Copyright © 1997 by the *Los Angeles Times.* Adapted by permission of the publisher.

Module 15

348: (TAT) From *Abnormal Psychology* by Barlow/Durand, 2/E, p. 79. Copyright © 1997. Brooks/Cole Publishing.

Module 16

370: (bottom, center) Redrawn from an illustration by John Tom Seetin in "Working Knowlege," *Scientific American, 277* (6), December, 1997, p. 132. Reprinted by permission of the illustrator. All rights reserved.

Module 17

380: Bar graph adapted from a figure in *The Developing Human: Clinically Oriented Embryology,* 4th ed., by Keith L. Moore. W. B. Saunders Co., Copyright © 1988 by Keith L. Moore. Adapted by permission of the author.

Figure/Text Credits

Module 18

407: Prom queen adapted from *Midterm Report*, by D. Wallechinsky, 1986. Viking Press. **413:** Ida and Christopher excerpt from *Parade Magazine*, July 14, 1991, pp. 6–7. Reprinted with permission from Parade. Copyright © 1991. **420:** Graph based on data from "Marital Happiness Cross the Family Life Cycle: A Longitudinal Analysis," by M. H. Benin and I. B. Robinson, cited in *Time*, August 25, 1997, p. 24. **420:** List adapted from "Preferences in Human Mate Selection," by D. M. Buss and M. Barnes, 1986, *Journal of Personality and Social Psychology, 7*, 3–15. American Psychological Association. **423:** (list center) adapted from "Mate Preferences in 37 Cultures," by D. M. Buss, 1994. In W. J. Lonner & R. Malpass (Eds.), *Psychology and Culture.* Allyn and Bacon. **423:** (list bottom) adapted from "International Preferences in Selecting Mates," by D. M. Buss, M. Abbott, A. Angleitner, A. Asherian, A. Biaggio, A. Blanoco-Villasenor, A. Bruchon-Scwietzer, H. Y. Ch'U, J. Czapinski, B. Deraad, B. Ekehammar, N. E. Lohamy, M. Fioravanti, J. Georgas, P. Gjerde, R. Guttmann, E. Hazan, S. Iwawaki, H. Jankiramaiah, F. Khosroshani, D. Kreitler, L. Lachenicht, M. Lee, K. Kiik, B. Little, S. Mika, M. Moadel-Shahid, G. Moane, M. Montero, A. C. Mundy-Castle, T. Niit, E. Nsenduluka, R. Pienkowski, A. M. Pirttila-Backman, J. P. De Leon, J. Rousseau, M. A. Runco, M. P. Safir, C. Samuels, R. Sanitioso, R. Serpell, N. Smid, C. Spencer, M. Tadinac, E. N. Tordorova, Z. K. Troland, L. Van Den Brande, G. Van Heck, L. Van Langenhove & K. S. Yang, 1990, *Journal of Cross-Cultural Personality, 21*, 5–47, and additional data from "Mate Preferences in 37 Cultures," by D. M. Buss. In W. J. Lonner & R. Malpass (Eds.), *Psychology and Culture.* Allyn & Bacon. **429:** (#13) List adapted from "International Preferences in Selecting Mates," by D. M. Buss, M. Abbott, A. Angleitner, A. Asherian, A. Biaggio, A. Blanoco-Villasenor, A. Bruchon-Scwietzer, H. Y. Ch'U, J. Czapinski, B. Deraad, B. Ekehammar, N. E. Lohamy, M. Fioravanti, J. Georgas, P. Gjerde, R. Guttmann, E. Hazan, S. Iwawaki, H. Jankiramaiah, F. Khosroshani, D. Kreitler, L. Lachenicht, M. Lee, K. Kiik, B. Little, S. Mika, M. Moadel-Shahid, G. Moane, M. Montero, A. C. Mundy-Castle, T. Niit, E. Nsenduluka, R. Pienkowski, A. M. Pirttila-Backman, J. P. De Leon, J. Rousseau, M. A. Runco, M. P. Safir, C. Samuels, R. Sanitioso, R. Serpell, N. Smid, C. Spencer, M. Tadinac, E. N. Tordorova, Z. K. Troland, L. Van Den Brande, G. Van Heck, L. Van Langenhove & K. S. Yang, 1990, *Journal of Cross-Cultural Personality, 21*, 5–47, and additional data from "Mate Preferences in 37 Cultures," by D. M. Buss. In W. J. Lonner & R. Malpass (Eds.), *Psychology and Culture.* Allyn & Bacon.

Module 19

450: (right TAT) From *Abnormal Psychology* by Barlow/Durand, 2/E, p. 79. Copyright © 1997. Brooks/Cole Publishing.

Module 20

467: Bar graph data from "Genes, Environment, and Personality," by T. J. Bouchard, 1994, *Science, 264*, 1700–1701. American Association for the Advancement of Science. Additional data from Bouchard & Loehlin, 2001. **468:** Bar graph data from "Genes, Environment, and Personality," by T. J. Bouchard, 1994, *Science, 264*, 1700–1701. American Association for the Advancement of Science. Additional data from Bouchard & Loehlin, 2001, Plomin & Crabbe, 2000.

Module 21

481: Text about Sandra Sullivan, adapted from an article by Sasha Nyary, *Life Magazine*, April, 1992 pp. 62–65. **483:** Situation list data from *USA Today*, August 19, 1987, p. 4D. **486:** List adapted from "The Factor Structure of Self-Reported Physical Stress Reactions," by J. C. Smith and J. M. Seidel, 1982, *Biofeedback and Self-Regulation, 7*, 35–47. Springer Netherlands. **490:** Scale: Reprinted from "Life changes scaling for the 1990s," by M. A. Miller and R. H. Rahe, *Journal of Psychosomatic Research, 43*, 279–292, Copyright © 1997, with permission from Elsevier Science. **490:** Text about Sandra Sullivan, adapted from an article by Sasha Nyary, *Life Magazine*, April, 1992, pp. 62–65. **501:** Graph data from "Body Temperature Changes During the Practice of g Tum-mo-Yoga," by H. Benson, J. W. Lehmann, M. S. Malhotra, R. F. Goldman, P. J. Hopkins & M. D. Epstein, 1982, *Nature, 295*, 234–235. **505:** (#19) Graph data from "Body Temperature Changes During the Practice of g Tum-mo-Yoga," by H. Benson, J. W. Lehmann, M. S. Malhotra, R. F. Goldman, P. J. Hopkins & M. D. Epstein, 1982, *Nature, 295*, 234–235.

Module 22

514: pp. 514–515: Syndrome titles from *Diagnostic and Statistical Manual of Mental Disorders*, Fourth Edition. Copyright © 1994 American Psychiatric Association. **518:** (bottom) Bar graphs data on phobias from "Panic and Phobia" by W. W. Eaton, A. Dryman & M. M. Weissman, 1991. In L. N. Robins & D. A. Regier (Eds.), *Psychiatric Disorders in America: The Epidemiological Catchment Area Study.* Free Press. **519:** Bar graph data from "Current Status of Pharmacological and Behavioral Treatment of Obsessive-Compulsive Disorder," by G. B. Stanley and S. M. Turner, 1995, *Behavior Therapy, 26*, 163–186.

Module 23

531: (Chuck Elliot) Adapted from "Breakdown into the Shadows of Mental Illness, " by C. Brooks, *San Diego Union-Tribune*, February 27, 1994, p. 4. **531:** (Michael McCabe) Adapted from "Shadowland: Three Profiled in Mental Illness Series Are Striving to Improve Their Condition" " by C. Brooks, *San Diego Union-Tribune*, February 27, 1995. **535:** (left) Excerpt from "Electroboy," by Andy Behrman. Copyright © 1999. Reprinted by permission of the author. **539:** Bar graph data from *Schizophrenia Genesis: The Origins of Madness*, by I. I. Gottesmann, 1991. W. H. Freeman & Company; with additional data from "The Epidemiology of Schizophrenia in a Finnish Twin Cohort," by T. D. Cannon, J. Kaprio, J. Lonnqvist, M. Huttunen & M. Koskenvuo, 1998, *Archives of General Psychiatry, 55*, 67–74. **543:** (#5) Bar graph data from "Current Perspectives on the Genetics of Unipolar Depression," by S. O. Moldin, T. Reich & J. P. Rice, 1991, *Behavior Genetics, 21*, 211–242. **543:** (#7) ECT treatment graph adapted from "Use of ECT with Treatment-Resistant Depressed Patients at the National Institute of Mental Health," by S. M. Paul, I. Extein, H. M. Calil, W. Z. Potter, P. Chodiff & F. K. Goodwin, 1981, *American Journal of Psychiatry, 138*, 486–489. **545:** Bar graph data from "The Diagnosis of Multiple Personality Disorder: A Critical Review," by T. A. Fahy, 1988, *British Journal of Psychiatry, 153*, 597–606; and "Multiple Identity Enactments and Multiple Personality Disorder: A Sociocognitive Perspective," by N. P. Spanos, 1994, *Psychological Bulletin, 116*, 1434–1465. **547:** Bar graph data from "Exercise treatment for major depression: Maintenance of therapeutic benefits at 10 months," by M. Babyak, et al., 2000, *Psychosomatic Medicine, 62*, 633–638.

Module 24

560: Therapy Session Adapted from "A Critique of So-Called Standard Psychoanalytic Technique," by S. D. Lipton, 1983, *Contemporary Psychoanalysis, 19*, 35–52. **564:** Therapy Session: Adapted from "Person-Centered Therapy," by N. J. Raskin and C. R. Rogers, 1989. In R. J. Corsini and D. Wedding (Eds.), *Current Psychotherapies*, 4th ed. F. E. Peacock. **565:** Therapy Session: Adapted from *Cognitive Therapy of Depression*, by A. T. Beck, A. J. Rush, B. F. Shaw & G. Emery, 1979, pp. 145–146. Guilford Press. **566:** Therapy Session: Adapted from *Clinical Behavior Therapy*, by M. R. Goldfried and G. C. Davison, 1976. Holt, Rinehart & Winston.

Module 25

592: Asch study based on "Effects of Group Pressure Upon Modification and Distortion of Judgements," by Solomon Asch, 1958. In E. Maccoby, T. M. Newcomb & E. L. Hartley (Eds.), Readings in *Social Psychology* (3rd Ed.). Holt, Rinehart & Winston. **606:** (#8) Bar graph data from "Improving the Academic Performance of College Freshmen," by T. D. Wilson and P. W. Linville, 1982, *Journal of Personality and Social Psychology, 42*, 367–376. American Psychological Association.

Name Index

Name Index

Name Index

Name Index

Subject Index

and stress management programs, 502
Approach-approach conflict, 492
Approach-avoidance conflict, 492
Arab people/cultures, 367, 471
Armstrong, Lance, 506
Arousal:
    and autonomic nervous system, 81
    and drug use, 175, 176, 177
    and emotions, 360, 361, 365
    and lie detector tests, 370–371
    and prosocial behavior, 595
    and REM sleep, 153
    and shyness, 449
    and stress, 483, 484, 485, 491, 493
    and test anxiety, 6
Arousal-cost-reward model of helping, 595
Artificial intelligence, 308
Artificial senses, 114–115
Asch, Solomon, 592, 593
Asian people/cultures:
    academic achievement, 448
    ADHD diagnoses, 29
    autism, 11
    autonomic nervous system control, 501
    cognitive processes, 321
    dental fears, 205
    drug use, 176, 185
    emotions, 367, 374
    gender roles, 399
    healing, 113, 572
    and intelligence, 283, 291
    mental disorders, 522, 546
    organ transplants, 603
    perception, 136
    and placebos, 31
    Suzuki method, 231
    weight, 337
Aspartame (Nutrasweet), 30
Assessment:
    mental disorders, 512–513
    personality, 9, 450–451, 474–475, 478, 512
    See also Diagnosis
Assimilation, 388
Assisted suicide, 427
Association areas, 78, 79, 97, 103, 125
Associations (memory), forming, 248, 249, 262, 265
Astrology, 475
Atkinson, John, 348
Atmospheric perspective, 131
Attachment, 377, 385
Attention:
    and brain structure, 76, 77
    and circadian preference, 155
    and consciousness, 148
    controlled vs. automatic processes, 148
    and drug use, 181, 192
    and emotions, 365
    and memory, 240, 241, 242, 243, 244, 245, 269
    and pain, 112, 113
    and perception, 135

and problem-solving, 309
and schizophrenia, 538
and social cognitive theory, 223, 225, 231
See also Attention-deficit/hyperactivity disorder
Attention-deficit/hyperactivity disorder (ADHD):
    controversies about, 27, 39
    and prenatal influences, 381
    research on, 28, 29, 30, 34, 35, 36–37
Attitudes, 588–591, 603
Attractiveness, 137, 582, 603
Attributions, 585–587, 604
Atypical neuroleptic drugs, 541, 542, 557
Audience, 591
Audition. See Hearing
Auditory association area, 78, 103
Auditory canal, 102
Auditory nerve, 103
Australia, 272
Australopithecus afarensis, 67, 69
Authoritarian parents, 413
Authoritative parents, 413
Authority, 593–594
Autism, 3
    behavioral approach to, 8
    behavior therapy for, 232, 568
    biological approach to, 6
    cognitive approach to, 7
    critical thinking exercise, 24
    cross-cultural approach to, 11
    and goals of psychology, 4
    humanistic approach to, 10
    psychoanalytic approach to, 9
    and savants, 7, 302, 311, 378
Automatic detector, 320
Automatic encoding, 248
Automatic processes, 148
Autonomic nervous system (ANS), 72, 81, 360, 484, 485, 501, 503
Autonomy vs. shame/doubt stage of psychosocial development, 393
Availability heuristic, 308
Aviophobia, 509, 524
Avoidance-avoidance conflict, 492
Awareness. See Consciousness
Axes (DSM-IV-TR), 514, 515
Axon membrane, 52, 53
Axons, 50, 51, 52, 540

B

Babbling, 314
BAC (blood alcohol content), 55
Backward conditioning, 202, 217
Bait shyness, 200
Balance, 102, 105
Bali, 572
Bandura, Albert:
    on aggression, 196, 224
    on anxiety, 493
    and behaviorism, 8
    on personality, 458, 459
    and Suzuki, 231
    See also Social cognitive theory
Barnum principle, 475

Bartz, Carol, 586
Basal ganglia, 60, 61, 150, 186, 541
Basic rules of grammar, 315
Basilar membrane, 103
Bear gallbladders, 31
Beauty, 137, 582, 603
Beck, Aaron, 565
Beck's cognitive theory of depression, 548, 549
Behavioral approach, 5, 8, 13, 223. See also Behavior therapy; Classical conditioning; Cognitive-behavioral therapy; Operant conditioning; Social cognitive theory
Behavioral genetics, 466
Behavior modification. See Behavior therapy
Behaviors:
    and attitudes, 588, 590
    and classical conditioning, 195
    defined, 4, 458
Behavior therapy, 566
    for ADHD, 39
    for autism, 232
    biofeedback, 233, 503, 568
    and child abuse, 401
    for motion sickness, 105
    operant conditioning, 216
    origins of, 555, 556
    systematic desensitization, 207, 567
    time-out, 230, 233
    See also Classical conditioning; Cognitive-behavioral therapy; Operant conditioning
Beliefs, 27, 30, 112, 135, 210, 258, 588, 590
The Bell Curve (Herrnstein & Murray), 290, 294
Bem, Daryl, 139
Benson, Herbert, 501
Benzodiazepines, 162, 163, 517, 525
Berkowitz, David, 536
Berry, Halle, 247, 281
Bias:
    and attributions, 586
        and brain size, 85
    in case studies, 30
    and deception, 40
    in IQ tests, 14, 290–291, 296
    and labeling, 516
    and memory, 265
    and perception, 124, 125, 135
    and person perception, 581, 583
    and schemas, 584
    in standardized tests, 34
    and surveys, 28, 29
    See also Discrimination
Bidirectionality principle, 401
Big Brothers/Big Sisters of America, 446
Big Five traits, 463, 467, 468
Bilingualism, 319
Binet, Alfred, 284, 285, 290
Binet-Simon Intelligence Scale, 285
Binge drinking, 44
Binocular depth cues, 129
Biofeedback, 233, 503, 568

Biological approach. See Biological factors
Biological clocks, 150–151, 155, 156, 157, 159
Biological factors:
    gender identity, 341
    hunger, 334, 335
    learning, 228–229
    memory, 263, 268–269
    mood disorders, 533
    overview, 5, 6
    personality disorders, 537
    schizophrenia, 539
    sexual behavior, 338, 339, 341, 343
    weight, 352
    See also Brain; Nature-nurture question; Neuroscience
Biological needs, 330, 332. See also Hunger; Sexual behavior
Biological psychology, 19
BioPsychoSocial approach to adolescence, 409
Biosocial theory of sexual behavior, 342
Bipolar I disorder, 311, 531, 532, 534
Birth control, 409
Birth defects, 379, 380
Bisexual orientation, 341
Blackouts, 182
Blindness, 93, 97, 98, 114, 144, 150, 161, 364
Blind spot, 96
Blinking, 241
Blood, as food, 110
Blood alcohol content (BAC), 55
Blood-brain barrier, 59
Boat people, 448
Bobo doll experiment, 196, 224
Body temperature, 155, 157
Bonobos, 323
Bowlby, John, 385
Brain, 67–91
    and biological clocks, 150, 155
    and classical conditioning, 201
    and concept formation, 307
    control centers, 74–79
    development of, 48, 314, 382, 391, 411, 441, 523, 539, 601
    and drug use, 73, 175, 188, 330
    effects of child abuse on, 401
    and endocrine system, 82
    evolution of, 69
    gender differences, 84, 85, 284, 321, 396
    and genetic factors, 68, 69
    head transplants, 64
    and hearing, 78, 103, 104
    hemispheres of, 7, 73, 76, 86–87, 321, 415
    and hunger, 335
    and intelligence, 85, 284, 297, 322, 323
    and language, 78, 313, 314, 316, 322, 323, 391
    limbic system, 80–81, 112, 161, 186, 362, 411
    and memory, 76, 80, 255, 263, 268–269

Subject Index

and mind-body question, 49
and nervous system, 72
neurons, 48–49, 50, 73, 269, 314, 540
and operant conditioning, 219
and pain, 112, 113
and perception, 125, 132
and phantom limb, 58
regrowth in, 49
size of, 50, 69, 85, 284, 297, 322, 323
and sleep deprivation, 157
and smell, 107
and speech, 78, 87, 229
and stress, 484, 485
structure of, 48
student activities, 83, 88–91, 620–621
study techniques, 70–71
and touch, 108
and vision, 79, 97, 99
See also Brain damage; Brain scanning/imaging; Cognitive neuroscience; Drug effects on nervous system; Executive functions of brain; Nervous system; Neuroscience; Neurotransmitters
Brain damage:
and drug use, 181
and emotions, 362
and lobotomies, 75
and memory, 239, 242, 245, 246, 265, 268, 278
recovery from, 49, 51
and smell, 107
and unconsciousness, 149
See also Neuroscience
Brain death, 90, 149
Brain scanning/imaging, 70–71. *See also* Neuroscience
Brain sides. *See* Hemispheres (brain)
Brain stimulation, 61
Breast cancer, 122
Breast feeding, 33
Breuer, Joseph, 555
Brightness constancy, 128
Broca, Paul, 284
Broca's aphasia, 78
Broca's area, 78, 229, 316
Browne, Sylvia, 139
Bulimia nervosa, 353
Buprenorhinenaloxone, 179
Burke, Chris, 288
Burma, 137
Burnout, 491
Bush, George W., 60
Bystander effect, 597

C

Caffeine, 178, 192
Calkins, Mary, 14
Calories, 334
Cancer, 33, 122, 195, 206–207, 506
Careers, 17–19
Care orientation, 412
Carey, Mariah, 491
Cartoons, 137

Case studies/personal profiles:
ADHD, 27
adolescence, 407
adoption, 377
adulthood, 407
Alzheimer's disease, 47
anencephaly, 67
autism, 3
behavioral genetics, 466
behavior therapy, 204, 224, 555, 566
blindness, 93, 98
brain damage, 67, 75
child abuse, 400
classical conditioning, 195
creativity, 305, 310
determination, 457
discrimination, 14, 457
drug use, 169, 174, 188, 464
dyslexia, 320
emotions, 359
fragile X syndrome, 67
Freudian psychologists, 440
hypnosis, 169
intelligence, 281
isolation experiment, 147
language, 305
learning, 213
lie detector tests, 370
memory, 239
mental disorders, 509, 531, 532, 544, 545
mild depression, 548
motivation, 329, 348, 350
olfaction ability, 107
panic disorder, 481, 500
Parkinson's disease, 60
perception, 121
personality, 417, 433, 470
prodigies, 378
psychic phenomena, 138, 139
psychoanalysis, 555, 561
school shootings, 523
severed limbs, 51, 58
spinal cord injuries, 51
split-brain operations, 86–87
stress, 481, 494
suicide, 426
systematic desensitization, 567
Case study approach, 28, 30, 35, 310
and Freudian theory, 561, 563
Catatonic schizophrenia, 538, 546
Categorization, 307
Catharsis, 605
Cattell, Raymond, 462
Causation vs. correlation, 33
CCK (cholecystokinin), 335
Cell body (soma), 50, 382
Central cues, 335
Central nervous system (CNS), 51, 72, 182
Central route for persuasion, 591
Central tendency, measures of, 611–612
Cephalocaudal principle of motor development, 383
Cerebellum, 35, 73, 186, 201
Cerebral cortex, 180, 186

Challenge appraisals, 482, 483, 494, 502
Chemical alphabet, 68, 382
Chemical senses, 106–107
Chemotherapy, 195, 206–207
Child abuse, 400–401, 537, 545, 568, 600
Childhood:
abuse during, 400–401, 537, 545, 568, 600
aggression, 604
behavior therapy, 568
classical conditioning, 205
cognitive development, 388–390
cognitive learning, 231
concept formation, 307
delay of gratification, 460
and dental fears, 205
development overview, 397
drug use, 187
dyslexia, 320
emotional development, 387
intervention programs, 298–299
language, 315, 316, 391
memory, 251, 258, 264
mentoring programs, 446
moral reasoning, 412
and nature-nurture question, 377
obesity during, 337
operant conditioning, 216, 219
and personality, 434, 436
sleep, 156, 163
social development, 392, 393, 394, 395
socialization, 522
See also Parenting
Chimpanzees, 69, 226, 229, 323. *See also* Primates
China, 11, 113, 136, 185, 337, 546. *See also* Asian people/cultures
Chi-square, 616
Chlorpromazine (Thorazine), 541, 557
Chomsky, Noam, 313, 315
Christie, Agatha, 320
Chromosomes, 68, 338, 378, 380, 382
Chunking, 243
Cigarettes, 33, 174, 178, 336, 381
CIPA (congenital insensitivity to pain with anhidrosis), 118
Circadian rhythms, 150–151, 155, 156, 157, 162
Citadel, 589
Clairvoyance, 138
Class. *See* Socioeconomic status
Classical conditioning, 195–211
adaptive value of, 200–201
and brain structure, 73
concepts in, 199
critical thinking exercise, 236
cross-cultural approach, 205
and emotions, 201, 204, 206
vs. operant conditioning, 217
procedure, 197–198
and stress, 489, 493
and systematic desensitization, 207, 567

theories of, 202
Classification, 390
Class notes, 16, 21
Claustrophobia, 518
Client-centered therapy, 564
Clinical assessment, 512
Clinical diagnosis, 513
Clinical interview, 512
Clinical psychologists, 17, 557, 558
Clinical scales, 474
Clinical social workers, 558
Clinton, Hilary, 318
Closure rule of perception, 127, 140
Clouser, Ronald, 274
Clozapine, 541
CNS (central nervous system), 51, 72, 182
Cocaine, 59, 175, 176, 177, 330, 381
Cochlea, 102–103, 104, 115
Cochlear implants, 115
Cochran, Floyd, 590
Cognitive appraisal theory of emotions, 360, 361
Cognitive approach:
aggression, 604
attitudes, 588
and classical conditioning, 202, 217
creativity, 310
defined, 305
depression, 548, 549
emotions, 360, 361
gender identity, 395, 396
group dynamics, 596
mental disorders, 510, 533, 548
motivation, 331, 350
overview, 5, 7
personality, 458, 459
psychotherapy, 565
See also Cognitive-behavioral therapy; Cognitive neuroscience; Language; Learning; Memory; Thinking
Cognitive-behavioral therapy, 559
aggression, 604, 605
and child abuse, 401
development of, 568
for drug use, 189
for eating disorders, 353
for insomnia, 162
mood disorders, 549
for phobias, 225, 524, 525, 568, 575
and social cognitive theory, 225, 461
stress management programs, 6, 502–503, 568
techniques for, 574–575
thought substitution, 574, 575
for trauma, 491
Cognitive development, 388–391
adolescence, 390, 410–413, 430, 523, 601
adulthood, 390, 415
and gender identity, 395, 396
Cognitive development theory of gender identity, 395, 396
Cognitive dissonance, 590
Cognitive factors. *See* Cognitive approach

Subject Index

Subject Index

and nature-nurture question, 377
sensory development, 382
sleep, 156
social development, 392, 393
Infatuated love, 419
Inferential statistics, 613–616
Inferior frontal gyrus, 320
Inferior parietal lobe, 297
Informational influence theory of the
    bystander effect, 597
Ingroup, 598
Inhibited/fearful children, 386, 387
Inhibited female orgasm, 344
Inhibitory transmitters, 54
Initiative vs. guilt stage of
    psychosocial development, 393
Innate language factors, 313, 316
Inner ear, 102–103, 104
Insanity, 509
Insects, as food, 110
Insecure attachment, 385
Insight, 226, 309
Insight therapies, 560–565
    client-centered therapy, 564
    cognitive therapy, 565
    overview, 559
    psychoanalysis, 555, 556, 559,
        560–563
    short-term dynamic psychotherapy,
        562
Insomnia, 162, 163, 332, 568, 575
Instinct theory of motivation, 330
Institutions, 495
Insula, 419
Integration, 492
Integrity (honesty) tests, 474
Integrity vs. despair stage of
    psychosocial development, 417
Intelligence, 281–303
    artificial, 308
    and brain size, 85, 284, 297, 322,
        323
    and correlation, 33, 85
    and creativity, 311
    cross-cultural approach, 282, 291
    definitions, 282–283, 292
    early measurement of, 284–285,
        296
    emotional, 369
    and intervention programs, 298–299
    IQ score distribution, 288–289
    IQ tests, 14, 286–287, 290–291, 296
    and music, 404
    and nature-nurture question,
        292–294
    new approaches, 297
    and race, 290, 294, 296
    and savants, 302
    student activities, 295, 300–303,
        627–628
Intelligence quotient (IQ), 282
    and cognitive development, 391
    and correlation, 33
    and emotional intelligence, 369
    and g factor, 282
    historical origins, 285
    and intervention programs,
        298–299

limitations of, 14, 290–291, 296
score distribution, 288–289
tests, 286–287
    See also Intelligence
Intensity:
    of emotions, 360, 367
    and perception, 123
Interactive model of sexual
    orientation, 341
Interference, 242, 265, 266, 267, 271
Internal attributions, 585
Internal locus of control, 459, 494,
    495
International Classification of Disease
    and Related Health Problems
    (ICD-10), 546
Interneurons, 56
Interpersonal conflicts, 492
Interpersonal therapy, 353
Interposition, 130
The Interpretation of Dreams (Freud),
    160
Interpreting function of attitudes, 589
Interval timing clock, 150
Intervention programs, 298–299
Interview research, 34
Intestines, 335, 485
Intimacy, 419
Intimacy vs. isolation stage of
    psychosocial development, 417
Intrinsic motivation, 331, 350
Introspection, 12, 13
Intrusive thoughts, 574, 575
Inuit people, 110, 161, 319, 367
In vivo (real) exposure, 525, 567
Ions, 52
IQ. See Intelligence quotient
Iris, 95
Isolation experiment, 147

J

Jagger, Mick, 417
James, William, 12, 360
James-Lange theory of emotions, 360
Japan:
    autism, 11
    dental fears, 205
    drug use, 176
    emotions, 367, 374
    gender roles, 399
    mental disorders, 516, 522
    organ transplants, 603
    perception, 136
    stress, 494
    Suzuki method, 231
    See also Asian people/cultures
Jet lag, 151
JND (just noticeable difference), 123
Job performance, 289
Journal of Cross-Cultural Psychology,
    11
Journal of Humanistic Psychology, 10,
    443
Journal of the American Psychoanalytic
    Association, 563
Jung, Carl, 440
Justice orientation, 412
Just noticeable difference (JND), 123

K

Kagan, Jerome, 386
Kanzi (bonobo), 323
Kasparov, Gary, 308
Kastak, David, 322
Kearins, Judith, 272
Keller, Helen, 115
Kelley's covariation model of
    attribution, 585
Kennedy, John F., 286
Kiedis, Anthony, 179
Killer whales, 236
King, Martin Luther, Jr., 443
Kinkel, Kipland, 523
KIPP (Knowledge Is Power Program),
    351
Kisspeptin, 408
Klinefelter's syndrome, 339
Koffka, Kurt, 13
Kohlberg, Lawrence, 412
Kohlberg's theory of moral reasoning,
    412
Köhler, Wolfgang, 13, 226
Koko (gorilla), 323
Konishiki, 335
Korea, 185. See also Asian
    people/cultures
Koresh, David, 594
Kroc, Ray, 310
Kume, Wakana, 603

L

Labeling, 516
Laboratory experiments, 34, 35
Laboratory settings, 34, 35
Laborit, Henri, 557
Lange, Carl, 360
Language, 312–316
    acquisition, 314–316, 391
    animals, 322–323
    and autism, 7
    and brain structure, 77, 78
    Chomsky's theory of, 313, 315
    defined, 305, 322
    dyslexia, 320
    and evolution, 69
    gender differences, 321, 396
    naming, 71
    oral vs. written, 253
    and personality, 459
    rules of, 312
    and thinking, 319
    See also Speech
Language stages, 314
Larynx, 316
LASIK surgery, 95
Latency stage of psychosexual
    development, 392, 439
Lateral hypothalamus, 335
Lateral prefrontal cortex, 297
Latinos, 14
Law of effect, 196, 214
L-dopa, 60
Lead poisoning, 381
Learned associations, 337
Learning:
    biological factors, 228–229
    cognitive learning, 196, 213,

223–226
and concept formation, 307
defined, 195
and gender differences, 84
observational, 223, 224–225, 459,
    493, 600, 601
and phobias, 525
student activities, 203, 208–211,
    227, 234–237, 624–625
Suzuki method, 231
types of, 196
    See also Classical conditioning;
        Operant conditioning
Learning-performance distinction, 224
Lee, Anne, 350
Leno, Jay, 320
Lens, 95
Leptin, 335, 336
Lesbians. See Homosexual orientation
Levels-of-processing theory, 249
Lewis, Jim, 466, 467
Lie detector (polygraph) tests,
    370–371
Lief, Harold, 250
Life expectancy, 424
Light and shadow, 131
Light therapy, 151
Light waves, 94, 96, 98
Lilly, John, 148
Limbaugh, Rush, 464
Limbic system, 80–81, 112, 161, 186,
    362, 411, 523
Limb reattachment, 51
Limitations, 491
Linear perspective, 130
Linguistic relativity, theory of, 319
Links to Learning. See Student activities
Lithium, 534
Little Albert case, 204, 224, 555, 566
Liver, 335, 485
Lobotomies, 75
Locus of control, 459, 495
Loftus, Elizabeth, 250
Loneliness, 497
Longitudinal method, 386, 417, 441,
    465
Long-term memory, 240, 244–246,
    268, 269
Long-term potentiation (LTP), 269
Lorenz, Konrad, 228
Lottery winners, 359, 366
Loudness, 100, 104
Loukaitis, Barry, 523
Lovaas, Ivar, 232
Love, 419–420, 423, 528
Love Lab, 422
LSD, 148, 169, 180
LTP (long-term potentiation), 269
Lu, Steve, 281
Lucky Man (Fox), 461
Lucy (Australopithecus afarensis), 67, 69
Lunesta, 162
Lung cancer, 33

M

Maathai, Wangari, 457, 458, 459
Magic, 138
Magic mushrooms, 180

Subject Index

Magnetic resonance imaging (MRI), 70, 321. *See also* Neuroscience
Mahadevan, Rajan, 239, 243
Maintenance programs (weight loss), 352
Maintenance rehearsal, 242, 249
Major depressive disorder, 532, 534, 547
Major life events, 490
Maladaptive behavior approach to mental disorders, 511
Male-female differences. *See* Gender differences
Mammograms, 122
Mania, 534
Manic-depression. *See* Bipolar I disorder
Marijuana, 186
Marriage, 332, 420, 422, 423
Maslow, Abraham, 10, 332, 443, 472. *See also* Humanistic theories; Maslow's hierarchy of needs
Maslow's hierarchy of needs, 332–333, 348, 443, 596
Mass hysteria, 520
Maturation, 383
McCabe, Michael, 531, 538, 539, 540, 541, 558
McCarty, Osceola, 595
McClelland, David, 348
McDougall, William, 330
MDMA (ecstasy), 181
Mean, 611
Measurement, 37, 369. *See also* Diagnosis; Intelligence quotient; Statistics
Measures of central tendency, 611–612
Measures of variability, 612–613
Median, 611–612
Medical marijuana, 186
Medical therapy, 559. *See also* Drug treatments
Medications. *See* Drug treatments
Meditation, 501, 503
Medulla, 73, 74, 182
Melatonin, 151, 159
Melzack, Ronald, 58
Memory, 239–259, 261–279
  adulthood, 415
  and Alzheimer's disease, 47
  amnesia, 172, 250, 307, 544
  biological factors, 263, 268–269
  and brain structure, 76, 80, 255, 263, 268–269
  and caffeine, 192
  cross-cultural approach, 253, 272
  definitions, 239
  and drug use, 181, 186
  and electroconvulsive therapy, 535
  and emotions, 247, 255, 267, 268, 362, 365
  encoding, 239, 244, 248–249
  and eyewitness testimony, 261, 266, 274–275
  false, 251, 258
  forgetting, 264–267, 278, 415
  impairment of, 239
  inaccuracy, 273

long-term, 240, 244–246, 268, 269
  mnemonics, 271
  organization of, 262–263
  and preparedness, 229
  repressed, 250–251, 265
  and senses, 107, 240, 241, 244
  short-term, 240, 242–243, 244, 245, 249, 268, 269
  and sleep, 153, 154
  and social cognitive theory, 225, 231
  student activities, 252, 256–259, 270, 276–279, 625–627
  and study skills, 20
  types of, 240
  unusual, 254–255
Memory-enhancing drugs, 271
Memory span test, 242
Men. *See* Gender differences; Gender roles; Sexism
Menarche, 408
Meniere's disease, 105
Menopause, 425
Menstrual cycle, 339, 379
Mental age, 285
Mental disorders, 509–529, 531–553
  anxiety disorders, 363, 514, 517–519, 522, 524–525
  assessment, 512–513
  cause theories, 510
  and creativity, 311
  cross-cultural approach, 159, 518, 522, 546
  definitions, 509, 511
  diagnosis, 513–516
  dissociative disorders, 9, 514, 544–545, 546
  frequency of, 516
  mood disorders, 311, 514, 531, 532–535, 547–549
  personality disorders, 515, 536–537
  schizophrenia, 514, 531, 538–542, 546, 557
  and school shootings, 523
  and social support, 497
  somatoform disorders, 514, 520
  student activities, 521, 526–529, 543, 550–553, 634–635
Mental grammar, 313
Mental processes, 4. *See also* Cognitive processes
Mental retardation, 218, 219, 285, 288, 290, 302
Mental set, 309
Menuhin, Yehudi, 378
Mescaline, 59, 181
Mesmer, Anton, 170
Message, 591
Meta-analysis, 559
Metabolism, 82, 336, 352
Methadone, 179
Methamphetamine, 175, 176, 177
Method of loci, 271
Methylphenidate (Ritalin), 27, 28, 30, 36–37, 39
Michelangalo, 310
Midbrain, 73
Middle ear, 102
Midnight-snack (food-entrainable)

circadian clock, 150
Midori, 281, 292
Mild depression, 548–549
Milgram's experiment, 593–594
Miller, George, 242, 243
Mind-body connection:
  and autonomic nervous system, 501
  and hypnosis, 112, 173
  mind-body question, 49
  and placebos, 31, 111
  and somatoform disorders, 520
  and stress, 487
Mind-body question, 49
Mind-body therapy, 487
Mindguard, 598
Mingus, Charles, 311
Minnesota model of drug abuse, 188
Minnesota Multiphasic Personality Inventory (MMPI-2), 474, 475, 512
Minorities. *See* Cross-cultural approach; Cultural Diversity feature; Race
Mire, Soraya, 346
Mirror neurons, 6, 369, 582
MMPI-2 (Minnesota Multiphasic Personality Inventory), 474, 475, 512
Mnemonics, 271
Mode, 611, 612
Modeling. *See* Observational learning
Modified frustration-aggression hypothesis, 601
Moniz, Egas, 75
Monoamines, 533, 534
Monochromats, 99
Monocular depth cues, 130–131
Moon illusion, 132
Moral reasoning, 412
Moral therapy, 556
Morning persons, 155
Morphemes, 312
Morphine, 113, 175, 179
Morphology, 312
Morton, Samuel George, 85
Motherese (parentese), 314, 316, 326
Motion parallax, 131
Motion perception, 131, 137, 140
Motion sickness, 105
Motivation, 329–357
  achievement, 329, 348–351, 448
  and brain structure, 80
  and creativity, 311
  and emotions, 365
  and group dynamics, 596
  hunger, 334–337, 352
  and needs, 330, 332–333, 348
  and sexual behavior, 339
  and social cognitive theory, 225, 231
  student activities, 347, 354–357, 628–629
  and study skills, 21
  theories of, 330–331
  unconscious, 434
  See also Hunger; Sexual behavior
Motivational therapy, 189

Motor cortex, 76
Motor development, 383
Motor (efferent) neurons, 56
Motor homunculus, 76
Motor responses:
  and brain structure, 73, 76
  and drug use, 182, 186
  gender differences, 84
  and schizophrenia, 538
Movies, 140
Mozart effect, 404
MRI (magnetic resonance imaging), 70, 321. *See also* Neuroscience
Mucus, 107
Mukhopadhyay, Tito, 7
Müller-Lyer illusion, 133
Multicultural perspectives. *See* Cross-cultural approach
Multinational studies. *See* Cross-cultural approach
Multiple-intelligence theory, 283
Multiple personality disorder (dissociative identity disorder) (DID), 9, 545, 546
Multiple sclerosis, 51
Muscles, 485
Music, 231, 378, 404
Myelin sheath, 50, 53
Myopia (nearsightedness), 95

N

Naming, 71
NA (Narcotics Anonymous), 189
Narcolepsy, 163
Narcotics. *See* Opiates
Narcotics Anonymous (NA), 189
Native American Church, 59, 181
Native Americans:
  and dreaming, 161
  and drug use, 59, 181
  emotions, 367
  language, 319
  traditional foods, 110
Naturalistic research settings, 35
Natural selection, 69. *See also* Evolutionary theory
Nature-nurture question, 292–294, 377, 378. *See also* Biological factors; Environmental factors; Genetic factors
Nausea, 195, 206–207, 568
Nazi Germany, 594
Nearsightedness (myopia), 95
Needs, 330, 332–333, 348, 443
Negative affectivity, 496
Negative correlation coefficient, 32
Negative punishment, 219, 230
Negative reinforcement, 218
Negative symptoms of schizophrenia, 541
Neglect, 400
Neglect syndrome, 79, 132
Neo-Freudian theory, 440
Neologisms, 538
Nerve impulses, 52–53, 96, 103, 177. *See also* Transduction
Nerves, 51
Nervous system, 47–65

Subject Index

imagined, 172
person, 582–584
vs. sensation, 93, 124–125
student activities, 134, 142–145, 622
subliminal, 122, 135
thresholds, 122–123
See also Senses
Perceptual constancy, 128
Perceptual sets, 137
Perceptual speed, 415
Perfect negative correlation
coefficient, 32
Perfect positive correlation coefficient,
32
Performance goals, 20
Peripheral cues, 335
Peripheral nervous system (PNS), 51,
72
Peripheral route for persuasion, 591
Peripheral theories of emotions, 360
Permissive parents, 413
Personal beliefs, 27, 30, 210, 258,
588, 590
Personal distress, 595
Personal factors, 458, 471
Personal identity (self-identity), 416
Personality, 433–455, 457–479
and academic achievement, 448
adolescence, 416
adulthood, 417
and aggression, 601
assessment, 9, 450–451, 474–475,
478, 512
and creativity, 311
disorders, 515, 536–537
and eating disorders, 353
humanistic theories, 442–446, 472
and hunger, 337
and mood disorders, 533
and obesity, 454
shyness, 449
social cognitive theory, 449,
458–461, 473
stability of, 465, 470
and stress, 494–497, 499
student activities, 447, 452–455,
469, 476–479, 632–633
study of, 18
theory overview, 472–473
trait theory, 462–468, 473,
474–475, 478
See also Freudian theory
Personality disorders, 515, 536–537
Personality psychology, 18
Personality tests, 9, 450, 512
Personal profiles. *See* Case
studies/personal profiles
Person-centered therapy (client-
centered therapy), 564
Person perception, 582–584
Person schemas, 584
Person-situation interaction, 464
Perspective, visual, 130, 131
Persuasion, 591
Pessimism, 495
PET (positron emission tomography)
scans, 71. *See also* Neuroscience
Pets, 445

Peyote, 59, 181
Phallic stage of psychosexual
development, 392, 439
Phantom limb, 58
Pharynx, 316
Phenomenological perspective, 442
Phenothiazines, 541, 542, 557
Phi phenomenon (apparent motion),
13, 140
Phobias, 509, 510
and classical conditioning, 195, 198
cross-cultural approach, 522
and emotions, 363
overview, 518
treatment for, 141, 225, 524–525,
567, 568, 575
Phonemes, 312, 320
Phonology, 312
Photographic memory, 254
Photoreceptors, 95, 96, 114
Physical abuse, 400, 600. *See also*
Child abuse
Physical appearance, 137, 141, 423,
582, 603
Physical fitness, 336, 352, 415, 547
Physical growth, 408
Physiological factors. *See* Biological
factors
Physiological reflexes. *See* Reflexes
Piaget, Jean, 388. *See also* Piaget's
cognitive stages
Piaget's cognitive stages, 388–391, 410
Pica, 218
Piloerection (goose bumps), 56, 485
Pineal gland, 151
Piriform (primary olfactory) cortex,
107
Pitch, 100, 104
Pituitary gland, 82, 408, 485
Placebos, 30, 31, 111, 112, 573
Placenta, 380
Place theory of pitch, 104
Pleasure principle, 436
PMT (Parent Management Training),
604
PNS (peripheral nervous system), 51,
72
Poe, Edgar Allan, 311
Polarization, 598
Polarized thinking, 565
Political correctness, 84
Politics, 318, 591
Polygraph (lie detector) tests, 370–371
Pons, 73, 74, 157
Ponzo illusion, 133
Porter, Cole, 311
Position, sense of, 105
Positive correlation coefficient, 32
Positive psychology, 495
Positive punishment, 219, 233
Positive reappraisal, 495
Positive regard, 445, 446, 564
Positive reinforcement, 218, 232
Positive symptoms of schizophrenia,
541
Positron emission tomography (PET)
scans, 71. *See also* Neuroscience
Postconventional level of moral

reasoning, 412
Postema, Pam, 585
Posterior pituitary, 82
Posthypnotic amnesia, 172
Posthypnotic suggestion, 172
Posttraumatic stress disorder (PTSD),
491, 510, 573
Poverty, 288, 298, 299, 351
Power rapists, 602
Prader-Willi syndrome, 332
Precognition, 138
Preconventional level of moral
reasoning, 412
Predicting behavior, 4, 33, 464
Predisposing function of attitudes,
589
Predispositions, 539, 540. *See also*
Genetic factors
Prefrontal cortex:
and ADHD, 35
adolescent underdevelopment, 411,
430, 523, 601
and aging, 415
and cognitive development, 391,
411, 415, 601
and dreams, 161
and emotions, 363, 371
and intelligence, 297
and meditation, 501
and memory, 242
and mental disorders, 533, 537,
540, 549
and moral reasoning, 412
and schizophrenia, 539
and school shootings, 523
Pregnancy, *See also* Prenatal period
Prejudice, 583
Premature (rapid) ejaculation, 344
Premo, Kate, 509, 514, 524, 567
Prenatal period, 378–381
Preoperational stage of cognitive
development, 389
Prepared learning. *See* Preparedness
Preparedness, 200, 229
Primacy effect, 245
Primacy-recency effect, 245
Primary appraisals, 482, 483, 499
Primary auditory cortex, 78, 103
Primary olfactory (piriform) cortex,
107
Primary reinforcers, 219
Primary values, 448
Primary visual cortex, 79, 97, 114,
161, 363
Primates, 49, 69, 229, 323
The Principles of Psychology (James), 12
Private practice, 17
Proactive interference, 266
Problem-focused coping, 499, 502,
503
Problem solving, 84, 226, 308–309,
604. *See also* Learning
Procedural (nondeclarative/implicit)
memory, 149, 246, 248, 268, 441
Processing speed, 415
Procrastination, 9, 21
Prodigies, 378
Progesterone, 339

Progressive relaxation, 503
Prohibition, 182
Projection, 437
Projective personality tests, 450–451,
474
Propranolol, 247
Prosocial behavior, 595, 597
Proteins, 68
Prototype theory of concept
formation, 306
Proximity rule of perception, 127
Proximodistal principle of motor
development, 383
Prozac (fluoxetine), 519, 534, 537
Psi, 138
Psilocybin, 180
Psychiatric nurses, 558
Psychiatrists, 17, 557, 558
Psychic hotlines, 139
Psychic powers, 138–139
Psychoactive drugs, 174. *See also*
Drug use
Psychoanalysis, 555, 556, 559,
560–563
Psychoanalytic approach. *See* Freudian
theory
Psychoanalytic Quarterly, 563
Psychobiologists, 6, 19. *See also*
Biological factors
Psychodynamic theory. *See* Freudian
theory
Psychokinesis, 138
Psychological assessment, 9,
450–451, 474–475, 478, 512
Psychological factors:
drug abuse, 183, 188
sexual behavior, 338, 340–341, 343
sexual problems, 344
weight, 352
See also Psychosocial factors
Psychological harm, 594
Psychologists, 17, 557, 558
Psychology:
careers in, 17–19
defined, 4
goals of, 4
historical approaches to, 12–13
modern approaches to, 5–11
Psychometric approach, 282, 310
Psychometrics, 19, 281. *See also*
Intelligence
Psychoneuroimmunology, 488
Psychopaths, 536–537, 552
Psychoses, 513
Psychosexual stages of development,
392, 393, 438–439
school shootings, 523
Psychosocial factors:
hunger, 334, 337
mood disorders, 533
personality disorders, 537
stress, 488–489, 497
See also Psychological factors
Psychosocial stages of development,
393, 394, 417, 440
Psychosomatic symptoms, 486–487
and autonomic nervous system, 81
and biofeedback, 233, 568

and burnout, 491
and hypnosis, 173
Psychotherapy, 555–579
 for anxiety disorders, 517, 524–525
 for child abusers, 401
 common factors in, 571
 cross-cultural approach, 572, 578
 for dissociative disorders, 545
 and dreams, 160, 435, 560, 561
 and drug use, 181, 189
 for eating disorders, 353
 effectiveness of, 559, 571
 and Freudian theory, 435, 555, 556,
  559, 560–563
 historical background, 555–557
 and humanistic theories, 446
 and hypnosis, 173
 insight therapies, 555, 556, 559,
  560–565
 mind-body therapy, 487
 for mood disorders, 534, 549
 for personality disorders, 537
 and psychology careers, 17
 and repressed memory, 250–251
 for sexual problems, 344
 for shyness, 449
 student activities, 569, 576 579,
  635–636
 for trauma, 491, 573
 types of, 558 559, 570
 virtual reality in, 141, 524
 See also Behavior therapy;
  Cognitive-behavioral therapy
Psychotic mental disorders, 514
PTSD (posttraumatic stress disorder),
 491, 510, 573
Puberty, 408–409. See also Adolescence
Punishment, 218, 219, 230, 233, 593
Pupil, 95, 485
Purposeful behavior, 459
PYY (hormone), 335, 352

Q

Quantum personality change, 470
Questionnaire research, 34, 155

R

Race:
 and achievement, 329, 348, 351
 and brain size, 85
 and eyewitness testimony, 274
 and intelligence, 290, 294, 296
 and mental disorders, 546
 and motivation, 329, 348
 and perception, 141
 and person perception, 582, 583
 racism, 14, 85, 291, 581, 583, 586,
  590
 and survey research, 29
Racism, 14, 85, 291, 581, 583, 586,
 590
Rader, Dennis, 509, 515, 552
Ramsey, Evan, 523
Randi, James, 138
Random selection, 36
Range, 612
Rape, 183, 602
Rape myths, 602

Rapid eye movement (REM) sleep,
 147, 153, 154
Rapid (premature) ejaculation, 344
Ratio IQ, 285
Rationalization, 437
Rat Man case, 561
Rave parties, 181
Rayner, Rosalie, 204
Reaction formation, 437
Reaction range, 293
Reaction time, 415
Reactive attachment disorder, 377
Reading, 320
Real (in vivo) exposure, 525, 567
Reality principle, 436
Real motion, 140
Real self, 444
Recall, 261, 264
Recency effect, 245
Receptors, 54
Recognition, 261, 264
Recovered memories. See Repressed
 memory
Reflecting, 564
Reflexes:
 and brain structure, 73, 74
 and classical conditioning, 196, 197,
  201, 217
 defined, 56
Rehearsing, 240, 242, 243, 245, 249
Reinforcement, 215, 216, 218–219
 and aggression, 604
 in behavior therapy, 232
 schedules of, 220–221
Relationships, 419–420, 422, 423, 497
Relative size, 130
Relaxation, 207, 501, 503, 524, 567,
 605
Relaxation response, 503
Reliability, 287, 451, 475, 614
Religion:
 and attitudes, 588
 and drug use, 59, 181
 and evolution, 69
 and personality, 433, 434
 and suicide, 427
 and suicide bombers, 471
REM behavior disorder, 153
Remote surgery, 141
REM (rapid eye movement) sleep,
 147, 153, 154
REM rebound, 153
Repair theory of sleep, 156
Replication, 139
Repressed memory, 250–251, 265
Repression, 250, 437. See also
 Repressed memory
Research, 27–45
 case study approach, 28, 30, 35,
  310, 561, 563
 choosing techniques, 34
 controversies, 27, 39
 correlation, 32–33, 85
 and discrimination, 84
 and ESP, 139
 ethical issues, 40–41, 60, 594
 experimental, 28, 34, 35, 36–37,
  500, 547

longitudinal vs. cross-sectional
 methods, 386
method overview, 28
and placebos, 31, 111
and psychoanalysis, 563
questionnaires, 34, 155
replication, 139
settings, 35
specialization areas, 18–19
statistics, 37, 610–617
student activities, 38, 42–45,
 619–620
surveys, 28, 29
See also Research Focus feature
Research Focus feature:
 achievement, 351
 ADHD, 39
 attributions, 587
 brain gender differences, 84
 circadian preferences, 155
 classical conditioning, 204
 drug prevention, 187
 dyslexia, 320
 EMDR, 573
 emotional intelligence, 369
 intelligence, 297
 marriage, 422
 memory, 247, 273
 note-taking strategies, 16
 operant conditioning, 230
 panic disorder, 500
 personality change, 470
 phantom limb, 58
 placebos, 111
 school shootings, 523
 shyness, 449
 subliminal perception, 135
 temperament, 386–387
Resiliency, 394, 415, 441
Resistance, 562
Resistance stage of stress, 487
Respiration, 485
Resting state, 53
Restoril, 162
Reticular formation, 73, 157
Retina, 95, 96, 99, 114, 128, 129,
 150, 159
Retinal disparity, 129
Retrieval cues, 265, 267, 271
Retrieving (memory), 239, 244
Retroactive interference, 266
Reuptake, 59, 175, 176, 177
Reward/pleasure center:
 and attractiveness, 582
 and drug use, 175, 177, 178, 181
 and emotions, 366
 and motivation, 330
 and reinforcement, 219
 and relationships, 419, 420
Rewards, 21, 331, 350. See also
 Operant conditioning
Rhino horn, 27, 31
Rhodopsin, 96
Rifkin, Joel, 536
Risk factors, 183, 427
Risk-taking behavior, 411, 413
Risky shift, 598
Risperidone, 541, 542

Ritalin (methylphenidate), 27, 28, 30,
 36–37, 39
Robotic surgery, 141
Rods, 96
Rogers, Carl, 444–445, 472, 564
Role schemas, 584
Rolling Stones, 310
Romantic love, 419, 528
Rorschach inkblot test, 450, 451, 512
Rotter, Julian, 459
Rules of organization, 126–127
Rush, Benjamin, 556

S

Sadistic rapists, 602
SAD (seasonal affective disorder),
 159, 532
Salem witch trials, 510
Salinger, J. D., 286
Saliva, 106
Salivation, 196, 197, 201, 202
Sanchez, George, 14
Sativex, 186
Savage-Rumbaugh, Sue, 323
Savants, 7, 302, 311, 378
Scandinavian countries, 205
Schachter, Stanley, 361
Schachter-Singer experiment, 361
Schedules of reinforcement, 220–221
Schemas, 420, 584
Schiavo, Terri, 90
Schizophrenia, 514, 531, 538–542,
 546, 557
Schizotypal personality disorder,
 536
School psychologists, 17
School shootings, 523
Scientific method, 36–37, 187
Scripts (event schemas), 584
Seasonal affective disorder (SAD),
 159, 532
Secondary appraisals, 499
Secondary reinforcers, 219
Secondary schools, 17
Secondary sexual characteristics, 408
Secure attachment, 385
Seizures, 86
Selective attention, 548, 565
Selective serotonin reuptake inhibitors
 (SSRIs), 491, 517, 519, 534
Self-actualization, 333, 442, 443,
 445. See also Self theory
Self-actualizing tendency, 444
Self-analysis, 459
Self-concept, 444
Self-defeating personality disorder,
 516
Self-efficacy, 460
Self-esteem, 349, 416, 549
Self-fulfilling prophecies, 30, 31, 40,
 135
Self-handicapping, 349
Self-help programs, 568
Self-identity (personal identity), 416
Self-injurious behavior, 219
Self-management skills, 8
Self-monitoring, 574, 575
Self-perception theory, 590

Subject Index

Subject Index

We'd like to ask you a small favor. We have worked very hard to make this book readable and stimulating and would like to know if we have succeeded. Would you take a few minutes to fill out this form and tell us your reactions to this textbook? We will use your comments, suggestions, and criticisms to improve the next edition of *Introduction to Psychology, 8th Edition*.

School: _____

Instructor's name: _____

1. What did you like most about *Introduction to Psychology*? _____
   _____
   _____

2. What did you like least about the book? _____
   _____

3. Were all the modules assigned for you to read? Yes _____ No _____ Which ones were omitted? _____

4. Did you use the Concept Review sections? Yes _____ No _____ Did you find them useful? Yes _____ No _____

5. How interesting and informative did you find the Cultural Diversity sections, which told you about behaviors in other cultures?
   _____
   _____

6. Did you use the Summary Test sections? Yes _____ No _____ Did you find them useful? Yes _____ No _____

7. How interesting and informative did you find the Research Focus? _____
   _____
   _____

8. Did you go to the Book Companion Website? Yes _____ No _____

   If so, did you use the quizzes or other activities? Yes _____ No _____

9. Did your text come with *PowerStudy*? Yes _____ No _____ Did you purchase it? Yes _____ No _____

10. How useful did you find *PowerStudy*? _____

11. In the space below (or in a separate letter) please make any other comments that you have about the book. (For example, did you like the way that photos and figures were integrated with the text?) We would really like to hear from you.
    _____
    _____
    _____
    _____
    _____
    _____
    _____

Many thanks for taking the time to fill out this survey.

Best wishes,
Rod Plotnik
Haig Kouyoumdjian

DO NOT STAPLE.   TAPE HERE.   TAPE HERE.   DO NOT STAPLE.

FOLD HERE

WADSWORTH
CENGAGE Learning

NO POSTAGE
NECESSARY
IF MAILED
IN THE
UNITED STATES

BUSINESS REPLY MAIL
FIRST-CLASS MAIL   PERMIT NO. 34   BELMONT CA

POSTAGE WILL BE PAID BY ADDRESSEE

Attn: *Rod Plotnik*
        Haig Kouyoumdjian

Cengage Learning

10 Davis Drive

Belmont, CA 94002

FOLD HERE

OPTIONAL:

Your name: _____ Date: _____

May we quote you, either in promotion for *Introduction to Psychology, 8th Edition* or in future publishing ventures?

        Yes: _____ No: _____

Sincerely yours,

Rod Plotnik

Haig Kouyoumdjian